American Life

MACMILLAN
INFORMATION NOW ENCYCLOPEDIA

American Life
A Social History

SELECTIONS FROM THE

Encyclopedia of American Social History

MACMILLAN LIBRARY REFERENCE USA

New York

Designed by Kevin Hanek

Macmillan Library Reference USA
1633 Broadway, 7th Floor
New York, NY 10019

Manufactured in the United States of America

Printing number
1 2 3 4 5 6 7 8 9 10

ISBN: 0-02-865015-8
LC #:

This paper meets the requirements of ANSI/NISO Z39.48-1992 (Permanence of Paper).

Table of Contents

Cover Image: **Spring** *by artist Emile Albert Gruppe brings to mind an early morning in the life of an American family. One could imagine an American family sitting down to breakfast before tumbling out the front door to start their day.* © Christies Images

Preface	vii

A

Adolescence	1
Chesapeake Migrants	2
Young Women in Slavery	7
Adolescent Morality	11
African American Music	12
A Variety of Instruments	15
African American Secular Music	19
Gospel Performance	22
James Brown and Aretha Franklin	28
Amusement and Theme Parks	30
The Roller Coaster and Carousel	32

C

Childhood and Children	39
Native American Children	40
Nineteenth Century Schools	42
John B. Watson	46
The City	51
The Public Health Movement	57
City Government	61
Chart: Population of Leading U.S. Cities	66
Clothing and Personal Adornment	67

Eighteenth Century Hairstyles	71
Female Attractiveness in the Nineteenth Century	74
The Cultivation of Beauty	76
Commercial Architecture	78
The Sun Building	81
The 1893 Columbian Exposition	83
The Evolution of the Shopping Mall	86
Communications and Information Processing	87
Concert Music	98
Early Twentieth Century Concert music	102
The Birth of "Bebop"	104
Country and Western Music	105
Minnie Pearl	110
Nashville	111
Courtship, Marriage, Separation, and Divorce	115
Bundling	116
The "New" Morality	124
"No-Fault" divorce	126

D

Death	131
Death of Children	133
The Mortality Gap	135
Funeral Practices in the Twentieth Century	137

F

Film	139
Nickelodeons	140
The Birth of a Nation	143
The Depression	148
Inquisition and Blacklist	150
Folk Song and Folk Music	154
Broadsides	156
Governmental Institutions and Folk Song Study	162
Foodways	165
Thomas Jefferson	169
Food Reformers	171
Scientific Housekeeping	175
Fraternal Organizations	177
Fraternalism as Entertainment	184
The Frontier	186
The First Americans	188
Whiskey Rebellion	192

H

Health Care	201
Public Medical Institutions in the Nineteenth Century	205
Housing	210
"Hall-Parlor" Houses	211
Climate and Housing Design	213
The First Suburbs	216
Humor and Comedy	221
Joel Chandler Harris	225
H. L. Mencken	227

Table of Contents

— J —

Journalism	235
Broadsides and Magazines	239
The Ethnic Press	240
The Rural Press	245
Censorship of the Press	248

— L —

Landscapes	253
The Forest Primeval	255

— M —

Manners and Etiquette	261
Rank and Status in the New World	263
The Laws of Etiquette	267
Women in the Workplace	269

— N —

National Parks and Preservation	273
Ecological Perspectives	277
Nightlife	280
Dance Halls, Cabarets, and Nightclubs	284

— O —

Old Age	293
Improvements in Longevity	296
Old Age and the Law	299

— P —

Parades, Holidays, and Public Rituals	305
Mother's Day and Other Holidays	308
"Harlem Is Also a Parade Ground"	310
The Plantation	313
"King Cotton"	318
Popular Entertainment Before the Civil War	323
Puritan Entertainments in the Eighteenth Century	327
Entertainments in Rural Communities	329
Popular Literature	337
The Age of Cheap Fiction: The 1830s to the 1950s	341
"Popular Trash" vs. High Art	344
"The Paperback Revolution"	347
Popular Music Before 1950	351
A Joyful Noise vs. an "Odd Noise"	352
Print and Publishing	358
Literacy in the Colonies	360
The Cause of "Useful Knowledge"	361
African-American Literacy	366
Ethnic Publishing in the Nineteenth Century	369
"The Best Reading"	373
Public Architecture	377
County Courthouse	383

— R —

Radio	387
The Distance Fiend	389
The Voice of America	393
Radio and Rock 'n' Roll	395
Rock Music	397

Rock and Roll: Mirror of Society	400
Punk Rock	406
Contemporary Rock and the African-American Express	408

— S —

Sexual Behavior and Morality	413
Sex and Reproduction	413
Native American Sexual Customs	416
Free Love	419
Pornography and Prostitution	422
The Fight for Reproductive Freedom	426
The Stonewall Riot	429
Sports Through the Nineteenth Century	431
Morton vs. Bradford	435
The Birth of Baseball	440
The "Y" Movement	442
Sports in the Twentieth Century	445
Modern Sports	446
Collegiate and Professional Football	452
The Suburbs	459
The Birth of the Suburb	460
Origins of Suburban Government	463
A Postsuburban Era?	468

— T —

Television	471
Sponsors	473
Television and Politics	475
Television News in the 1960s	479
Theater and Musical Theater	482
Pamphlet Plays	484
John Howard Payne	485
The Shuberts, Belasco, and the Fiskes	493
The Living Newspaper	496
Transportation and Mobility	502
The Way West	506
Travel and Vacations	513
Summer Camps	518
National Tourism	519
International Tourism	524

— U —

Urban Cultural Institutions	527
Literature and Enlightenment	528
History and Science	531
Art in the Twentieth Century	538
Urban Parks	543
The People's Park	547

— V —

Village and Town	551
The Pioneer Village	553
The Facade of the Small Town	556

— W —

Women's Organizations	561
The Women's Christian Temperance Union	565

Glossary	571
Index	589

Preface

ORIGINS

Social history has been variously defined: as "history from the bottom up"; as the history of everyday life; or as the history of groups and the power relationships between them. History from the bottom up immediately brings to mind images of the working class, black slaves, the poor. The history of everyday life chronicles change over time in the fabric of ordinary existence—sometimes minute and subtle, occasionally rapid and momentous. Social historians explore the relationships between diverse groups, but they also examine how people develop the cultures and ideologies that bind them together or set them at odds.

(from the Preface to the *Encyclopedia of American Social History*, 1993)

Those curious about American social history have learned to rely on the distinguished three-volume *Encyclopedia of American Social History* published by Charles Scribner's Sons Reference. Since its publication in 1993, consumers, historians, and students have expressed an interest in a single-volume version of this prestigious work, especially one that focuses on the ways in which groups of Americans lead their lives. The *Information Now Encyclopedia of American Life* is designed to fulfill that need.

CRITERIA FOR SELECTION

Grand in scope, *American Life* is organized in an A-to-Z format. Fascinating articles explore physical space (small towns, cities, and suburbs) and its impact on social life and structure as well as patterns of everyday life, centering on topics such as food, clothing, and housing. The encyclopedia also includes several essays on a wide variety of aspects of recreation and popular culture. Other articles consider aspects of social life arranged according to the phases of the life cycle, with a stress on age and gender.

In preparing this one-volume version of the *Encyclopedia of American Social History*, it was agreed that articles would be excerpted in their entirety and presented in a manner readers will consult first. Cross-references appear throughout the work in the margin and will assist readers as they explore the encyclopedia. A comprehensive index will provide further assistance.

FEATURES

To add visual appeal and enhance the usefulness of the volume, the page format was designed to include the following helpful features.

- **Cross-Reference Quotations:** These quotations, extracted from related articles in the volume and referenced with a specific page number, will lead to further exploration of the subject.
- **Cross-References:** Appearing at the base of many margins, "See also" cross-references also cite related articles to encourage further research.
- **Notable Quotations:** Found throughout the text in the margin, these thought-provoking quotations will complement the topic under discussion.
- **Definitions and Glossary:** Brief definitions of important terms in the main text can also be found in the margin and in the glossary at the end of the book.
- **Sidebars:** Appearing in a gray box, these provocative asides relate to the text and amplify topics.
- **Index:** A thorough index provides thousands of additional points of entry into the work.

ACKNOWLEDGMENTS

American Life contains over two hundred illustrations. Acknowledgments of sources for illustrations can be found in the illustration captions.

The articles herein were written for the *Encyclopedia of American Social History* by leading authorities at work in the field of social history. Mary Kupiec Cayton, Elliott J. Gorn, and Peter W. Williams of the Department of American Studies at Miami University of Ohio served as co-editors for the original set.

This book would not have been possible without the hard work and creativity of the staff at Macmillan Library Reference. We are grateful to all who helped create this marvelous work.

Editorial Staff
Macmillan Library Reference

ADOLESCENCE

Historical inquiry into American adolescence has been marked by a lively debate, kindled in the 1970s when several scholars took the position that adolescence did not exist, as a formal concept or stage of life, prior to the twentieth century. According to John and Virginia Demos and Joseph Kett, the terms "adolescence" and "adolescent" were rarely used before the 1890s. These words entered the popular lexicon only as Americans acknowledged the peculiar difficulties of coming of age in an urban industrial society: unlike colonial or early-nineteenth-century youths, "adolescents" lived in a world of rapidly changing ideals and expectations. Twentieth-century America measured the success of adults by their ability to perform in complex technological and bureaucratic settings; thus, "adolescents" endured prolonged dependency as they prepared for adulthood in extrafamilial educational institutions. "Adolescents" clashed with their elders, evincing such acute "storm and stress" that the older generation turned to experts in psychology, sexology, and medicine to explain the character and course of adolescent development. Finally, "adolescents" created their own subcultures, interacting with consumer industries that alternately invented and catered to their desires and spending habits.

Certainly, the experience of young people in colonial or antebellum America could not have mirrored that of modern adolescents. Nonetheless, the singular characteristics of twentieth-century adolescence should not prevent our recognizing the similarities between young people approaching adulthood in this century and those doing so in earlier times. Though they called this stage "youth" rather than "adolescence," Americans in the seventeenth, eighteenth, and nineteenth centuries acknowledged that young people in their teens and twenties were no longer children in mind, body, or capability. Parents demanded that their maturing offspring prepare deliberately for adulthood yet denied them full independence. Young people communicated the difficulties of growing up through antisocial conduct, indecision, and crises of identity. In turn, youths' struggles and rebellion provoked adults to devise a wide variety of coping strategies.

Adolescence has been a transitional and problematic stage of life in America throughout the past four centuries. Over time, adolescence has changed in response to transformations in the family, economy, and culture. Gender, race, region, ethnicity, and class have shaped the lives of adolescents, ruling out a single or inclusive definition of adolescence that holds for any particular time period.

The Colonial Period

Divergent patterns of development in New England and the Chesapeake created wide regional disparities in the experiences of seventeenth-century adolescents. The Puritans sailed from their homeland in family groups, hoping to create godly communities in the wilderness. Settling on the North Atlantic coast, they established productive agricultural villages and a patriarchal family system in which fathers directed the spiritual and worldly activities of wives, children, and servants. Puritans prized paternal guidance and filial obedience, yet perhaps because of their intense religiosity and strict behavioral expectations, they also knew the meaning of youthful uncertainty, crisis, and rebellion.

Although Puritan society was not rigidly age-graded, seventeenth-century New Englanders recognized the years from puberty to the twenties as a stage of earnest training for adult roles and of religious conversion. Young men and women were still dependents, required by law and custom to follow the dictates of their elders and excluded from marriage and from the economic and political roles appropriate to adults of their sex and social rank. Nonetheless, occupational choice and generational conflict were not entirely absent from their lives.

Most Puritan parents placed their offspring in the homes of other families during adolescence, hoping both to provide youths with necessary training and to undercut rebellious tendencies. Puritan girls were "placed out" as household servants in their early teens; they could not choose

Teenage interest in radio grew out of a technological change as well as social and cultural factors.

PAGE 395

A

ADOLESCENCE

The Colonial Period

*I've never
understood why
people consider
youth a time of
freedom and joy.
It's probably
because they have
forgotten their own.*

MARGARET ATWOOD

their future occupation and learned to become housewives like their mothers. Boys also were placed out to learn a trade or attend school, but for them occupational choice was an important step toward manhood. The Puritans believed that young men must choose a "calling," using their talents to serve God and society. Although fathers guided sons in discerning a calling, some boys were apprenticed to masters in several different trades before settling down.

If seventeenth-century fathers and sons sometimes worked together to overcome the quandaries of adolescence, in other instances Puritan youths actively questioned or repudiated the expectations of their elders. Unable to suppress their intense feelings of lust and willfulness as Puritan doctrine demanded, many young men and women experienced years of religious doubt, punctuated by periods of "exquisite anguish and inner torment," before surrendering unconditionally to God (Phillip Greven, *Protestant Temperament*, p. 95). Others attained adulthood without seeking conversion or church membership, prompting New England's religious leaders to devise the halfway covenant, establish church-sponsored young men's societies, and issue innumerable jeremiads denouncing youths' waning piety. The halfway covenant permitted adults who had never experienced "saving faith" to have their offspring baptized if they themselves had been baptized as children; however, "halfway" members of the church were denied communion and voting privileges.

Adolescent rebellion was social as well as religious, collective as well as individual. Roger Thompson's work on seventeenth-century Middlesex County, Massachusetts, shows that adolescents violated community norms through vandalism, drinking, theft, and premarital sexual experimentation. The participants were male and female; they were the sons and daughters of both elite and lower-class parents; and they were residents of college towns and farming villages. Although the youths were not highly organized, Thompson believes their activity shows that the "beginnings of . . . a distinct [youth] culture" may be traced "back to the middle of the seventeenth century" ("Adolescent Culture in Colonial Massachusetts," p. 141).

Although marriage marked Puritan youths' entry into adulthood, courting couples were frequently reminded of their abiding dependence on the patriarchal family. Males could not marry before inheriting land from their fathers, thus obtaining the means to establish an independent household. Most men married in their mid or late

CHESAPEAKE MIGRANTS
Long Terms of Indenture

In contrast with New England, where adolescence was shaped by the weighty presence of church and family, young people in the early Chesapeake came of age in a society notable for the light hold of these two institutions. Virginia and Maryland were more commercial than religious ventures, and most of the Chesapeake's initial migrants were unmarried Englishmen in their teens and twenties who came as indentured laborers to cultivate tobacco. They arrived without family ties and found it difficult to form them, encountering few female settlers. Moreover, disease ravaged the early Chesapeake, forcing it to depend on further immigration for population growth. The region's unbalanced sex ratio and high mortality rates undermined reproductive increase and family stability, preventing patriarchal authority from taking root until the eighteenth century.

Whether male or female, the status of young migrants in the early Chesapeake was uncertain, marginal, and paradoxical: they were not adults, but neither were they protected adolescents. The colonies' unmarried male laborers were free of parental intervention but deprived of parental aid. They looked after themselves, yet long terms of indenture and an unequal sex ratio prevented them from marrying and attaining independent status until their late twenties or thirties.

Young female migrants looked forward to a wide choice of marriage partners and an advantageous union. Because family and church were weak, females were able to engage in premarital sex without loss of reputation: more than one-third of the Chesapeake's immigrant women were pregnant at the time they wed. But, outnumbered by men and living as servants on plantations scattered about the countryside, young women were extremely vulnerable to rape. Moreover, the birth of an illegitimate child, whether the issue of forced or consensual sex, usually resulted in a heavy fine or a lengthening of the term of indenture.

twenties; their wives were typically a few years younger. Financial negotiations between the parents of young couples were central to Puritan marital arrangements, and courtship took place for the most part in public, under the watchful eye of the community. Still, New Englanders did per-

See also
Rock Music

mit young couples to engage in "bundling"—sleeping together while heavily clothed and separated by a wooden board. This traditional English custom gave young adults an opportunity to test their affection in a controlled setting; it was especially important to young women, who otherwise were passive in courtship.

The Chesapeake's first generation of native-born youths grew up within family settings, yet they, too, knew the meaning of an ill-defined and unprotected adolescence. Parental death was so commonplace in the early Chesapeake that most native-born children and youths lived in impermanent households, amid a succession of stepparents and stepsiblings. Erratic supervision and abuse were commonplace, and educational opportunities were meager.

Darrett and Anita Rutman contend that the Chesapeake's high rates of parental death undercut the emotional content of family life, forcing youths to mature early; young people passed into adulthood without experiencing adolescent turmoil or engaging in adolescent rebellion. But this interpretation assumes that adolescence exists only in a protective or watchful family setting. In contrast, Lorena Walsh argues that seventeenth-century Maryland's familial instability actually provoked an "adolescent crisis," at least for boys. Responding to the confusion in their homes, boys spent their inheritances unwisely, argued with their elders, avoided work, ran away, took up with dissolute companions, and got into scrapes with the law.

Over the course of the eighteenth century, the Chesapeake's mortality rate declined and its sex ratio reached a point of balance, permitting stable patriarchal families to assume a pivotal role in society. Yet even as the patriarchal family emerged in the Chesapeake and remained important in New England, diverse societal developments challenged its singular preeminence, altering the meaning of adolescence.

For white males of both British American and non-English parentage, adolescence became a stage of life associated both with widening opportunities for autonomous behavior and with heightened tension and ambiguity. Unmarried immigrant and native-born young men flocked to burgeoning commercial cities, seeking employment as storekeepers, clerks, insurance brokers, innkeepers, merchants, and laborers. They eschewed traditional apprenticeships, and the moral component of the master-apprentice relationship began to dissolve. Youthful rural-to-urban migration occurred even in New England as population growth outstripped the availability of inheritable lands, depriving Puritan fathers of the ability to secure their sons' futures.

Adolescent males faced the prospect, both exhilarating and frightening, of engineering their economic futures without paternal aid or direction; they might achieve prosperity or fall into the expanding ranks of the urban poor. Young men, Puritans especially, faced the additional challenge of weighing urban secular values against the competing ideals of their parents. City life exposed them to diverse cultures, to Enlightenment ideals emphasizing individual happiness, and to recreational drinking, gambling, and prostitution.

Fearing that the decline of patriarchal authority would produce a generation of dissolute young men, the colonies began to assign extrafamilial institutions more responsibility for managing and socializing adolescents. Elite parents and educators in New Jersey, New York, and Pennsylvania established colleges to provide the discipline and direction that families no longer offered. The select churchmen of Charleston, South Carolina, attempted to curtail youthful disorder by levying taxes to support foster homes, schools, and apprenticeships for the poor, and New England enacted strict laws against youthful disobedience.

Similarly, Puritan ministers condemned the wanton behavior of young men—night revels, filthy songs, tippling, and fornication—and urged youths to convert before encountering the temptations of secular society. Perhaps frustrated with the difficulties of achieving success in secular terms, many young men responded enthusiastically to calls for renewed religiosity; during the Great Awakening (1739–1744) the age of conversion for men dropped from the late twenties and thirties into the teens and early twenties.

Families also responded to the changing character of male adolescence, modifying their methods of parenting. As fathers acknowledged their diminishing authority and as Enlightenment values penetrated the home, parents placed new emphasis on affection, moderation, and liberty. Maturity was to be achieved not by forcing the male child or youth to submit to his parents, but by encouraging the development of self-control and autonomy. In addition, as independence and strength of will became prerequisites to male adulthood, parents began to accentuate gender differences, making sharp distinctions between appropriate "masculine" and "feminine" traits of character.

Discouraged from seeking "masculine" autonomy, adolescent girls nonetheless drew some ben-

The experience of wage earning gave working-class youths greater social and sexual autonomy than they had known in preindustrial economies.

PAGE 420

Wise parents know that fighting a teenager, like fighting a riptide, is inviting doom.

HAIM G. GINOTT
BETWEEN PARENT AND
TEENAGER (1969)

efit from the shift toward moderate parenting and greater gender-role differentiation. Eighteenth-century mothers perfected moderate parenting techniques, cultivating "egalitarian friendships" with their adolescent daughters. "Femininity"—tenderness, purity, and piety—was the crux of these friendships, their "invariable point of reference" (Norton, *Liberty's Daughters*, [1980] pp. 102, 111).

At the same time, however, the new trends exacerbated adolescent girls' apprehension about marriage, sharpening their awareness of the socially induced differences in temperament, role, and power that distinguished women from men. Increasingly, eighteenth-century society countenanced male sexual adventurism, provoking "good" women to protect themselves from unwelcome advances by claiming to be passionless. And while ambitious young men might carve out a future in the marketplace and the fledgling professions, young women looked to a future defined by marriage and legal subordination. Knowing that their fate—whether sorrowful or happy—lay in the hands of their prospective husbands, girls sought the advice of parents when choosing a spouse. They also turned to the church; young women's notable piety during the Great Awaken-

ing developed in response to anxieties about marriage and childbirth.

Yet if white males and females came of age in an era of diminished or moderated patriarchalism, the same cannot be said of African American youths. Patriarchal authority was central to the development of slavery; sentimentality may have obscured its operation within the white slaveholding family, but slaves felt its full force.

It was generally during adolescence that slaves began to experience and thoroughly comprehend the harsh reality of enslavement. White male slaveholders demanded more and more work of slaves as they reached physical maturity. By the age of sixteen most females and males worked from dawn to dusk in the fields; only a small minority were trained as house servants or craftsmen. The ability to assume a full workload frequently coincided with slaves' sale and forced separation from family; it was also during adolescence that slaves first felt the sting of the whip, usually for failing to complete a task satisfactorily. Finally, as they reached adolescence, slave girls became increasingly vulnerable to sexual harassment and rape by their white masters and overseers.

The slave community and family sustained and succored African American youths as they confronted the trials of adolescence. By the early eighteenth century slaves were reproducing in sufficient numbers to form families and resilient kin networks, especially on large plantations. The slave family taught youths how to resist and to cope with bondage. It also established clear patterns of normative behavior, discouraging promiscuous premarital sex and directing young men and women toward marriage, sexual fidelity, and church membership.

The New Nation

The political and ideological ferment of the American Revolution injected a new degree of self-awareness and self-assertion into the lives of American youths. Black slaves of both sexes and all ages used the war as an opportunity to escape servitude. White males began to employ the language of republicanism to challenge parents' intervention in courtship.

Young white women and girls also demonstrated their identification with republican ideology, revising the conventional script for women's coming of age. In the decades after the war, some young females repudiated marriage and embraced "blessed singleness." Others displayed a new assertiveness in courtship, demanding that suitors

ADOLESCENT SLAVES

Two slaves, part of the slave community and family that sustained and succored African American youths as they confronted the trials of adolescence.
HULTON-DEUTSCH COLLECTION/CORBIS

♦ **Antebellum**

Existing before a war, especially existing before the Civil War

treat them as equals and that parents respect their right to choose a partner without interference. Teenage girls also rejected an adolescence devoted entirely to domestic endeavors. Reflecting the nation's growing interest in female education, and hoping to learn how republican values might be incorporated into their future work as wives and mothers, America's "daughters of liberty" began to enroll in female academies in significant numbers.

Late-eighteenth-century parents tolerated, even applauded, their offspring's assertiveness, seeing in it the budding virtues of a republican citizenry. In contrast, by the 1830s and 1840s, Americans widely condemned male youths' contempt for authority, perceiving it as a grave threat to the public weal. College students rioted and rebelled against traditional rules of comportment. A much larger population of urban youths flouted authority and convention in their work and social relations. These young males "on the make" changed commercial and industrial employers frequently, taking years to settle into a trade or profession. They championed a rough-and-tumble democracy, joining nonhierarchical mechanics' clubs, fraternal organizations, and fire-fighting companies. More troubling still, most urban youths roomed in hotels or boarding houses and were completely free of adult supervision during nonworking hours. Devoting their leisure time to theater performances, gambling, and womanizing, they created a subculture that shunned sincerity and moral restraint.

America's disorderly young men were a frightening sign of fathers' declining ability to orchestrate their sons' transition to adulthood. Moreover, to traditionalists and critics of Jacksonian democracy, male youths were an apt symbol of national decline, of democracy gone awry. Their opportunism and disregard for virtue proved that the nation erred grievously in permitting mass politics, rampant economic speculation, the factory system, and urbanization to take root in republican terrain.

Significantly, the antebellum denunciation of urban males aroused Americans to deliberate analysis of youth as a life stage. Writing for the popular press, moral reformers and educators attempted to balance criticism with inquiry into the emotional, physiological, and mental characteristics of the young as they passed between childhood and adulthood. The emerging middle class rejected Calvinist notions about childhood; instead of seeing children as inherently sinful, parents viewed children as innocents who were responsive to systematic moral nurture. Set against

this vision of purity, antebellum authors depicted youth as a stage of moral dilemma. Susceptible to passion, overstimulation, and mental confusion, youths nonetheless faced a season of pivotal decision making; the course chosen in the teens and twenties determined the character of adult life.

Thus, in this view, urban males' uncontrolled individualism and sexual indulgence set them on a course toward moral depravity, poverty, disease, and possible insanity. In contrast, the thousands of young men who heeded the impassioned preaching of the Second Great Awakening in the early nineteenth century were destined for lives of robust health, prosperity, and moral rectitude. Both groups were susceptible to high emotion; according to purity reformers and educators, the critical distinction between them was their differing degree of exposure to principled adult instruction.

Not surprisingly, antebellum ideas about youth produced new extrafamilial strategies for socializing adolescent males and assuaging older Americans' anxieties about the new democratic and industrial order. Primary schools, secondary schools, and Sunday schools proliferated as Americans proclaimed a growing need for educational institutions to prepare young people, mentally and morally, for adulthood. Moral reformers founded houses of refuge and reform schools for impoverished and delinquent juveniles, both male and female. College administrators replaced old rules of student conduct with new procedures for judging academic performance, and thereby encouraged good behavior and self-control. Employers and managers urged young workers to develop more conscientious and productive habits. Finally, the Cadets of Temperance reinforced adolescent males' moral and religious sensibilities; and fraternal orders, including the Odd Fellows and Freemasons, promoted their identification with the competitive demands of the workplace.

Simultaneously, middle-class families adopted new methods for rearing their adolescent offspring. The urban "youth crisis" heightened parents' class consciousness, and families with means invested growing sums of money in education so that sons might develop skills and attitudes that would distance them from the "lower classes." Urban parents also prolonged adolescence, insisting that sons reside at home during their teens and early twenties to take advantage of educational opportunities and to avoid the temptations and pitfalls of working-class culture.

Most important, middle-class families promoted intense emotional and psychological bond-

The textile mills employed single farm girls sixteen to twenty-five years old who lived in a highly regulated and paternalistic community.

PAGE 57

A

In their struggle for financial security, parents saw children as wage earners rather than as students; thus, rather than keeping their children in school, the offspring were sent to work in their early teens.

PAGE 44

ing between mothers and sons, hoping that sentimental attachments would inspire youths to internalize an ethic of benevolent morality and self-restraint. As proponents of the nineteenth-century ideology of separate spheres, middle-class mothers emphasized the social value of gender difference, urging their sons to strive for "manly independence" while daughters aspired to "moral purity" and "true womanhood." But "manliness" need not conflict with virtue or devotion to the family, and young men were advised to look to their mothers rather than to their male peers for a moral standard of conduct. Maternal influence was especially critical to young men's sexual development; by offering their sons a compelling model of sexual purity, mothers hoped to convince them that sexual indulgence degraded women, the family, and the human spirit.

Whatever Americans may have gained by devising new strategies to manage adolescent males, they neither erased opportunities for youthful autonomy nor eliminated the tension between young men and their middle-class elders. The most carefully bred boy might rebel against a confining domesticity, dash his parents' expectations, break his mother's heart. Laboring-class and immigrant youths who encountered middle-class values only occasionally—in charity workers, employers, and fraternal associations—were even less likely to pass through adolescence without moral taint. A youthful working-class subculture continued to thrive in nineteenth-century cities, unconstrained by genteel ideals or pretensions.

Young women excited less public anxiety in antebellum America than did young men, being seen as less openly contemptuous of traditional values and authority. Nonetheless, the outpouring of advice literature on girls' manners, morals, and physical health suggests that middle-class Americans worried about young women's ability to travel the road to "true womanhood" without encountering dangerous obstructions or delays.

Middle-class girls confronted the problem of reconciling opportunities for education and employment with the antebellum emphasis on gender difference and female domesticity. In the decades prior to the Civil War, female academies multiplied rapidly, offering adolescent girls sex-segregated education at the secondary level. Simultaneously, the teaching profession opened its doors to young unmarried women with a secondary education, and textile mills offered jobs to adolescent girls from New England's farm families.

Certainly it was possible to fit these developments into the framework of domesticity. Mid-dle-class parents, educators, and reformers generally supported secondary education for teenage girls, believing that it prepared them to be better wives and mothers. They also defended young women's temporary employment as teachers or mill workers, deeming these occupations to be fully consonant with feminine capabilities and domestic interests. But the real experience of young females defied formulaic evaluations. Even as education and teaching encouraged young women to refine their skills in nurture and moral guardianship, they also taught them the value of self-esteem, mental stimulation, and independence.

Indeed, growing numbers of young women hesitated to give up the liberty gained through education and employment for marriage and a narrow home life. Of course, the vast majority of middle-class young women eventually married, knowing that they would be socially anomalous and economically insecure if they remained single. Nevertheless, they reluctantly withdrew from close circles of female friends and wondered whether marital happiness was possible in a society that required men and women to cultivate disparate mental, emotional, and behavioral traits.

Although working-class girls were less burdened by domestic ideology than were middle-class girls, they were also denied the opportunities for education and satisfying employment that their privileged sisters enjoyed. Many working-class girls spent their adolescence as subordinates in the "outwork" system, manufacturing clothing or other consumer products at home under the supervision of older relatives. Other working-class girls found employment as live-in domestic servants.

The constraints of subordinate status and familial obligation did not prevent working-class young women from carving narrow avenues of assertion into their overburdened lives. Discovering openings for unskilled hands in factories and workshops, native-born girls quit domestic service in droves, leaving this field of work to immigrants. The latter, knowing that the demand for servants was always greater than the supply, guarded their independence by moving on to new jobs whenever their mistresses became too demanding or judgmental. In New York City, growing numbers of wage-earning young women broke away from expected patterns of filial obedience and dependence, leaving their parents' homes to live with peers in boardinghouses and tenements. These girls became members of a working-class youth culture that flourished along the Bowery; seeking a rough equality with their

YOUNG WOMEN IN SLAVERY

Adolescents at Risk

More than any other group of antebellum female adolescents, young women in slavery were deprived of social autonomy, education, and satisfying employment. In addition, they directly confronted the underside of domesticity: nineteenth-century Americans honored the "pure" woman by setting up the "fallen" or "impure" woman as her foil. In the Northeast, female reformers tried to shorten the distance between the two classes of women, blaming lustful men for "innocent women's fall." By contrast, patriarchal planters in the slave South drove the two groups of women apart to excuse and camouflage their own sexual license; on the one hand, planters' rhetoric and rule stressed white women's "purity" and vulnerability; on the other hand, it emphasized the libidinous nature of slave "wenches."

Distressed and angered by the treatment they received from whites, slave girls struggled to preserve their integrity and well-being. From adult slave women, female adolescents learned to escape overwork by feigning illness, breaking tools, or disobeying orders. Just as important, the slave community's religious activities and courtship practices provided adolescent girls with a field of action outside the humiliating master-slave relationship, thereby boosting their self-esteem. But African Americans found it difficult to shelter girls from sexual molestation; young women who resisted the rape or abuse of a white master or overseer did so at great risk of punishment or sale.

male peers, they used casual sex and prostitution to finance autonomy, fancy clothes, and recreation.

Of course, working girls' self-assertion was neither unlimited nor free of danger. Whatever independence they found in adolescence, most young women confronted a future defined by severe economic constraints and marital dependency. Moreover, in boldly rejecting both working- and middle-class notions of female respectability, New York's Bowery girls risked family ostracism, rape, arrest, and placement in an industrial school for delinquent girls.

Urban Industrial America

During the late nineteenth and early twentieth centuries, American society reeled from the effects of change: the collapse of slavery and the rise of Jim Crow laws, urban growth, industrial consolidation and technological development, high rates of immigration, and the settlement of the West. The nation grew more heterogeneous and embattled than ever before, filled with the acrimonious debate of competing class, ethnic, race, and gender interests. The privileged fought to protect and enhance their status in the name of democracy; so, too, as partisans of democracy, the marginalized and dispossessed struggled to resist violence, deprivation, and discrimination. Amid this period of painful adjustment, adolescence acquired new experiential and cultural meaning. For young people of all backgrounds, adolescence emerged as an increasingly distinct stage of life; at the same time, class, race, ethnicity, and gender marked and fractured adolescence in significant ways.

Families of all kinds responded to the exigencies of urban industrial living by sharpening youths' dependency and sense of filial obligation. Realizing that young men could not become well-paid bureaucrats or professionals without acquiring specialized skills, growing numbers of middle-class parents sent their boys to high schools, professional schools, and colleges for training and formal certification. The child-centered Victorian family intensified the dependence of its adolescent girls in a different manner, keeping daughters at home to protect them from the perceived hazards of girlhood in late-nineteenth-century life: premarital romance and seduction, marketplace exploitation, and mental overstimulation.

In another pattern, impoverished immigrant and native-born white families sent millions of adolescents of both sexes into the industrial work force. Although these youngsters bore a heavy burden of responsibility for the welfare of their parents and siblings, they were not treated as adults; they were dependents, required to respond obediently to the dictates of their elders. And African American families in the urban South struggled to keep adolescent sons and daughters in school and out of a discriminatory job market, believing that education was the only authentic route to upward mobility.

Yet even as families sought to accentuate adolescents' dependency, young people elaborated distinctive forms of autonomy. Young unmarried black men and women migrated to northern cities, determined to lead their families out of the Jim Crow South. Although primarily in search of economic opportunity, these teenagers and young adults were also drawn to the excitement and cultural sophistication of northern city life.

Advice books, especially for teenagers and young adults in the postwar years, were full of specific prescriptions, all pointing to the same end.

PAGE 270

♦ **Anomalous**
Inconsistent with or deviating from what is usual, normal, or expected

The wage-earning sons and daughters of immigrants developed a subculture that pitted the autonomy and pleasure of the young against familial responsibilities. As champions of consumerism, adventurous heterosexuality, and self-assertion, they spent the wages needed at home on stylish clothes or commercial amusements, and indulged in heterosexual experimentation with their unmarried peers.

Similarly, male college students challenged their status as dependents, engaging in rowdiness and ritualized violence that offended the sensibilities of parents and violated the paternalistic rule of college administrators. White middle-class females also found ways to spurn the protective embrace of their families. Some gave voice to their discontent in self-destructive patterns, refusing food or cultivating physical fragility; others resisted dependency by pushing their way into higher education and the professions.

Southern black families responded to the migration of their young sons and daughters with pride, hope, and trepidation. Immigrant parents reacted to their adolescents' growing assertiveness with varying degrees of tolerance and moral outrage. White middle-class parents and their allies in Progressive reform criticized the "immoral" amusements of lower-class immigrant youths, worried that their own offspring would follow suit. In addition, they agonized over the meager ambition of their sons and the excessive ambition of their daughters, fearing that these developments signaled social collapse—that is, the collapse of the Victorian gender system and the demise of the Christian middle-class family.

Indeed, middle-class anxieties contributed directly to the formation of a modern ideology of adolescence. Anxious about the future of their children, middle-class Americans sought a "scientific" understanding of youth. G. Stanley Hall, president and senior professor of psychology at Clark University, responded to their call, synthesizing the research of dozens of physicians and psychologists and drawing on the theoretical models of Darwin and Freud to offer a systematic analysis of adolescence.

According to Hall's early-twentieth-century writings, the development of the individual from childhood to adulthood "recapitulated" the biological and cultural evolution of the human race. Much like "primitive" peoples who struggled to find a place for moral values amid the pressing demands of daily survival, adolescents experienced profound "storm and stress" as "old moorings were broken and a higher level attained" (G. Stanley Hall, *Adolescence*, vol. 1, p. xiii). Significantly, the conditions of modern life exacerbated adolescent stress by exposing immature minds and bodies to social and sexual disorder. Hall emphasized the importance of protective environments that discouraged "precocity," the assumption of adult behaviors and responsibilities; most important, adolescence should be a stage of idealism in which budding sexual impulses were sublimated in moral, athletic, academic, and artistic endeavors.

Hall's work provided inspiration and direction to a generation of middle-class parents and Progressive activists eager to reorganize adolescent life. Formal education became an important component of the adolescent experience within both

STRUCTURED TIME

American parents in the early twentieth century believed that adolescent life should be structured. Boy scouts, shown here doing calisthenics at a summer camp in 1925, offered athletic, social, and cultural programs to youths across the country.
MINNESOTA HISTORICAL SOCIETY/CORBIS

the working and middle classes as state laws were passed that prohibited the employment of children below specified ages. New state legislation also extended the age of compulsory full-time school attendance and required part-time attendance of working adolescents at continuation schools. Educators created age-graded vocational and comprehensive high schools for adolescents of disparate class and racial backgrounds. The high schools prepared adolescents for college, white-collar, and skilled industrial occupations; between 1890 and 1920 the number of adolescents attending public high schools rose from two hundred thousand to more than two million.

Simultaneously, adult-sponsored youth organizations including Boy Scouts, Girl Scouts, 4-H Clubs, settlement-house clubs, and the YMCA, YWCA, and YMHA offered structured athletic, social, and cultural programs to American youths in cities, towns, and urban villages around the country. Reformers, social workers, and psychiatrists developed special courts, probation programs, child guidance clinics, and state reformatories for juvenile offenders; they claimed that youthful delinquents acted in response to age-specific environmental stresses and mental conflicts that could be resolved with expert assistance in age-segregated settings.

Although Progressive Era reforms reduced the role of the family in the socialization process, they increased adolescents' dependency, enlarging the authority of unrelated professionals who provided instruction or supervision to adolescents and judged them on their performance and progress. Progressive reforms also prolonged adolescence: they discouraged early wage earning, made high school attendance a prerequisite to upward mobility, and restricted adolescents' informal social interaction with adults.

The institutional developments of the Progressive Era did not, however, eliminate modern youths' desire for or access to autonomy. Indeed, high schools provided fruitful ground for the further development of semiautonomous peer cultures. School administrators promoted extracurricular activities, hoping to foster greater homogeneity in culturally diverse student bodies, but discovered that high school peer groups were less malleable than desired: many peer groups developed normative patterns that subverted adult authority.

Certainly, high school peer cultures were not necessarily openly rebellious or contemptuous of adult values. According to Reed Ueda, the peer culture that developed in Somerville, Massachu-

setts, between 1890 and 1910 encouraged loyalty to the genteel culture of the students' Yankee parents. At the same time, however, by "transfer[ring] emotional ties from the family to the peer group," high schools prompted youths to express "independence from the codes of adults" (*Avenues to Adulthood*, p. 132). In suburban Somerville, students indulged in relatively superficial forms of rebellion: boys smoked in public, girls came to school without wearing hats, the student paper published cartoons that mocked social convention and propriety. In contrast, as William Graebner has shown, the student secret societies, cliques, and gangs that formed in inner-city working-class high schools developed rituals and codes of conduct that posed a serious challenge to school officials' authority.

Moreover, American adolescents continued to patronize the expanding world of consumer fashions and cheap amusements. They socialized in amusement parks, dance halls, and movie theaters, and tested the moral boundaries of their communities by smoking and drinking, wearing cosmetics and sophisticated clothing, and engaging in open heterosexual flirtation. Initially, immigrant working-class youths were far more engrossed in such activities than were adolescents from the white middle class, but by the 1910s white community leaders began to note the early signs of a sexual revolution among their own sons and daughters.

Just as early-twentieth-century adolescence was characterized by growing tension between dependency and autonomy, so adolescents felt the pressure of forces that both unified and divided them. Psychologists, settlement workers, and youth workers laid emphasis on the universal patterns in adolescents' emotional, psychological, and sexual development, and high schools brought adolescents of varied backgrounds into a common social and educational environment. In addition, the fashion and entertainment industries shaped the tastes and aspirations of adolescents whether they were rich or poor, black or white, immigrant or native-born. Nonetheless, adolescents' experience continued to be determined by race, class, gender, and ethnicity.

Expected to become the next generation's high-status professionals and community leaders, white middle-class boys took high school course work that prepared them for a business career or college study. The YWCA and the Boy Scouts encouraged these privileged young men to cultivate character and "go-ahead masculinity." By contrast, adolescent girls and boys from working-class, im-

Beginning in the 1950s, dance clubs increasingly responded to adolescent patrons' demands for rock and roll music, which had deep roots in both African American and working-class cultures.

PAGE 290

See also
Radio

*Rock and roll
taught adolescents
how to dance,
how to talk,
how to dress,
and how to date.*

PAGE 399

migrant, and nonwhite homes were commonly viewed by teachers and reformers as inferior students and potential delinquents or dependents. The public high schools generally steered these youngsters into vocational rather than academic courses, training them for "respectable" but low-ranking positions in the industrial, clerical, or domestic sectors.

Similarly, inner-city youth organizations focused on delinquency prevention, emphasizing social control rather than youthful creativity or ingenuity. And, unlike their middle-class counterparts, adolescents from working-class and immigrant districts faced the real possibility of legal sanctions for offending the moral sensibilities of parents, teachers, police officers, and community social workers. Adolescent girls were vulnerable to arrest and institutionalization for incorrigibility, promiscuity, and prostitution; boys were vulnerable to arrest for minor property damage or petty theft.

White middle-class young women's experience of adolescence reflected both the privileged ambitions of their class and race and the disadvantages of their gender. During the late nineteenth century, white middle-class girls fought for access to higher education, struggling against social and scientific critics who denied their capacity to withstand the rigors of college education and condemned their aspirations for an intellectual or professional life. Many young women who completed college experienced a crisis afterward as parents tried to engineer their reimmersion in domestic life and the elite professions barred them entry or advancement. By the first two decades of the twentieth century, the debate over higher education for women was dying down, but adolescent girls faced a new crisis about their identity and behavior: educators and psychiatrists fretted about the latent lesbianism in young women's friendships with one another, and they suggested that career ambitions might be further evidence of psychosexual perversion or deviance.

Modern America

During the 1920s, middle-class adults watched in astonishment as their sons and daughters threw off the shackles of Victorian sexual control en masse, flaunting heterosexual desire and defying the moral authority of their elders. Astonishment quickly hardened into opinion voiced in the pages of newspapers, popular journals, and advice books. "Progressives" applauded modern youths' vitality and rejection of "false standards," while "traditionalists" argued that the youth rebellion

must be put down before it destroyed the social order.

Historians agree that changes in the middle-class family lay at the heart of adolescents' unconventional conduct. The middle-class family defined itself increasingly as a "companionate" rather than as a hierarchical unit. Husband and wife embraced an ideal of mutuality and sexual fulfillment in their relations with one another. Similarly, parents put new emphasis on the happiness and emotional security of their offspring; they willingly funded adolescents' prolonged economic dependence but withdrew from directing youths' educational performance or vocational choices. Instead, parents left these matters to the high schools and colleges and focused on cultivating affectional bonds with their children—not realizing, perhaps, that they would have to compete with the bonds their offspring formed with each other.

Modern parents did not expect strict obedience from their adolescents. Still, they wanted to guide their sons' and daughters' social development and were unprepared for the youth rebellion of the 1920s, a rebellion that grew out of adolescents' unique degree of segregation from their parents and other adults. Schools and the new youth-oriented sector of the consumer market heightened adolescents' sense of separation from the adult world; students turned their backs on adults, celebrating the sensuality, the idealism, the style, and the daring of their peers. At the same time, prolonged residential and economic dependence on parents and long years of schooling sharpened adolescents' sense of indeterminacy, promoting anxiety about social and sexual identity and a keen desire for adult status.

Experts in family social work and psychology attempted to convince middle-class parents that America's "flaming youth" were less rebellious than they imagined. Indeed, historians have noted that adolescents' subculture, although resistant to adult rule, effectively socialized youths for modern adulthood. Peer groups enforced gender-appropriate behavior, heterosexuality, competitiveness, conformity to organizational demands, and consumerism. Their dating system recognized female sexuality and permitted necking and petting, but it established marriage rather than promiscuity as youth's goal. Far from upsetting the conventional inequality of the sexes, the dating system accentuated the social and economic prerogatives of men and the subordination of women.

Of course, not all adolescents participated equally in the youth culture of the 1920s. Working-class adolescents were active in urban youth sub-

See also
Childhood and Children

cultures at school and on neighborhood streets, but they lacked the clothes, cars, and cash required for full participation in the dating system. Small-town and rural adolescents participated in school-based subcultures, but they had little access to commercial amusements and were subject to closer community surveillance than were their urban counterparts. Black youths from middle-class and upwardly striving families were held to strict moral codes by parents who wanted to differentiate their offspring from those of the impoverished masses.

Despite adolescents' varying degrees of participation in youthful rebellion, the 1920s witnessed the emergence of a mass youth culture. Adolescents proclaimed a loyalty to values and a social identity all their own. Within their peer groups, adolescents offered each other protection from adult expectations; at the same time, as a mass youth culture took shape, generational conflict became an institutionalized and prominent feature of modern American culture.

The Great Depression temporarily interrupted American anxieties about youth. It placed severe financial constraints on middle-class families, and adolescents were denied the clothing, cars, and money for entertainment that made their distinctive life-style possible. The dating system continued, but on a straitened budget, and adolescent

dependency deepened in both middle- and working-class homes. Adolescents stayed in school longer, lived at home without employment after leaving high school, and postponed marriage.

World War II abruptly ended America's protracted encounter with the Great Depression, promoting a decisive increase in adolescents' autonomy and new freedom from economic constraints. Millions of young men left their parents' homes and joined the armed services; young women migrated to cities and found employment, lodging, and opportunities for socializing with their peers.

Middle-class parents believed that the practice of "going steady" would lead to premarital intercourse and to hasty marriages. More important, parents, members of Congress, and the U.S. Children's Bureau worried that a peer culture spread by comic books, television, radio, and the movies obstructed generational communication, promoting "lower-class" tastes, delinquency, and a disregard for family values. Just as the cold warriors of the 1950s tested the loyalty of government officials, so parents, politicians, and educators tested youths' loyalty to the values of white middle-class America. In both cases, the investigators declared themselves unhappy with their findings, having discovered substantial evidence of subversion and rebellion.

Widespread political and cultural activism drew its support and momentum from the baby boom generation; indeed, the countercultural revolution of the 1960s was in large part an adolescent rebellion more profound than any that had preceded it. Adolescents of the 1960s were determined to engineer (and often to delay) their own transition to adulthood. College students called themselves an oppressed group; they rejected as false their parents' and teachers' loyalty to a society that accepted the cold war but refused to acknowledge persistent inequalities of race, class, and age. Black and white adolescents proclaimed themselves committed to a new vision of peace, prosperity, and equality; by the end of the decade, many young people added tolerance for sexual diversity and gender equality to their list of revolutionary goals.

Rebellious adolescents encountered adversity and opposition in a variety of forms. The mass consumer market distracted them from political activism even as it helped to solidify their counter-cultural identity and supplied them with distinctive music, clothing, movies, and drugs. More significant, a conservative backlash developed, proclaiming itself loyal to traditional forms

I am sick and tired of eighteen-year-olds being coerced into bearing the burden of the failures of politicians to face the tough economic choices needed to end our dependency on foreign oil.

MARK O. HATFIELD
U.S. SENATOR (D-ORE.), 1974

ADOLESCENT MORALITY
A Casualty of War

World War II encouraged casual heterosexual experimentation among adolescents. Attracted to men in uniform and feeling a sense of high adventure, many adolescent girls engaged in promiscuous sex with GIs. Equally important, by drawing large numbers of young men and women into sex-segregated, nonfamilial environments, the war promoted the development of a distinct gay identity and gay subculture.

The sharp breakdown of community and familial controls during the war led to growing anxiety about adolescent immorality and delinquency. These sentiments intensified during the postwar era even as adolescents from both middle- and working-class homes demonstrated their adherence to the 1950s ideal of domesticity by endorsing steady dates and early marriage.

*Jazz is the only
music in which the
same note can be
played night after
night but differently
each time.*

ORNETTE COLEMAN

See also
Popular Music before 1950

of parental rule and opposed to government programs designed to redistribute opportunity, power, or wealth. Furthermore, by the late 1960s and early 1970s young people were splintered and distrustful of each other. They wanted to solve problems that defied easy resolution; their organizations were wracked by internal divisions and weakened by government infiltration. The rebellion of the 1960s injected new racial, sexual, familial, and gender values into American life, but it also provoked bitter opposition. Adolescents in the 1970s, 1980s, and 1990s have lived with the consequences of both of these developments.

Looking Ahead

In researching the years from 1920 through the 1960s, historians have amassed evidence of modern adolescents' distinctive agency, that is, their ability to be self-directing. Denied full independence, adolescents nonetheless acted as innovators. Taking advantage of their protected status and exclusion from adult responsibilities, they engineered the transition to adulthood on terms that were largely of their own choosing. But historians have only begun to study the meaning of adolescence from the 1970s to the early 1990s; their assessment of adolescents' agency may require modification as they analyze the impact of a declining capitalist economy on youths of all races from both middle-class and working-class homes. Our understanding of adolescents' identity and autonomy may also change as scholars investigate how adolescents have been affected both by feminist changes in the family and by rising resistance to a nontraditional gender system.

Young adolescents in the late twentieth century are still segregated from adults, and they continue to socialize within self-conscious semiautonomous subcultures. Undoubtedly many middle-class adolescents continue to demonstrate significant self-direction in making the transition to adulthood. However, high rates of divorce, a weak economy, and a faltering social welfare system have surely increased adolescents' exposure to adult worries and responsibilities, affecting their perceptions and options. Similarly, state efforts to restrict adolescents' access to abortion may have significantly eroded young girls' ability to postpone the obligations of parenthood. Finally, adolescents' increasing vulnerability to poverty, drugs, AIDS, and suicide, and their growing involvement in gangs and violent crime, point to growing indeterminacy and despair, declining idealism and hope. As historians study adolescence in the last decade of the twentieth century, they may need to take into account the mounting burdens of this life stage, the growing evidence of violence, distress, and chaos in youthful lives.

—RUTH M. ALEXANDER

AFRICAN AMERICAN MUSIC

The most popular and influential music in the late twentieth century is African American music. This music, which reflects the continuing creative vitality of a deep-rooted tradition, derives its dynamism from its African roots and illustrates both the persistence of fundamental African musical beliefs and practices and their ongoing transformation in the New World African diaspora. In colonial North America and later in the United States, particularly from the nineteenth century on, these patterns of persistence and of transformation have spawned a variety of genres and offshoots.

The contemporary significance of African American music is evident in its tremendous worldwide appeal and influence. Its historical significance encompasses the window it provides into the hearts and minds of African Americans; the focus here is the insight it offers into the historical development of distinctive forms of African American culture. The history of African American music has reflected, especially in the twentieth century, the tension between revitalization and assimilation as well as that between communalism and individualism. In each case, over time, the tension has become more, rather than less, complex. This situation, in turn, has further complicated the meaning of African American music in how it might illuminate African American identity, vision, and struggle. African American music is a critical arena of ongoing creative expression and cultural struggle. In our time, this music remains an important marker of African American ethnic/racial and cultural distinctiveness, in spite of assimilation, commercialization, and a notable measure of African American success in the mainstream music business.

Recognition of the importance of African American music has grown dramatically in the twentieth century, notably after World War II. While the judgments of musicians, ethnomusicologists, and critics have helped enhance this recognition, the cultural politics unleashed by the growing black assertiveness of the civil rights and black power movements has been equally pivotal.

Not only did these movements deeply influence culture and music, but the music itself revealed its irreducibly social essence by seeking more openly and directly to influence the struggle.

Why is unraveling this interpenetration between culture and politics so vital to an understanding of African American musical history? First, the African American musical tradition is a central ingredient in the development of modern American culture and music. Second, the meanings and functions of African American music depend heavily upon historical context. Third, a major reason for the tremendous influence of this music has been its openness and adaptability, its ability to integrate outside influences. Finally, worldwide United States cultural dominance and the commercialization and appropriation of African American music have added to its influence.

This historical analysis of how, why, and to what effect African American music has become so dominant is principally a close look at its origins and development. Examining the period between 1619 and 1865, the first section of this article discusses the social origins and functions of the music. The emergence of a distinctive African American musical idiom is the key issue in this period. Following the Civil War and emancipation, African American music has become far more complex, with important innovations unfolding, sometimes at a rapid pace. The article's second section emphasizes the creation of new forms and approaches, the vital role of innovators, the dialogue between tradition and change, and the factors of secularization and commercialization.

The explanatory model followed here for African American music's popularity and significance builds upon several interrelated themes. Broadly speaking, the music's impact emerges from the creative tension deriving from the syncretism of the various musical traditions informing its development, notably the African roots. This syncretic process enhances the music's organic and affirmative qualities. More narrowly, the music's resonance grows out of its profound conceptual and philosophical bases, which go far deeper than issues of specific aspects of African, European, or New World music making that contribute to the construction of African American music.

In other words, the music is much more than the sum of its primary components. Its power is based on the persistence of a traditional African orientation toward music as an inseparable and pervasive component of a social and cultural whole. While transformed in complicated ways among African peoples throughout the African diaspora, this conceptual structure can be seen in the United States in at least three interwoven ideas: music as affective; music as reflective of a spiritual or sacred worldview; and music as a multidimensional experience necessarily embracing cultural forms such as dance and poetry and, on a more elaborate level, ritual and ceremony.

"How I Got Over": African American Music Before 1865

In 1619, when the first twenty Africans set foot on the soil at Jamestown, they entered a new cultural milieu. It was literally a new world where the two Old World cultures—African and European—underwent an ongoing process of change and adaptation as they interacted with one another and with the culture of Native Americans. Over time, the nature and degree of these patterns of cultural contact and change have had enormous consequences for all involved. For each group, the result has been a complicated cultural history in that part of colonial North America which eventually became the United States; more specifically, for Africans it has meant the elaboration of syncretic African American cultures with significant commonalities and differences.

The emergence of African American music signified an integral development within the broader matrix of African American culture. Approximately four hundred thousand Africans, largely from a variety of West African states and ethnic groups, were brought here as slaves between the seventeenth and early nineteenth centuries. As involuntary migrants, typically forbidden and unable to re-create their lost political and economic worlds, they relied heavily on refashioning former beliefs and practices to fit the exigencies of their slave lives. Notwithstanding important cultural differences in language, kinship arrangements, and religion among enslaved Africans, they had many cultural traits in common. In addition, the unifying character of shared experiences over time facilitated the creation of a distinct African American identity incorporating a sacred worldview, a cyclical view of time, and a communal social ethos. Further, these preliterate Africans came from oral cultures that placed great emphasis upon the verbal arts, including song and storytelling. This traditional emphasis was echoed in aspects of both the European and the Native American cultures with which newly arrived

White America's sudden discovery of black rhythm and blues music was the result of the movement of large numbers of blacks from the South to large urban areas in the North and West during and after World War II.

PAGE 399

♦ Syncretism

The fusion of two or more original different inflectional forms

Africans interacted, and reinforced the commonalities among the groups.

The dialectic between slavery and resistance broadly defined the situation of African Americans before 1865 and influenced the evolving culture, especially the music. Not a great deal of evidence about African American music in the seventeenth and eighteenth centuries has been uncovered. Enough exists, however, to document clearly the coexistence of traditional African music, European music and instruments played by Africans, and the evolving outlines of a distinctive African American music. Certain defining characteristics set African music, whether traditional or hybrid, apart from European music. Continental and diasporan African music featured a basic complexity structured around one or more of the following: (1) antiphony, or call-and-response (responsorial exchanges within the music itself and among musi-

cians, singers, and other participants in the music-making process); (2) cross rhythms and polyrhythms providing an intricate pattern of beats and meter; (3) a communal or group basis; (4) improvisation; (5) functionality; (6) an integral association with dance and body language or movement; and (7) an emotive, at times ecstatic, mood.

Whereas European music emphasized melody, African music emphasized rhythm. In terms of singing style, in the African tradition this quality contributed to a percussive, as opposed to a lyrical, feel: singing emphasized intensity, emotional immediacy, and accents such as shouting, slurring, offbeat phrasing, falsetto, guttural tones, and trills (vibratory effects). Hand clapping, heel stomping, thigh slapping, "patting juba" (an intricate and rhythmic alternation of hand clapping and thigh slapping), head bobbing, and body weaving exemplified this percussive style and the relationship between music and body motion. Likewise, percussion often dominated instrumental music.

The overwhelming preponderance of the information about early African music in the colonies comes from Europeans who typically neither understood nor appreciated what they heard. Some did, however, recognize something extraordinary about slave music. Much of this music making, though, took place among the slaves themselves when whites were absent or few in number. In this context, slaves were far more comfortable and appeared to favor the traditional in music making. Even on those occasions when whites and blacks made music together, descriptions by whites make it clear that in important ways Africans and Europeans came from different cultures. Nonetheless, this situation did not seem to prevent Africans from musical expression in traditional modes.

While often ethnocentric, the white accounts are revealing. Variously described by many whites as uncivilized, uncouth, disgusting, sinful, and unharmonious, African American music clearly hit a nerve, epitomizing for innumerable whites an in-

ferior people lacking culture—defined as Western and European. Even among those like Thomas Jefferson, who thought that blacks were musically gifted or that certain features of African American music were estimable, racist attitudes toward African Americans persisted.

Regardless of how whites viewed African American music in the early period, for blacks it represented a central feature of the cultural world they created to sustain themselves. Exactly how African American music originated is unclear. There is written evidence of slaves in the colonies singing in various African languages and in mixtures of African and European languages. Much of this singing struck many white observers as unintelligible, ludicrous, or noise at best. Nevertheless, this melding of musical influences undergirded the transculturation process and enhanced the development of a shared musical idiom. Furthermore, early on instruments such as the drum, played in similar ways, functioned as a kind of common language or, more precisely, a common grammar. As musicians from diverse backgrounds played together, they simultaneously enhanced

A VARIETY OF INSTRUMENTS
Drum Language

A primary manifestation of early African American music was the use of a variety of instruments of African, European, and shared origins. Early on, the drum was the basic instrument, but European Americans were afraid of its power and its potential for promoting slave unity. Many slave owners were explicitly concerned that the drums might be used to assist in slave insurrection, a fear derived in part from the general white fear of slaves congregating for diversion, where music making and dancing predominated. Throughout the late seventeenth and eighteenth centuries, numerous laws sought to end these assemblies and to ban drums and other loud instruments that might be employed to plot resistance. The banning of the drum was most successful wherever whites took seriously the challenge of slave control. For those areas with large numbers of slaves, especially where blacks outnumbered whites (for instance, the coastal lowlands of South Carolina and Georgia), this challenge assumed a special urgency. Only in Louisiana, apparently, did open drumming persist to a significant extent. Elsewhere suppression appeared to be effective. Drum banning sent the practice underground. It also accelerated both the use of other

percussion instruments—tambourines, sticks, and bones—and the intensified percussive use of other instruments, notably banjos and horns, as well as the body and the voice. It deflected without deterring the emphasis on rhythmic complexity.

Drums aside, the banjo was the most common African instrument in the New World. Other popular instruments included rattles, bells, pipes, iron gong-gongs, castanets, keyboards (thumb pianos), horns, and small flutes and clarinets. In light of their familiarity with a wide variety of instruments, it is not surprising that Africans quickly became proficient on the European instruments most often encountered: violins, horns, and flutes. Because of the fundamental adaptability of African music, the cross-cultural impact of shared instrumental traditions proved enriching. African Americans learned to play European classical and folk music quite well, performing in elite and popular settings. Slave masters typically placed a high value on good slave musicians who entertained the whites at their dances, balls, and impromptu social gatherings. Similarly, slave musicians played trumpets, fifes, and drums in militia bands. Here again the music was principally European, but often African influenced.

♦ Diaspora
*People settled far from their
ancestral homeland*

A

AFRICAN AMERICAN
MUSIC

*"How I Got Over":
African American Music
Before 1865*

*Don't play
what's there, play
what's not there.*

MILES DAVIS

the development of a common language and culture.

The concept of "drum language" or "talking drums" is common in African music, going far beyond the idea of drums as instruments to send signals and codes. Skillful players can achieve a sound that vividly captures the meaning of spoken language. Because many African languages tend to be tonal, linguistic meaning can be created and varied within a piece of drum music through the deft use of pitch and similar inflections. Such a drumming style plainly illustrates that the instrument was played melodically and rhythmically. This highly advanced drumming sensibility was evident throughout the African diaspora and served to unify disparate African peoples and cultures.

Still, the question of how the music developed persists. Several intriguing bits of evidence provide tantalizing clues. The innumerable and often harrowing sounds of captured Africans during the traumatic process of enslavement revealed what European and some African observers described as an eerie musical quality. Indeed, beyond those exclamations which might be called "songs," shrieks, groans, moans, screams, and phrases welled up out of a consciousness in which spirited vocalizing was part of the traditional musical vocabulary. The awful experience of enslavement gave this vocalizing and singing added meaning. These demonstrative modes, drawing upon deep cultural wellsprings, would persist in various New World transformations, such as field hollers and street cries.

Likewise, there is significant evidence that on board slave ships African music was not at all unusual. Many slave captains indulged in a practice, sometimes referred to as "dancing the slaves," in which the ship's human cargo was ordered to dance and play drums and other instruments. Obviously they did so in African ways. This custom reinforced shared and compelling elements among the diverse musical traditions. Those Africans who survived the dreadful "Middle Passage" from Africa to the New World (the journey from Africa to the West Indies, the second leg in the so-called Triangle Trade) continued to experience enormous, often disorienting, changes. The continuation of a traditional worldview emphasizing a holistic and sacred social ethos might ease the pain of adjustment. Music typically played an essential role in the adjustment process.

Africans brought to the New World as slaves revitalized the spirit and memory of African music. In the early nineteenth century, however,

when the formal prohibition against importing slaves into the United States took effect, this direct invigoration dwindled significantly. Even during the previous century, when the importation of African slaves reached its peak, the music and culture were becoming increasingly a blend of New World influences with Old World African sensibilities. As more and more African descendants were born into slavery, that blending proceeded more rapidly. With fewer Africans arriving to reinvigorate the original spark of the culture, African Americans increasingly relied on memory to recapture the spirit.

Musicians who garnered favor among whites by skillfully playing European music often achieved notable status among blacks as well. Those who were proficient in African American musical idioms frequently achieved a higher status among the slaves. Skill in both musical traditions greatly enhanced a slave musician's status. An interesting index of the value slave masters placed on slave musicians is that newspaper descriptions seeking runaway slaves often mentioned their musical talent.

The integral relation between African music and dance continued in the New World. Many experts see the continuities between Old World and New World dance as among the most pronounced examples of African influence on African American and American culture. African dance featured flexibility, spontaneity, rhythm, gliding and dragging steps, smooth movements, pelvic action, little if any body contact among dancers, and animal imitations. European dance, however, emphasized more formal postures and approaches. Even when Africans took up European dances like jigs, fandangos, and Virginia breakdowns, they often reworked them in African idioms.

Intimately interwoven, African music and dance literally conflate. This inseparability between sound and motion—music and dance—is evident from patting juba and work songs in the early period to the contemporary explosive performance style of soul music innovator James Brown. Indeed, the practice of music as a social performance builds upon the interwoven quality of music and dance. The ultimate incarnations of this practice are the various cultural events—rituals, ceremonies, and festivals—at which African Americans utilize the expressive arts to affirm a sense of identity and to celebrate life and death. Music is an indispensable element of these events.

There are fascinating and revealing examples throughout the colonial and early national periods

16

of African American holidays and celebrations that include music and dance. These reveal the fundamental affective, spiritual, and multidimensional aspects of the music. Even in New England, where the percentage of African Americans in the population typically registered in low single digits, African Americans came together and celebrated in ostensibly African-derived ways. Two noteworthy examples were Election Day and Pinkster Day.

Election Day was a special holiday on which blacks elected their own leaders as part of a grand celebration. Taking place roughly between 1750 and 1850 and in May or June, the event often lasted several days. The highlights were a parade featuring the slaves in their best attire, the formal elections, and the subsequent series of parties. Surviving descriptions make it clear that the best singers, dancers, and musicians put on a spectacular show as African Americans celebrated in a rousing African-inspired mode.

Similarly, Pinkster Day, or Pentecost Sunday, celebrations featured serious merrymaking highlighted by vigorous singing, drumming, and dancing. Typically described as saturnalian, with African music and dance, these events attracted large numbers of participants and onlookers. At times, festivities lasted as much as a week after Pentecost Sunday. These celebrations were officially forbidden, and declined in the early nineteenth century.

Similar examples abound from the South. In areas of eastern North Carolina, African Americans observed the John Canoe festival from the eighteenth century until around 1900. As in similar Caribbean and West African observances, it included a series of informal festivities and stylized celebrations with ritual significance held during the Christmas-New Year holiday season and featuring elaborate masks and costumes. Playing a variety of instruments, singing, and dancing, the celebrants in one part of the event went from house to house seeking gifts. When a household was not generous, the singers responded with satirical improvised verse.

In the exceptionally diverse milieu of New Orleans, African cultural traditions thrived. Creolization proceeded in this setting in countless and untold ways. Still, the Africanness of African American culture here was extraordinary. Blacks, for example, danced and made music—most notably they drummed—in very African styles well into the nineteenth century. Long before the Civil War, there had been a tradition among the slaves of Sunday dancing, accompanied by thunderous drumming, in what was called Place Congo (now Louis Armstrong Park). Not surprisingly, large crowds, flocked to participate and to observe these stirring performances, which went on for several hours. Similar events had been prohibited and suppressed in other areas of the South in the previous century; in 1834 authorities outlawed Sunday dancing among African Americans in Place Congo. Nevertheless, this and similarly strong traditions of rhythmic music and dance persisted in less public contexts and strongly influenced the cultural history of New Orleans.

Scholars often point to New Orleans as well as the South Carolina and Georgia Sea Islands as the two most striking sites of African influence on African American culture in the United States. Whereas cross-cultural contact and cultural intermixture helped to shape African American music in New Orleans, the relative isolation of the Sea Islands gave music there the most vividly African flavor of any variety of African American music in the United States. The African cultural aesthetic thrived in this overwhelmingly black area where whites meddled comparatively little in black community life. The distinctive and demonstrably African-derived culture of this group, commonly referred to as Gullah after its unique language, fascinated outsiders, black and white. While the sacred and secular music of this region struck early observers as uniquely African and non-Christian, much of what survives today in the records is religious music that draws upon nineteenth-century African American Christianity. Nineteenth-century white collectors of black music typically found this religious music more compatible with their own tastes and outlooks. African Americans, especially the slaves, were ever wary of white motives and tended both to feed the collectors what they wanted and to prefer to sing religious music for them.

Spirituals were common in the early nineteenth century and proliferated in the revivals, in church services, in less formal worship settings, and even in ostensibly secular contexts. Many religious events brought together whites and blacks in an intensely soul-searching experience, especially during the waves of nineteenth-century antebellum religious revivalism often termed the Second Great Awakening. It was during this period that a significant proportion of the slave population combined traditional African religious beliefs with Christianity to create a distinctive slave religion and a distinctive African American Christianity. Unlike the Christianity of free urban blacks, slave Christianity reflected a more clearly

See also
Theater and Musical Theater

African-inspired sensibility. After emancipation, this kind of difference would enhance the complexity of African American music.

The importance of the spirituals cannot be overstated. In many ways this music accurately captures the essence of traditional black culture, especially its sacred core, and vividly reflects its affective, spiritual, and multidimensional qualities. That spirituals represent the bulk of the surviving musical record from the nineteenth century strongly suggests that blacks have treasured them. The spirituals have survived so well also because they so pointedly symbolize the black freedom struggle and the black quest for self-definition. In the spirituals, as in other vital modes of cultural expression, communal values—notably unity—dominate.

Lyrically the spirituals draw heavily upon traditional psalms, hymns, and vivid biblical and moral imagery. African American spirituals, as distinguished from white spirituals, however, transformed the texts, reworking various elements in a communal act of improvisational revitalization. Evolving out of a spontaneous, emotional, often ecstatic process of group composition and musical re-creation, African American spirituals fervently display their Africanness: antiphony, rhythmic complexity, repeat phrasing, uninhibited

vocals, and bodily movements. Rather than functioning as written texts to be followed precisely, the spirituals emphasize the folk process in which the group aurally re-creates a text within a flexible narrative musical format. This textual openness was crucial for a people most of whom could neither read nor write, but for whom verbal artistry, social interaction, and religion were central.

The spirituals signify hope, confidence, and transcendence, even in the face of seemingly insurmountable obstacles. Through this sacred music and the ethos it gives meaning to, the slaves identified strongly with the Children of Israel and their travail as God's chosen people. Indeed they envisioned the Israelites' deliverance from slavery through God's handiwork as emblematic of their own impending liberation. Likewise, they personalized their relationship to God and heroic religious figures, often referring to them in fictive kin terms. These songs were similar to white spirituals in revealing ways, including common origins in standard Protestant hymns sung in churches and camp meetings attended by whites and blacks. Common themes encompassed community, the eternal bliss of the heavenly afterlife, and martial imagery. Even more revealing, however, are the striking differences, including the African spiritual and musical imprints, more vivid biblical imagery, and the compelling sense of identification with God's chosen people. The slave spirituals were clearly a unique music which spoke profoundly to the slaves' experiences and needs.

African Americans, slave and free, preferred to worship apart from whites. When whites demanded that slaves attend joint services run by whites, slaves went and may even have been moved. Nevertheless, there persisted a vibrant tradition of separate—often surreptitious—slave worship services in secluded praise houses. In these secret meetings of the "slave church"—as opposed to the master's church—the spirit could reign unchecked. Shouting, weeping, moaning, even spirit possession were not uncommon. In this setting, the spirituals flourished, as did the ring shout (a religious dance performed in a counterclockwise-moving circle with a shuffling gait, picking up in vigor as the spirit intensified). In continental and diasporan African contexts, this kind of dance was a primary part of important rituals and celebrations.

Similarly, funeral customs often featured African forms of ritual celebration. Unlike the somber rites typical of many European American burials, those of African American slaves were frequently joyous, possibly featuring song and

**TRANSCENDENCE
AND HOPE**

*Spirituals symbolize the black
freedom struggle and the black
quest for self-definition. They
signify hope, confidence, and
transcendence in the face of
seemingly insurmountable
obstacles.*
CORBIS / BETTMANN

AFRICAN AMERICAN SECULAR MUSIC

A Unifying Cultural Tradition

While relatively little antebellum African American secular music has been preserved, enough accounts exist to show that this music was far more extensive and significant than the slender written record suggests. Drawing upon an African cultural framework in which music and work were interwoven, the secular music tradition was, not surprisingly, revitalized in America. It especially helped to define the various social affairs dedicated to leisure and entertainment.

Work songs, including industrial, domestic, and field work songs, are a particularly prominent element in the extant evidence. Tunes often accompanied maritime jobs such as roustabout and stevedore, and were sung as blacks worked the inland and coastal waters. Black watermen not only developed distinctive kinds of music but also played a vital role, notably in the antebellum period, in the dissemination of regional varieties of African American music. One of the most important factors serving to integrate such differences in the twentieth century is growing geographic mobility; in the antebellum era, however, mobility was quite restricted, particularly for slaves. Nevertheless, similar work song patterns evolved.

Field hollers, whoops, or water calls, in addition to city street cries, constitute an important yet neglected vocal musical tradition. The former are rare in the antebellum literature. Clearly improvised, functional, and multipurpose, they could range from a commentary on loneliness, to a plea for help, to a rhythmic work accompaniment. This mode of expression—notable for its variety, flexibility, mundane essence, and improvisational flair—is basic to African American music. Similarly, the street cries were extemporaneous and wide-ranging, yet direct. Originating with itinerant laborers seeking jobs and vendors hawking goods, they also influenced the developing musical tradition.

Although over time the distinction between sacred and secular music became more important, in the traditional antebellum world evidence of interpenetration abounds: the sharing of phrases, texts, tunes, and structures; the use of sacred songs in secular contexts; and the African-inspired musical aesthetic suffusing both.

dance as well as libations, animal sacrifices, and grave decorations. Highlighting the cultural importance attached to the afterlife and the ancestors, these customs vividly reflected the slaves' sacred worldview and social holism. The music ranged from the mournful to the ecstatic, but the context emphasized a positive spirit.

A remarkably similar spirit characterized antebellum African American secular music. In fact, the traditional worldview of African slaves in a sense recognized the sacred and the secular as more singular than dual. This relatively undifferentiated boundary between sacred and secular in the traditional ethos became more differentiated after emancipation as the freed people grew more literate and educated. As modernity—notably individualism, secularism, and urbanization—increasingly challenged tradition in African American culture, the tension between the spiritual and the worldly intensified. Similarly, the number and percentage of Africans born in the United States grew and as cross-cultural exchanges expanded, creolization increased. Growing Christianization added another layer of complexity to African Americanization. Emancipation enabled free and freed African Americans to accelerate the process of bridging their cultural differences with other Americans. Nevertheless, within the folk culture, especially the music, important unifying commonalities persisted.

Clearly music has been a vital element in the complex of cultural strategies African Americans have devised to endure and to rise above the hardships they have confronted. Beyond its function as a coping or adaptive mechanism, music has served in many ways to witness and to promote protest, even insurrection. For example, the many references in the spirituals to the liberation of the Hebrews as God's chosen people spoke plainly yet powerfully to the liberation quests of both slave and free African Americans. That songs like "Steal Away to Jesus" and "Follow the Drinking Gourd" functioned as a means of communication among runaway slaves within the Underground Railroad is likewise instructive. That music inspired and united revolutionaries such as Nat Turner and his followers is provocative. (Turner, a slave preacher, led an uprising in Virginia in 1831.) From the standpoint of the history of African American music, however, the primary point is the centrality of music to the culture. African American music helped African Ameri-

See also
Nightlife

In this time of growing consciousness of race prejudice, African American performers and composers achieved success beyond the traditional realm of black American music.

PAGE 104

See also
Concert Music

cans make sense of their often difficult lives, offering a sense of autonomy within an oppressive and restricted world.

"Soul Deep": African American Music 1865 to the Present

Emancipation appeared to offer much to African Americans. The fragile euphoria of the Civil War, emancipation, and Reconstruction years (1861 to 1877), however, gave way to the institutionalization of Jim Crow (discrimination against African Americans sanctioned by law or tradition) throughout the South at the turn of the twentieth century. Dashed hopes and dreams became more common as peonage increasingly ensnared massive numbers of blacks, although a modest African American urban middle class developed, primarily providing goods and services for their segregated communities. Given the persistent social, political, and economic gulf separating blacks and whites, it is not surprising that black culture and black music retained their distinctiveness.

Freedom, notwithstanding its contradictions, represented expanded cultural and musical horizons for African Americans. The "invisible institution" of the slave church came above ground, functioning as a spiritual and musical hothouse. Similarly, secular music found more public spaces in which to develop. Antebellum holiday celebrations had included (besides those previously mentioned) Christmas, New Year's Day, and, in the North, West Indian Emancipation Day (begun in 1834). After emancipation in the United States, that event itself was often the focus of a major celebration, as in the Juneteenth commemoration among black Texans.

A constellation of forces complicated the development of black music in the late nineteenth and early twentieth centuries. First, secularization accelerated the tension between the spiritual and secular realms. Second, rising rates of literacy and formal education meant intensified interaction between the traditional oral and modern literate aspects of the culture. Third, urbanization, particularly in the twentieth century, augmented the culture's parameters and directions, with a heightening of the interpenetration between the rural and the urban. Fourth, a growing measure of class differentiation resulting from a degree of African American social mobility enhanced the creative tensions between the folk culture and black middle-class culture. Fifth, in spite of racism and segregation, ongoing creolization enhanced cross-cultural musical influence.

Another factor—the expanding commercialization of American culture and African American cultural productions since the late nineteenth century—has had tremendous consequences for African American music. With the seemingly ever-expanding marketing of the music throughout the twentieth century, its hybrid qualities have become increasingly significant. As African American musicians have sought to broaden the music's scope and audience, the African taproot has grown deeper in some ways, less potent in others. Cross-pollination has enriched American music greatly, even though many underestimate and misconstrue this fact for a variety of reasons, including racism, ethnocentrism, and cultural nationalism.

White racial privilege has warped the inevitable process of cross-cultural musical influence, making the white appropriation of black music especially lucrative. Countless whites have preferred other whites performing assimilated black music, at best, and gross caricatures of black music, at worst, to blacks performing black music. In the late twentieth century, moreover, musical genres and styles have blurred in some instances to the point where African American music itself is no longer the special preserve of African American artists. In a world of equality and freedom, this would be a positive achievement. In our own real world of racial exploitation, though, where black music fuels significant white corporate wealth and many white musical careers, the white appropriation of black music is problematic.

Two nineteenth-century developments in particular heralded the expanding cultural complexity wrought by the phenomenal growth of black music. To begin with, even in the slave South, African Americans had created an impressive body of music. In the post-emancipation world, drawing upon that rich musical vocabulary, African Americans fashioned new and, in many cases, equally impressive musical languages. The importance of a musical tradition deeply rooted in social life and cultural practice cannot be overestimated; it constituted the essential building blocks for subsequent musical innovation.

Second, the place of nineteenth-century black music in the period's racial politics played a key role in shaping the music's development. The exceedingly complex patterns of ambivalence and ambiguity distinguishing race relations between whites and blacks have been both cultural and social. These patterns have proceeded in often unanticipated, ironic, and multifaceted ways. White power and privilege have remained substantial, but so have black endurance and transcendence. As whites controlled the political and economic high ground, blacks controlled the moral and spiritual high ground. On one level, in terms of a national culture, this dynamic has favored white tastes, styles, and productions over black ones. On a deeper level, it has given African American culture a broad and compelling impact.

Blackface minstrelsy vividly exemplifies the complicated quality of race in the nineteenth century. Beginning around the 1830s and 1840s, it grew out of white efforts to mimic and make fun of blacks for entertainment and for profit; it became the most popular form of mass entertainment in the nineteenth century. Minstrel tunes were a music of caricature and flattery, of ambivalent and tangled white feelings about blacks and their music. The supreme irony, of course, came when blacks appropriated this idiom and reinterpreted it. While white minstrelsy gave countless whites a racist white interpretation of black culture, the effect of black minstrelsy—given the inherent limitations of the minstrel form—was often no more enlightening or sensitive. Black performers could neither alleviate nor overcome the deeply disturbing racial politics of minstrelsy. Despite its popularity, blackface minstrelsy did not represent a central musical tradition. The more important musical forms came directly out of authentic African American worldviews and communities.

Following the brief gestational period of the immediate post-emancipation years, a series of innovations occurred within African American music that led to the maturation of distinctive yet inextricably interwoven genres. This creative outburst would help to shape twentieth-century American music and the burgeoning twentieth-century worldwide market for popular music. Gospel, blues, jazz, and rhythm and blues are the primary and most influential genres. The fundamental similarities among them reflect a common cultural aesthetic whose bedrock sensibility remains African. Two thematic clusters dominate: discontent and alienation, on the one hand, and struggle and affirmation, on the other. The best of these twentieth-century forms and their offshoots brilliantly capture the affective, spiritual, and multidimensional qualities so vital to the culture.

While the spirituals remained popular with African Americans in the new century, many—notably upwardly mobile assimilationists—saw them as quaint and embarrassing relics of the past. Middle-class blacks, including aspirants and supporters, typically displayed defensiveness and

ambivalence about any aspects of the folk culture—like the spirituals—that might not throw what they saw as the best light on African Americans and their progress since slavery. Similarly, as the outside world increasingly intruded upon African American consciousness, the sacred worldview that had given meaning and direction to African American life slowly came under attack.

Gospel music—"good news" or jubilee music—arose in the late nineteenth century among whites as well as blacks as a revivalist and evangelical response to the perception of rising immorality. This music stressed the joy of Christian salvation in the here and now as well as the benefits of a sanctified lifestyle. It was not simply fixated on the glories of the heavenly afterlife, as so many of its critics assumed. Among African Americans, gospel took root most firmly in the Church of Christ, Holiness, Pentecostal, and Church of God in Christ faiths with their strict evangelicalism and fervent religiosity. An awesome emotional intensity deeply influenced the maturation of black gospel, which was far livelier than white gospel during the early period. Black gospel took literally the biblical injunction to serve God with a "joyful noise." As rural southern blacks migrated north, they carried their music, especially gospel, with them. The countless northern storefront churches steeped in the evangelical tradition, as well as Baptist and Methodist citadels, furthered the spread and development of gospel music, especially in the 1920s and 1930s. By 1930 it had sur-

GOSPEL GREAT

Recipient of the title "world's greatest gospel singer," Mahalia Jackson was the first gospel singer to be given a network radio show in 1954, on CBS.
UPI / CORBIS-BETTMANN

passed the spiritual as the major African American religious music. By 1950 it had entered what some have regarded as its golden era (roughly 1945 to 1960).

Gospel music flowered in a spontaneous and expressive context comparable with that which had often served as the seedbed for the spiritual. Growing out of a process of group improvisation often featuring antiphonal give-and-take between the group and leaders, gospel music also featured holy dancing and shouting reminiscent of the ring about, especially in the rural South. The truly sanctified spoke in tongues (glossolalia), achieved spirit possession, and during Communion washed feet (as an act of humility). This multilayered and participatory worship experience enhanced the fiery depth of gospel music. Like the spiritual, early gospel music was typically sung a cappella. Soon, however, instruments were incorporated, augmenting the music's visceral power. Tambourines, pianos, organs, and guitars were common by mid century. Drawing extensively from other forms, notably jazz and blues, gospel music had also quickly added other instruments, such as horns and drums.

Lyrically, gospel music initially drew heavily upon a common stock of religious songs. Pioneer composers like Charles Albert Tindley (1856–1933) reworked these often raw rural expressions into texts. Within the gospel tradition, however, the text remains a malleable framework to be recast in accordance with the demands of the Holy Spirit. Still, the growing popularity of gospel music beyond the more evangelical faiths to the dominant Baptist and Methodist churches depended heavily upon the efforts of composers and popularizers like Thomas A. Dorsey (b. 1899). Personifying the cross-pollination between secular and religious music, Dorsey initially wrote gospel and blues tunes. An accomplished musician, he first achieved notoriety in the blues field as "Georgia Tom," the pianist for Gertrude "Ma" Rainey, a blues-singing sensation in the 1920s. He also had a four-year partnership with blues singer Tampa Red during this period that led to the writing and recording of the highly successful tune "It's Tight Like That." Not until the early 1930s did he succeed in the gospel vein. In addition to penning the classic gospel number "Precious Lord, Take My Hand," he became an im-

GOSPEL PERFORMANCE
A Spiritual Transformation

Above all else, gospel is a performance-based, live, social music. Whether in the church or the concert hall, the gospel performer participates in a musical incantation aimed at praising the Lord and promoting spiritual ecstasy, typically highlighted by shouting, hand clapping, oral antiphony ("Sing it!"; "Amen!"; "Praise Jesus!"), humming, moaning, body weaving, foot tapping, and head bobbing. Vocal pyrotechnics—melisma (stretching words and syllables across several notes), full-throated and lyrical textures, scintillating runs among low and high notes, bending notes, and screams, cries, and whispers—are common. Ultimately, if the musical ritual works, audience and performer become one, exemplifying the communal consciousness basic to African American music and traditional African American religious worship styles.

The famous gospel extravaganzas of the 1950s and 1960s featured a variety of performers—male quartets, women's groups, soloists, choirs—each vying to outperform the others. Success was judged by how well one captured and elevated the spirit. From the dress—fancy robes, gowns, and suits—to the dramatic touches—marching and swaying

choirs, dropping to one's knees, shouting, intense facial expressions, stirring monologues and dialogues, and the like—the goal was to deliver a spine-tingling and memorable performance. "Church wrecking" or "house wrecking"—achieving an incandescent spiritual peak throughout the audience or congregation—solidified the reputations of performers like Mahalia Jackson, the Sensational Nightingales, the Dixie Hummingbirds, Bessie Griffin, and Professor Alex Bradford. Particularly effective at church wrecking were the singing preachers, practitioners of the chanted or "performed" sermon, such as the Reverend C. L. Franklin.

In a sense, gospel music is the modern spiritual. The distinctive spiritual genre evolved from a rural, folk, preliterate sensibility, with an Old Testament bias. Gospel, which began as a transitional music signifying post-emancipation hope and affirmation, evolved in a context of movement away from the folk sensibility of the spirituals toward a more urban and polished sensibility, with a New Testament bias. Still, the emotional depth unifying spirituals and gospel blurs their differences.

See also

The Plantation

portant publisher and the composer of over four hundred gospel songs, a gospel publicist, and, with Sallie Martin (a pioneering and influential gospel singer in her own right), a cofounder of the National [Black] Convention of Gospel Choirs and Choruses.

Gospel's growing popularity also derived from its variety of formats and formidable vocal talent. There were male quartets early in the century; by the 1930s their numbers were growing dramatically. Among the most notable organized prior to 1940 were the Dixie Hummingbirds, the Soul Stirrers, and the Swan Silvertones. During the 1940s, women's groups achieved prominence, notably the Sallie Martin Singers, the Ward Trio, and the Angelic Gospel Singers. Among the outstanding soloists was Sister Rosetta Tharpe, who mixed blues-based guitar and sanctified music to gain a national following by mid century. She excelled as a rousing performer, taking the music to Carnegie Hall, jazz venues, or wherever it led. In addition, her records, such as her bluesy interpretation of Dorsey's gospel tune "Rock Me," sold well.

The most influential soloist of this period was Mahalia Jackson. Artfully combining a variety of early influences—Baptist hymns, gospel songs, spirituals, blues, and jazz—she created a contralto style notable for its fire, dignity, and rare beauty. A charismatic performer, she had an electrifying vocal and performance style that captivated audiences worldwide and inspired generations of admirers and followers. Jackson's 1947 recording of "Move on up a Little Higher" sold over a million copies—the first gospel million seller. In 1950 the National [Black] Baptist Convention selected her its official soloist. She was indeed the "Queen of Gospel." Her rising recognition among whites enabled her to achieve unparalleled fame for a gospel singer, including a recording contract with Columbia Records and appearances on television talk and variety shows.

Disagreement persists between those favoring a more or less rigid distinction between sacred and secular African American music. While the very strong disapproval within the gospel community of what was often called "the devil's music" has softened a bit with time, it continues to this day in many quarters. For many the problem is simple: the boundary between spiritual and secular pleasure has to be both maintained and solidified. In reality, however, this boundary blurs and proves permeable: musicians consciously and unconsciously cross it, often with provocative results. Sister Rosetta Tharpe's 1939 recording of Dorsey's

gospel number "Rock Me," for example, featured Lucky Millinder's blues band in the background and became a pop smash. Many found this objectionable. Nevertheless, a measure of gospel's vitality, like that of other genres, flows from an openness to borrowing outside elements and reshaping them along gospel lines.

Many have characterized the blues in particular as secular spirituals. In fact, many secular music artists, blues musicians included, began their musical immersion in the church. Much of the cross-referencing and cross-fertilization between the sacred and the secular, then, has strong religious roots. Ultimately, their mutual dependency has led to a fascinating paradox. This bond has both reinforced and blurred the distinction between them.

The blues vividly exemplifies this paradox. Indeed, compared with gospel artists, secular artists have appeared far less anxious about this issue, especially over time. Having been musically nourished in a tradition with a broad reservoir of forms and elements visible in both sacred and secular music, countless blues and jazz musicians have reveled in the resulting artistic possibilities. Many have consciously drawn upon the sacred musical grammar and vocabulary, included sacred music in their repertoire, and performed and recorded religious tunes. This same creative eclecticism has enriched later developments, notably 1960s soul music and post-1960s "progressive gospel."

Even more than those of gospel, the origins of the blues are hard to pinpoint. They clearly date at least as far back as the post-emancipation world of the late nineteenth century. The primary sources for this music are amazingly diverse. On the secular front, they include work songs, field hollers, urban cries, ballads, minstrel songs, ragtime tunes, and maritime music. Spirituals and revival hymns were the most influential religious music sources. Inspired, like gospel, by freedom and spatial mobility, the blues began as folk music. Throughout its history, it has maintained folk roots and forms even as many observers have lamented what they have interpreted as a decline in the blues as a folk music.

As a distinctive musical genre, the blues emerged as a personalized expression of the day-to-day experiences of ordinary folk. While still intimately wedded to a social ethos, the perspective is typically that of the self. Exploring the range of human emotions and feelings, the blues can be didactic, but above all else, they are a celebration of the human spirit: entertainment or "good time" music. The common mistake of confusing the

A jazz musician is a juggler who uses harmonies instead of oranges.

BENNY GREEN

Jazz came to America 300 years ago in chains.

PAUL WHITEMAN

popular definition of the word "blue(s)" as sad and mournful with the musical genre of the blues has thus been unfortunate and misleading. Although there are sad and mournful blues, they constitute only a slice of an emotionally rich pie. The blues run the emotional gamut from high to low, sometimes incorporating both in a single tune. This candid baring of the soul underscores the music's intrinsic realism and honesty.

Preeminently an aural and performance-based music, the blues evolved early on as improvisations building upon a common pool of lyrics and phrases. Improvisation took place largely as variations on a fundamental base: a twelve-bar form with a three-line verse and rhyming words. This flexible structure has yielded countless permutations. There are melodic and percussive styles. Essentially vocal music, the blues cull from the panoply of techniques typical of African American folk vocalizing, including moans, shrieks, cries, grunts, bends, slides, and dips; various textures and shadings, like vibrato and falsetto; and, most distinctive in the blues, falling pitches to express emotion. Early blues musicians favored a wide variety of accompanying instruments. While the guitar emerged as the favorite, the list encompassed the banjo, fiddle, piano, harmonica, washboard, jug, and kazoo.

The blues incubated in a variety of contexts: front porches, street corners, parties, juke joints, medicine shows, tent shows, vaudeville shows, clubs, taverns, red-light districts, and steamboats. Throughout southern and border states, in rural and urban areas, in places public and private, the blues gained players and supporters, as this singular yet diverse music came to speak so clearly and deeply to its hearers. The sundry themes—ranging from love to anger, from problem naming to problem solving, from accommodation to resistance—are universal. Several observers have cogently argued that feel and nuance are more important than lyrical integrity. A moving evocation of a mood, a place, an emotion—this is the stuff of the blues.

Given the diverse origins and wide—primarily southern—territorial domain of the blues, the early emergence of unique blues styles and varieties is not surprising. Most blues experts recognize three major types: down-home, rural, or country blues; classic blues of the 1920s, principally a black woman's genre; and urban blues. In the late 1920s and early 1930s, the most influential of the early down-home blues singers was "Blind" Lemon Jefferson out of Texas. His high voice and spare tone typified Texas blues. The most important regional variety of the down-home blues, however, came from the Mississippi Delta. Here a gritty approach prevailed, distinguished by a heavy rasping vocal quality, although there were high-voiced singers as well. Charley Patton, Eddie "Son" House, and Tommy Johnson epitomized this earthy style.

The most influential Mississippi Delta bluesman of this period, however, came on the scene a little later and met a violent death in 1938. Many argue that Robert Johnson, of "Terraplane Blues" and "Hellhound on My Trail" fame, was the greatest bluesman not only of his generation but in the music's recorded history. Legend and his superb yet limited recorded output reveal a compelling vocal and guitar talent whose disciples have included Muddy Waters and Elmore James. During his rediscovery in the 1960s, Johnson influenced many, including black folk singer Taj Mahal and white rock performers such as the Rolling Stones, and guitarist and vocalist Eric Clapton. His vocal and instrumental technique reflected a variety of influences transformed into a mesmerizing style. A self-assured player, he used falsetto howls, dramatic vocals, rapid bottleneck runs on the guitar, strong beat, lyrical detail, and aggressive delivery to create a gripping, if small, body of work. He skillfully presented powerhouse down-home blues while anticipating the urban, modern music still in the making.

In part, the impact of Johnson and other blues legends owes much to the tremendous growth of the "race records" market aimed at African American consumers. The extraordinary success of Mamie Smith's 1920 recording of "Crazy Blues" greatly advanced the commercialization of black music. The profits and wealth from this development, however, remained largely in the hands of white-owned record companies. Not until the postwar period, with the establishment of major black-owned record companies like Vee-Jay, Motown, and Philadelphia International, did this imbalance begin to shift measurably. Nevertheless, in the 1920s, records quickly outpaced traveling productions such as vaudeville shows as the principal method for the music's dissemination among blacks. Furthermore, records were far more important in this regard than published blues sheet music, like that of W. C. Handy. In addition, records gradually increased the popularity, among whites as well as blacks, of other kinds of African American music.

A significant result of the scramble among white-owned record companies to get into the race records market was the recording of a number of blues divas. The two most important were the "Mother of the Blues," "Ma" Rainey, and the "Empress of the Blues," Bessie Smith. While both got their start within the minstrel-vaudeville context, both soon emerged as overpowering solo artists in their own right. "Ma" Rainey's vocals tended in the folk direction, while Smith's went toward jazz. Smith rapidly became a huge success, eclipsing Rainey, whose records did not do justice to her strong and expressive voice. Smith's ability to combine blues intensity with jazz phrasing enabled her to handle jazz and blues material equally well. Among her stellar recorded performances are a 1925 duet with Louis Armstrong of "You've Been a Good Old Wagon" and her 1927 effort, "Back Water Blues." The proud and assertive posture of Smith and Rainey was an important contribution in the ongoing struggle of black women to speak for themselves from their own cultural world.

The blues necessarily encompassed much musical territory. This terrain incorporated early jug, string, and washboard bands; professional bands like Lucky Millinder's; and piano blues, most notably the irrepressible boogie-woogie with its firm left-hand rhythms and agile right-hand melodic and rhythmic lines. As with gospel, however, the end of the Great Depression, the entrance of the United States into World War II, and the growing militancy of the continuing black liberation struggle from the 1940s on, dramatically altered the blues. For one thing, urban blues became increasingly distinctive, with Chicago leading the way. Figures like blues harmonica pioneer John Lee "Sonny Boy" Williamson and the popular blues guitarist Big Bill Broonzy personified this trend.

The migration of hundreds of thousands of blacks out of the South during World War I, seeking jobs in northern cities like New York and Chicago, profoundly influenced African American culture and music. Similarly, during World War II blacks migrated in search of wartime jobs with corresponding cultural and musical results. This time hundreds of thousands headed west as well as north. Consequently, since 1945 African American music has witnessed a series of very rapid developments. Nowhere is this more evident than in jazz.

Like gospel and blues, jazz has a complicated and most likely irrecoverable prerecording history. Its origins go back at least to various kinds of music played around the turn of the century, including blues, brass band music, dance orchestra music, syncopated dance music, and ragtime. A unique piano music style in its own right, ragtime

was not an early jazz form. Rather, it—like other related but autonomous styles—contributed to jazz's early evolution. With its infectious steady left-hand beat and syncopated right-hand melody, ragtime spawned several important composers, most notably Scott Joplin, whose "Maple Leaf Rag" sold over a million copies in 1899 alone. Associated in the public mind at the time with the cakewalk, a turn-of-the-century dance craze based on moves first observed among slaves and popularized by minstrels, ragtime was a composed rather than improvised music. As such, while it led in directions that had influence in jazz, notably the stride piano style (so called because of the "striding" left hand that alternated between a chord on the off beat and a single note on the on beat) of Eubie Blake and James P. Johnson (also known as Harlem stride), it is best seen as a limited but distinctive form which served in addition as a tributary in jazz's early history.

Consistent with its diverse sources, jazz took root and flourished in various environments, especially that great musical polyglot New Orleans. The music sprouted in places throughout the urban South and Midwest—particularly Chicago, Memphis, and Kansas City—as well as New York City and points on the West Coast. Still, out of New Orleans came the acknowledged initial masters: the elusive cornetist Charles "Buddy" Bolden; Jelly Roll Morton, the first great jazz composer; and Louis Armstrong, the first great innovative soloist.

Not enough reliable information on Bolden remains to verify his turn-of-the-century reputation, but Morton left a solid recording legacy, notably his work with the Red Hot Peppers band (1926) and his fifty-two-record set made at the Library of Congress (1938). While considerable controversy has whirled around his flamboyant lifestyle, personality, and musical claims, his considerable jazz achievements have been well documented. First, his music is a unique and coherent blend of a variety of elements—blues, ragtime, and brass band music, with operatic touches. In fact, he effectively combined the heavily European-influenced music of the French Creoles of color with the more African-based music of the darker-complexioned uptown African American community. This he accomplished notwithstanding his own prejudice against African Americans darker than himself. Second, he convincingly met one of the central challenges of jazz: the integration of improvisation and composition. Third, his work demonstrates complexity on numerous levels, such as his successful negotiation of another

The basic difference between classical music and jazz is that in the former the music is always graver than the performance— whereas the way jazz is performed is always more important than what is being played.

ANDRE PREVIN

See also

Folk Song and Folk Music

major jazz challenge: blending solo and ensemble into a coherent whole. His musical legacy lives on through the numerous important works he contributed to the jazz repertoire, including "Black Bottom Stomp," "Smoke House Blues," and "King Porter Stomp."

Growing up poor and surrounded by music in his native New Orleans, Louis Armstrong (1900–1971) sang for small change alongside other children on the streets. After picking up the trumpet in 1914 during a stay at the (Colored) Waifs Home for Boys, he began a period of rapid musical study and growth. By the time he electrified the burgeoning jazz scene in Chicago and New York in the 1920s, he had imbibed a great deal from the extraordinary musical scene in New Orleans, especially from the honky-tonks of the notorious Storyville red-light district. Drawing upon a great trumpet tradition which included Buddy Bolden, Bunk Johnson, and King Oliver (an important early mentor as well), he soon developed his own unique style. Armstrong's greatness as a trumpeter resided in a complex of factors: superb technique (especially his marvelous tonal range), his innovative brilliance, bluesy passion, keen musical logic, and unparalleled ability to swing. And most of all, he was a wonderful entertainer. His musical contributions, as a result, are numerous and significant. Two of the most striking were his melodic creativity and his rhythmic artistry. Indeed those were crucial to his mastery of the swing aesthetic. The latter is notoriously difficult to explain, but it revolves around exploration of the myriad subtleties of rhythm. Much of subsequent jazz history has been deeply influenced by his melodic paraphrasing and his uncanny sense of swing. While his recording, performance, and show business careers stretched into the 1960s, he created his most innovative and influential work in the late 1920s and early 1930s. These pieces include "Potato Head Blues" (1927), "West End Blues" (1928), and "Weather Bird" (1928). Armstrong is widely acknowledged to have been one of the greatest musicians of this century.

Edward Kennedy "Duke" Ellington (1899–1974) grew up in middle-class surroundings in his native Washington, D.C., and by his high school years had demonstrated considerable artistic and musical talent. After leading several local bands as a teenager, in the 1920s he relocated in New York City where he honed his piano and band-leading skills, absorbing the rich influences of some of Harlem's most notable composers, arrangers, and musicians. A 1927 engagement at the Cotton Club launched him and his band on an extraordinary career. Ellington set the inventive standard for orchestra or big band jazz in much the same way that Armstrong did for solo jazz. There had been several notable bands prior to Ellington's, including King Oliver's Creole Jazz Band and Fletcher Henderson and His Orchestra. Both featured Armstrong for periods in the early to mid 1920s. Henderson and his early arranger Don Redman had pioneered the standard big band format, deftly mixing written parts, improvised solos, and call-and-response exchanges between sections of the orchestra. Ellington's greatness grew out of his innovative exploration of the central challenges in ensemble jazz that Morton negotiated so well. Going far beyond Morton, Fletcher Henderson, and his contemporaries, Ellington resolved the problems of integrating improvisation with composition, on the one hand, and the soloist with the band, on the other, through various creative blends and juxtapositions. These combinations relied heavily upon collaboration with first-rate band members, building upon their individual talents. This careful attention to the band's sonorous reservoir enabled Ellington to compose music with extraordinary harmonic range and beauty, and equally extraordinary color and texture. A prolific and talented composer and an indefatigable performer, Ellington (and his orchestra) contributed enormously to the popularity of 1930s big band jazz or swing jazz.

THE DUKE

A prolific and talented composer and performer, Duke Ellington and his orchestra contributed enormously to the popularity of big band jazz or swing jazz. UNDERWOOD & UNDERWOOD/ CORBIS-BETTMANN

Another aspect of Ellington's achievement was his ability to combine vernacular and elite forms and sensibilities. This is clear from his astounding body of around fifteen hundred works encompassing popular tunes like "Sophisticated Lady," "Satin Doll," and "Mood Indigo"; jazz orchestra works like "Harlem Airshaft" and "Ko-ko"; extended concert pieces like "Suite Thursday"; and operas, film scores, and ballets. Ellington was truly a creative giant and possibly the greatest composer America has ever produced.

Ellington's amazing achievements cannot diminish the outstanding contributions of many contemporary artists. Among the other great bands of the period, Count Basie's, coming out of Kansas City, merits special mention for bringing together the best of the midwestern variants of blues, boogie-woogie, and dance music. More squarely in the Henderson big band mold, Basie's aggregation distinguished itself with its exceptional swing capability, its bluesy boldness, and its strong solo tradition, personified by the legendary work of tenor saxophonist Lester Young. The preeminent jazz vocalist of the 1930s was Billie Holiday, whose work spanned the 1930s, 1940s, and 1950s. Typically surrounded by superb supporting musicians like Young, she excelled at creating and sustaining an intense musical moment, much like her acknowledged musical influences, Bessie Smith and Louis Armstrong. Her vocal artistry has been lavishly praised and she has influenced many, notably Sarah Vaughn and Dinah Washington. Particularly noteworthy were her melodic and rhythmic inventiveness, her ability to personalize a song, and her arresting emotional poignancy.

The 1920s and 1930s witnessed tremendous strides in jazz even as African American musicians and their efforts, like African Americans generally, remained subject to prejudice and discrimination. Jazz, in fact, initially often met serious opposition from some middle-class blacks who, like many whites, labeled the music sensual and barbaric. Even within the Harlem Renaissance (largely a literary and visual arts movement) of the 1920s, few realized the importance and potential of jazz. Nevertheless, the swing music craze of the 1930s greatly enhanced jazz's popularity. With whites, bands like Paul Whiteman's and Benny Goodman's were critical to this popular acclaim. Even black artists like Armstrong and Ellington found a growing measure of support among whites. Radio broadcasts, dances, concerts, and the overall development of the entertainment media in which jazz played a role—as well as jazz records—helped to expand the music's popularity. Depression America found a measure of release and joy in jazz.

The war years witnessed trends, most notably the intensifying black civil rights and black power struggles, that would seriously influence African American music. The rapidly growing black liberation struggle enhanced the move toward greater freedom of expression and experimentation throughout African American culture, especially within its music. This setting also fed the rise in black-owned music businesses, most notably record companies like Motown and Philadelphia International, aimed primarily at bringing black music to a larger audience. These efforts greatly expanded the impact of blacks throughout the music industry at all levels, from artists to executives, by skillfully exploiting the popularity and clout of African American music. Projecting themselves as both successful ethnic/race enterprises and authentic creators and purveyors of the music, these companies have reaped great success. In turn, the major white-owned record companies have effectively redoubled their efforts to dominate the market in African American music. The effects of this freedom, growth, and competition on the music can be traced in developments in the music, especially jazz and blues, since around 1945.

Gospel began to change most noticeably after the late 1960s when artists like the Hawkinses—Edwin, Walter, and Tramaine—and Andrae Crouch began to draw more confidently and openly upon secular music. This conscious and well-conceived blending of gospel and secular music is often referred to as "progressive" gospel, to distinguish it from traditional gospel. In the late 1980s one of the most popular gospel groups was Take 6, with its a cappella renditions steeped in jazz and gospel. Such cross-fertilization has revitalized interest in gospel among many and has generated countless new admirers in the United States and abroad.

The changes in the blues between the 1940s and the 1990s ranged from the minor to the cataclysmic. In 1949 the music industry via *Billboard*, its trade publication, changed the designation of popular music aimed at black audiences from "race music" to "rhythm and blues." This music encompassed a broad array of blues styles; its most characteristic features were its increased use of amplification and its steady beat. While country blues continued to be sung and played in rural areas, the rural blues became urbanized as blacks increasingly migrated to cities. Chicago artists like former Mississippi Delta bluesmen Muddy Wa-

Playing "bop" is like playing "Scrabble" with all the vowels missing.

DUKE ELLINGTON
AS QUOTED IN THE NEW YORK HERALD TRIBUNE
(JULY 6, 1961)

◆ **Funk**

Music that combines traditional forms of black music (as blues, gospel, or soul) and is characterized by a strong backbeat

27

What we play is life.

LOUIS ARMSTRONG

ters, Howlin' Wolf, and John Lee Hooker blazed this trail, bringing the country to the city with a stirring intensity.

In the blues band tradition, Louis Jordan's Tympani Five built upon its leader's jazz background to forge a highly popular and influential dance and "good time" music known as "jump." Guitarist T-Bone Walker proved influential as a bandleader, vocalist, and performer. His dazzling electric guitar work and show-stopping antics influenced artists such as B. B. King. Indeed, for countless fans in the 1990s, B. B. King still personifies the urban blues tradition, with its thrilling guitar runs and emotional immediacy.

As urban blues continued a distinctive line of development, other blues offshoots emerged in the 1950s from within the rhythm and blues rubric that spoke more plainly to both the changing status of African Americans and the emerging youth culture. Soul, as well as rock and roll, frequently crossed both musical lines and categorical boundaries such as age, race, class, and national origin. By the early 1990s, the most popular and influential music in the world was music that had

grown out of this blues or rhythm and blues matrix. As styles and forms increasingly mixed, the creole quality of the music also grew, this hybrid flavor greatly contributing to its worldwide impact.

Rock and roll emerged as a 1950s expression of rhythm and blues aimed initially at adolescent white audiences. While a number of the pioneering artists were black—Little Richard, Chuck Berry, and Bo Diddley—the breakthrough artist was Elvis Presley, a white Mississippian who combined blues and country music influences into a "rockabilly" mix and whose important work brought heavily black-influenced music to an ever-increasing white American and worldwide audience in the late 1950s and early 1960s. As the civil rights movement gained momentum, racial barriers fell, and blacks and whites did more soul searching, more and more black artists had crossover appeal. This diminished the practice of white artists covering black tunes, releasing denatured versions aimed at allegedly more refined white tastes. Interestingly enough, in the late 1960s, electric-guitar virtuoso Jimi Hendrix

JAMES BROWN AND ARETHA FRANKLIN

The Godfather and Queen of Soul

The music of James Brown and Aretha Franklin brilliantly captured the growing assertiveness and self-confidence of African Americans during the civil rights–black power years. As the "Godfather of Soul" and "the Queen of Soul," these singers, in their music, tapped into a revitalized black consciousness. When Brown sang "Say It Loud, I'm Black and I'm Proud," he contributed to a groundswell in black pride. When Franklin sang "To Be Young, Gifted, and Black," a stirring anthem by the "High Priestess of Soul," Nina Simone, people took notice.

Brown's work as a superb dancer, powerful vocalist, leader of a cutting-edge band, arresting conceptual artist, and legendary performer has exerted enormous influence on African American music. His driving rhythms and heavy bass line were basic to disco—the popular, more lightweight dance

music typically structured around less complex rhythms—and funk—the raw and hard-driving rhythmically based idiom he literally created. Furthermore, rap music draws liberally from his extensive body of work. Creole inventiveness at its finest, rap music employs the latest electronic musical technology to appropriate disparate musical riffs and phrases as a means of creating a unique musical mosaic. Highly developed and highly stylized verbal artistry in which rhyming lyrics are rhythmically delivered over music dominated by a pulsating beat characterizes this music.

Franklin's musical significance lies in her extraordinary vocal blending of the intense emotionality of both gospel and rhythm and blues. She imbibed the gospel tradition in the church of her father, the Reverend C. L. Franklin, and her best work in the soul idiom, like her classic first Atlantic album, *I Never*

Loved a Man the Way I Love You, is heavily gospel-laced. In addition, she personifies the tradition of black women vocalists who have greatly enriched African American music. The search for black women's contributions to modern African American music must encompass this diverse and potent vocal music tradition. Here, at least, the sexist and racist constraints they have endured in a male-dominated music industry appear to have been less restrictive, than, say, in the instrumental tradition. Stretching across musical boundaries and reflecting diverse points of view, the tradition of black women vocalists includes the likes of Bessie Smith, Mahalia Jackson, and Aretha Franklin. Most important, this wide-ranging tradition provides a most revealing window onto their private/personal world as well as their relationship to others both within and outside the African American community.

(1942–1970) forged a blues-based brand of high-voltage, flamboyant, and very influential rock and roll, which creatively explored the illusory yet resonant boundary between "black" rhythm and blues and "white" rock. Both, as his music shows, clearly derive from the blues tradition.

In light of the similarities among blues varieties, often the very idea of boundaries among them was dubious. Within the African American musical tradition, nevertheless, the rhythm and blues idiom spawned several innovations beginning in the 1950s. Chief among these were soul, which reigned supreme from around 1960 to the early 1970s, 1970s and 1980s funk and disco, and 1980s hip-hop and rap. Soul music features hard-driving rhythm and blues with a heavy gospel background. Its intensity draws heavily upon the deep emotional reservoir of both of these sources. Major innovators in this tradition have penetrated the interrelatedness between African American sacred and secular music traditions in highly influential ways. In the 1950s Ray Charles openly and effectively mixed traditional gospel melodic and lyrical frameworks with secular concerns and found a large white and black audience, notwithstanding the alarm of many who felt the mix was sacrilegious. Charles, a consummate artist, has also produced important work perceptively exploring the links between rhythm and blues and jazz, country and western, rock and roll, and mainstream popular song. He has truly stretched the idea of boundaries in African American and American music and culture.

In jazz, the shifts and changes since the early 1940s have been especially dizzying. The two most significant developments have been 1940s bebop and 1960s free jazz. Once again, both of the musics reveal a critical shift in African American consciousness and aesthetic values reflecting the accelerating black liberation struggle. In both movements, the artists approached their music with a seriousness that rejected popular notions of jazz as merely dance music or simple entertainment. Catering to their own creative muses rather than the dictates of popular taste, leaders in both movements forged music with uncompromising substance and impact, enhancing the popular conception of jazz as art music.

Bebop favored smaller groups over big bands and emphasized an aggressive and complex rhythmic charge fueling extraordinary harmonic imagination and melodic inventiveness. Alto saxophonist Charlie Parker, trumpeter John "Dizzy" Gillespie, pianists Thelonious Monk and Earl "Bud" Powell, and drummers Max Roach and Kenny Clarke were among those who pioneered bebop. In particular Parker's improvisational brilliance in melody, harmony, and rhythm mesmerized musicians and audiences alike. His best solos have been highly praised for their conceptual structure, technical acuity, and breathtaking execution. For many, including nonmusicians, who were alienated from mainstream American culture, he became a hero because of his iconoclastic personal and artistic style.

As bebop flowered out of innovations forged by artists such as Armstrong and Young, so free jazz evolved out of the harmonic innovations of bebop as well as the challenging work of musicians like pianist Cecil Taylor and bassist-composer Charles Mingus. The essence of the new jazz was radical harmonic freedom, best exemplified in the work of alto saxophonist Ornette Coleman, the late 1950s and early 1960s work of trumpeter Miles Davis, and the work of tenor saxophonist John Coltrane. Notwithstanding the enormous influence of the music of Davis and Coltrane, Coleman's innovations have proved to be even more compelling. In his albums and his performances, he surrounds himself with superbly supportive musicians. As a result, he has pioneered a music that has given each player unparalleled license to explore his own vision within a common musical ideal, beyond constraints of rhythm, key, and chord structure. At bottom, Coleman's music is a probing exploration of the social and collective possibilities of improvisation, typically using African American musical traditions as the launching pad.

In the 1990s, the lure of money and crossover success appear to threaten African American musical creativity, but there are hopeful signs. Beyond the extraordinary international success of popular music icons like Prince and Michael Jackson, both of whom draw heavily upon African American musical tradition, there are hip-hop and rap, both evolving out of urban African American vernacular culture. In addition, young jazz players, like the exceptional trumpeter Wynton Marsalis, are helping to restore popular interest in the whole of jazz's musical history, not just its most recent and often less significant popular expressions. Similarly, the continuing improvisational brilliance of veteran artists like tenor saxophonist Sonny Rollins and vocalist Betty Carter augurs well for the future. Finally—whether labeled sa-

If you don't like the blues, you've got a hole in your soul.

ANONYMOUS, SAYING

♦ Hip-hop

A subculture especially of inner city youths whose amusements include rap music, graffiti, and break dancing; also an element or art form prevalent within this subculture

cred or secular, classic or progressive, new or old, jazz, gospel, or blues—the music of contemporary groups like the World Saxophone Quartet, the Art Ensemble of Chicago, and Sun Ra's latest aggregation confirm that the powerful African American musical tradition endures.

—WALDO E. MARTIN, JR.

AMUSEMENT AND THEME PARKS

According to the social historian John F. Kasson, the phenomenon of the amusement park and its offshoots, in addition to symbolizing a displacement of genteel culture with a new mass culture, represented a "cultural accommodation to the developing urban-industrial society in a tighter integration of work and leisure than ever before." Ultimately, parks such as Coney Island led to a "passive acceptance of the cycle of production and consumption" and, as is certainly true today with the major theme parks, even the early amusement parks fostered an egalitarian spirit that led to a blurring of class differences and distinctions within American society.

Until the 1970s it was easy to distinguish an amusement park from a theme park, and a travel-

ing carnival from each of these. Coney island in its heyday was an amusement park, or rather a complex of three amusement parks, built in one location with a wide array of attractions, rides, games, and shows. Disney World and Six Flags over Texas were constructed as theme parks and were designed around one unifying theme or idea, or a series of related concepts. A carnival was a traveling amalgam of riding devices, shows or exhibits, and concessions, often providing, as they still do, the midway entertainment for small fairs, though some of the larger state fairs (like that of Texas) boast elaborate permanent midways that operate during the off-season as traditional amusement parks. According to the Outdoor Amusement Business Association, today there are still some five hundred carnivals in North America, employing fifty thousand individuals. In contrast to the nomadic existence of the carnival, the outdoor amusement park evolved as a permanent collection of rides, shows, and concessions.

Today it is more difficult to distinguish between theme and traditional amusement parks, once called iron or steel parks for the construction of their rides, always the main attraction. Early in the twentieth century, prior to the theme idea, traditional amusement parks existed in nearly every American city; they transported patrons into eclectic and exotic fantasylands. The Interna-

PRECURSOR

The World's Columbian Exposition of 1893 in Chicago is often cited as fostering the amusement park. Here visitors stroll through the Midway Plaisance with the giant Ferris wheel in the background.
LIBRARY OF CONGRESS/
CORBIS

tional Association of Amusement Parks and Attractions argues that in the 1990s every entertainment facility in the United States has some aspect of a theme park; thus in quoting a figure of approximately 600 active amusement parks in the United States in 1991 (compared with 1,500 in 1919), the only criterion used by the association is that of fixed-site amusement rides.

All profit-making outdoor entertainment forms operated as business ventures by professionals (as opposed to trade or agriculture fairs and expositions designed to demonstrate products and goods) have the same roots and ancestry. Elements of the American amusement park can be traced back to antiquity; its obvious precursors include various European traditions—the medieval fair and carnival (quite different from the later American version) and the seventeenth-century pleasure garden, common to England and France. Several similar gardens appeared on the East Coast in provincial cities prior to the American Revolution, providing patrons simple pleasures—food, drink, music, and some free variety acts, fireworks, or balloon ascensions.

Genteel amusements for a largely rural culture in a pastoral setting, however, gave way in the late nineteenth century to forms of amusement that mirrored the new urban, industrial age. Enterprising entrepreneurs—including hotel and resort operators, railway and trolley car executives, and brewers, who supplied the major refreshments to amusement venues—were quick to see the potential for profit. By mid century seaside resorts along the upper Eastern Seaboard, from the Jersey Coast to Maine, began to appear. At first catering to a wealthy and elitist clientele, their status changed rapidly as public transportation reached areas like Coney Island and Atlantic City in the 1850s.

The Amusement Park

The stimulus of the World's Columbian Exposition of 1893 in Chicago (with the Vienna World's Fair of 1873 as inspiration) and its Midway Plaisance and the development from 1895 of the Coney Island amusement parks are often cited as fostering the modern amusement park. As Richard W. Flint clearly demonstrates in "Meet Me in Dreamland," however, other entertainment precursors can be identified. Mechanical rides in this country, for example, date back to 1800 and were fairly common by the 1870s; many added excitement to otherwise tranquil picnic groves. The carousel or merry-go-round and the Ferris wheel, as well as the "switchback railway," an early, tame version of a roller coaster, were in limited circula-

tion by the 1880s. Resort areas, such as those on Lake Ontario serving Rochester, New York, were beginning to exploit a new working-class patron. By the turn of the century there were seaside resorts or picnic groves at Lake Compounce Park in Bristol, Connecticut (1846); Rocky Point, Rhode Island (1847); Jantzen Beach, Portland, Maine; Revere Beach outside Boston; and Gravesend Beach on Long Island, among others. Most of these could be reached only by the new trolley, and "trolley parks" developed by street-railway companies and seaside entrepreneurs extended the profit margin of the trolley by providing public transportation to these resorts in late afternoons and weekends.

CONEY ISLAND. Regardless of the number of pre-Coney Island attempts to establish an amusement park tradition, all are prosaic in comparison to the City of Fire, which was called by one religious leader, in a typical Coney Island-style overstatement, "a suburb of Sodom." From its beginning as a beach resort area in the 1870s (where it has been suggested the hot dog, or a version of the frankfurter, was invented in 1871 and the first United States antecedent of a roller coaster was built in 1884) up to its heyday before World War I, Coney Island set the example and pattern for the great twentieth-century versions of the amusement park. As John E. Kasson so vividly illustrates in his important social history of Coney Island, the development of this phenomenon marked the emergence of a new period in American history, one marked by changing economic and social conditions that contributed to a new mass culture. "Its purest expression at this time," writes Kasson, "lay in the realm of commercial amusements, which were creating symbols of the new cultural order, helping to knit a heterogeneous audience into a cohesive whole. Nowhere were these symbols and their relationship to the new mass audience more clearly revealed than at turn-of-the-century Coney Island" (*Amusing the Million*, pp. 3–4).

Coney Island owed much to both the 1876 Philadelphia Centennial Exposition and the Columbian Exposition of 1893. From the former came the Sawyer Observatory, a 300-foot (90-meter) observation tower with steam-powered elevators; it was moved to Coney Island, where it became the first mechanical amusement device on the island, standing until destroyed by fire in 1911. From the Chicago's World Fair came the idea of a midway and the demonstration of George Washington Gale Ferris's (1859–1896) famous wheel. Though similar devices had been

We act as though comfort and luxury were the chief requirements in life, when all we need to make us happy is something to be enthusiastic about.

CHARLES KINGSLEY

See also
Nightlife

*The mass
production of
distraction is now
as much a part of
the American way
of life as the mass
production of
automobiles.*

C. WRIGHT MILLS
"THE UNITY OF WORK AND
LEISURE," POWER, POLITICS
AND PEOPLE (1963)

built as early as 1872, this giant version (thirty-six pendulum cars, each with a sixty-passenger capacity, within a 300-foot-high and 30-foot-wide structure) once and for all established the phenomenal drawing power of mechanical rides, which Coney island so imaginatively exploited.

Three amusement parks were created at Coney Island between 1895 and 1903. A pioneer but largely unsuccessful effort called Sea Lion Park built by Paul Boynton in 1895 was followed two years later by George C. Tilyou's (1862–1914) "Steeple-chase Park" with its mechanical horses that sped passengers along a curving half-mile track in a half-minute. Then, in 1903, Elmer "Skip" Dundy and Frederic Thompson bought Boynton's faltering Sea Lion Park and rebuilt it at a cost of $1 million into a lavish version of Chicago's Midway Plaisance: Luna Park, a "blazing architectural jumble" with a widely eclectic environment of attractions, was considered by many to be the epitome of an amusement enterprise. Dreamland, built by real-estate speculator William H. Reynolds for $3.5 million, followed within a year across the street from Luna; it burned to the ground seven years later. While it lasted, Dream-

land, illuminated by one million incandescent lights, offered everything from a recreation of the Fall of Pompeii to three hundred midgets, girly shows, Venetian canals, a representation of hell, a leapfrog railroad, and a view of the first incubator, complete with babies.

Coney Island attracted one million patrons on one day in 1914. But soon Coney Island would begin its decline; before World War I, Dreamland burned down, Luna Park went bankrupt, and Tilyou died. By World War II, Coney Island's slide gained momentum, with the middle-class moving to the suburbs and fewer patrons making the subway trip from Brooklyn to the island. Today, the one remaining park, Astroland, part of a scant two-by-twelve-block entertainment area, is a gritty slum by the sea, fighting the ravages of poverty, crime, and blight.

POST–CONEY ISLAND PARKS. Nevertheless, while it lasted, the Coney Island model inspired countless other Luna Parks and Dreamlands all over America. The period following the Saint Louis World's Fair of 1904 marks the era of the greatest contribution of railroad, traction, and trolley car companies in building amusement

THE ROLLER COASTER AND CAROUSEL
A Thrilling Ride and a Nostalgic Experience

In the 1990s, voices of doom seem premature. Thrill rides, for example, have never been more popular. Roller coaster aficionados demonstrated the insatiable attraction of coasters by establishing in the late 1970s an organization called American Coaster Enthusiasts with its own publication, *RollerCoaster!* Choosing to place oneself on the edge of disaster has great appeal to lovers of thrill rides (although their danger is actually quite minimal). Amusement park entrepreneurs constantly rise to the challenge, creating new and more unbelievable thrill rides, especially roller coasters. A few 1991 examples will illustrate: "Mean Streak" ($7.5 million coaster) at Cedar Point in Sandusky, Ohio, claims to be the world's tallest and fastest wooden roller coaster (coaster addicts debate the advantages of old-style wooden coasters versus steel monsters) with a 160-foot (48-meter) hill, a 155-foot (46-meter) first drop, and a speed of 65 miles (104 kilometers) per hour; the $5 million "Anaconda" at Kings Dominion near Richmond, Virginia, boasts a 126-foot (37.8-meter) underwater tunnel; Kings Island near Cincinnati has added "Adventure Express," a special-effects coaster to its offerings; "Steel Phantom"

at Kenneywood near Pittsburgh claims the fastest steel coaster (80 miles [128 kilometers] per hour top speed); "The Viper" at Six Flags Magic Mountain, Valencia, California, is the largest looping coaster with seven loops. A new coaster is being developed that functions like a jet airplane with endless rolls in a pipeline construction. It is estimated that since 1985 some $135 million has been spent on thirty-seven new coasters.

In vivid contrast to the roller coaster, the traditional carousel has been the salvation for other sites. While the coaster serves as a dazzling reminder of modern technology and controlled violence, the merry-go-round remains an icon of a more relaxed, quaint, and remote past. Carousel animals today are valued collector items, some costing thousands of dollars. Some complete carousels have been declared landmarks; local groups have battled land developers and local governments to save amusement areas or at least to enshrine a number of the beautifully constructed older carousels still in existence. The number of hand-carved wooden carousels has dwindled from about 5,000 in the late nineteenth century to some 160 today.

parks. Ohio's Lakeshore Electric Railway, for instance, earned much of its revenue from fares to Cedar Point, which became a full-fledged amusement park in 1905; the Northern Ohio Transit and Light Company owned at least ten parks in Ohio.

With the 1920s came a tremendous upsurge in the development of mechanical rides, followed in the 1930s by the Great Depression and the introduction of parks to new patrons seeking inexpensive entertainment and brief escapes from their dreary existences. The final decline of the traditional amusement park dates from World War II when materials used by parks were needed for the war effort and patrons were growing bored with aging attractions. Natural disasters, vandalism, and other less tangible factors also contributed to the decline. Beginning in the late 1950s, a postwar baby boom brought a resurgence of interest in the amusement park business. Nevertheless, such historic parks as Palisades Park in New Jersey, Chicago's Riverview, Cleveland's Euclid Beach, and Massachusetts's Lincoln Park have closed since the 1960s and other urban parks are struggling to survive. In the 1970s and 1980s conflicting reports announced an upswing in amusement park business, the reaching of a saturation point, concern over the safety of rides, and the ultimate demise of amusement parks.

The Theme Park

The savior of the outdoor amusement business has been the theme park, a dynamic example of Madison Avenue advertising packaging at its most persuasive and often an astonishing example of organizational know-how. Conceived first by Walt Disney (1901–1966) in the 1950s, the concept of organizing amusement areas around one or several themes was a revolutionary idea, providing new methods of exploiting the amusement industry. Not all theme parks were successful (and some still are not), as the collapse of such early examples as Beanyland in Santa Monica, California, Freedomland in New York City, Magic Mountain near Denver, and Circus World in Barnum City, Florida, indicates. The World of Sid and Marty Krofft, in Atlanta, Georgia, one of the first attempts at an indoor amusement park, closed in 1976, only months after its opening.

However, since the 1955 opening of Disneyland in Anaheim, California, built by Walt Disney in his own backyard of Southern California on a fifty-five-acre tract with a $17 million investment, the theme park idea has spread throughout the United States and into other parts of the

world, with major Disney parks in Paris and Tokyo. Ironically, Disney, who chose a crowded urban setting for Disneyland, had no idea of the tremendous growth of this aspect of his empire. In the 1990s, in fact, plans to expand Disneyland in Anaheim have been restricted due to the lack of readily accessible land and expansion is planned elsewhere. Still considered by many to be the best amusement park in the world, in part because it was Disney's personal project, reflecting his taste, imagination, and style, Disneyland is organized around a central hub with the idea that the patron leaves the world of today and enters the worlds of yesterday, tomorrow, and fantasy (via seven themed areas: Main Street, Tomorrow, Fantasyland, Frontierland, New Orleans Square, Adventureland, and Critter Country).

The Disney empire has now grown into a diversified corporation with interests in film and television production, hotels (the designs of which have attracted some of the world's great architects, such as the postmodern architect Michael Graves), and extensive merchandising of the Disneyana. Even during difficult economic times (fiscal 1983–1987) Disney's annual revenues more than doubled, to $2.9 billion, with profits that nearly quintupled to $444.7 million. New schemes continue to be projected by the Disney team, from a new Disneyland in South America to an American theme-park based on the workplace as well as EuroDisney, which opened near Paris in 1992.

Although originally scoffed at, the idea of the theme park began to catch on by the 1970s; it attracted large corporations and businesspeople in contrast to the old-time showmen of the early amusement park era. Disney imitations appeared throughout the country: Astroworld in Houston; Cedar Point in Ohio; Hersheypark in Pennsylvania; Kings Island in Ohio; a revamped Knott's Berry Farm in Buena Park, California; Magic Mountain in Valencia, California; Opryland, U.S.A. in Nashville; the Six Flags circuit in Texas, Georgia, and Missouri (and later in New Jersey and Illinois); and, finally, in 1971, the giant of them all, Walt Disney World Resort in Orlando, Florida. Built on a site of over 27,000 acres (10,800 hectares) it has never ceased its expansion, adding to the original Magic Kingdom, EPCOT Center, Disney–MGM Studios theme park, and a complex of hotels, golf courses, and other service and entertainment components. From an initial 700 employees, Disney World now employs 33,000 and on its property includes shops (where everything from trash cans to trams

Idleness is as necessary to good work as is activity. The man who can take hold hard and to some purpose is the man who knows how to let go.

DR. FRANK CRANE

See also

Popular Entertainment before the Civil War

A

**AMUSEMENT AND
THEME PARKS**

The Theme Park

*Disneyland is
presented as
imaginary in order
to make us believe
that the rest is real,
when in fact all
of Los Angeles
and America
surrounding it are
no longer real.*

JEAN BAUDRILLARD

**LARGER THAN
LIFE**

*Disney character Goofy hugs
an admirer*

THE PURCELL TEAM / CORBIS

are constructed), a production department for live performances, warehouses, its own training school (called Disney University) and a separate company (Disney Development) responsible for hotels and service components outside of the amusement park areas proper. It all works with incredible precision and care, with no detail ignored or slighted. And, despite the uniformity demanded of all employees (including grooming and appearance regulations), Disney personnel appear surprisingly pleased with their positions, the operational procedures, and the Disney corporate image.

In many ways Disneyland and Walt Disney World illustrate how different the modern theme park is from the traditional amusement park. Other than having fixed rides, the theme park is often the antithesis of the older parks (though many of the survivors have been transformed into theme parks). For many patrons, the theme park is all they have known, and its extremely conservative, homogenized, hygienic ambience and the youthful, clean-cut appearance of the typical employee are taken for granted. In contrast, the older amusement parks were run with traditional showmanship, included gaming operations and pitchmen, and were often a bit seedy with their worn attractions. Many amusement parks grew with no preplanning or organizational scheme; theme parks revel in the designed plotting of their amusement areas, often with open spaces and generous landscaping added to create an aesthetically pleasing ambience.

Other than cleanliness, the greatest single difference between the two types of parks is location. Traditional amusement parks moved closer and closer to urban centers and attracted a fairly circumscribed clientele. Theme parks have sought isolation, though proximity to a major highway, an area devoted to tourism, or even an urban area is desirable. By the 1980s theme parks were often part of a larger leisure area. For example, north of the Great Smoky Mountains National Park in Pigeon Forge and Gatlinburg, Tennessee, a staggering array of commercialized leisure businesses can be found. The centerpiece is Dollywood, country singer Dolly Parton's park built around the theme of "Smokies Spirit" and country music, with forty-five musical performances each day. Clustered along Highway 441 through Pigeon Forge are such venues as Magic World, Treasure Ship Golf Course, Parkway Speedway, Wild Wheels & Waterbugs, Smoky Mountain Car Museum, Rockin' Raceway & Arcade, Hillbilly Village, Dixie Stampede, Museum of Reptiles, and dozens of additional attractions catering to tourists. A few miles away in Gatlinburg, once a small, quaint mountain hamlet, the main street is cluttered with such commercial attractions as Ober Gatlinburg, Mysterious Mansion, World of Illusions, the American Historical Wax Museum, Ripley's Believe It or Not, Haunted House, and the Guinness Hall of World Records. Just across the mountain range, Ghost Town in the Sky is located in Maggie Valley, North Carolina, and Santa's Land (with its Rudicoaster), billed as a fun park and zoo, is situated on the outskirts of Cherokee, North Carolina. Six Flags over Texas, in Arlington, Texas, between Dallas and Fort Worth, is situated in an area that also includes Arlington Stadium, home of the Texas Rangers baseball team; the Palace of Wax and Ripley's Believe It or Not; Wet 'n Wild (one of a growing number of water parks, totaling some 270 in the United States by 1991); and International Wildlife Park (a number of parks, such as Busch Gardens in Tampa, Florida, are theme parks with the veneer of animal preserves). Central Florida, with Disney World as its centerpiece, has spawned an enormous variety of entertainment venues, from Sea World (there are four Sea Worlds nationwide, each part of the Busch Entertainment Corporation) to Universal Studios, and a host of smaller leisure businesses scattered through the area.

If the theme park prefers isolation to an urban location (and there are exceptions—Busch Gardens in Tampa, Florida, and Disneyland, whose growth was curtailed because of its urban setting), the more successful parks draw on a national or even international patronage rather than the local clientele of the traditional amusement park. Even the smaller theme parks depend on regional rather than local business. And big business it is. In 1990 it is estimated that there were 243 million visits to amusement parks. Even related outdoor venues, such as miniature golf courses and water parks, did a large volume of business. The former attracted 120 million visits, while 49 million visits were made to water parks. Unlike the traditional amusement park, most theme parks have an entry fee or pass, costing in 1991, at Disney World, as much as $111 for a four-day adult "passport" and $88 for a child (ages 3 to 9). In 1991, a four-day/three-night visit, without airfare, could easily cost over $1,500 for a family of four.

When Disney World opened the EPCOT (Experimental Prototype Community of Tomorrow) Center in 1982, the theme park moved closer in intent to that of the world's fair or international exposition. Disney propaganda heralds:

*I love Mickey Mouse
more than any
woman I've known.*

WALT DISNEY, CARTOONIST

See also
Travel and Vacations

Journey through time and space, across the continents of the earth and beyond your wildest dreams in two dazzling and different worlds. At Future World you'll get an inspiring look at space-age technology and what lies ahead, while World Showcase will present you with the fascinating traditions and cultures of people from around the world.

Indeed, not unlike the New York World's Fair of 1939–1940, EPCOT attempts, as Andrea Dennett notes, "to challenge the patron to reinvestigate past achievements in order to grasp a better comprehension of future technological inventions." But Disney World, Six Flags, and other theme parks that claim to reflect history or to teach painlessly science and technology never lose sight that their first goal is to entertain a patron, usually a family unit, with plenty of money to spend. Consequently, history, science, and technology are handled in a way palatable for mass consumption and packaged in a fashion that will amuse and mesmerize as well as instruct. Indeed, the end result is often a kind of invented historical or scientific fantasy. In the realm of historical reenactment or representation, the product is rarely a realistic depiction but rather a utopian recreation (sometimes with automata) that reflects history based on a selectivity of detail, most frequently positive in attitude, politically conservative, and underscoring a belief in the efficacy of power and the correctness of capitalism. Marginalized groups, when represented, are idealized; all threats to existence are virtually ignored.

INDOOR FAMILY ENTERTAINMENT CENTERS.
The most recent development in the amusement industry, and arguably the newest amusement park mutation, is the Indoor Family Entertainment Center (FEC). Some limited areas set aside for amusement, usually with a few kiddie rides or a penny arcade, have existed in shopping centers and malls for decades. However, with the completion in 1985 of the West Edmonton Mall in Alberta, Canada, claiming as one component of its complex the world's largest indoor amusement park, the potential of the Indoor Family Entertainment Centers was realized, prompting other enterprising entrepreneurs to get on the bandwagon. Enclosed within the West Edmonton Mall, a shopping and entertainment complex covering 483,600 square meters, an area equivalent to 115 football fields, is Fantasyland, a full-sized amusement park complete with roller coaster. Although harking back to early trade fairs and expositions in large indoor halls or specially built

structures, such as the Crystal Palace constructed for London's Great Exhibition of 1851, the FEC is very much a contemporary phenomenon, made possible by current technology and building techniques that allow for highly automated attractions and rides to be constructed within massive covered indoor spaces. It is the amusement industry's response to what they see as an increasingly family-oriented marketplace. For years entertainment venues, such as bowling alleys, video arcades, theaters, ice- and roller-skating rinks, have been tenants at shopping centers but have not been considered major or anchor tenants. However, in the 1990s the FEC has begun to be seen as a "developer-produced and operated signature space." In what is seen as a soft market for retail nationwide, the FEC is one way to diversify market appeal, extend the stay of the customer, and even attract tenants during the initial leasing period.

The obvious advantage of an indoor amusement park is the protective environment, especially during inclement weather or in colder climes. And, the mall-related center has the added possibility of drawing business from other attractions in the complex. Unlike most theme parks, admission to the center is free, with the patron paying for individual games, attractions, and rides. Larger Indoor Family Entertainment Centers, either attached to other commercial areas or freestanding warehouse-like operations, are becoming major tourist attractions. The West Edmonton Mall, for example, draws 15 million visitors a year from Canada, the United States, and abroad. In the United States it is estimated that 97 million visits to Indoor Family Entertainments Centers took place in 1990.

To date, the United States' most prominent example of an FEC is Camp Snoopy (scheduled to open in 1992), as of this writing under construction by the Knott's Berry Farm organization at the future Mall of America in Bloomington, Minnesota (a cold climate similar to Alberta's). Within the center of this 4.2 million-square-foot (378,000-square-meter) facility will be a seven-acre FEC, its theme and contents similar to Knott's outdoor Camp Snoopy in California. Sixteen rides are proposed for this FEC, including a "Tivoli-style" steel roller coaster and a long flume twisting through a 70-foot (21-meter) high mountain. Illustrating the problem of definition of amusement and theme parks, Camp Snoopy is really an indoor theme park, as are most FECs. In this case it is the North Woods that creates the ambience, mirroring in an idealized fashion the Minnesota outdoors. The roof of the Minnesota mall is 100 feet (30 meters) high, 65 percent of which is glass, providing the interior of the complex with over 1.2 square miles (3 square kilometers) of sky light. With so much space available, Camp Snoopy will include a full acre covered in live landscaping, including trees 40 to 50 feet (12 to 15 meters) high.

Like the earliest amusement parks and carnivals, as well as theme parks such as Disney's EPCOT Center (built around an artificial lagoon), Camp Snoopy and virtually all FECs are arranged in a loop design that keeps traffic moving in a circular pattern, avoiding dead ends and guaranteeing that patrons pass all attractions, while allowing them to arrange their own programs in the environment.

Few FECs currently fall into the category of a Fantasyland or Camp Snoopy with a complete indoor amusement park. Most range in size from 20,000 to 150,000 square feet (1,800 to 13,500 square meters) with indoor ride- and show-based entertainment and participatory attractions, sports and food (and other merchandising facilities). These range from Neptune's Kingdom on the Santa Cruz, California, Beach Boardwalk—a $5.2 million indoor adventure entertainment center in a large building resembling an airplane hangar—to Fame City in Houston, a complex of hundreds of arcade games and kiddie rides combined with ten other major activities (roller-skating rink, bowling center, miniature golf, fun house, a laser maze, cinema); 49th Street Galleria, a 125,000-square-foot (11,250-square-meter) two-level complex in the Franklin Mills Mall (Northeast Philadelphia) and a 145,000-square-foot (13,050-square-meter) development in Salt Lake City, Utah (with more Gallerias planned); or "Celebration Station" in Baton Rouge, Louisiana, an FEC that caters to all ages, with redemption and video games, three types of go-carts, coin-operated mechanical animal rides for small children, and a 54-hole miniature golf course and nine batting cages for the sports-minded.

The amusement park industry, whose death, like that of the Broadway theater, is often predicted, has followed a natural course from trolley park and picnic grove to urban amusement park and the technologically superior theme park, including the current trend toward indoor family centers. It has grown prosperous along with America's increasing propensity for conspicuous consumption. Its current association with indoor malls is no coincidence. The new Mall of America in Minnesota, for example, expects to attract 40 million visitors annually by 1996, more than Disney World, and anticipates sales of $1 billion by that year. With home-entertainment centers ever more elaborate, the MTV generation will likely demand more sophisticated and spectacular attractions from the parks. Universal Studios in Florida, for example, in order to attract its clientele, has deemphasized its theme park identification and attempted to package itself more like a film and television facility, throwing the patron into a fantasized reality world, a center of special effects, and offering them a glimpse of a "hot" set, one that's ready to be filmed. It seems likely, therefore, that creative initiative, and stronger appeal to adults as well as children, will assure the industry's continuance well into the future.

—DON BURTON WILMETH

In our play we reveal the kind of people we are.

OVID
THE ART OF LOVE (C. A.D. 8)

Mankind is safer when men seek pleasure than when they seek the power and glory.

GEOFFREY GORER
IN THE NEW YORK TIMES
MAGAZINE (NOV. 27, 1966)

CHILDHOOD AND CHILDREN

Children's experience over the course of American history evolved in response to changes in the family and to new ideas about childhood as a stage of life. It also varied according to geographic location, gender, class, race, and ethnicity. While the current cultural category of childhood, with its assumptions about children's vulnerability, malleability, and dependence on parental love, is believed by many to be an invention of the early-nineteenth-century bourgeois family, throughout American history the experience of those younger than age twelve has always differed from that of other age groups.

The Colonial Era

Settlers of seventeenth-century New England towns recognized childhood as a separate stage of life. Preacher Gilbert Tennent noted four stages of life in a 1741 sermon: "old and aged Persons"; "middle-ag'd People, of thirty Years old and upwards"; "my younger Brethren, of fourteen years and upwards," and "little children, of six Years old and upwards," leaving out children under age six. In the seventeenth and eighteenth centuries, early childhood was brief, and historians find evidence of its end in changing patterns of dress: boys and girls, who had dressed in similar long robes that opened down the front, by age six or eight began to dress much like their parents.

Infant mortality rates varied by region in the seventeenth-century colonies. In the healthiest areas of New England, only one child in ten died before its first birthday, whereas in the Chesapeake region the rate was one infant in four. In the malaria-prone parts of the middle and southern colonies, as many as one child in three died in the first year of life.

In contrast, the likelihood of the death of an infant or the early death of a parent was a frightening dimension of seventeenth-century family life in the Chesapeake. The norm in the region was that one or both of their parents would die before the children were old enough to care for themselves. The death of one parent often led to remarriage by the surviving spouse, resulting in complex relationships between children and stepparents and stepbrothers and -sisters. Fear of infant mortality and early parental death created some emotional detachment, especially among parents in the South, where premature death was more common, but it did not prevent the emergence of the typical strong and loving bond between parent and child throughout the colonies during the seventeenth and eighteenth centuries.

In all of the colonies, most mothers breast-fed their infants for the first twelve to eighteen months. While very young, babies often slept in their parents' bed; later, they were transferred to their own cradle or to a trundle bed shared with siblings. New England Puritan families were quite large, with an average of eight children, and surrounding the infant with warmth and comfort. After the tranquility of the first year of life, the baby's existence was disrupted by two events: weaning and the arrival of a new sibling. Weaning is said to have been done quite abruptly after the infant's first year. Sometimes the mother applied a bitter substance to her breast to curb the infant's desire to suck; other mothers left the household entirely for several days in order to stop nursing. Then, by the time the infant was two, a new baby generally arrived, further shifting the mother's attention from the child.

Literature on Puritan child rearing emphasized the importance of curbing the child's will from roughly the second year of life. This process related to the centrality of ideas of original sin—the belief that newborn infants embodied sin and depravity—in the Puritan mind. Confronting a child's self-assertions and aggression was a crucial parental duty necessary to winning God's grace and achieving salvation for the child. This beating down of the child's early efforts at autonomy instilled a lasting sense of shame and doubt that left its imprint on the adult Puritan community. Less harshness is evident in the scant sources on child-rearing in the South, where parents tended to indulge their young children, delighting in their play and lavishing them with affection. White children in the South moved freely on the planta-

If children grew up according to early indications, we should have nothing but geniuses.

GOETHE

Most Puritan parents placed their offspring in the homes of other families during adolescence, hoping both to provide youths with necessary training and to undercut rebellious tendencies.

PAGE I

tion and enjoyed the companionship of neighboring children; all efforts were geared toward nurturing autonomous, self-reliant children.

Donning adult clothing between the ages of six and eight symbolized a new status for the child— the end of early childhood and the beginning of childhood proper. Though some historians contend that this transition marked the end of childhood and the initiation into "miniature adulthood," rich evidence suggests that childhood lasted until the stage of youth referred to by Tennant, when at age twelve or fourteen the child was prepared to leave home. The years from age six to the early teens were, however, less sheltered than childhood today, since children began to assume productive roles within the self-sufficient household economy by age six or seven. Boys learned farming and fence making from their fathers, and girls learned cooking, spinning, and cloth making from their mothers. Parents provided whatever academic training children received in these years,

with special emphasis on instruction in religion. Society's recognition of the immaturity of children roughly below the age of fourteen is indicated by the fact that it was highly unusual for preteenage children to experience a religious conversion signifying God's grace through personal faith. However, by age fourteen, or sometimes younger, children were "bound out" as apprentices to other families.

Changes in society in the eighteenth century led to important transformations in the experience of children. In New England, the strictly hierarchical Puritan social order gave way as population growth placed pressure on available land. This forced sons either to leave home to find land elsewhere or to enter the emerging commercial economy. These situations separated children from parents, both geographically and psychologically, weakening parental authority.

In addition, by the mid-eighteenth century the philosophers of the European Enlightenment

NATIVE AMERICAN CHILDREN
Producing Independent, Self-Reliant Adults

Childhood for Native American children in the seventeenth and eighteenth centuries differed from the experience of colonial white children. When the English settlers arrived in North America in the seventeenth century, there were between 850,000 and two million Native Americans living throughout the continent. Most Indian families were small because of high infant and child death rates and because the practice of breast-feeding babies for two or more years suppressed fertility. While the significance of other practices is disputed, some indicate the variety of Native American attitudes toward children: for example, in some tribes children were born in a special birth hut, located some distance from the family's home. Often, newborns were rubbed with animal oil or dipped in cold water. Infants of several months were initiated into their tribe in a special ceremony at which they were given their name. Some tribes also had rituals that included piercing the child's nose or earlobes.

In some Indian tribes, child rearing was the exclusive responsibility of mothers or grandmothers; in others, uncles, grandfathers, and other male relatives had a critical role as mentors and disciplinarians. Indians disciplined their children by praising and publicly rewarding good behavior, and shaming and ridiculing children for misbehavior. They believed these methods produced independent, self-

reliant adults and rarely used corporal punishment, which they felt created timid children. Indian children may have participated in work earlier than white children, since their play was modeled on their parents' work; very young boys learned to fish, hunt game, and gather fruits, berries, and nuts, while girls learned to sew by making doll clothes and to farm by raising corn and beans in miniature plots.

The growing-up process for both Indian girls and Indian boys was marked by puberty rites. At the time of their first menstruation, young girls were isolated for periods of time ranging from several weeks to a year, during which they were cared for by older women and instructed in the duties of adult womanhood. Boys underwent a more extensive series of initiation rites, marking their first tooth, first steps, and first game kill. In many tribes, when a young Indian boy approached puberty, he went alone to a mountaintop or into a forest to fast and seek a vision from a guardian spirit. When the boy returned to the community, he assumed adult status. Maturity for Native American children involved the acquisition of economic skills, cultural heritage, and spiritual awareness; and while these things were understood in ways that differ radically from a non-Indian conception, they nevertheless engendered self-reliance and courage.

See also

Sports in the Twentieth Century

promoted new ideas about the nature of children and childhood influencing parents throughout the colonies. In particular, notions of infant depravity gave way to ideas of the unique needs and impulses of children. Both John Locke's concept of the child's mind as a blank slate and Jean-Jacques Rousseau's celebration of childhood innocence emphasized the child's malleability. These ideas led parents to use the childhood years as preparation for responsible adulthood by developing their children's conscience and capacity for self-reliance.

The special children's toys and literature that appeared in the late eighteenth century reflected this new recognition of childhood as a distinctive stage of life. The use of pastel colors in furniture and pictures designed for children, with fantasy animals and images from nursery rhymes, all reflect the new concept of childhood as a time of play and innocence.

The early eighteenth century witnessed the importation of huge numbers of black slaves to the colonies. While in 1675 there were only 4,000 black slaves in the colonies, by 1780, 550,000 Africans had been forcibly brought to the mainland colonies. Improved health and an increasing proportion of female slaves enabled the black population to maintain itself through reproduction by the middle of the eighteenth century. Although slave marriage was not recognized by law, African Americans created a distinctive kinship system under slavery. Slaves conducted their own marriage rituals, and parents named children after themselves, grandparents, or other kin, passing down traditional African family names to their children. These naming patterns reinforced family bonds.

Black mothers in the eighteenth and nineteenth centuries spaced their children closely together and breast-fed their infants for at least one year. Newborn slave children were the center of attention and concern, attended by their mothers and sometimes by a midwife, and visited by their fathers, the parents' friends, and relatives in the slave community. The plantation overseer and mistress also immediately came to see the new infant, but in their case the visit was to view the plantation owner's new property. Slave mothers generally were granted from two weeks to one month "lying-in time," when they were free from plantation work and able to devote themselves entirely to the new baby. After the lying-in, mothers were permitted to return from the fields several times a day to suckle their infants. Children were nursed for at least a year. Once weaned, young children were cared for by female relatives while parents worked or, in many cases, in communal nurseries. Although in most nurseries children were left to their own devices, on one large Florida plantation an energetic woman ran the nursery like the kindergarten of today, telling stories and inventing imaginative games. At the end of the day, children joined their parents in their cabin and helped prepare the evening meal. In the evening they did chores such as washing, repairing furniture, gardening, sewing, and spinning.

According to some slave narratives, children were protected from the reality of slavery while they were young and often remembered the years before their induction into the master's work force as the happiest time in their lives. "As a barefoot boy," J. Vance Lewis recalled, "my stay upon the farm had been pleasant. I played among the wild flowers and wandered in high glee over hill and hollow, . . . and knew not that I was a slave and the son of a slave." The shelter of childhood ended when, youngsters of age five or six assumed responsibility for infant care; later, between the ages of ten and fourteen, slave children were forced to begin work in the fields. On some plantations, younger children were given lighter tasks advancing from "quarter-hands" to "half-hands" until they were grown and able-bodied and became "full-hands."

Still, slavery imposed serious stresses on the lives of slave children: squalid plantation living quarters often forced slaves to live with nonrelatives, and some children were moved to cabins separate from their parents at anywhere from age seven to ten. Families lived under the constant threat of breakup through sale, and children were frequently sold away from parents. Moreover, slavery undermined the authority of parents: children were forbidden to call their natural mother "mother," forcing them to call the plantation mistress by that title instead. When slave children were punished or abused by slaveholders, parents were unable to help them. In spite of this, parents managed to transmit a sense of family bonds to their children and endeavored to give their children the strength necessary to endure slavery.

The Nineteenth Century

In the North, a sharp drop in marital fertility rates in the early part of the nineteenth century profoundly changed the experience of white children. Several factors converged to create this trend toward fewer births. First, as the population grew, parents no longer had sufficient land to pass on to the next generation, creating an incentive for

Psychologists' "discovery" of children's play and adolescence in the late nineteenth century invested urban reformers with a theory by which to approach the hordes of immigrant children swarming American cities.

PAGE 449

parents to limit the number of children they had. At the same time, economic life became more specialized, families no longer functioned as economically self-sufficient units, and productive work increasingly occurred in shops and factories outside the home. This meant that children ceased to be economic assets in the agricultural home economy and became increasingly costly to raise. While a typical white woman in 1800 bore seven or eight children, by 1860 she bore only five or six. This decline in fertility continued until the end of the nineteenth century, when the average number of children born to white women declined to three or four. Overall, fertility in the United States declined by one-half between 1800 and 1900.

Smaller size families fit well with new ideas about the nature of childhood; the notion of childhood as a special, malleable stage of life encouraged greater attention to the proper care and development of the individual child. Having fewer children made it easier to nurture each one. With fewer births and the removal of much of domestic production from the home to the factory, women were now free to devote most of their time to rearing their children. Indeed, after 1800, when a father's labor shifted outside the home, the role of the paternal disciplinarian was replaced by that of the maternal nurturer, and child rearing emerged as married women's primary responsibility. The role of mother was glorified by the idea of "republican motherhood," created during the American Revolution, which charged mothers with the vital task of raising capable citizens—especially sons—for the new republic.

These shifts also freed northern white children from their household labors and led children to remain in their parents' homes until their teens and even early twenties. Childhood emerged as a time of leisure and prolonged financial and emotional dependence, devoted specifically to preparation for adulthood. In the model of nurturance that emerged by the 1830s, each mother manipulated the emotional bond between herself and her child to ensure proper behavior in the child. Her chief methods were maternal martyrdom and withdrawal of love. One mother explained to her three-year-old daughter the countless sacrifices she had made on the child's behalf, all the while "caressing her affectionately." Another mother, in an article in *Mother's Magazine* in 1833, described the effectiveness of withdrawal of love in curbing her son's disobedience. When she told her son, "I would not smile upon you, I should not receive your flowers, but should have to separate you from my company," her son responded, "I could not be

happy if you did not love me." In each case, obedience was ensured by provoking guilt in the child. According to advice written for mothers, moral nurturance demanded constant vigilance and supervision to be effective, as if to ensure that child rearing would take all of the mother's available time. Every aspect of the child's behavior was monitored by the mother, with the goal of lovingly shaping the child's conscience, instilling the preeminent middle-class values of honesty, industry, frugality, and self-control deep within the child's personality.

With children at home under their mothers' care and productive labor generally accomplished outside the family, children were socialized into the more sharply defined gender roles that began to characterize society. Daughters were prepared

NINETEENTH CENTURY SCHOOLS

Formal Settings to Teach Discipline

By the 1840s schools emerged as a setting for socialization, especially into adult occupational roles, mediating between the world of the family and the adult world of work. The need for this kind of socialization was particularly acute for boys. While prior to the 1830s and 1840s, rural boys and girls attended local "winter schools," leaving them free for field work in summer, by the 1840s public elementary schools emerged in Massachusetts, New York, Philadelphia, and the Midwest. Such early schooling was erratic, and by the 1830s reformers were calling for systematic education for all children between the ages of five and sixteen. By mid century, the majority of northern white children between those ages were enrolled in schools.

By the 1850s, schools for younger children had become increasingly formal settings for the inculcation of disciplined habits. Age-graded classes were introduced by mid century, and routines of rote learning were imposed on each age-group so that entire classrooms of children stood together as they chanted their lessons. Regimented classes permitted greater behavioral scrutiny and fostered conformity. Carefully graded lessons at school reinforced the mother's moral nurturance at home, and both were designed to enforce the "semi-mechanical' virtues of industry and regularity in middle- and working-class northern children.

See also

Adolescence

for marriage and the responsibilities of motherhood; they were reared to be chaste, delicate, loving, and emotional and to become self-reliant, nurturing, efficient caretakers. Girls attended school along with boys but grew up in a specifically female world of intense friendship and emotional intimacy. Boys, on the other hand, were raised to be aggressive and assertive in the public sphere but to exhibit gentlemanly self-control and self-restraint within the family.

The effect of such bourgeois socialization techniques was hardly uniform, and poor children living in northern cities in the 1850s missed its influence entirely. Such children never experienced the emotional world of the protected, private family with its intense maternal attention. Poor children at mid century lived in the public world of the streets, where they gained independence and economic responsibility as young as the age of six or seven; they were sent there by their parents to earn part of their keep and to contribute to the household economy.

The youngest of these children worked as scavengers, gathering salable trash such as cinders, coal, rope, metal, bottles, paper, and even kitchen grease and bad meat. These children learned how to use castoffs to "make something out of nothing" and either brought them home, sold them to neighbors, or peddled them to junk dealers. Older children worked at street peddling or huckstering, selling everything from tea cakes and sweet potatoes to matchsticks, scrub brushes, strings, and pins. Several low-paying trades were specially reserved for children; girls, for example, would sweep street crossings, and for boys it would be running errands, bootblacking, horse holding, and newspaper selling.

Children who worked in the streets far from adult supervision often strayed into illicit pursuits, such as petty theft and prostitution. Such shady activity drew concern from respectable parents who needed the income from their children's work and from reformers who disapproved of the habits of poor families. Street life became crowded and appeared increasingly depraved and dangerous to reformers, since the large influx of Irish and German immigrants in the 1840s made the poor a more visible presence in large cities. The presence of unsupervised children in cities—whether huckster boys whose taste of freedom led them to run away from home, orphans, or gangs of mischievous youth—rubbed sharply against the grain of middle-class notions of domesticity and a sheltered childhood. These children elicited a critique of working-class family life from social reformers, who endeavored to abolish poverty by teaching the poor the virtues of middle-class family life as a means to self-improvement. Charity workers viewed the poor homes they visited with disdain: "Homes . . . if it is not a mockery to give that hallowed name to the dark, filthy hovels where many of them dwell."

Reformers such as Charles Loring Brace, who established the Children's Aid Society in 1853, pioneered new institutional arrangements for dependent and delinquent children. So severe was the middle-class indictment of poor urban childhood that reformers considered the removal of a poor child from its parents to be in the child's best interest. In the 1850s, a new system of foster care placed urban children in rural homes, where they were supposed to not only learn the virtues of hard work by providing labor on the farm but also receive the morally strengthening influence of country life. This placing-out system was used where possible for orphans and juvenile offenders. Institutions that housed delinquents and orphans also underwent changes by mid century. Large houses of refuge established in the 1820s that used corporal punishment to reform youthful criminals were replaced by institutions that attempted to replicate family life through small residential cottages and an emphasis on education and hard work to reshape and reform the delinquent's character.

Another aspect of the late-century reformers' investigation of poor family life was an effort to protect children against family violence. While family violence was not restricted to the poorer classes, wealthier families were able to escape community attention, and in the late nineteenth century violence against wives and children was identified with poorer and immigrant families. Formal efforts at child protection began with the establishment of the first Society for the Protection of Cruelty to Children (SPPC) in New York City in 1874, with similar agencies opening in ten other cities by 1880. The society was created in response to both benevolent desires to protect children and fears among the wealthy, urban elite of social disorder brought about by poverty, drunkenness, and crime. In spite of the society's claim that it placed the protection of children above the preservation of families, parents were rarely prosecuted, and agents often upheld a father's authority by asserting that the "child deserved a beating." The SPCC did intervene in threatening situations and removed a significant number of children from abusive families. Although the agency's establishment represents an important step on be-

What's done to children, they will do to society.

KARL MENNINGER

half of the protection of children, efforts to identify and prosecute child abuse continued to be hampered because of strong cultural beliefs about paternal authority and the privacy of the family.

While middle-class families continued to try to insulate their children from the threatening and disorderly elements of urban life in the second half of the nineteenth century, the experience of children varied in newly settled regions of the country and among the different immigrant groups who brought their distinctive values and traditions to this country. In frontier towns, for example, childhood was hardly sheltered. Youngsters in these new settlements mingled freely among the adults in their midst, many of whom were single and transient, lusting after immediate gratification and seeking their fortunes in the West. The youngest boys and girls—sometimes as young as six—began to work panning gold or selling their mother's pies. Even on the frontier, as children got a little older, tasks were rigidly differentiated according to gender. Young girls began to work at the traditional domestic tasks of cooking, cleaning, and making clothes, whereas boys' work took them away from the household. By the age of twelve or thirteen, boys did the more menial work in mining towns, such as feeding pack mules and pounding out drills in a blacksmith shop, but

CHILD LABOR

Several low-paying trades were reserved for poor children of the 19th century. Boys sold newspapers and ran errands.
LIBRARY OF CONGRESS /
CORBIS

See also
Travel and Vacations

sometimes even took charge of businesses in the absence of the adult owner.

Work beginning at a young age, frequent contact between young and old, exposure to the seamier side of frontier life, and the difficulty of maintaining adult supervision all meant that frontier children grew up amid disturbing if not corrupting circumstances. In light of this, many parents worked hard to instill in their children habits and values similar to those of children living in the Northeast. Children were given moral and religious instruction in secular and sabbath schools, and parents, as soon they could afford it, pressed for formal education, libraries, and bookstores. In addition, many adults without families took an active interest in the education and upbringing of neglected children. Childhood in frontier towns was an imprecise blending of the realities of the roughness of life in these new communities and efforts both to live up to contemporary notions of child nurturance and to maintain some continuity with older moral lessons that parents had learned in their own youth.

Children of the immigrant groups who came to the United States in the late nineteenth century—Italians, Irish, Slavs, and Jews—were raised according to values and practices brought over from the old country, while both parents and children endeavored to adjust to the conditions of life in their new culture. Ethnic groups varied in birthrates, material circumstances, gender values, attitudes toward education and child labor, and the strength of parental authority over children. In general, first-generation immigrant families tended to have more children than did native-born parents but experienced higher infant mortality, due to inadequate diet and poor sanitary conditions. Decisions on whether to keep children in school or send them out to work reflected the varying values and the financial circumstances of the immigrants as they adapted to this country. First-generation Italians, for example, made the overall well-being of the family their chief priority. In their struggle for financial security, parents saw children as wage earners rather than as students; thus, rather than keeping their children in school, the offspring were sent to work in their early teens, and married women were not usually permitted to work. This pattern made sense at the turn of the century, when high rates of fertility and infant mortality among Italian families made it unreasonable to invest resources in individual children. By the 1930s, however, lowered infant mortality rates encouraged fewer births and made it possible for Italian parents to make greater investments in individual children, encouraging them to remain in school.

Jewish families, by contrast, were often better off financially in the first generation than were Italian families and thus could afford to forgo the earnings of their children, enabling them to remain in school. Like Italians, Slavic families depended on their children's wages and urged sons and daughters to acquire job skills rather than stay in school. For these children, contributing to family well-being took precedence over their individual success. Later on, in the mid-twentieth century, children of Chinese immigrants followed a pattern of high achievement in school similar to that of Eastern European Jews. Chinese families valued education and saw it as a route to upward mobility, keeping their children in school in spite of family poverty.

The Twentieth Century

Around the turn of the twentieth century, the rapid pace of social change gave rise to new public responses to children. Large-scale population growth, urbanization, and massive economic transformations such as the growth of heavy industry and corporate capitalism all created a desire for control and order and an anxiety about the future, encompassing concern about the well-being of children. These social and economic changes conjured fearful images of social dislocations, such as broken and inadequate families, poverty, dependency and neglect, crime, and immorality, each of which would affect children. The child-saving movement sought both to protect children from such threatening social transformations and to provide them with the benefits of recent discoveries in medicine and the social sciences. The resulting public reforms ranged from compulsory schooling laws, child labor laws, widows' pensions, and the creation of juvenile courts to the establishment of child health clinics, nursery schools, kindergartens, and playgrounds. These reforms combined two strategies—the Progressive tactic of addressing issues of class and urban life through community-wide efforts at broad social improvement and the implementation of programs nurturing individual differences.

The new system of juvenile justice that emerged in the late nineteenth century was designed to separate youthful from adult criminals and to treat young offenders on an individual basis. The first juvenile court was established in Chicago in 1899, although Massachusetts required separate hearings for children's cases as early as the 1870s. By 1920, all but three states had juvenile courts. The new penology that emerged from the juvenile court movement was designed to keep children out of institutions and to educate, treat, and rehabilitate young offenders. Courtroom procedures were informal and designed for "diagnosis" of the causes of criminal activity and the prevention of future crime. Age-segregated detention facilities were provided, and penal sanctions were imposed on neglectful or malicious adults.

Rehabilitative treatment, through the new probation system, centered on the child's home or family. Probation was designed to be educational and tutelary, and the instruction extended to the youth's family on the premise that the rehabilitation of the delinquent depended on the reeducation of the parents. In 1909, a psychiatric clinic was attached to the original Cook County juvenile court with the goal of using psychiatric and psychological insights into human behavior to prevent juvenile crime by investigating the causes of individual delinquency. While the new system of juvenile justice was a landmark achievement of the Progressive movement of the early twentieth century, juvenile crime persisted as a social problem.

With the passage of compulsory schooling laws, after the turn of the century nearly all children attended elementary school from age five to fourteen, and increasing numbers of children remained in school longer. By 1920, 61.2 percent of those age fourteen to seventeen were enrolled in school, and by 1930 the figure had risen to 73.1 percent. An even higher percentage of younger children was enrolled in elementary school. Progressive reforms of public schools accomplished by the 1930s included the use of uniform curricula, structured and expanded extracurricular activities, the decline of rote recitation, the introduction of attractive textbooks, flexible student groupings, and the hiring of better trained teachers. Public schooling emerged as a mechanism through which to fit individuals into the economy; educators believed that teaching specific skills and behavior patterns would create efficient workers and good citizens. Many scholars emphasize that urban school reform was imposed from above by business classes and directed at controlling poor and minority children in order to maintain their lower-class position in the industrial order. But in many communities, labor and immigrant groups played their own hands in school reforms and used education to enhance the economic welfare of their children.

Children have more need of models than of critics.

JOSEPH JOUBERT
PENSÉES (1842)

Children are not our creations but our guests.

JOHN UPDIKE

Federal efforts on behalf of children after the turn of the century included the White House Conference on Care of Dependent Children of 1909, which led to the creation of the Federal Children's Bureau in 1912. The Children's Bureau began with a focus on child labor legislation and broad issues of child health. The bureau's efforts culminated in the passage of the Sheppard-Towner Act in 1921. This landmark legislation extended the state's responsibility in matters of social welfare by providing federal funds for infant and maternal health care.

The child health movement of the 1920s, funded privately but promoted by the Children's Bureau, created local child health clinics that offered to children examinations and vaccinations and provided advice to mothers on caring for their children's health. Child guidance clinics emerged in the 1920s, as an outgrowth of the first court-affiliated psychiatric clinic. Child guidance clinics were initially designed to prevent mental illness by offering psychiatric and psychological examinations, but after the 1930s they became community facilities offering short-term psychotherapeutic treatment for normal children who exhibited mild behavioral or emotional problems. Taken together, all of these efforts significantly extended the authority of the state in the protection of children; they buttressed the role of the family as the proper place for the care and, if necessary, the rehabilitation of children, and they established novel institutions designed exclusively to meet the needs of individual children.

Within the family, fewer births and the infusion of new "scientific" child-rearing advice changed childhood and relations between parents and children. In 1890, more than half of families in all occupational groups had three or more children, although people in the professions and in business had fewer children than members of the other classes. By 1910, very large families were less common for every group, with small families of from one to three children most common among the middle class. This decline in the birthrate also meant a decline in the proportion of children in the population. The proportion of the total population that was under fifteen dropped from 34.4 percent in 1900 to 29.3 percent in 1930. Smaller families, fewer children and more adults per child in the general population paved the way for even more attention to be focused on the individual child. For most families, the distinctive features of early-twentieth-century childhood was that children lived at home longer and attended school longer. Childhood experience was increasingly uniform among children of the same age group—increasingly leisured, sheltered from adult life, and focused on preparation for adulthood.

After the turn of the century, new reactions to child death and campaigns to exclude children from the labor market indicated new attitudes toward children. Children were "sacralized," that is, invested with new religious and sentimental meaning, as they were set above financial considerations. While over the course of the nineteenth century the death of a child became the most painful and tragic of all deaths, tremendous public outcry at the accidental killings of children by au-

JOHN B. WATSON

Systematic Habit Training at an Early Age

The behavior of some parents in the early twentieth century was influenced by new scientific advice on child rearing offered by behavioral psychologist John B. Watson. Watson and other child study researchers accumulated data on "normal" child development and made popular a behavioral model of child rearing in the 1920s that offered the appeal of scientific approaches to parents anxious about raising children equipped to deal with modern life. Watson argued that the key to psychology was stimulus and response, and believed he had found evidence that children were born without definite instincts and that human nature at birth was more or less plastic. Thus, he asserted, the child's personality was shaped through systematic habit training early in life.

John Watson was the most severe of the behaviorists, asserting that families overindulged their children and that affection was responsible for social maladaptation. He counseled parents to curb their displays of affection, to shake their children's hands rather than to kiss and hug them, and never to let their children sit on their laps. Mothers were instructed to enforce a strict regimen of habit training and to resist their emotional responses to the child. While Watson's harshness limited his popularity, overall the behavioral emphasis on rigid adherence to "scientific" rules and schedules in feeding, toilet training, and discipline influenced the behavior of middle-class parents in the 1920s and early 1930s.

tomobiles and streetcars after the turn of the century indicated children's new sentimental value. Likewise, child labor laws after the turn of the century removed children from the market, in part because it became more efficient to educate children than to employ them but also because of new cultural definitions of legitimate and illegitimate forms of work for children. Acceptable work for children was now instructional rather than instrumental, and even poor parents were expected to subsidize their children's expenses by providing them with an allowance. The value of the new economically "useless" child was then measured in strictly emotional terms, in the parents' joy in a child's smile or goodnight kiss.

Consistent with the emotionally priceless child, relations between parents and children in these smaller families became more democratic. The formerly rigid roles that defined the interaction between parents and children were relaxed, giving way to more spontaneous expressions of emotion and affection throughout the family. The decline in the number of children per family and the focus on emotional satisfaction and nurturance made hierarchically defined relationships between parents and children both unnecessary and undesirable.

The economic stringency of the Great Depression forced many children to take on productive tasks both within and outside the household, reversing the trend of a childhood sheltered from adult responsibility. One important development of the Depression was that the shrinking size of the labor market increased the proportion of children remaining in school through high school graduation. Still, according to a sample of families from one community, children from both lower- and middle-class families faced with unemployment were often forced to take on new responsibilities at home or to find some kind of work to supplement family income.

Where possible, these tasks were assigned according to conventional gender definitions of acceptable "child work." Thus, girls took on housework and child-care responsibilities or earned wages by babysitting or working in neighborhood businesses. Boys were messengers, delivery boys, or dishwashers. In more economically comfortable families, children kept their wages for personal school expenses, clothing, and social activities, while in families facing the greatest hardship, some of the children's earnings went to basic household expenditures. The experience of boys working outside the home inculcated an early sense of independence, dependability, and mature

judgment about money, while girls who took on new household roles were reinforced in their domestic responsibilities and family obligations. Thus, the Depression placed children in responsible positions at younger ages and interrupted the pattern of complete dependence on parents; it also changed the parents' central focus, which had been responding to the needs of their children.

While public responsibility for poor and needy children has chronically fallen short of the mark in the United States, some concern for the welfare of children in the 1930s was manifest in the federal relief agenda of the New Deal. Limited federal daycare programs were established through the Works Progress Administration (WPA) in the 1930s and expanded significantly during World War II. The WPA also provided local school hot lunch programs and built playgrounds, swimming pools, and athletic fields, enhancing recreation facilities for children. The largest public maternity program in the United States to that time was the wartime Emergency Maternal and Infant Care Program, and the 1935 Social Security Act provided aid for rural, disabled and dependent children (ADC). The Federal Emergency Relief Administration (1933) worked on the assumption that poverty alone was not a sufficient reason to separate a child from his or her family and provided relief to enable poor families to remain together. In spite of these important precedents, American society's deeply held notions of the privacy of the family and the sanctity of motherhood have persistently interfered with the full assumption of public responsibility for child welfare.

The economic stringency and absence of fathers during World War II created unique conditions for children growing up in the 1940s. The wartime labor shortage led both servicemen's wives and young people to find jobs. This resulted in a relaxation of child labor and school attendance laws, enabling youths to assume adult responsibilities by age thirteen or fourteen. The scarcity of school personnel shortened school days and forced school closings in many communities, leading many young people to leave school. Women who headed their families while their husbands were overseas often moved in with their parents, resulting in further social dislocation for children and a dilution of parental authority.

The war shortened the sheltered childhood of many youths; it left children unsupervised and families stressed by separations, deaths, and financial constraint. Wartime anxiety over the neglect and premature independence of children was

If a child lives with approval, he learns to live with himself.

DOROTHY LAW NOLTE

♦ **New Deal**
The legislative and administrative program of President F. D. Roosevelt designed to promote economic recovery and social reform during the 1930s; also the period of this program

If there is anything that we wish to change in a child, we should first examine it and see whether it is not something that could better be changed in ourselves.

CARL GUSTAV JUNG
THE INTEGRATION OF THE
PERSONALITY (1939)

See also
Health Care

prompted by the disruption of the ideal of the nuclear family and sheltered childhood created by women's wartime participation in the labor force. The inadequacies of individual women, rather than society's failure to take responsibility for the trauma created by the war or the lack of public responsibility for child welfare, were improperly held to blame for the stresses on childhood in the 1940s.

Child-rearing literature in the 1940s continued to address the middle-class mother, at home full time. This writing returned to an emphasis on affection and emotional expression and on the importance of responding to the child's needs. Arnold Gesell's influential *Infant and Child in the Culture Today*, first published in 1943, avoided the entire issue of discipline and urged parents to follow rather than "force" the child's development. Parents were urged to recognize and respond warmly to their children's needs, on the theory that a satisfied child was a secure child. This renewed emphasis on affection and responsiveness to the child's needs may have been subtly geared to reinforcing an ideology that urged women to return to full-time mothering after their wartime participation in the labor force.

This indulgent advice to parents set the stage for the care of the postwar baby boom generation. The birthrate in the United States, which had steadily declined since 1800, made a dramatic turnaround after 1946. The birthrate went from a low of 18 per 1,000 population in the period 1930 to 1940 to a peak of 25 per 1,000 population in 1957, so that in the eighteen years after World War II (from 1946 to 1964) the nation's population increased more than it had in the fifty years before 1946. Perhaps the most important causes of the baby boom were a revitalization of family values after the war and a particular glorification of motherhood as women's proper social role, although postwar economic prosperity was another important cause.

Advice to parents set out in Benjamin Spock's *The Common Sense Book of Baby and Child Care*, first published in 1946, provided the underpinnings of the permissive child-rearing style in the postwar child-centered family. Spock endeavored to relieve anxious mothers by urging them to feel confident about their natural maternal responses to the child. He advised mothers to monitor their child's growth and development carefully and to offer the praise and encouragement that would enable the child to reach his or her full potential. *Baby and Child Care,* as Spock's book was called in its many later editions, stressed a cheerful and

congenial mother and a gentle and flexible intervention that would enable her to avoid conflict with her child. Feminists now claim that Spock undermined rather than affirmed a mother's confidence in her child-rearing ability by engendering guilt and suggesting consultations with childcare experts when problems emerged. His advice, however, was the template for the emerging 1950s ideal of the full-time, suburban, middle-class mother devoted exclusively to her children.

Postwar prosperity led to rapid housing construction that created new suburban communities, while government subsidies increased the rate of home ownership by 50 percent between 1940 and 1960. Suburban life was "child centered" in the 1950s, creating for some families a unique stage in the history of children. The most common reason given by one surveyed group of adults for moving from the city to the suburbs was "for the sake of the children." New suburbs promised children more space, fresh air, less traffic, and no neighbors in the same building. The suburbs offered parents child-centered organizations such as the Parent-Teacher Association (PTA), Girl Scouts and Boy Scouts, and the Little League. The needs of children dominated the life of the suburban family; postwar parents were ready to give their children "everything," which for some parents meant exclusively material indulgence; for others, the benefits of education; and for still others, thought and concern for their children's development and emotional well-being.

The carefree "Father Knows Best" suburban childhood of the 1950s was more a historical aberration than a long-standing pattern. Demographically, marriage and birth rates were exceptionally high, while the divorce rate was unusually low, making family life in the 1950s exceptionally stable. Families had more children than at any other time in the century, and more women devoted themselves exclusively to child rearing. Postwar prosperity and full-time mothering, combined with Dr. Spock's advice, led to children showered with maternal attention. Single-family homes gave families more privacy and allowed more permissive treatment of children. The conveniences of washing machines and diaper services permitted later and more relaxed toilet training. Central heating in homes made infants less dependent on heavy clothing for warmth, allowing them greater freedom of physical movement. The strong ideological emphasis on gender differences in the 1950s was translated into child-rearing practices, with particular concern that the child develop a firm sexual identity by identifying

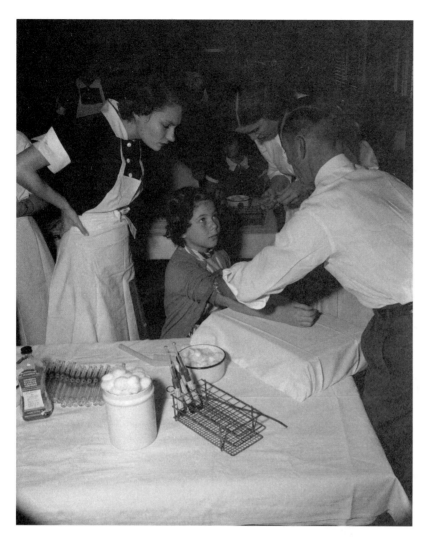

BOON TO HEALTH

*The most notable medical
advance for children's health in
the 1950s was the development
of the polio vaccine by Dr.
Jonas Salk.*
JACK MOEBES / CORBIS

with the parent of the same sex. Working-class parents placed greater emphasis on traditional gender roles than did middle-class parents of the 1950s, and they tended to be stricter in the treatment of their children.

The baby boom also challenged public schools to meet the demands of their swelling enrollment. Spending on public elementary and secondary education went from $5.8 billion in 1950 to $15.6 billion in 1960. Reforms in the public school curriculum in the 1950s were in part spurred by cold war political anxieties, which claimed that this nation's schools were inferior to those of the Soviet Union, leading to significant innovation in mathematics and science curricula. In addition, the 1954 Supreme Court decision *Brown* v. *Board of Education of Topeka* (Kansas) mandated racial desegregation of public schools, making schools an instrument to end racial discrimination.

Isolated in developments of single-family homes, suburban parents structured their children's leisure time so that children's lives were filled with endlessly scheduled lessons, sports teams, and clubs. All of these activities were supervised by adults, and children often had to be brought from home to school to after-school activities and home again by car. While parents encouraged these activities to foster the child's development, suburban childhood was more heavily supervised and scheduled than childhood had been in the cities a decade before. The safe and clean suburbs allowed children to ride bicycles to school, parks, and around their homes, but children were unable to explore beyond their residential neighborhoods without an adult, thus losing the opportunity for independent movement while they were young.

Medical advances of the 1950s improved the health of children. The most notable was the development by Dr. Jonas Salk of a vaccine against polio, which was approved by the federal government in 1955. While children of the 1950s have been called the healthiest, best-fed, best-clothed, and best-housed generation in this nation's his-

The largest selling book ever, next to the Bible, is Dr. Benjamin Spock's Baby and Child Care *(thirty-nine million copies in print by 1989).*

PAGE 338

C

*Most American
children suffer too
much mother and
too little father.*

GLORIA STEINEM
IN THE NEW YORK TIMES
(AUGUST 26, 1971)

tory, some children—notably poor and especially poor black children living in inner cities or in rural areas—were left out of the suburban dream entirely. While postwar housing growth created lower-class and working-class suburbs with neighborhoods populated by Irish, Italian, and Jewish families, restrictive covenants kept black families out of suburbs.

While postwar prosperity expanded the size of the middle class and actually reduced the percentage of poor in the population, the distribution of wealth in the postwar boom meant that the impoverished received an ever smaller share of the nation's resources. Government health care was poorly distributed after the war, to the detriment of the poorest families, and while overall infant mortality rates went down in the 1940s, for nonwhite infants the rate actually went up from 1950 to 1960. In the late 1980s, the United States ranked nineteenth among industrial nations in its rate of infant mortality. Moreover, children have been the slowest group to move out of poverty, since federal relief programs, notably Aid to Families with Dependent Children (AFDC), have been less effective in helping children than other groups. This is because American society views the care of poor children as primarily the responsibility of their parents. It is reluctant to support poor parents, since it represents "pauperizing" them. Thus, it limits its responsibility to poor children, creating a cycle of poverty that has been particularly devastating to children.

Recent History of Childhood

The type of sheltered childhood enjoyed by many privileged children who grew up in the 1950s and 1960s changed when a combination of feminism and the end of the postwar economic boom caused a series of transformations in the family. First, the birthrate fell from the late 1950s peak of 3.8 children per family to less than 2 in the late 1980s. Second, the divorce rate rose sharply: the number of divorces in 1988 was twice as high as in 1966 and three times higher than in 1950; by 1988 one-third of all marriages ended in divorce. This led to an increase in the number of single-parent households, and the number of female-headed households doubled between 1966 and 1988. Finally, married women entered the labor force in unprecedented numbers; in 1980, middle-income families were likely to have mothers in the labor force, and in 1988 more than half of all mothers with children in their first year were employed. Thus, by the late 1980s only 15 percent

of households were composed of a breadwinner father, a full-time housewife mother, and children, the pattern that described 70 percent of all households in 1960.

The fact that most mothers with young children now work full time and that many of these women are single heads of households have dramatically changed the experience of children. They have reduced the amount of time children spend with their mothers, though in some cases the father's involvement in child rearing has increased. While the issue of child care was previously identified only with poor families, increased labor force participation of mothers later linked it to families across the economic spectrum for the first time and challenged definitions of what constitutes quality child care and who should provide it. The traditional assumption that mothers alone can provide care that is essential for the well-being of young children was replaced by a widely held belief that what children need is responsible, responsive adult care that includes a relationship with at least one adult based on love and long-term commitment. This loving, responsible adult need not be the mother or any relative; the important point was the quality of the relationship between the adult and child.

Still holding to the notion that child care was primarily the private responsibility of parents, American society had yet to provide adequate public child care to meet the needs of dual-earning parents and single parents. This created stresses for both children and parents, especially for working mothers. Only in the most exceptional families with working mothers were family roles realigned so that both parents shared equally in child care and in household responsibilities. In such cases, children learned new gender roles—fathers who shared in nurturance and the expression of emotions and mothers who were equal contributors to the family economy. More typically, working mothers shouldered double obligations of family and job responsibilities, and both the quality and quantity of time children spent with parents were limited.

Children came to grow up in what are called "new families," which included families where both parents work full time, single-parent families, families with unwed parents, families with gay or lesbian parents, and families in which remarriage created a series of step relations. The process of divorce and the reconstituting of families had a range of effects on children. Children often blamed themselves for the breakup of their parents' marriage; they worried about the separation and their continued relationship to each parent and became anxious as they anticipated the new set of relationships that came with parental remarriage. Many children experienced temporary depression or anxiety or exhibited antisocial behavior, but the trauma of divorce and remarriage in many cases were mitigated by sustained and loving relationships with parents who were responsive to the child's needs, so that children emerged well adjusted after their parents' divorce.

The care children received in these newly configured families varied, but in general, children in new families experienced greater responsibility and independence at an earlier age than did children in conventional nuclear families. Some developed close relationships with several different adults and benefited from the variety of role models. Increased household responsibilities, when assigned with sensitivity to the child's developmental stage and needs, often strengthened the child; children derived self-esteem from the real contributions they made to the family and developed an enhanced sense of self-reliance and autonomy. Children who grew up in single-parent families may have been given even greater household responsibilities to relieve their overburdened parent. In these families there were risks that childhood may be foreshortened if children took on too much household responsibility or if the child became the emotional support and confidant of the single parent.

Those who grew up in female-headed households were often subject to special stresses since these families were frequently poor. One year after divorce, women and children experienced, on average, a 73 percent drop in the standard of living, while men experienced a 43 percent improvement. The feminization of poverty was due in part to fathers' noncompliance with child support awards after divorce and in general to the sex-segregated workplace in which women earn less than men.

The late 1980s and 1990s were a period of transition in gender roles and family composition that has changed the experience of children. The feminist movement, which led women into the labor market seeking equality in both the family and in society, also pressed for quality care for all children. Much of the progress in securing day care, maternity and paternity leaves, and part-time and flextime work were political achievements of the women's movement. The provision of adequate health care and quality day care for all children depends on society's willingness to take public responsibility for the well-being of all its children.

Throughout American history the stage of childhood has been sensitive to economic changes and to changes in the roles of women. The image of a childhood utterly sheltered from the adult world and under a mother's exclusive care has been idealized in our society. It was in fact rarer than is commonly assumed and was always associated with affluence; many theoreticians now question whether it is best for the child. Social anxiety over the quality of childhood has recurred frequently through our history; the current tension reflects a conflict between changes in women's roles and society's unwillingness to make child welfare a public responsibility, rather than a direct concern for the well-being of children. American society has yet to achieve what is best for all its children.

—MARGO HORN

THE CITY

From the earliest days of colonization to the present, American cities have been central places, providing a focal point for economic development, local government, culture, social reform, and technological innovation, and a site where newcomers clustered and became acculturated. A city is a site with at least twenty-five hundred residents that performs various specialized functions for itself and surrounding smaller communities and supports a cosmopolitan life-style. Organic entities that change over time, cities are composed of three major elements: physical structures (spatial dimensions, demographics, economy, and technology); organizational structures (class, ethnic, and racial groups, social institutions, and government); and value systems (attitudes, ideologies, and behavior). Their evolution can be categorized into four eras: the early American city (1630–1820), which comprised about 5 percent of the population; the walking city (1820–1870), which existed when urbanization occurred at its fastest rate and cities began to provide essential services; the industrialized radial city (1870–1950s), an entity of imposing physical dimensions inhabited by immense populations, a product of industrialization, immigration, and cheap mass transit; and the suburban metropolis (1945–1990s), characterized by the dominance of suburbia, the decline of the urban core, and the emergence of the Sunbelt.

Children are the living messages we send to a time we will never see.

NEIL POSTMAN
"INTRODUCTION," THE
DISAPPEARANCE OF
CHILDHOOD

♦ **Nuclear family**

A family group that consists only of a father, mother, and children

C

THE CITY

The Early American City

The Early American City

The first colonial cities, starting with Spanish Saint Augustine, Florida (1565), were clusters of concentrated populations, vanguards of settlement located on bodies of water, whose functions included defense, government, trade, and the support of religion and culture. Their importance transcended population. They were the most dynamic colonial places, and loci of an urbane and cosmopolitan lifestyle, and sites of key colonial institutions ranging from governments to churches. Their weak and often oligarchic governments provided few public services unconnected to commerce, relying instead on private initiative. Later cities learned from their experience, copying physical layouts, social organizations, and privatism.

Boston was the first English colonial city, founded in 1630 by the Puritans as a model settlement of Visible Saints who shared the same values and beliefs. Boston was an exceptionally homogeneous city, although the Puritan community weakened as the second and third generations were less likely to have a saving experience. By 1690 Boston had a population of seven thousand, which made it the fourth largest city in the British Empire. Philadelphia, New York, Newport, and Charleston, all compact ports, were the other major colonial cities. They were originally overwhelmingly English except for Charleston,

which by 1680 had become a haven for French Huguenots, who had first come to South Carolina in 1670, and New York, the cosmopolitan former Dutch colony of New Amsterdam, where eighteen languages were spoken. The early residents of the latter included Sephardic Jews.

Cities became more heterogeneous following Queen Anne's War (1702–1713), as indentured Germans and Scotch-Irish migrated to New York and especially to Philadelphia. After the French and Indian War (1754–1763), there was a substantial immigration of Irish and Scotch-Irish that temporarily halted during the Revolution and resumed afterward. The immigrants shied away from Boston because of its historic intolerance and limited economic opportunities for newcomers.

The colonial cities all had substantial black populations. In the early 1700s, Charleston's black and white populations were equal, and blacks comprised one-fourth of New York and one-sixth of Boston. As late as 1771, 15 percent of New York's adult male work force were slaves.

Colonial cities had a multilayered social structure. Ministers were at the apex of Boston's social structure until they were supplanted in the late seventeenth century by professionals and wealthy merchants who had the biggest homes and the most prominent church pews. Boston's merchants then controlled 40 percent of colonial shipping, but by the mid-eighteenth century they had lost their leadership because of an unproductive backcountry and the maturation of aggressive challengers, primarily Philadelphians who shipped wheat from the hinterland to Caribbean and transatlantic markets. Newport emphasized the slave trade; Charleston, rice; and New York, wheat and livestock.

The "better sort" enjoyed a high standard of living and dominated society and public affairs. In 1687 Boston's richest 5 percent controlled 25 percent of the city's taxable wealth, a figure that increased to 44 percent in 1771, about the same ratio as in other cities. The upper class was an open elite, and there were rags-to-riches stories, especially in New York, where 33 to 40 percent of the merchants in 1775 were self-made men. The rich owned elegantly furnished brick homes, rode in carriages, wore expensive clothing and powdered wigs, socialized at the finest coffeehouses, belonged to restrictive voluntary organizations like Philadelphia's Schuylkill Fishing Colony (1732), and married within the elite circle.

The "middling sort" composed about 70 percent of society. They had smaller homes, less

AMERICAN REVOLUTION SYMBOL

A 1900 view of Boston's Old South Meeting House, built in 1729, was a symbol of revolutionary Boston. Cities like Boston were instrumental in the American Revolution. LIBRARY OF CONGRESS/ CORBIS

property, and cheaper clothes. One-fifth of urban male workers were shopkeepers or other low-level nonmanual workers, and about half were self-employed or highly paid artisans who had a strong self-image as hard working, frugal, and competent.

At the bottom of the social ladder were the impoverished "inferior sorts": unskilled workers, indentured servants, and slaves, comprising 20–30 percent of urbanites in 1770. No permanent white proletariat existed because of opportunities to advance or move on, but the gap between rich and poor was growing. In 1687, 14 percent of Bostonians had no property; the figure had doubled to 29 percent in 1771. The poor mainly lived on the periphery in crowded housing and were increasingly insecure, disaffected, and less deferential.

Municipal governments had limited authority to tax or spend, and outside of New England were regarded as exclusive, elitist, tight-fisted, and insensitive to changing conditions. Their primary duty was to promote commerce rather than to provide essential services or social conformity. Three-fifths of all colonial cities were unincorporated, especially in New England, where they had considerable autonomy. Power there resided in the town meeting, where freemen (only 16 percent at mid century) enacted laws, levied taxes, settled disputes, and elected selectmen to run affairs between meetings. Under the British, New York was originally a royally chartered municipal borough run by a mayor and council dominated by merchants appointed by the governor, but charter reform in 1731 made it an open corporation with annual elections that forced the notables to be more responsive to the growing electorate. Political factions emerged over economic issues and conflicts between rival elite families. Philadelphia, whose government was one of only three closed corporations in the colonies, was run by an oligarchy with long terms, the prerogative to appoint successors, and, except for taxation, other wide-ranging powers. Charleston had no municipal government at all until 1715, when the provincial assembly appointed insensitive commissioners to supervise specific tasks.

Most new laws concerned economic matters because commerce was the cornerstone of urban economies. Municipalities regulated and supervised sites of mercantile activity like the wharfs and markets, and by 1690 all but Boston had a regulated market with standards of quality, weights, and measures. In Boston, however, economic laws comprised a mere 9 percent of all edicts. Bostonians believed that open markets provided opportunities for smaller purveyors and thus did not have a permanent public market until Faneuil Hall was built in 1742.

Cities did a poor job of coping with such public problems as morality, health, poverty, safety, and streets. Homogeneous Boston was the best-governed and most communally responsible city. Its earliest laws included fire-prevention measures, bans on garbage dumping, and penalties for Sabbath breaking and adultery. In 1701 over half of its ordinances dealt with public safety, order, and peace. Public services were paid for by license fees, fines, tariffs, lotteries, rents from public markets and wharves, and, later in the century, by property or poll taxes. There was also heavy reliance on private initiative. Streets received considerable attention because they were essential for commerce, created health hazards by draining poorly, and were dangerous for pedestrians and children at play. Boston had excellent paved streets and sewers, but it took other cities as long as forty years to catch up, mostly through relying on private efforts. Boston had some of the strictest fire regulations and best fire-fighting equipment in the world, yet there were severe fires in 1676, 1679, and 1711, after which the first volunteer fire company was established. The model for the future, however, was Philadelphia's elite Union Fire Company, formed in 1736 by Benjamin Franklin to fight fires and prevent looting.

Chronic poverty, particularly among women and children, materialized by the 1700s and was a major concern by mid century. In Charleston between 1751 and 1774, over 80 percent of people receiving aid were women and children. Impoverishment was frequently caused by the economic dislocations and bloodshed resulting from colonial wars. Thirteen percent of Boston's adult women were widows following King George's War (1744–1748), many of them left without any means of support or marketable skills other than sewing. Assistance to the deserving poor comprised a major portion of municipal expenditures, rising in New York from £250 in 1698 to £5000 in 1770, supplemented by private aid from philanthropists, churches, and voluntary associations. Most assistance was outdoor relief (money, food, clothing, and fuel) rather than indoor relief (institutionalization in almshouses).

Crime was less widespread and less severely punished in the colonies than in England. Homogeneous Puritan communities tried to prevent deviance through social pressure and regulation of public houses, but when necessary they relied on harsher methods such as banishment (the "antin-

THE CITY

The Early American City

During the colonial era the city was only of modest size, ten to fifteen thousand people.

PAGE 528

See also
Commercial Architecture

C

omian" Anne Hutchinson), whipping, and even execution (Quakeress Mary Dyer). As cities became more heterogeneous through the influx of outsiders like sailors, blacks, escaped felons, and runaway servants, the crime rate increased. The rise was accounted for primarily by morals violations, punished by fines and whippings. Policing was originally done by privately organized patrols—as late as 1690 New York was the only city with a paid watch—but by 1720 all the cities had copied the European system of municipally paid daytime constables and night watches to apprehend offenders, report fires, and maintain order against occasional riots caused by such lower-class grievances as impressment and soaring bread prices. Charleston and New York had the added special problem of potential slave insurrections. New York had a slave riot in 1712, and in 1741, when nearly one-fourth of the labor force were bondsmen, rumors of a slave revolt resulted in thirty-one executions.

Little was accomplished in the area of public health. Cities were hard-pressed to cope with the garbage dumped in the streets, which attracted hogs and stray animals. Boston had the cleanest streets, yet in 1711 the garbage on the streets caught fire. Infectious diseases were deadly threats, although port officials inspected and quarantined entering ships. Smallpox was particularly dreaded,

and there were three outbreaks in Boston between 1666 and 1702. After a fourth episode in 1721 that infected almost 6,000 and killed about 850, Cotton Mather and Dr. Zabdiel Boylston encouraged inoculation. The procedure gained acceptance only slowly, however, and was not widely applied until the 1760s.

Religion was the most important semipublic institution, and a church was usually the city's most prominent physical structure. Religion promoted morality and discipline, a message that became less salient with increased secularization, the worship of money and status, and the popularity of taverns, drinking, gambling, and blood sport. By 1737 Boston had 177 innkeepers and liquor retailers, one for every twenty-five adult males. Religious life was reinvigorated in the 1730s and 1740s by the Great Awakening, which promoted evangelical Protestantism and made thousands of converts. The revival led to higher moral standards and the formation of new churches, denominations, and seminaries that fragmented urban society.

Colonial cities were centers of a cosmopolitan lifestyle. In Puritan Boston children attended school to learn to read the Bible; future clergymen studied at the publicly supported Boston Public Latin School (1635) and went on to Harvard College (1636). By the mid-eighteenth century,

HARVARD COLLEGE

Harvard College, in Cambridge, Massachusetts, was founded in 1636, and by the mid eighteenth century had become a mark of status for classically trained elite sons.
CORBIS-BETTMANN

education was largely secularized, a mark of status for classically trained elite sons or vocational training for middle-class sons that ranged from apprenticeships to baccalaureate training at the College of Philadelphia (1755, now the University of Pennsylvania). Cities had weekly newspapers, beginning with the *Boston News-Letter* (1704), public and subscription libraries, bookshops, and other institutions like coffeehouses, mechanics' societies, and Philadelphia's American Philosophical Society (1743) that encouraged enlightened discourse.

Cities were instrumental in the coming of the American Revolution because they were the scenes of the greatest oppression and because they had the human resources and communication facilities (inns, coffeehouses, and print shops) to plan and implement resistance. Merchants led the opposition to George III's reassertion of royal authority, particularly following the Stamp Act (1765), to protect their rights as Englishmen. To secure repeal, leading Bostonians drew up petitions, organized boycotts and nonimportation agreements, established committees of correspondence, and allied with other social groups who staged organized riots. The Sons of Liberty subsequently led the opposition to the Townshend Acts (1767) and the Tea Tax (1770), culminating in the Boston Tea Party (16 December 1773). The Coercive (Intolerable) Acts then closed the port of Boston and revoked the charter of Massachusetts, thereby throttling commerce and liberty. Boston's Committee of Correspondence responded by appealing to other cities to organize a continental congress to coordinate collective action against the Crown. After independence and the defeat of the British, urbanites became the leading supporters of a strong national government to facilitate trade and promote economic stability. In 1787, when only 5 percent of Americans lived in cities, twenty of the fifty-five delegates to the Constitutional Convention were urbanites, and these cosmopolites saw the Constitution through to ratification.

The urban population over the next four decades remained at about 5 percent, although the number of cities with over ten thousand residents increased from five in 1790 to twenty-three in 1830. Twenty-five cities obtained more democratic charters, the franchise was liberalized, and most closed corporations like that of Philadelphia (1796) were replaced. An urban frontier emerged on the fringe of a rising national urban network, copying the methods older cities had employed to plat their sites and deal with emerging problems.

Towns like Pittsburgh, Louisville, and Cincinnati promoted economic growth at transfer points along navigable waterways like the Ohio River by centralizing and distributing goods and services. These cities also brought the accoutrements of civilization, including institutions of higher learning like Transylvania College (now University) in Lexington, Kentucky.

The Walking City

The era of most rapid urbanization occurred between 1820 and 1870, when the urban proportion of the national population reached 25 percent, a product of economic growth, the transportation revolution, and immigration. In the period 1830–1860 the number of cities with a population in excess of ten thousand quadrupled from 23 to 101. New York was the largest in 1860, with 813,600 residents, and eight others surpassed 100,000. These physically small cities seldom extended more than two miles in any direction, and consequently walking was the main form of locomotion. They were still primarily centers of commerce in which land uses were very mixed, although their populations became heterogeneous, divided into ethnic and class subcommunities. Municipal government grew increasingly powerful, often under the control of professional politicians, and began to provide essential public services.

The core of the walking city was the waterfront with its docks, warehouses, business offices, factories, and homes. The economic elite lived nearby in choice locations, particularly the healthier high land, while the poor resided in back lots, alleys, or shanties at the outskirts of town. The biggest cities were densely populated, led by New York with 135.6 persons per acre in 1850; slums were even more packed. Land was extremely valuable, not only in Manhattan, where property tripled in value between 1819 and 1836, but also in instant cities like Chicago. Growth and development were promoted primarily by speculators, businessmen, and politicians who stood to directly profit.

The transportation revolution had a huge impact on urban commerce. New York's emergence as the leading trade center after the War of 1812 was achieved through such innovations as the American Black Ball Line, a regular packet service to Liverpool (1818) that facilitated planning, auctions that cut out middlemen, steamship service via the Atlantic all the way to New Orleans, and the Erie Canal (1825). The city became the nation's financial and communications center, and the home of the finest lawyers, accountants, and

In the second and third quarters of the nineteenth century, thousands of tenement dwelling units were erected in New York, Philadelphia, and other growing cities.

PAGES 214–215

See also

Urban Parks

55

With the growth of cities in the nineteenth century, the responsibilities of municipal government grew markedly.

PAGE 382

other professionals. By 1841 New York controlled 59.1 percent of American foreign trade and dominated the hinterland.

The Erie Canal's success promoted a canal-building mania culminating with the Illinois and Michigan Canal (1848), which connected Chicago to the Mississippi River. Canals were soon surpassed, however, by railroads, introduced by aggressive Baltimoreans who established the Baltimore & Ohio Railroad (1828) to expand the city's nodal zone. Railroads carried freight and passengers rapidly, year-round, and wherever workers could lay tracks. Trackage rose from 2,800 miles in 1840 to 30,600 miles in 1860. The railroad was especially the key to western development. Chicago's emergence as a railroad hub in the 1850s enabled it to overtake conservative Saint Louis as the West's leading city.

The introduction of mass transit in the largest cities encouraged physical expansion by enabling residents to travel longer distances in the same amount of time. In 1827 the omnibus, a large, twelve-passenger vehicle drawn by two horses, was introduced in New York. The slow (three to four miles per hour), uncomfortable ride over fixed routes cost one shilling (12.5 cents), a sum limiting ridership to the middle and upper classes. Nonetheless, by 1853 New York had 683 licensed omnibuses transporting 120,000 riders. The omnibus accustomed people to ride to work, and led to the emergence of the commuter.

In 1832 the superior horse-drawn streetcar was introduced in New York. The forty-passenger vehicles rode on rails, resulting in faster (six miles per hour), cheaper, smoother, and safer rides. They operated under municipal franchises that specified terms of service in return for the right to lay tracks on public streets and long-term contracts. The streetcars were an enormous success, making journeys fast and predictable, and fit in well with a time-driven society. By 1860 at least nine cities had street railroads, led by Philadelphia with 155 miles of track. Philadelphia took advantage of the transportation revolution to annex its surrounding communities in 1854, thereby growing in size from 2 to 129 square miles.

The urban social structure became increasingly unequal. In 1833, Boston's top 4 percent had 59 percent of the city's wealth, and 64 percent in 1848, figures typical of major cities. A few made it from rags to riches, typically in new or smaller industrial cities whose economies were growing rapidly and where there was no entrenched elite. The rich segregated themselves by joining prestigious churches and restricted voluntary associa-

tions like the Union Club or a yacht club, and moving toward the periphery, into large mansions with such conveniences as indoor plumbing.

The middle class, 40 percent of the work force, were predominantly white-collar workers who had wide social contacts and belonged to voluntary associations; advocated such values as hard work, self-discipline, and domestic tranquillity; and limited leisure time to useful, moral recreations like baseball. They earned more than blue-collar workers and worked in clean and quiet settings. Under 10 percent were salaried clerks, salesmen, or bookkeepers—typically young men who could realistically expect substantially higher future incomes. The middle class lived in good neighborhoods near their jobs, in nicely furnished and carpeted homes with four to six rooms that provided privacy. Their wives shopped at specialty shops until mid century, when an important shift in merchandising occurred with the rise of large department stores with elegant interiors and huge inventories, like A. T. Stewart's in New York, which had two thousand salesclerks.

Blue-collar workers' standard of living declined as wages fell between 1830 and 1850, and it became harder to achieve a competency. Boston's propertyless rose from 44.6 percent in 1830 to 57.3 percent in 1860. At mid century, when the minimum budget for the average New York family of five was nearly $540, tradesmen earned only $300 a year, and wives and children had to work. One-third to one-half of the middle and lower classes were vertically mobile, accumulating property and advancing into better jobs. However, these gains were shaky because of boom-and-bust cycles, and required enormous familial sacrifices. Urbanites, especially young clerks and blue-collar workers, were geographically highly mobile, seeking better opportunities. Only one-third to two-fifths of urban residents remained in the same city for a decade between 1830 and 1860.

Cities were the locus of an emerging working-class community with a shared consciousness of interests, residential propinquity, and a common lifestyle. Manual workers unaccustomed to time-work discipline maintained an oppositional premodern culture largely expressed by leisure-time activities over which, unlike work, they exercised considerable control. These members of the male bachelor subculture enjoyed violent, socially dysfunctional, time-wasting participatory pleasures at gambling dens, groggeries, brothels, cockpits, boxing rings, and raucous theaters.

Manufacturing was mainly small scale in artisan-owned shops, but the rise of a national market

See also
Housing

at mid century encouraged entrepreneurs to increase production by employing the American system of manufacturing. The earliest factories, in small New England towns like Waltham (1813) and Lowell, Massachusetts (1822), harnessed the energy from fast-running rivers to operate machinery. The textile mills employed single farm girls sixteen to twenty-five years old who lived in a highly regulated and paternalistic community until, in the 1840s, they were replaced by unskilled Irish immigrants. The introduction of steam power enabled industrialists to locate in major cities near cheap labor, transportation, large markets, and sources of credit, information, and technological innovation. However, the urban occupational structure kept a preindustrial flavor because small-scale production lingered on, and many factories did not feature extreme division of labor. New York became the leading manufacturing center, but most plants had fewer than twenty workers. The great industrial boom came during the Civil War, to fulfill military requirements for munitions, food, and clothing.

Privatism slowly gave way to public efforts to deal effectively with urban problems beyond the scope of individual efforts. The movement for municipally sponsored services was advocated by boosters, businessmen, social reformers, and professional politicians. By mid century, state legislatures revised charters to empower municipalities to levy taxes and provide essential services. As local governments gained power, politics became a career for upwardly mobile men who belonged to emerging political machines like Tammany Hall that supported municipalization of services, which meant patronage.

Improved security was a prime requirement. The propertied classes were apprehensive about robberies, assaults, vice, labor unrest, and riots (there were thirty-seven in 1835 alone), which they attributed to lower-class Irishmen unable to cope with urban life; demands grew for deterrence, apprehension, and punishment. Municipalities responded by organizing professional police departments loosely modeled on the London Metropolitan Police (1829). Boston organized the first professional force in the United States (1838), but the prototype was New York's, established in 1844. The police were salaried, appointed and promoted by political connections, worked regular beats, exercised considerable discretion, and by the mid 1850s were armed and uniformed.

Fire protection was originally provided by middle-class volunteer fire companies, but by the

C

THE CITY

The Walking City

If you would be known, and not know, vegetate in a village; if you would know and not be known, live in a city.

CHARLES CALEB COLTON
LACON (1825)

THE PUBLIC HEALTH MOVEMENT
Improving Municipal Quality of Life

Physicians, journalists, and health faddists pressured municipalities to take greater responsibility for public health. Key problems included potable water; epidemics (cholera killed 10 percent of the population of Saint Louis in 1849); infant mortality, which surpassed 50 percent in New York at mid century; and clean streets. The first major action occurred in Philadelphia. The city had a history of yellow fever, and in 1798 established its own water system. New York followed suit in 1842, yet as late as 1860, one-fourth of major cities still relied on private water companies that inadequately serviced poor neighborhoods. Cities dealt ineptly with sewers and streets. As late as the 1850s, New York and Chicago still used pigs as scavengers, and only around 1860 were private street cleaning companies hired. Chicago dealt with the sewage problem in the late 1850s by raising street levels so the refuse would flow into Lake Michigan, the source of its water supply. At mid century, one-fourth of city budgets went to paving and cleaning streets, principally major commercial avenues, yet by 1880 only one-half of streets were paved, making street sweeping difficult. Seventy percent of cities had public street cleaning in 1880, but only one-fourth had municipal garbage collection.

The public health movement further advocated that cities provide breathing spaces for moral and health purposes. These needs were first fulfilled by private romantic cemeteries like Cambridge's Mount Auburn (1831), which had landscaped gardens, tree-lined walks, and lakes that provided picnickers an escape from urban hustle and bustle. A municipal park movement emerged in the 1840s to secure fresh air and sites for exercise to make workers healthier, develop choice new neighborhoods, and promote the reputation of cities. New York's secluded 840-acre Central Park (1858), designed by Frederick Law Olmsted and Calvert Vaux with rustic areas and formal gardens, became the model for future suburban parks.

*My ideal city would
be one long main
street with no cross
streets or side streets
to jam up traffic.*

ANDY WARHOL

See also
Public Architecture

1830s they had become lower-class fraternal and athletic clubs, centers of ethnic, occupational, or neighborhood gangs more interested in racing or in fighting than in quenching fires. Businessmen and fire insurance underwriters lobbied for tougher fire codes, advanced technology, and professionalized fire departments in order to improve fire-fighting capabilities. Most cities established professional fire departments by the 1860s, including Chicago (1858) and New York (1865)—usually following a disastrous fire.

Moral reform was largely in the hands of middle-class voluntary societies motivated by Christian morality and fears about the urban milieu. They advocated public education to promote order by indoctrinating immigrant children with traditional values and behavior and training them for jobs. Boston was the first major city to have a public education system (1818), followed by New York (1832) and Philadelphia (1836), and such systems were commonplace outside the South by 1860. The Children's Aid Society (1853) publicized the plight of homeless children and sent them to rural foster homes where they would have a good family environment, learn the work ethic, and become healthier. The temperance movement sought to curtail drinking, the reputed root of poverty, unreliable workers, and crime. Penal reformers promoted asylumlike penitentiaries to rehabilitate deviants by separating them from a bad environment and indoctrinating them with Christian morality, a work ethic, and respect for authority. Charity was limited to the deserving poor of high moral character. Thus pregnant women lacking proof of good moral character were turned away from New York's Asylum for Lying-in Women.

Reformers admired the home as the locus of female domesticity and a sanctuary from an increasingly dangerous outside world. Urban families were nuclear and smaller than in the past, but were frequently extended to include unmarried relatives, servants, or boarders. Women were expected to be exclusively homemakers, but poorer wives could not be, and at mid century about one-tenth held jobs, primarily as domestics. They comprised one-fourth of manufacturing workers. Schoolteaching, an extension of the domestic domain, was the only appropriate profession for middle-class young women. In 1860, they comprised nearly four-fifths of teachers in heavily urban Massachusetts. Middle-class women's activities outside the home were largely limited to shopping, often at massive new department stores

like A. T. Stewart's in New York, with their elegant interiors and huge inventories; to services at evangelical churches, where they comprised a majority; and to reformist voluntary organizations through which they extended their domestic role.

Cities were major destinations for Irish and German immigrants who came to America at mid century to escape poverty and persecution. More than two-fifths of New Orleans; over half of New York, Boston, and San Francisco; and over three-fifths of Saint Louis, Chicago, and Milwaukee were foreign born. The Irish settled mainly in eastern cities and the Germans in the Midwest, both groups in ethnic villages that helped to ease culture shock. Germans were geographically highly concentrated—in 1860, 83 percent in Milwaukee lived with their own kind, compared with 47 percent of the Irish and 53 percent of the native born. Their neighborhoods provided a full range of Old World institutions, including beer gardens, delicatessens, and turnvereins. Germans arrived with skills, literacy, and some capital, and fared far better than the poor, uneducated, and unskilled Irish, who got the lowest-level jobs. At mid century over half of New York's day laborers were Irish men, and three-fourths of Irish women were domestics. They endured deadly riots and other hostility from nativists because of anti-Catholicism, job competition, and political rivalries between native-born Whigs and Know-Nothings and Irish machine Democrats.

Antebellum blacks were the least urban ethnic group. There were sizable free African American communities in southern cities in the 1820s whose residents were relatively more skilled and dispersed than in the North. Three-fourths of free black Charlestonians in 1860 were artisans, primarily barbers, carpenters, and caterers, comprising 16 percent of the city's skilled workers. Northern blacks were overwhelmingly urban, encountered severe prejudice—they could seldom vote or serve on juries, were subject to race riots, and even expulsion—and lived in highly concentrated neighborhoods where segregation encouraged the establishment of a wide-reaching community including churches and mutual aid, educational, and fraternal societies seldom seen in the South except in New Orleans. About one-tenth of slaves lived in cities where they worked as servants, craftsmen, and factory laborers. They comprised over half of the work force in Charleston and Richmond, where feared contacts with freedmen and whites resulted in stringent restrictive laws and, after 1840, a stable slave population.

The Industrial Radial City

The United States emerged as an urban country in 1920, with over half the population (51.4 percent) residing in cities. The national culture was shaped by urban values, attitudes, and behavior, and cities became a focus of the federal government. Sixty-eight cities had over 100,000 residents, led by New York with 5.6 million. The post-Civil War city differed dramatically from the walking city because it was much bigger, had a larger and more heterogeneous population, enjoyed cheap mass transit, and had highly specialized land uses and industry-based economies. Radial cities were the locus of powerful political machines, impoverished slums, and ethnic villages that encouraged the rise of the Progressive movement to promote political democracy, social justice, economic opportunity, and moral order. These cities promised a better life for poor immigrants, rural dwellers fleeing boring small town society, and African Americans escaping Jim Crow laws.

Urban spatial relationships were reshaped by the emergence of cheap, rapid mass transit. The geographic distribution of businesses, industries, and homes was altered by soaring land costs in the old urban core and expansion toward the periphery made possible by improved transportation. By the mid 1880s, horse-drawn streetcars were used in three hundred cities, supplemented in fourteen major cities by cable cars. In 1888 fast (ten to twelve miles per hour), reliable electric trolleys were introduced, in Richmond, Virginia, and two years later there were 1,260 miles of electrified tracks, compared with 500 miles of cable car tracks and 5,700 miles served by horse-drawn vehicles. In 1902, 22,000 miles of urban tracks were electrified, including elevated routes over crowded downtown streets. Even more advanced were subways, built in Boston (1897), Philadelphia (1908), and especially New York (1904), which had a one-hundred-mile system by 1920. Traction lines required large capital investments for expensive equipment and consolidations, and great political clout (or bribes) to secure necessary franchises and rights of way; nevertheless, they generated substantial profits from millions of five-cent rides. Traction lines enhanced real estate values along their routes and facilitated urban sprawl, streetcar suburbs, annexations (Chicago in 1889 grew from 35 to 185 square miles and added 200,000 residents), and consolidations like the merger of Brooklyn and New York in 1898.

Streetcar traffic increased steadily until about 1923, when it began to encounter strong competition from automobiles. Several major cities, particularly Los Angeles and Detroit, dropped plans for subways, opting for better roads instead. By 1930, more than 50 percent of nonfarm families owned a car, typically the cheap Model T, and that ownership had an enormous impact on urban life. Riders traveled independently of fixed streetcar routes and schedules, could live in suburbia, and had greater leisure options, ranging from picnics to necking in the back seat. Furthermore, hundreds of thousands of jobs were created in production, repair, and related industries, and trucks greatly lowered freight costs.

The enhanced mass transit and skyrocketing realty values combined to create central business districts. In Chicago, for example, downtown property values rose by 700 percent between 1877 and 1891, making the old urban core too expensive for housing or factories. The central business district became the locus of administrative, financial, and commercial activities, cultural institutions, and light industry. Suburbanites worked in its office buildings, tourists and business travelers stayed at its hotels, and housewives shopped at its specialty shops and department stores. High land costs encouraged construction of taller structures, originally built with thick brick or masonry walls limiting interior space. An important improvement was the modern skyscraper. Chicago's ten-story Home Life Insurance Building (1885) was the first, employing a lightweight steel skeleton frame. Tenants of skyscrapers were independent professionals and major companies that centralized large bureaucracies in monumental structures erected for self-advertising, exemplified by Manhattan's fifty-five-story Woolworth Building (1913). New York was the site of nearly half of all American skyscrapers. Its skyline symbolized the city's stature, topped off in the early 1930s by the 102-story Empire State Building.

The central business district was surrounded by concentric rings of residential housing beginning with the slums—impoverished, densely populated, heterogeneous residential areas. Slums had inadequate municipal services and high rates of poverty, substandard housing, infant mortality, communicable diseases, and crime. Housing stock included cellars, shacks, lofts, subdivided warehouses and former mansions, and six-to-eight-story tenements constructed after the Civil War that housed up to 150 individuals—with a single water tap per floor, no ventilation, little light, and

THE CITY

The Industrial Radial City

Only in the late eighteenth and early nineteenth centuries did parks become identified with cities.

PAGE 544

59

*Commuters give
the city its tidal
restlessness; natives
give it solidity
and continuity;
but the settlers
give it passion.*

E. B. WHITE
AS QUOTED IN HOLIDAY
(APRIL 1949)

♦ **Endogamy**

*Marriage within a specific
group as required by custom
or law*

outdoor privies. Eighty percent of inner-city families had both parents present and were nuclear, although 20 percent included lodgers to help pay the rent.

Outside the slums were lower-middle and upper-lower-class residential neighborhoods, comprised mainly of modest single-family homes purchased with short-term mortgages from savings and loan associations. Residents included native-born craftsmen and second-generation blue-collar Germans and Irish. These urbanites worried about protecting what they had earned and feared the encroachment of slum dwellers into their communities. In the 1920s, they became prime candidates for Ku Klux Klan recruiters. Half of Klan members lived in cities of over fifty thousand, especially in the South and Midwest.

The final concentric ring was the suburban periphery. It was a safe, homogeneous, middle-class WASP area of large single-family homes with enclosed yards. Residents employed mass transit to travel to work, play, or shopping. Middle-class folk also lived in modest new apartments constructed along major streetcar routes. They were modeled on the luxury apartments of the rich located near the central business district in such exclusive neighborhoods as Chicago's Gold Coast. The rich also had other housing options, ranging from Fifth Avenue mansions to suburban estates.

Industry drove the economy of northeastern and midwestern cities, employing the American system of manufacturing and taking advantage of cheap labor, capital, consumer demand, and support services. Factories relocated to the outskirts or satellite suburbs like Gary, Indiana, where land was cheap, taxes were low, and bosses could exercise more control over their work force, particularly in company towns like Pullman, Illinois. By the 1910s several individual factories, including General Electric (Schenectady), International Harvester (Chicago), and U.S. Steel (Gary) had over fifteen thousand workers, and in the 1920s, sixty-eight thousand worked at Ford's River Rouge plant (Dearborn), the largest in the world.

The huge demand for low-paid unskilled and semiskilled workers was filled by immigrants who earned less than a family of four's minimal needs (fifteen dollars a week), and the entire family had to work at dehumanizing, dangerous, and boring jobs. Wives earned about half as much as their husbands, and children earned one-fourth. Advancement in the late nineteenth century was unlikely. Only one-fifth to one-sixth of manual workers, mainly native-born whites, were vertically mobile. Workers progressed by establishing a

savings account and acquiring property. Urbanites were geographically mobile, especially the native-born who moved to better themselves. One in four urban residents moved each year, and the ten-year persistence rate was typically around 50 percent.

The industrial city was a metropolis of immigrants and their children. In 1910, 41 percent of urbanites were foreign-born. Three-fourths of immigrants lived in cities, led by Russian Jews (89 percent), Irish (87 percent), Italians (84 percent), and Poles (80 percent). Milwaukee was nearly 90 percent first- or second-generation immigrant; New York and Chicago, 80 percent. The new immigrants came from traditional societies and were mostly uneducated, unskilled, and indigent, unprepared for urban America. Their goal was not to surpass their fathers but to get manly jobs, support their families, and purchase homes as insurance for old age. Jewish migrants were different because they had no homeland, were seldom formerly peasants, were more educated or at least respected scholarship, and had skills (tailoring) and an entrepreneurial tradition. Consequently, they were about two and a half times more likely to end up with a white-collar job than were other new immigrants.

The new immigrants lived in ethnic villages in slum neighborhoods where they reestablished old institutions like churches, maintained high rates of endogamy, and started mutual aid societies, social and athletic clubs, foreign-language newspapers, and parochial schools. Twenty to forty percent of school children in major immigrant cities attended Catholic schools. Children attended public school briefly because they were uncomfortable, parents feared Americanization, and their labor was needed. Immigrants were marginal people with one foot in each of two different worlds. Daughters were closely supervised but boys were not, and they often grew up tough and street smart. They frequently joined street gangs, hungry for recognition, excitement, money, and a sense of belonging. The gangs provided good training for future boxers and hoodlums.

On the other hand, African Americans, 90 percent of whom resided in the South, were the least urban group. In 1900 only 17 percent of black southerners were urbanites. The great migration north began in 1916, caused by the boll weevil's devastation of cotton fields, the availability of factory work, and aspirations for a safer and better life. Within five years the number of black men in major industrial cities more than doubled, but usually they worked in low-level, dead-end jobs; black women were predominantly domestics. They lived in slums that became ghettos because of white flight, discrimination, blockbusting, and violence against blacks who tried to move into white neighborhoods. African Americans had legal access to schools and public accommodations but encountered prejudice, embarrassment, lower-quality facilities, and brutality if they contested traditional exclusionary customs. Discrimination and ghettoization created opportunities for blacks to service their community's financial, cultural, recreational, and cosmetic needs, resulting in the emergence of such institutions as black insurance firms, newspapers, and baseball leagues. The concentration of black voters increased black political power, and in 1928 Chicago Republican Oscar De Priest became the first northern African American elected to Congress.

The city was the locus of a vibrant culture. A major city was expected to have several newspapers and such institutions of high culture as muse-

ums, a symphony, a public library, and universities. Popular recreation was cheap and accessible, enjoyed at such public sites as streets, parks, and beaches; semipublic facilities like amusement parks, arenas, ballparks, racetracks, dance halls, saloons, and vaudeville and movie theaters; and private social and athletic clubs. Urban recreation was largely class based until the 1920s, when higher wages and a shorter workweek democratized leisure. Until Prohibition, the saloon served as the poor man's club; workingmen also favored indoor sports like boxing, bowling, and billiards, and accessible resorts like Coney Island. Thereafter they could afford commercialized spectator sports and had greater access to municipal parks. In the 1920s crowds surpassing fifty thousand attended professional baseball and college football games, boxing championships, horse races, and the Indianapolis 500. However, the most popular entertainment was the movies, which had emerged from inner city nickelodeons in the early

THE CITY

The Industrial Radial City

CITY GOVERNMENT
Corrupt, Self-Serving Political Bosses

Lord Bryce (*The American Commonwealth*, 1888) and other early social critics described city government, run by corrupt, self-serving politicians, as the worst American institution. From the 1880s to 1914 nearly 80 percent of the largest cities had machine-run governments, at least for a brief period. They grew stronger over time; in the largest cities during the 1930s, one-third had been in power for over two decades. The boss usually operated from behind the scenes, but a few were also long-term mayors, like Martin Behrman of New Orleans (1900–1920, 1925–1926) and Frank Hague of Jersey City (1917–1947). Machines were not ideologically oriented but cranked out the vote with precision by providing patronage and other services to inner city constituents, or by fixing elections through payoffs or intimidation.

Bosses dispensed personalized government, providing help to people who could turn to no one else, ranging from fixing a traffic ticket to food, relief, and jobs. They sponsored outings, secured preferential treatment from the municipality for business allies, awarded utility franchises and valuable contracts to politically connected entrepreneurs, and gave organized crime a free hand. Boss Richard Croker of New York (1886–1895, 1898–1902) grew rich on "honest" graft, using inside information to make astute investments or securing stock and con-

tracts from firms seeking city business. His colleague George Washington Plunkitt distinguished this from "dishonest" graft, which was stealing from the city or taking payoffs to protect criminal activity.

Bosses centralized power and decision making, modernized city politics, and promoted urban development, building the urban infrastructure, albeit inefficiently and at a great cost. They were not omnipotent, however, as commonly believed. Tammany Hall, for instance, did not have complete control over New York's Democratic party until 1886, when a disciplined coalition of ward bosses was established on the basis of patronage and election victories. And even under Croker, Tammany did not win every major election, often because of scandals resulting from police corruption.

Furthermore, as David Hammack has pointed out, power in New York was so diffused because of ethnic, religious, and philosophical differences that neither machines nor urban elites could unilaterally postulate a coherent policy, much less act decisively. Finally, rural Republican control of state legislatures made it difficult for machine liberals such as Al Smith and Robert Wagner to repeal restrictive blue laws or enact such reforms as factory regulations or housing codes to improve conditions for their constituents.

C

THE CITY

The Industrial Radial City

A great city is that which has the greatest men and women.

WALT WHITMAN
"SONG OF THE BROAD-AXE,"
LEAVES OF GRASS

See also
Urban Cultural Institutions

1900s into luxurious, large downtown theaters a decade later.

Political corruption, urban pathology, growing anomie, and the need for improved public services encouraged the rise of urban reform in the late nineteenth century under the leadership of upper-class mugwumps, investigative journalists, Social Gospelers, the new professionals, and settlement workers. The reform impulse culminated in the Progressive movement (ca. 1900–ca. 1916), which sought to ameliorate life in impersonalized, segmented cities by promoting efficiency, social justice, political democracy, and economic opportunity.

In the 1880s, businessmen seeking efficient and honest government inaugurated the civic reform movement to investigate corruption, elect and promote "the best men," restructure government so as to weaken political machines, and improve sanitation, police, and fire services. They established local good government groups that affiliated into the National Municipal League (1894), which had moderate success electing reform candidates. Certain reform mayors, most notably Hazen Pingree of Detroit (1890–1897), did achieve major accomplishments. Pingree employed business principles to efficiently build parks and schools, reduce utility rates, and cut corruption while making no effort to impose Yankee norms on the new urban folk. Pingree's example was duplicated in the Progressive era by Samuel M. "Golden Rule" Jones (1897–1904) and Brand Whitlock (1905–1913) in Toledo and Jim Loftin Johnson (1901–1909) in Cleveland.

Since a few good men could not clean up corruption, reformers advocated structural changes including greater home rule, secret ballots, nonpartisan, at-large elections, and stronger administrative schemes, such as the city manager and the commission system in which experts administered urban agencies. Midwestern and western cities secured greater home rule under new charters that took power from councilmen elected from readily corruptible wards and gave greater authority to mayors. The commission system had its first major test in 1900 in Galveston, Texas, following a devastating flood that killed over 7,200 people. It was a success, and by 1917 had been adopted in nearly five hundred mostly small cities. The city manager system was first employed in Staunton, Virginia, in 1908, and within fifteen years 270 largely suburban cities had adopted it.

Settlement workers were among the most liberal Progressives. The first American settlement house was New York's Neighborhood Guild (1886); there were over four hundred by 1910, located in slums and staffed by idealistic middle-class men and women. Volunteers sought to identify neighborhood problems and then arrive at solutions. Settlements offered classes in English, civics, crafts, and job skills; employment bureaus; and recreational facilities ranging from gymnasiums to theaters. In addition, the workers promoted reforms in juvenile justice, playgrounds, housing, public health, and morality.

WASP reformers like Anthony Comstock of the Society for the Suppression of Vice (1873) tried to impose traditional middle-class behavior upon urbanites by fighting immorality. Crusaders expanded temperance into a prohibition movement against the ubiquitous workingman's saloon (New York had seven thousand in 1880), a reputed cause of poverty and broken families, and center of crime and political corruption. Ironically, the Eighteenth Amendment generated a boom in organized crime that had originated in late-nineteenth-century politically protected Irish crime syndicates involved in gambling and prostitution. Vice was rampant in urban slums and red-light districts like Chicago's Levee district, where gambling and prostitution operated freely. Occasional crackdowns followed investigations of police corrupted by gamblers and madams, and hysteric episodes over white slavery. Chicago closed its vice district in 1911, and about one hundred cities followed suit during World War I, most notably New Orleans (Storyville). However, vice soon reemerged in the slums and in working-class suburbs.

Progressive professionals advocated urban planning to address the quality of urban life while creating the efficient city. It began as the City Beautiful Movement, sought to enhance urban life by improving civic design, the impetus coming from Chicago's Columbian Exposition (1893), which influenced public architecture, municipal art, and planning. Fair coordinator Daniel Burnham's comprehensive Chicago Plan of 1909 marked a transition to the City Efficient Movement, directing environmental reform through spatial policies. Planners coordinated mass transit with planned land uses like garden cities, and employed zoning regulations for rational separation of incompatible land uses or buildings and protection of existing areas. New York in 1916 was the first city to introduce comprehensive zoning by establishing specific land use areas, limiting building heights, and restricting lot use to prevent the garment district from expanding toward Fifth Avenue. Ten years later, 591 cities had zoning codes.

The federal government first became deeply involved in the problems of cities during the Great Depression, when urban unemployment skyrocketed from 3.2 percent in 1929 to 15.9 percent in 1931 and 24.9 percent in 1933. In 1932, for instance, 1 million New Yorkers (30 percent), six hundred thousand Chicagoans (40 percent), and far greater proportions in industrial and mining cities (90 percent in Gary, Indiana) were out of work. By the end of 1930, the seventy-five largest municipalities appropriated $420 million for public works. Detroit's relief expenditures rose from $2.4 million in 1929 to $14.9 million in 1931. Cities tried to cope by borrowing, introducing sales taxes, and printing scrip to pay municipal workers. Little assistance came from the Hoover administration, save $300 million from the Reconstruction Finance Corporation.

Urbanites provided the backbone of Franklin Roosevelt's constituency, and the New Deal immediately responded with relief, recovery, and reform programs. Jobs were the biggest problem. The Federal Emergency Relief Administration distributed $500 million, mainly for work relief. In the winter of 1933–1934 about 8 million families received federal assistance, half from Civil Works Administration minimum-wage projects. The Public Works Administration (1933) promoted recovery through planned public works, especially in New York, where Robert Moses secured one-seventh of its allocations. The majority of Works Progress Administration (1935) grants went to the fifty largest cities, providing work relief (1936–1941) for nearly one-fifth of the workforce in public construction projects and in programs like the Writers' Project that supported the arts.

Housing was another major problem. Hundreds of thousands had lost their homes (in 1933 there were one thousand home foreclosures a day), and the construction industry was moribund. The New Deal promoted recovery by establishing the Home Owners' Loan Corporation (1933) to stabilize the mortgage business, and the Federal Housing Administration (1934) to refinance private loans at 4 percent for up to thirty years. The Public Works Administration financed slum clearance and public housing, and the U.S. Housing Authority (1937) helped the neediest with $500 million for loans and grants for slum clearance, and 47,500 new low-cost rental units.

The New Deal instilled public confidence in Washington's ability to cope with major problems and shape the direction of urban development. The federal government provided services once supplied by machines but did not supplant the bosses, who became brokers between Washington and their constituents, doling out jobs, relief, and construction projects.

Urban America in the Suburban Age

The postwar metropolis was the locus of enormous change, much of it fostered by federal programs. The most important developments were suburbanization, the expansion of inner city ghettos, the decline of the northeastern and midwestern Rustbelt, and the emergence of the Sunbelt. The postwar city was an exciting and dynamic site of opportunity with industry prospering because of pent-up demand, the needs of baby boomers (consumer goods purchases tripled in fifteen years), and housing shortages. Hundreds of thousands of white veterans moved their growing families to suburbs using their government benefits, while central cities became increasingly black ghettos. By the 1960s, as the economy shifted into a postindustrial phase, the promise of the old industrial cities began to fade as problems mounted with the loss of jobs, fleeing taxpayers, growing impoverishment, spiraling disorder and violence, increasing needs for expensive public services, and an aging infrastructure. Thereafter the most dynamic areas were the suburbs and Sunbelt cities that became the desirable places to live.

As late as 1950, only one of the ten largest cities was located outside the Northeast and Midwest, but by 1980 half were in the booming Sunbelt. New York and Chicago had fewer residents in 1970 than twenty years before, and Saint Louis in 1980 had declined to the level of 1890! Columbus, Ohio, was the only major northern city to grow in the 1970s. The decline in the Rustbelt was tied to white flight to suburbia and the loss of industrial jobs through automation and factory relocation to suburbs and the Sunbelt—and abroad by the 1970s. In the latter decade the number of jobs in the Sunbelt rose by 40 percent, compared with 12.4 percent in the North. New York and Philadelphia alone lost 16 percent of their jobs between 1960 and 1972. The Sunbelt first boomed because of the need during the cold war for military bases and defense-related high-tech industries. It soon attracted an aging population who retired to warm climates (especially after the introduction of air conditioning), and lured industrialists, real estate developers, and entrepreneurs in leisure businesses because of weak unions, low taxes, cheap land, and improved roads and jet travel.

In order to relieve street congestion, Boston, New York, and Chicago built elevated train tracks calls "els" in the late nineteenth century.

PAGE 509

C

Thirty million Americans lived in suburbia in 1950 and seventy-six million by 1970, when the suburbs surpassed central cities in population (37.6 to 31.4 percent). These were mainly bedroom suburbs made accessible by such federal programs as G.I. loans, FHA mortgage insurance, and highway funding acts (1947, 1956), and by the low cost of cars and gasoline. Mass transit ridership peaked shortly after the war, but the automobile became so ubiquitous that by 1958 ridership on public transportation fell below the rate in 1900. Families left cities for privacy, lower taxes, escape from declining neighborhoods and rising crime, and a higher quality of life that included better schools, parks, and other public services. The new suburbs included totally planned communities like Levittown, New York, and Park Forest, Illinois, where mortgages cost less than rent. Among the fastest growing was Anaheim, California, located at an exit on the Santa Ana Freeway and home to Disneyland, which increased from 17,267 residents in 1952 to 91,100 seven years later.

Urban leaders after World War II encouraged development and the protection of assets by improving highways, ports, and airports, and revitalizing central business districts. Physical expansion was impossible in eastern and midwestern cities because there was no room outside their old boundaries. Pittsburgh and Philadelphia provided

a model by employing insurance company capital to refurbish the central business district through cleaning and brightening it up, and enhancing accessibility with buses and underground parking. Pro-development businessmen worked with like-minded politicians, including reformers like DeLesseps Morrison in New Orleans, bosses like Richard Daley of Chicago, and professional politicians like Robert Wagner of New York, who hired able administrators and secured revenue for capital improvements.

There was far less cooperation from conservative, self-interested business leaders, especially in Sunbelt cities like Dallas, Houston, and Los Angeles, who used their power in publishing, banking, and insurance to shape major policy decisions according to their personal interests. These cities had considerable space available for expansion, mainly through annexation (Phoenix thereby grew from 17 to 187 square miles), that promised greater efficiency and prestige. Consolidations, on the other hand, were quite rare, most notably the Miami/Dade County metropolitan federation (1957), established to avoid duplication of governmental services.

Civic leaders usually focused on the central business district, giving less attention to the needs of residential neighborhoods. One-fifth of urban homes were substandard after the war, and cities began to rely on Washington for assistance. The

CORPORATE INFLUENCE

Cities like Los Angeles had considerable space available for expansion after World War II. Business leaders used their influence to shape major policy decisions like development according to their personal interests.

Housing Act of 1949 sought to eliminate substandard areas and provide decent homes and environments through slum clearance, public housing, and an expansion of FHA mortgage insurance. However, FHA hurt working-class neighborhoods by recommending that developers build homogeneous tracts and redlining inner city areas by refusing to guarantee loans in localities that had older homes or were likely to experience black encroachment. Stable lower-class areas were ruined because mortgages became unavailable, homeowners could not get loans for home improvements, and merchants had a hard time getting affordable insurance.

Developers were expected mainly to construct low-cost public housing on the cleared sites, but frequently they evaded the spirit of the law by building luxury apartments, parking lots, shopping malls, or even factories that urban boosters applauded, anticipating an enhanced tax base and revitalization of decaying areas. It was expected to take six years to build 810,000 new units, but it took twenty. Meanwhile, about three times as many units were abandoned or razed for highways or urban renewal. The new public housing failed to promote communities as originally planned, and became places to hide the urban poor. Huge multistory developments like Chicago's Robert Taylor Homes, built in the early 1960s, became dangerous places where residents were intimidated by gangs and afraid to leave their apartments.

Working-class communities got another jolt in 1954 when Washington changed its emphasis from redevelopment to urban renewal. The new goal was to fix up decaying neighborhoods to attract more affluent residents, revitalize investment opportunities, and protect the central business district. Neighborhoods that residents considered alive and worth protecting, like Boston's West End, were bulldozed for urban renewal or highways with little concern for dislodged residents. Viable or potentially viable communities were replaced by public or semipublic institutions such as university campuses (University of Illinois on Chicago's Near West Side), baseball parks (Dodger Stadium in Los Angeles's Chavez Ravine), convention centers, and hotels. Displaced residents and small businesses seldom received adequate assistance.

Major development plans after the 1960s continued to focus on the central business district in hopes of encouraging confidence, investment, resettlement, and tourism. Municipalities improved public transportation with downtown bus malls in Portland and Minneapolis, and subways in San Francisco (1972) and Washington (1976); constructed major symbols of progress like arches, domed stadiums, convention centers, and malls; and supported private restorations of historic but run-down waterfronts like Baltimore's Harborplace and dilapidated markets like Seattle's Pike Place Market. Local governments also supported refurbishment of older inner city housing to attract affluent youthful taxpayers seeking exciting, safe, and convenient neighborhoods. Gentrification began in the 1960s at Philadelphia's Society Hill and Washington's Capitol Hill, and thereafter spread to most major cities, improving their tax base but showing little consideration for those displaced.

The combination of declining industrial employment and the migration of the middle class to suburbia resulted in a major shift in urban demographics and social structure. This was exemplified in the 1970s by the first decline of median family income among urban core residents. The flight of the middle class was crucial because they paid the taxes; supported businesses, cultural institutions, and schools; and promoted social and political reform. Public school demography dramatized the changes: two-thirds of New York's public school students were white in 1957; 14 percent were white in 1987. People had lost their confidence in the city and no longer believed that its problems could be solved. Cities tried to raise taxes to make up for lost revenues, and to defer maintenance and services, which encouraged more businesses to leave. New York's infrastructure began to collapse in the late 1960s: buildings were abandoned, and one out of eight residents was on welfare. The outcome was financial collapse in 1975, and a bailout by Washington.

The people left behind and the new immigrants were increasingly poor people of color. A second great black migration had occurred during World War II, and it continued after the war. By 1970 three-fourths of African Americans lived in cities, comprising the majority in Washington, D.C. (71.1 percent), Newark, Gary, and Atlanta. One decade later, they were a majority in Detroit, Baltimore, New Orleans, and Birmingham as well. Nearly all of the increase between 1950 and 1966 (86 percent) occurred in central cities at a time when 70 percent of white increase was in suburbia. There was also a postwar boom in Spanish-speaking urban populations. New York's Puerto Rican population rose from 61,000 in 1940 to 613,000 in 1960. Ten years later the city was 10 percent Puerto Rican. Substantial Puerto Rican

Colonial versions of European high-style architecture . . . eventually lent larger cities such as Boston and Philadelphia a character similar to contemporary London.

PAGE 78

♦ **Gentrification**

The process of renewal and rebuilding accompanying the influx of middle-class or affluent people into deteriorating areas that often displaces earlier, usually poorer residents

THE CITY

*Urban America in the
Suburban Age*

*There are eight
million stories in
the naked city.
This has been
one of them.*

MARK HELLINGER
FOR FILM, THE NAKED CITY
(1948), AND USED AS A
SPOKEN AFTERWARD AT THE
END OF EACH EPISODE OF
THE 1958-1962 TV SERIES,
NAKED CITY

Population of Leading U.S. Cities

1690		1800		1950		1988	
1. Boston	7,000	Philadelphia	69,000	1. New York	7,891,957	New York	7,352,700
2. Philadelphia	4,000	New York	60,000	2. Chicago	3,620,962	Los Angeles	3,352,710
3. New York	3,900	Baltimore	26,000	3. Philadelphia	2,071,605	Chicago	2,977,520
4. Newport	2,600	Boston	25,000	4. Los Angeles	1,970,358	Houston	1,698,090
5. Charleston	1,100	Charleston	20,000	5. Detroit	1,849,568	Philadelphia	1,647,000
				6. Baltimore	949,708	San Diego	1,070,310
1850		**1900**		7. Cleveland	914,808	Detroit	1,035,920
1. New York	515,500	New York	3,437,202	8. Saint Louis	856,796	Dallas	987,360
2. Philadelphia	340,000	Chicago	1,698,575	9. Washington	802,178	San Antonio	941,150
3. Baltimore	169,600	Philadelphia	1,293,697	10. Boston	801,444	Phoenix	923,750
4. Boston	136,880	Saint Louis	575,238	11. San Francisco	775,357	Baltimore	751,400
5. New Orleans	116,375	Boston	560,892	12. Pittsburgh	676,806	San Jose	738,420
6. Cincinnati	115,435	Baltimore	508,957	13. Milwaukee	637,392	San Francisco	731,600
7. Brooklyn	96,838	Cleveland	381,768	14. Houston	596,163	Indianapolis	727,130
8. Saint Louis	77,860	Buffalo	352,367	15. Buffalo	580,132	Memphis	645,190
9. Albany	50,763	San Francisco	342,782	16. New Orleans	570,445	Jacksonville	635,430
10. Pittsburgh	46,601	Cincinnati	325,902	17. Minneapolis	521,718	Washington	617,000
11. Louisville	43,194	Pittsburgh	321,616	18. Cincinnati	503,998	Milwaukee	599,380
12. Buffalo	42,260	New Orleans	287,104	19. Seattle	467,591	Boston	577,830
13. Providence	41,573	Detroit	285,704	20. Kansas City	456,622	Columbus	569,750
14. Washington	40,001	Milwaukee	285,315				
15. Newark	38,890	Washington	278,718				
16. Rochester	36,403	Newark	246,070				
17. San Francisco	34,776	Louisville	204,731				
18. Chicago	29,963	Minneapolis	202,718				
19. Detroit	21,019	Indianapolis	169,164				
20. Milwaukee	20,061	Kansas City	163,752				

Sources; Carl Bridenbaugh, *Cities in the Wilderness: The First Century of Urban Life in America, 1625–1742* (1964), 143; Marshall A. Smelser, *The Democratic Republic, 1801–1815* (1968), 22; Howard P. Chudacoff, *The Evolution of American Urban Society* (1975), 56; *World Almanac and Book of Facts, 1989*, 538–539; *Information Please Almanac, 1991*, 787.

communities were also established in mid-sized industrial cities in the metropolitan New York region and in Philadelphia, Cleveland, and Chicago. By the late 1980s Miami had a Hispanic majority. It has elected Puerto Rican and Cuban mayors, and the social climate is set by its Cuban immigrants, who have made it the economic capital of the Caribbean. On the West Coast, one-third of Los Angeles in 1980 was Hispanic, and one-tenth Asian.

These newcomers generally ended up in ghettos like New York's Bedford-Stuyvesant, Chicago's West Side, or Los Angeles's Watts, whose populations greatly increased and whose boundaries expanded. White residents in zones of emergence used various methods to prevent integration, including neighborhood improvement associations that promoted solidarity and political pressure on elected officials, restrictive covenants (illegal since 1947), zoning laws to encourage stability, and violence. The ghetto residents lived in decayed, overcrowded housing, had substandard educational and health facilities, high unemploy-

ment, few well-paying jobs with advancement opportunities, and high rates of crime.

Widespread frustrations, epitomized by the black power movement, provided the underpinnings for the eruption of racial hostilities in the summers of 1964 through 1968, when there were about seventy-five "commodity riots." These involved the destruction of neighborhood shops and property, largely white-owned, whereas race riots encompassed interracial conflict over contested turf. About 10 percent of local residents looted white-owned neighborhood stores that symbolized oppression and the unfulfilled expectations of the civil rights movement. The worst violence occurred in Detroit in 1967; forty-three died and two thousand were injured. The riots drew national attention to the problems of the black ghettos and led to increased federal assistance to the inner city.

The black power movement energized the community into grassroots political activity ranging from New York's local school district elections to campaigning for mayors. The first African

American mayor of a major city was Carl B. Stokes of Cleveland (1967), who promoted public housing and urban services. By 1970 there were black mayors in fifty cities, primarily those with large African American populations, and by 1990 African Americans had been elected mayor in New York, Chicago, and most of the largest cities, generally because of exceptionally strong black turnouts at the polls.

The riots were an important reason that cities in the 1960s received renewed positive attention from Washington under Democratic administrations already influenced by the "discovery" of poverty in Michael Harrington's *The Other America* (1962). Lyndon Johnson's $390 million Great Society program comprised a variety of initiatives to fight the War on Poverty. In 1964 the Office of Economic Opportunity established such programs as the Job Corps, Head Start, and the community action programs that empowered neighborhood service agencies. Johnson expanded food stamp and urban housing programs and established the Model Cities program (1966), which targeted federal funds for thirty-six neighborhoods, relying on local involvement to coordinate programs to enhance education, housing, health, and jobs. By 1969, total federal expenditures for cities soared to $14 billion, and the number of Americans below the poverty line was cut nearly in half. Under the Nixon administration funds nearly doubled by 1974, but the administration sought to reduce Washington's role in local affairs, first by cutting allocations and reducing or eliminating programs, and later by New Federalism (1972), which gave local governments policy planning responsibilities.

While the federal share of local budgets rose from 15 percent in 1960 to 25 percent in 1975, revenue sharing ended up mainly benefiting suburbia. Ghetto conditions seem to have gotten worse rather than better. African American males have a hard time finding employment (black teenagers' unemployment nearly doubled between 1965 and 1980, to 46.9 percent, reflecting their poor education and lack of access to jobs), and black female-headed households are nearly the norm, rising from about 20 percent in 1960 to 43 percent in 1988. The result is pervasive hopelessness and gang violence among a young and seemingly permanent underclass.

The Future of the City

Cities are likely to remain the focal point of economics, government, culture, and innovation for residents of metropolitan districts. Institutions like corporate offices and sports arenas may move to greener pastures, but museums, libraries, and universities are less mobile. Long-term efforts to sustain historic institutions and enterprises by protecting and rebuilding the central business district remain important. Cities will also have to attend to their infrastructure before highways and bridges begin to crumble. These are difficult tasks as revenue sources dry up, historically powerless and voiceless people with their own agendas gain political power, and the gap between the haves and have-nots broadens. Low levels of academic achievement, rising crime rates, and growing proportions of female-headed households provide the potential for a frightening future. Scholars and planners believe there needs to be a balanced metropolitan vision for the future based on a pluralistic symbiotic model with greater shared responsibilities. Yet even more basic is the enormous need for jobs and development in the urban ghettos before conditions become so intolerable and unacceptable that anarchy emerges.

—STEVEN A. RIESS

CLOTHING AND PERSONAL ADORNMENT

Clothing and personal adornment are the most immediate means human beings have of communicating personal identity and social position, and the study of dress and appearance leads inevitably to a consideration of the complex and changing relationships of gender, class, and power. Attitudes toward men and women, work and leisure, success and failure, youth and age, health and sickness, beauty and sexuality, are all reflected in America's concern with personal appearance. This concern has from colonial days supported a fashion industry that, in advising us how to acquire the right hair, face, body, and clothes, claims to tell us not only who we can be, but who we ought to be.

Native Americans

When Europeans visited America in the sixteenth and seventeenth centuries, they sent back accounts of a myriad of native peoples with varying customs in dress and adornment. In many regions, Native Americans made clothing from well-dressed skins, but some groups also used woven textiles made from wild cotton (in the South-

See also
Urban Parks

west), cedar and spruce bark fiber (in the Northwest), grass, or animal hair. Typical garments included breechclouts (or, for women, short skirts), belts and leggings, moccasins, and robes or mantles, but how much was worn depended on weather and occasion. While utilitarian clothing might be left plain, many garments were elaborately decorated with painted figures, quillwork, feathers, copper disks, beads, or fringe, according to local custom. Some tribes oiled, painted, or tattooed their bodies. Head hair was greased and blackened with charcoal, and, among men, varied widely in cut and style. Body hair was pulled out. Both men and women wore necklaces, earrings, headbands, and other adornments, ornamented with wampum, feathers, animal claws and teeth, turquoise (in the Southwest), or pearls.

European settlers appreciated the comfort and practicality of Indian snowshoes and moccasins, and moccasins became a permanent feature of American dress, not just where other shoes were unavailable but as house slippers, carriage boots, and, in altered form, modern leisure shoes. In a similar vein, the Indians admired European wool and linen textiles, and as their traditional hunting lands were lost, they added more and more woven garments to their wardrobe. But these were integrated into Indian patterns of dress rather than being worn in European style. Blankets (their

barter price in beaver skins woven as stripes along the selvage) were used as mantles, for example, and shirts were belted and worn over breechclouts and leggings rather than tucked into trousers. Trade beads were assimilated into traditional Indian ornamentation. Even when the basic garb is European, as it appears in many mid-nineteenth-century photographs, Indian men and women maintained a distinctive culture by adding the blanket mantle and traditional necklaces and headgear.

The Seventeenth Century

Information about the clothing of colonial Americans is thin compared with the wealth of data available on clothing worn after 1800. We do know what styles were fashionable in England, and it is fair to assume that American dress was similar, since most textiles and many made-up garments were imported from the mother country. Contemporary American portraits (especially of women) provide but equivocal evidence since many sitters were depicted in ambiguous draperies. Where clothing is distinct, there is seldom proof that the sitters were painted in their own clothes. Little actual clothing survives from the colonial period. We have a few accessories owned by seventeenth-century Americans, but nothing like a complete outfit. A number of eighteenth-century dresses and suits exist, but the majority are made of rich materials and have been altered several times. Given the ambiguity of portraits and the scarcity of surviving clothing, scholars interested in early American dress must depend heavily on the written word.

Inventories tell us that the basic garments for seventeenth-century women were (1) the shift (a knee-length white linen undergarment with high or low neck and long or elbow-length sleeves); (2) the skirt (known as a petticoat or "cote"), of which several might be worn, the upper one often tucked up to show another of contrasting color beneath; and (3) a fitted bodice (usually called a doublet or waistcoat), boned when intended for formal wear. With these were worn stockings, garters, and shoes, a cap to cover the hair, and a cloak for warmth. Women of greater means might also own one or more gowns (a one-piece dress). To this basic wardrobe were added white linen neckerchiefs, collars and cuffs, gloves, fans, ribbons to trim the sleeves, masks to protect the complexion from the sun, silk hoods, and jewelry, including rings, necklaces, and earrings.

The typical man's wardrobe consisted of (1) the shirt (a linen undergarment corresponding to a

**WELL-DRESSED
MAN**

The typical 17th century man's outfit included a shirt, breeches, coat, jacket, waistcoat and doublet, complemented by stockings, garters, leather shoes or boots, a collar, hat, cuffs, gloves, and maybe muff, cane and rings.
CORBIS-BETTMANN

woman's shift); (2) breeches (knee-length pants cut in many variations of fullness but never very tight); and (3) coats, jackets, waistcoats, and doublets (upper-body garments that are difficult to distinguish but that seem to have been worn in layers and that sometimes matched the breeches). To complete the outfit, a man wore stockings with garters, leather shoes or boots, a collar, cuffs, a hat, gloves, and sometimes a muff, cane, and rings.

Except for the linen shirt and shift, the most common material used for clothing was wool of varying weight and quality. Summer garments were sometimes made of linen. For common clothes, solid colors were typical, but utilitarian striped and checked patterns were also used. Printed textiles, however, were still very rare. In more prosperous families, the outer clothing was made of better quality wool or of silk, the latter sometimes woven with complex multicolored designs. Good fabrics were trimmed with gold, silver, or silk braid and ribbon loops and bows. Collars and cuffs of fine linen were trimmed with lace. The wealthiest might own a jeweled hatband. Military men frequently wore hard-wearing doublets of buff leather, which afforded some protection in battle.

Seventeenth-century Americans wore fabrics of every color, and in the clothing of the well-to-do, glittering braids and lace-edged linens created dramatic contrasts. While the Puritan settlers of Massachusetts disapproved of excess in dress, it is not true that they dressed primarily in black and gray. Tans and browns were probably the most common colors, being practical in a period when outer clothes were seldom washed, but red petticoats, green stockings, and green or blue aprons were a common sight among women of all classes. The "sad" colors often mentioned in inventories do not imply melancholy or gloom. "Sad" is etymologically related to "sated" and signifies being fully saturated with dye, resulting in a dark shade rather than a light one. But a sad (dark) color can be of any hue, and green, purple, orange, and various shades of brown are specifically mentioned.

What diversity there was in colonial dress arose more from class than from region, since Americans everywhere continued to import most of their fabrics and garments from England. Mice Morse Earle does mention a visitor to New York in 1704 who noted that middle-class Dutch women, unlike the English, tended to "go loose," that is, without corsets, and that they liked earrings and wore a different style of cap. Otherwise the differences were chiefly economic.

HEMMED IN

Fashionable dress in the mid to late nineteenth century restricted movement in every way. The layers of heavy petticoats, full sleeves and tight waistline of this nineteenth century dress severely hindered mobility. HULTON-DEUTSCH COLLECTION / CORBIS

Surviving correspondence proves that Americans took a lively interest in fashion, but in New England the picture was complicated by Puritan religious principles. Like all seventeenth-century Americans, the Puritans who settled New England brought with them the assumption that fine clothing was an appropriate way of displaying rank and wealth. But for them dress was also a visible sign that revealed the spiritual health of both individual and community. Since the division between rich and poor was part of God's plan, the classes ought to be distinguished by their dress, but since everyone, rich or poor, was supposed to be working toward the good of the community as a whole rather than individual self-aggrandizement, it was not appropriate to compete to see how many luxuries could be acquired nor to spend an inappropriate proportion of one's income on clothing. New fashions were objectionable because they made the old ones unwearable before they were worn out and encouraged competition in wasteful luxury. It was also inappropriate to use clothing as a means of sexual display. Thus the first laws regulating dress, passed in 1634 and 1636, little more than a decade after the first Puritan settlement, targeted "new and immodest fashions" and any garment judged to be "uncomely [meaning inappropriate rather than unattractive] or prejudicial to the common good."

Inappropriate fashions included certain items made with silver, gold, silk, lace, or needlework,

♦ **Breeches**

Short pants covering the hips and thighs and fitting snugly at the lower edges or just below the knee

*Teenagers
underwent rapid
change as they
adopted the British
rockers' music,
haircuts, and
clothing styles.*

PAGE 402

♦ **Sumptuary**
*Designed to regulate
extravagant expenditures or
habits especially on moral or
religious grounds*

and garments that wasted material by being cut with unnecessarily full sleeves or by being slashed. Slashing was a decorative technique in which a garment was slit to allow puffs of the linen shirt or shift beneath to be pulled through the gap. The Puritans tolerated moderate slashing roughly equivalent to leaving a sleeve or bodice seam open. But sometimes fabrics were entirely covered with a pattern of tiny slits. Such fabrics must have ripped and worn out quickly and been difficult to reuse, making them a particularly wasteful example of conspicuous consumption.

The lack of contemporary references to cosmetics or face patches suggests that these European vanities were little known in America. The immodest fashions most often mentioned were women's low necklines and sleeves that left the arm bare below the elbow. Bare arms apparently possessed the erotic attraction that any customarily covered body part may acquire when newly exposed. Female modesty was enjoined by the Bible and felt to be necessary under the Calvinist principle that men and women were predisposed to sin and therefore needed restraints. Modern readers should not confuse this with prudery. In a century when husband, wife, and children all slept together in the same bed, with servants of both sexes in the same room, prudery could hardly exist, while prudence might welcome the support of modesty.

Men were the targets of sumptuary law chiefly in the matter of long hair, which the Bible branded as "shameful." The dislike of long hair extended to the very long and elaborately curled men's wigs that came into widespread use in the 1660s and 1670s. Seventeenth-century preachers racked their brains for words strong enough to express their disapproval (John Eliot called the periwig a "luxurious feminine protexity"), but the fashion gradually spread until wigs were a necessary part of any respectable man's appearance.

In 1651, a new Massachusetts law acknowledged that excess in dress was still a problem, "especially amongst people of mean condition, to the dishonor of God, the scandal of their profession, the consumption of estates, and altogether unsuitable to their poverty." The solution was to forbid silk hoods, thigh-high boots, gold and silver, and other luxuries to any family whose estate was less than £200. Anyone who held public office, who was well educated, or who had been well off in the past was exempt from the ban. Where the earlier laws had touched both rich and poor and been enforced by the churches, this law regulated only the poor and was enforced by the town constables—

the temporal authorities were enforcing the privileges of the upper class.

By the middle of the seventeenth century, Puritan society had begun to show signs of change. The rigors of the early years had eased, and increasing prosperity allowed people to acquire more than the bare necessities. The great exodus of Puritans from England had ceased when the Civil War (1642–1652) gave them a cause to fight at home, and the younger generation had difficulty duplicating the same depth and intensity of religious experience known by its parents. Under these conditions, people found it more difficult to accept restrictions in dress. Hannah Lyman of Northampton, Massachusetts, not only wore a forbidden silk hood, but she brassily wore it into court when she was presented to the judge. The last sumptuary laws appeared during the Indian war of the 1670s, an upheaval perceived as divine punishment for a spiritual decay visibly symbolized by the inclination toward luxurious dress. But in spite of bare arms and silk hoods, ribbons and wigs, the Indian threat was turned back, and after the middle 1680s the laws seem no longer to have been enforced.

The Eighteenth Century

In the seventeenth century, rich and elaborate clothing had often appeared in startling contrast to the relatively primitive living conditions. But in the growing culture of consumption in the eighteenth century, fine clothing found a more fitting setting in fine houses with elaborate furnishings, and the importance of being in fashion became a recurring theme in American social life. The Puritan paradigm whereby both rich and poor dressed with restraint but according to their condition had been replaced in the later seventeenth century by the older and simpler idea that costly dress was a privilege vested only in people of wealth and rank. After 1700, that privilege began to be perceived as an obligation to dress well. Taking pains with one's dress (and suffering them too) was a way both of showing respect and of receiving it.

The importance of clothing and fashion in eighteenth-century society resonates throughout the personal diary of Samuel Sewall. In 1720, his third wife having died, Sewall (then aged sixty-eight) began to court a wealthy widow, Madam Winthrop. On 12 October, he found her barricaded behind a piece of black needlework, but when at last it was taken away, "I got my Chair in place, had some converse, . . . [and] Ask'd her to acquit me of Rudeness if I drew off her glove. Enquiring the reason, I told her 'twas great odds between handling a dead goat, and a living Lady. Got it off." It is hard not to smile at Sewall's note of triumph, but Madam Winthrop wore gloves indoors not primarily to keep suitors at a distance but to prove that she could afford servants to do all but the most refined and unnecessary needlework. On another visit Sewall was pleased to receive courteous treatment but noted that Madam Winthrop was "not in Clean Linen as sometimes." The implication is that she had not taken any special care in her dress to please or impress him—not a good sign. Madam Winthrop was apparently embarrassed by Sewall's personal appearance: "she spake somthing of my needing a Wigg." Sewall abominated wigs and told her that since God, his "best and greatest Friend," had given him the hair he had, he had no heart to go

to some lesser person for a wig. Madam Winthrop, countering with an argument from a book Sewall himself had given her, "quoted him saying 'twas inconvenient keeping out of a Fashion commonly used." Few of Madam Winthrop's contemporaries would have considered her point of view inappropriate or frivolous—even "Col. Townsend spake to me of my Hood: Should get a Wigg." Sewall continued to visit Madam Winthrop for a time, but by 7 November "I did not bid her draw off her glove as sometime I had done. Her Dress was not so clean as somtime it had been." And with these eloquent messages in the language of costume, Samuel Sewall's courtship came to an end.

The adoption of wigs in the later seventeenth century coincided with a broader change in men's clothing. The doublet disappeared, and the ancestor of the modern three-piece suit—breeches, coat, and vest (waistcoat)—came into use. As the century passed, the knee-length vest shortened, the coat became slimmer, and the breeches tighter. The formal coat was cut so as to require a very straight posture, with shoulders drawn back. For less formal occasions, the looser and more comfortable frock coat was worn, and for private moments at home, coat and wig could be replaced by a loose dressing gown and cap. Farmers protected their clothing with a large, shirtlike linen or wool coverall (also called a frock), while laborers doffed their coats and waistcoats in hot weather.

Women's clothing also changed around 1700. Over the linen shift, a woman now put on separate boned stays that created a stiff, cone-shaped torso. One or more petticoats were worn, the top one meant to show, and for most of the century, fashion required that these be supported by a hoop. Over these garments, the fashionable woman wore an unboned gown open down the center front from neck to hem and made so that the front edges did not meet. The gap was filled at the bottom by the petticoat, and at the top by the stomacher, a triangular piece of material, often elaborately decorated. Working women omitted both hoop and gown and instead wore a hip- or thigh-length, front-opening bodice. Some were form fitting and were worn over stays. Others, called bed gowns or short gowns, were cut loose enough to require no stays, allowing the freedom of movement necessary for heavy work.

The chief materials continued to be linen for undergarments and wool or silk for suits and gowns. Where summers were hot, people wore unlined linen, and as the century progressed, printed cottons were increasingly fashionable for

EIGHTEENTH CENTURY HAIRSTYLES

Elaborate and Uncomfortable

Wigs in a myriad of styles were worn by every man with any pretense to fashion or respectability until late in the century. The voluminous wig of 1720 diminished only slowly. By the 1780s, many men merely powdered and curled their own hair to make it look like a wig, and in the next decade powder was gradually abandoned; but some conservative men wore wigs into the nineteenth century. Women's hair was relatively simple until about 1770, when elaborately built-up styles came into fashion. Anna Green Winslow described hers in her diary for May 1773: "I had my HEDDUS roll on, Aunt Storer said it ought to be made less, Aunt Deming said it ought not to be made at all. It makes my head itch, & ach, & burn like anything." This "head roll" was made of cow tail, horsehair, and human hair carded together and formed into a cushion. Anna's natural hair was combed up over it, pomaded, and probably powdered and augmented with extra curls. From hairline to the top of her cap, twelve-year-old Anna's hairstyle measured an inch longer than her face. In Europe, elaborate powdered hairstyles appeared above faces enameled with dangerous white lead paints and cheeks flaming with rouge. This extreme of artificiality was probably rare in America, but rouge, pearl powder, and patches were known.

Beware of all enterprises that require new clothes.

HENRY DAVID THOREAU
WALDEN

gowns. Silk weaving reached high levels of sophistication in the eighteenth century, and fine silk dresses were so highly prized that they were remade and passed down for generations. Men's suits for special occasions were beautifully embroidered in colored silks, and the buttonholes were outlined with metallic braid. None of these stylish materials were made in America. Northern colonial communities did raise sheep and cultivate flax, producing woolens and linens suitable for sheets, towels, blankets, and common clothing. Virginia cloth, a southern-made cotton fabric, was used to clothe slaves. But silk, fine linen, broadcloth, and other quality wools had to be imported.

Along with imported fabrics came imported fashions. Some Americans kept their measurements with London agents, but most depended on local tailors and dressmakers to keep them in the mode. Imported shoes, silk stockings, hats, gloves, fans, and laces rounded out the American wardrobe. The desire to be in fashion was an entirely respectable concern for both sexes. Since men took care of business and were more likely to travel to London or correspond with London agents, they were often the ones who selected fabrics and accessories for their families. When shopping was done by proxy, personal taste was difficult to consult, and Americans tended instead to stipulate that whatever was purchased be in the latest fashion. This, coupled perhaps with the fear of appearing provincial, resulted in Americans' dressing even more elaborately than their counterparts abroad, a fact noted by many travelers. In 1784 Abigail Adams wrote from London, "I am not a little surprised to find dress, unless on public occasions, so little regarded here. The gentlemen are very plainly dressed, the ladies much less so than with us. . . . There is not that neatness in their appearance which you see in our ladies" (quoted in Earle, *Two Centuries of Costume*, p. 733).

Americans recognized their dependency on foreign manufactures as a weakness, especially when England began to tax them. From the 1760s through the 1780s, it became patriotic to spin and wear homespun rather than enrich England by wearing imported fabrics. Anne Hollingsworth Wharton's 1897 biography of Martha Washington mentions visitors to Mrs. Washington in 1777 who "felt rebuked by the plainness of her apparel and her example of persistent industry, while we were extravagantly dressed idlers, a name not very creditable in these perilous times" (p. 117).

The eighteenth-century day was divided into morning and afternoon. Relatively informal and comfortable clothing was permitted until dinner, but genteel folk dressed formally for the afternoon. The midday change of clothes is recorded by a London merchant who, visiting Mount Vernon in 1785, found George Washington coming from his farm in morning "undress" (plain blue coat, white cassimere waistcoat, black breeches, and boots). After chatting, the General excused himself. He returned dressed for his three o'clock dinner wearing a clean shirt, a drab coat (probably a good deal tighter than his blue one), a white waistcoat, white silk stockings, and powdered hair. Another Mount Vernon story related by Wharton describes some visiting young girls who neglected to dress for this midday meal, only to be surprised by the arrival of several young French officers. Hastily requesting leave to go up and dress properly, they were mortified to be told by Mrs. Washington to "remain as you are, what is good enough for General Washington is good enough for any guest of his." The girls' morning dress was probably loose and cool (it may not even have required a corset), while to dress formally meant to look attractive but feel uncomfortable, a combination that signified both self-respect and a desire to please others. To eyes accustomed to the rigidly controlled body shapes of corseted women, the loose look appeared slatternly and undisciplined. Thomas Jefferson wrote to his daughter Patsy on 22 December 1783:

Some ladies think they may under the privileges of the dishabille be loose and negligent of their dress in the morning. But be you from the moment you rise till you go to bed as cleanly and properly dressed as at the hours of dinner or tea. A lady who has been seen as a sloven or slut in the morning will never efface the impression she then made with all the dress and pageantry, she can afterwards involve herself in.

CHILDREN'S CLOTHING. Children's clothing underwent a number of changes during the eighteenth century. In the seventeenth century, infants were swaddled for the first four to six weeks and thereafter were dressed very much like their mothers until age five or six, when boys changed their skirts for breeches. Beginning in the early eighteenth century, however, swaddling was replaced with diapers and dresses made too long to be kicked off. These were shortened when the baby began to walk. At two or three, children were put in adult clothing, but, as before, there was no distinction of gender until the boys were breeched. Even little children's dresses had stiffened bodices or were worn over stays. Padded caps called puddings protected the head from falls, and leading strings attached to the shoulders kept little ones from straying.

The influence of Jean-Jacques Rousseau's *Émile* (1762) brought a gradual relaxation in the style of children's clothing. Young children were allowed loose muslin dresses sashed at the waist, a style that was eventually extended to older girls as well. Boys old enough to be breeched were put in "skeleton suits," consisting of a tight jacket with two rows of buttons on the front rising over the shoulders and a pair of ankle-length pants.

The Nineteenth Century

The early nineteenth century saw significant changes in both men's and women's dress. For men the most visible were the replacement of knee breeches by trousers and the loss of ornamentation and color. Black gradually replaced other dark and neutral colors until, by 1860, all business and formal coats and trousers were black wool, and waistcoats were limited to black and white. The monotony was relieved somewhat by the new casual sack suits, made of pronounced checks and plaids in the 1850s and 1860s and of tan and brown tweeds toward the end of the century. Nineteenth-century masculine models included two opposing figures. The first was the businessman (a gaunt Yankee early on, later a portly entrepreneur), whose conservative clothes reflected his success through expensive materials and tailoring, and his obsession with work in their avoidance of color and ornament. The second was the dandy or masher, who specialized in conspicuous and time-consuming dressing and other behaviors redolent of idleness. The desirable male look was clean-shaven except for sideburns in the early nineteenth century, but by the 1860s beards and mustaches were becoming indispensable, suggesting that the ideal had shifted toward older men.

Women's clothing about 1800 permitted a new degree of naturalness and comfort inspired by classical models. Whereas eighteenth-century dress had imposed a highly artificial shape on the body, now the body gave its shape to the clothes. Hoops were discarded, along with the large-scale floral silks that had spread over them. Stiff stays were replaced with lighter corseting, and softly gathered white cotton dresses revealed the moving body beneath. High-heeled buckled shoes gave way to flat sandals, and hairstyles so diminished that some women cropped their hair. The new fashions required little material and less trimming, so they were available to nearly all

classes. Some Americans deplored the new styles as immodest, others criticized any emulation of foreign fashions as unbefitting a free nation, but these skimpy, high-waisted dresses were nevertheless universally worn and are the first garments that commonly survive with American documentation and minimal alteration.

The freedom of classical styles did not last very long. Shortly after 1820, the waistline dropped, tight lacing returned, and skirts became fuller. Over the succeeding decades fashionable dresses managed to restrict movement through every possible means: sleeves or skirts too wide for doorways and hats to match, armholes cut so that one could not raise the arms, sleeves too tight to bend the arms, sleeves that dragged in the soup, bonnet brims so deep one could see only straight ahead, layers of heavy petticoats, bulky trains that swept the streets, tied-back skirts in which it was difficult to take a normal step, bodices so heavily boned and tightly fitted that they became second corsets.

Burdensome fashions persisted in ironic contrast to the improvement in women's condition in other areas. By century's end, many women enjoyed the benefits of secondary and college education, and the traditional occupations of domestic service and needlework had expanded to include teaching, factory and clerical work, social work, and nursing. Women had increasing impact on public life through their participation in the abolition, temperance, and women's rights movements, community social work, and women's clubs. But most women clung doggedly to the latest fashion, no matter how uncomfortable. In 1851 feminist leaders introduced the bloomer, a kind of Turkish trouser worn under a matching dress of ordinary style except for being knee-length. It provoked a storm of abuse, as if women in trousers were ready to expropriate the entire male domain, leaving emasculated men home with squalling babies. The bloomer was soon abandoned for public wear, but it continued a covert existence in the health dress worn at spas and the gym suits girls wore for single-sex sports. Later reformers advocated lightening or discarding corsets, redesigning underwear, and reducing the oppressive weight of clothing. "Aesthetic dress" advocates rejected the fashionable stiff bodice and draped skirt in favor of softly gathered classical dresses with Pre-Raphaelite details.

Most women did not benefit from these new ideas until the twentieth century, but other changes did find widespread acceptance. The thin footwear of the early nineteenth century gave way to more

Women dress well in countries where they undress often.

FRENCH SAYING

See also
Rock Music

Fashion is made to become unfashionable.

COCO CHANEL

substantial leather boots after 1860. In the 1890s young women adopted the shirtwaist, a white, tailored blouse worn with a simple skirt and optional tailored jacket, which allowed greater freedom of movement than the heavily boned fashionable bodice. This style, based on men's suits, was associated with "The Gibson Girl," a new and distinctive American type with freer manners and a more active lifestyle than her mother. Shirtwaist suits were worn on the street, by clerical workers at the office, and while participating in the new fads for tennis, golf, and bicycling.

The nineteenth century continued to observe the division between tight-fitting public and more comfortable private forms of dress. Women wore loose wrappers at breakfast, while doing housework in the morning, and in their own rooms (a refuge women often sought in the summer heat); and from the 1880s a tighter version called a tea gown could be worn at home in the afternoon. But a corset and fitted bodice were required when receiving visitors or appearing in public, for loose clothing out of its limited sphere suggested immorality, slovenliness, or lack of self-respect. As the century progressed, etiquette became even more complex, and different activities required different clothes. The latest canvas shoes, chic at Newport, had no place on the street in New York, and attention to such distinctions were as much a symbol of wealth and leisure as were more ostentatious kinds of display. Dressing well, which in the eighteenth century had been an upper-class

obligation, now became a female obligation, partly because men's clothing had become so dull.

There was little regional variation in women's dress within the United States, partly because all new fashions emanated from one source—Paris. If anything, this fixation on Paris intensified through the century with the rise of highly publicized designers like Charles Worth and Jacques Doucet, to whom rich American style-setters went for their clothes. Conformity to fashion was encouraged by a growing system of transatlantic and coastal packet ships and a network of canals and railroads that sped new textiles, accessories, and fashion information to increasingly remote areas. Beginning with *Godey's Lady's Book* in 1830, American magazines began to include fashion plates (copies of French designs, not indigenous American styles), and their wide circulation helped bring all classes into the fashion mainstream.

The great exception, of course, was field slaves, who were provided coarse cotton clothing of extremely simple cut. House slaves, being more visible in public, tended to be better dressed and were more likely to receive castoff clothing as gifts. Some slaves were able to buy bright accessories to help individualize their holiday dress. Among free people, what deviation there was from mainstream fashion was found chiefly among sects like the Quakers, Shakers, and Mennonites, who dressed "plain" on religious principle. People in California and other parts of the Southwest that were under Spanish or Mexican rule

FEMALE ATTRACTIVENESS IN THE NINETEENTH CENTURY

Beauty as Duty

Middle-class women were also strongly admonished by etiquette books and popular magazines to take pains with their dress. Clean, well-fitting, becoming, and above all appropriate clothing was an important part of female attractiveness, and being attractive was the source of a woman's power (or "influence," as it was called in the nineteenth century). Only beauty could draw men, inclined by nature to "baser passions," into a domestic circle where they could be "influenced" by wives and mothers stronger than

they in moral sensibility and religious sentiment. According to the magazine *Demorest's* in 1883, "many a man's heart has been kept from wandering by the bow on his wife's slipper." Beauty was duty, and the lesson was taught from earliest childhood. Jefferson had warned his six-year-old daughter Maria "not to go out without your bonnet because it will make you very ugly and then we should not love you so much" (20 September 1785). Pale skin, considered beautiful and ladylike everywhere, acquired additional importance in the South, where children of

mixed blood lived on every plantation. Obvious rouging of the cheeks ended soon after 1800, but the English traveler Frances Trollope noted in *Domestic Manners of the Americans* (1832) that in the late 1820s the ladies of Cincinnati "powder themselves immoderately, face, neck, and arms, with pulverised starch; the effect is indescribably disagreeable by day-light, and not very favourable at any time" (1949 ed., p. 300). Later in the century, skin washes and lotions were used, but other cosmetics were supposed to be unobtrusive.

also wore distinctive styles until those regions were overrun by American culture in the 1840s. Otherwise most differences reflected economic class and, to some degree, climate. Immigrants, encouraged to adopt American customs as quickly as possible to speed their assimilation, rarely retained elements of national dress beyond the first generation. Only very close-knit groups such as the Hasidic Jews kept distinctive garments in daily wear.

Although the United States continued to look to Europe for new fashions, it became increasingly independent in its manufactures. The cotton gin (1793) made southern cotton profitable, encouraged slavery, and supplied the New England textile mills founded after the Revolution. Some mills specialized in coarse "Negro cloth" to clothe field slaves, and most emphasized quantity rather than quality. Not until April 1863 did *Godey's Lady's Book* note that "in previous seasons [Lowell calicoes] have been very nice, common, cheap goods, not remarkable for beauty. But this season they are equal to any English prints." Repeated attempts to establish silk culture were unsuccessful, and silk weaving took hold only after heavy duties were levied on imported silks during the Civil War.

The sewing machine transformed the early ready-made clothing industry in the 1850s and was widely used by dressmakers and in homes by the 1860s. It was also the first step in mechanizing the shoe industry, which by century's end not only provided this continent with footwear of every grade but was a significant exporter as well. Pattern drafting systems simplified and standardized the art of cutting out clothing and made paper patterns in graduated sizes available to the general public by the late 1870s. By 1900 most American men were wearing ready-made clothes. Women could buy ready-made cloaks, underwear, wrappers, and accessories, but because fashion required an exact fit in the bodice, most dresses were still custom-made.

CHILDREN'S CLOTHING. Nineteenth-century children did not wear fully adult styles until their teens, suggesting it was now desirable to prolong childhood. Little boys were given suits with skirts, and older ones wore suits with knee pants before graduating to adult trousers. Girls' dresses were gradually made longer as the wearer approached maturity.

The Twentieth Century

The acceptance of loose, unstructured clothing in the 1910s permitted the success of ready-made dresses and made the private dressmaker obsolete. The new styles also eliminated the traditional division of the day into private and public times according to whether loose or tight clothing was worn. Evening wear was signaled instead by fabric, decoration, décolleté, or archaic elements such as long skirts that were no longer found in daytime clothing.

The twentieth century was the first to see the development of a specifically American style, emphasizing sportswear. It grew out of an increasingly informal lifestyle and found its models in the movies. In the 1930s, New York stores began to recognize and feature American designers (who had been working incognito for years), a development given further impetus when World War II cut New York off from its fashion sources in Paris. The century was also noteworthy for the use of artificial fibers and materials. Rayon came into wide use by the 1930s, and nylon stockings became a staple at the end of World War II. These were followed by acrylics, polyesters and related fibers, tubular jerseys, bonded knits, and permanent-press fabrics. In spite of domestic technological advances, many textile and apparel industries were lost to foreign countries with less expensive labor.

Regional differences in dress, never very distinct, were further discouraged in the twentieth century by the explosion of nationally distributed images in movies, television, and magazines and by the mobility of the population. The clearest exception occurs in the western hats, boots, and fancy belt buckles men wear in Texas and the Southwest, but there are also subtle differences in taste elsewhere in the country. These have less to do with cut than with what styles are chosen for what occasions. Life in New York and Washington requires more formal clothing than in Boston. Like Boston, California is informal, but it is far more flamboyant and experimental in color and style.

Men's business and formal suits changed only in detail in the twentieth century, gaining minimal variety through the use of wide or narrow trousers with or without cuffs, double- or single-breasted coats with wide or narrow lapels, and more or less shoulder padding. Richard Martin and Harold Koda suggest that while men's basic garments are not subject to dramatic seasonal style changes, there are persistent stylistic types that fall into twelve categories (including jock, nerd, businessman, and rebel). Although reinterpreted over time, these types remain recognizable from decade to decade.

It is easy to be beautiful; it is difficult to appear so.

FRANK O'HARA

See also
Manners and Etiquette

*Most feminist
comics dressed like
cartoon characters.*

PAGE 231

*The Lord seeth
not as man seeth;
for man looketh
on the outward
appearance, but
the Lord looketh
on the heart.*

THE BIBLE
SAMUEL

See also
Nightlife

More important than changes in cut has been the creeping informality in dress. As early as 1900, women's magazines inveighed against the "shirt-sleeve habit" indulged in by men who went coatless at home and even on the street, looking slovenly beside their corseted wives. By century's end, many businesses that once would have expected their male employees to appear in three-piece suits now required only trousers, buttoned shirt, and tie. Non-matching coats and trousers became acceptable and vests were increasingly omitted altogether. Sportswear cut loose from traditional khakis and tweeds and was made in every bright color, a trend echoed faintly in formal clothes as well. Early in the century and into the 1920s, men wore knickers and kneesocks (often bright tartans) for sports, with perhaps a sweater replacing the vest. Informal shirts were often colored and patterned, and the collar gradually became lower and softer. Beginning in the 1930s, men began to wear swimsuits without tops, shorts that bared the leg, and short-sleeved, knitted "sport shirts." From the knit sport shirt, the next step was the "T-shirt," which by the 1960s was made in colors and by the 1970s and 1980s was printed with mottoes and pictures so that it looked less like underwear.

Not only did women enjoy greater informality in the twentieth century, they saw the basic cut of their clothing change radically as well. The first steps were to loosen the bodice and to shorten the skirt to the knee. Once a skintight fit was abandoned, corsets became less necessary for creating the fashionable line. The introduction of pantyhose gave the coup de grace to the gartered foundation garment and made possible the miniskirts of the 1960s. These changes allowed real freedom of movement but were offset by the persistent fashion for extremely high heels. Women's hats, a necessary component of decency for two centuries, fell out of use in the 1960s except for functional headgear. In the 1930s, pants and shorts came into common use, at first for sports and loungewear but gradually for more occasions, until they went nearly everywhere by 1975. The wearing of trousers, so controversial in the nineteenth century, simply seemed practical after two world wars in which women had worn them while employed in war industries. The 1970s and 1980s saw revivals of 1920s and 1930s styles, with a

THE CULTIVATION OF BEAUTY

A New Emphasis on the Body

Aside from the tendency toward informality and the adoption by women of men's garments, the most important long-term trend in the twentieth century is the fashion emphasis on body rather than clothes. The roots of this development are complex. The moral superiority claimed for women in the nineteenth century had justified many advances in women's position, but it also required eschewing personal indulgence and putting family (or substitutes like schoolchildren or the urban poor) before self. As middle-class women spent less time immured at home and more time in the world, such restraints perhaps came to seem unfair. At any rate, moral superiority was rarely claimed or conceded by the 1920s. This allowed women greater freedom in a climate of self-indulgence, but it also left personal attractiveness as the chief criterion of female distinction. Whereas in the nineteenth century the essential female grace lay in the inner character, and careful grooming and dress were recommended chiefly as means of attracting men to the benign domestic sphere of female moral influence, now physical attractiveness was an end in itself. The cultivation of beauty became for women a means of personal aggrandizement, and the acquisition of beautiful women became for men a symbol of status and wealth. The growing prevalence of divorce may well have put pressure on women to preserve a youthful and attractive appearance.

An attractive appearance came to be defined less in terms of clothing than of the body itself. This was encouraged by the tendency toward informality in dress and the relaxation of etiquette, so that clothes simply became less important, and also by the tendency to wear fewer and scantier clothes for many occasions. As short skirts, sleeveless and backless dresses, and increasingly brief bathing suits revealed more and more of the body, the body itself inevitably became the focus of attention. Beauty parlors had already become common by the 1890s, specializing not only in hair care but in manicures, wrinkle removal, massages, face peeling, and even rudimentary plastic surgery. Makeup began to come out of the closet soon after 1900, and by the 1920s lipstick and powder were applied in public. With the popularity of short skirts, sheer stockings, and sleeveless dresses, women of the 1920s routinely began to shave leg and underarm hair.

growing emphasis on broad shoulders and narrow hips that was interpreted by some as an attempt to minimize the waist, by others as an attempt to ape masculine body lines. The "dress for success" books for businesswomen of the period recommended masculine-style jackets worn with skirts and heels to establish the wearer's gender, suggesting that symbolism in dress was still far more important than practicality.

When women bobbed their hair in the 1920s, they symbolically discarded the burden of traditional femininity in favor of boyish freedom. But our culture is not nearly so disturbed by women borrowing masculine traits as by men taking on feminine qualities. Thus when young men adopted long hair in the 1960s, middle America was outraged. In that same decade many black Americans stopped straightening their hair and wore it in natural "Afro" styles. These styles were widely imitated by whites in the 1970s, reflecting the new acceptance by both races that "black is beautiful."

After 1900, a new generation of women's magazines, including *Vogue* at the couture end and *Ladies' Home Journal* for the middle class, depended for their survival more on advertising than on subscriptions, and at present women's magazine advertising is dominated by perfumes and skin- and hair-care products. This change grows partly out of the emphasis on beautiful bodies, but it also reflects the fact that makeup, unlike clothing, is not really essential, so that manufacturers must market not only the product but the need for it. Doing this requires massive advertising. Thus a symbiotic relationship developed between women's magazines and beauty product manufacturers that conspired to teach women that unembellished looks were ugly and that "natural" beauty is possible only with the aid of art. During this same period, photographs gradually replaced drawings in both fashion articles and advertising. At first the new images of real bodies with their ordinary waistlines and big feet clashed with the idealized drawings. This conflict was solved not by moderating the ideal but by idealizing the models. Real women, chosen for their height and slenderness, carefully posed, and cleverly photographed, create an exemplar more powerful than any drawing because they prove that the ideal can actually be attained and thus impose on women the obligation to attain it.

Feminists have protested the exploitation of women in advertising as in pornography, but Rita Freedman in *Beauty Bound* suggests that by teaching personal control through assertive behavior, feminism may have encouraged women to reshape their lives by reshaping their bodies. Certainly by the 1980s, the traditional emphasis on dieting had expanded to include physical fitness, and women are now expected to develop their muscles like men. This change is often described as a liberation from traditional models of dependent femininity, but the implication that natural female bodies are unacceptable still entraps all too many young women in masochistic behaviors such as anorexia and compulsive fitness training.

Men have not escaped this growing emphasis on the beautiful body, although it has taken longer to show pernicious effects. Twentieth-century models of male attractiveness have in general been more athletic than those fashionable in previous centuries. Portliness went out in the 1890s, and now a slim, athletic build implies health and strength. Transient models such as the hippie radical or the sensitive male of the 1960s and 1970s did not counter the general expectation of physical fitness in men. By the 1980s, a barrage of images of heavily muscled cartoon heroes, movie stars, and athletes created such pressure for a powerful body that young men felt obligated to spend hours working out with weights, and many took drugs to build their muscles artificially, a kind of self-destructive behavior formerly associated with women. The pressure on both sexes to have lean and muscular bodies has inflated the market for diet programs, special foods, expensive equipment, and special clothing for exercise. As a result, "attractively fit" bodies have become a status symbol, along with overdesigned, high-priced athletic shoes and tight exercise leotards and bicycling pants whose elastic materials allow freedom of movement and yet reveal every nuance of muscle.

CHILDREN'S CLOTHING. Children's clothing has also changed dramatically in the twentieth century, reflecting the prevailing trend toward increased informality. In the early twentieth century, rompers became available to toddlers of both sexes, and dresses were abandoned by boys out of infancy. In the last several decades, children's dress has become increasingly gender-specific. For fancy occasions, even tiny boys wear suits and girls dresses. Everyday clothes differ less in cut, but a rigid color code, beginning with pink for girls and blue for boys, was established by 1950. In spite of the interest in unisex dress in the 1970s, children's clothing clearly reflects contemporary concern with establishing gender identity from a very early age.

—NANCY REXFORD

COMMERCIAL ARCHITECTURE

The history of commercial and industrial architecture in the United States is integrally connected with the emergence and development of the most characteristic attitudes, values, and ideals of middle-class Americans. While important facets of the national psyche are reflected in American civic and residential architecture, it is in commercial and industrial building that the most cherished precepts concerning the relationship between private and public enterprise have been dynamically interwoven and expressed.

The Atlantic colonies were established in large part for mercantile purposes. Although many inhabitants had other reasons for settling in the New World, the mercantile impulse was germane to the culture and politics of the new land. Although in 1789 government was constitutionally separated from religion, its fertile relationship to private enterprise, cultivated from the outset of the colonial period, was affirmed. This relationship has remained so vital that in the twentieth century, commercial architecture emphatically represents such national cultural ideals as individualism, ambition, wealth, success, and personal power, as well as social and economic power, the growth of urbanization, and the rise of a market economy.

Freedom, pragmatism, ingenuity, functionalism, and technological progressiveness are among the obvious qualities associated with American commercial and industrial architecture; however, these qualities only began to generate an identifiable architectural expression in the early nineteenth century. Prior to that they had borrowed forms and images from both the civic and residential spheres. Early colonial commercial architecture reflected a mixture of medieval traditions and more urbane seventeenth-century English and continental architectural taste. Retail and small commercial ventures were often managed as family businesses and installed in residences or buildings of residential character, such as the Paul Revere House (1677) in Boston. Trade restrictions imposed by Britain inhibited the development of mill or industrial building, although European visitors often found American applications of wind- and waterpower in smaller projects to be ingenious and more frequent than in Europe.

Colonial versions of European high-style architecture, based in large part on pattern books, available materials, and incidental local craft, were first introduced in governmental, religious, and residential structures. These eventually lent larger cities such as Boston and Philadelphia a character similar to contemporary London. As the familiar vocabulary was adapted for the agencies of finance and commerce, a uniquely American urban character began to evolve.

One of the earliest examples of such an adaptation is Faneuil Hall (1740), given by Peter Faneuil to the city of Boston to enclose and improve the farmers' market on Dock Square. The plans were prepared by the portrait painter John Smibert (1688–1751), which indicates the absence of professional architects in mid-eighteenth-century America. It was constructed of red brick with an arcade around the first-floor market space and sash windows admitting light to the second-story public meeting hall, an arrangement generally derived from European models. The whole block was covered by a gabled roof surmounted by a cupola and loosely resembled the familiar New England meetinghouse. The adjacency of market and meeting room reinforced the fact that Faneuil Hall was a popular forum where town worthies informally exchanged opinions on public matters while shopping.

In 1760, land in Newport, Rhode Island, was dedicated to the construction of a market building which, like Faneuil Hall, had an open trading area on the first floor surmounted by two stories of flexible space used for storage, offices, and shops. The Brick Market (1772) was designed by Peter Harrison (1716–1775), a British-born merchant whose intense interest in architecture had caused him to collect the largest library of treatises and pattern books in the country. His scheme was based on a design by Inigo Jones, who had introduced Italian classicism to England in the late sixteenth century and whose work had been in revival since the early eighteenth century in England.

Although Harrison was no more than a gifted amateur, professional architecture was encouraged and supported by the country's other great amateur, Thomas Jefferson, as a mark of sophistication and wise planning. Commercial architecture began to profit from professional architectural services upon the immigration of Benjamin Henry Latrobe (1764–1820) from England in 1796. The Bank of Pennsylvania (1798–1800; razed 1860s) in Philadelphia is a distinguished example of his early work. It exhibited masonry construction, including interior vaulting for both structure and architectural effect. Temple porticos fronted both ends of a block supporting a low pantheonic dome, beneath which was located the banking room, generously illuminated by daylight. The design established a standard of elegance and efficiency that was followed in banking and commercial buildings throughout the country.

William Strickland (c. 1787–1854), who was a talented designer and Latrobe's pupil, won a competition in 1818 for the Second Bank of the United States (1819–1824) in Philadelphia. Faced with Pennsylvania marble, this was the first public building to derive from the Parthenon and signaled the advent of the Greek Revival, the style with which Americans identified nationally after the War of 1812. The Greek Revival style was also employed by Strickland in his design for the Merchants' Exchange (1832) in Philadelphia which converted irregularities of the city plan to advantage. The wedge-shaped site was terminated at its narrower end by a semicircular Corinthian portico surmounted by a lantern modeled on the choragic Monument of Lysicrates of late classical Athens. A similar dependence on classical models characterized the Merchants' Exchange (1836–1842) in New York by Isaiah Rogers (1800–1869). Its exterior Ionic colonnade on a high podium screened a brick-vaulted exchange room 80 feet (24 meters) in diameter.

Such references were certainly signs of sophisticated architectural taste and erudition on the part of designers; but they also directly reinforced popular sentiments about the manifest destiny of the United States as the modern descendant of ancient democratic Greece. This was particularly important during the period of Jacksonian expan-

sionism when the drive westward was envisioned as bringing civilization to the wilderness as well as taking advantage of the limitless natural resources of the Great Plains and western mountains. Towns founded during this period often took Greek names as symbols of this spirit: Athens, Syracuse, Sparta, Utica, Ithaca, Arcadia, Alexandria, Delphos, Troy, Memphis, Corinth. Commercial architecture along the principal streets of these and similar towns was often of a reduced neoclassicism, thus serving as an understated context for more prominent civic, religious, and residential structures in Greek Revival style.

With British restrictions on manufacturing removed by the Revolution, the United States sought to achieve economic independence through the development of industry. In the late eighteenth century, structures based on existing sawmills in New England began to house waterpowered machinery for producing textiles. The earliest mills employed traditional materials and structural techniques, amplified around the turn of the century with the malleability, permanence, and strength of cast iron.

Probably the first building to be planned and constructed as a textile mill was the 1793 spinning mill designed by Samuel Slater (1768–1835) in Pawtucket, Rhode Island. Based on his experience and familiarity with English textile production, the machinery was housed in a frame structure whose proportions and noble simplicity were consonant with the residential context. The main requirements—large, continuous interior spaces in a two-story block, adequate daylighting, and a structural system rigid enough to stabilize the building against vibrations from the power mechanism and machinery—were all satisfied functionally without sacrificing basic architectural principles or pleasing design. Such a successful integration of social, commercial, and architectural values by manufacturers allayed the fears of many agrarian-minded citizens that industrialization would contaminate the morality of the nation.

The rapid growth of manufacturing in the period between 1810 and 1820 began to alter the size and form of mill buildings. Mills became larger in all dimensions and were increasingly constructed in stone or brick masonry for rigidity and fire protection. They acquired clerestory-light monitors to make their attic spaces more useful, as in the Lippitt Mill (1809–1810) in West Warwick, Rhode Island. With cupolas holding bells to call the workers to their jobs, mills became increasingly important as the focus of community life, especially in small towns.

COMMERCIAL ARCHITECTURE

We shape our buildings; thereafter they shape us.

SIR WINSTON CHURCHILL

See also
The City

79

TRADITION AND
TECHNOLOGY

*A view of the Chrysler
Building in the year it was
completed (1930). Art Deco
style reconciled the continuing
taste for ornament and traditional materials with a growing interest in technology as a
form of power.*
LIBRARY OF CONGRESS/
CORBIS

In the first four decades of the nineteenth century, manufacturing moved beyond the limits of local capital and mechanical skills. To increase output capacity, the textile industry was gradually transformed by an investment and managerial structure geared to efficient production and the organization of a large labor force. Mill buildings evolved to meet new safety needs and production realities. Large lateral towers added for circulation, fire containment, and vertical mechanical runs separated the mill from the meetinghouse typologically, as in the woolen mill by Zachariah Allen (1822; enlarged 1839) in Allendale, Rhode Island. Landscape design, reliance on neoclassical architectural principles to govern a complex of buildings, and a concern for appropriate living quarters for single men and women as well as for families transformed factories from isolated objects into planned communities, sometimes of compelling visual appeal. In the Crown and Eagle mills (1825, 1829, respectively) by Learned Scott in North Uxbridge, Massachusetts, boardinghouses, dormitory structures, and row housing, along with the factory buildings, began to reshape the urban fabric in conjunction with waterways and green areas.

While manufacturing before the Civil War frequently remained rural due to the necessity of locating mills and factories where waterpower could best be harnessed, retail architecture was decidedly urban and more directly responsive to changing technology and economics as well as fashion. The shopping arcade or *passage*, inaugurated in France in 1790, appeared in the United States in Philadelphia (1827) and Providence, Rhode Island (1828–1829). Designed by John Haviland (1792–1852), the Philadelphia Arcade had streetfront arcades while the Providence Arcade, designed by Russell Warren (1783–1860) and James C. Bucklin (1801–1890), had a glass-roofed interior.

The Gothic Revival, a romantic phenomenon that followed on the heels of the Greek Revival, produced a few retail buildings, for example, the step-gabled and pinnacled Oak Hall on North Street in Boston, a frame structure of mid-century date. The use of wood for such highly detailed ornamental buildings was actually facilitated by the invention of the jigsaw during this period, a byproduct of the industrial revolution.

In the end, neither the Greek nor the Gothic Revival lent itself to the economic or spatial exigencies of retail building. Rather, in the late 1840s the Palazzo style began to dominate retail and office buildings, where rows of arched windows separated by engaged columns in the manner of sixteenth-century Venetian palaces defined the stories. Stewart's Downtown Store in New York (1845), executed in white marble, was the first to apply this generalized Renaissance style, whose main advantage was its ability to be extended both horizontally and vertically over a large commercial facade.

THE SUN BUILDING

The First Cast-Iron Exterior

The rapid spread of the Palazzo style in the 1850s and 1860s was encouraged by the development of cast iron as a finish material as well as a structural component. Pioneered in the United States by James Bogardus (1800–1874), an inventor and foundry owner, iron appeared in the Baltimore Sun Building (1848), which he designed in collaboration with R. G. Hatfield, and in his design for the Harper Brothers Building in New York (1854). The Sun Building had two iron fronts that had been cast in sections at the Bogardus foundry, shipped to the site, and assembled with bolts as a prefabricated building skin. Iron thus made the repetition of facade units entirely practical as well as far cheaper than building in conventional materials and methods. Cast iron was normally rendered in forms that imitated stone and, because it needed to be painted to protect against weathering, it could be given any color the architect or patron desired. Flexible, practical, and cheap, the popularity of cast-iron components spread rapidly from urban centers to towns and villages to become the first identifiable commercial vernacular architecture.

Perhaps more important, Bogardus used iron as a system of cast columns and wrought beams in the Sun Building. The slender columns, which eliminated the need for heavy masonry-bearing walls, afforded unprecedented interior space as well as lightness and rapid construction by semiskilled labor. Iron also lent itself to other building components such as stairways and railings. It thus set the stage for the concept of a structural cage in which loads could be carried on continuous columns from top story to foundation. This system was utilized already in the A. T. Stewart Store in New York (1862) by John Kellum, one of the largest cast-iron buildings anywhere. Its central rotunda was surrounded by galleries beneath a skylight and contained a pipe organ for the entertainment of the customers.

See also
Public Architecture

C

COMMERCIAL ARCHITECTURE

Soon movie theatres were constructed in cities across the nation as luxurious, mammoth halls, resplendent with colorful ushers, plush carpeting and seats, and ornate decor with Greek or Oriental motifs.

PAGE 145

Architecture is inhabited sculpture.

CONSTANTIN BRANCUSI

Bogardus pushed his system further when he constructed a shot tower for the McCullough Shot and Lead Company of New York (1855). A metal frame served as the structure of the tower with brickwork used merely as infill, thus adumbrating the emergence of the steel skeletal frame in Chicago and New York some thirty years later. In addition to the employment of cast iron, the Haughwout Building (1856) in New York by John P. Gaynor and Daniel Badger incorporated the first passenger elevator. Invented by Elisha Otis, the elevator became the second stimulant of vastly increased height in commercial buildings throughout the country.

Cast iron was also used widely in other commercial building types. The Crystal Palace (1853) in Bryant Park by Carstensen and Gildemeister brought both the materials and the concept of the London Exposition and its Crystal Palace of 1851 to New York. A twenty-minute fire that destroyed the gossamer exposition building in 1858 proved that the major disadvantage of iron was its low melting point. The train shed of the first Grand Central Station (1871) in New York by John B. Snook used a metal skeleton carrying glass panels, as did many other railroad stations. These were superseded by less-combustible steel structures after about 1875 due to the spread of the Bessemer steel process, invented simultaneously in England by Henry Bessemer and in Kentucky by William Kelly in 1856.

Rapid commercial growth after the Civil War produced the most important developments in commercial and industrial architecture. Skyrocketing land values in urban centers demanded that technology address higher density and concentration in commercial buildings. The powerful combination of profit and prestige became the driving motivation for ever-taller buildings. Never before had the largest, tallest, and most dominant buildings in an urban skyline represented the private power of the commercial, financial, and industrial enterprises of a society rather than the power and authority of its religious or governmental institutions.

In New York, the Tribune Building by Richard M. Hunt and the Western Union Building by George B. Post (both built from 1873 to 1875) announced the success of private investment in mass communication. Yet by extending their Victorian masses upward through picturesque clock towers without giving up traditional bearing-wall masonry, they remained only on the cusp of stylistic and technological change. But in the frantic effort to rebuild Chicago after the disastrous fire

of 1871, the technological and engineering advances begun by James Bogardus and others came to fruition. Large quantities of concentrated office space were needed to house the growing legions of white-collar workers and secretarial staffs required by the administrations of the vastly expanding business enterprises there. The advantages of metal and glass radically altered the engineering and design of the new fireproof buildings that mushroomed in the Loop to meet the demand.

The first Leiter Building (1879) by William Le Baron Jenney (1832–1907) used cast-iron columns for both interior and peripheral loads, situated columns next to the brick envelope of the facade, and substituted huge plate-glass windows for bearing walls. Jenney, who had been trained as a civil engineer in France, took the next step toward skeletal engineering in the Home Insurance Company Building (1883–1885), which is considered the first skyscraper. Although some bearing masonry continued to support peripheral load in the first two stories, a combination of cast-iron columns and wrought-iron girders established a true skeletal frame for the upper eight stories.

Unfortunately, Jenney's engineering genius far surpassed his abilities in architectural design, where he remained bound to historical precedent and uninspired eclecticism. The question of an appropriate expression for the shell, an expression of contemporary social, economic, and cultural conditions, was taken up by other firms. That Chicago architects were dissatisfied with the initial expression of the new technology in a cloak of revivalist styles is partially attributable to the tradition of practical thinking that began with Thomas Jefferson, Charles Bulfinch, and Benjamin Henry Latrobe, manifesting itself in mill and factory design. It continued under the impulse of sculptor and critic Horatio Greenough, who in his writings had called for an organic relationship between the form of a building and its internal realities.

Among those who took up the search for appropriate expression was the firm of Burnham and Root. Although he was in command of the technology at his disposal, John Wellborn Root (1850–1891) was equally concerned with the functional and aesthetic accomplishments of his buildings. The Rookery Building (1885–1886), framed in steel with masonry outer walls, addressed several practical problems by introducing a hollow core in its block-square volume. The resulting light-well permitted the handsome lobby to be brightly illuminated through skylights and

82

insured that all offices on the inside of the upper stories would have the benefit of adequate light and ventilation. The exterior composition was additive and eclectic, a manner that Root rejected in the unornamented Monadnock Building (1889–1891), the first tall building to be treated as a slab in one continuous upward sweep. The steel cage of the Reliance Building (1894–1895) was protected against fire with terra-cotta cladding using Gothic motifs; but its vast expanses of plate glass "Chicago windows" projected the impression that its exterior was truly an expression of the frame and the interior space.

Contemporaneous with the Rookery, Henry Hobson Richardson (1838–1886), one of the foremost architects on the East Coast, designed the Marshall Field Wholesale Store (1885–1887) in Chicago. The structure consisted of a mix of terra-cotta-clad, cast-iron columns on the first three floors and wood framing typical of New England mill buildings on the floors above. The understated exterior, however, made an enormous impact on Chicago architects who saw in it an appropriate solution to the form of a modern commercial building. In his religious, civic, and private commissions, Richardson had popularized an energetic neo-Romanesque style. For the Field Wholesale Store, he abandoned all romantic qualities of the revival mode in favor of a severe treatment that projected unity, integrity, economy, and rationality.

Among those most influenced by Richardson were Dankmar Adler and Louis Sullivan (1856–1924) who designed the mixed-use Auditorium Theatre Hotel (1887–1889), an important turning point in their work. Retaining their characteristic finish, ornament, and detail, especially on the interior, in their final scheme they incorporated numerous qualities of the Field Store design, including its solidity, its understatement, and its reliance on the arch as an organizing device. Sullivan developed a personal philosophy about balancing the engineering aspects of the skyscraper with the poetry of ornament derived from geometry and plants. In a series of structures for Saint Louis, Missouri (Wainwright Building, 1890–1891), Buffalo, New York (Guaranty [now Prudential] Building, 1895), and Chicago (Gage Group, 1898–1899) he envisioned tripartite vertical compositions articulated by organic ornament. Perhaps his most notable accomplishment was the Schlesinger and Mayer (now Carson Pirie Scott) Store in Chicago (1899–1904), a celebration of the social aspects of shopping, in which he enclosed the steel cage with a subtle terra-cotta skin that contrasted with an elaborate two-story band of florid wrought-iron ornament enframing the display windows and entrances at pedestrian level. After this tour de force, Sullivan spent his late career designing small banks and thrift institutions as essays in organic ornament for midwestern towns such as Grinnell, Iowa, Owatonna, Minnesota, and Sidney, Ohio.

In New York, the technology of steel framing reinforced rising land prices and led to ever higher buildings and more conservative design. When it was erected, the impressive Woolworth Building by Cass Gilbert (1910–1913) in Lower Manhattan was the tallest in the world at 792 feet (238 meters). Its terra-cotta cladding was cast as Gothic ornament, which inspired the nickname "cathe-

---

THE 1893 COLUMBIAN EXPOSITION

A European Revival

In 1893, the World's Columbian Exposition opened in Chicago. Planned by Daniel H. Burnham (1846–1912) and landscape architect Frederick Law Olmsted (1822–1903), the Exposition was envisioned as a symbol of American industrial, commercial, and social progress four centuries after the arrival of Columbus. McKim, Mead, and White, Richard Morris Hunt, and other architects from the East Coast were invited to join stylistically conservative Chicago designers such as Burnham to create a complex of classical-revival buildings in the manner of the École des Beaux-Arts in Paris, all in an artificial setting replete with Venetian canals and a lagoon on the lakefront. They succeeded in raising consciousness about architectural and urban-design values, especially among midwesterners of limited background, who saw in the "White City" a model of urbanity. Yet they also sent a powerful message about the venerability of historical revival architecture derived from Europe—in contrast to the emerging Chicago School of commercial building—as the appropriate vehicle to express commercial, industrial, and social progress as well as national identity.

The impact of the Columbian Exposition can be measured in the spread of the City Beautiful movement, a trend toward improved urban design related to Burnham's master plan for Chicago (1909), and in the continued dominance of revival styles for commercial as well as civic architecture throughout the country.

See also
The Suburbs

C

COMMERCIAL ARCHITECTURE

dral of commerce" for the corporate headquarters of Frank Woolworth's chain of variety stores.

By contrast, Sullivan's protégé, Frank Lloyd Wright (1867–1959), had designed an innovative office building for the Larkin Soap Company administration in Buffalo, New York (1903). Avoiding historical references altogether, Wright produced an environment derived not only from the utilitarian realities of the building and the formal precedents of Chicago commercial architecture but also from the need for programming the tasks and duties of a large secretarial staff and managerial team, for social interaction, and for a sense of dignity in the workplace. Nevertheless, apart from the circle of Sullivan and Wright, functionally based architecture without historical ornament remained limited in large part to industrial structures where it could be justified as an expression of economy and efficiency.

Perhaps the clearest indication of this dichotomy is in the architecture produced for the automobile industry. Having experimented with several alternatives to conventional mill construction in the design of factories for automotive production, the Detroit architect Albert Kahn (1869–1942) began to employ reinforced concrete as a structural system in 1905. Commissioned by Henry Ford in 1909, Kahn designed a huge assembly plant in Highland Park, Michigan, in which concrete stabs and steel-girder beams afforded not only strength, safety, and permanence but adequate clearspan space for production. In 1912–1915, the plant incorporated a continuously moving assembly line, the basis of most factory production ever since.

Kahn continued to improve the architecture of factories, creating dramatic forms based on clearly analyzed functional relationships. Vast expanses of glass in industrial framing, jagged roof lines, rows of columnar smokestacks rising out of power plants, and complex truss systems for clearspan space became his trademarks, especially in huge complexes such as the Ford River Rouge Plant in Dearborn, Michigan, begun in 1916. Yet when General Motors commissioned him to design its headquarters in Detroit, Kahn turned out an impressive structure based on classical revivalism.

The General Motors Building (1922) is an early example of the expression of a corporate culture, rather than the expression of the taste and power of an entrepreneurial individual or family. Rising from an arcade of show windows to display its products at street level, separate tower-like elements are connected to a slab at the back, the whole crowned by a classical colonnade at the top.

The location of executive offices at the top level and the general composition of the structure metaphorically suggest the gathering of the five automotive companies into one corporate body. Research and development was housed in a lower block just behind the main building, reflecting its supportive but less prominent character.

The extent to which eclectic architectural vocabularies continued to connote grandeur and magnanimity in the minds of patrons can be judged by the Chicago Tribune Tower competition of 1922 in which a neo-Gothic design by John Mead Howells and Raymond Hood took first place over a group of some two hundred entries. Yet the second-place entry by Eliel Saarinen, a tower dynamically telescoping itself skyward with a limited amount of abstract ornamental detail, made its impact on countless office buildings throughout the United States and Canada, even influencing Hood and Howells in their subsequent design work, and paved the way for the important changes in skyscraper design.

The first of those changes was the Art Deco style, which reconciled the continuing taste for ornament and traditional materials with the growing interest in new industrial metals, in technology as a form of power, and in air transportation, electricity, and radio waves as symbols of progress. Art Deco also exploited architecture as a form of advertising, partly in pure verticality and partly in the identifiability of a building profile in the urban skyline. The Union Trust Building by Smith, Hinchman, and Grylls in Detroit (1929) and the Chrysler Building by William Van Alen in New York (1930) both used night illumination to enhance their presence; and the Empire State Building (1931) by Shreve, Lamb, and Harmon in New York relied on its 101-story height to dominate most of midtown Manhattan. These qualities began to disappear as the impact of the Great Depression cautioned corporation presidents and boards of directors to seek ways of representing fiscal responsibility in architectural form.

The Philadelphia Saving Fund Society building (1933) by George Howe and William Lescaze was the first corporate tower to draw on contemporary German functionalist design in order to make the structure as maintenance-free as possible and to prevent shareholders from suspecting unnecessary expenditure. During the 1930s and 1940s, the Moderne style, a softer version of functionalism influenced by French sources, was especially popular in retail and smaller commercial buildings. In gasoline stations, grocery markets, drugstores, barbershops, beauty salons, and variety stores, it implied an architectural connection with the culture of large-scale business enterprise.

In reaction to European functionalism and the Moderne, Frank Lloyd Wright offered his own solution to the office building and corporate headquarters in the Johnson Wax Administration Building (1939) in Racine, Wisconsin. Its smooth brick surfaces rest on reinforced concrete platforms resembling lilypads and its fenestration consists exclusively of glass tubing held in place by steel spacers. As in the Larkin Building, Wright designed not only the architecture but also the furnishings. The final effect of the whole building was to inspire the workforce into a stronger sense of social cohesion.

In an effort to generate electric power, raise living standards in rural areas, provide jobs during the Depression, and implement a policy of long-range regional planning, the federal government initiated a series of hydroelectric dam projects during the 1930s. The most extensive of these, the Tennessee Valley Authority (TVA), begun in 1933, consisted of eight dams along a seven hundred-mile waterway between the Appalachians and the Ohio River. It was echoed in other projects in the Pacific Northwest, the West, and the Southwest. The architecture of the TVA was cast into the Moderne style and was considered important enough by the Museum of Modern Art in New York to deserve a special exhibit in 1938.

Meanwhile, the rise of the automobile after World War I brought countless other changes to commercial architecture. In the 1930s, freeways had already begun to change the face of Los Angeles. Cross-country travel and truck transport was facilitated and encouraged by a growing system of state and federal highways, along which service stations and tourist cabins sprang up. The motor lodge or motel was geared to travelers on the move in private vehicles. Motels were accompanied by an entirely new culture of culinary establishments offering low- to medium-priced fare for people of modest means who were in transit. Diners, sometimes literally converted from railroad cars, connoted both the convenience and transitory quality of eating on the road and inadvertently acknowledged the demise of rail transportation which was in decline after 1914. Public transportation was supplied by the development of bus lines that installed terminals in towns and cities but relied on service stations and stores as stopping places in rural areas. The mobile home also emerged at this time as a kind of updated Conestoga wagon that permitted owners to pull their shelter on the road after them.

The impact of the automobile and the general rise of consumer culture between the world wars was documented by the Chicago World Fair of 1933 and the New York World Fair of 1939. In contrast to the Columbian Exposition of 1893, exhibits representing transportation, electrical power, industry, communication, consumer products, and entertainment at both the 1933 and 1939 fairs were contextualized in architectural environments designed with the collective intention of looking stunningly futuristic. This was accomplished in large part by the use of dramatic lighting and water displays and, at the New York fair, by elevated walkways and curvilinear buildings, imparting a sense of free movement. Although the fair buildings were no more than imaginative variations on the Moderne and functionalist styles, they popularized the equation of technology with progress and confirmed the notion of architecture as a vehicle of public relations and advertising.

One of the most important effects of the automobile during this period was its implementation of suburban development. Liberated from having to live near their workplaces, Americans began to move from central cities to newly subdivided neighborhood developments at the edge of or outside city limits. Flourishing central business districts began to be eroded, imperceptibly at first, by decentralized commercial strips and shopping districts. The Country Club Plaza in Kansas City, Missouri, developed by J. C. Nichols and designed by Edward Beuhler Delk (1922–1925), offered a master-planned commercial quarter that responded to the rapid growth of the city southward and set a standard for similar developments elsewhere. The use of a neo-Spanish colonial architectural idiom, the concentration of parking in designed areas, and tight controls placed on signage, lighting, and future development, not only preserved the image Nichols planned but made environmental control serve private enterprise in a way that had rarely been seen before.

After World War II, a wave of Modernist influence swept through American business and commercial architecture, due in part to the immigration of several leading European architect-educators to the United States in the late 1930s: Ludwig Mies van der Rohe, Walter Gropius, and Marcel Breuer. Their influence brought about a strong school of commercial building represented by pace-setting structures such as the Lever House by Skidmore, Owings, and Merrill (1952) and the Seagram Building by Mies van der Rohe with Philip Johnson (1957) in New York City.

C

COMMERCIAL ARCHITECTURE

In the business district office blocks of beef-red brick rose two or three stories, a modest but dignified vernacular architecture.

PAGE 553

See also
Urban Parks

High land costs encouraged construction of taller structures, originally built with thick brick or masonry walls limiting interior space.

PAGE 59

THE EVOLUTION OF THE SHOPPING MALL

Interiorization of Commercial Architecture

Suburban shopping strips of less pretension in the 1920s, 1930s, and 1940s offered convenience to motorists who could easily park their cars while doing light shopping. The success of strips eventually led to the development of the supermarket as well as several other concepts, including the drive-in restaurant, drive-in movie theater, and drive-through store. It also led to the shopping center, a concept first articulated in the 1950s by Victor Gruen, an immigrant Austrian architect who saw in it a way to bring a desirable quality of public interaction to the highly decentralized life of the American suburb. Early examples such as Northland Center (1954) in Southfield, Michigan, were treated as elaborate complexes of retail establishments connected by covered sidewalks, interspersed with parklike elements such as fountains, benches, and plantings, and surrounded by parking lots. They thus drew on the imagery of urban and civic life while remaining totally private developments. Their popularity even had the reflexive impact of causing towns such as Richmond, Indiana, and countless others to eliminate automobile traffic from their principal commercial streets and convert them into pedestrian zones in hopes of revitalizing their commercial districts. The enclosure of Southdale Center (1956) in Edina, Minnesota, to avoid inclement weather created the first self-contained shopping concourse.

The evolution of the regional shopping mall, especially from the late 1960s on, exploited the ambiguity of a private domain open to the public. Excluding whomever its owners wished and eliminating truly civic interaction, malls became paradises of consumerism in contrast to the increasingly empty and dangerous urban centers. Fairlane Town Center (1976) in Dearborn, Michigan, developed by the Taubman Company, is a consummate example of the interiorization of commercial architecture around atrium courts with corridors of shops strung between large anchor stores. It is also an example of design that alters the users' perceptions of space, time, and movement as retail strategy. Festival marketplaces, an outgrowth of regional malls and open markets, have been developed by James Rouse in Baltimore, New York, Boston, Miami, and many other cities. Usually directed toward leisure activities, these marketplaces often incorporate outdoor dining and entertainment, and are frequently sited on rivers, shores, or harbors.

These understated minimalist slabs expressed corporate identity through machine precision and the elegance of tinted glass in a light curtain-wall skin that has no support value and serves only as an insulating envelope. In contrast to earlier complexes such as Rockefeller Center (1931–1933 and later) in New York in which a group of buildings was organized around a public plaza where outdoor activities could be centered, these buildings were conceived as objects isolated by set-back plazas, a concept related to the Modernist urban-planning principle of functional separation and zoning.

Modernist concepts likewise dominated such other areas of commercial architecture as transportation. In the Lambert Air Terminal (1956) in Saint Louis, Missouri, Minoru Yamasaki covered large waiting rooms with thin concrete shells whose lightness and curvilinearity for the first time metaphorically suggested aerodynamic forces. Similarly Eero Saarinen engaged the air terminal as a serious architectural problem in his reinforced concrete sculptural design for the Trans World Airlines Terminal at Kennedy Airport (1962) in New York. By contrast, the United Airlines Terminal (1988) by Helmut Jahn at Chicago's O'Hare Airport contextualizes the high technology of air transportation in reminiscences of the rail transportation buildings of the nineteenth century.

In the early 1960s, the main concourse of Grand Central Terminal (1913) by Reed and Stem with Warren and Wetmore in New York nearly faced demolition when the Pan Am Building (1963) by Emery Roth, Pietro Belluschi, and Walter Gropius was proposed to replace it. The struggle to save Grand Central and the failure to preserve New York's Pennsylvania Station (1910; demolished 1963) by McKim Mead and White were early signs of the conflicts that would continue to emerge in the 1960s and later over the preservation of historic buildings in American cities. In some cases, preservation activities were directed against developers who sought to redevelop the potentially lucrative sites of historic buildings more densely; in others, preservationists fought for historic buildings as the last vestige of history and stability in decaying urban centers.

The preservation movement began just as the sociopolitical base of architectural Modernism came under attack during the postmodern revolution. Postmodernism is associated with broader cultural changes in the United States during the 1960s and 1970s that are also coincidental with the rise of consumerism and late capitalism. In some cases, it fosters the revival of historical styles; in others, it manipulates Modernist architectural language for commercial purposes. The commercial typologies of this period include signature office buildings—whether corporate or speculative—atrium hotels, regional and urban shopping malls, and festival marketplaces: buildings that frequently project the image of public domain but are completely controlled by private interests. They are often generated by public/private partnerships in which market success and architectural imagery ambiguously mix with political values.

The earliest example of a postmodern signature office building is the AT&T Building (1976) by Philip Johnson in New York; it sent shocks of reaction through both architectural and business communities when it was announced. Long the champion of architectural Modernism, Johnson offered AT&T a revivalist granite-clad slab topped by a pediment. In his design for the Humana Building (1985) in Louisville, Kentucky, the winner of a national competition, Michael Graves explored his interest in abstraction fused with classicism through sensuous color and traditional materials. Ironically, the luxurious building denotes health care as a successful business just at the time that health care was in crisis nationally. In these and other cases, the name of the architect and his personal style have become as important an asset as the real estate itself.

The burgeoning suburbs eventually attracted another typology: the office building built on speculation. Found usually along main thoroughfares and often at the exits of interstate freeways, suburban office complexes are predominantly horizontal rather than vertical, often include atrium courts, and are always accompanied by parking decks or surrounded by parking lots. They usually lease space to small businesses, sales personnel, and professional firms, offering them the convenience of suburban location along with an image derived from the signature tower.

Commercial architecture had already lent its image to other building types during the twentieth century. The Nebraska State Capitol (1916–1928) in Lincoln by Bertram Grosvenor Goodhue replaced the prevailing classical dome with a

vertical tower in the manner of a skyscraper. The Shrine of the Little Flower (1929–1936), a large Roman Catholic church by Henry J. McGill and Talbot F. Hamlin in Royal Oak, Michigan, reflected Art Deco commercial architecture in Detroit and New York. Even more radically, however, the State of Illinois Center in Chicago (1988), a state office building designed by Helmut Jahn, incorporates a mall into its atrium lobby and encloses it in a curtain-wall structure that rejects all conventional civic imagery and substitutes for it the commercial marketplace. The most public part of the building, the hearing chamber, is buried under the sidewalk near the entrance. Similarly, Philip Johnson's design for the Garden Grove Community Church, the "Crystal Cathedral" (1987), in Garden Grove, California, adopts the reflective-glass skin of nearby suburban office buildings to cover its surfaces.

Historically, the dominant institutions of any culture have determined an architectural language that has been assumed by related or subordinant institutions. On that basis, it may be argued that by the end of the twentieth century, capitalism in the United States is embodied in a variety of related building types possessing a vocabulary that has been assimilated by other sectors of the culture that were formerly considered dominant, especially the religious and the civic. Apparently, this vocabulary stimulates and bears enough meaning, power, and authority that it is an acceptable vehicle to express the values of contemporary religious and political institutions for a large number of citizens of the late capitalist social order. At the least, commercial and industrial architecture have established the visual appearance of American cities and suburbs in the twentieth century; and by the last decade, they have also determined the shape and character of the buildings and spaces in which American public life is formed, ordered, and takes place.

—ROBERT ALAN BENSON

COMMUNICATIONS AND INFORMATION PROCESSING

Of all the forces that have shaped American society in the past four centuries, few have had a more palpable influence on the pattern of everyday life than the remarkable transformation in the means of communication. But until quite recently, few

The art of architecture studies not structure in itself, but the effect of structure on the human spirit.

GEOFFREY SCOTT
THE ARCHITECTURE OF
HUMANISM (1914)

See also
Village and Town

C

COMMUNICATIONS AND INFORMATION PROCESSING

Contexts for the Study of Communications History

Men have become tools of their tools.

HENRY DAVID THOREAU

See also
Journalism

historians devoted much attention to just what this transformation entailed. Eponymous inventors like Samuel Morse, of course, received detailed treatment, as did major inventions like the telegraph. Yet most historians regarded these developments as little more than disconnected bits of information, mostly of the "famous first" variety, that bore little relationship to the critical turning points in the making of the modern world.

In the past few years, all this has begun to change. For a growing number of scholars—whose ranks include not just historians, but also historically inclined political scientists and sociologists—the means of communication has become a historical actor in its own right. While no synthesis of this literature has yet appeared, four recent books can be taken as representative of the main lines of inquiry: Ian K. Steele's *English Atlantic* (1986); Richard D. Brown's *Knowledge Is Power* (1989); William J. Gilmore's *Reading Becomes a Necessity of Life* (1989); and James R. Beniger's *The Control Revolution* (1986). Steele explores the pattern of communications in the British Empire in the eight decades following the Restoration (1660), with implications far broader than its title might suggest; Brown and Gilmore analyze the epochal "communications revolution" that occurred between the American Revolution and the Civil War; while Beniger furnishes a stimulating, if highly speculative, survey of technological innovations in communications between the coming of the railroad and the present day.

These four books share the premise that the history of communications is best understood not as a chronicle of famous firsts but as a social process involving the relationship between ordinary people and the large-scale institutions that have come to play such a prominent role in their everyday lives. Thus far, there is no general agreement as to just what this process ought to be called. For Steele, the preferred term is "circulation"; for Brown, "diffusion"; for Gilmore, "dissemination"; for Beniger, "control." That each has adopted a slightly different terminology is hardly surprising. Each has chosen a term that aptly describes this process in the particular historical epoch with which he is primarily concerned.

This matter of definition is of no small moment since concepts have a way of carrying their etymologies with them forever. For the purposes of this essay, the most semantically neutral term for this process is "transmission." Alternatives include "processing" or even "access." None of these terms, of course, is entirely free from multiple as-

sociations. Nonetheless, they do serve to highlight the shared concern of communications historians with the pattern of collective behavior in language capacious enough to embrace the whole sweep of the American past.

Contexts for the Study of Communications History

COMMUNICATIONS, MODERNIZATION, AND THE STATE. Perhaps the most distinctive feature of recent scholarship in communications history is its preoccupation with questions of *process* and *scale*. Like the practitioners of the new social history, communications historians use theoretical models borrowed from social science to link the recorded experience of large numbers of people to patterns of collective behavior. Above all, they seek to answer a number of rather specific questions about how information was transmitted at specific points in the past: How geographically extensive was the process? How far did it penetrate into the social order? Whom did it exclude? What were the major trends over time? Indeed, just as the new social history has come to be distinguished from the more purely descriptive old social history, so too the new communications history might well be distinguished from an old communications history that chronicled the life and times of inventors and inventions.

The similarities between the new communications history and the new social history extend beyond their shared commitment to social science. Both draw on models of social change associated with modernization theory—that is, with the large body of sociological literature that seeks to chart the transition from tradition to modernity in terms general enough to embrace the United States, western Europe, Japan, and the postcolonial nations of the Third World.

That communications historians should draw on modernization theory is hardly surprising. Few models of social change assign communications a more fundamental role in the making of the modern world. Ever since 1953, when Karl Deutsch published his *Nationalism and Social Communication*, modernization theorists have stressed the role of communications technology in the social-psychological transformation that hastened the shift from tradition to modernity. According to Deutsch, the global penetration of communications technologies such as newspapers, radio, and television would encourage the spread and eventual worldwide triumph of the cosmopolitan mind-set that, or so Deutsch believed, had already gained ascendancy in the West.

Such conclusions are hardly implausible. Yet it is worth noting that today most social scientists would question Deutsch's interpretation of the relationship between technology and culture. Few would reject out of hand the proposition that changes in communications technologies have cognitive consequences. Yet none would assume that these technologies *necessarily* promote the ascendancy of the cosmopolitan mind-set that Deutsch so obviously admired. Indeed, the recent rise of Islamic fundamentalism in the Middle East suggests a rather different scenario. In a world in which the followers of the Ayatollah Khomeini smuggled back to Iran tape-recorded messages that their leader prepared while exiled in Paris, the cognitive consequences of new communications technologies have come to seem, at least to most Western observers, far more unpredictable and far less benign.

The limitations of modernization theory are by no means confined to its oversimplified account of the relationship between technology and culture. An even more basic limitation is its implicit premise that, in accounting for social change, socioeconomic processes are, in some subtle yet ineluctable way, more fundamental than processes set in motion by public policy. Or put somewhat more abstractly, that *society* is more fundamental than the *state*.

The limitations of such a society-centered perspective—and the possibilities of an alternative, state-centered perspective—are especially evident in the historical study of communications. The state has almost always fixed the boundaries of the prevailing pattern of information transmission, while most new communications technologies—from the postal system to the computer—have either been sponsored outright by the state or powerfully shaped by its influence. It is thus one of the principal contentions of this essay that, however refurbished, modernization theory—and, by implication, the society-centered explanatory strategies favored by the new social historians—provides too limiting a conceptual framework for historians intent on exploring the role of communications in shaping the pattern of the past.

THE NEW COMMUNICATIONS HISTORY AND THE TORONTO SCHOOL. While historians of communications have drawn extensively on modernization theory, they have thus far mostly neglected the contributions of the so-called Toronto school of media theorists, whose most prominent members include Harold A. Innis, Marshall McLuhan, and Walter J. Ong. In 1975, Harry S. Stout observed that, for historians interested in communications, the insights of the Toronto school provide "vast opportunities for integrative studies of social change" ("Culture, Structure, and the 'New' History," p. 223). Yet in the ensuing years, surprisingly few historians have chosen to follow Stout's lead.

Innis, McLuhan, and Ong are best known for their provocative, wide-ranging, and unfailingly stimulating ruminations on the relationship between communications technology and culture. Unlike modernization theorists such as Deutsch, the Toronto school focuses less on the content of a given communication than on its form. For McLuhan, the act of silently scanning a printed page is far more consequential than the ostensible information its author sought to convey. It is precisely this preoccupation with the form, or medium, of communication rather than with its content, or message, that inspired McLuhan's famous adage "the medium is the message."

Among the more provocative of the Toronto school's contributions is its expansive conception of the role of communications technology as an agent of change. Following Innis, McLuhan and Ong go so far as to periodize the whole course of human history around technological transformations in the means of communications. For Ong, these technologies include writing (the "most momentous" technology of all), the printing press, and the computer; for McLuhan, the telegraph, Sputnik, and television. According to Innis, who has done the most to work out the implications of this perspective, each communications technology—whether it be the newspaper, radio, and stone tablet, or the human voice—exerts a palpable influence, or "bias" on the political order. Newspapers and radio are easily transmitted over long distances; as a consequence, they promote the establishment of large, territorially bounded empires. Stone tables and the human voice are far more difficult to transport; as a consequence, they discourage the establishment of political units larger than the city-state.

The Toronto School's preoccupation with the role of communications technology in the historical process often verges on the baldest kind of technological determinism. It is almost as if, like the tin soldiers in *The Nutcracker*, the famous firsts in communications history have suddenly sprung to life. Especially problematic in this regard is McLuhan's cursory understanding of the process by which information got transmitted from place to place. Mechanical contrivances like the printing press command McLuhan's attention; yet he dismisses the postal system, a key element in the

Do not fold, spindle, or mutilate.

ANONYMOUS INSTRUCTIONS ON PUNCHED CARDS USED WITH EARLY COMPUTERS

*What hath God
wrought!*

SAMUEL F. B. MORSE
ELECTRIC TELEGRAPH
MESSAGE, MAY 24, 1844

communications infrastructure, as little more than a "charming relic of the hardware age."

These limitations notwithstanding, the Toronto school does offer historians a host of valuable insights on the relationship between technology and culture. And in at least one regard, it offers a useful corrective to the new communications history. With few exceptions, the new communications history has devoted far more attention to the consumption of information than the production of knowledge. The Toronto School, if anything, errs in precisely the opposite direction. McLuhan may be rather vague about precisely how information gets transmitted yet, like Innis and Ong, he has quite definite notions about where all this information is coming from. For McLuhan and Ong, the source is ultimately religious, or, more precisely, Christian: in the beginning was the Word, and the Word was with God. For Innis, the source is more likely to be rooted in the political order.

The Toronto school may well have come up with the wrong answers—few historians, after all, are likely to embrace the avowedly theological, quasi-millennial ruminations of McLuhan and Ong—yet its members have asked fresh and imaginative questions, and historians would do well to follow their lead. It may, in short, be time to pay more attention not merely to who is getting the message, but to who is spreading the word, and perhaps even to why it is being sent.

Communications and Empire

Until quite recently, few American historians would challenge the assertion that, in the pre-electronic era, transatlantic communication was slow, infrequent, and hazardous. Or that it was, in a word, bad. Recent scholarship on the pattern of information transmission in the colonial period, however, points in an altogether different direction. In this period, as Ian Steele has observed, the Atlantic Ocean was anything but a "vast social moat" separating the New World from the Old. If anything, it functioned instead as a convenient thoroughfare for an immense multitude of people, goods, and information.

How could historians have gotten the story wrong for so long? The answer lies partly in the assumption that maritime empires are somehow "unnatural." For the period before the nineteenth-century revolution in land transportation, this assumption is dubious at best. The Dutch, the Florentines, the Venetians—and, for that matter, the Greeks and the Romans—had all established far-flung domains that were organized primarily, if

not exclusively, around water rather than on land. So too had the English.

This new perspective has prompted a new way of thinking about the prevailing patterns of information transmission. These patterns fall into three main phases: 1607 to 1660, 1660 to 1763, and 1763 to 1781. In the first phase, which stretched roughly from the first permanent European settlement at Jamestown in 1607 to the restoration of the Stuarts, the settlers found themselves largely cut off from the main currents of European civilization. For a period of time, at least, America was truly a strange new world.

Yet even during these early decades, the settlers' isolation is easily exaggerated. Consider the case of Puritan New England, the most demographically self-contained of all the settlements. Despite the Puritans' many quarrels with English society, they retained an abiding interest in English politics, about which they managed to stay exceedingly well-informed, and maintained an extensive correspondence with their friends and relations back home. A similar pattern prevailed in the Chesapeake, the other principal area of settlement. At no point did the settlers completely lose contact with the European world from which they had come. As David D. Hall has remarked, America was "*never* really a frontier society with culture radically dispersed into local units; the technology . . . was derived from a metropolitan tradition, and most of the books . . . had originated in centers such as London, Edinburgh, Boston, or New York" (*On Native Ground*, p. 322).

This point is worth stressing since, in the 1970s, several prominent historians questioned the importance of long-distance communications in the colonial past. Drawing on the scholarship of the cultural anthropologist Clifford Geertz, these historians posited that, in the colonial period, community life was "primordial"—which is to say that it more closely resembled the world of the nonliterate Balinese villagers that Geertz had so evocatively described than the technologically sophisticated world of the present.

In the 1980s a reaction set in. While historians have by no means abandoned their interest in the small-scale communities of the colonial past, they have become far more sensitive to the differences between the inhabitants of colonial America and the villagers of Bali. In particular, they have come to distinguish rather sharply between what Ong terms the "primary orality" of nonliterate peoples like the Balinese and the "high oral residue" of the white settlers of colonial America. The mental universe of even illiterate colonists, it is now assumed, had been so fundamentally transformed by their intimate familiarity with the ways of the literate world that it may best be described as "verbal" rather than "oral." As Ong observes: "It takes only a moderate degree of literacy to make a tremendous difference in thought processes" (*Orality and Literacy*, p. 50).

However isolated the colonists may have been during the opening decades of the seventeenth century, with the restoration of the Stuarts this first phase of colonial communications came to a close. The second phase owed its impetus to the crown: like the financial revolution of the 1690s, it was part of the crown's broader effort to consolidate its authority over its far-flung imperial domain.

This effort succeeded, at least for a time. In the century between the Restoration in 1660 and the Treaty of Paris in 1763, the prevailing pattern of information transmission reinforced—and, indeed, helped to forge—the links between the inhabitants of British North America and Great Britain. The colonists were becoming, as it were, not "Americanized," but "Anglicized." As this process went forward, it became increasingly plausible for them to conceive of themselves as the inhabitants of a single, transatlantic society, whose boundaries were defined not by the largely inaccessible, and still mostly unexplored, North American continent, but by the oft-traveled and familiar English Atlantic. To the extent that the settlers' identity was informed—or, as Innis would say, biased—by the prevailing pattern of information transmission, then, in this period, its trajectory was decidedly imperial.

Of the various crown ventures that helped to institutionalize this new pattern, the most notable included the reorganization of the imperial postal system in 1711—which, for the first time, brought the postal network in British North America under direct crown control—and the permanent establishment, under government supervision, of the colonial newspaper press, beginning with the *Boston News-Letter* in 1704. Both of these institutions were designed primarily to facilitate communications between Great Britain and British North America. The imperial orientation of the postal system was especially marked. As late as 1761, Benjamin Franklin, the crown-appointed deputy postmaster general for British North America, could state matter-of-factly that the inhabitants of Amboy and Burlington, New Jersey, should not be expected to send many letters through their respective post offices since they engaged in "little or no foreign trade." The

newspapers displayed a similar orientation. To the eternal frustration of colonial historians, who have assiduously searched their pages for information about local life, these newspapers were overwhelmingly preoccupied with European affairs. Rather than the distillation of local gossip, newspapers in this period were, in Steele's apt phrase, "paper windows on the world."

To be sure, in the eighteenth century the scope of these institutions remained quite limited. Only in the nineteenth century would the postal system and the press come to exert a palpable influence on the pattern of everyday life. As late as the 1760s, probably no more than 5 percent of the population had more than the most incidental contact with either institution, though thus far too little work has been done on this topic to say for certain. Most of these individuals were public officers, merchants, or ministers living in the port cities on the Atlantic seaboard. And, needless to say, almost all were white men.

To highlight these limitations is not to suggest that the situation was markedly different in Great Britain. Indeed, the expansion of the postal system and newspaper press in both places is probably best regarded as part of a single, integrated process. The newspaper press in British North America resembled quite closely its provincial counterpart in Great Britain. Much the same could be said for the postal system: in 1765, there were roughly as many post offices per capita in British North America as in England and Wales.

Perhaps the most remarkable feature of communications in this period, at least from a twentieth-century standpoint, is the extremely limited nature of the demand for translocal information. The diffusion pattern was strictly top-down: that is, information from overseas typically came first to the provincial gentry, who would then pass it along on a "need to know" basis. Members of this gentry, such as Boston merchant Samuel Sewall (1652–1730), rarely shared information with members of the lower orders. If one word were to describe this process, it might well be circulation. Within the charmed circle of the gentry, information traveled freely. Only rarely did it travel downward to the common people, a circumstance that might have been expected to generate at least a modicum of concern. Yet it apparently did not. Outside of the gentry, no one really seems much to have cared.

Following Great Britain's victory over France in the Seven Years' War, which was formalized by the Treaty of Paris in 1763, the prevailing pattern of information transmission entered a third dis-

*All progress has
resulted from people
who took unpopular
positions.*

ADLAI E. STEVENSON

See also
Radio

*Television, as
Marshall McLuhan
observed in 1964,
increased the visual
at the expense of the
aural; it increased
the importance of
the vicarious at the
expense of direct
experience.*

PAGE 482

tinct phase. For the first time, large numbers of provincial Americans began to embrace the momentous proposition that the widest possible circulation of information ought to be regarded, in and of itself, as a public good.

Despite the enormous outpouring of scholarship on the coming of the War of Independence, this pivotal transformation in prevailing assumptions regarding the proper role of communications in the political culture remains obscure. A number of questions suggest themselves. Precisely why did this transformation emerge at this time? How did it affect the prevailing pattern of information transmission? Could it have contributed to the emergence of an organized opposition to the crown?

One hypothesis points to the role of imperial legislation like the Stamp Act (1765) in galvanizing the provincial gentry to reconsider the traditional relationship of knowledge and power. This legislation inspired an unprecedented flurry of pamphlets and newspaper articles, including the impassioned attack upon all monopolies of knowledge that Massachusetts lawyer John Adams penned in 1765, and which would later become known as the "Dissertation on the Canon and Feudal Law."

An alternative hypothesis fixes the spotlight on the mid-century religious revivals, the Great Awakening. According to Harry S. Stout, the extemporaneous, emotionally charged sermons of itinerant evangelicals like George Whitefield (1714–1770) inspired thousands of ordinary people to secure for themselves the kind of scriptural knowledge that Whitefield had so impressively displayed. In the language of Walter J. Ong, Whitefield had interiorized the Bible, providing his audience with a compelling example of how direct access to print could challenge the status quo. It was this impulse, Stout contends, that created the social world that would render plausible the "typographic ideology" of the revolutionary-era pamphleteers.

The role of novel preaching styles in the coming break with Great Britain remains hotly contested. One obvious problem with Stout's hypothesis is the question of timing. The revivals had mostly petered out by the end of the 1740s; the revolutionary movement did not get underway until 1765. According to Jon Butler, the true significance of George Whitefield lay in neither his message nor his medium. Rather, it lay in his utilization of recent improvements in the communications and transportation infrastructure, which greatly facilitated his ability to travel about

the countryside and his followers' ability to participate in the revival meetings that he so elaborately staged. In either scenario, one conclusion seems clear: poor communications did not bring on the war.

Communications in the New Republic

Following the defeat of the British at Yorktown in 1781, the successful revolutionaries sought to institute a communications policy for the newly established republic. The policy they devised was far more expansive than anything that had ever been attempted by the crown. Despite the crown's support for the postal system and the press, it had retained tight control of constraints on the transmission of public information. Following the ratification of the Constitution, all this would change. Under the leadership of the Federalists, who included most of the framers of the Constitution, a government was instituted that was explicitly committed to broadcasting news of its ongoing activities throughout the land.

The Federalists justified their communications policy on two principal grounds. First, following President George Washington, they contended that the widest possible diffusion of information regarding the operations of government would counterbalance the centrifugal forces that might tear the republic apart. Nowhere was the importance of such a policy more obvious than in the far-flung transappalachian West. Washington feared especially that the paucity of certain information regarding the newly established central government might encourage malcontents to circulate wild rumors that could undermine its legitimacy. By making public information easily accessible, Washington hoped, as the editor of the official government newspaper, the *United States Gazette*, made plain, not only to enable the citizenry to monitor its activities, but also to "tranquilize" the public mind.

The second rationale was articulated most forcefully by the Philadelphia physician Benjamin Rush (1745–1813). If Washington intended the government to *diffuse* authoritative information, Rush hoped it would *disseminate* practical knowledge. Rush's vision, like Washington's, was basically political. By disseminating knowledge—through newspapers, public schools, and, or so Rush hoped, a national university—the government would promote the creation of a virtuous, public-spirited citizenry that would protect the republic from internal decline and external assault.

Rush's bold agenda for the future is often contrasted with his later disillusionment over his failure to get this agenda translated into law. With respect to communications, this juxtaposition is misleading. For much of Rush's communications policy—and, in particular, his commitment to the widest possible circulation of political newspapers, those "centinels of our liberties"—would become institutionalized in the 1790s, with far-reaching consequences for the future course of American history. Indeed, it may not be too much to suggest, as would James Madison—a leader of the Republican opposition, as well as a major architect of the Constitution—that in the new nation this policy worked powerfully to consolidate the authority of "public opinion" as a political force.

The Federalists' communications policy was, quite literally, unprecedented in the history of the world. Never before had popular access to information regarding the ongoing activities of government been presumed to be not a privilege but a right. Never before had a government been founded on the premise that an informed citizenry was fundamental to its very survival. For the first time in world history, a politics of vigilance has supplanted a politics of trust.

The creation of an informed citizenry was by no means identical with the task of informing the population-at-large. Excluded from the citizenry were Indians, slaves, and women, as were those men who failed to meet the various property requirements established by the individual states. Even so, the task of keeping the propertied, white male population informed posed an enormous challenge for the fledgling administrative apparatus of the new republic.

To meet this challenge, Congress moved quickly to upgrade the major elements in the communications infrastructure: the postal system and the press. The upgrading of the postal system—the principal pre-electronic long-distance communications technology—was accomplished with the passage of the Post Office Act of 1792. This act had two main features. First, it required postal officers to admit newspapers into the mails at rates far below their actual cost of delivery. Second, it mandated that henceforth the postal system would expand into the hinterland virtually without regard for the possible impact of this policy on postal finance. Both of these policies had major consequences for the press. The former guaranteed it a market; the latter ensured that this market would expand with the population. The consequences of this policy were little short of astounding. In 1792, the postal system consisted of some 250 offices; in 1800, 903; in 1860, 28,498.

Press coverage of public affairs expanded in a parallel fashion. It may be something of an exaggeration to declare, as the historian J. R. Pole does, that, during the whole course of the colonial period, "nowhere and at no time . . . did any newspaper or magazine report one single assembly debate." Yet it remains undeniable that, in the period prior to the ratification of the Constitution, press coverage of public affairs was distinctly limited. In the 1790s, this coverage would expand enormously, thanks to a variety of public policies that included, in addition to those already mentioned, generous press subsidies, the opening of Congress to the public, and, perhaps most important, the constitutional guarantee of a free press.

The Communications Revolution

The communications policy established by the Federalists exerted an enormous influence on the subsequent history of the United States. Indeed, it may not be too audacious to suggest that it marked the opening chapter in the communications revolution that has proceeded more or less without interruption from the 1790s to the present day.

At no time were these changes more dramatic than in the half-century following the ratification of the Constitution. Of the numerous changes that occurred in this period, perhaps the most notable was the extraordinarily rapid increase in the volume of books, religious publications, public documents, and newspapers. In the book trade, the period marked the crucial transition from a world of scarcity to a world of abundance. A parallel shift occurred in religious publishing. By the 1820s, the American Bible Society (founded 1816) and the American Tract Society (founded 1825) were distributing so many publications that they have been aptly described as having created the first American mass media. Equally impressive, though often overlooked, was the enormous expansion in the publication of public documents. Taken together, the federal and state governments constituted by far the largest publisher in the United States. In 1830, these two sources accounted for 30 percent of *all* the imprints in the United States.

Nowhere was this incredible expansion in the volume of printed matter more obvious than in the newspaper press. In 1790, there were 92 newspapers in the United States; in 1800, 242; in 1860, 3,725. Beginning in 1833 with Benjamin Day's New York *Sun*, the cheap "penny dailies" would take advantage of the steam press to expand enormously not only the potential audience for news-

The real cause for dread is not a machine turned human, but a human turned machine.

FRANZ F. WINKLER
MAN: THE BRIDGE BETWEEN
TWO WORLDS

See also
Print and Publishing

C

*In the age of
television, image
becomes more
important than
substance.*

S. I. HAYAKAWA

♦ **Pluralism**

*A state of society in which
members of diverse ethnic,
racial, religious, or social
groups maintain an
autonomous participation
in and development of their
traditional culture or special
interest within the confines
of a common civilization; a
concept, doctrine, or policy
advocating this state*

papers but also their coverage of urban news—and, perhaps above all, of crime. For what may have been the first time in the history of the republic, a publisher had flatly rejected Rush's hortatory mission and had put out a newspaper purely to entertain.

The social consequences of this communications revolution remain highly uncertain. Did the explosion in printed matter democratize knowledge by destroying existing monopolies over the transmission of information? Or did it merely make possible new controls on popular thought? What other consequences might this process have entailed?

For the moment, answers to these questions must necessarily be tentative. Part of the problem is empirical. Only recently have historians begun systematically to gather data on the influence of printed matter on the pattern of everyday life. More fundamental still are the methodological questions that arise once the data are assembled.

Thus far, as discussed above, the principal theoretical model that historians have drawn upon is derived from modernization theory. Like the social theorist Karl Deutsch, they have tended to focus above all on the consequences of the communications revolution for social psychology. For Richard D. Brown and William J. Gilmore, the communications revolution represents a net gain for the common man—and, in particular, for the propertied, white male citizenry whom the Federalists' communication policy was intended to reach. For Brown, the communications revolution fostered a commitment to the discernibly "modern" values of competition, pluralism, and individual choice. No less important, it encouraged thousands if not millions of Americans to believe that knowledge is power: that is, that improvement in popular access to information translated readily into the democratization of knowledge. For Gilmore, the communications revolution ushered in an age of reading in which, for the first time in world history, lifelong reading became, at least for the farmers of northern New England, a cherished ideal.

The consequences of the communications revolution for groups on the periphery—for women, children, and slaves—were far more ambiguous. The emergence of periodicals like *Godey's Lady Book* that were aimed specifically at the burgeoning market of middle-class women introduced their female readership to the cosmopolitan world of fashion and genteel deportment even as they accentuated their exclusion from the male-dominated world of politics and commerce. Children

lucky enough to have access to books designed specifically for their use—the children's book was largely a nineteenth-century innovation—were encouraged to embark upon imaginative journeys to worlds far removed from the everyday affairs of their parents. Slaves took advantage of improvements in transportation to devise remarkably elaborate communications networks linking far-flung plantations, yet as all but a tiny minority were illiterate, the communications revolution increasingly left them behind.

The consequences of the communications revolution extended far beyond their impact on individuals. For the white men who were its primary beneficiaries, the physical act of reading a newspaper served not merely to encourage a heightened sense of individualism, but also to encourage a new vision of community. It is this vision that the French traveler Alexis de Tocqueville so brilliantly analyzed in his *Democracy in America* (1835; 1840) and that the genre painter Richard Caton Woodville so evocatively depicted in his *War News from Mexico* (1848). In Woodville's painting, the citizenry of the village—all white, all male—are assembled at the local post office to discuss the affairs of the day. On the fringes of the scene, a woman and a free black listen in. Yet it is clearly the men who are at center stage. For these men, newspaper reading serves less as a means of generating knowledge than as a ritual that reinforces a distinctive, emphatically fraternal, vision of community.

The role of newspapers and other forms of political discourse in creating new visions of community was extremely complex. Often it worked less to foster consensus, as George Washington might have hoped, than to encourage dialogue. Sometimes this dialogue was heated and acrimonious. Still, the very fact that it was taking place at all worked, at least in the short run, to promote a vision of community that extended beyond the locality and the state to embrace the entire nation.

This national vision was, of course, imagined. It existed not in a specific place, like a New England town, but rather in the minds of large numbers of people, most of whom would never meet. Yet it was very real for those many people who thought of themselves not just as members of a specific region, or religion, or class, or race, or gender, but as Americans.

The creation of this national community inevitably involved a complex process of exclusion and inclusion. The extension of citizenship to virtually all white men hastened the stigmatization of noncitizens and especially of Indians and blacks. This process, in turn, was powerfully reinforced by the virulently racist, and typically Democratic, mass-circulation newspapers and magazines that flourished, beginning in the 1830s, in the urban centers of the North.

The process of creating a national community met with opposition even from some of the groups it was supposed to embrace. Beginning in 1810, male Evangelicals, joined behind the scenes by women, opposed a government policy that required the delivery of the mails and the opening of the post offices on the Sabbath. In the 1830s, northern anti-abolitionist mobs destroyed abolitionist presses and murdered the antislavery printer Elijah P. Lovejoy. In the same decade, white southerners took a variety of legal and extralegal steps to prevent the distribution of abolitionist literature. In July 1835, a mob backed by former South Carolina governor John Lyde Wilson ransacked the Charleston, South Carolina, post office and publicly burned in the town square a bundle of abolitionist tracts that the New York–based American Antislavery Society had attempted to send through the mails.

Yet what is perhaps most remarkable about this process of community creation is the extent to which it has since come to be regarded as perfectly natural and indeed almost foreordained. In the half-century following the ratification of the Constitution, an imperial community spanning the English Atlantic had been transformed into a national community that more or less coincided with the middle-third of the North American continent. This transformation was neither predictable nor inevitable. Indeed, as the recent history of the postcolonial third world makes plain, it may well be the exception rather than the rule. Yet its consequences were profound. For by creating a vision of a national community, it may well have provided the impetus for those many thousands of northerners, women as well as men, black as well as white, who, in 1861, when the South chose to secede, dedicated themselves to saving the union by winning the war.

The Information Society

From the perspective of the late twentieth century, what is perhaps most striking about the nineteenth-century communications revolution is the extent to which it marked, for contemporaries no less than for historians, a genuine democratization not merely of information but also of knowledge. It is almost as if Benjamin Rush's republic of knowledge had reached its apotheosis in Tocqueville's America.

Today the relationship between information and knowledge is far more complex. The rise of the professions, the modern corporation, the government agency, and the whole panoply of organizations that make up what has come to be known as the information society have enormously widened the gap between the information conveyed by news or entertainment and the knowledge necessary to command the levers of power. In an age in which the management of public relations has become a major industry, it is by no means clear that the simple act of reading a newspaper, or of watching the news, bears any obvious relationship to the exercise of power or authority in government, business, or everyday life. In short, it is no longer plausible to conflate the *consumption* of information with the *production* of knowledge.

The origins of the information society date back to the second half of the nineteenth century. It was during these decades that, for the first time in the history of American business, information processing became a key element in corporate strategy. The catalyst for this striking development, as James R. Beniger explains, was the "crisis of control" occasioned by the general speeding-up in the processing of goods and services that began in the 1850s with the expansion of the railroad into the transappalachian West. The crisis was resolved when corporate managers devised new accounting techniques and related communications technologies to coordinate the myriad activities of

**FIRST TELEGRAPH
LINE**

Samuel Morse established the first electric telegraph line between Washington and Baltimore in 1844. The telegraph allowed corporate managers to coordinate the activities of geographically diverse enterprises.
LIBRARY OF CONGRESS/
CORBIS

*Most important,
in response to
television's
popularity, radio
stations adopted a
strategy that they
had previously
rejected:
specialization.*

PAGE 396

geographically extended enterprises like the Pennsylvania Railroad. If there were one word to describe this process, it might be control.

Of these new technologies, by far the most important was the electric telegraph. Following the establishment of the first line between Washington and Baltimore by Samuel Morse in 1844, the electric telegraph was quickly extended throughout the United States, reaching New Orleans by 1851 and San Francisco in 1861. Funding for the Washington-Baltimore line had been provided by Congress, which, for almost three years, left open the possibility that it might purchase Morse's patents outright and place the industry under the authority of the postmaster general. Despite Morse's fervent commitment to government ownership, his lobbying efforts failed, and the industry went private. By 1866, a single firm—Western Union—would come to dominate the industry. Capitalized at over forty million dollars, Western Union was not only the largest firm in the industry, but the largest single business enterprise in the United States.

The patrons of the electric telegraph were largely, if not almost exclusively, merchants, newspaper editors, and corporate managers. Corporate managers came to rely on it to coordinate their increasingly far-flung operations. Newspaper editors used it to obtain the nonlocal, time-specific information about politics and commerce that is commonly called news. And merchants took advantage of its capacity to provide them with the most up-to-date information regarding the often volatile international markets for agricultural commodities such as cotton and wheat. Most other Americans, including virtually all women, would continue to rely on the postal system as their principal long-distance communications technology and would continue to do so until well into the twentieth century, when it would become supplemented—but never entirely replaced—by the telephone.

From the standpoint of everyone other than the commercial and editorial elite, the electric telegraph marked far less of a turning point in the history of communications than the postal reform act of 1845. In this landmark piece of legislation, Congress for the first time reduced the rate of letter postage to a level that eliminated the cost of the postage as a major constraint. Henceforth, letter writing was no longer confined merely to politicians (who under federal law could send and receive most of their letters without charge) and the well-to-do. Indeed, it was the postal system—more than any other institution, and certainly

more than the electric telegraph—that created the technological preconditions that would make possible the extended friendships by letter between family and friends—and, perhaps above all, among women—that were such a prominent feature of popular culture in Victorian America.

In the twentieth century, information processing has become, if anything, even more central to American business. Rapid improvements in telecommunications have rendered nineteenth-century technologies such as the electric telegraph virtually obsolete. Of these new technologies, perhaps the most ubiquitous was the telephone. Invented in the 1870s, the telephone system was extended from New York to Boston by 1884, and coast-to-coast by 1915. By that year, the industry had become dominated by a single firm and a single individual. The firm was American Telephone and Telegraph (AT&T) and the individual was Theodore M. Vail. As the president of AT&T, Vail, a former superintendent of the railway mail service, dedicated the firm to the attainment of "One System, One Policy, Universal Service," a motto that reflected Vail's familiarity with postal policy. This goal would soon help to make the telephone almost as common a feature of daily life as the posted letter.

To attain his objective, Vail committed AT&T to the deliberate strategy of using long-distance communications to subsidize local service. While this strategy reduced somewhat the firm's short-term profitability, it increased considerably its base of popular support within Congress and the electorate and, in this way, protected itself against the possibility of hostile government legislation in the future. Vail's strategy kept long-distance rates high and, therefore, mostly confined to business until well after the Second World War (much as postage had been in the period before 1845). Local service, however, was subject to no such constraint and expanded accordingly. In 1891, fewer than one American in a hundred had a telephone; by 1921, that number had expanded to almost thirteen per one hundred. By 1925, AT&T would emerge as the largest corporation in the United States, just as Western Union had been in 1866.

If the telephone was the most ubiquitous of the new technologies, then the most far-reaching in its political and economic implications was the digital computer. The first computers were invented during the Second World War as the product of a notable collaboration between government, business, and the university. Like so many communications technologies—including the postal system and the electric telegraph—it was, at least initially, less the product of market forces than of political fiat.

In the post-Second World War period, the computer has revolutionized the storage, retrieval, and analysis of data. In certain instances, it has facilitated the performance of tasks that antedated its invention, such as the taking of a business inventory or the compilation of the federal census. In other instances, it has made it possible to embark on unprecedented new ventures such as high-energy physics and space travel. By the 1980s, even small businesses had come to rely upon sophisticated computing and telecommunications technologies in conducting their routine operations. For the multinational corporations that have increasingly come to dominate the world economy, telecommunications have made it possible for them to conduct their operations on a truly global scale. And the explosion of the internet has made it possible for nearly anyone to launch a global business on a shoestring.

The impact of the computer upon ordinary Americans, however, is more ambiguous. As corporate managers have increasingly turned to computers to monitor the production process, the size of the semiskilled blue-collar work force has decreased, undermining the influence of the traditional blue-collar unions. In addition, the proliferation of public and private data banks containing detailed financial and medical information about millions of ordinary Americans has raised troubling questions about confidentiality and the potential for abuse.

Few communications innovations better illustrate the complex relationship between private enterprise and public policy than commercial radio. The origins of the industry date to the 1910s, when radio buffs began to experiment with homemade receivers. By the end of the decade, however, the buffs found themselves outmaneuvered by the military and a number of major corporations, which began to consolidate their control over the all-important wavelength. In the 1920s, thanks in part to this corporate sponsorship, a radio boom began: in 1922 there were 30 broadcast stations; in 1923, 556. By 1933, a radio could be found in fully two-thirds of all homes in America.

Throughout the 1920s, public officials remained deeply ambivalent about the prospect of permitting the radio industry, like the newspaper, to be financed out of advertising revenue. It is "inconceivable," declared Secretary of Commerce Herbert Hoover in 1922, that "we should allow so great a possibility for service to be drowned in advertising chatter." The establishment of two major radio networks—NBC in 1926 and CBS in 1927—doomed Hoover's hopes.

Now that radio commanded a national audience, advertisers redoubled their efforts to reach this vast new market. Before long, they would largely succeed. With the exception of unusual ventures such as National Public Radio, which receives partial funding from the federal government, most radio programming since the 1920s has been funded neither by the government nor by the locally oriented ethnic, religious, labor, and public groups that had flourished briefly before the rise of the networks, but rather by the national—and, increasingly, multinational—corporations that had the financial resources to foot the bill.

The early history of television followed a similar pattern. The first public television program dated from 1947; the television boom began in 1949. By 1953, television had found its way into twenty million American homes. Once again, advertisers saw their opportunity and, once again, neither the federal government nor local groups proved either able or willing to check their rise. By 1970, 97 percent of all American households had at least one television. Like radio, the new technology was overwhelmingly dominated by its corporate sponsors—whose advertisements, in turn, encouraged lavish and often wasteful patterns of mass consumption that hastened, at least in the minds of some of its more radical critics, the "commodification" of desire.

The regulatory regime that emerged with radio and television was hardly inevitable. In other countries, different arrangements prevailed. Radio could conceivably have remained in the public sector or, alternatively, it might well have been obliged to provide greater popular access to the airwaves. Television, similarly, might have been encouraged to feature more special-interest broadcasting, just as has occurred since the 1980s with the emergence of cable television. Yet few Americans seem aware of the possible alternatives, at least partly because broadcasters so repeatedly invoke the myth that the industry is controlled ultimately by its audience rather than by the major corporations—or, as it were, by the consumers of information rather than by the producers of knowledge.

Corporate control of the mass media ought not to obscure the fact that its influence on ordinary Americans can be extraordinarily complex. Sometimes, as in the nineteenth century, the mass media could reinforce an attachment to the national

Technology is the science that produces more and more inventions and less and less mechanics to service them.

EVAN ESAR

See also
Television

The first American newspaper was printed at Boston in 1690 by a bookseller and publisher, Benjamin Harris.

PAGE 235

It continued for some time to be in the best interest of colonial printers to keep controversy out of their papers.

PAGE 362

community. More recently, its influence has often been more divisive. Ethnic and religious groups routinely use the mass media to promote their distinctive agendas. Often these agendas work to fragment the national community into diverse and often antagonistic camps. In Chicago during the 1920s, the impact of mass culture—radio, movies, and records—upon the mostly immigrant, working-class audience worked less to promote cultural homogeneity, as social scientists have often assumed, than to reinforce a sense of shared class or ethnic identity. Italian immigrants who listened to the records featuring the great Italian tenor Enrico Caruso or to the radio broadcasts prepared especially for their benefit by the Italian dictator Benito Mussolini, might well take away from the experience a heightened sense of their own distinctiveness. Given the extraordinary heterogenity of the American people, such outcomes are to be expected. What is perhaps more notable is the extent to which, two centuries after the founding of the American republic, the vision of a national community continues to retain its undeniable allure.

Conclusion

Over the course of the past four centuries, the means of communications have had an enormous influence on the pattern of everyday life. Nowhere has this influence been more far-reaching than in the ever-changing relationship between state and society. In the period between 1660 and 1765, communications strengthened ties between Britain's North American colonies and the crown. Following the ratification of the Constitution, it helped to create a national community. In the twentieth century, it has simultaneously hastened the internationalization of business and the revitalization of intranational conflicts rooted in ethnicity and religion. Each of these processes has occurred over an extended territory whose boundaries have been shaped less by social circumstances than by political fiat. Thus, they can best be understood by adopting a national—or, more precisely, transnational—perspective that is sensitive to the role of state-formation in the making of the modern world.

—RICHARD R. JOHN

CONCERT MUSIC

The history of American concert music is a story of interactions between "cultivated" and "vernacular" traditions. These interactions often suggest a variety of comparisons: between, for example, the music of the concert hall and opera house, on the one hand, and more indigenous folk musics (including jazz), on the other; between the established styles of European composers and performers, and the unproven talents of American musical artists; and between the idea of music as an art and as an accompaniment to work, religious expression, or celebration.

These comparisons were often the source of tension between arbiters of "good taste," who advocated continuing or imitating European models in order to create good American music, and those who searched for an authentic American idiom in the music of everyday life. For most critics prior to World War II, American concert music lay at the margins of artistic respectability, and the tendency of American composers to interpolate the vernacular traditions of their own country into pieces written for the concert hall only exacerbated the tendency to view our music as something less than serious. Since World War II, the increasing internationalization of musical culture has blurred many of the national and class lines upon which these distinctions relied; in this period American concert music has achieved distinction in its own right.

The earliest music heard in North America was likely not considered art at all but an integral part of religion, history, or celebration. Native Americans sang and chanted to worship and celebrate and to record the histories and myths of their various tribes. These musical traditions were transmitted orally, and many early writers on American music assumed there was nothing interesting in this music and merely classified it as "aboriginal," part of the prehistory of music on the North American continent.

The settlers who arrived in North America in the seventeenth and eighteenth centuries brought with them a European musical heritage, along with political and social traditions. Once the early exploration and settlement had begun, this music became a part of everyday life. Wealthy planters in the southern colonies who could afford to import music and musicians were consumers of the finest products of Europe's secular culture, while music in the lives of the less ostentatious New England Congregationalists took the form of psalm-singing and chanting in the meetinghouse. The New England Puritans valued religious sincerity over musical performance, and the psalms were chanted to metrical and melodic patterns set down in books such as *The Whole Booke of Psalmes*

Faithfully Translated into English Meter (1640), also known as the Bay Psalm Book, which was the first English book printed in America. Sometimes the patterns were "lined out" or chanted one line at a time by an adventurous worshiper. As memories of the tunes faded over time, though, psalm-singing apparently became a cacophony. Defenders of "Usual Singing," in which every worshiper sang as he or she pleased, argued for the preservation of religious fervor over musical harmony; advocates of "Regular Singing," on the other hand, favored teaching simple musical notation. These reformers—among them Cotton Mather—argued that when it came to singing God's praises, no haphazard group singing would suffice: the proper religious standard could only be met by creating a higher musical standard. Thus arose the first American debate over cultivated and vernacular musical traditions.

The American Revolution provided quite different opportunities for musical expression, in the form of patriotism. Texts mocking the British or supporting the American cause were set to familiar tunes and disseminated by word of mouth, newspapers, or broadsides. Thus, the British musical salvo against the colonial military commander Benedict Arnold went, "Arnold is as brave a man who ever dealt in horses / He now commands a num'rous band of New England jackasses"; American troops, on the other hand, parodied this song by rewriting it as "Yankee Doodle." William Billings (1746–1800), a Boston tanner who composed music for worship and for the Revolution, wrote an anthem, "Chester," which became quite popular. Other musical amateurs, among them Francis Hopkinson, Thomas Jefferson, and Benjamin Franklin, contributed to the musical life of the new nation as amateur composers, consumers, and inventors of new musical instruments.

After the Revolution, musical life in American cities began to thrive as prohibitions against instrumental music in churches and musical theater were relaxed, and immigrant composers, performers, and entrepreneurs established themselves. Alexander Reinagle (1756?–1809) in Philadelphia, Benjamin Carr (1768–1831) and James Hewitt (1770–1827) in New York, and Johann Christian Gottlieb Graupner (1767–1836) in Boston were among the new Americans who composed, performed, taught, and published music in large urban centers. Graupner was part of the group that founded the Handel and Haydn Society in Boston in 1815. The society's purpose was to provide performances of music by established European composers for elite urban audiences.

In smaller communities, musical activity flourished in local churches. The musical settings that amateur composers such as Daniel Read (1757–1836), Timothy Swan (1758–1842), and Jeremiah Ingalls (1764–1838) used for hymn and psalm texts reflected the distance of their local audiences from the current trends in European composition that were popular in American cities. Their musical work was in the tradition of Billings, who had written that "every composer should be his own Carver," and their musical settings often preserved the unpolished qualities of the earlier tunes. Musical reformers Andrew Law (1749–1821), Samuel Holyoke (1762–1820), Oliver Holden (1765–1844), and John Hubbard (1757–1810), however, decried popular musical expressions of religious feeling as undignified. They advocated order rather than chaos in religious music, and they published devotional music by Handel, Haydn, and Mozart that would, they argued, inspire spiritual uplift as well as education in the "best" European musical models. This was a continuation of the Usual versus the Regular Singing debate with an added element of tension between rural traditionalists and more urban and urbane musical reformers.

The careers of Anthony Philip Heinrich (1781–1861), William Henry Fry (1813–1864), and George Frederick Bristow (1825–1898) reflect the American composer's dilemma of seeking a uniquely American musical idiom while

See also
Theater and Musical Theater

C

CONCERT MUSIC

struggling for acceptance within prevailing European traditions. Like the generation of post-Revolutionary composers, all three earned a living in music, but not as composers. Heinrich was a conductor and impresario who successfully staged performances of European symphonies in the hinterlands of Kentucky and used the history and culture of Native Americans as inspiration for some of his compositions. Fry, a critic for the *New York Tribune*, lectured and wrote in support of an American declaration of cultural independence, even as he wrote traditional symphonies. And Bristow, a violinist in New York, composed an opera based on Washington Irving's "Rip Van Winkle." Each of these proponents of American music sought inspiration for romantic symphonic music in his own country rather than in the European countryside, long-distant past, or myth and fantasy.

The music of African Americans has consistently resided far outside the European high-culture tradition. Nineteenth-century or antebellum work songs, spirituals, and musical expressions of religious faith were integral to daily life. The traditions were oral, and the music was improvised rather than performed. In slave communities, there were song leaders who could capture the emotions of the moment, often to the accompaniment of a fiddle and banjo, but music was not a discrete art or occupation.

The same was often true for white settlers in small towns, on the frontier, or in urban ethnic enclaves for whom music provided a way to pass time and to chronicle the events of family, class, and community. Appalachian murder ballads and other storytelling songs (many of which were descended directly from English traditional ballads), the descriptions of cowboy life on the plains, and the music of new immigrants (such as the Irish in the 1840s and 1850s), contributed to a rich and varied popular music that was largely ignored or denigrated by arbiters of high culture and good taste.

Louis Moreau Gottschalk (1829–1869), a pianist whose style resembled that of Franz Liszt, saw in the music of the slave quarter, popular art songs, and patriotic celebrations the seeds of an American concert music. He quoted liberally from African American, Caribbean, and popular music in his piano and symphonic pieces. In the 1840s and 1850s, Gottschalk was wildly popular with American audiences, who recognized in his elaborate fantasias Stephen Foster songs such as "Camptown Races" and various patriotic tunes—from "Hail Columbia" to "Yankee Doodle" and

"The Star-Spangled Banner." Although he cannot be said to have created an American music for the concert hall, he did recognize the importance of folk and popular traditions in the development of an American art.

As Gottschalk's popularity increased, Boston's John Sullivan Dwight (1813–1893) spoke out against the influences of popular music. From 1852 to 1881, he argued in *Dwight's Journal of Music* that Americans should listen to the music of the best European composers rather than to the popular tunes of their own nation. Dwight was an Associationist and a transcendentalist reformer who was close to Ralph Waldo Emerson and other Brook Farm residents. He ascribed to fine music the power to create good citizens and to inspire order in a democracy that might otherwise succumb to popular tastes and opinions. Dwight had little faith in popular culture—he was convinced that the songs of the Mexican and Civil wars brought out the worst passions in human beings—and in the music of victory celebrations and the Fourth of July he heard little more than injurious noise.

Prior to the Civil War, orchestral music was available to a relatively small audience and live performances were confined mainly to traveling minstrel shows that parodied high culture to eager audiences. As a result, middle-class Americans created a genteel musical culture at home. The Civil War period saw an increase in popular musical creativity to meet the needs of the moment with new songs about battle and heroes, along with sentimental ballads about mothers, wives, and sweethearts left behind. In addition, art songs by such American composers as Stephen C. Foster (1826–1864) and Henry Clay Work (1832–1884) reached middle-class households in the form of piano-vocal sheet music. These songs, written by trained composers, were about nature, love, and other "proper" subjects for middle-class audiences. An emerging genteel tradition encouraged young women to acquire basic piano-playing skills. Songs with simple accompaniment—for example, Foster's "Jeanie with the Light Brown Hair"—found a place next to the hymnals on the upright piano in many homes, and came to serve as family entertainment.

The emergence of the United States as a growing economic power after the Civil War generated capital that could be invested in culture. The New York Philharmonic Society, which had been presenting concerts since 1842, was followed by the New York Symphony in 1878, the Boston Symphony in 1881 (under the sponsorship of Major

Henry Lee Higginson), the Chicago Orchestra (later the Chicago Symphony) in 1891 (with the support of local businessmen who were eager to promote their city as the new cultural capital of the nation), and the Philadelphia Orchestra in 1900. With the exception of the New York Philharmonic Society, which was founded as a cooperative, symphony orchestras were supported by men of new wealth, whose ability to purchase culture quickly made them pillars of local society. American orchestras performed to please their patrons, and concert programming was characterized by a predominance of tried and true European "classical" compositions. Music by American composers rarely found its way into such programs, except perhaps as a novelty.

During the last third of the nineteenth century, as the United States assumed a more prominent role in the world, the nation took many opportunities to celebrate its democratic past and promising future. From 15 to 19 June 1869, Boston bandmaster Patrick Sarsfield Gilmore (1829–1892) staged the National Peace Jubilee and Music Festival "in Honor of the Restoration of Peace and Union Throughout the Land." The festival, with its orchestra and chorus of five hundred performers each, attracted most notably President Ulysses S. Grant. Among its innovations were the use of synchronized church bells and fifty cannons firing live ammunition triggered by an electrical switch installed in the conductor's stand. Gilmore staged another peace jubilee in 1872 to commemorate the end of the Franco-Prussian War. In keeping with the cultural assumptions of the day, the music he chose came from the pens of European rather than American composers.

American accomplishment was the theme of the Philadelphia Centennial Exhibition of 1876, which featured the five-thousand-horsepower Corliss Engine and Alexander Graham Bell's telephone. Music for the exhibition included the "Centennial Hymn" composed by John Knowles Paine (1839–1906), the first professor of music at Harvard University and the most respected American concert-music composer of the late nineteenth century at that time. Church-music composer Dudley Buck (1839–1909) wrote the music for Sidney Lanier's cantata, "Centennial Meditation of Columbia." But the exhibition's Women's Committee, which sponsored the musical events, sought to engage the services of a famous European composer to create the musical showpiece of the summer. As a result, it was Richard Wagner, rather than an American composer, who was

commissioned to write the "Centennial March" to celebrate the hundredth anniversary of the Declaration of Independence.

The four-hundredth anniversary of Christopher Columbus's voyage occasioned another celebration, the World's Columbian Exposition in Chicago in 1893, whose theme was the industrial and commercial progress of the United States. Conductor Theodore Thomas, who was famous for his orchestral performances of the music of Richard Wagner, was again engaged to plan the concert programs and conduct the orchestra, as he had done for the Philadelphia Centennial. Paine composed the "Columbus March and Hymn" especially for the Chicago exposition. Several concerts featured music by American composers, including Paine, Arthur H. Bird (1856–1923), Charles C. Converse (1823–1918), Arthur Foote (1853–1937), Edward MacDowell (1860–1908), and Margaret Ruthven Lang (1867–1972); but the audience for these American composers was small and elite compared with the thousands who toured the midway in search of more popular entertainments. At the end of the nineteenth century, concert music remained the preserve of the wealthy who could subsidize orchestras and pay to hear the best European standard repertoire; and the country's major orchestras and opera companies were still dominated by European performing and conducting talent. To be accepted, an American composer had to compose music that sounded as though it had been written in Vienna or Berlin.

In the early twentieth century, new ideas about the nature of art rapidly produced new approaches to creating music—so rapidly that composer Edgard Varèse was prompted in the mid 1920s to describe music as nothing more or less than "organized sound." But the end of the nineteenth century did not signal a leap into modernity in American concert music; rather, the challenge to nineteenth-century musical traditions took many forms as American composers joined in the search for new ways to organize sound.

American versions of the European art song, the marches and arrangements of European symphonic pieces by John Philip Sousa and a generation of bandmasters who brought middlebrow American music to hometown audiences, and music for the vaudeville stage and musical theater were integral to the life of middle- and working-class white audiences. African American music had distinctly rural and urban flavors, from southern work songs, hollers, and spirituals to the urban blues of northern cities, which were sung to

The gospel performer praises the Lord and promotes spiritual ecstasy by shouting, hand clapping, oral antiphony, humming, moaning, body weaving, foot tapping, and head bobbing.

PAGE 22

See also
Folk Song and Folk Music

C

See also

African American Music

EARLY TWENTIETH CENTURY CONCERT MUSIC

Forging a National Identity

Early in the century, a small group of American concert music composers looked to popular music specifically to express a national identity in their symphonic music. Henry F. B. Gilbert (1868–1928), Arthur Farwell (1872–1952), John Powell (1882–1963), and others used Native American melodic fragments, African American rhythms and familiar tunes, and the ballads of rural southern whites. Edward MacDowell's "Indian" Suite (1897) is typical of this approach to musical nationalism. It uses a brief horn call and a few fragments from music of the Iowa and Kiowa tribes in a symphonic musical context.

At about the same time, Charles Ives (1874–1954) quoted popular hymns, patriotic songs, and music by other composers. Unlike his contemporaries, however, Ives placed his familiar quotations in a polytonal and/or a polyrhythmic context in which they often sound both modern and American. Ives was not embarrassed to bring the most mundane musical images, such as small-town marching bands and church choirs, into the concert hall. Only late in his life, long after he had stopped composing, was Ives's music recognized as significant to the development of modern American music. Ives was unique in his willingness to experiment with a variety of musical sounds and textures. His goal was to evoke scenes from the New England of his youth. In doing so, he often created dissonant, modern-sounding music.

the accompaniment of the trumpet, piano, and other instruments of European origin. In New Orleans, black marching bands performed for funerals and festivals the syncopated rhythms that would soon become familiar as early jazz. Scott Joplin (1868–1917) and Charles Lamb wrote piano pieces for indoor performance, and the cakewalk, a dance performed in music in "ragged time" became the rage in black urban enclaves. White and black popular musical traditions coexisted without influencing each other or American concert music to any great extent.

When, in the first decades of the twentieth century, many African Americans migrated from agricultural to urban, industrial regions of the north, the outdoor bands came with them. The locus of jazz activity shifted from New Orleans to Chicago, Kansas City, and New York; as performances moved indoors, jazz ensembles modified their instrumentation to include a piano rather than a tuba and stationary percussion rather than a portable bass and snare drum. Groups such as Jelly Roll Morton's Red Hot Peppers and King Oliver's Creole Jazz Band (including the young Louis Armstrong), recorded in a style that featured "hot" solos and simultaneous improvisation. After World War I, Armstrong (1898?–1971) recorded a number of pieces in this early Chicago style with a group called the Hot Fives and, later, the Hot Seven.

In elite musical circles and in the press, the rise of anti-German sentiment precipitated by World War I prompted a debate over the importance of culture and its relation to patriotism. For many critics, high culture was presumed to have German origins—*Kultur*—and some feared that the demand for "100 percent Americanism" would result in the elimination of most if not all of the repertories that concert and opera audiences paid to hear. A furor over the Boston Symphony Orchestra's refusal to play "The Star-Spangled Banner" at a concert in Providence, Rhode Island, in 1917 contributed to a severe criticism of German *Kultur.* BSO conductor Karl Muck was arrested, interned, and eventually deported on suspicion of disloyalty—partly due to his insistence on separating art and politics and partly because he haughtily denigrated the quality of the American song (which became the national anthem in 1931).

In effect, the war forced orchestras to expand their concert repertories. In place of the romantic symphonic music by German, Austrian, or Hungarian composers, the mainstay of most concert programs became music by modern French, Russian, and even American composers, who often were receiving their first hearing. For a brief period, orchestra audiences heard more music by American composers (they even saw the employment of the first American-born concertmaster in Boston); but with the end of hostilities, these same elite audiences were quick to demand music by German, Austrian, and Hungarian composers.

Although the American composer's move into the American concert mainstream was short-lived, after the war many young American composers sailed for Europe. There was nothing unique about the presence of Americans in European studios and conservatories, but now some were traveling to study new techniques with Arnold Schönberg (1874–1951) and other nontonal composers in Vienna, while others—notably

Aaron Copland (1900–1991) and Virgil Thomson (1896–1989)—went to study with Nadia Boulanger at the American Academy at Fountainebleau in Paris. The war had seen the arrival of American jazz and dance in France when James Reese Europe's orchestra performed with dancers Vernon and Irene Castle. In the 1920s, inspired by American jazz, a number of French, Russian and German composers—including Darius Milhaud (1892–1974), Erik Satie (1866–1925), Igor Stravinsky (1882–1971), and Adolph Weiss (1891–1971)—wrote modern compositions employing sounds recognizable to devotees of American popular music.

By the mid 1920s, concert music composers in America as well were beginning to explore ways to synthesize jazz and symphonic music. In 1924, for example, the Paul Whiteman Orchestra performed George Gershwin's "Rhapsody in Blue," orchestrated by Ferde Grofé. That piece—an example of symphonic jazz in which the influence of the composer's early years as a Tin Pan Alley song plugger (a pianist who performed the latest songs seated in a store window in order to sell more sheet music) was apparent—as well as his "An American in Paris" and " 'I Got Rhythm' Variations" foreshadowed the use of jazz idioms by Aaron Copland in the 1930s and Leonard Bernstein (1918–1990) in the 1950s. The popularity of all three composers attests to the significance of bringing jazz into the concert hall to create an American symphonic style.

Starting in the 1920s, the development of radio technology brought American music into American homes; audiences could hear bluegrass and country music, symphonic and operatic performances of standard works (performed by Arturo Toscanini's [1867–1957] NBC Symphony and the Metropolitan Opera Company), and popular dance orchestras. Radio leveled many of the class distinctions of the concert hall: anyone who could afford a radio set could bring European high culture—along with dance band music, country songs, and the World Series—into his or her home.

This democratizing trend was dealt a blow by the Great Depression, which brought hard times for American musicians and American music. Public schools ran out of money for music curricula, performers had fewer opportunities, and composers—rarely able to support themselves on their creativity, in any case—now found themselves facing even bleaker prospects. The Federal Music Project of the Works Progress Administration, however, created useful work in the form of concerts and teaching projects, as well as by sponsoring the cataloging of American folk music and the copying of many new works to prepare the parts for performance.

During the depths of the Depression, many American concert music composers and songwriters developed an interest in the history, ethnic diversity, and current plight of the American people. Singers Woody Guthrie (1912–1967) and Hudie Ledbetter ("Leadbelly" [1885–1949]) created songs from both white and black folk traditions, and composers such as Copland and Elie Siegmeister (b. 1909) incorporated everyday music into symphonic works; of these efforts, Copland's "Billy the Kid" (1938), "Rodeo" (1942), and "Appalachian Spring" (1943–1944) are the best known.

In the late 1930s, the music of working people and the cultural history of labor struggles inspired members of the Composers' Collective in New York, which included Charles Seeger (1886–1979), Earl Robinson (b. 1910), Copland, Siegmeister, and Marc Blitzstein (1905–1964). They wrote songs and rounds for two *Workers Song Books* (1934, 1935) and debated the most appropriate form of workers' music in *New Masses* and *Modern Music*, the journal of the League of Composers.

INNOVATOR

Leonard Bernstein (1918–1990) used many jazz idioms in his composition, helping to create what is known as an American Symphonic style.
LIBRARY OF CONGRESS/
CORBIS

In this time of growing consciousness of race prejudice, African-American performers and composers achieved success beyond the traditional realm of black American music. White audiences had long applauded the musically "correct" arrangements both of spirituals set by Harry T. Burleigh (1866–1949) and those sung by such groups as the Fisk Jubilee Singers. In the 1930s, Paul Robeson (1898–1976) was popular not only as a performer of spirituals but as an actor and singer in several languages. When Marian Anderson (b. 1902) was denied permission to sing in Washington's Constitution Hall by the Daughters of the American Revolution, her performance to an audience of more than seventy-five thousand on the steps of the Lincoln Memorial in the spring of 1939 brought the interrelation of race and high culture to the American public. In 1955, Anderson made her belated Metropolitan Opera debut. However, it was only in the decades after World War II that African Americans crossed the high-culture barrier as successful singers and symphonic performers in significant numbers.

Concert music audiences were no less patriotic during World War II than they had been in the previous world war, but the issue of American nationalism had receded considerably—one could listen to music by German composers and still remain loyal to the United States and its war aims. By this time, European refugee composers, including Béla Bartók (who taught at Columbia) and Paul Hindemith (at Yale), had influenced the development of modern American music. Once again, audiences heard first performances of compositions by Americans, but the composers' names were far from obscure, and the likelihood of subsequent performances of new American works was much greater than it had been in 1917–1918.

After World War II, American composers again joined in the search for new musical effects. Like their European counterparts who experimented with *musique concrète* and electronically produced sounds, American composers benefited from the technology that had given radio and television to the larger culture. At first, their efforts were isolated in universities and special centers for new music, as the postwar realization of Varèse's "organized sound" did not sound anything like music to most audiences. Harry Partch (1901–1974) found it necessary to invent his own instruments to create sounds that diverged from the Western tempered scale. John Cage (b. 1912) organized notes and rhythms randomly, and even created a silent piece. Electronic music composers

♦ **Musique concrète**

A recorded montage of natural sounds often electronically modified and presented as a musical composition

Mario Davidovsky (b. 1934) and Vladimir Ussachevsky (b. 1911) generated sounds mechanically and made the stopwatch and tape recorder integral to their musical performances.

Although the first synthesizers of electronic sound occupied entire rooms and were used exclusively for composition, synthesized sound generated by portable computerized instruments had by now become commonplace, especially in the commercial and popular music realms. The same public that disdained electronic music as too esoteric and too far removed from understandable melody and rhythm now hears electronically synthesized music every day, albeit in catchy and singable melodies not common to more experimental modern music.

After World War II, American musicians saw this country's major cities, especially New York, as major cultural centers on par with the capitals of Europe. As an important locus of the new television industry, New York was the site of innovative

THE BIRTH OF "BEBOP"

A Unique Musical Style

In popular music, swing held sway during and after World War II, but in the early 1940s a group of young black musicians struck out on their own to create a musical style that was less tied to the convention of the twelve-bar blues or the thirty-two-bar popular song. The result was "bebop," a challenging musical style based on the creative art of the soloist, which Charlie Parker (1920–1955), Dizzy Gillespie (b. 1917), Max Roach (b. 1924), and Curly Russell made popular. The small size of bop groups created opportunities for extended flights of soloist virtuosity, and bop musicians often pushed their instruments and voices to the limits of their capabilities. Bop was "hot"; it demanded attention and could not be considered background or dance music. It was most popular with young people who felt that swing band music had become tired. The early 1950s saw a creative reaction to the intensity of bebop in the form of "cool" jazz; this style, pioneered by Miles Davis (1926–1991), Thelonious Monk (1917–1982), and Lenny Tristano (1919–1978), was no less creative or intense, but it was quieter. Early bop and cool jazz performers were analogous to the creators of electronic and modern music, in that they all experimented for its own sake and cared little for audience acceptance.

broadcasting by the New York Philharmonic under Leonard Bernstein's direction. Young People's concerts and special programs narrated by the conductor were broadcast to millions of homes all over the country. Orchestral music and, later, opera were made accessible to citizens who otherwise might never have attended a concert because of their distance from a concert hall or lack of resources. High culture was, in a sense, democratized; and the advent of public television in the early 1960s expanded these opportunities for concerts broadcast live and simultaneously on radio (a "simulcast").

By the late 1960s, rock musicians, influenced by blues, jazz, and music from all over the world were creating eclectic works that were inappropriate because of their length or their verbal content for standard AM radio play. A 1966 ruling by the Federal Communications Commission created large blocks of FM airtime, which was quickly filled with albums and songs that were too long or too sexually or politically explicit for the AM band. While the FCC's goal had been to free the FM band from the dominance of "sister" AM stations, the effect was to create more room for college and independent stations to play music that appealed to young, affluent audiences. FM radio quickly became the medium through which young people heard the latest music. This so-called album-oriented radio (AOR) continues to provide a venue for unconventional styles (fusion, crossover, and experimental); and FM radio continues to be the medium of choice for most classical music broadcasting.

The 1970s and 1980s saw the emergence of musical minimalism, a style that relies extensively on repetition of rhythmic patterns and chord structures. Philip Glass (b. 1937) and Steve Reich (b. 1936) are often cited as exponents of this style, which, in its relative simplicity, bears some resemblance to some rock music. Glass, Reich, performance artist Laurie Anderson (b. 1947), and the underground rock band Sonic Youth have all recorded pieces that blur generic boundaries and bear the "crossover" label. A variety of crossover neoromanticism is apparent in New Age music, some of which includes instruments and tonal effects of non-Western—particularly Tibetan and Japanese—cultures. The New Age phenomenon has offered a successful multicultural synthesis of Western concert instruments and musical forms with melodic ideas and inspiration from non-Western cultures.

In concert music, the latter decades of the twentieth century saw debates among composers over the continued viability of varieties of modernist musical thought. Composers for whom melody has remained more important than rhythmic invention continue to create accessible modern music, which is sometimes labeled "neoromantic." David Diamond (b. 1915) integrated neoclassic and romantic musical sounds into some of his compositions, as did William Schuman (b. 1910), composer of symphonies and an opera, "The Mighty Casey," based on the popular poem. Elie Siegmeister composed "I Have a Dream," a cantata based on the life of Martin Luther King, Jr., and Ned Rorem (b. 1923) set to music the work of American poets as diverse as Walt Whitman and Sylvia Plath. Elliott Carter (b. 1908) and Leonard Bernstein have been strong propagandists for American music, Carter in an academic context and Bernstein in his many books, lectures, and television appearances. Although composing and conducting have long been the province of men, the work of countless women composers, including Louise Talma (b. 1906) and Miriam Gideon (b. 1906), and such famous conductors as Sarah Caldwell (b. 1924) has contributed to the development of American concert music for a broader public.

American music is not confined to a set of national tunes, myths that inspire great symphonies, or a single folk music tradition. It reaches small avant-garde audiences in the academy, millions of fans through concerts and recordings, and almost everyone in the form of more or less ambient music piped into public and private architectural spaces. Indeed, in the last decades of the twentieth century, Virgil Thomson's assertion that American music is simply music written by Americans is being realized through the variety of the American musical product itself. Earlier cries for a higher standard of European culture in the music we hear in this country have given way to a plethora of approaches to composition that rely on no national label. In its diversity and availability through electronic media, concert music in the United States has assumed a place in the mainstream of American culture.

—BARBARA L. TISCHLER

COUNTRY AND WESTERN MUSIC

In forty years of rapid modernization after 1920, much of the southern-eastern United States was transformed from a rural, agricultural society to

The notes I handle no better than many pianists. But the pauses between the notes—ah, that is where the art resides!

ARTUR SCHNABEL

See also
Rock Music

C

*"Young Charlotte"
is an example of
a widely sung
sentimental ballad.*

PAGE 160

an urban, industrial one. During this time the region also endured a severe economic depression, contributed heavily to a world war, and accommodated new government programs designed to commercialize agriculture, import new economic systems, and improve home life. One by-product of these changes was a dramatic increase in migration throughout the region and subsequent economic displacement, divorce, and social disruption among families. This situation was congenial to the rise of a popular music focusing on personal hardship or invoking nostalgia for a more orderly way of life imagined as the region's rural past.

Dramatic social change was common in southern society during the early twentieth century. In Appalachia, where a novel form of rustic musical entertainment was invented in this period, nineteenth-century family farming was made obsolete by industrial urbanization and agricultural modernization. First came timber cutting, then coal mining, textile mills, commercial manufacturing towns, railroads, highways, land acquisition for national parks, tourism, and government flood-control and hydroelectric projects. So much Appalachian land was removed from private ownership by these incursions that during the downside of boom-and-bust cycles government welfare programs were required by almost half the mountain population before World War II. A similar displacement occurred throughout the South. Between 1920 and 1960 sharp increases in mechanized farming and related changes in southern agricultural regions had unprecedented demographic effects. Jack Temple Kirby estimates that if each 1920 southern farm household consisted of five persons, in the forty years before 1960 nearly eight million people migrated from farms and nine million people left the region altogether. This extraordinary migration precipitated both urban and nationwide markets for country and western music.

During the same forty years that southerners were displaced from rural environments, complex institutions to promote popular entertainment were built in the South. New technologies were essential to this process. Radio broadcasting, phonograph recording, and electrical amplification equipment used in concerts made it possible for large numbers of people to hear intricate levels of nuance in singing and instrument playing. Paved highways, automobiles, and bus transportation allowed enterprising performers to be booked in concerts throughout the region and beyond. Concerts became both a source of major income

and an important setting where entertainers could build emotional relationships with their fans by singing of personal hardship or pain, love traumas, memories of family and kin. Movies, television, music festivals, and concert tours spread this musical subculture widely in the 1950s and 1960s. Combining a fortunate location in the middle South with business entrepreneurship and investment capital, Nashville, Tennessee, became a major center for the nationwide marketing of country and western entertainment by 1960.

An Emerging Star System

In the early 1920s recording-company entrepreneurs began packaging mountain string music into rustic formats with market appeal. A style that would later come to be known as "hillbilly" music began in June 1922 when Alexander Campbell "Eck" Robertson and Henry Gilliland, old-time fiddlers from Texas and Oklahoma, were recorded at Victor studios in New York City. Radio broadcasting quickly embraced rusticity. On 24 January 1923 station WBAP in Fort Worth, Texas, aired the first radio program of hillbilly string music to an extremely receptive audience that responded with telephone calls and telegrams of praise. Successful radio barn-dance programs were soon begun in Chicago, Atlanta, Nashville, and other cities.

Recording companies responded to radio's success with string-band music by offering an alternative—solo vocalists. Marion T. Slaughter is often cited as the most important of these. A graduate of the Dallas Conservatory of Music and a figure of the New York light opera stage, Slaughter was an ironic candidate for success as a hillbilly; he had also recorded songs in black dialect for the "race" market. In 1924 he began making records in New York City under the pseudonym Vernon Dalhart—a recording persona constructed from the names of towns in Texas where he had once worked as a cowboy. His 1924 version of "The Prisoner's Song," the first hillbilly vocal to sell a million records, was a guitar- and viola-accompanied ballad about loneliness and separation from a lover. Slaughter followed his hit record with numerous releases having sentimental themes.

Hillbilly records were made in several cities in the 1920s. Although New York City was the earliest recording site, formative events that would lead to a popular-music industry took place in Tennessee. In the summer of 1927 Ralph Peer, a young entrepreneur working with the Victor Talking Machine Company, went to Bristol, Tennessee, to make field recordings. He was searching for hillbilly entertainment that would boost record sales for Victor. An arrangement would soon emerge that would allow his music publishing company to receive royalties on songs copyrighted and performed by the artists he selected; this would encourage Peer to give much attention to his stars.

Peer advertised for local musicians; he would record their work for fifty dollars per song plus royalties. Spread by a newspaper story, this offer attracted much notice. According to Charles Wolfe, in about two weeks at Bristol, Peer made over seventy recordings of pop and vaudeville, fiddle, banjo, and gospel music (*Bristol Sessions*, vol. 1, liner notes). Among the many acts responding to Peer were two that would become the earliest national stars in country and western music: the Carter Family and Jimmie Rodgers.

THE CARTER FAMILY. This trio had a pervasive influence on subsequent performing styles. Probably most important for the formation of country music instrumental styling was Maybelle Addington Carter, a creative guitarist and alto singer. A. P. (Alvin Pleasant) Carter, Maybelle's brother-in-law, sang bass and managed the act. A. P. Carter and Ralph Peer may have initiated the practice of copyrighting and recording songs that were collected from many sources and adapted to a particular group's playing style. Sara Dougherty Carter, A. P.'s wife, sang lead and played the Autoharp in an unusual way, picking an instrument designed for strumming a rhythmic accompaniment.

Signature innovations of the Carter Family in the late 1920s were crucial to their commercial success and influence. Maybelle Carter perfected a distinct guitar style by playing melody on bass strings with her thumb while chording rhythm on treble strings. A. P. Carter's song arrangements reduced complicated traditional melodies and accompaniments to standard vocal lines sung in a repetitive fashion against a regular rhythm of basic chords. These two innovations may have been developed partly under the influence of Leslie Riddles, a black guitarist and songwriter from Kingsport, Tennessee. Riddles's periodic travels with A. P. Carter influenced the latter's method of song collecting.

Carter Family music is marketable popular music featuring lyrics with broad appeal for a changing society. While the trio adapted many kinds of music to their format, a main theme was personal hardship and emotional responses to it. In their first six songs recorded at Bristol, a daughter sentimentalizes her mother's Bible reading, a young woman pines for unrequited love, a mother longs for her wandering boy, lovers pledge loyalty in a lament over pending separation, blessings are asked for poor orphan children, and a bride complains of constraints in married life. The lives of Carter Family members suggest that such themes may have been derived from personal experience. Always maintaining jobs other than music in order to make a living, they were frequently separated because family members worked as far away from their Scott County, Virginia, homes as Detroit or Washington, D.C. Marital life was problematic: in 1933 A. P. and Sara separated; in 1939 they were divorced, and Sara married A. P.'s cousin in Texas. Yet despite personal problems they recorded consistently between 1927 and 1941, releasing more than three hundred songs.

Carter performing style was readily distinguished from that of previous hillbilly artists—it was precise in execution, emotionally exciting, and repetitive—and could be imitated or elaborated upon by other musicians. The Carters got important airplay during the three years they spent in San Antonio and Del Rio, Texas, in the late 1930s making transcriptions for radio stations licensed in Mexico as XEG, XENT, and XERA. These border radio stations were built beyond the reach of American law by colorful figures who had violated American radio regulations and power limits by zealously promoting a startling array of money-making schemes. The Carters' promoters recognized the audience appeal of rustic music and used it heavily; consequently, the Carter Family received nationwide exposure virtually every evening at a time when radio listening was America's novel form of popular entertainment.

With both radio and record exposure the Carter Family was able to create enduring music that both inspired future entertainers and nurtured a popular market for them. Although the family act disbanded in 1943, Maybelle Carter remained an influential musician well into the 1970s. The Carter name remained prominent through the marriage of Maybelle's daughter, June, with Johnny Cash, as well as through the Carters' touring with Cash's show.

JIMMIE RODGERS. The brief recording career of Jimmie Rodgers also began in Bristol, Tennessee—he first performed for Peer two days after the Carter Family. Rodgers was the first major success story of Peer's promotional arrangement with Victor. The attention Peer ac-

A man who loved "country" before "country" was cool.

HILLARY RODHAM CLINTON ON PRESIDENT CLINTON'S FONDNESS FOR COUNTRY MUSIC

♦ Hillbilly music

Country music

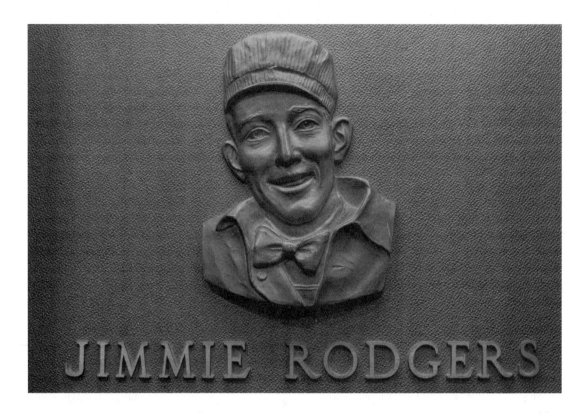

corded Rodgers (and all his stars) gave him reason to remain loyal to Peer. Rodgers was an enduring role model for male stardom and a symbol
of individual wealth and popular acclaim, and his
performance innovations helped to define a
"western" musical genre.

In 1927 Rodgers, an itinerant railroader from
Mississippi, was working as a part-time cab driver
and as a deputy for the Asheville, North Carolina,
police. Recently diagnosed with tuberculosis and
wanting to leave the railroad, Rodgers was sleeping in an Asheville firehouse and singing with a
hillbilly band at a local radio station. He discovered the Peer recording sessions accidentally during a visit to Bristol. Just before recording for
Peer, Rodgers split with his band in a billing dispute and chose to sing solo. Peer recorded two of
Rodgers's songs; he performed each in a slow
tempo and sang them from a woman's point of
view. "The Soldier's Sweetheart" was a popular
World War I song, a lament about a lover lost in
battle. "Sleep, Baby, Sleep" was a mother's sooth-
ing lullaby to an infant. It included a novelty
item—a variation on the Swiss yodel that had
been a stage feature of vaudeville. Peer detected
commercial possibilities in Rodgers's yodel and
soon recorded him at Victor studios in Camden,
New Jersey.

In a contribution analogous to the Carter
Family's innovations in rhythm and instrumenta-

tion, Rodgers combined the yodel with the blues
to create his signature "blue yodel." Rodgers had
learned blues from black workers during his fourteen years on the railroad, beginning as a teenage
water boy. When he brought together the yodel
and blues traditions, Rodgers was able to express
personal emotion, particularly the pain of vaga-
bond living or turbulent love relationships, in a
novel way. The blue-yodel phenomenon was popular in an era that also produced jazz, and it had financial results that impressed aspiring musicians.
In 1928 "Blue Yodel" ("T for Texas") became the
first hit record of modern country music.

Jimmie Rodgers died of tuberculosis complications at age thirty-five in 1933. In only six years of
recording he had become the first pop superstar of
country and western music. His signature blue yodel appeared a dozen times among 111 recorded
titles. He also recorded sentimental ballads, popular and novelty songs, jazz, blues, Hawaiian music,
and songs with, variously, an orchestra, a jug band,
a whistler, and a musical saw. He was one of the
first white performers to record with black artists.
Despite this varied repertoire Rodgers had a
memorable styling that greatly influenced the
tone of later country and western music. Nolan
Porterfield reports that Rodgers, instructing his
musicians at a rehearsal to play in a distinctive
manner, said, "It's gotta have pathos. Make folks
feel it—like we do, but we gotta have the feelin'

ourselves first. This is supposed to be pathetic" (*Jimmie Rodgers*, pp. 75–76). Rodgers pressed this point so far as to record songs about his own terminal illness, such as "T. B. Blues" and "Jimmie Rodgers' Last Blue Yodel." His emphasis on pathos tapped much popular feeling during the Great Depression years; by the year of his death he had sold almost twenty million records.

The blue yodel and pathetic themes cannot, however, fully account for Rodgers's success. In another innovation he modeled a stage demeanor that would be elaborated upon by later singers who understood that the emerging star system required performers to provide stage entertainment well beyond singing. In his apprenticeship Rodgers worked medicine shows, minstrel shows, tent shows, schoolhouses, beer joints, and street corners, perfecting a personal style that touched his listeners' emotions. His mature stage manner was extremely relaxed and unaffected, and his usual stage attire and props were informal; he often appeared alone with his guitar. Rodgers lengthened or shortened words for emotional expression, and during performances he carried on a stream of verbal comments to encourage other players or to enliven his audience—more adaptations from blues stylists. Rodgers's vivacity was memorable. He became the first country and western star to have a fan club operated entirely by his followers, and in 1961 he was the first performer voted into the newly formed Country Music Hall of Fame.

After the example of Jimmie Rodgers the performance style of many country and western stars favored individual singing, guitar playing, informal interaction with fellow musicians and the audience, expressive voice innovations, emotional styling, and lyrical themes invoking pathos about the hardships of life and love. While some entertainers copied virtually everything Rodgers did, including his novelty sounds, most used his example to establish their own innovations. Depictions of the American West that had long been a staple of American popular culture were partly responsible for the emergence of western music, but Rodgers influenced the genre as well.

At the height of his popularity Rodgers built a home in Texas. He had posed for photographs in cowboy garb and used western themes in his music. Looking for a signature style and inspired by Rodgers, Gene Autry found it in a yodeling cowboy persona. Between 1929 and 1933 Autry recorded twenty-four Rodgers titles, launching his own rise to record and movie stardom and substantially advancing western imagery. Other male stars affiliated with western music have paid tribute to Rodgers. In 1932 Ernest Tubb (The Texas Troubadour) began a half-century career that after Rodgers's death earned the blessing of Rodgers's widow and the gift of Jimmie's guitar.

The Grand Ole Opry, Radio, and the Music Business

Jimmie Rodgers never appeared on the *Grand Ole Opry*, yet during his lifetime this vaudeville show developed from a "radio barn dance" by an entrepreneurial newspaper reporter was already becoming a major institution. Today the *Grand Ole Opry* is America's longest-running radio program; its stage is a shrine for country and western fans, a focus of aspiration for many performers, and the centerpiece of impressive commercial activity reaching into tourism, cable television, and other aspects of American popular culture.

In 1923 George D. Hay, a reporter and radio editor for the *Memphis Commercial Appeal*, began broadcasting over the newspaper's radio station. The following year he moved to Chicago, where he began the *National Barn Dance* on station WLS and won a national poll naming him the most popular radio announcer in America. In 1925 the National Life and Accident Insurance Company opened a thousand-watt radio station in Nashville, designated WSM for the insurance company's sales slogan, "We Shield Millions." Hay joined WSM that year to host a new barn dance from studios in the insurance building.

Hay had a shrewd grasp of the emerging radio audience for sentimentalized rural experience in an era when rural life was being permanently transformed. He readily moved to Nashville, which was well located for his promising market, and from the beginning of his work at WSM, he positioned his entertainers carefully. Hay sought performers who could project primitive rural images and material with nostalgic themes. He appeared to favor performers of advancing age who could impart wisdom and a feel for tradition. Although only thirty, Hay presented his own *Opry* persona as the "Solemn Old Judge." With marketing wit he renamed his barn dance the *Grand Ole Opry* to contrast with a symphonic music program broadcast just ahead of it—music he said was far from earthy realism because it was taken from grand opera.

Many of Hay's early performers were staged as rustics or curiosities. The first to perform on the evening Hay christened his *Grand Ole Opry* program was DeFord Bailey, a black man who played blues harmonica through a megaphone and was

There remained millions of Americans to whom the music of the last generation of Tin Pan Alley composers did not appeal— most blacks, as well as the whites of rural America.

PAGE 358

See also
Concert Music

called by Hay the "Harmonica Wizard." Bailey was an elevator operator in the insurance company's building who became quite popular and was kept with the program until the early 1940s. Another act reflecting Hay's early emphasis was a musical physician from the county just north of Nashville who headed Dr. Humphrey Bate and His Augmented Orchestra. Hay dressed Bate's group in exaggerated rural garb and named it The Possum Hunters. Other acts were similarly styled as the Fruit Jar Drinkers or the Gully Jumpers to project rural nostalgia.

The first solo singing star of the *Grand Ole Opry*, Uncle Dave Macon, was a symbol of age and tradition. A vaudeville performer, banjo player, and gospel singer, Macon joined the *Opry* in 1926 at the age of fifty-six, then toured and performed regularly until three weeks before his

MINNIE PEARL

The *Opry* has featured a long series of vaudeville-style comedians who portray zany images of rural life. In the minstrel tradition country comics focus on the foibles of country people, especially their alleged inability to cope with modernity or their naive observations about it. Comics have had an important influence on country and western stage shows. Most prominent among them has been Sarah Ophelia Colley Cannon, whose character Minnie Pearl first appeared in 1940, when Colley was twenty-eight years old. A graduate of Ward-Belmont College in Nashville, she studied stage technique. After Colley's family lost their Tennessee lumber business in the Depression, she taught drama and dance until she joined the *Opry*. She based Minnie Pearl on a rural woman she met in north Alabama. *Opry* insiders feared that this act might be disliked as a negative image of rural life, yet the first airing drew hundreds of positive cards and letters. After more than fifty years in entertainment, in the early 1990s Sarah Cannon was still personally answering fan mail; she believes that comic performers serve country and western fans by providing relief from the music's main focus on unhappiness. Minnie Pearl was elected to the Country Music Hall of Fame in 1975.

death at age eighty-two. A fully modern *Opry* star, clearly influenced by both Jimmie Rodgers's stage manner and Carter Family musical styling, first appeared in 1938. A former semiprofessional baseball player who had learned to play fiddle while recovering from sunstroke, Roy Acuff came to the *Opry* with his band, The Crazy Tennesseans, to fill in for a canceled act. Acuff's nostalgic and rhythmically precise gospel rendition of "The Great Speckled Bird" received an outpouring of adoring mail, and his version of the Carter Family's famous railroad song, "Wabash Cannonball," brought him national attention as the *Opry* audience expanded with the advent of radio broadcasting networks. Billed as the "King of Country Music," Roy Acuff was still singing Jimmie Rodgers's blues on the *Opry* in the 1990s.

George D. Hay's radio formula of rural rusticity, string-band music, country singing stars, vaudeville comedians, and aging images of tradition had a strong audience appeal that commercial advertisers found attractive. The National Life and Accident Insurance Company saw the value of its insurance policies quadruple between 1925 and 1940. The R. J. Reynolds Tobacco Company, Pet Milk, Royal Crown Cola, Coca-Cola, Rudy's Farm Country Sausage, and the Standard Candy Company (makers of an item whose name invokes imagery of unrestrained infants seeking treats, the Goo Goo Cluster) have been prominently associated with the *Opry*. Between 1945 and 1949 Martha White Flour expanded its sponsorship of WSM programs from one P.M. to eight P.M., and its unit sales for that period tripled. In 1945 each sponsored musical program was estimated to increase flour sales for that year by 152,062 units. Commercial advertising has been so intrinsic to this musical subculture that many stage acts have been named for products that sponsored them.

Tuned to prospects for building a new music business, WSM and radio broadcasters helped establish country and western music's other basic institutions. In 1934 WSM created the Artist Service Bureau to help stars book lucrative personal appearances and tours. In 1939 a dispute over license fees charged to radio stations as a way of collecting royalties for songwriters resulted in broadcasters' forming their own licensing agency; Broadcast Music, Inc. (BMI), was set up—in competition with the American Society of Composers, Authors and Publishers (ASCAP)—to support country, western, blues, and jazz songwriters. Bill Ivey, director of the Country Music

Foundation, regards the creation of BMI as the event most important to the professionalization and commercial success of the country and western music business. After broadcasters had assured a fiscal foundation for the new music, record companies moved south. In 1946 Nashville's first permanent studio, Castle Recording Company, opened. Soon studios of major record labels such as Capitol, RCA, and Decca were established in Nashville.

Major Trends and Stars

Since the 1950s country and western music has become a sophisticated commercial enterprise. Yet it has continued to emphasize themes of personal hardship and emotional trauma consistent with its social origins. As a musical tradition it, like the blues, has evolved distinct conventions. To become a star, a performer must devise a novel way to address traditional themes and musical styling—through voice innovations, creative instrumental motifs or special dexterity, elaborations on stage manner and performing style, or modification of existing genres to create a new one. Country and western musicians are highly conscious of one another, and the work of a successful performer influences that of aspiring ones. These relationships and conventions are illustrated in the careers of six artists whose achievements suggest notable trends in the music.

WESTERN SWING: BOB WILLS. Early southwestern swing music modified by popular dance-hall bands and broadcast nationally by radio networks in the late 1930s and early 1940s came to be known as western swing. Bob Wills was among its most significant innovators. As a child in migrant labor camps Wills, the son of a country fiddler from Texas, listened to blues musicians and other ethnic performers. As an adult he admired Bessie Smith as well as the dance orchestras of Tommy Dorsey, Count Basie, Bob Crosby, and Glenn Miller. Famous for a signature blues fid-

*Country music is
folk music in
overdrive.*

ALAN LOMAX
MUSICOLOGIST

NASHVILLE

The Business of Popular Culture

Since World War II, Nashville and country music have emerged as a notable financial and cultural force. In 1960, for example, Nashville studios produced singles that hit number one on *Billboard* magazine's top hits chart for twenty-eight out of fifty-one weeks. Two years earlier the Country Music Association had been formed to promote country and western music at a time when rock and roll—a derivation that many regarded as heresy—threatened its popularity. In another response to rock and roll, innovative producers like Chet Atkins at RCA Victor Studio B developed the Nashville sound as smoother country pop stylings aimed at new listener markets. By the 1980s, at the height of its popularity, country and western music grossed over $500 million annually—about 15 percent of the $3.8 billion market for all popular music then recorded in the United States. It was also being played full time on more than twenty-two hundred radio stations. Since that time, the business has increasingly em-

phasized restoration of traditional styling in the promotion of its stars.

The solid position of country and western music in American popular culture since the 1980s is indicated by its continuing impact in urban radio markets, where it competes well with easy-listening music and frequently surpasses in popularity other established genres such as rock, blues, and jazz. The culture associated with country music has spawned clothing fashions, music palaces, bars, hotels, theme parks, trade publications, movies, novels, and museums, and it has been the subject of both popular and scholarly writing. Its most vivid contemporary symbol is an elaborate theme park fittingly named Opryland U.S.A. A showcase of American popular music, this vast tourist attraction occupies four hundred acres adjoining a Nashville outer freeway loop and the Cumberland River, where the park operates a 285-foot riverboat, the *General Jackson*. Opryland, which had an attendance of 2.35 million in 1989, features a 1,070-room

resort hotel, syndicated cable television on The Nashville Network (reaching more than twenty million homes), and an array of tourist attractions. One of these, an annual event called Fan Fair, attracts almost twenty-five thousand people to the Tennessee State Fairgrounds each June, where they may see thirty-four hours of stage shows and visit booths where the stars provide personal thanks to their supporters. Replacing the Ryman Auditorium to become the sixth official home of country and western music since the 1920s, a fifteen-million-dollar Grand Old Opry House opened at Opryland in 1974 with a guest piano performance by President Richard Nixon. (Nixon was the first of several American presidents, including Jimmy Carter, Ronald Reagan, and George Bush, to publicly affiliate their politics with country and western music and its fans.) In 1983 the Opryland complex was sold for $270 million to a national media company based in Oklahoma.

dling with a string band that yielded a jazzy swing, Wills added woodwinds, horns, and drums so that his Texas Playboys could perform numbers ranging from Jimmie Rodgers's blues to popular dance-band and jazz renditions to Rossini's "William Tell Overture." By 1938 Wills's band could play almost thirty-six hundred pieces, yet despite this crossover virtuosity he retained a strong interest in western themes and in the 1940s appeared in many western movies. After World War II he moved his operation to the West Coast, where a potential audience among southwestern migrants was growing; although his national popularity declined, he remained influential into the 1960s.

Merle Haggard, who describes his own distinct sound out of California as a form of jazz, has called Bob Wills a national hero and honors him often in performance. Wills fused several pop traditions into the country and western idiom, and in turn he influenced country pop styling as well as other popular music. Bing Crosby recorded his "New San Antonio Rose" in 1941; it became a gold record, selling 1.5 million copies. Wills was voted into the Country Music Hall of Fame in 1968.

HONKY-TONK: HANK WILLIAMS. A country and western subgenre, honky-tonk music is especially characterized by themes of turbulent love, romantic anguish, and excessive drinking. Hiram "Hank" Williams greatly extended the popularity of this music after World War II. A gifted songwriter, he used an approach directly in the Jimmie Rodgers tradition—his signature songs spoke with great emotion of the hardships of life, and he

had a charismatic stage manner. The son of a lumber company railroader from rural south Alabama, Williams learned music from Cade Durham, an old-time fiddler who worked in a local shoe shop, and from Rufe "Tee Tot" Payne, a black street singer who probably introduced him to whiskey as well as to the blues when he was a teenager in the mid 1930s. After an apprenticeship in Alabama honky-tonks, in 1946 Williams came to Nashville, where his songwriting impressed Fred Rose of Acuff-Rose Publishing, and he was signed to a contract. Williams appeared on the radio barn dance *Louisiana Hayride* at Shreveport in 1948. By the spring of 1949 his records became so popular that he was invited to appear on the *Opry*. In a repeat of Rodgers's instant success story, at the end of the 1940s and into the early 1950s Williams's hits dominated both country and pop charts, selling millions of records.

But success pressed Williams severely. Alcohol and drugs, phobias, and the effects of painkillers for spina bifida affected his work. A dramatic divorce followed. He soon became an erratic performer and was fired by the *Opry* in August 1952. That year Minnie Pearl described him as a "pathetic, emaciated, haunted-looking tragic figure" (Koon, *Hank Williams*, p. 45). The date of Williams's death has become a matter of considerable investigation. Either on the last day of 1952 or the first of 1953, Williams died of a heart attack in the back seat of his Cadillac while being driven to a concert in Canton, Ohio. Public response to his death was reminiscent of the death of Jimmie Rodgers—he was so widely memorialized that his legend greatly extended his lifetime fame.

Williams's influence on other male singers was important. In an impressive vocal career George Jones, in particular, has kept Hank Williams's examples of honky-tonk singing (and personal behavior) alive. In the early 1990s popular young male singers are creating innovative stage personas in the honky-tonk genre: Clint Black, Garth Brooks, Alan Jackson, George Strait, Randy Travis, Dwight Yoakam.

BLUEGRASS: BILL MONROE. Bill Monroe created a modern style of string-band playing and vocal harmonizing that has attracted numerous followers to an elaborate country and western subgenre known as bluegrass music. As a boy Bill Monroe worked on his father's 655-acre farm in Kentucky, where he witnessed timber cutting, sawmilling, and coal mining. A loner with poor eyesight, he gravitated toward the music played by his older brothers. His uncle, Pendleton Vandiver, taught him rhythm and timing through old-time fiddle playing, and a black fiddler and guitarist, Arnold Shultz, taught him the blues. Monroe's later stylistic innovations were in part a blending of these traditions.

At age eighteen Monroe migrated to Indiana, where he began working in an oil refinery near Chicago. There he collected hillbilly string-band records, listened to radio barn dances, and performed with his brothers, Birch and Charlie, for an audience of Appalachian migrants. The Monroe Brothers had a Gary, Indiana, radio show by 1934; turned professional to perform full time in Iowa and Nebraska; moved to the Carolinas in 1935; and made best-selling records during the next two years. In 1938, in Atlanta, Monroe formed the Blue Grass Boys; this band gave its name to a new type of string-band music and trained many of the musicians who spread it. Monroe's bluegrass used five instruments: mandolin (played with great dexterity by Monroe), fiddle (played in a jazzy and soulful manner), banjo (played in a charismatic picking mode introduced to this audience by Earl Scruggs), guitar, and bass. By 1939 Monroe was on the *Grand Ole Opry*, where his first performance was an adaptation of Jimmie Rodgers's blue yodel "Mule Skinner Blues."

Bluegrass is a distinct style within country and western music. Its rhythms stress offbeats, tempos are usually quite fast, vocal harmonizing is intricate and high-pitched, and instrumental virtuosity is prominent. Lyrics are conventional, focusing on home, family, love, hard times, work, and religion. Bluegrass invokes a potent tone of nostalgia for the rural past. In the late 1950s and early 1960s national magazines promoted bluegrass; during the "folk" movement Monroe played college campuses, and in 1963 he headlined the Newport Folk Festival.

There were more than a hundred bluegrass festivals by 1975, as well as record companies and magazines catering to an avid audience. Young *Opry* stars such as Ricky Skaggs and comedian Mike Snider, as well as the syndicated television program *Hee Haw*, actively promote rustic imagery and bluegrass music. A patriarch in his eightieth year, who in 1991 still performed as "The Father of Bluegrass Music," Bill Monroe was elected to the Country Music Hall of Fame in 1970—the same year as the Carter Family.

COUNTRY POP: PATSY CLINE, LORETTA LYNN, DOLLY PARTON. After World War II, many significant country and western music stars sought a broad audience by adopting variations of a country pop sound and image. Patsy Cline, Loretta Lynn, and Dolly Parton are important female stars who exemplify this phenomenon. None came from privileged circumstances, all were devoted to a successful professional career, and each promoted a signature identity related to changing gender roles in America. They provided an important artistic precedent for many younger women singers.

Patsy Cline was born Virginia Patterson Hensley near Winchester, Virginia, in 1932. Her parents separated when she was fifteen. By then Cline was a radio singer; at sixteen she dropped out of school to work by day and sing in clubs at night. In 1954 she got a recording contract, and three years later won national attention on a network television show, *Arthur Godfrey's Talent Scouts*. Intensely ambitious and an admirer of female pop singing stars as well as of Hank Williams, Patsy Cline devised a sound produced by Owen Bradley that was close to mainstream popular music and a precursor of the Nashville sound. This came at a time when, as an antidote to rock and roll, Nashville was recruiting an audience of American pop music lovers. Meanwhile, divorce rates were rising and a mystique praising faithful women in nuclear families was evident in popular culture. Despite Cline's own reportedly audacious personality, her musical signature was slow-tempo songs about the painfulness of unquestioning and compliant femininity, done in renditions richly backed by harmonic vocals and strings. Cline was an emerging *Grand Ole Opry* star with several hit songs lamenting male behavior in romantic relationships when she died in a plane crash in 1963. Paul Kingsbury quotes Robert K. Oermann's description of her as "the first great country torch singer" (p. 330) who influenced many later female artists. In 1973 she was the first woman solo artist voted into the Country Music Hall of Fame.

Loretta Lynn was the second of eight children in a coal miner's family of Butcher Holler, Johnson County, Kentucky. Born in the mid 1930s (she won't say when), married at fourteen, and eventually mother of six, Lynn began singing in bars near Custer, Washington, where her husband had migrated to find work in the timber industry. In the early 1960s she won a talent contest in Tacoma hosted by Buck Owens, made a hit record, moved to Nashville, and appeared on television as well as the *Grand Ole Opry*. Lynn's musical signature may have responded more to Patsy Cline's personal life than to Cline's singing; Lynn wrote and sang of women who openly object to men who cheat romantically. With a soulful voice featuring a tearful quality and singing titles such

♦ **Honky-tonk music**

Of, used in, or being a form of ragtime piano playing performed typically on an upright piano

*There are songs that
come free from the
blue-eyed grass.
From the dust
of a thousand
country roads.*

ROBERT JAMES WALLER

See also
African American Music

as "You Ain't Woman Enough to Take My Man," "Your Squaw Is on the Warpath," "Fist City," and "The Pill," Lynn built an image as an assertive, noncompliant female whose behavior defends traditional family values.

This formula was highly attractive in American popular culture of the early 1970s. In 1972 Lynn became the first woman named Entertainer of the Year by the Country Music Association, and in 1973 she received honorable mention in a Gallup poll of the world's ten most admired women. By the mid 1970s she had over one hundred music awards, and in 1988 she was elected to the Country Music Hall of Fame. Her life story was told in a movie intended as an accurate depiction that would personalize the country music business; *Coal Miner's Daughter* (1980) includes several actual stars playing themselves in places where life events occurred. Lynn and her husband own a chain of western clothing stores, the nation's largest rodeo, three publishing companies, and a 1,450-acre ranch and theme park near Nashville. This park pays nostalgic homage to Lynn's youth, featuring a replica of her childhood home.

Dolly Parton is a precocious product of Holiness church-singing as well as the offspring of a musical mother and a grandmother who played harmonica. Born in 1946 into a family of twelve children at Locust Ridge, Tennessee, Parton appeared on a television variety and radio show in Knoxville by the age of ten and on the *Grand Ole Opry* at fifteen. She moved to Nashville immediately after completing high school and formed a recording partnership with *Opry* star Porter Wagoner. They won the Country Music Association Vocal Duo of the Year award in 1968, 1970, and 1971.

In a variation on Loretta Lynn's gender themes, Dolly Parton's stage persona exaggerates her ample feminine characteristics to attract audience attention while singing songs that invoke conventional values; music critic Ken Tucker has described the effect of Parton's wig, bustline, and high heels as a deliberate cartoon sex symbol. Her signature titles about the hard times of her family—"Coat of Many Colors," "My Tennessee Mountain Home," and "The Bargain Store"—reinforce the image of a poor girl whose cultivated femininity can be marketed to improve her economic and social status. With a vivacious stage presence, a soprano voice capable of virtuoso coyness, and a powerful imagination that has produced over thirty solo albums with hundreds of her own compositions, Parton has become one of popular music's most commercially successful artists.

Named CMA Entertainer of the Year in 1978, Parton has starred in a television variety show, had important roles in five movies, and earned six-figure salaries in Las Vegas. In 1986 she opened a multimillion-dollar theme park named Dollywood in Pigeon Forge, Tennessee. A candid proponent of gender imagery, Parton achieved ultimate crossover status when Gloria Steinem honored her in *Ms.* magazine as a woman who "has turned all the devalued symbols of womanliness to her own ends" (p. 66).

Country and Western Music and Social History

Country and western music emerged in the late 1920s partly as a reaction to modernization—it provided musical images of rural rusticity on radio programs and promoted recording stars who expressed emotions typical of the personal hardships and romantic traumas evident during social change. It also took advantage of technological innovations in electronics, communication, and travel to build a national music subculture radiating from Nashville, Tennessee. This hastened regional modernization through the financial success of a modern music business, its stars, and its commercial sponsors. The themes of country songs, however, remained close to the impulses that initiated them; in its first six decades of growth to a multimillion-dollar enterprise, country and western music has offered traditional agrarian values to an audience for whom rural life probably functions more as nostalgia than as lived experience.

Perhaps partly because of this, the country and western subculture is usually associated with the white majority in America, and most of its major stars have been white males. Yet many of its important instrumental and vocal innovations were inspired by the art of minority musicians. By adopting blues and jazz motifs such as persistent rhythms, improvisational instrumental features, and emotionally expressive vocal renditions, country and western musicians played a role in bringing musical motifs associated with nonwhite Americans to the general popular culture, and influenced the early era of rock and roll.

Country and western music has illustrated but not embraced the changing roles of women in America since World War II. It has typically rewarded female stars who, in their art, may elaborate upon but not deviate fundamentally from conventional gender expectations. While a few women singers challenged gender boundaries during the 1980s and 1990s as a nationwide women's movement gained strength, and important female artists have achieved much popularity since the 1960s, the masculine perspective has dominated this musical subculture. Of sixty-one members elected to the Country Music Hall of Fame between 1961 and 1991, only seven were women—and three of these were solo artists. One was a comedian whose famous character, Minnie Pearl, nicely satirizes but does not threaten accepted roles.

There is no lack, however, of certain sexual themes. Lovers of this music praise its plain speaking—usually called "sincerity—because so many songs speak convincingly of emotions arising from fragmented or failed love relationships. A study by Jimmie N. Rogers of the four hundred most popular country and western songs from 1960 to 1987 found that 75 percent of them were love songs. Most of those were about unhappy, hurting, or lost loves; next most frequent were songs about cheating situations; and least frequent were songs of happy love. Dorothy Horstman found country and western songwriting to be a complex literature "full of death, sadness, and self-pity." This persistent pathos of wasted love complements themes of fading rusticity and nostalgia for lost rural life.

Rustic imagery, adaptations of jazz and blues motifs, conventional gender roles, and pathetic themes of broken hearts are central features of country and western music. They resonate with a tacit assumption: the proper way to confront hardships in a difficult world is to live in a monogamous marriage with traditional family life and conventional religion. Even though country and western stars are often unable to meet this standard themselves, they persistently elaborate upon an art that celebrates it. Fans know this. Perhaps they admire in their stars this elusive striving for a stability not characteristic of their historical experience. Regarded this way, despite its modernity, country and western music in American life amounts to a conservative critique of modern society and a very human resistance to social change.

—CURTIS W. ELLISON

COURTSHIP, MARRIAGE, SEPARATION, AND DIVORCE

There are no universally accepted definitions of the terms "courtship," "marriage," "separation," and "divorce," but working definitions can be es-

tablished in the context of American history and tradition. Courtship is the process of identifying and testing potential marriage partners and of selecting the best candidate. Marriage is the alliance of a man and a woman, of them and the state, and of two sets of kin in a socially and legally legitimized union. This union regularizes a couple's sexual relationship and childbearing, and it creates an economic unit that will support the married pair and any children they produce. Marriage usually begins with a public announcement, some sort of ceremony, and a legal document, all of which assume a degree of permanence in the marriage. Often, marriage confers adult status on the new spouses in their own eyes, and those of their families and of society.

Separation and divorce are processes that dissolve and dismantle the legal and emotional ties a married couple create. Although a marriage remains legally intact during separation and is totally nullified in divorce, both processes must provide for division of joint property, care of children, support of a financially dependent spouse, and financial arrangements in case of illness, disability, and retirement. In addition, separation and divorce must address the dissolution of kin ties—for example, grandparents' right of access to their grandchildren.

During the course of American history, these institutions have modified in several significant ways. Today the most noticeable trends are an increase in the number of people who contract several marriages of limited duration and an increase in the number of people who resort to divorce as a solution to marital problems. Most Americans think of their ancestors as people who formed enduring, stable families, but serial marriage and widespread divorce were present early in the nation's history.

Colonial America, 1607–1776

American Indian customs and laws were diverse and well established when the first permanent European settlers arrived in 1607. Native practices included patriarchal and matriarchal families; patrilineal and matrilineal descent; patrilocal and matrilocal residences; polygamy; and relative ease of divorce. Anthropologists estimate that perhaps as many as one-third of Indian tribes were matriarchal, matrilineal, and matrilocal; polygamy and ease of divorce appear to have been more widespread.

Early settlers, who of course brought their own beliefs and practices with them, frequently commented upon and criticized these native customs.

C

COURTSHIP, MARRIAGE, SEPARATION, AND DIVORCE

Colonial America, 1607–1776

Country rock (also known as rockabilly) emerged from the country and western tradition of Hank Williams, Roy Acuff, and other Grand Ole Opry stars.

PAGE 398

See also
Popular Music Before 1950

C

**COURTSHIP,
MARRIAGE,
SEPARATION,
AND DIVORCE**

*Colonial America,
1607–1776*

Most Europeans believed that all marriages and families should be patriarchal, patrilineal, and patrilocal. They expected marriage to involve one man and one woman, bonded by a religious sacrament into a lifetime union. Some Europeans, however, accepted the idea of separation in cases of physical abuse and divorce in cases of adultery or other serious violations of the marriage compact.

Puritan settlers in what became the Massachusetts colony were the first to break with some of these accepted ideas regarding marriage. Because they had adopted Martin Luther's and John Calvin's belief that marriage was a civil rather than a religious concern, Plymouth officials formally declared in 1620 that marriage was a civil matter. As the colony's second governor, William Bradford, explained, marriage was to be "performed by the magistrate, as being a civil thing." Puritan leaders in other colonies also adopted this philosophy. By removing marriage from the jurisdiction of the church, they hoped to create strong, state-regulated families that would serve as the keystone of their society. They expected well-ordered, religiously oriented, patriarchal families to bring about their dream of a harmonious community in the wilderness.

BUNDLING

Family members, friends, ministers, and officials could not always oversee courting couples. Sometimes necessity dictated that they be left alone while others worked, worshiped, or slept. At bedtime, a young woman's family might bundle her and her swain, both fully dressed, into the same bed. Often a board was placed between them. The rest of the family could then bank the fire and retire for the night. The custom of bundling was not a Puritan invention; it had roots in cultures all over the world, including the British Isles and American Indian civilizations. But it was controversial. Its supporters maintained that it was an innocent practice, while its critics argued that it led to fornication and pregnancy before marriage. Certainly, court records indicate that a significant number of Puritan marriages were contracted as the result of fornication which led to pregnancy. In the New Haven colony (later part of Connecticut), the sin of fornication could lead to marriage even if no pregnancy occurred.

Because effective mate selection was crucial to stable marriages, courtship was a public affair that involved not only the courting couple but their families and neighbors as well. Romantic love was not a high priority. Rather, a couple was to be well matched in abilities, ambitions, backgrounds, and beliefs. Once they married, established a productive economic unit, and produced children, conjugal love would develop.

Like courtship, marriage was a public concern regulated by social expectations, church rules, and community law. Both men and women were expected to marry. Typically, men married between the ages of twenty-five and twenty-eight. Young men who delayed marriage, or were unable to find a mate due to the high ratio of men to women, often were subject to a bachelor tax levied by their townships. During the seventeenth century, the greater number of men than women put pressure on women to marry while in their teens. During the eighteenth century, however, women customarily married between the ages of twenty and twenty-two. In 1692, Puritan minister Cotton Mather declared in *Ornaments for the Daughters of Zion*, "For a woman to be praised, is for her to be married." It is little wonder that nine out of ten women married at least once in their lifetime. Women who did not marry lived with their nearest male relatives, performed child-care duties, and did spinning—and as a result were usually known as spinsters.

Despite their rejection of marriage as a religious concern, Puritans, like other European settlers, favored the patriarchal family form in which the husband was the head of the family. He was to make decisions for his wife and children as well as to direct and oversee their behavior. He also owned any wages they earned. But a husband also faced certain restrictions. He was, for example, liable for his wife's support, responsible for her crimes and debts, and required to leave at least one-third of his land and one-third of his movable property to her in his will. He was also supposed to be faithful sexually to his wife, to live with her in peace and harmony, and to avoid abusing her.

Puritans considered a wife the "weaker vessel" who owed submission to her husband. Guidebooks titled *A Good Wife, God's Gift* and *Marriage Duties*, both published in 1620, spelled out a married woman's duties. Although before marriage she might hold the legal status of *feme sole*, which allowed her to manage her own affairs and even establish a business, after marriage she shifted to *feme covert*, which made her part of her husband's legal and political identity and prohibited her from conducting her own affairs. This change in status derived from the civil death concept early settlers brought from England. Civil death, summarized in Sir William Blackstone's *Commentaries on the Laws of England* (1765–1769), prescribed that a married woman had no legal, political, or social identity apart from her husband. She could not sign contracts, had no right to her own earnings, was not able to own property, could not vote on civil or religious matters, and lost her children in case of separation or divorce. In actual practice, however, many wives were partners in family businesses, ran their own enterprises, or took over a husband's business in case of his absence, illness, or death.

As with courtship, not all Puritans obeyed the rules concerning marriage. New England church records indicate that wayward spouses were regularly brought to trial and punished. Puritan ministers usually rebuked the erring mate and ordered troubled couples to reconcile, but many feared that forcing embattled couples to remain together would undermine the social harmony they hoped to achieve. They especially feared adultery, which minister John Robinson called a "foul and filthy sin." Adultery also threatened property rights, for if a man impregnated another man's wife, the other husband's property might go to a child not his own.

As a result, New England officials sometimes followed the English practice of granting "divorces of bed and board," or legal separations. In this arrangement, a couple remained married but lived separately. The husband was expected to support his wife, and both were barred from remarriage. This solution was usually unsatisfactory because husbands often missed payments, while wives, because they were still married women, could not start their own businesses or marry men who could better support them.

In certain cases, divorce seemed a far better solution than forcing spouses to remain legally wed. After divorce, women returned to *feme sole* status or could remarry. Consequently, in 1639 the Massachusetts Bay Court of Assistants granted the first divorce in America to a woman who claimed her husband was a bigamist. The second divorce occurred in 1643, when Anne Clarke charged her husband with living with another woman. As these cases suggest, divorce involved a court trial in which one party sued the other. The plaintiff had to prove fault on the part of the defendant. Property, support, and child custody awards were made by the court, which typically favored the injured party. As a result, a woman who could prove her husband's sins had a far better chance of a favorable settlement than a woman whose husband proved her guilty of a marital misdeed. It is little wonder that by the early 1700s, more women than men sued for divorce in America, a situation that has continued to the present day.

Surviving court records indicate that Massachusetts magistrates had granted nearly one hundred divorces by the time of the American Revolution, a rather high number for a society dedicated to the family and in an early stage of experimentation with divorce. Also, these figures omitted nonwhite people. American Indians were left to tend to their own marital disputes, and African Americans seldom sought, or were granted, white legal sanctions. A rare African American case occurred in 1758 when free black Lucy Purnan successfully charged her husband with extreme cruelty, including kidnapping and selling her as a slave.

Other New England and middle colonies experimented with separation and divorce. Each jurisdiction defined its own grounds for divorce, which included adultery, bigamy, willful desertion, extended absence, and nonsupport. Divorces might be granted by local courts or the governor of the colony. Some officials condoned physical and even mental cruelty as a substantiating charge, thus laying the basis for later generations' acceptance of cruelty as a ground for divorce. Of these colonies, only Connecticut appears to have surpassed Massachusetts in the number of divorces granted relative to the size of its population.

In the southern colonies, marriage and divorce differed slightly from other regions. Marriage was patriarchal, while law and custom restrained husbands from abusing their power. Such early guidebooks as *A Godly Form of Household Government* admonished husbands to "seldom reprove" and "never smite" their wives. Wives were supposed to be agreeable and obedient mates, capable and energetic household managers, and prolific and loving mothers.

Personal letters, family and court records, and similar documents indicate that numerous southern couples enjoyed devoted relationships, while others destroyed their unions with arguments and abusive behavior. But, unlike the situation in New England and in some of the middle colonies, estranged couples could only seek separations. In the colonial South, every government maintained a belief in the long-standing Anglican practice of granting only divorces of bed and board. But implementing such divorces was problematic be-

C

COURTSHIP,
MARRIAGE,
SEPARATION,
AND DIVORCE

*Colonial America,
1607–1776*

Drive-in theatres were an invitation to young couples to bring children to the cinema in the privacy of their cars, or to young couples to use moviegoing as part of a courting ritual.

PAGE 151

C

COURTSHIP, MARRIAGE, SEPARATION, AND DIVORCE

The New Nation, 1776–1861

Married women's leisure was "segregated from the public realm and not sharply differentiated from work, but was sinuously intertwined with the rhythms of household labor and the relations of kinship."

PAGE 283

See also
The Frontier

cause the southern colonies lacked the ecclesiastical courts necessary to give such decrees. Consequently, courts of chancery (courts of equity rather than common law) filled the void by giving separate maintenance orders to disgruntled spouses. Following English ecclesiastical court procedure, chancellors ordered husbands to continue to support wives who were to live on their own. They also prohibited both parties from remarrying.

Women initiated virtually all separate maintenance requests. Such orders brought desperately needed financial support to women who had absent, cruel, adulterous, and bigamous husbands. Aggrieved husbands had little to gain through such orders because they could separate from their wives without paying anything, or paying only what they thought sufficient.

The legal system of marriage and separation in the southern colonies excluded African American slaves. Slave owners usually decreed whether slaves could marry or part, and frequently ordered them to do so. In other cases, slaves turned to their churches or communities for approval of their matings and partings. The only notable laws regulating African Americans' marital behavior—whether they were slave or free—were miscegenation provisions prohibiting black women and men from marrying white mates. Such laws had their roots in color prejudice and fear of "race suicide." Soon local prohibitions were enacted into colonial codes of law. Although these laws, which persisted in some states until the 1960s, were not always observed, essentially two systems of marriage developed in the colonial South, one white and one black.

The New Nation, 1776–1861

By the time the American colonies declared independence from Great Britain in 1776, a wide range of social and economic factors had modified the institution of marriage. Certainly the emergence of a market economy, new forms of production, and technology had already begun to alter the family's role as the basic unit of production. As early as the mid 1770s, the economic partnership of spouses in producing agricultural and other goods began to decline. In addition, the growing mobility of Americans and the gradual development of a trend toward western migration placed severe stresses on marriages and families. During the 1760s and 1770s, existing social and economic stresses were exacerbated by an expanding rhetoric of individualism, a philosophy which argued that liberty, justice, and the pursuit of hap-

piness were American rights—both politically and personally. Then the Revolutionary War itself created temptations for spouses at home or at the front, encouraged people to marry without forethought, and called into question women's usual roles within the family.

When leaders in the new states hastened to write constitutions and enact codes of laws, they had to decide how each of the thirteen new states would regulate and order the marital status of citizens under their jurisdiction. At first, most simply integrated existing practices and laws into their constitutions and laws, but in the years following the Revolution, states began to change and expand the rules. As a result, the thirteen states developed thirteen different sets of rules governing marriage.

When the United States Constitution created a federal government, which went into effect in 1789, the diverse legal patterns might have been standardized if the Constitution had given the new government the power to regulate the marital status of Americans. But each colony had controlled the marital status of its own citizens since the beginning of settlement in 1607, and the new states resisted losing this, or any other, power. Thus, individual states retained the right to regulate marital status within their boundaries. In 1792 the U.S. Congress tried to bring harmony to the situation by passing a "full faith and credit" bill reinforcing a statement in the Constitution that each state was required to give full faith and credit to the acts of other states. In the matter of marital status, however, this was a practical impossibility because states still refused to relinquish their sovereignty in this matter; it was eventually adjudicated by the Supreme Court.

Marriage was further complicated by the fact that Americans exhibited all three of the basic forms of family structure. The nuclear family consisting of two parents and their children gradually became the idealized form in the new nation. But some people chose the extended family in which two or more nuclear families were affiliated by parent-child relationships, or the polygamous family in which two or more nuclear families were affiliated by plural marriage, usually one husband and several wives. The extended family was often used in cases of scarce resources. For instance, western settlers lived together to pool goods and services. Polygamy was a preferred form for a number of practical and religious reasons among Mormons, who moved westward during the mid nineteenth century, first to Nauvoo, Illinois, and then to Utah.

Diversity occurred in other ways as well. In Philadelphia and Boston, New York and Virginia, during the 1780s and 1790s, for example, close kin marriages were commonly used to solidify family wealth and power. And while such northeastern states as Massachusetts and Connecticut refused to give wives a measure of protection from husbandly abuse or mismanagement by recognizing a married woman's right to hold property, southern states did so through prenuptial agreements. Such contracts usually stipulated that the property of a bride-to-be would be held in trusteeship for her exclusive use and that she could not be held liable for her husband's debts. One example was an 1824 agreement between Henry M. Armistead and Mary Robinson of Virginia, stipulating that the bride-to-be's "considerable" land, slaves, and other personal property would be held by a trustee for her sole use throughout her lifetime. Although such agreements were usually negotiated by wealthy families, they were widely used in some areas of the South. For instance, in Louisiana, people of many backgrounds, races, and ethnic origins signed them. During the early 1830s in Louisiana, an Irish widow protected her plantation and slaves with a contract, and two free African Americans, who held 7 acres (2.8 hectares) between them, made their marks on a premarital agreement.

During the post-Revolution period, American marriage altered in yet another way. The traditional view of patriarchal marriage was increasingly under attack. An emerging ideal of companionate marriage—a partnership of equals and companions who would respect each other in a reciprocal, loving manner—challenged the customary idea of male-headed, male-dominated unions. Articles, essays, speeches, and sermons spoke of the need for spouses to give each other respect, reciprocity, and romance during both courtship and marriage.

Wives, who had long been taught to respect their husbands, especially began to ask for more consideration. As early as 1776, political wife and farm manager Abigail Adams argued that wives should be helpmeets rather than slaves and should be free from husbandly "tyranny." The wife-slave analogy was a popular one during these years. But in 1831, an essay in *Godey's Lady's Book* informed readers that tyranny was now "out of fashion" because men were becoming "more enlightened and more rational."

Women's rights advocates especially called for respect in marriage. Abolitionist and feminist Sarah Grimké claimed in *Letters on the Equality of the Sexes* (1838) that God intended wives as "companions, equals, and helpers" rather than as servile housekeepers. In 1843 and 1845 transcendentalist Margaret Fuller argued that wives should be companions and equal members of "household partnerships."

Reciprocity was another key ingredient to successful marriage. In 1874 popular novelist Timothy Shay Arthur explained that marital "felicity" meant that spouses tried to please each other whenever possible. And when reformer Robert Dale Owen married Mary Jane Robinson in 1832, he released a statement on reciprocity in marriage. In it, he repudiated his "unjust rights" that "an iniquitous law tacitly give over the person and property of another," and he labeled a husband's legal right the "barbarous relics of a feudal, despotic system." Later a few other couples, such as reformers Lucy Stone and Henry Blackwell, attempted to create equal marriages by issuing similar statements.

The third component of marriage was heightened romantic love. Letters of courting couples from this period clearly exhibit an intensified interest in romance rather than in practical matters. Many mentioned that they had the right to reject parental advice regarding their choice of mate, for how could another person judge the presence of true love?

The theme of romantic love also appeared in thousands of essays, stories, and novels. In 1785 an essay in *Boston Magazine* encouraged unmarried people to resist parental advice. Instead, they were to "avoid sacrificing a life of happiness" by bending to their parents' will. T. S. Arthur also advised couples to marry for love. In *The Stolen Wife* (1843), he told the story of a woman whose true love carried her off half an hour before she was to wed the man her parents had chosen.

Of course, the three r's—respect, reciprocity, and romance—did not immediately eclipse longstanding beliefs regarding courtship and marriage. Writers of innumerable guidebooks, such as *The Young Wife*, which was popular between 1800 and 1860, argued that wives must be submissive, pure, and domestic. The home was, after all, wives' "proper sphere." Husbands were the center of women's lives, for women lived best in "the regions of sentiments and imagination." Women's sphere also included motherhood. A growing idealization of republican motherhood—mothers who raised virtuous citizens for the new republic—reinforced the customary view that motherhood was the be-all and end-all of women's lives. In 1842, Margaret Coxe unequivocally stated that

C

COURTSHIP, MARRIAGE, SEPARATION, AND DIVORCE

The New Nation, 1776–1861

A man and a woman marry because both of them don't know what to do with themselves.

ANTON CHEKHOV

C

**COURTSHIP,
MARRIAGE,
SEPARATION,
AND DIVORCE**

*The New Nation,
1776–1861*

*Within individual
families, necessity
caused women to
assume new roles
and take on tasks
that had formerly
been the exclusive
responsibility
of men.*

PAGE 195

See also
Rock Music

motherhood was the "most important channel through which woman was to direct her special moral agency" (*Claims of the Country on American Females*, p. 37).

This dual system of values bewildered many people. Was marriage to be patriarchal or was it to be companionate? How could a person select a suitable mate in this situation? In 1850 novelist Nathaniel Hawthorne described the confusion that reigned in many romantic relationships. In *The Scarlet Letter*, distressed women come to Hester for advice about marriage, but she can only soothe them by predicting that love and marriage will be easier in the future: "At some brighter period. . . . a new truth would be revealed, in order to establish the whole relation between man and woman on a surer ground of mutual happiness."

Other observers of the situation took a far different stance. Some reformers argued that marriage itself was the culprit. As early as 1826, Frances Wright's utopian community, Nashoba, Tennessee, rejected the concept of marriage entirely. Wright and her supporters argued that love and respect, rather than legal ties, should bind couples. When love and respect disappeared, couples could simply separate. As a consequence, public outrage rose against Wright; her critics accused her of being a free-love advocate. On July 4—Independence Day—of that same year, Robert Dale Owen declared that no one should be trapped in a distressing marriage. In his view, only marriages that resulted in equality and companionship ought to continue.

Other utopian communities also experimented with marriage. Under the leadership of Ann Lee, Shakers established their first socialist Christian community at Watervliet, New York, during the mid 1770s. In hopes of hastening the millennium, Shakers advocated and practiced total celibacy. As Shaker communities multiplied, problems arose when one spouse wanted to join the Shakers and the other did not. Shaker leaders were afraid their communities would become havens for runaway husbands and wives. Accordingly, they refused to accept a married person without his or her spouse unless they were legally separated or divorced.

Also in New York, the Oneida Community, founded by John Humphrey Noyes in 1848, followed the practice of "complex" marriage in which every woman in the community was married to every man, and every man to every woman. The goal of complex marriage was to eliminate competition, jealousy, and inequality between men and women. Noyes hoped mates would no longer feel "ownership" of their spouses, so the need for

divorce would disappear. In 1850 an Oneida tract described marriage as "contrary to natural liberty," as "a cruel and oppressive method of uniting the sexes," and as a "huge Bastille of spiritual tyranny where men and women have the power to debar each other from their rights . . . " (Oneida Community, *Slavery and Marriage: A Dialogue* [1850], pp. 7–13).

Most Americans rejected these and other criticisms of traditional, white, middle- and upper-class marriage. Religious leaders, notably Episcopalians and Catholics, spoke in favor of marriage as a lifetime religious sacrament. By the 1820s and 1830s, when European immigration began to increase significantly, immigrants who brought their strong religious and family beliefs with them reinforced the conservative position. But definite changes were occurring as well, especially concerning women's legal position in marriage. In 1839 the state of Mississippi passed the first Married Women's Property Act, allowing wives to own and control property. In 1848 the New York legislature adopted a similar bill; Pennsylvania and several other states soon followed suit.

As the American debate regarding the future of marriage accelerated, cases of marital dissatisfaction also multiplied. Apparently the new, freer, romantic courtship was failing to help people select partners they could love for a lifetime. Moreover, Americans' rising expectations of marriage were complicating an already difficult situation at the same time that industrialization was placing unthought-of demands on marriages. Among the middle and upper classes, women remained at home while their husbands spent long days at offices in town. Among the working classes, both spouses often went to work, but at different workplaces. Working women usually were still expected to take care of domestic chores and arrange for child care. Consequently, numbers of separations and divorces rose. When the Frenchman Michel Chevalier toured the young nation during the early 1830s, he commented that marital connections were far more easily dissolved in America than in Europe. The most noticeable change had occurred in the South, where legislatures, except in South Carolina, radically revised their divorce policies beginning in 1790. The first divorce in the South was granted by members of the Maryland General Assembly in 1790 after John Sewall proved his wife had borne a mulatto child. By the mid 1830s the Maryland legislature was granting over thirty divorces each year. But in 1842, legislators passed a bill placing primary jurisdiction for divorce in the courts. The legislators felt overburdened by the volume of divorce petitions and distracted from their other work. In 1852 the Maryland constitution prohibited legislative divorce entirely. For better or worse, divorce was now in the hands of the courts.

A similar process occurred in other southern states. As states ended their confusing dual systems of divorce by lodging jurisdiction in courts only, divorce began to expand and become easier to obtain. Divorces of bed and board were still available, but growing numbers of people sought the finality of divorce instead. In so doing, they brought a plethora of causes, complaints, and requests to judges who gradually extended the number of acceptable causes—or urged the state legislature to do so—and made a wide variety of decisions concerning alimony, property, and child custody. In particular, judicial pliancy led to a broader definition of the ground of cruelty.

As divorce developed in the Northeast—the former New England and middle colonies—similar patterns emerged. One was the gradual abolition of legislative divorce, and another, a steady expansion of lists of grounds for divorce. Of the northeastern states, Connecticut created the most comprehensive divorce laws. In 1843 legislators added habitual intemperance and intolerable cruelty to an already generous list of grounds. In 1849 they added life imprisonment, committing an infamous crime, and the omnibus provision citing "any such misconduct as permanently destroys the happiness of the petitioner and defeats the purpose of the marriage relation."

During these years, new western states and territories tended to copy existing practices and laws, often adding refinements of their own. Divorce became more flexible and easier to obtain than in the East. For instance, in 1825, Illinois lawmakers restrained a guilty party from remarriage for two years rather than for life, allowed either wife or husband to obtain a divorce of bed and board for cruelty or intemperance, and efficiently divorced two couples (rather than one) with one legislative bill. In this land of mobility and haste, residency requirements for divorce were sometimes as low as ninety days, a situation that soon made western regions attractive divorce meccas for those who could afford temporary relocation.

Unfortunately, from divorcing women's point of view, little was done during these years to regulate and stabilize alimony, property, and child custody decisions. Most states referred such matters to judicial discretion, making settlements a lottery

C

COURTSHIP, MARRIAGE, SEPARATION, AND DIVORCE

The New Nation, 1776–1861

SPOUSAL ABUSE

Intolerable cruelty, such as wife beating, was one of the grounds for divorce in 1843 Connecticut, which had the most comprehensive divorce laws in the Northeast at the time.
CORBIS-BETTMANN

C

No laborer in the world is expected to work for room, board, and love— except the housewife.

LETTY COTTIN POGREBIN

See also
Nightlife

at best. Still, the effect of divorce upon early American women is unclear. While there is some evidence that New York and Louisiana provisions made it difficult for women to obtain divorces, the growing number of female petitioners in such states as Connecticut and Tennessee dispute the contention that divorce was punitive to women and difficult for them to obtain. American women of the early 1800s did have more recourse than their mothers and grandmothers.

At the time, Americans disagreed on the subject of divorce. Congregational minister Benjamin Trumbull in 1788 expressed his outrage when he learned that 390 couples had divorced in Connecticut during the preceding half-century. But in 1795, Judge Zephaniah Swift complimented Connecticut policymakers on their "temperate" divorce policies, which were conducive to "the virtue and happiness of mankind." Opponents of divorce believed the spread of divorce indicated decay and evil in society as well as breakdown in the family. They feared for the future of the nation and its people. Supporters argued that divorce dissolved dysfunctional marriages and released spouses to make better matches. They also believed freedom and happiness were rights of all people living in a democratic country.

Civil War to World War I, 1861–1914

Like all wars, the Civil War encouraged couples to marry in haste before men left for the battlefront. The war also created distances that heightened people's sense of romance. One young northern soldier claimed that only thoughts of his wife sustained him through battle, while a southern officer wrote to a friend that he avoided the pain of war by dreaming of the "fair and gentle wife" he would pursue once war ended.

During the postwar period, romance retained its hold on courting couples, but the nature of courtship itself gradually changed. Growing numbers of young women and men leaving home for college, young working women who lived in boardinghouses on their own or with other women, and finally the invention of the automobile caused the demise of the custom of men "paying calls" upon women. By the end of the nineteenth century, few women still had the power to decide if a man could come to her home and meet her family. Instead, he tendered the offer of a date, took her away from the safety of her home, paid for the date, and often expected at least a kiss in return. As the historian Beth Bailey put it, courtship was in the process of moving from the

front porch of a woman's home to the backseat of a man's automobile.

The post–Civil War era brought a number of significant modifications in American marriage as well. For one thing, the emancipation of African American slaves beginning in 1863 created an opportunity for newly freed slaves to register their marriages with legal authorities. Despite the widespread belief that slaves cared little about marriage, large numbers of freed blacks reported their marriages, and others searched for mates taken from them by sale. By the 1880s, African American marriages showed the same proportion of husbands present—approximately four out of five—as did those of white Americans of the same social classes and occupational categories.

Prejudice and discriminatory laws, attitudes, and practices, however, continued to discourage, or legally prohibit, black-white marriages. Both blacks and whites argued against interracial marriage because they feared the demise of the autonomy and integrity of their own race. But others argued for marriage between the races as a way of solving differences; blend black and white into one, and prejudice would disappear.

Marriage among whites was also a source of controversy and debate during the postwar years. By the late 1880s and 1890s, a rash of self-help books and marriage manuals appeared that revealed the pressing concerns of the day. Typical advice told people to marry for love rather than wealth or status, to pick someone with compatible interests, to avoid marrying someone to save him or her, and to institute mutual decision making and open communication in marriage. In 1909, Anna B. Rogers warned potential husbands and wives to avoid "the latter-day cult of individualism; the worship of the brazen calf of Self." She especially counseled women to remember that marriage was "their work," and to get "the germ of divorce"—selfishness and individualism—out of their veins (*Why American Marriages Fail* [1909], pp. 6–7, 16).

Novelists and essayists also dissected marriage, often supporting the traditional view. In 1880, Nathan Allen maintained in the *North American Review* that American individualism was destroying marriage, for it was a "supreme selfishness" that drove mates apart ("Divorces in New England" [June 1880], pp. 558–59). In 1902, *The Outlook* decried the breakdown of marriages because of the havoc wreaked on children who, through no fault of their own, were torn away from their mother or father and lacked any redress or rights to offset their suffering ("Children's Side of Divorce" [February 1902], pp. 478–80).

During the late 1800s and early 1900s, religious leaders joined the fray. Episcopal Bishop William C. Doane of Albany, New York, helped organize an Inter-Church Conference on Marriage and Divorce that met in 1903. At this conference, representatives from twenty-five religious denominations supported the ideal of lifetime marriage. Early in 1905, the Inter-Church Conference sent representatives to plead with President Theodore Roosevelt for help. In January of that year, President Roosevelt assured the committee that "questions like the tariff and the currency are of literally no consequence whatsoever when compared with the vital question of having the unit of our social life, the home, preserved." He proclaimed that "one of the most unpleasant and dangerous features of our American life is the diminishing birth rate, the loosening of the marital tie among the old native American families." Roosevelt declared that "no material prosperity, no business growth, no artistic or scientific development will count if the race commits suicide" (quoted in U.S. Department of Labor, *Marriage and Divorce*, 1861–1906 [repr. 1978], vol. 1, p. 4).

Certainly, Americans continued to believe in marriage. Even women who hoped to pursue a career now thought it was possible to be married as well. Although earlier generations of career women, such as Frances Willard, had eschewed marriage because of its demands and limitations, her successors married in greater numbers, worked toward companionate relationships, and continued to work. These college-educated women, however, bore no children or limited their childbearing.

In fact, after the Civil War the birthrate in general had begun to show signs of decline, especially in urban areas and among native-born women. Among immigrant women, first-generation women tended to produce large numbers of children, but second-generation women reduced their childbearing. Both birth control devices and abortion were responsible for the decline.

In 1873, the Comstock Law, which grew out of the American Medical Association's and the Young Men's Christian Association's campaign for the "suppression of vice," attacked both birth control and abortion. The Comstock Law prohibited "trade in, and circulation of, obscene literature and articles of immoral use." This included mail-order pessaries that women used to avoid conception. The act additionally banned "any arti-

cle or thing designed or intended for the prevention of conception or procuring of abortion." Because the birthrate failed to rise after its passage, it is likely that the Comstock Law did little more than anger many people and drive birth control and abortion underground.

At the same time, other people worried far more about the divorce rate than the birthrate as the inexorable forces of industrialization, urbanization, changing gender roles, and rising expectations of marriage continued to disrupt American marriages. In 1860, 1.2 of every 1,000 marriages ended in divorce; in 1864, 1.4 did so; and in 1866, 1.8 did so. Undoubtedly, the Civil War was partially responsible for this increase, but figures later collected by the U.S. Census Bureau showed that the number of divorces continued to increase even after the war ended. Between 1872 and 1876, divorces rose 17.9 percent over the late 1860s, and between 1877 and 1881, they rose 30.3 percent over the early 1870s.

During the post–Civil War period, Horace Greeley's *New York Tribune* aired a long-running divorce debate, women's rights' leader Elizabeth Cady Stanton spoke on behalf of divorce and free love, and the McFarland-Richardson divorce case of 1867 stunned the nation with its sex, intrigue, and blood. In 1872, esteemed minister Henry Ward Beecher was implicated in one of the most sensational divorce trials in American history. And during the 1880s and 1890s, South Dakota, North Dakota, and Oklahoma Territory spent fleeting moments in the limelight as divorce mills.

In 1881 the New England Divorce Reform League was organized; it soon became the National Divorce Reform League, and in 1896 the Family Protective League. Under the leadership of Congregational minister Samuel W. Dike, the league urged Congress to collect marriage and divorce statistics so the extent of the problem would be clear. The resulting statistics did nothing to calm people's minds. They showed plateaus in the divorce rate, but they also showed an overall upward trend. Many reformers believed a uniform national divorce law would at least stop migratory divorce and lower the divorce rate somewhat. Although Dike had doubts about how much migratory divorces contributed to the total, he worked for this cause until his death in 1913. Others carried on the campaign until 1947, but the states were unable to agree on a uniform set of laws and unwilling to give up their power to the federal government. In addition, women's rights leaders, divorce reformers, and social scientists argued for

Courting couples had little privacy and were seldom out of sight of family members in the small, crowded houses in which all members of the household often slept in the same room.

PAGE 414

C

**COURTSHIP,
MARRIAGE,
SEPARATION,
AND DIVORCE**

*World War I Through
World War II, 1914–1945*

THE "NEW" MORALITY

By 1910 a wave of "new" morality seemed to be sweeping America. Progressives and feminists called for freedom of choice in entering and leaving marriages. Socialist reformer Emma Goldman argued insistently for equality and free love, branded marriage obsolete, and advocated birth control six years before Margaret Sanger began her campaign. And in 1913, a middle-class woman named Sara Bard Field left her husband to live with attorney and reformer Charles Erskine Scott Wood without benefit of marriage.

By this time, Nevada had gained public attention by combining lax divorce laws, leisure pursuits, a pleasant climate, a six-month residency requirement (reduced to six weeks in 1931), and a long list of grounds for divorce. The city of Reno especially gained notoriety as a divorce mill. Eastern lawyers established branch offices there and advertised widely. The rich and famous—as well as average couples—responded, providing fodder for every journalist and reformer in the nation.

divorce as a protective device for wives and as a citizen's right in a free society.

World War I Through World War II, 1914–1945

By the time World War I erupted in 1914, further alterations were in the offing for American courtship and marriage. Social scientists began to argue that love and mate selection were at the mercy of such factors as propinquity, membership in ethnic and racial groups, and prospective mates' educational levels. Psychologists began to maintain that personality played a larger role in courtship than previously thought. In their view, if a person could reestablish the personality dynamics of his or her own home and parents with another person, they were likely to select that person despite his or her overall suitability as a mate. It seemed, then, that underlying forces directed the course of courtship and married love in the United States.

But the nature of courtship and marriage was altered far more by the birth control revolution than by scientific studies. In 1916, public health nurse Margaret Sanger founded the first birth control clinic in the nation. Although her oppo-

nents argued that birth control would lead to "race suicide," increased promiscuity, and lessened respect for motherhood, in 1921 Sanger organized the American Birth Control League to disseminate birth control information. By 1930, fifty-five birth control clinics existed in fifteen states. And by 1937, all states except Massachusetts and Connecticut permitted doctors to dispense birth control information to their patients. If they wished, married couples could now legally attempt to regulate family size.

America's entry into the war in 1917 fostered yet other revolutions in family life. Before men left for the front, many couples married in haste. And with so many men leaving the labor force, the federal government urged women—whether single or married—to take jobs, especially in war-related industries. By 1918 many women workers felt confident enough to seek better-paying positions, join labor unions, and participate in strikes and other militant actions.

When the war ended, conflict was inevitable. Because returning veterans wanted their jobs back, women workers experienced mass layoffs. While many women stayed in the labor pool by taking lower-paying jobs, others returned home, often grudgingly. During the 1920s, an emphasis on consumerism that raised people's expectations regarding standards of living and the material goods marriage should involve helped further erode marital satisfaction. By 1929 approximately one out of every six marriages ended in divorce, an all-time high.

Many Americans believed that people's increasing affluence and mobility, coupled with the availability of easy divorce in certain jurisdictions, contributed to the breakdown of marriages. Social scientists, psychologists, statisticians, social commentators, and novelists suggested other root causes of marital breakdown, including rising expectations of marriage, industrialization, decline in economic functions of the family, weakening of religious tenets, and the decreased stigma of divorce. Women's changing roles were especially blamed for divorce. Supposedly the leading culprits were woman suffrage, women's employment, the rising number of working mothers with small children, and the growing availability of birth control devices.

Statisticians attempted to test these hypotheses, but the figures proved fickle. Arranged one way, divorce statistics supported one assumption; arranged another way, they proved the validity of a different cause. The erratic collection of statistics also hampered analysis. Although govern-

See also
Adolescence

ment officials hoped to collect marriage and divorce statistics every ten years, the nation's entry into World War I in 1917 coincided with, and disrupted, the next scheduled survey. Data collection remained erratic until 1958, when the U.S. Census Bureau established divorce registration areas to facilitate the process.

After World War II, 1945–1991

After World War II, courtship and marriage took on a staid and traditional tone for over two decades. The back-to-the-home movement for women and a return to a belief in customary gender roles served as a buffer against a world marred by memories of the Great Depression and world war, by fear of nuclear weapons, and by anticommunist hysteria. To many Americans, stable family life, located in suburban sprawl and characterized by stay-at-home wives, seemed to be a hedge against the disintegration of the modern world.

During these postwar decades, more Americans married than in previous ones: single people accounted for 31 percent of the population in 1940, a figure that dropped to 23 percent in 1950, and to 21 percent in 1960. In both courtship and marriage, men were dominant figures; they proposed dates and marriage, earned and controlled money, and made a couple's larger decisions. Despite the increasing availability of birth control devices, the average American family produced two to four children, thus creating a "baby boom."

But when the "boomers" reached young adulthood, they questioned, and often rejected, their parents' beliefs and practices. By 1970 these young women and men, who, unlike their parents, had grown up in stable financial and political times, created and engaged in a plethora of protest activities, including the feminist movement. The baby-boom generation soon changed the face of courtship and marriage. For instance, women took some of the initiative in the courting process. During the late 1960s, American women began to go out in groups or alone, go to bars without male escorts, and join singles' groups. By the early 1990s, more women than men placed personal advertisements for dates and mates in newspapers and utilized dating services. Women's growing dedication to jobs and careers, and the resulting increase in their work hours, suggest that this trend will continue as they actively look for companionship through a quick and safe means.

Many Americans "courted" by living together before marriage. In 1988 the Census Bureau estimated that the number of unmarried couples living together, which included never-married,

divorced, and widowed people, had reached 2.3 million. Seven hundred thousand of these couples were raising children. Another 1.5 million same-sex couples were cohabiting, 92,000 of them with children.

Despite these changes in courtship, mate selection during the 1980s and early 1990s failed to be any more effective than in earlier times. Studies demonstrated that cohabiting couples tended to divorce sooner than couples who had not lived together before marriage. In 1989 a University of Wisconsin study indicated that 38 percent of cohabiting couples divorced within ten years, while only 27 percent of noncohabiting couples did so.

Psychologists argued that courtship had to take a different direction if it was to be effective, a direction that relied less on romance and more on common sense. In *The New Male-Female Relationship* (1984), psychologist Herb Goldberg recommended man-woman relationships based upon "authentic friendship, companionship, and sexuality" rather than "the romantic, illusion-filled approach to courtship and marriage" that dominated American culture.

Despite this advice, love continued to be the byword in marriage during the postwar period. Spouses valued each other's personal qualities above all other considerations. Once married, they often found themselves embroiled in arguments, but these were different arguments than their parents and grandparents had had. Two-

C

**COURTSHIP,
MARRIAGE,
SEPARATION,
AND DIVORCE**

*After World War II,
1945–1991*

A happy marriage is not so much how compatible you are, but how you deal with the incompatibility.

GEORGE LEVINGER
ESSAYIST

BABY BOOM

Following World War II, the average American family produced two to four children, thus creating the "baby boom."
CORBIS-BETTMANN

See also
Sexual Behavior and
Morality

C

**COURTSHIP,
MARRIAGE,
SEPARATION,
AND DIVORCE**

*After World War II,
1945–1991*

*Hit records praising
religion, marriage,
the family, parents,
individualism, and
America abounded
on the rock charts.*

PAGE 400

earner families argued over division of household tasks and child care, duties that in an earlier era would have fallen automatically in the woman's realm. Many wives expected to participate in financial decisions and planning, and demanded a voice in frequency and quality of sexual relations. In return, they expected their husbands to participate in disciplining and playing with children.

At the same time, effective and fairly reliable birth control, notably contraceptive pills, allowed couples to eliminate or to limit childbearing if they chose. For the first time in history, sexual relations and conception were separated into two functions, each with its own norms and expectations. In addition, by the late 1970s and early 1980s, women especially began to believe they did not need husbands to have children. Significant numbers of both poor, lower-class women *and* educated, middle-class women had babies without getting married. One-person and single-parent households mushroomed. By 1970, 17.1 percent of all American households consisted of only one person; by 1985, this figure reached 23 percent. In addition, single-parent families more than doubled. In 1985, single-parent families included 893,000 custodial fathers.

A growing tolerance for interracial marriages brought further diversity to the American family. In 1967 the U.S. Supreme Court struck down the last remaining miscegenation law in the United States, thus allowing black and white people to marry legally anywhere in the nation. Marriages that were mixed in terms of religion, ages, and other factors also increased and gained some acceptance. By the early 1990s, mixed marriages still exhibited a higher degree of stress and breakdown than homogamous matches, while the pattern and stability of homogamous marriage differed from group to group. Among Hispanics in the southwestern United States, for example, nearly 78 percent of Hispanic women between thirty-five and forty-four had a husband present, compared with approximately 68 percent among African Americans.

Americans tended to be far less tolerant of lesbian and gay couples who began to demand their right to legal marriage during the 1980s. Opponents called same-sex marriages outrageous and immoral, while supporters pointed out that Americans should be able to marry whomever they wished. In 1990 a special feature in *Newsweek* magazine noted that numerous same-sex couples were raising children without benefit of marriage. These children had been born in previous marriages, conceived by artificial insemination, conceived with a third person, or adopted. Clearly, the number of gay and lesbian couples who "married" during the early 1990s and the legal tangles

"NO-FAULT" DIVORCE

In 1970 California implemented no-fault divorce. No longer was divorce to be an adversary procedure in which the plaintiff had to blacken the reputation of the defendant. Other states soon followed California's lead. In 1971 Iowa became the second state to adopt no-fault divorce. By late 1977, only three states retained adversary divorce: Illinois, Pennsylvania, and South Dakota. Fifteen states had established irretrievable breakdown of a marriage as the sole ground for divorce, and sixteen had added irretrievable breakdown to existing grounds. By 1985, only South Dakota had fault divorce.

No-fault divorce changed divorce from the punishment of an offending spouse to a remedy for unendurable situations, made collusion between spouses unnecessary because one no longer had to "sue" the other, and provided relief to dissatisfied spouses on nonjudgmental grounds. Still, it was not the nirvana that reformers hoped it would be. In 1986

an article in the *New York Times Book Review* declared "no-fault" was "no fair." Its author reviewed several books that revealed the destructive effects of no-fault divorce on women and children, wives' lack of redress for a husband's adultery and defection from the marriage, and the failure of judges to offset women's low earnings with proportional alimony and property awards.

During the 1980s, experts tried to determine how legislators had adopted no-fault divorce without a searching analysis of what it might mean to women and children. Sociologist Lenore Weitzman explained that in the feminist flush of the late 1960s, legislators had envisioned wives as full economic partners. In practice, however, few wives earn as much as their husbands; many earn no cash income at all. The tragic result of no-fault divorce has been a contribution to the growing poverty of women and their children in the United States.

surrounding their children would soon demand adjudication and perhaps an adjustment in legal codes.

Many significant changes occurred in divorce after the end of World War II. In 1949 South Carolina ended its prohibition of divorce. In 1966 New York expanded its list of grounds for divorce from only adultery by adding cruelty, abandonment, confinement in prison, and living apart for two years. Separation also became a precondition for divorce in many states. Even conservative South Carolina accepted a couple's separation for two years as a ground for divorce.

One of the most revealing symptoms of these changing attitudes toward marriage and divorce was the growing self-help literature. In 1945, marriage manuals were common and divorce books were few. Typically, marriage manuals of the 1940s described marriage as a lifetime undertaking and advised wives to cater to their husbands to keep their marriages intact. Authors who did address the issue of divorce did so in dismal terms. They referred to divorce as the nation's "number one social problem" and declared that women who allowed it to happen to them would be shunned by family and friends. The postwar back-to-the home movement, the teachings of Dr. Benjamin Spock, and such popular magazines as *Life* reinforced the view that women were meant to be wives and mothers; any other choice would bring them only despair and disdain.

By the 1960s, however, such traditional ideas were under attack. In 1961 President John F. Kennedy created the President's Commission on the Status of Women, and in 1963 Betty Friedan's *The Feminine Mystique* exposed the frustrations women felt regarding domestic life. Self-help literature responded accordingly. Although women's emancipation was linked to the divorce rate during the 1920s, writers now sharply indicted women as culprits. Working wives were too aggressive, unable to combine work and marriage, and ready to dispute their husbands' every word. Should they divorce, however, that same aggressiveness would stand them in good stead, for they could expect to receive satisfactions from their work that other women derived from marriage.

During the 1970s, conventional wisdom concerning marriage and divorce expanded even more. Responding to the feminist call for marriage based on equality and communication, self-help authors urged wives and mothers to become independent beings who deserved respect and reciprocity in marriage. A host of books such as Jerry Greenwald's *Creative Intimacy* (1975) instructed readers, who were primarily women, how to achieve the ideal marriage. From self-counseling to biofeedback, from no-fault marriage to creative aggression, self-help manuals offered ways to avoid divorce.

By the mid 1970s and early 1980s, a huge number of divorce manuals had appeared. They carefully shunned the word "failure" and emphasized a practical approach to divorce instead. Because no-fault, community property, and other recent developments had complicated divorce, they explained its intricacies and included charts, worksheets, checklists, and time schedules. Still others specialized in emotional advice. Written largely by marriage counselors and psychotherapists, the books offered approaches developed through counseling patients and leading workshops. They stressed personal growth through divorce and the ability to find happiness as divorced people. Another new line was the emphasis on getting professional help—lawyers, accountants, and counselors. Marriage and divorce were no longer matters to be handled by the individual. Nor was divorce any longer a matter of embarrassment and shame.

The 1990s and Beyond

During the early 1990s, the great American debate concerning marriage and divorce continued. Some studies claimed that the marriage rate was rising—that marriage was back in style—while others predicted the end of marriage in the twenty-first century. At the same time, some studies maintained that the divorce rate continued to rise, while others argued that it was receding somewhat. Due to the variations and difficulties in methods of computation, statisticians were unable to agree upon one position or the other. Even after the U.S. Bureau of the Census established divorce registration areas in 1958 as a way of collecting necessary data, statistics remained erratic due to state inconsistencies in reporting and the common practice of including annulments and separations in divorce statistics. And as improved collection methods and computer analysis developed, it was soon clear that every means of computing the divorce rate had its weak point. For instance, comparing the number of divorces with the number of marriages in a given year ignores the fact that most divorces are of marriages contracted in previous years. And if the number of marriages in a given year is unusually low, the divorce rate will appear high. Or if the number of divorces is compared with the population in a given area and the population contains a large

The proper time for divorce is during the courtship.

DR. REUBEN HILL

See also
Manners and Etiquette

C

*At the time,
melodramas
depicted their
heroines in
situations that
often compromised
the dominant
ideals of marriage
and the family.*

PAGE 147

*I have great hopes
that we shall love
each other all our
lives as much as if
we had never
married at all.*

LORD BYRON
IN LETTER TO
ANNABELLA MILBANKE,
WHOM HE MARRIED A
MONTH LATER. SHE LEFT
HIM AFTER A YEAR.

number of children under marriageable age, the divorce rate will appear low. In other words, there is no such thing as a valid, conclusive divorce rate.

But what is clear, despite the method of computation, is that the overwhelming majority of Americans marry—and remarry—and remarry yet again. Marriage rates have held steady between 8 and 10 per 1,000 each year. Although the marriage rate drops during times of economic depression, it hovers around 10 per 1,000 during stable periods. The censuses of 1980 and 1990 indicated that the rate had held stable at around 9 to 10 per 1,000.

It was also clear that the overall trend in the divorce rate is upward. The rate rose after World War I, dropped somewhat during the Great Depression (although the number of desertions may very well have increased), rose after World War II, settled on a plateau between 1955 and 1963, and then began to rise again. Figures also show that since the end of World War II in 1945, urban areas continue to have more divorce than rural areas; African Americans divorce more frequently than other racial groups (although the divorce rate of Mexican Americans and Asians is rising); growing numbers of women employed outside the home seek divorces; an increasing number of families with children dissolve; and the West has the highest rate of divorce, the South is second, and the Northeast third.

If the divorce rate continues to rise, family relationships will become incredibly complicated. Statistics show that the more frequently a person divorces, the shorter the duration of his or her next marriage. In 1983 the average duration of marriage for all divorcing couples was 9.6 years; for the once-married, 10.8 years; for the twice-married, 7.0 years; and for the thrice-married, 4.9 years for women and 5.1 years for men. It may eventually become mandatory for remarriers to negotiate and sign prenuptial agreements to protect property and children.

Divorce has become more acceptable than ever before; it is commonplace in the media and in daily life. In 1990, "Mister Rogers" commented on the effect of the growth of divorce on his widely aired children's television program: "If someone told me twenty years ago that I was going to produce a whole week on divorce, I never would have believed them."

By 1990, another attitudinal change was evident. Although religious and other groups continued to support lifetime marriage and to oppose divorce, the numbers of divorces convinced them to recognize and attempt to deal with its exis-

tence. Most Catholic parishes, for example, required extensive premarital counseling, offered marital counseling and marital enrichment workshops, and organized workshops and other programs for separated and divorced Catholics.

Today, approximately one marriage out of two will end in divorce. Of course, this statistic neglects multiple remarriers and divorcers. It also overlooks the fact that people live far longer than they did during the nineteenth century; thus, divorce terminates a marriage that would have ended in the death of one spouse in earlier eras. It might also be speculated that given the modern system of computers, social security numbers, and other identification, it is more difficult for a spouse to desert than formerly. Perhaps a number of potential desertions become divorces instead.

This summary of courtship, marriage, separation, and divorce might well be interpreted as a distressing picture of the American family, one that seems to portend destruction and despair. Or it might be seen as a hopeful scenario. Because old norms are being challenged and changed does not necessarily indicate decline and social ills. It is far more likely that American society is in a transition phase—an evolution to new forms and mores. After all, in other contexts, Americans are fond of calling rapid change and lack of permanence by the name of progress.

Rather than bemoaning these changes, it is more helpful in the long run to devise constructive coping strategies. Courtship could be improved by counseling and education so that it functions as effective mate selection. Marriage and remarriage would benefit from increased community support, such services as child care, and extensive counseling resources. Separation could be used as an exploration and counseling period rather than as a road to divorce. And divorce could be accepted as a long-term historical trend, an integral part of American life that can be made into a more positive, healing institution than it is now. The old and continuing problems of support for a dependent spouse, division of property, and custody and care of children must be addressed more thoroughly and dealt with more effectively.

During the next few decades, diversity in American marriage and dissolution practices will surely continue. Many Mexican Americans, for example, are likely to cling to more traditional ideas, while Hollywood stars and other public figures will continue to engage in multiple marriages and divorces. American society may also find itself creating and accepting new forms of marriage and dissolution. Some couples have tried open marriage and cooperative marriage in recent decades. Many have tried no-fault divorce with a wide range of results. During the twenty-first century, however, contract marriage may become commonplace. And at time of divorce, one court may grant a dissolution while another may decide custody and financial arrangements. Premarital and post-divorce counseling may become mandatory.

Despite the potential changes, the historical record indicates that the American family will survive. Marriages may be short in duration, long-distance, two-career, or gay or lesbian, but Americans will continue to court, marry, and remarry in huge numbers. Perhaps it is fallacious to judge marital success by the length of a marriage. In coming years, marriage may increasingly be judged by the success it achieved while in force, the fulfillment of mates' expectations, and the harmony and positive nature of its dissolution, should it end.

—GLENDA RILEY

♦ **No-fault divorce**

Of, relating to, or being a divorce law under which neither party is held responsible for the breakup of the marriage

DEATH

Historical interest in death and dying has grown considerably since the 1960s. Both demographic and cultural studies of death and dying in the past have enriched the understanding of American social history and have provided a useful perspective for dealing with these issues in the present. Most of the studies of death and dying have been focused on colonial and nineteenth-century America with much less attention to developments in the twentieth century. Moreover, the monographic studies of death and dying often appear in obscure and hard-to-find publications so that it is difficult for the general reader to access them. As a result, despite the considerable expansion of literature on this topic, much of it has not been thoroughly integrated into the broader syntheses of American social development.

Colonial America

Earlier historians such as Oscar Handlin (1959) argued that death rates were high throughout colonial America and that this made stable family life nearly impossible. For their information on mortality rates, these scholars relied almost exclusively upon contemporary literary accounts, which reported high death rates in both the North and the South. According to these historians, the high death rates meant that few parents could expect to survive long enough to raise their own children. Coupled with the other disruptions of coming to the New World, the early settlers therefore created institutions such as churches and schools in order to overcome the problems created by the disruption of family life in the American wilderness.

More recent demographic studies of early America, including those by John Demos, Philip Greven, and Kenneth Lockridge, provide a very different picture—especially for New England. Using lists of births, deaths, and marriages and employing the technique of family reconstitution, demographic historians have provided much more accurate estimates of colonial mortality. Infant and child mortality rates were quite high in New England, but adult death rates in rural areas were surprisingly low. In colonial Andover or Plymouth, Massachusetts, for example, twenty-year-olds could expect to live more than another forty years. While adult death rates in larger towns such as Boston or Salem were considerably higher than in the countryside, more than 95 percent of the population lived in the smaller towns. As a result, family life in New England was much more stable demographically than previously suggested and most children even had the opportunity to know and interact with their grandparents.

Some analysts contend that female life expectancy in New England was considerably lower than that of males because of the dangers of childbearing. Certainly some women did die giving birth, but the overall evidence suggests that the extent of maternal mortality has been exaggerated. Nevertheless, colonial women greatly dreaded the dangers of childbearing, since death under those circumstances was particularly gruesome and painful. Moreover, Puritan ministers, in urging pregnant women to acknowledge and repent their sins, often reminded them that they were likely to die during childbirth—thereby reinforcing the impression that maternal mortality was very high in early America.

Even if adult mortality rates in colonial New England were lower than had been suggested, infant and child mortality remained high. Since most families had large numbers of children, high infant and child mortality meant that most families experienced the loss of at least one member of the household during the childbearing years. Moreover, periodic epidemics in both rural and urban areas contributed to the sense that life was short and unpredictable. In 1721, for example, during an outbreak of smallpox in Boston, about 10 percent of the entire population died. Puritan religion also placed great emphasis on death and dying and reinforced the notion that death was always imminent for both children and adults. Consequently, most adults in early New England underestimated their actual life expectancy and thought that they were likely to die at any moment—even though most of them survived for many more years.

I don't want to achieve immortality through my work. I want to achieve immortality through not dying.

WOODY ALLEN

D

Unlike the somber rites typical of many European American burials, those of African American slaves were frequently joyous, possibly featuring song and dance as well as libations, animal sacrifices, and grave decorations.

PAGES 18-19

Initially, Puritans did not devote much attention or many resources to burying their dead. The dying person was cared for at home and given a simple funeral. (Puritans buried their dead in both cemeteries and churchyards.) Over time, however, funerals became more elaborate and expensive. The practice of distributing gifts of gloves, rings, or scarves at funerals became so widespread that colonial legislatures tried unsuccessfully to curtail it. Funeral sermons, which earlier had been either avoided altogether or kept very simple, now became common and expected. The simple, wooden gravemarkers of the early seventeenth century were replaced by elaborately carved gravestones with symbolic illustrations of death. The image on many of the early gravestones was the death's-head, while on later ones angel's heads and weeping willows predominated. While historians are still debating the exact meaning or the significance of the changes of the symbols on New England gravestones, there is little doubt that by the eighteenth century the nature of the Puritan funeral had changed dramatically.

If adult death rates in rural New England were lower than earlier scholars had guessed, those in the South were as high as had been first suggested. Based upon extensive demographic studies of the Chesapeake region, it appears that because of the unhealthy climate, death rates in the seventeenth-century South were very high, for both children and adults. The life expectancy of twenty-year-olds in the Chesapeake was only another twenty to twenty-five years—about half that of their rural counterparts in New England. High mortality rates, combined with a great excess of males over females, made family stability difficult in the South. In seventeenth-century Middlesex County, Virginia, only 46 percent of children age thirteen had both of their parents alive and that figure dropped to 31 percent by age eighteen. While mortality rates appear to have improved in the second half of the seventeenth century, they continued to be much higher than in New England.

Given the high mortality and family instability in the Chesapeake, settlers looked for alternative ways to care for orphaned children. Unlike the situation in New England, most of the early settlers to the Chesapeake did not come with any kin who might take care of their orphans in an emergency. High adult mortality rates also meant that few children had any living grandparents to care for them if their parents died. Instead, the roles of godparents were expanded as they were expected to look after the orphans. In addition, special courts were set up to protect the estates of young children who had lost their parents.

The high adult mortality in the Chesapeake also discouraged the early planters from importing African slaves; it was more economical to bring short-term white indentured servants who were less expensive and therefore presented a smaller loss to the planter if they died. Once mortality conditions in the Chesapeake improved, however, it became profitable to import African slaves; even though the initial cost of an African slave was considerably higher than that of an indentured servant, the slaves worked for the planter for the rest of their lives, and their children remained the property of the master. Partly as a result of the improvements in mortality rates in the South, the proportion of African slaves in the population increased rapidly in the late seventeenth and early eighteenth centuries.

Throughout colonial America, widows found it difficult to survive unless their husbands had left them an unusually large estate. Therefore most widows with young children tried to remarry as quickly as possible in order to support their families. Remarriage was much easier in the South because of the greater shortage of women there than in the North. Older women and those with young children found it more difficult to remarry than younger widows with no children. Widows who were unable to remarry had to support themselves by working or receiving assistance from their relatives or neighbors. Those who were unable to sustain themselves were forced to rely upon the very limited and inadequate local town or county poor relief. Despite continued public professions about the importance and value of families, colonial Americans often were willing to separate indigent widows from their children if this reduced the welfare burden on the rest of the community.

Nineteenth-Century America

There is considerable disagreement on the course of mortality in nineteenth-century America. Some scholars think that mortality increased in the antebellum period as the United States became more urbanized and industrialized while others maintain that it decreased as per capita incomes rose. Much of the disagreement stems from the use of inadequate and faulty eighteenth- and nineteenth-century life tables (actuarial tables based on age-specific mortality statistics). The most commonly used life tables of the period, the Wigglesworth Life Table of 1789 or the Jacobson Life Table of 1850, are methodologically seriously flawed and misleading. Moreover, most of the existing life tables are based only upon Massachusetts, which was more urbanized than the rest of the nation and therefore not representative of the country as a whole. Several recent studies, however, have provided more accurate life tables for that period. For the New England area, for which the best evidence exists, mortality rates seem to have been fairly stable from the late eighteenth century to the Civil War. After the Civil War there appears to have been a gradual improvement in life expectancy.

Despite the worsening of environmental conditions in some American cities owing to population concentration and the negative health effects of early industrial development, public health measures such as the introduction of sewage disposal and the improvement of the drinking water helped contain or even reduce mortality levels. Concerns about high rates of infant mortality also led to efforts to sanitize the milk supply—though most of these public health improvements came only after 1900. It is clear that by the 1890s mortality was declining in both rural and urban areas throughout most of the United States.

Antebellum Americans were concerned and fascinated with death, but their images of death became softened and muted over time, as people became more optimistic that they might be among the saved and would go to heaven when they died. Dying people continued to be cared for at home and most of the funeral preparations were carried out by friends and neighbors. Only in the larger cities after the Civil War did funeral directors emerge as a specialized profession to help to dispose of the dead.

A great deal of attention was paid to how one died. The ideal ritual occurred at home with the dying person saying goodbye to family and friends. He or she was also expected to reflect calmly on past deeds and express confidence of soon entering heaven. When the idealized death rituals were followed, the survivors sometimes published these accounts as a guide for others. Pressure was placed on the dying person to suppress any fears or anxieties about the future and to acknowledge the supremacy and wisdom of God. When the dying person did not follow the prescribed steps, however, those present were usually confused and embarrassed. Compared to the early colonial period, nineteenth-century clergymen played a more active role in officiating at both the bedside of the dying person as well as at the grave.

Having a proper funeral was deemed especially important. A great fear of many, especially mem-

bers of the lower classes, was that they might die alone and unattended or be buried as a pauper. Special programs were set up to provide for burial insurance, some by the many fraternal lodges, especially those for immigrants and members of the working class. While some efforts were made to purchase life insurance to support the widow and surviving children, most nineteenth-century Americans either were not interested in such policies or could not afford them.

Whereas cemeteries in colonial America had not attracted much attention or care, in the nineteenth century much more effort was made to landscape and maintain a rustic burial site. A few widely publicized rural cemeteries, like Mount Auburn (established in 1831) just outside Cambridge, Massachusetts, were established, which permitted the living and the dead to share pleasant surroundings. These rural cemeteries captured the imagination of contemporaries and historians have devoted considerable attention to them. Yet most people continued to be buried in more traditional and less expensive cemeteries, while the poor and minorities were often still relegated to an ignominious burial in a potter's field.

Fears of dying in childbirth continued into the nineteenth century, but the social context of that experience was altered. Increasingly in northern cities, male doctors replaced midwives in superintending the birthing process. Gradually the male doctors tried to eliminate the female friends and relatives from the scene so that pregnant women now had to face this ordeal isolated from their traditional sources of emotional support and comfort. Yet it was only in the early twentieth century, as children were increasingly delivered in a hospi-

DEATH OF CHILDREN

There is considerable debate over how emotionally upset colonial and nineteenth-century Americans were over the deaths of very young children. Some scholars have maintained that given the high infant mortality of the period, parents did not immediately invest emotionally in their newborn children and therefore did not grieve very much if their children died young. Although grieving parents were often restrained by religious and societal conventions from expressing themselves fully, there is considerable evidence to suggest that most parents deeply mourned the loss of even young infants.

See also
Parades, Holidays and
Public Rituals

Life is a great surprise. I do not see why death should not be an even greater one.

VLADIMIR NABOKOV

tal, that male doctors finally gained full control over the birthing process and eliminated the presence of close female friends and family. While the health care professionals who replaced the friends and family provided better medical treatment, they were not as attentive to the emotional needs of the expectant mother.

Widowhood continued to be difficult for most women in nineteenth-century America. Poverty and the difficulties of raising children by themselves led most widows to remarry if possible. Widows who could no longer provide for their young children were likely to enter an almshouse or have their children placed in an orphanage. According to a study of Petersburg, Virginia, during the period 1784 to 1860, wealthier widows who could maintain themselves economically were reluctant to remarry as reentering matrimony meant giving up some of their new freedoms from male dominance.

Historians have often minimized the role of wars in affecting the life course of Americans. Indeed, social historians specializing in the nineteenth century have almost entirely ignored the importance of the Civil War, even though the number of men who died in that conflict alone (nearly 620,000) is almost larger than the combined total number who died in all other American wars. Compare the approximately 50,000 American troops who died in the Vietnam War or the 400,000 killed in World War II. The relative devastation of the Civil War becomes even more apparent when death rates are compared: while there were approximately 2 deaths per 10,000 population in the Vietnam War and 30 deaths per 10,000 population in World War II, there were 180 deaths per 10,000 in the Civil War. Nearly 10 percent of the white military-age population in 1860 died in the Civil War. The losses were particularly high in the South, where almost one out of every five white southern males between thirteen and forty-three in 1860 died. While relatively few African Americans were allowed to fight for their freedom in the Civil War, those who did were more likely to die than their white counterparts in the northern armies.

The impact of the war not only decimated the male population, but it also left large numbers of widows. One estimate is that in 1890 there were about 195,000 Civil War widows—or about 10 percent of all widows at that time. Special orphanages were often created by states to care for the surviving children, and an elaborate and expensive pension system was devised for Union widows. An analysis of rural and urban widows in

Massachusetts and Michigan suggests that those receiving federal pensions were less likely to be compelled to join the labor force than those who were ineligible for such assistance. Since federal pension benefits were revoked if the widow remarried, the system may have also encouraged some of them to remain single. Overall, the federal pension system to surviving Union veterans or their widows was a very large and expensive program. In 1893, for example, more than 40 percent of the entire federal budget went for pensions for Union veterans or their widows. Although a few Southern states in the late nineteenth century provided some pensions, most Confederate widows did not receive any pensions (and those who did received only a small amount). Only in 1958 were federal benefits made available to Confederate soldiers and their survivors.

Not only did the Civil War affect America demographically, it also may have had a profound effect on the ways in which Americans viewed death. Before the Civil War, they were comfortable and open in their discussions, but the great loss of men during the war made it more difficult for many Americans to deal forthrightly with death. As a result, a preliminary study of mentions of death in short stories in popular magazines revealed a dramatic drop during the Civil War; afterwards, the total number of mentions of deaths in the short stories never recovered to pre–Civil War levels. Moreover, when there were mentions of death in the short stories after the Civil War, they were less explicit and direct; usually they referred to death and dying only euphemistically.

Twentieth-Century America

Compared to the mortality data for the seventeenth, eighteenth, and nineteenth centuries, the information for the twentieth century is much more plentiful (though the data for the early twentieth century are not as reliable as those for the mid twentieth century). Therefore, it is possible to document the rapid improvements in mortality rates during the past ninety years.

There was a great improvement—indeed, a great revolution—in life expectancy at birth. In 1900 the average child born could expect to live 47.3 years; that figure jumped to 59.7 years by 1930 and to 69.7 years by 1960. In 1986 the average life expectancy at birth was 74.8 years—or 27.5 years more than in 1900.

Most of the increase in life expectancy at birth was due to the great reductions in infant and child mortality. In 1915 the infant mortality rate was 99.9 deaths per 1,000 live births; in 1930 the rate dropped to 64.6 deaths and in 1960 the rate was down to 26.0 deaths. In 1987 the rate of infant mortality is only 10.1 deaths per 1,000 live births. While the United States continues to have a higher rate of infant mortality than most other advanced nations, there has been a tremendous improvement since the turn of the century.

Improvements in life expectancy at older ages have not been as dramatic as at younger ages. For example, in 1900 the average white male at age twenty could expect to live another 42.2 years, while in 1986 he could look forward to another 53.4 years. Similarly, in 1900 the average white male at age sixty could expect to live another 14.4 years, while in 1986 his remaining life expectancy was 18.2 years.

THE MORTALITY GAP

While the gap in life expectancy between whites and African Americans has been declining, the differential between women and men has been actually increasing, for both African Americans and whites. In 1900 female life expectancy at birth was 48.3 years (against 46.3 years for males). In 1986 female life expectancy at birth had risen to 78.3 years (against 71.3 years for males). In other words, while females at birth could expect to live two years longer than their male counterparts in 1900, that differential increased to seven years by 1986.

Notably, maternal mortality has declined. In 1915 there were 60.8 maternal deaths per 10,000 live births; in 1930 that figure had risen to 67.3 deaths, but dropped to only 3.7 deaths in 1960 and a relatively rare 0.7 per 10,000 births in 1986. While maternal mortality rates for African Americans continued to be twice as high as for whites in the 1990s, for neither group was the likelihood of dying in childbirth as large or as frightening as it had been in colonial and nineteenth-century America.

The explanations for this revolution in mortality are complex, but fundamentally Americans experienced an epidemiologic revolution during the twentieth century. In 1900 the leading causes of death were pneumonia-influenza-bronchitis, tuberculosis, and diarrhea and enteritis. Today, degenerative and man-made diseases are the major causes of death with heart disease, cancer, and stroke leading the field.

Race and gender differences in life expectancy continued in the twentieth century. In 1900 the life expectancy at birth of African Americans was 33.0 years (against 47.6 years for whites). By 1986 the life expectancy of African Americans had risen to 69.4 years (against 75.4 years for whites). Thus, while there continued to be differences between the races, the size of the gap in life expectancy at birth narrowed from 14.6 years in 1900 to 6.0 years in 1986. Concern about the differences in mortality continued into the 1990s, with particular attention to the higher rates of mortality among African American infants and the growing number of homicides among African American young males.

Not only was there a great decrease in death rates during the century, but birth rates fell as well. The combination has had a great impact on the likelihood of children experiencing the loss of a family member. Peter Uhlenberg has calculated that the likelihood of children experiencing the loss of one or both parents before age fifteen dropped from 24 percent in 1900 to 5 percent in 1976 ("Death in the Family," pp. 313–320). Moreover, the probability of that same child experiencing the loss of a nuclear family member (parent or sibling) decreased dramatically from 50 percent in 1900 to 10 percent in 1976. Finally, the changes in mortality have also affected the likelihood of having grandparents. In 1900 less than one out of five children at age fifteen had three or more grandparents alive, whereas in the 1990s that figure had risen to 55 percent. Thus, whereas death was a common and integral part of growing up in the early twentieth century, it has become much less salient for most children in the late twentieth century.

The decrease in death rates also greatly affected single-parent households. In the past, most single-parent households were the result of the death of either the father or the mother. Even as late as 1970, 18.5 percent of children living in a single-parent household resided in ones created by the death of a father. Yet in 1986 only 1.4 percent of all children under eighteen lived in a single-parent household headed by a widow; and of all children living in single-parent households, only 6.7 percent of them were due to the death of one of the parents. In other words, whereas single parenting in the past resulted mainly from the death of one of the spouses, in the 1990s death accounted for only a tiny fraction of single-parent households.

The provision for the care of widows and orphans has also changed greatly in the twentieth

See also
Old Age

century. In colonial and nineteenth-century America, widows were expected to take care of themselves and their children. If they could not support themselves, they risked being sent to a poorhouse or having their families broken up, with their children sent to an orphanage or apprenticed to some employer. In the late nineteenth and early twentieth centuries, however, there was a concerted movement to keep dependent children in their own homes rather than sending them to any institution. As a result of this new emphasis on the importance of home care, efforts were made to find alternative ways of helping widows with children.

One very popular and innovative program was the development of mothers' pensions. Illinois passed the first state mothers' pension program in 1911, which provided assistance for widowed, deserted, and never-married mothers with children. The mothers' pension programs were quickly adopted by many other states. Reactions against the provision of assistance for divorced and never-married mothers meant that the bulk of the money went to widows, who made up 82 percent of all those receiving assistance in 1931. African American widows were eligible for these benefits, but they were less likely to receive them than their white counterparts. While in theory the mothers' pensions were intended to allow women to stay at

home with their children, in practice most widows were expected to enter the labor force and contribute to the family income. Nevertheless, despite the small amounts of money available and the continued discrimination against certain categories of needy mothers, the state mothers' pension programs were an improvement over the colonial and nineteenth-century forms of welfare assistance.

With the collapse of the funding for many of the state programs during the Great Depression, the federal government stepped in to assist poor mothers and their children under the Social Security Act of 1935. The Aid to Dependent Children portion of this legislation was modeled on the state mothers' pension programs and explicitly provided financial assistance for children of widows as well as for those of divorced, separated, and never-married mothers. The number of families receiving such assistance doubled within two years compared with those who had received aid through the state mothers' pension programs. While the Social Security Act of 1935 provided for equal treatment of children regardless of the status of the mother, the revision in 1939 reversed this policy and privileged the children of widows.

Children of widows in the 1990s continued to enjoy a significant differential in income compared to other single-parent families. In 1982 the

**CIVIL WAR
DECIMATION**

*The Civil War decimated the
male population and left large
numbers of widows. Rows of
white grave markers fill a large
Civil War cemetery, shown
here, in Alexandria, Virginia.*
U.S. ARMY MILITARY
HISTORY INSTITUTE / CORBIS

See also
Transportation and Mobility

FUNERAL PRACTICES IN THE TWENTIETH CENTURY

Although funeral directors came into being in some urban areas in the second half of the nineteenth century, it was only in the twentieth century that they came virtually to monopolize the disposal of the dead in the United States. While many view the role of funeral directors as comforting and helpful, others have denounced them as unnecessary and exploitive. Jessica Mitford's best-selling *The American Way of Death* caused a sensation in 1963 by ridiculing how Americans buried their dead and attacking the funeral directors for taking advantage of people during their period of grief. While her overall analysis of the American way of death was more anecdotal than analytic and based upon an inadequate understanding of the history of American practices, her calls for reforming the funeral industry were heeded by the Federal Trade Commission.

In other societies burials are not always the preferred way of disposing of the dead. In Japan, for example, over 90 percent of those who die are cremated. While cremation was advocated by some American reformers in the late nineteenth century, it has not attracted a sizable following in this country though there is a slight increase in its popularity today. In 1976 about 7 percent of Americans who died were cremated, while by 1985 the figure had risen to almost 13 percent. Nevertheless, more Americans were trying to reduce the costs of their burials by joining memorial societies, which provide consumer education and alternatives to traditional funerals. During the 1960s and 1970s memorial societies grew rapidly in the United States and it is estimated that in 1983 there were approximately 175 such societies, with a total membership of about 500,000.

American concerns with death and funerals in the twentieth century were not confined to human beings. A surprising number of Americans are concerned about the disposal of their pets. The oldest pet cemetery in the United States, the Hartsdale Canine Cemetery, was established in 1896 in New York, and today there are over five hundred pet cemeteries in operation.

total cash income of widows was $17,799 in mother-only white families, while their counterparts in divorced ($13,845), separated ($10,122), and never-married ($7,812) families had much lower income. In large part this disparity was due to the fact that benefits provided through the Survivors' Insurance were much higher than those available through the Aid to Families with Dependent Children (AFDC).

If the demography and economics of death and dying have changed in the twentieth century, so have the institutional and cultural settings. In colonial and nineteenth-century America, most people died in their own homes or those of friends. In the late twentieth century, however, most people died in some institution. In 1949, 49.5 percent of deaths took place in an institution; in 1958 that figure increased to 60.9 percent, and in 1968 it rose to 68.1 percent. Moreover, in urban areas like New York City the percentage of deaths occurring in an institution was even higher. As the scene of dying shifted from a home to an institution, the dying person was isolated from friends and relatives. Professionals replaced close acquaintances in the last moments and the separation of the dying from the rest of society made it easier for people to deny the existence of death. Whereas deathbed scenes were central to the rit-

ual of dying in colonial and nineteenth-century America, today many Americans die without any last-minute interactions with their loved ones.

During most of the twentieth century, Americans were reluctant to discuss or even acknowledge the presence of death and dying. Since the 1960s, however, there has been much more public and scholarly attention given to dying people, much of it due to the efforts of Elisabeth Kübler-Ross, who popularized the idea that people should interact with the dying rather than trying to pretend that they do not exist.

Her best-selling book, *On Death and Dying*, argued that dying patients went through five stages: denial and isolation, anger, bargaining, depression, and acceptance. While her pioneering work did much to encourage people to treat the dying person as a human being, she may have unwittingly created a twentieth-century model of the "good" death that is at times counterproductive. Although Kübler-Ross claimed that her five-stage model was based upon careful, scientific clinical work with dying patients, closer scrutiny suggests that her research was inadequate and impressionistic. Critics of Kübler-Ross have pointed out that many dying patients do not experience the five stages or go through them in the sequence suggested by her model. The danger is that some

*We feel and know
that we are eternal.*

SPINOZA

*In nineteenth
century America, the
family doctor would
be fetched for births
and deaths and saw
it as his role to
comfort the family.*

PAGE 202

health practitioners have accepted Kübler-Ross's stages as not only descriptive but also prescriptive. Dying patients who do not follow the prescribed model are sometimes castigated by health professionals as being deviant and forced into adjusting their behavior to the Kübler-Ross model. As a result, just as the nineteenth-century rituals of dying were both a source of comfort and difficulty for the dying person, so Kübler-Ross's twentieth-century model proved to be both helpful and problematic.

Despite the growing awareness of death and dying in the 1990s, many Americans still found it difficult to discuss or even acknowledge the presence of death. Moreover, while there were some significant improvements in the clinical understanding of the bereavement process, American society as a whole was not very emotionally supportive of those who have lost a loved one. As a result, Americans still did not handle bereavement as well as their colonial and nineteenth-century ancestors, who regarded death as an inevitable and natural part of life.

—MARIS A. VINOVSKIS

FILM

In 1872, Leland Stanford, a former California governor, wagered $25,000 that a galloping horse lifted all four legs from the ground simultaneously and hired Eadweard Muybridge to shoot an experimental set of photographs to prove his point. The first experiment failed, but five years later, the two men tried again. At a Sacramento racetrack in 1877, they set up a track equipped with trip wires connected to twenty-four cameras, so that the horses set off the cameras' shutters as they galloped past, momentarily airborne.

The Invention of the Movies

The resulting set of photographs—which looked much like the minutely changing still frames on a strip of twentieth-century celluloid movie film—won Stanford's bet for him. Stanford's experiment with Muybridge also, inadvertently, proved to be a major innovation in the scientific study of motion and the development of the motion-picture camera. Muybridge's series of still photographs created an illusion of motion that impressed the French scientist and inventor Étienne-Jules Marey. Marey had previously worked with photography to re-create action, but never with Muybridge's success. It was Marey who made the technical breakthroughs that gave rise to the motion-picture camera in 1882.

The American inventor Thomas A. Edison pushed the new inventions further toward an entertainment medium. Working with his assistant, William K. L. Dickson (an often-unacknowledged contributor to the cinematic inventions attributed to Edison), the famous inventor attempted to devise a means of projecting the film sequences that captured an illusion of motion. In-

♦ **Trip wire**

A low-placed concealed wire used especially in warfare to trip an enemy or trespasser and usually to trigger an alarm or explosive device when moved

LEADING TO MOVIES

Muybridge's series of photographs created an illusion of motion that impressed the French scientist and inventor Étienne-Jules Marey, whose technical breakthroughs gave rise to the motion picture camera in 1882.
LIBRARY OF CONGRESS / CORBIS

*The cinema is not
an art which films
life: the cinema is
something between
art and life.*

JEAN-LUC GODARD
DIRECTOR

terestingly, Edison's first experiments with motion pictures were attempts to coordinate moving images with sound as a visual accompaniment for his new invention of the phonograph. The synchronization of the aural with the visual was quickly abandoned, however, as a futile effort, and Dickson's endeavors turned toward perfecting silent motion pictures. It took approximately thirty more years—until 1927—for sound to accompany the moving pictures.

In 1891, Dickson discovered how to make motion-picture film by perforating the celluloid so that it moved through the camera. Later that same year, he invented a boxlike machine through which the images could be projected. Looking through an opening in the top of the machine, an individual viewer could see the pictures move. By 1891, Edison had been granted a patent for both Dickson's camera, the kinetograph, and his projecting device, the kinetoscope.

What emerged in the 1890s, as inventors in several countries competed to perfect the motion-picture camera, was a primitive entertainment device. The first "movies" were projected in peep shows, not on the large screens associated with the cinema today. In April 1894, Edison first demonstrated the kinetoscope on Broadway in New York for the relatively high price of twenty-five cents. There, peering through a binocularlike lens, a single spectator could see tiny figures juggling balls or ocean waves washing toward the shore. It was an instant success with audiences, who waited eagerly to see the tiny living pictures.

But Edison's greatest ambition was a more realistic projection of moving pictures on a human scale. Unlike the inventor-scientist Marey, Edison was a shrewd businessman and self-promoter who turned the new discovery into profitable entertainment for the masses. Edison's earliest films were simple, nonnarrative documentations of the fact that motion could be preserved on film. In 1903, *Electrocuting an Elephant* illustrated the death of a circus elephant that had gone berserk. One of the first uses of trick photography in film was in a short titled *The Execution of Mary, Queen of Scots* (1895), in which an actress was filmed walking to the block. A dummy was then substituted for the beheading, and the resulting footage spliced together. Such early films were already purveyors of sensationalist entertainment.

In films usually running under ninety seconds, the earliest motion pictures thus simply entertained vaudeville theater audiences with the magic of the new invention. Dickson began shooting short segments of the era's variety-show acts, such

as Annie Oakley, Buffalo Bill Cody, and the dancer Ruth St. Denis. Other film promoters shot prizefights as a means of making the new medium popular and profitable in peep shows.

It was in Paris in 1895, however, that motion pictures were first projected to a large audience who paid for the entertainment. The brothers Auguste and Louis Lumière had experimented with motion-picture equipment in France; they expanded on Dickson's kinescope and kinetograph, developing a projector they called the *cinématographe*. It is in this term that the current word "cinema"—from the Greek for "motion"—has its origins. The cinématographe was capable of projecting film on a screen, allowing many people to view motion pictures at once.

The invention of what we currently know as "the movies" is thus the product of many inventors. Once both the camera and the projection equipment had been invented, entrepreneurs quickly scrambled for a way to make the new motion pictures profitable. Edison, rapidly working from the ideas of the Lumière brothers, developed his own projector, called the vitascope. In the spring of 1896, he premiered his invention at Koster and Bial's Music Hall in New York. The showing included short films of women dancing,

NICKELODEONS
The First Movie Theaters

It was not long before audiences grew tired of the novelty of watching simple pictures move. The next step forward in the development of the entertainment medium was its evolution as a narrative form. When, around the turn of the century, films began to tell stories, another important development in the evolution of the motion picture occurred: theaters rose that devoted their bills solely to film.

Called nickelodeons, after the five-cent price of admission, the new storefront theaters sprang up in cities all over the country. By 1905, neighborhood theaters were finding increasingly enthusiastic audiences, pushing their coins across box office windows to watch an entire bill of short, often one-reel, films. It was not long before thousands of nickelodeons existed throughout the United States; in 1907, one estimate figured that five thousand of the theaters were in operation, drawing primarily working-class audiences.

a comic portrayal of a boxing match, and—most popular of all—scenes of high waves breaking dramatically on a shore.

Soon, motion pictures were running on the bill of vaudeville programs, where they followed comedy acts or song-and-dance skits. Such films typically ran at the end of live vaudeville shows, becoming known as "chasers"—the act that signaled it was time to leave.

The First Narrative Films and the First Studios

One of the most sophisticated motion pictures of this period is *The Great Train Robbery*, directed by Edwin S. Porter in 1903. In his use of close-ups and parallel editing, Porter created a visual sense of suspense and action that made his film a popular success. Using many shots of both interior and exterior scenes, the film raced quickly from one action to the next, following the railroad bandits through the countryside with heightening drama. While Porter's techniques brought new life to the cinema, his themes also captured an important element of America—the legend of the West in all its violent lawlessness.

Porter's development of film techniques, especially the sophistication of his editing, provided important building blocks for the new art form. At the time of Porter's greatest success, Hollywood had not yet been born as the location of America's "dream machine." Several factors created the West Coast mecca for the movies: it had an ideal climate and it offered raw, dramatic scenery unavailable at the studios on the East Coast. Most important, however, the Hollywood site, with its distance from the East Coast and its proximity to Mexico, offered independent film companies some modicum of protection from Edison's Motion Picture Patents Company (MPPC), commonly known as the Trust.

In 1908, Edison had formed a group of nine film-producing companies and one importer, all agreeing to share the patents that each company held. In an effort to dominate the industry, the ten companies made an agreement with Eastman Kodak (the nation's only manufacturer of raw film stock) that the Kodak product would be sold only to MPPC members. To further consolidate their control, the Trust companies licensed only select distributors and exhibitors for their films. They thus threatened both to outlaw all other companies and to prevent new ones from forming. Edison's shrewd business tactics paid off handsomely; his annual profits skyrocketed after the formation of the Trust.

Several renegade film companies fled to the West Coast and set up business in the inviting climate of southern California. It proved to be a lucrative move for the independents. The competition between the independents and the Trust, however, had several positive results for the film industry. In order to compete with the MPPC, the independent companies took risks and experimented in ways that the conservative Trust members did not need to. Independents such as Carl Laemmle, with his Independent Motion Picture Company (1909), invested in the quality of their films, so that by 1915, when the MPPC was broken up after the Supreme Court's *Mutual Film Corporation* v. *Industrial Commission of Ohio* decision, the Independent motion pictures were generally of better quality than the lower-budget, short MPPC pictures.

In 1909, Laemmle tried one of the most enterprising tactics of all when he initiated a phenomenon that later film audiences would take for granted—the star system. Prior to the rise of the star system, the actors and actresses in early silent films remained uncredited, and the anonymous stars were identified by fans simply by titles such as the "Girl with the Curls" or as "Little Mary," the character often played by the actress who would later become famous as Mary Pickford. Recognizing the curiosity that audiences had for the anonymous early film "stars," Laemmle made the unprecedented move of releasing personal information about the actress Florence Lawrence. The shrewd film producer first gave false information to the press about the actress, claiming that she had been killed in an accident. The resulting outcry from fans proved Lawrence's box office appeal. Laemmle quickly retracted the information, and brought Lawrence before a new set of adoring, curious fans. When Lawrence had worked for Biograph Pictures and then with Laemmle's Independent Motion Pictures, she was known only as the "Biograph Girl" or the "IMP Girl."

Following the release of Florence Lawrence's name, the surge of public interest in the actress made the identification of featured actors and actresses commonplace—and launched the star system. The new celebrities provided audiences with fantasy figures, and it was not long before fan magazines and posters catered to the curiosity of moviegoers. As the American public looked to the larger-than-life figures on the screen for their ideals of human perfection and romantic fantasies, the stars became valuable commodities. Salaries of actors and actresses quickly skyrock-

FILM

The First Narrative Films and the First Studios

The Mercury Theatre troupe was soon lured to Hollywood where it scored its greatest triumphs, the watershed motion pictures Citizen Kane *(1941) and* The Magnificent Ambersons *(1942).*

PAGE 497

See also
Rock and Roll

eted to as much as $10,000 a week for Charlie Chaplin in 1916. As their power increased within the industry, actors and actresses even began to form their own companies, the biggest being United Artists, established in 1919 by Mary Pickford, Charlie Chaplin, Douglas Fairbanks, and D. W. Griffith.

One of the most important outcomes of the competition brought on by the Trust was the creation of the feature film. In order to draw more middle-class audiences and to secure respect for the often-criticized new entertainment form, independent filmmakers began to experiment with longer motion pictures. During the Progressive Era, feature films, such as those made by IMP, slowly began to rival the MPPC's one-reelers and bill of shorts with a single movie attraction.

A lesser-known film than Griffith's famous southern epic is the black cinematic response to it. Booker T. Washington and his assistant, Emmett J. Scott, felt that the best protest would be for a black motion-picture company to make a film that would be a counterpoint to *The Birth of a Nation.* After many months of fund-raising and organizing (during which Washington died), *The Birth of a Race* was released in 1918. Its makers were a panoply of filmmaking interests including the white Selig Polyscope Company and Daniel Frohman, a vaudeville producer. Unfortunately,

neither the film company nor its final product were what Booker T. Washington had originally hoped to achieve. The makers were not the all-black company he and Scott had worked so hard to establish. The result was virtually two films—shot independently by both Selig and Frohman—and was blasted by critics who thought the two halves haphazardly pasted together.

While *The Birth of a Race* was a critical failure, it succeeded in one important area: it inspired black filmmakers to work all the harder to secure a powerful cinematic voice. In 1915, the Lincoln Motion Picture Company had been formed by the African American actor Noble Johnson, who, with his brother George, began to make films that bolstered the position of blacks in society. Lincoln's first film, *The Realization of a Negro's Ambition,* showed an Alabama farm boy graduating from Tuskegee Institute and then heading west to work in the oil business. He is first denied a job because of his race, but he heroically saves the boss's daughter from an accident and is hired. Soon, he is prospecting for oil, and by the film's end, he has found wealth and happiness with the girl of his dreams. In 1916, the Lincoln Company released *The Trooper of Troop K,* which portrayed a black soldier who rises in society by performing heroic military acts. Essentially, many of the films made by the black companies urged black audi-

BOARD OF DIRECTORS

United Artists was formed by (l–r) actor Douglas Fairbanks, producer Samuel Goldwyn, actress Mary Pickford, and actor Charlie Chaplin. This photograph was taken in 1935 as Alexander Korda (far right) joined the Board of Directors.
UPI / CORBIS-BETTMANN

THE BIRTH OF A NATION

Technically Advanced; Thematically Retrogressive

One of the most famous and technically influential early features was David Wark Griffith's controversial *The Birth of a Nation*, released in 1915. New York City was the original base for Griffith, one of the most important directors in the history of the medium. He came to the filmmaking business in 1907, leaving behind his acting career in the New York theater in an effort to make more money. At Biograph Studios, Griffith experimented with cinematic technique in a way that would later influence directors all over the world, particularly the Russian filmmaker Sergei Eisenstein. Griffith's films, *The Birth of a Nation* (1915) and *Intolerance* (1916), provided glimpses of the technical achievements possible for the new medium. The rapid cross-cutting of parallel editing so that two narrative events could be presented simultaneously heightened the suspense of Griffith's films. The extreme close-ups he used in *The Musketeers of Pig Alley* (1912) brought a new, gritty realism to the urban characters and conflicts of the film.

It is ironic that *The Birth of a Nation*, one of the greatest early motion pictures, should be so progressive technically, yet so thematically retrogressive. A Kentuckian by birth, Griffith wanted to extol the ideals of the Old South and its concept of white racial supremacy. Based on *The Clansman* (1905) by Thomas Dixon, Jr., Griffith's melodramatic epic reveals the origin of the Ku Klux Klan as if its leaders were heroic saviors of the white women of the South during the Reconstruction era. Except for those loyal to the white families, former slaves are depicted as demonic creatures going berserk with their new freedom. Yet Griffith told the saga of the Deep South so dramatically that many audiences found its visual images emotionally compelling, despite what was, for the era, an extraordinarily long running time of over two and a half hours. It was, stated Woodrow Wilson after he saw *The Birth of a Nation* in a private screening at the White House in 1915, "like writing history with lightning": such was the power of the cinema to blend propaganda with historical fact and make it appear to be objective truth. The rapid building of suspense and tension played on the emotions, even discouraging analytical thought.

Not everyone, of course, was so favorably impressed with *The Birth of a Nation* as Woodrow Wilson—though many were emotionally affected. In protest of the showing of the racist film, riots broke out in Boston. It was, perhaps, the first time that the visceral power of the motion picture was so publicly recognized. (Griffith was appalled at what he deemed the misunderstanding of his intention. [He had felt that his cinematic portrayal of loyal former slaves was respectful.] In response to the protests, he immediately began making *Intolerance*, a lengthy historical film in four parts that campaigned against intolerance in any form throughout history.)

F

FILM

The First Narrative Films and the First Studios

The family in Woody Allen's film Radio Days *(1987) represents radio audiences.*

PAGE 397

ences to aspire to membership in the rising bourgeoisie in America; the films' typically happy endings told moviegoers that such aspirations would be amply rewarded.

Thus, during the Progressive Era, many films designed for black audiences celebrated hope and perseverance—and the heroism that seemed the only path out of the blacks' oppressed circumstances. Since many of the early nickelodeons were segregated under the nation's Jim Crow laws, films such as *The Realization of a Negro's Ambition* or *The Trooper of Troop K* played in theaters catering to black audiences. The films are testimony to the power of the cinema to speak to the needs of a community. This was especially important during a time when white film companies usually showed blacks in positions of comic servitude—if they portrayed black people at all.

MELODRAMAS OF REAL LIFE. When the black companies were formed in the early Progressive Era, however, white audiences often saw another portrayal of what it meant to be a struggling American. Countless melodramas explored what life was like in urban tenements or in sweatshops or mining communities. Often, what the films concluded was that a surrender to "destiny" was the protagonist's only recourse.

Chief among the creators of this sort of film was Griffith. During his early years Griffith influenced cinematic themes as well as techniques. When he began work as a director at the Biograph Company in 1908, Griffith walked the streets of New York looking for subject matter for the one-reelers he might typically shoot in a week's time. What he found—alcoholism, poor tenement conditions, child labor, unemployment, disease, sweatshops, police corruption—all became themes in his melodramas.

One of Griffith's best early films, *The Musketeers of Pig Alley* (1912), was shot on the streets of

♦ Nickelodeon

An early movie theater to which admission usually cost five cents

*Since films and
television have
staged everything
imaginable before it
happens, a true
event, taking place
in the real world,
brings to mind the
landscape of films.*

ELIZABETH HARDWICK
BARTLEBY IN MANHATTAN
(1983)

New York, with close-ups and unusual camera angles to heighten the dramatic tension, as well as extraordinary depth of focus. The story centers on a working-class couple played by Lillian Gish and Walter Miller, who struggle to survive in the corrupt ghetto; it ends with a gesture that indicates that the police are as corrupt as the street gang that victimizes the couple.

While the silent-film era is often stereotyped as a period of clowns, vamps, or mustache-twirling villains, the movies of the Progressive Era reflected the nation's controversies just after the turn of the century. In numerous melodramas and comedies, socialism, female suffragism, temperance, and even the push to legalize birth control, were explored and turned into sources for both entertainment and political persuasion.

This was an era in which women were often able to find work as directors and editors in Hollywood. Directors such as Lois Weber made countless acclaimed films during the silent era, especially prior to the 1920s. Weber even made films that crusaded for the cause of the legalization of birth control, *Where Are My Children?* (1916) and *The Hand that Rocks the Cradle* (1917). The latter film was based on the trials of Margaret Sanger, the famous nurse and birth-control activist whose jail sentences for releasing information about birth control had put her in the public spotlight.

Dorothy Gish, already famous as an actress, occasionally directed her own films—including a woman suffrage comedy called *The Suffragette Minstrels*, in which dancing women use their short skirts and shapely legs to persuade men to give them the vote. Earlier, in 1912, Anita Loos was already writing the humorous scripts that would make her famous in the twenties. Her comedy, *A Cure for Suffragettes* (1913), ended with the title card "Even a suffragette can be a mother."

During the period, such "crusading" films—masquerading as popular entertainment—were not unusual. Leading woman suffragists such as Emmeline Pankhurst, Elizabeth Cady Stanton, and Jane Addams collaborated with Hollywood filmmakers to turn out melodramas that would also serve as propaganda for their cause. Such films as *Votes for Women* (1912) and *What Eighty Million Women Want*—? (1913) circulated through the nation's movie houses much as ordinary film releases did.

At a time when the film industry was still shaping itself, it is not surprising that special-interest groups sought access to the new medium to promulgate their causes. The cinema was not seen as a closed-off, inaccessible force. Perhaps in a way akin to the current uses of the home-video camera, some Americans saw the motion pictures as a form that they, too, could use for their own concerns.

Since the early films drew audiences of primarily working- or lower-middle-class people, at least one frightened critic worried that the films would actually teach anarchists and revolutionaries how to overthrow the government. At the time, film was a new invention with potential repercussions that were feared by would-be guardians of society. The new entertainment form might become "the daily press of . . . Socialism, syndicalism, and radical opinion," warned Frederic Howe, in an article in *The Outlook* on 20 June 1914. The attempts at censorship of the new medium revealed the tensions in American society, as a controversy raged about the immorality and socialism shown in motion pictures—especially to working-class audiences who might be most vulnerable to their message.

For instance, a 1913 drama called *Why?* shocked many people with its scenes of Manhattan workers pleading to their boss, who sat next to a sack of gold, and children laboring—literally—on treadmills. The film ended with the protesters burning down the Woolworth Building, in hand-painted red flames. *Why?* suggested that there was no easy solution for the discontent of many workers, and it refused a "happy ending." These were the films that roused concern among those who would censor the motion picture. Films, believed such reformers, should educate and "uplift," in the spirit of the Progressive Era.

The crusade of state censors was given further credibility in 1915, when the Supreme Court ruled in its *Mutual* decision that film censorship was permitted under the First Amendment. The Court found that motion pictures were "a business, pure and simple," to which free speech was not guaranteed. The result was that states, on an individual basis, continued to establish which scenes might be viewed by film audiences.

Yet, for every social problem film that championed the liberal causes that many censors feared, such as labor unionism or birth control, another melodrama suggested the evils of such movements. Many comedies satirized the idea of the votes-for-women movement or portrayed melodramatic heroes defeating striking miners. While most films remained simply escapist, many motion pictures offered a cinematic forum for the social and cultural issues of the time. Entertainment helped negotiate the cultural changes of the Pro-

See also

Humor and Comedy

gressive Era by bringing volatile issues into a public forum and resolving them within the conventions of melodrama or comedy.

During that period, Charlie Chaplin shuffled his way into the hearts of American moviegoers with his famous character the Little Tramp. Chaplin's famous character was an everyman, an often-bullied, long-suffering hero whose large spirit and dogged determination became his way of survival in the cold, mechanized world in which he found himself. Chaplin's own liberal political sensitivities made their way into his films. In the 1917 comedy *Easy Street*, the Little Tramp demonstrated sympathy for a large working-class family, which obviously suffered the consequences of the era's laws making birth control a crime. Later, the comedian directed and starred in important cinematic statements against industrial mechanization and fascism with his films *Modern Times* (1936) and *The Great Dictator* (1940).

The Studio System and the Ritual of Moviegoing

During the early years of Chaplin's career, the film industry underwent changes that slowly turned moviegoing into the familiar ritual we know today. Motion pictures were becoming longer, generally running from an hour to ninety minutes—closer to the feature length that we now associate with the average running time of the movie. Most films were shown on a double bill, replacing the old bill of shorts in a run-down neighborhood nickelodeon. In 1914 the Strand Theater on New York's Broadway opened as the first movie "palace," elevating the moviegoing experience into a grand fantasy that took place not only on the screen but in the immediate surroundings as well. Soon movie houses were constructed in cities across the nation as luxurious, mammoth halls, resplendent with colorful ushers, plush carpeting and seats, and ornate decor with Greek or Oriental motifs. During the Great Depression, such fantastic movie halls took on even more special importance, allowing audiences to escape the drudgery of everyday life.

The rise of the feature film and the film "palace" revolutionized the filmgoing experience and drew increasing audiences from the middle and upper classes—audiences that helped make the cinema a more "respectable" form of entertainment. Films were made with higher budgets, and a new generation of film directors began to experiment with the medium.

Entrepreneurs also began to experiment with the industry. With the coming of World War I,

the film industry underwent significant changes. The structure of the industry began to shift in ways that would alter the entire face of Hollywood for decades by giving rise to the studio system. In 1914 a leading Hollywood mogul, Adolph Zukor, initiated the "vertical integration" of the industry—a system through which film manufacturers also distributed and exhibited the films they made. This created a monopoly within the film industry, as film companies not only produced motion pictures, but also had power over their national distribution and their exhibition in local theaters.

Between 1919 and 1921, Zukor oversaw the control of at least three hundred theaters across America for the exhibition of Paramount films. Thus was born the theater designed to show only a certain company's films—of which the neighborhood "Paramount Theater" is one typical example. Zukor's concentration of power in the hands of film producers was the beginning of Hollywood's studio system. Later, in the 1930s, the major studios—Warner Bros., Paramount, RKO (Radio-Keith-Orpheum), Metro-Goldwyn-Mayer, and Twentieth Century–Fox—consolidated their control over distribution and exhibition. With power over most of the nation's first-run movie houses, the big studios set the trends for the kind of motion pictures produced in America. Individual moguls such as Zukor, Sam Goldwyn, David O. Selznick, Louis B. Mayer, Jack Warner, and Irving Thalberg wielded tremendous power over the films that moviegoers saw. It is perhaps noteworthy that many of Hollywood's most successful producers were Jewish immigrants who personified the "American Dream."

This monopoly of the big studio was to continue for decades, until the Supreme Court decided that such vertical integration constituted an unfair economic monopoly with the *United States v. Paramount* decision in 1948. Under the studio system, Hollywood's "classic" period lasted from about 1930 through the 1950s, when the system's dismantling finally began in earnest.

THE WESTERN. As the studio system began, film genres evolved into more sophisticated fare. By the 1920s, the Western was a popular draw at the box office. (*The Great Train Robbery* had proven as early as 1903 that the genre held a popular appeal for film audiences.) In 1917, a young Irish-American director named John Ford had made his first film, and, by the 1920s, he was finding his métier in formulating various versions of the Western genre. Later, with such classics as *Stagecoach* (1939), *My Darling Clementine* (1946),

FILM

The Studio System and the Ritual of Moviegoing

"*More than a year passed before we again visited a movie theater,*" recalled one man after the purchase of the family's first television set in 1950.

PAGE 474

*All Americans born
between 1890 and
1945 wanted to be
movie stars.*

GORE VIDAL
THE SECOND AMERICAN
REVOLUTION AND
OTHER ESSAYS

See also
Theater and Musical Theater

She Wore a Yellow Ribbon (1949), and *The Searchers* (1956), Ford established a career as an "auteur" director of Western films. (After World War II, French critics developed the notion of the director as "author" of the motion picture to indicate that films may be seen as artistic visions of a single creative spirit.) Ford also helped to establish the career of a premier "auteur actor"—John Wayne, who starred in many of Ford's Westerns.

The Western was rich in contradictions that held the potential for social commentary. "Good" versus "bad" might be represented as "civilization" versus "savagery," "white" versus "Indian," "farm or garden" versus "wilderness or desert," and "community" versus the "individual."

Yet, in the early Westerns, the freewheeling independence of a young nation giddy with its own rapid economic development is present; so is the violence of the frontier. In the classic Westerns of the 1930s and 1940s, much of the concern lies with settlement of the frontier, set largely in the period from 1870 to 1890, when the major Indian wars were fought and the territories were still open. In general, the hero is presented as an unambiguous good guy, fighting to preserve both the rights of the community and his own individualism. In a classic Western such as Ford's *Stagecoach*, for instance, all the elements of the struggle between settlement and lawlessness are present—and are resolved in a fashion that offers an unambivalent closure to the conflicts.

Later, in the 1950s, the Western hero became increasingly complex, and sometimes likely to have neurotic characteristics. In 1956, with *The Searchers*, Ford presents John Wayne's character as a man fanatically obsessed for years with finding his niece, captured by the Indians. Once his mission is completed and he has reunited his family, he turns his back on the community and leaves again for the frontier. The hero was less a one-dimensional, white-hatted "good guy" and more an increasingly disturbed protagonist who revealed the dark side of his character.

In the 1950s, the Western also came to serve as an analogy for the terrible clashes that ruptured the nation during the McCarthyite red scare. In the films *High Noon* (1952) and *Johnny Guitar* (1954), for instance, the directors Fred Zinnemann and Nicholas Ray found covert ways to make political statements about the hysteria in American society. As a traditional American genre celebrating deep values of individualism and freedom, the Western lent itself well as a vehicle for subversive statements about the loss of freedoms during the decade. At about the same

time, with Delmer Daves's *Broken Arrow* (1950), Robert Aldrich's *Apache* (1954), Sam Fuller's *Run of the Arrow* (1957), and, later, Ford's *Cheyenne Autumn* (1964) and Kevin Costner's *Dances with Wolves* (1990), Hollywood films began to portray the Indian as the "good guy."

Along with the more positive portrayal of the Indian, Westerns revealed more psychological complexities in their white "heroes," as Wayne's character in *The Searchers* had indicated in 1956. Issues of individualism came to represent, at times, America's role in the world. For instance, an intrepid hero who knew that "a man's gotta do what a man's gotta do" reflected America's image of itself as the post–World War II leader of the free world. Later, however, the Western hero in Sam Peckinpah's Vietnam-era film *The Wild Bunch* (1969) was a member of a self-serving, greedy band of entrepreneurs whose morality could not be taken for granted. The unquestioningly good, individualistic hero was already in decline, however: in 1960, John Sturges's extremely popular film, *The Magnificent Seven*, depicted a hired gang of gunslingers with as much interest in the pay they received for their skills as in keeping order. In the 1970s, as the Western became more self-conscious as a genre, the conventional contradictions became a source of nostalgia, as in Don Siegel's *The Shootist* (1976).

SOPHISTICATES AND CENSORS. During the 1920s, however, the Western was not yet so complex a genre. The Roaring Twenties was a period when other motion-picture genres, such as the melodrama and the slapstick comedy, were causing would-be censors to rise up in protest that the sexuality and violence on the screen would corrupt the nation's morals. This was an age when Clara Bow emerged as the " 'It' Girl," in all her unbridled, jazz-age hedonism; even "America's sweetheart," Mary Pickford, cut her adolescent golden ringlets in the early 1920s to star in *Rosita* (1923), directed by Ernst Lubitsch.

Hollywood in the 1920s saw the influx of foreign film directors, notably Lubitsch and Erich von Stroheim, who brought with them more sophisticated, European social values. Lubitsch's *The Marriage Circle* (1924) and *Lady Windermere's Fan* (1925) contained the comic celebrations of free-wheeling hedonism present in his later sound pictures. The confusion and uncertainty of his characters' feelings often left simple resolution impossible. With his European elegance and wit, Lubitsch transcended the Victorian melodramatics that had so thoroughly suffused many Hollywood films. In a somewhat similar vein, the films of Stroheim, such as *Foolish Wives* (1922) and *Greed* (1925), portrayed characters with more complicated psyches than were seen in the usual Hollywood fare of the period.

In the early 1920s, a Hollywood scandal involving the comedian Roscoe "Fatty" Arbuckle had helped to create a popular suspicion of Hollywood as a scene of moral debauchery. In 1921 the rotund Arbuckle was accused of raping and then causing the death of the young actress Virginia Rappe in a San Francisco hotel.

Along with other negative publicity, the resulting uproar and a drop in movie attendance so frightened filmmakers that they inaugurated their own internal "watchdog" organization. In 1922, the Motion Picture Producers and Distributors Association (MPPDA) was formed. To further legitimate the MPPDA, Will Hays, a former postmaster general of the United States, was signed on to serve as the promoter of "right" values and mores in Hollywood film. Hays, acting as a sort of public-relations specialist, initiated a list of "Don'ts and Be Carefuls"—including sexuality and controversial political issues—which he circulated among the film community. At the same time, Hays crusaded against more formal, outside censorship of the movies.

As disturbing as censorship was, however, it was not the biggest challenge faced by the film industry in the 1920s. In October 1927, Warner Bros. released an innovative film called *The Jazz Singer*, starring Al Jolson. What made the film unusual was its use of sound. Warners' gamble paid off richly: *The Jazz Singer* was an immediate success with audiences in New York, and soon moviegoers across the country were demanding talking films. The experiment thrust Warner Bros. into the forefront of the film industry.

The coming of "talkies" thoroughly revolutionized the industry. Once the popularity of the sound films was established, the change within the industry was rapid and irrevocable. Though sound was an innovation that would destroy the careers of some actors and actresses, the film industry in general went through a renaissance. It was not long before Depression-era moviegoers flocked to see Warners' spectacular Busby Berkeley musicals such as *Forty-second Street* (directed by Lloyd Bacon) and *Gold Diggers of 1933* (directed by Mervyn LeRoy). Movies had become a genre virtually unthinkable without sound.

The outcries of the Roman Catholic church's Legion of Decency—formed in 1934 to protest "immoral" entertainment—had become so vociferous that Will Hays capitulated to their growing power. He joined with the Legion to establish the Production Code Administration in 1929. The resulting Production Code (1930) established a rigid, eight-page set of conventions for American films, stating that family values must be upheld at all times and forbidding the showing of detailed violence or sexuality.

The earlier suggestions of the Hays office had failed to curtail the sexual suggestiveness of many of the era's films. At the time, melodramas (sometimes called "women's weepies," made largely for female audiences) depicted their heroines in situations that often compromised the dominant ideals of marriage and the family. For instance, in 1932 the earliest version of Fannie Hurst's classic melodrama *Back Street* (directed by John M. Stahl) revealed the heroine engaged in a lifelong affair with a married man. While the protagonist of such melodramas typically paid dearly for her choices, she was nevertheless presented as a sympathetic and understandable character.

Mae West also titillated audiences with her witticisms and sexual allusions. In 1933, *I'm No Angel* and *She Done Him Wrong* were filled with her bawdy humor and salty one-liners. At the same time, W. C. Fields's acerbic wit and the anarchic play of the Marx Brothers challenged the censorial push for obedience to rules and order.

Other motion pictures of the early 1930s also tested the tolerance of many religious and community groups. The gangster film's violence celebrated the criminal as a new American antihero. In Mervyn LeRoy's *Little Caesar* (1930), William Wellman's *The Public Enemy* (1931), and Howard Hawks's *Scarface* (1932), American audiences saw a sordid underside of life in America, in which gangsters often seemed to be a product of the chaotic world around them. Such films increased the movement toward censorship. In 1934, after protests and threats of boycotts from religious groups across the country, the Production Code's restrictions were, finally, fully enacted. In that year, Hays put Joseph Breen, a prominent Catholic layman, in charge of administering the Production Code's rules. Motion pictures had to pass the code's standards before they were released to public audiences. By 1934, even married couples could not be shown in the same bed.

The taming of Mae West's screen persona ended her best film performances. And the genre of the gangster film underwent a modification of its most overt violence. One response to the Production Code was the rise of the G-man film, which championed the government law official as its hero. In William Keighley's *G-Men* (1935),

FILM

The Studio System and the Ritual of Moviegoing

The only way to get rid of my fears is to make films about them.

ALFRED HITCHCOCK
DIRECTOR

*The director is
simply the audience.*

ORSON WELLES
DIRECTOR

James Cagney leaves the underworld of organized crime to join the FBI; one year later, in Keighley's *Bullets or Ballots*, Edward G. Robinson played a policeman who breaks up a mob ring. The gangster-hero deplored by the Breen code was replaced, in part, by a series of films celebrating the law-enforcement official.

SCREWBALL COMEDIES. In the field of comedy, an ingenious response to the Production Code appeared: the screwball comedy. While avoiding overt sexuality, the screwball comedy typically portrayed an upper-class woman in a romantic liaison with a working-class man (and, often, vice versa). Frank Capra's *It Happened One Night* (1934) starred Clark Gable and Claudette Colbert in a very successful comedy (it was the first film to win all five major Oscars) that also spoke to the economic crisis of the time. By bringing together a couple from radically different class backgrounds, the comedy suggested that the nation itself could perhaps heal the wounds of class conflict, and that American democracy could survive despite the decade's economic calamities. Screwball comedies also offered audiences sexual suggestiveness without actual breaking of the code; in so doing, they freed women from the bedroom, and put them in newspaper offices and corporate boardrooms. The genre often depicted women as assertive, independent heroines, such as Rosalind Russell in Howard Hawks's *His Girl Friday* (1940) and Ruth Hussey in George Cukor's *The Philadelphia Story* (1940). Katharine Hepburn was at her feisty best, for instance, in Hawks's *Bringing Up Baby* (1938), and opposite Spencer Tracy in later screwball comedies such as George Stevens's *Woman of the Year* (1942).

ANIMATED FILMS. Depression-era moviegoers could also readily find escapist entertainment at their local theaters. The 1930s was a decade of innovations made in the most fantastic cinema of all—animation. With the development of Betty Boop, the Fleischer brothers—Dave and Max—created one of the most popular cartoon characters of the period. At the Fleischer studio, animation achieved new, complicated heights with surrealistic portrayals of Betty Boop in *Snow White*, complete with a jazzy soundtrack provided by Cab Calloway's band. Such sophisticated cartoons were intended more for adults than children, and were a success with audiences.

At the same time that the Fleischer brothers were making cartoons with an anarchistic spirit, the Walt Disney Studio was perfecting the art of animation with a painstaking attention to detail. Mickey Mouse evolved from a rodentlike creature in his second film, *Steamboat Willie* (1928) (in his first, *Plane Crazy*, he had appeared under the name Mortimer) to a more human, lovable character during the 1930s, and became the first Disney "star." Disney's typically sweet characters and moral tales captured the hearts of moviegoers.

With the use of color and sound, the Disney cartoons grew more sophisticated through the decade, though the content remained that of idealized fantasy. In contrast to the anything-goes Fleischer cartoons, the Disney films were often morality tales in which the world had rules that must be obeyed. In the late 1920s, censorship was still such a strong force that Disney was ordered to remove the udder from an animated cow, and—while the late 1920s cartoons were wilder and more primitive—during the 1930s, the Disney cartoons became increasingly mild and inoffen-

THE DEPRESSION

The film industry itself weathered the Depression only after terrific struggles to win back the audiences that had flocked to the movies soon after the coming of sound in 1927. Declining attendance plagued theaters in 1931 and 1932. In response, theaters offered double bills, "Depression glass" favors, and more emphasis on the escapism offered by the elaborate movie palace. By 1934, the economic crisis had largely been survived, despite the additional threat of the Production Code. Americans still needed the movies. Even former President Herbert Hoover suggested that the unemployed should be given movie tickets as a sort of "dole," so that potential unrest might be kept to a minimum. At the time, however, several motion pictures were made to portray the plights of the unemployed or the victimized.

In 1932, Mervyn LeRoy's *I Am a Fugitive from a Chain Gang* starred Paul Muni as a hero whose life was completely out of his own control. Through false implication in a robbery, the hero is imprisoned and his parole repeatedly denied. By the end of the grim tale, he has escaped and stands wild-eyed in the darkness, telling his former lover that he must survive by stealing. Such films suggested the powerlessness of the individual, and the terrible abuse of authority taking place in America's legal system.

sive portrayals of conservative American values. Even in the depictions of dark fairy tales and the evil that threatened Snow White or Bambi, the protagonists never lost their innocence or purity—and the films remain largely sentimental.

HORROR FILMS. Audiences who attended the cartoons of the 1930s escaped to the mild fantasies offered in animation. In the era's horror films, however, audiences escaped the realities of the Depression to a very different fantastic landscape—one that was filled with nightmarish images of a world gone hopelessly awry, in which strange forces had been set loose. In Tod Browning's *Dracula* (1931), the horror came not from the known, "civilized" world of London, but from the mysterious, vampire-inhabited realm of Transylvania. In a world in which little seemed to be under human control, the films allowed audiences to see their terrors in physical form. In 1933, audiences paid to see a berserk giant ape terrorize Manhattan in *King Kong*. Part of the film's message warned of the danger in tampering with the unknown, in bringing "monsters" to civilization from the wild islands of the Pacific.

Other horror films of the decade emphasized a similar moral: scientific experimentation could lead to threats to the human race. Such was the message of the film that made Boris Karloff a star—James Whale's *Frankenstein* (1931). Despite censorship problems over a scene in which the monster throws a little girl into a lake, *Frankenstein* was Universal's biggest box-office success in 1932. (The excised scenes were restored in 1987.) One of the most unusual of the decade's horror films was Tod Browning's *Freaks* (1932), set in a circus and cast with actual sideshow performers. The film portrayed the deformed characters as a community of survivors who band together to rid themselves of an evil interloper. The Depression-era horror films allowed audiences to see their worst fears expressed, and, finally, contained in a way that reassured them that society would survive and humankind ultimately prevail.

The Promise of the Forties

By the end of the thirties, of course, not only had the movies survived, but new genres and brilliant directors had emerged from Hollywood. Many European film talents, such as Michael Curtiz, William Dieterle, William Wyler, and Lubitsch, had found a new creative home in Hollywood. Their films carried the innovations of Europe and of German Expressionism to California.

Such directors were integrated into the studio system, and by the late 1930s the big studios determined the fate of their countless stars such as Joan Crawford and Bette Davis, as well as new directors. David O. Selznick, Samuel Goldwyn, and Louis B. Mayer, for instance, were tycoons who controlled their studios with a sometimes tyrannical hand. When Selznick began the production of his mammoth *Gone with the Wind* (1939), it was with an absolute control over decision-making that he wielded until the film was finally wrapped. *Gone with the Wind* was already practically a legend by the time its world premiere was held in Atlanta, largely because of the fame of Margaret Mitchell's novel and the publicity over Selznick's meticulous attention to the details of his epic production, particularly his search for the perfect Scarlett O'Hara. Despite the enormous success of the film, however, it would be the last of such huge cinematic enterprises until after World War II.

The war years were a time of internal turmoil and also technical experimentation for Hollywood. With budgets drastically cut for the war effort, directors were forced to find inexpensive means of making cinematic innovations. Creative minds found a way to reach beyond the funding cuts—using actual streets or buildings instead of elaborate sets. Working in black-and-white, many film-makers made use of unusual camera angles and lighting to attract the eye. Often, oblique angles fractured the scene and created a sense of restlessness. Heightening the uneasiness might also be shadows that obscured a character's face while the light illuminated inanimate objects.

It was a foreboding, even ominous, film style that French critics, seeing the Hollywood films for the first time after the war had ended, dubbed *film noir* (black film). The term alluded both to the black-and-white quality of the films and their dark dramatic themes. Often inspired by the hard-boiled detective novels made popular by writers such as Dashiell Hammett and James M. Cain (and later Mickey Spillane), the films delved into the perverse side of human nature, exploring violence, greed, and existential loneliness. Such films as Edgar Ulmer's *Detour* (1945), Billy Wilder's masterpiece *Double Indemnity* (1944), and Howard Hawks's *The Big Sleep* (1946) epitomized the *noir* style of filmmaking. Orson Welles's classic *Citizen Kane* (1941) used striking *noir*-like lighting techniques and camera angles that helped to convey the greed and paranoia of its rags-to-riches American hero, based on William Randolph Hearst.

Many elements of German Expressionism also shaped the making of that body of films charac-

FILM

The Promise of the Forties

Some films are slices of life; mine are slices of cake.

ALFRED HITCHCOCK
DIRECTOR

See also
Television

INQUISITION AND BLACKLIST

The HUAC Investigations

Internally, wartime Hollywood was shaken by the technical workers' efforts to unionize. It was a community divided by conservative forces such as Walt Disney and Jack Warner, who created the Motion Picture Alliance for the Preservation of American Ideals (MPA). One of the chief purposes of this group was to defend the Hollywood filmmaking community against infiltration by Communists. Men like Disney and Warner were deeply threatened by the liberalism they saw in the development of trade unionism and by the ensuing empowerment of the workers within the industry. The film community that survived the traumas of the Great Depression had new forces tearing at it during the 1940s.

Not the least of these elements came from Washington. In 1940 the head of the then-temporary House Committee on Un-American Activities (HUAC), Martin Dies, journeyed to Hollywood to make the first of what would become a wave of inquisitions into liaisons between the film industry and the Communist party. At that time, he found a Hollywood united against his efforts. For the most part, producers refused to listen to his accusations that the Screen Writers Guild and Screen Directors Guild were primarily Communist fronts, and the first investigation thus failed.

Several years later, however, the existence of the MPA gave the HUAC investigation a vehicle into conservative Hollywood. Hollywood trade unionism had divided the entertainment community with strikes, and when Rep. J. Parnell Thomas called the first "friendly witnesses" before the committee in 1948, the witnesses—among them Ronald Reagan, Gary Cooper, Louis B. Mayer, Jack Warner, and Walt

Disney—were willing to "name names" of those suspected of being Communist sympathizers.

The hysteria began in earnest, as both the famous and the relatively obscure were brought before the committee and questioned about their membership in the Communist party. During the 1930s, when communism had been seen by some as a viable alternative to both the fascism rising in Europe and the failure of capitalism in the West, there had been a lively interest in the party among some members of the Hollywood community. In the 1950s, when the horrors of Stalinism had been revealed and the cold war was in deadly earnest, they paid dearly for their past interest. When the group known as the "Hollywood Ten" were called before the committee, they refused to testify on the grounds of both self-incrimination and free speech. Convicted of contempt of Congress, the ten—mostly directors and screenwriters such as Ring Lardner, Jr., Edward Dmytryk, Herbert Biberman—were all sentenced to serve prison time. Ironically, Lardner served time with J. Parnell Thomas in a minimum security prison in Danbury, Connecticut. Thomas, who had tried to appear so loyal to American causes as he led the inquisition, had been accepting kickbacks from the members of his staff.

The effects of the HUAC inquisition on Hollywood during the 1950s were devastating. The hysteria from Washington left a divided, suspicious community, with many of its most talented members blacklisted. Hollywood lost some of its greatest talents. Charlie Chaplin grew disgusted with American conservatism (and high taxes) and, in 1952, left for Switzerland, never to work in America again. (His last two films, *A King in New York* [1957] and *A Countess from Hong Kong* [1967] were made in Great Britain.)

The censorship of free speech put some filmmakers in the position of making films that became covert statements against the mentality of paranoia and hysteria in the country. In 1952, Fred Zinnemann's *High Noon* (written by the later blacklisted Carl Foreman) poignantly depicted a sheriff (Gary Cooper) who could not win the support of the townspeople in fighting off returning criminals. The film was a subtle allegory about the nature of betrayal and deception and the loss of integrity. Such pictures were the only vehicle for safely expressing protest against the prevailing mood. Even in allegory, however, artists were not always safe in making criticisms of the political climate. Upon his release from prison, Herbert Biberman directed *Salt of the Earth* (1953), a film about striking miners in New Mexico that was financed by a miners' union. The film was blacklisted and shown in only one American theater, though it received critical success in Europe. Over ten years later, in 1965, *Salt of the Earth* was finally distributed in the United States. Even Arthur Miller's historical play, *The Crucible* (1953) caused him to be called before the committee for investigation.

terized as *film noir*, such as the sense of bleak, fatalistic despair and shadowy, sinister dramas.

Film noir was, perhaps, a reflection of the wartime disorientation and confusion about what the future held for the nation, though it was not limited to the wartime necessity imposed by limited budgets. The dark films continued into the early 1950s, growing even bleaker with their portraits of human despair and evil. In 1955, Robert Aldrich's adaptation of a Mickey Spillane novel, *Kiss Me Deadly*, contained a frightening vision of a society in which nuclear power is bandied about in a black box. Aldrich's Mike Hammer is one of the darkest protagonists of the era. Other heroes or heroines bordered on the psychotic as the later cinema of *film noir* explored the dark undercurrents in the human psyche. Nicholas Ray's *In a Lonely Place* (1950) captures the hero's inner turmoil and self-destruction. (His *Rebel Without a Cause* [1955], though not an example of *film noir*, cynically portrayed the underside of the American family through James Dean's confused adolescent hero.) Many of the fears of the era—atomic warfare, the cold war, and the paranoid grip that the McCarthyite red scare had upon the nation during the 1950s—were brought to the screen in the form of *film noir*. The *noir* techniques, born of wartime hardships, survive to influence filmmaking and television in the 1990s.

The war effort made its demands on Hollywood in other ways as well. Frank Capra, who established his career in the 1930s and 1940s with homespun populism in *Mr. Deeds Goes to Town* (1936), *Mr. Smith Goes to Washington* (1939), *Meet John Doe* (1941), and his widely seen Christmas classic *It's a Wonderful Life* (1946), set to work for the government. His *Why We Fight* series (1942–1945) comprised a number of influential propaganda films.

The Threat of Television

In addition to the HUAC investigations, Hollywood faced other challenges during the 1950s.

The advent of television threatened motion pictures as American families found its accessibility attractive. In the age of the postwar "baby boom," television quickly became a popular entertainment form. The film industry responded in various ways. To enhance the appeal of the movies, color began to be used increasingly, with a number of cheap new processes eventually supplanting the expensive original Technicolor. Various widescreen systems, such as Cinerama and Cinema Scope, three-dimensional effects, and stereophonic sound were developed to emphasize the theatrical experience. In addition, drive-in theaters began to spring up across the country to compete against television. They were an invitation to families to bring children to the cinema in the privacy of their cars, or to young couples to use moviegoing as part of a courting ritual.

Metro-Goldwyn-Mayer began to turn out elaborate musicals to win audiences away from their television sets. After sponsoring an audience survey, the studio discovered that American moviegoers wanted to see musical comedies more than any other genre. In the late 1940s, Vincente Minnelli's lavish *The Pirate* (1948) had proved that musicals could be exhilarating escapism for audiences, and the survey respondents indicated that they wanted more of the same.

MGM was quick to react to the findings. Musicals such as Stanley Donen and Gene Kelly's *Singin' in the Rain* (1952) became huge popular hits. In 1953, Fred Astaire starred in Minnelli's *The Band Wagon*, continuing his screen persona that had evoked wonder from the days of such Depression-era musicals as *Swing Time* (1936). Astaire's fantastic dancing gave a sense that the physical world could be surmounted and even transcended in joyous play of body and spirit. The musicals presented a kind of utopian society in which characters might break into song and dance at any minute, rupturing the mundane world of the taken-for-granted. Like the Warner Bros.' musicals of the 1930s, these lavish musicals offered a happy face for America—fantasies in which troubles could be forgotten and innocence regained.

In the 1950s, the melodramas of Douglas Sirk also pushed the genre of the "woman's film" to a new level of sophisticated social commentary. With films such as *All That Heaven Allows* (1956), *Written on the Wind* (1956), and *Imitation of Life* (1959), Sirk presented an unsettling portrait of the American family, and particularly of the narrow-minded ideals and values that restrict independence for women. Just as Fred Zinnemann

FILM

The Threat of Television

Conditions in the [movie] industry somehow propose the paradox: "We brought you here for your individuality, but while you're here we insist that you do everything to conceal it."

F. SCOTT FITZGERALD

See also
Radio

*. . . the movies spoil
us for life; nothing
ever lives up
to them.*

EDMUND WHITE
FROM HIS BIOGRAPHY OF
JEAN GENET

used the Western genre as a means of conveying a larger statement about American culture in *High Noon*, so Sirk exposed the underside of American traditions and family values through the melodrama.

The era's horror films also reveal the underside of the prosperous 1950s. While the horror films of the 1930s typically portrayed a monster coming from outside America—from a shadowy landscape in Transylvania or South Sea islands—in Don Siegel's *Invasion of the Body Snatchers* (1956), the monsters came mysteriously in the form of giant seed-pods. As the pods evolved into humanoids who resembled the inhabitants of the town of Santa Mira, it was the average American who became the "monster." The film was a warning against the peril of communism and the vulnerability of even small towns to its insidious takeover. Yet *Invasion of the Body Snatchers* can also be interpreted in an opposite way—as a protest against mass hysteria and conformism.

By the decade's end, Alfred Hitchcock signaled the coming of a new age in horror films with *Psycho* (1960). The "monster" no longer comes from outside America, or outside us. Rather, it resides in the very structure of our family, and in the madness the family generates in the human psyche.

Changes in the Sixties

By the 1960s, several factors were changing the shape of the film industry. Censorship restrictions had begun to lift during the 1950s, so that by the 1960s, partial nudity and violence became more prevalent. In 1966, the Motion Picture Association of America selected Jack Valenti, a former aide to President Lyndon Johnson, as its head. Valenti's first job was to initiate a ratings system to guide audiences about the nature of the less-restricted film content. Originally, there were four categories: G for general, M for mature, R for restricted, and X for no one admitted under age eighteen. Though Valenti's rating system has gone through many revisions—and the content of films that warrant certain ratings has changed drastically—the system's basic concept has remained in place.

In addition, the old studios declined as vertical integration was thoroughly dismantled. According to the Supreme Court *Paramount* decision of 1948, the unification of production, distribution, and exhibition was finally outlawed. The result was that the film companies were taken over by corporate empires, an action that put the ultimate power over filmmaking decisions in the hands of

business executives who primarily understood only the profit-making end of the industry. TransAmerica bought United Artists; Gulf and Western bought Paramount; and Kinney took over Warner Bros.

The big corporations, however, inherited the financial problems that the studios had suffered during the previous decade. As profits at the box office fell during the 1960s, the emphasis was increasingly placed on the blockbuster hit. Epics such as Joseph L. Mankiewicz's elaborate *Cleopatra* (1963) and musicals such as Robert Wise's *The Sound of Music* (1965) were high-stakes gambles at winning the jackpot at the box office, and one outcome of the emphasis on big-budget films was that smaller, independent films were neglected by the large corporate interests.

One important producer of low-budget films during the sixties was American Independent Pictures (AIP), which provided experimental vehicles for young directors and actors. Among those directors was Roger Corman, who went on to form his own studio and distributorship, New World Pictures, in 1970. Many of Hollywood's best talents of the 1980s and 1990s—among them Jack Nicholson, Martin Scorsese, Robert De Niro, and Jonathan Demme—got their starts with AIP and New World in the 1960s and 1970s. Corman had made a name for himself with extremely low-budget films such as *A Bucket of Blood* (1959) and *The Little Shop of Horrors* (1961), which was shot in two days. Though both films have the plots of horror movies, they are also quirky social satire—and even parody the horror film genre.

In part because of Corman's low-budget successes, the cult film began to burgeon by the late 1960s. George Romero's *Night of the Living Dead* (1968) and Jim Sharman's British-made *The Rocky Horror Picture Show* (1975) captivated American audiences, who went to see the films time and again, often at midnight showings.

Another important event in the 1960s was the rise of film studies as a serious area of scholarship in the nation's universities. In college towns and cities across the country, "art" movie houses that exhibited foreign or independent films flourished, exposing young people to the cinema of foreign directors like Ingmar Bergman, Federico Fellini, and the French New Wave directors such as François Truffaut and Jean-Luc Godard.

A further consequence of the establishment of university film studies was that many current directors received their training not on Hollywood studio lots but in film schools. Young directors of the 1970s, among them Steven Spielberg, George

Lucas, Francis Ford Coppola, Brian De Palma, and Martin Scorsese, attended such film production schools as the University of Southern California, New York University, and the University of California–Los Angeles. The late 1960s were a time of transition as the older, studio-educated filmmakers saw the rise of a generation of directors just out of film school. Increasingly, it is the film school that provided the aspiring director's entry into professional work in Hollywood.

The Counterculture and After

Late in the tumultuous decade of the 1960s, several successful films, among them Arthur Penn's *Bonnie and Clyde* (1967) and Mike Nichols's *The Graduate* (1967), reflected the confusion and alienation of many young people. In 1969, Dennis Hopper's *Easy Rider* proved that lower-budget films about the era's counterculture could be smash hits, and also demonstrated the economic power of what was called "the youth generation" at the box office. Attendance at theaters began to rise substantially; the "youth market" had been successfully tapped.

The phenomenal success of the younger directors carried over into the seventies, as Robert Altman's *M*A*S*H* (1970), Coppola's *The Godfather* (1972) and Lucas's nostalgic *American Graffiti* (1973) brought critical raves as well as solid revenues. But it was Lucas's *Star Wars* (1977) and Steven Spielberg's *Jaws* (1975) and *Close Encounters of the Third Kind* (1977) that focused attention on the special-effects blockbuster. While such films cost a great deal to produce, they also paid off handsomely.

By the end of the 1970s, successful films spawned not only imitators, but, increasingly, sequels. In 1976, John Avildsen's *Rocky* starred Sylvester Stallone as a model of a simple American hero rising to fame and wealth in his career as a boxer, and established a formula for the subsequent *Rocky* films. Stallone's model of an uncomplicated super-hero carried over into his portrayal of *Rambo*, the machine-gun–toting warrior-soldier who promised to resurrect the pre-Vietnam era values of militaristic glory. The success of the first *Rocky* led to five more movie versions of the boxer's attempts at championships. The Stallone films, however, were not the ultimate representative of the sequel phenomenon—that unlikely distinction fell to the horror series, *Friday the 13th*, which, by 1988, had seven versions. The film found most of its audience among young adolescents willing to return time and again to witness the latest horrors of Jason. Similarly, *A Nightmare on Elm Street* (six versions by 1991) had young fans returning to watch Freddy Krueger, the villain who invades young people's minds.

At the same time, Hollywood finally began to come to terms with the Vietnam War, with such films as Michael Cimino's *The Deer Hunter* (1978), Hal Ashby's *Coming Home* (1978), and Coppola's *Apocalypse Now* (1979). Instead of the heroics of World War II dramas, these films portrayed the complexity and darkness of war and its aftermath at home. In the following decade, the Vietnam conflict would become the focus of many motion pictures, most of which portrayed the horror of war rather than the glory of battle.

The emphasis on megabucks films continued into the 1980s, to the extent that smaller films were seen as a greater risk. By the end of the 1980s, several successful directors felt the impact of Hollywood's skittishness about smaller motion pictures. Robert Altman, who received financial backing from Twentieth Century–Fox for such "small" films as *Three Women* (1977) and *A Wedding* (1978), by 1990 had to rely on European funding to make his *Vincent and Theo*, based on the life of Van Gogh.

In the late 1980s, Spike Lee proved that a film made by a black director could be a lively, controversial—and lucrative—statement on American culture. With *Do the Right Thing* (1989), alluding to the actual killing of a black man by a white police officer in Brooklyn, he created a cinema that both white and black audiences found visually compelling as well as provocative. Released in 1990, Charles Burnett's *To Sleep with Anger*—a compelling portrait of a black family in south-central Los Angeles—received less promotion, and, consequently, less critical attention and box-office revenues. Burnett's film, however, is a powerful, sometimes comic, portrait of what happens in a black family when a relative arrives from Louisiana, with all the folklore and superstitions of that region. Such quieter films, however, are often overlooked as producers and distributors concentrate on blockbusters.

A phenomenon that began in the 1970s permanently changed the film industry in the 1980s: the video revolution. More Americans enjoyed the convenience of watching movies at home with the entire family as the videocassette recorder became a household item. The rise of the demand for videotaped movies provided another market for films, which might slowly make most of their profits from video rentals.

Regardless of the inroads made by video, the early 1990s saw both the continuation of the Hol-

FILM

The Counterculture and After

The Disney empire has now grown into a diversified corporation with interest in film and television production, hotels, and extensive merchandising of the Disneyana.

PAGE 33

See also
Country and Western Music

**FOLK SONG AND
FOLK MUSIC**

*Folk Song as a
Representation
of American Culture*

I don't want life
reproduced up there
on the screen. I want
life created!

SIDNEY LUMET
DIRECTOR

Throughout the
silent film era and
the talking pictures
of the 1930s and
1940s, American-
made comedy films
swept to mass
popularity.

PAGE 228

lywood blockbuster and the circulation of independent films that speak to quieter subjects and
smaller audiences. Lucrative Hollywood motion
pictures continued to generate imitators—the
phenomenon of the sequel attested to the avoidance of risk taking by big producers. Many of the
most inventive films, however, are produced outside the mainstream, by independent producers
and directors. Whether mainstream or independent, however, the cinema has proven itself
throughout the decades of American film history
to be both a vital reflector of cultural values and a
creator of national trends.

During the twentieth century, America became a nation of moviegoers who, even through
the crises of the Great Depression and the advent
of television in the 1950s, never lost their devotion to the cinema. It was on the big screen that
the latest fashions and romantic role models were
discovered. While the ritual of moviegoing has
shifted through the decades, from the early era's
multiple shorts and the later double bill—when
one might enter the film in mid-screening and
stay through to the next showing—its function as
an element of courtship and a social rite has remained virtually unchanged for audiences attending contemporary feature films. It is in the nation's moviehouses that modern audiences, like
their early counterparts, find themselves entertained with their deepest hopes and horrors.

—KAY SLOAN

FOLK SONG AND
FOLK MUSIC

Folk Song as a Representation
of American Culture

Folk song and folk music are constantly changing
as ever-varying cultural representations of the society in which they are performed and perpetuated. Political boundaries do not necessarily de-
lineate a cohesive culture, so it is not surprising
that folk song and folk music in the United States
have always consisted of a wide variety of styles
and forms. Only since the latter half of the twentieth century has there been an interest in the entire spectrum of folk music, most of which had
been ignored previously in favor of the more
highly valued Anglo-American tradition. Consequently, although this essay is restricted to the
study of folk song that originated in the British
Isles and has been perpetuated in American En-

glish, the reader should keep in mind that the
United States always has included diverse folk
song cultures: Latino, African American, Cajun,
and French-Canadian, to name but a few. Every
group that has come to America has brought its
own music, songs, dances, and instruments, and
these unique musical heritages were continually
refashioned by the American experience. That experience not only altered the various types of imported folk songs, it also forged new folk groups
that developed their own ever-changing repertoires. American workers—such as miners, sailors,
lumbermen, and cowboys—sang folk songs that
reflected their work experience. Because categories
of women's work gained validation only recently,
most studies and recordings of workers' songs have
focused on men rather than women.

Folk songs tell us about how various social,
economic, religious, and political issues were perceived by the people who sang them. Such issues
have always been topics of folk songs either directly or indirectly. Songs about orphans, young
girls who went wrong only to be murdered by
their sweethearts, or noble Indian maidens who
took their own lives, all of which abound in this
country's repertoire, tell us as much about our social history as do songs concerning presidential
assassinations, railroad disasters, shipwrecks, or
cowboy heroes.

Assumptions Behind Folk Song
Studies in America

Until the second half of the twentieth century,
most people assumed that the "genuine" folk
traditions of the United States were Anglo-
American, despite the fact that numerous indigenous peoples already were living on this continent
when Europeans first settled here. It is incorrect
to think that the complex of cultures that make up
the United States has been influenced mainly by
Anglo-American settlers. The monolithic view of
American culture was perpetrated by those who
held power, themselves products of a generalized
European worldview and a part of an Anglo-
Celtic tradition.

American folk song scholarship had its roots,
just as did early anthropology, psychology, and sociology, in the social Darwinism that dominated
Europe and the British Isles at the end of the
nineteenth century. This theory of culture postulated that all societies developed through a series
of stages, and that northern European and British
cultures were deemed superior to all others. By
the end of the 1800s, American scholars who
were self-conscious about the nation's lack of his-

torical tradition simply assumed that the Anglo tradition was America's authentic one. Such a view identified this country with "superior" cultures and effaced the unsophisticated image of the United States.

Genres of American Folk Song

THE CHILD BALLADS AND OTHER BALLADS. The folk songs that first drew the attention of scholars in this country were those now known as the Child ballads, named after Francis James Child, the Harvard University, professor who compiled and systematized them. Child's most important work was the multivolume *English and Scottish Popular Ballads*, which was published between 1882 and 1898. Child's criteria for inclusion of a song in his work were closely linked to the social Darwinism of the day. He included narrative songs that he believed had an oral tradition in either England or Scotland.

Child organized by number what he judged to be distinct ballad narratives, clustering the versions that he believed were related and publishing them under the title and number of the version that he felt was the oldest. In all he found 305 basic ballad stories. When field collectors of folk song in the United States later came across versions of these ballads, they listed them in their own collections using Child's numbering system. For example, "The Wife of Usher's Well," a representative example of the ballad genre, became known as Child no. 79:

1 There lived a wife at Usher's Well,
   And a wealthy wife was she;
He had three stout and stalwart sons,
   And sent them oer the sea.

2 They hadna been a week from her,
   A week but barely ane [one],
When word came to the carline wife
   That her three sons were gane.

3 They hadna been a week from her,
   A week but barely three,
When word came to the carlin wife
   That her sons she'd never see.

4 'I wish the wind may never cease,
   Nor fashes [fishes] in the flood,
Till my three sons come hame to me,
   In earthly flesh and blood.'

5 It fell about the Martinmass,
   When nights are lang and mirk,

The carlin wife's three sons came hame,
   And their hats were o the birk.

About half of the 305 distinct ballads to which Child gave numbers crossed the ocean and gained currency in the English-language tradition of American folksingers. For almost three quarters of a century following the publication of *The English and Scottish Popular Ballads*, collectors combed the United States looking for versions and remnants of Child ballads, often ignoring other vital types of folk song that surrounded them. These songs were interpreted as poems by Child and the many others who studied Anglo-American ballads through the 1950s. Attention was paid to the poetic devices by which the lyrics developed the story. Not until the publication of Bertrand Bronson's *The Traditional Tunes of the Child Ballads* (1959–1972) was this neglect of the music partially redressed. Today we recognize that ballad texts are inseparably bound to the tunes to which they are performed.

The study of English and Scottish ballads became the earliest and, until recently, the most enduring type of folk song scholarship in America. Among the poetic devices that were valued by scholars in folk ballads were a specific stanzaic form (4-3-4-3 with a-b-c-b rhyme); understatement; leaping and lingering (on only the most important elements of plot); the advancement of narrative through dialogue; repetition; focus on the most important elements of plot; beginning the story in the midst of the action; the use of commonplace word groups and stanzas (that appear in other ballads); and the lack of a personal narrator (an "I" who editorialized).

Today numerous ballad traditions are studied in addition to the Child canon. Students now analyze the folk song narratives of occupational, ethnic, and regional groups, and study outlaw ballads, war ballads, and other specific types of folk songs. Malcolm Laws, in his work *Native American Balladry*, offers a classification system for "ballads which have originated in the United States and the Maritime Provinces of Canada" (Laws 1964: 9).

LYRICAL SONG. The lyric folk song has no narrative but instead presents a feeling or mood, much like the blues. There is no system of classification or exhaustive study of Anglo-American lyrics in the United States, probably because these songs have extremely malleable texts. For example, a song that could express high-spirited courting humor as a dance song could also be sung in a different mood by the same singer to indicate that life is a dreary and tragic existence. Both rendi-

Singers Woody Guthrie (1912–1967) and Hudie Ledbetter ("Leadbelly" [1885–1949]) created songs from both white and black folk traditions.

PAGE 103

See also
African American Music

BROADSIDES

A broadside is a sheet of paper that has a message usually printed on one side. The broadside song, dating from the earliest days of movable type, usually contained only text. Quite often the text was accompanied by a graphic woodcut, not necessarily related to the contents of the song itself, which helped sell the broadside much as covers on books do today. The title of the song was usually followed by the name of a well-known tune to which it could be sung. These songs were hawked by street vendors who often established small stalls on which they displayed the ballad sheets. Sometimes the printers varied the color of the paper, printed two songs on a single sheet, changed the size of the paper, hand-colored the accompanying woodcuts, or added elaborate borders to the texts.

> On one bright summer's morning,
> the weather being clear,
> I strolled for recreation down by
> the river fair.
>
> I overheard a damsel most
> gracious-like complain
> All for an absent lover who
> plowed the raging main.
> (Laws, 1957:221; Laws N 36,
> 'John (George) Riley I')

Even though the broadsides were often described as "ballads," many of these songs did not tell a story. They could have been lyric songs, nonsense songs, or other non-narrative texts. Many of the broadsides did tell stories, however, and they often were the source of information about the latest scandal, disaster, strange occurrence, or other community news. During slow news times, broadside writers would recast the stories of the folk ballads currently in oral circulation. The printed word and the tradition of oral transmission were intertwined.

Broadsides were a tradition in numerous countries and cultures. Great Britain had a thriving broadside press, as did the United States. Philadelphia, New York, and Boston were early centers where broadsides could be bought, and they continued to be well into the twentieth century. Rural America also had its own broadside writers, performers, and hawkers. Small books called "songsters," which could fit into one's pocket, were an offshoot of the need for both news and song texts. With the rise in literacy the personal songbook, printed, handwritten, and perhaps pasted with clippings of songs from publications, became popular as a handy reference for individual singers.

The textual style of the broadside ballad is different from that of the sparse Child ballad. The rhyme schemes, usually a-b-c-b or a-a-b-b, were followed with such strictness that forced rhymes often resulted. The texts told the listener how to feel about the events and, unlike the Child ballads, were presented using the first person as narrator. Some broadsides are called "Come All Ye"s, since those words were part of the first line of the text, sung by the hawker to attract an audience of prospective customers.

Broadsides tell us much about American culture, since many of them either were gleaned from folk tradition or entered (and reentered) the oral tradition. They had a great influence on all of American folk song tradition.

tions are lyrics in the sense that they express emotions while they lack a narrative thread, but they vary greatly in mood. Most lyrics that have been collected in the United States express sadness, usually over a loss.

Although the lyric does not have a narrative, the listener often thinks that a story has been told, because the lyrics imply a narrative. These songs often contain stanzas that begin "If I were . . ." or "When we were . . . ," thus implying, but not telling, of past or future events. "Floating stanzas" are added or removed as the singer wishes. Varia-tions of the following two stanzas, for example, are found in many Anglo-American lyric songs:

> Dig my grave both wide and deep;
> Put a tombstone at my feet,
> And on my heart carve a turtle dove
> To tell the world I died for love.
>
> If I had wings like a turtle dove,
> I'd fly away to the one I love.
> I would fly away to the one so dear
> And talk to him while she is near.

See also
Country and Western Music

If I had the wings of a turtle dove
I would fly away to the one I love,
I would fly to the one I love so dear
And talk to him while she is near.

(Belden: 479)

I wish that I had never been born
Or died when I was young
And never lived to wet my cheeks with tears,
Oh, for the love of another woman's son.

(Belden: 482)

Singers of lyric songs have a vast repertoire of these floating stanzas that they can alter and insert while singing so as to better express the emotion they wish to convey.

The lyric folk song, unlike the Child ballad, makes wide use of metaphor, similes, tropes, and other symbolic devices, although their stanzaic form is much like that of the Child ballad. The lyric aims to create a mood, even if, at times, the tune may be one usually associated with a contrary feeling, like the fast dance tune sung as a lament.

Entire stanzas that are sung to a particular tune one day may be replaced the next with floating stanzas or lines that the singer prefers to sing on that day. The determination of what is "the song" is thus rendered "subjective" in terms of the singer, and is almost always a subjective call on the part of the collector who does not ask the singer about the identity of the song sung. Most collectors did not ask for titles, but rather gave titles to lyric songs as they transcribed them.

DIALOGUE SONG. The dialogue song develops its mood or story entirely through the use of dialogue. The "action" usually takes place in a dramatic dialogue between speakers who usually alternate verses, and the story is revealed retrospectively through the dialogue. If there is a digression from the alternating voices, it usually comes in the introductory verse that sets the scene.

'O where ha you been, Lord Randal, my son?
And where ha you been, my handsome young man?'
'I ha been at the greenwood; mother, mak my bed soon,
For I'm wearied wi hunting, and fain wad lie down.'

'An wha met ye there, Lord Randal, my son?
And wha met you there, my handsome young man?'
'O I met wi my true-love; mother, mak my bed soon,
For I'm wearied wi huntin, and fain wad lie down.'

Some of the "ballads" that Child collected fall into this category, although he might have felt that they were narratives in time. His rationale for labeling them as ballads might well have been based in the belief that oral tradition had eroded the rest of the story line, leaving only the dialogue. Be that as it may, certainly "Lord Randal" (Child no. 12) and "Edward" (Child no. 13) are such songs, as are the Anglo-American songs "Paper of Pins" and "Oh No John." Dialogue is an important device that advances the action of ballad narratives, and so it is possible that some dialogue songs are related to earlier ballads. It is also probable that many dialogue songs were composed by a singer to be just that, dialogue songs.

WORK SONG. While songs have been identified as belonging to certain "genres" or types by their textual characteristics, scholars have also defined genres by the function that they served or by the groups that sang them. There are numerous folk songs whose subject matter and use were at the heart of people's livelihoods. The most collected of these songs were those of work groups who both lived and worked together.

Come, butter, come!
De King an' de Queen
Is er-standin' at de gate,
Er-waitin' for some butter.
An' a cake.
Oh, come, butter, come!
(Scarborough, 215. Woman's butter-churning song; one of the few examples of women's work songs found in American collections of the early twentieth century.)

There were three kinds of work song. First there were the songs in the worker's general repertoire that were not specifically about the singer's work experience. These were usually sung at general gatherings when there was no work to do. The second type, sung mostly for entertainment in the same context, were songs about the work itself. This group might include songs about disasters, heroes, or humorous incidents on the job. Among the third type were those songs that literally helped the workers with the task at hand. Most often these were songs that had a set rhythm and allowed a group of workers to coordinate effort—to hoist a sail, to coordinate blows of hammers, or to hoe a field in unison. (Vocal expressions that border between song and speech were used by groups to communicate important information, such as the call to "mark twain" on riverboats or the calls that cowboys used to soothe cattle at night.)

Some of these work songs originated in the United States, while others owe traits, themes,

F

FOLK SONG AND FOLK MUSIC

Genres of American Folk Song

Music is my weapon. I believe in music, in its spirituality, its exaltation, its ecstatic nobility, its humor, its power to penetrate to the basic fineness of every human being.

HENRY COWELL

*Joan Baez also
helped introduce the
public to another
young folksinger
who would provide
a major voice for
social change in the
1960s and early
1970s—Bob Dylan.*

PAGE 404

See also
Popular Music before 1950

and even entire texts and tunes to foreign song traditions. American lumbering songs have ties to both the Australian folk song tradition and to Irish folk music. Cowboy ballads show a range of influences as wide as the vastly eclectic mix of persons who became cowboys, "from the folksong repertoires of African Americans or Latinos working the range, to those of the popular-song tradition of the day" (Thorp: 20, 23). Sailor's songs, both from the Great Lakes and the ocean-going ships, reflect the lumbering, farming, and immigrant traditions.

As the concept of work has changed since the 1970s books have begun to appear that address the wider question of how an occupation can be seen reflected in the folk songs both of workers and of other groups. The extensive folk song tradition of coal miners in the United States has been studied by Archie Green, and Norm Cohen has shown the major significance of railroading in both American life and song.

TOPICAL SONG. Topical songs are those that deal with issues of immediate importance to a group. The tradition of writing topical songs is at least as old as the earliest broadsides of the fifteenth century. They concern themselves with social, economic, and political issues such as disasters (storms, shipwrecks, floods, earthquakes), movements (temperance, abolition), wars, local community issues (including murders and scandals), or labor strife. There are a few reasons why a topical song could persist as part of the folk song tradition long after the particular incident upon which it has been based has occurred. The issue that the song addresses may still remain unresolved and of importance to the group; the song might be regarded as a historical song (such as songs about past presidents and their assassinations); or the song may have been changed or reinterpreted so that it has become meaningful in a context different from that in which it originated.

> Come, listen, fellow-workingmen, my story,
>   I'll relate,
> How, workers in the coal-mines fare in
>   Pennsylvania State;
> Come, hear a sad survivor, from beside his
>   children's graves,
> And learn how free Americans are treated
>   now as slaves.
>
> They robbed us of our pay,
> They starved us day by day,

> They shot us down on the hillside brown,
> And swore our lives away.
>
> (Foner: 202)

The topical song is of ideological importance to the singer and listener. Its goal is to enact change or allow catharsis. Many topical songs are written by those who have suffered harm or feel they are in jeopardy. Thus, while topical songs may be considered folk songs, they are perhaps the only folk songs that have as a goal their own demise, since they seek the elimination of the causes for which they are written and sung. In this sense, songs urging women's suffrage became obsolete after women were granted the vote.

The words to topical songs are written by persons familiar with the immediate situation, and the tune is often one commonly known by both singer and audience. Either popular or folk tunes are used. This flexibility in the use of different melodies is also characteristic of religious folk songs, as is the attempt to create change or intensify feelings relating to group identity (social, religious, political, and so forth). In fact, Joe Hill, the famous songwriter and organizer of the IWW (Industrial Workers of the World, whose members were known as "Wobblies"), often used hymn tunes for his topical songs. And it was not infrequently that the Wobblies found themselves singing their songs on a city street corner within distance of competing religious groups such as the Salvation Army.

The words of topical songs that are set to borrowed tunes are often similar to the lyrics of the original song, a fact that makes these songs parodies of a sort, since they rely on a referent text for their impact and often for their humor. At times the use of familiar tunes and texts allows for "sing-along" topical songs. Such songs could inspire a group to act. At other times a topical song might be sung to impart a story. However, not all topical songs are built on other folk songs. Some are original compositions that serve the group's needs. When labor began to organize in this country toward the end of the nineteenth and the beginning of the twentieth centuries, repertoires of topical labor folk songs developed with it. Groups both adapted existing folk song texts for their own use and created new songs to carry their message and help with the activities of the labor movement.

"It Isn't Nice" is an example of a song that inspired action, sitdowns, and other peaceful resistance, first in the 1960s in the San Francisco area and in many other places thereafter. This song was sung widely in the 1960s. Judy Collins and others have recorded it, including its writer and composer, Malvina Reynolds.

> [Verse 2]
> It isn't nice to carry banners
> Or to sit in on the floor,
> Or to shout our cry of Freedom
> At the hotel and the store,
> It isn't nice, it isn't nice,
> You told us once, you told us twice,
> But if that is Freedom's price,
> We don't mind.

> [Verse 5]
> It isn't nice to go to jail,
> There are nicer ways to do it
> But the nice ways always fail.
> It isn't nice, it isn't nice,
> But thanks for your advice,
> Cause if that is Freedom's price,
> We don't mind.

As with any repertoire of songs, topical folk songs developed a set of commonplaces, terms that had a shortcut meaning for the listener. Calling someone a "brave young comrade" in a song about the mining troubles in Harlan County, Kentucky, in the 1930s was a way of saying that the person in question was a fighter for the people and a martyr. One can often date topical songs by their commonplaces.

At times it is the context that defines a topical song. During the civil rights movement of the 1960s, the religious folk song "We Shall Overcome" was used by marchers to express their feelings. Although the song's text was little changed from what was sung in church, the singing of it during a civil rights march provided a context in which it became a protest song. Thus, any song, if sung in the right cultural context, is a potential protest song. Likewise, it can be said that a topical song, once it has lived past its historic and social contexts, can become popular with a different group of singers than those intended by the original writer or singers. This occurred with Woody Guthrie's "This Land Is Your Land."

In her history of topical songs in this country in the 1930s through the 1950s, Robbie Lieberman points out that "This Land Is Your Land" "was written as a [left-wing] parody of Irving Berlin's "God Bless America" (the first version was "God Blessed America for Me"). [Today] schoolchildren do not learn the more militant verses, such as this one:

> Was a big high wall there that tried to stop me
> A sign was painted said: Private Property
> But on the back side, it didn't say nother—
> This land was made for you and me.
>
> (Lieberman: 163)

In other words, Guthrie literally meant that we, not just monied and politically powerful people, should own the United States. Lieberman's insightful work is very much beholden to the pioneering scholarship of Richard Reuss, who began the trend toward careful study of the interrelationship of twentieth-century American left-wing politics and topical song.

SENTIMENTAL SONG. It is not a great step from the style of the broadside to the style of the sentimental or "parlor" song. Both are transmitted through the complex interaction of print and oral tradition. The sentimental song, a product of the lower- and middle-class parlors of the nineteenth century, used commonplaces that were the clichés

Joe Hill, the Wobbly Troubador, taken shortly before his arrest and execution. Salt Lake City, 1915.

of the time. These songs employed the imagery of Victorian moralism, and described events and their consequences with a heavy hand. Because the aesthetic of such songs was associated with the lower classes, people who regarded their tastes as more refined were reluctant to pay attention to them. Scholars considered them subliterature and not worthy of study.

"Young Charlotte" is an example of a widely sung sentimental ballad. It warns young women against vanity, dancing, not heeding parents, and the frivolities of youth.

> *Young Charlotte lived by the mountain side*
> *In a wild and dreary spot*
> *With no other dwelling for miles around*
> *Except her father's cot[tage].*

> *On many a cold and wintery night*
> *Young swains would gather there;*
> *Her father kept a social board,*
> *And she was young and fair.*

[On a bitterly cold Christmas Eve she wants to go to a nearby dance.]

> . . . .
> *When dashing up to the cottage door*
> *Young Charles in his sleigh appeared.*

[Mother warns daughter to wrap in blankets in sleigh.]

> *"Oh, no, no," the daughter said,*
> *And she laughed like a gypsy queen.*
> *"To ride in blankets all muffled up*
> *I never will be seen."*

[She freezes to death as they drive, but Charles realizes it only as they reach the dance.]

> *He bore her out into the sleigh*
> *And with her he drove home;*
> *And when he reached the cottage door*
> *Oh, how her parents mourned!*

> *They mourned the loss of a daughter dear,*
> *And Charles mourned o'er his doom,*
> *He mourned until his heart did break—*
> *They slumber in one tomb.*

(Belden: 309–310)

But despite this historical social stigma, these songs about gray-haired mothers being led to the poorhouse, of orphaned and blind children, of dying nuns, and of loyal Indian maidens held as honored a place in the repertoires of traditional singers as did the older imports from the British Isles. A few early collectors such as H. M. Belden and Vance Randolph recognized that sentimental songs were as much a part of America's folk song tradition as were the Child ballads, and they included them in their collections.

RELIGIOUS SONG. Religious folk songs are identified as those sung during the services of groups that practice folk religion, or as songs that have religious events or stories as their central theme. During colonial times both psalms and hymns were sung by congregations through the technique of lining out. The preacher would sing a line and the congregation would repeat that line after him. This technique was especially helpful where books were scarce or where the congregation was not able to read.

During the Great Awakening in the mid 1700s spiritual songs appeared in congregations that wished to incorporate group singing into the church service. These new songs often took current secular folk tunes and combined them with new words to make religious texts. With the advent of camp meetings in about 1800, large numbers of people traveled great distances to set up "camp" in order to hold church services over a period of days or weeks. These meetings produced a simpler spiritual song, one whose words and stanzaic form allowed for greater group participation than occurred during the Great Awakening. The camp meetings were part of the religious movement known as the Second Awakening, during which the religion preached was far more personalized than that of the earlier period. The Second Awakening was primarily a rural phenomenon, and its activities were scorned by urban populations, because of the unlettered who participated and the ecstatic states to which they rose.

As the urban centers swelled after the Civil War and toward the end of the nineteenth century, the social gospel developed in the cities. This religious movement preached the "City of God on Earth," where material rewards can be had in this rather than the afterlife, which had been the focus during the Great Awakening. Religious folk songs consequently changed with the times, taking on the trappings of the urban popular music that had been forged through a mixture of many different cultural influences. The result was the gospel song, a modification of the earlier camp meeting songs in an urban context. The gospel song incorporated the developing ragtime sound, an upbeat rhythm, and words that depicted a far more intimate relationship to God or Christ than did earlier religious folk songs.

With each turn in this country's religious history, new instruments and folk instrumental styles found their way into church services and church music. With the development of string bands and the country music industry in the early twentieth century, religious songs were sung in hillbilly, bluegrass, and other singing styles. Folk groups such as the Carter Family were welcomed by the commercial recording and music industry.

The Carter Family was a southern mountain family singing group. They were one of the most popular commercial country music groups from the late 1920s through the early 1940s, whose records and regular radio appearances were very popular. They sang both religious and secular songs, wrote many of their own pieces, and came to represent the American family and pristine morals (Malone: 63–65).

OTHER GENRES OF AMERICAN FOLK SONG.

Genres of American folk song are not delineated just by textual form or by function. Some kinds of American folk song have been accepted as genres simply because there has been a good deal of scholarship or public attention devoted to them. Because of this inclusiveness, the list of American folk song genres could be long. Various other types of folk song in the United States might include children's songs, game and play-party, songs, dance songs, bawdy songs, nonsense songs, dialect songs, and patriotic songs.

Performed Folk Song

Folk song is a complex of elements far beyond simple text. In the same manner that a movie is not only its screenplay, or a stage play is not only its text, folk song must be seen as a total performance. Each element of that performance is learned traditionally, and each is judged by a traditional aesthetic. Every folk group has a folk aesthetic by which it judges text, music, and style of performance. What one culture values is not necessarily what another one will. Only when we examine folk songs in terms of these elements can we begin to understand the folk songs of a culture.

TEXT. Cultures recognize certain arrangements of words as texts to given genres of folk song. Texts have various characteristics, most of which are derived from the study of written poetry. A text can be analyzed, for example, in terms of its meter, stanzaic form, rhyme scheme, point of view, or themes. In order for a song to be considered good, all of its textual elements must meet aesthetic criteria learned traditionally within the group that perpetuates it.

MUSIC. A folk song's music, like its text, contains elements that are immediately recognizable to its composers, players, and audience. There is a culturally learned musical vocabulary used with each genre, and the performer must know the limits of individual choice and creativity when choosing and performing a song. For example, southern mountain traditional singers seldom used instrumental accompaniment to sing the old ballads. They often sang them without a "regular" rhythm and strove for a high, tense pitch, sometimes called a "high, lonesome sound." This music seems understated to current urban American audiences, especially since this traditional musical aesthetic emphasizes limited use of dynamics (loudness and softness).

STYLE OF PRESENTATION. When referring to style of presentation, we should be aware that there are separate styles for texts and for music. What is meant here by style of presentation is the way in which different types of songs are performed in different manners. Style of presentation is essentially what is done by the voice, the body, and the instruments that makes a song performance a definite "type" of song. There are vocal and instrumental techniques as well as appropriate gestures (or lack thereof) that good traditional singers learn and master and that can be varied within culturally condoned limits. There are folk standards of good and bad folk performance just as there are of popular and classical performances.

There were two distinct styles of a cappella folksinging presentation brought to this country from the British Isles. One was a generally plain, unornamented vocal style that had virtually no vibrato, used no dynamics, and had a varying rhythm. The sound was produced by a nasal or throat effect. This style is primarily English. The second style was an ornamented one, often with a set rhythm, which featured a glottal vibrato without pitch alteration, and dynamics often unrelated to the text. This style is primarily derived from the Scottish and Irish tradition. In addition, there were definite instrumental styles that were brought to America and further developed here.

Two of the best-known European American instrumental styles to develop in this country are the string-band musical styles of bluegrass and "old timey" (a precursor of bluegrass). Instruments such as the Autoharp, the five-string banjo, and the southern mountain dulcimer were Americanizations of instruments brought to this continent from Europe, Africa, and Scandinavia. For the most part, however, the Americanization of music had more to do with the manner in which instru-

Beyond its function as a coping or adaptive mechanism, music has served in many ways to witness and to promote protest, even insurrection.

PAGE 19

***

See also
Rock Music

161

ments were played than the development of entirely new instruments. Fiddle-playing in Texas in the 1800s sounded very different from the violin playing of "classical" musicians in Boston of the same period, even if each performer was playing a physically identical instrument.

FUNCTION. In a given culture, singers learn what songs to sing, when, where, and why to sing them, and with whom or to whom they can be performed. This knowledge is a vital part of folk song; it constitutes the function of the song or music. To know these particulars means that a singer has an understanding of the proper context

in which a song may be sung or must be altered. A judicious choice of a song or a sequence of songs can be as creative an act as a remarkable performance.

Once a folk song is learned, each singer makes changes that best suit her or his aesthetic and the situation in which the song is to be sung. The folksinger can change any aspect of the song as long as the audience will tolerate the change. Considering the potentials for variation in all the elements of a folk song, the folksinger in the United States has extensive opportunities for creativity.

GOVERNMENTAL INSTITUTIONS AND FOLK SONG STUDY
American History Through Music

Early academic interest in folk song began in America in the last half of the nineteenth century. It was centered in the Northeast, with Francis James Child, his student George Lyman Kittredge, and Phillips Barry as the major proponents. At Harvard, where Child and Kittredge worked, many of this country's folklore and folk song scholars began their careers. Although neither Child nor Kittredge did any fieldwork, and although neither showed an interest in the performance of folk song, they were responsible in part for later folk song scholars who were.

One of Kittredge's students was John A. Lomax, who traveled to the western United States in order to record cowboy songs. In 1910 he published *Cowboy Songs and Other Frontier Ballads*, one of the earliest and most popular firsthand collections of what he believed were genuine American folk songs.

John Lomax was accompanied in much of his fieldwork by his son Alan Lomax, who took up his father's vision of presenting to the United States its own folk song legacy. To a large extent through publications of commercial collections such as his *Folk Songs of North America* (1960), his extensive issuing of field recordings for labels such as Columbia and Atlantic, and through academically affiliated projects such as that which forms the core of his work on folk song style, Alan Lomax has been one of the most influential persons in the twentieth century to spur the development of both academic and popular interest in American folk song.

Among the recordings that were used by city singers to learn new songs during the folk song revival of the 1960s were the field recordings that are still issued commercially by the Archive of Folk Song

in the Library of Congress. This archive was established in 1928, and scholars such as John A. Lomax, Benjamin A. Botkin, and Alan Lomax were among its first directors. Today that archive is known as the Archive of Folk Culture. In 1976 it was placed under the umbrella organization of the congressionally established American Folklife Center. This organization remains located in the Library of Congress. The Library of Congress, along with the National Endowment of the Arts' Folklife Programs and the Smithsonian Institution's Folklife Program, are the central governmental organizations devoted to ongoing research and presentation of American folk life.

The primary forum for both scholars and nonscholars of folklore is the American Folklore Society, founded in 1888, whose periodical, the *Journal of American Folklore*, has continuously published for over a century. In addition, numerous regional folklore societies and publications flourish throughout the country.

Major universities in the United States offer advanced degrees in the study of folklore. A doctorate in this field is offered by Indiana University, UCLA, the University of Texas at Austin, and the University of Pennsylvania. These universities and numerous others offering master's degrees in folklore often cooperate in projects with the governmental institutions. In addition, governmental organizations also help fund regional and state folklife centers, which have flourished throughout the country since the 1970s. Local historical societies and arts boards, privately funded, state run, or supported by the National Endowments of the Arts and Humanities, also employ folklorists and encourage the study and presentation of American folklife and folk song.

Commercialization of Folk Song and the Folk Song Revival

The earliest commercialization of folk music undoubtedly occurred through whatever early institutions were considered the mass media of the time. European and British troubadours, as well as the broadside press, certainly spread folk songs. There is a constant interaction among potentially fixed aspects of song performance (those that can be spread by mass media and recorded in some manner, such as the text of a tune) and elements of folk song that are passed on through the performance itself. A pure oral tradition probably never existed during the time humans made written records. The extent to which a folk song has been "commercialized" is not a measure of whether or not the song is a folk song in any given context. The transmission of a song (all four elements) within a group, without reference to a fixed source for continual correction, constitutes a folk song.

It is only recently that the concepts of "commercial" and "folk" have seemed contradictory. In the early days of professional entertainment in the United States, the vaudeville stage, traveling tent shows, medicine shows, and minstrel shows all contributed to and received from general popular tradition. From the beginning, radio broadcasts used local talent. Right before the Great Depression, the recording industry, then in a slump and sensing the threat of the new radio technology, sent scouts to the southern mountains to seek out local musicians. In the 1920s Ralph Peer, talent scout and recording director for a number of record companies, introduced to the commercial recording industry both African American and Anglo-American folksingers. He discovered Mamie Smith and Fiddlin' John Carson among others, and he was a key player in establishing the commercial country and western music industry. This industry catered to an underclass that longed for music from "back home."

In the 1930s and 1940s folk songs were brought to the attention of urban middle-class audiences through the federal government's Works Progress Administration (WPA) and by left-wing political groups who felt that "people's songs" were most appropriate as a vehicle for political ideology. For left-oriented urban singers of folk songs, the "folk" meant the "people" or the working classes (farmers and the industrial workers). Folk songs and folklike songs were sung at political rallies, union meetings, and at hootenannies. The urban "hoot" of the mid-twentieth century was usually an advertised event with featured artists who espoused left-wing causes. They would perform from a stagelike area and sing songs with clear political messages, many of which were selected (and written) so that the audience could join in the singing.

Were it not for the political left wing of the 1930s and 1940s, urban middle-class America might never have known Woody Guthrie, Leadbelly, Sarah Ogan Gunning, and other traditional folksingers. And if it were not for the persistence of urban singers who believed in the principals of the left-wing ideology of the day, such as Alan Lomax, Peggy Seeger, Burl Ives, Pete Seeger, Will Geer, and Ronnie Gilbert, American mass media and popular culture never would have seen many major talents.

In the 1950s there was a burgeoning interest in folk song outside of political circles. Some performers, such as Pete Seeger and the group in which he sang, the Weavers, felt the need to carry their political messages to new audiences, especially those that were developing on college campuses. Seeger's and the Weavers' brilliance as musicians and performers allowed them a wide range of expression, and their audience was extensive. In their commercial recordings they presented an apolitical repertoire; by the early 1950s they had numerous hit records such as "Good Night, Irene," "On Top of Old Smoky," and "The Midnight Special," and they had performed at Carnegie Hall. However, blacklisting during the anticommunist McCarthy era removed the

FOLK SONG AND FOLK MUSIC

Commercialization of Folk Song and the Folk Song Revival

♦ **Broadside**
A sizable sheet of paper printed on one or both sides and folded or not; something (as a ballad) printed on a broadside

TRADITIONAL FOLKSINGER

Leadbelly, photograph 1966, and his music came to the attention of the 1930s and 1940s urban audiences at political rallies, union meetings, and at hootenannies.
UPI / CORBIS-BETTMANN

*The Hutchinson
Family Singers
performed songs
with a social
conscience based
on a typically
American faith in
social progress.*

PAGE 355

See also
Concert Music

Weavers, collectively and individually, from public media.

To understand the urban folk song world of the 1940s, 1950s, and 1960s, one needs to make a distinction between traditional folksingers and singers of folk songs. The former includes those singers who learned all elements of folk song from traditional sources, while the latter encompasses those musicians whose repertoires relied on regional folk song collections. The texts and tunes that singers of folk songs performed originated with traditional groups. These singers performed for urban audiences in a recast style of presentation and with a function particular to their urban needs. Eventually some of these singers and others would begin to write their own texts and tunes based on a folklike model.

In 1958 the folksinging Kingston Trio hit the charts with "Tom Dooley," a song they learned from the recording of a traditional folksinger. For almost twenty years thereafter popular song would be heavily and directly influenced by Anglo-American and African American folk song. It was this introduction of various aspects of folk song into the mainstream of American popular music that allowed for the drastic shift in the popular aesthetic that occurred by the 1970s and had blossomed earlier with Bob Dylan and other singers and songwriters of his generation, such as Joan Baez, Judy Collins, and Tom Paxton.

The folk song revival flourished throughout the decade of the 1960s. Basically four kinds of singers emerged during this period, some of whom found more in common with the currents of preceding decades and some of whom foreshadowed the sound and style of the decades to come.

The first kind of singer that formed the basis of the folk song revival of the 1960s was the "traditional" performer or "folksinger" who had learned all four elements of folk song through the culture in which he or she was raised. Such performers were invited to sing at folk festivals, on college campuses, and in coffeehouses. Before the 1960s, urban audiences had not been prepared to hear their style of presentation. The major folk song element that each of them had to alter in his or her performance, which seriously distorted their art, was the function. It was virtually impossible to present accurately in an urban setting songs that originally had been performed in an entirely different context. This affected texts, tunes, and style of performance. Many traditional singers began to "urbanize" their performances, increasing the tempo of the songs that they sang

for urban audiences, adding accompaniment to their previously a cappella traditional performance style, and dropping local references from their texts. Nevertheless, the difference between what they presented and what their audiences were accustomed to hearing was startling. It raised basic questions in the minds of urban audiences about what standards should be used to judge "good" songs and performances. Typical of this kind of singer were Sarah Ogan Gunning, Mississippi John Hurt, and Glenn Ohrlin.

It is interesting to note that the two kinds of traditional folksingers who were in demand in urban America at this time were poor white southerners and poor rural African Americans. These were the same groups sought by the early recording industry. One seldom heard other groups in the urban revival, despite the fact that audiences were rarely composed of poor whites or African Americans. The audience of the urban folk song revival in the 1960s was primarily white middle-class youth from urban suburbs.

The second type of performer in the 1960s urban folk song revival was the emulator. These performers were, like their audiences, mostly white middle-class suburban or urban young people who chose to immerse themselves in both the music and culture of the traditional singers. The emulators found profound meaning in both the traditional texts and music, as well as in the style of presentation. Many of the performers became so versatile at emulating a traditional folk song style that they were accepted as traditional by the cultures that they sought to emulate. Some of them were not only able to imitate, they were able to create. The one element that they found most difficult to master, however, was function. Among those of this type were the New Lost City, Ramblers, Dave Van Ronk, the Greenbriar Boys, and the Jim Kweskin String Band.

The third kind of singer in the urban revival was the utilizer. These performers were singers of folk song who took traditional texts and music and set them to a style which, in the early 1960s, was acceptable to the established aesthetic of mainstream urban audiences. These singers appealed to the urban "pop" sound (the music of the Kingston Trio, for example), and the urban "art" sound (represented by those such as Alfred Deller and Richard Dyer-Bennet).

The fourth kind of folksinger in the 1960s urban folk song revival was the singer who personified the new revival aesthetic. These singers differed from utilizers in that they did not remold the material in terms of an aesthetic that already existed. This group of singers attempted to blend traditional and urban aesthetics in their performance. They developed a new way of accommodating the inevitable tensions that existed among various song styles in nonurban and urban cultures. They and their audiences synthesized new aesthetic criteria for all four elements of folk song. The sound of this group was one that blended folk, classical, jazz, and pop styles. Almost all of the revival aesthetic singers performed with accompaniment. They crafted ways to harmonize the modal traditional tunes, and they created what at the time was a new effect in their performances.

It was this sound of the revival aesthetic that became the sound of the urban folk song revival of the 1960s. It was Joan Baez; Peter, Paul, and Mary; and Bob Dylan. The days of the popular crooner who had reigned during the 1940s and 1950s were replaced by the sounds of these new singers and their derivatives. Pete Seeger, one of the most gifted arrangers, creators, and performers of this revival aesthetic, was a leading influence in developing a new popular music in the United States. With the urban folk song revival, mass media developed a commercially successful new sound of the 1960s. It was one that would influence generations to come. Popular taste was dramatically altered, and listening skills were expanded.

The opening of aesthetic choices in the 1960s led the way to a new diversity and inclusiveness in popular music suited for the coming age of global communications. It also gave many singers in urban centers a new repertoire and a new folksinging tradition. This urban tradition has yet to be studied with the enthusiasm of America's earlier rural traditions, although it presents just as rich an area of cultural expression. Folksinging is now recognized as a viable form of expression in modern urban America, for which we are indebted to both commercial interests as well as to the scholars of the multifaceted American folk song.

—ELLEN J. STEKERT

FOODWAYS

Arugula, big macs, barbecue, C rations, caviar, chitterlings, chop suey, Gerber's strained peaches, jambalaya, johnnycakes, kielbasa, matzoh balls, Moon Pies, pemmican, sauerkraut, and Weight Watchers frozen pizzas are all food items that have been consumed at one time or another in the United States of America. Though some foods, such as the humble but omnipresent hamburger, transcend lines of age, class, and geography, preferences for others clearly correlate with historical period, region, social class, gender, age, occupation, race, and ethnicity. Foodways—the manner in which groups of people select, prepare, and ingest edibles—are thus a valuable source of information about the character of the various social groupings of the United States and their interrelations at any given time. Although the term is most commonly used by ethnologists and ethnologically influenced students of folklore and folklife in examining "folk" societies and subcultures, the following essay will focus on the role of food in American society more broadly.

The Columbian Exchange

The story of North American foodways begins with the "Columbian exchange," the process that began in 1492 with the European arrival in the New World, through which the natural and human ecologies of the two broad cultural zones began to become inextricably intertwined. European newcomers were faced with the absence of indigenous sources of food—such as wheat bread—to which they had been accustomed. The English "Pilgrims," near starvation after their arrival at Plymouth on coastal New England in 1620, were happy enough to incorporate the maize (corn), beans, and squash offered by the native peoples into their diets, together with the wild turkey, venison, and abundant seafood that the new land offered. The Spanish also reluctantly learned to make do with manioc or cassava as substitutes for wheat in Central and South America until more familiar patterns could be reestablished.

Prior to the coming of the Europeans, the diet of the indigenous North American peoples had varied by region, but was broadly based on locally available fish and game and the three vegetable staples of maize, beans, and squash, together with nuts and berries. As a result of the Columbian exchange this diet also was altered, as were the broader life patterns of the native peoples, who became employed in the cultivation of bananas, sugarcane, rice, and coffee—all of them Old World imports, though now for centuries associated intimately with the Americas. In addition, the Spanish introduced Iberian staples such as wheat, olives, and wine grapes into those areas where they could be successfully cultivated. (Junípero Serra and the Franciscans who organized the California Indians into mission colonies in the late eighteenth century attempted to Europeanize their charges in part through the cultiva-

He who would be the tongue of this wide land/ Must string his harp with chords of sturdy iron/ And strike it with a toil-imbrowned hand.

JAMES RUSSELL LOWELL
ODE (1841)

tion of these crops.) A major result of this importation of European food plants and animals and their rapid flourishing was the creation of a living environment both materially and culturally hospitable to succeeding waves of Old World colonists.

Where pre-Columbian native peoples had raised little livestock other than poultry for food, they accepted the introduction of pigs and cattle much more readily than they did most European food plants. Native peoples living near the northern edge of New Spain in what is now the southwestern United States—the Navajo, Pueblo, and Apache—eagerly turned to cattle raising. The horse, previously unknown in the New World, was used more in the raising of cattle and other food animals than for food itself. Its introduction revolutionized the cultures of the Plains peoples through its usefulness for transportation and warfare as well as pursuit of the bison and wild cattle. In the longer run, Spanish cattle and horses paved the way for a western culture featuring latter-day vaqueros (cowboys—sometimes a role ironically played by Indians under the Spanish) and a fierce American appetite for beef. The overall result, according to biohistorian Alfred W. Crosby, Jr., was "so successful . . . that . . . [it was] probably the greatest biological revolution in the Americas since the end of the Pleistocene era" (*The Columbian Exchange*, p. 66).

Anglo-American Colonial Patterns

English-speaking colonists began early in the seventeenth century to fashion their own sets of foodways, which combined regional English patterns of cooking and eating successively with locally available foodstuffs, foods transplanted from England, and, eventually, imports from a wide variety of foreign locales. Borrowings from Native American and other neighbors, together, in some cases, with religious and ideological considerations, further influenced Anglo-American patterns. William Bradford describes the earliest patterns of interaction and adaptation in *Of Plymouth Plantation* for the year 1621:

[In April] they began to plant their corn, in which service Squanto stood them in great stead, showing them both the manner how to set it, and after how to dress and tend it. Also he told them except they got fish and set with it (in these old grounds) it would come to nothing. . . . Some English seed they sowed, as wheat and peas, but it came not to good, either by the badness of the seed, or lateness of the season, or both. . . .

They began now [in September] to gather in the small harvest they had. . . . Others were exercised in fishing, about cod, and bass, and other fish, of which they took good store, of which every family had their portion. All the

CARVING DINNER

*A woman dressed in American
Colonial attire shows how seventeenth century colonialists
butchered meat.*
RICHARD T. NOWITZ / CORBIS

summer there was no want. And now began to come in store of fowl, as winter approached, of which this place did abound when they came first (but afterward decreased by degrees). And besides water fowl, there was great store of wild turkeys, of which they took many, besides venison, etc. Besides they had about a peck of meal a week to a person, or now since harvest, Indian corn to that proportion. Which made many afterwards write so largely of their plenty here to their friends in England, which were not feigned, but true reports.

The alternating abundance and want that characterized these and subsequent years in New England gave rise to days both of thanksgiving and of fasting and repentance, the only occasions other than the Sabbath that constituted Puritan collective ritual observance for many decades.

THE NEW ENGLAND DIET. Cattle from England had been introduced into the Plymouth Colony by 1624, thus reducing the necessity for hunting, an occupation or recreation alien to the British "middling" classes. (John Winthrop, the leader of the much larger 1630 settlement of the Massachusetts Bay Colony, was not averse to an occasional expedition with his fowling piece, though.) Wheat and rye supplemented the indigenous maize, and chicken, hogs, and fruit trees were also introduced into New England before long. The Puritan "plain style"—a cultural aesthetic based on a religious objection to overelaborateness, whether in preaching, clothing, or cooking—combined with circumstance to produce what David Hackett Fischer has called "one of the most austere foodways in the Western world" (*Albion's Seed*, p. 135).

The resultant cuisine has endured as part of the New England diet to the present day. After they had overcome their initial aversion to the giant lobsters that abounded in coastal waters, New Englanders appropriated the aboriginal custom of holding clambakes, in which clams, other shellfish, and later accompaniments were cooked while buried in sand with heated rocks. Such affairs were easily turned into communal and, eventually, commercial ventures. Succotash, a mixture of beans and Indian corn, derived both its name and its character from Algonkian usage. Cornmeal yielded various edible products such as samp, a coarse hominy now sold by the Vermont Country Store as a semiexotic, seminostalgic regional item; johnnycake (journey cake), a baked or fried kind of cornbread suitable for taking along on travels; and Indian pudding, made with milk and mo-

lasses, and now served at restaurants featuring regional cuisine such as Boston's Durgin Park.

Other aspects of the New England diet that arose from necessity and were later regarded as embodiments of frugal virtue were baked beans, described by Lucy Larcom in the nineteenth century as the "canonical dish of our Forefathers" (Fischer, p. 136), and prepared in advance to avoid cooking on the strictly observed Sabbath; the New England boiled dinner, based on carrots, potatoes, cabbage, and corned beef, that is, meat "corned" with salt as a preservative, then boiled in unseasoned water; and codfish balls or cakes, made from the ubiquitous fish enshrined in a six-foot model at the Massachusetts State House as the "Sacred Cod" in tribute to its role as provider of both food and commercial value. The expansion of trade with Britain, the West Indian colonies, and other ports that did so much to create many coastal mercantile fortunes also enriched the regional diet with molasses, rum, and citrus fruits from the West Indies; tea, coffee, chocolate, spices, and sugar from the East Indies; tapioca from Latin America; dates from the Middle East; wine, brandy, and raisins from the Mediterranean; ginger from China; and rice and corn from the southern colonies. Farther north, those intrepid settlers attempting to eke out a living in the mountains of what would become Vermont and New Hampshire found domestic uses as well as external markets for maple sugar, and a confluence of cultural patterns with nearby French Canada led to other regional adaptations. Pies, an English institution and ubiquitous to all parts of New England, were sometimes fried in Vermont. (Part of Yankee folklore, or perhaps "fakelore," has it that a Yankee is simply anyone who eats pie for breakfast.)

Patterns of food preparation in New England were derived primarily from East Anglia, the region of origin of the majority of the earliest English settlers. Dark English beer was the beverage of choice in the seventeenth century, and was later augmented by fermented apple cider and the universally popular rum, some of it home-brewed from cherries. Pork and beef were the preferred meats. (An abundance of meat and dairy products distinguished the diet of the "middling" classes from their poorer neighbors, and imported products such as tea were at least at first a mark of luxury.) Boiling and baking were the most common means of food preparation. The latter operation could be done in iron kettles or, as circumstances began to permit, in the more elaborate brick ovens that soon became common. Food preparation was

FOODWAYS

Anglo–American Colonial Patterns

The very discovery of the New World was the by-product of a dietary quest.

ARTHUR M. SCHLESINGER, JR.
PATHS TO THE PRESENT
(1949)

See also
The Plantation

F

strictly gender-typed, and women managed domestic gardens and chicken coops in addition to buying food and preparing meals.

OTHER BRITISH COLONIAL FOODWAYS. New England's culture has received extensive scholarly attention, and provides a useful example of the social and ecological complexities involved in foodways. There were, of course, other sorts of British colonial societies in North America. Virginians also continued English foodways, but more according to the customs of southwestern England. The great planters were the closest thing the colonies produced to an aristocracy, and their ample means and conservative tastes produced the closest the era came to a haute cuisine. "Dining," observed the eminent historian Edmund Morgan, "was a fine art in Virginia," and dinners offered by the plantation elite were major social occasions (*Virginians at Home*, p. 75). In such grand households, kitchens were separate from the main building, and meals were prepared there by slaves or servants. Humbler Virginians had to be content with one-dish "messes" of greens and salt meat seasoned with wild herbs, and ample doses of cornmeal mush. Unlike their more austere New England cousins, Virginians of all classes enjoyed ample seasonings in their foods.

David Hackett Fischer, in *Albion's Seed*, argues that two other cultural zones emerged in the English-speaking colonies that reflected as well the foodways, as well as other folkways, of still other

parts of Britain from which they were originally settled. The Delaware Valley Quakers, who hailed primarily from the North Midlands and Wales, were as similar to the New England Puritans in their pragmatic and rigorously antisensual approach to cuisine as they were in their "work ethic." Boiling was the preferred cooking technique, with dumplings and puddings as regional favorites. Sugar came to be shunned, since it was produced by slave labor, a practice abhorrent to Friends' humanitarian principles. Some interchange also developed with the nearby "Pennsylvania Germans" (or, incorrectly, "Dutch") as both groups produced versions of scrapple, a fried mixture of cornmeal and finely chopped miscellaneous parts of the pig or cow.

A more widely spread and perhaps even more enduring approach to food preparation was that of the "backcountry." This was the piedmont and mountain region west of the original coastal zones of settlement, populated originally and primarily by emigrants from the northern British borderlands, many of whom came to be categorized as Scotch-Irish (that is, Scottish lowlanders or transplants in Ulster). These people came culturally prepared to be frontier settlers. Their culinary staples included oats, which in the New World yielded to maize in the form of hominy grits; pigs, which similarly replaced the Old World sheep; potatoes, accepted in Britain only as the fare of simple people; clabber, made from sour milk, curds, and whey; and various sorts of unleavened flat cakes cooked on a griddle. Whiskey—first Scotch, then bourbon—was the backcountry beverage of choice. Vegetables indigenous to North America rounded out the regional diet. It is clear enough how many of these elements combined in various ways to form the bases of a generic southern regional style.

SLAVE FARE AND ITS INFLUENCE. The other side of the southern social spectrum was reflected in the fare of slaves, who frequently subsisted on the three M's—meat (sow belly), meal (corn), and molasses. Several African foodstuffs and descriptive words entered the regional repertoire. Okra (Ashanti, *nkru*; in other West African languages, *nkru, nku, ruma,* or *nkruma*) is a pod containing seeds and a thick, gluey substance eaten fried or in gumbo (Bantu, *ngombo*), a synonym for okra also used in Louisiana Creole and Cajun cuisine to describe a variety of soups or stews thickened with okra or *filé* (French for "threads") powder made from dried sassafras leaves. Goober (Kongo, *nguba*) remains a regional synonym for peanut, transplanted from South

See also

Childhood and Children

THOMAS JEFFERSON

America's First Gourmet

The social and economic polarization of the South was reflected in its foodways as they took shape during the early nineteenth century. Thomas Jefferson was widely known as one of America's first gourmets, a distinction which earned him Patrick Henry's denunciation for unrepublican culinary elitism. Jefferson acquired a firsthand knowledge of continental European foods and techniques for their preparation during his sojourns abroad. A widower at an early age, he employed his daughters, granddaughters, and slaves in the elaborate process of food selection and preparation at Monticello, and utilized inventions of his own such as dumbwaiters to minimize eavesdropping by servants at his frequent elaborate dinners for highly placed guests. His introduction of French chefs and their fare into the White House and the enormous "bar bill" for French wines and champagne—five hundred bottles a year of the latter—generated in the course of official entertaining placed an enormous strain on his resources. Jefferson's largess reflected not only his own expansive temperament but also the tradition of southern hospitality that had originated among the planter class as a means of entertainment among widely scattered plantations, a service to travelers, and a visible means of demonstrating status through conspicuous consumption.

America to Africa and then back to the North American colonies. Corn (maize) and yams (a word of mixed African origins) also played a major role in southern black fare; like the goober, yams were also introduced from South America to Africa in the sixteenth century by Portuguese traders. The experience many slaves acquired in food preparation facilitated entry into the broader economy after the Civil War; among the few niches in the workforce open to them for many decades were jobs as cooks, waiters, and, in the armed forces through World War II, mess stewards. Aunt Jemima and Uncle Ben persist to this day as commercial emblems of nurturing slaves associated with bountiful food service. Interestingly, the Nation of Islam (called Black Muslims), which became influential in many urban black ghettos in the 1950s and 1960s, adopted a dietary code very loosely based on that of traditional Islam, which banned on religious grounds most

items associated with soul food; instead, they promoted—ironically, given their ideology—a diet favoring foods characteristic of the white middle-class norm.

The sorts of foods eaten by slaves and, later, sharecroppers were by no means restricted to blacks; rather, a diet based on pork, corn, and such other vegetables as sweet potatoes and cowpeas emerged early as characteristic of the South as a whole, and has persisted with a staying power far in excess of that of most other parts of the country. The earliest stages of settlement saw a heavy reliance on game—deer and bear, as well as smaller animals such as squirrels, opossums (from Virginia Algonkian, *apasum*) and raccoons (Algonkian, *arahkun*). Indian corn rapidly established itself as a primary food, giving rise to innumerable popular derivatives such as hominy (Algonkian, *rockahominie* or *rokahamen*), produced by treating ripe corn with lye; grits (or hominy grits), made of finely ground hominy; cornmeal mush; hush puppies, fried balls of cornmeal and, sometimes, onions; and hoecake and other forms of cornbread. (Wheat bread was eventually introduced into the region, but never displaced cornbread in popularity.) Cowpeas and greens—collard, turnip, and others—were boiled (with frying, a favorite form of preparation) and eaten, with the remaining pot likker (liquor) relished for sopping as well. Chicken was a favored food for special occasions among the poorer classes, while pork was the standby. Little of the pig was wasted, with even such parts as the chitterlings or chitlins (intestines) entering the repertory of blacks in particular. Beef and lamb were not disdained, but the expense, particularly of the latter, relegated them to the wealthier classes. Catfish—fried and served with hush puppies and cole slaw—remains a favorite among southerners of all sorts and conditions.

SOUTHERN FOODWAYS. Although these foods have remained popular throughout the South, other foods were abundant more locally and helped to shape a more restrictedly regional cuisine. Seafood was plentiful in coastal areas, and attained a special place in the closely related cuisines of the Creoles (American-born descendants of Europeans or, locally, any residents of New Orleans) and Cajuns (displaced French-speaking Acadians from Nova Scotia who settled amid the bayous of southern Louisiana). New Orleans was particularly a cultural and culinary melting pot, with French, Spanish, African, and Native American elements enhancing its complexity and giving rise to a mixture of spices unacceptable

> Gardens appeared
> on the East Coast
> in provincial cities
> prior to the
> American
> Revolution
> providing simple
> pleasures—food,
> drink, music, and
> some free variety
> acts, fireworks, or
> balloon ascensions.
>
> PAGE 31

to most Yankees. (Gumbo, mentioned earlier, was built around celery, tomatoes, and bell peppers, with andouille [ANN-dooey] sausage, chicken, or seafood sometimes added.) Cajun foodways built on abundant seafood such as crawfish and redfish; in the 1980s, this hitherto obscure regional culture received national attention through the work of the New Orleans chef Paul Prudhomme, and blackened redfish—as well as blackened almost everything else—began to grace fashionable restaurant menus across the country. (Zydeco music, a similar regional cultural blend, also attained a national following in this period.)

Following the Civil War, the gradual entrance of the South into a national market economy led to mixed consequences. Once antebellum agriculture had become established, according to Joseph R. Conlin, slaves on the better plantations consumed over four thousand calories a day. After the war, though, as Joe Gray Taylor notes, heavily milled corn and fatback (fat meat from the back of the hog) from the Midwest rather than bacon undermined the nutritional value of the diet of rural people. A similar decline in the quantity of fruits and vegetables they consumed further made them vulnerable to malnutrition-related diseases such as pellagra and hookworm. The resultant endemic poor health nurtured the image of a "lazy South" filled with "tobacco roads" of poor, illiterate, disease-ridden sharecroppers.

Though this stereotype was not entirely baseless, reflecting economic circumstances more than character, southerners have expressed a typical ambivalence toward their past in their enshrinement of regional foodways, even as they began to participate fully in a national culture and economy. Coca-Cola (regionally pronounced Koh-KOH-lah) originated in Atlanta in 1886, and ultimately became an international symbol of American national culture and mass marketing. ("Cocacolonization" has emerged as a synonym for such commercial hegemony.) RC Cola is a more localized taste and is linked with the Moon Pie, a marshmallow sandwich invented in Chattanooga around 1918. Another favorite regional confection is the Goo Goo Cluster (Nashville, 1912). Ice(d) tea is the drink preferred in genteel circles, while corn likker—originally a convenient way of transporting corn in highly condensed and remunerative fashion—is a beverage reflecting another side of regional taste (together with its more sophisticated counterparts, Jack Daniels and Rebel Yell sour mash whiskeys).

National franchising elevated Colonel Sanders' Kentucky Fried Chicken to transregional emi-

nence, making that staple of fine southern cooking an attenuated regional counterpart of the aregional McDonald's and Burger Chef. (Harland Sanders opened his first stand in Corbin, Kentucky, in 1956, but was later bought out by a national syndicate.) Other chains such as Stuckey's, Po' Folks, and Cracker Barrel now market regional cuisine of greater or lesser authenticity along interstate highways within and beyond the South itself, each capitalizing on a "countrified" image in the manner of the Grand Ole Opry and the television program *Hee Haw*. Traditional southern cooking, whether perpetuated through family oral tradition or "yuppified" à la *Southern Living* magazine, retains its hold on the indigenous populace more perhaps than in any other extended cultural region in the United States to this day.

THE GREAT AMERICAN STEAK RELIGION. The crude, pork- and corn-based food habits of the frontier South were also characteristic of the broader frontier of the earlier nineteenth century. European travelers viewed with alarm the monotonous diet of heavy, greasy foods consumed by the locals and offered to these sojourners as well, and noted that dyspepsia—a severe, chronic form of indigestion no longer common—was a widespread problem. (Modern-day truckstops offer similar fare, making it clearer why fast-food franchises have become so popular.) Once family farms had become established, the diet of countryfolk became more varied and salubrious, but continued to be heavy and abundant to generate the energy necessary for strenuous outdoor work. John Mack Faragher, in his *Women and Men on the Overland Trail*, describes a typical midwestern farm family's daily provender at mid century as including two kinds of meat, eggs, cheese, butter, cream, corn, bread, several vegetables, jellies, preserves, relishes, cake, pie, milk, coffee, and tea (p. 52; cited by Conlin, p. 8). Conlin estimates that Americans at the time consumed an average of four thousand calories per day, a startlingly large amount compared with a late-twentieth-century average of about half that, or with the barren diet of contemporary British and Continental laborers and peasants. (Many of the poor, however, consumed far less, often from foods of dubious nutritive value, and malnutrition and its related diseases were scarcely unknown in both rural and urban areas.)

Though corn and pork remained popular especially in the South, it was midwestern beef and wheat that began to rival and eventually surpass them as national dietary staples, especially as the railroads and new agricultural technology made their growth and distribution rapid and economical. The preference for beef, more plentiful in the United States than in any part of the world except perhaps Argentina, would persist as a distinctive character of an emergent national taste, and would later be characterized by food reformer Frances Moore Lappé (*Diet for a Small Planet*, 1971) as the "great American steak religion." The *Statistical Abstract of the United States* (1980) indicated that approximate daily consumption of beef by Americans rose from 2.4 ounces (67 grams) in 1910 to 4.2 ounces (118 grams) in 1976, which accounted in part for a 28 percent increase in fat consumption during that period. (Pork consumption declined slightly from 2.7 to 2.6 ounces [76 to 73 grams] during the same period.) A similar preference for white over whole-grain bread was also in this period emerging as a not entirely wholesome dietary preference. Diurnal alcohol consumption also yielded during the early nineteenth century to coffee and tea, stimulants conducive to the disciplined effort that a nascent national market economy demanded.

Immigration and Ethnic Foodways

The quest for a better diet was a primary motive for the vast immigration that altered American society so dramatically during the entire nineteenth century. The potato, another example of the Colombian exchange, was first exported from the highlands of South America to Europe in the sixteenth century, but was originally categorized as an aphrodisiac, a cause of leprosy, and the fare of peasants. Though it eventually became a staple, especially of eastern European folk society, its introduction into Ireland during the later years of the 1500s transformed the diet of that nation and promoted an extraordinary growth in population in the ensuing centuries. This growth came to an abrupt halt in the 1840s, when a devastating blight on the potato crop combined with other political, economic, and demographic factors to result in massive famine and emigration, primarily to the northeastern coastal cities of the United States. (The typical Irish diet had consisted of up to 10 pounds [4.5 kilograms] of potatoes per day, often with little else but milk.) The rapid assimilation of the initially despised but English-speaking Irish militated against the perpetuation of a fare that was basically a variant on a broader northern European peasant theme. Though corned beef and cabbage remains an ethnic favorite on Saint Patrick's Day, this is a residual reminiscence of a vanished folk culture characteristic of many deracinated ethnic groups attached more in nostalgia than in everyday behavior to their ancestral past. (Jiggs's attachment to the dish in the comic strip "Bringing Up Father," however, was a sign of his passive resistance to the hectoring Maggie's attempts at assimilation and social climbing.)

FOOD REFORMERS

Healthy Eating in the Nineteenth Century

This seemingly relentless progress toward a heavy, calorie-laden diet, whether based on pork and corn or beef and wheat, was not without its challengers. A Puritan reformist strain was manifest in the urgings of Catharine Beecher, in *A Treatise on Domestic Economy* (1841), toward a temperate regimen eaten deliberately. She cited physical as well as spiritual health as primary rationales. Beecher's contemporaries also denounced excessive seasonings and fried foods with a similar mixture of motives. One of the most influential reformers of the era was the Presbyterian minister Sylvester Graham (1794–1851), whose name has ever since been connected intimately with the cracker made from the unbolted flour he promoted. Utopian experiments, ranging from Bronson Alcott's vegetarian Fruitlands (1844–1845) to the herb-loving celibate Shaker communities, similarly practiced variations on the theme of a simple, natural diet that contributed physically to a lifestyle harmonious with higher laws. (Thoreau's primitive urge to devour a woodchuck raw was only an apparent exception to this tendency.) Religious motives were also prominent in the Seventh-Day Adventist movement, which arose out of the Great Disappointment over William Miller's unfulfilled millenarian prophecies in the mid 1840s. Influenced by Graham as well as the Adventists, both John Harvey Kellogg (1852–1943) and C. W. Post (1854–1914) contributed to the quest for a salubrious, natural, precooked food in their respective development of the cornflake and the grape nut. The heavily sugared cold cereals favored by children in the later twentieth century were a far less healthful variation on the Post-Kellogg theme characteristic of the child-oriented consumer culture promoted especially by television commercials.

See also
Amusement and
Theme Parks

The heavy diet of the German immigrants who streamed into first the middle colonies and then Ohio and other parts of the Old Northwest in the days of the early republic was similarly characteristic of the agrarian folkways of northern Europe. Like the Poles and other Slavs who swelled the ranks of America's newcomers during the latter decades of the century, Germans consumed prodigious quantities of pork together with potatoes, beets, cabbage, and other vegetables that kept well without refrigeration. This fare, which has never gained culinary esteem because of its lack of variety and seasoning (apart from salt, sugar, and vinegar), was developed to its fullest among the misnamed Pennsylvania Dutch. These sturdy people were in fact German Anabaptists drawn to southeastern Pennsylvania through the appeals of their pacifist counterparts, the Quakers, beginning in the late 1600s. Abundance rather than subtlety characterizes this regional cuisine exemplified in such traditional dishes as shoofly pie, chicken corn soup, schnitz (seasoned ham) and apples, scrapple, and the variety of preserved fruits and vegetables that make up the proverbial "seven sweets and seven sours."

NEW IMMIGRANT FOODS. The "New Immigration" of the decades from the 1870s through the outbreak of World War I enriched the American diet in a number of ways. Central and eastern European fare, again, did not gain a wide audience outside of a few highly spiced items such as kielbasa (Polish sausage) and Hungarian *gulyas* (goulash). Much more influential beyond the limits of particular ethnic communities was Italian pasta- and tomato-based fare such as spaghetti, lasagna, and, of course, the pizza that has become omnipresent in the mass culture of the later twentieth century. (Tomatoes were also introduced into Europe as a result of the Columbian exchange, but were grown in Britain until the nineteenth century only as an ornamental plant. These "love apples" were feared as poisonous in some places until the turn of the twentieth century.) Ironically in retrospect, many New Immigrants were derided as "garlic eaters" by native-born Americans unaccustomed to highly seasoned foods.

As Evan Jones has pointed out, the presence of Italians in California from the time of the gold rush launched their cuisine into American life through their cultivation of plants and vineyards characteristic of their traditional foodways and also through their involvement in the restaurant business. The durum wheat from which Italian pasta was made began to be grown in Kansas on a large scale through Department of Agriculture encouragement, and the shutting off of European imports by World War I gave further impetus to domestic cultivation. The introduction of the pizza to the United States is a topic of contention perhaps second only to the discovery of America in some circles, but many favor the hypothesis that Wooster Square, New Haven—the old center of that city's strong Italian population—deserves the honor. (Nearby Louie's Lunch is sometimes credited with the introduction of the hamburger as well; other schools of thought give it a German origin, imported via the English Salisbury steak and popularized at the Saint Louis World's Fair in 1904.) The dramatic popularity gained by what was originally known as the "pizza pie" following World War II is a prime example—together with the hamburger, fried chicken, and tacos—of the assimilation of selected items of ethnic diet into the mainstream of popular culture through mass production, franchising, and aggressive advertising and merchandising.

The Greek immigrants who constituted another major wave of the New Immigration have been particularly distinguished as restaurateurs, originally gaining an economic niche through providing food to urban workers seeking a quick lunch on their breaks from the office and factory work that dominated the new economic order of the early twentieth century. Greek proprietors later capitalized on a growing demand for a more distinctive cuisine, providing moussaka, *pastitsio*, and a variety of lamb dishes from the old country in Greektown restaurants and the diners that proliferated in the urban Northeast. A distinctive Greek-American contribution is Cincinnati "five-way" chili, made from ground beef and a complex combination of flavorings (including cumin, allspice, and unsweetened chocolate), served over pasta with grated cheese, kidney beans, and onions. Developed locally in the 1920s, this culinary hybrid later began to encroach on the broader popularity of the Tex-Mex chilis that themselves represent an adaptation and indigenization of Mexican traditions. Though Greek Americans, like most groups of New Immigration provenance, have become increasingly assimilated into the middle-American culinary and broader cultural mainstream, events such as the annual *panegyri* held at many Greek Orthodox churches feature traditional foods—together with music, dancing, and folk costumes—as occasions in which traditional folkways are still honored, if only in the breach.

The Jews who emigrated from the ghettos and shtetls of central and eastern Europe during these tumultuous decades illustrate the complex relationship between ethnicity, cultural adaptation, and religion in their foodways as well as in other aspects of their lives. What has come to be known as Jewish cooking—that characteristic of urban delis—is a variation on the foods of Germany, Romania, Hungary, and the Slavic-speaking countries in which Jewish culture flourished prior to the devastation of the Holocaust, and includes pastrami, corned beef, latkes (potato pancakes), and borscht. Other foods, like matzoh (flat, crisp unleavened bread), are used especially on ritual occasions, and are uniquely Jewish. Also governing the foodways of observant Jews are the kosher (ritually clean) laws, which among other things prohibit the consumption of pork and the mixing of milk and meat products. The maintenance of these customs has been a major issue between Orthodox or Conservative Jews who have chosen to be faithful to tradition, and Reform or secular Jews who reject such practices as obsolete. Roman Catholics, among whom were many Irish, Italian, German, and eastern European immigrants, maintained a similar distance from the dominant American Protestant and secular cultures through their observance of "fish on Fridays," a practice made optional (except during Lent) after the Second Vatican Council of the early 1960s.

Another set of foodways is that of Spanish-speaking peoples—who, in fact, are a wide variety of different groups united mainly by variants on a common language. West Indian (Cuban and Puerto Rican) cuisine varies considerably from that of Mexican Americans, whose poverty, language, and frequent illegal status have helped to preserve traditional foodways longer than those of immediately European origin. In the barrios of southern California and Texas, the tortilla—the traditional flat maize cake—is still a dietary staple, together with salsas (sauces) made from tomatoes and chilis, all reminders of the pre-Columbian regimen. Variations on these themes have led not only to the simplifications purveyed by Taco Bell and other fast-food chains, but also to the hominy-based *posole* of New Mexico and the barbecue (from West Indian, *barbacoa*) that characterized pre-Anglo California and, in endless varieties, Texas and the South.

Forces of Standardization

In striking contrast with the diversity of ethnic foodways in the history of American food patterns was the simultaneously emergent force of standardization. A major factor in the growing homogenization of national foodways that began

to take shape during the middle decades of the nineteenth century was technology. Beginning in the 1830s, expanding railroad networks provided rapid transportation of goods between city and country, with each being gradually transformed as a result. The availability of a wider and less expensive variety of foodstuffs in urban kitchens and dining rooms was particularly accelerated by the development of the refrigerator car, which permitted the slaughter and processing of animals near where they had been raised and their subsequent distribution virtually anywhere in the world. Large-scale fortunes were made beginning in the 1880s by industrialists such as Gustavus Franklin Swift and Philip Danforth Armour, whose names later attained a nearly generic status as synonymous with meats. Refrigeration also made possible the development of large-scale cultivation of a wide range of vegetables and citrus fruits in Florida and California that had until then played only a limited role in the general American diet, but could now be easily brought to distant markets.

Another technical innovation of long-range importance was quick-freezing. Early in the twentieth century, Clarence Birdseye—better known today as a brand name than as an inventive and eponymous individual—developed a technique for preserving foods through rapid freezing, which precluded decay by not generating the large ice crystals that could destroy cellular walls. Such freezing was the culmination of a whole series of innovations over the course of a century or so, which began with improved canning techniques and continued through Gail Borden's perfection of a condensed form of milk shortly before the Civil War. Corresponding developments in domestic technology, including the refrigerator, the home freezer, and the microwave oven, which permitted rapid defrosting, made possible the widespread use of these preservation techniques from the farm to the kitchen.

By the 1920s, "scientific" advertising had united with aggressive new marketing strategies and techniques of mass distribution to alter national patterns of food selection dramatically. Brand names such as Swift, Birds Eye, and Betty Crocker—a fictional personage whose image is periodically updated—became fixed in shoppers' imaginations as synonymous with uniform, dependable, and reasonably priced products. The supermarket, exemplified by the Great Atlantic and Pacific Tea Company (A&P), began during the 1930s to displace locally owned stores—sometimes by incorporating them into national chains—

There is no love sincerer than the love of food.

GEORGE BERNARD SHAW

♦ **Borscht**
A soup made primarily of beets and served hot or cold, often with sour cream

F

More die in the United States of too much food than of too little.

JOHN KENNETH GALBRAITH
THE AFFLUENT SOCIETY
(1958)

with new, seemingly giant emporiums featuring self-service and a vast variety of fresh and processed foods and other household goods.

Fast-food chains were a variation on the theme. Their symbiotic relationship with other modernizing forces was exemplified in the monopoly obtained by Howard Johnson's for food service on the Pennsylvania Turnpike, which in 1940 opened as the nation's first interstate highway. HoJo's, as the orange-roofed purveyor of updated versions of traditional New England fare later came to be known, had been founded in 1925; in the 1970s it began to yield to newer, still more efficient chains, such as Ray Kroc's dramatically successful McDonald's. Kroc, the son of a Bohemian immigrant, who rivaled Henry Ford as an archetypal American rags-to-riches entrepreneur, took over a local California drive-in in the 1950s and developed an inordinately successful formula: the easily recognizable golden arches trademark; a national chain of clean, standardized franchised outlets; headquarters at Hamburger Central in Oak Brook, Illinois; a restricted, unsubtle range of products, broadly based in appeal; minimum-wage employees, mainly teenagers; aggressive advertising and public relations campaigns; sophisticated but easily operated standardized equipment; and strategic locations designed to attract travelers, teenagers (since the 1950s, possessed of vast discretionary income), and inner-city dwellers. By the 1990s, ecological and nutritional concerns were successfully pre-

vailing upon McDonald's and other fast-food chains to minimize nonbiodegradable packaging and to decrease the fat content of their usually fried products. The introduction of salad bars at such establishments was also indicative of heightened consumer health consciousness.

THE INFLUENCE OF GOVERNMENT. In counterpoint with business and technology as agents of standardization were government, science, and education. The distrust of fresh vegetables and milk that was commonplace through the early decades of the nineteenth century gradually yielded to advances in bacteriology and new processing techniques such as pasteurization. These enabled children especially to take advantage of these vital sources of nutrients, vitamins, and minerals without risk of acquiring mortal diseases spread through improper sanitation. Outrage over widespread unsanitary conditions in food processing was epitomized in the public outcry that followed the publication of Upton Sinclair's *The Jungle* in 1906. The Pure Food and Drugs Act passed by Congress the same year was the first of a long series of measures through which the government sought to regulate the condition of the public diet. This law brought to the federal level the movement among state and local governments to ensure a supply of pure milk that had been in progress since the 1880s. Larger producers, who were in these same years banding together into trade associations, tended to welcome such regulation as enhancing their own efforts to rationalize their industries and squeeze out smaller competitors.

Other governmental involvements played major roles in the standardization of the national diet as well. Just as the Civil War had accelerated the phenomenon of mass production in its demand for rifles with interchangeable parts, it also stimulated demand for vast quantities of edible, palatable, and nutritious foods in standardized form. Gail Borden capitalized on this demand by creating a network of licensed plants throughout the country to provide the Union forces with the condensed milk he had recently perfected. The usual soldier's ration of salt beef or pork and hardtack—a baked mixture of flour and water—was neither appetizing nor salubrious, however. Plentiful coffee was a more popular staple of the military diet. Unpleasant as the regimen of the Union troops may have been, the scarcity of any food at all among their opponents doubtless hastened the collapse of the Confederacy. Growing nutritional knowledge, the "embalmed beef" scandal of the Spanish-American War, and new techniques of

SUCCESSFUL FORMULA

Ray Kroc, founder of the McDonald's Corporation, developed a successful formula: a recognizable brand (golden arches) and clean, strategically located franchise outlets that served a limited but popular menu.

CORBIS-BETTMANN

SCIENTIFIC HOUSEKEEPING

The Growth of Home Economics

Still another source of standardization was the "scientific housekeeping" movement that arose among middle-class women in the late nineteenth century. Laura Shapiro, though deploring its bland culinary consequences, interprets it as an attempt by women to attain a new professional dignity and sense of usefulness, while not simultaneously appearing radical. This they attempted by elevating a traditional woman's sphere to a more exalted status. Manifestations of this were the "home economics" movement—the name was first adopted in 1899—which placed many women in university positions, and the cooking schools exemplified by the Boston Cooking School of 1879. The latter, originally aimed at providing working-class girls with commercially and domestically useful skills, soon grew popular with middle-class women as well.

The most distinguished graduate and later director of the Boston Cooking School was Fanny Farmer, whose *Boston Cooking School Cook Book* of 1896 had sold over a third of a million copies by the time of her death in 1915. Although recipe books had been in circulation since the colonial era, Farmer's was the first to approach food preparation with an enthusiastic but no-nonsense practical attitude, utilizing, for example, standardized spoon-and-cup measures that had recently become available commercially. (Farmer's work foreshadowed many later variants, such as Irma S. Rombauer's prodigiously successful *The Joy of Cooking* of 1931.) The overall effect of this movement was the promotion of a nationally standardized cuisine prepared from identical recipes with identical equipment, a development that probably advanced nutrition while certainly abetting the success of brand-name foods and related products in a national market system.

> *If you're going to America, bring your own food.*
>
> FRAN LEBOWITZ
> HUMORIST, IN SOCIAL
> STUDIES (1981)

food preservation led in subsequent wars to a better and more varied diet, including the C and K rations of World War II, and the once universally reviled Spam, a canned pork product improved in later years.

In addition to war, poverty was a potent factor in mobilizing a variety of institutional forces toward the transformation, the improvement, and, as a byproduct, the standardization of the national diet. The muckraking interests that had galvanized public interest in the purity of foods also called attention to the miserable nutritional condition of the poor, especially urban immigrants and the rural native-born, and more especially their children. The Great Depression of the 1930s was a further spur to federal extension and educational work by a number of agencies in promoting better knowledge of preventive nutrition and wholesome techniques of food preparation.

Postwar Transformations

The prosperity that many Americans enjoyed during the decades following World War II made possible suburban lifestyles whose followers sought appropriate culinary expression. Outdoor patio living saw new uses for the previously regional barbecue, an adaptation symptomatic of the prestige that California customs now began to exert across the nation. The popularity of the hibachi, a small grill, and of rumaki, an hors d'oeuvre consisting of chicken livers, water chestnuts, and bacon, testified to the new influence of Japanese culture mediated in various ways to North American shores. "Gourmet" cooking, however, was largely synonymous with the culinary Francophilia of a tradition-minded elite, and "American" restaurants tended toward the chophouse, the supper club, the neighborhood family establishment, and the corner bar and grill.

THE POLITICS OF FOOD. The social, cultural, and political ferment that swept the nation beginning with the civil rights and antiwar movements of the 1960s had complex ramifications in the realm of foodways. The alarm over the contamination of foods by pesticides sounded by Rachel Carson in her 1962 *Silent Spring* not only led to growing pressure for increased government regulation of agribusiness; it also helped promote a new enthusiasm for organically grown food among counterculturalists and other, more mainstream middle-class Americans concerned with the purity of their diet. For the more radical, the purity of food was not simply rooted in a concern with physical health, but became as well a metaphor for a broader preoccupation with social, political, and spiritual integrity. Macrobiotics, a dietary regimen based on whole grains, beans, and vegetables, attracted many followers, especially in avant-garde enclaves in academic communities and on either coast.

Later twentieth-century food reform, usually based on a call to simplicity of diet, had its roots

Rations, given out weekly, generally consisted of three and a half pounds of bacon and a peck (fourteen pounds) of cornmeal for each adult, with lesser amounts for children.

PAGE 321

♦ **Cognoscenti**

People who are especially knowledgeable in a subject: connoisseurs

in the reform movements of the pre–Civil War era. Beginning in the late 1960s, food also became associated with political causes. The feminist movement helped focus attention on both the physical and psychological dimensions of women's health, and promoted a growing awareness among adolescent and younger women in particular of eating disorders such as anorexia—deliberate self-starving in an attempt to attain a fashionably though unhealthily thin figure—and bulimia, consisting of bingeing followed by bouts of self-induced vomiting. A less excessive dieting that found continuing favor among both genders was motivated by a desire to be physically attractive, the irrepressibly American cult of youthfulness as an escape from the ravages of mortality, and a more sensible desire to promote health and longevity through the avoidance of excessive strain on the heart and other organs. Feminism for some has become associated with a vegetarianism based on animal rights, a linkage expounded in Carol J. Adams's *The Sexual Politics of Meat* in 1989. Still other political issues involving food were boycotts of grapes, lettuce, and other crops harvested by migrant workers striving to achieve better pay and working conditions; protests against the sale of infant formula in third-world countries by American firms; and the adequacy of nutrition supplied by school-lunch and other programs in inner-city neighborhoods.

THE EXPANSION OF GOURMET DINING. The social and political concerns that focused on food use during these years were paralleled by other developments of somewhat different import. It was this same period that witnessed the transformation of "gourmet" dining from the preoccupation of a small, well-to-do elite into a much broader middle-class phenomenon. Since Lorenzo Delmonico's founding of his celebrated establishment in New York around 1830, French cuisine had enjoyed—with other aspects of that culture—a place of honor among the cognoscenti. *Gourmet* magazine (1941) was the first of what would later become a proliferation of glossy magazines devoted to food and its preparation; it and Julia Child, the Cambridge-based "French Chef" of television fame, helped introduce home preparation of food in the approved manner to growing audiences.

By the early 1970s, something of a revolution had begun to take place in the social functions of food as a mark of status, as well as in its acceptable modes of preparation. Food columns, such as Craig Claiborne's in the *New York Times*, now appeared in lifestyle rather than women's sections

and advocated a wide variety of cooking styles. The introduction of a variety of Chinese regional cuisines, especially those of Szechuan and Hunan provinces, began to displace the primacy of the blander Cantonese and Chinese American dishes that had been the staples of chop suey joints for the previous century, begun originally by Chinese employed to feed logging and railroad crews. Other cuisines—*nouvelle* French, north Italian, regional Mexican, Vietnamese, Thai, Cajun—proliferated bewilderingly as trendy foods among a new consumer culture of "yuppies" eager for novelty and the prestige of seeming to be in on the latest trends. Restaurants, including many formula-following, modish "fern bars," flourished in an industry known for rapid changes of fashion and a correspondingly brief life expectancy for new establishments.

Both regional magazines, such as *Southern Living*, and less sedate rivals of the long-established *Gourmet*—*Bon Appetit, Food and Wine, Cook's* magazine—aimed at an audience of aspiring upper-middle-class clientele desiring sophistication in the purchase, preparation, and consumption of food as an entree into a breathless new social world. Such glossies aimed at an audience of men as well as women. Formerly associated with professional chefs and gay men, cooking skills now became a necessity both for fathers of young children expected by working wives to share in domestic duties, and for both married and single men wishing to flaunt this newly prestigious social skill. New cooking equipment such as the food processor filled kitchens as well as shops and mail-order catalogs designed for an upscale audience. A cultivated taste for wine—California-produced as well as the traditional French—was an important adjunct to this quest for sensual experience and enhanced status.

An American Diet?

American foodways have often been cited as a particularly good example of the melting pot metaphor once hailed as the essence of American society and culture. The long procession of foods discussed above indicates that this image is not groundless; many Americans today consume regularly a wide variety of edibles reflecting a similarly wide variety of cultures in both their modes of preparation and their ultimate sources. However, some nuances must be added for a more accurate picture.

The food consumption patterns of most Americans in the latter part of the twentieth century reflect a linear progression from the regional

British foodways imported during the colonial period to the patterns of mass production and distribution and standardized preparation exemplified in today's supermarkets and fast-food restaurants. In continual tension with this axis have been the variant ethnic, regional, and class-associated foodways that, beginning with the basic crops and game of the aboriginal Native Americans, have interacted with and modified the transition from early modern Britain to the postindustrial United States. Americans today do not so much partake of a common diet as eat within a common matrix, in which certain choices favored by the middle classes are easier to make but others are available as well, though with greater effort or expense. Beef is still plentiful and popular, and the fast-food chains have promoted the consumption of beef, cheese, and wheat flour for hamburger rolls and pizza dough as well as bread. Tea and especially coffee continue as favored daytime beverages suitable to a competitive work force, and their popularity remains strong to the point of addiction. Fresh fruit and vegetables are a still-increasing part of the diet of a health-conscious middle class in which women strongly influence patterns of food selection and preparation.

As the food critic Raymond Sokolov laments, regional foodways are going, but are fortunately not yet gone. Social class and income level push some Americans toward "gourmet" restaurants and others toward government surplus commodities. "Real men" may prefer steak to quiche, and women may choose the salad bar over red meat. Middle-class blacks may occasionally pine for soul food at homecomings, as Italian Americans long for pasta with traditional "gravy" at *feste* and family gatherings. Handmade tortillas may still be the everyday fare of Mexicans isolated in the barrios of southwestern cities. Few, however, are immune to the lure of the hamburger and the pizza. American foodways, in sum, are neither unilinear nor immutable; they are, however, as recognizable as the blue jeans and rock music by which non-Americans, for better or worse, see ours as a distinctive culture.

—PETER W. WILLIAMS

FRATERNAL ORGANIZATIONS

In late-nineteenth-century United States, fraternal orders such as the Masons and Odd Fellows grew to enormous size and influence. Paralleling them was an array of mutual benefit associations that sought to offer both financial security and group identity to members of immigrant communities and to black Americans. Moreover, fraternalism was a widely used form for the organization of trade unions, agricultural associations, and nativist and racist groups. Despite its ubiquity in the social, cultural, and political life of American communities, it is only recently that scholars have made a concerted effort to explain fraternalism's popularity through a recognition of its specific appeal.

The term "fraternal" commonly refers to those organizations that approximate the Masonic model of a secret society with elaborate rituals and degrees or levels of membership. More broadly, fraternalism may designate any organization that organizes the practice of mutual aid around the metaphor of kinship. Mutual benefit societies were found throughout the population, while Masonic fraternalism was, in general, most influential among native-born populations of British and northern European descent, and among African Americans, where secret societies were a fundamental part of community life.

As fictive kinship groups, fraternal orders used ritual to effect bonding, and presented family as metaphor for relations of mutual support and unselfish concern. Additionally, fraternalism implies a brotherhood, a society of men. Most, though not all, lodges have excluded women, but they vary in the extent to which the articulation of masculinity is symbolically central, the more highly ritualized Masonic tradition being most adamant about its all-male character. By 1900 most fraternal orders had parallel or auxiliary organizations of women attached to them. These women's groups, like the Order of the Eastern Star and the Daughters of Rebekah, are most properly designated fraternal auxiliaries rather than sororal organizations, since they functioned primarily within the framework of the male fraternal world rather than within the broader sisterhood of nineteenth- and early twentieth-century women's organizations. Since the 1940s the fraternal world has been in decline in both size and prestige, but during the late nineteenth and early twentieth centuries, fraternal associations were the largest national secular membership organizations.

From Colonial Era to Civil War

The principal fraternal organizations of this period, the Masons and the Odd Fellows, both originated in Britain. Of these, Freemasonry is partic-

FRATERNAL ORGANIZATIONS

From Colonial Era to Civil War

A dog starv'd at his master's gate Predicts the ruin of the state.

WILLIAM BLAKE
AUGURIES OF INNOCENCE

♦ **Schismatic**

*Of, relating to, or guilty
of schism (discord,
disharmony, or formal
division in, or separation
from, a church or religious
body)*

ularly important, not only because the Masonic institution was itself large, well-known, and long-lived but also because Masonic fraternalism functioned as the implicit model for so many subsequent organizations. The Masonic model may be defined in terms of three characteristics. First, its ritual is organized around degrees or levels of membership, which are ascended one by one, in separate initiation ceremonies. For example, the neophyte Mason begins as an Entered Apprentice, then becomes a Fellow Craft, and a Master Mason, with numerous higher degrees, up to thirty-two in Scottish Rite Masonry, as a further option. Second, orders operating within this model all adhere to the Masonic concept of the order as a moral system directed toward the edification of the individual member. Finally, quasi-Masonic organizations claim to disregard "worldly" identity, stating that occupation and class position, like religious and political views, are irrelevant to the brotherly bonds of the lodge.

Freemasonry originated in the seventeenth century, when British gentlemen began to request admission into the lodges of practicing stone masons, and then to adapt and refashion the traditional rituals of operative masons in their own autonomous or "accepted" lodges. In the American colonies, it began as an organization of the elite, composed primarily of wealthy merchants and professionals. By the time of the Revolution, the

membership base had broadened, prompted by a schismatic dispute between rival factions of Ancients and Moderns in which the newer and more inclusive Ancients recruited significant numbers of the era's upwardly mobile, newly assertive artisans. The first black fraternal order also was founded during the revolutionary war when Prince Hall, a minister, and fourteen other African American residents of Boston were initiated as Masons by British soldiers. Their Masonic credentials were thus completely regular, recognized as such by the Grand Lodge of England, despite their rejection by the white Masons of Massachusetts.

Masonry emerged from the revolutionary war with enormous prestige, derived in part from its association with Washington and other Revolutionary heroes. At the same time Masonry provoked hostility and suspicion because of its secrecy, its elite pretensions, and the belief that Masons favored each other in business and politics. The order also drew opposition from Evangelicals and Calvinists, who disliked Masonic optimism and worldliness, and from women, who may have seen its claims of masculine moral sufficiency as an attack upon the emerging canons of domesticity. Thus in 1826, when William Morgan of Batavia, New York, sought to publish an exposé of Masonic secrets, his kidnapping and alleged murder by Masons, coupled with an at-

**CONVIVIAL
SOCIETY**

*The Odd Fellows began as a
convivial society, much closer
to the traditional journeyman's
society than to the Masonic
model.*

tempted cover-up by sympathetic local authorities, crystallized earlier suspicions and led to the emergence of Anti-Masonry as a major political and social movement.

The social base of Anti-Masonry remains unclear. Earlier scholars portrayed it as the reaction of economically and socially marginal farmers to modernizing trends. More recent research suggests the opposite: that Anti-Masonic activism drew its support from flourishing commercial centers that were also centers of evangelical religion and civic voluntarism. What is uncontested is the effect of the Anti-Masonic movement in decimating the fraternity. In New York, for example, membership plummeted from between twenty thousand and thirty thousand to 1 to 15 percent of that figure (sources conflict); in Vermont and Illinois all lodges ceased operation for a time. While Anti-Masonry as a political movement was ineffective by 1834, its condemnation of Freemasonry continued to have a social impact; in most regions normal Masonic activities were resumed only in the 1840s.

The Masons were a multiclass organization that transformed artisanal rites and customs into a highly elaborated system of rituals articulating moral ends. In contrast, the Odd Fellows began as a convivial society, much closer to the traditional journeyman's society than to the Masonic model. Yet by the 1840s, white American Odd Fellowship had been transformed into something much closer to Masonry—a multiclass organization espousing morality and the promotion of individual self-improvement. At the same time (1843), the Grand United Order of Odd Fellows received its charter of origin from one of the English Odd Fellows' organizations, thus establishing Odd Fellowship among African Americans.

During the 1820s, educated, middle-class reformers began to join the white Odd Fellows. Their attack on conviviality, or drinking in the lodge room, was accompanied by restrictions on fraternal mutual aid practices and, most important, by revision and expansion of the ritual. The new rituals invested the order with a sense of decorum and moralism that was intended to attract higher-status members while promoting in the "industrial classes," its traditional base, an ethos of discipline and self-improvement.

The Golden Age: Fraternalism After the Civil War

The Civil War represents a watershed in the history of American fraternalism. Before the war, fraternal growth meant primarily the expansion of the Masons and Odd Fellows, the organizations that largely defined the boundaries of social fraternalism. After the war their membership increased, not just steadily but exponentially. In the state of Missouri, for example, membership of white Odd Fellows grew from 4,000 in 1866 to 93,000 in 1914. By 1907 national membership of the white Masons and Odd Fellows reached over one million each, while black Odd Fellows numbered 270,000 and black Masons 100,000.

Equally important, however, was the creation of many new fraternal organizations. The *Cyclopaedia of Fraternities* (1907), a directory of fraternal secret societies, identified some three hundred fraternal organizations. The years from 1864 to 1884 were the crucial period when the Knights of Pythias (1864), the Benevolent and Protective Order of Elks (1868), the Ancient Order of United Workmen (1868), the Ancient Arabic Order of the Nobles of the Mystic Shrine (or Shriners, 1867–1872, variously), the Knights of Honor (1873), the Royal Arcanum (1877), the Knights of the Maccabees (1878), and the Modern Woodmen of America (1883) were among the major orders established. The new orders spread rapidly, so that a town of fifteen thousand, like Belleville, Illinois, which had only Masons and Odd Fellows' lodges in 1868, was home to thirty-five lodges of sixteen different national organizations by 1884. By 1900, contemporary observers estimated that from 20 to 40 percent of the adult male population belonged to at least one lodge; if that is correct, then an even larger proportion must have belonged at some point in their lives, making the fraternal order a truly massive presence in late-nineteenth-century popular culture and community life.

The fraternal world became not only larger but also more variegated. The founding of the Ancient Order of United Workmen in 1868 marked the creation of the first insurance fraternity, which offered a death benefit to members along with a ritual experience. Many new organizations of this period were insurance fraternities, and some older orders felt compelled by the competition to offer an insurance option to members. The offering of insurance extended fraternalism's practical side by transforming the traditional death and sick benefits into something more substantial and rationalized.

Two other fraternal innovations, the playground lodge and the military branch, sought to elaborate the pageantry and ritualism of the lodge movement. The quintessential playground lodge was the Ancient Arabic Order of the Nobles of

♦ Journeyman

A worker who has learned a trade and works for another person, usually by the day

the Mystic Shrine, an organization whose membership is restricted to Masons of the highest degree. Shriners became known for their comically
exaggerated titles, lavish parades, and red fezzes;
because they are today the most visible remnant of
the fraternal movement, they are often mistakenly
seen as representative of what fraternalism means.
The idea of the military branch was much more
successfully disseminated through the nineteenth-
century fraternal movement. Military branches
were parade units, drill teams elaborately costumed and trained to march with military precision. Yet they represented something more than
pure spectacle, for they were quasi-military organizations. Military branches surely drew upon
nostalgia for the Civil War, but it seems equally
significant that they emerged during an era of intensified nativism and unprecedented labor unrest.

Women's auxiliaries, including the Order of
the Eastern Star, the Daughters of Rebekah, and
the Pythian Sisterhood emerged during these
decades. Important black orders like the Independent Order of St. Luke were established, while
the Prince Hall Masons and the Grand United
Order of Odd Fellows experienced significant
growth, facilitated by the ending of slavery and
the consequent greater ability of southern blacks
to engage in civic and community activities. The

Patrons of Husbandry, commonly known as the
Grange, was organized in 1867 as a social, political, and self-help association for farmers, and the
Knights of Labor was created in 1869 to advance
the interests of workers. They, like many other political and labor organizations, made intentional
use of fraternal ritual to create solidarity among
their members.

Inclusion and Exclusion

CLASS COMPOSITION. The fraternal world,
if we can talk about one world, reflected and reinforced divisions of class, race, and gender.

In terms of class composition, fraternal orders
were somewhat heterogeneous. Some scholars
have characterized mainstream fraternal orders as
middle class in composition and ethos, while others have seen them as working-class institutions
contributing to class solidarity. Analysis of the
membership of lodges in a variety of locales consistently finds that they were mixed-class organizations. The Masons, always the most selective
group, tended to be primarily middle class, but
even Masonic lodges typically contained an identifiable minority of blue-collar workers. Other orders, such as the Odd Fellows and Knights of
Pythias, contained many more working-class
members than the Masons. Individual lodges
were often skewed in their composition, but core

membership was drawn from the ranks of small proprietors and skilled workers, with significant representation among professionals, clerks, salesmen, and factory operatives as well. Most significantly, even the most class-homogeneous local lodge was symbolically a part of a heterogeneous national organization whose members were united in ritual brotherhood. Indeed, the irrelevance of class was a central tenet of fraternal ideology: "Every good citizen, be he laborer in the streets, or a judge, a farmer, mechanic, or capitalist, stands on a footing of exact equality in the Modern Woodmen of America" (Clawson, *Constructing Brotherhood*, p. 176).

ETHNICITY. It is generally assumed that the white Masonic-type fraternal orders were ethnically as well as racially homogeneous, composed almost wholly of native-born white Protestant men of British or northern European descent. Groups like the white Masons and Odd Fellows often appeared to be strongholds of nativist sentiment; there is, for example, evidence that Masonic lodges served as recruiting grounds for the Ku Klux Klan during the 1920s. Yet evidence from an earlier period suggests a more complex history, with significant variation in fraternal policies toward immigrants.

From the 1860s through the 1880s, most orders not only accepted immigrants as members but also allowed local lodges to operate in languages other than English and even provided foreign-language versions of their rituals. German immigrants were undoubtedly the most numerous beneficiaries of such policies; almost every town with any significant German population had German-language lodges of Masons, Odd Fellows, and Pythians. During the 1880s a nativist upsurge, coinciding with the beginnings of large-scale immigration from southern and eastern Europe, led to the abolition of foreign-language lodges. While none of the major orders enacted policies of outright ethnic exclusion, the changing character of immigration, the increasing articulation of nativist sentiments, and the polarization created by the interaction of fraternal anti-Catholicism and Catholic antifraternalism resulted in the abandonment of whatever degree of cultural pluralism had characterized earlier years.

Immigrant groups formed two sorts of fraternal associations. Local mutual benefit societies organized on the basis of province, region, or city of origin were common among southern Italians, Poles, Russian and Polish Jews, and Czechs, who brought their European associational experience to the United States. These small, localized bene-

fit societies were not usually ritualized secret societies, but they were fraternal in their adherence to the principle of mutual aid and their conception of themselves as a logical extension of kin-based networks of exchange governed by norms of reciprocity, rather than by notions of charity or benevolence. To traditions of self-help and mutuality brought from their societies of origin was added a sense of ethnic identity, a sense that in organizing for their own survival, immigrants were acting to preserve a cultural heritage.

In addition, most immigrant groups formed national fraternal organizations, such as the Ancient Order of Hibernians (1836) and the Order of Sons of Italy (1905). Some of these organizations followed in the benefit tradition by offering insurance to members; others engaged in charity fund-raising. Often, as secret societies with initiation rituals, they resembled Masonic fraternalism. They differed from the localized benefit societies in their concern to articulate a sense of nationality or national ethnic identity—but as an ethnic group *in America*, whereby ethnicity began to be seen as a form of Americanism. In this sense the decline of local ethnic benefit societies and the growth of these national ethnic organizations in the 1920s and 1930s indicates a growing assimilationism.

One obstacle to the incorporation of immigrants into the Masonically oriented fraternal movement was its proscription by the Roman Catholic church. As early as 1738 the church had condemned Freemasonry as a type of natural religion that denied that divine grace and revelation are necessary to lead a good and moral life. Furthermore, the church opposed the possibility that Catholics could join with non-Catholics in secret societies. In the late nineteenth century, papal condemnation was extended to the Odd Fellows and Knights of Pythias, and American bishops frequently wrote and preached against Catholic participation. These admonitions, coupled with anecdotal evidence in lodge records and numerous attempts to create Catholic fraternal societies, suggests that Catholic participation in proscribed orders was common and regarded by the church as a serious problem. This Catholic ethnic presence probably diminished in the early twentieth century in response to increased nativism and the creation of visible Catholic alternatives.

The Knights of Columbus, established in 1882, became the preeminent Catholic fraternal order, including members from all ethnic groups. Although the organization was created by a priest and consistently sought ecclesiastical approval, a

FRATERNAL ORGANIZATIONS

Inclusion and Exclusion

Trust men and they will be true to you.

RALPH WALDO EMERSON

See also
Village and Town

F

*Those mausoleums
of inactive
masculinity are
places for men
who prefer
armchairs to
women.*

V. S. PRITCHETT

few bishops disapproved of it in the early years because of its parallels with Masonry. Indeed, the intent of the organization, with its signs, passwords, and ritual of three degrees, was to offer Catholics a fraternal alternative. What is most striking about the Knights of Columbus is its assimilationism, a movement away from ethnic identity toward a religious one, and the articulation of that religious identity as a form of Americanism within a pluralistic society.

RACE. Masonic fraternalism was inconsistent in its approach to ethnic and religious difference; alternative ethnic and religious brotherhoods emerged in response to its openness as much as to its policies of exclusion. About race there was much more consistency; indeed, racial exclusion was a hallmark of mainstream American fraternalism from its inception. The enforcement of white racial purity was accomplished not simply on a de facto basis, which could have been done through the blackball, but by formally requiring that prospective members be white and by denigrating black orders. This was particularly true of the white Masons, who persisted in viewing Prince Hall Masonry as an irregular or "clandestine" body that was not "genuinely" Masonic—despite its "regular" origins and recognition by the Grand Lodge of England.

Challenges to the all-white character of orders, usually from the position that it violated claims of fraternal universalism and brotherhood, surfaced periodically in fraternal debate. National policies mandating white racial status as a prerequisite for membership allowed such challenges to be quickly and summarily suppressed. Fraternal orders existed in and reflected the values of a racist society. The public commitment of the national organizations to racial hierarchy worked to suppress oppositional tendencies by making loss of fraternal legitimacy the price for any attempt, however minimal, to breach or weaken the color line. The national groups thus worked not only to reflect but also to enforce racial boundaries, to serve as one institutional resource, however small, for the organized defense of a segregated society. Black fraternal orders consistently rejected these values even as many sought to use the cultural apparatus of white fraternalism to build their own communities.

Fraternal societies have been extraordinarily important in African American communities, perhaps even more so than in white ones. Earlier generations of white scholars tended to devalue black lodges as largely expressive in function, giving otherwise powerless people the opportunity to enact hierarchical relations that severed them from the larger community and reinforced acceptance of the status quo. It is clear that black people, like their white counterparts, delighted in the enactment of fantastical ritual dramas that may seem bizarre or laughable today; these may have carried an especially powerful symbolic charge to individuals who were denied so many public roles.

Organizations that placed themselves directly within the traditions of white Masonic fraternalism were the largest and oldest black fraternal orders. They attracted a membership of largely middle- and upper-working-class men, and provided their members with the pleasures of ritual, fellowship, and mutuality. Black Masons, Odd Fellows, Knights of Pythias, and Elks used the same rituals but were not recognized by the white-only orders. This replication of the rituals and practices of organizations that were flagrantly racist might seem like a bizarre act of identification with the oppressor. Yet if the exclusion of blacks sought to convey that adult manhood, as defined and ratified by fraternalism, was not available to black males in American society, then the organization of such parallel groups may have represented one way of denying this claim, through the assertion of a right that white groups sought to deny.

Black orders displayed a self-conscious concern for the welfare of the race, which they articulated through increasingly politicized actions. In 1926 the Improved Benevolent and Protective Order of Elks established a Civil Liberties Department, which engaged in litigation against racial segregation. The Prince Hall Masons pursued similar ends through a policy of contributing to the National Organization of Colored People. Thus their allegiance to the forms of a racially exclusive institution was coupled with an explicit rejection of its racist tenets.

Through practices of mutual aid, fraternal associations in black communities, like those in white communities, contributed to the marshaling of collective resources needed for everyday survival and improvement among the economically marginal. Moreover, benefit societies and fraternal orders provided their participants with leadership roles and experience in managing money, speaking in public, directing meetings, and engaging in concerted collective action. A study of postbellum Richmond, Virginia, finds that virtually every black political and union activist had a history as an officer of multiple lodges and benefit societies. "These societies provided the necessary social foundation to address black issues collectively" (Rachleff, *Black Labor in Richmond*, p. 33).

Black local mutual benefit societies in many ways paralleled the ethnic benefit societies described earlier, but differed in that female societies were more common. This was true as well of national benefit societies; such organizations as the Grand United Order of Galilean Fishermen (1856), the International Order of Twelve Knights and Daughters of Tabor (1872), and the United Brothers of Friendship (1861) and the Sisters of the Mysterious Ten (1878) were established as both-sex organizations or as parallel but closely related men's and women's groups. These groups, several of which included up to one hundred thousand people by 1900, were created within the black community. They had internally generated traditions, some of which may have had African antecedents, incorporated into the fraternal vocabulary that was so current throughout nineteenth-century America.

WOMEN'S ORDERS. The emergence of fraternal women's auxiliaries as organized entities occurred in the last third of the nineteenth century, a period that saw the development of many mass women's organizations, including suffrage groups, the Woman's Christian Temperance Union, and the women's club movement. In contrast with these autonomous women's organizations, which barred or discouraged male participation, women's fraternal auxiliaries were defined by their connection to existing male societies. To join the Order of the Eastern Star, for example, a woman had to be the wife, mother, sister, or daughter of a Master Mason. Though women were excluded from the ceremonies and lodges of Masons and Odd Fellows, men could become members of the women's organizations; indeed, the Eastern Star and Daughters of Rebekah (now the International Association of Rebekah Assemblies) required male participation, with certain offices reserved for men. With their rituals focusing on the feminine virtues of fidelity, purity, and domesticity, these organizations might seem to have been created by men to placate their women relatives at a time when women were increasingly demanding participation in public life. Yet, as with black orders, such an analysis of women's auxiliaries is too simple, for it ignores both the depth of male opposition and the commitment to feminine advance that characterized their proponents.

Degrees for wives had been suggested within the Masons and established by the Odd Fellows before the Civil War. These degrees, however, were envisioned by their creators as honorary titles, awarded as a device to reduce feminine antipathy to the all-male lodge by symbolically in-corporating women into it. They were not intended to establish separate women's organizations, which developed and grew from the initiative of women, frequently against the opposition of men. When women recipients of the Daughters of Rebekah degree, for example, began to form their own lodges, the Odd Fellows' Grand Lodge initially tried to suppress them. But women continued defiantly to hold meetings until 1867, when they were incorporated into the order. Subsequently, women in Rebekah lodges sought to expand their autonomy, gradually gaining the right to hold meetings without men present, to head local lodges and preside over meetings, and to be represented at the state level of the male organization.

Similarly, women in the Order of the Eastern Star, the organization for women relatives of Masons, sought to transfer power from the Grand Patron, who was necessarily a man and a Master Mason, to the Grand Matron, the highest woman officer, who was originally placed in the role of an assistant. The Grand Matron eventually became the executive officer of the lodge, but the Grand Patron remained the central ritual figure, in whom resided the sole right to confer degrees. Eastern Star lodges thus based their identity on Masonic involvement, even as membership was predicated upon a willingness to acknowledge the legitimacy of women's exclusion from Masonry.

Masculine opposition to the auxiliaries was, in the nineteenth century, widespread and persistent. The Knights of Pythias, for example, did not recognize the Order of Pythian Sisters as an official Pythian organization until 1904, twenty-seven years after it was first proposed. The Masons have never officially acknowledged the Order of the Eastern Star as Masonic in character, despite its hundred-year existence. Yet the twentieth century witnessed an accommodation in which the male orders increasingly accepted the energy and support of the auxiliaries while guarding their symbolic separation.

Why Fraternalism?

The immense popularity of fraternal organizations, like other types of voluntary associations, was the product of massive economic and social changes transforming the postbellum world: the growth of commerce and manufacturing, the increasing urbanization of the population. Urbanization was particularly important in facilitating mass fraternal participation, for rural people could not easily be active in organizations that met weekly, usually in the evenings. Time was as much

Shall we judge a country by the majority or the minority? By the minority, surely.

RALPH WALDO EMERSON
CONSIDERATIONS BY THE
WAY, IN THE CONDUCT OF
LIFE (1860)

See also
Women's Organizations

a factor as was proximity. Fraternal participation assumed the regular availability of "free time" and, for those who had such time at their disposal, a diverting way to use it.

BENEFITS. Lodges offered a range of practical social and economic benefits to members. The society's high rates of geographic mobility made membership in a national organization advantageous, for an Odd Fellow or Pythian could arrive in a strange community and be guaranteed access to the local lodge with the opportunities for acquaintanceship it represented. Many must have hoped that fraternal membership carried with it not only social recognition but also the possibility of preferment in business and politics.

Lodges also offered material benefits through the practice of mutual aid. Traditionally these were relatively modest sums, distributed by the local lodge on the occasion of a member's death or disability. Societies like the Ancient Order of United Workmen and the Modern Woodmen of America extended the idea of fraternal mutuality to the dispensing of life insurance, paying out larger, predetermined sums derived from assessments levied on the entire state or national membership rather than on the local lodge. Access to insurance could be a valuable service, and even the smaller disbursements of traditional lodge practice often represented important aid to needy members or their survivors. Yet the value of such economic benefits does not explain why they were so often obtained through the medium of a ritualized fraternal organization. This requires consideration of the social and cultural meanings that were at the heart of fraternalism's popularity.

FRATERNALISM AS RELIGIOUS EXPRESSION. The ritual practices and moral claims of fraternal orders must have been experienced by members and interpreted by outsiders as religious in character. This was especially so when lodges claimed responsibility for public ceremonies like funerals, which were traditionally the province of religious authority. As contemporary scholars have begun to recognize fraternalism as a mode of religious expression, a variety of interpretations have been advanced. Tony Fels (1985) characterizes Masonry as the bearer of popular Enlightenment traditions of religious rationalism and an ameliorism that located virtue in individual character-building and benevolence toward needy brethren. Lynn Dumenil (1984) sees Masonry as a nonsectarian extension of American Protestantism, dominated by the tenets of religious liberalism but encompassing a range of theological views. In contrast, Mark Carnes (1989)

FRATERNALISM AS ENTERTAINMENT

If fraternal ritual partook of the sacred, it also served as entertainment. The initiation rite is in essence a drama, a miniplay in which the initiate takes on a role, undergoes a test of courage, and demonstrates that he is worthy of acceptance into the brotherhood. In the highest Pythian degree, for example, the initiate braves skeletons, snakes, a black-clad Pluto, and the demand that he prove his courage by jumping onto a bed of nails. Participation in such a drama worked to generate "an emotional response not unlike the visceral excitement teenagers find so compelling in horror movies" (Carnes, p. 55). Fraternal leaders consciously used ritual to attract members, changing it at will if it proved ineffective or unappealing. Almost every order went through some revisions: the Odd Fellows in 1835, 1845, and 1880; the Knights of Pythias in 1866, 1882, and 1892; the Elks "several times" from 1866 to 1895. Lodge officials sought interesting effects and catchy themes, and hoped to attract attention through the creation of elaborately costumed parade units, thus extending fraternal theatricality into the public sphere of the street and the civic event. In the increasingly competitive environment of late-nineteenth-century fraternalism, both an appealing ritual and a colorful public image were deemed essential in the contest for members.

The nineteenth-century lodge bears a marked resemblance to more traditional forms of popular culture in that it was a vehicle through which members made their own entertainment, participating as actors rather than spectators in the ritual performance. At the same time, it was a highly standardized entertainment, specified to the last detail of words and costume by the national order. In this sense, it anticipated twentieth-century mass media entertainment. The national fraternal organization was a social technology that made possible the marketing and consumption of a standardized entertainment product through organizational rather than electronic means.

argues that fraternalism articulated an implicit critique of both rationalist and evangelical Protestantism, with the eerie displays of skulls and skeletons, ubiquitous in fraternal ritual, portraying an ominous God and a depraved and mortal humanity. Most important in this view, the lodge, as an exclusively male institution, represented a masculine response to the feminized theology and social milieu of the era's Protestant churches.

RESPONSE TO CAPITALIST TRANSFORMA-TIONS. The popularity of fraternalism has been explained as a traditionalist response that asserted the value of kinlike relations in opposition to the impersonality of the market and the dislocations of capitalist development. Mutual benefit societies sought to guarantee their members protection against the threats of death and illness, functioning as a type of insurance. Yet mutual benefit societies differed symbolically from commercial life insurance, which was widely rejected because it transformed relations of trust and solidarity into market relations and subjected the worth of human life to a strictly financial calculus. Fraternal insurance dealt with this moral dilemma by defining insurance provision as a system of mutual aid based in quasi-kin relations rather than in commodity exchange. As a result, it was immensely popular, outselling the offerings of commercial life insurance companies in the 1890s despite the greater security the latter offered. In its use of kin-based imagery, fraternalism invoked the moral community of the family, proposing a model of social life that was noncontractual and anti-individualist, that resisted the subordination of human relations to market mechanisms.

Yet fraternalism did not represent a simple rejection of capitalist development in the name of tradition; rather, its symbolic structures combined accommodation and resistance, legitimation and critique. Masonic ritual, and others inspired by it, affirmed the worth of economic productivity, using artisans' tools to symbolize morality and imbue members with the virtues of industriousness and self-discipline. Systems of degrees or levels of membership presented members with an idealized model of class structure, to be ascended over time. They thus maintained that upward mobility was available to all industrious men who cared to seek it.

Fraternalism defined the lodge as a cross-class institution that bound men together, regardless of who they were. By constructing bonds of loyalty across class lines, it argued for the irrelevance of class as a social identity and envisioned a social order founded on harmonious class relations. Yet fraternal membership was itself a commodity, a form of modern leisure marketed aggressively but available only to those who could afford to pay for it.

While the degree structure proclaimed the inevitability of success for all, fraternal mutuality, the obligation to assist needy brothers, implicitly conceded that some would fail. Fraternalism thus recognized the social dislocations precipitated by individualistic, market-oriented relations and proposed voluntary association, the construction of a compensatory moral community outside the sphere of production, as the means to alleviate the costs of change.

FRATERNALISM AND MASCULINITY. Fraternalism was centrally "about" the articulation of masculine identity. Its rituals idealized relations of brotherhood between men and established the lodge room as an exclusively masculine space. As a cultural institution that maintained solidarity among white men, Masonically oriented fraternalism offered gender, along with race, as a central category for the organization of collective identity A variety of reasons may be adduced to explain its appeal.

Fraternal initiation rituals may have offered a means for young middle-class men to attain a problematic masculinity, to reconcile themselves with a paternal authority that was increasingly distant in the nineteenth century, as child rearing became more feminized and adult men more remote, more embedded in an economic sphere separate from the home. Alternatively, fraternal ritual could serve to proclaim the moral self-sufficiency of men, and masculine social organization, in an era that emphasized the spirituality of women and men's moral dependence upon them. Fraternalism could also represent a response to perceived attacks on spheres of male camaraderie or masculine control of public social space. To those who experienced the church as a feminine realm, the fraternal order offered a ritual sphere that belonged to men alone. But lodges could also serve as more casual, but no less important, institutions of male sociability. This was especially significant for men who were answerable to the moral suasion and social pressures of the temperance crusade, and thus deprived of the tavern as a sex-segregated, male-only social space. Finally, for many men the benefit and insurance features of lodge membership promised security for their families and helped to consolidate their view of themselves as good providers, able to live up to the era's dominant masculine ideal.

The Decline of American Fraternalism

By the late twentieth century, the fraternal movement was for most people only a memory. Membership declined steadily in the post–World War II era and precipitously from the 1960s on. Well before this, however, in the early twentieth cen-

One thing I know: the only ones among you who will be really happy are those who will have sought and found how to serve.

ALBERT SCHWEITZER

tury, informed observers had noted a loss of momentum, a declining commitment, as the fraternal ideal was replaced by other models of social life.

By the 1920s and 1930s, commercial life insurance easily outsold fraternal insurance, even in those ethnic communities which had been its last stronghold. Government provision of benefits beginning in the 1930s dealt a further blow, as did growing assimilation within ethnic communities. Among middle-class men, cross-class social fraternalism was weakened by the vogue of service clubs such as Rotary and Kiwanis, organizations that restricted their membership to proprietors and professionals. While the creation of service clubs did not lead immediately to a wholesale exodus of businessmen from fraternal orders, it offered a new and prestigious rival for their energy and commitment.

Changes in social relations between men and women also reduced the appeal of the male-only fraternal order. The ideal of companionate marriage was accompanied by new expectations of a more gender-integrated social life, beginning with dating and courtship and continuing throughout married life. These expectations posed a challenge to the fraternal orders' defense of masculine camaraderie. The orders that experienced the greatest growth in the twentieth century were those like the Elks, which deemphasized ritual and offered a more couple-oriented sociability to their members.

Finally, the lure of new forms of commercialized recreation, such as movies, radio, and television, greatly reduced the entertainment value of the lodge. The drama of fraternal ritual could not hope to compete with the technical sophistication and thematic variation of the new mass media products, which would, moreover, become central to the conduct of the twentieth century's more gender-integrated social life, in which new rituals of courtship and family life were organized around new diversions available to both women and men.

In their rediscovery of fraternalism, scholars have interpreted it in strikingly varied ways. It has been seen as religious expression, popular entertainment, an early form of trade union organization or life insurance provision, a means of constructing masculine identity or racial and ethnic solidarity, a vehicle for sociability, self-improvement, or self-aggrandizement. Fraternalism offered the metaphor of kinship as a way of conceiving and thus creating social solidarity. Like "family," "fraternity" was an elastic concept, capable of containing and reconciling contradictory elements into a highly resonant whole.

—MARY ANN CLAWSON

THE FRONTIER

"The Frontier" is a troublesome term for historians. On the one hand, it evokes one of the most important processes in American history, the movement of European peoples across the American continent. It encompasses exploits of heroic exploration and violent warfare and, less dramatic but no less significant, the spread of settlements and social relations. Unfortunately, the notion of the frontier has become encumbered with many misleading images based on assumptions of racial and national superiority. Above all, the dislocation and destruction of native tribes in the face of European American advance has often been taken for granted as an inevitable, even necessary, step in American history, the price of "progress." The bias built into the story of the frontier has been regularly reinforced, not just in popular fiction and film but also in the work of professional historians.

The foremost, if not the first, historian to focus scholarly attention on the American frontier was Frederick Jackson Turner. While still a young professor at the University of Wisconsin, he wrote a path-breaking essay, "The Significance of the Frontier in American History" (1893), that became a classic work in American historical writing. Indeed, over the course of the next half-century, Turner and the disciples of his "frontier thesis" formed one of the most prominent schools of historical thought in the United States. Turner identified the frontier as a "fertile field for investigation," a distinct conceptual category that could "be isolated and studied as a factor in American history of the highest importance." More to the point, he argued that "American history has been in a large degree the history of the colonization of the Great West. The existence of an area of free land, its continuous recession, and the advance of American settlement westward, explain American development" ("Significance of the Frontier," p. 1). The frontier was, in short, the most important element in the evolution of the United States, the critical factor that made the American people culturally unique. From the earliest days of colonial settlement, westward movement to successive frontiers promoted the "steady movement away from the influence of Europe" and thus helped Americans develop new standards of democracy and equality. As long as people had the prospect of moving west to free lands, they could "escape from the bondage of the past" and "escape to the free conditions of the frontier." Unfortunately, Turner argued, that prospect had dimmed by the end of the nineteenth century: "the frontier has gone, and with its going has closed the first period in American history" ("The Significance of the Frontier," p. 38).

Turner was a remarkably creative and insightful historian, but his "frontier thesis" was seriously flawed. Throughout the first half of the twentieth century, and especially in the 1930s and 1940s, other scholars refined or rejected his argument, challenging both his scholarship and his historical vision. According to Turner's critics, he overstated the effect of the frontier environment on the development of democracy and individualism, and he offered rather loose and imprecise definitions of those terms. He took little or no account of the impact of urbanization and industrialization on American society. Moreover, his emphasis on American exceptionalism overlooked or obscured the continuing significance of European influence on American culture. In general, by the 1950s, Turner's "frontier thesis" had become if not a ruin, then certainly a relic. It still stood as an impressive monument to an important academic achievement, but it no longer formed a stable foundation for future scholarship.

One issue that was not resolved by the scholarly debate over Turner's frontier thesis was the very idea of "the frontier" itself. Both Turner and his critics used the term freely, sometimes arguing about its precise definition but seldom questioning its inherent assumptions. Yet it is important to note that "the frontier" is an ethnocentric notion that has meaning primarily from the standpoint of Europeans or European Americans, but not from that of Native Americans, the people Europeans called Indians. Turner, for instance, described the frontier as "the outer edge of the wave—the meeting point between savagery and civilization" ("Significance of the Frontier," p. 3). Even when stripped of its most obvious cultural bias—the distinction between Indian "savagery" and European "civilization"—the description of the frontier as "the outer edge of the wave" still adopts the point of view of the advancing (or, indeed, invading) culture. For those native inhabitants resisting or retreating before that advance, the idea of the frontier had a very different meaning—or, more accurately, no meaning at all.

For that reason, recent historians have attempted to develop alternative terminology or at least to take a more multicultural approach to the study of the frontier. Rather than describing the frontier as a line or an edge of cultural division, many scholars prefer to talk of "contact zones" of intercultural exchange. In this sense, the emphasis is on the plurality of frontier regions in North America, and not just on the Anglo-American wave of westward expansion. More important, the emphasis is not so much on place as on process, the patterns of interaction between different peoples. Again, plurality is important; there was no single, predictably repeated process of frontier interaction. Historians now seek to understand the varieties of interaction among different groups at different times in different places. Indians and Europeans frequently engaged in warfare and violent conflict, but they also cooperated as allies and trading partners. Whatever the case, neither group remained unchanged by extended contact with the other. The recognition of the two-way relationship helps break down the distinction between "savage" and "civilized," and offers a more complex and ultimately more compelling history of human interaction on the North American continent.

The major European colonizers of North America—the Spanish, French, Dutch, and English—shared a common goal of extracting wealth from the New World, and the pursuit of that goal

HISTORIAN OF THE FRONTIER

Frederick Jackson Turner, the foremost historian to focus scholarly attention on the American frontier, wrote a path-breaking essay that became a classic work in American historical writing.
CORBIS-BETTMANN

THE FIRST AMERICANS

Frontiers Before European Colonization

The early period of intercultural contact makes one point clear: just as one cannot talk of a single frontier, much less a single frontier experience, neither can one talk of "Europeans" and "Indians" as single, monolithic entities. Both groups included people who exhibited significant differences in language, identity, and interest.

On the eve of European colonization, the native population of North America was both large and diverse. Descended from nomadic groups that crossed the Bering Strait from Asia over thirty thousand years before, Indian people had been well established in North America for thousands of years. Thus they, rather than Europeans, were not only the original discoverers of America but also the first settlers. Indeed, some North American Indians, like the Hopewell culture of the Ohio Valley or the Mississippian culture, had developed complex and sophisticated societies and then, long before the advent of Europeans, had begun to decline. Population estimates for the area north of Mexico in the pre-European period vary widely, ranging from a low of around one million to a higher (and more recent) figure of over ten million.

The Indians of North America comprised hundreds of linguistic and societal groups. Some, like the Siouan peoples of the Great Plains, were primarily nomadic hunters, but far more were comparatively settled agriculturists. In the desert Southwest, for instance, the Hopi and Zuni cultures had developed elaborate irrigation systems to facilitate farming in their arid region. Moreover, their villages of substantial, multiroom, apartment-like houses (called *pueblos* by the Spanish) stood as monuments to the people's persistence. To the east, especially along the Atlantic seaboard and in the interior piedmont region, people of the Muskogean, Algonkian, and Iroquoian language groups combined hunting, gathering, fishing, and farming.

Numbering about half a million and divided into dozens of kinship networks, chiefdoms, and confederacies, Indians of the eastern woodlands lived in villages within distinct tribal territories. Unlike Europeans, they did not emphasize individualism or private property but tended to share land and other natural resources communally among members of the village or tribe. Men and women shared a greater degree of equality than was common in European culture. Like Europeans, however, eastern woodland tribes had sometimes cordial but often conflicted relations with groups outside their own. They traded extensively with each other, but they also fought ferociously to avenge violations of tribal territory or honor. Indeed, long-standing antagonisms between some tribal groups mirrored the traditional rivalries of the European powers and contributed to the complex military and diplomatic alliances of the early North American frontier.

led them into fierce competition. Indeed, they fought against each other as much as against the Indians; their New World settlements became imperial outposts in a broader struggle for economic and military supremacy on both sides of the Atlantic. Even their maps of the New World were designed to reflect not so much geographical accuracy as imperial policy. Cartographers often claimed much more territory than military men could hope to acquire, and the maps of the major European colonizers almost always showed competing claims to vast expanses of the North American interior. Moreover, when Europeans actually settled on the land, their respective modes of colonization revealed strikingly different strategies of social and economic development. Those strategies had long-term implications not only for the continuing competition among the European powers but also for their relationships with the natives of North America.

The Spanish, for instance, did not make a significant attempt to establish large-scale, well-populated settlements inhabited by emigrants from their own country. Rather, they sought to continue along the path of plunder that had taken them through South and Central America, extracting the riches of the New World to send back to Spain. Lured northward by their lust for gold and silver, sixteenth-century Spanish explorers laid claim to large parts of what is now the southern United States, from Florida and the Gulf of Mexico to the coast of California. One conquistador, Francisco Vásquez de Coronado, pushed as far north as present-day Kansas in his search for the fabled Seven Cities of Cibola. He never found the gold he sought, nor did the other Spaniards in North America. Still, by the end of the sixteenth century, they had set up numerous small military garrisons and Catholic missions, from which they managed to impose considerable control over the

See also

Landscapes

economic and religious lives of the native peoples. Moreover, they used these outposts as bases of military operations against other European powers. Although their numbers were never very large, the Spanish played an important role in North America well into the nineteenth century.

Similarly, the Dutch and French established a significant presence in North America without sending over large numbers of settlers. Both nations developed an extensive fur trade with native tribes, and during the first half of the seventeenth century they did a lively and lucrative business in beaver pelts. From their main settlement at New Amsterdam (present-day New York City), the Dutch dominated trade in the Hudson, Connecticut, and Delaware river valleys. In the third quarter of the seventeenth century, however, a series of wars between the Dutch and the English resulted in the loss of Dutch territory and trade on the North American mainland.

The French, by comparison, maintained control of an increasingly extensive North American trade network. They established fishing operations along the northern Atlantic coast in the sixteenth century, and beginning in 1534, the explorer Jacques Cartier led expeditions up the Saint Lawrence River. The Saint Lawrence soon became the first major area of French influence in North America. In 1608, Samuel de Champlain established a small settlement at Quebec, and by the 1620s French traders had ventured into the North American interior as far as the Great Lakes. In the 1670s and 1680s other French explorers—most notably Louis Jolliet, Father Jacques Marquette, and René Robert de La Salle—pushed west well beyond the Missouri River and south to the mouth of the Mississippi River. By the end of the seventeenth century, then, the French claimed a huge expanse of territory that reached from southern Canada to the Gulf of Mexico and covered roughly the middle third of what is now the United States. Like the Spanish, they reinforced their claim by creating a network of trading posts, military garrisons, and Catholic missions. Still, the number of French colonists in North America in 1700 totaled little more than ten thousand.

The English adopted a much different strategy for North American colonization. They were comparative latecomers to New World exploration and settlement, and they did not establish a permanent foothold on the North American mainland until 1607, with the creation of Jamestown in Virginia. Like the other European colonizers, the English sought to extract the abundant riches of the New World—fish, furs, and, if they were fortunate, gold and silver—but they did more than set up forts and trading posts. They planted permanent agricultural communities populated by English and other European emigrants. From the staple-producing plantations in the South to the quasi-communal farming villages of New England, these colonists quickly spread over the landscape in their quest for land.

By the 1750s, England's North American colonies reached from present-day Maine to Georgia and as far west as the Appalachian mountain chain. Although this area was quite small compared with the vast territories claimed by Spain and France, it held a comparatively large population of nearly a million and a half English subjects. This approach to colonization had important implications for the future of the Anglo-American frontier: unlike the Spanish and French, the English sought not only to subdue the native tribes but also to remove them.

This process of removal had begun in the first period of contact. Everywhere they went, Europeans carried with them diseases—especially smallpox, diphtheria, and measles—against which North American natives had no natural or acquired immunity. Long before the main force of European colonizers arrived in North America, imported illnesses had swept the native peoples, devastating tribes in every region and depopulating some by as much as 90 percent. Especially along the eastern seaboard of North America, in the region ultimately dominated by the English, Indians suffered a demographic catastrophe that greatly undermined their ability to resist European invasion. Thus the early colonizers accomplished more through this unwitting germ warfare than they could ever have achieved through force of arms.

Frontier Warfare before 1800

Force of arms did, of course, play a critical role in the longer history of the North American frontier. Warfare on the frontier was seldom a clear-cut contest between European invaders and Indian resisters. The European colonizing powers fought among themselves, and so did native tribes. Both Europeans and Indians took advantage of the other's animosities, creating complex intercultural alliances out of overlapping layers of long-standing hostility. They used those alliances to further their own diplomatic and military ends, and when making new alliances served their purposes, they did so.

THE FRONTIER

Frontier Warfare before 1800

My reason teaches me that land cannot be sold. The Great Spirit gave it to his children to live upon.

BLACK HAWK
CHIEF OF SAC AND FOX
TRIBES, AUTOBIOGRAPHY
(1833)

MOHAWK LEADER

Joseph Brant (1742–1807), Mohawk leader who supported the British in the French and Indian War and the American Revolution.
CORBIS/BETTMANN

In the seventeenth and eighteenth centuries, the imperial wars of the European powers brought Indian-European diplomacy into play on a broad scale. Although the contest in the colonies was essentially a sideshow to the larger, long-lasting Old World conflict, the American frontier increasingly became both battleground and prize in the struggle among the European powers.

For instance, in the major imperial struggle of the colonial era, the Seven Years' War—or the French and Indian War, as it was called in the British American colonies—Great Britain established dominance over a huge expanse of territory on the American frontier. This conflict began with a series of clashes on the Pennsylvania frontier in 1754 and spread throughout North America, from Canada to the West Indies. Within a few years, almost thirty thousand British regulars joined colonial militia units to combat a much smaller French force aided by a substantial number of Indian allies.

Both the British and the French attempted to gain Indian support. In the early years of the conflict, a few hundred Mohawk and Cherokee warriors fought briefly for the British as mercenaries, but they were hardly loyal or long-standing allies. The Iroquois confederacy, of which the Mohawk were a part, chose for the most part to adopt a position of neutrality, letting the Europeans fight between themselves while accepting gifts from both. Only when the military situation began to shift in favor of the Anglo-Americans—especially after their victories over the French at Louisbourg in 1758 and at Quebec in 1759—did the Iroquois tilt toward the British side.

In the South, the Cherokee turned toward the French after their limited alliance with the British turned sour, and after 1758 they posed a serious threat to Anglo-American settlers in the southern backcountry. They attempted to bring the powerful Creek into the war against the Anglo-Americans in a multitribal alliance with other southern Indians. But the Creek, like the Iroquois, played one European side against the other for favorable trade concessions. In the end, this position of neutrality proved beneficial. The Iroquois and Creek emerged from the European conflict with their trade relations and tribal lands intact; the Cherokee suffered because of the loss of French trade goods, and they had to accept territorial boundaries imposed by the victorious British.

By 1763, at the end of the war, the British had greatly expanded their North American territories. Above all, the removal of the French presence from the trans-Appalachian interior promised new opportunities for Anglo-American expansion, and thousands of land-hungry settlers looked forward to moving west.

But almost immediately two obstacles rose to stop them, or at least impede them. In 1763, a chief of the Ottawa tribe, Pontiac, led the tribes of the Great Lakes region in a resistance movement to stop Anglo-American encroachment. Pontiac's forces attacked and destroyed several British garrisons, and they threatened to drive the British army out of the area. By 1764, war-weary British regular troops, just returned from fighting the French in the West Indies, managed to break up Pontiac's forces and maintain a presence in the Northwest. Still, the volatile situation in the region led British policymakers to try to prevent further conflict between Indians and Anglo-Americans by keeping white settlers out of Indian territory. While Pontiac's uprising was still in progress, the government in London imposed the Proclamation of 1763, which prohibited settlers from moving west of the Appalachian Mountains. The British army was too sparsely stationed to enforce the policy effectively, and thousands of whites simply ignored the ban and moved west anyway. Nonetheless, the policy seemed oppressive to many potential migrants, and the government's attempt to restrict access to the trans-Appalachian West was one of the many tensions contributing to the antagonism between Britain and its American colonies.

The American War for Independence had important implications for the future of the frontier. It created a new North American nation that took over not only the territory formerly held by the British but also the lands of native tribes. As was the case in the Seven Years' War, Indians were considered valuable allies in frontier fighting, and both the British and their rebellious colonists sought to recruit them. In the North, tribes of the Iroquois confederacy fought on both sides, sometimes attacking each other and often suffering devastating losses. Once the war was over, the Iroquois confederacy was weakened almost beyond repair, and its leaders were forced to concede a large area of western land to the victorious United States in the Treaty of Fort Stanwix (1784). In the South, the Cherokee fought for the British—or, more properly, against American expansion. Like the Iroquois, they suffered greatly from retaliatory expeditions, and at war's end they, too, had to surrender territory to the new American republic.

The Struggle for Order on the American Frontier

The acquisition of western land both from the native tribes and from the British fueled expansionist fever among white Americans. Having been legally limited by the Proclamation of 1763, settlers and speculators now eagerly sought to take advantage of the opening of new lands in the Old Northwest. One of the main tasks (and few successes) of the American government under the Articles of Confederation was the organization of orderly settlement in that region. Beginning in 1785, government surveyors divided the territory into a grid-work of townships, each six miles square with thirty-six one-mile-square sections of 640 acres, which could be subdivided into smaller lots and sold. (In fact, this straight-line design became the model for the government's land policy of the west throughout the nineteenth century.) The assumption was that, once populated with productive settlers, these western territories would enter the Union as new states, thereby adding to the size and strength of the new nation.

But the imposition of an orderly plan on the western territories did not guarantee control. Although the British were required by the Treaty of Paris (1783) to relinquish their military garrisons in the Northwest, they did so very slowly. The United States government, with its army demobilized and somewhat demoralized at the war's end, could do nothing to hurry the British on their way. The Spanish likewise caused trouble in the West. They held New Orleans, which they had acquired at the end of the Seven Years' War, and thus controlled the outlet from the Mississippi River to the Gulf of Mexico. In 1784 they closed New Orleans to American shipping, denying frontier farmers access to foreign markets and discouraging the commercial development of the trans-Appalachian interior. To make matters worse, Spanish agents were reported to be encouraging western settlers to break away from the United States and ally themselves with Spain. At the same time, native tribes throughout the trans-Appalachian region, from the Ohio country to Georgia, resisted further white expansion and attacked settlers who encroached on tribal lands.

By the time the first federal government under George Washington took office in 1789, the western frontier of the United States was a vast but extremely vulnerable appendage to the original thirteen states. Foreign intrigues and Indian unrest made the region a source of national insecurity, and the government's claims to control rang hollow. Washington himself—who had had extensive experience in the western country as a military leader and who still held a sizable financial interest there as a land speculator—made securing the frontier one of the main items on his political agenda. There was little he could do militarily to oppose Britain and Spain, but he could take action against North American inhabitants.

Washington committed a large armed force to combat native tribes in the Northwest Territory, and in 1794, at the Battle of Fallen Timbers in northern Ohio, United States troops under Major General Anthony Wayne gained a decisive victory against a combined force of Shawnee, Ottawa, Ojibwa, and Pottawatomi warriors. In the same year, Washington sent (and for a while personally led) a huge military expedition into western Pennsylvania to suppress the Whiskey Rebellion, an uprising of local farmers opposed to the Washington administration's excise tax on whiskey, a marketable commodity crucial to the local economy. The rebellion broke up before Washington's army arrived, so there was no climactic battle like that against the Indians. Still, by dispatching federal troops to assert governmental authority, Washington made clear his resolve to put down frontier unrest, whether it came from Indians or whites.

The Whiskey Rebellion points to a phenomenon that had long been part of Anglo-American frontier relations: intracultural, as well as intercultural, conflict. That is, Anglo-Americans not only fought against Indians and other Europeans for control of the frontier, they also fought among

THE FRONTIER

The Struggle for Order on the American Frontier

The encounter between invader and aborigine was disastrous for the latter, resulting in the near-total obliteration of antecedent landscapes as Native American populations were severely decimated and demoralized.

PAGE 253

♦ **Garrison**
A military post, especially a permanent military installation; also the troops stationed at a garrison

F

THE FRONTIER

The Struggle for Order on the American Frontier

The history of most countries has been that of majorities— mounted majorities, clad in iron, armed with death, treading down the ten-fold more numerous minorities.

OLIVER WENDELL
HOLMES, SR.

WHISKEY REBELLION

Whiskey Rebellion (1794). The American backcountry in the 1790's was intensely democratic in its views and resented the way in which Secretary of the Treasury Alexander Hamilton's fiscal policies concentrated power in the hands of the upper classes. Other grievances accentuated western resentment, notably the failure to open the Mississippi River to navigation, the dilatory conduct of the Indian wars, the speculative prices of land, arduous and ill-paid militia duty, scarcity of specie, and the creation of a salaried official class. The excise law of 1791, which taxed whiskey—the chief transportable and barterable western product—furnished a convenient peg on which to hang these grievances, and for three years the opposition to this measure increased.

The fact that noncomplying distillers from western Pennsylvania had to go to York or Philadelphia for trial (a procedure that would cost the value of the average western farm) formed so legitimate a grievance that in May and June 1794 Congress passed a measure making offenses against the excise law cognizable in state courts. While the bill was in Congress the U.S. District Court of Pennsylvania issued a series of processes returnable to Philadelphia. The fact that these processes were not served until July, six weeks after the easing measure was passed, angered the citizens of the southwestern counties. A federal marshal was attacked in Allegheny County while serving a process, and on July 17 several hundred men, led by members of a local "Democratic society," attacked and burned the home of Gen. John Neville, the regional inspector of the excise.

The attackers would probably have stopped with this action, but certain leaders robbed the mail and found in the stolen letters expressions that they used in stirring up the people to attack Pittsburgh. A muster of the southwestern militia was called at Braddock's Field for Aug. 1. The citizens of Pittsburgh were so alarmed that they exiled the odious townsmen, including Neville, and thus averted the wrath of the recalcitrants. The militia march on Pittsburgh on Aug. 2 was carried through without violence. Nevertheless, on Aug. 7 President George Washington issued a proclamation ordering the disaffected westerners to their homes, and calling up the militia from Maryland, Virginia, Pennsylvania, and New Jersey.

On Aug. 14–15 delegates from the Monongahela Valley met at Parkinson's Ferry, but were prevented from drastic measures by the parliamentary tactics of the moderates. A committee appointed by Washington met with a western committee and arranged that the sentiment of the people of the western counties concerning submission be taken on Sept. 11. The vote was unsatisfactory, and Washington set in motion the militia army that had meanwhile been gathering in the East. The western counties were occupied during November, and more than a score of prisoners were sent to Philadelphia. All of them were acquitted or pardoned, or the cases were dismissed for lack of evidence.

The result of the rebellion was simply to strengthen the political power of Hamilton and the Federalists, and circumstantial evidence seems to indicate that Hamilton promoted the original misunderstanding and sent the army west solely for that purpose. It is likely also that the defeat of the democrats encouraged investors to accelerate the economic development of the region that they had already begun.

themselves. This conflict manifested itself dramatically in a series of armed insurrections, the most notable of which were Bacon's Rebellion in Virginia (1676), the Land Riots in New York (1766), the Regulator movement in North Carolina (1766–1771), and the Regulator movement, or Shays's Rebellion, in Massachusetts (1786–1787), and then the Whiskey Rebellion. In each case backcountry settlers felt themselves economically and politically oppressed by their fellow countrymen, both the elite in their own frontier regions and the merchants and officials in the more established regions to the east. When their pleas and petitions to the established authorities brought no positive result, they rose up in arms to seek redress of their grievances. Even though these frontier insurrections were usually suppressed by the superior military might of the government, they still represented a recurring threat to the established order of Anglo-American authorities.

On a lower, less dramatic scale, frontier folk frequently lived in tension with those lawmakers and landowners who sought to impose their notions of spatial, social, and economic order on the process of settlement. Elite proprietors of backcountry tracts hoped to populate the frontier with sturdy, stable, hardworking farmers who would improve the land (and land values) and produce a marketable commodity. They also wanted settlers who would pay proper respect to the landowning elite. For this reason proprietors often tried to attract German and Swiss immigrants, ethnic groups that were thought to fit the profile of the productive settler.

Yet large landowners often found that the people who actually settled (and sometimes squatted) on their land were not the people they had planned for. The early American backcountry attracted an ethnically diverse group of settlers, not only sturdy Germans but, more often, Scotch-Irish immigrants who had been driven out of Ireland and were hardly more popular in the American colonies. The Scotch-Irish made up a sizable proportion of the emigrants who swept down the Shenandoah Valley of Virginia in the middle of the eighteenth century. Members of the Virginia gentry found these new inhabitants of the western lands to be hardly the decent and deferential sort they had expected. Instead, these newcomers tended to be independent-minded people who had their own ideas and expectations about making their way in the wilderness. Rather than making the kinds of permanent improvements needed for commercial development, these settlers lived off the natural bounty of the environment. Rather than engaging in such gentlemanly forms of competition as horse racing, dancing, and dueling, they took sport in cockfights and brutal gouging matches. Rather than accepting the orderly religion of the Anglican church, they lived according to the spiritual, almost supernatural, intensity of enthusiastic, evangelical religion.

Bound together by mutual need and mystical belief, people in the Virginia backcountry and elsewhere on the American frontier formed their own communities that existed outside of, and even in defiance of, the control of elite landowners. Accordingly, those landowners increasingly came to scorn these settlers as disorderly, slothful people who, according to the common complaint, lived like Indians. In fact, the term "white Indians" became a common slur cast against these settlers by members of the Anglo-American elite. In their eyes, these "white Indians" represented obstacles to orderly development, and therefore they, no less than "red" Indians, had to be subdued or removed.

National Expansion and Military Conquest

In the first half of the nineteenth century, the United States government pursued an aggressive policy of territorial expansion, acquiring huge tracts of land by both peaceful and violent means. The first and most dramatic step came with President Thomas Jefferson's purchase of the Louisiana Territory from France in 1803. Although he acted without proper constitutional authority, Jefferson bought over eight hundred thousand square miles of land that reached from the Gulf of Mexico as far north as the headwaters of the Mississippi River and as far west as the Rocky Mountains—for less than two dollars a square mile. In addition to being a remarkable bargain, the Louisiana Purchase created great opportunities for future frontier farmers. Indeed, the expansion of an agrarian republic was one of the main motivations behind Jefferson's move to acquire the Louisiana Territory.

Expansion would first require exploration, and Jefferson acted quickly to send expeditions into the newly acquired territory. In 1804, a team of explorers led by Meriwether Lewis and William Clark left Saint Louis, on the Mississippi River, to begin a two-year trek northwest across the northern Plains and the Rocky Mountains to the Oregon Territory and the Pacific coast—far beyond the bounds of the Louisiana Purchase. While Lewis and Clark were heading northwest, the government sent Zebulon Pike to explore other regions of the American frontier. In 1805, Pike led an expedition northward from Saint Louis along the Mississippi River to what is now Minnesota. In 1806, Pike set out on a second trip westward to the southern Rocky Mountains and south into Mexico before returning to Louisiana. In the years following these early exploratory expeditions, the United States government established a handful of military outposts west of the Mississippi River. In the first two decades of the nineteenth century, then, the path had clearly been prepared for the massive migration of white settlers into the western frontier.

In the 1820s, several thousand of these settlers moved out of the United States into Texas, a Mexican possession. Mexico, which had gained its independence from Spain in 1821, encouraged settlement of its northern borderlands by offering generous inducements to immigrants. Farmers from the American South, many of whom were slave owners, responded eagerly to this opportunity to acquire new lands for cotton production. By the end of the decade, settlers from the United

The province of Techas will be the richest state of the Union without any exception.

THOMAS JEFFERSON
LETTER TO JAMES MONROE
(MAY 15, 1820)

♦ **Agrarian**
Of or relating to fields or lands or their tenure

F

THE FRONTIER

*National Expansion
and Military Conquest*

*Go west, young
man, go west.*

JOHN B. L. SOULE
(1851)

States far outnumbered Mexicans in the Texas Territory. At that point, the Mexican government attempted to curtail their influence in the region by outlawing slavery and blocking additional immigration from the United States. The resulting tension between the Mexican government and the North American emigrants developed into armed conflict in 1835–1836, during which rebellious settlers defeated a Mexican army and declared Texas an independent republic. For nine years thereafter, expansionist political leaders in the United States government pushed for the annexation of Texas, and finally, in 1845, Texas entered the Union.

The annexation of Texas accelerated the engines of expansion. Claiming that the nation had a divine mission, or "manifest destiny," to control the whole continent, expansionist politicians and their allies in the press promoted a final push to the Pacific. In 1844 the Democratic party had made acquisition of the Oregon Territory a major plank in its platform, and the Democrats took a very aggressive stance toward Great Britain, which disputed the United States' territorial claims. In 1846 James K. Polk, the Democratic president, negotiated a treaty with Great Britain that compromised American territorial demands but nonetheless gave the United States its first foothold on the Pacific. In the same year, lingering tensions over Texas brought the United States into war with Mexico, and the American victory two years later forced the Mexican government to cede a huge expanse of land stretching from Texas to California.

In less than half a century, the results of expansionist policy proved dramatic. Between 1803 and 1848, the United States had tripled its original territory and, in the minds of many of its citizens, had fulfilled its manifest destiny to reach from the Atlantic to the Pacific. Moreover, warfare and diplomacy had reduced the power and presence of Spain, Britain, and Mexico in North America, and the United States faced no foreign competition for its continued conquest of the continent.

Foreign powers were not, of course, the greatest obstacle to national expansion. Native tribes had occupied much of the North American interior for hundreds, even thousands, of years, and they would not easily accede to the more recent claims of the United States. Indeed, in the earliest years of nationhood, the federal government adopted an official policy of recognizing traditional tribal lands as legitimate territorial possessions that could be acquired only through treaties. At the same time, however, the young agrarian

nation's demands for new land increasingly led political and military leaders to exact territorial concessions from Indian tribes through warfare rather than diplomacy.

In the years after the Battle of Fallen Timbers, for instance, the United States government continued to push for land cessions from tribes in the Old Northwest, especially in the Indiana and Michigan territories. In response to this growing pressure from whites, two Shawnee leaders, Tecumseh and his brother Tenskwatawa ("the Prophet"), began to organize widespread resistance among Indian people, and established a sizable confederation of tribes in the region. In response to the Indians' threat to white expansion, the territorial governor of Indiana, William Henry Harrison, sent an armed force against Tecumseh's warriors. In two decisive engagements, the Battle of Tippecanoe (1811) and the Battle of the Thames (1813), Harrison defeated the tribal confederacy and killed Tecumseh. The destruction of the confederacy reduced Indian resistance in the Midwest and opened the Indiana and Michigan territories to rapid white settlement. Harrison's victories also provided him with a claim to military fame as a frontier fighter that proved useful in his campaign for the presidency in 1840.

In the South, a similar pattern of conquest was played out in the first four decades of the nineteenth century. The Creek tribe, which inhabited much of present-day Georgia and Alabama, sought to stop white encroachment onto tribal lands. Beginning in 1813, they carried out a series of devastating raids on recent settlers. Whites reacted with horror and hostility, and another future president, Andrew Jackson, organized a punitive expedition of militiamen from Kentucky and Tennessee and Indian warriors from tribes hostile to the Creek. Over the spring and summer of 1814, Jackson won decisive victories, most notably at the Battle of Horseshoe Bend in Alabama. Then, having subdued the Creek militarily, Jackson demanded land cessions of more than twenty million acres in the Southeast. Like William Henry Harrison, Andrew Jackson built his political career on a foundation of his fame as a frontier Indian fighter—a new kind of American hero.

Even those tribes which chose not to resist forcibly suffered eventual defeat. The Cherokee, who had supplied fighters for Jackson's campaign against the Creek, attempted to maintain friendly relations with the United States. During the first three decades of the nineteenth century, they even developed a society which mirrored that of the whites, with settled farms, African slaves, a written alphabet, and, in 1827, a tribal constitution modeled on the state constitutions of their white neighbors.

But nothing appealed to whites so much as Cherokee land. During the 1820s, several southern states, most notably Georgia, began to push the federal government to remove Indians to lands west of the Mississippi River. Moreover, in response to the framing of the Cherokee constitution, the Georgia legislature declared it invalid and laid claim to all Cherokee land within state boundaries. The Cherokee were to be considered nothing more than "tenants at will," with no legal right to call the land their own. Playing by the white man's rules, the Cherokee challenged Georgia's action in the United States Supreme Court, which ruled in favor of the Cherokee in *Worcester v. Georgia* (1832).

But Andrew Jackson, the former Indian fighter who had been elected president in 1828, had little regard for either the Cherokee or the Supreme Court, and he refused to enforce the Court's ruling. Indeed, Jackson had already promoted the Indian Removal Act (1830) in Congress, giving the federal government the power to force the Cherokee and other tribes to exchange their tribal lands for territory in the West. Between 1831 and 1839, thousands of Chickasaw, Choctaw, Creek, Seminole, and Cherokee people were forced to move to reservations in what is now Oklahoma—an area of vast plains that scarcely resembled the eastern woodlands they had known. The Cherokee's forced migration along the "Trail of Tears," which claimed the lives of nearly a fourth of the tribe, underscores one of the most unfortunate features of frontier history: like whites, Indians also moved west, but seldom of their own accord and almost never with the prospects of a better future.

The Emigrants' Experience

The westward migration of white Americans did not result in the same degree of cultural dislocation as that of the native Americans, but it was not without its share of social, familial, and individual crises. There was, in fact, no single pattern of "frontier life" for whites moving west, but a complex and often conflicted interplay of expectation and experience.

Throughout the first half of the nineteenth century, the image of the West took on a decidedly romantic tinge in the minds of many Easterners. Popular writers—most notably James Fenimore Cooper, but also scores of other novelists and journalists—depicted the frontier as a region of danger, drama, and heroic deeds. Similarly, in the era before photography, prominent painters such as George Catlin and Albert Bierstadt offered eastern audiences vivid eyewitness views of the West and its native inhabitants. The result was that people setting out for the West often began their journey with a great sense of anticipation and adventure.

Along the way, however, the trail exacted its toll on settlers' spirits, and the romanticism of the East eventually faded in the face of the realities of the West. The trip west proved a difficult test of endurance, both for individuals and for the social units they formed. Most emigrants traveled in groups, and their caravans became short-term communities of necessity, mobile models of the established social order. At least at the outset, the social organization of migrant trains tended to reinforce the standard gender roles and power relationships of the white American family. Even the decision to move west reflected different perceptions. What might have seemed to men an opportunity for a new life often seemed to women the loss of an old life, a separation from the relationships of kinship and community left behind. Once under way, migrant communities generally replicated the division of labor according to customary notions of "separate spheres." Men took primary responsibility for driving and defending the wagon train, while women cooked, cared for the children and the sick, and generally provided the emotional support that kept the family—and the migrant community—together.

As the trip wore on, internal conflict often threatened to drive the migrant community apart. The arduousness of the journey caused roles to change and relationships to become strained. Men argued among themselves about who should determine the route and pace of migration; sometimes these disagreements boiled over into open power struggles that ultimately resulted in the division of the migrant community into two separate caravans, each going its own way. Within individual families, necessity caused women to assume new roles and take on tasks that had formerly been the exclusive responsibility of men. In the end, the long, difficult trip not only tarnished people's expectations about the adventure of moving west, it also challenged some of their basic assumptions about fundamental human relationships.

Once they reached their destination, migrant groups generally sought to re-create the familiar patterns of community life they had known be-

Your father never sold his country— never forget my dying words. . . . This country holds your father's body. Never sell the bones of your father and mother.

JOSEPH
NEZ PERCÉ CHIEF, TO HIS
SON JOSEPH, 1871

♦ **Caravan**

A company of travelers on a journey through desert or hostile regions

THE FRONTIER

The Emigrants' Experience

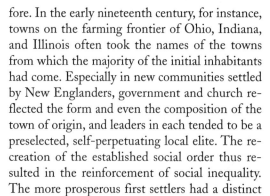

fore. In the early nineteenth century, for instance, towns on the farming frontier of Ohio, Indiana, and Illinois often took the names of the towns from which the majority of the initial inhabitants had come. Especially in new communities settled by New Englanders, government and church reflected the form and even the composition of the town of origin, and leaders in each tended to be a preselected, self-perpetuating local elite. The re-creation of the established social order thus resulted in the reinforcement of social inequality. The more prosperous first settlers had a distinct advantage in being able to acquire land and set down permanent roots. Their poorer counterparts, not to mention those who came later, often stayed only a comparatively short while and then moved on, looking for land and better prospects elsewhere. While the towns on the midwestern frontier included some people in their strong ties of community, they excluded others—as had been the case in the New England towns from which they originated.

In the settlements farther west, the familiar social patterns were more fluid and fragile. For instance, in the wake of the discovery of gold in California in 1848, thousands of migrants swarmed west, most of them young, single, and eager to get rich. Almost overnight, they created dozens of little mining camps inhabited largely by prospectors and prostitutes. With men outnumbering women sometimes by more than ten to one, life in these new communities tended to be volatile and violent, and there were few churches, schools, or other institutions of moral guidance and social control. In time, however, with the growth of commercial centers such as San Francisco and Portland, the cities of the West began to offer at least a pale—or sometimes quite gaudy—reflection of the genteel life of the urban East.

The western replication of eastern society and culture was not simply a matter of popular preference, it was also an important question in national politics. Throughout the second quarter of the nineteenth century, westward expansion heightened the conflict between two competing models of eastern society: the free labor system of the North and the slave labor system of the South. Both northerners and southerners came to believe that the expansion of their particular way of life was crucial to the future of their respective regions, and therefore the future of the frontier became especially crucial to both. From the acceptance of slavery in Missouri in 1820 to its rejection in California in 1850, political leaders had attempted to reach a compromise on the issue in the new states created out of the western territories. Compromise, rather than offering a complete resolution of the controversy, increased tensions over the future of the territories.

That tension turned to open violence in 1854, soon after Congress passed the Kansas-Nebraska Act, which had been sponsored by Senator Stephen A. Douglas of Illinois. Douglas's original intent had been primarily to promote a northern route for a proposed transcontinental railroad, not to add more fuel to the debate over slavery. But to gain southern support, he agreed to open the question of slavery in the Kansas and Nebraska territories to the doctrine of "popular sovereignty," the notion that the inhabitants of the territories, and not Congress, should have the right to decide on slavery for themselves before entering the Union. When the Kansas-Nebraska Act passed, thousands of pro-slavery and anti-slavery settlers rushed into Kansas, each faction intent on shaping this rich farming region according to its particular social system. The conflict quickly turned to armed struggle, and "Bleeding Kansas" became the scene of small-scale but brutal civil war. In-

deed, the violence on the farming frontier foreshadowed—and, to some degree, triggered—the larger, bloodier struggle that would engulf the whole nation in 1861.

Integrating the Western Frontier into Industrial Society

While the North and South were locked in civil war, the United States government adopted two policies that would have a profound effect on the future of the West. First, Congress passed the Homestead Act in May 1862, to encourage settlement and development of the western frontier. Any settler could get 160 acres of land essentially for free, on the condition that he cultivate it and live on it for at least five years. Although unscrupulous speculators succeeded in turning the law to their own advantage, thousands of actual settlers were lured west by the promise of free land.

Two months after Congress passed the Homestead Act, it authorized massive land grants and other benefits to railroad companies to promote the construction of a transcontinental railroad. Two companies started working toward each other, the Union Pacific moving west across the plains from Omaha, Nebraska, and the Central Pacific heading east through the Sierra Nevada. After years of back-breaking and often deadly labor by ethnically distinct work forces—the Irish of the Union Pacific and the Chinese of the Central Pacific—the two lines of track met at Promontory Point, Utah, in May 1869. Technology and human toil had finally forged an iron link between the Atlantic and the Pacific. Thus, in the post–Civil War era, uniting the rapidly growing West with the industrializing East became as important a process as reuniting the North and the South.

The combination of cheap land and easy transportation spurred a remarkable surge of settlers to the West. A trip that once took up to six or seven months by wagon train now took six or seven days. Those who came west on the railroad, like those who built it, added greatly to the ethnic diversity of the region. Recent immigrants from almost all parts of northern and eastern Europe—England, Ireland, Scandinavia, Germany, Poland, Russia—joined native-born settlers in the search for new farmland. Often they formed distinct ethnic communities, and in some territories, like Minnesota and Wisconsin, the concentration of Scandinavians and Germans created an immigrant culture that shaped the future of the states.

No matter where they settled, or with whom, the new immigrants faced a difficult struggle to

THE FRONTIER

Integrating the Western Frontier into Industrial Society

What treaty that the White man ever made with us have they kept? Not one. When I was a boy the Sioux owned the world. . . . Where are the warriors today? Who slew them? Where are our lands? Who owns them?

SITTING BULL

See also
National Parks and Preservation

*The prospects
appeared even more
grim than for the
first winter. Again,
the two greatest
concerns were food
and fuel sufficient to
carry us through the
terrible months.*

RACHEL CALOF
IN RACHEL CALOF'S STORY:
JEWISH HOMESTEADER OF
THE NORTHERN PLAINS

♦ **Harrow**

*A cultivating implement set
with spikes, spring teeth, or
disks and used primarily for
pulverizing and smoothing
the soil*

secure a living from the soil. Although the land of the Great Plains was generally fertile, it was also quite dry and bare. Such discouraging environmental conditions challenged even the most committed and courageous farm family. Sometimes living in miserable huts made of prairie sod and always contending with violent weather and voracious insects, many families soon gave up in one place and moved on to another. In some midwestern regions, the rate of persistence from one decade to the next was well below 50 percent, and in some cases was even below 30 percent.

Those who stayed, however, eventually managed to make a decent if sometimes precarious living. Building modest yet handsome frame houses, schools, and churches, they made the Midwest the mythical as well as the geographical center of the nation, America's heartland. Moreover, using new agricultural technology developed in the middle of the nineteenth century—more efficient plows and harrows, large, horse-drawn reapers and threshers—grain farmers made the Midwest one of the most productive agricultural regions of the nation, America's breadbasket. The high cost of modern farm equipment encouraged most farmers to specialize in one main crop, usually corn or wheat, that had a high market value. Connected to large milling operations by the railroads, frontier farms in the newly opened parts of the West soon provided a significant part of the foodstuffs needed to feed an increasingly industrialized East.

So, too, did western cattle ranches. Although cattle ranchers and farmers were usually bitter enemies in the competition for access to prairie lands, they played a similar role in the national economy. Cowboys drove huge herds to new stockyards adjoining railroads in Kansas, and from there the cattle were shipped to slaughterhouses, the largest and most technologically advanced of which were in Chicago. After the cattle had been killed and sent through a "disassembly line," the meat could be shipped in refrigerated railroad cars to eastern cities. About half the beef consumed in the United States originated on the western cattle ranches. Here again, the inhabitants of the West—including the cowboy, the highly romanticized but very hardworking and low-paid laborer in the cattle industry—helped feed those who worked in the offices and factories of the East.

Along with cattle and grain, the third critical contribution the West made to the economic development of the industrializing nation was its vast mineral resources. Mining operations ex-

tracted gold, silver, copper, lead, zinc, and other valuable minerals from the high plateau west of the Great Plains. Rich discoveries in the Rocky Mountains and the Sierra Nevada created new gold and silver rushes to rival that of the 1848 California boom. As had been the case earlier, some of the rough, rapidly growing, and predominantly male mining camps soon turned into sizable—and surprisingly civilized—towns, complete with elegant hotels, restaurants, and theaters. They did so, in part, because of the increasing concentration of wealth in the hands of a few mine owners. Individual prospectors usually sold their claims to large entrepreneurs, and mining became part of industrial capitalism, with high-priced machinery and low-paid workers.

Native Resistance to National Integration

Throughout the post–Civil War era, the settlement, development, and national integration of the western frontier may have seemed an inexorable process, but it did not go unopposed. Despite the extensive claims of the United States government, the trans-Mississippi West was still home to more than three hundred thousand Indians, dozens of tribal groups that inhabited the region from the Great Plains to the desert Southwest to the coastal Northwest. These native inhabitants of the West lived in a variety of ways—some farmed, some fished, some followed the buffalo—but despite their diversity, all eventually faced the common fate of encountering the huge influx of white settlers. As had been the case more than two centuries before, in the first period of Indian-white contact on the eastern coast of North America, new diseases decimated the Indian peoples of the trans-Mississippi regions. Some tribes were repeatedly devastated by the sicknesses brought by white settlers, and they were virtually helpless to resist the steady encroachment of white society. Other tribes resisted forcefully and, for a while, successfully. Eventually, however, even the most warlike tribes were reduced by disease and military defeat, and had to accept being limited to life on government-controlled reservations. The struggle and ultimate subjugation of the western Indians in the second half of the nineteenth century remains one of the most dramatic and tragic chapters in the history of the American frontier.

The majority of these western Indians lived on the Great Plains, and there the buffalo became the source, or certainly the symbol, of the conflict between Indians and whites. For over three centuries—ever since the Spanish had introduced horses to North America—Plains Indians had been skilled, wide-ranging hunters who depended on the buffalo for their survival. They used the meat for food, the hide for clothing and shelter, and virtually all parts of the animal for some purpose, including ceremonial dress and religious symbols. In the post–Civil War era, whites developed an apparent need for the buffalo, but more for show than for survival. Seeking skins for blankets and heads for trophies, whites hunted the buffalo for sport and profit. So extensive was the hunting by the end of the 1870s that the once-vast herds were near extinction, the number of buffalo having dropped from the tens of millions to only a few thousand in the space of less than two decades. The decline of the buffalo spelled the decline of the Indian as well.

The native inhabitants of the Great Plains faced not only a devastating decline in the buffalo population but an equally threatening increase in the white population as well. The United States government's policy of promoting orderly settlement and economic development in the West did not allow Indians their accustomed access to the land. Rather, Indians were to be restricted to reservations, far removed from the railroad routes and new farming communities, where they could be regulated by the government's Bureau of Indian Affairs and reformed by Christian missionaries. Some Indian tribes accepted removal to reservations without open resistance. Others, however, refused to accommodate themselves to the demands of the white man, and they fought back in a bitter warfare. From the Apache in the Southwest to the Nez Percé in the northern Rockies to the Sioux, Cheyenne, Comanche, and other tribes on the Great Plains, Indians' resistance made white expansion a costly and deadly process.

The Sioux played the most dramatic role in this war for the West. Although several western Sioux tribes in the Dakota, Montana, and Wyoming territories of the Upper Midwest and the northern Rocky Mountain region had been assigned to a reservation by the Treaty of Fort Laramie (1868), many Sioux refused to be limited to the reservation. Moreover, the discovery of gold in the Black Hills of South Dakota, which was part of the Sioux reservation, prompted a rush of white prospectors into Indian territory. To push the Sioux onto the reservation and thereby to promote settlement by white miners and farmers, the United States government sent a military expedition to the region in 1875. Government troops led

by a flamboyant young general, George Armstrong Custer, suffered a crushing defeat at the hands of the Sioux leader Sitting Bull at the Little Bighorn River in the Montana Territory in June 1876. The massacre of Custer's force frightened white Americans and encouraged Native Americans, but it proved to be the exception rather than the rule in the war between the Sioux and the United States. Over the next five years, the United States Army stalked and eventually subdued the Sioux, forcing them not only to return to their reservation but also to cede about a third of their land to the government.

In 1889, however, the Sioux once again rose up in resistance. Reservation-bound Indians began to practice a new ritual, the Ghost Dance, which reinvigorated their sense of their culture and created a new sense of defiance. Concerned federal officials saw the implications inherent in this ritual of resurgence, and they used armed force to put an end to the Ghost Dance movement. The results were disastrous for the Sioux. The government's attempt to take Sitting Bull into custody ended in his being shot and killed. Two weeks later, on 29 December, a detachment of the Seventh Cavalry—Custer's old regiment—rounded up some 350 Sioux at Wounded Knee, South Dakota; and when someone fired a shot, the soldiers massacred about 300 Indians in a matter of minutes.

The slaughter at Wounded Knee was not the last step in the suppression of Indians—some tribes still engaged in armed struggle against the United States government well into the twentieth century—but it did signal the end to Sioux resistance. Moreover, it symbolized a more widespread defeat for Indian peoples throughout the West. By 1890, the reservation had become virtually their only recourse. The superintendent of the 1890 census declared that the process of white settlement had spread so completely across the continent that "there can hardly be said to be a frontier line." That simple bureaucratic pronouncement inspired the historian Frederick Jackson Turner to see the "closing of a great historic movement" ("Significance of the Frontier," p. 1). Indeed, the "closing" of the American frontier led to the opening of a new area of interest in the writing of American history.

The Enduring Significance of the American Frontier

It is difficult for historians to declare the frontier truly closed. The frontier is, as noted at the outset, an ambiguous, often deceptive, concept. Yet the

THE FRONTIER

The Enduring Significance of the American Frontier

The red man was pressed from this part of the West/ He's no more likely to return/ To the banks of the Red River where seldom if ever/ Their flickering campfires burn.

ANONYMOUS
THIRD VERSE OF COWBOY
SONG HOME ON THE RANGE,
1860S OR EARLIER

F

THE FRONTIER

The Enduring Significance of the American Frontier

Land of opportunity, land for the huddled masses—where would the opportunity have been without the genocide of those Old Guard, bristling Indian tribes?

EDWARD HOAGLAND

notion of the frontier has become so deeply embedded in American culture that it cannot be dismissed no matter how inaccurate or anachronistic it may be. From the fiction of James Fenimore Cooper and other popular novelists to nineteenth-century "Wild West" shows and twentieth-century "westerns," the frontier has been a powerful mythic symbol of unfettered individualism, a place where a person could live, perhaps thrive, without the standard constraints of society. In a word, the frontier represented freedom.

For many people, the promise proved to be true, at least to a degree. Not only white men but black men as well rode the ranges as cowboys. African Americans could never fully throw off the burden of prejudice in American society, but in the West they could escape the institutionalized racism that prevailed in the South (and often in the North). Similarly, women could not completely overcome the legal and cultural restrictions imposed on them, but in some western states they gained the right to vote almost fifty years before woman suffrage became the law of the land. Moreover, in an era when it is no longer easy, as Huck Finn put it, to "light out for the territory," many people in twentieth-century America still long to escape "civilized" society by going to the "wilderness," whether in the vast spaces of Alaska, in the relatively confined and well-designed recreational areas of national and state parks, or in the even greater comfort of a motor home.

But as the experience of Indian peoples made clear, the history of the frontier is not a chronicle of openness and opportunity for all. Indeed, whatever freedom most Americans gained as a result of national expansion came at the expense of

the freedom, even the very existence, of Native Americans. The remnants of tribes restricted to reservations in the twentieth century now struggle to preserve a culture that once covered the continent.

The fate of Indian peoples mirrors that of the land itself. The ever-expanding resource demands of industrial capitalism have led to the exploitation and near-extinction of the wilderness. Beginning in the nineteenth century, nature writers began to express concern for the future of the American wilderness, and at the turn of the century the naturalist John Muir issued a clear call for the preservation of the natural beauty and grandeur of the western landscape. Accordingly, state and federal governments began setting aside parks and nature preserves in the nineteenth century, and today there are still vast wilderness areas that remain essentially undeveloped. But even these are not safe from the nation's increasing need for timber products, minerals, and water. Alaska, for instance, is now connected to the "Lower Forty-eight" by a lengthy oil pipeline, a controversial project that has brought both economic benefits and environmental disaster to the "last American wilderness."

The debate over the Alaska Pipeline is merely the latest, and certainly not the last, chapter in a history of human and environmental interaction that began on the North American continent thousands of years ago. The experience of the past, with all its promise and pitfalls, is still the best guide to the proper path to whatever frontier may yet exist in America's future.

—GREGORY H. NOBLES

H

HEALTH CARE

The history of America's health system is deeply intertwined with the social and political history of the nation. America's hospitals are an amalgam of institutions whose function and sponsorship reflect the diversity of the country's ethnic, religious, political, and racial groups. Similarly, American financing of health services is a mixture of public and private sources, organized through state and local regulatory agencies and nonprofit and for-profit insurance companies. Like its hospital system, which reflects the idiosyncratic histories of the nation's diverse populations, the health care financing system reflects the varieties of local political and economic circumstances of the country's regions and populations. For the past two hundred years, the health care system has adapted to enormous changes in the social, economic, political, and medical landscape, and its heterogeneity in organization, mission, and patient base reflects the diversity of the communities and interests it serves. Here we explore the historical culture in which hospitals, physicians, the insurance industry, and governmental regulatory functions have developed, however inadequate their responses may sometimes be to the changing needs of society's dependent and sick.

Those familiar with American history need little reminding that for most of the country's history life revolved around small communities and narrow personal contacts. The wide variety of groups that made up the city, while close to each other, nevertheless lived in highly structured communities separated by culture, ethnicity, and language. Until after the Civil War the vast majority of health services was provided through informal networks of caretakers, families, and friends whose views of what constituted health care reflected local customs, social practices, and beliefs. Care for society's dependent was provided in the home, the community, or not at all.

During much of the nineteenth century it was widely recognized that medical knowledge was inexact at best; professionals often engaged in bitter and highly publicized disagreements about the causes of disease or its proper management. Consequently, the treatment chosen was often a reflection of the customs and medical beliefs of a particular community or group of practitioners rather than of a standardized professional or scientific consensus. The medicine practiced in one section of the country or by a particular group of practitioners was often quite different in form and theory from that of another area or group. In much of rural America, lay people combined local folk customs with information gleaned from medical dictionaries and popular medical texts to arrive at their own idiosyncratic body of therapeutic practices. Similarly, doctors, who were not yet an elite professional group, were generally trained locally through a combination of formal medical school preparation and apprenticeship. The many medical schools were generally proprietary institutions organized to profit local practitioners in which students, often from lower-middle-class or lower-class backgrounds, paid to attend lectures of dubious worth. Formal medical education, largely unregulated and nonstandardized, could vary in length, content, and structure and was, from 1847 when the American Medical Association was formed, criticized for its lack of standardization of practice.

Few during the nineteenth century could agree on what might constitute appropriate practice among the myriad individuals who ascribed to the wide variety of schools of medicine. Furthermore, most practitioners and educated laymen of the period were skeptical of those who sought to unify practitioners under any one therapeutic umbrella. Throughout much of the nineteenth century, the disparate demands of different groups in various areas of the country created a diverse body of therapeutic knowledge and practice. Accordingly, medical training differed for rural and urban practitioners, homeopaths, allopaths, eclectics, Thomsonians, and a host of other practitioners of the art of medicine. Even those treating different classes and ethnic groups within the population were forced by the realities of the medical marketplace to adjust their practices.

This disparity between the educational requirements of various schools was reflected as well in differences between medical nosologies, views,

In the malaria-prone parts of the middle and southern colonies, as many as one child in three died in the first year of life.

PAGE 39

◆ **Nosologies**
Classifications or lists of diseases

Infectious diseases were deadly threats, although port officials inspected and quarantined entering ships.

PAGE 54

and theoretical positions. Different groups of practitioners generally identified with their own schools or "sects" of medicine.

Unlike today, when patients have little meaningful control over or choice of the types of therapies used, patients in nineteenth-century America could choose from among a host of practitioners and a fairly wide variety of therapies. By and large, doctors were family or community practitioners who were engaged in general medicine. Although a small number of doctors specialized in surgery, ophthalmology, or other areas, specialization was largely tangential to the practices of most physicians.

Family practitioners, who made up the bulk of the profession, generally lived within the communities where they practiced, providing health services either at the homes of their patients or in the doctors' offices, which were generally located in their own houses. They served a patient population that typically lived within a neighborhood and were often members with their patients of the same church or other local community clubs and organizations. The family doctor would preside at the significant events in peoples' lives. He would be fetched for births and deaths and saw it as his role to comfort the family; it was not unusual for him to move into a patient's house for the duration of an illness.

The relationship between doctor and patient was not necessarily the product of a deep-seated intellectual or professional belief in democracy nor in the importance of trust and understanding in the therapeutic process. Rather it was in large measure an outgrowth of a professional environment wherein practitioners working in an era of significant medical uncertainty with regard to procedures and outcomes were in severe competition with each other for clients. An abundance of doctors turned out by a large number of loosely organized and unregulated medical schools combined with loose licensure requirements uncontrolled by the state or the profession to produce a surfeit of practitioners. Without the options now available of research positions in universities, hospitals, and institutes, and before the era of highly specialized forms of practice, doctors depended on the goodwill of their patients for their economic survival. The competition among practitioners for patients, which was fierce by the end of the century, made familiarity, dress, demeanor, courtesy, cultivation, and common understanding essential qualities for the successful practitioner. What might have been lacking in scientific rigor and detailed knowledge was made up for by the intimacy of the practice itself. The authority of the practitioner rested as much on his social relationship to his patient as upon the consistency or scientific base of his therapeutics.

In the decades surrounding the turn of the century a significant reform movement arose within medicine that held as its guiding principle the need to standardize medical education. Underlying this reform effort lay a notion that, by standardizing the training of physicians and by controlling entrance into the profession through specific licensure procedures, medical practice would become more uniform. This movement culminated in the now-classic 1910 Carnegie Foundation bulletin known as the Flexner Report, which called for the reorganization of the medical school curriculum. The Flexner Report, named for its primary author, Abraham Flexner, was the end product of a long, involved process among medical educators, predominantly within the American Medical Association's Council on Medical Education, to standardize American medicine. But it was successful only in certain narrow respects. Although medical practice remained a field filled with uncertainty and nonstandardized procedures performed by individual practitioners, the standardization of the social background of medical practitioners was achieved. By the end of the nineteenth century, the eclectic nature of the practice of medicine and the largely unregulated environment in which medicine had developed had created a large, diverse set of educational institutions catering to women, blacks, and poorer students. By 1900 there were sixteen women's medical schools and ten black medical colleges, primarily in the southern states. The majority of medical students attending the various proprietary medical colleges was of a lower- or lower-middle-class social background. By 1916, however, only one women's college and two black schools remained, and many of the proprietary institutions that had once catered to part-time and working students had gone out of existence.

Reformers saw little need for protecting these poorly endowed institutions, in part because of their belief that a future era of scientific medicine would make social diversity within the ranks of those in medicine unimportant. If the physician of the future was to become a scientist treating patients irrespective of their social class, then there was little practical justification for protecting certain groups in medicine. Doctors were to treat organs rather than people and were to cure diseases irrespective of the social, racial, and class characteristics of the bodies the diseases attacked. In Flexner's model for the new science of medicine it mattered little who the practitioner was as long as he trained in modern scientific institutions. If what was seen to be the best also turned out to be white, upper middle class, and male, so much the better, for the general social position of medical practitioners would then be enhanced as well. Flexner's discussion of the future roles of the "poor boy," women, and negroes in medicine showed a simple and, from today's perspective, naive belief in the ability of medical science to solve the issues of equity and equality that became the central concerns of health planners and professionals in the 1960s and 1970s.

The Growth of Institutional Care

Before the Civil War, only a handful of hospitals existed. Philadelphia's Pennsylvania Hospital (1751), New York Hospital (founded 1791), and Boston's Massachusetts General Hospital (1811) were the oldest nongovernmental institutions in the nation. They were generally governed by lay trustees, many of whom were descendants of the earliest Dutch and English settlers. Bellevue Hospital in New York City, the largest of the public facilities, evolved as an adjunct to an eighteenth-century almshouse. The few pre–Civil War facilities were large institutions that often served as long-term-care establishments for the city's dependent poor, travelers, and the mentally ill. Others, such as Kings County Hospital in Brooklyn, were municipal institutions.

After the 1870s, hospitals began to be built in large numbers throughout the growing cities of the Northeast and Midwest. Generally, these institutions were diverse and served a wide variety of social and medical needs. Very often the elite of a community, generally its merchants, local businessmen, and members of the clergy, would initiate and sponsor the formation of what were known as charity hospitals to serve the working class and the dependent poor. Such hospitals generally differed in their religious and ethnic orientations, sources of financial support, size, medical orientation, and the types of services they provided. Most of these hospitals reflected the particular nature of the community they served. Specific hospitals catered to different groups of Jews, Catholics, Italians, Germans, and blacks. Children's hospitals arose to care for orphaned children. Maternity hospitals, often located in working class neighborhoods, were as much shelters for unwed mothers as they were maternity medical services. In communities with a significant number of elderly and dependent persons, local merchants often organized a home or hospital for supposedly incurables or for the chronically ill.

Most of the health-care institutions that developed around the turn of the century were small, locally sponsored charity facilities serving working-class and poor patients almost exclusively. Be-

HEALTH CARE

The Growth of Institutional Care

NINETEENTH CENTURY SURGERY

An operation at Bellevue Hospital in the 1870s. New York's Bellevue is the largest public institution built before the Civil War.

CORBIS-BETTMANN

See also
The Frontier

H

*The Growth of
Institutional Care*

*The first wealth
is health.*

RALPH WALDO EMERSON

cause they reflected the social diversity of their ethnic and religious sponsors and working-class patients, no "typical" hospital can be said to have existed. Many in fact looked and functioned like homes or churches and were therefore not readily distinguishable from other establishments and organizations within the community.

The hospitals that developed during the early period of growth before the 1920s were organized around various notions of purpose and function. For one thing, there was little interest or concern with establishing a standardized institution. In fact, most of the hospitals were tiny in comparison to even the smallest of today's institutions and were established in a seemingly haphazard manner. Many institutions exhibited a degree of spontaneous organization characteristic of the fluidity of nineteenth-century social organization. Small hospitals of fifty beds or fewer showed an average life span of little more than five years, often being organized and disbanded with a frequency that would shock modern observers.

The small late-nineteenth-century institutions were not only liable to closure at any moment but were also in danger of immediate eviction. During the late nineteenth century, the typical East Coast city underwent fundamental changes in economic and social organization that placed tremendous pressures on charitable institutions, not only forcing them to adjust to new demands for services but also making them relocate and adjust to changing uses of land and space. As older, pedestrian-oriented communities gave way to new industrial and commercial centers, the land upon which many institutions sat often became more valuable. Streets were widened, electric trolley lines laid down in many cities, elevated train lines introduced, and new means of personal transportation such as the bicycle and later the automobile brought in that forced city governments to pave and clean their streets. Once-sleepy commercial shopping districts that had aimed to serve local neighborhood clientele suddenly emerged as busy, bustling downtowns with large department stores, massive traffic jams, and crowded streets. Pressure for space arose from newly established stores, warehouses, and government establishments in growing downtown commercial areas. Older communities were destroyed as people moved out to new "streetcar suburbs" that began to develop on the peripheries of central-city neighborhoods. As the new economically segregated city arose, its institutions adopted class-specific identities that tended to undercut their older ethnic identifications.

The relative variability in the nature of the nineteenth-century hospital might seem a sign of weakness or instability, but this would be only partially accurate. While individual institutions were subject to tremendous social, demographic, and economic pressures that often forced them to move or go out of existence, the system as a whole flourished. Charity hospitals increased in number throughout the period, and the system continued to experiment with form and function. The tremendous variety of institutions that served the dependent poor in nineteenth-century America gave the system as a whole a dynamism and stability that is remarkable.

The turn-of-the-century institutions under discussion were not solely medical facilities. Rather they were institutions that provided shelter, food, and care to those in need. Because upper-class community leaders and the middle class were generally cared for in their own homes, hospitals treated the working-class residents who were forced to become dependent on the larger society during times of hardship. The forms that this hardship took varied significantly from one segment of the working-class community to another. Sometimes dependence was created by illness, but often it was social circumstances that caused the growing dependence of a class of the population. The urban hospital can in fact be understood to have its origins in the variety of forms that dependence—not illness—took in the later nineteenth century.

Within this context the nineteenth-century institution played a varied, ambiguous role. It functioned simultaneously as a health-care facility, a social service provider, and an agent of social control. Admission to one of numerous hospitals depended less on a patient's medical situation than on a determination by wealthy patrons that the patient's physical and social circumstances made him or her an appropriate candidate for admission to it.

In many ways nineteenth-century hospitals reflected the diversity of the communities that sponsored, organized, and populated them. Often the values of the trustees, patients, and workers were incorporated into the very order of an institution. Assumptions regarding the meaning of dependence and disease, their moral context, and their relationship to poverty or a patient's occupation were active factors in shaping the diverse institutions that addressed the special needs of particular neighborhoods, religious groups, occupations, and races. In short, institutions differed from each other in much the same way as the diverse communities that founded them differed.

The moral and political objectives of these diverse nineteenth-century institutions had a profound impact on their internal order and organization. In general, the use of large, undifferentiated wards with many beds, which was the usual form of housing in the nineteenth-century hospital, met the needs of an institution trying to supervise and control patients confined there for long periods of time. Having the ward's beds lined up along its walls allowed nurses or attendants to watch many patients simultaneously and guaranteed strict supervision of potentially disruptive or untrustworthy poorer "inmates." Such a ward arrangement also allowed patients to socialize in an institution that in practice substituted for a home. And ambulatory patients could learn good work habits by serving as orderlies or nurses and by helping nearby patients who were incapable of helping themselves. By performing assigned and necessary tasks, patients made the administration of the hospital less complex and in effect paid for

---

PUBLIC MEDICAL INSTITUTIONS IN THE NINETEENTH CENTURY

Patient Diversity

The only social characteristics used to separate patients in wards were their sex, age, and medical condition. Although the institutions of the period were often administered by particular religious or sectarian orders, most trustees believed in a moral obligation to admit poorer patients regardless of race or religion. In fact, with their strong missionary zeal many trustees understood the inclusion of a wide range of religious, racial, and ethnic groups to be an important indication of the usefulness of the institution. Furthermore, the missionary function of some facilities dictated that the hospital not merely accept poor patients who presented themselves but also seek out and welcome such people. The annual reports of the various hospitals of the time remarked regularly on the wide variety of races, religions, and nationalities of those who appeared in their beds. Even the architectural detail of many such institutions reflected an overriding concern with social and moral objectives, as many of these facilities were built to resemble churches, mansions, and homes rather than prisons, schools, or factories.

---

their stay. At the same time, they learned the value of work by performing vital tasks for their fellow patients.

The organizational changes that overtook city hospitals during the early years of this century profoundly affected the relationships between trustees and their medical staffs. In part the new relationships were forced on all concerned by the changing social conditions under which both medical and hospital care now functioned. And the changing internal economy of these institutions altered the pattern of traditional paternalistic control that trustees had exerted over their institutions. While it is sometimes said that the voluntary hospital has become a workshop for the physician, closer inspection of the history of trustee-physician relationships shows that the modern professional and administrative structure of the hospital is the product of a series of profound compromises and adjustments in the running of the facility.

To understand the changing relationships between trustees and their medical and administrative staffs it is necessary to review briefly some of the central elements of the crisis in hospital financing that overtook American hospitals in the late nineteenth century. For most of that period, the country's charity hospitals were inexpensive institutions that could run on relatively small sums of money per year. In New York in the 1890s, for example, nearly all of the voluntary charitable institutions in the city spent less than $30,000 each to provide care. Partly because they were small institutions, rarely having more than 150 beds, partly because patients provided much of the labor, and finally because medical care then was a decidedly low-tech enterprise, these institutions generally spent less than $1.50 per patient per day. Funded by the institutions' benefactors, by a variety of state and local government sources, and by minimal patient payments, these institutions ran at modest deficits every year, which were generally covered by trustee contributions.

By the end of the century, however, costs for patient care began to increase substantially as advances in medical technology and changing standards of cleanliness began to affect the care provided. Also, philanthropists who had formerly supported hospitals now faced competing demands from other agencies, and as the number of poor increased substantially, hospitals found themselves strapped for funds. Increasingly, as hospital trustees were forced to make hard choices about the futures of their charitable enterprises, they began to turn to new, untested sources of in-

As had been the case more than two centuries before, in the first period of Indian-white contact on the eastern coast of North America, new diseases decimated the Indian peoples of the trans-Mississippi regions.

PAGE 198

See also
Death

H

HEALTH CARE

The Growth of Institutional Care

Consider the deference which is everywhere paid to a doctor's opinion. Nothing more strikingly betrays the credulity of mankind better than medicine.

HENRY DAVID THOREAU

See also
The City

come: private middle-class patients. In order to attract paying patients into charity hospitals, however, their trustees needed to change both the types of services and the administrative structure of their facilities. They needed to bring into their facilities private community practitioners who had previously been excluded, for it was they who largely controlled the loyalties of paying patients. Without the private practitioner there was no mechanism to attract the patient who could afford to pay for his or her own care. Along with this, hospitals had to underplay their traditional image as facilities for the poor. Furthermore, they had to introduce the new services and amenities that would be expected by a wealthier clientele. During the decades before the Great Depression, many hospital trustees faced wrenching decisions about whether or not to fundamentally restructure their facilities.

For many institutions the introduction of private practitioners into their voluntary institutions was the most troubling aspect of the restructuring. Before this period, hospitals' trustees had previously run very closely controlled institutions in which most of the workers, patients, administrators, and even "house staff" physicians lived together in a closed environment. Within the older closed "houses" in which a limited number of physicians were younger "house staff" who depended upon the paternalistic authority of the trustees, the institutions' leaders generally didn't hesitate to reprimand, limit, and even dismiss rebellious doctors. For example, as late as the 1890s, protests by physicians in Brooklyn over living and working conditions resulted in the dismissal of the entire staff. In another facility, doctors who protested their treatment at the hands of the head nurse and who demanded her dismissal were themselves dismissed by indignant trustees. As late as 1900, hospital trustees believed that the efficient functioning of an institution depended more on its nursing staff than its medical staff. In institution after institution, trustees reluctantly and slowly opened up their facilities to practitioners from the private community.

For many trustees facing the challenge of private practice in their previously closed houses, the answer lay in organizing two parallel systems of health services. The trustees sought to protect traditional charitable institutions from entrepreneurial private practitioners by giving local doctors only visiting privileges rather than staff appointments in their institutions. By keeping local practitioners outside the formal structure of their facilities, trustees believed they could shield

charitable hospitals for the deserving poor from the commercial aspect of private care. Thus, trustees organized private wings, wards, and rooms within their institutions as much to shelter charity patients from the commercialization of medical care that paying patients, private practitioners, and private services represented as for reasons of care. As part of this process, care became structured around the patients' social class, with the poor or uninsured being served in wards by ward staff and paying patients being served by attending or visiting physicians in private or semi-private rooms.

The tensions that plagued hospital administrators reflected larger pressures affecting the very leadership of such institutions. After World War II, trustees lost sight of their earlier commitment to charity and community, as traditionally defined. The growing involvement of the federal government in financing research, construction, and medical education altered the relationships between institutions and their local communities. Furthermore, the long, historical evolution of private practice medicine into the hospital and out of the private office significantly changed the internal culture of health-care institutions as their trustees lost their role and legitimacy as guardians of the poor, the dependent, and the sick. As the social-class makeup of these institutions changed, their commitment to traditional religious, ethnic, and economic constituencies slowly lessened. In their place a newer commitment to communities of professionals—most notably of doctors—developed. With such new communities came abandonment of older, traditional rationales of social service and the development of new, if vaguer, definitions of success. Medical definitions of disease came to replace the older social definitions of dependence as the reason for the existence of the institution, and less specific community needs took a backseat to medically defined priorities. Institutions now relied less and less on the decisions of trustees who understood little about medical technology and medical decision making. Trustees became solely concerned with the finances of their institutions.

The very idea of community was significantly altered in the aftermath of World War II. While earlier generations of trustees and patients often shared certain religious or moral assumptions, the development of highly stratified communities divided along lines of class or race made the whole concept of community more nebulous. As the interstate highway system spurred the growth of wealthy suburbs and then hastened the economic decline of the inner cities, health facilities' trustees found themselves more and more removed, socially and physically, from the communities of the poor they ostensibly served. The social origins of patients in hospitals became mere abstractions amid larger efforts by trustees and administrators to maintain the economic integrity of institutions dedicated to medical care rather than social service. By the mid 1960s, as hospitals responded to calls for unionization, the notion of health care institutions being closely connected to their communities seemed like a romantic remnant from a prescientific era. Health planners and activists alike began to call for community-based services as the very institutions that had once appeared to be central to community life now appeared ever more remote. Federal programs through the Office of Economic Opportunity were organized under the rubric that health was a "community affair" that demanded the creation of neighborhood health centers to respond to locally defined needs. At the very time there was a rebirth of interest in locally based health services, hospital leaders seemed increasingly distant, perhaps even antagonistic, to such efforts. In some communities, such as New York City's South Bronx, Bedford-Stuyvesant in Brooklyn, and elsewhere, the hospitals that had once been the cornerstones of community social service were perceived as the enemy and on occasion even occupied in demonstrations. The growing distance between community leaders and hospital trustees spoke to the tremendous historical journey that community hospitals have set out upon during the twentieth century. Along with hospitals' abandonment of community came the growth of national standards to measure progress and success.

Women in the Changing Twentieth-Century Hospital

Throughout the late nineteenth and early twentieth centuries, when most hospitals were considered part of the extensive network of charity institutions, most hospital administrators were women. Especially in the numerous smaller charity institutions scattered throughout the nation many nurses, nuns, or laywomen who functioned as caretakers within the facilities rose through the ranks to assume major roles as ward or institutional managers. Until as recently as 1929, women made up nearly 40 percent of all chief hospital administrators. A 1929 survey of superintendents of 7,610 health institutions in the United States and Canada by Michael M. Davis reported that 20 percent were nurses, 8 percent were sisters, and 11 percent were laywomen. Of the 61 percent remaining, 37 percent were male physicians, 10 percent were laymen, and the remaining 14 percent were unspecified.

The significant role that women have played in shaping modern health administration has hardly been recognized. In the years when the health system was growing dramatically, the administration of the hospital and the clinic was seen as the natural preserve of largely single middle-class women whose social role was to maintain the harmony, stability, and cohesiveness of their communities. Just as married woman ran households, single women—who were often sisters in Catholic institutions or nurses and laywomen in smaller ethnic facilities—were thought appropriate candidates to run the community's voluntary institutions. In these generally smaller institutions, such women were responsible both for providing care and for managing the business functions of their facilities. For a large part of the first third of this century, caregiving and financial management abilities were seen as coequal qualities considered necessary in hospital administrators. Therefore, women, with their claim on the running of the household and on the emotional lives of the community, made excellent candidates for administrative positions and shaped institutions' goals as

UNDERVALUED OCCUPATION

Nurses have continually found themselves caught between one image as the handmaiden to physicians and another as professionals with skills, status, and an identity of their own.
TED STRESHINSKY / CORBIS

*There was a great
improvement—
indeed, a great
revolution—in life
expectancy at birth.*

PAGE 134

their administrators. The importance of women in the administration of many early twentieth-century health institutions grew out of the unique blend of moral, religious, medical, and social services hospitals were expected to provide. While sickness was one major form of dependence that increased the demand for health care, it was the social surroundings of a community's life that made these institutions the appropriate centers to care for the poor or for immigrants. In such settings, women's traditional role as caretaker could merge with their career aspirations to create career paths that were unavailable in the male-dominated outside world. Women, locked out of many of the professions, government service, and business, found a relatively welcoming field in hospital administration.

Women's traditional role as the protectors of the moral life of the nation added a degree of legitimacy to their positions as hospital administrators. In late nineteenth- and early twentieth-century urban society, where dependence, poverty, and illness were often interpreted as interlocking indications of the general morality or immorality of patients, medical care was seen as intimately linked to the success of moral reform within the health care institution. Hence the administrator, as the person responsible for the total life of the institution, largely controlled the program designed to teach patients acceptable standards of moral behavior.

Internally, the institution's facilities reflected the underlying moral goals of the program's originators and of the head administrator. The superintendent was responsible for the daily running of the institution, and he or she functioned as a patriarch or matriarch of the extended family that the hospital was supposed to resemble. The entire structure of the administration of the facility was modeled on the ideal of the middle-class family of late nineteenth- and early twentieth-century America. The superintendent or matron served as father or mother. Nurses, sisters, long-term patients, and young house-staff physicians played the roles of older children who had varying degrees of responsibility for the housekeeping chores needing to be done in the institution. Newly admitted patients not yet socialized into the life of the institution were in effect infants, in need of constant guidance and supervision by parents and siblings. Only the trustees, the institution's spiritual leaders, escaped the confining environment of the "house," as it was called.

Women's role as administrators augmented their other positions in hospitals, most notably as nurses. From the very earliest moments of hospital history, nurses were central to the care of patients. Yet because their role was so defined by the mission of caregiving, women were placed in ambiguous and ambivalent positions within the institution's hierarchy. The origin of nursing in the traditions of charity and volunteer work has led to a significant undervaluing of nurses' role and status. Despite repeated historical attempts to professionalize nursing fundamentally, nurses have continually found themselves caught between one image as handmaidens to physicians and another as professionals with skills, status, and an identity of their own.

Despite the fact that schools particularly for nursing were opened in the late nineteenth century, the system of nursing education was fractured and multilayered. More often than not, nurses were seen as a source of unskilled labor by hospital trustees eager to keep costs low and to maintain the charitable aura of the institution. The nursing schools associated with hospitals were built to produce an inexpensive labor force, not to create a cadre of skilled professionals. Similarly, physicians, whose role in the hospital expanded greatly during this period, rarely allowed nurses autonomy, thereby reinforcing their image as adjuncts to the male-dominated medical profession. Drives by institutions to lower costs and a concomitant increase in hospital-based nursing schools then created an oversupply of nurses that also served to fragment the profession.

Throughout the twentieth century, tension has existed within the nursing field. Those interested in autonomy have striven to decrease the output of nursing programs, thereby creating a nursing shortage, and have sought to professionalize the field by increasing the skill levels to those associated with highly trained professionals. Yet the ideology of professionalism has come into conflict with the division of labor within medicine that gives authority and responsibility to a medical profession that lacks interest in ceding control to a new group of professionals.

The Rise of Private Health Insurance

While caregivers and hospitals have been central components in the health system of this country, it seems fair to say that the system for financing health services is probably its single most problematic aspect in the minds of millions of poorly insured or uninsured Americans. A chronic issue that affects nearly everyone at one time or another, the system of health insurance has throughout the twentieth century led to repeated calls for governmental involvement. Yet despite the unhappiness of millions with existing private, nongovernmental health financing, calls for national or compulsory health insurance programs have been regularly sidetracked or delayed. For instance, in the early twentieth century a movement for the creation of statewide plans to finance health care, modeled along the lines of workers' compensation, was defeated. In the middle years of the Great Depression, health insurance was specifically left out of the Social Security Act. In the 1940s and 1950s, despite apparent presidential support, attempts to pass national health insurance legislation were defeated. Only in the 1960s did Congress pass Medicare and Medicaid, two programs to fund care for the elderly, the disabled, and the desperately poor.

To comprehend the ability of a widely criticized insurance industry to withstand these pressures for change and even grow in the midst of ongoing public discontent demands understanding on both the political and the cultural levels. To do so it is necessary to appreciate the traditional resistance that has existed to governmental involvement in the provision of health insurance and also American laborers' traditional interest in self-help, the ideal of establishing programs, services, and benefits through voluntary or nongovernmental forms. Furthermore, it is critical to understand the long-held distrust of both management and government control over these programs by many elements in the labor movement.

After wages and hours, the provision of health and welfare benefits has always been central to the struggles of labor and management to control the workplace. Throughout the nineteenth and twentieth centuries, both management and organized labor have sought to sponsor programs aimed at providing health and welfare benefits to workers. In the early nineteenth century, paternalistic textile mill owners in Lowell, Massachusetts, initiated what became known as the Lowell Plan. Late in the century, railroads, logging, and mining companies began to contract with physicians to provide minimal health services to workers. Into the 1920s, welfare capitalists at U.S. Steel, International Harvester, and other such companies developed welfare plans. Throughout, labor has distrusted employee benefit plans that were not under their own control.

While the various health and welfare programs were portrayed by management as paternalistic responses to the felt needs of the work force, most union representatives saw them as a means of undermining worker- and union-based initiatives to improve working conditions. These management-initiated programs were seen as attempts to make workers dependent upon the goodwill of the company, thereby creating a nonmilitant, acquiescent labor force. The programs were thought to be inadequate and temporary at best. At worst they were perceived as tools in management's attempts to cover up the dangers of the workplace and to hide deaths or disabilities caused by unsafe, unclean working environments. Because of the general lack of availability even of management programs and in light of dismal experiences and widespread distrust of management's motivations, workers and unions organized their own health and benefit societies, self-insurance and disability compensation programs, old-age pensions, and even clinics and hospitals. In the late eighteenth and early nineteenth centuries, many workers organized mutual aid and benevolent societies. By the mid-twentieth century, there were well over two hundred group health plans in the country. Among the more important employee-sponsored plans were the hospital and medical care program of the United Mine Workers of America's welfare and retirement fund, the Union Health Center, the International Ladies Garment Workers Union, and the Sidney Hillman Medical Center of the Male Apparel Industry of Philadelphia of the Amalgamated Clothing and Textile Workers, members of the CIO.

The 1930s are a critical period for understanding labor's changing attitude toward what labor leaders considered their long support for voluntary (union initiated) health and welfare programs. During this time, under the financial pressures of the Depression, the development of the New Deal administration in Washington, and the impact of specific pieces of pro-labor legislation such as the 1935 National Labor Relations (Wagner) Act, and because of splits within the labor movement itself, labor showed a willingness to consider new models to provide health and welfare services to their members.

During the Depression, organized labor faced innumerable problems as millions of its workers found themselves unemployed and dependent. Also in that era the longstanding supremacy of the American Federation of Labor was challenged by organizing drives in heavy industry that were spurred by the Committee for Industrial Organization (later the Congress of Industrial Organizations). With the development of the CIO in the second half of the 1930s, organized labor faced not only an internal schism in its ranks but also a split over its long-held belief in self-help. Many of

The incidence of long-term disability and chronic disease increases with age. The last stage, demographers report, is characterized not so much by sickness as by frailty.

PAGE 293

See also
Childhood and Children

the new CIO unions saw themselves as in close alliance with New Deal government politicians and administrators, especially in the years following the passage of the Wagner Act. In fact, many unionizing drives used the image of a pro-labor president and sympathetic congressmen in their organizing literature. For the first time in labor history, significant sectors of organized labor looked to the national government for support, protection, and sometimes even advice. In the context of the Depression, as the new CIO became deeply involved in organizing millions of workers, significant portions of the labor movement supported governmental programs in the areas of social welfare, protective legislation, and even working hours and wages. Walter Reuther and the United Auto Workers, along with other leaders of the CIO, even went so far as to endorse various calls for national health insurance.

This was a dramatic break with the traditions of the American Federation of Labor regarding self-reliance and voluntarism in the development of critical labor programs. Here for the first time labor accepted the notion of third-party intervention. This change proved important in the more conservative postwar years, when Blue Cross emerged as a viable, nongovernmental, and non-management-oriented insurance alternative.

One important factor affecting labor was the previously mentioned passage in 1935 of the National Labor Relations Act, specifically its mandate for management and labor to engage in collective bargaining. Collective bargaining had always existed in industrial and labor relations, but this act greatly expanded the number of industries that could now reach agreement on any number of management-labor issues. The development of nonpartisan or third-party insurance schemes at the same time collective bargaining was spreading gave tremendous impetus to both labor's and management's interest in this new approach. During World War II, wage raises were restricted and many unions thus turned to expanding their members' fringe benefits. The years following World War II saw the rapid expansion of third-party health insurance systems, most notably the Blue Cross program, which grew by the infusion of funds into welfare and health programs established through collective bargaining agreements.

For most of this century, voluntary institutions such as hospitals and nongovernmental insurance companies have dominated the health system. But the end of the century is a critical time for health care because now, for the first time in many decades, the field has become increasingly responsive to forces outside the traditional nexus of care providers, patients, politicians, and institutions. Today corporations and consulting firms control vital elements of the health care system. Others are organizing what are termed "preferred provider organizations" or "health maintenance organizations" for corporations. In these new settings it remains unclear whether the culture of health services, with its focus on profit rather than care, will be capable of withstanding the growing political and popular impatience with a system that is a central factor in determining a health professional's identity. Fifty years from now, we may look back at this period and note how it was a period of change when the basic contours of health care were altered by demands for new services from the elderly, AIDS patients, an increasingly dependent population of sick, poor people, and an insurance system that could not meet even the most basic needs of the population.

—DAVID ROSNER

HOUSING

Americans' need for housing has been satisfied by an impressive diversity of house forms. This essay will identify some characteristic configurations of housing, consider what kinds of households used particular kinds of dwellings, and look at the ways that climate, materials, designers, builders, and construction methods created these houses. The diversity of ethnic heritages, the range of resources available for building, the historical moment, and the class position of dwellers all have affected the form of American housing.

This overview of American housing is organized chronologically. The first section, on seventeenth- and eighteenth-century houses, emphasizes regional differences, since both climate and European settlement patterns strongly influenced the shape of early houses. The second section, on the nineteenth century, focuses on new national trends, emerging class demarcations, and the effects of industrialization on house forms. The twentieth-century section considers the diversity of house forms within each income level, and closes with some indications of future directions in housing.

The Colonial Period

The future United States was colonized independently by several European nations in the late sixteenth and seventeenth centuries. Spanish,

See also
Old Age

French, Dutch, and English colonists were sent to the New World to secure parts of North America for their home countries' economic benefit. They arrived to find a landscape inhabited by Native Americans speaking a wide variety of languages, living in a variety of structures, and with unfamiliar community organizations.

New England and the Chesapeake region were the focus of English colonization. The shelters the colonists made upon first arrival were rude constructions: tree branches, twigs, and bark created a wigwam; a hollow in the earth protected new arrivals from the weather. Colonial efforts at creating housing depended primarily on settlers' knowledge of house types, room arrangements, and building practices brought with them from their countries of origin, combined with the building materials available on New World sites. When woodworking skills and tools imported from England combined with a ready supply of wood in New England, timber-framed houses sheathed in overlapping clapboards and roofed in shingles resulted.

Many one-room houses were erected in New England and the Chesapeake by and for ordinary farmers and townspeople. A common type had wood posts planted directly in the ground—called earth-fast construction—supporting a pegged-together timber frame. Sheathed and roofed in wood, unpainted, often with a clay-covered wooden chimney, such houses could easily last for at least a decade or two. Owners of such structures may have planned to move on when agricultural opportunities called them elsewhere, or to return to the mother country after improving their fortunes. Such dwellings constituted the largest number of Anglo dwellings in the seventeenth and eighteenth centuries.

A one-room house had to contain all the persons and activities of the household that required shelter. When feasible, some activities were pushed outdoors. For example, a cooking fire with a tripod-suspended pot served as outdoor kitchen. Sleeping, socializing, and work spaces all could occupy a single room, activities changing with times of day. A one-room house might have extra space under the roof—a rough attic reached by a ladder served many people as a bedroom. For the poorest, one-room structures continued to provide housing through the nineteenth century both on the traditionally understood frontier, and in urban settings where poverty allowed no other choice.

The middle states of New York, New Jersey, and Pennsylvania were early homes for German

"HALL-PARLOR" HOUSES

Permanent Dwellings in New England

New Englanders intending to create permanent towns built wooden houses on stone footings to protect the wood from decay; they constructed stone or brick fireplaces and chimneys to secure the wood structure from fire. They carefully cut mortises, tenons, and a variety of other timber joints to create a lasting structure, and added onto the house as family size and resources expanded. The hall-parlor plan represents a well-known organization of the main spaces in a seventeenth-century New England house. The main floor was divided into two rooms set left and right of a front door. The hall was the all-purpose room in which cooking and daily meals, spinning, and small-scale household production took place. Furniture was sparse, and tables and benches could be pushed against the walls to allow multiple activities to take place. The parlor was reserved for the finer household goods, special meals, visiting, and the parent's bed.

The exterior of the New England hall-parlor house reflected its internal organization. A massive chimney rose through the middle of the roof, signaling the presence of one chimney core opening into fireplaces in the hall, in the parlor, and perhaps toward the rear if there was a kitchen across the back of the house. Such a kitchen was often the first addition made by a growing family, and the extended roof that covered it gave New England houses their characteristic saltbox profile. On the floor above the hall and parlor might be additional rooms, named "hall chamber" and "parlor chamber" for their location, and used both as sleeping spaces for the children and servants or apprentices living in the household and for storage.

and Dutch settlers as well as the English. Dutch settlers occupied New York's Hudson Valley, and nearby New Jersey and Long Island in the mid-seventeenth century. Houses were constructed of wood, framed with heavy timber anchor-beams visible on the interior. These knee-braced beams supported the high ceilings of rooms often arranged in linear fashion, each room having its own front door. Limestone or brick sheathed the exterior; dates, initials, or geometric patterns were sometimes introduced into the brick courses. In-

See also
The Plantation

creasing prosperity allowed the Dutch to expand originally one- or two-room houses into multiroom long bar, **L** shape, or square plans.

In Pennsylvania, German immigrants arrived in the later seventeenth and eighteenth centuries. They built freestanding houses in farmstead settings. The preferred exterior wall materials for German house builders were stone or exposed timber framing with clay or masonry infill. The characteristic house form had as its principal ground-floor rooms the kitchen with a cooking fireplace and the *stube*, or entertaining room, with a heating stove and built-in seats along the walls. Like the early Anglo houses, German houses had exposed ceiling beams. Second-floor chambers complemented one or two ground-floor bedrooms. Stone cellars contained insulated storage rooms for food, and sometimes, a spring. In the eighteenth century, German settlers migrated south into Maryland, the Valley of Virginia, and North Carolina, where they continued to build stone and half-timbered houses.

Settlers in Maryland and Virginia built houses to suit a warmer climate. While the earliest established planters erected large houses with many rooms, by the eighteenth century it was common for a prosperous planter to construct multiple buildings clustered together instead of a single house. These forms were influenced by the southern commitment to an agricultural economy based on slave and indentured labor. One building provided a home for the planter and his immediate family. Slaves and servants had separate outbuildings in which to sleep. The kitchen, with its overheated atmosphere and hazardous sparks, occupied a building of its own. Additional storage and utility buildings dotted the near landscape, such that travelers described the planter's house as looking like a little village.

The houses erected for slaves in the South tended to provide minimum space for each household group—usually a single room for a family. The slaves built their housing with materials that were inexpensively acquired; sometimes leftovers from a more important piece of construction were handed along to them. A slave house might contain two or more households, each with one room on the main floor and an attic space above, the several households separated by partitions. A small window or two let in light; a door could create cross-ventilation; the fields served as privy. The slaves' scanty possessions were sometimes secreted in storage holes in the earthen floor.

Slave houses were located close to the work sites; a small cluster would be built near the fields where the slaves worked, creating a quarter apart from the owner's house. Sometimes slave houses were lined along a drive near the master's house, contributing to the townlike appearance of the planter's domain. If near the main house, slave dwellings were likely to have a coat of paint or other exterior finish, to give visual appeal to the planter's home grounds. If located at a greater distance, slave houses were made weatherproof but otherwise left unfinished on the exterior.

Ambitious families built houses in brick on both rural and town sites in Maryland, Virginia, and the Carolinas. They created symmetrical structures of two or three stories, sometimes extended laterally with wings or dependencies. The wealthiest looked to England for stylistic potential, adapting late Renaissance classical details for exterior door and window ornament, and for interior mantelpieces, moldings, door and window frames, elaborated staircases, and paneling. But they still relied on the aggregation of mostly wooden buildings to contain all the functions of the agricultural year, as did the majority of less prosperous planter households.

The French settlers arrived on the eastern shores of Canada and moved westward to the Great Lakes in the seventeenth century. Settlements followed the path of the Mississippi River; two of the original French foundations are the modern cities of Detroit and Saint Louis. Driven from Canada, French-speaking Acadians became Cajuns in the New Orleans-Delta region of Louisiana.

The French building traditions brought to America include the tall roof of northern Europe, the exterior veranda used for circulation, exterior staircases to the second story, and timber building methods such as *poteaux sur solle*—squared-off logs standing on a horizontal sill of wood. The spaces between the vertical logs were filled with clay and a binder such as hair or straw, or stones and mortar.

In the warm and wet Delta region, the raised creole cottage provided a convenient ground floor for services, relatively crudely finished, able to withstand an occasional flood, and a principal floor one level above ground where finely crafted woodwork would stay dry. A surrounding veranda that served the principal rooms was reached by a broad flight of steps in the country or smaller exterior stairs in urban settings.

Spanish settlers first colonized Florida in the late sixteenth century, then California, New Mexico, and the rest of the Southwest. Houses set flush with the street helped to create an urban clarity of definition for plazas and rectilinear street grids—features of the Spanish town plan prescribed by guidelines for the creation of colonial towns, the 1873 Laws of the Indies. In Florida, simple houses of two rooms, expanded by adding rooms in single file, were built of wattle and daub or boards and roofed in thatch. More sophisticated builders used coquina, a local stone made up of compacted seashells, or "tabby," a kind of cement mixture of shells, sand, lime, and water. Favored building materials in the Southwest were adobe (sun-dried brick) combined with local wood for ceiling beams, door and window frames, and veranda framing. In a dry climate, adobe was long-lasting, cheap to build with, and easily repaired with a periodic coat of clay to seal the surface.

The Spanish house was often a single range of rooms wrapped around a courtyard, sometimes with a second story. Extended roofs sheltered verandas and patios, characteristic of hot-climate architecture; outdoor courtyards and indoor rooms were equally essential in providing for the household's space needs. Elaborated wooden screens and grilles allowed Florida builders to encourage the passage of breezes through houses. The Spanish tradition of tile as a surfacing material gave color to the more expensive houses.

The Nineteenth Century: Immigration and Industrialization

The coastal settlements of the early period expanded as a growing population moved inland, after the 1785 survey of western lands, to find new farmland, to found new towns, and to exploit new resources. The original settlers were joined by immigrants from Germany, Scandinavia, Ireland, Russia, and elsewhere. Land made available to settlers by the United States government through the Homestead Act of 1862 and other legislation drew new arrivals west of the Appalachians and across the Mississippi.

Well established before the nineteenth century, the single-family house continued to serve American households. For new arrivals on the frontier, migrant or immigrant, one-room houses satisfied the need for speedily erected and economical shelter, just as they had for seventeenth- and eighteenth-century settlers. In the longer-settled areas, prosperous planters, farmers, and merchants built showplace single-family houses with many rooms.

Houses were directly affected by industrialization, which added many new possibilities to the nineteenth-century repertoire of house ideas. New materials were mass-produced and shipped around the country by rail; these included sawn lumber, nails, ornament in wood or cast iron, and prefabricated dwellings. New town forms developed with characteristic new housing types: the company town added tenements and boardinghouses, communitarian utopias developed collective dwellings, and commuter suburbs served the burgeoning middle class with variations on the single-family home at all prices.

A long-mythologized house form of this period was the log house, associated with the self-reliant economy of the frontier. The log construction method was indeed widely used during the period of western migration as a conveniently and quickly erected, inexpensive house that made use of on-site materials. It afforded housing to rural people with small resources. While an individual, casually built log house might not last more than a generation, the tradition of building them persisted for many generations in rural areas. Small, one-room log houses could be assembled quickly with round logs, the gaps between them chinked with mud and straw.

The slaves on the plantation lived in simple quarters some distance from the plantation house, in single cabins or double houses of wooden boards or shingles with a chimney in the middle and occupied by two families.

PAGES 320–321

See also
Public Architecture

CLIMATE AND HOUSING DESIGN

Variations in the Colonial Era

Climate played an important role in forming the configurations of colonial-era houses. In warm-climate areas, greater use was made of outdoor spaces than in the colder regions. Thus outdoor kitchens in separate buildings were used by French builders in the lower Mississippi Valley, Spanish settlers in Florida, and Anglo settlers in Virginia. Hispanic houses of the Southwest and Florida displayed a similar attitude to outdoor spaces with their second-story porches and courtyards. Outdoor passages from one part of the home grounds to another were common; one walked outdoors from the planter's main house to a subsidiary library or schoolhouse, often with bedrooms above; or one went onto the veranda of a creole cottage to get to the next room instead of using an interior hallway. Colder-climate architecture tended toward steep roofs, small window areas, and entranceways that faced south. Additional space in the attic above the parlor and hall was used as a sleeping area for household members and for storage.

By the early nineteenth century, water-pow-
ered mills were turning out mass-produced sawn
lumber, nails, textiles, and other goods; mill workers settled near these workplaces, creating new
towns and giving rise to new housing needs.
One such new form was the company town.
Housing produced by companies to house their
workers ran from single-family cottages to two-
and three-story houses for managers and tenements for single workers or for poorer families.
Management-owned housing was rented to
workers, and sometimes the rent was subtracted
from the paycheck before payday.

At Lowell, Massachusetts, in the 1820s, the
cotton company built boardinghouses where single women workers lived communally, sharing
bedrooms and eating centrally prepared meals in
group dining rooms; there was a housemother to
guarantee propriety. Next to the cotton mills in
Baltimore's Jones Valley, mill workers could live in
company-sponsored two-family houses; each
household had two rooms on each floor of a two-
story house located within a block or two of the
mill.

The elaborate and much-publicized company
town of Pullman, Illinois, built in the 1880s, provided single-family, two-family, and four-family
houses, tenements, boardinghouses, and a hotel.
Workers at the vast Pullman railroad car plant

lived in these many housing types, according to
their means, across the street from the factory
buildings in a nicely landscaped town with public
market buildings, church, stables, and a park. Exorbitant rents caused the state to divest George
Pullman of his interest in the town. The houses
remain in good condition and are still inhabited.
The town, now part of Chicago, is a historic site.

In cities of the industrial era, multifamily
housing rather than houses for single families became the norm. At the turn of the nineteenth
century, older houses that had been built for single families "filtered down" and were subdivided
for renters at rates affordable to workers. The
demolition and rebuilding that characterized urban centers in the 1830s and 1840s decreased this
housing stock, leaving poor families in need of
specially designed cheap rental quarters—tenements. The name "tenement" was applied to any
house in which three or more households shared a
common roof but lived in separate quarters. As
urban housing after about 1830 took on distinctive class differences, "tenement" came to refer to
a building for working-class, immigrant, or poor
tenants; the term "apartment" came into use as the
name for a middle-class family unit in a multifamily dwelling.

In the second and third quarters of the nineteenth century, thousands of tenement dwelling

units were erected in New York, Philadelphia, and other growing cities. The physical form of early tenements was varied. Often built of wood, some resembled private houses, while others reminded contemporaries of huge barracks. Tenement landlords rarely supplied their tenants with pure water or sanitary facilities. Wood construction made tenement living a fire hazard, one not alleviated by the tendency to make fire escapes out of wood. High death rates in tenement districts drew attention to the health problems created by their unsanitary conditions, leading to legislative efforts to control their design in the 1850s, 1860s, and 1870s.

A typical tenement built for profit in the last quarter of the nineteenth century in New York was sited on a lot 25 feet by 100 feet (7.5 by 30 meters). It was called a dumbbell tenement after the shape of the plan: the plan narrowed in the center to create a light well, while at the front and back it spread to the full-lot width. Each tenement house had five floors with four units on each floor. Family units in such buildings usually had no more than three rooms—a living room used for cooking, eating, washing, income-producing work, and socializing, and two bedrooms, used for sleeping but also for income-producing piecework. Families frequently took in unrelated boarders to help pay the rent, so parents, children, and boarders all slept in proximity to each other—a lack of privacy that early social workers found threatening to morality. When there were indoor toilet facilities, they were limited to water closets in the public halls; bathtubs were not supplied in tenements. However, for those who wanted to bathe, public baths were common in larger cities after 1900.

Only two or three apartments per floor rather than the standard four was a variant of the tenement for tenants who could afford higher rents. Fewer units per floor meant that each family gained square footage. Two apartments per floor in a 25-foot-wide (7.5-meter) building each ran from front to back in a long string of rooms. When these apartments had no interior hallways, a space-saving device, they were called railroad flats because one walked from room to room as if going through the cars on a train.

Charitable organizations and individual philanthropists participated in the building of workers' housing. Alfred Tredway White promoted "5% philanthropy," the idea that public-spirited investors could put their money into progressively conceived workers' housing projects and still make a modest 5 percent return on the investment. White assembled large plots of land the size of an entire city block, and built model tenements such as the Tower and Riverside buildings, in Brooklyn, which provided three- or four-room units in two-room-deep perimeter-type buildings. These structures were built to wrap around the edge of the lot, leaving the land inside free to be used for recreation, laundry, and children's play. Every apartment had cross-ventilation and ample sunshine from both the street and courtyard sides. Unlike privately sponsored tenements, whose owners were bent on saving money, philanthropic housing often included bathtubs in the basement and private water closets within each household space.

The mid-nineteenth century saw the definition of an American middle class with boundaries in part articulated by housing form. Farmers, the backbone of the American economy, built improved farmhouses with the aid of advice in agricultural journals. The modern farm included a house with heating and cooking stoves, a pump drawing running water into the kitchen sink, and many rooms to differentiate receiving company from work-related tasks or from the family's sitting and sleeping rooms. The activities of the farm, and therefore the specific spaces of the farmhouse and its linked, work-related buildings, were often divided by gender between husband and wife, their male and female children, and their farmhands. The women's sphere included the kitchen, the dooryard, and adjunct spaces for readying butter and eggs for market; the men's sphere was the barn, the barnyard, and adjunct spaces for tending to farm animals and crops.

Some farm families built larger and more refined log structures with several rooms. Building techniques such as finely cut corner notching, found throughout the Midwest and the South, exhibit highly developed building skills exercised with elaborate tool kits. In the upland South a double-pen log house (the dogtrot form) comprised two one-room log structures separated by an open passage and joined under a single roof. The open-air passage served as circulation (that is, the path of movement for residents), as an outdoor protected sitting area, and for the ventilation needed in hot southern summers. Nineteenth-century "improvements" led to sheathing log houses in clapboards or some other modern finish and enclosing the open-air passage, creating a center hall, often with stairs to an added second story. Such alterations sometimes made the log house look like a framed central-passage house.

'Mid pleasures and palaces though we may roam,/ Be it ever so humble, there's no place like home.

JOHN HOWARD PAYNE
HOME SWEET HOME,
SONG FOR THE OPERA CLARI,
OR THE MAID OF MILAN
(1823)

In the northern Midwest, immigrant Finns, Swedes, and Norwegians brought northern European, refined corner-notching techniques to build houses of one and two stories with logs. As their farms prospered, their houses grew to several rooms, with interior walls notched into the exterior log structure. Often a porch was part of the basic plan. Logs for these houses were carefully squared off and the bark removed before the corner joints were cut. The logs were closely fitted and the internal walls plastered for a smooth finish.

Another new housing idea of the nineteenth century emerged from the flourishing utopian and religious communities in which the believers often lived in large collective dwellings rather than single-family houses. The Shaker community at Hancock, Massachusetts, created a large, collective dwelling form, the Brothers' and Sisters' House, which contained rooms for all the males and rooms for all the females of the group, spatially segregated from each other. The Shaker dwelling house included sophisticated built-in cupboards and drawers to accommodate the residents' need for storage and to free the floor from

THE FIRST SUBURBS

More middle-class families took up living in suburbs from the 1850s on. The first suburbs arose with the first transportation lines. Railroads and ferry boats linked urban downtowns with new residential districts created as bedroom communities for middle- and upper-middle-income households. Commuting husbands went to city workplaces while homemaking women and children spent the day in the healthy fresh air and greenery of the suburb. A profusion of illustrated architectural books from the 1840s on promoted ornamental cottages in landscaped settings as the American single-family ideal.

By the 1880s trolley lines reached out from many American downtowns to open up new residential areas for middling families whose budgets might allow them to live in half of a two-family house or one floor of a triple (three-flat) house in a "streetcar suburb." The wide availability of factory-cut lumber gave rise to a proliferation of moderately priced wooden houses for members of the emerging middle class in towns and suburbs.

extra pieces of furniture. At Salem, North Carolina, a settlement of Moravians created large, gender-segregated collective dwellings for their single members, constructed using German half-timbering with brick infill. Married church members moved into single-family houses for raising families, and ultimately went to their final rest in gender-segregated cemeteries.

Apartment houses for middle-class tenants provided another version of the collective dwelling in mid-nineteenth-century cities. This type first appeared under the name "hotel" in Boston about 1860. The conveniences provided by a hotel, including meals, maid service, central heating, gas or electric light, and security, tempted the well-to-do to renounce private houses and turn to apartment living. First called "flats," "French flats," or "Parisian dwellings," because they reminded early observers of the apartment-house tradition of middle-class Parisians, apartment houses designed expressly to preserve family privacy yet provide the pleasant services vices of a hotel were under construction in the late 1860s in New York, and in the 1870s in Washington, Chicago, and elsewhere.

Apartment houses for the middle class developed first as smaller buildings not too different in external appearance from large private houses. Inside, each floor was built to be a separate family unit. Early (1870–1880) apartment house designs of four or five stories made use of staircases rather than elevators. Servants slept on the topmost floor, and rents were adjusted so that those who had to climb the most stairs paid the least.

Much larger apartment houses of eight to ten stories appeared in the 1880s along with elevators, elaborate lobbies, doormen, and other service staff. Tall apartment houses in Chicago, Washington, Boston, and New York presented a new architectural image to passersby—one poised among the architectural conventions for a private house, a hotel, and an office building of the period. These buildings were constructed using new steel-cage engineering techniques, and were decorated on the exterior with stylish historical ornament in stone and terra-cotta.

The interior planning of an apartment unit was grounded in middle-class standards of family privacy and the sociable display of consumer goods. A formal parlor provided the space for receiving guests and placing the best furniture. Apartments for the wealthy, such as the 1883 Central Park Apartments in New York, had additional reception rooms—a library, a drawing room, and even a billiard room. Dining rooms were standard for all middle-class apartments. Family bedrooms ranged from one or two to eight or more; in addition there were always servants' rooms, either within the family unit or in attic or basement spaces. Apartment buildings set the standard for central heating, gas and electric lighting, telephones, refrigerators, and other technological household advances in the 1890s.

Private houses of the wealthy in the early nineteenth-century city were often four or five stories high, with a basement half aboveground. In the basement were a kitchen and family dining room. It was important for the kitchen to have immediate access to the backyard, where a cistern or pump was located and where garbage could be dumped. On the first floor, raised somewhat above sidewalk level by a flight of steps, were the reception rooms—a front and back parlor, and perhaps a formal dining room. The upper floors contained bedrooms and family sitting rooms. At the top, in the attic, were servants' rooms, storage, and workrooms.

Some early houses also contained a "counting room" or office in which the male head of the household conducted business. However, one aspect of improvement in house design of the nineteenth century was purging the house of explicit business and income-producing activities, so the counting room did not persist. Of course, the house served to enhance a family's income-producing potential because it secured extended family and social connections so necessary for the successful conduct of business, certified the social rank of the inhabitants, and itself increased in value.

At the same time, the home was increasingly mythologized as a refuge completely separated from work. A middle-class woman was told—in household magazines, manners manuals, and fiction—that her primary role was to be the moral force in the household, educator of her children, and example to her husband. She represented honorable values untainted by the commerce that weakened the moral fiber of the working world beyond the home. This framing of women mystified the real work that went on inside the household and the cash relations that underpinned the existence of servants and housewives.

Wealthy families continued to live in private houses in the cities of the later nineteenth century, but often possessed at least one country house as well. Philadelphians built summer homes on the Atlantic coast of New Jersey in towns such as Elberon; a winter home in Manhattan was complemented by a summer home at Newport, Rhode Island, or Asheville, North Carolina. Country houses for the well-to-do displayed familiarity with European architectural styles, which were inventively interpreted in wood, brick, or stone. Popular styles were the Greek revival in the 1830s and 1840s, Italianate and Gothic revival in the 1840s and 1850s, French Second Empire in the 1860s and 1870s, Victorian in the 1870s, and Queen Anne in the 1880s. Information on up-to-date architectural styles was available to architects, clients, and builders in mass-distributed books—another influence of industrialization. All these styles allowed American builders to display ornamental vocabularies, both inside and outside, adjusting the use of lavish materials to suit the wealth of the patron.

The spaces provided for a wealthy family in a country house of the later nineteenth century included several reception rooms—drawing room, library, parlor, sitting room, billiard room, boudoir; a dining room and perhaps a separate breakfast room; family bedrooms, typically grouped together on the second floor; a service suite of rooms including the kitchen, several pantries, food storage rooms, laundry rooms, servants' dining room, servants' bedrooms; several bathrooms, located separately for family members and for servants; and additional services located in the basement, stable, and carriage house.

The kinds of activities and meanings the American house had to support changed with time, climate, ethnicity, gender, and economics. Such changes were evident even on the simple level of function. For example, the late-nineteenth-century middle-class urban dwelling, whether in a single-family or multifamily configuration, tended to include a kitchen and a bathroom, and to exclude the income-producing work site. In a Virginia farmhouse of the early nineteenth century, the reverse was the case: separate kitchens were in independent back buildings, frequent baths were not part of people's behavior, and income was produced by work done in the house and its immediate landscape.

Twentieth-Century Dwellings

The twentieth century continued to use many of the nineteenth century's innovations—apartment houses, suburbs, and multiroom single-family houses. The automobile affected both the location of houses and their design: garages became part of the home. Most influential was the increased role of the state in housing production and distribution, seen in areas as diverse as zoning law, publicly subsidized housing for the poor, and federal

Faculty lived in two-story pavilions with their living quarters above and classrooms below; each pavilion illustrates a different example of classical architecture.

PAGE 379

See also
The City

H

HOUSING

*Twentieth-Century
Dwellings*

*Middle-class folk
also lived in modest
new apartments
constructed along
major streetcar
routes.*

PAGE 60

mortgage insurance. The state's negligence was also visible in the rise of homeless individuals and families.

Regional and climate characteristics so evident in houses of the eighteenth century continually diminished in the wake of industrialization. Modern building materials such as steel and concrete were used in every region, and inventions such as air-conditioning made climate-specific design solutions unnecessary. Manufactured housing increased rapidly since the 1970s, providing already-built houses that were trucked to sites all over the country and priced for households with very modest incomes. Such houses were designed for generic buyers; only after installing them were climate-specific adjustments made.

The twentieth century saw the distribution and incorporation of utilities into houses on a scale never before experienced. Most Americans since World War II lived in dwellings that had electricity for lighting and appliances, gas for cooking, stoves or furnaces for heating, indoor plumbing and sanitary facilities, and hot and cold running water. Before 1850 many of these conveniences were unavailable; some could be had only by the wealthiest households. Middle- and upper-class households that once had servants to light fires and lamps, cook meals, and empty slops now had plumbing and heating systems, power tools, and appliances to accomplish these housekeeping tasks. These same systems, tools, and appliances came to be a normal part of low-cost housing.

As immigrant populations moved into American cities, older generations, now Americanized, sought new homes, either in apartments or in single-family houses built for low-income households. Small houses priced to meet low-to-middling budgets and sized for the economy of servantless housekeeping were offered in diverse markets. In the first decade of the twentieth century, a house could be contracted for with a builder, or purchased already built from a developer. Mail-order houses such as Sears, Roebuck's could be purchased either as a set of plans and specifications that a local builder would follow, or as a complete house shipped as precut parts with instructions, to be erected on the site of one's choice, perhaps with one's own labor. Small, one-story houses with four rooms, called bungalows, were built nationwide, popularized by specialized magazines and even in songs. A living room, a kitchen, a bathroom, and one or two bedrooms provided lower-income families with homes of their own. Financing assisted those without savings to achieve independence. Manufacturers or developers offered special rates and installment payments at the turn of the century, a financial support system taken up later by banks and other thrift institutions, and subsidized by the federal government.

Early twentieth-century housing also included multifamily alternatives located away from the center of the city in peripheral or suburban settings. Garden apartments emerged as a popular form of low-rise, three-to-five-story housing, set back from the street in landscaped grounds. Generous courtyards provided residents with recreational and even gardening possibilities. Apartment units were placed so that every one had generous light and cross ventilation; occupants of several units shared laundry equipment, garages, and storage rooms. Such apartment developments were sponsored by businesses that wanted sound investments, such as insurance companies, or by organizations working to improve the lot of their membership, such as labor unions.

Downtown housing accommodated households that did not fit the standard American family model. Single people, both male and female, found city housing to their taste in hotels or single-room-occupancy, apartments. One or two rooms with a private bath located close to cultural attractions and downtown workplaces satisfied those who had no need for larger apartments and who rejected the life-style of the suburbs. At the turn of the century many "bachelor flats" were built for this group, whose special needs were not much acknowledged at the end of the century.

Company towns sponsored by corporations and erected for their workers continued in the twentieth century. Companies located away from population centers had to make special provisions for bringing workers to the job site; a new town near the site was an obvious solution. An example is Copperton, Utah, built in the 1920s by a copper mining company next to a vast open mine. The town of several square blocks contained schools and playgrounds, public meeting spaces, and single-family houses built according to five different plans. Exterior gables, porches, and window details combined with varied colors and material finishes to give the houses a good deal of individuality. Four-car garages at the rear corners of four contiguous lots were the only collective features; each house had its own front and back yards, clothesline, and driveway.

Suburban homes were widely believed to be superior places to bring up children for both physical and moral health reasons. The outer edges of cities were built up as automobile-era suburbs in the 1920s and 1930s, each house with its own garage, front yard, and back yard. The model suburban town of Radburn, New Jersey, was built in 1929 to demonstrate the latest in planning theory for the automobile era. A commuter suburb, the town was located near railroad lines but was also structured around the private car. Modest three-bedroom houses were finished in brick, wood, and stucco using half-timbered and other historical motifs. Houses faced onto two circulation systems: the back of the house and its garage faced an automobile street; the front of the house and its entrance faced a paved pedestrian route. Car traffic near houses used cul-de-sac streets with a low speed limit; larger collector streets took traffic through town and linked it to highways. All the pedestrian paths crossed automobile paths by means of bridges and underpasses, to protect pedestrians (especially children) from accidents. Every house was linked by a network of walking paths to the school and to a small shopping district.

The expansion in population after World War II gave rise to a demand for more single-family housing subsidized by federal loan programs. Huge numbers of houses were erected by developers such as the Levitt brothers, whose Levittowns in New York, Pennsylvania, and New Jersey became synonymous with repetitive and homogeneous suburban housing developments. Their houses, built by the thousands using traditional masonry and carpentry techniques, had minimum square footage, maximized the appliances and services that made for modern housekeeping, and were intended for future expansion. The company provided ideas to transform carports into garages, and garages and attics into bedrooms.

In the 1930s public housing began to redress problems created by the Great Depression. Poor but employed families were preferred as the tenants in federally produced row houses and low-rise apartments built all over the country. The best of these included playgrounds and landscaping; family unit sizes were kept to the minimum, and low-rise configurations meant that districts of subsidized housing did not reach the high densities that more prosperous neighborhoods found threatening.

After World War II, migrations of formerly rural Americans, especially southern African Americans, into cities pointed up the need for increased modern urban housing. Decades of suburban housing production had taken attention away from inner-city conditions. There, tenement buildings that had been constructed in the 1870s and 1880s still served poorer families in densely spaced, ethnically homogeneous enclaves. Houses once built for single families after the Civil War continued to serve as inner-city housing, subdivided to create two, three, or more apartments. Such housing lacked up-to-date plumbing and wiring and was often in serious disrepair. Neighborhoods, once identified as slums, were not thought worthy of the investment necessary for upgrading. The oldest, most decayed housing had always been inherited by those least able to pay; to city administrators and urban planners of the

♦ **Ticky-tacky**
(n) Sleazy or shoddy material used especially in the construction of look-alike tract houses; also something built of ticky-tacky; (adj.) of an uninspired or monotonous sameness

TICKY-TACKY TRACT
The Levitt brothers' Levittown, which became synonomous with repetitive and homogenous suburban housing developments, and which led to a new noun and adjective: ticky-tacky.
UPI / CORBIS-BETTMANN

*When I can no
longer bear to think
of the victims of
broken homes,
I begin to think
of the victims of
intact ones.*

PETER DEVRIES
THE TUNNEL OF LOVE

See also
The Suburbs

1950s, this old housing looked too decayed to serve anyone. "Urban renewal" policies were formulated to demolish and replace it, rebuilding center-city neighborhoods with the most up-to-date dwelling units equipped with modern plumbing, heating, lighting, and other services. The tower form was preferred because it used less land and initially appeared to be cheaper to build.

The replacement housing planned in these years was government-sponsored, but the state had never been widely supported as a housing initiator. Many critics still felt that housing was the rightful province of private enterprise, and in the absence of full commitment, public moneys did not achieve the amount of replacement housing originally intended. Building costs far exceeded estimates, and high-rise housing turned out to be far more costly than the low-rise units developed in the 1930s. Such small row and single-family houses continued to be erected in rural and suburban settings under federal programs, such as the 1950s and 1960s housing found on Indian reservations.

An example of public housing erected in this era is the 1958 Pruitt-Igoe redevelopment neighborhood in Saint Louis. Dwelling units were organized in thirty-three towers, each eleven stories high. Family units included large windows, several rooms, and fully equipped kitchens and bathrooms. Apartments were reached by elevators which stopped on every third floor. The fresh paint and services seemed to create the atmosphere for successful home life, but the project as a whole was ill managed.

Housing such as Pruitt-Igoe concentrated large numbers of poor households in too limited an area rather than mixing varied income households or dispersing smaller housing projects for the poor in several neighborhoods. So many people without resources could not keep their dwelling units in good repair, and city officials did not invest in the necessary maintenance of the public spaces—halls and elevators, parking lots and playgrounds—that should have been their responsibility. Pruitt-Igoe was finally demolished in 1972 after it proved unrepairable. In many cities, tower public housing has been closed awaiting reuse plans or has been sold to middle-class buyers as condominiums; some projects are being reduced in height to create more domestically scaled environments.

Housing for the wealthy in the twentieth century has few characteristics besides size and location that differentiate it from that of the middle-income and the poor. A full array of services has been a feature of expensive housing since 1900, but has been available to middling and poor households as well since World War II. Since the 1930s, architect-designed modernist houses of one story with an open plan and walls of glass have satisfied wealthy clients willing to take an artistic risk. Suburban houses in historical styles, popular in the nineteenth century, have remained the most popular in well-to-do, exclusive suburbs outside many American cities. Zoning laws have been used to require very large lot sizes and costly houses in neighborhoods allocated to the wealthy. The phenomenon called gentrification characterized efforts to reclaim inner-city buildings for housing in the 1970s and 1980s. The historic preservation movement, having raised appreciation of historic architecture among the upwardly mobile, provided a counter to urban renewal by demolition. Late-nineteenth-and early twentieth-century houses were sold to willing renovators who treasured the urbanity and historic character of aging city neighborhoods. Preserved blocks of such houses, now inhabited by wealthier owners, drove up real estate prices in areas previously deemed slums. In urban downtowns housing commanding high rents or sale prices has been created from underutilized older office and factory buildings, and sometimes even philanthropic tenements have been converted to high-priced condominiums.

High-rise towers have also been used for expensive apartments across the country, located in urban neighborhoods associated with social success. The sizes of household units for the wealthy can be much larger than units in middle-class or publicly subsidized apartment towers, and the material finishes are finer; the construction techniques and utilities and service systems use the same technologies. As in the nineteenth century, well-to-do people often possess more than one home, and a small urban apartment often suits their needs when combined with a large country house. The cost of renting or owning even a small apartment, however, depends significantly on location. Two rooms in the "best" building may cost as much as a dozen rooms in a less desirable place.

Since the 1970s some shifts in house form have suggested that developers and legislators acknowledge that household form is more diverse than the single-family standard. Municipalities recognized the need for families to incorporate an elderly parent into the household by structuring zoning laws to allow "mother-in-law" apartments attached to single-family houses. Apartment buildings were designed to allow two unrelated individuals to share one unit while each maintained a separate social life. Both bore the costs of rent on a shared kitchen and living room, services and utilities, and each had a personal bedroom and bathroom. Recognizing that many families were headed by a single parent, some multifamily dwellings were organized around collective day care for children. Housing forms were needed that recognize the many alternatives to a standard family that comprised households.

Near the end of the twentieth century, striking similarities between house forms for all classes and regions pointed up the triumph of modern construction techniques and services over ethnic and regional variants. Tall apartment towers served all income levels; they were just erected in different neighborhoods to serve different classes. The costliness and quality of materials and the square footage distinguished a single-family suburban house for a wealthy client from one for a poor client, but both were likely to have paved roads and driveway, gas and electric power, appliances, heat, cooking equipment, and indoor plumbing.

What Americans lacked was equal access to these house forms and to the comfortable and secure life they promise. Regional imbalances in price led to mansion price tags on four-room bungalows in some areas. Young middle-class or poor people could never expect to amass a down payment to buy their own house in inflated real estate markets. Low-income families who could only afford to be tenants found that income tax breaks were given to those who buy housing but not to those who rent. Racial discrimination in housing, although illegal, still prevented some from living in the district or the building of choice. The success of constructing and servicing houses must be followed up by economic and social structures that give everyone access to housing.

—ELIZABETH COLLINS CROMLEY

HUMOR AND COMEDY

What is so funny about American humor? How have its forms evolved? Does American comedy fairly articulate American humor? Does American humor afford a measure of the nation's true character? Can we, in this pluralistic society, even define humor and comedy as American, or should we consider the nation's diverse communities of laughter separately?

The problem with such questions is that humor resists investigation, as do a number of its sources. Humor evaporates in the heat of critical examination, vanishing altogether whenever its thrusts cease to be timely or friendly. Example and analysis must contend in dramatic tension to uphold the context for laughter to erupt. Race, gender, age, ethnicity, and social role and status prescribe the commonplace categories of America's humor. Language, folklore, family life, religion, and politics establish its convenient frames of reference and modalities of communication. No form of native expression covers the spectrum of popular utterances and tastes more thoroughly. American humor spans the conceivable possibilities from crude and vulgar outbursts to elite literature and dramatic comedy. Native Americans, European colonists, indentured servants, African slaves, immigrants, and contract laborers all contributed to folkloric humor and to humor and comedy in the popular culture. Although not all Americans were originally Englishmen and American humor was not necessarily English humor, the styles and usages of literary humor had deep roots in British culture, as Mark Twain observed, undergoing major transformations in the New World environment. Today's humor reflects the social changes of our times. Its contents and purpose have been shaped by mass media, which have overwhelmed the original characteristics of American humor.

History and theory help to explain. Pressures of class, sex, race, ethnicity, religion, politics, and role have shaped popular humor over time into divergent modes of expression, and bequeathed disparate styles to subsequent generations.

Early Wit

In colonial America, there was laughter of course, earlier than studies of humor can demonstrate or explain. Children gleefully mimicked adults. Europeans mocked the Indians, who retaliated in kind. Englishmen burlesqued Dutchmen, the Dutch ridiculed the English. Slaves raked their masters. In Georgia, people took care not to be overheard giggling at the proprietor's funny name, General Oglethorpe. Older settlers tried out tall tales on newcomers, and both understandably laughed at their plight. Frontier struggles gave birth to native traditions of American humor. Hopes and dreams could break against harsh realities in the wilderness, but laughter afforded a sure avenue away from despair. Humorous storytelling grew out of real experiences. A proclivity for hilarious exaggeration rang true enough by 1670 to make its way, along with astronomical, naviga-

It's hard to be funny when you have to be clean.

MAE WEST

H

HUMOR AND COMEDY

Democracy's Voices

tional, astrological, and calendrical data, into New England's proliferating almanacs.

Homely, coarse, often earthy, embodying a peasant shrewdness, the colonial almanacs imported the tradition and styles of English country humor, thereby enriching the indigenous propensity for wit. Almanac humor profiled village and rural life: the distinctive but mutually dependent roles of man and woman, the power and majesty of the law offended by the plague of lawyers, the farmer and his animals, the youth and his damsel, the clergymen bewitched by a seductive widow. Scatological humor frequently appeared, and bawdy jingles competed for the reader's attention, as in Daniel and Titan Leeds's almanac of 1714: "Dick on the hay doth tumble Nell/ Whereby her Belly comes to Swell." The quality of almanac humor scarcely improved over the years, except in the output of the Ames and Franklin families. Dr. Nathaniel Ames of Dedham, Massachusetts, and his namesake son, likewise a physician, wrote elegantly humorous essays. James S. Franklin launched Poor Robin's *Rhode-Island Almanack* several years before his younger brother Benjamin's *Poor Richard's Almanack* (1732–1758) appeared in Philadelphia. Poor Robin's philosophy ("Some tell us Money is a curse. So 'tis, but want of Money's worse.") anticipated Poor Richard's copybook maxims to encourage enterprise, diligence, and thrift. Ben Franklin helped to invent America's longest-lasting comic figure as a fount of common sense—the homespun, uneducated, artless provincial, the teller of tall tales, and somehow our most enduring joke about that type. Franklin's Poor Richard satirized authority, false piety, and deceitfulness, expounding wittily about adultery, prostitution, excretion, and such unsavory subjects in a foreshadowing of black humor. William Cobbett, an outspoken Tory turncoat, castigated him as a deist, quack, fornicator, and infidel. Unchastened by such attacks, Franklin comforted himself that "there's more old drunkards than old doctors." Franklin's style of humor spread north, south, and west.

Since American humor was at once old and new, literary humorists and storytellers strove to strike the right note between colonial import and native local color, between personal idiosyncrasy and national significance. The Connecticut Wits, a loosely linked ring of poets active in the late eighteenth and early nineteenth centuries, aimed satirical epics at dissenters or backsliders from New England's upright standards of liberty and morality. The examples set by its members John Trumbull (M'Fingal), Joel Barlow, Timothy

Dwight, David Humphreys, and Lemuel Hopkins reappeared in Washington Irving's *Knickerbocker's History of New York*, "Rip Van Winkle," and "The Legend of Sleepy Hollow," and still later in Oliver Wendell Holmes's wonderfully ironic "The Deacon's Masterpiece" about the "one-hoss-shay" and James Russell Lowell's acerbic *Biglow Papers*. Diedrich Knickerbocker's *History of New York* (1809), a purportedly serious account of Dutch life in New Netherlands, stands out as both a burlesque of history and a satire of the politics of Washington Irving's time and place. Knickerbocker's *New York* forecast great humor to come. Laughter would serve the white, male, upwardly aspiring forces of democracy as an avenging sword in the youthful republic, where ambition and pretension far outdistanced achievements. Laughter combined that same hostility toward intellect with a blessing for uneducated common sense that the almanacs had featured. Simon Suggs's judgment (1840) prevailed: "Booklarnin spoils a man if he's got motherwit, and if he ain't got that it don't do him no good." The people themselves and the wilderness confronting them abundantly supplied the comic materials for humorists. Writers and lecturers, usually eccentric literary figures and traveling showmen, jollied their audiences while fostering their own careers. More often than not, when geographical differences and telltale accents still distinguished one part of society from another, they relied on dialect humor for surefire laughter. Through the regional and ethnic speech patterns of rural New England and the frontiers of the West and Southwest, augmented in published form by bizarre typographical devices and spelling grotesqueries, they could depend on everyday incongruities to stimulate laughter.

Democracy's Voices

Mark Twain's Library of American Humor (1888), a guidebook for our purposes, compiled selections from forty-six authors. "Smack of whom it would," William Dean Howells enthused, "it has always been so racy of the soil that the native flavor prevails throughout, and whether Yankee, Knickerbocker, Southern California, refined or broad, prose, verse, or newspaper, it was and is always American" (*Twain's Library*, p. x). In 1906, however, Samuel Clemens (Mark Twain) concluded that his anthology was by then nothing but "a cemetery," though he seemed self-satisfied at the durability of his own output against the literary demise of most of his contemporaries. Twain's favorite ploys—understatement, black dialect, hy-

See also
Theater and Musical Theater

perbole, burlesque, incongruity, straight-faced vernacular, and others—had been employed by humorists before him. Concentrating on politics at first, their slyly derisive commentaries pointed out one direction to follow, while the grotesquely exaggerated exploits of their tall tales indicated another. Twain endured because he surpassed his competitors in all of their specialties. Masterfully he blended and shaped their techniques into an oral-sounding style that raised him into the highest rank of prose writers. He mixed his somber moods so subtly with folk wisdom that he educated generations of comic writers about humor's profoundest possibilities. But the scandal-ridden officeholders of the Gilded Age overwhelmed his relish for political humor: "If I could keep my faculty for humor uppermost, I'd laugh the dogs out of the country. But I can't. I get too mad" (Dunne, Philip, eds. *Mr. Dooley Remembers*, 1963, p. 260). Fortunately, other humorists persisted. Gleeful mockery of politicians' pretensions articulated the democracy's doubting voices.

Since 1830, when Seba Smith of Portland, Maine, founded his *Courier*, the first daily newspaper in Maine, and published letters he himself was writing (purportedly from Jack Downing, an innocent rustic), a beguiling political humor began to appear on a regular basis. Downing blundered into the legislature and, in his quaint vernacular, commenced writing to his friends back home of the strange doings there. Smith's plan proved highly successful. His scope widened. "Major" Jack Downing in Washington became a confidential adviser to presidents from Andrew Jackson to Franklin Pierce. Soon newspapers everywhere were imitating Jack Downing's bizarre depictions of public affairs. Even Downing's character was appropriated by other writers. The *Letters of Jack Downing, Major*, written by Charles Augustus Davis for the New York *Advertiser*, gained wide acclaim for a time, owing to the sharp bite of their satire. The immortal Sam Patch (1807?-1829) postulated that "some things can be done as well as others," while Jack Downing himself knew there was "an *outside* as well as an inside to everything," politics included.

There was much more. Comic tellers of local-color stories flourished. Foremost were the makers of the Davy Crockett myth. David Crockett's real self is lost in legend, but his prodigious reputation as a Tennessee frontiersman, three-time member of Congress, tall-story teller, and martyred hero of the Alamo perpetuated itself in popular history. Davy's motto, "Be sure you're right and then go ahead," caught the spirit of the times.

MASTER HUMORIST

Humorist Mark Twain, who surpassed his competitors in all of their specialties by blending and shaping their techniques into an oral-sounding style that raised him into the highest rank of prose writers.
CORBIS-BETTMANN

The coonskin humor in the Crockett anecdotal books and almanacs most likely emanated from an array of unsung authors exploiting his fame. Whoever wrote his "Coon Story" captured the flavor of frontier electioneering. Campaigning for Congress, Colonel Crockett grins the bark clean off a large knot on a tree branch to demonstrate to onlookers that his smiling opponent might likewise, if they were unwary, grin them out of their sound judgment on election day.

The Crockett myth played upon credulity, as Carroll Smith-Rosenberg points out in "Davy Crockett as Trickster." The mythic tale was actually a joke. Jokes and myths alike distort their subjects to conjure up illusions of truth. By inversion or comic reversal, the Crockett tales challenged middle-class respectability by opposing a wild West to the East that was too terrifying to abide. The Crockett depictions of women, for example, parody gentility, as with the young woman boldly disrobing herself except for a petticoat woven of brier bushes. "I could not come near her without getting stung most ridiculous," Crockett related. "I would as soon as have embraced a hedgehog." Panicked, he fled, leaving his coonskin cap behind.

Bemused or amused at safe distances, eastern readers devoured the comic works of nineteenth-century western storytellers: Augustus Baldwin Longstreet, Thomas Bangs Thorpe, Phillip B. January (Obe Oilstone), William Tappan Thompson, Johnson Jones Hooper, John S. Robb, and Joseph G. Baldwin stand out. They all imparted

> *I do think that a sense of humor gets you much farther in the movies than it does in real life.*
>
> TOM HANKS

See also

Radio

an exuberance to their descriptions of regional life. Longstreet's *Georgia Scenes* (1835), his earliest and most influential book, related true episodes modified to suit his narrative purposes into "fanciful *combinations* of real incidents and characters." Thorpe's masterful tall tale "The Big Bear of Arkansas" (1841), about a futile hunt for a creation bear, an "unhuntable bear," who died "when his time came," is spun by Jim Doggett aboard a Mississippi River steamboat before "a plentiful sprinkling of the half-horse and half-alligator species of men, . . . who appear to gain a livelihood simply by going up and down the river." January, a contributor to *The Spirit of the Times*, a magazine of indigenous humor, repeatedly demonstrated that the events of a tale mattered less than the manner of its telling. Thompson is remembered for his Georgia cracker dialect stories collected in several volumes, including *Major Jones's Courtship* (1843) and *Major Jones's Chronicles of Pineville* (1843). Hooper's Simon Suggs, a comic rogue ("It is good to be shifty in a new country."), resembles James Russell Lowell's Birdofredum Sawin and foreshadows W. C. Fields's roles as a confidence man.

Meanwhile John S. Robb (Solitaire), in Philadelphia, the author of "Swallowing an Oyster Alive" (1845) and Streaks from *Squatter Life, and Far-West Scenes* (1847), caricatured the westward movement as continuous hilarity. Robb depicted Old Sugar, "the standing candidate" in 1844 for elective office in Missouri's Niauga County, as brilliantly comic but never ludicrous, luring "sniggers" from his whiskey-drinking clientele. Robb's outlines of character were soft, wilderness crudity blending into urbane civilization. Like Andrew Jackson, Old Sugar lifted his glass to national unity: "Here is to the string that binds the states; may it never be bit apart by political rats!" Somewhere, perhaps, Old Sugar keeps a watchful, if bloodshot, eye on the American people. "Whar politicians congregate," quoth he, "I'm always thar at any rate." Baldwin's Ovid Bolus, Esquire, a lawyer like himself, in *The Flush Times of Alabama and Mississippi* (1853) elevated lying ("The truth was too small for him.") to the art form Mark Twain would make his own—for instance, characterizing Markiss as such a compulsive liar that his mendacious reputation obliged a coroner's jury to discredit his handwritten suicide note and enter a verdict of death by foul play at unknown hands.

Some humorists escaped both local-color and western categories. James Russell Lowell, a Massachusetts blueblood penning comic verses in parallel vein, was one such exception. His antislavery convictions led him to oppose westward expansion. In Lowell's *The Biglow Papers* (collected 1848), the principals are Hosea Biglow and his father, both ordinary but sensible farmers; Birdofredum Sawin, a volunteer soldier fighting in Mexico, the twisted incarnation of Manifest Destiny; and Homer Wilbur, an elderly clergyman epitomizing New England's cautious facets of personality and pedantry "with an infinite capacity of sermonizing muscularized by long practice." Lowell's satires suffered from excessive zeal. His humor, unlike Downing's, betrayed his lack of sympathy for its targets, an all-important element in democracy's laughter. George Washington Harris's *Sut Lovingood Yarns* (1867) featured a loud-mouthed, sex-driven Tennessee mountaineer, a brutal practical joker, a prototype scatologist and pornographer, a specialist in hell-raising. George Washington Cable, in the New Orleans dialects of his *Old Creole Days* (1879), captured the incongruities between the city's culture of French and Spanish whites and the state's Protestant Anglo-Saxons, which, ironically, irritated both the Creoles and Cajuns but won him admirers in the North and East.

Midway to Maturity

Charles Farrar Browne, influenced by Jack Downing, created Artemus Ward, a traveling showman and writer of comic tales. Showman Ward paraded his "moral wax figgers" and certain "sagashus beasts" before crowds of gaping rustics with comically mixed results. Couched in the semiliterate prattle of small-town America, Artemus Ward's sketches of his experiences appeared in *Vanity Fair*, "the grate komick paper" launched to compete with London's *Punch*. Lincoln read to his cabinet Ward's "High-Handed Outrage at Utica," a wildly plausible report of an indignant citizen's seizing of the show's effigy of Judas Iscariot. On the platform, Ward's humorous disquisitions depended on his masterful timing punctuated by shattering anticlimaxes. Like Mark Twain, who learned from him the tricks of the lecturing trade, Ward's appearance of personal distress and ignorance, his electrifying flashes of interest stalled by recurrent despair, his deadpan earnestness, and his meandering vagueness could not be duplicated in print. Unlike Downing, Ward devoted only part of his talent to politics, where he could be cunningly neutral. His classic shilly-shally compels conviction: "My perlitical sentiments agree with yourn exactly. I know they do, becaus I never saw a man whose didn't." In his

JOEL CHANDLER HARRIS

Popularizing African-American Humor

Joel Chandler Harris was, according to Lawrence Levine, "the most effective single force" to popularize the humor of African American culture. "All over the South, the stories of Br'er Rabbit are told," Octave Thanet (Alice French) noted in 1892. "Everywhere not only ideas and plots are repeated, but the words often are the same; one gets a new vision of the power of oral tradition." In his early volumes particularly, Harris, a Georgian, faithfully transcribed themes and speech from the humorous animal tales, songs, and folk traditions he heard recounted by former slaves. If in centering too much on Br'er Rabbit's comic misadventures Harris overemphasized the trickster tale, he nonetheless celebrated the victory of the weak over the strong. Decades would have to pass, however, before white men and women of the civil rights generation could appreciate the profound nature and functions of the laughter bubbling up from the repressed minority of blacks in their midst.

POPULARIZER

Joel Chandler Harris, who was the most effective single force to popularize the humor of African American culture.
LIBRARY OF CONGRESS / CORBIS

celebrated "Interview with President Lincoln," Artemus Ward avowed: "I have no politics. Nary a one. I'm not in the bizniss . . . I'm in a far more respectful bizniss nor what pollertics is." Yet the secret of success was the same everywhere. Once, in heralding his traveling show, he played his high card. "You scratch my back," he proposed, "& Ile scratch your back."

In fact, the humorists of the Civil War and Reconstruction era scratched a lot of backs. Georgia's Charles Henry Smith (Bill Arp) blended genial humor, forceful satire, and common sense in his "rebellious" letters to "Mr. Abe Linkhorn": "I'm a good Union man—'so-called'—but I'll bet on Dixie as long as I've got a dollar." Arp backed up his convictions: "I joined the army and succeeded in killing about as many of them as they of me." In the Confederacy's darkest days, it was said, he kept southern hearts from breaking.

David Ross Locke (Petroleum Vesuvius Nasby), editor of the *Findlay* (Ohio) *Hancock Jeffersonian*, wrote serialized letters presenting diverse views, opinions, and prophecies of Nasby, who claimed to be the late pastor of the Church of the New Dispensation, the chaplain to the president, and postmaster at "Confederit X Roads which is in the State uv Kentucky." Petroleum Vesuvius Nasby's initial success lay in recognizing the widespread fear among northern workingmen

that any emancipation of the South's slaves would release a flood of unwanted African American immigrants into the North. With deadly irony, Nasby contrived to "support" a petition to keep blacks out of Ohio, and leading journals throughout the country soon were reprinting his views. And in 1866, while "swingin' round the cirkle" with Andrew Johnson, a Unionist Democrat electioneering for favored congressional candidates, Nasby caricatured the president's supporters as sporting "a large proportion uv red noses and hats with the tops off." Nasby loved his party for its right, through election, to distribute the spoils of office. President Johnson could buy Nasby and his tattered ilk on easy terms, but he would have to furnish their ammunition. "Will he do it?" worried Nasby, who wanted a postmastership for himself. "That's the question a hundred thousand hungry soles, who hanker even ez I do, are daily askin'."

Not all Gilded Age humorists were memorable. The reputation of Robert Henry Newell (Orpheus C. Kerr), once ranked with Downing, Ward, and Arp, rests on his Civil War "papers," but his punning on "office seeker" was the funniest product of his wit. Henry Wheeler Shaw (Josh Billings) tried several careers before turning into a comic essayist and lecturer. Charles Farrar Browne persuaded his publisher to collect

See also
Popular Literature

Billings's pieces in *Josh Billings, His Sayings* (1865), which led to nine more compilations and prompted Abraham Lincoln to rate Billings's aphorisms second only to Shakespeare's. Charles Heber Clark (Max Adeler), a Philadelphia local-color journalist who lightened the gloom of an odd corner in "My First Political Speech," sketched the dilemma of stolen thunder for those speakers unlucky enough to appear last on a program. Edgar Wilson Nye's political humor followed the pattern set by Downing, Ward, and Nasby, and later by Will Rogers, who would be compared with him. "Bill" Nye's letter accepting the postmastership at Laramie, Wyoming Territory, "a great triumph of eternal truth" published in the *Laramie Boomerang*, brought him widespread acclaim. Nye often lectured with the Hoosier poet James Whitcomb Riley, against whose bathos his humor shone. Riley's way of retelling old favorites was superb platform art. His rendition of "The Old Soldier's Story" was "about the funniest thing I ever listened to," Mark Twain recalled.

The problem is that Twain's *Adventures of Huckleberry Finn* (1885) overshadows all else, not only his other works but also his contemporaries' works and his appraisals of them. Southwestern humorous fiction furthered the literary context for many of Twain's writings, as did local colorists and rural humorists. In time, their reliance on back-country speech, folkways, and local idiosyncrasies rendered them inaccessible to cosmopolitan readers; Twain escaped such constraints by mastering the main currents of American literature.

The Assault of Laughter

At this stage, humor and comedy underwent significant transformations. Southern blacks and waves of immigrants from Europe, including masses of Jews from eastern Europe, moved into the cities of the Northeast, carrying in their cultural baggage their own forms and usages of humor. Nasby's bigoted neighbors moved into urban complexes. So did the smug, onetime small-town elites Mark Twain vilified in "The Man That Corrupted Hadleyburg" (1900) and the pretenders to godliness he uncovered in "The Mysterious Stranger" (1916) as well as in "To the Person Sitting in Darkness" (1901). Alienated, self-detached humor had always been around, but its normal genialities fast became outweighed by newly belligerent absurdities expressed in racial, ethnic, sexual, religious, or political terms for urban readers and audiences. Filled with skepticism,

derogation, and cruelty yet aloof from serious protests or revolutionary manifestos, humor's new strain afforded, in Jesse Bier's mind, "a means of perspective between exaltation and destruction." It explains Robert Benchley's insistence that "Sheer madness is, of course, the highest possible brow in humor." Will Rogers would be a significant exception.

Often humorists were journalists or columnists at odds with governmental excrescences, hypocritical moralizing, patriotic pieties, and warfare. Ambrose Bierce (1842–1914?), the most bitter of them all, self-schooled in the dark recesses of Poe, was a twice-wounded veteran of the Civil War. In *The Cynic's Word Book* (1881–1906), renamed The *Devil's Dictionary* (1911), and his *Fantastic Fables* (1899), Bierce's satanic mordancy and misanthropy outdid Twain's final efforts. To appreciate his definitions required a special sort of sanity. Thus: "BELLADONNA, *n.* In Italian, a beautiful lady; in English, a deadly poison. A striking example of the essential identity of the two tongues." And "PATRIOT, *n.* One to whom the interests of a part seem superior to those of the whole. The dupe of statesmen and the tool of conquerors."

Mr. Martin Dooley, Chicago columnist Finley Peter Dunne's immortal saloonkeeper and public oracle, exuded an immigrant aura all his own. Dooley dispensed a satirically rich, jocose, and waggish humor in an amalgam of all the brogues of Ireland. Dooley's Irishness supplied an insider's insight into urban machine politicking and an underdog's perspective of American society with its democratic pretensions and nativist contradictions. At first, Dooley's opinions centered on local politics, as had Seba Smith's Downing letters, but soon he was capturing the excitements of the days of Cleveland, Bryan, McKinley, and the war with Spain. Merrily he discoursed on "Raypublicans," "Dimmycrats," and Populists, on the relationship of marriage and drink to politics, Christian Science, the Supreme Court ("th' supreme coort follows th' illiction returns"), and the vice presidency ("it isn't a crime exactly"). Politics was a great game, though never critical. "If ye don't win fair, ye may win foul," Dooley averred. "If ye don't win ye may tie an' get the money in the confusion."

From Chicago westward, in the 1890s whimsy and Bierce-like savagery flourished, paced by (Frank) Gelett Burgess, Eugene Field, and George Ade. In San Francisco, Burgess and his collaborators launched *The Lark*, a forerunner of the little magazines of the 1920s (including the comic *Life, Judge, College Humor, Captain Billy's*

Whiz-Bang) and the zany *Mad* and *National Lampoon* of the present. In the first issue, Burgess published "The Purple Cow":

> I never saw a Purple Cow
> I never hope to see One
> But I can tell you, anyhow
> I'd rather see than be One.

Before winning renown for sentimental poems, Field composed mock Old English ballads, destroyed actors and plays in caustic one-line drama reviews for various newspapers, and contributed ghoulish burlesques of children's primers to the *Denver Tribune*. "This is a Cock Roach," wrote Field. "He is Big, Black, and Ugly. He is Crawling over the Pillow. Do not Say a Word, but lie still and Keep your Mouth open. He will Crawl into Your Mouth and You can Bite him in Two. This will Teach him to be Discreet in the Future." Ade's fables in slang were both gentle and corrosive. Ade implied sarcasm while jumping back

---

H. L. MENCKEN
The Sage of Baltimore

Henry L. Mencken (1860–1956), the sage of Baltimore, lampooned popular politics and personalities in the *Baltimore Sun* for nearly half a century. A formidable critic of the arts and lexicographer (like Bierce, whom he admired extravagantly), Mencken bombarded his readers with well-chosen words. He excoriated President Harding's inaugural address as the worst example of English writing he knew. He assailed his fellow citizens as mediocrities: the dubs, oafs, yahoos, galoots, wowsers, trimmers, stoneheads, plus the booboisie's storied boobs, boob-bumpers, boob-squeezers, and other feeders at the public trough. Although puritanism—"the haunting fear that someone, somewhere may be happy"—had poisoned the soil ages ago, the nation's fundamental problem was democracy. Fact and theory, in Mencken's judgment, disputed Jefferson's tenet that wisdom lay in an electoral majority. Might one hope for improvement by urging men to seek office? Definitely not, Mencken thundered. This made no more sense to him than trying to halt prostitution by filling bawdy houses with virgins. In Mencken's jaundiced view, the man of culture was suffocating between the moneygrubber and the peasant. Not surprisingly, Mencken was both hated and adored.

---

and forth from sympathy to vituperation. Like Dunne, whom he greatly admired, he invariably concluded with a note of absurdity. His sixteen "Stories of Benevolent Assimilation" (1899) derided the intentions of Americans to transform the Filipinos into Asiatic reproductions of themselves as almost too ridiculous for words. "Give the people what they think they want," he sneered—and, for all his equivocations, Ade did just that.

Ethnoracial Subversion and Survival

New technological innovations began to carry humor and comedy to mass audiences: newspaper comic strips, motion pictures, radio, and television. If comedy can be defined as tragedy that happens to somebody else, this definition nowhere fit more neatly than the movies and the standardized formulas of radio and television humor such as the situation comedy or "sitcom." Much of the explanation lay in ethnicity. During the twentieth century, with the lingering exception of the comic strips, humor by Jews and blacks exerted profound influences on American popular culture.

People more than likely have always ridiculed those unlike themselves. In America, ethnic humor first expressed feelings of superiority by well-favored English-speaking, Protestant whites toward newer immigrants, especially if they were Roman Catholic Germans, Irish, Italians, or Poles, and against black slaves and freedmen, Hispanics, their children and their children's children. Ironically, derisive stereotypes became adopted by their victims in self-mockery, then, in revenge, were turned against the tormentors. Economic and social distinctions perpetuated the joking form of slurs to reveal the dynamite underlying agonizing differences within America's increasingly pluralistic society. Certain roots and characteristics of ethnic humor were imported long ago from far away. European Jewish immigrants introduced centuries-old habits of humor, while the humor of blacks, with identifiable African folklore ingredients, matured in resistance to slavery and racist suppression.

The Jewish Purim play annually featured irreverent humor and raucous buffoonery. Droll figures—the schnorrers (moochers), schlemiels (simpletons), and luftmenshen (luckless dreamers), Yiddish-tongued precursors of countless stand-up comedians—fled among the throngs migrating from east European ghettos. Humorously and invariably, these fools—indignant, righteous, and victimized—won out in the end.

Comedy is the last refuge of the nonconformist mind.

GILBERT SELDES

*In the field of
comedy, an
ingenious response
to the Production
Code appeared: the
screwball comedy.*

PAGE 148

See also

Popular Entertainment
before the Civil War

Already, to the barbs of older stock Americans (Why is the wheelbarrow the greatest invention ever made? It taught a few Irishmen to walk on their hind legs.), Irish comedians were retaliating in kind. Likewise Jewish ethnic humor, taking advantage of vaudeville and burlesque stages, built on its origins. (*Priest*: When will you give up those silly dietary laws? *Rabbi*: At your wedding, excellency.) Minstrelsy was a case in point: even Jews donned burned cork, their blackened faces guaranteeing immunity from customary restraints. Sophie Tucker, Al Jolson, George Jessel, and Eddie Cantor were minstrel stars who later triumphed on radio and the silver screen. The Marx Brothers carried comic Jewish dialogues into vaudeville, brandishing madcap nihilism against established institutions. Jewish entrepreneur's operated many theaters, so Jewish comics flocked onto the stages to test their talents and chutzpah. Analysts Sigmund Freud and Theodor Reik emphasized the historic tendency of Jews toward skepticism and self-criticism, the springing of mirthless wit at a flash of subjective truth or profound insight.

Defiant in their survival after the Holocaust, Jewish humorists and comedians broke loose from their cultural bonds to inject massive doses of their ethnocentric wisdom into all corners of American life. The best included radio stars Jack Benny and George Burns, as well as Sid Caesar, Milton Berle, Mort Sahl, Mel Brooks, and novelist Philip Roth. Never again would American humor be the same.

Blacks responded differently. Skin color and the terrible heritage of slavery set them apart. James Weldon Johnson, black novelist and poet, recalled his stint as a teacher among his people in backwoods Georgia: "Their deep genuine laughter often puzzled and irritated me. Why did they laugh so? How could they laugh so?" Black poet Claude McKay agreed: "How can they consent to joy and mirth/who live beneath a world of eternal ban?" Blacks shared with Jews, women and others despised, the humor of the oppressed. Blacks retaliated against their fate with laughter. Inwardly their laughter could mock themselves. Outwardly their humor both attacked and concealed. Black comedians were aggressive, even acrimonious: cursing ironically, relying on double meanings, ethnic put-downs, and trickster ploys. Often blacks' humor and gallows humor were one and the same.

Springing from sub-Saharan sources, African American humor rode its vehicles for laughter along two major avenues. Externally it functioned, and functions, as a mechanism for accommodation to a hostile white society. The John-Master slave stories, an oral tradition, humorously and in coded language vented helpless anger. John ridiculed his owner if he felt like doing so, which was only when the master was up at the big house and John was laboring down in the field. In the animal trickster tales—parodies of white society in Lawrence Levine's verdict—rabbit masked the slave, yet rabbit also displayed the slave driver's tyranny. White minstrels in blackface makeup stole this style of humor to convulse white audiences with their blatant stereotypes of Jim Dandy, an effeminate hustler, and Jim Crow and Sambo, who were slow-witted buffoons. To perform before whites, black comedians had to caricature themselves. Bert Williams presented separate routines to white and black audiences. Either way, "Jonah Man" Williams, helped by "Nobody," drew his laughter from his people's sorrow. Stepin Fetchit (Lincoln Perry) and Rochester (Eddie Anderson) prolonged the time-honored accommodating character for movies and radio, respectively.

Out of the civil rights movement and the urban turmoil of the 1960s and 1970s, black stand-up comics and writers joined Jewish and other ethnic laughmakers to jar and delight white middle-class audiences with their folk commentaries fortified by anthropological insight. Dick Gregory, from the back of his segregated bus, hit especially hard. (*Restaurateur*: "We don't serve Nigras!" *Gregory*: "That's cool. I don't eat them.") "Do you realize," Godfrey Cambridge inquired, "the amount of havoc a Negro couple can cause just by walking down the street on a Sunday morning with a copy of the *New York Times* real estate section under the man's arm?" Scourging Sambo, Redd Foxx confided that "Boss" spelled backward meant "double S.O.B." Comedienne, writer, and film producer Jackie "Moms" Mabley, and later screen actor Richard Pryor, revisited folk sources for earthy soul food to nourish laughter in those most weary and heavy laden. The phenomenally popular Bill Cosby, on the other hand, virtually deracialized the characters in his situation comedies into a utopian, if incredible, harmony with their white neighbors.

Mass Media and the Masses

Throughout the silent film era and the talking pictures of the 1930s and 1940s, American-made comedy films swept to mass popularity. The movies rejuvenated traditional jesting and clowning and, as the carnivals, circuses, medicine shows,

minstrel acts, theatricals, and burlesque shows had done, comedy films journeyed up and down the land, even crossing the oceans. Knockabout improvisations came first, followed by Mack Sennett's introduction (1912) of his satirically sharp, slapstick counterculture. Sennett introduced the Keystone Cops, bevies of bathing beauties, Fatty Arbuckle, cross-eyed Ben Turpin, Louise Fazenda, Harry Langdon, Marie Dressler, Charley Chase, Buster Keaton, and, briefly, Charlie Chaplin and Harold Lloyd. Chaplin left Sennett to launch his own company, developing his Little Tramp into the folk hero of the world. Chaplin and Keaton were alike in that both were at odds, the one with society and its defenders, the police, the other with his amazing props or the absurdity of life itself. Lloyd's "glass character," ill equipped for life, and his "human fly" stunts won him tremendous acclaim. Eventually, in catering to increasingly sophisticated theatergoers, Hal Roach outpaced Sennett by strengthening story lines and structures over and beyond visual gags.

Many performers with different styles were just as funny. The Micawber-like W. C. Fields, a longtime comic juggler on stage, repeatedly demonstrated man's helplessness in a world where inanimate objects, children, and dogs thwart one's innocent intentions. In *The Bank Dick* (1940) and other successes, Fields moved warily through life, protected by his flamboyant braggadocio, until he ran afoul of superior forces and invariably became obsequious or hostile to all who got in his way. Stan Laurel and Oliver Hardy—"two fools of God," Marcel Marceau called them—portrayed a physical contrariety that placed them beyond normal restraints. Laurel's forays into magic, such as igniting his thumb into a cigarette lighter, would lift him momentarily to leadership. Otherwise Hardy's "You after me Stanley" syndrome, abetted by his necktie twiddle and soul-deep resignation, pronounced his simpleminded conviction of his own superiority. Their derby hats inevitably switched themselves, expanding the confusion.

Again technology transformed the popular medium for humor and comedy. Motion picture theaters added animated cartoon comedies featuring "Silly Symphonies," "Betty Boop," "Looney Toons," and Walt Disney's incomparable Mickey Mouse to their short subjects. Although many vocally deficient comedians of the silent screen found themselves sidelined, Hal Roach sailed ahead into all-talking pictures with Laurel and Hardy, Charley Chase, and the rough-and-ready boys and girls of Our Gang. Likewise, for other producers, W. C. Fields, Charlie Chaplin, the madcap Marx Brothers, slow-burning Edgar Kennedy, Wallace Beery and Marie Dressler of *Tugboat Annie* fame, big-mouthed Joe E. Brown, sizzling Mae West, and Will Rogers made the transition.

COMIC DUO

Stan Laurel (r) and Oliver Hardy performed a style of recognizable, physical comedy and contrariety that kept audiences laughing through many successful movies.
CORBIS-BETTMANN

Audiences also loved screwball comedies—fast-action, romantic farces featuring witty dialogue by the leading characters, who were often drawn from disparate social classes but overcame their initial antipathy to fall magically in love. Frank Capra's *It Happened One Night* (1934), starring Claudette Colbert and Clark Gable, launched the genre, which went on to include *The Thin Man*, *Theodora Goes Wild*, *My Man Godfrey*, *Mr. Deeds Goes to Town*, *The Awful Truth*, *Nothing Sacred*, *Holiday*, *You Can't Take It with You*, *His Girl Friday*, and *The Philadelphia Story*. Screwball comedies suited the escapist spirit of the Great Depression, then subsided with World War II. For home amusement, the radio networks introduced weekly comedy shows starring, among others, Eddie Cantor, Jack Benny, Fred Allen, Fanny Brice, Joe Penner, and Bob Hope. Commercial sponsors fed faithful listeners a weekday diet of fifteen-minute episodic comedies led by *Lum and Abner*, *Vic and Sade*, and others. Enormously popular, *Amos 'n' Andy* commanded prime time nightly for the misadventures of their blackface Fresh Air Taxicab Company, though most blacks were not amused.

Will Rogers, beloved cowboy humorist, mastered all of the media. He dispensed folksy commentaries on the news, especially on politics, while performing rope tricks in the *Ziegfeld Follies*, and later as a columnist for the *New York Times* syndicate and as a Sunday evening radio network broadcaster. In films, he starred as a fatherly problem solver humorously upholding the homely virtues in screwball comedies. Rogers was never sharper than when discoursing on the Great Depression. He patriotically offered his services for the campaign to restore confidence. "But you will have to give me some idea where 'Confidence' is," he insisted, "and just what you want it restored to." Of President Hoover's Valley Forge appeal for patience, Rogers commented: "He found somebody that was worse off than we are, but he had to go back 150 years in history to do it." And in 1931 he summed up the situation: "We got more wheat, more corn, more food, more cotton, more money in the banks, more everything in the world than any nation that ever lived ever had, yet we are starving to death. We are the first nation in the history of the world to go to the poor house in an automobile."

After Rogers's untimely death in 1935, there were only Mencken's twilight essays, Westbrook Pegler's rare mellow moments, and Langston Hughes's sensitive cameos about blacks through his Dooley-like characterization of Jesse B. Sim-

ple. In time, hopes for a successor to Rogers as the nation's court jester concentrated on television's promise. It was claimed that televised programs could be distributed for repeated enjoyment as easily as humorous lectures and radio broadcasts. Not until television and the VCR became commonplace did this dream come true.

Until then, *The New Yorker* magazine, abetted by big-city newspaper columnists, films, and stage comedies, dominated America's output of humor. Harold W. Ross, an unlikely genius, launched *The New Yorker* in 1925, "not for the old lady in Dubuque" but for sophisticated Manhattanites. A number of the Algonquin Hotel's Round Table wits lent their names as advisory editors and contributed scattered bits, but Ross soon learned that Dorothy Parker was the only member of that group on whom he could rely. He therefore recruited self-conscious urbanites who ranged along a lunatic fringe from Don Marquis, the creator of Archy, a lower-case, free-verse cockroach, and Mehitabel, an amoral cat, to Franklin P. Adams of "The Conning Tower," to the flippant, surreal Ring Lardner. Their Freudian denominator was a reliance on abnormal traits of personality, which Adams spoofed but Marquis and Lardner wholeheartedly accepted. The cartoonists were deliciously neurotic. Helen Hokinson's silly club women became fixtures, as did Peter Arno's voluptuously dizzy blondes and lecherous magnates. Otto Soglow and Mary Petty joined them, as later did Whitney Darrow, Sam Cobean, Charles Addams, George Price, and Saul Steinberg, and still later George Booth, Edward Koren, and William Hamilton. Alexander Woollcott condescended to write "Shouts and Murmurs" as a regular feature. Ogden Nash penned nonsense verses. Frank Sullivan invented the wonderful Mr. Arbuthnot, the cliché expert. And Clarence Day's stories accumulated into *Life with Father*. E. B. White, James Thurber, Robert Benchley, and S. J. Perelman completed *The New Yorker's* madhouse. Thurber was the funniest madman of them all.

Humor from All Sides

After 1945, radio and film comedies continued to make their enormous audiences laugh, and so did musical comedies. But the longtime training schools for comedians, burlesque and vaudeville, with the exception of the Jewish Borscht Belt (Catskill Mountains) resorts or offbeat night clubs in Chicago and San Francisco, gave way to television. Radio and film stars had led the way into the electronic medium: Fred Allen, Jack Benny, Bob Hope, Amos and Andy, Abbott and

See also
Film

Costello, and Groucho Marx. Yet these luminaries soon found themselves overshadowed by television's comic geniuses, including Sid Caesar and Imogene Coca, Ernie Kovacs, and Steve Allen. Television proved too visual for radio-style, imaginative comedy, and too demanding for stage or film actors and producers to keep up. Only Bob Elliott and Ray Goulding, who on radio for forty years hilariously parodied radio as though it were made for them, hung on to the microphone to get drivers through dense traffic, students ready for exams, and all listeners through long weekends. Who can forget Wally Ballou reporting a parade while facing the wrong way?

In contrast, Sid Caesar's timid sponsors sidelined him for lampooning sacred cows, while the hypercautious unities of the 1950s red scare squelched the tradition of jesting at the nation's leaders. Even Adlai E. Stevenson, Jr., the Democrats' presidential nominee, drew criticism for joking at public concerns. Thurber blamed the frightful hazards of living in the nuclear age—next door to catastrophe "on the brink of Was," he put it. Mort Sahl worried that he could not be certain if the unidentified aircraft approaching would "drop a hydrogen bomb or spell out Pepsi Cola in skywriting." "It is not expected that we will soon recover," Thurber went on about the witch-hunting of Senator Joseph McCarthy, "and contribute to a new and brave world literature of comedy." Satire, he judged, in words that raised protests from dairymen and threats to investigate his loyalty from congressmen, had declined until it reminded him of a drink of milk: "It won't hurt anybody, but who likes it?"

Humor recovered mightily in the civil rights struggles of the 1960s and the ensuing women's movement. Segregation's absurdities came to the surface through underlying veins of despair and moral indignation. Stand-up comedians assailed the hollow rhetoric, the principles betrayed, the meanness, the ignobility, and crass pieties. Laughter once again began to succeed where other weapons were failing. Ethnic comics counterattacked where their forebears—blacks, immigrant Jews, Italians, and Poles—once served as laughter's scapegoats. Dick Gregory ridiculed segregation. Mort Sahl hoped there were no groups he had not offended, trampling them all "anyway onward." Together they pressed their case against the waspish, prudish, stand-pat Americanism in their way. Knowingly or unknowingly, they were following the examples of Twain, Bierce, Mencken, Lardner, Thurber, Benchley, and Hughes. Lenny Bruce, the new era's heroic antihero, defined his fellow citizens in Jewish idiom as "schmucks." A schmuck, as Bruce saw him, believed in Uncle Tom and Santa Claus and labored in vain to sing "The Star-Spangled Banner," and brought up his hapless children to do likewise. Imported from Britain, on stage and screen, the anti-establishment mockeries of Peter Cook's *Beyond the Fringe*, Benny Hill's music hall vulgarity, and *Monty Python's Flying Circus* intensified the bedlam.

Sexuality in contemporary humor (other than the timeworn format for dirty jokes) was a product of the new feminism of the women's movement. Sex is to women's role in society as skin color and racist repression are to black personality. Feminist humor by women comedians supplied a fresh fount of laughter wherever there was an audience willing to listen. In films and nightclubs, Joan Rivers, Phyllis Diller, and Lily Tomlin became nationally known. Fran Lebowitz brilliantly and somewhat acidly analyzed womanhood in a male-dominated society. Erma Bombeck, the leading specialist on the funny side of motherhood, wrote a syndicated column, "At Wit's End," ultimately carried by several hundred newspapers. However, most feminist comics dressed like cartoon characters and quarreled aggressively on stage with the shortcomings of their own bodies and the men or women in their lives. To monologues on menstruation, intercourse, gynecologists, masturbation, toxic waste, and bureaucracy, they brought a grotesque carnival aura. Their humor was frightening, and it was meant to be.

To explain such public manifestations, anthropologist Mahadev L. Apte reminds us that for the greater part humor is culture-based, and that the humor of a people can supply vital insights toward understanding them. In the United States, as Apte observes, humor is a big business, pervading every walk of the nation's life. Film comedies playing at theaters are advertised as "howlingly funny," "sidesplitting," "wacky," "whimsical," and "hilarious." Television programming is dominated by comedy shows, especially situation comedies, such as *Seinfeld*, a show about "nothing." *M*A*S*H*, about a behind-the-lines hospital in the Korean War, and *Hogan's Heroes*, about Allied soldiers in a German prison camp, cleverly made light of grisly situations. The sitcoms give way around midnight to talk shows starring wisecracking hosts such as Johnny Carson, David Letterman, and Jay Leno. There are also the once-a-week skits of *Saturday Night Live*, which most memorably starred Chevy Chase and Gilda Radner.

Newspapers feature dozens of syndicated comic strips, which, over almost a century since

The only honest art form is laughter, comedy. You can't fake it . . . try to fake three laughs in an hour—ha ha ha ha ha—they'll take you away man. You can't.

LENNY BRUCE

H

HUMOR AND COMEDY

Humor from All Sides

the introduction of Richard Felton Outcault's "The Yellow Kid," have come to include both "funnies" and adventure dramas. Seldom bound by time's constraints, comic strips rely on theatrical conventions including dialogue, dramatic gesture, scene or backdrop, a rectangular frame, and props or stage devices. The comics, moreover, anticipated numerous film techniques, such as montage, angle views, panning, cutting, framing, and close-ups. Favorites like "Blondie," "Peanuts," "Beetle Bailey," and "Garfield" appear in about two thousand papers. Foreign-language adaptions travel around the world. The intellectually ironic "Peanuts" by Charles M. Schulz succeeded Walt Kelly's "Pogo" to captivate the 1960s. Gary Trudeau's "Doonesbury," with its counterculture philosophy, topped the 1970s. The leading comics of the 1980s and 1990s, except for the fantasy of Bill Watterson's "Calvin and Hobbes," Berke Breathed's "Bloom County," and Gary Larson's "Far Side," chronicle real-life problems and affronts, as Cathy Guisewite does for her perplexed, mistreated, and humiliated "Cathy." Images of comic strip characters as well as humorous maxims adorn shirts, household and recreational wares, toys, bumper stickers, watch dials, stationery, and many other products.

Newspapers also feature sharp editorial cartoons and witty columnists. Masters of the one-note message, the cartoonists upholding the satir-

ical tradition of London's James Gillray (1757–1815) and Thomas Nast (1840–1902) of *Harper's Weekly* are Herblock, Paul Conrad, Jeff McNelly, Mike Peters, Tony Auth, Doug Marlette, Pat Oliphant, Don Wright, and Jules Feiffer. Art Buchwald, whose talent for punch lines resembled Mr. Dooley's, and Russell Baker lead the humorous columnists. Technology has widened distribution. Copy machines and facsimile networks speed jokes, clippings, and graphic humor to all accessible points on a round-the-clock basis.

Humor and comedy bubble up everywhere. Stand-up comedy, long the backbone of vaudeville, burlesque, and the variety theater—for example, Earl Carroll's *Vanities*—has spawned an industry of its own in hundreds of comedy clubs. The comedy clubs present a lengthy bill of comedians and would-be comedians who briefly, through exclusive control of the microphone, carry on the hallowed ritual of public joking, trying to make their audiences laugh. The social context and the procedures followed are as important as the text of the joke itself. Nevertheless, the laughter shared by a comedian and the crowd celebrates their agreement on whatever it is that merits mutual ridicule or sustains their common beliefs and behavior. The appeal of comedy clubs is tribal in composition and ritualistic in nature. A more familiar style of gently funny storytelling flourishes as well. Beginning in 1974, Garrison Keillor, a champion of small pleasures, broadcast his radio show, *A Prairie Home Companion*, before live audiences. His anecdotes brought to life a comically fascinating array of the folks of Lake Wobegon, Minnesota, an authentic fictional village, "where all the women are strong, the men are good looking, and all the children are above average." Keillor's collected essays, many of them having appeared previously in *The New Yorker*, remind readers of Mark Twain, George Ade, Ring Lardner, and Peter DeVries. More than most humorists, Keillor's comic light, though truthful, is soft and compassionate.

The best American comic fiction since the 1950s has come from Vladimir Nabokov, Joseph Heller, Philip Roth, Kurt Vonnegut, Jr., and Peter DeVries. Nabokov, a Russian-born novelist, poet, playwright, and critic, displayed his astonishing verbal facility, seasoned by exquisite dashes of irony, in his highly acclaimed *Lolita* (1955) and *Pale Fire* (1962). Joseph Heller's weird and poignantly funny novel *Catch-22* relates the imaginative efforts of Captain John Yossarian to survive World War II, to outwit somehow the merciless logic of a regulation that stays one step ahead

SMALL PLEASURES

Broadcaster and writer Garrison Keillor, whose radio show, A Prairie Home Companion, *features gently funny storytelling before live audiences.*

UPI / CORBIS-BETTMANN

of his schemes. Philip Roth wrote *Goodbye, Columbus, and Five Short Stories, Portnoy's Complaint, Our Gang* (an outcry of rage against Nixon's Watergate), and the autobiographical Zuckerman trilogy. Roth, a Jew, has been castigated by Jewish spokesmen as anti-Semitic, while various critics have denounced him as a pornographer and traitor. Both Portnoy and Zuckerman, Roth's alter ego, star in comedies of entrapment—burlesques of psychic processes wherein irreverence and explicitness shock the pieties that protect inner sensitivities against unwanted turmoil.

Kurt Vonnegut, Jr., who as a prisoner of war experienced the firebombing of Dresden, has frequently combined science fiction with hilarious comedy in the satirical fashion of Aldous Huxley and Evelyn Waugh, sometimes as pure slapstick and sometimes for belly laughs, yet invariably to attack social ills. In *Player Piano, Cat's Cradle, Slaughterhouse Five,* and *Breakfast of Champions,* Vonnegut moved from wildly absurd frameworks to sanitary outcomes. His visions were so horrific that indignation could provide a basis for rejection, except for the laughter that for the moment allows one to manage. Peter DeVries, in terms of high-level productivity and sustained achievement, was for a time the greatest American comic novelist. Renowned as a punster with tongue firmly in cheek while acidly satirizing his fellow citizens, his triumphs numbered *The Tunnel of Love, The Blood of the Lamb, Let Me Count the Ways,* and *Mrs. Wallace.* The comic novels of Kingsley Amis, David Lodge, and Tom Sharpe, imported from Britain, enriched readers' amusement.

More visible in filmmaking, television, and stage productions, though outstanding as comic writers themselves, were Woody Allen, Mel Brooks, and Neil Simon. Woody Allen's collected humor, his stories, his screenplays, and his own acting performances demonstrated his comic talent. He is best known for his movies *Annie Hall, Sleeper, Radio Days, Love and Death, Hannah and Her Sisters, Broadway Danny Rose,* and *The Purple Rose of Cairo.* In a short story, "The Kugelmass Episode," Allen transports his hero into the pages of Flaubert's *Madame Bovary,* where he conducts a lively affair with Emma, to the confusion of readers and scholars everywhere. Mel Brooks (Melvin Kaminsky), comedian, writer, actor, and film director and producer, created such acclaimed films as *The Producers* and *Blazing Saddles.* A onetime social director at Catskills resorts who was inspired by the stand-up comedians he encountered, Brooks later wrote television skits for Sid Caesar's *Your Show of Shows.* The public learned to expect riotous comedy from him. Brooks and straight man Carl Reiner created that living witness to the history of mankind, the Two-Thousand-Year-Old-Man, a hilariously opinionated medical miracle. Neil Simon, a onetime comedy writer in succession for Goodman Ace, Phil Silvers, Garry Moore, Jackie Gleason, Red Buttons, and Sid Caesar, went on to write a string of popular comedies and musicals. His successes are legendary: *Barefoot in the Park, The Odd Couple, Sweet Charity, Promises, Promises, Last of the Red Hot Lovers, The Sunshine Boys, Plaza Suite, California Suite, Brighton Beach Memoirs, Biloxi Blues,* and *Broadway Bound.* Simon once defined his goal as "to make a whole audience fall onto the floor, writhing and laughing so hard that some of them pass out." He has often come close.

With the Watergate scandal over President Nixon's countenancing burglary, his obstruction of justice, and finally his resignation in disgrace, all restraints ended for political humorists. Jokes and tall tales abounded, affording comedians an undreamed-of opportunity. Even "Nixon's the One," the slogan used to reelect him, came to indict the faltering champion. Stand-up commentator Mark Russell hoped that the Watergate affair would never end. "If it does, I'll have to go back to writing my own material. Now I just tear it off the news service wires." And John Kenneth Galbraith decided that "We've passed from the age of the common man to the age of the common crook." With more than a touch of anger, presidents Ford, Carter, Reagan, and Bush, along with other public figures, were mocked unsparingly.

"Throughout our history," former President Gerald R. Ford, the only chief executive to put together a book on humor, wrote in *Humor and the Presidency* (1987), "humor and the laughter it brings has [*sic*] carried us over many different obstacles and through many difficult times." Ford, who often made himself the butt of his own jokes, recalled such an occasion: "I gave a speech in Omaha. After the speech, I went to a reception elsewhere in town. A sweet, little old lady came up to me, put her gloved hand in mine, and said, 'I hear you spoke here tonight.' 'Oh, it was nothing,' I replied modestly. 'Yes' the little, old lady nodded, 'that's what I heard.'"

All humor studies should begin and end with the problem set forth ages ago in Ecclesiastes 2: "I said of laughter, 'It is mad,' and of mirth, 'Of what use is it?'"

—ARTHUR POWER DUDDEN

To appreciate nonsense requires a serious interest in life.

GELETT BURGESS

See also
Television

J

JOURNALISM

The first printing establishment in the North American colonies was set up in Cambridge, Massachusetts, in 1639. Printing there and elsewhere in the seventeenth century was devoted largely to religious works along with job printing for business, legal, and governmental purposes. Journalism, if by that we mean the regular, periodic publication of information about contemporary affairs, did not exist until the very end of the seventeenth century.

Not until the beginning of the nineteenth century did daily newspaper publication make journalism a part of everyday life even for urban Americans. Not until the middle of that century did newspapers hire their own reporters and begin to establish journalism as an occupation or profession. Not until the twentieth century did the First Amendment protection of press freedom become a living tradition in the courts. Yet from its earliest days, American journalism has been an important institution for expressing democratic ideals and for embodying communal sentiment. Even in the late nineteenth century, when metropolitan daily newspapers became industrial giants, with leadership linked to money and power, another journalism flourished in the literary underbrush closely connected to ethnic communities and social movements. As a political institution and as a cultural form and forum, journalism has long been a key part of American life.

The Colonial Press

The first American newspaper was printed at Boston in 1690 by a bookseller and publisher, Benjamin Harris. *Publick Occurrences Both Forreign and Domestick* indicated in its first issue its modest ambition to publish once a month (oftener only if "any Glut of Occurrences happen") a faithful account of those "considerable things as have arrived unto our Notice." For the next seventy-five years, this would be the scope of news reporting in the American press—no affirmative gathering of news, only the making available of newspaper columns for what might fall into the printer's lap.

Because Harris failed to obtain permission from the governor and council of the Massachusetts Bay Colony, his paper died after one issue. The next paper, and the first successful one in the colonies, was the *Boston News-Letter*, begun by John Campbell in 1704. Campbell took news to be "recent history" and tried to keep his news printed in chronological order. However, because he had so little space to reprint news he received from London newspapers and occasional correspondents, he fell further and further behind. He caught up by printing more often but, even at that, he had little sense of urgency. In May 1719 he claimed that he was printing news from Britain up to the first week of March and other European news only as recent as October 1718.

The notion that news should be as timely as possible was not well established in the early eighteenth century. Even the notion that the newspaper should be devoted to accounts of recent events was not self-evident. Samuel Keimer, a Philadelphia printer, began publishing *The Universal Instructor in All Arts and Sciences: and Pennsylvania Gazette* in 1728. He saw the newspaper as an instrument of instruction and enlightenment and so chose to print serially Ephraim Chambers's *Cyclopaedia*, A through Z. In 1729, however, while Keimer was still working through the A's, Benjamin Franklin bought the paper and discontinued the encyclopedia project. He introduced a mode of journalism more literary and satirical on the one hand and more engaged in civic affairs on the other, something he learned not only from English literary models but also from his own experience in Boston as an apprentice at his brother James Franklin's *New England Courant*. James Franklin had begun his paper in 1721, despite the counsel of friends who said they thought the paper not likely to succeed, "one newspaper being in their judgment enough for America."

All this suggests that the first colonial newspapers were a motley group in their aims and directions, and that the history of journalism in the United States must take up the development of the cultural category of "news" as well as the story of its institutional embodiment in weekly and

As a medium for information, broadsides carried official announcements, advertised the printer's inventory, recorded colonial laws, and commented on local events.

PAGE 339

♦ **Sedition**

Incitement of resistance to or insurrection against lawful authority

POPULAR FORM

Pamphleteering, a popular form of political journalism, reached its heyday with the publication of Thomas Paine's Common Sense *in 1776.*

CORBIS-BETTMANN

daily newspaper publication (and later radio and television broadcasting).

The format of colonial papers as four-page weeklies was relatively standard, and their contents, after a time, tended toward a common model. Newspapers presented readers an assortment of local advertising, occasional small paragraphs of local hearsay, and larger chunks of European political and economic intelligence. Much of this news, concerning, for instance, disputes between central European monarchs, would seem very far removed from the interests of the colonists. What this model meant is obscure. Stephen Botein suggests that the newspapers may have been providing a kind of global mapping of Protestantism versus Rome, but he confesses that this is a highly speculative observation. More likely, he concludes, the printers operated by an economic rather than a political or ideological strategy: wanting to avoid offending their readers, they sought out remote foreign news that mattered little to people and would arouse no controversy, a practice known in journalism as Afghanistanism.

If this is so, much of what early colonial papers printed fit neither the criterion of timeliness nor that of interest or utility to readers. Local political

COMMON SENSE;

ADDRESSED TO THE

INHABITANTS

OF

AMERICA,

On the following interesting

SUBJECTS.

I. Of the Origin and Design of Government in general, with concise Remarks on the English Constitution.

II. Of Monarchy and Hereditary Succession.

III. Thoughts on the present State of American Affairs.

IV. Of the present Ability of America, with some miscellaneous Reflections.

A NEW EDITION, with several Additions in the Body of the Work. To which is added an APPENDIX; together with an Address to the People called QUAKERS.

N. B. The New Addition here given increases the Work upwards of one Third.

Man knows no Master save creating HEAVEN,
Or those whom Choice and common Good ordain.
THOMSON.

news and political news of other colonies rarely appeared. Though the printer of the *New-York Weekly Journal*, John Peter Zenger, was tried for sedition for his paper's attacks on the royal governor and found not guilty by a jury in 1735, he was thereafter a tame journalist. Even though it set no legal precedent, the Zenger verdict gave support to popular sentiment in favor of liberty generally and liberty of the press specifically; but printers seemed impressed more by Zenger's harassment than by his exoneration. Zenger had been prudent to attack the governor rather than the legislature: throughout the colonial period, the legislatures, in defense of parliamentary privilege, were more likely than the governors or courts to suppress free expression, written or spoken. Even after licensing requirements for newspaper publication were withdrawn, colonial assemblies took publication of their votes or proceedings to be a breach of privilege. There is not much to suggest that many newspaper proprietors in the first part of the eighteenth century were strongly motivated to print political news and views; when they were, there were major constraints to doing so.

As economic enterprises, colonial papers were generally family affairs. Benjamin Franklin apprenticed with his older brother. Elizabeth Timothy, who became the country's first woman publisher by taking on the management of Charleston's *South Carolina Gazette* in 1738, was the first of at least fourteen women who ran colonial print shops, usually after the deaths of their husbands. The newspapers were not self-sustaining. Most printers of newspapers also conducted job-printing businesses that accounted for the larger share of their income.

While newspapers grew in number and importance, there was little magazine journalism in the colonial period. The first magazines in the colonies were *American Magazine*, issued by the Philadelphia printer Andrew Bradford, and *General Magazine*, issued by Benjamin Franklin, both begun in 1741. (The ubiquitous Franklin also began the colonies' first foreign-language paper, the *Philadelphische Zeitung*, which lasted only two issues.) But none of the eighteen magazines published before the end of the revolutionary war survived to see the founding of the new nation; only a few lasted as long as a year. Their content tended toward coverage of contemporary political or religious affairs, and they did not leave much of a mark on their times.

The political orientation of the press began to change in the 1760s. With the colonies on the brink of breaking with England after the Stamp Act controversy of 1765, colonial printers were compelled to choose sides. Reluctantly they did so, and modest print shops became hives of political activity. In the late seventeenth century and early eighteenth century, colonial politics had been a relatively private matter. The press generally avoided politics, and when an occasional pamphlet did take up a political issue, it was addressed to the colonial assembly, not to the general population. But pamphleteers became more active in political campaigning by the 1740s in the major colonial cities of New York, Philadelphia, and Boston. Although many conservative leaders objected to pamphleteering, they found themselves obliged to resort to it. The pamphleteers reached their height of influence with Thomas Paine's publication of *Common Sense* in 1776. At that time, the newspapers of largest circulation sold no more than two thousand copies of a weekly issue. The typical pamphlet was printed once or twice in editions of just a few thousand copies. *Common Sense* was reprinted twenty-five times in 1776 alone, and altogether it sold an estimated 150,000 copies. Paine, like other professional pamphleteers of his generation, addressed the general populace, but he extended and perfected the practice. He dropped esoteric classical references for familiar biblical ones, seeking a language the general population understood. His style, his own lowly social origins, and his political republicanism combined to make him the leading political pamphleteer of his day.

Newspapers took on a more and more active political role in the years leading up to the Revolution. John Dickinson's *Letters from a Farmer in Pennsylvania*, beginning in 1767, were among the articles attacking British legislation that appeared in newspapers and helped prepare for the break with England. Patriot journals began to print news, and rumor, of the offenses of British soldiers. The colonists advanced their economic boycotts of British goods by having the names of violators published in the newspapers.

Newspapers remained small in size (the four-page format was unvarying), few in number, and precarious in rates of survival. Of thirty-five papers in existence when the Revolution began in 1775, only twenty survived to the war's end in 1783, although thirty-five new ones were established in the same period. Print technology did nothing to further newspaper development; the technology of the wooden flatbed press was essentially unchanged since Gutenberg.

The Political Press in the Early Republic

The press in the new nation grew rapidly. *The Federalist Papers*, a series of political essays written by Alexander Hamilton, John Jay, and James Madison to persuade New York to ratify the Constitution, were published serially in several New York newspapers and widely reprinted in other parts of the country (without, as it happens, winning the hearts and minds of the New York legislature). The first daily newspaper, the *Pennsylvania Evening Post and Daily Advertiser* of Philadelphia, appeared in 1783. Although it did not survive long, by 1800 Philadelphia had six dailies, New York had five, Baltimore had three, and Charleston had two; altogether, there were 241 newspapers in the United States, 24 of them dailies. Noah Webster's *American Minerva* boasted in 1793, "In no other country on earth, not even in Great-Britain, are Newspapers so generally circulated among the body of the people, as in America." This was certainly true. *Porcupine's Gazette*, a Philadelphia daily, had a circulation of two thousand in 1799, as large a circulation as any newspaper in England. Foreign visitors—Crèvecoeur, Tocqueville, Trollope, and others—were repeatedly astonished in the next half-century by the widespread habit of reading, especially newspaper reading, in America. Edward Dicey, an English journalist visiting during the Civil War, claimed that the American might well be defined as "a newspaper reading animal." The two hundred papers of 1800 had become by 1830 more than seven hundred, including sixty-five dailies. By 1850 there were over two thousand newspapers, more than two hundred of them dailies. Not all European visitors found the spread of newspaper reading that these numbers reflected a good thing. One visitor, Thomas Hamilton, observed unhappily that newspapers "penetrate to every crevice of the Union." Since even the lower classes could afford papers, he observed, the newspapers catered to them and so grew "indifferent to refinement either of language or reasoning."

In the first decades of the new nation, newspapers were identified with the editorial voice. Intensely partisan, they were frequently founded as weapons for party or faction, like Alexander Hamilton's *New York Evening Post*, begun in 1801 to recoup Federalist power after the loss of the presidency to Thomas Jefferson. Reporting of news was incidental, unorganized, and obviously subordinated to editorial partisanship. John

JOURNALISM

The Political Press in the Early Republic

Were it left to me to decide whether we should have a government without newspapers, or newspapers without a government, I should not hesitate a moment to prefer the latter.

THOMAS JEFFERSON

The publication of newspapers was primarily an economic move for most colonial printers, with little or no sense that the circulation of information might fill any particular civic need.

PAGE 362

◆ **Vituperation**
Sustained and bitter railing and condemnation: vituperative utterance

Fenno, in the *Gazette of the United States*, spoke semi-officially for the Federalists and traded barbs with Philip Freneau at the *National Gazette*, the voice of the Jeffersonians, during the brief flourishing of that paper in the early 1790s. Journalistic vituperation was chilled by the Alien and Sedition Acts of 1798. The Sedition Act made it a criminal offense to print "any false, scandalous and malicious writing . . . against the Government of the United States." While there were relatively few prosecutions under the act, it was a partisan bone of contention and expired after Jefferson came to power in 1801.

Politicians objected to the other party's papers but still held a favorable attitude toward the press in general. The Postal Acts of 1792 and 1794 are instructive: all parties assumed that newspapers should have preferential mailing rates. While it cost six cents to mail a one-page letter up to sixty miles, a newspaper could be mailed up to a hundred miles for a penny. Publishers could use the mails free to exchange copies of their papers with other newspaper establishments. Subsidy of the press, like federal support for the building of roads and canals, seemed taken for granted, as both leading parties favored nationalization. Washington and Jefferson agreed that postal rates should be low. Jefferson, in his first annual message, even advocated abolishing newspaper postage "to facilitate the progress of information." Newspaper circulation, especially beyond an immediate locale where private news distributors could be employed, relied on the postal service. Thus from the republic's earliest days, the press was the beneficiary of federal laws intended to ease or to enlarge the newspaper business.

Thomas Jefferson, well known for his statement that he would prefer newspapers without a government to a government without newspapers (1787), was a prime target for the vituperation of the Federalist press. It is not surprising that, despite his vigorous defense of the role of the press in a democratic society, he also said in 1807, "The man who never looks into a newspaper is better informed than he who reads them, inasmuch as he who knows nothing is nearer the truth than he whose mind is filled with falsehoods and errors." Editors attacked one another as viciously as they attacked politicians, and sometimes carried rivalries into fistfights and duels in the street.

But by the 1820s newspaper competition began to express itself in less primitive fashion. Several New York papers began to send small boats out to incoming ships to get the news from London faster than their rivals. This was indicative of

a turn toward reportage in newspaper work. The War of 1812 had precipitated a gradual shift to domestic news, although foreign intelligence still predominated. Some technological changes also began to affect the work of printers. Iron presses began to replace wooden ones at the turn of the century. The Fourdrinier papermaking machine, patented in 1799, significantly improved the production of paper. Hand-powered presses began to give way to steam-powered ones, and flatbed presses to the much faster cylinder presses. The first steam-powered cylinder press was used to print the *London Times* in 1814, turning out sheets at about four times the rate of the best flatbed hand press. However, it took much greater skill to use, the quality of the printing produced was low, and its productivity outstripped the needs of most printers.

By 1833 the American newspaper was well established as a vehicle for political parties and a bulletin board for the business community. Advertising was abundant: papers devoted half or more of their space to advertisements, including most or all of what we think of as the front page. (There is evidence that editors of the day judged the outside pages as a kind of cover, less important than the inside pages, notably the editorial column that ordinarily appeared on page 2.) Still, efforts to attract advertising were haphazard. Circulation grew, but even in 1833 the largest paper had a circulation of only 4,500—more than double the typical city paper's circulation. The newspaper was barely distinguishable in many cases as an independent venture. While the newspaper was by 1830 differentiated from the post office and distinguishable from the print shop—at least in some cases—it was not easily separable from the party, faction, church, or organization that it served. Journalism was certainly not yet an identifiable occupational path. Few papers hired reporters; what was called a correspondent was just that, a friend or acquaintance of the editor, an unpaid amateur who would write an occasional letter to the paper. Newspaper proprietors were publishers, editors, and editorial staff at once. Often they regarded their posts as stepping-stones to political office or at least the political largess of government advertising when their party came to power.

A New Breed of Papers

Journalism participated in the major social changes in American life of the Jacksonian era. As property qualifications for voting were repealed in the states, as lawyers came under attack as a kind

BROADSIDES AND MAGAZINES

Information Sources in the Early Republic

From 1780 to 1830, newspapers were not alone as a source of current information and views. Broadsides—any item printed on one side of a single sheet—were important, representing about 20 or 25 percent of all imprints before 1800. New England records suggest that before 1830 the broadsides most often concerned politics, music, secular ballads, reports of strange or supernatural happenings, and literature. The broadsides typically circulated locally and were published in runs of five hundred to fifteen hundred copies (and rarely went through more than two runs). Treated very much like newspapers, judging from the fact that they were only occasionally saved in family libraries, they seem to have been superseded by the increasingly successful newspapers early in the nineteenth century.

Magazines flourished in the early national period, too, despite the fact that the Post Office Act of 1792 provided very low rates for newspapers but not for magazines. In 1794 there were five magazines, twelve in 1800, and nearly a hundred by 1825, both weeklies and monthlies. The most important general magazine was Philadelphia's *Port Folio*, devoted to both politics and literary criticism, known for the lively wit of its editor, and gathering contributions from leading (Federalist) figures of the day. This period saw the beginning of the first specialized periodicals in the country, including the New York *Medical Repository*, a medical journal that lasted from 1797 to 1824. Magazines flourished more readily after Congress lowered postage rates for periodicals in 1825. The largest circulation magazine before the Civil War was *Godey's Lady's Book*, founded in 1830 by Louis Godey (as *Lady's Book*) and edited from 1837 to 1877 by Sarah Josepha Hale. Its circulation reached 150,000 by 1860 and may have come close to 500,000 at its height in 1869. While often remembered as an influential advocate of domesticity and a supporter of a "separate sphere" for women, *Godey's* was at the same time a strong voice for the support of women's education both in formal institutions and at home.

of "aristocracy" and the examination and certification requirements for admission to the bar in many states were repealed, as reform movements for the abolition of slavery, for women's rights, and for rights of the working man flourished, journalism, too, experienced a democratic revolution. Beginning with the *New York Sun*, edited by the printer Benjamin Day and first published in 1833, a new breed of newspaper sought commercial success and a mass readership.

Between 1833 and 1835, in New York, Boston, Baltimore, and Philadelphia, venturesome entrepreneurs began "penny papers" selling for a penny an issue rather than the six cents at which papers were commonly priced. Moreover, the new penny papers were hawked on the streets by newsboys instead of being available exclusively by subscription, although it is likely that subscription remained the predominant form of distribution. The penny papers were typically more aggressive than their six-penny rivals in seeking out local news, assigning reporters to the courts, and even covering "society." They aggressively solicited advertising at the same time that they engaged in vigorous competition to get the "latest" news as fast as they could. For instance, James Gordon Bennett's *New York Herald* hired horse express riders who beat those of the most aggressive mer-

cantile papers, the *Courier and Enquirer* and the *Journal of Commerce*, in getting Andrew Jackson's annual message to New York from Washington in 1835. Bennett also jumped into the newsboat competition that had developed in the 1820s and hired several newsboats to go out to sea to meet incoming European ships, get their newspapers, and bring them back to port ahead of the ships. By 1840 he organized an express service from Washington that was faster than the mails, and by 1844 another express service that met British mail boats in Boston and brought their news to New York ahead of regular mail delivery.

The great circulation gains of the penny papers were made possible not only by low price and aggressive distribution and marketing but also by aggressive use of recently developed technologies. The *Sun* began the penny-press revolution with a traditional hand-run flatbed press. Within a few months, however, Day bought a cylinder press that made a thousand, rather than two hundred, impressions an hour. In 1835, when it was already selling twenty thousand copies a day, the *Sun* became the first newspaper in the country to purchase a steam-driven press. The penny papers were also the most aggressive papers in making use of the telegraph. The *Baltimore Sun* made early use of telegraphic communication, and its

J

JOURNALISM

A New Breed of Papers

It is a newspaper's duty to print the news and raise hell.

THE CHICAGO TIMES

239

example helped encourage both press and public acceptance of the invention. During the war with Mexico in 1846, penny papers in New York and Philadelphia made the first and fullest use of the telegraph. The two-cylinder Hoe press, which became standard for much of the nineteenth century, was first used by a penny paper, the *Philadelphia Public Ledger*, in 1847. Technology was available, but it took the peculiar disposition of the competitive, news-hungry, circulation-building penny papers to make quick use of it.

The *New York Herald* was the penny paper with the most sustained commercial success. The editor, James Gordon Bennett, was a portent of changing times: unlike Day and most newspaper proprietors of the times, he had never worked as a printer. Educated for the Roman Catholic priesthood in his native Scotland, he emigrated first to Canada, where he worked as a schoolteacher, and then to the United States, where he was a clerk in a publishing and printing establishment in Boston; then a proofreader in New York, then an editorial assistant for the *Charleston* (South Carolina) *Courier*, where he translated foreign news from Spanish and French; then a freelance writer for the *New York Enquirer* and other papers; and then as an associate editor for the *Enquirer*, writing on politics and society from Washington, Albany, and Saratoga Springs. After several years at the *Enquirer*, he bounced from one party newspaper to another before establishing the *Herald* in 1835, sympathetic to the Democrats but without personal ties or allegiances to any party. The penny papers typically proclaimed their independence from party—prematurely, one might add—but they proved to be the beginning of a modern press for which economic goals supersede political loyalties.

While the leading edge of journalistic innovation, commercial vigor, and competitive newsgathering was the penny press, the most widely circulated sorts of papers before the Civil War were country weeklies or other nondailies with local or regional circulations. These papers, with generally small circulations, nonetheless could have sizable readerships because a copy of one paper could have ten to twenty readers. The country press, whatever its political predilections, was invariably a booster of economic development in its own towns and regions.

Horace Greeley, like many other journalists of his day, began work on one such small weekly, the *Northern Spectator* of East Poultney, Vermont. He moved from his printing apprenticeship there to Erie, Pennsylvania, and to New York in 1831,

looking for the main chance. If it is misleading to take New York journalism as representative of all journalism, it is nevertheless hard to exaggerate its influence as the radiating center of American communications. In New York, Greeley found himself in a world of journalistic ferment and change. Setting up his own printing business within a few years, by 1834 he began issuing the *New Yorker*, a magazine of literature, reviews, and politics with a circulation that reached nine thousand. In 1840 he ran the Whig campaign paper,

THE ETHNIC PRESS

The pluralism of American society in the 1830s, spurred by renewed immigration, particularly from Germany and, in the 1840s, from Ireland, was reflected in the newspapers. In 1834 the Jacksonian New York *Staats-Zeitung* was founded, a paper that survived well into the twentieth century. Other German papers, mostly Democratic, emerged as immigration grew in the 1850s (by 1860 the 1.3 million German-born represented more than a quarter of all foreign-born citizens). In 1828, the *Cherokee Phoenix* was the first Native American newspaper, published in English and Cherokee. The African American press began with *Freedom's Journal*, published by John Brown Russwurm and Samuel E. Cornish in New York from 1827 to 1829, and later the *Colored American*, a New York paper that ran from 1837 to 1841. Frederick Douglass began the *North Star* in Rochester in 1847, changing the paper's name in 1850 to *Frederick Douglass' Paper*. The African American-run papers before the Civil War were a part of the abolitionist movement, whose most famous journalistic leader (apart from Douglass) was William Lloyd Garrison and his Boston-based *Liberator*, first published in 1831. The abolitionist press not only reached its own adherents with news and argument but also sought to propagandize others. In 1835 the American Anti-Slavery Society launched a major propaganda effort, shipping out more than a million pieces of abolitionist literature, directed especially to the South. Postmasters refused delivery and mobs burned sacks of mail in hysterical reaction. The onslaught of print convinced proslavery forces North and South that the abolitionist cause, still a very small and poorly funded set of political groups, was a vast and threatening mass movement.

See also

Popular Literature

the *Log Cabin*, for William Henry Harrison (with a circulation of up to eighty thousand for its brief run) and in 1841 began his own penny paper, the *New York Tribune*. Quickly reaching a circulation in excess of ten thousand, this Whig paper was strongly antislavery and clearly showed itself a journal of ideas, reporting on women's rights and socialist experiments. Not an advocate of women's rights, Greeley nonetheless hired Margaret Fuller in 1844 as the first woman to be a regular staff employee on a major American newspaper. He hired Karl Marx as a European correspondent. The paper never rivaled the *Herald* in circulation, but the *Weekly Tribune* Greeley established to circulate outside the city was lucrative and for decades was widely known in rural communities throughout New York, New England, and the West. (The *Tribune* in 1924 bought the *Herald* and the merged *Herald Tribune* remained a leading paper until its demise in 1966, survived only by the Paris-based *International Herald Tribune*.)

News Gathering and News Agencies

Newsgathering was growing as the central function of the newspaper, but political reporting in the early nineteenth century was at first anything but taken for granted. The Senate did not make its proceedings public until 1795. Only two state constitutions made legislative sessions public. Congress did not officially keep its own records until the 1820s, nor did any newspaper outside Washington regularly cover Congress until this period. The *National Intelligencer*, founded in 1800, provided the best Washington news, especially after gaining the right to take notes on the floor of Congress in 1802. Reporting suffered from inadequate stenographic skills—only the *Intelligencer*'s Samuel Harrison Smith apparently had the requisite skills, and when he (frequently) left the city for reasons of health, government news essentially stopped. What did get reported, as Washington reporting became more competitive in the 1820s, did not necessarily resemble what was actually said in the Congress. Reporters and politicians developed a cooperative relationship that took for granted that the journalists would rewrite and improve upon what was originally said. There was not much regard for what one journalist called "unfeeling accuracy."

As late as 1846, only Baltimore and Washington papers assigned special correspondents to cover Congress. But as politics heated up in the 1850s, more than fifty papers hired Washington correspondents. State capitals also began to receive greater coverage. Still, most Washington correspondents wrote for half a dozen or more papers and earned further salary as clerks for congressional committees or as speechwriters for politicians. The occupational world of journalism was narrowly differentiated from politics.

A new journalistic enterprise, the wire service, began in the mid-nineteenth century when New York newspapers joined in 1848 to establish the New York Associated Press (later the Associated Press) as a way to make better, and cheaper, use of new telegraphic services. The AP was a cooperative and gathered news for member newspapers with its own correspondents and part-time stringers. For hundreds of American newspapers with limited resources for their own newsgathering, most national and international news still comes from wire services in the 1990s. During the Civil War, Associated Press clients in the Midwest began to resent the control of the organization by the New York press. A subsidiary organization, the Western Associated Press, sought independent access to European news sources but quickly returned to the fold. The rival United Press began in 1882 but died in 1897. Publisher E. W. Scripps sought to create a rival wire service in 1907 with a new United Press, and William Randolph Hearst organized his own International News Service in 1909. The new services merged under Scripps-Howard ownership in 1958 as United Press International. By the 1980s UPI was struggling to survive and filed Chapter 11 bankruptcy before reviving, precariously, under new ownership.

Despite the proud independence of the penny papers, the intimate link between journalism and political parties, established in the early 1800s as electoral competition between Federalists and Jeffersonians, dominated through mid century. It was taken for granted that journals were political, that they were financially and literarily supported by one side or another, and that their task was more one of rousing the party faithful than of reporting the news. Not only parties had newspapers; so did factions of parties and so, sometimes, did individual politicians. But the connection between paper and party began to weaken late in the nineteenth century. The penny papers' economic success was the first sign of change, followed by new institutions self-consciously dedicated more to making profits than to promoting policies or politicians. In 1861, Abraham Lincoln began using the AP rather than an official or semiofficial newspaper as administration spokesman. This followed the establishment in 1860 of the Government Printing Office, whose existence cut

J

JOURNALISM

News Gathering and News Agencies

The circulation of information increased astonishingly: New York news, which in 1790 took three weeks to reach Ohio, arrived in 1830 in six days or less.

PAGE 505

away at the official status of the press and the patronage link between government and newspaper.

After the Civil War, development away from a political press accelerated. Newspapers rapidly expanded as profitable businesses, the biggest of them larger than all but a few other kinds of industrial operations. By 1870, every major daily in New York had at least one hundred employees. Competition over news grew more intense, the war having stimulated consumer expectations and demand for news. In the 1870s and 1880s, liberal reformers, first in the Republican party and then in the Democratic party, began to criticize the notion of party loyalty. These reformers promoted new forms of electoral campaigning, urging an "educational" rather than a participatory or "spectacular" campaign, moving from parades to pamphlets, and arguing that the exercise of the franchise be the making of a rational choice among candidates, parties, and policies rather than a demonstration of emotional and traditional allegiance to a party label. Newspapers at the same time became more willing to take an independent stance. Horace Greeley and Whitelaw Reid's *New York Tribune*, and the *New York Evening Post*, the *Springfield Republican*, the *Chicago Tribune*, the *Cincinnati Commercial*, E. L. Godkin's *Nation* (founded 1865), and George William Curtis's *Harper's Weekly* (founded 1857) dared to dissent from party loyalty and helped direct the reform effort. By 1890, a quarter of daily newspapers in northern states, where the reform movement was most advanced, claimed independence of party. The largest papers were especially likely to be independent—nineteen of twenty-eight papers with circulations over fifty thousand.

Big-Business Newspapers and Syndicates: The Mass Audience

Newspapers in the last two decades of the nineteenth century saw a great increase in the size of their circulations. The development of wood pulp, rather than rags, as a paper source after the Civil War helped push the price of paper down from eight cents to two cents a pound in the course of a generation and encouraged newspapers to be more generous with white space and to use larger type sizes. The development of curved stereotype plates made it possible for papers to abandon the column rules that held type in place on the press and kept headlines, pictures, and ads from extending beyond one column. Typesetting was no more efficient in 1880 than it had been for Gutenberg, but Ottmar Mergenthaler's invention of mechanical typesetting in Baltimore in 1884 increased the

speed of typesetting four or five times. Photoengraving of line drawings replaced and greatly improved upon wood engraving in the late nineteenth century. *The New York Daily Graphic*, begun in 1873, was the first heavily illustrated daily in the world and a pioneer in halftone photoengraving. Illustrations grew larger and more numerous in many papers, advertisements began to use display type, headlines became bigger and more informative; by 1900 technological improvements brought halftone photographs into the daily newspaper. Papers initiated campaigns to promote circulation and aggressively courted new audiences (particularly women). The newspapers were major enterprises in a rapidly industrializing nation. Advertising became a more central source of income. Between 1880 and 1900 the ratio of editorial matter to advertising shifted from about 70:30 to 50:50 or lower. Advertising income represented a growing proportion of total revenue. Paradoxically, this increased rather than diminished the importance of circulation for revenue because circulation became the measure of a newspaper's competitive standing. Circulation became less a private source of income and more a public (and audited) indicator of the newspaper's serviceability to potential advertisers. The department store became a major source of advertising income; as cities became integrated economically and knit together by new forms of public transportation, the newspapers became more indispensable than ever. As the mass medium with the widest coverage, they remained the likeliest source for advertising of nationally branded products as an integrated, national market in consumer goods expanded.

A key figure in the developing big-business model of the newspaper was Joseph Pulitzer, an Austrio-Hungarian Jewish immigrant who came to the United States in 1864. Though admitted to the bar in Missouri, his limited facility in English was a factor in keeping him from practice, so instead he became a reporter for a German-language newspaper in Saint Louis, the *Westliche Post*. He bought the *St. Louis Post* in 1878 and merged it with the *Dispatch*, serving as publisher, editor, and business manager. He made the crusade a constant feature of the paper. In 1883, he bought the failing *New York World*, which then had a circulation of fifteen thousand. By 1887 its circulation was more than 250,000. By 1895 the *World* was the biggest paper in the country with twelve hundred employees in circulation, production, editorial, advertising, and accounting departments. While some dailies retained the old

♦ **Stereotype (plate)**

A plate cast from a printing surface

four-page format, the *World* was normally twelve to sixteen pages on weekdays and three or four times larger on Sundays.

Pulitzer's success can be attributed to both business and editorial innovations. On the business side, he lowered the *World*'s price to a penny (and forced other papers to lower their prices to stay competitive), sold advertising space on the basis of actual circulation, and in other ways rationalized the relations between newspapers and advertisers. He helped open the way to advertisers who wanted display ads using illustrations or breaking column rules. Before Pulitzer, newspapers regarded such advertising skeptically. James Gordon Bennett had laid down the law that advertisers should gain from what they said, not how their ads were printed or displayed. Charles Dana, editor of the *New York Sun*, the paper with the largest circulation in the city until Pulitzer came to the *World*, thought that advertising was a waste of space; as late as 1878 he hoped to do without it altogether. The new comradeship with advertising was marked by the establishment in 1887 of the American Newspaper Publishers Association, the main concern of which in its early years was to regulate commissions paid to advertising agencies and to standardize the ways in which advertising rates were calculated.

Editorially, Pulitzer brought his crusading Saint Louis journalism and an intensified atten-tion to local news. What he added to these far from unique features was a variety of forms of self-advertisement for the newspaper. He used illustration, both sketches and political cartoons, lavishly. He played up any stories that the *World* had gained exclusively. Relatively simple words, content, and sentence structure, as well as the illustrations, helped reach the thousands of immigrants in New York. By 1880 New York had 479,000 foreign-born citizens and by 1890, 640,000, about 40 percent of the city's total population. If technological and economic changes made the new mass journalism possible, and the prospect of profit made it desirable, the changing habits and inhabitants of the cities made it necessary in the eyes of ambitious publishers.

Pulitzer intended his paper to be "a daily school-house and a daily forum," as he put it; but it was also a daily carnival, incorporating a growing acceptance of the newspaper as a form of entertainment. In 1842 only one New Yorker in twenty-six bought a Sunday paper; in 1850, after heavy Irish immigration, it was one in nine. During the Civil War, more papers developed special Sunday editions with war news, which helped accustom people to the idea of a Sunday paper; but even by the early 1880s only a hundred newspapers nationwide published on Sunday. Pulitzer helped change that, introducing a Sunday paper brimming with entertainment features—for

**SAVVY
BUSINESSMAN**

*William Randolph Hearst, a
businessman who saw the press
as a political agency as well as a
lucrative moneymaker through
the use of sensationalism.*
CORBIS-BETTMANN

women, for young readers, for sports fans. By the end of the decade, half of New Yorkers bought a Sunday paper, nationally there were more than twice as many Sunday papers as there had been at the beginning of the 1880s, and there were more Sunday than daily newspaper readers. The Sunday papers, lavishly illustrated, were the first to adopt color comic strips and the first to develop special women's pages. The new mass-circulation papers promoted a consumerist orientation in the press and, no doubt, encouraged a consumer culture in the public as well.

If Pulitzer began this new-style mass journalism, it was his rival, William Randolph Hearst, who took it to its most notorious extreme. Like Pulitzer, Hearst was a businessman but not only a businessman. He, too, saw the press as a political agency and not just a lucrative business. Taking over his father's *San Francisco Examiner* in 1887, he bought the *New York Journal* in 1895, the *Chicago Evening American* in 1900, and the *Chicago Examiner* in 1902. At the *New York Journal*, he hired away many of Pulitzer's *Sunday World* writers and artists and the cartoonist Richard Outcault, whose "Hogan's Alley" featured a character known as the "Yellow Kid"—who, according to journalistic lore, gave "yellow journalism" its name. Within a year of buying the *Journal*, Hearst had added pages of comics, sensational news coverage, a self-promoting crusading spirit, and several hundred thousand readers. Battling the *World* for the biggest share of New York's mass readership, Hearst, followed somewhat more gingerly by Pulitzer, pushed for a war with Spain and sent correspondents to Cuba to cover the developing crisis. The war coverage was a high-water mark of sensationalism. Still, the popular view that yellow journalism "caused" American intervention owes a lot to Hearst's delight in taking credit for the war. Many other leading papers, including those with the greatest influence in elite circles, opposed American intervention.

Indeed, at the same time that Pulitzer and Hearst were competing for the largest number of newspaper readers, Adolph Ochs, a Knoxville printer's devil who rose to become publisher of the *Chattanooga Times*, bought the *New York Times*, a paper of fine pedigree but having a circulation of 9,000 at a time when the *World* sold 600,000, the *Journal* 430,000, and the *Herald* 140,000. In his famous declaration "to give the news impartially, without fear or favor, regardless of any party, sect or interest involved," Ochs set the paper on the path to its becoming the national paper of record and, perhaps, the finest newspaper

in the world. Journalism in the 1890s and after was more differentiated than global references to an "era of yellow journalism" suggest. Newspapers were increasingly orienting themselves to market-defined rather than party-defined population segments. Advertising agents by the 1890s distinguished the "mass" from the "quality" audience. Newspaper competition for advertisers in both mass and quality papers led to the unsavory practice of "puffing," in which newspapers would present as news favorable information about the products of their advertisers. The independence that economic self-sufficiency brought to newspapers divorced from party threatened to become—and often enough did become—its own form of servitude.

Magazines addressed to a mass audience also flourished. *The National Police Gazette*, begun in 1845 in New York as a reporter of crime news, moved on to a special focus on sex crimes after the Civil War, diversified to include attention to theater and sports, and reached a circulation of 150,000 by the 1880s. The largest circulation success of the late nineteenth century, however, was *Youth's Companion*, founded in 1827—a magazine for young people that kept up its subscription list with aggressive campaigns offering premiums for both new and continuing subscribers.

Not all "mass" journalism, clearly, measured down to the sensationalist standards of Hearst. Hearst was not alone, of course, in a self-conscious insistence that newspapers could and should be entertaining as well as informative. Melville Stone, editor of the *Chicago Daily News*, insisted on three functions for the newspaper: to inform, to interpret, and to entertain. Pulitzer certainly offered a different model. So did E. W. Scripps, who developed newspapers aimed at working people in Cleveland, Cincinnati, Detroit, and Saint Louis in the 1880s. Scripps, who pioneered chain ownership of newspapers, held to an editorial policy sympathetic to labor and reform politics. His papers supported Theodore Roosevelt for president in 1912 and Robert La Follette in 1924.

Outside the Mainstream

The world of journalism of the late nineteenth century and early twentieth century, like that of the antebellum period, was remarkably pluralistic. Besides the general commercial papers, newspapers flourished as agents of various special communities—religious groups, ethnic groups, political organizations, and social movements all fielded many newspapers. There were, for instance, hundreds of Populist weeklies. The *Topeka Advocate*, with a circulation of 80,000 in 1894, was the largest newspaper in Kansas. *Appeal to Reason*, a radical paper, reached a national circulation of 100,000 by 1900, and 450,000 a decade later.

There were, it is estimated, about 800 non-English-language newspapers in 1884 and close to 1,200 by 1910, reaching a high point of 1,300 by 1917. Thereafter, the number declined, especially the German papers—with 627 papers in 1910 but only 258 in 1920. The German papers' decline was not exclusively war-related; the number of German newspapers and magazines reached a high in the 1890s and began to drop off as immigration slowed and second-generation Germans switched to English. But the war put German Americans and their newspapers in a difficult position, and some readers avoided harassment by stopping their subscriptions. Moreover, the Trading with the Enemy Act (1917) required foreign-language newspapers to provide the Post Office with translations of any news concerning the war. Exemptions could be granted to papers that proved their loyalty, but this itself was a form of soft censorship. Some papers reduced their war coverage. Some went out of business. Most of the foreign-language papers were weekly or semi-weekly. Non-English-language dailies reached a peak of 140 in 1914—a third of these were German-language papers; twelve each were French, Italian, and Polish; ten, Yiddish and Japanese; eight, Spanish and Bohemian. In ethnically concentrated areas, the influence of foreign-language newspapers could be significant. In the 1890s there were five or more German daily newspapers in Milwaukee, Chicago, Saint Louis, Cincinnati, Philadelphia, and New York. As late as 1940 there were four Yiddish dailies in New York (the last of them, *Forverts*, became a weekly in 1983).

Still, the opportunity for the mass-circulation English-language dailies was that many of the foreign-language papers were edited by European intellectuals whose ideas of journalism were modeled on European journals of politics and opinion. The foreign-language press proved most successful when it imitated the sensational or popular style of the English-language papers. Abraham Cahan, editor of the *Jewish Daily Forward*, pruned his Yiddish paper of difficult expressions, introduced English words his readers would be certain to have picked up, and tried to make the paper bright, simple, and interesting, as he had learned to do while working with Lincoln Steffens on the New York *Commercial Advertiser*.

The black press reached a high point of size and influence in the first half of the twentieth century. Black dailies attained large circulations, none larger than the *Pittsburgh Courier*'s (founded 1910) 300,000 in the 1940s. *The Chicago Defender*, a weekly founded in 1905, had a paid circulation of 230,000 by 1915, two-thirds of it outside Chicago. It was the first African American publication with a broad, national circulation. The editor, Robert S. Abbott, wrote regularly about

THE RURAL PRESS
News for the Community

A small-town and rural press persisted alongside the urban papers. While in some cases aspiring to the news-centered model of the commercial urban press, most of these papers adopted a different view of what a newspaper should be, much more a kind of community cheerleader than a community tribune. Hometown boosterism has characterized this press, both past and present: local sports teams are cheered in the sports section, local real estate news is almost exclusively public relations rather than reporting. Local businessmen, in the boosterist press, are taken to be and are encouraged to be in business for the good of the community. The concept of news in the rural and small-town press, in the community press serving specific urban neighborhoods, and in much of the suburban press emphasizes building community as much as relaying information. The community press has typically emphasized good news over bad, has celebrated routine events (births, marriages, graduations, business openings, holiday pageants and celebrations), and has catered to community values of propriety and privacy. Politics in the small-town press, while typically an establishment politics, has especially in the twentieth century been a minor element in the papers. William Allen White, a celebrated editor of the *Emporia* (Kansas) *Gazette* from 1895 to the 1930s, wrote in his first editorial that his paper would be Republican and support Republican nominees "first, last, and all the time." But, he added, "politics is so little. Not one man in ten cares for politics more than two weeks in a year. In this paper, while the politics will be straight, it will not be obtrusive. It will be confined to the editorial page—where the gentle reader may venture at his peril" (William Allen White, *Autobiography*, p. 261).

See also
Television

♦ **Muckraking**
Searching out and publicly exposing real or apparent misconduct of a prominent individual or journalist

the opportunities for blacks of living in northern cities; the *Defender* is credited with great influence in stimulating black migration north, not only in its editorial content but also in its efforts to help southern blacks form clubs to get group railroad rates. The black press during World War II urged on readers a "Double V" campaign—victory over the Axis abroad and victory over racism domestically. After the war, however, the black press was in decline as the mainstream press began to cover racial issues, the white-run media began to hire black journalists, advertising support weakened, and a growing black middle class left the inner city and its newspapers.

After mid century there was a revival of the ethnic press, and by 1975 there were an estimated 960 non-English-language newspapers. Non-English-speaking broadcasting, with Spanish-language broadcasting the most notable, also appeared. Univision, the largest Spanish-language television network, had over four hundred affiliates in the 1990s, and thirty-one television stations broadcast entirely in Spanish. The black press survived, with nearly two hundred newspapers in 1986, only three of them dailies, and these had much smaller circulations than the black press had had a generation or two earlier. Magazines, however, were a different story, with *Ebony*, founded in 1945, gaining a circulation of more than a million and a half by the late 1980s. A religious press continued, and there were radio and cable television stations owned by evangelical and other Christian groups.

Reporters and Muckrakers

Reporting was increasingly the center of newspaper life from the late nineteenth century on. Reporting became a self-conscious activity and reporters a self-conscious community in the larger cities with their own formal organizations and informal gathering spots and watering holes. While an occasional black journalist wrote for the mainstream press, newsrooms were effectively white. In Washington, reporters organized the socially exclusive Correspondents' Club in 1867 and another exclusive club, the Gridiron Club, in 1885; Washington journalists writing for African American papers set up their own organization, the Associated Correspondents of Race Newspapers, in 1890. In 1879, Washington correspondents formed the Standing Committee of Correspondents to control access to the congressional press galleries. The committee's rules sought to prevent journalists from acting as lobbyists. The rules also limited access to Congress to reporters

whose salary came primarily from sending telegraphic dispatches to daily newspapers. This effectively eliminated black and women reporters, all of whom wrote for weeklies or sent dispatches by mail. Frederick Douglass, for instance, sat in the press galleries in the 1870s but no black reporter did so after him until 1947.

Reporters' status and income rose steadily in the 1880s and 1890s as reporting became more often a regular, full-time job and the custom of relying on freelance reporters paid "on space" declined. Still, most newspapers paid their Washington correspondents only during months that Congress was in session, and it was common practice for reporters to supplement their newspaper income by working as clerks or secretaries in the Congress. Popular acclaim for dashing reporters—Elizabeth Cochrane Seaman (Nelly Bly) going around the world in eighty days, Henry Morton Stanley finding David Livingstone in Africa, the handsome Richard Harding Davis reporting on war and on football—added to the élan of the field.

The work of reporting became much more than stenography or observations and sketches. Reporters began to conduct interviews as a routine part of their work and to publish verbatim quotations or even whole question-and-answer stories. With only isolated exceptions, this was unheard-of before the Civil War and remained relatively uncommon into the 1880s. At that time, members of Congress were likely to refuse comment when questioned on the record by reporters; they had no special orientation toward the press for use in their own public relations. But increasingly the reporters pressed to do interviews, both with political leaders and with sports or entertainment celebrities. There was in this a spirit of enterprise and a sense of combative achievement in getting an interview or in tricking an interviewee into a surprising or embarrassing revelation. Foreign observers looked askance at the American interviewing habit, seeing it as crude, perhaps crudely egalitarian, and overemphasizing reporting at the expense of analysis and commentary. Interviewing spread more slowly among European journalists but was boosted by the prevalence of American reporters in Europe during World War I.

If interviewing was one sign of the new assertiveness of the reporter, muckraking was another. The rise of mass-circulation monthly magazines with national readerships and an appreciative middle-class audience in the 1890s helped the rise to prominence of muckraking. "Muckrakers" (so named by Theodore Roosevelt in a sizzling attack on their negativism) investigated illegal and unsavory practices of capital, labor, and state and local government. The most celebrated of them worked for *McClure's Magazine*—Lincoln Steffens, Ida Tarbell, David Graham Phillips, Ray Stannard Baker—as well as for *Cosmopolitan* and *Munsey's*. These three journals cut the price of an issue to ten cents in 1893 and circulation zoomed upward, *Cosmopolitan's* growing from sixteen thousand to four hundred thousand in five years. The muckraking, crusading strain in journalism has been traced back to the eighteenth century, but certainly investigation, rather than polemical pronouncements or argumentation, was a rarity until the late nineteenth century. The *New York Times* pursued Tammany Hall with reportorial as well as editorial diligence in 1871, but the reportorial exposé became an art form, a circulation booster, and a routine political tool only after the 1880s.

Public relations developed apace in the early twentieth century, stimulated in part by muckraking attacks on business, in part by the general growth and rationalization of corporate enterprise. World War I was a major contributor to the advance of public relations after the war, as wartime propaganda provided a model for business and government public relations. Journalists complained in the 1920s that they were suddenly outnumbered by public relations agents, an entirely new occupation catering to the power of journalism. Where nineteenth-century reporters could naively believe that reporting consisted in gathering facts, now they could see that facts rained down on them not from "reality" but from interested parties. Two philosophers of democracy and public discourse, Walter Lippmann and John Dewey, pointed to the rise of public relations as the most significant change in the political life of the twentieth century.

Journalists' growing sense of the partiality, subjectivity, and manipulability of information, advanced by their awareness of public relations and their own experience in World War I as propagandists, led to important changes in journalism in the 1920s and 1930s. The most visible and important change was the institution of the political column. Until the 1920s, the only regular newspaper columnists were humorists and the occasional dispensers of gossip and advice. In the 1920s, David Lawrence, Mark Sullivan, Heywood Broun, Walter Lippmann, and others wrote regular political columns for leading newspapers; soon their columns were syndicated across the country.

When Robert and Helen Lynd studied Muncie, Indiana, in 1925, the local papers carried two columnists; ten years later the morning paper had five columnists and the afternoon paper four.

There was a more subtle change in the same era in the writing of basic political news. While nineteenth-century coverage of political events could be, and usually was, highly partisan and highly colored, it could also be, and often was, highly routinized. For instance, newspapers that reported on important state papers or speeches generally would print the document verbatim. This is the way papers of various stripes reported the president's annual message (the State of the Union address) through much of the nineteenth century. Commentary was reserved for the editorial page. Only beginning in the early twentieth century did journalists highlight and summarize the main points of the presidential message in a news story. By the 1920s, correspondents not only summarized what they took to be the most important points of the presidential speech but also noted what the speech omitted or pointed to what it said "between the lines." This practice seemed to recognize and accept a need to interpret the complex world of national politics just as it accommodated the growing autonomy of reporters. In 1913 managers of the two main wire services, the Associated Press and the United Press, debated journalistic philosophy at a university symposium, the AP arguing for unbiased reporting and the UP claiming that there is no such thing. Oddly enough, both views influenced journalism. By 1934, the UP view had convinced the American Society of Newspaper Editors to devote more space to "interpretive news." At the same time, an explicit faith in "objective" news reporting had become part of the toolkit of the journalist.

The recognition of interpretive news was sometimes taken to be a concession to readers overwhelmed by the world's complexity. It was also a type of marketing. Newspapers competed to make news more accessible to readers. *Time* magazine, begun in 1923, helped stimulate this competition. Newspapers began to concern themselves more with layout. They introduced news summaries. The *Baltimore Sun* was among the first to package news by putting related items together on a page rather than randomly scattering them through the paper.

This does not mean that journalism was fully institutionalized or professionalized, but certainly there were moves in those directions. Journalists in the nineteenth century had no formal training. Journalists in the twentieth century might be

♦ **Polemical**

Of, relating to, or being a polemic (an aggressive controversialist)

CENSORSHIP OF THE PRESS
Government Interference and Judicial Support

One outcome of World War I was a new recognition of how manipulable information is. A related outcome was the recognition of—and in the courts, resistance to—the most overt and malicious forms of manipulation: censorship practiced by government. While the First Amendment, adopted as part of the Constitution in 1791, proclaimed that "Congress shall make no law . . . abridging the freedom . . . of the press," this had not prevented the Alien and Sedition Acts of 1798 from doing just that. Generally speaking, freedom of the press in the nineteenth century went unchallenged by government and little of a judicial tradition protecting press freedom developed until World War I and after. At that point, freedom of the press became a public issue. In 1917 Congress passed the Espionage Statute, which was used to suspend the mailing privileges of dozens of radical journals and resulted in the imprisonment of radical journalists. In 1918 the Sedition Act made prosecution of journalists easier still. Repression seriously damaged the American socialist movement, with many of its leaders in prison and many of its journals silenced. German-language publications, regardless of their politics, and black papers were intimidated. In the *Chicago Defender*, Robert Abbott vigorously attacked the segregation of and discrimination against black soldiers; he escaped imprisonment under the Espionage Statute only by consenting to promote the purchase of war bonds in the *Defender*.

While a "red scare" continued even after the war, several Supreme Court decisions established for the first time a tradition of defense of the First Amendment. The court, in *Abrams* v. *United States*, found against five New York radicals imprisoned for distributing pamphlets attacking American intervention in Russia, but Oliver Wendell Holmes, joined in dissent by Louis Brandeis, argued that "free trade in ideas" should be the guiding rule and that "the best test of truth is the power of the thought to get itself accepted in the competition of the market." In 1925, in the vital case of *Gitlow* v. *United States*, the court again upheld a conviction of radical pamphleteers, but acknowledged for the first time that First Amendment guarantees applied to the states under the Fourteenth Amendment. In 1931, *Near* v. *Minnesota* struck down a Minnesota "gag law" that permitted the suppression of malicious and scandalous publications. The *Near* decision held that prior restraint of publication was unlawful and suppression a greater danger than journalistic irresponsibility.

trained in one of the journalism schools, or journalism or communications departments that emerged after World War I (a bequest in 1903 from Joseph Pulitzer established the most famous journalism school, at Columbia University, which opened in 1912) and developed on a large scale, particularly in the state universities of the South and Midwest, after World War II. But young people may enter journalism with bachelor's degrees in English or history as well as in journalism, and relatively few journalists have advanced degrees.

Corporate Journalism

Larger and larger corporate entities reaped the benefits of the press freedom that was often tested by lone individuals or small publications. Chain or group newspaper ownership, begun around the turn of the century by Scripps, Hearst, and others, grew enormously in the twentieth century. At its peak, in 1935, Hearst's empire included twenty-six daily newspapers with a seventh of the total circulation in the country and a quarter of Sunday circulation, as well as a fleet of magazines, radio stations, a features syndicate, and motion-picture companies. By 1980 two-thirds of 1,700 daily newspapers commanding three-fourths of total daily circulation were group-owned. City by city, newspaper competition fell off sharply, so that the number of cities with competing daily papers dropped from 181 in 1940 to 29 in 1986. The largest chain, Gannett, in 1982 founded a new national newspaper, *USA Today*, that by 1987 had a circulation of more than 1.5 million. It was a model of technological, if not journalistic, brilliance, printed at thirty-two different sites, produced by satellite transmission of copy, and making more use of color and attractive graphics than any other newspaper. Media critics might observe that some of the dailies that died were not paragons of journalistic virtue, and certainly many independent papers taken over by chains upgraded their product as a result. But the growing concentration of ownership in the media caused concern in a society in which the competitive marketplace is seen as a testing ground of truth.

See also

Radio

Newspapers not only competed with new technologies but also used new technologies. Mechanical typesetting was replaced by cold type or photocomposition, and by the 1980s most newspapers used computerized systems in which reporters and editors could write and edit stories on word processors.

A major new influence on postwar journalism was television. Television borrowed personnel and style from radio for its journalism. Television news consisted of "talking heads" from its beginnings in the 1950s until the mid 1960s. On a separate track, documentaries and news-style programming, most notably the news shows of Edward R. Murrow, contributed to the shaping of American journalism. Maturation of television news presentation came with the expansion of the standard evening news program from fifteen to thirty minutes in 1963, a year in which the Roper poll found that, for the first time, more Americans claimed to rely on television than on newspapers as their primary source of news. (Whether their claims were true is open to some doubt. When asked what news source they actually examined

the day before, more people said newspapers than television.) Three television networks produced national news programs beginning in the early 1960s. *60 Minutes*, an hour-long program of investigative journalism, began in 1968 and in the 1970s became the highest-rated program in the country. ABC began a late-night news program in 1980 called *Nightline*, and it became a regular part of the broadcast news diet.

The rise to prominence of television news was aided significantly by President Kennedy, who began holding live televised press conferences, and by the Vietnam War, during which television news coverage took on a symbolic centrality for both Washington elites and the public at large. Political campaigners measured their success as much by seconds on the evenings news as by polls; presidents, notably Lyndon B. Johnson and Richard M. Nixon, became obsessed with the television screen. Specific political events also promoted television as a news source. Walter Cronkite's personal interest in space exploration helped propel national news coverage of satellite (and later space shuttle) launchings. Cable News

GLOBAL VILLAGE

A family gathers in front of the television to watch the funeral of John F. Kennedy on November 25, 1963. Television unified the world during coverage of this event and its aftermath.
UPI / CORBIS-BETTMANN

*News is the first
rough draft of
history*

PHILLIP L. GRAHAM
(1915–1963) PUBLISHER OF
THE WASHINGTON POST

See also
Print and Publishing

Network's growing international linkups during the late 1980s led to its eminence in covering the Persian Gulf War in 1991.

But, historically, nothing so established the symbolic centrality of television or its substantive national importance as the television coverage of the Kennedy assassination. Few people learned of the assassination first from television, but by the evening of 22 November 1963, millions of people were glued to their sets. They saw, on live television, Jack Ruby shoot Lee Harvey Oswald on 24 November, and they sat before their sets watching the Kennedy funeral procession, listening to the solemn beat of the drum, watching the riderless horse lead the way. The experience many people had in World War II of listening to Edward R. Murrow's live radio reports from London under aerial bombardment was amplified with the television coverage of the Kennedy funeral. It was the first media event to serve as a distinctively new form of modern, collective, participatory ritual, even if the participation is a kind of action at a distance.

Television news received some credit for stimulating the civil rights movement in the 1950s and 1960s. The civil rights movement occasioned a great benefit to journalism by giving rise to the case that transformed libel law by bringing all state libel laws under the restraints of the First Amendment. This was *New York Times* v. *Sullivan* (1964), in which an Alabama sheriff sued the *New York Times* for printing a political advertisement that he believed libeled him. The Supreme Court held that a public official, to show libel, must demonstrate that the news institution published something it knew to be false with "malice" or "reckless disregard" of its truth or falsity.

In 1970, the television networks had no competition—only 10 percent of American homes had cable systems. By 1989 the proportion had risen to 53 percent and the networks' share of total television viewership was in decline. Moreover, the cable industry began C-SPAN (in 1979) as a public-service gesture; while C-SPAN has a tiny audience, its presence in Congress has affected the conduct of public affairs, especially with live reports from the House (1979) and Senate (1986) floors. Cable News Network, begun in 1980 by the millionaire Atlanta businessman Ted Turner, provided news around the clock and quickly established a reputation for responsible reporting. In the Persian Gulf War in 1991, people who had never watched CNN tuned in to watch Peter Arnett, the last reporter for an American network in Baghdad. The Public Broadcasting System began

the *MacNeil-Lehrer News Hour* in 1975. Radio, though never again the key source of news it was in pretelevision days, continued to be important. In 1970 National Public Radio was formed, launching *All Things Considered* in 1971. With only seven million listeners, NPR is small but much more than a headline service. NPR journalists are seen on television as well as heard on radio and command respect in their profession.

Journalism as a Political Issue

Increasingly in the 1970s and after, television became a political issue, not just a political observer. In reporting the war in Vietnam, the media ran increasingly into direct confrontation with the government. Presidents Kennedy and Johnson both objected to the *New York Times's* reporting of the war in Vietnam, and during the Johnson administration the press drew attention to what was called the "credibility gap," administration lies and half-truths about the war that reduced the believability of any government claims. During the presidency of Richard Nixon, all-out hostility emerged between the press and the president. Nixon came into office with a chip on his shoulder, regarding the media—particularly the eastern establishment media of the three networks, the *New York Times, Time, Newsweek*, and the *Washington Post*—as his enemy. He attacked television in particular for its "instant analyses" of presidential addresses in 1969. Proponents of the Vietnam war effort criticized what they saw as television bias against the war and, indeed, blamed the failed American war effort on demoralization caused by the onslaught of television scenes of bloodshed in Vietnam. While the research seems irrefutable that general public support for the war remained high until after the Tet offensive in 1968, that most television stories on the war remained more neutral or upbeat than critical until after Congress was much divided about the war, and that most stories on the war broadcast on television downplayed rather than emphasized the bloodshed, the network news programs became prominent public scapegoats.

Two moments in the early 1970s brought the press a new prominence, reporters a heightened status, and the *Washington Post* a new national position as the leading rival to the *New York Times* for national journalistic authority. In 1971, the *New York Times* published the first installment of the "Pentagon Papers," a classified Defense Department history of the Vietnam War that a one time Pentagon insider and Rand Corporation whiz kid, Daniel Ellsberg, copied and released to the newspaper. Nixon sought by court injunction to prevent further publication, but when an injunction succeeded against the *Times*, publication was taken up by the *Washington Post* and then the *Boston Globe*, the *Chicago Sun-Times*, and other papers. The Supreme Court found in favor of the newspapers, and the affair cemented the enmity between the press and Nixon.

It also made the aggressive new editor of the *Washington Post*, Benjamin C. Bradlee, feel intensely competitive with the *New York Times*. He had his opportunity to steal a march on his rival in 1972 with "Watergate," the collective term for the illegal campaign practices, burglaries, unauthorized wiretaps, use of intelligence agencies for domestic surveillance, use of the Internal Revenue Service to harass political opponents, and ultimately the lying, bribery, hush money, and perjury authorized by the president or his close associates to obstruct justice. Watergate was a milestone for the press. Though Watergate activities were uncovered by Congress, the courts, and federal administrative agencies, they were originally disclosed by the *Washington Post* and kept in the public eye by the *Post* and other news agencies. Investigative reporting was already rapidly expanding in leading newspapers, and even at the wire services, because of the growing distrust of government and other leading institutions in the Vietnam War years. Watergate served as the sym-

bolic capstone to the newly aggressive journalism. Bob Woodward and Carl Bernstein, two *Post* reporters, became celebrities, and their account of Watergate became a popular film with Hollywood stars Robert Redford and Dustin Hoffman playing the brash, gutsy young reporters. In the 1980s, print reporters became celebrities of sorts, regularly appearing as panelists on television news talk shows, particularly in Washington. Enrollments in journalism and communications schools at colleges around the country had begun to grow rapidly in the mid 1960s, and the notoriety of Watergate may have kept enrollments high a little longer or at least given journalism courses a more focused identity (although enrollments in the advertising and public relations sections of these academic programs grew faster than enrollments in news and editorial).

At the same time, the ensuing convulsions in government and the resignation of Nixon were so traumatic that leaders of journalism almost instantly began to warn of too much investigative reporting. While Watergate stimulated a new interest in the muckraking tradition in American journalism and provoked a deeper skepticism in Congress about executive activities that led to new investigations and new scandals, government and media cooperation did not disappear by any means. Responding to the urging of CIA director William Colby in 1973 and 1974, investigative

**PRESS
MILESTONE**

*Bob Woodward and Carl
Bernstein,* Washington Post
*reporters whose account of the
Watergate scandal served as the
symbolic capstone to the newly
aggressive journalism and
made them celebrities.*
UPI / CORBIS-BETTMANN

For fifteen years
(1961–1975)
television newscasts
brought to American
homes the
"living room war"
in Vietnam.

PAGE 479

reporter Seymour Hersh sat on a story on the *Glomar Challenger* expedition (a secret operation to recover a sunken Soviet submarine), believing that revealing what he knew could put national security at risk. The *Washington Post* routinely provided CIA and other administrative spokesmen the opportunity to make a case that a given story threatened national security, leading to the delaying and modifying of news reports throughout the 1980s. Still, as government and media conflict over the reporting of the Grenada invasion (1983) and the Persian Gulf War (1991) indicated, tension between government and the fourth estate remained. Presidents continued to have "honeymoons" with the press. If the press was more self-confident and powerful as an institution, the executive was more savvy about the uses of the media.

Since the 1960s there has been a growing national consciousness about and nationalization of the news media. While various interest groups continue to spawn their own media, both print and broadcast, there has been a growing sense inside and outside mainstream journalism that the networks and leading newspapers have a public responsibility and should be answerable to public criticism. This sense of the public responsibility of the press has been most effectively demonstrated in the challenges women and minority groups have mounted to media coverage, media stereotyping, and media hiring practices. Before the 1960s, for instance, women journalists wrote about fashion and society and rarely anything else, although there were isolated exceptions of distinguished women foreign correspondents. The National Press Club admitted women only in 1971, and as late as the mid 1960s a *Newsweek* bureau chief turned down a woman reporter for a job, explaining, "What would you do if someone you were covering ducked into the men's room?" Women, and to a lesser extent minorities, are more numerous and more visible in journalism than they were, and their presence in newsrooms has made a real difference in what is covered and with what emphasis. And there is a sense, despite the status of media entities as private enterprises—often monopoly private enterprises—that the tradition of a free and independent press responsive to citizens as citizens, not just as consumers, is a tradition to which both journalists and critics of journalism as it is practiced today can legitimately appeal.

Within journalism, practitioners worry about improving coverage of minorities and improving representation of minorities in the newsroom. They worry about attracting more readers and point to alarming evidence that newspaper readership is especially low among young people, who are not adopting the newspaper-reading habits of their elders. They debate whether to emphasize investigative reporting or whether to err on the side of caution in patrolling the line between public and private life that investigative work sometimes challenges. Outside journalism, looking in, social groups from business leaders to religious, ethnic minorities or lesbians and gay men challenge what they see as inattention, inaccuracy, or ways of framing that belittle, marginalize, or trivialize their concerns. Media criticism is a small growth industry in universities. Despite the death of the critical journalism reviews that sprouted in the late 1960s, organized groups of media criticism like Accuracy in Media, on the right, and Fairness and Accuracy in Reporting, on the left, monitor political and cultural bias in the news. All this critical attention to journalism is the result in part of real growth in media power and prominence. It also owes much to the crisis of political legitimacy during the Vietnam War and particularly to efforts of the Nixon administration, which effectively painted "the media" as an autonomous source of power, and subversion, in American life. It is also a consequence of the rise of television news, which has stimulated new thinking about the meaning, function, and value of "news" in journalism, in cultural criticism, and in popular culture. This rethinking of the news media in the present encourages reconsideration of the role of journalism in the American past, too.

—MICHAEL SCHUDSON

L

LANDSCAPES

The landscapes of the United States are peculiarly American and decidedly unlike those of the nation's ancestral societies. Minimally constrained by the complexities of an Old World past, these man-made, or man-modified, ensembles of terrestrial objects are the purest expression anywhere in our contemporary world of the central dictates of capitalist economics, if modulated somewhat by the singularities of imported and commingled European cultures. In any event, the activities of European settlers and their progeny have transformed a vast territory into something radically different from the aboriginal scene.

Aboriginal Landscapes

The newcomers who began entering the future United States more than four centuries ago encountered a land already distinctly humanized over the millennia by some millions of Native Americans. Only locally, in portions of New Mexico and Arizona, were the inhabitants fully sedentary farmers. The great majority of aborigines subsisted by combining cropping systems with hunting, fishing, and gathering along the Pacific Coast and in Alaska; in the more thinly settled tracts west of the 100th meridian (running from the Dakotas to central Texas), they pursued only the latter.

The range and variety of cultural systems were considerable in pre-Columbian America, and the same was true for the resultant landscapes, although our knowledge of their actual appearance is quite fragmentary. House types and village patterns differed markedly from place to place, but most settlement was transient because of the prevailing system of shifting cultivation. The human impact on what appeared wild to the European pioneer was considerable. Substantial evidence indicates that repeated burning, for hunting and other purposes, had created the extensive grasslands of the central United States, while agricultural activity was responsible for the many openings punctuating the eastern forests, those "Indian old fields" that European farmers eagerly exploited. Furthermore, selective harvesting of vari-

ous trees, shrubs, annuals, and other organisms certainly modified the biota of early America.

Perhaps the most crucial landscape-related factor in aboriginal life, as far as later dealings and misunderstandings with Caucasians were concerned, was a total absence of European concepts of private ownership of land or the precise delineation of property lines. Insofar as there was any thought of proprietorship, it was along communal lines; and boundaries between neighboring communities had always been vaguely defined or nonexistent. Be that as it may, the encounter between invader and aborigine was disastrous for the latter; among the unfortunate results was the near-total obliteration of antecedent landscapes as Native American populations were severely decimated and demoralized, shunted from place to place, and eventually confined to reservations where little of their material culture was left intact. Today perhaps the only remaining aboriginal landscapes with any semblance of authenticity are found in a few New Mexican localities.

The European Transformation

When the first wave of European settlers arrived—in the late sixteenth century in the Southwest, and along the Atlantic seaboard a few decades later—their automatic impulse may have been to re-create the traditional societies and landscapes of their homelands, but pioneer conditions in the New World seldom rendered such faithful transcription feasible. A spectacular abundance of usable land, virtually free for the taking, and the weakness of political and legal controls made it quite difficult to implement any sort of planning. In place of the orderly, compact, regularly aligned rural and urban settlements envisioned by the various grantees favored by the British, Spanish, Dutch, and French regimes, the actuality turned out to be much messier: scattered, often isolated farmsteads and a string of small seaports and even smaller inland trading centers with little pretense of regularity in layout or elegance in appearance. This statement applies equally well to New England, where, common myth to the contrary notwithstanding, clustered villages were the rare exception before the late

*They arrived to find
a landscape
inhabited by Native
Americans speaking
a wide variety of
languages, living
in a wide variety
of structures.*

PAGE 211

See also
The Frontier

L

LANDSCAPES

The European Transformation

Land of extremes. Land of contrasts. Land of surprises. Land of contradictions.

FEDERAL WRITERS' PROJECT
ARIZONA: THE GRAND
CANYON STATE (1956)

eighteenth century. Approximations of European models, such as some of the Hispanic outposts in the Southwest, or New Orleans, Boston, Philadelphia, and Savannah, were few in number.

Building styles in early America tended to be generalized, simplified versions of Old World folk practice. Regional patterns did gradually emerge in the design of houses, barns, churches, cemeteries, and other visible features but, given the frequent mixing of peoples and influences from varied European localities and the impact of a novel environment, simple duplication of any specific Old World scene could hardly occur. Only much later, as wealth and sophistication grew, did individual homes and estates come to resemble what had become fashionable in Europe.

Many a foreign visitor recorded his or her impressions of the early American scene, including the frontier zone, and aside from occasional mild compliments for a major city or two and some of the older, more flourishing farming areas, they were uniformly taken aback by the pervasive physical crudities of town and countryside, a prodigal wastefulness in resource exploitation, and the jarring visual disharmonies in what they generally beheld. As David Lowenthal has noted, what struck them most was the vastness, wildness, and formlessness of a future-oriented land characterized by extravagant extremes. The passage of time has not canceled these early characteristics; indeed, just the reverse has happened in terms of formlessness and incongruous contrasts. As social disparities have widened, as the ranks of both the wealthy and the poor and underprivileged have grown substantially, we often find their two utterly irreconcilable landscapes existing side by side in some of our larger cities.

If the vestiges of aboriginal occupancy were negligible and if the shaping of the colonial and subsequent American scene has been essentially that of European peoples and ideas operating under new, unfamiliar circumstances, there remains one other set of influences, at least in the American South, that is still poorly understood: African influences. Cultural transfers from the Old World in African American church buildings and domestic architecture, yard treatment, agricultural and burial practices are quite plausible in light of the physical evidence despite the paucity of documentation.

The evolution of the American landscape from pioneer days to the present has been largely a matter of applying a series of ever more advanced technologies, along with the necessary investment of capital, to a varied set of places and resources,

all in fulfillment of certain cultural and economic drives, as often as not unspoken and unwritten. The former set of forces—the technological and financial—may have altered greatly over the years, but the latter—those internalized imperatives which energize both individuals and the larger society—have remained remarkably consistent over time. As basic a principle as any is the supreme value of individualism and thus a vigorous, if not always productive, competition and the sacredness of private property. In landscape terms this article of faith finds expression in many ways, including the isolated farmstead, the detached, single-family urban or suburban home set on its own lot, the multitude of small burial plots in the countryside, the world's largest proliferation of church denominations and their buildings, weak or nonexistent control of commercial land use, and, consequently, that duplication and excess of facilities so fully embodied in the present-day commercial highway strip. It is the infrequent counterexample, most notably the Mormon communities of Utah with their compact, well-ordered, theocratic landscapes, that reminds us how extreme the general American case really is.

Allied to this powerful streak of individualism is a degree of mobility—obviously spatial, but social as well—that animates American life and landscape to a level no other country can rival. The acceptance—indeed, the celebration—of rapid change quite logically accompanies American individualism and mobility. The landscape results include endless turnover in land use and structures or their remodeling, frequent juxtaposition of building styles from different eras, a high incidence of abandoned farmland, derelict urban neighborhoods and ghost towns, a never-ending series of new highway projects or the relocation or improvement of existing roads, and, except during deepest economic depression, a great amount of construction at various stages of completion in favored localities.

Undergirding so fluid and seemingly anarchic a scene is the most basic principle of all: the sanctity of the profit motive for both individual and business firm. But if a creed common to all of modern Western society happens to be expressed most nakedly in a United States lacking the burden of ancient tradition, there is another facet of the American ethos (one possibly derived from the English cultural system) that is exceptional: an antiurban bias. (The pastoral urges of Americans also find expression in another British heritage, the homeowner's passion for lawns.) Cities may be necessary evils in the furtherance of economic aims, but, unlike the situation in continental Europe, the American metropolis is, with few exceptions, an unloved creature. The results of such disaffection are visually obvious in the cities themselves, as well as in the extraordinary extent of suburbanization and exurbanization. A less direct but nonetheless genuine expression of this mind-set is the propensity to select smaller towns for state capitals and rural or small-town settings for colleges.

THE IMPACT OF TECHNOLOGY. In a country of such daunting size, the means for transporting people and goods have always been primary determinants of the material framework of American life and livelihood. The changes over time in the morphology of American cities clearly reflect this fact. For the first two hundred years or so of European settlement—certainly until the 1840s or 1850s—towns were relatively small, compact pedestrian places (with access to horse-drawn carriages limited to the more prosperous) that, with rare exceptions, were tied to waterborne commerce and thus oriented toward wharves and docks. They were also places with minimal spatial segregation of economic functions, classes, or ethnic groups.

The introduction of the steam railroad had a profound impact upon urban form and landscape and, eventually, on the countryside as well. Besides fostering vigorous growth in city size, commerce, and manufacturing, the new mode of transportation transformed the outward appearance of much of the city. There were new depots, freight houses, marshaling yards, maintenance facilities, associated hotels, bridges, and tunnels accompanied by the evisceration of much of the old urban fabric to provide space for tracks and all the other rail-related activities. New factory and warehouse districts arose at rail side, sometimes on a massive scale. By the close of the nineteenth century, the building of commuter and light-rail interurban lines enabled the city to sprawl outward in an unprecedented way, as did the installation of electric trolley service within the expanding metropolis.

Aside from the immediate physical stigmata—the many cuts and fills executed across all but the most subdued of surfaces, defoliation of rights-of-way, creation of parallel telegraph lines and signal systems, and the erection of innumerable small-town depots and ancillary structures—the indirect effects of inserting so many tens of thousands of miles of rail into the countryside were ultimately both visually and socially significant. The presence of an extended "metropolitan corridor" meant availability of city goods, information, and ideas in many formerly isolated villages and hamlets as well as the start of that gradual coalescence, or interdigitation, between town and countryside that has become so prominent an aspect of contemporary America. It is no coincidence that the onset of a standardized way of life became noticeable in the 1850s, just when the railroad began to monopolize long-distance transportation. It was then that some magazines acquired nationwide readership, that a mass market developed for many types of mass-produced merchandise, and

THE FOREST PRIMEVAL

Trees in the Early American Landscape

Among the environmental circumstances molding the American landscape, few are more noteworthy than the initial superabundance of trees in so much of the eastern half of the country and a good portion of the far West. It was both curse and blessing. Clearing a fifty- or one-hundred-acre (20- or 40-hectare) farm could mean an entire working lifetime of literally backbreaking labor for the homesteader, and the outcome for another generation or so might be unsightly, stump-filled fields and pastures. But the forest also provided absolute necessities: raw materials for house, barn, other outbuildings, fencing, furniture, vehicles, and tools, and, of course, fuel for warmth, cooking, and industrial processes. The fact that so many thousands of sawmills sprang up along the frontier illustrates the centrality of wood and lumber to American life. Rural and much of urban America, early and late, then, has been wood-dominated. Even today the woodlot remains on many farms.

In the past and to a surprising extent today, wood has been the preferred material for houses, churches, school buildings, shops, mills, bridges, and much else. In a land where labor has been dear and lumber cheap, the adoption of brick, stone, and other materials for construction has come about only gradually, locally, and incompletely. So deeply ingrained in the American psyche did the preference for wood become that when the settlement frontier entered the treeless Great Plains, other expedients, such as the sod house, were quite temporary; lumber, even entire prefabricated wooden buildings, were shipped in at considerable expense.

See also
National Parks and
Preservation

that fashions in house design and landscape architecture (including park cemeteries) showed signs
of becoming uniform coast to coast thanks to
widely circulated manuals and preachments such
as those of Andrew Jackson Downing.

Dramatic and pervasive though the effects of
the new railroad system may have been, there
were many other innovations, less well publicized,
that helped modify the American landscape during the latter half of the nineteenth century:
barbed-wire fencing, cheap paint, indoor plumbing, mass production of portland cement, the
mail-order catalog, the balloon-frame house, electric elevators, and streetlights. Equally important
though less celebrated were advances in earth-
moving devices and technology and, most especially, the invention and large-scale use of dynamite. In any event, remarkable alterations came
about in the topography of American cities.
Rough terrain was leveled (as happened in Manhattan), entire surfaces lifted (as in Chicago), dry
land created out of swamps (as in Washington),
and waterfronts remade (as in New Orleans). In
many instances, as in Boston, the changes have
been so thoroughgoing that if a seventeenth-
century resident were to be resurrected, it is
doubtful whether he or she would find any part of
the metropolitan area or its harbor recognizable.

No major American seaport, and few lake or river
ports of consequence, have escaped extensive
physical revamping.

Another crucial shaper of the landscape has
been the automobile. The easy availability, since
the early decades of the twentieth century, of personal vehicles to all but the very poorest, along
with great numbers of trucks, buses, motorcycles,
and other motorized conveyances as well as access
to almost any point, have profoundly reordered
the settlement structure and landscapes of America in ways that are still not fully appreciated. As
far as the city is concerned, there has been a
remarkable outward explosion of population,
businesses, and traditional urban functions. In a
number of cases, the old urban core has lost its
dominance as suburbs, or even virtually autonomous "edge cities," have sprung up along the
periphery. The feasibility of long-distance commuting and the new flexibility in delivering materials and information have facilitated the redistri-
bution of enterprises and employees into what
were once remote locations. The urbanization of
the countryside is proceeding inexorably. One of
the more visible aspects of the phenomenon has
been the proliferation of second homes and seasonal housing in environmentally attractive locales within commuting range of major popula-

tion centers—or, for the airborne affluent, almost anywhere in the country.

Within the more or less contiguous built-up area we still call a city, the imprint of the automobile is hard to ignore. Immense acreage is given over to paved streets and parking lots; multiple-lane, limited-access highways within and around the city with their massive interchanges, bridges, overpasses, and outsize signage and lighting have done more to revise the physiognomy of urban places than even the most imperious of railroad barons could have dreamed of doing. And the interstate highway system and similar projects, with their commercial clusters arising around every interchange, have transformed the face of much of rural America. Every self-respecting modern dwelling has a one- or two-car garage and an ample driveway; along every thriving commercial street we find not just filling stations, auto showrooms, parts dealers, repair facilities, and perhaps some motels but also an endless array of retail establishments geared to the drive-by and/or drive-in trade and a great swarm of often large, garish advertising signs designed to engage the attention and urges of the passing drivers. As symptomatic as anything of the new order is the profusion of auto-oriented shopping malls in city and suburb, a development that gives every indication of becoming the central social institution of our times.

Important as airborne passenger, mail, and freight traffic may have become, the landscape impact of the airplane has been much less profound than that of the automobile or truck. Nevertheless, one of the more striking localized features of present-day America is the airport complex on the outskirts of major metropolises with its mix of office, motel, and high-tech industrial facilities as well as the considerable acreage devoted to the airport proper.

THE IMPACT OF CULTURAL AUTHORITY. Ultimately rivaling the significance of technology as a shaper of the American landscape have been the workings of central authority, even though it was initially rather weak. A leading item on the agenda of the colonial proprietors and, later, the provincial, state, and national regimes was the rapid disposal of land to settlers through sale or other means. Until the early years of national independence, there was little regularity in the ways real estate was surveyed or bounded. The prevailing pattern throughout the original thirteen states is known as the metes-and-bounds systems, one that relied largely on natural features for designating property lines. The resulting highly irregular mosaic of parcels contrasts with the long-lot sys-

tem used in areas of early French and some Spanish settlement, one in which long, narrow strips of property ran back at right angles from riverfront or road.

Such relatively casual modes of carving up the American land vanished in the late 1780s when the young republic adopted a rigidly rectangular survey system for the vast, as yet unsettled national domain to which it held title. Moving in advance of permanent settlers, federal surveyors laid out six-by-six-mile townships with straight-line boundaries oriented to the compass. Each township consisted of thirty-six sections, each containing 640 acres, or one square mile (256 hectares, or 2.6 square kilometers). Public roads and virtually all subsequent property lines and field boundaries within sections were aligned north, east, south, and west along or parallel with section lines, and most later urban street layouts followed suit. The result for the nearly 75 percent of American territory so marked off (not counting national parks and forests, early French and Spanish grants, and Indian reservations excluded from the system) is a remarkable geometric repetitiveness in the settlement fabric. It is a checkerboard regularity that can be discerned from the ground but appreciated fully only from the air. The federal example was emulated by several states that controlled unsettled lands not included in the national domain, notably Texas, Georgia, Pennsylvania, New York, and Maine, though their survey methods were not quite as rigorous as in the national case.

The rationale for such a relatively simple method for partitioning the American land was obvious enough: it made good business sense. Henceforth it would be easy to describe, advertise, sell, resell, subdivide, or combine parcels with a minimum of legal fuss and expense. But if the effects of the federal rectangular survey have been deep, widespread, and enduring, other visible evidence of the existence of a relatively underdeveloped central government was scarce during the first several decades of national existence. Perhaps the occasional fort, lighthouse, or customhouse was then the only visible token that some sort of national entity was ruling the land. The visible effects of state and local governments were even more difficult to detect.

The net balance of power and sentiment, as between government and the governed, and thus its landscape expression, began to shift substantially from the time of the Civil War onward, but certain deeply ingrained attitudes persist. Americans have always felt uneasy about centralized

*Although the land
of the Great Plains
was generally fertile,
it was also quite
dry and bare.*

PAGE 198

See also
Transportation and Mobility

*The dramatic
topography of
the Sierra Nevada
and the Rockies
fired the popular
imagination.*

PAGE 274

governance and the bureaucracy, or indeed any form of external interference with the exercise of property rights or the pursuit of wealth—thus the late, slow, reluctant acceptance of planning and zoning or other land-use regulations. But where controls have been effective, the contrasts between juxtaposed jurisdictions can be quite dramatic—for example, between the landscapes of the District of Columbia and those in its Maryland and Virginia suburbs or the differences between the roadsides of Vermont and those in adjacent states. But even though planners may enjoy their minor triumphs, the larger reality is that entrepreneurs, whether individual or corporate, have been the dominant creators of a landscape whose crevices the homeowner can modify only modestly. Perhaps nothing more vividly illustrates their hegemony than the ways they have contrived suburban housing developments and shopping centers.

However ambivalently Americans may regard control by distant government agencies, there is no escaping its necessity in a modern economy; and with the strengthened central regime a modern citizenry finds itself necessarily imbued with nationalist notions. Inevitably such collective loyalties and such concentrated political power take recognizable form in the landscape. Official architecture is the most obvious point of entry. Governmental edifices in Washington, especially from the 1850s on, and their facsimiles in various state capitals, not to mention the ubiquitous standardized post offices of the twentieth century, set standards that were copied not only by counties and municipalities but also by builders of commercial and residential structures. This is especially striking in the case of the long-lived popularity of various classical revival styles. And even without official sponsorship, nationalist sentiment shows up unmistakably in the persistence of colonial revival designs since the 1880s and all the many buildings reminiscent of Independence Hall.

The federal presence has manifested itself in many ways other than building styles. The American land is punctuated by a great many military installations, some of them quite extensive, and their inevitable offshoots: veterans' clubhouses, Veterans Administration hospitals, and military cemeteries—all readily recognizable. To a marked degree, the historical monuments that began to appear in the 1850s have been as nationalistic in tone as in other lands. But what makes the United States truly exceptional among modern nation-states is the unparalleled profusion of flag display,

by private individuals and businesses as well as by official installations, along with a remarkable prevalence of eagles (the national totem) and the national colors (red, white, and blue) in every conceivable venue. A complete inventory of the impress of central authority would require more space than is available here, but certainly one cannot overlook the interstate highway system, the array of rather standardized national parks and forests, the countless accomplishments of the Army Corps of Engineers in their reordering of America's hydrology and much else, and the highly visible feats of the Tennessee Valley Authority and other federal dam projects, some of gargantuan magnitude. Since the New Deal era, we have had the many tangible deeds of the Works Progress Administration, Civilian Conservation Corps, and other agencies and the immediately identifiable federal housing projects in numerous cities.

If the power and prestige of the national regime have generated so many notable signs and symptoms on the American scene, another kind of centralized authority—that of the more successful national or regional business firms—has produced something of a parallel phenomenon. The earliest such expression may well have been the standardized facilities of the major railroad lines, but the trend has fully blossomed more recently with nationally uniform designs for filling stations, hotel and motel chains, and a great assortment of look-alike franchised eating and retail operations.

SALVAGE AND PRESERVATION. Although economic, technological, and political forces have been the prime determinants of America's humanized landscapes, certain counterforces have been in evidence. In large part they have been energized by the mistakes and excesses of the past. Exploitation of American soils, waters, forests, and mines for immediate gain was intense, rapid, and all too often totally heedless of ultimate cost or consequence. So thorough has been the assault upon the habitat that, taking plant cover as an example, the survival of any patch of original prairie is improbable, and genuine virgin stands of forest are exceedingly rare, as are streams in anything like their original condition. Virtually everything sylvan that seems wild is actually second- or third-growth forest at best. In some instances one can argue that human intervention may have improved conditions in both substance and appearance. But the contrary situation is much easier to document, a notorious example being the cutover area of northern Michigan, Wisconsin, and Minnesota. The clear-cutting of the once splendid forest in the late nineteenth century, along with many subsequent fires, has yielded a scraggly semidesert of scrub vegetation with no prospect of regeneration for a good many decades.

It was only toward the close of the 1800s that an organized conservation movement was born. It was led by elite members of society who were primarily concerned over the future availability of resources (for both economic and recreational use) and only incidentally, if at all, with the visual aspects of the problem. The same statement applies to the soil conservation programs that began to be implemented seriously in the 1930s. In any event, the question of appearance, of the integrity of manmade or man-modified landscapes, has come to the fore slowly and gradually, in part as a result of the historic preservation movement. From a halting start in the mid-nineteenth century with campaigns to safeguard especially memorable single buildings, the movement broadened to embrace entire early settlements and urban neighborhoods of a certain venerability and charm as well as the more significant American battlefields. No doubt sensibilities have been sharpened by such scathing jeremiads against uglification as those by Peter Blake and Ian Nairn, and issues involving both preservation and the look of the land and the works of man have gradually crept onto the political agenda.

Serious problems remain unresolved. Is it possible or desirable to keep these places frozen in a state of suspended animation? Should these localities be museumized or (like Charleston's Historic District or New Orleans's Vieux Carrée) allowed to change ever so slowly? How is genuine authenticity to be attained? How does gentrification of older city neighborhoods fit into the preservation picture?

Another recent movement, the environmental, may have even greater long-term consequences for the American landscape. Pursuing as their most central objective the preservation or restoration of wilderness and various fragile ecosystems, since the 1950s and 1960s the leaders of the movement have gained much popular support and perhaps catalyzed what seems to be a mass conversion to "green," or organic, consciousness. The effect on the landscape is incidental but potentially important. In a parallel development, beautification projects are no longer uncommon in American municipalities, and some cities have gone out of their way to encourage public art.

We must reckon with still another set of forces, those which mold our collective mental landscape

images and thus, indirectly but meaningfully, the ways in which we manipulate our environs. Through the media of fiction, verse, landscape painting, calendar art, photography, movies, and television, we have charted a constellation of ideal landscapes in the mind's eye. They include the New England village; the antebellum southern plantation; the idyllic yeoman farm; the Middle American Main Street (so cleverly miniaturized and embalmed in a sanitized Disneyland) with its elm-lined residential streets; the western ranch; the South Sea island paradise; and perhaps others. Much of today's commercial and residential design is a matter of life imitating art.

SCHOLARLY APPROACHES. If an awareness that landscapes or, more generally, the visual aspect of shared spaces are items of common concern were to dawn upon the general public quite belatedly, the academic community has been equally slow in recognizing the value of landscape study. Although for many years geographers in the United States and abroad have debated the definition of the term "landscape," or its equivalent in other languages—with meanings ranging from simple scenery or vista to such abstractions as entire regions—it is only recently that anything resembling a serious school of landscape analysis has emerged. Human geographers have been the most conspicuous members of this loose fraternity, one that also includes historians, landscape architects, and folklorists. The essential premise, eloquently expounded by Henry Glassie and Thomas Schlereth, is that the ensemble of material objects (the relevance of sounds and smells remains moot) we call the landscape represents a priceless archive, a deeply layered palimpsest, the richest sort of means for gaining a deep understanding of human societies past and present. It is interesting and important not just in and of itself but even more for its implicit messages. The contention is that the documentation furnished by the landscape, including the testimony of those large groups of humanity who leave no written records, offers a much more comprehensive view of human life, thought, and ideals than the paper trail traditionally exploited by historians.

If there has been any central figure in this enterprise, it is undoubtedly John Brinckerhoff Jackson, who through his essays has given the landscape school a certain philosophical coherence and who, through the journal *Landscape*, which he founded in 1951 and edited for many years, has provided practitioners a major forum. The agenda for geographers and other students of the American (and other) landscapes is enor-

Diners sprang up along the highways, some resembling gleaming railroad dining cars, others wacky reproductions of giant coffee pots, milk bottles, or Dutch windmills.

PAGE 511

See also
Housing

L

LANDSCAPES

*The European
Transformation*

*If a man owns land,
the land owns him.*

RALPH WALDO EMERSON

◆ **Exegesis**
*Exposition, explanation,
especially an explanation or
critical interpretation of a
text*

mous, a task involving both description, or inventory, and subsequent analysis. More often than not, they have barely begun taking up the challenge, but what has been achieved justifies the claims of the landscape advocates.

At this point one can only briefly sketch what has been done and the long list of future chores. Data and understanding are fullest when it comes to rural houses, farmsteads, barns, and bridges; students of them may have already passed the point of diminishing returns. There has been some progress in studying cemeteries, parks, fencing, roads, roadside architecture, lawns, and gardens, but a great deal remains to be learned. For a large number of other landscape components, our organized knowledge is quite skimpy or entirely lacking. The list includes vernacular church buildings, factories, office buildings and office parks, yard and porch ornaments, field patterns, hospital and school buildings, monuments, shopping malls and commercial structures in general, the entire array of items associated with sport and recreation, trailer parks, abandoned spaces, and, not least, refuse dumps.

Finally, beyond the task of assembling so much needed data there looms the challenge of adequate interpretation of finding and answering the many urgent questions embedded in the many material microworlds we have created or transformed. The potentials of such landscape exegesis appear in Banham's work on Los Angeles, Duncan's account of a Westchester County village, Zelinsky's treatment of the Pennsylvania town, or the essays on the historical geography of the American landscape edited by Michael Conzen.

Such publications suggest that landscape analysis may play an important, perhaps vital role in addressing the grander issues that have begun to engage social historians and social scientists—such as the meaning of community and the operations of power, class, ethnicity, and gender in American life. In any event, there is little prospect that even the most enterprising set of students can bring to closure any time during the foreseeable future an exciting, ever-expanding research agenda.

—WILBUR ZELINSKY

MANNERS AND ETIQUETTE

To suggest the full significance of etiquette in American history, it is perhaps best to approach the subject obliquely, looking first to one of the central struggles in American history—the struggle over race. D. W. Griffith intended his epic film *The Birth of a Nation* to plead a case: the "birth" he envisioned was the reuniting of North and South, an Anglo-Saxon nation standing against the twin threat of blacks and immigrants. He meant to leave the white middle-class audiences of 1915 cheering as the white-robed Ku Klux Klan rode to the rescue of Anglo-Saxon civilization.

Griffith set up his argument carefully, with predictable scenes that portray black men sexually menacing white women. But Griffith also gave great weight to another scene, clearly intending it to raise the ire of proper audiences. The hero, a southern gentleman, walks along a sidewalk with a lady. They encounter the ambitious mulatto Silas Lynch, who not only does not relinquish the right of way to his "betters" but insists upon being "recognized" by them. While this scene lacks the raw racist charge of a black man sexually threatening a white woman, Griffith clearly intended it as a piece of emotional evidence. Lynch's claims were an egregious breach of etiquette—meant and understood as a challenge to social order. Modern audiences see the "Little Colonel" (the Civil War nickname for our gentleman hero) fuming over this affront and are vaguely puzzled. Audiences in 1915 saw the challenge as significant because they, like Griffith, lived within a system of etiquette that was closely tied to fears about social order and disorder.

The scene does not work with modern audiences partly because we do not know the rules Lynch is breaking. They have passed from our behavior; they have disappeared from the etiquette manuals. The middle-class man or woman today is thoroughly ignorant of the myriad rules of etiquette that would have defined his or her middle-class status fifty or one hundred years ago.

The term "etiquette" itself has fallen out of favor. It sounds quaint—like the system of manners it is most often used to describe. Etiquette, in contemporary American society, most often surfaces in rituals that lay some claim to formality, such as weddings, and in exhortations to politeness based on common good sense. But while the term remains attached to a tradition of rules and manners developed, elaborated, and overelaborated in the nineteenth century, we live within systems of etiquette no less complex and arcane.

Etiquette has played a complex and important role in American history. It is not just that, in Erving Goffman's words, "the gestures which we sometimes call empty are perhaps the fullest things of all" or, in the social historian John Kasson's words, that "the rituals of everyday behavior establish in important measure the structures by which individuals define one another and interact." Both points *are* important: a people's manners—the rituals of their everyday behavior—are full of meaning and of information. We can read manners as ritual and learn much.

But ritual is not the whole story, for manners and etiquette are not interchangeable terms. The term "manners" describes behavior, however unmannerly that behavior might be. Etiquette, on the other hand, is prescriptive. Etiquette is the code of manners, the set of rules, the definition of proper behavior. The relationship between manners and etiquette is complicated and often tense. It is in that tension, which prevents the perfect correspondence of manners and etiquette, that we often learn most.

Etiquette, in addition, is instrumental. In the course of American history, etiquette has often served as a tool—even as a weapon—in struggles over social change in America. Etiquette has often been concerned with drawing lines between people and boundaries between groups—most importantly, between social classes in the nineteenth century and between men and women in the twentieth century (the role of race remains complicated throughout). In observing etiquette, Americans enacted rituals of power and exclusion while claiming them to be natural manifestations of "taste" or of "breeding." But etiquette has also

Within this world of urban amusements, young women dressed in the latest finery, attended dance halls and amusement parks unescorted, and often picked up young men to pay their way once they arrived.

PAGE 425

M

MANNERS AND ETIQUETTE

Early Codes

♦ **Aboriginal**
Being the first or earliest known of its kind present in a region

provided means to claim inclusion and served as a forum for testing conflicting claims about the nature and form of civility.

Many different systems of manners and of etiquette have existed in America. A modern high school might have an elaborate but local code of etiquette that, though unwritten, structures daily interactions. Immigrant groups brought the manners and etiquette of their home countries to the United States, and those systems changed through contact with other groups. The fine points of social usage differed between Charleston and New York, Des Moines and Dallas. And in terms of etiquette, the past truly is another country.

Etiquette is a prescriptive system and never fully matches behavior. Even the most universally prescriptive system of etiquette is mediated by factors like religion, race, ethnicity, class, region, gender, and profession. Nonetheless, the observance of appropriate etiquette has been a precondition for participation in public life, and etiquette has worked both to determine social status and to structure relationships between individuals. Of course, what was "appropriate" etiquette was often contested.

While many have claimed otherwise, there is nothing timeless about etiquette—neither the behaviors prescribed and proscribed nor the definitions of the term. A nine-year-old boy in the mid-1960s declared: "I have good manners. I say good night and good morning. I say hello and goodbye, and when I see dead things lying around the house I bury them." His implicit definition and practical interpretation strain the bounds of credulity less than those of many older and better-known advisers. In the pages that follow, I will attempt to offer an overview of the changing definitions of etiquette and to analyze the significance and utility of etiquette in American history.

Early Codes

Those who journeyed to the New World carried with them, in addition to the supplies they thought would be useful in the unknown land, a vast store of cultural baggage. They brought to the new continents old ways of seeing, habits of behavior, and systems of manners: sets of assumptions so deeply rooted as to be unconscious and unremarked upon. The culture they transplanted did not flourish unchanged in new soil, but the manners and mores of these new Americans were marked as much by persistence as by change.

The development of American manners is not a story of creative synthesis through cultural contact: the colonists dismissed the aboriginal inhabitants of the new world as "barbarians," and the newly named "Indians," in other languages, thought pretty much the same of the settlers. The Europeans would never have survived in the new landscape without knowledge gained from the Indians, and contact with Europeans radically transformed the lives and culture of Native Americans. But the two groups came from very different worlds and assigned very different meanings to similar acts. What seemed to the Europeans to be trade, for example, was to the tribes of the eastern woodlands often gift-exchange, a ritualized system that served to create and maintain allegiances between tribes. Overall, Europeans tended to describe Native Americans as existing in a state of nature (meaning they were uncivilized), and Native Americans, though drawn into European trade networks and desiring firearms and other European goods, had no desire to wear European-style clothes, live in stuffy houses, or adopt the manners of "Christian people."

The British settlers of North America came from a highly rank-ordered society, and brought with them a belief in the naturalness of hierarchy. Such traditional forms did not serve the settlers of Jamestown well. In England, "gentleman" designated one who did not earn his living through manual labor, and in Jamestown the gentlemen refused to work until John Smith, Gent., subverted proper form and forced them.

For the early settlers in Massachusetts Bay, rank and hierarchy were crucial. The colonists saw their settlements as small and fragile centers of Christian civilization clinging to the edge of a vast and menacing wilderness. The death rate was high, support from England not certain, winters harsh, and food scarce. Order was crucial, so that the community not succumb to chaos within. Order, to these seventeenth-century men and women, entailed hierarchy. John Winthrop, the governor of the colony and a gentleman, wrote in *A Modell of Christian Charity* (1630): "God Almighty in his most holy and wise providence hath so disposed of the condition of mankind as in all times some may be rich, some poor, some high and eminent in power and dignity, others mean and in subjection."

Many of the rules of etiquette transferred to the colonies were concerned with rank and status. The colonists dealt with the issue of hierarchy in ways that seem exceedingly direct to twentieth-century Americans, used to reading class and status in subtler signs. Titles designated status: "Mister" was reserved for gentlemen (a status determined not by behavior but by social position);

the wives of gentlemen were addressed as "Madam." Those of commoner clay were called, as in England, "Goodman" and "Goodwife" (or less formally, "Goody"). In America, though, the title of gentleman lost some of its social significance, for a good-man might ascend to the "gentry" if he were elected captain by his peers in the local militia, or if he were chosen to hold a town office such as justice of the peace. In the New World, unlike the Old, a man without substantial fortune, education, or lineage might be addressed as a gentleman.

The general manners of the people can be surmised from their surroundings. While the wealthiest colonists had begun to stock their homes with luxuries imported from Europe, most people lived very humbly. In the Chesapeake Bay area in the seventeenth century, for example, only one-third of the families had chairs or benches in their homes. Homes were small, with little separation of space or function. Few had real beds at first, but those who did kept them in the main room. Families slept together, welcoming travelers into the common bed. Privacy was seen neither as a good or necessary commodity, nor as a requisite for polite behavior.

To eat, common people gathered around a board laid on trestles. Hierarchy remained important: adults and guests sat "above the salt" (the salt cellar placed in the middle of the table) and servants and children below. They shared trenchers and cups, and freely dipped their hands into common serving bowls. European travelers were often appalled at the promiscuous sharing, as common cups became fouled with spit and grease, and bits of tobacco floated in the common drink. As late as 1827, Margaret Hunter Hall wrote home to England, "They are a nasty people, the Americans, at table; there is no denying that fact."

It was not only the common folk or lesser ranks whose concepts of privacy and proper deportment were shocking. The advice offered in the conduct or courtesy books popular in colonial America is telling. "Spit not in the room but in the corner, or rather go out and do it abroad," advises Eleazar Moody's *School of Good Manners*, the most popular of American courtesy books published in the eighteenth century. George Washington, at fifteen, copied out the following in his commonplace book: "Kill no Vermin as Fleas, lice ticks &c in the Sight of Others . . . " and "Being set at meat Scratch not neither Spit Cough or blow your Nose except there's a Necessity for it." Such rules were derived from conduct guides written for nobles at court in the fifteenth and sixteenth centuries; even here we see standards of proper behavior changing, for these versions had dropped proscriptions against "relieving" oneself before the doors of "court chambers"—this advice no longer had to be stated. Still, in colonial and early national America, it was deemed polite to blow one's nose not on the tablecloth but in one's fingers—as long as it was not the hand with which one was eating.

RANK AND STATUS IN THE NEW WORLD

Rank was assumed as the most natural way of ordering a group of people. Students at Harvard and Yale were listed in order of family standing until 1772, when an alphabetical system was adopted. The change, significantly, seems to have stemmed less from a rise of democratic feelings than from increased difficulty in determining rank and the grumbling of parents who did not agree with the college's determination of their status.

Even in religious services colonists did not assemble as an undifferentiated community of worshipers. Pews were assigned according to community consensus on the social rank of each family, and services offered a ritual enactment of hierarchy and status. Still, rank-order was sometimes contested. Town records tell of shoving matches in the aisles, and of one Goody Elizabeth Randall who claimed the place she believed rightfully hers, pushing and scrambling her way over pews with backs four to five feet tall.

The passing of sumptuary laws in the various colonies also testifies that the boundaries of rank and status were stretched in America. "One end of apparel," according to Urian Oakes (1631–1681), president of Harvard College, "is to distinguish and put a difference between persons according to their places and Condition." But the Massachusetts General Court felt it necessary to register its outrage "that men or women of mean condition, should take upon them the garb of Gentlemen," requiring that one must possess property equivalent to £200 in order to wear "gaudy apparel." The Virginia House of Burgesses had passed similar legislation in its first session. The law was violated, but offenders were rarely convicted.

♦ **Trenchers**
Wooden platters for serving food

Articles, essays, speeches, and sermons spoke of the need for spouses to give each other respect, reciprocity, and romance during both courtship and marriage.

PAGE 119

The South and the North

The manners of colonists differed by region—both because of the accidents of geography and because of the different traditions of polite behavior that served as models. Northern society looked to the moralist strand of English courtesy books, and, in revising them for American consumption, enhanced the religious component. Southerners looked to the landed gentry, reading works in the courtly tradition. Richard Allestree's *The Whole Duty of Man*, first published in London around 1660, was owned by both George Washington and Thomas Jefferson. Allestree presented a model of comportment based on the ideals of chivalry and hierarchy, emphasizing the criteria that made gentlemen. "Gentlemen," he insisted, "sweat only at the Engagement of their Sports," while the lesser ranks must live by the sweat of their brows.

Southern etiquette was based on a chivalric code of honor that was, as Bertram Wyatt-Brown argues in *Southern Honor*, "inseparable from hierarchy and entitlement, defense of family blood and community needs." The code of honor applied to all southern whites, though its proper manifestation differed depending on rank in society and upon gender. The southern code, though never so romantic or so "civilized" as it has been portrayed in retrospect, suffused southern life. In contrast, northern society, with its early emphasis on mercantile pursuits followed by its transformation into an urban-industrial society, developed an ethic and code of manners based on conscience and secular economic concerns.

Honor was enacted, in its most extreme form, through the highly ritualized performance of the duel (which one historian has described as men "killing each other according to strict rules of etiquette"). Dueling was introduced to America by French and British aristocrats serving (on different sides) during the Revolutionary War and was taken up in the ranks of America's military. But dueling became widespread in the postcolonial South, where, in spite of strong opposition, the *code duello* became a part of the gentleman's life.

Duels were fought in defense of honor. If one man insulted another's personal honor, custom and community opinion urged that the matter be resolved through a duel. Duels were governed by an etiquette, though many duelists were not clear on proper form; John Lyde Wilson, a former governor of South Carolina, compiled a "blue book" of dueling etiquette.

Dueling, in keeping with the hierarchical nature of the code of honor, was restricted to gentlemen; one did not challenge or accept a challenge from a social inferior. While a small percentage of southerners qualified as gentlemen in the strictest sense (for example, in 1860, 11,000 families, or 0.75 percent of the southern population, owned fifty or more slaves), a much larger number of white men laid claim to that status as officers in local militias. In a culture noted for its physical violence and hotheadedness, dueling may have served to mediate extremes of violence, for the proper duel offered cooling-off time as the rites of challenge and response were observed, and official intermediaries were sometimes able to settle matters with honor and without violence.

Southern etiquette was also tightly enmeshed with the South's peculiar institution. Deference was expected from slaves. In the physical embodiment of honor, according to Bertram Wyatt-Brown, southern culture linked honor to the body: "the eyes witnessed honor and looked down in deference or shame." Thus a slave who met the gaze of a white person was impudent. Travelers were sometimes confounded by the workings of hierarchy in the South. One young woman, overwhelmingly modest in her relations with white men, undressed freely in the presence of a male slave. His status rendered him unimportant—his race canceled the significance of his sex. The not-uncommon relations between white masters and slave women were also covered by the code of honor. The sexual union itself was no violation of honor or of etiquette, but if someone "violated good taste" and spoke of the liaison directly to any member of the man's family, the entire family was disgraced. In such matters, silence was polite.

While southern manners and etiquette remained rooted in the traditions of hierarchy and honor well into the nineteenth century, in the North both manners and the claims of etiquette had undergone a revolution. The sources of change are two: the rise of democratic sentiment in the wake of the American Revolution, and fundamental changes in the social and economic organization of the nation.

Much of our description of American manners comes from European travelers who were quick to attribute virtually everything to the effects of democracy. "Nothing does democracy more harm than its outward forms of behavior," wrote Alexis de Tocqueville (1805–1859) in a chapter called "Some Reflections on American Manners" in *Democracy in America*, for "many who could tolerate its vices cannot put up with its manners." It

See also
Clothing and Personal Adornment

was the presumption of equality that rankled the most with Frances Trollope (1780–1863), who made herself very unpopular in America with the publication of her *Domestic Manners of the Americans* (1832). Mrs. Trollope experienced the friendliness of a Cincinnati neighbor as a "violent intimacy," and contact with members of the lower classes was infinitely uncomfortable. "I am very far from intending to advocate the system of slavery," she wrote. "I conceive it to be essentially wrong; but so far as my observation has extended, I think its influence is far less injurious to the manners and morals of the people than the fallacious ideas of equality, which are so fondly cherished by the working classes of the white population in America."

Some Americans rejected the European styles, as did a clergyman who argued that "we have already suffered much by too great an avidity for British customs and manners; it is now time to become independent in our maxims, principles of education, dress, and manners, as we are in our laws and government." Others made the point more directly, as did one Cincinnati lodging-house keeper, who turned Mrs. Trollope away because she did not want to take tea with the other lodgers. When she tried to apologize, explaining that she was not familiar with the manners of the country, he replied, "Our manners are very good manners, and we don't wish any changes from England." Still, travelers told tales of being fawned over by the members of local society, all of whom wanted reassurance that their manners, customs, furnishings, and entertainments matched those of Europe.

Foreign observers cast American etiquette as a drama of democracy, and to some extent it was. What was the proper role in a republic for a system of manners rooted in the chivalric tradition of European court life, of rules of behavior meant to maintain and reinforce hierarchy and fixed place? Formal systems of etiquette, however, did not decline in the face of democratic rhetoric and its limited reality. Instead, etiquette grew in importance as a means of control and a measure of stability in the often confusing and threatening urban-industrial-capitalist society that emerged in nineteenth-century America. An increasingly elaborate code of etiquette mediated the effects of the market economy and the relative mobility and anonymity felt keenly by our ancestors. This allowed newly useful boundaries to be drawn between the realms of public and private, and between people whose place was no longer fixed and whose status no longer secure.

Middle-Class Respectability

John Kasson, in his wonderful work *Rudeness and Civility*, argues that the redefinition of the term "genteel" in the nineteenth century "epitomizes enormous changes in economy and society," as the emerging urban-industrial-capitalist system replaced the rank-ordered society of colonial America. "Gentility," in colonial America, designated status; it referred to the well-born. By the 1830s, "genteel" referred to qualities of politeness and grace.

Central to the transformation of the concept of gentility—and to the crucial importance of etiquette in nineteenth-century American society—was the emergence of middle classes. As Kasson emphasizes, the emergence of the industrial-capitalist system did not create a more economically equal society, nor did it offer unlimited mobility. But the diminished importance of inherited rank, along with geographic mobility (especially the move to the rapidly growing cities), combined with the emerging system to offer new possibilities. The new economic system demanded new sorts of workers—clerks and managers, people who did a variety of white-collar work and who, no matter what the reality, defined themselves as upwardly mobile and who sought the trappings and manners of "respectability." While offering many the means to live in comfort, the new industrial-capitalist order left many in desperate poverty. It also created vast fortunes and intense jostling for social position, as money contested name for precedence.

In the ferment of change, all seemed possible. "It is not here, as in the old world," wrote one nineteenth-century adviser, "where one man is born with a silver spoon, and another with a pewter one, in his mouth. You may all have silver spoons, if you will." She was referring not solely to material wealth, but also to the outward signs of gentility. Any man might be a gentleman; any woman a lady. "You may be whatever you will resolve to be," exhorted yet another adviser.

In the flood of writing about society and manners, the "best society" was increasingly defined as middle class—and presented as attainable. "You have it in your power to fit yourselves by the cultivation of your minds, and the refinement of your manners, for intercourse, on equal terms, with the best society in the land," promised the influential writer Catharine Sedgwick (1789–1867). The manners that marked one as a gentleman or lady could be learned. One could master the rules and forms of etiquette and purchase the increasingly available accoutrements of gentility.

Manners require time, as nothing is more vulgar than haste.

RALPH WALDO EMERSON "BEHAVIOR," IN THE CONDUCT OF LIFE (1860)

M

MANNERS AND ETIQUETTE

Middle-Class Respectability

Manners are the happy way of doing things. . . . If they are superficial, so are the dewdrops which give such depth to the morning meadows.

RALPH WALDO EMERSON
THE CONDUCT OF LIFE

See also

Courtship, Marriage, Separation, and Divorce

The flood of etiquette and advice books that appeared in the nineteenth century offered entree to the world of respectable middle-class behavior. In the 1830s, because of major developments in the technologies of printing and book publishing, books, magazines, and newspapers became much more widely available and much less expensive than before. Etiquette and advice books occupied a prominent place in the offerings of nineteenth-century publishers. According to Arthur Meier Schlesinger, an average of three new etiquette manuals appeared each year between 1830 and the decade of the Civil War, and from the 1870s through World War I, five to six new manuals appeared annually. This staggering number does not include reprints and new editions. Etiquette books were sold by sales agents who went door to door and in direct-mail advertisements in magazines and newspapers. Some were massive and expensive—encyclopedic in form—and others were short and inexpensive "dime books," designed for a mass market. While the forms of etiquette developed in the cities, they were copied by "respectable" folk in small towns and villages throughout the country. The majority of these works were American in authorship and addressed to the middle classes, broadly defined.

These works were very much "how-to" in spirit—self-improvement books—frequently with a heavy dose of moral exhortation. Readers were told, in precise detail, how to sit, how to stand, how to receive a guest, and how to decorate a parlor. No detail was too small for attention: "The general positions for the arms are about the level of the waist, never hanging down or being quite stiff, but being gently bent, the elbow a little raised, the fingers not stretched out stiffly, but also a little bent, and partially separated, or the hands half crossed one over the other, or placed in each other, &c.," offered a volume titled *A Manual of Politeness, Comprising the Principles of Etiquette, and Rules of Behavior in Genteel Society, for Persons of Both Sexes* (1837).

The promise of social mobility and the availability of such helpful advice made gentility, in Kasson's words, "increasingly available as a social desire and a purchasable style and commodity." By the second quarter of the nineteenth century, gentility seemed not so much a product of birth as the result of striving, of solid middle-class effort.

A knowledge of etiquette, no matter how arcane and complex, could serve as a tool for advancement in society. According to the best advisers, the effort involved was considerable, but it paid off. The rituals of etiquette, once mastered,

were inclusive. They paved the way to an *attainable* middle-class gentility—and the phrase "middle-class gentility" did not seem contradictory. The importance of etiquette in the nineteenth century, in substantial measure, was a sign of the era's optimism. The rigors of etiquette were born of a sense of possibility.

But nineteenth-century American etiquette had mixed parentage: as it was inclusive, it also worked to exclude; as it grew from optimism, it was also an expression of profound social fears. Karen Halttunen, in her pathbreaking and sophisticated book *Confidence Men and Painted Women*, reads in nineteenth-century urban middle-class culture a "crisis of social identity faced by . . . men and women who were on the move both socially and geographically." As they aspired to gentility and to higher social status, they feared a world where other people were not what they seemed. Halttunen argues that such fears coalesced around the figures of the confidence man and the painted woman, hypocrites who "poisoned polite society with deception and betrayal by dressing extravagantly and practicing the empty forms of false etiquette."

In Victorian America, an etiquette of gentility came to be largely synonymous with an exceptional delicacy about matters physical or sexual. Frances Trollope wrote with disgust of American women's "ultra-refinement." Frederick Marryat, another traveler, claimed to have seen, in a seminary for young ladies, a piano with its legs—or limbs—covered by "modest little trousers, with frills at the bottom of them!" Hiram Powers's (1805–1873) statue *The Greek Slave* was dressed in calico blouse and flannel trousers for its exhibit in Cincinnati. Etiquette books advised ladies to avoid questions in polite conversation, for questions might lead to embarrassing subjects. One adviser rather breathlessly told of a lady who inquired of a gentleman what sort of medicine he practiced, only to discover that he was a doctor of "midwifery." This pretentious delicacy is comical in retrospect, but it is important to understand that, as Christopher Mulvey explains in *Transatlantic Manners*, this behavior was meant to demonstrate social status and good breeding as much as or more than to manifest an essential prudery. Refinement was the essential characteristic of respectability.

The formal dinner party was perhaps the greatest test—though of course one had to have passed as "acceptable" in order to be invited. While in the early nineteenth century Americans commonly ate with a two-prong iron or steel fork

THE LAWS OF ETIQUETTE

A "Polite Fiction"

Advice and etiquette books stressed sincerity as the heart of etiquette, insisting that the empty forms were meaningless—even destructive—but nonetheless furnishing detailed instructions on how to comply with those very forms. This paradox, Halttunen argues, was resolved through what she calls a "genteel performance," in which the complexities of etiquette were navigated and performed in a "sincere" manner. The genteel performance was a "polite fiction," presenting "the courtesy of those ladies and gentlemen who adhered to the hundreds of rules governing parlor conduct" as the result of "right feelings and not . . . of the painstaking study of etiquette manuals."

The fiction was fragile; its existence depended upon the collusion of those who participated. Thus its existence depended upon exclusion. Those who threatened the magic of the performance by recognizing it as performance must be excluded. Those who were insufficiently genteel to play their proper roles must be excluded. While a plethora of manuals told people how to be genteel—how to pass—many of the rules they were mastering detailed the art of "polite" exclusion. As Charles William Day's *Hints on Etiquette and the Usages of Society* (1844) explained:

> *Etiquette is a barrier which society draws around itself as a protection against offences the "law" cannot touch; it is a shield against the intrusion of the impertinent, the improper, and the vulgar,—a guard against those obtuse persons who, having neither talent nor delicacy, would be continually thrusting themselves into the society of men to whom their presence might (from the difference of feeling and habit) be offensive,*

and even insupportable. (Halttunen, pp. 111–112)

The laws of etiquette provided a series of tests, or measures, of social acceptability. That someone could observe all the complex rules of etiquette and do so "sincerely," seemingly without effort, seemed to be a guarantee of "breeding" or, more accurately, class background, in a society that was both socially and geographically mobile.

EMILY POST (1872–1960)

Well-known American etiquette columnist, whose first book was Etiquette in Society, in Business, in Politics, and at Home. LIBRARY OF CONGRESS / CORBIS

and a knife, using the rounded blade of the knife to carry food into one's mouth, by the 1830s eating had become a much more complicated business. In the 1830s, Andrew Jackson's White House dinners offered guests a choice of two forks, one silver, one steel. By the 1880s, successful silverware companies like Reed and Barton offered tableware in many patterns—most of which included specialized serving pieces, and up to ten different kinds of knives; twelve different kinds of forks (including those intended specifically for terrapin, for mango, for oyster, and for ice cream);

and twenty different kinds of spoons. Knowing which fork to use was not so easy, and making one's way through a formal dinner with no breach of etiquette was a formidable task. Washington society commonly noted which new congressmen from the provinces attempted to eat the doilies, and it was said that President Lincoln, when asked by a waiter at his first state dinner whether he would have white wine or red, replied, "I don't know. Which would you?"

"Calling" was the central act of the "genteel performance," and worked most directly to dem-

*Nothing more
rapidly inclines a
person to go into a
monastery than
reading a book on
etiquette. There are
so many trivial ways
in which to commit
some social sin.*

QUENTIN CRISP

onstrate social status and to test and reinforce social boundaries. The ritual of calling was controlled by women, who played important roles in advancing families' social status. Most middle- and upper-class women designated a specific day "at home" for receiving callers. Callers presented calling cards to the maid who answered the door, indicating their intentions by the ways the cards were folded. By bending the right-hand corner of the card, one indicated that he or she was only paying respects and did not ask to be received; by bending the whole right-hand side of the card, one asked to be received. The upper left-hand corner, when bent, signaled "congratulations," the lower left-hand corner "condolences." Gender played a role: a man was not to call on a woman without her express invitation. Thus young women had the sole right of initiative in courtship—for it was deemed most important that women be able to exclude unwanted attentions and unsuitable admirers.

Those seeking to be received were either ushered into the parlor or told that the lady of the house was "not at home." This might or might not be strictly true: she might not be receiving that day—or she might be signaling the social unacceptability of the caller. Etiquette books advised their readers to keep strict account of their calls—of whether or not calls were returned, of where they were received and where turned away. Such an accounting offered a clear statement of one's social status (or, in appropriate cases, one's romantic prospects). With characteristic overstatement, the influential writer Mrs. Sherwood (Mary Elizabeth Sherwood, 1826–1903) explained the importance of the calling system in nineteenth-century America: "The [calling] card may well be noted as belonging only to a high order of development. No monkey, no 'missing link,' no Zulu, no savage, carries a card. It is the tool of civilization, its 'field-mark and device.'"

Part of the exclusionary nature of the system stemmed from the competitive struggle for social status. The middling classes meant to demonstrate respectability, but also to advance socially just as they advanced economically. At the same time, those in the upper reaches of society enacted a more stringent form of exclusivity. Caroline Astor, with her aide Ward McAllister, worked to hold the line of society against the claims of the nouveaux riches who flooded New York in the last half of the nineteenth century. Ward McAllister coined the term, "The Four Hundred," in trying to explain why only four hundred were invited to Mrs. Astor's annual Patriarch's Ball (the real rea-

son was space limitation). "There are only about four hundred people in fashionable New York Society," he explained. "If you go outside that number you strike people who are not at ease in a ballroom or else make other people not at ease." Mrs. Astor's invitations determined who belonged to "society," and her insistence on proper form and ritual structured her particular brand of social exclusivity. Still, by the end of the century younger social leaders like Mrs. Stuyvesant Fish and her aide Harry Lehr mocked the strict forms of society, giving dinners that they called "vaudevilles" and that Mrs. Astor publicly called "undignified."

All this genteelly couched jostling for social position lay at the heart of Victorian etiquette. But at the less genteel gut of the system was a great sense of vulnerability. The genteel performance was enacted in controlled spaces—in middle-class parlors with doors kept by maids, in private dinners and balls and parties to which no one came without invitation. This protected world existed in tension with the new world of the industrial city, a city larger, more anonymous, more frightening than before. Money served to cushion existence; those who could afford it kept carriages and drivers, attempting to stretch the boundaries of the private to the public world. But the experience of walking down a city street, subject to the stares of strangers, the importunities of the ill bred, the insults of the common, the dirt and disorder and chaos—all contributed to the importance of etiquette as a system that stressed strict control of one's own body and emotions and of physical space, in an assertion of the importance of privacy and an emphasis on the ability to exclude the unsuitable.

Of course, the "unsuitable" had their own systems of etiquette. Immigrant groups carried the manners of their old countries, and though no etiquette manual seems directly addressed to immigrants, much of the material that was aimed at Americanization or assimilation dealt with points that might well be described as etiquette. And in the foreign language press, leaders and writers such as Abraham Cahan (1860–1951) of the Yiddish paper, the *Jewish Daily Forward*, spoke of the significance of manners and mores. Black leaders advised others of their race on matters of character and etiquette, most notably in a manual called *The Negro in Etiquette: A Novelty* (1899). But while all African Americans were lumped together in common disdain by most whites, blacks were divided by class, by skin color, and by place of origin. Black society, epitomized in the late nineteenth century by the Society of the Sons of

See also
Nightlife

New York, guarded its gates against newcomers as carefully as did the originators of the Patriarch's Ball.

While the etiquette of Victorian America seems extremely rigid, changes in social organization continued to strain established forms. New technologies were often the impetus for change in social form. The telephone, for example, fit uneasily into the pattern of calling (the telephone was patented in 1876, and by 1900 approximately 1.5 million were in use in the United States). Advisers agreed that it was a greater assertion of intimacy to telephone than to arrive at the door and present a calling card. If "on a certain footing of intimacy," one explained in 1907, a man might telephone the lady of the house to see if it were all right to call that evening. Eventually, of course, the hierarchy of intimacy would reverse.

The automobile also would present new difficulties as the old system of etiquette tottered. Virginia Scharff argues in *Taking the Wheel* that "the cultural gap between social status and control of technology" caused great concern for the owners of the new machines. Men who drove their own automobiles were cautioned to differentiate themselves from professional drivers (chauffeurs) through dress and manner. Some worried about

WOMEN IN THE WORKPLACE
New Challenges in Etiquette

The new technologies of American business also began to transform social etiquette. Typewriters, for example, introduced in the late 1800s, brought a flood of respectable young women into business offices. Women who typed were dubbed "typewriters" after the machines they operated. This label gave rise to the predictable joke ("Here I sit, my typewriter on my knee"), but the increasing presence of women in business complicated other traditional forms. What degree of deference based on gender did an employer owe a secretary? Did the forms of polite society transfer to business relations between the sexes? As more and more "respectable" women entered the public world, attending college, working in offices or stores, moving unchaperoned in public, the existing lines between men and women, public and private, genteel and unacceptable, were necessarily redrawn.

the amount of power and control vested in a chauffeur, especially when his passenger was a woman. (In French slang, the phrase *chauffer une femme* meant "to make hot love to a woman.") But at the same time, the automobile promised women privacy and protection from unwanted intrusions. The Detroit Electric Car was advertised so: "To the well-bred woman—the Detroit Electric has a particular appeal. In it she can preserve her toilet immaculate, her coiffure intact. She can drive it with all desired privacy, yet safely—in constant touch with traffic conditions around her."

The etiquette of gentility broke down as the entire Victorian worldview, with its insistence on the absolute polarities of civilization and savagery, of good and evil, of men and women, began to crumble. More and more of those who came of age in the late nineteenth century felt stifled by the weight of gentility and the rigidness of form—some rebelling in profound ways and with profound results, others frivolously. But to a great extent, the breakdown of Victorian etiquette and the genteel performance came through those who were not afraid of the city, who found the intense *publicness* of the private world—attending dances with the same people, conducting polite conversations in genteelly appointed parlors—suffocating. They sought the privacy that the public world of the city offered in its anonymity. They sought the excitement of mixing with people of different conditions and backgrounds. And they sought a form of sexual freedom in the companionship of the opposite sex, exploring the new cabarets and restaurants, escaping into the world of the city that had so terrified their parents.

The Etiquette of Gender

If the etiquette of the nineteenth century centered on issues of class, the etiquette of the twentieth century coalesced on issues of sex and gender. The problem of defining relations between the sexes had, in many ways, replaced the problem of defining relations between the classes. Gender etiquette offered a means of controlling the relationships between men and women and of reinforcing the "natural" barriers between the sexes that seemed increasingly under siege in the twentieth century.

We see the shift from class to gender etiquette in the rise of the dating system and the elaboration of dating etiquette in the twentieth century. The calling system, as it operated in courtship, still centered upon class. As an invitation to call was an invitation into one's home, the calling system granted women and their parents the right of

I don't mind if you don't like my manners. I don't like them myself.

HUMPHREY BOGART

The English are polite by telling lies. The Americans are polite by telling the truth.

MALCOLM BRADBURY

♦ **Necking**

Engaging in amorous kissing and caressing

initiative, thus allowing them to screen out the unsuitable suitor. Dating transferred initiative to men and shifted the focus of etiquette from the barriers between classes as demonstrated in genteel performance to the roles of the sexes and the importance of gender politics.

The practice of dating originated in American cities in the last decade of the nineteenth century as young people of the working classes, pushed out of overcrowded tenement apartments and drawn to the new urban amusements that catered to them, took flirtations and courtship into the public realm. Their term "date" (which had referred to the temporal liaison with a prostitute) indicated the centrality of money in the relationship: the man paid for entertainment and the woman owed him something in return—flirtatious gaiety, quiet admiration, some degree of sexual intimacy. The practice of dating was taken up, in modified form, by the fast set of "society" youth who were drawn to the possibilities of the city, and filtered its way into middle-class conventionality by the mid-1910s to 1920s.

The new custom was confusing, as dating and calling coexisted for some years. A joke from the 1920s told of the young man who went to call on a young woman of his acquaintance only to find that "she had her hat on." The hat signaled that she expected to go out, and so he took her out, spending his scarce savings on their entertainment. Advisers in mass circulation magazines, such as Mrs. Burton Kingsland, who wrote the column "Good Manners and Good Form" for the *Ladies' Home Journal* in the early years of the twentieth century, attempted to make sense of the new system. The date, these advisers concurred, was an invitation into the man's world. The man was responsible for the expense, and thus claimed the right of initiative: only the man could ask for a date. The system of dating etiquette, as it developed, coalesced on the basic fact of men's money.

Whereas nineteenth-century manuals specified rules of chaperonage or simply assumed them, twentieth-century advisers more and more often discussed the etiquette of sexual relationships. In the 1930s, *Parents* magazine advised parents to deal with the issue of "petting" "dispassionately as being much more a matter of etiquette than of morals." A popular 1930s etiquette book for college women, *Coediquette*, offered information about how a girl should "conduct herself at a football game" and behave at a "rush tea." But the author's credentials were telling: traveling to forty-three universities, she had "dated college men and learned to know them

by their lines." Another work linking etiquette and sex, Nina Farewell's *The Unfair Sex* (1953), begins, "Ever since the author's eighteenth birthday, when she surrendered her virginity because she was afraid to seem rude, she has felt a crying need for a handbook for girls—a manual on How to Cope with Men." Others offered very specific information about the etiquette of necking and petting: "for gallantry's sake a man is not in a position to withdraw from petting even should he very much want to," one adviser insisted. Women, according to the laws of etiquette and of nature, were to be the limit setters. Advisers differed in the etiquette of limit-setting: "Dear Abby," in the 1960s article "Blue Jean Biology," suggests a "stereophonic slap" to discourage a "mad lover"; a 1940s advice book suggested "excusing yourself from the room in a flustered way to adjust your hair with a 'Gracious, how I must look!' manner."

While etiquette played a role in the control of nonmarital sex, it was perhaps most important as it came to define qualities of masculinity and femininity. "Good etiquette, for a man, is whatever makes a woman feel more like a woman, without making her feel weakminded. . . . Good etiquette, for a woman, is whatever makes a man feel more like a man, without making him feel more harassed and put upon than he normally does anyway," explained Peg Bracken in *I Try to Behave Myself* (1959). It was the barriers between the sexes that seemed most beleaguered by midcentury, and scholarly journals and popular magazines alike were full of analyses of the problems of masculinity and femininity, both allegedly under threat of extinction in modern society. Masculinity and femininity seemed not things inherent, securely linked to one's physical sex, but a set of attributes to be achieved—largely through observing an elaborated and overelaborated gender etiquette.

Advice books, especially those for teenagers and young adults in the postwar years, were full of specific prescriptions, all pointing to the same end. Women, the system of rules made clear, were constantly to demonstrate their submission and need for protection, avoiding acts that they could perform perfectly well (like opening doors or ordering from menus) but that became "aggressive" and "competitive" in the company of a man. Men were to demonstrate control and dominance. As *Esquire Etiquette* declared in 1953: "When she's with you, etiquette renders her helpless. You're It." Not all young people, boys especially, conformed to the rules of etiquette—often much to the disappointment of teenage girls, who expected the conventionalized "perfect" date. But the newly developed teen magazines of the postwar years stressed etiquette (sometimes conflating it with "personality"), and teen advice books for girls spent a good deal of time offering strategies for "subtly" teaching their escorts proper behavior. A 1954 high school etiquette text reminded readers that the boy or man should walk on the outside, closest to the street. "Don't ignore the situation." If he walks on the inside, this book advised girls, "slip around" at the first opportunity.

The etiquette of masculinity and femininity did provide a comfortable script (in that the rules were clear) for a society in which dating was a central ritual that brought together strangers in a fairly intimate situation. The rules of etiquette offered protection, smoothing awkward encounters on those nights better spent washing one's hair, and turning others into the fairy tale stuff of teen magazines. But the etiquette of masculinity and femininity had greater significance than these uses suggest. It was born of deep-seated fears about changing relations between the sexes and served to reject—at least in the "private" world of romantic relationships—women's claims to greater roles in the public world. The etiquette of

masculinity and femininity expressed social fears every bit as profound and conservative as the class-based fears that structured the genteel performance of the nineteenth century.

The shift from class to gender in the new etiquette books of the twentieth century does not mean that class lost all importance in American etiquette. The small points of etiquette still serve as signs of "breeding" and background and are easily read by those who seek to exclude others. But as Emily Post discovered from the response to her first etiquette book, published in 1922 under the unwieldy title *Etiquette in Society, in Business, in Politics, and at Home*, her readers were not interested in climbing the social ladder to challenge the ascendancy of the "Worldlys" and the "Well-borns." They were interested in more modest social mobility; they wanted not advice on the protocol of exclusive gentlemen's clubs and entertaining with a staff of twelve, but instead information about the rituals of middle-class inclusiveness—the luncheons and showers and dinners and weddings they intended to invest with grace and propriety.

There was still the threat of exclusion, and advertising played on fears of insufficiency. An ad-

MANNERS AND ETIQUETTE

The Etiquette of Gender

A NIGHT OUT

The practice of dating was taken up by the fast set of "society" youth of the city and filtered down to middle-class conventionality by the 1920s.
CORBIS-BETTMANN

Relatively informal and comfortable clothing was permitted until dinner, but genteel folk dressed formally for the afternoon.

PAGE 72

vertisement for Doubleday's *Book of Etiquette* read: "Again She Orders—'A Chicken Salad, Please!'" (thus betraying to her date that she could not pronounce the French words that filled the menu). Many a suburban housewife pored over books of etiquette for the table setting that would convince her husband's boss that he had the right social stuff for a promotion. But much writing on etiquette, especially in the post–World War II era, aggressively assumed that America was a middle-class nation, and that all were subject to the same middle-class rules. And the new media taught etiquette in more pervasive fashion than etiquette manuals ever did: advertisements pictured the good life (and justified hiring female "admen" to make sure the ads showed correct table settings, for example); television shows like *Leave It to Beaver* portrayed the polite middle-class family dinner for all to watch and learn.

This middle-class inclusivity masked real barriers in American society, the most obvious, of course, being predicated on race. But the rhetoric of cultural inclusivity through participation in a common middle-class culture was strong, and the forms of etiquette were tightly bound up with this comforting vision. Thus when cultural rebels in the 1960s attacked the forms of politeness and civility, they had found a good target, partly because the etiquette of gender had become increasingly overelaborated and stifling. Proper etiquette also embodied a respect for authority that necessarily supported the status quo. Some of the prevailing forms of etiquette were tightly bound up with inequality, and some people violated these norms in attempts to create a more democratic society. Others simply rebelled against what they described as "uptight" behavior. However, to cultural conservatives, these attacks on civility seemed to be attacks on civilization itself.

The forms of etiquette have changed drastically in the past half-century. But despite the rejection of much of what passed for polite behavior in earlier decades, Americans have not abandoned the rules of etiquette. Society does require rules or codes, be they informal or formal, for its continued functioning, and many people seek some method of smoothing the travails of social interaction. The enormous popularity of Judith Martin, who writes as "Miss Manners" in a column syndicated in over three hundred newspapers and whose book *Miss Manners' Guide to Excruciatingly Correct Behavior* (1982) has become a classic, witnesses contemporary ambivalence about etiquette. Her authority lies in irony and wit, and while she may refer to "Dear Queen Victoria" her voice and her advice are firmly rooted in the late twentieth century. And, most importantly, her advice is taken seriously.

Prescriptive literature as a serious genre is three decades out of favor in America. But as Miss Manners's surprising success shows, a filter of irony can ease the rigors of etiquette into the modern age. Perhaps even more indicative of the advent of a new system of etiquette in the 1990s is the rise, most notably on college campuses, of whole new codes of civility, codes that are most directly concerned with race, gender, and sexual preference, and that are hotly debated. These codes take up many of the thorny problems of etiquette—the problems that underlie many of our historical systems of etiquette—and this time recognize the problems as political.

—BETH BAILEY

See also
Sexual Behavior and Morality

NATIONAL PARKS
AND PRESERVATION

Contrary to popular understanding, the national parks of the United States do not exist solely to protect tracts of wild, unspoiled nature like Yellowstone and the Grand Canyon. While preservation of nature was an important historical reason for their establishment, national parks preserve not only wilderness areas but also significant cultural landscapes and historic sites, like industrial structures in Lowell, Massachusetts. These twin purposes—preservation of nature and conservation of heritage—have shaped the evolution of the idea of the national parks.

Originating in a nineteenth-century quest for a distinct American identity, the idea of national parks was transformed by twentieth-century interest in the country's ecological and cultural heritage. Initially, the national parks were designed to afford legal protection to areas considered significant for their scenic, patriotic, or recreational value. Recently, calculations about the utility of parks only to people have been supplemented by biocentric considerations of a park's contribution to ecological stability and continuity. Increasingly, national parks in the United States are seen as biological preserves and heritage landscapes as much as scenic playgrounds.

The Shifting Philosophy of Preservation

No grand design guided the growth of the national park system. It developed as a random collection of natural, historical, and recreational properties, and the American philosophy of preservation evolved similarly, in fits and starts.

The haphazard origins of the park idea are illustrated by the ambiguity of identifying the first national park in the United States. While Yellowstone National Park (1872) is usually accorded the distinction, federal action had previously established two other natural reserves. As early as 1832, the national government had set aside an Arkansas hot spring as a "reservation," chiefly for its medicinal value. And, in 1864, Congress ceded the Yosemite Valley and the nearby Mariposa

Grove of giant redwoods to the state of California for permanent management as a state park, a public assertion of a national interest in scenic preservation.

In its original usage, the designation "national park" resulted from bureaucratic convenience rather than a federal commitment to nature preservation. The term was first applied to the Yellowstone reserve created in the territories of Wyoming and Montana in 1872. Since no state government existed to which park administration might he shifted, as in the case of the Yosemite cession, responsibility devolved to the federal government for the preserve it carved from the territorial public domain. The burden was assumed rather grudgingly. At first no federal funds were allocated to administer the new national park, and, for its first forty-four years, the preserve was managed by the United States Army, until the National Park Service was created within the Department of the Interior in 1916.

Many people believe that national parks were created to protect wilderness. While this motive is a common rationale for national parks today, it was by no means the initial—and certainly not the only—reason for the American interest in nature preserves. Nationalistic pride, a new landscape aesthetic, the conservation movement, a recreational revolution, and ecological perspectives all shaped the evolving philosophy of nature protection. Preservation of historic and cultural resources followed a related but distinct route into the national parks.

PATRIOTISM AND AMERICAN IDENTITY.
The impetus for national parks was rooted in the preoccupation of nineteenth-century Americans with their cultural identity as a nation. Originating shortly after the Revolution among intellectual and social elites, the search to define national distinctiveness became an exercise in patriotic virtue in the course of the century. To those drawing transatlantic comparisons, the United States lacked the traditional monuments of high culture from which European societies derived a sense of collective identity and history. But under the influence of European romanticism and American transcendentalism, cultural critics proclaimed

Pursuing as their most central objective the preservation or restoration of wilderness and various fragile ecosystems, the leaders of the environmental movement have gained much popular support.

PAGE 259

N

NATIONAL PARKS AND PRESERVATION

The Shifting Philosophy of Preservation

Men as a general rule have very little reverence for trees.

ELIZABETH CADY STANTON
DIARY ENTRY (1900)

A tree is a tree—how many do you need to look at?

RONALD REAGAN
SPEECH (1965)

natural scenery a source of American uniqueness and therefore pride. The timelessness of nature's monuments might compensate for the absence of civilization's antiquities.

As war and diplomacy extended the national boundaries to the Pacific by midcentury, curiosity about the rugged geography of the Far West became a potent incentive for nature preservation. The dramatic topography of the Sierra Nevada and the Rockies fired the popular imagination. Thus, when Congress debated the Yosemite cession and the Yellowstone reserve in the 1860s and 1870s, interest focused on scenic marvels like the majestic drop of Yosemite's waterfalls and the thermal novelty of Yellowstone's geysers. Congressional proponents (and their railroad allies, anxious to stimulate tourist interest in the West) argued that such "natural curiosities" were national treasures to be protected for public enjoyment. Significantly, in terms of the development of a philosophy of preservation, the scenic—not the wild—qualities of the landscape were identified as worthy of national recognition.

The public domain of the West provided the means, as well as the inspiration, for the American invention of the national park. The sheer size of the public lands made possible nature preserves of remarkable scale, two million acres in the case of Yellowstone. Well into the twentieth century, the creation of a national park could involve a transfer of land from one federal agency to another, rather than an expensive real estate purchase.

Outside the West, the absence of public lands retarded establishment of national parks, and, as a result, private philanthropy played a crucial role in the authorization of the first national parks in the East and the South. The first eastern park, Acadia on Maine's Mount Desert Island, was not established until 1919 and was a gift from wealthy summer residents of the Bar Harbor area. In the South, Great Smoky Mountains and Shenandoah parks were both authorized in 1926 and established in the 1930s. At Acadia, Great Smoky, and Shenandoah, the philanthropy of John D. Rockefeller, Jr. (1874—1960), augmented the campaigns for public subscriptions. Rockefeller continued to underwrite public (and even federal) efforts at park creation through the 1950s.

Curiosity and pride in the scenic and geological wonders of North America have provided the most consistent rationale for nature preservation in the United States. The appeal of visually spectacular topography animated the earliest proponents of the national park idea, and it has continued to inspire Americans to set aside mountain peaks like Hawaii Volcanoes (1916) and North Cascades (1968), gorges like Zion (1909) and Canyonlands (1964), and surrealistic landforms like Bryce Canyon (1923) and Badlands National Monument (1929).

A TASTE FOR WILDNESS. In the circumstances surrounding the creation of Yosemite National Park (1890), a new and powerful rationale for preservation emerged: the idea that wilderness itself was useful and therefore worth protecting. As much as anyone in his generation, the California naturalist John Muir (1838–1914) encouraged Americans to identify wild nature as a complement to civilization. Like transcendentalists earlier in the century, Muir found contact with nature rejuvenating to the body and enlightening for the soul. In contrast to most transcendentalist writing, however, Muir's nature essays were bestsellers. A "back to nature" impulse had seized many middle-class Americans by the turn of the century. The panoramic landscapes painted by Albert Bierstadt (1830—1902) and Thomas Moran (1837—1926) of the Rocky Mountain school, the new art of landscape photography pioneered by William Henry Jackson (1843—1942) and Carleton Watkins (1829—1916), and sundry works of exploration and nature fiction by John Wesley Powell (1834—1902) and Ernest Thompson Seton (1860—1946), among others, all testified to the discovery of wild nature in American popular culture.

Those who expressed enthusiasm for wildness did not face it from the perspective of the homesteader or lumberjack. They were people who could visit it voluntarily and temporarily and did not have to make a living there. As much as anything, it was the ability to contemplate wild nature from the safety and comfort of the city that diluted traditional animosities about wilderness. Rather than the antithesis of civilization and progress, raw nature became an antidote and complement to modern life. The taste for wildness was also rooted temporally, in nostalgia. The celebration of wild nature occurred as Americans contemplated the closing of the frontier, a historical and geographical boundary that many, including the historian Frederick Jackson Turner, had come to associate with the formation of the national character. Through nostalgic mists, preservation of the disappearing wilderness seemed to promise a living link with the pioneer past.

These emerging sensibilities offered receptive ground for John Muir's appeals for wilderness preservation. In 1890 Muir published a series of articles in *Century* magazine that urged protection of the Sierra Nevada high country beyond the previously reserved Yosemite Valley. The Yosemite National Park created in 1890 at Muir's urging was not the first national park in the country, nor even the first park in the Yosemite region, but it was the first park consciously designed to protect wilderness as a valuable quality in its own right.

In the late twentieth century, the Yosemite precedent culminated in three pieces of landmark legislation: the Wilderness Act (1964), which sought to protect undeveloped and roadless regions throughout the public domain; the Wild and Scenic Rivers Act (1968), which established a national system of free-flowing rivers; and the Alaska National Interest Lands Conservation Act (1980), which set aside 104 million acres of the Alaskan wilderness. The Alaska lands act alone doubled the size of the national park system and illustrated how preservation of wilderness had become an American priority by the eve of the centennial of Yosemite National Park.

THE CONSERVATION MOVEMENT. A major misconception about national parks is that they enjoy protection "forever"; in fact, the boundaries, acreage, and uses of national parks are transitory. This quality of impermanence is a legacy of the turn-of-the-century conservation movement and its utilitarian approach to natural resources.

The distinction between national parks and national forests is an important difference that illuminates much about the place of national parks within the history of conservation. While both are federal reserves, each is rooted in a separate resource philosophy: preservation of unaltered nature in the case of national parks, use of natural resources in the case of national forests. Unlike national parks, with their emphasis on outdoor recreation, national forests are "lands of many uses" that permit lumbering, mining, reclamation, and grazing, as well as recreation (including hunting, which is prohibited in national parks).

For turn-of-the-century conservationists like Theodore Roosevelt and his chief forester, Gifford Pinchot, national forests embodied the best of the utilitarian conservation idea: wise management of the public domain through the planned and efficient development of natural resources. Utilitarians operated within a materialist framework that viewed nature as a collection of commodities useful in production. While preservationists like John Muir spoke of forests as cathedrals where people went for spiritual insight and refreshment, utilitarians like Gifford Pinchot

(1865—1946) regarded forests as factories that should produce lumber in an efficient and rational manner.

The national parks have been a bureaucratic entity separate from the national forests for some time, but the utilitarian doctrine nevertheless affected the politics of parks by tempering the tendency to absolute preservation. To meet the argument that productive land should not be locked up, advocates of national parks have been obliged to point out the economic marginality of the lands they sought to preserve. The complex compromises that preceded establishment of parks reflected this utilitarian perspective. Resource development clauses have been routinely inserted in the enabling legislation of major national parks to permit activities like mining, reclamation, forestry, grazing, railroads, or settlement, should it eventually be decided that such land use was in the national interest.

Perhaps the most celebrated instance of society redefining parklands occurred in 1913, when the federal government authorized a dam and reservoir in the Hetch Hetchy Valley of Yosemite National Park. Similar controversies have occurred in other parks in subsequent decades, as in a proposal in the 1960s to permit a reservoir to flood the Colorado River in the Grand Canyon. Despite the widespread public impression, preservation of nature in the United States has seldom represented permanent protection, even in the national parks.

CIVILIZATION COMPLEMENT

The naturalist John Muir (1838–1914) encouraged Americans to identify wild nature as a complement to civilization. This photograph shows Muir with conservationist Theodore Roosevelt at Yosemite National Park.
CORBIS-BETTMANN

See also
The Frontier

*In the first half of
the nineteenth
century, the United
States government
pursued an
aggressive policy
of territorial
expansion,
acquiring huge
tracts of land by
both peaceful and
violent means.*

PAGE 193

OUTDOOR RECREATION AND AFFLUENCE.
Closely tied to the nation's conservation battles and the emergence of a wilderness aesthetic were social changes that linked outdoor recreation with the good life. By the 1920s the growth in real wages, the invention of the annual vacation, and broadening automobile ownership permitted the middle class to appropriate the national parks. Heeding Theodore Roosevelt's exhortations about the utility of "the strenuous life" in an over-civilized world, hardy urbanites formed mountaineering groups, adventuresome youth joined the Boy Scouts, and countless others embraced the pleasures of tenting and automobile tourism.

The national parks themselves changed to accommodate the growing numbers of hikers, campers, and tourists. Initially nature tourism was the prerogative of the few, the rich, and the well-born, who traveled to stylish railroad hotels near the most notable scenic wonders. In contrast, middle-class visitors, who arrived in national parks by car, wanted good roads and convenient campgrounds.

The task of recreational development fell to the National Park Service. The Park Service had been created in 1916 to provide for the public in the parks, while also conserving the scenery. Some of the wild rawness of parks disappeared, as the Park Service fashioned highways and trails to provide safe and democratic access, erected interpretive facilities to educate and inform city folk, and built accommodations to feed and house the millions who eventually made the pilgrimage to parks each summer. In time, popular demands introduced tourist villages, complete with carnival amusements like bear feedings and the night illumination of scenic wonders.

While it has become commonplace today to point out that recreational development in parks has triumphed over sound biological management, it is important to remember that visitors provided a base of popular support and an economic rationale for the nascent national park system. The first director of the National Park Service, the influential Stephen Tyng Mather (1867—1930), was an enthusiastic advocate of mass recreation who worked assiduously to promote visitation and to cultivate a constituency for parks. When permission for automobiles to enter parks stirred debate in the 1910s and 1920s, Mather endorsed their use because cars got people to the parks and the entrance fees provided a source of government revenue. To accommodate wide-ranging public tastes, Mather encouraged private concessionaires to build hotels, stores, and

transportation systems, as he championed the growth of a western tourist industry. The visitor, the automobile, and the concessionaire were democratizing forces that opened the national parks as never before.

But this legacy has been problematic. The modern paradox that Americans are loving the national parks to death reflects both the popularity of outdoor recreation in an affluent society and the institutional reluctance of the Park Service to ignore popular demands. The dilemma became especially acute following a period of recreational expansion in the 1950s and 1960s. Postwar affluence and population growth intensified demographic pressures on parks, and the Park Service responded with its traditional policy of accommodation, in the form of a massive ten-year construction program known as Mission 66. Completed in 1966 to mark the fiftieth anniversary of the National Park Service, the project attracted criticism for its enormous budgets, recreational overdevelopment, and even its abandonment of the rustic style popularized in park architecture by the Civilian Conservation Corps in the 1930s. By the 1970s and 1980s, many environmentalist critics had become convinced that parks-built-for-visitors threatened to uproot and replace parks-built-by-nature.

CULTURAL PRESERVATION. Protection of unaltered nature was not the only form of preservation associated with the national parks. Heritage conservation—the preservation of historic and cultural resources—has been a responsibility of the national park system since the turn of the century. Today the role of the National Park Service in the field of historic preservation has broadened to include not only stewardship of the built environment of national parks but also administration of federal heritage programs unrelated to the parks, such as the National Register of Historic Places.

Federal involvement in cultural preservation evolved reluctantly, stimulated initially by patriotic pride and misgivings about vandalism on the public domain. In the 1890s, in response to pressure from veterans' groups, the War Department began efforts to set aside commemorative landscapes like Civil War battlefields and military cemeteries. Only slightly earlier, in 1889, Congress had authorized protection of a site in Arizona to protect its prehistoric ruins from looters.

Systematic federal protection of historic sites, though, began with passage of the Antiquities Act (1906) and establishment of Mesa Verde National Park (1906). As with the campaign on behalf of

ECOLOGICAL PERSPECTIVES

Preserving Biological Environments

The authorization of Everglades National Park in 1934 marked an important turning point in the history of the national parks. In the Florida Everglades, a national park was created primarily for reasons of biological preservation, to protect the wildlife and vegetation of a forty-mile-wide "river of grass." Habitat and animate scenery, rather than the physical endowments of visually striking landscapes, provided the pretext for preservation. Although land acquisition was slow in the new park and its borders never encompassed the entire watershed, Everglades suggested a fresh attitude toward nature preservation.

The idea of establishing national parks to protect ecological systems for their own sake has gained considerable currency in recent years. In debates over the future of the public lands of Alaska in the 1970s, for example, advocates of wilderness preserves argued that the proposed parks should have biological integrity. They lobbied for scientifically meaningful boundaries that would enclose whole watersheds and entire animal migration routes. The ecological perspective is also evident in discussions to reserve natural systems illustrative of all North American life zones. The prairies and plains of mid America, for instance, are preserved nowhere in the national park system. That "representative" areas should be considered for national parks testifies to how far the philosophy of nature preservation has moved since nineteenth-century proponents made their case on the distinctive scenic qualities of Yosemite and Yellowstone.

Within existing parks, biocentric management has also attracted attention. As early as the 1930s biologists began pointing out that public recreation was compromising the protection of park wildlife, but the so-called Leopold Report of 1963 stirred the most discussion. The report urged a fundamental shift in thinking about parks, from a preoccupation with inanimate resources (like scenic vistas) to a program of managing ecological processes (through a proposal to restore the pre-European biology of major national parks). No such sweeping commitment was subsequently made to turn back the clock on four hundred years of environmental change, but incremental efforts at ecological restoration are evident in projects to reintroduce native species, as well as the current view of forest fires as a benign natural phenomenon that should not be suppressed in national parks. In these ways, the philosophy of preservation has been recently interpreted as a mandate for restoration.

Yellowstone in the 1870s, the immediate stimulus for federal action was concern about private appropriation of what was seen as a valuable national treasure, in this case the recently discovered cliff dwellings and artifacts of precontact Indian societies in the Southwest. The Antiquities Act prohibited destruction of historic and prehistoric objects on the public lands and authorized the president to preserve archaeological, historic, and scientific sites as national monuments. By 1933, when a number of federal preserves were consolidated under the jurisdiction of the National Park Service, the historic properties in the national park system were largely commemorative sites associated with great deeds and famous men: revolutionary war and Civil War battlefields, military cemeteries and forts, presidential birthplaces, and memorials like Ford's Theatre and the Washington Monument.

Depression in the 1930s moved the federal government more vigorously into the field of historic preservation. New Deal legislation envisioned a significant federal responsibility for protecting the country's architectural heritage and authorized a number of labor-intensive projects to carry out this enlarged role. Through the Historic American Buildings Survey, for example, one thousand unemployed architects were hired for a nationwide inventory of vernacular and elite buildings. Similarly, the Civilian Conservation Corps employed hundreds of historians and technicians for its restoration projects at historical parks. Particularly significant was the Historic Sites Act of 1935, which defined an expanded mission in cultural preservation for the National Park Service, especially to survey, acquire, research, restore, and operate historic sites and structures. The act decisively shaped the historic preservation movement in the United States and conferred a leading role on the National Park Service.

The National Historic Preservation Act (1966) grew out of concern about the impact of urban renewal and the federal interstate highway program on American cities. While this far-reaching act did not focus on the national parks specifically, it

See also

Landscapes

did involve the National Park Service in new and significant ways in historic preservation, particularly through its administration of the National Register of Historic Places. As the nation's official list of cultural properties worthy of preservation, the register was to be a potent incentive for heritage conservation both nationally and locally. Amendments in 1980 to the National Historic Preservation Act called for a set of cultural parks within the national park system, an endorsement of a trend that began in the 1970s when a number of urban sites and cultural landscapes were set aside, such as in Lowell National Historical Park (1978) and Ebey's Landing National Historical Reserve (1978).

The Varieties of Parks

The role of parks in the stewardship of the nation's natural and cultural heritage broadened dramatically in the late twentieth century, transforming the conventional meaning of the national park idea. The traditional focus on wilderness areas and commemorative shrines linked to political and military events has expanded to include an array of cultural landscapes that seek to preserve the social and industrial heritage of the entire nation. As the philosophy of preservation has broadened, so, too, have the strategies and methods of protection. Reflecting both the fiscal constraints of tightening budgets and a desire to manage parks with a degree of local participation, the National Park Service has experimented with cooperative land use agreements, as it has eschewed acquisition and outright ownership of parklands.

The national park system is composed of almost four hundred natural, historical, and recreational units that run the gamut from parkways to an international peace garden, all arranged into a plethora of administrative categories that make subtle distinctions between a battlefield and a battlefield park, for example, or a park and a preserve. For a history of the national park idea, though, seven types of reserves under the jurisdiction of the National Park Service illustrate the most significant trends within the shifting preservation impulse: national parks, national monuments, historic sites, urban recreation areas, national historical parks, national historical reserves, and national heritage corridors.

NATIONAL PARKS. Traditionally, national parks have been areas afforded federal protection through an act of Congress, in recognition of their dramatic topography, wild character, or biological significance. The term "national park" was first used to designate the geysers and canyons of the

Yellowstone region in 1872, and this reservation inspired the creation of large parks primarily in the American West for over a century. Today, about 90 percent of the acreage of the national park system is set aside as wilderness parks and preserves. Opportunities for creating nature reserves in the United States on the Yellowstone model began to recede in the 1980s, following the creation of Great Basin National Park (1986) in Nevada and the establishment in Alaska of twenty-five new wild and scenic rivers, twelve new national parks and preserves, and eleven new wildlife refuges.

NATIONAL MONUMENTS. The Antiquities Act of 1906 provided that national monuments could be designated by presidential proclamation to protect sites on federal lands with scientific or historical significance, as in the cases of the first two national monuments, Devil's Tower in Wyoming (1906) and Mesa Verde in Colorado (1906). Not until 1933 were all national monuments consolidated under the jurisdiction of the National Park Service. Generally, the designation "national monument" has been used to protect sites prior to their establishment by Congress as national parks. An unwritten sense of hierarchy distinguishes the two categories; thus, a national monument, like the Grand Canyon, set aside by Theodore Roosevelt in 1908, was "elevated" to national park status in 1919 by Congress. The most dramatic, recent use of the Antiquities Act occurred in 1978, at the height of the debate over the public lands of Alaska, when President Jimmy Carter reserved 56 million acres in seventeen new national monuments.

HISTORIC SITES. Large numbers of historic sites were first added to the national park system in the 1930s. Through presidential order in 1933, military sites administered by the War Department and national monuments managed by the Forest Service were transferred to the National Park Service, and the resulting properties were officially designated "the national park system." The addition of historic sites located predominantly in the eastern United States had two important consequences. First, it complemented the existing collection of western nature preserves, making the park system truly national in scope. Second, it emphasized the role of the National Park Service in preserving both the cultural and natural heritage of the United States. Today roughly half of all properties in the park system are sites preserved primarily for their historical significance.

URBAN RECREATION AREAS. Urban recreation areas go by a number of names: national

See also
Urban Parks

lakeshore, national seashore, national recreation area. Although the first recreation area and seashore were authorized in the 1930s, most of the urban-based recreation areas in the national park system were established in the 1960s and 1970s. These include metropolitan open spaces like Indiana Dunes National Lakeshore (1966) near Chicago, Gateway National Recreation Area (1972) in New York and New Jersey, and the Cuyahoga Valley National Recreation Area (1974) near Cleveland. The idea of locating national recreation areas near cities sprang from congressional interest in urban reform and a desire to bring "the parks to the people," in response to the charge that national parks were remote and elitist preserves for the white middle class. The federal role in urban recreation has remained controversial, both for its redefinition of the national park idea and the hefty price tags associated with land acquisition. (Occasionally this expense has been minimized through land transfers, as in Golden Gate National Recreation Area [1972] in San Francisco.)

NATIONAL HISTORICAL PARKS. Some thirty or so national historical parks have been added to the national park system since establishment of the first at Morristown (1933), a revolutionary war site in New Jersey. One of the most unusual national historical parks was authorized in 1978 within the city of Lowell, Massachusetts, to facilitate the preservation of the country's early industrial heritage. Through innovative public-private partnerships and cooperative agreements, the National Park Service and community groups have sought to adapt the national park idea in new directions designed to stimulate urban redevelopment through rehabilitation of heritage structures, while minimizing federal ownership. The Lowell model has become a much-studied example of how historic preservation can promote both economic revitalization and heritage tourism.

NATIONAL HISTORICAL RESERVES. One of the first national historical reserves was established by Congress at Whidbey Island, Washington, in 1978 to preserve the agricultural landscape associated with a nineteenth-century rural community. In a novel arrangement, the National Park Service will administer the Ebey's Landing National Historical Reserve only temporarily. When land-use restrictions have been developed, the reserve will be turned over to a unit of local government for management and administration. Most of the land in the reserve will remain as farmland, in private ownership.

Vice was rampant in urban slums and red light districts like Chicago's Levee district, where gambling and prostitution operated freely.

PAGE 62

See also

Rock Music

NATIONAL HERITAGE CORRIDORS. The heritage corridor represents an effort to integrate preservation of significant cultural landscapes into regional planning and economic development, particularly along the nation's historically industrialized waterways. The first national heritage corridor was established in 1984 outside Chicago, along the Illinois-Michigan Canal. There, and in similar corridors elsewhere, a federally appointed commission seeks to coordinate the interests of landowners and local governments, while encouraging economic development that protects the region's historic and natural resources. As in the Lowell National Historical Park, on which the heritage corridor is modeled, the National Park Service chiefly provides technical assistance, with a minimum of ownership and long-term management.

Future Directions

If their history is any guide to future directions, national parks will continue to evolve, as society deems new aspects of its ecological and cultural heritage worthy of preservation. The idea of a national park has proved a flexible concept, and there is every reason to believe that Americans will continue to find it useful for enhancing the quality of modern life, as they add parcels of natural systems not yet represented in the park system, create international parks that transcend traditional political boundaries, or expand the definition of wilderness to include, perhaps, ocean environments.

—ROBERT R. WEYENETH

NIGHTLIFE

When the sun set and evening fell across late-nineteenth- and early-twentieth-century American cities, gas, and later electric, lights illuminated the alluring world of nighttime amusements. Many entertainment opportunities enticed the city dweller at night, including bars, cabarets and nightclubs, and dance halls. Each offered some combination of diversion and relaxation. These enterprises varied widely, depending on location, size, and nature of clientele. Music performance and dance, which were available in many of these venues, contributed to their sensory appeal. Alcohol often provided additional stimulation for the evening's fun.

Seeking recreation at night was a well-established pastime for many Americans throughout the nineteenth century. Before and after the Civil War, commercial spectator entertainment grew as people patronized theaters, circuses, minstrel shows, music halls, and institutions like P. T. Barnum's American Museum. Americans found time for these activities as industrial work discipline strictly divided their time between work and play. Leisure that offered a chance for physical or emotional relaxation might help one escape the dulling effects of routinized labor. Urban areas provided large enough markets for entrepreneurs to offer ever-increasing entertainment choices; in less populated areas Americans continued to rely more on their own devices for creating fun.

Although these diversions had potential appeal for any urbanite, many amusements were popular primarily with the working class, and entertainment choices often reflected ethnic preferences. Certain activities, such as sporting events, cockfights and ratbaiting, gambling, and prizefighting were part of a male-dominated subculture centered on the saloon. Elliott Gorn has noted that "Cliques of men created informal but stable brotherhoods in particular bars, where politics were argued, grievances aired, heroes toasted, sports discussed, legends told, songs sung, and friendships cemented" (*The Manly Art*, p. 133). Men were well aware that their participation in rough sports, prostitution, and saloon life challenged the dominant Victorian expectation that people would remain disciplined in work and play. Those who made all or part of their living by participating in sports, especially boxing, knew that the "very word 'sport' implied social deviance" (p. 139).

Eventually, those urban entertainment areas most associated with "sporting" activities became legally, or were, by custom, defined as vice districts. San Francisco's Barbary Coast, New York's Bowery, and New Orleans's Storyville became spatially distinct worlds promising sensual mysteries as well as seedy dangers. In them, many saloons, gambling houses, dance halls, and brothels operated. Because prostitutes sometimes lit red lamps to signal their location, these neighborhoods were called red-light districts; guidebooks advertising sexual services also directed patrons to houses of prostitution.

Those Americans who identified with Victorian strictures against "wasted" time frowned on any dissipation of energy and wages in the saloon or other amusement spots. Advocates of genteel values encouraged leisure-time pursuits that improved the mind and promoted "good" company. They valued self-control for themselves and encouraged it in others. By the turn of the century, however, bars, nightclubs, and dance halls attracted a new middle-class, and in some cases female, clientele that challenged Victorian strictures against immoral entertainment. Nighttime amusements continued to inspire considerable public debate and discussion, however, because reformers, law enforcement agencies, employers, and parents believed controlling leisure would ameliorate various social ills.

As the nineteenth century progressed, sophisticated mass-marketing strategies evolved to attract customers. Location, architecture, interior decor, and music helped set a nightclub or barroom apart from working life. The activities of bars, clubs, and dance halls were increasingly structured by the needs of entrepreneurs, as well as by zoning restrictions. For the price of a drink or the cost of the cover charge, patrons purchased entertainment as a commodity. Some opportunities for defining one's own free time always took place in these locations. One might dance, flirt, drink, gamble, or socialize. Except for establishment employees, people came for fun—an activity defined by the relaxation of physical and emotional restraints. Nightlife institutions also served an important function in helping successive generations of Americans define immigrant, ethnic, peer, and gender cultures. In some cases, the settings helped Americans break down class and racial boundaries.

Early-Twentieth-Century Nighttime Leisure

As industrialization and urbanization dramatically changed the nature and size of cities after the Civil War, saloon proprietors found that city dwellers were less likely to make their own alcoholic beverages. Previously, public consumption of alcohol took place primarily at inns or other establishments near major thoroughfares. Otherwise, citizens tended to drink at meals, on social occasions, and with friends in their homes.

By the late nineteenth century, Americans purchased beer or whiskey, as they did many other consumer products, from commercial manufacturers (through the saloonkeeper). Saloons offered the most common public setting for nighttime amusement, and they quickly became a ubiquitous feature of even the smallest towns. A few establishments catered to the wealthy elite, but most affluent drinkers joined private clubs. Consequently, the saloon tended to service working-class men.

Leisure and consumption patterns changed in tandem with the transformation of work. Beginning in the early nineteenth century, increasingly large and complex industrial manufacturing enterprises gradually replaced the artisan's shop and household-based production. In this process, employers were partially successful in keeping workers from consuming alcohol at the workplace. Previously, workers could correctly assume that drink would be a part of the daily regimen, especially when grog or some other alcoholic beverage was provided as part of the compensation.

But industrialization was accompanied by the growing influence of bourgeois values; employers encouraged sobriety because it would help workers exercise self-control at work and at home. Supervisors assumed this discipline encouraged greater productivity. Furthermore, since industrial manufacturing increasingly relied on machines that required workers to perform at a faster pace, the drink that might help one cope with the numbing effects of repetitive labor could also dull one's attention to potential workplace hazards. Drinking on the job could easily be perceived as both a moral and an occupational hazard by working-class Americans.

Industrial work discipline affected far more than the conditions of the shop floor, however; and when workers had increased leisure time, and in some cases greater discretionary income, the saloon proved an inviting location for sharing the joys and frustrations of the job. Away from the employer's gaze, a bar afforded some measure of privacy for workers who lived in densely populated urban neighborhoods. Since conversation during the production process declined with industrialization, the saloon offered a much-needed place to talk. Drinking rituals, such as buying successive rounds of drinks to treat one another, "embodied a resistance of sorts to the transformation of social relationships into 'commodities'—a means of preserving reciprocal modes of social interaction within a capitalist world" (Rosenzweig, *Eight Hours for What We Will*, p. 60).

Saloons opened as early as 5:30 or 6:00 A.M. and closed late at night, thus providing workers with a location for drinking and socializing before and after work. In addition, patrons stopped in for the free lunch served in many establishments. Transients relied on the saloon not only for food and drink but also for sanitary facilities, warmth, and, in some cases, a place to sleep through the night. Saloonkeepers might cash checks, receive mail, or write letters for their patrons, and many provided free newspapers. Saloons also sold liquor, particularly beer poured into "growler" buckets, to be taken off the premises.

NIGHTLIFE

Early-Twentieth-Century Nighttime Leisure

And the night shall be filled with music.

HENRY WADSWORTH
LONGFELLOW

Patrons shaped a saloon culture within a context strongly influenced by brewers, distributors, and saloonkeepers. Seeking to maximize their market share, brewers designated particular saloons as outlets for their products. Some owned bars, or operated them, at or near their production facilities. Others rented fixtures, helped retailers pay licensing fees, and eventually paid the rent or mortgage. In the late nineteenth century, brewers, like other industrialists, competed in a volatile market where hundreds of saloons opened every year. Vertical integration of production and distribution facilities helped them manage their share of the market, and in the process they controlled many aspects of bar culture.

The taps, mirrors, and lighting rented or sold by the brewers were only one aspect of saloon decoration. Bars varied in size and quality of decor. Tables provided in the earliest saloons offered men an opportunity, for relaxed conversation, card games, and neighborhood camaraderie. Saloons located on major transportation routes were, by contrast, most likely to increase their standing room for commuting clientele. The largest venues might have a barroom in front and a room with tables, billiards, and (where legal) a dance floor in the back.

Other notable features included sawdust and drip mats on the floors, brass rails, spittoons, and pictures of sporting men (and women). Massive wooden bars, defining the location as a bar, dominated some saloons. The most elegant were made from expensive wood and were backed by ornate gilded mirrors. Prizefighter John L. Sullivan's portrait graced thousands of saloons—a legacy of earlier times, when saloons sponsored bare-knuckle fighting. The Anheuser-Busch Brewing Company distributed a popular print, *Custer's Last Fight*, which celebrated "military pugilism" on the frontier.

For recently arrived immigrants, the saloon could represent a reassuring connection with the Old World. Irish American drinking songs and rituals bore a strong resemblance to those in Dublin, for example. German Americans opened beer gardens and encouraged family-style saloons in their neighborhoods, and in many communities German brewers became prominent businessmen. Saloons also helped immigrants find out about jobs in their new neighborhoods, and the saloonkeepers might well speak one's native tongue. Since many bars were patronized almost exclusively by members of one ethnic group, the saloon became a cohesion-building social institution. Outsiders might receive a chilly reception.

Saloons in western cities developed in the earliest years of settlement, particularly where mining towns or cattle-drive depots dotted the mountains and prairies. Saloons survived when towns weathered boom-and-bust cycles. Like establish-

MULTIPURPOSE

Saloons in western cities developed in mining towns or cattle-drive depots. They often served as bank, post office and hotel until other institutions took root.
CORBIS-BETTMANN

ments in the East, the western saloon was multifunctional; it served as bank, post office, and hotel until other institutions took root.

Regardless of its geographical location, the saloon was a haven for working men; women patronized bars in much smaller numbers. One main reason for this gender segregation was the strong association of bars, especially the "low-class" dives and barrelhouses, with prostitution. Women who danced or offered other entertainment acts as part of barroom fare were typically labeled "scarlet women," and presumed to be guilty of lewd behavior. Even in cities where the activities of the bar or saloon were clearly restricted to the provision of drink, a risqué aura surrounded saloon life—particularly at night.

Women's employment patterns shaped their leisure choices. Women who worked in domestic service, or those tied to household chores for their own families, had far less freedom to patronize saloons than did men. Married women's leisure, according to historian Kathy Peiss, "tended to be segregated from the public realm and was not sharply differentiated from work, but was sinuously intertwined with the rhythms of household labor and the relations of kinship" (*Cheap Amusements*, p. 5). Women might "rush the growler" by buying a bucket of beer and carrying it home. Most female socializing—with or without male companionship—tended to take place at neighborhood social clubs, on street corners, or on house stoops. Occasional family excursions to the theater or an amusement park included women, but these adventures were luxuries for working-class families with tight budgets.

The saloon remained central to many working-class neighborhoods despite its limited accessibility for women. It served as a neighborhood communication center, which contributed to its importance as a location for political and, in some cases, union organizing activities. Politicians made the rounds of saloons to pitch their messages, often buying drinks for patrons. Nighttime entertainment became important for organizing and funding political life. Some saloonkeepers went on to become well-known political leaders—for example, "Bathhouse" John Coughlin and Michael "Hinky-Dink" Kenna in Chicago, and Tom Anderson in New Orleans.

The variety of services provided by the saloon did not change its primary function: it provided alcoholic beverages to men who could easily squander their paychecks and ruin their health behind the swinging doors. Temperance reformers lobbied against excessive alcohol consumption

throughout the nineteenth and early twentieth centuries. Most temperance activists considered bars and their nightlife culture to be the scourge of stable and harmonious working-class life. The worker who exhausted his paycheck at the neighborhood bar might well deprive his family of food and shelter—a scenario vividly drawn when temperance literature and speeches portrayed drunken fathers as profligate spenders prone to domestic violence.

Even though prohibitionists were alarmed at drinking among all social classes, the public saloon was a more visible target than the private clubs of the elite. Saloon opponents were interested not only in the effects of alcohol on individuals and their families, they also felt the saloon fostered collective social ills, particularly prostitution, gambling, and political corruption.

The reputations of the worst saloons colored public opinion about many others. Vice raids did close down numerous saloons where illegal or violent activities had taken place. The most notorious dens of vice were "concert saloons," multi-room enterprises that featured separate rooms for gambling, dancing, drinking, and (often) prostitution. Bars figured prominently in campaigns against prostitution and gambling. Fears that young women were being lured into prostitution, or the "white slave trade," against their will proved well-grounded when a Chicago saloon operator and corrupt policemen were implicated in a prostitution ring. Such activities led to the Mann Act (1910), which made it a federal offense to transport females across state lines for immoral purposes.

All cities—even some young frontier towns—had temperance activists who fought for sobriety. National organizations like the Anti-Saloon League and the Women's Christian Temperance Union (WCTU) were joined by dozens of local groups. Their attempts to regulate the activities of the saloon often began with the use of moral persuasion through temperance lectures or religious sermons. Eventually, municipalities regulated saloon growth by limiting the number of licenses issued or by zoning restrictions on drinking establishments.

Critics resorted to other tactics to restrict the saloon, such as lobbying for municipal ordinances that abolished Sunday hours, reduced the number of licenses granted, or restricted activities like dancing on the saloon premises. When cities restricted the number of saloons, some brewers and saloon-keepers benefited because such ordinances favored established businesses. New suburbs

After World War II, American musicians saw this country's major cities, especially New York, as major cultural centers on par with the capitals of Europe.

PAGE 104

See also
Popular Entertainment before the Civil War

NIGHTLIFE

*Early-Twentieth-Century
Nighttime Leisure*

*Whoever thinks of
going to bed before
twelve o'clock is
a scoundrel.*

SAMUEL JOHNSON

sometimes incorporated as dry territories to set themselves off from their wet metropolitan neighbors, thus emphasizing the continued association of the inner city with salacious nightlife.

Settlement-house workers and other Progressive reformers tried to control working-class leisure, including saloon behavior, by providing alternatives to the services offered by the saloon. Some opened coffee houses or built facilities for hungry and weary urban dwellers. Numerous organizations, including the Young Men's and Young Women's Christian Associations, provided athletic facilities and reading rooms. Other reformers lobbied for improved parks and recreation. Settlement house leaders endorsed family outings as an antidote to destructive male drinking. Labor unions, sensitive to the accusations of vice lodged against the saloon, established their own lodges or halls where drinks might be provided.

But the regulation of bars and saloons could have unexpected consequences. For example, the licensing of liquor establishments eliminated many home-based "blind pigs" (a place where intoxicants are sold), a change that encouraged men to leave their families and drink with other men in saloons. In some places, fights over saloon regulation intensified class tensions. Workers defended the saloon as an example of their freedom to choose leisure-time activities—a realm of experience they did not feel outsiders should control. Saloon regulation did not necessarily reduce the amount of drinking that took place in public bars; it merely altered its social and economic context.

The saloon did not provide welcome leisure-time activity for all Americans; young people, especially young women, wanted alternatives. In the early twentieth century, young unmarried women increasingly sought nondomestic labor outside the home. When they found jobs as secretaries, clerks, or factory workers, more evening leisure time was available to them. Women tended to patronize new commercialized entertainment venues such as dance halls, amusement parks, and movie theaters—which were not perceived to be exclusively male worlds.

As Kathy Peiss has documented, young women considered these "frivolous" activities exciting. They could wear stylish clothes and escape the supervised and restrictive worlds of family and

---

DANCE HALLS, CABARETS, AND NIGHTCLUBS
Nightlife Alternatives

Beginning in the 1910s, many major cities across the nation reported a rapidly increasing number of dance halls that attracted young men and women: "In Chicago alone, in 1911, it was calculated that 86,000 young people attended dance-halls every evening—many more than attended movies or pursued any other forms of recreation" (Nye, "Saturday Night," p. 15). Observers in cities like New York, Cleveland, and Boston concurred. The smallest dance halls held only one or two hundred patrons, but lavish ballrooms, such as New York's Manhattan Casino, held six thousand people. Like movie and vaudeville "palaces," the ballroom entrepreneurs sought to create an awe-inspiring alternative to boring daytime environments. Live music, in some cases at least two bands, provided a heady atmosphere. Commercial dance halls proved especially desirable for the young because they provided a relatively safe atmosphere in which to meet strangers away from the knowing eyes of chaperons.

Dance halls were not an entirely new institution in American communities; some saloons had spaces set aside for dancing, and many neighborhood and ethnic clubs held dances in rented halls. Sensitive to the associations of saloon dancing with prostitution, most twentieth-century dance halls posted rules and provided some supervision to ensure greater respectability. "Taxi-dance halls," where the sexual services of young women might be procured, still operated, but most of the new dance halls avoided any connection with prostitution.

Two other nighttime enterprises developed alongside the dance hall: cabarets and nightclubs. Building upon certain aspects of the saloon, such as the provision of alcohol and the use of elaborate decorations to shape patrons' leisure experiences, nightclubs were closely tied to commercial entertainment entrepreneurs who invested in them and sometimes acted as agents for performers. A nightclub or cabaret sold an entertainment experience for people who might be drawn from any part of town; it was not the neighborhood refuge typically offered by the bar or saloon.

work in a dance hall or club. "A woman could forget rattling machinery or irritating customers in the nervous energy and freedom of the grizzly bear and turkey trot [popular dances]" (*Cheap Amusements*, p. 45). Like male co-workers in the saloon, women often based their leisure-time social networks on relationships developed at work. Some women used nights on the town as courtship opportunities. Women were acutely aware of their financial dependence on men, who generally earned higher salaries and wages, to treat them to a good time.

The treating that took place in saloons implied a mutual camaraderie for men, but treating for young women underscored hierarchical social divisions. As Peiss observes, "The culture of treating was reinforced in the workplace through women's interactions with employers, male workmates, and customers, particularly in service and sales jobs" (p. 54). Thus, although women sought entertainment as one way to create some autonomy in their lives—away from the control of families and bosses—they found their choices shaped by many situations in which male peers had more power than the women.

Beginning in the late nineteenth century, restaurant entrepreneurs experimented with seating, floor design, and decorations that would attract upscale customers. Some of the earliest cabarets opened atop hotels or near theaters, places where middle-class patrons already felt comfortable. Restaurant owners, primarily motivated by financial considerations, transformed their businesses to attract more of these affluent customers. As long as dining remained the stated function of their enterprise, owners avoided theater licensing fees.

At the heart of the cabaret experience, entrepreneurs created what historian Lewis Erenberg described as "action environments." Diners were seated on the same level as musicians or the floor show; the proscenium stage and obstructive pillars of earlier, more formal decor were removed; and an intimate space was created that encouraged greater performer-audience interaction.

Increased participatory performance took place in several ways. Popular dancers Vernon and Irene Castle entered the floor from a table in the audience, for example, thus using their proximity to add excitement and informality to their dance routines. Comedians assimilated unsuspecting audience members into their acts. Singers, including many of the legendary blues women like Alberta Hunter, circulated among the tables to collect tips, thereby bringing the audience into greater contact with the performer.

The most ambitious cabaret owners drew on the examples of the music hall and theater by featuring Broadway revues and chorines in their clubs. Here, too, some kinds of intimacy could be staged, as when the "Balloon Girls" at Ziegfeld's Midnight Frolic moved among the tables, allowing men with cigars or cigarettes to pop the balloons attached to their costumes. Men and women generally attended the cabaret as couples, thus expanding the opportunities for public entertainment available to middle-class women. Reformers, suspicious of this gender-mixed audience, worried about women being exposed to "unrefined" amusements.

But even though the cabaret broke with the more formal decorum of an earlier era, interactions in these clubs were carefully staged and managed. Waiters brought people their drinks; a cabaret did not have the free-ranging ambience of a saloon. Since couples made up the majority of the clientele, unescorted women were often discouraged or barred from the premises. Tables brought patrons close to a dance floor or performance space, but they also provided barriers between patrons, thus obviating too much communal socializing.

Nightlife in the Jazz Age, the Depression, and World War II

Nighttime entertainment faced new restraints following World War I. Prohibitionists enjoyed a significant victory with the Volstead Act, which banned the manufacture and sale of beverages containing more than 0.5 percent alcohol and forced saloon owners to close their doors. The statute was ratified to enforce the Eighteenth Amendment in 1919. Many saloon owners had already experienced hardship because of state temperance laws, World War I rationing and hours restrictions, and increased competition from private home sales. German saloon operators and brewers were particularly hard hit in the war years because of anti-German sentiment.

Adaptable owners operated "speakeasies," so named because one might need a password to gain entrance. Many nightclubs had ties to members of organized crime; some of the decade's most notorious criminals, such as Chicago's Al Capone, amassed fortunes by supplying nighttime drinkers. Bars and saloons were relegitimated when the Twenty-first Amendment was ratified in 1933. In the meantime, prohibition did not dis-

You ought to get out of those wet clothes and into a dry martini.

MAE WEST

See also
Country and Western Music

N

*Nightlife in the Jazz Age,
the Depression,
and World War II*

*For the first time on
a large scale, whites
living in cities
outside the South
could listen to black
music in bars.*

PAGE 399

See also
The City

courage nightclub patronage—in fact, clubs multiplied during the 1920s.

Early cabarets appealed to a primarily middle-class clientele, but nightclubs diversified as their popularity grew. Some clubs continued to be located in hotels, but others opened underground or in similarly dark and womblike settings. Often the setting for new musical acts, smaller clubs had a bar and a dance floor, perhaps a short menu of food. Large, lavish clubs offered expensive fare and glamorous shows.

The name and decor of a nightclub helped establish it as a refuge or escape from daytime activities. Some clubs still had the aura of the tenderloin, and were called Bucket of Blood or Spider's Nest. Others pandered to fantasy or the interest in "exotica" by sporting names like Plantation, Dreamland, Pekin, and Elite. Club Alabam and Plantation Club suggested the Jim Crow South, and for potential black patrons the names proved accurate. Only the very lightest-skinned African Americans would be allowed inside—even though famous black band leaders like Duke Ellington and Cab Calloway graced the bandstand. "Black and tan" clubs, which tolerated a racially mixed clientele, challenged the racist limits of social respectability, and as a result became the targets of police harassment.

The Cotton Club, a premier entertainment haven in Harlem, was representative of the nightlife in 1920s nightclubs. Gangster Owney Madden opened it in 1923, and by building on the reputations of earlier clubs at the site, the Douglas Casino and Club Deluxe, created a new marvel. Designed to attract an affluent white audience to Harlem, the seven-hundred-seat Cotton Club featured an elegant interior with two tiers of seats around the performance space.

The Cotton Club built its floor show around Broadway-style revues. Musicians, tap and troupe dancers, comedians, and other acts were combined into one show. "Primitive" and "exotic" themes—which generally meant graphics depicting trees, drums, and scantily clad "African" natives—decorated the menus, walls, and stage props. Performers' costumes also reflected these ideas. Duke Ellington's accomplished jazz orchestra was reputed to play a "jungle sound," heavy with syncopated bass and drum accents.

Few white revelers at the Cotton Club protested the exclusion of African American guests. Some undoubtedly agreed with Jimmy Durante's sentiments: "It isn't necessary to mix with colored people if you don't feel like it. You have your own party and keep to yourself. But it's worth seeing.

How they step!" (Durante and Kofoed, *Nightclubs*, p. 114). Other white patrons believed the nightclub provided access to "liberating" African American culture that could serve as an antidote to the ills of overly regimented industrial society. When whites went slumming in black neighborhoods, they participated in what historian Nathan Huggins described as "a means of soft rebellion for those who rejected the Babbittry and sterility of their lives, yet could not find within their familiar culture the genius to redefine themselves in more human and vital terms" (*Harlem Renaissance*, p. 91). Unfortunately, when white visitors purchased illusionary nighttime visions of "exotic" black life, they failed to develop an accurate appreciation of the sobering daytime realities of African American life.

African American club owners opened their own establishments, some of which became popular after-hours spots for entertainers performing on Broadway or in whites-only Harlem clubs. Participants in the Harlem Renaissance patronized some of the clubs, using them as meeting and socializing centers. Nightclubs and fancy-dress balls also became part of the lesbian and gay subculture of Harlem, particularly as young homosexual migrants to the city sought to shape an entertainment world of their own.

Claude McKay depicted many of the conventional "primitive" motifs in his description of the Congo, a fictional Harlem nightclub: "Drum and saxophone were fighting out the wonderful drag 'blues' that was the favorite of all the low-down dance halls. In all the better places it was banned. Rumor said that it was a police ban. It was an old tune, so far as popular tunes go. But at the Congo it lived fresh and green as grass" (*Home to Harlem*, p. 36). McKay captures the participatory flavor of the music to convey the controversial reputation of the club. Other writers, such as Langston Hughes, found inspiration for their novels and poetry in blues and jazz, as well as cabaret dancers.

Ordinary nightclub patrons might hope to receive a whiff of the excitement associated with famous nightclub patrons, who brought some of the glamour of urban America's intellectual, sporting, and entertainment circles into the dusky club confines. The most exclusive nightclubs became places where one's reputation as a socialite could be legitimated. Many cities witnessed the arrival of these enticing opportunities: "Seattle, Salt Lake City, San Antonio, Cincinnati, Buffalo, Akron, Albany, Omaha, Miami, Syracuse, Baltimore, Pittsburgh, Cleveland and Denver experienced the expansion of vibrant nightclub entertainment with floor shows and bands" (Erenberg, "From New York to Middletown," p. 766). In Los Angeles, one might rub shoulders with stars from the film colony.

Nightclubs provided entertainment for patrons, but that was only one of their functions. Musicians and other employees experienced other aspects of these institutions. Unlike the saloons, in which the owner and saloonkeeper made many key decisions, a large nightclub brought together dozens of players. Owners, bartenders, cooks, performers, agents, doormen, and others put together the glitzy reality of the club. Some musicians felt that the ties to gangsters made 1920s nightclubs dangerous places to work. Jazz musician Earl "Fatha" Hines remembered that Al Capone was a frequent visitor to the Grand Terrace club in Chicago. Capone, Hines said, "liked to come into a club with his henchmen, order all the doors closed, and have the band play his requests" (Shapiro and Hentoff, *Hear Me Talkin' to Ya*, p. 130). In many cities, the capital provided by the men with connections to organized crime may have helped refurnish and improve nightclubs, however, and even raise salaries. Ronald Morris, who studied the relationships between gangsters and jazz, asserted that the underworld-influenced "cabaret owners of the 1920s transformed an otherwise lowly amusement palace into an occasionally lucrative business whose capabilities for self-promotion, in addition to showcasing jazz music, were far-reaching" (*Wait Until Dark*, p. 103). At the same time, the increasingly violent criminal activities associated with the gangsters continued to give an immoral reputation to nightclubs.

Jazz became the music most associated with the cabaret and nightclub in the 1920s. Large nightclubs showcased big bands with twelve- or fifteen-piece jazz ensembles, while smaller ones might host improvisational jam sessions. Intimate clubs allowed the audience to feel a part of the music being made, without any distracting staging. But in the next decade, economic pressures resulting from the Great Depression forced many club designers to eliminate the "facades and excesses of the architecture associated with failure" (Erenberg, "From New York to Middletown," p. 770). Jazz, especially swing, gained a wider following from the mid 1930s to World War II, when it became the preferred sound for many clubs, dance halls, and ballrooms.

Most dancing establishments were racially segregated, and black dancers were allowed in the predominantly white ballrooms only on specific nights—if at all. But because swing-style jazz was the most common music in the urban dance palaces, whites were exposed to African American musical culture even if they paid to see and hear predominantly white musicians. White jazz band-leader Benny Goodman, for example, was reputed to be unhappy unless "the floor was filled with activity. Dancers worked up to an ecstatic state in which, through a physical activity, they could leave this earth and fly through the air"; the combination of improvisational music and wild dance steps created the message that "ecstasy and personal freedom still existed in the modern world" (Erenberg, "Things to Come," p. 232).

African Americans were most welcome at the halls and ballrooms that opened in black neighborhoods. Musicians performing in the clubs catering to recent migrants from the South credited the dancers with helping to influence the style of music performed. Pianist Willie ("the Lion") Smith described how newcomers from the South Carolina Sea Islands helped shape the dance music: "The Gullahs would start out early in the evening dancing two-steps, waltzes, schottishes; but as the evening wore on and the liquor began to work, they would start improvising their own steps and that was when they wanted us to get-in-the-alley, real lowdown" (*Music on My Mind*, p. 66).

Recent migrants found clubs and ballrooms places in which to preserve some of the dancing traditions they had known in rural and small-town "jooks." As Katrina Hazzard-Gordon has

HARLEM SHRINE

A couple dance the night away at New York City's Savoy Ballroom in Harlem, the "Home of Happy Feet," which hired the best bands in the country and became something of a shrine.
UPI / CORBIS-BETTMANN

NIGHTLIFE

Nightlife in the Jazz Age, the Depression, and World War II

A man hath no better thing under the sun than to eat, and to drink, and be merry.

THE BIBLE
ECCLESIASTES 8:15

See also
Amusement and
Theme Parks

documented, "Dances in the jooks included the Charleston, the shimmy, the snake hips, the funky butt, the twist, the slow drag, the buzzard lope, the black bottom, the itch, the fish tail, and the grind" (*Jookin'*, p. 83). Many white, as well as black, urban social dancers enjoyed later variations of these styles, which were based on vigorous physical abandon rather than the more restrained dancing of earlier generations.

Ballroom entertainers provided more than dancing music. Jazz cornetist Louis Armstrong remembered his ballroom gigs as a combination of dance music and comedy: "The Sunset had Charleston contests on Friday night, and you couldn't get in the place unless you got there early. We had a great show in those days with Buck'n' Bubbles, Rector and Cooper, Edith Spencer and Mae Alix, my favorite entertainer, and a gang of now famous stars" (*Hear Me Talkin' to Ya*, p. 111). Variety troupes toured ballroom circuits across the country in the 1930s and 1940s.

Some ballrooms acquired great fame. Chicago's Sunset and New York's Savoy, for example, created legendary environments that seemed to offer an almost sacred sanctuary from the outside world:

> *The Lindy Hop reached its height of sophistication at the Savoy Ballroom in Harlem, the "Home of Happy Feet," which hired the best bands in the country and became something of a shrine. It was cavernous, a block-long structure with a half-lit, cathedral interior and two altar-like bandstands. Patrons coming in off the street for the first time discovered a sumptuous wonderland with its thick carpets, uniformed attendants, broad expanses of mirrored walls reflecting a large cut-glass chandelier, and an ornate, marble staircase leading to the crowded dance floor. (Leonard, Jazz, p. 167)*

Malcolm Little (later Malcolm X) was one of the patrons impressed with the Savoy's ambience in the 1940s. He "went a couple of rounds on the floor with girls from the sidelines" while listening to Lionel Hampton and Dinah Washington (*Autobiography of Malcolm X*, p. 74).

The clientele of the Savoy changed its composition throughout the week. Malcolm X recalled that Thursday night was Kitchen Mechanics' Night at the Savoy. He wrote, "there were twice as many women as men in there, not only kitchen workers and maids, but also war wives and defense worker women, lonely and looking" (*Autobiography*, p. 74). The Savoy used a variety of ploys

to attract dancers, including "bathing beauty contests, and a new car given away each Saturday night" (p. 82).

Depression-era migrants moving from the South across the Southwest and West brought an important dance institution with them. The "honky-tonk," a rural saloon much like the jook, was a common feature in many southwestern states. Country-western music historian Bill Malone described its intense appeal:

> *Amidst the din and revelry there had to be, for both the dancer and the passive listener, a steady and insistent beat which could be felt even if the lyrics could not be heard. The music became louder: "Sock rhythm"—the playing of closed chords, or the striking of all six strings in unison in order to achieve a percussive effect— was applied to the guitar; the string bass became a fixture in the hillbilly band; and in rare cases drums were used. (Country Music, U.S.A., pp. 163–164)*

In Texas, the 1930s oil boom brought in many new workers who patronized these small joints, which often were located on the outskirts of town.

As these workers and other families migrated west, they took their taste for western swing and country music with them. Bands like the Light Crust Doughboys, Bob Wills's Texas Playboys, and Al Dexter and His Troopers became popular in dance clubs. Agricultural migrants in California considered honky-tonks one of the institutions, along with evangelical Christian churches, that connected them to the homes they had left behind. "Every San Joaquin Valley town had its Pioneer Club by the end of the 1930s," wrote James Gregory. "There the flipside of the Oakie population congregated: daring women, single men, married men with a taste for liquor and independence" (*American Exodus*, p. 222). The honky-tonk atmosphere became memorialized in hundreds of "cry in your beer" country-western songs that testified to broken love affairs.

By World War II, honky-tonk acts traveled an expansive dance club scene across the West, and country-western dance styles followed suit. In them, as in many others, ever-louder music was needed to reach large audiences. Electric guitars often replaced acoustic ones to meet the need.

Nightclubs and bars in the West had long promoted frontier themes in their decor, and the association of gambling with western nightlife intensified in the 1930s and 1940s after Nevada legalized casino gambling in 1931. Gambling was common in mining town and lumber camp saloons and brothels. Nevadans hoped that the legalization of gambling would attract people and capital in the midst of the Depression. Las Vegas grew quickly during World War II when investors, sometimes with ties to organized crime syndicates, funded the building of hotel-casinos.

The windowless casinos used artificial lighting, free food and drink, and many other amenities to create a world encouraging indulgent behavior. By the 1980s, casinos had added individual musical acts and revues, circuses, zoo animals, and spectacles like exploding volcanoes to their premises. Gambling resorts sold the pleasures of nighttime entertainment twenty-four hours per day.

Nightlife in Postwar America

Following World War II, more Americans than ever made drinking, dancing, and socializing central to their nighttime activities. The institutional structure as well as patron practices changed in several important ways. America shifted toward a managerial and service-oriented economy, and many Americans enjoyed unprecedented amounts of leisure time as the workweek shortened. A baby boom exploded following the war, and it produced a huge generation of young people who would define many entertainment trends between the 1950s and 1980s. Widespread ownership of phonographs, radios, television sets, and video-cassette recorders provided mass-marketed music and entertainment that consumers could enjoy at home, which dramatically reduced the need to seek out public entertainment. Nighttime leisure reflected the tensions created when new generations of pleasure seekers questioned the homogenization and complacency that accompanied many of these postwar developments.

Bars and cocktail lounges became a common feature of American society, with every conceivable institution, including hotels and restaurants, laundromats, and airports, offering some sort of alcoholic fare. Corner pubs still served some functions of the saloon, especially where new groups of immigrants and urban migrants looked for places to congregate, watch television, shoot pool, and play video games. The bar continued to serve as an important location for individuals to meet friends or potential companions. Unescorted women were more welcome in bars after World War II, though bars often continued to be spaces in which men had considerably more freedom than women.

Specialized bars served college and university populations, conventioneers in large hotels, and tourists. Bars became important meeting places for lesbians and gay men because they offered one of the few public places where homosexual socializing might be tolerated. In some cities, gay bars helped galvanize the early gay liberation movement, particularly the Stonewall Rebellion of June 1969, when working-class gay youth resisted a punitive police raid at the Stonewall Bar in New York City.

Rarely outlets for local beers, most late-twentieth-century bars featured mass-marketed products and national name brands. Some bars or bar-and-restaurant combinations were parts of regional or national chains. Bars continued to be criticized as environments encouraging inebriation and a lack of control, particularly when happy hours and other events featuring bargain drinks were promoted. The pervasiveness of the automobile in many cities added new urgency to the demands to control drinking. Many states raised the drinking age to twenty-one, and others passed stiff penalties for drunk driving.

In some cases, bar owners and bartenders found themselves legally liable for the behavior of drunken or abusive customers. Heightened public awareness of the costs of alcohol-related leisure

♦ **Iconoclastic**
One who attacks settled beliefs or institutions

BEAT POET

Iconoclastic poet Allen Ginsburg, inspired by bebop jazz, who read verse to beatniks in coffeehouses and small clubs.
HULTON-DEUTSCH
COLLECTION / CORBIS

It is awfully easy to be hard-boiled about everything in the daytime, but at night it is another thing.

ERNEST HEMINGWAY

♦ **Beatnik**

A person who rejects the mores of established society (as by dressing and behaving unconventionally) and indulges in exotic philosophizing self-expression

activities led to new nighttime habits such as designated drivers and the creation of "dry" alternatives, especially for teens.

As the bar culture became more widely disseminated in the 1950s and 1960s, nightclubs and dancing establishments became more specifically focused on the young. Particular countercultural movements were associated with nightclubs, discotheques, and concert venues. In the late 1940s and early 1950s certain New York City nightclubs on West 52d Street became the center of avant-garde jazz, which broke away from the swing-band music of the 1930s. Bebop jazz, featuring the harmonic improvisation of musicians like Charlie Parker and Dizzy Gillespie, was performed in coffeehouses and small clubs. The music helped inspire iconoclastic poets like Allen Ginsberg, who read verse that railed against the regimentation and materialism of postwar America to small beatnik audiences.

Beginning in the 1950s, dance clubs increasingly responded to adolescent patrons' demands for rock and roll music, which had deep roots in both African American and working-class cultures. Like jazz in the 1920s, rock was attacked by adults who feared that its raucous sounds and values would harm young morals. Teenagers defiantly responded by embracing the music as a language voicing rebellion against restrictive authority figures, including their parents. Rejecting much of the social conformity promulgated during the cold war, teenagers danced to live and recorded music blasting with the raw sexual energy of performers like Elvis Presley, Chuck Berry, and Bill Haley and the Comets.

In addition, when young people became activists in the civil rights, antiwar, and women's liberation movements during these decades, music and dance helped convey their grievances. A growing commitment to bridging the distances between different racial, ethnic, and regional social groups was often articulated through folk, soul, and rock music. George Lipsitz points out that the music scene in Los Angeles was particularly representative of the growing merger of white, African American, and Chicano musical influences. Performers like Hannibal and the Headhunters, Ritchie Valens, and Johnny Otis represented young people who "identified themselves as a self-conscious and rebellious social group, they made music that reflected an unprecedented crossing of racial and class lines." As young Americans rejected the conformity and inequality, associated with the status quo, and

formed an enthusiastic audience for the new music, they created a "calculated foolishness" that was "quite serious; its imagination and sense of play went a long way toward transforming American culture from the domain of a privileged elite into a 'land of a thousand dances' " (Lipsitz, "Land of a Thousand Dances," p. 267).

The pluralistic dancing Lipsitz described took place in increasingly large pavilions and ballrooms during the 1960s. Strongly associated with the hippie subculture, these venues witnessed evenings that combined sound-and-light shows, powerfully amplified hard rock music, and mind-altering drugs that underscored hedonistic pleasure. The Jefferson Airplane, the Jimi Hendrix Experience, and Janis Joplin played to wildly enthusiastic crowds. Some young people structured their lives around the concert tours of prominent groups like the Grateful Dead. For them, leisure dominated their lives; it was no longer a way to spend nonworking hours.

By the 1970s discotheques and nightclubs varied in accordance with patrons' tastes. For example, disco music in the 1970s, and hip hop and rap music in the 1980s, swept urban clubs. Each originated with black dance music, although disco clubs attracted a primarily white, and often male homosexual, crowd. The latter two dance and music phenomena drew on the leadership of disc jockeys, who spun the records at the clubs. Nightclubs continued to offer teenagers the opportunity to "play" with dress and behavior associated with music styles as diverse as heavy metal, punk, and top-40 pop hits. Prestigious clubs in New York and Los Angeles employed doormen, or bouncers, to screen patrons for dress deemed stylish. The lucky entrants enjoyed their upscale triumph at the expense of others waiting in line. Thus, the nightclub served as a vehicle for conspicuous consumption.

Conclusion

Nighttime entertainment trends resulted from a complex mixture of patron tastes and desires, the commercial aspirations of leisure entrepreneurs, and regulations set by local, state, and federal agencies. Many evening pastimes were determined by the changing nature of work. Shortened hours and workweeks made it possible to find more time for relaxation on weekends, and in some cases during the workday. The bar or dance hall ceased to offer a rare escape from alienating labor, particularly as activities like movies came to compete with live entertainment. Nighttime leisure lost much of its local flavor during the twentieth century as increased corporate control of bar, restaurant, and nightclub chains standardized entertainment experiences in many communities.

Still, young people often treated the dance floor or concert venue as a place where they could try to assert political and sexual autonomy from dominant adult values. Some bars and clubs continued to serve a clientele restricted on the basis of race, class, gender, or sexual preference; these patrons considered their entertainment spots reassuring havens in the face of an impersonal society. At the same time, jazz clubs, swing ballrooms, country-western honky-tonks, and rock and roll discotheques helped break down social and regional barriers. In addition, when youngsters mixed African American, white working-class and ethnic, and Hispanic music and dance styles, they nurtured pluralistic cultural trends in the face of increasing standardization of leisure through film, radio, and television.

By the late twentieth century, nightlife continued to appear as a clearly demarcated world, promising an exciting alternative to everyday experience. Americans continued to seek escape from the regimented aspects of their lives by finding places where they could raise an elbow at a brass rail or stamp their feet on a dance floor. Nightlife remained a process of negotiation in which revelers chose from a wide array of mass-media offerings, such as movies and television, and the continuing enticements of dance halls, ballrooms, nightclubs, gambling resorts, and music performance venues.

—KATHY OGREN

See also
African American Music

OLD AGE

The meanings and experiences of growing older and being elderly in postindustrial America are both remarkably similar to and strikingly different from circumstances in the colonial period. To appreciate the novel dimensions of old age in the contemporary era, one first must understand why the universals of age matter greatly.

Universals of Aging

THE BIOLOGY OF SENESCENCE. For centuries people have acknowledged that senescence is in part a biological phenomenon. Elderly men and women are more likely than youth to have wrinkles and gray hair. The incidence of long-term disability and chronic disease increases with age. The last stage, demographers report, is characterized not so much by sickness as by frailty. People over sixty who fall are a hundred times more likely to suffer adverse physical consequences than those under sixty. Death ineluctably marks the end. Such realities have always colored images of the elderly.

Early in recorded history, adventurers and scholars sought the secret to prolonging life. Mesopotamian and Hindu legends hold that hags were transformed into damsels by bathing in oil-slick waters. Juan Ponce de León (1460–1521) searched for the Fountain of Youth. Charles E. Brown-Séquard (1817–1894), a French-American physician, regularly injected himself with an extract of ground dog testicles. None of these permanently effaced the marks of age.

Scientists have not discovered an elixir that rejuvenates the long-lived. Nor are they yet able to separate cause and effect in changes associated with aging. Many bodily functions decline with advancing age. Hardening of the arteries, however, does not cause senescence. Nor does digestive putrefaction or alterations in the endocrine system—though some American researchers around 1900 advanced theories of aging based on these symptoms. The mechanisms of senescence remain a mystery.

Recent biomedical discoveries have given rise to immune theories of human aging. Experiments show that human regulatory functions decline gradually, accelerating when normal aging processes are diseased. Yet lower forms of life, which lack specialized immune systems, also manifest functional declines at the cellular level. Immunological errors are associated with senescence, but they do not explain its developments.

Biological aging, according to the best research available, is partly played out at the genetic level. If all of one's biological parents and grandparents survive(d) past seventy, one's likelihood of living to a ripe old age is good. In addition, random degradations in DNA and at the cellular and organic levels affect basic processes. Decrements accumulate, impairing homeostasis.

Evolutionary advantages, moreover, go to species with comparatively large brains. Researchers believe that the capacity to learn, store, and retrieve information resides in brain neurons, which in humans are long-lived but finite. There is no indication that there has been any prolongation of the life span of neurons over time. This immutable biological limit helps to explain why there has been no change in maximum human life potential over several centuries.

"My spirit shall not abide in mortals forever, for they are flesh," says the Lord in Genesis (6:3), "but their days shall be one hundred and twenty years." That number approximates what scientists presume is the chronological limit to the human life span. Veterans' records and Social Security files do not challenge the figure. Nor do studies of centenarians. Life expectancy beyond age one hundred has increased by less than a year during the twentieth century.

Not only did Old Testament writers rightly understand that there is a natural boundary to human existence, but they also acknowledged physiological variations late in life. "The years of our life are threescore and ten, and even by reason of strength fourscore," observed the Psalmist (90:10). "Yet their span is but toil and trouble; they are soon gone, and we fly away."

Two points made in this verse apply directly to the American experience. First, most people do not survive to the maximum life span. The 1990 life expectancy for white infants was

I hope I never get so old I get religious.

INGMAR BERGMAN
DIRECTOR

♦ **Senescence**
The state of being old; the process of becoming old

O

OLD AGE

Universals of Aging

Age imprints more wrinkles on the mind than it does on the face.

MONTAIGNE

around seventy-five. Black infants could expect to live sixty-nine and a half years. These figures are close to the biblical seventy. Changes in life expectancy at birth, at forty, and at sixty, have altered the meanings and experiences of old age, particularly during the twentieth century. That said, the biblical notion of when one is old seems quite modern.

Second, the Psalmist stipulated that at least two physical states exist within old age. Mounting adversity sooner or later plagues the latter stage. This typology conforms to a distinction made since Elizabethan times between a "green old age" (which is healthful and vital) and "senectitude" or the "second childhood" (in which a person requires care). The twofold categorization remains salient. Gerontologists often distinguish between the young-old (people between the ages of fifty or fifty-five and seventy-five) and the old-old (those over seventy-five or eighty).

Throughout America's history, the chronological boundaries of old age have remained quite stable—and demarcated in a broadly similar fashion. There has never been a consensus in American culture about which birthday, if any, signals the onset of late life.

Invoking European traditions, colonial writers sometimes referred to 63 as the "grand climacteric," the magical product of multiplying 7 and 9, numbers fraught with symbolism. The 1935 Social Security Act, corporate pensions, and other public policies have made age sixty-five a trigger for entitlements in recent decades. The complementariness of such thresholds challenges the myths that once upon a time in America old age began at forty, and that it rose thereafter as life expectancies rose.

Yet age sixty-five is not the only benchmark for old age. Other birthdays have been proposed: fifty-five, sixty, sixty-two, sixty-four, sixty-seven, seventy, seventy-two, and seventy-five. Few have suggested a figure below fifty or over eighty, though Bernard Baruch in late life claimed that "old age is always fifteen years older than I am." Old age in the American experience might be said to begin at sixty-five, give or take fifteen years. This has always been the case.

THE SOCIAL CONSTRUCTION OF OLD AGE. Such looseness in defining chronological parameters suggests that senescence is not just biologically determined. Old age is also socially constructed. Many of the heterogeneous physical, mental, psychological, and social characteristics ascribed to the "old" in America today hark back to ancient roots. Competing conceptions of late

life have long shaped norms and expectations affecting the elderly.

No single image captures the diversity of old age. Scripture, for instance, extols the elders' wisdom. Moses listened to Jethro, and Ruth took Naomi's advice; both grew wiser over time. But Noah and Lot acted foolishly in late life, when inebriated. Patriarchs were not always paragons of virtue. Nor were "hoary heads" always revered.

Although older men in the Bible were considered past their prime, they nonetheless contributed to the well-being of the community. Levites retired at fifty but still assisted in rituals. Octogenarians served as advisers. The early body Christians were led by "elders"—whose efforts were opposed by senior members of the Jewish ruling council.

Older women also played vital roles. Leviticus 27:1–7 indicates that, at every stage of life, women were valued less than men of the same age. Yet the differential narrowed past sixty. Some elderly women prophesied. The Israelites made special provisions for aged widows. In early Christian congregations, widows over sixty ministered to the sick and poor, and helped with religious ceremonies.

Greco-Roman culture provided the other major wellspring of ideas about old age and aging in America. Themes in modern-day jokes about dirty old men and constipated old women date back to motifs that fill Greek tragedy and Latin poetry. *Oedipus at Colonus* and the *Odyssey* reflect a wide range of intergenerational dynamics, universally shared. The myth of Tithonos—the comely prince granted long life but not eternal youth—inspired Juvenal, Jonathan Swift, Oscar Wilde, Aldous Huxley, Alfred Lord Tennyson, and contemporary science fiction writers. The nascent nineteenth-century American medical opinion that old age is a disease recalls Seneca's dictum, "Senectus morbidus est" (Old age is a disease).

Late-life experiences, which were as varied as images of old age in classical times, provide precedents for understanding how phenomena as diverse as senior power and elder abuse evolved in America. Older men with wealth often wielded considerable power. Militaristic Sparta was ruled by a *gerousia*, a council of twenty-eight elders. *Senex* was a term of respect for the *paterfamilias*. Emerson and Longfellow borrowed themes from Cicero's *De Senectute* in their paeans to old age. Yet the Romans also had a tradition of throwing off bridges those over seventy who had become burdens. Widows and old slaves, marginal in the best of times, suffered socioeconomic hardships.

Over the centuries positive and negative images of old age, as well as the contradictions and ambiguities ascribed to late life, were embellished. Venetian doges presided over a gerontocracy at roughly the same time Chaucer and Boccaccio mocked crones' lust and the cuckolds' plight. Medieval iconography, which stressed Father Time's associations with old age and death, later inspired American folk art depicting the stages of life. Shakespeare's characterization of Lear—complete with insights into insanity and power in impotence—has influenced portraits of late-life styles as different as those offered by Erik Erikson and May Sarton.

No single text transmitted all Western traditions concerning old age. But it is worth noting that in the colonial era John Bunyan's *Pilgrim's Progress* (1678–1684) was the most widely read tract on aging as a spiritual journey. True to its genre, the book is a treasure trove of ideas about age. It abounds in biblical allusions and references to Reformation ideals. Divided into two parts, it highlights basic differences between the ways men and women grow older. Christian makes his way alone to the Celestial City. Christiana, in contrast, takes her children along; she travels with a group following a less direct route. Such differences (instrumental/cooperative; solitary/nurturing) resonate in contemporary discussions of age and gender.

The social construction of old age in American history thus builds on centuries of motifs, folk wisdom, reinterpretations of classical texts, and "scientific" observation. It also reflects the fears, hopes, struggles, successes, failures, and adaptations that people through the ages have felt and experienced in growing older. Biological processes shape key parameters of late life. But the meanings and experiences of old age that have prevailed in any period of American history are malleable. They reflect and result from a concatenation of broader demographic, economic, political, social, and cultural forces in society at large.

There has never been a revolutionary shift in old-age history—no dramatic, sudden change in attitudes or behavior. Nor does modernization theory help much to explain significant shifts in how Americans perceived and experienced late life. Industrialization, declining fertility rates, and new political institutions all affected the lives of the aged, to be sure. And conceptions of older people's roles changed as society changed. But turning points in the history of old age in America do not dovetail neatly with watersheds in American economic and political history.

Demographic Patterns

FERTILITY, MORTALITY, AND MIGRATION. Population structures are shaped by three demographic factors: changing fertility and mortality rates, and shifts in (im)migration patterns. Of the three, rising and declining birthrates are the most important in determining the relative size of the elderly age group. Periods of high fertility produce a relatively youthful population. The proportion of elders rise as birthrates fall.

By this logic, the proportion of older people in the United States should have risen steadily throughout the national experience. Fertility rates had been high in the colonial period, reaching their peak in 1790. Since then, there has been a net decline in birth rates for white native-born women, particularly marked during wars, the Great Depression, and after 1964. Black fertility rates, higher than those of whites, have fallen strikingly since the 1870s. The same downward pattern obtains for women of various ethnic groups. Even so, there were not dramatic increases in the numbers of older people until the twentieth century.

Throughout the colonial period, proportions of the elderly remained quite stable. Based on extant town and county records, less than 2 percent were over sixty-five in 1790. A century later, the figure stood at 4 percent; the 1990 census reports that about 13 percent were over sixty-five. There was a 59 percent increase in the relative numbers of older men and women between 1870 and 1920, compared with a 115 percent increase between 1920 and 1970. During the 1970s and 1980s, the population over sixty-five grew three times faster than the group under sixty-five.

Comparable trends obtain if the "old" are defined as those over sixty. Older men and women constituted anywhere from 1.7 percent to 6.4 percent of the population according to scattered eighteenth-century records. It is unlikely that the proportion over sixty grew more than 1 percent between 1790 and 1830 (when the federal census first reported numbers of aged whites). The percentage over sixty rose from 4.1 percent in 1850, to 6.4 percent in 1900, to 10.4 percent in 1950. By 2050, the percentage is projected to soar to 27.7 percent.

The increasing proportion of older Americans has altered the distribution of children and elderly in the population. There were forty people under the age of eighteen for every four over sixty-five in 1900. By 1980, the ratio had fallen to twenty-eight to eleven. By 2050, demographers anticipate, there will be twenty-two senior citizens for every twenty-one children and youth.

O

OLD AGE

Demographic Patterns

A man is not old until regrets take the place of dreams.

JOHN BARRYMORE
ACTOR

♦ **The Reformation**
A sixteenth century religious movement marked ultimately by rejection or modification of some Roman Catholic doctrine and practice and establishment of the Protestant churches

The aging of the population has not affected the nation's dependency ratio—the proportion of people under nineteen *and* over sixty-five to the working-age population—as much as declining fertility rates have. There were 111 "dependents" for every 100 "prime age" Americans in 1870. The ratio fell to seventy by 1940. By 1970, it had risen to ninety-one. The ratio is not projected to reach pre-1900 levels until the middle of the twenty-first century.

Such data suggest that the aged have not been, and are not likely to be, burdens on society—as various media depict them. The young have typically been the nation's costly dependent class. But

IMPROVEMENTS IN LONGEVITY

A Twentieth Century Phenomenon

Demographers estimate that two-thirds of the improvement in longevity since prehistoric times has occurred since 1900. Most gains have improved life expectancy at younger ages. Children born in 1790, for instance, had as much likelihood of surviving to age one as children born in 1970 have of reaching age sixty-five. Babies born in 1900 could expect to live an average of forty-seven years; those born in 1985 are expected to live to be seventy-five.

Besides improvements in infants' and children's mortality rates, there have been notable gains in adult longevity. The average life expectancy of men aged forty in 1940 was only a year greater than for men aged forty in 1790. Forty-year-old women in 1940 on average could expect to live three years longer than forty-year-old women in 1790. Since then, thanks to better diets, reduced smoking, and medical interventions, there have been dramatic gains throughout the adult life course.

Americans who turned sixty-five in 1985 can expect to live another seventeen years, compared with the additional twelve that those who were sixty-five in 1900 on average might have enjoyed. Whereas the average sixty-five-year-old woman could expect to live only a few months longer than her male counterpart in 1900, there was a four-year differential in life expectancy by 1985. The gap has narrowed somewhat since then—in part because more adult women than men now smoke.

children have futures; the elderly are near the end of their lives. Perhaps it is the expected rate of return on outlays, and not the actual costs, that affects the calculus of the debate over generational equity.

Why did the growing numbers of older people not become more visible in the United States until the twentieth century? The answer lies in the dampening effect of mortality and (im)migration trends on falling birthrates. Both have made the population more youthful.

Some gains in longevity mean that more people will live to old age. According to the life tables for 1949–1951, only two-thirds of all babies would live to age sixty-five; in 1990, almost 80 percent are expected to do so. As a result, there are more young and middle-aged people alive than might have been expected. This makes the American population younger, but more age conscious.

Similarly, (im)migration patterns tended to make America "young" in the 1800s. People are most likely to move between the ages of eighteen and forty-five. Successive waves of newcomers in the 1830s and 1840s, between 1880 and 1920, and after the mid-1960s rejuvenated the population. As the immigrants produced children, the percent of Americans in younger age groups grew proportionately.

DIVERSITY AMONG THE ELDERLY. Besides influencing the relative size of the elderly population, the interplay of fertility, mortality, and (im)migration rates historically ensured considerable racial, ethnic, and regional variations within the ranks of the old.

There has always been a smaller proportion of all blacks than of all whites past the age of sixty-five. In 1890, 2.9 percent of all blacks were over sixty-five, compared with 3.9 percent of all whites. This disparity has widened since the 1920s. In 1985, the figures stood at 8 percent and 13 percent, respectively.

Differential fertility rates account for the black : white difference. Black rates, historically higher, have fallen more slowly than white rates since Reconstruction. Black immigration, minimal since the early nineteenth century, had no discernible effect on the age structure.

Mortality rates for blacks persistently have been, and remain, higher than those for whites. Blacks typically have had poorer diets, living conditions, and medical care. The mortality gap has been narrowing, however. From 1929 to 1931, there was roughly a thirteen-year difference in life expectancy at birth between whites and blacks; by 1983, the gap had narrowed to six years.

Whites generally live longer than blacks. In 1985, sixty-five-year-old blacks on average could expect to live another fifteen and a half years, about eighteen months less than whites. Those blacks who reached eighty-five, on the other hand, could expect to live another seven years, a year longer than whites of the same age. This reversal in life expectancy at advanced ages, some speculate, results from racial differences in diet and adjustment to old age.

The most interesting alterations in the foreign-born component of the elderly American population reflect variations in immigration patterns. Roughly a fifth of the older population was foreign-born in 1870. Most were of German and Irish descent, people who had come to America in the 1830s and 1840s. By 1900 the proportion of foreign-born aged exceeded 30 percent. This increase doubtless fueled nativist sentiments against old-age dependents, particularly in cities like Boston with large numbers of foreign-born residents. The percentage did not begin to fall below 25 percent until 1940. By then, older persons both in southern and eastern Europe were prominent in the ethnic pool—reflecting late-nineteenth-century immigration patterns.

The long-term effect of laws passed since the 1920s, which were designed to reduce and regulate the influx of foreign-born persons into the United States, has been to swell the proportion of all foreign-born people who are old. In 1920, 9.7 percent of all foreign-born whites were over sixty-five. The number soared to 33.5 percent by 1960.

The number of Hispanic elders will grow in the twenty-first century. Between 1970 and 1980, the Hispanic population grew by 61 percent, compared with a 7 percent increase for the non-Hispanic population. Although only 3 percent of the current aged population are Hispanic, in some places—notably southern California, Texas, Chicago, and New York City—aging Hispanics already exercise significant political and economic power.

REGIONAL DISTRIBUTIONS. Not surprisingly, states with the largest populations tend to have the largest concentrations of older people. Regional variations in the distribution of the elderly, however, also reflect differential fertility rates and internal migration patterns. The northeast section of the country has always had a high proportion of men and women over sixty-five due to comparatively low fertility and high out-migration rates. Frontier areas usually have lower percentages of senior citizens than do older settlements.

Even sparsely populated areas, like the Southwest, boast remarkable ethnic diversity. There, Hopi, Pueblo, Apache, and Navajo tribes, Mormons, descendants of Spanish-speaking explorers, Mexican émigrés, and easterners established their own cultural norms and social systems. Each ethnic group treated its old differently.

Because they are less likely than younger people to move, most older Americans have aged in place. As nineteenth-century youth moved to the cities, their elders stayed on the farms and in villages. As late as 1970, 27 percent of all aged Americans lived in small towns.

Since the 1930s, there has been a growing concentration of the old in established urban areas. Cities like Buffalo and Pittsburgh, which have experienced absolute declines in population, have larger elderly populations than "newer" cities like Houston and San Diego. Not until 1980 did more older people live in suburbs than in central cities. Even then, they resided in suburbs developed before 1914, places with lower average resident income levels, more rental housing, and lower home values than communities that attract yuppies.

Although people in their twenties are six times more likely to move than those over sixty-five, Sun-belt states have experienced notable population aging. Especially since World War II, large numbers of well-off elders have moved to temperate climates. Florida is now the state that has the highest percent (18 percent) of people over sixty-five in its population; in absolute numbers, it ranks third in the nation. California, Texas, and Arizona also are favorite retirement destinations.

Before 1945, there was no such concept as "retirement community." The first housing development exclusively for senior citizens was called

NEW PHENOMENON

Retirement communities are a relatively new phenomenon. Since World War II, large numbers of well-off elders have moved to temperate climates.
CHARLES E. ROTKIN/CORBIS

See also
Health Care

O

OLD AGE

Social Patterns

As a result, family
life in New
England was
much more stable
demographically
than previously
suggested, and most
children even had
the opportunity to
know and interact
with their
grandparents.

PAGE 131

"Youngstown," completed in 1954. Its success inspired Del E. Webb to commit $2 million in 1959 to construct his first retirement housing project. By 1975, there were more than seven hundred mobile-home parks housing three hundred thousand senior citizens. Sun City, Arizona, and its imitators represent themselves as age-segregated communities that take pride in their recreational as well as their health care facilities. Sun City now houses more than 40,000 residents over 60.

THE SIGNIFICANCE OF SEX AND GENDER. Men and women grow older in such divergent ways that some scholars think two theories of human aging are required to take account of the range of experiences observed in later years. Some differences are sex-specific: they are due to biochemical or reproductive factors. Others are gender-specific: they reflect different values and treatment in the marketplace or the private sphere. Unlike sex-related variations, these gender-specific manifestations vary over historical time. Still others—like smoking habits and thinking patterns—result from the interplay of both.

On average, women historically have lived longer than men. Although there are slightly more males at birth, three females for every male survive past seventy-five. Recent demographic trends have made older women more visible in America. Before 1870, there was little difference in the male-female ratio. A century later, only 8.5 percent of all men, compared with 11.2 percent of all women, were over sixty-five. The progressive effect of higher male death rates at each stage of life has widened the gender gap.

Despite a comparative advantage in longevity, women suffer a greater incidence of disease, which disables them for longer periods. Historical changes in chronic disabilities cannot be documented. Death records indicate, however, that women over forty have been less likely than men to succumb to coronaries and other fatal, acute maladies.

Divergent life expectancies have created differences in marital status. Older men have been more likely to be married than older women: in 1986, the figures were 77 percent and 40 percent. In the same year, half of all women over sixty-five were widows, five times greater than the number of widowers. As divorce has become more acceptable in the twentieth century, the percentage of divorced older persons has risen. Fewer reach old age nowadays never having married.

Living arrangements have changed over time. The husband-wife unit has long been the core of the American family, notwithstanding vicissitudes

such as death, separation, illness, or accidents. In the 1890s more than 75 percent of all males over sixty-five were heads of household. With advancing age, the proportion of men reported living with a child, in-law, or sibling increased. Few went to an almshouse or a stranger's home.

Institutional statistics have changed surprisingly little over time. Never has more than 5 percent of the population over sixty-five been in institutions at any moment. An individual over sixty-five, however, has long had a 25 percent probability of entering an institution before death.

Older women's behavior historically differed from that of elderly men in two respects. The number of female heads of household increased as the number of "wives" decreased; the proportion never exceeded a third of the female population, however. Furthermore, women have been more likely than men (to be able) to turn to kin with advancing age.

Perhaps the most important trend has been the dramatic rise in the number of older people living alone. Roughly 40 percent of all women and 15 percent of all men over sixty-five lived alone in 1986. These figures represent a 68 percent increase since 1970, and nearly 300 percent since 1900. The decline in coresidency, however, does not necessarily signal a decline in intergenerational exchanges.

Social Patterns

DEFINING OLD AGE. Increasing numbers have made the elderly more visible. Demographics, however, have not been the sole force shaping images of old age. Far more important has been the historical interplay of social, economic, legal, cultural, and political currents.

Reinterpretations of the values and meanings of late life in America have tended to accentuate negative features of growing older. A deep strand of ageism has manifested itself in divergent ways over time. In recent decades, however, an effort has been under way to engineer positive ideas about late-life potential, building on earlier notions.

Antebellum Americans were not blind to the physical, psychological, and social liabilities of old age. Disparaging remarks often were made. Nonetheless, almanacs and magazines extolled the value of the aged in performing domestic duties, preserving the revolutionary spirit, and instilling appropriate values in the new nation.

Thomas Cole (1801–1848) portrayed old age as the ultimate stage of human existence in his painting *Voyage of Life* (1848). Though the vessel was battered and the scene gloomy, the old navigator at last had witnessed all there was to experience in this world and was prepared to meet his Maker. Sentimental images flourished in the antebellum period. Stephen Foster sold 130,000 copies of "Old Folks at Home" ("Swanee River") between 1851 and 1854. Currier and Ives's popular folio *Old Age* (1868) idealized the relationship between youth and age.

New ideas about age, associated with trends in commerce and science, gave rise after the Civil War to less flattering images. In the 1840s youthful politicians called themselves "Old Fogies" to signify a commitment to defending the wisdom of their elders. Later in the century the term referred to the obsolescence of age. Elders were not perceived to be at the cutting edge of progress. They suffered from "senile" disorders. "Geezer" and "fuddy-duddy" entered American speech in the latter quarter of the nineteenth century. Corporate managers, impressed by evidence suggesting that productivity began to wane after forty, selected sixty-five and seventy as ages appropriate for no-longer-efficient, but faithful, employees to receive pensions.

Around the turn of the century, old age came to be defined as a "problem." In some ways this reconception was a positive step, since it focused expert attention on "curing" or at least ameliorat-

OLD AGE AND THE LAW

The law also shaped definitions of old age. In colonial times, men over sixty were typically exempted from military service and road repair work, though not from political office. Federal and state constitutions discriminated more against youth than against age in eligibility for voting and holding office. (Such provisions rarely acknowledged the status of older women. Large numbers of elders thus were rendered invisible.)

Statutes based on Elizabethan poor laws held family members responsible for kin who were infirm or dependent. Yet before 1914 no state made specific reference to aged relatives. There was little case law. Decisions in Colorado, Ohio, and Kentucky, which around 1900 made negligence of elders a criminal offense, set the foundations for elder law. Courts nowadays consider a wide range of cases, ranging from age discrimination and right-to-die appeals to elder abuse.

ing difficulties ascribed to late life. I. L. Nascher published *Geriatrics* (1914), borrowing from the strategy physicians and caregivers had developed half a century earlier to make pediatrics a specialty. Social reformers began focusing on old-age dependency. G. Stanley Hall's *Senescence* (1922), a compendium of ideas about the vitality of people over fifty, set the stage for gerontology.

In due course, however, viewing old age as a problem itself became problematic: it unduly emphasized the negative. In the 1950s, a new set of euphemisms—senior citizen, golden-agers—came into vogue. These conceptions glossed over significant racial, class, and gender differences within the population. Images of age, to be faithful to late life's diversity, had to be ambiguous, subject to multiple and supple interpretations.

Charities and philanthropies have also shaped images of age. Early on, local elites contributed funds to provide institutional support and financial relief for certain segments of the aged population—spinsters, widows, or hitherto self-sufficient citizens down on their luck. Especially after 1865, Protestant denominations; Irish, German, Polish, and Italian parishes in the Roman Catholic church; and Jewish congregations built old-age homes for members of their communities. Religious groups operated more than 40 percent of all old-age social services in 1900.

Foundations underwrote research on aging. In Cleveland, Benjamin Rose left money for this purpose. The Josiah Macy, Jr., Foundation advanced biomedical research in the 1930s, and provided support that led officials in the Public Health Service to create a unit on gerontology. The Rockefeller and Ford foundations sponsored work in the social sciences, especially dealing with the economics of aging. The topic was increasingly timely as America became an advanced industrial country.

Economics of Aging

WEALTH AND POVERTY IN LATE LIFE. Generations of Americans have been inspired by the dream of rising from rags to riches. Until lately, most children could expect on average to enjoy a better standard of living than their parents. But against the promise of upward mobility lies the reality that few Americans of modest means have died rich in old age. Poverty has always threatened the old, especially women and minorities.

Tracing accumulations of wealth historically over the life course reveals that people tend to possess their greatest wealth in their fifties. People

♦ Gerontology

The comprehensive study of aging and the problems of the aged

O

*Only in the 1960s
did Congress pass
Medicare and
Medicaid, two
programs to fund
care for the elderly,
the disabled, and
the desperately poor.*

PAGE 209

then begin to dissave, though on average they have more in their sixties than they had acquired by age thirty. Even so, around the Civil War, roughly a quarter of all elderly men left estates worth less than one hundred dollars. Most aged blacks died penniless. Nineteenth-century native-born elders tended to be better off than their foreign-born counterparts. Since Social Security, the extent of old-age poverty has declined, although improvements in the economic status of the aged vary by sex, race, and occupation.

Because of differences in marital status, working careers, and cultural norms, it is harder to generalize historically about women's wealth. Colonial inheritance laws varied, but by 1710, most widows could expect to receive a third of the estate for life. Prior to 1900, women were far less likely than men to have probated estates and wills. Such gender-specific differences made older women more economically vulnerable than older men. Higher rates of female old-age poverty persist today.

The magnitude of the threat of old-age poverty has long colored intergenerational relations. Coresidence, particularly among the poor and those who were economically vulnerable, often became an economic necessity. Since colonial times, fear of want has made older people fearful of yielding control of property. That choice has precipitated social advantages and psychological bruises.

Even today, issues surrounding presumed generational inequities make for good politics. Born of the Great Depression, the architects of the Social Security Act (1935) hoped to relieve hardships among the young and middle-aged by addressing the problems of the oldest members of society. (The omnibus legislation also provided aid to dependent children, expanded state-level unemployment compensation programs, assisted the blind, and augmented public-health services.) In addition, Social Security enabled workers to contribute to their own retirement pensions. Social Security has relieved adults of some of the responsibility of caring for their parents. For most Americans it is *the* major source of their old-age security. While financing provisions were amended during the 1980s, the system was never any more shaky than any other American retirement vehicle. Medicare has serious financing problems, but Social Security is not likely to go bankrupt.

Even so, yuppies who chafe under the program's high taxes deride their elders as "greedy geezers." There is genuine (if not well-founded) fear among those currently middle-aged that the system will not be there for them when they are old. Grandparents today give the young more than they receive—contrary to much of the rhetoric about intergenerational transfers. They have the wherewithal to assist with mortgages and tuitions. Yet in the absence of adequate insurance, nursing-home care and medical emergencies can still wipe out fortunes.

INVENTING RETIREMENT. The word "retirement" did not always have age-specific connotations in America. Colonial farmers "retired" from wintry storms. Youth in the early years of the Republic "retired" to their studies.

For two hundred fifty years, most men expected to work until they died. Farmers managed more and labored less with advancing years. Many older mechanics and journeymen disengaged in an equally informal manner. Occasionally they took a cut in pay and performed less taxing tasks. Annuities (sometimes called "tontine insurance") were sold in the nineteenth century. Prudent workers were more inclined to purchase disability or life insurance to cover the greater risk that they would be maimed or dead long before reaching sixty-five.

Retirement patterns of older women differed from those of men because of variations in their career histories. Women typically entered the labor force as youths and remained there only until they married. With widowhood, some reentered the labor force—taking in boarders and lodgers, working as clerks or nurses, tending bar, or doing some other service-related task—to make ends meet. Some ethnic groups frowned upon even this limited involvement outside the home.

In 1875 American Express permitted workers over sixty to receive some compensation for quitting work. The Baltimore and Ohio Railroad stipulated minimum age (sixty-five) and service (ten years) criteria in 1884. The pension movement grew slowly. Only 159 companies inaugurated programs before 1915. No more than 15 percent of the labor force qualified for old-age retirement plans by 1935. Fledgling labor unions concentrated on bread-and-butter issues for workers in their prime. In any case, the Great Depression wiped out most of these corporate plans.

Title II of the Social Security Act (1935), which established a retirement fund to which both employees and employers contributed, made it possible for more and more workers to provide for their old age. After the war, steel and auto unions demanded that pensions be included in collective bargaining. Coverage increased. By 1960, 30 percent of the labor force were covered by private plans; 80 percent of all workers were insured under Social Security.

Virtually all workers now contribute to Social Security. The Employee Retirement Income Security Act (1974) was enacted to regulate private pensions. Roughly 70 percent of all full-time workers are covered by company retirement plans in addition to Social Security. With the expansion and liberalization of public and private plans, overall old-age poverty has fallen from 50 percent in 1935 to 33 percent in 1961 to 12.4 percent in 1986. More than ever before, older people can afford not to work if they so desire.

THE NEW OLD: ONE CLASS OR TWO? Labor force statistics indicate that the sharpest decline in older workers' participation in the marketplace has occurred since the 1940s. About 42 percent of all males over sixty-five were in the labor force in 1940, 29 percent in 1960, and 16 percent in 1986. Although the increase in gainful employment of females is one of the major trends of American history, older women remain less likely than men to be in the labor force. Never have more than 10 percent of all women over sixty-five been gainfully employed; 7 percent were in the labor force in 1986.

Researchers disagree about trends before 1935. Assuming that a significant number of all older men were disabled, probably no more than 75 to 80 percent of males over sixty-five were actually able to work. Some scholars claim that shifts in employment opportunities and ageism depressed labor-force percentages, possibly as early as the 1840s. By adjusting census data, others contend that opportunities probably opened up for older workers in the early phases of industrialization and commercialization. If so, the labor force participation rates of aged men may have risen slightly. Still others argue that there were merely fluctuations in older people's labor status until they were forced out of the marketplace. This occurred when Social Security was used by public officials and corporate managers as an instrument of social control.

In any case, whereas retirement was once a luxury, it is now perceived as a right. A 1978 survey reported that nearly two-thirds of all retirees had left work before sixty-five. Even so, 75 percent would like some kind of paid, part-time work after retirement; roughly a fifth of all retirees find such work within three years of collecting a pension. Trends point toward part-time, part-year "unretirement."

Healthier and more affluent than any cohort of old people in American history, many today take their senior-citizen discounts and head off to their retirement homes. Advertisers are noting their consumer patterns and leisure habits. Being old has begun to resemble a class distinction.

Not all elderly persons are so fortunate. More than a fifth were poor or near-poor in 1986. Economists estimate that without Social Security two-thirds of all senior citizens would have incomes less than 125 percent of the official poverty level. Older women are twice as likely as older men to be poor. A quarter of all who live alone or with nonrelatives are poor. That more than two-thirds of all black elderly women are poor suggests the baleful effects of racism, sexism, and ageism.

To the extent that smiling, white-haired couples in their kelly-green golf sweaters personified the new face of age in the 1980s, the stereotype hardly applied to a significant minority whose poor health, low income, and lack of basic amenities made their old age miserable. Old-age politics used to focus on old age as a problem. Now those who represent the interests of aging America have had to adjust to the paradox of being unable to grapple with economic and health-care needs that fester amid unprecedented affluence.

Old-Age Politics

FROM POOR LAWS TO OLD-AGE WELFARE. The federal government has dominated old-age politics since 1935—and vice versa. Many under fifty-five think of pork-barrel politics in terms of debates among silver-haired, golden-tongued senators. Some recall that it was two senior members of the Senate—Ernest Gruening and Wayne Morse—who cast the only two votes against the Gulf of Tonkin resolution that justified escalating the Vietnam War. At center stage in the 1980s was the oldest man to occupy the White House. Ronald Reagan may or may not have embodied the wisdom of age, but the septuagenarian's ability to survive an assassin's bullet and several operations affirmed the vigor of today's old.

More senior citizens are willing and able to serve in politics. Seniority gives advantages to incumbents. But this is not the first generation of older people to participate in politics. While we extol "the young men of the Revolution," it is worth remembering that the first five presidents of the United States were at least sixty-five when they left office. John Quincy Adams served in

For age is an opportunity no less/ Than youth itself, though in another dress,/ And as the evening twilight fades away,/ The sky is filled with stars invisible by day.

HENRY WADSWORTH LONGFELLOW

♦ **Septuagenarian**
A person whose age is in the seventies

O

OLD AGE

Old-Age Politics

Congress after his presidency, dying on the House floor at age eighty-one. Older men filled various high-ranking city, county, and state posts.

Little is known about older women's leadership role in politics. Many of the most widely known took over their husbands' seats as widows or, like Eleanor Roosevelt (1884–1962), achieved worldwide recognition late in life by acting on deeply held convictions. Some like Lucretia Coffin Mott (1793–1880) and Martha Griffiths (1912–) remained active as reformers at advanced ages. Still others worked behind the scenes.

For most older Americans, government was less a source of employment than a resource for relief. Throughout most of American social history, local communities, counties, and states have paid for provisions that individuals, families, and friends could not pay for themselves. The elderly's safety net resembled a patchwork quilt. Institutional support and quality of care varied. Some elders were treated with respect in almshouses; many were committed to insane asylums because there was no alternative. Although private groups built old-age homes, it was not until 1903 that Homer Folks, commissioner of charities in New York City, converted a public facility for paupers in New York specifically into a home for the aged and infirm.

Ironically, although Congress rejected pleas that it address old-age dependency, the federal government did more for the elderly indirectly than any other agency managed to do directly. In 1818 it provided relief for Revolutionary veterans in need; most who were eligible were at least sixty-five.

Thereafter, each cohort of survivors could anticipate some delayed benefit for their military service. Union soldiers and their widows ultimately received eight billion dollars, twice as much as it cost the North to fight the war. (Some economic historians claim that the burden of caring for Confederate veterans through old age was one reason why the South took so long to modernize.) Veterans' benefits cost eight times as much as outlays for the Spanish-American War. Older people clearly benefited: in 1929, 82.3 percent of all beneficiaries of any private or public pension plan were recipients of veterans' benefits.

Since 1935, an impressive federal network to aid the aging has been created. The struggle for Social Security galvanized activities through the nation. States like California, Pennsylvania, and New York established commissions in the late 1940s. Massachusetts created a cabinet-level post in the 1970s. Michigan funded university research

institutes and sponsors an annual senior-citizen rally on its capitol steps. The federal Administration on Aging was established in 1965, the same year that Medicare, Medicaid, and the Older Americans Act were enacted. As part of its Great Society initiatives, policymakers turned to the needs of older people after they had tackled problems of unemployment and training for minorities, the rural poor, and youth. The National Institute on Aging was chartered in 1974 to support basic research on aging. More than three hundred federal agencies now supervise programs that affect the lives of older Americans in one way or another.

THE GRAY LOBBY. When old age became perceived as a social problem, the elderly began to mobilize their efforts. Self-help social and educational groups emerged in the 1930s to "salvage" old age. In the Depression, Francis E. Townsend and Upton Sinclair capitalized on the fears and needs of the aged. Their radical politics affected the scope of federal and state old-age pension legislation, as did George McLain's movement to improve pensions in California a decade later. Early manifestations of a gray lobby tended to organize around a single issue under a charismatic leader.

The American Association of Retired Persons (AARP), founded in 1958, began similarly. It started as a modest effort by Ethel Percy Andrus, a retired Los Angeles principal. Now boasting more than thirty-six million members, it is the largest social group in America after the Roman Catholic church. Besides offering low-cost pharmacy services and travel discounts, AARP maintains an impressive network of policy analysts and activists in Washington and in each state. Local chapters disseminate information and mobilize members when necessary. To the extent that they join in activities and benefit from lobbying, AARP members (all over fifty) become more conscious of their power as an age group.

Whereas AARP mainly appeals to middle-class interests, the National Council of Senior Citizens has strong ties with labor. The National Council on the Aging was a product of the 1961 White House Conference on Aging. With initial support from the Ford Foundation, it is a federation of agencies helping the elderly. The Gray Panthers try to bridge the interests of young and old. Founded in 1970 by Maggie Kuhn, a sprightly woman now in her eighties, the Gray Panthers have been successful in capturing media attention with radical protests reminiscent of the Yippies. More than one hundred other national organizations cater to specialized needs within the elderly population.

Future Research

This article has emphasized the diversity of images and experiences associated with late life. It builds on interpretations published in the 1970s which offered overviews of major trends and modal tendencies. It complements subsequent work which has emphasized the significance of gender, race, and class.

This essay has stressed discontinuity in recent social patterns. Whereas pioneering studies highlighted revolutionary shifts in attributes between 1780 and 1820, or later in the nineteenth century, developments in the twentieth century attract the most attention here. This is because the aging of America's population has accelerated during this century. The most dramatic exodus of males from the labor force has occurred since the enactment of Social Security. Old-age welfare politics now raises the specter of generational rivalries at the federal level.

Subsequent reconstructions of the social history of old age in America will pay even greater attention to women. To what extent do males and females develop in separate spheres as they grow older? To what degree have matters of gender affected women's ways of aging independent of issues of class, race, or ethnicity? To raise such questions is to underscore the pluralist perspectives of the new social history. While we are only beginning to understand the history of all elderly subgroups, we are woefully ignorant about the feelings and experiences of Hispanics, blacks, southerners, people on the frontier, and the very old.

Although they were marginal for most of the nation's history, a case can be made for viewing our elders as pioneers, leading us into the postmodern era. The choices older Americans are making, and the constraints that shape their lives, provide an exhilarating if sobering glimpse at our future selves.

—W. A. ACHENBAUM

OLD AGE

Future Research

One of the reasons old people make so many journeys into the past is to satisfy themselves that it is still there.

RONALD BLYTHE

PARADES, HOLIDAYS, AND PUBLIC RITUALS

Introduction: Days Off

Holidays by definition are times out of time, when the familiar rhythms and practices of everyday life are temporarily suspended and replaced, often dramatically, by other possibilities, experiences, and sensations. Holidays of all sorts (official and unofficial, spontaneous and planned, secular and religious) are "days off" from the disciplines and demands of work, the usual relations among family members and friends, the familiar geography and ecology of everyday life, and even from what regularly passes as a person's normal self.

The variety of American holidays, from Memorial Day solemnities to the green-dyed hilarities of Saint Patrick's Day, have generally been interpreted as events of cohesion and integration. The great celebrations of civic life are viewed as the sacred liturgies of the nation's civil religion, while the festivals of immigrants are presented both as the way that the uprooted preserved and passed on their cultural traditions to their children and, at the same time, that both generations were connected (or connected themselves) to the national narrative. In a diverse, pluralistic society, according to these arguments, holidays and holy days have maintained the integrity of the different peoples of the United States as they have brought them together into one nation and a common civic culture.

But as countless reform-minded citizens have pointed out over the years, men and women do not behave on holidays the way they should (and normally do). Public festivals derive their peculiar energies from the tensions and conflicts between generations, classes, and cultures that surface in the absence of the restraints of routine. Popular rage and frustration with the discrepancies between the world as it is said to be and the world as it is experienced at work and at home have frequently erupted during civic and religious festivals. Furthermore, the institution of each major

American public holiday was attended by social dissension—the controversies over whether or not to create a holiday in honor of Martin Luther King, Jr., are only the most recent example—adding to their complexities. The suspension of the ordinary makes holidays potentially very dangerous times.

From Calendar to Covenant

The men and women who risked the North Atlantic crossing in the mid-seventeenth century to establish a pure church in a godly society on New England's shores had left behind them a world in which the passage of time was measured by holy days and saints' feasts, many of which had pre-Christian roots and were linked to the cycles of the agricultural year. The Puritans rejected this calendar and this way of being in time. They celebrated none of the old "popish" holidays, not even Christmas and Easter, both of which went scrupulously, almost ostentatiously, unobserved in New England. These were days like all others, which meant that God's will could be best served on them not by resting and merriment but by sharing the tasks of building the new world together in the wilderness.

New England's days-out-of-time reflected the Puritans' foundational commitment to the godly labor of the covenant. The special relevance of the word of God for New England was explicated by the clergy each week on the Sabbath, a day set aside by piety and law. Fast days were called by ministers and magistrates in response to troubles like war, epidemics, and internecine conflict that imperiled the very survival of the community and seemed to indicate divine displeasure; days of thanksgiving were proclaimed when God granted the covenanting people a reprieve. All work stopped on these days as the people gathered in their meetinghouses to fortify the bonds of the threatened covenant.

But the "grandest spectacles" of Puritan New England were public executions. The Puritans put to death murderers, adulterers, religious dissenters, witches, men accused of consorting with animals, and pirates in hugely attended public rit-

The clearest case of a European seasonal festival surviving the passage to the New World intact is Louisiana's Mardi Gras, though New Orleans did not officially recognize the event until 1857.

PAGE 324

See also

Amusement and Theme Parks

uals. The "criminals" on the gallows (some of whom were hapless men and women snared in webs of godly suspicion and pettiness) had endangered the success of the New England way by their transgressions, and this demanded reparation and revenge before the eyes of the community. Tension mounted as the crowds strained to see if the condemned would repent. If he or she did, in a reenactment of every Puritan's inner passage from terror to something like assurance, then the assembled saints enjoyed the satisfactions of having their cosmology sanctioned by the scaffold, and printers did a brisk business in subsequent weeks hawking the spiritual capitulations of the doomed. But if the man or woman under the rope refused to play the part assigned, as some hardy and indignant souls did, then the crowds left troubled and uneasy, their world shaken a little by this unexpected and vexatious gallows obduracy.

A People Free and Enlightened

The first American secular holidays took shape amid deepening tensions with England in the 1750s and 1760s, when the dangerous hilarities of medieval and Elizabethan festival traditions fused with the intensity of colonial republican ideology to constitute brilliant and powerful public political theater. The Stamp Act, for example, passed

INAUGURATION FESTIVITIES

The celebration is on as General George Washington is inaugurated as the first president of the United States on April 30, 1789, in New York City.
LIBRARY OF CONGRESS/
CORBIS

by Parliament in 1765, unleashed a yearlong series of demonstrations. One of the first, in Boston, was organized with the assistance of the men responsible for the annual excitements of Guy Fawkes (or Pope's) Day. Realistic-looking effigies of stamp distributors were paraded in carts and then desecrated by crowds throughout the colonies; in subsequent years, patriots met together to commemorate this moment of resistance in further celebrations. In this way, by means of provocatively worded toasts, hanged effigies, public choral singing, and fireworks, the colonists celebrated themselves into revolution.

These political excitements were recalled but vastly outdone by the huge and brilliantly choreographed national parties that attended first the events of the war's end and then the ratification of the Constitution and Washington's inauguration in 1789. The festivities centered largely on Washington himself, whose two long journeys, homeward from the battlefields and later to New York and the presidency, became occasions for the outpouring of national sentiment (although some Americans protested what they saw as a monarchical or even "popish" quality to the proceedings).

The people were not so much celebrating their enthusiasm for the nation in these festivities as they were constituting it—"observing themselves," as Kenneth Silverman has written, "in the process of defining themselves." Men of diverse occupations and ranks marched side by side in ratification parades, carrying the tools of their trades (and sometimes stopping to demonstrate their skills to the crowds), with their feet making the case for civic republicanism.

Surprising Conversions

Washington's epochal journeys were anticipated almost half a century earlier by another itinerary that generated almost as much excitement and enthusiasm. Evangelist George Whitefield's ride through the colonies on his second visit from England in 1739–1741 fanned the flames of a religious revival that had been flickering in New England and the Delaware Valley since the 1720s. The grandchildren of the founding generations, living in a more heterogeneous and fragmented society, were forced to find new idioms for religious experience and new sources of consolation; their response was protracted public gatherings in which neighbors moved from anxiety to reassurance—if not quite together, then at least side by side and within sight of each other. Revival meetings in this way resembled the earlier generations' public trials and executions, only now the mourners' bench replaced the scaffold as the site of the drama of conversion.

Revivals became one of the central instruments of American popular religion, shaping Protestant experience, identity, and participation, particularly in periods of internal migration. A second awakening, beginning at Cane Ridge, Kentucky, in 1801 (where more than fifteen thousand people assembled for six days of religious excitement) accompanied the expansion of the westward frontier; later in the century, eastern and midwestern evangelists organized similar gatherings in Texas and the Southwest.

Long and uproarious revival meetings, held outdoors under the trees either in the summer or at the end of the harvest season in the early fall, drew isolated farm and ranch families from miles around, offering them some sacred, and many more profane, encounters. Revivals were the early nation's most popular regional gatherings and the ancestors both of the state fairs of the late nineteenth century and of tourist attractions, like the Memphis Cotton Carnival and West Fargo, North Dakota's Pioneer Review Days, concocted by ingenious local boosters in the twentieth.

Outdoor religious meetings were also among the few occasions that African American slaves could come together apart from work and away from the scrutiny of their overseers. Initially ignored by white Protestants (and even forbidden conversion by their masters), slaves were swept up in the enthusiasms of the Great Awakenings. At camp meetings, which were segregated by race (and gender), slaves congregated behind the preacher's stand; but African Americans from different plantations often stole away at night to meet in hidden "hush harbors" where they forged a unique and powerful synthesis of revival Christianity and African religious sensibilities.

Storm-Tossed Celebrations

As the rift between the North and the South widened in the 1830s and 1840s, civic holidays which only a generation earlier had served as engines of national identity become spectacles of fear and regional hostility and mistrust. One of Georgia's representatives, Wiley Thompson, rose during the bitter and protracted congressional debate over how to celebrate the centenary of Washington's birth in 1832 to warn that the removal of the first president's remains to the capital would mean that in the event of secession, the great Virginian would repose "on a shore foreign to his native soil." Southern Fourth of July oratory in these

DIVINE ANGELS

In the 1930s Father Divine's white-robed angels carried placards in processions to proclaim God resident in the community through the streets of New York City.
UPI / CORBIS-BETTMANN

years progressed inexorably from fulsome evocations of the national spirit to darkening predictions of conflict and heated apologiae for slavery, and finally to calls for secession, while in the North abolitionists turned the day into a forum for attacks on the peculiar institution. Not surprisingly, the popularity of this American holiday reached its nadir in the decade before the war.

Regional loyalties have always been important in determining the American calendar. For much of the nineteenth century, folks outside of New England resisted the celebration of a national thanksgiving, scorning it as a "Yankee" holiday and preferring instead locally rooted harvest home festivals. There are competing northern and southern versions of the origins of Memorial Day, and southern states continue to commemorate the heroes and events of the Confederacy. Indeed, there is, properly speaking, no truly "national" holiday in the United States, since congressional jurisdiction over the calendar is limited to the District of Columbia and federal employees, with each state retaining authority for its own cycle of holidays.

The Country and the City

In the years after the Civil War, millions of Americans, black and white, moved from farms and

See also
Manners and Etiquette

What moistens the lip and what brightens the eye? / What calls back the past, like the rich pumpkin pie?

JOHN GREENLEAF WHITTIER
THE PUMPKIN (1844)

small towns to cities and factories, a vast internal migration with profound and lasting consequences for the texture of everyday life. People who were raised amid the smells, sounds, and rhythms of the countryside found themselves in the harsh, confusing, and competitive environment of the industrial city during the brutal heyday of American capitalism. The era's public gatherings and celebrations took shape in this break between worlds, as men and women struggled to keep body and soul together in daunting material circumstances. Dwight L. Moody's revivals at the end of the nineteenth century and Billy Sunday's in the early twentieth offered transplanted country folk the opportunity to reencounter the religious world of their childhoods until the summers, when they could make pilgrimages back to the old places for homecomings, family reunions, and church picnics. African American migrants came together in intimate Pentecostal congregations in small spaces just off the cold streets of northern cities, the urban equivalents of the hush harbors, where they could share powerful currents of feeling with people they greeted in the language of kinship.

Holidays of the Huddled Masses

Immigrant celebrations also took place between worlds. Men and women from southern and eastern Europe, Ireland, Mexico, and Asia brought the calendars of their homelands with them to these shores and continued to keep the special times of the old worlds, as much as the changed circumstances of their new lives and work would allow—and sometimes even when they would not. The premodern European calendar of holy days reappeared as the American Catholic population steadily increased during the nineteenth century, and Jewish immigrants brought an even more ancient cycle of days to the industrial city. In the familiar rituals of the Sabbath or a saint's feast day, immigrants could experience another kind of time than the regimented and closely monitored minutes of their workplaces.

The nation's cities, which seemed bizarre enough in these years to longer-established residents, became even more foreign and strange on important days in other calendars. Chinese immigrants in San Francisco and New York danced dragons in the streets to celebrate the start of their new year, and Jews threw breadcrumbs representing their sins into rivers shining with industrial effluvium on the first day of their year. In adjoining neighborhoods, Italian (or Portuguese, Puerto Rican, or Mexican) Catholics carried the statues of saints who had protected their crops, fishing boats, and villages in their home countries out into city traffic, dollar bills fluttering on their brocaded gowns.

MOTHER'S DAY AND OTHER HOLIDAYS

The peculiar strains of the post–Civil War period on the transplanted urban middle classes, among whom desire and denial colluded to shape a culture of sentimentality, gave rise to a new holiday. In 1907, Anna Jarvis, a West Virginian who had migrated to Philadelphia, was moved by her mother's death back home two years earlier to begin a national campaign to celebrate the image of the old-fashioned mother. This appeal to nostalgia and innocence proved widely compelling at a time when many American mothers were staring for ten hours a day, in poorly ventilated and badly lit factories, at the pulsing needles of sewing machines or grinding through mounds of piecework at home, and others were seeking broader roles for themselves in public life. By 1912, Mother's Day was observed in every state. But the ultimate fate of sentimentality is cynicism, and the times quickly overwhelmed Jarvis's vision. She had wanted the day marked by church services, home-cooked meals, and small tokens of filial piety; by 1961, $875 million was being spent on the holiday, which had become a showcase for the powers of the advertising industry. Jarvis had disappeared from public awareness long before this; deeply disappointed by what had happened and defeated in her strenuous efforts to prevent it, she died alone and destitute.

More realistically, American workers managed to claim some time off for themselves (and their mothers) in the long stretch between the Fourth of July and Thanksgiving. The socialist New York Central Labor Union organized a parade and picnic in September 1882 to raise funds for a labor newspaper. More than ten thousand workers came out to march around Union Square and then up Fifth Avenue to Forty-second Street in a declaration of the power of unions. Labor Day was a legal holiday in all states but one by 1928.

See also
Nightlife

All of this was a nightmare to the descendants of the Puritans, an almost unbelievable return of the repressed, and they fought back in kind. An organization grimly called the National Security League began promoting Constitution Day (17 September) in 1914 as a way of Americanizing immigrants, and the tricentennial of Forefathers' Day was celebrated in 1920 with particular enthusiasm. The old civic holidays were charged with a new agenda: in 1915, for example, the commissioner of immigration at the port of New York, Frederick Howe, asked that the Fourth of July be celebrated as Americanization Day.

These efforts to diminish the threat of the immigrants' otherness were welcomed by the ethnic middle classes, eager to find some connection to the society around them. Neighborhood doctors, lawyers, funeral directors, and high school teachers promoted holidays in honor of Pulaski, von Steuben, and Columbus as declarations of their own pride and achievement. The immigrant working classes could not always recognize themselves in these grandiloquent re-creations of what they were told was their history and culture—southern Italian immigrants, for example, knew more about the tax policies than the glories of Rome—so tensions over the right way to celebrate the tradition often erupted between classes within ethnic communities. The ethnic clergy often encouraged these middle-class "reforms" as a way of asserting church power over unruly popular devotions.

Ethnic holidays were not carried across the ocean like baggage. Instead, they became the occasion in this country for a troubled and anxious engagement with the difficult challenges of migration and for the enactment and experience of competing versions of the past and present between classes, men and women, insiders and outsiders, and generations. American-born children often found themselves forced to participate in these events by their parents and grandparents, who sought to secure through the discipline of family and community gatherings the younger generation's submission to an ethos it could not possibly share. Especially fierce hostilities centered on the daughters of immigrants, who during festivals risked what was ordinarily forbidden them—going out or talking to boys—which is why so many second-generation romances were begun on these days.

Festivals of Collective Obscenity

Between January and May 1919, five black men were burned alive in separate incidents in Arkansas,

Florida, Georgia, Mississippi, and Texas, before large and excited crowds. The lynching of African Americans and the desecration of their bodies became one of the central public spectacles of the South in this ugly year.

Lynch mob leaders used the language of holiday entertainments to describe the tortures they intended for the bodies of their victims; and when the crowds, which included men, women, and children of all social classes, had been sufficiently excited and amused by these promises, they torched the pyres. The noise of the flames competed with the crowds' roars of approval and shotguns fired in celebration. Afterward souvenir sellers picked through the smoking ashes for prizes, the most coveted of which were bits of rope and pieces of the victims' charred bodies.

Although these grim "holidays"—"festivals of collective obscenity" in Max Gluckman's phrase (quoted in Lincoln, *Discourse and the Construction of Society*)—were rooted in the pathologies of racism and the social organization of southern society in the early years of the twentieth century, they also recall the public executions of Puritan New England and the later colonial desecration of effigies, and in this way raise the broader issue of violence and American public celebrations. The Fourth of July has been a particularly gory feast: in 1908, to take just one year's statistics, more than six thousand people were killed or wounded during the "annual orgy of fire" (in the words of the National Fire Protection Association).

Each occasion of festival violence must be examined separately because these rituals of destruction and brutality, like other kinds of human performance, take on resonance and meaning in specific social and historical circumstances. The crowds scanning the faces of the condemned or rooting through the ashes of rope and flesh seem literally to have been looking for something, practicing a nervous divination. The social worlds around the scaffolds were under pressure from hidden forces when these carnivals of desecration became an important feature of local popular culture; men and women could feel in their everyday experiences that what they called reality was cracking, and violence may have been the effort to articulate the old order of domination and seal it with the fixative of the blood of outsiders. The desecrated body of the victim represented, through ritual inversion, the fantasy of the social order restored.

But arguments like these, which are useful up to a point, ignore an essential feature of holiday violence: it was a source of pleasure, amusement, and satisfaction for many people. Fourth of July revelers went looking for bloodshed and took pleasure in the risk of gunpowder and brawls; in the more carefully sublimated domestic world of the middle classes, these thrills were found in antiquarian reconstructions of Wild West shootouts, Indian massacres, and Civil War battles that have been popular regional tourist attractions since the nineteenth century. The old paradigm of

"HARLEM IS ALSO A PARADE GROUND"

African-American Festivals

African Americans who migrated to the great black metropolis of the North found there a heterogeneous community of varied African American and African Caribbean classes, cultures, religious faiths, and political aspirations. But Harlem's many different peoples shared its streets in common, and these served as the theater of the community's richness and complexity, where people went to observe and be observed.

Harlem took its protests into the streets. In the summer of 1917, eight thousand Harlemites marched down Fifth Avenue in complete silence to the sounds of muffled drums to express their outrage and sorrow over the July massacres in East Saint Louis; in later summers, street protests against racism, police brutality, and economic exploitation took more violent forms. Harlem also took pride into the streets. On 17 February 1919 the 369th Infantry, Harlem's Hellfighters, which had fought with distinction under the French flag, returned in a glorious parade up Fifth Avenue to Harlem. And Harlem took its different and competing hopes into the streets: Marcus Garvey's followers paraded up Seventh Avenue in dress uniform in the early 1920s, and in the 1930s Father Divine's white-robed angels carried placards in processions to proclaim God resident in the community. On Sunday mornings, as James Baldwin remembers them in *Go Tell It on the Mountain* (1953), Christian men and women walked proudly past the shipwrecked survivors of Saturday night, making clear that there was another way to live than this. The young Baldwin knew, though, that Saturday night in Harlem (and around the country) had pleasures undreamed of (or denied) by Sunday folk, most of them on display, along Seventh Avenue.

sacred liturgies and ritual integration was clearly off: holidays of all sorts have more often permitted men and women to experience the delights of violence as they performed their rage in the streets.

The Movement for a Safe and Sane Fourth

The Fourth of July has always been a troubled holiday, if not for the dullness of its soporific oratory (which was already the butt of national ridicule by the 1830s) then for the intensity of its excitements, noise, and smoke. But in 1903 the *Journal of the American Medical Association* began publishing casualty counts for the day, and as these rose, so did national revulsion with the holiday. The Progressives set out to improve it.

The campaign for a "Safe and Sane Fourth" was initiated in 1909 by the Playground Association of America at its annual meeting in Pittsburgh. The enterprise was widely supported by fire and police departments (which began refusing permits for the sale of fireworks) and by medical doctors, who each year had to attend the horribly painful deaths of scores of adults and children from an affliction called "patriotic tetanus" or "Fourth of July tetanus," which developed in the infected wounds inflicted by fireworks. Reformers proposed in place of this annual patriotic firefight a "New Fourth," observed with civic pagents, alcohol-free picnics, and the revival of edifying oratory. In a widely reported and highly regarded model celebration at Springfield, Massachusetts, in 1908, people of Swedish, English, Scottish, Irish, Greek, Italian, French, Chinese, Armenian, Syrian, Polish, and African American heritage marched in a parade of nations led by Buffalo Bill Cody's Wild West troupe.

But the motives of the reformers were not unmixed. They wanted the Fourth of July to be safer, more restful, and family-centered, but above all they wanted it to be quiet. Holidays articulate their discordant messages in many voices; in the case of the Fourth, the explosion of firecrackers eloquently tossed over the high fences surrounding the homes of factory owners delivered a clear enough greeting. As Roy Rosenzweig shows in his discussion of the holiday in Worcester, Massachusetts, at the turn of the century, the town's elite had become disturbed not only by the noise and violence of working-class festivities but also by their unmistakable political content. In the days of labor struggles the Fourth of July was threatening to become the nation's annual *charivari*, and when reformers called for a "safe" Fourth they meant safe for themselves as well as for other people's children.

"Sane" refers to something else. One of the sponsors of the campaign, Mrs. Isaac L. Rice, encouraged "those of us who know what the day means" to "endeavor to make it both memorable and illuminating to those who do not," by which she meant the children of "the poor and ignorant, of the distressed and disheartened alien within our gates" (quoted in Cohn, "Popular Culture and Social History," p. 177). A version of America's past and present, free of class struggle, racial hatreds, and regional hostilities, had to be constructed for these new Americans, although Mrs. Rice was not confident they would understand.

From Covenant to Consumption: Movable Sales

The United States had become an ambivalently, often anxiously, modern society by the third decade of the twentieth century, increasingly dedicated to an ethic of consumption that many feared was subverting the nation's traditional religious and cultural values. The story of American holidays in the twentieth century both reflects this development and serves as a counterpoint to it, because as everything solid was melting into air, some Americans used their days out of time to celebrate and test the possibilities of the new, others to exploit them, and still others to resist what they saw as the end of a Christian society.

The signs of a new national ethos were evident by the 1920s. Church activities which had once absorbed so much American time were competing, less and less successfully, with new and tantalizing secular opportunities for leisure such as movies and baseball, and the lure of Sunday outings in the family automobile seemed to spell the end of the traditional American Sabbath. Even the faithful who stayed behind could not help comparing their minister's all-too-familiar voice and well-worn morality with the mellifluous blandishments of radio preachers, peddlers, and crooners.

As Anna Jarvis discovered to her dismay, commercialism had come to dominate the seasonal round of American calendrical holidays. Beginning in the early 1920s, huge Thanksgiving Day parades sponsored by department stores like Macy's in New York and Hudson's in Detroit, consolidating their victories over smaller competitors, ushered in the frenzied Christmas retail season. The new advertising industry, wielding techniques of mass motivation perfected during the propaganda campaigns of World War I, trans-

formed even relatively minor holidays like Valentine's Day into feasts of sales for the retailers of gifts and tokens.

Gradually, over the middle years of the century, consumption, and not commemoration or recollection, became the point of most American holidays. Patriotic pageantry diminished and civic parades were shortened or canceled as Americans took to the beaches, amusement parks, and, more recently, the malls rather than to their village greens, on their days off, a shift in holiday observance that reflects a broader trend in these years away from the public sphere and toward more private and domestic concerns and interests. Increasingly people wanted to spend their holidays in their own backyards, where they could watch holiday pageants or ball games on television; and the topography of the suburbs, which had no central meeting spaces other than stores, built this reorientation of the common life into the landscape.

Citizenship was being redefined as life-style; excitement and enthusiasm drained from the public square. The ebullient and hilarious partisanship that had once characterized the nominating conventions of the two major political parties and their subsequent campaigns were associated now with mass-marketed sporting events like the Super Bowl. And as the public meaning of holidays waned, the connection between specific dates and events in the nation's past (Lincoln's birthday, for example) and the holidays marking them was severed. Holidays are now routinely moved from their traditional locations on the calendar and reaffixed to convenient weekends to facilitate retail sales and private leisure activities, making all American civic celebrations into movable feasts.

Although these developments have permanently altered the character of American holidays, they did not proceed at the same pace around the country or go unchallenged. Several traditional holidays of the white South, like the birthday of Robert E. Lee and Confederate Memorial Day, retained strong historical and regional meanings. The African American festival Kwanzaa, which runs from 26 December to 1 January, was established in 1966 in part to provide black families with an opportunity to exchange gifts, enjoy family gatherings, celebrate their African heritage, and reaffirm community values in a less commercial atmosphere than that associated with Christmas. Ceremonies honoring local veterans, especially those who fought in the Vietnam War, became important events in small towns around the country during the 1980s, and there are signs that the patriotic Fourth has enjoyed a revival.

There are fascinating and revealing examples throughout the colonial and early national period of African American holidays and celebrations that include music and dance.

PAGE 16-17

See also
Popular Entertainment before the Civil War

P

PARADES, HOLIDAYS, AND PUBLIC RITUALS

'Tis the Season . . .

It ought to be solemnized with pomp and parade, with shows, games, sports, guns, bells, bonfires, and illuminations from one end of this continent to the other, from this time forward forevermore.

JOHN ADAMS
IN A LETTER REGARDING
THE ESTABLISHMENT OF
INDEPENDENCE DAY
(JULY 3, 1776)

'Tis the Season . . .

Fierce public debates have erupted in the past several years over the place of Christmas in a secular and pluralistic society dedicated to the separation of church and state. That government offices and many schools and businesses are closed for two Christian holy days, Christmas and Good Friday, seems to be generally tolerable; but battle lines have been drawn over the issue of placing Christian holiday symbols in government spaces like post office lobbies or the corridors of city hall. Indeed, the appearance of civil liberties lawyers in court to argue against such displays has become almost as regular a feature of the American Yuletide as the descent of Santa Claus into shopping malls.

Some people have argued that the Christmas tree is a folkloric symbol drained of specific religious content that has become the common property of all Americans; others have attempted to balance Christian imagery in government spaces with holiday icons of other faiths, a gambit known as the "menorah defense"; a minority have defended the display of Christian symbols on the grounds that the United States is in ideals and history a Christian nation, however religiously diverse it has become. But civil libertarians and the nation's courts have found these arguments unpersuasive, and many religious citizens consider the arguments reductive of the integrity of their traditions. The debate over the appropriate place of religious imagery in a secular, tolerant society continues, however, making Christmas into an ongoing examination—and, obliquely, a celebration—of the First Amendment.

American diversity has more recently led to the reimaging of another popular holiday. Halloween was originally intended as a mockery of the pieties and spiritual comforts of the two days following it in the Christian calendar, All Saints (November 1) and the Day of the Dead, All Souls (November 2). In the United States it has always been mainly a children's festival, with only the faintest trace of the night's subversive possibilities lingering in its macabre costumes and in the rougher pranks of older children.

As Americans cut their ties to the public sphere and cities became more dangerous places, this holiday waned; parents were warned to inspect the candy their children had collected trick-or-treating for harmful objects inserted by unknown people out there in the empty and so threatening public square, and children were encouraged to limit their rounds to family and friends. But while the children's holiday shrank, another more adult and playfully subversive celebration appeared in its place. Halloween had already had an underground appeal as being one occasion when gay men and lesbians could publicly express and explore at costume parties the identities they otherwise had to guard. In the 1970s and 1980s, as gay and lesbian political activists pressed for recognition of their civil liberties and political rights, Halloween costume parades in New York and San Francisco became public celebrations of the nuances of gay identity and pride; more recently, the darker idioms available on Halloween have offered a way of expressing grief and mourning for friends and family lost to AIDS.

Recapitulations

The public spectacles of the 1950s and 1960s, some of which appeared strange and radical at the time, recalled many of the themes and traditions of earlier American festivals. The prurient fascination with the Rosenbergs' last moments, including the grisly details of Ethel Rosenberg's prolonged agony, offered an anxious nation the familiar satisfactions of revenging the betrayed covenant. The televised rituals of grief during the days after John F. Kennedy's assassination resembled the spontaneous outpourings of national sorrow at the deaths of Abraham Lincoln and Franklin Roosevelt. Even the bitter polarization of holidays like Memorial Day and Veterans Day during the Vietnam War was not new, as the history of the Fourth of July shows. The ritual-makers of the 1960s took these varied traditions and reassembled them into powerful and evocative forms; the improvisation of public rituals—sit-ins, teach-ins, "summers of love," and people's parks—became one of the decade's most accomplished arts. The greatest improvisations rose out of moral and political passions. The weary feet and rested souls of civil rights marchers, the angry demonstrations and riots in northern ghettos, and the street rallies of the Nation of Islam contributed to the beginnings of the remapping of relations between black and white, while the anti-Vietnam moratoriums and demonstrations helped end a war and a presidency.

What was truly new in this period was the technology of communications. The chant of protesters that "the whole world is watching" signaled a new age of public ritual. Millions looked on while cities burned and children ran from police dogs; now hundreds of millions watch football games and revolutions. Public spectacles have been transformed into global events.

Conclusions

Holidays exist in counterpoint to the world of work. The temporal rhythms of work, the impact of particular jobs on the postures of the body, and the psychological demands of different workplaces are fundamentally constitutive of the worlds of holidays, from harvesttime revivals to the sit-ins that freed students from exams. This is why such occasions seem endless, and why some people try to extend the oblivion with alcohol and drugs while others fling their bodies into unaccustomed excitements.

These liberated laborers then go to work on their worlds. The rituals and practices of holidays do not reflect or legitimize social practices and cultural styles; they create them. Worlds are made and unmade during holidays, and because the power of these days is so elemental, sex and violence in complex patterns of creation and destruction are inevitably a fundamental part of them.

Furthermore, holidays create and "decreate" worlds with many different tools, the least important of which, despite what all those sorry hours of oratory might suggest, are words. Protests, parades, homecomings, and saints' feasts are marked by particular smells, sounds, tastes, and textures. The power of these days works deeply in people, at the level of their senses, beneath their awareness: Americans abroad scour souks for cranberry sauce that they will not eat on Thanksgiving, and patriotism in the United States will always smell of the library paste that public school students used to make their collages of cherry trees, log cabins, and Pilgrims.

Finally, "public" does not adequately demarcate the terrain of such days and experiences. Revival meetings and ethnic festivals, for example, derive their power from the interplay between what happens in the tent and street and what happens at home. It is impossible to draw a clear line between public and private at such events; instead, they work their power in the interplay between the two spaces, just as they do between past and present, meaning and hope, desire and denial.

—ROBERT A. ORSI

THE PLANTATION

Of all the characteristic components of the society and civilization of the Old South, by far the most important was the plantation. This institution largely influenced virtually every aspect of southern existence—political, judicial, social, cultural, economic, and religious. Southern planters (those with twenty or more slaves, the number that commonly qualified one as the proprietor of a plantation), while constituting little more than a tenth of the slaveholders in 1860 but owning over half the slaves, held most of the important political offices—local, state, and congressional—as well as the top judicial posts. They also established social and cultural mores for southern society in general and determined the economic posture of the antebellum South, with its commitment to large-scale agriculture and the considerable neglect of other aspects of the economy, such as industry, commerce, and banking. And with the exception of the backcountry, they were the leading members of most of the churches.

Neither small slaveholders (owning fewer than twenty slaves) nor nonslaveholding yeomen felt uncomfortable with the large measure of power and influence in the hands of the planters. They realized that the planter class, by producing the exportable surplus of southern staples, raised the living standard of all southerners. Less than 7 percent of the 1860 cotton crop in Mississippi, for example, was produced by free labor, with the major portion being grown by the big planters with fifty or more slaves. Slaveless farmers in Virginia produced only 5 percent of the tobacco crop. And hemp in Kentucky was characterized as a "nigger crop," with virtually the entire crop produced by slave labor.

The social structure of white southern society was relatively fluid, with small slave owners by dint of thriftiness, hard work, and a little luck very often able to move up to the planter group. Even a slaveless farmer could, by using a surplus bale or two of cotton, move up the economic stairway to first become a small slave owner and then possibly achieve the prized position of planter. By 1860 the number of landholdings qualifying as a plantation (in excess of 500 acres, 200 hectares) varied from only 2 percent in North Carolina to almost 9 percent in Mississippi and to more than 10 percent in South Carolina, which had the largest average-size landholding of any state in the United States.

A number of these plantations were held by self-made men. For example, a propertyless man in eastern North Carolina by great industry and thrift was able to acquire the farms of ten to twelve small owners and thus become the greatest landed proprietor in his area, living in style in an elaborate plantation house. Sometimes even overseers became plantation owners. President James K. Polk's overseer, Ephraim Beanland, accumulated enough land and slaves in Mississippi to elevate his family to a point where one son could

P

THE PLANTATION

Many slave owners were concerned the drums might be used to assist in slave insurrection, partly from their fear of slaves congregating for diversion, where music making and dancing predominated.

PAGE 15

♦ **Bondsperson**
Bondman (slave, serf)

become a physician and the others could achieve positions of standing in their communities.

Whether the southern landowner was slaveholder or nonslaveholder, planter or farmer, he achieved a great measure of self-respect and independence from being able to farm land that he could call his own. With the exception of South Carolina, where there was a virtual caste system—especially among the low-country chivalry of rice and the sea island cotton planters, where one's standing was based almost entirely on one's family affiliation and holdings in land and slaves—there was no common discrimination of slaveholders against nonslaveholders or planters against farmers in the antebellum South. Nor did any of these groups consider fieldwork degrading for white men. During emergencies even large slaveholders were sometimes forced to work in the fields, and their sons normally did so during college vacations. And in areas with few slaves, any farmer (slaveholder or not) could be elected to local offices, especially that of county sheriff.

Across the antebellum South planters committed themselves to a paternalistic ethos that was based on the concept of reciprocal responsibilities for master and bondsperson and the implicit recognition of the slave's humanity. Thus, the plantation provided a composite unit, where master and slaves could pool income and resources within the slaveholding household. Such a household always included the plantation house, outbuildings, fields, gardens, and slave quarters. The size, complexity, and comfort of the buildings varied considerably from one plantation to another, as did the size and variety of fields, gardens, pasture, orchard, and forest.

By gender the master assumed principal responsibility for the household, maintaining an appropriate balance between the care and safety of his dependents and the economic efficiency of the plantation. He determined what crops to plant and when, the work cycle on the plantation, the disciplining of field hands (especially male), the marketing of the crop, and any other responsibilities that tied the household to the market or to the outside world. Managing his black dependents—who were to him an extension of his family or in effect his own children—consumed the greater part of his time.

The plantation mistress, normally the planter's wife but sometimes his widow, mother, daughter, or sister, operated within the world of ruling lady, a position assigned to her by gender and class. She was the recognized superior of all other women of the household. The mistress oversaw the running of the plantation house, flower and vegetable gardens, and dairy. She carried, as a symbol of her status as supervisor of feeding and clothing members of the household, keys to the domestic buildings and the various plantation storehouses. She supervised the plantation infirmary and aided in childbirth. And should the master be absent from the plantation for any great length of time, the mistress assumed full control of the operation, although generally with some difficulty. Her training would have included little pertaining to the internal workings of the plantation or to its affiliation with the outside world. The male-dominated plantation hierarchy could never quite accept her as being anyone other than a delegate of the master and male authority.

Pooling of income and resources within the plantation household brought the slaves little opportunity to determine their own lives, relations, and culture. As property of the master, they could not legally hold property themselves. While they had some control over the composition of their subhouseholds, they had no legal rights there. Only in a marginal way could slaves affect the income that they received in way of food, clothing, and shelter. Most of their food came from crops and livestock they produced themselves. Much of the clothing was made by slave seamstresses. And slaves built their own cabins.

The relationship between master and slave was always one of give-and-take. Wise masters would accommodate a measure of slow work, pilfering, faked illness, or even running away. They also allowed the slaves to tend their own gardens and livestock and generally gave them Saturday afternoon and Sunday off to care for these. On the other hand, slaves had little say over the master's use of their labor or in how they should be compensated for it. Slaves justified their stealing from the plantation storehouses in terms of "taking" what should have been theirs already—in short, they were simply providing for a fairer distribution of the plantation's resources. While the slaves could never accept the master's justification for keeping them as permanent dependents, they realized that the success of the plantation determined the basic income and resources for themselves as well as for the planter's household. Thus, if the master were more prosperous, some of the prosperity might trickle down to them.

The Formative Period

The earliest antecedent of the southern plantation seems to have been the sugar estate of ancient India, characterized by extensive commercial acreage and a large labor force divided into clustered villages under centralized control. Arab traders introduced the Indian mode of operation to the eastern Mediterranean, especially the Levant, in the seventh century, whence it was carried to the western Mediterranean by the Crusaders of the eleventh and twelfth centuries. The Spanish and Portuguese imported black African slave labor to their plantations in the Iberian Peninsula and the Canary, Madeira, and Cape Verde islands in the 1400s and thence to their great sugar empires in the Caribbean and Central and South America the following century. Great Britain entered the overseas world of sizable sugar estates with massive slave forces in the 1640s in Barbados. By 1680 hundreds of Englishmen had developed virtually all the arable land of Barbados as sugar plantations, averaging 200 acres (80 hectares) of sugar fields with one hundred slaves who cultivated provision crops during the off-season of sugar.

The initial beginnings of the plantation in British North America were in the Chesapeake tobacco country of Virginia and Maryland. John Rolfe developed a sweet-smoking variety of tobacco at Jamestown in about 1612, and within a year or two tobacco was being shipped to England. Production of good-quality tobacco re-quired painstaking care and mature judgment in performing a variety of operations; consequently, tobacco was generally produced on small units with a handful of highly skilled workers.

Indentured servants provided the principal labor force for the small tobacco plantations from the beginning; black Africans, although brought to Jamestown as early as 1619, numbered only about 2,500 as late as 1680. In the 1680s, however, with indentured servants becoming less and less available because of improved economic conditions in England and African slaves readily obtainable at affordable prices as a result of the saturation of the Atlantic slave trade, an increasing number of Chesapeake planters turned to slaves as a more dependable and economical means of labor. Nevertheless, the need for indentured servants who could perform skilled and managerial labor existed in the Chesapeake through the time of the American Revolution.

Out of the West Indian setting, however, a more mature plantation pattern was introduced to the American South. The saturation of sugar production in Barbados by 1680 prompted a number of the planters—at least 10 percent of the 175 wealthiest planters (with sixty or more slaves) and an even larger number of the lesser gentry (with twenty to fifty-nine slaves)—to seek large land-

SLAVE LABOR

This print depicts slaves producing tobacco. Slaves had little to say over the master's use of their labor or in how they should be compensated for it. HISTORICAL PICTURE ARCHIVE / CORBIS

P

*Slavery is founded
in the selfishness of
man's nature—
opposition to it, in
his love of justice.*

ABRAHAM LINCOLN

holdings in South Carolina. This semitropical locale, it was thought, would provide the advantages of Caribbean agriculture in the more wholesome environment of the North American mainland. Thus, these West Indian planters brought to South Carolina two things of major importance: the most extensively developed plantation system in British America and slavery on a massive scale.

However, it was not sugar that gave rise to the southern plantation but rice, although it proved to be exceptionally difficult to develop as a crop. While the Spanish in Central and South America, the Portuguese in Brazil, and the Dutch in the West Indies had all developed a highly successful rice culture, there is no evidence that any knowledge of rice planting was brought from any of these areas to South Carolina. Thus, rice production there, beginning about 1685, was largely through trial and error, even though 330 tons (2,000 to 2,200 barrels of 350 pounds [29.7 metric tons] each) were exported in 1700, according to Edward Randolph, surveyor of customs for North America from 1691. Recent scholarship has indicated that black African slaves from Madagascar and West Africa (a portion of which was called the Rice Coast) in the 1690s and early 1700s taught the white South Carolinians (whom they outnumbered by 1708) the techniques of rice growing as practiced in their homelands. With the application of irrigation to the rice plants by about 1724, half a century after the colony's founding, the rice industry needed only the successful development of suitable facilities for threshing and polishing the crop to reach full maturity.

Between 1685 and 1720, in conjunction with the rice industry, there had been a blending in coastal South Carolina of three factors essential to a plantation system: the land use system begun in the Levant and transplanted to the western hemisphere, a viable commercial crop suited to the plantation mode of production, and the development of a frontier colonizing project in conformity with the British concept of "plantation" as applied to their colonizing of Ireland in the sixteenth and early seventeenth centuries. In Ireland extensive landholdings had been granted by the British crown to English and Scottish settlers, and were manned by large labor forces (men of arms and their families brought over) committed to agriculture. Each family was assigned a "planting" (field), and a collection of these constituted a "plantation," sometimes as large as 12,000 acres (4,800 hectares).

The first half-century in South Carolina saw considerable use of both free and indentured labor

and a limited use of native Indian slave labor, more than in any other English mainland colony. After 1720, however, the rice plantation complex necessitated large importation of black African slaves (especially those with experience in rice culture), to the extent that perhaps as many as 40 percent of the slaves brought to British North America entered through the port of Charleston. In addition, highly sophisticated techniques of plantation management (generally associated with plantations of the antebellum era) were developed; the plantations constituted literal "factories in the field," with few limitations in the way of economies of scale in either acreage or labor force.

The scarcity of shipping during the War of Jenkins's Ear (1739–1743) and King George's War (1744–1748) led to a glut in the Charleston rice market and a precipitous drop in rice prices—by 40 percent in the first conflict and down to 10 shillings per hundredweight by 1746, less than one-seventh of the peak prices of 1738. Among the alternatives open to the rice planters was the development of a second staple, more valuable for its size, to cope with the scarce shipping. Out of this circumstance indigo, grown on a small scale in the early years of the colony, was successfully developed as a crop by Eliza Lucas (Pinckney) in 1744 and produced in considerable quantities (spurred by a British bounty to compensate for loss of access to high-quality French West Indian indigo). It accounted for 10.39 percent of the value of the colony's exports by 1748 (compared with 54.78 for rice).

The period after 1750 (with peace restored and rice prices back up to 63 shillings per hundredweight) was one of exceptional prosperity for the rice planters. They now produced two staples, with each slave able to grow two acres (0.8 hectares) of indigo (produced on the higher areas of the plantation, in a work cycle that dovetailed well with that of rice) along with three acres (1.2 hectares) of rice (grown in the swamplands, which could be periodically flooded). A number of planters amassed enormous holdings of land and slaves. Henry Middleton and Gabriel Manigault accumulated 50,000 acres (20,000 hectares) of land each; Henry Laurens, 20,000 (8,000 hectares); and John Stuart, 15,000 acres (6,000 hectares). Middleton possessed 800 slaves; Laurens, 500; Manigault, 300; and Stuart, 200. Manigault and Laurens, as was common among the South Carolina aristocracy, were heavily involved in merchandising, to the extent that they were the two wealthiest men in the colony. Indeed, these four and a number of others were truly the elite of American plantation society, with their wealth based on the firmest footing anywhere in the British mainland colonies. In fact, these Carolina planters were virtually equal in prosperity and prominence with their Barbadian counterparts.

Rice culture spread from South Carolina northward to the Cape Fear River in North Carolina in the 1730s and southward to Georgia along the Savannah, Ogeechee, and Altamaha rivers in the 1750s. While rice never achieved much status in North Carolina, remaining throughout the colonial period as only an adjunct of the naval stores industry, along with indigo it achieved considerable proportions in Georgia, once the restrictions on landholding and slavery were removed in 1750. By the time of the American Revolution, a number of Georgia planters rivaled those of South Carolina in holdings of land and slaves.

On the eve of the revolutionary war tobacco plantations in Virginia and Maryland were much smaller than rice and indigo plantations in South Carolina and Georgia. The greatest planters—the Byrds, Carrolls, Carters, and Dulanys—who owned many thousands of acres of land and slaves by the hundreds, divided their operations into numerous "quarters" where the work force seldom exceeded a dozen or so laborers. This was necessitated by the closely supervised and highly regimented labor format used in tobacco culture. Robert Carter of Virginia, for example, dispersed his 500 slaves over eighteen widely scattered plantations, as opposed to Henry Middleton's 800 slaves who were densely congregated along the Ashley River above Charleston.

Perhaps as much as 35 percent of the tobacco in the Chesapeake was produced on small farms employing no slave labor, whereas virtually all of the rice and indigo was produced on large units employing dozens of slaves. Thus, tobacco did not enjoy the economy of scale of rice and indigo in either acreage or work force. And while per capita tobacco exports from the Chesapeake by 1770 averaged about £3 for each free resident, the exports of rice and indigo from South Carolina brought £9 per white. Nine of the ten wealthiest men who died in the English mainland colonies in 1774 made their fortunes in South Carolina.

The post-Revolutionary era saw considerable change in the southern plantation system. Indigo, with the loss of the British bounty (essential to its profitability) and market (England now turned to the East Indies for its supply), and the invasion of the indigo fields by a destructive caterpillar in about 1780, virtually ceased to exist as a commercial crop. But it left behind a social structure and labor routine perfectly adaptable to the production of a new staple, sea island cotton, so called because it thrived best in the Sea Islands along the coastline of Georgia (to which it was introduced in 1786) and South Carolina.

The variety of cotton, with a silky fiber of from 1^1/$_2$ to 2 inches (37.5 to 50 millimeters), was used principally for the fine cambric and laces of the wealthy. Consequently it fetched premium prices, sometimes as much as $1.25 per pound but more commonly from 20 to 40 cents—two to three times the price of upland, short-staple cotton, of which the fiber was only an inch (25 millimeters) or less. The bulk yield of sea island cotton was about half that of the short-fiber, and it was considerably more difficult to produce and process for market. However, the higher prices and the suitability of sea island cotton as a replacement for indigo more than compensated for the difference. Profits were high, sometimes as much as 10 to 12 percent, with virtually the entire crop produced by large-scale slave labor.

Whereas climate confined sea island cotton to the littoral of South Carolina and Georgia and middle Florida (where its production was developed in the 1850s), upland cotton, once Eli Whitney had perfected an inexpensive and workable gin in 1793, could be profitably produced anywhere the growing season was at least two hundred days and the annual rainfall 20 inches (500 millimeters)—on virtually any kind of soil, on flat or hilly land, and on a small scale by one-horse farmers or in massive amounts by large planters with dozens or hundreds of slaves.

The Antebellum Plantation

By the early 1800s, and especially after the War of 1812, Atlantic seaboard farmers and planters with badly worn soils and declining incomes—especially those of South Carolina and Virginia—moved west and southwest to the Black Belt of Alabama, to central Tennessee, to the lands along the Mississippi River from Arkansas and west Tennessee to the Gulf of Mexico, and eventually to east Texas in search of cheap, fertile lands—by then the price was $1.25 an acre (0.4 hectare) for government-owned land—and a new stake in life. With the insatiable British demand for cotton to fuel their booming textile industry keeping prices high, southern cotton production doubled about every ten years between the War of 1812 and the Civil War—from less than 150,000 bales (averaging about 450 pounds [202.5 kilograms] each) in

As I would not be a slave, so I would not be a master.

ABRAHAM LINCOLN

♦ **Hectare**

10,000 square meters (approximately 2.47 acres)

A resistless feeling of depression falls slowly upon us, despite the gaudy sunshine and the green cotton fields.

W. E. B. DU BOIS
THE SOULS OF BLACK FOLK
(1903)

♦ **Hogshead**

A large cask or barrel

♦ **Nabob**

A person of great wealth or prominence

"KING COTTON"

It was cotton—more than all the other staples put together—that dominated southern society, economy, and politics. Cotton could be produced with some profit by small independent farmers holding few, if any, slaves (more than half the landowners in the Cotton Kingdom owned no slaves at all); however, the greatest prosperity (especially in the 1850s) was enjoyed by the three thousand to four thousand big planters who owned most of the land and slaves and received as much as three-fourths of the annual cotton income.

Natchez, Mississippi, became the great mecca of cotton wealth, with perhaps a third of the millionaires in America in 1860 clustered there; and they made their great affluence visible in the hundred or so grand mansions that arose in and around the city. Individual landownerships and yields in the Natchez area were amazing. In 1859 (the crop year for the 1860 census) Levin R. Marshall, a Natchez banker who either owned or had a share in more than 25,000 acres (10,000 hectares) in Louisiana, Mississippi, and Arkansas, produced 4,000 bales; Stephen Duncan, with six cotton and two sugar plantations and 1,018 slaves (plus 23 at his residence near Natchez), 4,000 bales; John Routh, once called the "largest cotton planter in the world" but who by this time had settled much of his land on his children, 3,500 bales; and Frederick Stanton, with five large plantations in Louisiana and a small holding in Mississippi comprising 15,000 acres (6,000 hectares) and 444 slaves, 3,000 bales. Cotton sold in 1860 for 11 to 12 cents per pound. An average bale of 450 pounds (202.5 kilograms) would thus be worth about $50.

In Louisiana in 1859, Meredith Calhoun in Rapides Parish produced 3,800 bales on his plantation of 5,000 improved and 10,000 unimproved acres (the largest number of bales produced in the South on a single plantation), along with 531 hogsheads of sugar and 30,000 bushels of corn for the plantation's 700 slaves; Alfred Davis of Concordia Parish, 3,400 bales; and Joseph A. S. Acklen of West Feliciana Parish, 3,100 bales. Nine other Louisiana planters produced between 2,000 and 3,000 bales. In Georgia, Joseph Bond of Macon produced 2,199 bales in 1859, making him the largest producer in that state.

1814 to over 4,500,000 by 1860, the value of which amounted to 57 percent of the total exports from the United States.

Indeed, the Cotton Kingdom of the antebellum South stretched for a thousand miles (1,600 kilometers) from South Carolina westward to Texas, with a breadth from north to south of some two hundred miles (320 kilometers) in Carolina and Texas and 600 to 700 miles (960 to 1,120 kilometers) in the Mississippi Valley—a total of about 400,000 square miles (1,040,000 square kilometers). On the periphery the other great staples were produced—tobacco across the upper South (with more production west of the Appalachians by 1860 than east), hemp (used principally for cordage and bale cloth) in Kentucky and Missouri, sugar in Louisiana, and rice along the lower reaches of some seventeen tidal rivers on the South Atlantic coast from the Cape Fear River in southeastern North Carolina to the Saint Johns River in northern Florida.

Among the producers of the other staples, only the great rice nabobs of South Carolina and the sugar magnates of Louisiana could rival the cotton lords in ownership and production. The rice princes were Nathaniel Heyward of Colleton District, largest of the rice planters, with 5,000 acres (2,000 hectares) of improved land and 30,000 unimproved acres (12,000 hectares) on seventeen plantations and over 2,000 slaves; Joshua John Ward in Georgetown District, with 3,000 improved and 7,000 unimproved acres (1,200 improved and 2,800 unimproved hectares) on seven plantations and 1,100 slaves; and William Aiken of Colleton District, with 700 slaves on his Jehossee Island plantation of 4,000 acres (1,600 hectares), 2,000 (800) of which were improved (Aiken and Meredith Calhoun of Louisiana were the only planters in the entire South in 1860 with as many as 700 slaves on a single plantation). The value of their crops rivaled or exceeded that of the largest cotton planters. The largest sugar holdings were those of John Burnside of Ascension and St. James parishes, comprising about 7,500 improved and 22,000 unimproved acres (3,000 improved and 8,800 unimproved hectares) on five plantations and 950 slaves. Samuel Hairston, with numerous plantations in both Virginia and North Carolina and 1,600 slaves, was the only tobacco planter of this magnitude.

Not only did these great planters build stately mansions adorned with colonnaded Greek Revival porticoes, finely furnished and surrounded by lush gardens, they also built or purchased expensive town houses in Charleston and New Orleans. Samuel Hairston beautified his plantation house and grounds with such lavish splendor that a neighboring minister described paradise as being "as beautiful as Mr. Hairston's."

As a result of the great holdings of these and lesser planters, the South in 1860 had 83 percent of the farms in the United States with 500 or more acres (200 or more hectares), fifty counties with populations of over 75 percent slaves, and the twelve richest counties in the country; Adams County, Mississippi (of which Natchez was the county seat) was the richest of all and had a slave population of more than 90 percent.

By 1850 the southern plantation system had reached maturity, with cotton plantations (those producing five or more bales) numbering 74,031; tobacco (raising 3,000 pounds [1,350 kilograms] or over), 15,745; hemp, 8,327; sugar, 2,681; and rice plantations (producing 20,000 pounds [9,000 kilograms] or more), 551. The fact that such a small quantity of production was needed to qualify a unit as a plantation doubtless means that many thousands of small cotton and tobacco farms with but one or two working hands were included in these numbers. One field hand could produce five bales of cotton, the normal yield from ten acres (4 hectares); two slaves could grow 3,000 pounds (1,350 kilograms) of tobacco, the average output of five acres (2 hectares); and two laborers could raise ten acres of rice, which should produce 20,000 pounds. Even including these many small units, there were only 101,335 plantations out of a total of 569,201 farms and plantations, slightly less than 18 percent.

With respect to the kind of staple produced, the number of slaves generally was inversely related to the number of plantations growing that kind of crop. The superintendent of the 1850 census estimated that 2.5 million slaves of all ages were directly engaged in agriculture: 60,000 in the production of hemp, 125,000 in rice, 150,000 in sugar, 350,000 in tobacco, and 1,815,000 in cotton. Thus, the rice plantations in 1850 would have 226 slaves per estate; sugar plantations, 55; hemp, 7; tobacco, 22; and cotton, 24.

What largely determined the physical size of the plantation was the walking distance from the slave quarters to the most distant field. Planters did not want this to exceed an hour or so; consequently, the middle-sized plantation consisted of 1,000 to 1,500 acres (400 to 600 hectares). While most planters used a portion of the improved land to produce provisions for their own use and that of the slave force, the principal function of the plantation was to produce a commercial crop for export. Thus, it was essential that it be located along a suitable transportation route (most often a river) and have fertile soil.

Planters in general were scientific farmers, as evidenced by their subscriptions to agricultural journals and the large number of articles written by planters for these journals. They practiced crop rotation to preserve soil fertility, and where practical and feasible they used fertilizing materials such as marl and guano and planted winter cover crops. Planters adapted agricultural procedures to their slave labor, using the latest techniques of planting and the most advanced machinery, tools, and implements. They were constantly striving to improve the quality of their seeds, draft animals, and livestock. And the planters wrestled with the problems of slave management, avidly reading the advice on such matters in the agricultural magazines and often writing responses.

The Culture of the Plantation

The antebellum plantation constituted a composite community. The bulk of the slave population consisted of field hands used directly in producing the commercial staple and the provision crops, such as corn (the most widely grown crop in the South), oats, peas, and potatoes. However, each plantation had another group of slaves employed in nonfield pursuits. They included animal raisers, baby keepers, barbers, blacksmiths, bricklayers, butchers, butlers, carpenters, coachmen, cobblers, cooks, coopers, engineers, gardeners, ginners, laundresses, maids, millers, nurses, seamstresses,

PORTICOS AND GARDENS

The typical antebellum plantation house and grounds was colonnaded with Greek Revival porticoes and surrounded by lush gardens.
CORBIS-BETTMANN

*All spirits are
enslaved which
serve things evil.*

SHELLEY

shoemakers, tailors, tanners, valets, waiters, and weavers. Many of these skilled slaves were trained to perform two or more trades and could also double as field hands during critical labor periods such as the harvest. After accounting for the young, old, and infirm (who could do no more than a quarter to half the work that a prime hand could do), gender differences (women could do three-fourths as much as a prime hand), and days lost to illness (generally from one to two a month), the planter's slave numbers were reduced in prime worker equivalency to little more than half. Thus, a plantation with one hundred slaves of all ages could expect the work of only fifty to sixty prime hands.

The focal figure in administering the plantation was the overseer, who had complete charge of the plantation for the period of his contract (usually a document written in January for the calendar year). He was consequently responsible for the labor and well-being of the workers, the maintenance of the property, and, most important, the success of the crop, on which the renewal of the contract very often depended. Although in 1860 there were 46,274 slaveholders with enough slaves (20 or more) to justify the employment of an overseer, William K. Scarborough (in *The Overseer*) was able to find only about 25,958 overseers in the entire South at that time. Rice plantations, whose owners were away from the plantation during the malaria season (May to November), needed overseers, as did most of the large sugar plantations. Apparently many large cotton and tobacco planters, disgusted at bad experiences with overseers, who generally came from the small farmer or poor white classes, chose to administer their own plantation. Bennet Barrow of West Fe-

liciana Parish in Louisiana, for example, supervised his plantation with two hundred slaves, using a slave foreman, or "driver," as assistant. Overseers were normally paid $500 to $700 annually, but those on large rice and sugar plantations often made $1,000 to $1,500; on his massive Jehossee Island rice plantation in South Carolina, with a slave force of seven hundred, Governor William Aiken paid $2,000. The tenure of an overseer was generally about three and a half years.

Below the overseer in the plantation hierarchy was the driver, who had direct responsibility for the day-to-day performance of the workers. The driver got the slaves to the fields in the mornings, organized the work gangs for the day, and excused them upon the satisfactory completion of the day's labor. He also generally administered plantation discipline. In addition, the driver was responsible for proper decorum in the slave quarters. He had certain perquisites: better food, clothing, and housing than was the lot of slaves in general; freedom from physical toil; and the prestige and authority accompanying the position of supervisor. At the same time the driver operated under a number of handicaps. His workday was longer than that of other slaves; he often experienced considerable difficulty in being fully accepted by the other slaves in the quarters; and he was buffeted by demands from the owner and overseer above and the slaves below. Planters generally selected a driver for each fifty slaves and considered the services of a good driver more important than those of the overseer; consequently the tenure of the driver normally was much longer than that of the overseer.

The slaves on the plantation lived in simple quarters some distance from the plantation house,

SLAVE QUARTERS

The slaves on the plantation lived in simple quarters some distance from the plantation house, in single cabins or double houses of wooden boards or shingles and occupied by two families.

LIBRARY OF CONGRESS /
CORBIS

in single cabins or double houses of wooden boards or shingles with a chimney in the middle and occupied by two families. There was also a "sick house," where the plantation nurse cared for slaves suffering from various maladies and fevers (and occasionally from such deadly diseases as cholera). She administered the medicines prescribed by the doctor who looked after the health of the slaves on a number of plantations at once, normally under contract for $1.25 to $1.50 per year for each slave in his care.

Clothing was issued twice yearly to the slaves—in late April or early May for the summer season and in late November or early December for the winter. In addition, the winter issue included blankets. Rations, given out weekly, generally consisted of three and a half pounds of bacon and a peck (fourteen pounds) of cornmeal for each adult, with lesser amounts for children. The slave family was usually given a piece of land for a garden to supplement its diet and was allowed to raise its own chickens and pigs. The planter also attended to the religious welfare of his slaves by employing local ministers to preach and encouraging the holding of religious classes on the plantation, and by allowing them to attend churches of their faith, usually Baptist or Methodist, in the general neighborhood.

The labor system on most plantations was that of gang labor, with individual squads working under the supervision of the driver or a squad leader from sunup to sundown. The exception was on the rice plantations, where discipline would have been virtually impossible without the task system. Because the planter was gone from early May to the killing frosts of November, leaving only the overseer and slave drivers to control affairs, a labor format was needed in which the slaves could largely direct themselves. The task system provided for an assignment that the poorest worker could complete in eight to nine hours. In practice, however, most slaves finished their tasks by midafternoon and could devote the rest of the day to working in their gardens, farming small tracts of rice of their own, looking after their livestock, or hunting or fishing. More than anything else, the task system kept lonely slaves on the isolated rice plantations from becoming restless and rebellious.

There was little interchange between rice slaves and those from the other plantations. Tobacco or cotton slaves would have difficulty acclimating to the isolated existence of the rice plantation and adjusting to the rice diet and the task system of labor. Thus, new hands on rice plantations were generally acquired from other rice plantations where sales were necessitated by the planter's overextension, by the breakup of the estates, or by slaves being too refractory to retain. The natural increase of slave numbers on rice plantations was normally about 5 percent. Conversely, rice slaves would not adapt very easily to the gang labor system of the cotton, tobacco, or sugar plantation.

Southern planters, with a considerable amount of fixed capital in their slaves, attempted to use their work force in the most efficient and profitable manner. Thus, they planted a much greater acreage in cash crops than in food crops (mainly cotton versus corn) and committed a larger share of the labor time of slave households to market production than was generally true for free families (mainly women doing fieldwork instead of housework). They could collectivize such household duties as food preparation and child care, thus freeing additional labor for fieldwork. The off-season of the commercial staple left ample time for the slaves to grow sufficient provisions; otherwise, as a fixed labor supply, they would have had little to do during much of the year.

As a result of these factors, slave labor was probably more efficient than free labor. The household economy of the plantation, with the work force able to produce great quantities of the staple, ample provisions, and most of the commodities needed on the plantation, doubtless contributed to the plantation's profitability. While most planters provided little more than bare subsistence in the way of food, clothing, and shelter for the slaves (as compared to what they took from the plantation profits for their households), there is ample evidence to demonstrate that planters well understood the correlation between fair treatment and the willingness of the slaves to work. In short, the masters who treated the slaves the best generally got the most efficient labor from them. Conversely, masters who were cruel to the slave force in the main found the slave labor output declining accordingly. Thus, the measure of treatment was a major factor in slave discipline on the plantation, generally of more effect than the constant threat of punishment. However, even the most generous master occasionally had to punish disobedient slaves to keep order among his work force.

While the plantation system brought high per capita incomes to individual planters (recent studies have demonstrated that plantation profitability was at least as much as the earnings of stocks and bonds in the North—6 to 8 percent—and sometimes considerably more), it ensured that the South, with its commitment to large-scale pro-

Where slavery is, there liberty cannot be; and where liberty is, there slavery cannot be.

CHARLES SUMNER

♦ Collectivize

To organize by collectivism, a political or economic theory advocating collective control especially over production and distribution; also a system marked by such control

P

*Wherever anyone is
against his will,
that to him is
a prison.*

EPICTETUS

duction of a few agricultural commodities in world demand, was dependent with respect to manufacturing (except for the household production on the plantations), merchandising, and banking. Southern planters showed little interest in internal improvements or in developing urban centers of manufacturing. However, while the South had only about twenty thousand manufacturing establishments in 1860, compared with one hundred thousand in the North, the gap is narrowed considerably when such facilities as cotton gins and rice and sugar mills on the plantations are considered in the South's overall manufacturing.

With respect to cultural matters, the southern planters put great stock in education to prepare their sons for public service and the professions. Accordingly, a large number of excellent academies sprang up throughout the southern states, and the area had the largest number of college students in the United States. At the same time, the planter elite saw little need to educate the masses, thus preventing much in the way of public schools. From the standpoint of religion, they supported the Episcopal church, whose ministers not only preached the gospel of slavocracy but often were slaveholders themselves (Leonidas Polk, the Episcopal bishop of Louisiana, owned four hundred). Some planters were Presbyterian or Roman Catholic (mostly in Louisiana), while the populace in general subscribed mainly to the Baptist and Methodist faiths.

The great planters buttressed their economic domination with political power. They produced great leaders such as John C. Calhoun, Robert Toombs, and Jefferson Davis, and exercised virtually total power at both the county and the state level (every governor in all the southern states in the 1850s was a slaveholding planter) and a large measure of control within national circles, especially in Congress and on the Supreme Court. At the same time, they drew together in support of such issues as the tariff and the westward expansion of slavery, developing the extreme doctrines of nullification and ultimately secession—a measure of how far the ultraconservative political views of South Carolinians had come to influence the section.

In alliance with the Old Northwest, the southern planters controlled the Democratic party from 1830 to 1860 and largely shaped the policies of the national government. They were able to force the lowering of the tariff in the nullification controversy of the 1830s and were in large part responsible for the Mexican War, fought to acquire

new lands for the expansion of slavery and the plantation system westward to the Pacific. However, their insistence that all the newly acquired territory be open to slavery, and that Cuba and Central America were possible targets for annexation, alienated their western allies and ended their control of the party. The election of a Republican president committed to containment of slavery in 1860 made the threat of secession a reality, bringing on the Civil War.

The Plantation Legacy

Although the invading Union forces wreaked massive destruction upon the plantation facilities and the slaves were ultimately freed, the plantation system largely survived intact but with a vastly different labor format. Probably as many as half of the plantations changed hands over the following ten to fifteen turbulent years. The planters, labor lords before the war, were now landlords and thus forced to accommodate the demands of the emancipated blacks for more control of their lives and conditions of work. At first they tried to operate with a cash wage system, with the blacks living in their former slave cabins and subject to plantation discipline under the newly enacted black codes. However, this plan did not work well for either group. The planters could not force the blacks to work as hard as they had when they were slaves, nor could they be certain of how dependable the blacks would be to see the crop through. In addition, little capital was available to the planters, and where it was, the interest rates were prohibitive—2.5 to 3 percent a month. From the blacks' standpoint, the wage system resembled slavery too much and gave them little say in their own working lives.

Cotton and tobacco planters soon came up with a sharecropping system under which the blacks would be rented certain portions of the land (to which they would move, thus getting away from the distasteful slave quarters) and share in decision making with the owners. To the blacks the new system brought a large measure of independence; to the planters it brought a more dependable and cheaper labor supply. Generally, the planter furnished workers with land, seed, fertilizer, draft animals, and tools, and in exchange took half to two-thirds of the harvested crop.

Under this new organization the plantations survived with little change until the 1930s, but not without great difficulties. The cotton crop of 1875 equaled that of 1859 in amount but not in profits. A saturation of the world supply of cotton

See also
African American Music

depressed prices (by the mid 1890s they were little more than a third of the inflated prices of the late 1850s), and the resulting economic hard times created as much havoc for cotton planters as the Civil War had. Indeed, the antebellum cotton planters would have fallen on hard times had there been no war nor emancipation of the slaves.

Other staples fared less well. The sugar crop in Louisiana was back to its prewar level by 1879, but the plantations is largely survived through outside capital, with about half of them owned by northerners.

Rice made the poorest recovery of all. The former slaves were not willing to go back into the snake- and mosquito-infested swamps, nor were they willing to do the "mud work" of cleaning out ditches and repairing banks. Outside capital was not available, and competition soon developed on uplands in Louisiana (led by Dr. Seaman A. Knapp, president of Iowa State College, and a group of midwestern grain farmers), with powered irrigation and harvesting machinery too heavy for the soggy swamplands of the Carolinas and Georgia. The new competition, coupled with a series of very destructive hurricanes around the turn of the century, spelled the death knell for the old rice coast. The plantations were converted to residential housing, resorts, and wildlife refuges, or allowed to return to their natural state.

The New Deal of the 1930s dealt a sharp blow to the plantation system. What may be called an "American enclosure movement"—like the English movement of the 1500s that turned fields into sheep pastures, driving out agricultural workers—encouraged the displacement of sharecroppers and tenants (generally whites who had lost their small farms in the 1890s and early 1900s, and by now out-numbered the black sharecroppers), the expansion of home farms cultivated by family members rather than sharecroppers, and more reliance on hired labor. The concomitant development of mammoth farm machinery, including mechanical cotton pickers and tobacco harvesters, and the effective use of chemical herbicides and pesticides led to such a reduced need for labor that blacks and whites were forced to migrate in droves to the cities of the Northeast and Midwest to seek new employment. Thus, by the 1970s the plantation, the focal point in shaping southern life for three centuries, was little more than a memory, shrouded in such nostalgic distortions of the *Gone With the Wind* variety that it very often was difficult to separate the mythical from the real.

—JAMES M. CLIFTON

POPULAR ENTERTAINMENT BEFORE THE CIVIL WAR

The Evolution of the word "entertainment" between 1600 and 1860 suggests a broad outline for the social changes described in this essay. The verb "to entertain" was once closely allied to the verb "to maintain." It implied an obligation owed to a guest under one's roof and even extended to the legal responsibilities that came with the employment of domestic labor, as in "I entertained five ploughmen on my property." Over the course of the eighteenth century, however, this sense of personal obligation became muted, so that any form of social treating could be called an entertainment. Tavernkeepers now "entertained" their guests, even though the guests paid for the privilege. By the time of the Civil War, an entertainment could be any form of freestanding commercial amusement.

This change in the word's meaning reflects the rise of a popular market for leisure pursuits over the period, indeed a striking transformation; by the late nineteenth century, most entertainments were provided *for* families rather than *by* them. The change also suggests the transformation of early notions of duty and respectability into some fairly mercenary social practices. This moral reevaluation can be seen even more clearly in the parallel development of the concept of "amusement." "To amuse" once carried only negative connotations. It suggested planned trickery, as in a military general's sending out troops to amuse an enemy. Again, by 1860 Americans were using the term, almost with approval, to describe a whole range of popular recreations. Through amusement and entertainment, one might relieve the pressure of work or the anonymity of the city.

These shifts in meaning determine a dual agenda for those who wish to study the social history of American entertainment. One approach is to track the passage of leisure, however broadly defined, into an urban, commercial marketplace, noting the many new forms of amusement made available to an increasingly diverse and growing population. A second avenue is to highlight the problem of values, both moral and political, in this extension of popular entertainment. As various groups began to develop their own distinctive styles of amusement, there inevitably arose com-

Another strand included the eighteenth-century commercial proprietors who opened private parks, modeled on London's pleasure gardens, for outdoor entertainments.

PAGE 544

P

**POPULAR
ENTERTAINMENT
BEFORE THE
CIVIL WAR**

*The Colonial and Early
National Periods*

*If you have ever
been an actor . . .
why it just about
ruins you for any
useful employment
for the rest of
your life.*

WILL ROGERS

peting claims and doubts about the worth of these different forms of recreation in a single, virtuous republic. Far from being a neat linear description of ever-growing choice, the history of American recreation may appear as fractured and as problematic as the story of American political party formation. Without this second, evaluative task, the subject of recreation might remain inherently lighthearted, perhaps confirming G. R. Elton's remark that the social historian often appears as "second cousin to the tabloid journalist."

The Colonial and Early National Periods

The narrative must begin awkwardly, by questioning the very notion of "American" recreation in the colonial period. It is difficult to claim that before about 1840 the United States had a national cultural outlook as expressed by its amusements; most musical and theatrical life, for example, remained local in character until the 1820s. Americans' amusement customs reflected citizens' different ethnic and religious affiliations. In addition, the demands of regional farming and market patterns caused rural populations to have varying degrees of acquaintance with urban forms of pleasure. New England farmers tended to be more self-sufficient in meeting their needs for food than were their neighbors in the Middle Atlantic states and thus had less opportunity to come together in marketplaces that might have provided opportunities for popular amusements. In the South, the draconian demands of single-crop cultivation, especially of tobacco, severely limited the occasions for socializing and amusement for most residents.

Despite such variation, certain generalizations may be made about the place of entertainment in the overall fabric of colonial life. The most obvious point about early American society was that it was predominantly agricultural; indeed, the rural population increased as a percentage of the whole through most of the eighteenth century, and only 5 percent of the national population was urban as late as 1820. The leisure activities of most Americans during the colonial period and the early years of the republic revolved around the yearly cycle of agricultural work, with the traditional European celebrations of May Day, marking the arrival of spring, and Harvest Home (celebrating the gathering of the crops) being recast in local forms. In New England, the spring-training days for militias, despite their serious intent, took on the aspect of a "Maygame" (11th-century English phrase for "Mayday"), and the religious Thanksgiving celebration retained older images of abun-

dance and sexual promise. The clearest case of a European seasonal festival surviving the passage to the New World intact is Louisiana's Mardi Gras, though New Orleans did not officially recognize the event until 1857.

Such holidays may have been traditional in the sense that the forms were ancient, but their social context in the infant society was new. Travelers observed that the most distinctive American entertainments were those connected to communal work. Because of the relative shortage of male labor in the early years of settlement, a premium was placed on cooperative effort, occasioning such "frolics" as cornhuskings and barn and house raisings. The social aspects of such work, especially the liberal treating to food and drink, were necessary for securing the labor of the villagers and added to the density of kinship and community ties upon which credit and livelihood depended. One of the more interesting aspects of these frolics is that they were viewed as such a necessary social ritual that even the most frugal farmers seldom registered the cost of these events in their account books. To refer back to the initial sense of the word, one's obligation to "entertain" still carried a sense of maintaining property and social standing. In addition to work-related frolics, families were also expected to treat the community on the occasion of births, baptisms, weddings, and, before the rise of the early-nineteenth-century vogue for protracted mourning, funerals as well.

Two other forms of amusement, though not strictly entertainments, were judged by both visitors and residents to have taken on distinctive qualities in the New World. The traditional field sport of hunting was immeasurably enhanced by the presence of plentiful and, for Europeans, unusual game. As James Fenimore Cooper recounted in the pigeon-shooting scene in *The Deerslayer* (1841), hunting soon became as much a form of recreation as a necessity, as settlers in all sections took to the woods and fields. The popularity of mass "coon" and squirrel hunts, turkey shoots, and deer draws (the use of horses to flush animals from cover) cannot be explained solely by the need to provide sustenance or to protect crops. The enthusiasm for hunting may have had much to do with the novel absence of aristocratic game laws and the greater availability of firearms among all social classes. As George Alsop, an indentured servant, observed in seventeenth-century Maryland, "Every Servant has a Gun, Powder and Shot allowed him, to sport with all on all Holidays and leasurable times."

See also
Urban Parks

P

**POPULAR
ENTERTAINMENT
BEFORE THE
CIVIL WAR**

*The Colonial and Early
National Periods*

WORK AND PLAY

*In the nineteenth century,
hunting was as much a form of
recreation as it was a necessity.*
HULTON-DEUTSCH
COLLECTION / CORBIS

Quarterly training and annual election-day gatherings also drew the attention of travelers and the magistracy. Though both events were seen as central to the maintenance of colonial order, both also attracted their share of high jinks and drunkenness. Booths serving food and drink were often placed on the periphery of the marching ground at training sessions, and some seventeenth-century New England accounts record the presence of Native Americans as onlookers. (The interaction between the races in terms of amusements remains a remarkably unexplored subject.) Training days usually ended with informal target-shooting contests, wrestling matches, and foot-races, as well as music and dance. Such festivities provided a welcome break from the rigors of work and offered a convenient occasion for young men to "keep company" with young women.

Frolics, bees, musters, and hunting were all later celebrated, especially in nineteenth-century genre painting, as occasions when American society was at ease with itself and most cohesive in character. Yet amusements could just as readily express the inequalities in the social structure. The most persistent fracture in the world of colonial recreation occurred along the lines of gender. Women's leisure remained tied to the domestic sphere, and despite the sewing parties, quilting bees, flax pullings and scrutchings, or celebrations organized around family rites of passage, women's recreations were probably more solitary and sparse than those of men. Laurel Thatcher Ulrich's wonderful account of New England women, *Good Wives* (1991), contains little about leisure, since domestic production remained paramount. Literature of the period suggested that women could not be both productive and ornamental at the same time, although during the eighteenth century thinking advanced to the point that it was conceded that a gentlewoman might take tea with her friends, polish the silver, and embroider lace. Recent studies of rural women have found that an increase in what might be termed women's discretionary time did not lead to a broadening of their social role; rather, it led to an increasingly ceremonial meaning of housekeeping, requiring further embellishment of the garden and the table.

Social class further regulated the access to, and the meaning of, entertainment. Most servants in early New England society were prevented by laws of indenture from visiting taverns and other places of resort, and since fully one-third of the men arriving in the northern colonies were under some form of servitude, their opportunities for regular recreation must have been fewer than those of free-holders. The class patterning of amusement was even more evident in the South. There large landowners adopted the ideals of the

See also
African American Music;
The City

P

**POPULAR
ENTERTAINMENT
BEFORE THE
CIVIL WAR**

*The Colonial and Early
National Periods*

*Songs, riddles,
jokes, fortune-
telling, and
abridged versions of
chivalric romances
and the popular
English novels
of the day were
printed in
chapbooks.*

PAGE 339

♦ **Magistracy**
*The district under a
magistrate*

English gentry that linked the enjoyment of leisure with social prestige. The provision of entertainments to guests and workers conferred a sense of honor, and from the mid eighteenth century on, writers such as the indentured John Hammond promoted the South as a region given over to leisure and material abundance.

In hunting, the southern planter class differentiated itself from the commoners by emphasizing the chase rather than the kill and by preferring sports, especially horsemanship and fencing, associated with the aristocracy. The most glaring archaism was the popularity of ring tournaments, which referred back to the medieval pageantry of royal jousts. "Knights," often military cadets, had to scoop up with their lances rings suspended from posts, with the most skilled performer ending up as a "king." The gentry were certainly not above promoting and enjoying rougher sports; indeed, their position as judges and patrons of wrestling matches, cockfights, and eye-gouging contests further emphasized their social standing.

The class lines evident in patterns of amusement in the South were made much stronger by the presence of slavery, and most of the original work on American popular culture has been influenced by recent debates on the autonomy of slave religious and cultural practices. In contrast to the neo-abolitionist historians, who stressed the physical and psychological confinements of plantation slavery, most recent studies have documented the ways that slaves maintained both cultural identity and a sense of self-worth through family life, religion, and amusement. Even allowing for hyperbole among the later apologists and memorialists, many planters did "entertain" their slaves with a form of patriarchal benevolence. Most owners granted slaves the traditional Christian holidays and the sabbath, as well as Saturday afternoons and extra time after harvesting and planting. In addition, the provision of extra meat and drink for celebratory barbecues appears to have been customary. Historians Eugene Genovese and John Blassingame have detailed the ways in which slaves used this free time: securing passes to visit towns and other plantations, engaging in rural sports, and performing traditional African styles of music and dance, especially "patting juba." Disagreement arises, however, over the social and psychological consequences of such benevolence by slaveholders. From Frederick Douglass onward, many commentators have taken the provision of leisure to be little more than a cynical means of exercising social control. For Genovese, the granting of "entertainment"

generated a curious double bind, characteristic of other aspects of master-slave (and, indeed, class) relationships. "Treating" permitted the masters to proclaim their benevolence as well as to allow slaves the social space to develop their own oppositional culture; on the other hand (and more problematic), the slaves' "acceptance" of entertainment tied them into their own domination.

After studies of the Old South, the recreational practices of Puritan New England have gained most scholarly attention, perhaps because the Calvinist emphasis on work spawned a debate about the danger of social pleasure that continues into the present. The role of amusements has also figured in the perennial debate over whether Puritan society suffered a decline, with a growth in hostility between sinners and saints, or whether it maintained its social cohesion at the local level, as manifested in relatively low rates of crime and of social deviance.

Puritanism in England emerged as a reformation in manners rather than as a distinct theological strain within Calvinism; the revelries associated with Guy Fawkes Day, Christmas, May Day, and Saint Valentine's Day were symptomatic of the popular culture that Puritans wished to escape in coming to America. Puritan society was also invested, to an unusual degree, in the adult and the patriarchal. All people—apprentices, children, servants, and wives—had to live within the firm government of the family. Sermons and conduct books contained long lists of prohibitions on the enjoyment of cards, dice, alehouses, and taverns.

Yet studies of New England towns have now shown that there was an embarrassing gap between rhetoric and practice and, moreover, that this gap widened during the eighteenth century. Folly and lewdness at harvest time continued despite the many warnings against such practices. As Roger Thompson has shown, though there was nothing quite like the "Abbeys of Misrule," a traditional opportunity for young folk to go on a spree, there was nevertheless a good deal of youthful revelry, usually at the festival times that Puritans formally abhorred. Young men who found a red ear of corn were allowed by custom (more American Indian than English) to kiss any women they chose, leading to predictable excesses and lawsuits. What is more surprising is that the magistracy displayed a certain degree of latitude in indictment and in sentencing, either because leniency is often the best way of maintaining hegemony or because Puritan theology contained a sophisticated conception of sin as a condition of

PURITAN ENTERTAINMENTS IN THE EIGHTEENTH CENTURY

Nathaniel Hawthorne was right about the gap between rhetoric and practice regarding revelry at Marymount—indeed, there was a riot in Middlesex when a maypole was erected—but he was probably wrong about the gray joylessness that appeared in its place. We know that Puritans sang, danced, and drank and that ministers were tolerant of secular music and approving of man's dominion over fish and fowl as expressed in hunting. It was in fact a passionate society; the problem was that passion could so easily become lasciviousness.

Over the course of the eighteenth century, the practice of keeping "holy watchfulness" over neighbors' behavior eroded. Increasing geographical mobility militated against social control by patriarchs or community, and a number of studies have charted the changes brought on by a growing population, land shortages, and the search for new opportunities. New kinds of secular information and enjoyment were prized under such conditions. In addition, as historian William Rorabaugh has shown, plentiful supplies of both domestically produced grain spirit and imported rum affected both work and leisure pursuits.

the person, rather than as a proscribed set of behaviors.

In the towns, the mercantile elite threw off much of the productivist ethos that had bound its more religious forebears. By mid century, most cities held formal assemblies for the wealthy, and even Boston established regular social evenings for dancing and music after 1740. Charleston's Saint Cecilia Society founded the first subscription ball in 1762. The arrival of theatrical performances open to all sections of the public, however, formed the most distinctive change in entertainment in the towns. One Richard Hunter, sometime between 1699 and 1702, petitioned the corporation of the City of New York to permit him to stage a play, though there is little evidence that the show actually opened. Other bands of players occasionally performed in mid-Atlantic and southern towns throughout the early eighteenth century, but it was not until a troupe of actors led by Lewis Hallam arrived in New York in 1752 that any American city witnessed something that approached a full season of theatrical enter-

tainment. New York gained its first permanent theater, on John Street, in 1767, and Philadelphia, on Chestnut Street, in 1794; Boston, in 1794, opened the Federal Street Theatre after a riotous crowd protested the closing of an unlicensed performance.

Despite New Yorkers' habit of calling the John Street Theatre "Old Drury," after London's major playhouse licensed by royal letters patent, or their briefly renaming lower Broadway "The Mall," in the hope of creating a formal promenade, the scale of refined urban entertainments was minute compared to those conducted under aristocratic patronage in European capitals. The John Street Theatre could contain only four hundred people at a time, and no American place of entertainment could accommodate more than one thousand people until 1810.

In response to the growing secularization of leisure in the towns, local ministers initiated moral-reform societies and pushed for formal "sabbatarian" legislation (no secular amusement on Sunday), raising the pitch of their anti-entertainment rhetoric. The reformation of psalmody in New England after 1720, for instance, has been seen as a central exercise in ministerial control over unruly congregational practices, and the Massachusetts General Court's 1750 act banning "public stage-plays, interludes, and other theatrical entertainments" was only a timely (and perhaps desperate) restatement of codes already on the books. Yet the greatest ideological challenge to the rise in secular entertainment came from less traditional sources of authority. The arrival of the English evangelist George Whitefield and the spread of the Great Awakening of the 1740s emphasized in a new way the emotional and personal side of salvation and called for a more active monitoring of personal pleasure; evangelicals resurrected the criticism of many amusements as representing a waste of time and a dissolution of self-control. Only by the beginning of the twentieth century would the notion of consuming pleasures or products come to mean anything other than the using up of resources that would be better saved for later.

On the other hand, it is possible to claim that evangelical revivalism accelerated the creation of a national, popular culture. Both amusement entrepreneurs and evangelicals stressed American innovation over European tradition, and competition over orthodoxy. Whitefield's use of advance publicity, paid puffs, and cheap pamphlets set new standards for the infant commercial culture. Since evangelicals did not allow one's standing as a

P

POPULAR
ENTERTAINMENT
BEFORE THE
CIVIL WAR

*The Colonial and Early
National Periods*

*Slave masters
typically placed a
high value on good
slave musicians
who entertained the
whites at their
dances, balls, and
impromptu social
gatherings.*

PAGE 15

See also
Sports through the
Nineteenth Century

P

**POPULAR
ENTERTAINMENT
BEFORE THE
CIVIL WAR**

*The Rise of Commercial
Entertainment*

*Drinking,
gambling, and
many of the
pastimes of Old
England flourished;
and hunting,
fishing and fowling,
sports of the
privileged back
home, could be
enjoyed by all.*

PAGE 433

Christian to rest on baptism only, a succession of public declarations of faith was required. Revivals were seldom spontaneous; they had to be—and were—worked up using the most modern forms of promotion available. By the time of revivalist Charles Grandison Finney's sweeps through New York in the late 1820s, the performative values of a protracted meeting, with its use of the anxious bench, certainly matched the melodramatic productions that were being staged in the new urban theaters. The rhetoric traded between ministers and amusement entrepreneurs was so hostile because both helped forge, and claimed as their own, the new American public of social actors who could be equally "recreated," regardless of class or background. When in the 1840s ways were found to link piety and commercial entertainment, as in showman P. T. Barnum's moral plays or moralist Timothy Shay Arthur's temperance tales, a profitable and enduring amalgam was created that survives to the present.

Through the revolutionary and early national periods, evangelical piety combined with notions of republican simplicity and virtue to steady the growth in commercial amusement. Suspicious of the theater's historical association with European courtly corruption and wary of the practical fact that the British officer class and monarchists were the theater's avid devotees, the Continental Congress banned troops from attending staged performances throughout the War for Independence. Local revolutionary assemblies were more direct; Philadelphia's patriotic leaders, for instance, issued edicts against the theater, card playing, and dancing assemblies. One positive result of this republican fervor was a general movement, as in the promotion of shape-note musical notation (a simplified notation that was readily comprehended), to make cultural learning less arcane and more available to the average citizen. Physician Benjamin Rush suggested that republican citizens should be directly educated through the eyes rather than by the classical learning of the past, leading artist Charles Willson Peale to experiment with "moving picture" and transparencies at his Philadelphia museum. The vogue for panoramas and dioramas after 1790 also answered the call for innovative, virtuous ways to blend instruction and amusement. Some cultural leaders even believed that public virtue might well deserve public funding. Merchant and philanthropist John Pintard petitioned the New York legislature to turn an old almshouse building into an institution encompassing the Tammany and Historical societies, an art gallery, studio space, and a music

school. New York theatrical manager William Dunlap dreamed of a time when the theater, under state ownership and control, might be turned into an "engine" of virtue, and Boston's Joseph Haliburton presented a plan for an enormous octagonal superdome that would provide space for public functions such as Harvard commencements as well as a place where indigent women could sew clothes.

Despite these modest efforts to hitch cultural forms to the bandwagon of internal improvements, almost no state sponsorship of recreation occurred, except for the movement to establish city parks, until the Progressive Era. To an unusual degree, considering religious and political concern about unproductive activities, the free market was left to provide for all forms of recreation with hardly any legal intervention; for example, New York City possessed no formal system of theater licensing until 1823.

The Rise of Commercial Entertainment

Between 1800 and 1850 the customary patterns of leisure for most Americans underwent a transformation within a dynamic and unregulated commercial setting; the impact of a tremendous increase in population and improved transportation, as well as the complex of social changes that accompanied urbanization, came together to forge a new amusement culture. The change was more than just a matter of scale and involved a decided and perhaps irreversible change in vector. Everywhere amusement for profit grew at the expense of customary pastimes and introduced a division of leisure activities by social grouping as marked as that of labor.

The transformation in the scale and vector of commercial culture in the towns is most evident in the theater. As late as 1820, New York had only one theater, the Park, which was opened in 1798 by Lewis Hallam and John Hodgkinson to replace the John Street Theatre. In 1850, New York possessed six legitimate theaters operating during the winter season, four summer gardens, and at least sixty other places of minor amusement. Even Pittsburgh, which still had a population under fifty thousand at mid century, claimed eleven places of commercially staged entertainment, as well as nine bookstores and four music shops. Chicago gained its first theater in 1847, with eight more opening before 1860. Whatever index is examined, the increase in commercial staged amusement outpaced the growth rates in urban population.

ENTERTAINMENTS IN RURAL COMMUNITIES

Theater, Fairs, and Circuses

Although the innovation in recreational forms began in the cities, social change, and awareness of change, must have been most dramatic in rural society. The new turnpikes brought many more itinerant troupes of performers and sundry shows to farming regions, making their people's acquaintance with commercial amusement something more than just a seasonal experience. By 1829, according to Philip Jordan, the National Road was carrying several good-sized caravans of living animals and skilled performers, and the Mississippi and Allegheny rivers had flatboat theaters in operation before that date. Scott Martin has found that even in the communities of deepest rural Pennsylvania, entertainments were being provided after 1820. Harvest festivals, for instance, began to incorporate point-to-point horse racing with organized betting, in violation of a state ban on such equestrian contests. The arrival of planned agricultural fairs may offer the best way to date local changes in amusement practices. Promoter and agriculturalist Elkanah Watson organized the first formal fair for Massachusetts in 1810, which, though it professed an educational mission, immediately attracted a range of booths offering liquor, performances, and food. Most counties in the Northeast and Middle Atlantic regions had regularly scheduled fairs by the late 1820s, and the South developed its state fairs through the 1830s. These developments meant that itinerant showmen could now plan on having routes, audiences, and profits.

While there continued to be communitywide activities, a host of voluntary associations and orders now provided organized amusement specifically for their membership. The number of Masonic lodges multiplied tenfold between 1780 and 1820, and after 1820 the vogue for incorporating literary, singing, and philosophical societies brought new kinds of cultural knowledge to the countryside while at the same time further eroding whatever commonality of leisure existed.

The meaning of such changes for rural society remains to be charted. Studies of popular amusement beyond the cities are still few and far between, though there exists a wealth of information to be mined in the many county histories published at the turn of the last century. There is no general work on popular recreation for the antebellum period equivalent in its range and seriousness to Robert Malcolmson's study of leisure activities in England. Nevertheless, it is clear that the commercialization of recreation helped to differentiate the world of work from the pursuit of leisure. Though frolics and bees continued well into the nineteenth century, especially among the poor, the arrival of commercial amusement at the taverns and the fairs no doubt lessened their appeal and adjusted their frame of meaning. Recreation no longer oscillated within the rhythms of work but was to gain its own place in the commercial setting. Further, the same movement that lifted much entertainment out of its earlier community setting also allowed for a privatization of leisure pursuits. The advent of mass-produced musical instruments and sheet music allowed people to narrow their social sphere of entertainment rather than take their pleasures at increasingly anonymous sites of public performance. Parlor theatricals became popular within middle-class households after 1830, at the same time that the commercial theater gained a large working-class patronage.

Moreover, the cost of access to the expanding world of popular entertainment decreased as the century progressed. In 1820, admission to major American theaters usually cost one dollar for the boxes, seventy-five cents for the pit, and fifty cents for the upper gallery, prices that excluded all those below the ranks of regularly employed skilled artisans. By 1850, admission prices had been generally cut by half, despite inflation. All theaters, except for those offering opera and other costly spectaculars, then held to a scale of "fifty cents top." Entrance to the minor forms of minstrelsy, pantomime, and variety could be gained for as little as five pennies. High volume and low admission prices became the surest formula for success; elaborate subscription plans, which had supported America's first theaters, gave way to cash taken at the door or at ticket outlets distributed throughout the cities. The era of the common man, at leisure and in politics, had arrived.

This impressive expansion in the market for what was, by the Civil War, termed "the show business" was also dependent upon an ever-broadening range of amusements offered. As with other forms of commercial enterprise, curious divisions of labor and specializations occurred within the entertainment field. The late-eighteenth-century stage had hosted all manner of perform-

See also
Humor and Comedy;
Theater and Musical Theater

**POPULAR
ENTERTAINMENT
BEFORE THE
CIVIL WAR**

*The Rise of Commercial
Entertainment*

*After the
Revolution, musical
life in American
cities began
to thrive as
prohibitions against
instrumental music
in churches and
musical theater
were relaxed.*

PAGE 99

See also
Parades, Holidays and
Public Rituals

ance: tragedy, comedy, vocal and dance acts, sleight of hand, and equestrian dramas and other animal acts. All these were performed before a socially heterogeneous audience distributed within the auditorium according to rank and degree; the wealthy families occupied the boxes, younger elite men sat on benches in the pit, and the common folk crowded into the inexpensive upper galleries. During the summer, when the indoor theaters closed because of the heat, a similar mixture of performance and audience could be found in the summer gardens. By 1800, New York possessed two such gardens specializing in musical performances, fireworks, and transparencies.

In both theaters and gardens, the irregular performance values issuing from the stage were matched by the untidy behavior of all sections of the audience. Before about 1830, a "long run" seldom lasted more than a few days, and it was not unusual for stock actors to perform in six different plays over a week. An evening at the theater included a "double bill" of a tragedy and a comedy separated by an entr'acte of a vocal or choreographic nature. Though performances rarely ended much before midnight, customers seldom felt it necessary to sit through the entire evening's presentation, as the house bars were open all evening and one could also secure a pass to visit neighboring hostelries. A constant shuffling among the audience, together with the ad-libbing of the actors, audible prompts from the wings, and outright disasters, such as might occur when an elephant urinated into the orchestra pit, added to the excitement. Since the performers themselves hardly presented a finished piece, the audience felt free to add its own interpolations of original wit and local allusion. It also felt entitled to close the performance down altogether by hissing and throwing oranges, chairs, and other projectiles if the management departed from customary practice or if the featured actor made unpatriotic statements. At least five British actors had their American tours terminated by such interference between 1825 and 1850. Under these conditions one can understand why actors deferred to the audience as their patrons and masters.

After about 1825, however, as the towns began to sustain more than one permanent theater, both sides of this audience/performance equation changed. In New York, which has always possessed the most active market in commercial recreation, the new Bowery Theatre, opened in 1826, began to specialize in lively melodramatic plays, in contrast to those presented at the Park, which continued to stage Shakespeare and genteel

British comedy. By 1830 the Bowery had become known not only for its distinctive staging, which incorporated all the latest technology, but also for the raucous artisanal audiences who flocked to its presentations. Observers invariably tagged the most active section of the Bowery crowd as "Byronic" because of its appreciation of the daring, manly feats on stage and its overtly republican interjections. In its new popular form, melodrama presented a general social radicalism owing little to its "music and mime" origins in eighteenth-century France. No matter what the setting—gothic castles, republican Rome, or secluded forests—melodrama always specialized in male heroes who overcame the forces of nature, the state, or sheer evil. Most of the new American plays, including John Augustus Stone's *Metamora* (1829) and Henry M. Milner's *Mazeppa* (1831), featured a recognizably Jacksonian lead character who stumbled, drenched in blood, toward a magical resolution of injustice and inequality. By mid-century, melodrama had become a byword for the merely popular, a theatrical form that pandered in its blood-and-thunder routines to the lowliest newsboy and mechanic. Foreign visitors were advised to avoid theaters other than the Park, and by 1840 most elite New Yorkers had relinquished their patronage of any staged drama.

As noted, there was nothing new about social distinction and exclusivity in the exercise of leisure, even in republican America. The gentry and mercantile elite had always spent their discretionary time in ways different from the common folk; indeed, only the elite possessed leisure of a nominally elevating kind, since others were bound to the world of daily work. Yet there are two aspects to the exercise of cultural distinction in the Jacksonian period that are strikingly novel. First, class separation in entertainment practices acquired a spatial reality in the growing cities. In New York, for instance, almost all of the new popular forms of amusement first appeared on the Bowery, in a narrow strip adjacent to the largest concentration of working-class housing. More-refined amusements followed their wealthy patrons out of the heavily congested commercial downtown into what then constituted the suburbs. Though this may be taken as a simple matter of real estate markets, a degree of planning was involved. For instance, the Astor family on occasion "seeded" its residential developments with low-cost leases for high cultural institutions to improve the social tone of the locale.

New forms of entertainment were also developed beyond the suburbs. Improved transportation led to a reconceptualization of the benefits of "nature," or rather allowed the temporary pursuit of older values celebrating the rural life. Wealthier New Yorkers, for example, developed and patronized a number of local resorts after 1810, especially Hoboken and the Rockaways, as Bostonians were to do at Nahant. Though such extraurban resorts initially attempted to offer relaxation in a pastoral setting, commerce soon moved in. By midcentury Hoboken offered horse racing, ox roasts, fortune telling, and any number of spectaculars, such as a buffalo hunt staged by Barnum. As in the case of the theater, the wealthy largely abandoned these sites in the face of such popularization. By 1830 it was practical, and socially advantageous, to summer in the Berkshire hills in Massachusetts or in Newport, where one might hobnob with other regional elites or, in the case of Saratoga, with southern gentry as well. It has been estimated that upward of fifty thousand southerners vacationed annually at northern spa resorts in the decade before the Civil War, and the Yankee elite returned the flow by popularizing White Sulphur Springs, in West Virginia. As part of this discovery of extramural enjoyment, the seaside vacation was invented. Seawater had first been recommended by doctors for its therapeutic properties as a drink, but following aristocratic fashion, in which the nobility had followed the Prince Regent (later George IV) down to Brighton, polite Americans took to the surf. By the second decade of the nineteenth century, Far Rockaway, New York, and later Long Branch, New Jersey, featured bathing machines and other technologies for pleasurable paddling, such as devices to hide women's legs as they descend into the surf. The middle classes did not patronize coastal resorts much until after the Civil War.

Added to this spatial separation of recreation was the advent of new ethical and aesthetic claims for refined entertainments at the same time that the plebeians were gaining increasing access to all forms of dramatic and literary production. This movement to establish an ethical hierarchy in forms of entertainment was most marked in musical activity. Before about 1830, no American city had managed to sustain a permanent site for secular concert performances; the only regularly scheduled concerts featured sacred works, usually with a large choral component. In 1840, however, the Boston Academy of Music dispensed with its chorus and set about winning the support of the public for the classical secular canon centered on Beethoven. Behind this change in programming lay two assumptions about the nature of the

Academy's public. First, the Academy could count on subscription support, for the first time, from a large sector of Boston's mercantile elite, including the Appletons, the Lawrences, and the Stoddards. Second, it claimed that the public attending the concerts possessed a certain discriminating taste. "Taste" indeed became a key word, shifting in meaning from an instant sensation, as in a taste of food, to an aesthetic understanding resident in a person. Concert music, claimed Samuel Eliot, the Academy's president, was no longer mere entertainment, something to be tasted occasionally; rather, music possessed a transcendent value that reached into the very soul of the listener and remained as part of that person's moral character. In one sense, since Eliot had trained to be a Unitarian minister, music became a necessary adjunct to formal religious experience.

Similar claims, redolent of German idealism, also issued from critics writing in the newly specialized musical and literary journals. Certain forms of music, poetry, and fiction apparently had an ethic of moral gravity, in contrast to the levity of the overtly popular amusements. In New York much ideological work was devoted to raising the opera out of the plane of amusement and into this sacralized sphere. Four attempts to found a permanent site for the opera after the notable arrival of the García troupe in 1825 failed until the opening of the Astor Place Opera House, with Astor family support, in 1847. The *New York Herald* noted that this opera house was the "first authentic organization of the upper classes . . . of the city." Yet, for those involved in the enterprise, the elite character of the patronage was not as important as their claim that opera, unfettered by a literal understanding, could ascend to a plane of moral purity untouched by the topicality of local theater.

Enthusiastic critics of music and opera claimed to be in tune with Jacksonian democracy to the extent that the common man was supposedly amenable to taste and cultivation, something eighteenth-century gentry might not have acknowledged or thought desirable. However, in practice the price of entry into the world of refined taste was high, and the social distance between self-consciously artistic performances and the popular stage broadened over the second quarter of the century. Opera houses and concert halls were the first performance spaces to introduce numbered seating and uniformed ushers and to demand a sense of decorum among the audience. Male patrons were expected to remove their hats (by 1830), refrain from eating, and withhold

Ben Franklin's Poor Richard satirized authority, false piety, and deceitfulness, expounding wittily about adultery, prostitution, excretion, and such unsavory subjects in a foreshadowing of black humor.

PAGE 222

P

**POPULAR
ENTERTAINMENT
BEFORE THE
CIVIL WAR**

Urban Popular Culture

*These libraries
catered to a whole
new reading
audience in the
decade and a half
prior to the
Revolution:
individuals, many
of whom were
women, who read
for entertainment.*

PAGE 361

See also
Concert Music; Print and
Publishing

their applause until the end of the act. Music and opera, as well as Shakespearean tragedies, required an aesthetic sanctity and coherence that could not be violated by audience members shifting or gesticulating in their seats—behavior in which all social classes had engaged before 1830. Some critics, such as Walt Whitman, continued to dream of a genuinely popular operatic and concert life in America, yet by the Civil War most cultural nationalists had relinquished their fond hopes for a progressive elevation of taste through such forms. Taste might indeed improve, yet it was thought unlikely to reach deep down into the mass of society. Instead, the career of taste gravitated toward formal education, as American colleges after 1840 began to incorporate musical instruction and the study of contemporary literature into classical notions of humanistic education, taking what had been undergraduate enthusiasms and making them part of a broader understanding of cultivated character. Indeed, by the Civil War, the word "culture" was vying in popularity with "virtue" to describe the central principle of a civilized society.

Urban Popular Culture

While new notions of high cultural attainment were being developed in the domestic parlors and concert and opera houses of the urban elite, the vernacular, urban amusements were also being cut loose from their traditional moorings. Inexpensive places of public resort, especially saloons, increased dramatically after 1820. Bars and hotels set aside spaces for an ever-changing mix of music, dance, fantoccini (a form of puppet show), legerdemain, and ventriloquism. At the same time, genres that had been floating within the mixed offerings of the late-eighteenth-century stage also won their own dedicated sites. An inexpensive menagerie and hippodrome opened on the Bowery in 1833 for animal acts, and two halls to display dramatic panoramas opened a year later. There was little innovation in this embryonic variety entertainment, however, until the depression of 1837, during which the older tradition of the "free and easy," in which the landlord supplied free modest entertainment in hopes of increasing the bar trade, became reenergized and gave rise to new forms. Patrons were now invited to give their own renditions of native songs, to try their hand at feats of skill, or to provide other impromptu performances. In New York, for the 1841 season at the once-genteel Vauxhall Garden, an energetic manager named P. T. Barnum advertised "Grand Trials of Skill at Negro Dancing" and asked the public to witness enactments of such city types as "The Fireman," "The Fulton Market Roarer," and "The Catherine Market Screamer." Prizes for amateur slack-rope-walking and beauty contests rounded out the bill. Barnum and others thus began to appropriate, at very low cost, entertainments that had previously had their life in the streets and markets of the cities. Through the 1840s, various ethnic and local acts such as "Dutch" (German), Irish, and Bowery b'hoy sketches were transferred onto the commercial stage.

The most notable innovation of the period, however, was the rise of "negro" characterizations. Dressing up in blackface was not new to the antebellum era; indeed, the slave lyric had been a feature of sentimental drama in England during the late eighteenth century. After about 1820, however, at the same time that melodrama was becoming the dominant tragic mode in popular theater, a new kind of blackface appeared as a comic entr'acte in which subversive dandy figures—Zip Coon, Jim Crow, and Dandy Jim—poked fun at the enthusiasms of the day. In the hands of gifted actors like Thomas D. Rice these occasional sketches were extended into small-scale operettas such as *Oh, Hush!* (1833) and *Bone Squash* (1835). Finally, during the 1837 panic, as theater prices plummeted, minstrelsy proper arrived, in the form of multipart olio entertainment usually performed by at least four actors; credit for the first true minstrel troupe is usually given to the Christy's Minstrels' act at New York's Branch Hotel in 1843. By 1846, an old Bowery free and easy named the Melodeon became the first specialized "Ethiopian opera house," and through the Civil War blackface minstrelsy remained the most popular urban staged entertainment.

The dimensions of minstrelsy's popularity are, however, easier to chart than its meaning. Scholars have argued over whether the form was simply racist at its root or stood in opposition of mainstream culture as a form of commercial charivari in which social hierarchy was turned on its head. In addition, there are varied opinions on what blackface owed to an authentic urban black culture, by way of dance forms and vocalizations, or how the predominantly white male audiences may have understood the portrayals of boisterous, sexually charged "black" figures.

Eric Lott's recent work promises to bring these diverging emphases into better and more sophisticated alignment. On the one hand, much of the fun of minstrelsy undoubtedly came from viewing the buffoonery of "inferior" people; the audience laughed "at" black people, and the performers certainly played up the distance between themselves and the personae they characterized. Yet overlaid onto this social distancing were attempts by the black characters to ape and critique the pretensions of white gentlefolk. Minstrel routines specialized in mock lectures on phrenology and lampoons of operatic stagings; in this frame of reference audiences laughed "with" the blackface performers at the claims of the cultivated tradition. Minstrelsy was a curious admixture of sympathy and distortion; it worked within a series of confusions that contributed to its continuing popularity.

The difficulties in recovering the meaning of popular forms such as minstrelsy will no doubt occupy scholars for years to come, especially since these entertainments gained their "life" only in the course of a performance before an audience that will never return. The best one can do is to emphasize their place within an expanding landscape of popular amusements and how they attracted or expressed the sentiments of a particular sector of the population. For while so much of respectable culture, especially as it unfolded in a host of polite monthlies after 1840, specialized in the domestic, the pious, and the literal, much of the popular stage worked with the aggressive, the transgressive, and the metaphorical.

Along with melodrama and minstrelsy, a third popular stage genre, travesty, was largely supported by working-class audiences. By 1850 almost all cities had a theatrical house that regularly offered "burlesques" and "extravaganzas." As the name suggests, travesty worked by violating and mocking theatrical convention. For instance, in John Brougham's *Hamlet* (1843) the tragic hero had to contend with a blue fly buzzing around his head while he asked the question, "A bee, or not a bee?" Any genre or enthusiasm could be cut down to size: Gaetano Donizetti's opera appeared as *Lucy Did Lamm Her Moor*, and Fanny Elssler's balletic *La Tarantule* ended up as *La Mosquito*. The results were so laughable that their effect hardly depended upon any exacting familiarity with the original. Nevertheless, like minstrelsy, travesty had to appeal to a certain sense of cultural entitlement and knowledge among the working classes. Travesty stood the revised cultivated tradition on its head and returned it to the popular audience; it continued the vitality of the stock company's relationship to a vigorous audience at the same time that high cultural production demanded a new decorum.

POPULAR FORM

Minstrelsy became a popular form of entertainment during the mid- to late nineteenth century. White entertainers dressed up in blackface and poked fun at enthusiasms of the day. HULTON-DEUTSCH COLLECTION/CORBIS

One further feature of travesty indicates that more than just class referents played a part in the making of this new popular culture. All female lead characters were played by men, and even a deadly serious figure such as Lady Macbeth found herself speaking in double entendres and innuendo (indeed, her unruliness was hinted to have issued from a lack of sexual relations with the king). Thus, as in other areas of American society, the rhetoric of gender had a central role in framing popular amusement. The culture of the Bowery and other popular entertainment zones was overwhelmingly male in character, whereas much of the monthly press and the lecture circuits placed the "woman's influence" at the center of moral value. Popular stage culture was so insistently masculine in its themes that it is tempting to see it as the mirror image to "the feminization of American culture" as outlined by Ann Douglas.

Demography and geography partly account for this male modality. It has been estimated that from 1840 to 1860, at least 30 percent of male, urban workers lived outside regular family arrangements in northeastern cities and that this work force was unusually young compared to a standard distribution across age groups. The wards adjacent to the Bowery contained the largest concentration of boardinghouses in the city. The new spaces for working-class leisure—bars, theaters, and billiard halls—provided informality and con-

See also

Popular Literature; Popular Music before 1950

P

**POPULAR
ENTERTAINMENT
BEFORE THE
CIVIL WAR**

*Entertaining the
Middle Class*

*Royall Tyler's
comedy* The
Contrast *(1878),
the first American
comedy to be
professionally
staged, introduced
"Jonathan," the
prototype for a long
line of theatrical
Yankees.*

PAGE 485

viviality for those with modest means and were firmly linked with older forms of masculine sociability. The Bowery Theatre, for instance, maintained its own militia company and band, and at least four New York volunteer fire companies had portraits of theaters and actors gracing their engines.

Fire-company antics, staged fistic duels, minstrel quarrels, and "fireladdy" plays all stressed physical prowess to such an extent that a demographic account seems hardly sufficient. The area around the Bowery produced a version of the upper-class "sporting life," though with a distinctly plebeian caste. Almost all of the traditional rural sports, save fox hunting, were incorporated into the urban scene. Mass pigeon shooting, rabbit coursing, gander pulling, cockfighting, and ratting, though banned in many cities through the 1830s, gained new commercial life. At least three animal pits in the backrooms of bars in lower Manhattan were in regular operation throughout the 1840s, untouched by police interference. It was the proliferation of these rough sports in urban settings that led to the formation of the ASPCA, with its own independent police powers of enforcement, in 1866.

Some scholars have seen this urban extension of rural sports as a form of compensation for a sense of power lost through the immiserization, or, the deskilling of artisanal work. Yet many leading figures on the sporting scene were drawn from regulated public trades, notably butchering, that had not experienced the introduction of machine technology or the breakdown of the apprenticeship system. Rough sports, dares, and physical prowess proved an effective way of claiming and appropriating public power and of rubbing shoulders with upper-class aficionados.

One of the most noted, though unexamined, features of the period is the way in which mass party politics and the popular amusement industry emerged in lockstep, often sharing the same personnel, constituencies, and routines. Part of the genius of early Jacksonian democracy was the way in which it absorbed traditional festivities such as the barbecue and recast them as techniques for securing loyalty and as demonstrations of popular support. In their "log cabin and hard cider" campaign of 1840, the Whigs outdistanced the Democrats in appropriating older communal customs; throughout the country, Whigs encouraged their supporters to raise an emblematic "barn" and to treat participants and onlookers to cider. Though these scenes referred to ideas of community, their significance was now totally

changed, as ironically noted in William Sidney Mount's genre picture "Cider Making the Old-Fashioned Way." Such jubilees no longer celebrated community effort but rather partisan support; indeed, the lineaments of party affiliation reached deep into those areas of public life once known for neighborliness and cohesion as rural taverns declared allegiance and urban parades, illuminated arches, and liberty poles became rallying points for the faithful. Scott Martin has found that the party organization of leisure occurred within even the rural Pennsylvania German population.

Popular politics shared personnel as well as routines with the infant entertainment industry. In 1836, the famous American actor Edwin Forrest was asked by the New York "loco foco" wing of the Jacksonian Democrats to run for the Senate. That he declined the nomination is of less importance than the notion that an actor was this early seen as a "natural" for high political office. Both actors and politicians had begun to see their road to success not in patronage but in popular acclaim; both worked the crowd and possessed a vision of a career that moved on to larger and larger "stages." In New York the "platform" performances in Tammany Hall were judged to be so similar to the melodramatic stage that it was easy to move between the promotion of politics and the arena of amusement. At least three figures who had been free-and-easy proprietors on the Bowery during the same time as Barnum—Tom Maguire, David Broderick, and George Wilkes—later went on to have successful, if tortuous, careers as politicians and promoters in California.

Entertaining the Middle Class

While this account has so far stressed a bifurcation in commercial entertainment between the growing vernacular tradition and the cultivated tradition—between what was later termed "high" and "low"—in retrospect, the development of a middle ground of leisure activities, neither overly refined nor rowdy, is the perhaps most significant development in entertainment over the antebellum period. For every elite opera attendee or raucous Bowery b'hoy, there must have been many more who assented to Horace Greeley's pleas in the *Tribune* for earnest self-improvement. By 1850 almost every town with over ten thousand people possessed a mechanics' institute or lyceum, and most of these lecture sites were integrated into circuits, allowing intellectual luminaries such as Ralph Waldo Emerson to garner over ten thousand dollars per annum in fees. Lesser "professors" circulated promotional materials that promised illustrated talks on every subject from foreign travel to the reproduction of bees. On average, New York City offered five lectures every week night at mid century, in halls whose total capacity matched that of the commercial theaters. The centrality of the lecture in the formation of American culture has yet to gain the appropriate attention of scholars, despite the fact that writers, no matter their field, were able to gain more cash from lecturing than from book publication and often, like Mark Twain, viewed the former as a way of achieving the latter.

The social parameters of this middle ground of popular entertainment can be expressed in a simple formula: the absence of alcohol and the presence of families. The temperance movement, which possessed a much broader social base than abolitionism, profoundly shaped popular culture through the 1840s and after. Unlike earlier moral-reform and temperance societies, which were led by the established clergy, the Washington Temperance Society, which was active after 1840, promised a reconciliation of social advocacy with popular cultural forms. The Washingtonians did not demand an instant conversion in Christ or rely on the distribution of pamphlets and home visits but rather enticed potential pledges through torchlight parades, song recitals, and highly dramatic testimonial lectures, such as those offered by temperance lecturer John Gough. They realized, in other words, that the new commercial culture centered on saloons and cheap theaters had to be reformed by militantly public means. Most towns possessed a temperance hotel and an ice cream salon by 1850, and at least two genres—the temperance play and the singing "happy" family such as the Hutchinsons (1843)—became viable forms in their own right on the regular stage. W. H. Smith's *The Drunkard* (1844, revived in 1850) was the first play in America to achieve a run of one hundred consecutive performances. In the field of literature, both Walt Whitman and Timothy Shay Arthur gained reputations as temperance storytellers, although they had no formal connection to any temperance organization.

No career better illustrates this conscious fusing of domestic piety; temperance, and popular entertainment into a successful amalgam than that of P. T. Barnum. After offering distinctly lowbrow entertainment, plus drink, at the Vauxhall Gardens, in 1842 Barnum moved downtown, buying the old Scudder's American Museum at a Depression price and turning it into arguably the most active site for amusement in the United States. In terms of style and audience, some of the Bowery traveled with him to this respectable location. Barnum festooned the front of the museum with glaring transparencies illustrating its permanent attractions. He placed a powerful Drummond (lime-burning) light on the roof, thereby dividing New York, according to guidebooks, into "above" and "below" Barnum's. He also employed a wind and brass ensemble to play on the balcony in hopes of luring customers inside. No building had so insistently imposed itself on an American city before.

Inside, Barnum employed a series of "transient attractions" such as the Feegee Mermaid, General Tom Thumb, and bearded ladies the likes of which had been the mainstay of itinerant showmen for decades. Now, however, they were bound to a "museum" complex that also claimed to educate citizens in the wonders of natural creation. The Linnean classifications that had informed American museum arrangements from Peale's museum onward were punctuated with a host of oddities, so that the typical oscillated with the idiosyncratic.

These changes produced almost a travesty of the museum form, yet Barnum's efforts were also directed at the creation of a moral environment in which all people, regardless of gender or class, could feel at home. In 1844 he opened a "lecture room" intended for "all those who disapprove of the dissipations, debaucheries, profanity, vulgarity, and other abominations, which characterize our modern theatres." into this hall he imported the proven vehicles of the temperance cause, such as singing families (eleven in all) and Smith's *The Drunkard*; he also allowed Shakespeare and minstrelsy "shorn of their objectionable features." The most remarkable innovation lay not in the forms but in their mode of presentation; in 1846 he invented the idea of the continuous performance to attract a new public, which he tagged "the family audience." The terms of entry into this new public were generous, yet exact: no alcohol or profanity were to be allowed.

Barnum's unending search for the largest, though respectable, audience found its greatest success in his management of Jenny Lind's tour in 1850–1852. Many European stars had traveled to the United States in search of cash before, yet almost all had fallen prey, in an era of heightened cultural nationalism, to their Old World, and potentially corrupt, origins. Dancer Fanny Elssler (1840) was criticized for her "aristocratic" sexual relations; violinist Ole Bull (1845) apparently pandered to the elite; and tragedian William

P

**POPULAR
ENTERTAINMENT
BEFORE THE
CIVIL WAR**

*Entertaining the
Middle Class*

In this way, by means of provocatively worded toasts, hanged effigies, public choral singing, and fireworks, the colonists celebrated themselves into revolution.

PAGE 336

335

If you would understand your own age, read the works of fiction produced in it. People in disguise speak freely.

ARTHUR HELPS

See also
Nightlife; Urban Cultural Institutions

Charles Macready was driven from the country by the Astor Place riot of 1849 for making antirepublican statements. In Lind, however, Barnum found a perfect object for his promotional genius, for though she possessed a fine operatic voice, she had developed a reputation for piety, charity, and republican sentiments made all the greater in Barnum's advance publicity. After her arrival, he carefully steered his valuable property to all the important New York institutions in a conscious orchestration of the city's competing cultures. He restricted the elite's access to her while allowing fire companies to parade before her hotel, and to further forestall accusations of favoritism he came up with the idea of auctioning the tickets to the concerts (of course, he also sold tickets to the auction).

By the standards of the time, the Lind tour was a great success, producing over half a million dollars in revenue for Barnum alone. Above all, it proved that mammoth productions need neither offend the respectable nor pander to the rowdy. Lind's image and her repertoire remained constant throughout her tour. She brought assured standards of production and moral value to a host of local stages. Lind carried an almost religious aura that demanded the use of an older religious word—"celebrity." The advent of such international celebrities, together with touring musical virtuosos such as Ole Bull and Henri Vieuxtemps,

set new professional standards for entertainment for the whole nation. By the Civil War, localisms had become merely a mark of the vernacular, and ethnic acts appeared not as the product of genuine immigrant cultures but as a way of recycling cultural differences for national market returns.

By 1860, then, most American cities possessed some form of commercial entertainment that would be recognizable to us today—large stages with long runs, concerts for the masses, multiple sites for variety acts—while rural areas experienced increasing acquaintance with all forms of commercial pleasure, usually shaped by the standards and tastes of the eastern cities. The creation of this amusement landscape was a matter of some self-congratulation. Hawthorne observed in his *Passages from the French and Italian Notebooks* (1871) that in contrast to Europe, where amusements were staged by the aristocracy to blind people to the nobility's exercise of power, Americans crowding to their entertainments reflected the true spirit of democracy in action. This coupling of entertainment and democracy provided the dominant, positive story of American popular culture as documented by the American-studies movement after World War II.

However, the expansion of commercial amusement was not the simple unfolding of the promissory note of democracy. At every level, entertainment reflected and informed the tensions of race, gender, and class as the United States moved into the industrial age. Doubt could also be raised about the extent to which such developments were restricted to America, offering another case of American exceptionalism, for there was little in the popular forms themselves that was uniquely native. At least 80 percent of the staged dramas followed European scripts, and as late as 1850, 30 percent of "American" actors were British-born. Even something as apparently homegrown as minstrel and Yankee acts were quickly incorporated into a transatlantic repertoire of popular culture. Thomas D. Rice returned triumphant and wealthy from an 1837 display of "breakdown" dancing in London, the Hutchinson family claimed to have netted $30,000 from a European tour in 1845, and P. T. Barnum was the only entertainment figure to have secured three private audiences with an amused Queen Victoria. Laments about the current American hegemony over popular culture in the world have to be tempered by the observation that the appetite for any national novelty was there from the beginning.

The American case does appear exceptional, however, in that the domain of the "popular" spread out in an unusually free market. Much commercial amusement in England and France, because of the active power of the state, was thrown at its inception into the arms of working-class dissent. Lacking established institutions of cultural certification and state censorship, American popular culture has been left to draw its own boundaries between the respectable and the prurient, in a constant series of negotiations and contests as to what falls within such categories. Perhaps the very lack of state authority, rather than the informing presence of old Puritan traditions, accounts for the continued energy Americans expend on issues raised by the morality of popular amusement. The early nineteenth century left an especially strong legacy of linkage between respectability and the domestic sphere of feminine and family influence. No matter how free the market, issues of sexual representation therefore still remain matters of enduring public, and occasionally state, concern.

—PETER G. BUCKLEY

POPULAR LITERATURE

The concept of "popular literature" as one half of a bifurcated literary universe emerged in the United States in the second half of the nineteenth century and became widely acknowledged in the twentieth. In this view "popular literature" designates the reading tastes of the common reader, "the masses," in contrast with the "serious" literature of an educated, cultured elite. Popular literature under this rubric is mass entertainment; serious or elite literature is art. Popular literature is distinguished from literary art both quantitatively (its greater audience) and qualitatively (its dependence on formula, on sensationalism, on stereotype, on accessibility); from the standpoint of sociology, it reaches a significantly wider range of social and economic classes. So considered, popular literature is the product of a culture industry; elite literature is the product of genius. Through the 1960s this division was accepted by most cultural historians across the political spectrum; they disagreed not in describing "popular literature" but in interpreting its uses. Conservatives damned popular literature for its degradation of taste; leftists, particularly those involved with or influenced by the Frankfurt school, damned it as an element in a manipulative, hegemonic "mass culture"; liberals celebrated it for contributing to a democratic culture within which individuals chose from a range of options according to their personal tastes.

Complications of the simple division between high and low, popular and elite, have often been noted: the popular writing that is granted literary merit (Mark Twain's fiction is the classic case in the United States) or the literary novel that becomes a best-seller (John Updike's novels are recent examples). But the division itself has become increasingly problematic, as literary scholars and historians have shifted their attention from aesthetics to the material conditions of book production and to the experience of reading. "Popular literature" has come to signify less a body of writing to be studied than a cluster of issues to be investigated: the complex relationships through history among authors, publishers, texts, readers, and the modes of production, distribution, and marketing. In order to reflect its current status as a field of study, "popular literature" ought perhaps to be written as "popular literature?" or, better yet, " 'popular'? 'literature'?"—the terms themselves often being the subject of investigation. On the one hand, to call into question the concept "literature" is to ask what distinguishes supposed literary texts from other kinds of writing—from daily journalism, private letters, personal journals, oral narratives. Such questioning challenges the distinction between "literature" and "popular fiction," with its assumption that writers of genius are somehow exempt from the pressures of the marketplace and the prevailing modes of production. It also challenges the privileged status of "literature" more generally, to the extent that some scholars have insisted that the study of popular literature ought to include not only best-selling novels and genre fiction but also posters, graffiti, T-shirt slogans, campaign buttons, billboards, the backs of cereal boxes—the entire universe of print that confronts us daily.

To call into question the concept of the "popular," on the other hand, is to raise the issue of whether literature is a popular medium at all. Through most of its history literature in whatever form has been relatively expensive, available, for economic reasons, to varyingly small portions of the population. Reading necessarily depends on literacy, which until the beginning of the nineteenth century, was largely restricted to an educated, prosperous, predominantly male elite. Most recently the supplanting of print by the electronic media as source of both entertainment and information has relegated literature increasingly to the margins of American culture.

Nonetheless, if understood as a relative rather than as an absolute term, popular literature has a long and important social history in the United

P
POPULAR LITERATURE

Erma Bombeck's The Grass is Always Greener over the Septic Tank (1976) is only one of many imaginatively titled volumes on suburban living that have been published since the 1950s.

PAGE 459

♦ **Hegemonic**
Having preponderant influence or authority over others; domination

*Reading, like
prayer, remains
one of our few
private acts.*

WILLIAM JOVANOVITCH

States as the literature "of the people," in both the demographic and the political senses of that term. In its production popular literature has most fundamentally been "cheap" literature; in its consumption popular literature has usually served to entertain and to inform rather than to provide moral instruction or to elicit aesthetic appreciation (the primary criteria by which "serious" literature has been distinguished from "popular"). And in content it has been primarily fiction. A tradition of popular poetry can be traced from such writers as Lydia Sigourney and Henry Wadsworth Longfellow in the early to mid nineteenth century, through the newspaper poets (James Whitcomb Riley, Ella Wheeler Wilcox, Edgar Guest) in the late nineteenth and early twentieth centuries, to Rod McKuen and Judith Viorst most recently. But popular poets have been popular only in relation to other poets; even at its most popular, poetry's audience has been a fraction of that for fiction. Popular literature also includes a varied tradition in nonfiction ranging from devotional tracts and Indian captivity narratives in the colonial period, to political tracts before and during the Revolution, true-crime stories and populist economic treatises in the nineteenth century, celebrity biographies and self-help manuals in the twentieth. Nonfiction books have periodically outsold the fiction from the same period. The largest-selling book ever, next to the Bible, is Dr. Benjamin Spock's *Baby and Child* Care (thirty-nine million copies in print by 1989). In the early nineteenth century the *New England Primer* and Noah Webster's *American Spelling Book* were the greatest best-sellers after the Bible. Nonetheless, the hunger of "the masses" for fiction, which as recently as the late nineteenth century was a cause for intellectuals' condemnation, is basic to a historical understanding of the popular.

This essay, then, will focus chiefly on popular fiction. Its history in the United States entails not just a history of taste but also histories of printing and print technology, of literacy, of distribution and marketing, of postal and copyright laws, of permissiveness and censorship, of the profession of authorship, of reading and readers. Within these contexts the nature and most basic meaning of "popular literature" has changed over time. In the United States the period from the 1830s to the 1950s marks what might be considered the golden age of American popular literature, the time when printed fiction reached the broadest audience and figured most prominently in American lives. The period from the seventeenth century through the early national period marks a

long prehistory, to this golden age; the decades following the 1950s have seen, paradixocally, the triumph of the "blockbuster" novel at a time when print has declined as a popular medium.

The Age of Scarcity: 1607–1830

The popular culture of early modern Europe, as documented by social historians, consisted of rural sports and urban amusements in which the common folk sought their private and public pleasures. "Popular" culture in this sense is virtually equivalent to "folk" culture; that is, it was created by the people themselves for their own uses. To speak of the "popular literature" of early modern Europe is more problematic. While anyone could dance around a maypole, only a relative few wrote broadsides and chapbooks, and fewer yet printed them; more, yet still a small minority, could read them. Insofar as there was a "popular literature" in early modern Europe, it was a literature listened to in groups rather than read individually.

Within major constraints (Puritan restrictions in New England, reduced free time during periods of economic scarcity, the many necessities inherent in taming a wilderness), European popular culture crossed the Atlantic with the settlers of Massachusetts and Virginia in the seventeenth century. Faced with more pressing material needs, they brought few books with them; those they did bring were primarily religious or practical. That some of the founders brought as many as they did, and immediately began to import more, are the surprising facts. When John Harvard donated his personal library in 1636 to the college named for him in 1638, his collection numbered four hundred titles. Although the first printing press in the colonies was also established remarkably early, also in 1638, the majority of books read by Americans continued to be imported from England throughout the colonial period. But a vigorous colonial press nonetheless thrived. The first work printed in what is now the United States was a broadside, "The Freeman's Oath" (1639). The second was *An Almanacke for New England for the Year 1639*. In 1640 the first book was published, *The Whole Booke of Psalmes*, more commonly known as *The Bay Psalm Book* (sometimes identified as the first American bestseller). The literary production of the colonial press, in addition to such almanacs, broadsides, and religious tracts, included newspapers, medical handbooks, practical manuals of various kinds, "ready reckoners" (for computation), primers, hymnals, sermons, and chapbooks. Of these, almanacs, broadsides, and chapbooks can be considered, in relative terms, colonial America's popular literature. They were much cheaper than bound books, they were ephemeral (literally "read to pieces," as numerous commentators have noted), and they were the most widely read or listened to.

Almanacs and broadsides were local and topical, produced by a printer with a press and distributed, usually by peddlers, throughout the more or less immediate region. Almanacs, originally single sheets with eight pages to a side, began as practical guides—calendars and projections of the weather—but beginning in 1687 with the almanacs of John Tulley, they increasingly provided entertainment as well. Popular science and remarkable events, proverbs, and jokes, all copiously illustrated, were thrown together with useful facts to blur the distinction between information and entertainment. Broadsides (printed on one side of a single page) and broadsheets (printed on both sides) were abundantly produced in the colonies from the middle of the seventeenth century until the end of the eighteenth, when newspapers assumed their function. As a medium for information, broadsides carried official announcements, advertised the printer's inventory, recorded colonial laws, and commented on local events. After 1760 and through the Revolution, they became a primary source of information on political debates and major events. As entertainment, broadsides provided gossip, commentary on fashions, funeral eulogies, and news of more sensational sorts: slanderous attacks on various figures, confessions of criminals on the eve of execution, as well as lurid accounts of crimes, natural and unnatural disasters, and monstrosities. A small portion of the broadsides were written in verse, "literature" in the more conventional sense.

Chapbooks, finally—small (3.5 inches by 6 inches), paper-covered pamphlets, usually sixteen or thirty-two pages long, printed on coarse rag paper, often with crude woodcuts—were widely printed from the early eighteenth to the early nineteenth century. Chapbooks were the cheap books of the period and, as such, the forerunners of dime novels and inexpensive paperbacks. In content they ranged from devotional tracts to cookbooks and household manuals, to melodramatic tales of pirates and highwaymen. Songs, riddles, jokes, fortune-telling, and abridged versions of chivalric romances and the popular English novels of the day were printed in chapbooks. Because they were longer than almanacs and broadsides, and thus posed greater economic risk to the printer, the majority of chapbooks were imported from England up to the Revolution. But at least one native type, the Indian captivity narrative, was prominent among the colonial printers' offerings. In the case of both broadsides and chapbooks, even when the content was lurid or sensational, most of this writing remained essentially religious: captivity narratives, criminals' confessions, and descriptions of prodigies and portents were invariably presented as the workings of Providence.

Information on the culture and commerce of colonial printing is meager, and scarcer yet on ephemeral forms such as almanacs, broadsides, and chapbooks. Few copies exist today; titles often are known only through the surviving inventories and advertisements of a handful of printers. But it is nonetheless possible to sketch out the place of this popular literature in colonial and early national America, relative to the books that were available only to the most prosperous classes. It appears that about half of the males in New England were minimally literate (able to sign their name) in the middle of the seventeenth century, and nearly all by the end of the eighteenth;

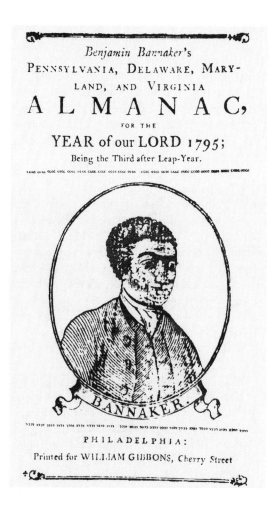

POPULAR FORM

Title page to Benjamin Bannaker's Almanac, *1795. Almanacs, a popular form of literature in the colonial period, provided practical advice, calendars, proverbs, jokes, and popular science.*
CORBIS-BETTMANN

See also

Humor and Comedy

Within a decade,
Life, Look,
Collier's, *and* The
Saturday Evening
Post *had ceased to
exist as mass-
circulation weekly
magazines.*

PAGE 476

literacy was lower outside New England and among women. Given the possibility that the ability to read preceded the ability to write, these estimates may have to be revised upward, and the inability to read did not preclude access to print material transmitted orally. But whatever the precise figures, compared with the generations after 1830, reading played no large part in most colonial Americans' lives.

Access to print was limited. Although considerably less centralized than it would become after the triumph of industrialization, printing was more concentrated in New England than in the South, in major cities such as Boston, Philadelphia, and New York than in villages and the countryside. Imported books and pamphlets also were unevenly available. Distribution of books—chiefly through bookshops and peddlers (hawkers or chapmen)—was largely local, at best regional. Social libraries (with use of books restricted to members) began in the 1730s and circulating libraries (with books rented to the larger public) in the 1760s, but the first were prohibitively expensive for the majority, and both served chiefly the urban population in a nation that by the end of the eighteenth century was still 95 percent rural. The public library, did not become a significant institution until the 1830s.

And print was costly. According to Cynthia Z. and Gregory A. Stiverson, in mid-eighteenth-century Virginia an inexpensively bound book cost twice the daily wage of a common laborer. A shortage of rags for making paper continued to be a major problem well into the nineteenth century. Before the development of steam presses, rotary presses, and other mechanical improvements, printing was slow. Until the invention of stereotyping and electrotyping in the first half of the nineteenth century, later printings of books or pamphlets that sold well had to be completely recomposed and proofed again. All these factors contributed to the expense of books.

The high cost, small quantity, and limited access to print meant a popular culture that, according to Rhys Isaac (p. 233), was predominantly oral yet "contained within a book-defined cosmology"—that is, the information in books, preeminently the Bible, was available to common folk and shaped their consciousness. Even by the end of the eighteenth century, few families owned more than a few books: a Bible, an almanac, and perhaps a speller (Noah Webster's, most likely) or a devotional tract. Only 8 percent of the family libraries in a study of rural New England contained more than fourteen books. Thus the relative pop-

ularity of almanacs, broadsides, and chapbooks must be viewed within this context of scarcity. The so-called best-sellers of colonial America—primarily religious in orientation and probably printed as inexpensive chapbooks—can be characterized as "steady sellers," as opposed to the almanacs and broadsides that were more instantly popular and local in circulation, but short-lived. Lawrence C. Wroth notes (p. 40) that in 1766 Benjamin Franklin's press, assumed to be typical, printed books in editions of four hundred to five hundred copies, and broadsides in editions of two thousand to twenty-five hundred. Printings of almanacs ranged from ten thousand to sixty thousand.

Popular fiction began to reach a significant segment of the reading public only in the final quarter of the eighteenth century. The rise of popular fiction was tied to the emergence of a literate, largely urban, to some degree secularized middle class; diffusion of popular fiction throughout American society had to await the development of mass-production and mass-distribution technologies. As novels began to dominate popular reading taste, they were repeatedly attacked in intellectual journals as immoral, fallacious, and frivolous—the perennial disdain of the popular. By the beginning of the nineteenth century, reading remained the activity of an elite, but within these narrow limits a "popular" novel-reading public was emerging as the percentage of readers expanded. The rise of novel reading during this period meant less a transformation of popular literature, however, than a preview of the transformation that was to come.

STORY PAPERS AND DIME NOVELS. Popular literature can be either widely read types of literature or widely read individual titles; this is the distinction today, for example, between Harlequin Books' romances and the latest best-seller by Stephen King or Judith Krantz. The print revolution in antebellum America produced popular literature of both kinds as the broadsides and chapbooks of the colonial period became the story papers and cheap novels of the nineteenth century.

This revolution began with the penny press in the 1830s, not just a cheaper newspaper but a new kind of newspaper: one aimed at the expanding urban middle classes. The penny papers commercialized journalism and to some degree democratized it, reaching an audience until then outside the universe of print. Among the new cheap papers were literary weeklies that capitalized on the lower postal rates for newspapers than for magazines (until the completion of a railroad system in

THE AGE OF CHEAP FICTION: THE 1830S TO THE 1950S

In the first half of the nineteenth century, the technology of printing was transformed, making this the most remarkable period in the entire history of print after the initial revolution of the fifteenth century. The building of an iron press in England in 1795 marked the beginning; American versions were developed over the first quarter of the new century. Steam-powered presses appeared in the 1820s, cylinder presses shortly after. Stereotyping was introduced in the United States in 1811, electrotyping in 1841—the major processes by which impressions were made from set type, so that subsequent editions could be made from the original plates. The first papermaking machine was patented in England in 1799; the first book printed on American machine-made paper appeared in 1820. The shortage of linen and rags for papermaking, which led to experiments with as many as five hundred alternative substances, was finally solved and put into practice around 1860 by the development of effective processes for making paper from wood pulp, of which American forests offered a seemingly limitless supply.

Thus was laid the industrial foundation for a massive proliferation of print beginning in the 1830s, and the centralization of publishing in a handful of northern cities. Nearly universal white literacy, the growth of a mercantile middle class and an upward-aspiring working class with tastes for entertaining fiction, the expansion of public schooling, and development of public libraries created vast audiences for the print that now could be produced more cheaply and abundantly. The United States remained a predominantly rural nation, 93 percent in 1830, 85 percent in 1850. And the local printer remained the chief source of print for small towns and the surrounding farms until mid century. But new technology, coupled with new social forces, led to the first mass-produced American popular literature in the 1830s and gave rise to the first large publishing companies, concentrated in New York, Boston, and Philadelphia. Beginning in the 1860s, comparable developments in transportation and distribution completed the creation of a truly national popular readership.

the 1860s, distribution of print was dependent on the mails). Such papers as the Philadelphia *Saturday Courier*, the *New World*, and *Brother Jonathan* copied fiction from competitors, pirated English novels, and eventually developed a source of native material, creating both the first generation of professional American authors and the first "mass" audience. These literary weeklies quickly evolved to eight-page, nearly all-fiction story papers (with bits of humor, advice, correspondence, and editorials). The papers with the largest national circulations emerged in the 1850s: first Robert Bonner's *New York Ledger*, transformed in 1855 from a merchants' paper to a fiction weekly, then Street and Smith's *New York Weekly* in 1859. The story papers both created and thrived on star authors (for the *Ledger*, Fanny Fern, Sylvanus S. Cobb, and Mrs. E.D.E.N. Southworth; for the Weekly, T. S. Arthur, Horatio Alger, "Ned Buntline" [E. Z. C. Judson], and Mary J. Holmes). Exclusive contracts with such writers were immensely profitable to both publishers and authors (ten thousand dollars annually for Southworth, for example, and eventually more than two hundred thousand dollars annually for Bonner). Writers for the story papers, and later for the dime

novels, were the least respected yet most financially successful authors in America. They were also the most prolific: Sylvanus Cobb wrote 122 novels or "long stories" for Bonner over a 30-year career; Southworth's output was comparable. Between 1839 and 1901, more than fifty different weekly story papers were published; the circulation of the *Ledger* reached four hundred thousand by 1860 but, more important, numerous lesser story papers far exceeded one hundred thousand in circulation. Collectively the papers reached their zenith in the 1870s, just before their sudden decline in the 1880s.

The story papers thus introduced the mass-produced, widely distributed cheap fiction that was continued by dime novels from 1860 to the 1890s, by pulp magazines from the 1890s through World War II, and by inexpensive paperbacks in the 1940s and 1950s. Dime novels both succeeded and competed with the weekly story papers for the late-nineteenth-century cheap-fiction market. Dime novels were latter-day chapbooks: originally 4-inch-by-6$\frac{1}{4}$-inch pamphlets of about one hundred pages, in yellow covers, printed on pulp paper, selling for a dime; later 8$\frac{1}{2}$-inch-by-12-inch newsprint magazines selling for as little

See also
The Suburbs

A best-seller is the
golden touch of
mediocre talent.

CYRIL CONNOLLY

as a nickel. In all, more than 130 dime novel series appeared between 1860 and 1912, with circulations of a handful of the most successful ones approaching one million. They contained complete novels rather than serials and were aimed more toward juvenile readers than families. They were both a little more sensational and a little less respectable than the story papers, but their variation in content was in fact minimal, and prolific hacks of the day such as "Ned Buntline" wrote similar stories for both markets.

The most important fact about all of these forms of popular fiction was their cost. The six cents for a weekly story paper, the dime (or nickel) for a dime novel, later the ten or fifteen or twenty cents for a pulp magazine and the quarter for the early paperbacks made them affordable to readers otherwise excluded from the literary marketplace. This inexpensive fiction was also readily available: it was the publishers of story papers and dime novels—Robert Bonner, then the Beadle brothers and Frank Tousey and Street and Smith—who developed the marketing strategies and methods of distribution that revolutionized the commerce of literature. In ways that now seem crude they advertised their publications and accepted paid advertising within them. They pioneered in national distribution through the American News Company with its network of newsstands (the ANC held a virtual monopoly on periodical distribution from its creation in 1864 until 1904). The cheap-fiction publishers also developed techniques for building circulations: scholarships for top salespersons, premiums for subscriptions and renewals.

To emphasize the economics of cheap fiction is not to ignore the fact that the publishers were also the innovators of popular literature in matters of form and content. What we recognize today as the conventional genres and formulas of popular fiction were adapted in the story papers and dime novels from European models and then refined and augmented, particularly in the pulps. Gothic and sentimental romances, sins-of-the-city melodramas, work-and-win success stories, and heroic tales of the noble laborer or working girl dominated the story papers. To these the dime novelists added the Western and the detective story. All of these were simply variations of either melodramatic adventure or sentimental romance: the perennial literary motifs of heroism and villainy, disguise and hidden identity, predicament and rescue, repeatedly adapted to the concerns of a highly unstable industrializing and urbanizing society, and simplified and intensified for an expanding,

minimally literate, relatively undiscriminating audience.

The audience for cheap fiction in the nineteenth century included both the working class and the expanding middle class, between which there was considerable mobility and no clear demarcation. Whether it included the lowest economic group is uncertain. The audience for popular literature in the United States at any period has always been, in a loosely defined way, "middle class," but the range of that middle-class audience was greatest for the cheap fiction available from the 1830s to the 1950s. The effects of this popular fiction on readers, its cultural uses, have been widely and loudly debated, the extreme positions claiming that popular literature has functioned as social control (the "containment" model) or as social liberation (the "subversion" model).

Popular fiction has always been rooted in formula: the patterns of plot and character that are conventional within a culture and thus familiar to readers. Variation and innovation are essential, but only within the framework of the recognizable formula. And cheap fiction has always been more rigidly formulaic than other kinds of popular literature, the best-selling novels and fiction in upper-middle-class magazines to be discussed shortly. Yet story papers and dime novels were also less observant of Victorian propriety and social convention than were these more respectable literary forms. In *Adventure, Mystery, and Romance,* John G. Cawelti asserts that at the heart of American formulaic fiction in both the nineteenth and the twentieth centuries has been a conflict between what might be considered conventional values and subversive desires. Thus, a typical conflict in a woman's romance: the heroine's choice between marriage and family, on the one hand, and erotic abandon or self-serving career, on the other. Thus also, a typical conflict in a Western: the violence of the lone male versus the domestic stability his violence makes possible. The resolution of such conflicts is inevitably an affirmation of conventional values—thus formulaic narratives' political conservatism, their possible "containment" of disruptive or utopian desires. But cheap fiction, as a mark of its lower cultural status, also has always explored more openly the boundaries of the forbidden—thus its "subversive" or liberating potential.

The models of both containment and subversion are text centered; how actual readers have read and responded to formulaic fiction is largely unknown. If answers are elusive, however, issues of ideology remain important. It is significant that class and gender are considerably less stable and narrowly defined in nineteenth-century cheap fiction than in the more respectable literature of the period. While the resolution of the stories with working-class heroes, for example, invariably was conservative—the poor but noble sewing-machine girl marries her employer, the honorable laborer is handsomely rewarded for solving a crime or rescuing his benefactor's child—the realities of class, and the attendant antagonisms and discontents of social inequality, are nonetheless acknowledged in these narratives. Whatever "containment" of class resentments resulted from reading such stories must have been partial at best; whatever "liberation" for readers, equally incomplete. While the actual power of such narratives is uncertain, their value as a social record is undeniable.

MAGAZINES AND BEST-SELLERS. It is essential to recognize a plurality of popular reading publics rather than a single mass audience. Story papers and dime novels represent only one aspect of popular literature in the late nineteenth century. The story papers can be viewed as one end of the spectrum of the era's periodical literature, for which there was a range of audiences (as there were varied reading publics for the story papers themselves). Like literature generally, magazine reading had been largely restricted to an educated, prosperous elite from the appearance of the first American magazine in 1741 until the second quarter of the nineteenth century. The publication of the first fiction weeklies in the 1830s and 1840s coincided with a dramatic expansion in the circulation of general-interest magazines. *Godey's Lady's Book, Graham's Magazine,* and *Ladies' National Magazine* (renamed *Peterson's Magazine* in 1848) all thrived in the antebellum period as major sources of belles lettres for the expanding middle classes. In the 1850s *Harper's New Monthly Magazine* (1850), followed by *Putnam's* (1853) and *Atlantic* (1857), emerged as the first great general-interest monthlies, joined after the Civil War by *Scribner's, Century, Lippincott's,* and *Galaxy Harper's Weekly* and *Frank Leslie's Illustrated Newspaper* were the great general-interest weeklies of the period. Women's magazines (*Godey's* and *Peterson's* maintaining their popularity, to be joined and soon surpassed by *Woman's Home Companion* and *Ladies' Home Journal*), men's sporting journals (from *Spirit of the Times* to *National Police Gazette*), children's magazines (chiefly *Youth's Companion,* followed later by *St. Nicholas*), and a wide range of specialized magazines (of which the agricultural journals were the greatest sellers) also had large circu-

lations. The age of cheap fiction was also an age of periodical literature more generally.

While the contents of these magazines varied, most included at least some fiction and can be said to have contributed to the popular literature of the period. The magazines differed in price, in circulation, and in level of sophistication, each a factor in determining their audience. As a group the weeklies were the cheapest and had the largest circulations and least sophistication; they were followed by the monthlies and then the much more exclusive quarterly reviews. Among the weeklies the story papers were cheaper, more widely circulated, and less sophisticated than the major general-interest magazines; among the monthlies the editors of *Atlantic* strove for a more literate, less popular audience than the readers of, say, *Leslie's Popular Monthly.* In the 1870s and 1880s the largest circulations were those of mail-order weeklies such as *People's Literary Companion,* whose editors claimed half a million subscribers by 1871. The large number and variety of periodicals with circulations of at least one hundred thousand suggests most concretely a multi-layered popular audience.

Within this proliferation of periodicals, the democratization of the general-interest magazines—their increasing availability to a wider economic range of readers—was perhaps the most significant development for popular literature. At a typical price of thirty-five cents in the 1860s and 1870s, the major general monthlies—*Harper's, Atlantic, Century,* and so on—excluded readers below the upper middle classes. In the 1880s and 1890s, however, the prices of these magazines dropped to twenty-five, twenty, fifteen, even ten cents, in order to compete with a new generation of cheap monthlies led by *McClure's, Munsey's, Everybody's,* and *Cosmopolitan.* When *Saturday Evening Post* appeared as a newly redesigned family weekly in 1899, it sold for a nickel, the cost of *New York Ledger* and *New York Weekly* a generation earlier. Postal acts of 1874 and 1885 reduced the rates at which magazines could be mailed; new cheap techniques of photoengraving dramatically reduced production costs for illustrated magazines. But the most important factor was the replacement of copy price by advertising as the primary source of revenue. By 1900 magazines were becoming a primary medium of advertisement for emerging national brands of consumer goods. The printing of advertisements on the same page with stories and serials also created a new environment for the reading, or consumption, of popular literature.

*Reading is
sometimes an
ingenious device for
avoiding thought.*

ARTHUR HELPS

♦ **Belles lettres**
*Literature that is an end in
itself and not merely
informative; specifically,
light, entertaining, and
often sophisticated
literature*

> *Having your book turned into a movie is like seeing your oxen turned into boullion cubes.*
>
> JOHN LE CARRÉ

The fiction in nineteenth-century magazines ranged from the extreme sentimentalism and melodrama of the story papers to the subtler sentimentalism and nascent realism of the literary monthlies, all part of the era's popular literature with its overlapping reading publics. The major novelists and short-story writers of the era—Henry James and William Dean Howells; Bret Harte, Sarah Orne Jewett, Mary Eleanor Wilkins Freeman, George Washington Cable, Kate Chopin, and the rest of the local-color school—supported themselves as writers by routinely publishing their fiction in magazines before it appeared in book form. The boundary between the "popular" and the "literary" has often been blurred in the United States, but particularly in this golden age of general-interest magazines.

A comparable range, with comparably overlapping audiences, is apparent in the popular books of the period. The paper-covered dime novels, at a nickel or a dime, reached a far wider readership than cloth-bound books selling for one dollar and a dollar and fifty cents (half the cost of books in the late eighteenth century, yet still equal to the average worker's daily wage). Among the relatively costly books, with their narrower, more educated, and more prosperous readership, it is necessary further to distinguish expensively bound volumes from cheaper reprints, in either cloth or paper, often in the publishers' "libraries" that became widespread in the second half of the century. In such editions appeared pirated novels by the most popular English writers, the serialized fiction from the story papers, and cheap reprints of native best-sellers. The best-sellers tended to be exceptionally pious and conventional, the story-paper serials more wildly melodramatic. The fact that reprints of both appeared in the cheap libraries suggests once more the overlapping of popular reading publics. The best-seller appeared at mid century: first Susan Warner's *The Wide, Wide World (1850)*, followed by such spectacular successes as Harriet Beecher Stowe's *Uncle Tom's Cabin* (1852), Maria S. Cummins's *The Lamplighter* (1854), and Augusta J. Evans's *Beulah* (1859). Before 1850 there had been popular novels: gothic and sentimental romances and picaresque tales beginning in the late eighteenth century, the historical romances of James Fenimore Cooper and others beginning in the 1820s, preeminently the popular English novels that thrived until the Copyright Act of 1891 brought the United States into compliance with the Berne Convention and removed the financial advantages of publishing them. But the 1850s saw a spectac-

ular leap in sales of native-authored novels of a certain type: the extraordinarily popular domestic romances that marked the decade for early social historians as the "feminine fifties."

Before 1850 the only commercially successful American writer of belles lettres was James Fenimore Cooper. Beginning in the second half of the nineteenth century, more authors with literary ambitions became able to support themselves with their writing (usually through serialization of their novels in popular magazines). But with the rise of authorship as vocation rather than avoca-

---

"POPULAR TRASH" VS. HIGH ART

Commercial Success in the 19th Century

For literary critics, the 1850s became known as the high point of an "American Renaissance"—the age not of *The Wide, Wide World* and *The Lamplighter* but of *The Scarlet Letter*, *Moby-Dick*, *Walden*, and *Leaves of Grass*. Nathaniel Hawthorne's famous complaint to his editor, William Davis Ticknor, about the "damned mob of scribbling women" whose sales dwarfed his own, has been repeatedly quoted as a sign of the literary artist's newly heightened estrangement from a marketplace now dominated by trivializing popular fiction. In another much-quoted document in the brief against popular trash, Herman Melville complained to his friend Hawthorne, "What I feel most moved to write, that is banned,—it will not pay. Yet, altogether, write the *other* way I cannot. So the product is a final hash, and all my books are botches."

Although Hawthorne and Melville correctly perceived the consequences of marketplace conditions for American literature, what was different in the 1850s was not the commercial failure of serious literature but the dramatic success of popular books. From its rise in the eighteenth century, the novel had always been a "popular" genre in the sense that it provided entertainment for the newly emergent middle class. The mid-nineteenth century marks the period in the United States not when a new kind of popular novel appeared but when the audience for popular novels significantly expanded, at the same time that certain writers, acknowledging the novel's preeminence among literary genres, attempted to transform what had been essentially a popular genre into art.

tion, such writers as Henry James felt more keenly the tensions between art and the marketplace. Antebellum reviewers had made two primary demands on the novel: that it entertain and that it morally instruct. Not until the 1870s and 1880s did such writers as James and William Dean Howells begin articulating a theory of the novel as art. In the 1850s, then, Warner's *Wide, Wide World* and Hawthorne's *Scarlet Letter* were held to the same standard: judged for their fidelity to life, the typicality of their characters, their morality, their narrative interest and power. Middle-class readers found *The Wide, Wide World* more satisfying on these grounds.

And publishers found an expanded market for popular novels. The best-sellers of the second half of the nineteenth century were predominantly sentimental domestic tales, historical romances, instructive stories with either religious or secular messages. Together with the most respectable magazines of the era, they were fundamentally conservative, their general narrative strategy to reaffirm or consolidate traditional values in the face of troubling challenges. In contrast with the broad range of readers of cheap fiction, their presumed audience was more narrowly "respectable" and primarily female—the latter a fact with which male authors had to contend. A masculinist revolt in the 1890s and early twentieth century produced a "strenuous age" in American writing, in which novels of Western and international adventure competed for popularity with romances of business and nostalgic novels of simple rural life—a cacophony of responses to a rapidly modernizing world.

PULPS AND SLICKS IN THE TWENTIETH CENTURY. In the decades following the 1830s, then, there emerged a vast world of print within which "popular literature" signifies not a single body of writing but possibilities within a range of print media including books, magazines, and newspapers. This range, and the varied forms within this range, continued into the twentieth century. The appearance of the cheaper general-interest monthlies created a greatly expanded audience of magazine readers at the turn of the century. In 1885 there were only four general monthlies with circulations greater than one hundred thousand; at twenty-five to thirty-five cents a copy, their aggregate circulation was six hundred thousand. In 1905 twenty such monthlies had circulations over one hundred thousand; at ten to fifteen cents a copy, their aggregate circulation exceeded five and a half million. The new leaders emphasized journalism over belles lettres, but short stories and serialized novels remained a staple. A new generation of popular weeklies, led by the revived *Saturday Evening Post* and later by *Collier's*, continued to feature fiction by favorite writers.

The content of popular magazine fiction in the nineteenth century had been governed to a considerable degree by the literary and moral tastes of editors and publishers; in the twentieth century, as the magazines' "popular" readership expanded to become a "mass" audience (the circulation of the *Post* reached two million by the end of World War I), and as advertising revenues replaced copy price as their financial foundation, new kinds of market considerations became all-important in determining content. The new breadth of audience dictated an appeal to "middlebrow" (as opposed to both "highbrow" and "lowbrow") taste; the dependence on national advertisers dictated content not at odds with the basic values of corporate business. Publishers and editors came to think about their readers, at least in part, as potential consumers of their advertisers' goods and services. Cyrus H. K. Curtis, publisher of *Saturday Evening Post, Ladies' Home Journal*, and *Country Gentleman* (which together attracted a third of the national advertising revenue in the 1920s), initiated marketing research in 1911; under the editorship of Ben Hibbs, *Post* readers in the 1940s were polled twenty-six times a year on their reading preferences.

Successful magazines tended to develop distinctive editorial formulas; Theodore Peterson observes (p. 73) that each issue of *Collier's* in the 1930s, for example, included articles on politics, economics, sports, and a women's issue; a celebrity profile; two serials (usually with an emphasis on mystery or romance) and three short stories, one of them less than a page long; an editorial, a column of miscellany, and several cartoons. Magazines came to be distinguished less by the personality of their editors, as had been the case earlier (Richard Gilder at *Century* for twenty-eight years in the late nineteenth century, George Horace Lorimer at *Saturday Evening Post* for thirty-seven years, Edward Bok at *Ladies' Home Journal* for thirty years), than by these editorial formulas. Whether the fiction embedded in this new magazine environment became significantly less diverse than in the nineteenth century (when publishers, editors, and writers came overwhelmingly from similar social backgrounds) has not yet been documented. The key to a successful magazine came to lie in the publisher's ability to target an audience, devise a formula for attracting it, and

*Even bad books
are books and
therefore sacred.*

GÜNTER GRASS

See also
Film

*The Tabloids make
eavesdroppers of
reporters. . . .*

ABDEN KANDEL
(1927)

sell the concept to advertisers. The "popular" in this sense, ironically, came to include the specialized: magazines such as *Popular Mechanics*, *American Rifleman*, and numerous others with large yet narrow audiences.

The typical contents of an issue of *Collier's* suggest a still-important role for fiction in popular magazines, a situation that changed dramatically after World War II. Human-interest features and celebrity profiles usurped much of fiction's place; the immensely popular confessional magazines (beginning with *True Story* in 1919), true-crime magazines (beginning with *True Detective* in 1924), movie magazines, and men's adventure magazines became other alternatives. But popular fiction flourished more widely than ever in the pulps, the cheap-fiction end of the twentieth-century magazine industry. The story papers and dime novels died in the 1880s and 1890s, but in 1896 Frank Munsey, one of the major publishers of late-nineteenth-century cheap fiction, began the pulp era when he converted his *Argosy* to an all-fiction magazine for adults, printed on rough wood-pulp paper and selling for a dime. Several other major producers of nineteenth-century cheap fiction, most notably Street and Smith, as well as a new generation of cheap publishers, soon followed Munsey into the pulp market. The story papers and dime novels, initially printed on rag paper, both turned to news-print in the 1870s. The pulps differed from their cheap-fiction predecessors in size and format: they were bound magazines with slick covers, much thicker (generally 150 to 200 pages), eventually well illustrated. They continued both the family- and male-oriented appeals of the story papers and dime novels; like the dime novels in particular, they grew more sensational over time. With perhaps ten million regular readers the pulps reached a smaller audience than nineteenth-century story papers, and considerably smaller than twentieth-century slick magazines, which by 1946 were read by 68.7 percent of Americans fifteen years old or older. Yet in the unprecedented quality of at least some of their writing, and in the particulars of their relationship to readers, the pulps represent the zenith of the age of cheap fiction.

For writers the pulps provided not only regular income (as the fiction weeklies and dime novels had done) but also, for some, an apprenticeship in literary craft. A handful of pulp authors—including Dashiell Hammett, Raymond Chandler, H. P. Lovecraft, Ray Bradbury, and Isaac Asimov—were the first writers in the cheap-fiction tradition to break through the walls of critical condescension. For readers the pulps provided a steady output of narrative fiction in immediately recognizable genres, for the publishers' offerings responded directly and immediately to readers' desires as expressed in newsstand sales. Although the first generation of pulps emphasized adventure of a general nature, specialized publications appeared as early as 1906 with *Railroad Man's Magazine*. By the late teens, as pulp publishers discovered the marketing advantages of targeting specific audiences, first *Detective Story Magazine* (1915), then *Western Story Magazine* (1919), established two of the most popular and enduring pulp genres (romance, beginning most notably with *Love Story Magazine* in 1921, was the third). *Snappy Stories* (1912), *The Thrill Book* (1919), *Black Mask* (1920), *Weird Tales* (1923), *Sport Story* (1926), and *Amazing Stories* (1926) were major innovators in the genres of sex, fantasy, hard-boiled mystery, horror, sport, and science fiction. The superhero pulps of the 1930s—magazines featuring Doc Savage, the Shadow, the Spider, and numerous others—crossed several genres while becoming a transgeneric genre in themselves.

The pulps were published weekly, bimonthly, or monthly. No individual title approached such magazines as *Saturday Evening Post* in circulation; like the dime novels and story papers, their numerical popularity was collective. Also like dime novels, the pulps were sold chiefly on newsstands and depended for their revenues on cover price rather than advertising—this last an important fact for assessing their function as popular literature in an age when aspects of the publishing business were being transformed. The myriad ads in *Saturday Evening Post* were intended to construct their readers as consumers; with few ads, for nonmainstream products, the pulps affected their readers more exclusively through their formulaic narratives.

Though tied to generic convention, the pulps were the form of cheap fiction least bound by standards of propriety (considerably less bound than the contemporary slicks). At their best the pulps challenged the too-narrow boundaries of middle-class respectability; at their worst they wallowed in extremes of violence and perversion. In matters of form as well as of content, the pulps had an unprecedented license for innovation and risk. Besides the major genres of mystery, Western, and romance, publishers tried the market with numerous others that failed to catch on: short-lived railroad pulps, gangster pulps, sea-story pulps, aviation pulps, Civil War pulps, firefighter pulps, and so on. With cheap production (small profits were possible even if half the copies were unsold), and with publishers carrying as many as thirty titles at a time (the unsuccessful ones quickly disappearing), the pulps thrived on an unusually close relationship between publisher and reader. By not buying certain titles readers said "no" to publishers; by buying others in abundance they said "yes." Individual writers often produced stories in a variety of pulps, adapting the same conventions of plot to only superficially dif-ferent genres. But the variety as well as the same-ness of the pulps must be acknowledged. Whether truly subversive or merely degenerate, the pulps were less ideologically narrow than the more re-spectably middle-class, mass-circulation slick magazines.

PAPERBACKS AND BEST-SELLERS. The pulps flourished between the world wars and then died quickly from a variety of causes: internal problems (a decline in quality and misguided at-tempts at respectability) as well as external factors

---

"THE PAPERBACK REVOLUTION"
Affordable Literature for All

The "paperback revolution" that began in 1939 with the publication of the first ten Pocket Books describes not a new kind of popular book, then, but the transformation of both the publishing industry and the reading habits of a vast popular audience. The keys to the spectacular success of the new paperback publishers were price and distribution. At twenty-five cents Pocket Books were nearly as affordable as pulp magazines; more important, the new paperbacks were sold not as books were traditionally sold (chiefly through book-shops) but as periodicals were sold (through the magazine distribution system). Paperbacks ap-peared on racks in department stores, chain stores, stationery stores, drugstores, and eventually news-stands, reaching out not to a relatively small book-buying readership but to an immense magazine-buying public.

The first paperbacks had none of the marks, or the stigma, of cheap fiction. Pocket Books' initial ten titles began with James Hilton's best-selling novel of 1935, *Lost Horizon*, and included a volume of five of Shakespeare's tragedies, Dorothy Parker's poems, the children's classic *Bambi*, and a self-improvement book, in addition to five more novels: both classics (*Wuthering Heights* and *The Way of All Flesh*) and popular contemporary works (Thorne Smith's *Top-per*, Agatha Christie's *The Murder of Roger Ackroyd*, and Thornton Wilder's *The Bridge of San Luis Rey*). This list of ten provides a revealing case study in ed-itorial selection and the construction of a middle-class popular audience in the mid-twentieth century. Clearly, different books were meant to attract differ-ent readers, and the strategy succeeded: by 1941, 302,000 copies of *Wuthering Heights* had been sold (compared with 239,000 copies of *Lost Horizon*). Avon Books, created in 1941 not by a publisher but by a magazine distributor, the American News Com-pany (after Pocket Books abandoned it for inde-pendent distributors), included in its initial twelve ti-tles novels by Sinclair Lewis and William Faulkner, in addition to the mysteries that became one of its sta-ples. A third early contributor to the paperbacking of America, the Armed Services Editions published be-tween 1943 and 1947 for distribution to soldiers, was oriented even more toward "quality" fiction.

The paperback emerged, then, not as a competi-tor to the pulps but as the "cheap" alternative to hardcover best-sellers, whose audience was ex-panded by the creation of book clubs in the 1920s and by a flourishing system of public libraries. In content the best-selling novels between the wars re-flect an American middle class groping to come to terms with deeply disturbing changes. The pastoral innocence of pre-World War I best-sellers by Gene Stratton Porter, Harold Bell Wright, and Booth Tark-ington partially gave way in the 1920s to social criti-cism (Sinclair Lewis's *Main Street* and *Babbitt*) and tentative explorations of the new sexual permissive-ness (the fiction of "flaming youth"). But these new voices never drowned out the old, in novels cele-brating traditional values of self-reliance, religious feeling, and rural virtue. The hardcover bestseller has always been more conservative than the cheap fic-tion of any period. The most conspicuous best-sellers of the 1930s—*The Good Earth*, *Anthony Ad-verse*, and *Gone With the Wind*, each topping the lists for two years running—reaffirmed traditional values more emphatically than ever. In general, while hardcover best-sellers and the various forms of cheap fiction have equally affirmed the mainstream middle-class values of the day, cheap fiction has di-rectly or indirectly challenged those values more daringly before ultimately affirming them. Best-sell-ers have more obviously functioned to accommo-date change to traditional verities.

See also
Television

> *Journalism allows
> its readers to
> witness history;
> fiction gives its
> readers an
> opportunity to
> live it.*
>
> JOHN HERSEY

(increased production costs due to paper quotas during World War II and competition from comic books and the new slick adventure magazines, beginning in 1945 with yet another metamorphosis of *Argosy*). Perhaps the chief factor was the appearance in 1939, and then proliferation through the 1940s and 1950s, of a new generation of inexpensive paperback fiction. Fiction in paper covers is at least as old as the chapbooks; the first complete paperback novels published in the United States date from 1829 and were available intermittently through the nineteenth century until the Copyright Act of 1891 put an end to cheap pirated reprints. Various attempts at paperback publishing in the 1920s and 1930s were unsuccessful for several reasons, most often problems with distribution.

The modern paperback that appeared in 1939 was a hybrid: a book marketed as a magazine. Initially it was tied to neither the hardcover bestseller nor the formulaic genres of cheap fiction. By the end of the 1940s, however, it had acquired more and more of the characteristics of the cheap-fiction tradition. It increasingly specialized in mysteries and Westerns, the popular genres at the center of both pulp publishing and the cheap-reprint trade of the 1930s. Chiefly through their brilliantly lurid cover illustrations, paperbacks acquired the reputation for prurience and sensationalism that clung earlier to both the dime novels and the pulps. But the paperbacks also remained books, their popularity tied to individual titles, not to publishers or publications, and some titles sold as few novels had sold before. Margaret Mitchell's *Gone With the Wind* (1936) made hardcover publishing history by selling more than a million copies in its first seven months; the paperback made such extraordinary figures nearly routine. The first million-seller was Dale Carnegie's *How to Win Friends and Influence People* (1936, paperback 1940); by 1945 an additional twenty Pocket Books, including twelve works of fiction, had reached that figure (seven were mysteries, one a Western). More significant, with print runs ten times those of typical hardcover books, every paperback was a best-seller by traditional book standards.

The success of Pocket Books quickly spawned competitors: Avon in 1941, Pocket Library in 1942, Dell in 1943. It is significant that although Pocket Books was started by men from book publishing, Avon was created by a magazine distributor, Pocket Library by a pulp publisher, and Dell by a magazine publisher—clear signs of the paperback's mixed parentage. With its cheap-fiction

aura, the paperback remained the somewhat embarrassing and scorned stepchild of the book trade until the 1970s, its publishers collectively, and sometimes individually, torn by the competing demands of art and the marketplace. In the 1950s, for some intellectuals the paperback embodied their hopes for democratic culture by making the classics available to millions of readers. For others the paperback threatened to debase Western culture by pandering to vulgar tastes. Congressional probes into the paperback, comic, and magazine industries in 1952, and the well-publicized obscenity trials of publishers of *Lady Chatterly's Lover*, *Tropic of Cancer*, and *Fanny Hill* focused additional attention on the morality of paperbacks generally. Within this climate of intense scrutiny, the appearance of handfuls of "highbrow" literary titles on publishers' lists, alongside truckloads of Westerns, mysteries, and sexual potboilers, points to the paperback's continuing existence in a netherworld between the traditional book and sensational cheap fiction.

Through the paperback American popular literature has been transformed since World War II. In 1939 three million paperback books were sold; in 1950 the total was 214 million, by 1960, 280 million. And in 1960 the offering of stock in Pocket Books, the acquisition of Alfred A. Knopf by Random House, and the purchase of New American Library by the Times Mirror Company signaled yet another fundamental restructuring of the publishing industry. But an event outside the literary world had a more immediate impact on readers. The emergence of television in the 1950s would have doomed the pulp magazines if other factors had not already done so; the spectacular growth of the new medium after 1960 did not kill the best-seller or the paperback, but it had profound consequences on the place of reading in American culture. Although not immediately apparent, the simultaneous rise of television and accelerated transformation of publishing from a cottage industry to a corporate business created a distinctively new era in the history of American popular literature.

The Age of the Blockbuster: The 1960s to the 1980s

In 1987, 6,298 separate works of fiction were published in the United States, 2,632 of them mass-market paperback titles (two and a half times the number in 1960). In both 1985 and 1986, five hardcover books exceeded one million copies in sales; in 1987, fifty-two works of fiction and seventy-two of nonfiction sold at least one hundred thousand copies. By 1989 there were 14.5 million paperback copies of J. R. R. Tolkien's *The Hobbit* in print, 12.8 million of George Orwell's 1984, 12.4 million of William Peter Blatty's *The Exorcist.* By virtually any measurement the growth since 1960 was impressive.

Yet these figures can mislead. The years since 1960 did not see steady growth in the publishing industry but a series of short-term booms and recessions. The 1960s began impressively. Trade paperbacks opened up bookstores to paperbacks generally; the growing use of paperbacks in classrooms created another huge market. Yet in 1969 an essay in the *New York Times Book Review* asked if the paperback revolution had ended: total sales were not much higher than in 1959, while the population had increased by 15 percent. No sooner was the question asked than the 1970s saw a new boom in which paperback titles selling eight million copies became common. A slump in the early 1980s, followed by mid-decade recovery, followed by hints of another decline as sales for 1988 and 1989 fell behind the 1987 figures, confirmed that book publishing had become a particularly volatile business.

This volatility, and the economic forces that underlay it, had important consequences for popular literature and the reading public. One more set of figures is necessary for comparative purposes: through the 1940s paperbacks cost twenty-five cents; in 1960 the average price was sixty-nine cents. In 1988 the average mass-market paperback cost $4.55, an increase since 1960 nearly double the rise in the cost of living; the age of cheap fiction had ended. Even in 1987, the industry's high point, although more books were sold than ever before, it seems almost certain that the audience for popular literature was a significantly smaller percentage of the population than during the era of the pulps and the cheap paperbacks. Television most obviously replaced cheap fiction in providing narrative entertainment for the largest popular audience (a revealing development: nonfiction best-sellers permanently passed fiction in sales during the 1950s). Magazine circulations reached astonishing figures—16.5 million for the monthly *Reader's Digest* in 1989—but fiction nearly disappeared from the large-circulation magazines. Sensational journalism—the *National Enquirer, True Story,* and so on—continued the popular tradition of the penny papers and the *Police Gazette* in which supposed fact was indistinguishable from sensational fiction; and hardcover novels, if measured simply by sales, achieved their greatest popularity ever. But the

TABLOID PRECURSOR

A Police Gazette *cover, May 11, 1889. Today's supermarket tabloids continue the sensational journalistic tradition of the penny papers and the* Police Gazette *in which supposed fact was indistinguishable from sensational fiction.*
CORBIS-BETTMANN

meaning of "popular" itself changed. The popular literature of this period was distinguished by a double paradox: an unprecedented quantity of books published yet a narrowing of options for readers, an unprecedented quantity of books purchased yet a decline in the importance of popular literature. This paradoxical expansion and contraction was epitomized by the overwhelming predominance of generic paperbacks and "blockbuster" novels.

Both of these developments resulted to a considerable degree from the restructuring of the book industry. Publishing houses had come and gone, as profits rose and fell, since the beginning of mass-market publishing in the mid-nineteenth century, but the concentration of ownership that began in the 1960s led to major changes within the industry that had equally profound consequences for readers. Private companies went public; publishing houses emerged; publishers of hardcover books purchased paperback houses; large conglomerates acquired publishing houses that became minor assets within the corporate structure. Although it became too easy for critics to romanticize traditional publishers for their love of literature, and to vilify the new corporations for their single-minded commitment to profits, a less extreme shift of this sort did occur with incorporation. As profits became the driving force behind

♦ Tabloid

Of, relating to, or characteristic of tabloids, especially featuring stories of violence, crime, or scandal presented in a sensational manner

*New technological
innovations began
to carry humor
and comedy to
mass audiences:
newspaper comic
strips, motion
pictures, radio
and television.*

PAGE 227

publishing as never before, genre fiction and blockbuster best-sellers narrowed the range of popular literature as never before.

The latest genre fiction—the mysteries, romances, Westerns, men's adventure tales, fantasies, and science fiction that closely followed a limited number of formulas—continued a tradition in popular literature that began with the story papers and dime novels of the nineteenth century and continued with the pulps and paperbacks of the twentieth. But compared with the golden age of the pulps in particular, the range of genres markedly shrank. Pulp publishers virtually created hard-boiled detective stories and science fiction; they sustained minor genres such as sports and aviation fiction; they continually experimented with new genres, most of which proved unsuccessful but all of which contributed to a breadth of possibilities for readers. Publishers of genre fiction in the 1970s and 1980s perfected the marketing of a handful of popular genres, but they neither supported less profitable minor genres nor created new ones.

In one sense, the latest genre fiction was more popular than ever, in that it probably commanded a greater share of the entire fiction market than ever before. Women's romances alone, supplanting Westerns as the dominant genre in popular fiction by the end of the 1970s, claimed 40 percent of the domestic paperback market. But in other ways the new genre fiction was less "popular." Whereas pulp publishers and pulp readers in effect collaborated in the creation of popular literature—publishers trying new lines, readers buying or not buying them—the relationship was now more one-way, despite seemingly contrary developments. Publishers polled readers of romances for their preferences and devised techniques for determining the demographics of their audience, but their intention was to develop a few formulas with the broadest appeal, not many formulas with something for everyone. And just as postal regulations and copyright laws significantly affected popular literature in earlier periods, so the 1979 ruling by the United States Supreme Court that books held in inventory could not be depreciated contributed importantly to the emphasis on fast-selling titles and a short life for all other books.

Genre fiction also was no longer cheap. Initially a hybrid, a book marketed like a magazine, the paperback became more fully a book, and the relationship between clothbound and paperbound books became increasingly complex. By the 1950s the practice of issuing paperback editions of reasonably successful hardcover books, within a year

or two of initial publication, became the norm. Paperback publishers, the stepchildren of the publishing industry, purchased the rights from the original publishers for relatively small fees. The second-class status of the paperback began to change in the 1960s, however. Modest hardcover sellers like *Catch-22* sometimes became spectacular successes in paperback; fees for paperback reprint rights during a frenzied period in the late 1970s were auctioned for astounding sums (Judith Krantz's *Princess Daisy* topped all records, selling for $3,208,875 in 1979). Established book publishers consequently purchased paperback companies in order to control the price of subsidiary rights more effectively; "paperback originals" offered publishers a way to avoid reprinting fees altogether. Novels appeared simultaneously in cloth and paper; paperbacks appeared in both more expensive trade and less expensive mass-market editions. For readers all these developments meant that they now encountered popular fiction in books rather than in periodicals, and that the particular form of that book was most likely a paperback.

Readers also encountered books in an altered environment. The incorporation of book publishing was part of a larger restructuring of the book trade. The growth of huge bookstore chains (by 1983 B. Dalton and Waldenbooks were selling half of the books purchased in the United States) made them not just outlets for books but also arbiters of what kinds of books should be published and how large the printings should be. The chain stores turned the quiet bookshop into a supermarket, displaying certain books prominently in order to snare impulse buyers, turning their inventory over rapidly. Books that did not sell within a few weeks were returned to the publishers; return rates approached 50 percent. The possible "steady seller," a book that might gradually acquire a popular audience, disappeared, leaving the shelf space to instant best-sellers and quickly disappearing failures. With two hundred new paperback titles appearing each month, publishers aggressively competed for rack space in the chain stores and other outlets, and for the displays that leaped out at potential buyers as they entered the stores. When, in 1985, publishers began distributing hardcover best-sellers in supermarkets and discount stores, the book's increasing status as a commodity was only confirmed.

The emergence of powerful literary agents, who orchestrated the astonishingly lucrative royalty agreements and reprint auctions for a handful of novelists, introduced another new force into the book world. Together with the agent came the book tour, pioneered by Jacqueline Susann in 1966 with *Valley of the Dolls*, following the earlier discovery (beginning in 1960, as the *Tonight Show* made bestsellers of books by Alexander King and Harry Golden) that appearances on television talk shows could boost sales spectacularly and transform the right authors into celebrities. Finally, the increasingly complex relationship between books and other media, particularly television and movies, made the popular novels part of a multifaceted package. The resulting "blockbuster complex" meant that a handful of popular novels sold more spectacularly than ever before but then disappeared from readers' consciousness as new blockbusters appeared. The profits from the blockbusters enabled publishers to print novels that would not succeed financially, yet the concentration of resources on the potential best-seller almost guaranteed the other novels' commercial failure. Huge advances and paperback rights drove up the prices of books beyond levels affordable for many groups that had been readers in earlier periods. Popular literature thus simultaneously expanded and contracted.

The blockbuster complex created a new cultural environment for the popular novel: certain books were now encountered as cultural phenomena rather than more simply as literary narratives for personal pleasure. Popular literature became part of a much larger network of popular entertainment, its own role diminished even as the audience reached by the varied aspects of this total network became the largest ever. Women's romance narratives, for example, became available in both brand-name lines (Harlequin, Silhouette) and best-selling novels by celebrity authors (Danielle Steel, Rosemary Rogers, Janet Dailey), as well as in daytime and primetime soap operas and television miniseries. A little-read novel called *First Blood* led to the blockbuster series of *Rambo* movies, which in turn created a new audience for the original book. A reversal of the book-to-movie norm, the "novelization" of popular movie scripts was most spectacularly successful in 1982 and 1983, when first *E.T.: The Extraterrestrial Storybook* and then *Return of the Jedi* topped the hardcover best-seller lists. The marriage of book and movie spawned many offspring: action-figure toys, board games, promotional give-aways at fast-food restaurants, Saturday-morning cartoon shows. Whether as the original narrative or as an intermediate product, the popular novel reached the smallest audience of all these cultural forms.

The most basic question about popular literature that emerges from examining the current literary situation is whether "popular literature" even continues to exist. One answer must be an emphatic "yes." The concentration of publishing in huge, diversified corporations and the increasing dominance of the bookstore chains have almost totally driven out the traditional elitism of the book trade. The distribution of books through supermarket-like stores in shopping malls and the overwhelming emphasis on genre books (the traditionally popular forms) also contribute to what would seem a thorough democratizing of literature. The popular reigns nearly unchallenged. Certainly the most passionate spokesmen for high culture today fear the disappearance of great literature under an avalanche of popular schlock. But the narrowing of the popular audience to a smaller segment of the middle class (large enough, however, for blockbuster sales), the narrowing of choices compared with what was available during the age of cheap fiction, the diminished role of print itself in an electronic age—all these factors suggest a more tentative "no." The most reasonable response is to recognize that popular literature survives, but with new meanings for both "popular" and "literature." The future may reveal that we are now in the early stages of a third print revolution, following those of the fifteenth and nineteenth centuries, a third major restructuring of popular literature's place within Western cultures.

—MICHAEL ORIARD

POPULAR MUSIC BEFORE 1950

Popular music differs from classical music in its greater simplicity and its accessibility to large sections of the population. Unlike folk music, popular music begins life as written music, and its styles are usually neither regional nor ethnic. There is an inescapable element of commerciality in popular music, which is composed for the purpose of being sold. The greater the distribution, the greater the profit, with the result that popular music can be defined, particularly in recent years, as mass-disseminated music.

The Colonial Period

The first book published in the American colonies was in this sense popular music, though it contained no printed notes, probably because no

Gone with the Wind *was already practically a legend by the time its world premiere was held in Atlanta, largely because of the fame of Margaret Mitchell's novel.*

PAGE 149

♦ Schlock
Of low quality or value

On January 24, 1923, Fort Worth, Texas, radio station WBAP aired the first program of hillbilly string music to an extremely receptive audience.

PAGE 106

♦ Psalmist
A writer or composer of especially biblical psalms

one could engrave the plates. *The Whole Booke of Psalmes Faithfully Translated into English Metre*, more commonly known as the *Bay Psalm Book* (1640), featured every psalm rendered into one of six metrical patterns and indicated to which of forty-eight tunes each should be sung. The same principle was observed in the broadside ballads hawked on the streets of England and America at this time, for they too contained lyrics only; customers were expected to know the melody.

The Pilgrims had brought the Ainsworth psalter, which included music as well as words, with them on the *Mayflower*. There was evidently a high level of musical literacy and ability among early Pilgrim singers, as Edward Winslow recalled of their Leyden sojourn: "Wee refreshed ourselves after our teares with singing of Psalmes, making joyfull melody in our hearts, as well as with the voice, there being many of the Congregation very expert in Musick." As the decades

A JOYFUL NOISE VS. AN "ODD NOISE"

Sacred Music in the Eighteenth Century

Though the Psalmist had enjoined a joyful noise, by 1718 Puritan clergyman Cotton Mather found that the singing had become an "odd noise." Another observer in 1721 complained that the psalm tunes "are now miserably tortured, and twisted, and quavered, in some Churches, into an horrid Medly of confused and disorderly Noises." The tempos had evidently slowed down considerably, and the length of the services was effectively doubled by the practice of "lining-out," in which a deacon would speak or sing each line of the psalm and wait for the congregation to repeat it. The abler singers had to wait for the dawdlers to catch up and passed the time improvising flourishes, grace notes, and turns. One witness reported, "I myself have twice in one note paused to take breath." On one occasion, a deacon, apologizing to his flock for his failing eyesight, announced, "My eyes, indeed, are very blind." Like sheep, the congregation faithfully sang the line back, thinking it was the first line of the psalm. Trying to explain, the deacon added, "I cannot see at all." Same response. In amazement, he exclaimed, "I really believe you are bewitched!" They sang this back, too, as they did his final despairing words: "The mischief's in you all!"

passed, however, there was a considerable falling off; later generations at Plymouth found the Ainsworth tunes too difficult, and few could read music. In addition, the Massachusetts Bay inhabitants were never as musically knowledgeable as the first Pilgrims had been. The *Bay Psalm Book* that was eventually adopted throughout the colony represented a significant impoverishment compared to the Ainsworth psalter. Whereas the Ainsworth psalter had featured fifteen types of meter, the *Bay Psalm Book* had only six. The ninth edition of the *Bay Psalm Book* (1698) included music for the first time and is the first known book with music to be printed in the colonies. It contained but thirteen tunes, one-third the number in its imported predecessor, the Ainsworth psalter.

In a pattern that would be repeated throughout the history of American music, gentility sought to improve upon rural backwardness. Bostonians grew embarrassed at what they perceived to be uncouth behavior, and a movement arose to replace "lining-out," which was essentially singing by ear, with "regular singing," or singing by note. Eventually the urban progressives won the day, and the practice of lining-out retreated to the remoter hinterlands, surviving to the present in isolated pockets of the Appalachians. But the A.R.S.es (a Harvard pun of the time on "Anti-Regular Singers") put up a fight, for they did enjoy the freedom and self-expression that lining-out provided. Their improvisations had the spontaneity of the jazz of a much later generation, and they resented the straitjacket their "betters" wished to impose on their singing. Ironically, those who stifled native expression, the more closely to imitate European practice by singing only what was printed on the page, were actually farther from the desired model than were the ornament-loving lining-outers. For the ability to play around with a note was at that time prized among European classical musicians as a most valuable skill. It would have been a poor performer indeed who sang a line of Handel exactly as written.

The rough democracy that lining-out encouraged emerged again in the "fuguing tunes" of William Billings (1746–1800). Fuguing tunes began with hymnlike homophony, after which a wild polyphony set in, as Billings put it, "each part striving for mastery and victory. The audience entertained and delighted, their minds surprisingly agitated and extremely fluctuated, sometimes declaring for one part and sometimes for another." Harmony was restored in the third and final part of the fuguing tune, which returned to the homophony with which it began. Though he had done his best to learn the rules of composition, autodidact Billings's naive polyphony violated strictures against parallel fifths and did not shy away from dissonance. Yet it was exhilarating and, at least for a while, popular. He did not after all invent fuguing tunes, but exploited what was already a popular pastime.

When Cotton Mather publicly complained that something had to be done about the poor quality of psalm-singing, Boston bookstore owner Samuel Gerrish, who had printed Mather's pamphlet, seized the chance to profit by publishing the first music instruction book in America, John Tufts's *Compleat Treatise of Singing* (1721). Tufts's method replaced notes with the letters F S L M (for *fa so la mi*, a simplification of the traditional solmization, or use of syllables to represent notes) to indicate the pitches and used dots to indicate the rhythm. This system had earlier appeared in the 1698 edition of the *Bay Psalm Book*, though accompanied there by notes. Tufts's book soon sold out and ultimately went through seven more editions. The fifth edition (1726) included a new song that some scholars have attributed to Tufts; thus "100 Psalm Tune New" may be the first piece of published music composed by an American. Or that honor may go to James Lyon, who included six tunes of his own composition in *Urania* (1761), a collection that also featured British tunes as well as hymn texts by Isaac Watts and John Wesley. In 1801 *The Easy Instructor*, by William Little and William Smith, introduced a shaped-note system of notating *fa so la mi* that achieved wide popularity among rural Americans.

By the second quarter of the eighteenth century, a singing-school movement was flourishing. Young people of both sexes, despite the severe disapproval of their elders, who preferred the old lining-out tradition, gathered in churches or taverns throughout New England two or three evenings a week to study Tufts's instruction manual, under the tutelage of a singing master who made sure they bought the books and sufficient manuscript paper. These were evidently mirthful occasions, as one Yale student wrote of "going to a singing meeting tonight and indulging myself a little in some of the carnal pleasures of the flesh, such as kissing & squeezing." Enthusiastic graduates of the singing schools moved to the front pew of their congregations to lead in the singing of psalms; thus were American church choirs born.

The Puritans had allowed only psalms to be sung in church, since only they were scriptural; hymns could be sung only in family and private devotions in the home. The Great Awakening of the early 1740s, which itself was made possible by the waning of Puritan fervor, changed all this. Evangelist George Whitefield introduced the hymns of Watts and Wesley to his American converts and even persuaded the fiery revivalist Jonathan Edwards to adopt them in his church. Watts's hymns enjoyed yet another surge of popularity in the Second Great Awakening of the early nineteenth century and exerted a significant influence not only on white but on black American folk hymnody as well. Gospel singer Mahalia Jackson spoke affectionately of the "old Doctor Watts songs" she heard as a child in black churches in South Carolina and Georgia, and Tony Heilbut suggested that one Watts hymn in particular, with "its mood of desolation and loss" and a metrical structure that anticipated the sixteen-bar form, "became an ancestor of the modern blues."

The Massachusetts patriot Samuel Adams was a singing master, and he organized the workmen of Boston into choruses that fomented revolution. At a banquet in 1769, 350 Sons of Liberty sang John Dickinson's words to a popular English tune by William Boyce: "In Freedom we're born and in Freedom we'll live, / Our purses are ready. / Steady, Friends, steady. Not as slaves, but as Freemen our money we'll give." Billings's "Chester," with its opening words of defiance—"Let tyrants shake their iron rod"—was a rousing favorite with American soldiers during the Revolution. Broadsides, too, contributed to the revolutionary spirit. "Yankee Doodle" was originally sung by British redcoats, often just outside churches, to make sport of the Americans and to disrupt the psalm-singing within, but the colonists adopted the song as their own and took delight in playing it at British General Charles Cornwallis's surrender at Yorktown. Sigmund Spaeth points out that "Yankee Doodle" is practically the only humorous national air in existence and "is certainly more characteristic of our people, in its comic nonchalance and quiet effrontery" than are more serious patriotic songs. Perhaps only in the confidence of extreme youth is such a healthy self-deprecation possible.

The Post-Revolutionary Period

Popular music in eighteenth-century America was based on English tunes, and English popular music in the last quarter of the century was barely distinguishable from the classical repertoire of George Frideric Handel, Thomas Arne, and Johann Christian Bach, "the London Bach." Amer-

Some experts claim
the roots of rock
music can be traced
to the back-country
ring shouts
of African
American slaves.

PAGE 398

See also
Country and Western Music

*During the 1940s,
women's groups
achieved
prominence, notably
the Sallie Martin
Singers, the Ward
Trio, and the
Angelic Gospel
Singers.*

PAGE 23

ican song publishing, which really began only after the Revolution, borrowed heavily from collections of songs of the type popular in London's Vauxhall Gardens. In 1788, gentleman amateur Francis Hopkinson, a signer of the Declaration of Independence, published his *Seven Songs for the Harpsichord*, one of the earliest collections of secular music in the newly formed United States, written very much in the Arne style. Other American composers in the post-Revolutionary era were recent immigrants James Hewitt, former music director at the court of George III, Benjamin Carr, and Alexander Reinagle. The music of Hopkinson and his contemporaries was not, however, truly popular. Too pretentious, genteel, and imitative of European models, it could not reflect the American frontier and revolutionary experience.

Very little of the popular music written in the first decades of the nineteenth century has retained its popularity today. An exception is "Home, Sweet Home" (1823), with words by John Howard Payne and music by Henry R. Bishop, which was composed for the ballad opera *Clari, or The Maid of Milan*. The British style remained the predominant influence, although Irish and Scottish melodies attained great popularity with the publication of *The Scots Musical Museum* (including "The Blue Bells of Scotland") in 1787 and Irish poet Thomas Moore's *A Selection of Irish Melodies* (with "Believe Me If All Those Endearing Young Charms," "The Last Rose of Summer," and "The Minstrel Boy"), published in folios at intervals from 1808 to 1834. Irish tunes exerted a fascination on Britons and Americans for some of the same reasons that black music did in later decades. The music of these oppressed people was perceived as uncouth yet weirdly evocative. One could look down on the singer yet appropriate the song for one's own purposes, including that of expressing longings repressed in one's own culture. The poet Moore complained in a preface to his book that it was impossible to notate Irish music in an authentic manner, because the tunes rebelled against the strict rhythm that the printed notes implied they should have.

Italian bel canto opera exerted a disproportionate influence on American popular music of the first half of the nineteenth century, given the fraction of the population that was Italian. Operas by Gioacchino Rossini and Vincenzo Bellini were performed to capacity crowds, and arias from the operas were published with English texts and sung in parlors throughout the country. Singer and songwriter Henry Russell, who had studied with Rossini, made a fortune touring the East Coast from 1833 to 1841, performing his Italianate songs on such topics as motherhood ("The Old Arm Chair"), madness ("The Maniac"), and nostalgia ("Woodman Spare That Tree"). It is noteworthy that Louis Moreau Gottschalk's piano piece "Columbia, Caprice Américain" (1860), though essentially a meditation on Stephen Collins Foster's "My Old Kentucky Home" (1853), gives equal time to a ravishing melody from Charles-François Gounod's *Faust* (1859)—as if good, singable tunes from European opera (in this case French) could be immediately adopted as American. Giuseppe Verdi was "American" enough in this sense for music from *Rigoletto* to be played at Lincoln's first inaugural, and Union soldiers marched to the beat of "La Traviata Quickstep." As Lawrence Levine has pointed out, this lowbrow infatuation with Italian opera fell victim in the second half of the nineteenth century to the "sacralization of art," by which highbrows called for "standards" to stamp out popular enthusiasms, turning to northern Europe, in particular Germany, for their inspiration.

The desire to correct the musical behavior of others, already evident in the battle over how psalms should be sung, was the guiding force in the career of Bostonian Lowell Mason (1792–1872), who did well by his efforts, becoming one of the first American composers to make a fortune from his music. He may have done some good as well, through his efforts to bring musical education into the public schools and his composition of some hymns still widely sung today ("My Faith Looks Up to Thee," "When I Survey the Wondrous Cross," "Nearer, My God, to Thee"). But his contributions came at the cost of practically wiping out New England psalmody and fuguing tunes and seriously endangering the development of a native American hymnody. Fasola and shaped-note singing stayed alive on the frontier, blossoming into what came to be known as *Sacred Harp* music, after the title of an 1844 collection. It was a raw, vigorous, participatory hymnody characterized by independent three- and four-part singing, with the melody—as had been common before 1800—in the tenor. By contrast, Mason's bland hymns were part of the general trend toward the sentimentalization of Christianity. Indeed, the transfer of the melody from the tenor to the soprano not only represented a harmonic submission (with the three other parts now merely serving to accompany the top line's melody) but may also have incarnated what Ann Douglas has described as the feminization of

American culture. Women in the early nineteenth century were beginning to greatly outnumber men in the churches; a revivalist hymn such as "Jesus Is Tenderly Calling" presents a maternal vision of God strikingly at variance with the wrathful judge depicted by Jonathan Edwards. Indeed, Gilbert Chase reports that in the late eighteenth century, when men still held the melody, women enjoyed screaming out the high notes to such a degree that it "may have been a compensatory means of feminine self-assertion."

In 1797 the tiny frontier town of Washington, Kentucky, later to be the site of the slave auction that would inspire Harriet Beecher Stowe to write *Uncle Tom's Cabin*, saw an amateur production of the British comic opera *The Padlock* (1768), featuring Mungo, a drunken character played in black-face. A sign of things to come in American popular musical entertainment, Mungo would soon be reincarnated in countless minstrel performers in circuses and stage productions in the early decades of the nineteenth century. In 1828 Thomas Dartmouth ("Daddy") Rice introduced his song *Jim Crow*, inspired by a crippled stable hand he saw singing at his work in Louisville. The genre took on an ensemble aspect with the Virginia Minstrels in 1843 and developed into an entertainment form that would retain its popularity for several decades. Minstrel music became an important resource for the sheet music industry, though writing down the songs for the American parlor involved an inevitable loss of rhythmic subtlety. The immense popularity of the "Ethiopian business" in white America must in part be explained as a way of salving bad conscience over slavery: slaves were portrayed as happy children. Yet other factors may have been at work, too: delight in seeing urban sophistication lampooned by country folk wisdom, the innate attraction of black music (much of which must have come through even when played by whites), and an increasing nostalgia among city dwellers for a lost rural past.

The songs of Stephen Collins Foster (1826–1864) play upon that evocation of loss, of homesickness for an Old Kentucky Home that never was, yet for a virgin landscape that had indeed once been—a regret for lost innocence in industrial America. The Pittsburgh of his birth was already dark with factory smoke, though its isolation from Europe protected him from the foreign influence to which Lowell Mason had pledged allegiance. His childhood there and his youth in Cincinnati gave ideal exposure to the mix of North and South, to the vanishing frontier, and to

the African American music of church and levee alike. Foster's music shows the influence not only of black music but also of the Irish tunes and Italian opera that had been so popular earlier in the century.

At about the same time that the Virginia Minstrels rose to fame, the Hutchinson Family Singers of Milford, New Hampshire, achieved considerable success with what was in many ways a diametrically opposed approach. In 1842, when the three brothers added their sister to the act, what had been a local amateur group became an international phenomenon. The fad had begun with singing families who came from the Alpine regions of central Europe in the 1820s, and American imitators soon sprang up, particularly from New England. But none could match the success of the Hutchinsons, who performed songs with a social conscience based on a typically American faith in social progress. They lent themselves to the abolitionist cause, most spectacularly with "Get Off the Track," a controversial song that represented the emancipation of the slaves as a freedom train.

Despite the nation's optimism in the years before the Civil War, American popular songs were steeped in sadness and grief. Maudlin and morbid, they sentimentalized the death of the beautiful and young, broken families, maternal grief, and disasters such as fires and storms ("Ship of Fire" managed to combine the latter into one horrendously effective performance). Songs on the stage were valued for their drama, and songs sung in the home, for their decorous gentility. Young

POET/LYRICIST

A late portrait of Julia Ward Howe (1819–1910) whose poem "Battle Hymn of the Republic" celebrated the justice of the Union cause. Set to music, it was one of an estimated ten thousand songs inspired by the Civil War. LIBRARY OF CONGRESS/ CORBIS

*I care not who
writes the laws of
a country so long
as I may listen to
its songs.*

GEORGE JEAN NATHAN,
THE WORLD IN FALSEFACE
(1923)

ladies in middle- and upper-class homes inevitably studied the piano, which became increasingly popular as the development of upright models brought prices down significantly by 1860. The demand for sheet music consequently increased, and the invention of the cylinder power press in 1850 helped disseminate the material by lowering the cost of publication. The sheet music industry came into its own during the Civil War, which inspired the composition of what has been estimated as ten thousand songs. Some celebrated the justice of the cause ("Dixie," "The Battle Hymn of the Republic"), but many, perhaps most, allowed the soldiers to express love of home and family ("Who Will Care for Mother Now?") and fear of a sudden and lonely death ("All Quiet Along the Potomac Tonight"). "Weeping, Sad, and Lonely" sold over a million copies, though Union generals banned it for fear it would lower morale.

In the wake of the originality and tragic sensibility evinced by Civil War-era songs, popular music in the Gilded Age reverted to pale imitations of European culture and shallow sentimentality. Song texts, as Spaeth observed, were based on thoughts of "mothers' graves, girls' names and tender associations with mills, lanes, gates and other possible rendezvous." And such songs as "In the Gloaming," "Silver Threads Among the Gold," and "When You and I Were Young, Maggie," reveal, as Hughson Mooney put it, "the social thinking of a nation dominated by males and built upon the sanctity of marriage, prenuptial chastity and perennial passivity of women."

But other influences were at work. Blacks now joined the minstrel stage in troupes of their own. James Bland, the first black composer to succeed in the sheet music industry, published "Oh, Dem Golden Slippers," "In the Evening by the Moonlight," and "Carry Me Back to Old Virginny." The Fisk Jubilee Singers achieved international renown with their highly polished performances of Negro spirituals. The minstrel show would eventually be replaced by vaudeville, whose roots may be traced back to Tony Pastor's Opera House, which opened in New York's Bowery in 1865. While the songs and dances and comic skits of minstrelsy drew upon rural southern culture, those of vaudeville grew out of the developing urban culture of the North. Popular songs such as "The Bowery" (1892) and "The Sidewalks of New York" (1894) began to depict life in the city. The intense nationalism of the late nineteenth century found fulfilment in the stirring marches of John Philip Sousa, who sold his music to as many as ten

thousand military bands in 1889, a figure that would grow to eighteen thousand by 1900. Between 1890 and 1910 band concerts were the country's most popular musical entertainment. If Stephen Collins Foster and those who loved his music felt threatened by the coming industrialization of America and sought solace in nostalgia for a vanishing rural past, Sousa's listeners, as Wilfrid Mellers has observed, embraced the mechanized present with an adolescent bodily joy.

The American music industry mechanized itself to a significant degree in the 1880s when Thomas Harms and M. Witmark began to specialize in popular music and to treat it as an industrial product. The new firms conducted market research and commissioned songs by their in-house composers to conform to what they thought would sell. Tin Pan Alley acquired its name from the tinny-sounding pianos everywhere audible on West 28th Street, where Witmark relocated in 1893 and was soon joined by a raft of other publishers. By the late 1890s, thirteen hundred dollars was spent to launch a typical Tin Pan Alley song, including publication, advertising, and a five hundred dollar payment to a singer to perform it regularly. Less than half these songs paid back their investment, but on average one out of twenty made a considerable profit. Charles K. Harris's "After the Ball" (1892), for example, sold more than five million copies, which means that nearly one out of every thirteen Americans bought one. The Gay Nineties acquired their name partly as a consequence of the new role that marketing now played in the music business, as publishers made the conscious decision to banish sad themes and reality in general from popular music. In waltz time, Tin Pan Alley songs such as "The Band Played On" (1895), "Let Me Call You Sweetheart" (1910), and "Down by the Old Mill Stream" (1910) satisfied a perceived desire for entertainment as a respite from the rigors of daily life. The birth of Tin Pan Alley followed the passage of an 1891 copyright law that finally gave protection to European music and thereby changed the face of the American music publishing industry. Since 1790, foreign music had been free for the taking, and American publishers had always thrived on piracy; thanks to the new legislation, the proportion of published music in the United States that was of native origin rose from 10 percent in the early nineteenth century to 70 percent by its close.

Despite the false gaiety of American popular music at the turn of the century, intense commercialization did allow expression of popular senti-

See also
Folk Song and Folk Music

ments. The patriotism inspired by America's imperial adventures and its sense of manifest destiny, as noted, surfaced in Sousa's marches, as well as in songs like "America, the Beautiful" (1895) and George M. Cohan's "You're a Grand Old Flag" (1906). Hughson Mooney's analysis of lyrics of the period detects, in addition to this new nationalism, an affirmation of the common man, American-style, in the way love songs replaced old European "poetical" stereotypes with language of the street in such songs as "Little Annie Rooney" (1889) and "The Bicycle Built for Two" (1892). A third wave of popular expression was an almost libertine hedonism that can be attributed not only to a revolt against elitist morality but also to the increasing freedom experienced by women as they left the restraints of home and hearth and migrated to jobs in the cities. The rise of ragtime songs, with their fairly licentious lyrics featuring aggressive women and frank descriptions of physical love, allowed white men and women to break free, at least vicariously, from culturally imposed proprieties by pretending for a moment to be black. The progress of the sexual revolution in mainstream popular song can be measured by the distance traversed from the kiss that for decades had been the farthest imaginable limit to 1894's "Their Heads Nestle Closer Together" to 1904's "Won't You Fondle Me?" and 1910's "Cuddle Up a Little Closer." The new freedom afforded by the invention of the automobile was reflected in "You May Go as Far as You Like with Me, in My Merry Oldsmobile" (1906).

Though rhythmically related to the ragtime song, ragtime piano music was a separate phenomenon—according to Rudi Blesh and Harriet Janis, "remarkably nonerotic." Whereas the former was a purely American and proletarian expression, the latter was a marriage of Victorian parlor piano music with black folk-dance forms. Scott Joplin, whose "Maple Leaf Rag" sold over a million copies within seven years of its 1899 publication by John Stark of Sedalia, Missouri, studied composition with a German-born teacher. Tin Pan Alley was astounded by the popular success of this obscure product of Middle America, especially because the music was too difficult for most amateur pianists to play. The success of ragtime piano sheet music was all the more remarkable for the fact that there were no lyrics. Buyers associated it, of course, with the ragtime songs for which there were words, but other factors in its popularity were its ubiquity on player pianos (which constituted one out of every eight pianos manufactured in 1909 and three out of five in

1921); the meticulous precision and marchlike regularity ragtime piano shared with the music of the still-popular John Philip Sousa; and music lovers' admiration for the virtuosic razzle-dazzle of black ragtime pianists such as Eubie Blake and Luckey Roberts, easterners who did not obey Joplin's repeated stricture to "play it slow." The invention of the phonograph helped increase the popularity of instrumental music, since the first machines in the 1890s were too primitive to accurately record the human voice, and hence contributed to the wide diffusion of ragtime played by woodwind and brass ensembles. Ragtime represented a way to defuse pomposity, as the work of European masters (such as Felix Mendelssohn's "Spring Song") was subjected to syncopated "ragging" arrangements. The delightful discovery was soon made that Antonin Dvorak's "Humoresque" could be played as a countermelody to Foster's "Old Folks at Home" in ragtime.

The vast improvement in sound reproduction brought about by electric recording and the replacement of the cylinder by the disc meant that by the mid-1920s a song often sold more records than sheet music. The development of commercial radio, dating from the first commercial broadcast by Pittsburgh's KDKA in 1920, offered still more competition to the music publishing industry, since the mainstay of radio programming was popular music. When Hollywood turned to sound in 1927 and developed the musical film by the mid-1930s, millions more who could not read music could hear it. The parlor piano was being replaced by the Victrola, and the passive listener eventually came to predominate over the performing amateur among the consumers of American popular music. Even popular music itself took on a languid passivity, as the technology of radio and electrical amplification encouraged a new style of singing, impossible before, in the "crooning" style of Rudy Vallee in 1928 and Bing Crosby in 1931 (preceded by Jack Smith, the "Whispering Baritone").

The popular music industry developed, in the period between the two world wars, a remarkably sophisticated style, influenced by such classical European composers as Claude Debussy, Sergei Rachmaninoff, and Edvard Grieg. As the English, the Irish, the Italians, and the African Americans had made their marks on popular music in previous decades, during the war years Jewish New Yorkers made an immense contribution to American culture through the music of Irving Berlin, George Gershwin, and Jerome Kern (Cole Porter, from the American heartland of Peru, In-

The development of radio technology brought American music into American homes.

PAGE 103

See also
Nightlife; African American Music

In the 1930s and 1940s folk songs were brought to the attention of urban middle-class audiences through the federal government's Works Progress Administration and by left-wing political groups.

PAGE 163

See also
Rock Music; Concert Music

diana, was a significant exception). They brought European sophistication and the minor tonalities of synagogue cantors (no Stephen Collins Foster song, sad as some may have been, was ever written in a minor key). Their music has the sense of ongoing movement toward climax and release, of an underlying musical logic in which each piece contributes to the effect of the whole, that had always been characteristic of classical music but until then had not been found in popular song. The simple chords of an earlier era were enriched by lush harmonies of added sixths, sevenths, and ninths and by canny modulations to distant keys. In two examples from the early 1930s, "Body and Soul," by Johnny Green, moves from D-minor to D-flat major and Jerome Kern's "Smoke Gets in Your Eyes," though it shifts abruptly from E-flat major to B-major in the middle section, eases gently back into E-flat for the close.

The Great Depression of the 1930s left its imprint on the lyrics of popular songs, which no longer embodied the rebellious spirit of the ragtime era or the energy of the twenties but offered relaxation and solace to the battered soul. Far from the participatory and communal experience popular music had been in the nineteenth century when every home had a piano or a guitar, during the 1930s this music increasingly became not only a passive but a solitary experience, as each listener tuned into his or her private radio, drifting away to the despair-tinged words of "Stardust" or "Solitude" or "Blue Lovebirds Die Alone."

There remained, of course, millions of Americans to whom the music of the last generation of Tin Pan Alley composers did not appeal—most blacks, as well as the whites of rural America who had their own popular music traditions. The growth of radio and the recording industry, however, did encourage the development of these other forms of popular music (see *Country and Western Music* and *African American Music*). During the 1920s and 1930s recording companies targeted eastern European groups with polkas and other ethnic music as well. Yet much of blues singer Billie Holliday's repertoire was made up of songs by Gershwin, Kern, Porter, and other Tin Pan Alley composers, as was that of such black jazz bands as those led by Count Basie, Cab Calloway, and Louis Armstrong. The "swing" style of the big band era, from 1935 to 1945, represented a fresh influx of black-inspired music into the American mainstream.

The nation's entry into World War II did not greatly change the melancholy mood of popular lyrics, nor did the war inspire many patriotic songs. Even World War I had generated only a few (such as Cohan's "Over There" and Berlin's "Oh! How I Hate to Get Up in the Morning"), for in the Tin Pan Alley era songs did not usually reflect the events of the day as they had in the years before and during the Civil War.

When the big bands declined in popularity at the end of World War II, the vocalists they had always featured in a minor role—singing the slow ballads while the bands alone shone on the fast, rhythmic numbers—now took center stage. The decade from 1945 to 1955 might be called the era of the big singer. The bands played a background role to the personal styling of vocalists such as Frank Sinatra, Perry Como, Nat "King" Cole, Mel Tormé, Dinah Shore, Peggy Lee, and Ella Fitzgerald. As the nearly fifty-year hegemony of Tin Pan Alley began to fade, popular music in the forties acquired more variety, if not quality, as novelty ("Pistol Packin' Mama"), Latin ("Tico-Tico"), and country and western songs ("Deep in the Heart of Texas") took to the radio airwaves. At the same time, cynicism was beginning to be replaced by warm images of family and home. The Broadway musical *Oklahoma!* (1943), with its celebration of old-fashioned American agrarian values, set the tone. Such late 1940s and early 1950s songs as "Buttons and Bows," "Dear Hearts and Gentle People," "On Top of Old Smoky," and "Oh, My Papa" continued the strain, preparing the country for the withdrawal into conservative orthodoxy that would characterize the McCarthy years of the early 1950s. These same songs and others like them would also prepare America to welcome the sea change that rock and roll would bring.

—RANDOLPH PAUL RUNYON

PRINT AND PUBLISHING

Print is a technology for communication. Like all technologies widely adopted by cultures, it has come to shape human interaction as much as it has been shaped by it. The printed word engenders particular kinds of thinking, and the presence of print in a culture supports the development of certain cultural biases: the valuing of rational, analytic, and precise thought; the decontextualization of knowledge that we have come to call "objectivity"; a separation of past from present, logic from rhetoric, academic learning from wisdom. As Walter Ong puts it, writing—and print as a special case of writing—is "a technology that restructures thought."

Print has been part of the experience of the American peoples since the European migration to the continent, but has only recently attracted the attention of historians as a force in the shaping of society. It is a truism in the history of ideas that people come to reflect self-consciously about the mental structures that make thought possible only as those structures are threatened, or as clear alternatives to them arise. The explosion of the electronic media in the twentieth century—television, radio, film and video, and sound recording—has made the role of print in contemporary America more problematic than in the past, giving rise to a historiography about its role in American culture.

That role has always been intimately tied to its position in the market economy. For if print is a vehicle for the transmission of ideas and the reproduction of culture, it has always been a business as well. As economies of scale have developed, both what people have been able to say through print and how they have been able to say it have changed.

Print in an Era of Scarcity

Perhaps not half of the early European migrants to North America were literate, yet the cultures they brought with them were not primarily oral. Whether or not particular individuals were able to read, they had come of age in a culture profoundly influenced by writing, books, and the printed word. Since its invention by the goldsmith Johannes Gutenberg in about 1440, the movable-type printing press had spread rapidly throughout western Europe, making books the first modern-style, mass-produced commodity. By the sixteenth century, Stephen Gardiner thought reading books "such as few can skill of, and not the hundredth part of the realm," with clergy, merchants, and large landowners the chief possessors of the ability to read (quoted in Cressy, p. 43). But literacy was becoming an increasingly widespread and valuable skill among the English. Those who could not read—approximately 70 percent of the English in the 1640s, according to one estimate—were frequently the beneficiaries of reading aloud by those who could. By the seventeenth century, a network of distribution had been well developed whereby printed ballads, broadsides, chapbooks (small volumes of tales and poems), and religious works reached town and countryside. In circular fashion, the availability of printed matter, some of it cheap enough to be widely affordable, spurred the rise of literacy and, in turn, growing numbers of literate people stimulated the market for print, so that literacy rose gradually during the seventeenth century and the quantity of printed materials grew. Febvre and Martin estimate that, during the seventeenth century alone, somewhere between 150,000 and 200,000 editions of books were published in Europe.

One colonial response to the presence and valuing of literacy was the early establishment of the printing trade in British North America. As early as 1638, at a time when authorized printing in England was restricted to a handful of printers in London, Oxford, and Cambridge, the Reverend Jose Glover brought the first printing press to the British American colonies. Although Glover died on the transatlantic voyage, his wife engaged Stephen Daye, a locksmith, to set up the press. In 1640 the press published the first book to issue from a British American printing establishment, *The Whole Booke of Psalmes Faithfully Translated into English Metre*, or the Bay Psalm Book. Printing spread slowly to other British American colonies, constrained by the expense of imported paper, type, and ink; scarce labor; and the relatively small market for printed materials in the colonies. In 1685, William Bradford, a London émigré, set up the first press in Philadelphia; by

The first American printing press, brought to America by Stephen Daye and established at Harvard in 1640.
CORBIS-BETTMANN

♦ Catechisms

*A manual for catechizing;
specifically, a summary of
religious doctrine often in
the form of questions and
answers*

LITERACY IN THE COLONIES
Religious and Economic Necessity

Migration to the New England colonies in British North America drew disproportionately on literate groups from East Anglia and the environs of London. In 1660, about 61 percent of men and 31 percent of women in New England could sign their names to wills, a rudimentary measure of literacy that historians have used, based on our knowledge that reading was generally taught before writing in both English and New England culture. By 1710, that figure would rise to 69 percent of men and 41 percent of women, and by 1760, to 84 percent and 46 percent. Although literacy figures for the southern colonies were somewhat lower, with about 50 percent male signature literacy in the mid-seventeenth century and 67 percent in the mid-eighteenth, the rates were still no worse than those for much of England and probably a bit better than those for most European rural areas. Clearly, by the eighteenth century, the largely rural British colonies on the North American continent had a literacy rate among the highest in the world, comparable to that of cosmopolitan, commercial Amsterdam.

Moreover, New Englanders committed themselves to engendering literacy skills among the young, especially among young men. The Massachusetts Bay Colony mandated basic literacy education through the school law of 1647, "it being the chief project of that could deluder, Sathan, to keepe men from the knowledge of the Scriptures" (quoted in Hall, *Worlds of Wonder*, p. 38). Children were taught rudimentary reading skills by women—frequently mothers—in households, using oral repetition of passages from the Bible, primers, and catechisms. "Dame schools," overseen by women, taught ciphering and writing skills, while male schoolmasters in "grammar schools" taught Latin grammar to boys with an expectation of progressing in the professions. Although girls were expected to read as a way of achieving piety and conformance to God's will, writing was a skill particularly valuable for those engaging in business—hence, for boys. The Puritan emphasis on direct reception of the word of God through pious reading may be one explanation for the emphasis on virtually universal literacy; equally plausible as an explanation, however, was the necessity from the beginning of the colonial experience of dealing with a variety of legal documents, including land titles and transfers. Moreover, mercantile activity demanded the ability to read. In both a religious and an economic sense, literacy was a crucial skill, particularly for men.

1688 he had opened a bookstore and by 1690 (in partnership with Samuel Carpenter and William Rittenhouse) had established the first paper mill in America. (Bradford fled to New York in 1693 after printing a pamphlet for Quaker dissident George Keith, becoming the first printer in that colony as well.) By 1810, the printer and publisher Isaiah Thomas estimated that about 195 paper mills existed. These produced hand-manufactured, rag-based paper for use in the colonies. Until the invention of the papermaking machine in 1798 and the development of the technology for manufacturing paper from wood pulp in the 1850s, however, the American appetite for paper was dampened by the expense of the final product.

Throughout the first half of the eighteenth century, printing spread slowly from colony to colony. Printers usually located themselves at seats of government, since appointment as printer to the government or the reception of state-sponsored jobs usually made the difference between making a go of things financially and failing. Economically, printing remained a somewhat tenuous proposition in colonial America. In a land marked by scarcity of labor, the labor-intensive work of printing made print an expensive commodity. Typesetting and the inking of type were done by hand. The state-of-the-art "two-pull press" required two experienced pressmen to operate and at full speed could produce only about two hundred sheets per hour, printed on one side only. Although American printers produced a variety of work prior to the introduction of more efficient methods in the early nineteenth century, the common denominator among printed materials was that they were short. American presses produced blank forms, laws and other government publications, short godly books or works of religion, almanacs, ballads, broadsides, newspapers, and, by the later eighteenth century, even short works of fiction. Anything longer was imported from England, or sometimes Germany.

Throughout the colonial era, the book trade centered in London. Booksellers arranged with printer-publishers there to import books of interest to their clientele. Colonial booksellers were peripheral to the London trade, however, and often found themselves the dumping grounds for "remaindered" works that did not sell well in England. Like printers, booksellers in the colonial era found it impossible to specialize; they frequently carried a variety of merchandise related in some way to written and print communication, including stationery, blanks, paper, ink, quills, and sealing wax. Sometimes they branched out further, selling items such as tinware, patent medicines, cloth, and jewelry to supplement their income. It was not uncommon for printers to operate a bookstore as a side enterprise or for printers or booksellers to function as postmasters for particular locales.

Books were expensive and so were generally limited to those with some degree of wealth—clergy, lawyers, planters, merchants, and others among the professional and well-to-do. For example, Thomas Ruddiman's *Rudiments of the Latin Tongue*, a schoolbook, cost the equivalent of two pairs of shoes or half a hog in Virginia in 1760. This sum represented two days' work for a common laborer or one day's work for a more highly paid artisan such as a carpenter. Tobias Smollett's fifteen-volume history of England would have cost a common laborer half a year's earnings, and a skilled artisan three months' pay. Not surprisingly, book ownership became not

only the prerogative of a gentleman, but the sign of one.

People of modest means often owned books of specific kinds; Bibles and testaments, psalmbooks, small godly works, and schoolbooks formed a list of "steady sellers." Bibles alone accounted for 20 percent of all book importation by bulk in Philadelphia in the mid-eighteenth century. Those either blessed with more considerable resources or spurred on by professional need might accumulate a more substantial personal collection. David Hall has found that in seventeenth-century New England, ministers on average owned libraries of about one hundred books each, with Cotton Mather's three-thousand-volume collection being one of the most extensive in the colonies at this time. Lawyers, physicians, and scholars might also accumulate relatively extensive holdings for use in their work.

Attitudes Toward Reading

During this early era of print scarcity, books generally embodied knowledge considered authoritative for the culture. Moreover, the oral repetition of the Bible and other religious works as a technique of literacy training established these texts as reading prototypes. As a result, certain characteristic attitudes and practices regarding reading and literacy developed. Printed matter was often

THE CAUSE OF "USEFUL KNOWLEDGE"

Libraries in the Eighteenth Century

In some areas of colonial America, the demand for books coupled with their expense led to the establishment of libraries, which made available a variety of printed material to subscribers at a fairly modest cost. The first libraries consisted of no more than a few hundred volumes and were generally inaccessible to the public, serving colleges such as Harvard and William and Mary. In a few locations—probably no more than ten or twelve by the end of the Seven Years' War (1754–1763)—book collections viewed as public property were established during the first two-thirds of the eighteenth century. Particularly in the South, the Society for the Propagation of the Gospel established parochial collections for the dissemination of religious literature. These relatively accessible institutions were supplemented by a number of commercial endeavors designed to moderate the cost of book use for particular groups. For example, during the half century prior to the Revolution, privately formed proprietary groups founded some twenty social libraries, jointly owned and acquired to advance the cause of "useful knowledge." The most famous of these, the Library Company of Philadelphia, was the brainchild of Philadelphia printer Benjamin Franklin in 1731. Geared mainly to the needs of men in the trades, it offered its members access to a collection comprising primarily works on history, literature, and science. A second category of restrictive collection, the commercial circulating or subscription library, charged users a modest fee to borrow books. Fueled by interest in novels, which came to form a substantial portion of these circulating collections, these dozen or so libraries catered to a new reading audience in the decade and a half prior to the Revolution: individuals, many of whom were women, who read for entertainment. Unlike the other types of libraries, subscription libraries actively encouraged women to borrow.

*Almanacs and
broadsides were
local and topical,
produced by a
printer with a press
and distributed,
usually by peddlers,
throughout the
more or less
immediate region.*

PAGE 339

See also
Television

shared through reading aloud; hence, reading on the whole was not yet particularly experienced as a private, solitary activity as it would later become. The scarcity of print coupled with the emphasis on the authoritative meaning of most works available led to a style of reading a number of historians have termed "intensive." A text was to be tasted slowly, its meaning to be savored for its truth value. Knowledge depended less on the accumulation of information and participation in interpretive discourse than on an explication of those authoritative sources already believed to contain the marrow of truth. For most people in the colonies prior to the mid-eighteenth century at least, print served mainly to confirm their status in a revealed and well-articulated social order.

Some historians and cultural critics have argued that this situation began to change in the first half of the eighteenth century. Print began to contribute substantially to the emergence of a public sphere of discourse that encouraged individuals to define themselves as citizens to whom public institutions had particular responsibilities, rather than primarily as subjects with divinely mandated responsibilities to established authority. Beginning in England in the late seventeenth century, a coffee-house culture of discussion and debate based on printed resources—newspapers, pamphlets, and books—began to develop, according to Jürgen Habermas. In this culture, print became mainly a vehicle for questioning and reinterpreting social identity and institutions, rather than merely a way of confirming their legitimate authority. The subsequent role of print in catalyzing new notions of the public sphere and of public discourse can be seen concretely in the development of the newspaper press in the three-quarters of a century prior to the American Revolution.

Newspapers in the English colonies first appeared in 1704 with the publication of John Campbell's *Boston News-Letter*. There was no expectation that they would publish controversial opinion—or, indeed, opinion of any sort. An expansion of a commercial newsletter service offered privately to government officials and merchants, Campbell's newsletter provided little by way of either local news or controversy. Newspapers were gradually recognized by colonial printers tottering on the brink of financial insolvency (like Campbell) as relatively ephemeral, consumable commodities capable of generating consistent revenue and repeat business. By 1739, according to Ian Steele, thirteen newspapers were being printed in English America, serving mainly

the commercial community—in Bridgetown (Barbados), Kingston (Jamaica), Charles Town (South Carolina), Williamsburg, Philadelphia, New York, and Boston. Boston, with its wealth of readers and its burgeoning commercial economy, was second only to London in the Atlantic empire in the number of newspapers published.

Thus the publication of newspapers was primarily an economic move for most colonial printers, with little or no sense that the circulation of information might fill any particular civic need. And with a limited clientele and with support frequently provided in part by government printing contracts, it continued for some time to be in the best interest of printers to keep controversy out of their papers. Indeed, in colonies such as Virginia, the printing trade itself had been actively excluded from the life of the young colony until 1730 for fear that printing would spread divergent opinion and lead to the creation of sects and social disorder.

There were exceptions that presaged the emergence of a new ethic. In 1721 James Franklin established his *New-England Courant* to criticize explicitly the powerful clergy of Massachusetts for advocating inoculation of the population against smallpox. Franklin was eventually imprisoned and his paper banned, but not before his younger brother Benjamin received valuable experience, both in the printing trade and the politics of controversial authorship. In 1732 a political faction in New York led by lawyers James Alexander and William Smith commissioned one of William Bradford's partners, John Peter Zenger, to publish a newspaper in opposition to the regime of Governor William Cosby. Like Franklin, Zenger threatened to undermine a social order based largely on status by taking on the legitimacy of the standing order; like Franklin, he was imprisoned for his seditious libel against the government.

Unlike Franklin's, Zenger's case became a cause célèbre when it came to trial. Under English law the truth was not considered a defense against libel. Zenger's lawyer, Andrew Hamilton, urged the jury to throw out the law on the implicit principle that (as Michael Warner puts it) "censure of an official is an exercise of virtue rather than a violation of status." The jury returned a verdict of not guilty; "freedom of the press" became the power to exert oneself in civic affairs. Print was becoming legitimized as an arena for public controversy.

Nevertheless, despite the gradual decline of raw censorship, printers still had the withdrawal of patronage or support to fear and therefore im-

P

PRINT AND
PUBLISHING

Attitudes Toward Reading

**RIOTING
COLONISTS**

*Undated illustration depicting
the burning of John Peter
Zenger's "weekly Journal" on
Wall Street, November 6, 1734.*
CORBIS-BETTMANN

The first printing establishment in the North American colonies was set up in Cambridge, Massachusetts, in 1639.

PAGE 235

♦ **Masthead**

The name of a publication (as a newspaper) displayed on top of the first page

posed a form of self-censorship. "Open to all parties, but influenced by none," as a typical masthead slogan of the time had it, printers for the most part pledged themselves to accommodate all rational public discourse without discrimination. Just as the market promoted an impersonality of exchange of goods and currency, print (as it came ideally to be conceived) grew to be a place where what was assumed to be an impersonal, rational, and impartial exchange of ideas occurred.

By the time of the Revolution, this notion of an open press as the primary locus of public discourse had become so culturally embedded that the press was seen as critical to the maintenance of good government. Rather than keeping political discourse and discussion out of the newspapers they published, printers were obliged—for reasons of civic responsibility as well as of economy—to ensure that all rationally expressed opinion had fair access to their journals. The ideology followed what was just good business sense for colonial printers, who, after all, looked to the newspapers they published to turn a profit. In a limited market, it paid to open the press to a wide variety of opinions. To adopt a particular political position oneself, however, was to run the risk of alienating precious customers.

The 1765 Stamp Act, which placed a tax on every half-sheet of newspaper, every advertisement, and every almanac, blew this world apart. Not only was it an economic blow to printers already just barely in the black, but also it virtually destroyed any room that the printer-publisher might have had to claim a neutral ground. To adhere voluntarily to its provisions conveyed the impression that the printer had adopted a Tory point of view. Not to do so, however, conveyed endorsement of the patriot position. Printers who had habitually assumed a middle ground were faced with a decision in which no middle ground was possible.

The result was a forced abandonment of any notion of "neutrality of the trade" and adoption of party identification by the press, although many printers tried to maintain a nonpartisan posture for as long as they could sustain it. Eventually twice as many newspapers exhibited patriot sympathies as Tory. One of the major legacies of the Revolution, as far as the character of print in American culture is concerned, was the large-scale transformation of the print medium into the principal vehicle for public discourse, discussion, and polemic. As printed matter, particularly newspapers, took blatantly partisan political (and eventually religious) positions, the number of

newspapers published increased enormously. In the dozen controversial years after 1763, for example, the number of newspapers published in the colonies seems to have about doubled, from the twenty-one published in the year of the Treaty of Paris. By 1800 more than a hundred fifty public journals were published in the United States. Isaiah Thomas, renowned printer, publisher, and historian of the trade, could write in 1810 that "there are now more newspapers published in the United States, than in the United Kingdom of Great Britain and Ireland" (quoted in *History of Printing*, p. 14).

The rise in number correlated directly with the heightened stature of the newspaper as the principal vehicle for political discourse. In 1803 the Reverend Samuel Miller marveled in his *Retrospect of the Eighteenth Century* at how greatly the station of print in general and newspapers in particular had changed. "Instead . . . of being considered now, as they once were, of small moment in society," he wrote, "they have become immense moral and political engines, closely connected with the welfare of the state, and deeply involving both its peace and prosperity" (quoted in *History of Printing*, p. 18). Prior to the Revolution, the only essential printed document in most colonial households was a Bible; for the post-Revolutionary generation, the newspaper became an indispensable connection with the outside world.

Print in the Era of Market Expansion

With the expansion of the market during the first half of the nineteenth century, the scope and reach of print grew enormously in the United States, particularly in the North and West. Although raw numbers and statistics do not adequately convey the qualitative difference that print made in people's lives, they do suggest the magnitude of the growth in some print-related endeavors.

PRINTING AND PUBLISHING. By 1859, the number of printing shops in the United States had risen to about four thousand, from about fifty in the mid-eighteenth century. Additionally, about four hundred publisher/capitalists financed, coordinated, and supervised production and distribution of books and other printed matter.

NEWSPAPER PUBLISHING. By 1854, 254 dailies circulated, supplemented by a vast array of weeklies, biweeklies, and triweeklies. In 1800, only 15 dailies and 220 papers of any sort had appeared regularly. The number of papers produced per capita per year was just under 22 in 1850, up from an average of about four in 1810. The largest circulation newspapers by this time averaged sales of between 10,000 and 40,000 copies daily.

PERIODICAL PUBLISHING. In 1850, American publishers issued about six hundred different periodicals geared toward a variety of interests and audiences. During the entire first half century of American periodical publication (1741–1791), American printer/editors had produced only forty-five periodicals, with the majority of these short-lived and appearing only sporadically.

POSTAL DELIVERY. In 1845, 14,000 post offices for the transmission of written and printed communication existed, up from 75 in 1789.

This tremendous growth in the presence and availability of the printed word can be accounted for by a number of factors. First, the dynamic growth of the United States population during this period resulted in a larger pool of potential readers. Between 1790 and 1860, the population of the United States grew eightfold and the nation's geographical area more than tripled. The printing press—and its ubiquitous adjunct, the newspaper—accompanied white settlement of the Ohio and Mississippi valleys. Boosters used the press to tout the presence of prime lands and a lucrative business environment to potential settlers.

Technological development and innovation in the fields of printing and papermaking also undeniably contributed to the print explosion of the early nineteenth century. These enabled print, printed images, and reading matter to be produced relatively cheaply and disseminated widely.

As the increased demand for print became obvious from the mid-eighteenth century on, entrepreneurs had incentive to develop domestic sources of the printing essentials, including paper mills, type foundries, and press and ink manufactories. By the first quarter of the nineteenth century, rapid changes in printing technology, spurred on by the increased consumer appetite for print, led to a revolution in the printing industry. The two-pull wooden press gave way to iron presses strong enough and large enough to print a newspaper page with one pull of the platen. This Stanhope press (so called after its inventor) was first imported to the United States in 1811, and Philadelphian George Clymer invented an improved iron lever press within five years of the Stanhope press's introduction. In the 1820s printers experimented first with horsepower then with steam, as ways of powering presses. At about the same time, some large, urban print shops had begun to use the recently invented process of stereotyping (and later electrotyping). These allowed the production of relatively permanent metal plates from set type that could be saved for subsequent editions. The invention of lithography, the mechanization of some aspects of the binding process, the introduction of the cylinder press (1846), the mechanization of paper-making (widespread by the 1830s), the ability to manufacture paper from wood pulp instead of rags and to produce it in continuous rolls instead of sheets (1854)—all of these contributed substantially to the growth of the print industry. Moreover, the innovations of the transportation revolution, including the development of roads, canals, steam-powered ships, and finally railroads, gave entrepreneurs both the incentive to produce for wider markets and the ability to do so.

But as significant as was the introduction of new technologies to the widespread dissemination of print, it would be a mistake to view technology as the only—or even necessarily the primary—prod to the development of print as the dominant vehicle for the transmission and reproduction of culture during this era. Indeed, expansion of print's influence had begun in substantial ways *before* the widespread introduction of the major new technologies. Literacy rates rose notably, particularly among women in the North, during the early nineteenth century. Female literacy, only about 50 percent in New England in 1790, rose to a stable rate of about 85 percent, even in rural areas, by 1830. By 1840, when the cheap penny press was still in its youth, illiteracy rates were consistently less than 10 percent in the North and about 20 percent in the South, where as recently as 1800 they had hovered between 40 and 50 percent. The self-reports of the 1850 census on literacy indicated that the chief gaps in literacy existed between native-born whites on the one hand and nonwhites and foreign-born whites on the other.

Ideologically, print and literacy had come to occupy a key position in the continued health and prosperity of the new nation. The ability to read, to educate oneself on public issues, and to take advantage of developments in the area of useful knowledge were regarded as vital to both citizenship and effective participation in the economy. In addition, print followed the lines of market development, encouraging people to keep track of what happened at a distance. Faraway events and processes became increasingly of interest as they were perceived as having an impact on individual lives—politically, religiously, and economically. Not surprisingly, as part of the bargain, the new abundance of print made newspapers, novels, periodicals, pamphlets, and tracts into consumable

♦ Electrotyping

Making a duplicate printing surface by an electroplating process

commodities good not only for providing vital information and spiritual edification, but for furnishing entertainment as well.

Literacy was now viewed as essential to full functioning in society; illiteracy, rather than being seen as a fact of life, was labeled a social problem. In the religious sphere, many Protestant evangelical leaders hoped that in a less close-knit social environment, printed religious materials would act as the glue to hold together socially diverse and geographically far-flung people in a cohesive Christian union. Organizations such as the American Education Society (1814–1815), the American Bible Society (1816), the American Tract Society (1825), and the American Sunday School Union (1824) trained ministers, provided basic literacy skills, and distributed materials designed to form Christian character and maintain piety. Methodists especially took the lead in the West. There they distributed Bibles, tracts, books, and pamphlets, acting as the major supplier of printed materials in the region. In 1784 they had founded their own publishing house, the Methodist Book Concern; by the time of the Civil War, they would be joined by the American Baptist Publication Society, the Presbyterian Board of Publication, and the Lutheran Publication Society, among others. In the East, organizations like Arthur Tappan's New York Tract Society tried to provide each citizen of the city with a new tract every month.

Moreover, during an era of increasing denominational contention, religious journalism became an important vehicle for solidifying denominational identity. Practically nonexistent in 1800, the religious press by 1830 had become a staple of daily life. In Jacksonville, Illinois, for example, over half of all subscriptions recorded by the post office during the years 1831 and 1832 were for religious periodicals. Although the steady sellers (such as John Foxe's *Book of Martyrs* or John Bunyan's *Pilgrim's Progress*) that formed the backbone of pious colonial literature declined in importance, the amount of religious material as a percentage of total print output seems to have increased in some areas.

In the secular sphere, republican ideology spurred widespread efforts to provide common schooling for an informed citizenry. The Northwest Ordinance of 1787, for example, encouraged the establishment of common schools, although it did not formally provide for their support. In practice, the lack of a firmly established tax base, particularly in sparsely settled areas, meant that practice sometimes lagged far behind the ideal.

AFRICAN-AMERICAN LITERACY

Many free African Americans recognized that literacy had become key to full participation in American society. Although barred in most places from attending schools established for European Americans, and without reliable means of support for schools to meet their own needs, African Americans in the North pursued the ability to read and to write in a variety of ways. Adult literacy education took place most often in groups organized principally to serve other purposes, such as the benevolent and mutual aid societies formed to provide social and economic security, and in the black churches. Still, as late as 1840, nonwhite seamen in Philadelphia had an illiteracy rate of about 75 percent, as compared with 30 percent for white males in that group, according to Lee Soltow and Edward Stevens. Black illiteracy overall did not begin to decline dramatically until the end of the century. In the South, where gatherings of free blacks were often restricted or schools illegal, literacy education took place sporadically. Slaves for their part seem to have been almost entirely illiterate, having been prohibited access to literacy skills because of white fears of revolt and insurrection.

Women, responding to the claims of the ideology of republican motherhood, took up the pursuit of literacy in order to be able to provide a proper education in republicanism for their children. Common schools increasingly began to accommodate them as students.

In the wake of this dramatic rise in emphasis upon reading, schoolbooks, particularly of an indigenous variety, were among the printed commodities most in demand. Noah Webster's textbooks, for example, were widely distributed throughout the nation. But other new genres also captured the popular imagination as some of those formerly in demand fell by the wayside. For example, the novel, feared by the clergy as the supplanter of moral and socially useful literature, replaced chap-book versions of romances and fairy tales and found an audience particularly among women. Newly popular periodicals such as *Godey's Lady's Book*, *Graham's*, and *Peterson's* published the work of "literary domestics" such as

See also
Radio

Mrs. E. D. E. N. Southworth, Fanny Fern, Mary Virginia Terhune, and Harriet Beecher Stowe, serializing their novels and disseminating their short stories and sketches to an eager public. By the 1850s, this "damn'd mob of scribbling women," as Nathaniel Hawthorne called them, held a powerful place in the American literary market. *The Scarlet Letter*, Hawthorne's commercial success, sold 6,800 copies in its Ticknor and Fields editions of the 1850s. In contrast, Parton sold 70,000 copies of her *Fern Leaves from Fanny's Portfolio* in about the same period of time. By 1871, three-quarters of all American novels published were written by women.

Magazines and Periodicals

This era also saw, in addition to the novel, an explosion in the number of magazines and periodicals. The two principal early genres included the religious magazine and the literary miscellany. Such periodicals as the *North American Review* (1815), *Knickerbocker Magazine* (1833), and *Graham's Magazine* (1840) published serious essays, commentaries, and reviews, often touting the work of American authors such as Washington Irving, James Fenimore Cooper, and Edgar Allan Poe. Articles on female virtue and clothing styles and, later, fiction were staples of magazines directed primarily toward women, with *Godey's Lady's Book*, edited for some forty years by Sarah Josepha Hale, the most prominent of them all.

Periodicals such as *Youth's Companion* (1827) catered to younger audiences, while adjuncts of large publishing houses, such as *Harper's New Monthly Magazine* (established in 1850) and *Putnam's Monthly Magazine* (1853), covered a variety of topics from public affairs to household matters. Espousing middle-class values, their goal was to appeal to all members of the family.

In the area of newspaper publication, the single most striking event of the era was the emergence of the penny press. Some historians, such as Dan Schiller, argue that the penny press emerged out of a nascent working-class press of the 1830s. Newspapers such as the *Mechanics' Press* and the *Working Men's Advocate* showed particular sensitivity to issues of class in an era when many artisans and mechanics were losing independence and autonomy within their trades. Others, such as Michael Schudson, have seen the penny press as the result of the emergence of an egalitarian middle-class ethic of the period, a response in part to increased participation in an abstract market that did not distinguish among individuals in its operation.

Whatever the case, the penny press, enabled in part by the new technology that lent itself to mass production, was innovative in a number of respects: it refused to be financed by party patronage, as the press had been since the era of the early republic; it relied on advertising not as a subsidiary means of gaining revenue but as its major

PRINT PROLIFERATION

The nineteenth century produced an explosion of the number of magazines and periodicals. People preferred to read large amounts of material, thereby accumulating a large fund of information and experience from which to reason, judge, and act.
LIBRARY OF CONGRESS/ CORBIS

means of self-support; and it valued an ethic of objectivity and factuality, seeming thereby to deal evenhandedly and impartially with the truth for all comers. Professional managing editors and reporters supplanted the printer as collector of information and the party hack as manager.

In large part, the penny press was successful because it was cheap, reaching out to working-class and immigrant audiences. Whereas an older, established paper would have sold for six cents, the penny press, as its name implies, sold for a penny. The older, established press had been distributed mainly via subscription; the penny press reached its audiences in large part through street hawkers who sold individual papers. Blessed with a persisting reputation for sensationalism, largely due to the tenor of its advertising and its extensive coverage of crime, the penny press expanded the paying audience for news dramatically. For example, the *Philadelphia Public Ledger* (1836) reached ten thousand readers after eight months in business. The largest prior circulation of a paper in that city was two thousand copies. Benjamin Day's *New York Sun* (1833), the first of the penny dailies, had a circulation of thirty-eight thousand by 1843.

The penny press was most successful in the larger cities of the North—and later, the West. In the South, by the time of the Civil War, only two major penny papers existed: the New Orleans *Picayune* and the *Richmond Dispatch*. The South had fewer paper mills, less well-developed means of transportation, and fewer newspapers overall. In smaller towns and villages throughout the country, local papers responded to the competitive pressure of the large urban dailies by increasingly turning to the publication of local news.

As individuals gained access to greater amounts of printed material and wider varieties of it, their cultural preconceptions about reading changed as well. In place of the early "intensive" approach to reading—concentrated attention on a few key texts—an ethos emphasizing "extensive" reading gradually came to dominate. People now thought themselves best advantaged by reading large amounts of material relatively quickly, thereby accumulating a larger fund of information and experience from which to reason, judge, and act.

The valuing of access to large amounts of printed material during this period stimulated the growth of libraries of a variety of sorts. Circulating libraries—book-rental agencies, in effect—originated in bookstores but quickly spread to a variety of sites governed only by their accessibility to the intended clientele. These included general

stores, drugstores, dry goods stores, confectionaries, taverns, and brokerage firms. Such new book outlets provided fiction to those willing to pay the required subscription fee, but also supplied increasing numbers of works on politics and belles lettres. Since women had come to constitute a very large audience of readers, circulating libraries run by women principally for women operated in places such as millinery shops.

For men, the advent of privately owned subscription reading rooms, operated for profit, provided the opportunity to read a variety of materials, particularly newspapers. The Postal Law of 1792 had provided that printers might exchange copies of newspapers with others for free. These exchange newspapers often ended up in coffeehouses, which provided reading space for their customers. Sometime in the first decade of the nineteenth century, however, particularly in the West, the need for more formal reading space gave rise to for-profit subscription reading rooms. These facilities provided clients, mainly those involved in commerce, with access to current business information. During the 1820s and 1830s, mechanics' and mercantile libraries arose to meet other needs. Mechanics' libraries grew out of the workingmen's benevolent organizations founded in large cities to provide financial aid and assistance to the families of mechanics in distress and comprised mostly works of "useful knowledge." Mercantile libraries, in contrast, catered to the needs of young clerks and merchants. Eventually, mechanics' libraries became viewed principally as a way to keep young apprentices off the street, while mercantile libraries were an institution through which young men learned the attitudes, values, manners, and behaviors appropriate to their class status. Both, however, made printed materials widely available to individuals who could not or would not otherwise have bought them. Free African Americans were by and large excluded from societies organized by whites, so they organized their own debating and literary societies, lyceums, and prose reading groups in cities such as Boston, Brooklyn, and Philadelphia.

Eventually, all of these proprietary reading establishments gave way to the tax-supported public library, first established in New York State in 1835. Linked with school districts but not constituted as school libraries, these institutions supplied mainly works of nonfiction to adults (fiction still being considered of specious social value). These libraries were supplemented by a variety of philanthropic endeavors, including Sunday school libraries, which provided young people with "didactic fiction," and Young Men's Christian Associations collections. In 1852 the establishment of the Boston Public Library marked the beginning of a large-scale trend toward public support of the nation's reading habit that by 1900 provided most Americans with access to printed works.

Innovations in Marketing and Distribution

Widespread demand for printed materials was both the cause and the result of a major reorganization in book and periodical production that took place between 1790 and 1840. During that era, full-fledged publishers arose, responsible for coordinating production, distribution, and marketing and for maintaining a primary relationship with authors. Prior to this time, book production had been financed principally by the author, with the printer usually receiving either a flat fee or a percentage of the profit to cover costs. Occasionally, printers had functioned as publishers, holding final financial responsibility and oversight over the work. Often, in order to ensure that costs would be covered, books were published only after a certain number of subscriptions had been taken, indicating that there would be an adequate market for them.

The new publishers introduced innovations in marketing and distribution that quickly led to the demise of the old printer/publishers. The first American publisher worthy of the name, Irish immigrant Mathew Carey, abandoned the trade of master printer early on in his career to establish an extensive sales network of agents, contacts, correspondents, and "adjutants" (as they were called) from his headquarters in Philadelphia in the late 1790s. With the assistance of Mason Locke Weems, an itinerant bookseller and ordained Episcopal minister from Maryland, Carey was able to tap a new market in the Upper South, supplying people there with cheap, popular works. Engaging a well-developed network of distributors to take subscriptions for Carey works or sell them on consignment, Weems and agents like him helped to establish the Carey firm as a dominant national presence for almost half a century.

As large firms like J. and J. Harper—later Harper and Brothers—discovered, dealing in large volume and developing a widespread distribution network would become the keys to successful publishing in the nineteenth century. Harper's emerged as the largest publisher in America in the 1840s by experimenting with strategies to minimize risk and maximize produc-

ETHNIC PUBLISHING IN THE NINETEENTH CENTURY

Some European-American ethnic publishers had a good deal more success than did African Americans. For example, by the 1840s a German book trade was well established, having existed in North America since the mid-eighteenth century. Centered in Philadelphia, Cincinnati, Saint Louis, Boston, and New York, the trade produced books that by the 1840s were status symbols among intellectuals and students enamored of German romanticism. German and bilingual newspapers flourished after 1830, when genres roughly equivalent to those published in English proliferated wherever substantial numbers of German speakers settled. The first Hebrew press was established in the United States in New York by Henry Frank, a Jewish German immigrant, in 1849 or 1850. His firm produced prayer books and other scholarly and devotional works.

In addition, a small American Indian press addressed the needs of Native Americans. Sequoya, a member of the Cherokee tribe, recognized the need for literacy as a way for Indians to gain power with respect to white society. In 1809 he invented an eighty-six-character alphabet whose use spread rapidly among the Cherokee. In 1828 the *Cherokee Phoenix*, a bilingual newspaper, began publication in New Echota, Georgia. The Cherokee, Chickasaw, Choctaw, and Creek peoples published newspapers and periodicals by and for an Indian audience in a number of states during the nineteenth century.

tion. Founded as a job printing firm in 1817, Harper's quickly adopted state-of-the-art technological innovations (such as stereotyping and the newly invented steam-driven press) that required a greater initial outlay of capital but that resulted in the ability to produce in volume a list of books that could be reprinted and issued in new editions if demand warranted. After the passage in New York of legislation establishing school district libraries, Harper's took advantage of the new library market by initiating "library" series designed to be purchased in toto, especially by these new public institutions. The Harper's Family Library, the Library of Select Novels, Boys' and Girls' Library, the Classical Library, and the School District Library all attempted to establish appropriate

A classic is a book that has never finished saying what it has to say.

ITALO CALVINO

*Newspapers saw
radio as a
competitor, since
radio news
bulletins could
reach people before
newspapers could.*

PAGE 393

See also
Journalism

standards of reading taste and culture. The motive was not—or not only—altruism or civic responsibility. Grouping the books together into a canonical set meant that Harper's imprint would stand for desirable cultural values, an incentive to purchase for certain audiences.

Other major publishers, such as D. Appleton, Putnam's, A. S. Barnes and Company, Scribners, D. Van Nostrand, and E. P. Dutton and Company, also operated on a large scale, sometimes producing specialized lists in areas of science or educational materials. Many of the publishers of the period from about 1830 to 1870 were, like Harper's, family-owned and -run businesses that valued maintaining a certain personal quality in their relationship with authors. Most too were located in the New York—Philadelphia nexus. These cities, the endpoints of important transportation routes to the West and South, were the earliest to be able to take advantage of economies of scale. Through the 1830s, most New England publishers continued to reach only local audiences; authors who wanted to accrue a national reputation were well advised to seek New York or Philadelphia publishers for their works.

The large New York and Philadelphia publishing houses solidified their hold on national markets by acting increasingly as wholesalers, distributing to retailers rather than directly to customers. A publisher such as Harper's might send its sheets to another city for local binding or might sell or rent plates to local printers so that one work might be published under multiple imprints, thus realizing a profit while minimizing transportation costs. Although Carey-type book agents, peddling door-to-door, remained active until at least the end of the century, most of the action began to take place within the book trade itself. Trade sales, parcel sales, and book fairs funneled new books, bound or in sheets, to booksellers and jobbers.

A few black book publishers existed in the antebellum period, with most (like the AME Book Concern, formed in Philadelphia in 1817, and the African Methodist Zion Publishing House, formed in New York in 1840) affiliated with a particular religious denomination. Within the black community, publishers faced obstacles in acquiring capital and in getting their books reviewed. In addition, the small number of literate African Americans in this period, and their relative poverty, meant that the mass market that sprang up for books produced by European-American publishers did not exist for African-American publishers. Black periodicals fared somewhat better, but even here, only three out of

eleven African-American-produced periodicals in the antebellum era lasted more than five years. Many of these early periodicals encouraged self-improvement and education. Meanwhile, the infant African-American press, having sprung out of the abolitionist movement with Samuel E. Cornish and John B. Russworm's *Freedom's Journal* in 1827, tended to be explicitly reformist in tone, urging the uplift and empowerment of blacks.

As the publishing industry became well established, two important developments shaped the industry. First, the ability of printers to act as independent editor-publishers and entrepreneurs eroded as their social status declined. As the size of the average print shop increased and printing increasingly became absorbed into the larger world of publishing, tasks within the printing trade became more segmented and routinized. Wages and status plummeted. Artisans and mechanics, who before had had a claim on the work of ideological production through editing and publishing, now became industrial cogs in the larger publishing machine.

In addition, competition to produce books more cheaply and to disseminate them more widely led to the introduction of the cheap paperback book. In 1839 New York journalists Park Benjamin and Rufus Griswold produced *Brother Jonathan*, a weekly periodical that serialized pirated British fiction in a format that looked like a newspaper. If it looked like a newspaper, they reasoned, the publication might take advantage of cheap postal rates for newspapers. In 1840 *New World* followed suit. Such "story papers," as they were called, could be bound together to form a book. Yet as it became apparent that novels in their entirety might be published before serialization was complete, cutting into sales, these penny-paper publishers began to issue "extras" or "supplements" containing the entire text of a novel just off the boat. The cost of these supplements might be a little over a dime, compared with a dollar or two for clothbound editions. In 1843 Congress changed postal regulations to prohibit the practice of marketing books in the guise of newspapers, but not before competition within the book industry drove prices down.

Throughout the nineteenth century as well, property rights vested in texts were continually at issue among publishers and authors. The United States copyright law of 1790 gave the copyright holder, usually the author, the sole right to print, publish, and distribute a work for a period of fourteen years, renewable for another fourteen. As publishing firms came to dominate the book business, authors increasingly sold copyrights to their publishers in return for fixed royalties. Because the law extended only to works published domestically, however, the copyright law had important implications for American authors. Until 1891, when the United States agreed to abide by international copyright law, works of foreign publication could be—and were—pirated without compensation to the original publishing firm or author. Thus American authors were simply more expensive to publish than were European. Gradually, out-and-out piracy moderated, as a practice known as "courtesies of the trade" (or "the Harper rule") came to govern the interactions of domestic with foreign publishers. Domestic publishers made arrangements with foreign publishers to reprint material and in return provided some agreed-upon compensation for the right to do so. Other domestic publishers, in their turn, had a gentleman's agreement to respect the relationship of a domestic publisher with its foreign counterpart or with a foreign author unless either of the foreign correspondents expressed an interest in changing the agreement. The "courtesies of the trade" were effective only during periods of "business as usual," however; when competition heated up, they were largely disregarded as the market became flooded with cheap reprints.

Print in the Era of Mass Commercial Culture

In the second half of the nineteenth century, three principal forces thoroughly transformed the market for print in the United States: standardization in the production of certain kinds of printed materials; the shift to advertising and away from circulation as the major source of periodical income; and coordinated methods of print distribution. Each of these factors was meant to maximize the profit of publisher-entrepreneurs involved in a notoriously chancy business with historically low returns. However, as T. J. Jackson Lears has noted elsewhere in this encyclopedia, who pays the bill makes a difference in what gets said. Rationalized methods for production, financing, and distribution meant substantial changes in the forms and genres of printed materials available to the new mass audience—and in their overall tone and tenor.

While family-owned houses, such as Harper's, Putnam's, and Ticknor and Fields (established 1843), continued to maintain a paternalistic and noncommercial ethos and to generate genteel literature designed for family reading, a new breed of more commercially oriented publishers turned

fiction writing into an assembly-line business. In 1859 the firm of Beadle and Adams adapted the format of the cheap, paperbound music books they had been publishing to the realm of fiction. The new works, bound in yellow and selling for a dime, encompassed both reprints and new stories. So successful were they that by 1865 Beadle and Company (helped by a brisk trade among Civil War soldiers) had published over four million of these "dime novels." Irwin and Erastus Beadle's effort spawned a number of imitators, nearly all of whom had begun in the printing trades but had sought out new avenues of opportunity as skilled craftwork was downgraded and routinized through industrialization. By the 1870s, firms had begun to issue whole "libraries" of sensational adventure and detective stories, sentimental romances, frontier and western fiction, and city stories.

As the appetite for cheap fiction grew, publishers discovered that generating a standard format and standard procedures would not only ensure customer loyalty to their product, but also would lower the costs of production. Beadle and Adams were the first to standardize manuscript lengths and payment rates for authors. Subsequent dime-novel publishers reserved the right to change the manuscript in any way they felt appropriate in order to fit the recognizable format of the firm's line. In addition, famous "library" characters such as Deadwood Dick, Ned Buntline, and the Old Sleuth became publishers' (not authors') property, as did the pseudonyms under which authors wrote. By the 1880s, standardization of characters, plots, and manuscript lengths had become so common that the production process has been likened to a factory system.

Even among the gentlemen publishers who clung to an older ideal, the expansion and rationalization of production led to an increasing gap between author and publisher. By the 1880s and 1890s, firms began to divide into specialized divisions, each of which had a separate budget and staff and produced a different list. Publishers in these large-scale enterprises found themselves increasingly playing the role of businessmen responsible for coordinating all facets of acquisition, production, and distribution. The bulk of the face-to-face work with authors and potential authors fell to the lot of a new middle manager, the editor. Whereas under the older system many houses prided themselves on the personal quality of their relationship with their authors, the new system dictated a more distant and businesslike relation. Literary agencies sprang up in New York in the 1870s and 1880s to handle negotiations be-

A good newspaper . . . is a nation talking to itself.

ARTHUR MILLER

*Printing links the
present with forever.*

NEIL POSTMAN

tween author and publisher. In addition, a number of writers' organizations and "unions" arose to gain leverage for authors in their dealings with publishers.

The new impetus toward mass production culminated in the printed mass product par excellence, the general-interest mass-market magazine. Although family magazines had begun to flourish in the decades before the Civil War and the number of magazines published annually had nearly quintupled between 1865 and 1885, the 1890s saw the beginning of an explosion of magazines with very large circulations. By the end of World War I, *McClure's* magazine would boast circulation figures of over half a million, *Cosmopolitan* and *Collier's* of over a million, and the *Saturday Evening Post* of over two million. What accounted for this incredible increase in the volume of circulating printed materials was neither a dramatic rise in the literacy rate nor a discernible rise in consumer affluence, although marginal increases in each of these areas may have had some effect. Some portion of it can also be explained by the increasing use of attractive illustration, made possible through chromolithography, halftone photoengraving, and electrotyping. Perhaps more instrumental in the industry's shift into overdrive, however, were the introduction of organizational rationalization into the industry and the move to advertising as the major source of revenue. And these, in turn, had their effects on the ways in which authors who published in mass-market periodicals defined themselves.

The shift came first in the newspaper industry. Joseph Pulitzer's New York *World* (revived in 1883) and William Randolph Hearst's New York *Journal* (1895) enjoyed rapid rises in circulation and posed a challenge to older, more established newspapers such as the *Times* (1851), the *Herald* (1835), and the *Tribune* (1841). Lowering their price to a penny, the World and the *Journal* turned to advertising revenue for the bulk of their financial support. Before this time, advertisements tended to be small and unobtrusive; under Pulitzer's and Hearst's regimes, advertising became bold and flashy and eventually took up nearly 50 percent of print space. Standard advertising rates were established based on circulation figures.

At the same time, the two papers concentrated on entertaining readers through sensational stories and self-promotion. Commuters on trains and omnibuses increasingly turned to attention-grabbing headlines and garish illustrations to amuse themselves on the way to work. The elite

got its information (particularly business news) from information-oriented newspapers such as Adolph Ochs's *New York Times*. The rest got theirs from the new papers, whose explicit goal was to entertain the reader. Pulitzer's Sunday supplement to the *World*, first published in the 1880s, emphasized the role of newspaper reading as leisure activity. Comics, in-depth articles, and a large volume of advertisement all contributed to the sense that a newspaper was as much for lingering over with a second cup of coffee as for procuring information.

Newspaper circulation shot up. The combination of the low price and the orientation to entertainment was a formula borrowed by magazines that had to compete with this new kind of story-oriented newspaper for audiences and revenue. In the 1870s these same magazines had utilized premiums and club combinations to boost circulation. Now their strategy was to liken themselves explicitly to the new genre of newspaper in order to appeal to potential customers. "A good magazine is a good newspaper in a dress suit," George Horace Lorimer, the editor of the *Saturday Evening Post*, said of his own endeavor (quoted in Tebbell and Zuckerman, *The Magazine in America* p. 67). New muckraking magazines, such as *McClure's, Everybody's, Munsey's,* and *Collier's,* hired reporters to uncover sensational instances of corporate or government wrongdoing. Professional editors ensured that the product was delivered in a standardized format and commissioned stories to fit their need rather than merely waiting for them to be volunteered or delivered by free-lance writers. Although the genteel magazines of the Harpers and the Scribners survived, magazines sponsored by chains increasingly displaced them in popular influence. The latter aimed to entertain rather than to edify. Moreover, as part of marketing groups, they had access to large advertising revenues that lowered the cover price, raised their profit, and contributed to high circulation figures. The Curtis group (*The Ladies' Home Journal, The Saturday Evening Post, The Country Gentleman*), the Hearst chain (*Cosmopolitan, Hearst's Magazine, Good Housekeeping*), and the Crowell-Collier group (*Collier's, American Woman's Home Companion,* and *Farm and Fireside*) were the most important of these.

Along with the general interest magazines, a host of special interest magazines sprang up. Directed at women, children, farmers, and professionals of all stripes, some were more specialized than others. The "Golden Age of Magazines" temporarily destroyed the dime-novel business.

(It would reemerge in the 1930s as the paperback trade.) In its stead, a hybrid product emerged that dealt with dime-novel themes and contained mainly fiction but that also contained advertisements, letters from readers, and a host of other features. These pulp magazines, invented in 1896 by dime-novel and mass-market publisher Frank Munsey, became a staple for the juvenile audience.

The new regime resulted in changes for both authors and readers. Newspaper and magazine writers sometimes seemed less like authors in the old-fashioned sense and more like employees of large, bureaucratically organized corporations. The standardized format and expectations of the industry frequently dictated more about the shape of an article or story than the author's own preferences. Yet the pretense of objectivity among these new "reporters" masked a world in which certain facts were presented and marketed in certain predictable ways to sell advertising space and magazines or newspapers. The news was not manufactured out of whole cloth, but it was cut and tailored to serve particular commercial purposes.

Audiences for their part could no longer imagine being addressed by authors as "gentle readers." Rather, they were now consumers—not only of the printed word, but also of the products whose manufacturers financed their access to the printed word. Women were particularly targeted as potential purchasers as they became identified as the chief consumers for the family. Advertisers flocked to publications such as Cyrus Curtis's the *Ladies' Home Journal*, with its formula of household hints, celebrity profiles, and short fiction, and in 1900 helped make it the first of all the million-seller magazines. Indeed, so powerful has been the link between advertisers and women's magazines that the feminist magazine *Ms.* dropped its connections with all advertisers in 1990, complaining that they demanded too much control over the magazine's content. Although radio and television later came to take the place of print as the dominant media of mass entertainment, the mode of commercial sponsorship developed in the mass-market magazines has endured.

Because it could not appeal to as large a mass market, the black periodical press suffered by comparison. Initial optimism about the advent of legal equality during the Reconstruction period gave way by the 1880s to the clear realization that social equality was nowhere on the horizon. As a result, the African-American periodical press enjoyed a revival during this period, for the most part existing to combat racial stereotypes and to emphasize the importance of education to racial uplift. Literacy among blacks grew considerably between 1870 and 1910, from 20 percent to 70 percent. Along with the small urban middle classes, these new readers provided new audiences for black newspapers such as T. Thomas Fortune's *New York Age* (1887–1937) or the *Washington Bee* (1882–1922).

"THE BEST READING"
Libraries as Arbiters of Taste

Not everyone saw the spread of the often-sensational wares of the mass market as an unbridled good. Librarians in particular, organized professionally in 1876 as the American Library Association, fought to protect the older patrician culture from the pernicious influences of the newer, cheaper dime novels and pulp fiction. ALA founders, including individuals such as Melvil Dewey, Charles Cutter, and William F. Poole, were by and large middle-aged Protestants whose families had migrated to the New World four or more generations back. Although they were dedicated to providing (as the ALA motto had it) "the best reading for the largest numbers at the least cost," the class bias in their understanding of what the "best reading" might be was clear from the very beginning. Designed to ameliorate class friction during a period of high tension by making "good" reading materials democratically available, the style and values of the public libraries of the period often left members of the working classes cold. Nor did Andrew Carnegie's famous gifts for use in the construction and establishment of public libraries help matters much; many members of the working class saw his beneficence as part of an elitist and paternalistic scheme of social control and resisted using the new facilities. For middle-class, white women, however, the new system of public libraries provided professional opportunities heretofore unavailable. And professional librarians did have room to exercise social power as censors of inappropriate reading materials, particularly novels. The Comstock Law of 1873, designed to check the spread of pornographic and salacious printed materials, was an additional manifestation of the tendency of the middle class to fear and censor printed materials that challenged bourgeois norms.

♦ **The Reconstruction**
The reorganization and reestablishment of the seceded states in the Union after the American Civil War

*For most
Americans,
television replaced
friends, the print
media, radio, and
the movies as their
primary source of
both entertainment
and news.*

PAGE 471

If white-owned magazines were sold in large numbers on newsstands, black-owned and -oriented magazines had to depend largely on subscription agents to ensure circulation. Although black commercial magazines, following the trend of the age, turned to advertising from both black businesses and white-owned corporations to support themselves, a large percentage of African-American periodicals were sponsored by the black churches and other established nonprofit organizations, such as the Afro-American League (1890), the National Association of Colored Women (1896), and the National Negro Business League (1900). In contrast to the mammoth white-owned mass-market periodicals, the two largest black publications at the turn of the century were the *Colored American* (17,840 peak circulation) and the *Voice of the Negro* (about 15,000 at peak). The influential *Crisis*, affiliated with the National Association for the Advancement of Colored People and edited by W. E. B. DuBois, reached a circulation of about 35,000 in 1915.

The distribution of printed materials also underwent a revolution during the late nineteenth and the early twentieth centuries. Founded in 1864, Sinclair Tousey's American News Company (ANC) came to hold a virtual monopoly on the distribution of mass-market magazines and paperbound novels to newsstands, railway stations, and hotel lobbies through the 1930s; eventually its operation would spread to chain stores (including grocery and drug chains). Buying periodicals at discount and selling them to local dealers, the ANC operation succeeded because it provided a high-profit, no-risk situation to retailers. Retailers received a certain percentage of the cover price of each magazine sold; they were not charged for unsold magazines.

Publishers of books faced a greater challenge in coordinating marketing and distribution. Books have always been tricky commodities to sell because of their variety and because of the lack of what might be called a "general audience." In order to compete in the new mass-market environment, publishers needed to come up with new and effective strategies for distributing what would come to be called the mass-market "best-seller." The book trade began to publish information about what was selling and what was not with the founding in 1895 of the trade journal *Bookman*. Best-sellers of the early twentieth century included mainly novels. In the 1910s and 1920s such works as Eleanor H. Porter's *Pollyanna* (1913), Edgar Rice Burroughs's *Tarzan of the Apes* (1914), Sinclair Lewis's *Main Street* (1920), and Edith M. Hull's *The Sheik* (1921) began to reach large audiences. Two important innovations in sales and distribution, however, brought book sales into the age of mass marketing: the mail-order book club and the mass-market paperback trade.

Established in 1926, Harry Scherman's Book-of-the-Month Club was the first modern mail-order distributor to advertise through the mail using "bait" premiums and considerable discounts to purchasers. A staff of editors sought out "middle-brow" works and offered them on a regular basis to consumers, who presumably got into the habit of buying. Utilizing such mass-production techniques as standard packaging and direct mail, book clubs quickly captured the largest segment of United States book sales, with a hundred fifty different clubs responsible for more sales than all U.S. retail outlets in 1980 (Stevens and Garcia, p. 113). All but two of the books to make the best-seller list in the twenty years following the establishment of the Book-of-the-Month Club were book club selections.

At about the same time that the book club phenomenon was catching on, a variety of publishers began to produce a series of cheap, rack-sized books that could be sold at a variety of retail outlets. Inspired by successful German and English precedents, Robert Fair de Graff (with financing help from Simon and Schuster) began to publish the Pocket Books series in 1939. Paperbound versions of hardback best-sellers selling for a quarter a copy, these portable books could be distributed easily to newsstands, grocery stores, or other mass-market outlets. As a result of the introduction of Pocket Books, people began to buy (rather than borrow) a greater percentage of the books they read. In short order, additional paperback houses sprang up, among them Bantam, Avon, Dell, New American Library, and Popular Library. In time, not only would new material begin to be produced in paperback form; but also hardcover publishers such as Doubleday (which created its Anchor Books division in 1953), Alfred A. Knopf (Vintage Books), and E. P. Dutton (Everyman Paperbacks) would find it necessary to get into the trade paperback publishing business to continue to compete in the market.

With its headlong entry into mass-market publishing and distribution, the book trade increasingly became less the province of a well-read gentry at family-owned publishing houses willing to take a loss on good literature, and more a subsidiary enterprise of massive multinational conglomerates concerned with the bottom line. Be-

See also
Popular Literature

ginning in the 1950s, a number of the older family houses either merged with others or were bought outright by larger entertainment enterprises. Although publishers of all sorts were subject to mergers, takeover attempts, and buyouts during this period, the fortunes of Macmillan (parent company of the publisher of this Compendium) illustrate the kinds of financial transformations wracking the book industry during the middle and later decades of the twentieth century.

The Macmillan Company was originally a British-owned publishing firm that opened an independent partnership in the United States in 1890. In 1960 Crowell-Collier, which had risen to prominence as a publisher of encyclopedias and mass-market magazines, took over Macmillan when the latter ran out of capital to invest in the new and lucrative textbook market. The new company, known as Crowell-Collier and Macmillan, Inc., began to buy properties in areas outside its own fields, such as music publishing. By the 1970s, the company had become simply Macmillan, Inc., a large conglomerate acquiring new properties and struggling to fight takeover attempts from nonbook conglomerates. In the heady business climate of the 1980s, Macmillan acquired the old-line house of Scribners, which had itself acquired Atheneum. In 1988, Maxwell Communication Corporation, part of British publisher Robert Maxwell's empire, acquired Macmillan, Inc., making it part of an even larger and more diverse multinational enterprise; this empire, however, collapsed after the death of founder Maxwell in 1991 and ensuing revelations of financial irregularities. Although Macmillan may be a particularly prominent example of corporate vertigo in publishing, similar changes in status have befallen a number of the family-founded houses in the latter half of the twentieth century.

In the area of retailing, the privately owned and run bookstore has also given way to new economies of scale. While many small, independent booksellers have gone out of business, the total number of bookstores in the United States has risen in the past few decades, mainly due to the dominance of shopping mall-type chain stores. Waldenbooks and B. Dalton, currently the two largest bookselling chains, focus mainly on the sale of bestsellers. Computer-controlled inventories maximize sales and minimize risk by ensuring that retailers are aware of mass-market tastes and trends at any given moment. Although the number of bookstores has multiplied, the large chains tend to stock the same few titles at stores across the country. The number of titles offered for sale

RISING NUMBERS

Shoppers look at books through store window. The total number of bookstores in the United States has risen in the past few decades.

E. O. HOPPÉ / CORBIS

*Freedom of the
press is guaranteed
only to those
who own one.*

A. J. LIEBLING

*The job of the press
is to encourage
debate, not to
supply the public
with information.*

CHRISTOPHER LASCH

on the retail book market has perhaps decreased as a result.

Print in the Electronic Age

In the twentieth century, the new audiovisual and electronic media have had as great an effect on print, literacy, and reading as has the rise of the mass market—but historians and cultural observers still disagree about the extent of those effects and their implications for the future of print. Those who see more radical changes argue that the introduction of radio, film, the phonograph, and especially television has undermined the primacy of print in American culture and is leading to a decline in literacy and in reading in general. Those who see the changes wrought by the electronic revolution as more modest in scope argue that new computer and data communications technologies have made print more important than ever as a vehicle for information transmission.

From the 1860s through the 1910s, print was the dominant source of information and entertainment for most Americans. At the beginning of the century, an estimated 90 percent of households, for example, regularly purchased and read newspapers. Literacy was nearly universal among the native-born white population. Even with the advent of radio as a source of mass entertainment in the 1920s, per capita spending on reading materials (controlled for inflation) continued to climb—except for a small decline during the Great Depression—until 1979, when it began to slip.

Different sectors of the print economy began to feel the impact of television, introduced on a national scale in 1947, at different times. The first to sustain damage were mass-market magazines, whose advertising revenues and circulations began to decline in the 1950s. There were two reasons for television's tremendous impact on the magazine industry. First, it provided an alternative vehicle for advertising. Second, it provided Americans with an alternative source of entertainment. *TV Guide* became the mass-market magazine with the largest circulation.

The magazine industry in the early 1960s fought back by trying to boost circulation figures. Cutting prices and offering special premiums and package deals to subscribers, magazine publishers hoped to lure back advertising dollars that had migrated to television. Such moves were by and large disastrous, failing to boost circulation and resulting in lost revenues. More successful magazine publishers learned to target their products to

specialized audiences whose needs would not necessarily be served by the general audience programming of television. Advertisers, more concerned with who, rather than how many, got the message, returned to these specialized vehicles. New periodicals sprang up for working women, the politically radical, gay men and lesbians, foreign-language speakers, African Americans, sports fans, environmentalists, and other market segments.

Newspapers showed some of the same effects of television's ubiquitousness. As network news shows expanded to a half-hour format and increasing portions of network budgets were devoted to information programming, television became the dominant source of news for most Americans by the 1960s. In response, some newspaper entrepreneurs turned to specialization as well, with suburban and specialty newspapers an area of growth since the 1960s. Major dailies suffered, however, with newspaper buying declining following the peak year of 1960. By the 1980s many major cities were left with only one substantial newspaper of any size; mergers and buyouts meant that many metropolitan areas were left with only one major printed news source. The number of people who said that they read a newspaper regularly declined from the levels of the 1960s as well, with older people more likely than younger ones to read.

Meanwhile, the number of people who claim to be book readers has held constant over the past half century at 20 to 25 percent of the American population. Women read more than men, younger people more than older, whites more than nonwhites, and the middle class more than the working class. Much of the book reading that takes place in the United States is a leisure activity, although individuals also report reading for information, for religious inspiration or self-improvement, for critical cultural commentary, or for alternatives to the dominant cultural perspective.

Have literacy levels dropped in recent years? It depends on how one defines literacy. By census self-report measures, 99.5 percent of the United States population older than fourteen years of age can read. A number of studies indicate, however, that perhaps 20 percent of that population has difficulty comprehending enough to accomplish certain basic cultural tasks—that is, about 20 percent are estimated to be functionally illiterate. Functional illiteracy is not distributed randomly across the population; it is highest (according to National Institute of Education figures) in black urban youth (47 percent) and Hispanic youth (56 percent). Several contemporary critics have also lamented another type of illiteracy that they call "cultural illiteracy," meaning an unfamiliarity with the basic knowledge necessary for informed cultural participation.

The glass that is half empty from one perspective is half full from another. Electronic publishing, photocopying, word processing, data bases, and computer software have democratized the production of information and the printed word—at least for those able to afford or have access to the necessary equipment. Indeed, far from becoming extinct as a medium for communication, printed material is increasing in quantity so rapidly that a major new cultural challenge has been the control and management of information generated through print. In many countries today, including the United States, Japan, Canada, and the nations of the European Community, information-making, -managing, and -processing industries account for about half of the gross national product. If people seem to read less for entertainment, they are likely to have to read much more in the course of their work performance. The danger is that a literacy gap based mainly on class will yawn wider between those who can manipulate printed sym-

bols and those who cannot—between those who inhabit the ranks of the relatively well-to-do and those consigned to a low-paying service economy with few employment options. Although Americans are not in danger of becoming a nation of illiterates anytime soon, there is a danger of clear and growing class divisions based on literacy and the ability, or the lack thereof, to process printed information.

—MARY KUPIEC CAYTON

PUBLIC ARCHITECTURE

American public architecture is a physical symbol, often on a monumental scale, of the definition of government and its role in American society. It is within public buildings that the drama of a democratic government has taken place. "Public" architecture can be variously defined. In the broadest sense, any building that is open to all people or contributes to establishing the public face of a city can be considered public. However, the essence of public architecture is composed of those buildings

COLONIAL LANDMARK

The Capitol in Williamsburg, Virginia, an important landmark because of its towering two-story cupola, was atypical by colonial American standards in its commanding presence and articulation of functions.
DAVID MUENCH / CORBIS

*Form ever follows
function.*

LOUIS HENRI SULLIVAN

that are built by the people to serve fundamental needs of society, particularly those of government and education. It is these two central categories of public buildings which will be examined here.

Colonial Buildings

Before the American Revolution, the goals of public architecture were quite different from what would be sought after 1776. Rather than defining a new nation, public architecture at first was a colonial extension of the imperial ambitions of European governments. The Palace of the Governors in Santa Fe, New Mexico (1610–1614), was a tiny outpost on the edge of the Spanish world, which sought to provide administrative order to the Christian missionary efforts directed at the Native Americans. This building is atypical among colonial civic buildings in the New World in that the Spanish learned from Native American building techniques and utilized the Pueblo material of adobe. This is in sharp contrast to the public buildings of the English colonies, where native traditions in building were ignored in favor of transplanted European ideas and forms.

In Puritan New England, it was the meetinghouse that first emerged in the seventeenth century as the major public building in a community. These typically large, square, and very plain wooden buildings on the town's common were built primarily for religious services, but they also served as a convenient gathering point for town meetings. A less pious but more convivial setting for holding discussions about the welfare of a community was the local tavern, where government officials often chose to meet. In New Amsterdam, the City Tavern (1641–1642) was even converted in 1653 into the Stadt Huys (city hall), since it was one of the largest and most prominent buildings in the Dutch settlement on the island of Manhattan. This tradition continued into the eighteenth century as can be seen in Williamsburg, Virginia, where the Raleigh Tavern was a center of political discussions second only to the Capitol.

The emergence of a civic architecture beyond meetinghouses and taverns was rather slow and limited during the seventeenth century. Boston's first Town Hall (1657–1658, destroyed 1711) was a rough wooden building with medieval gables exhibiting little architectural pretension other than two belfries that crowned its roof, denoting that the building was a place of assembly. Continuing a medieval tradition, the open first floor of the structure was a market, which added to the importance of the building within the lives of the

people of Boston. This market also suggests one of the British government's primary hopes for the colonies as a promising economic venture.

The largest buildings built in the English colonies were colleges, reflecting the importance that education held for colonial society. American colleges throughout their history were often perceived to be ideal communities providing on a small scale a model of what society could be. At first a single building, looking like an enlarged house, was built to contain all of the functions of the college, including dormitories for the students, and sometimes housing for the faculty. The earliest college buildings follow this pattern, such as the Old College at Harvard in Cambridge, Massachusetts (1638–1642, demolished 1678), and the College of William and Mary in Williamsburg, Virginia (1695–1699, rebuilt 1705–1715). A common type of college building emerged during the Georgian period of the eighteenth century and is exemplified by Nassau Hall (by Robert Smith and William Shippen, 1754–1756) of the College of New Jersey (later Princeton University). A large symmetrical block is given distinction through a central pavilion and cupola, and stands grandly on a large open, green space, in contrast to the tight, cloistered enclosures of England's Oxford and Cambridge.

When new capital cities were laid out according to a plan, such as Philadelphia (1682), Annapolis (1694), and Williamsburg (1699), care was taken to provide prominent central locations for major public buildings that would create an architectural climax at the end of central avenues. In the plan for the new capital of Virginia, Williamsburg, the College of William and Mary and the Capitol anchor opposite ends of the town's major street, the Duke of Gloucester Street. Adjoining the center of this east-west street is a secondary axis running north: the palace green terminating with the Governor's Palace. At the crossing of these two axes stands Bruton Parish Church. Williamsburg's plan diagrams a balance of the institutions of education, religion, and government with the palace of the crown governor standing at the head of this colonial capital for the British empire.

It was through the Capitol in Williamsburg (1701–1705; rebuilt 1928–1934) that the judgments of royal authority were dispensed to the people of Virginia. The towering two-story cupola asserted this building as an important landmark. The open arcade at its center provided a welcoming gesture to the public. The **H** plan of the building architecturally expressed the bicameral nature

See also
Urban Cultural Institutions

of colonial government, with the House of Burgesses in the east wing and the Governor's Council in the west wing. Another major chamber within the Capitol was the General Court. By colonial American standards, the Virginia Capitol was atypical in its commanding presence and its articulation of its functions. The more common solution for a major civic building (or college building) was to design along the lines of a great house as seen in Richard Munday's Old Colony House at Newport, Rhode Island (1739–1741), where only the building's size, cupola, and isolated position on a central site set the building apart from the general residential fabric of the town. The most monumental and prominent urban landmarks in colonial cities were church spires. The Old State House in Philadelphia (Independence Hall; Andrew Hamilton and Edmund Woolley, 1731–1753) is a prime example of the dilemma of definition of public architecture in colonial America. A large Georgian block, reminiscent of a house, is fronted by a churchlike tower; however, the building does not appear to be a church since the tower is placed on the broad side, rather than on the traditional narrow end. American society in the English colonies was not one of monumental institutions. The dominant architectural forms of the time were the house and the church. Public and educational buildings tended to be hybrids and transformations of these more prevalent types. Colonial public architecture suggests that it was built for a society whose ultimate political control lay elsewhere, with the crown and parliament back in England.

Building for the New Republic

With the revolutionary war and the establishment of the United States of America, the role of public architecture had suddenly and dramatically changed. New edifices needed to be conceived to house the just-created democratic institutions of the nascent country. One figure who was especially sensitive to the important role that architecture could play in the definition of a nation and its people was Thomas Jefferson, who was a gentleman-amateur architect, along with his numerous other talents. He played a key role in having the capital of Virginia moved from that symbol of the British crown, Williamsburg, to Richmond, where a fresh start further west could be made. While he was the American minister to France, he designed a new capitol with the assistance of C.-L. Clérisseau. Jefferson modeled his new State Capitol (1785–1798) after an ancient Roman temple, the Maison Carrée in Nimes. Jefferson had created a truly monumental and grand structure unlike any American colonial public building. The order, scale, and nobility of a rectangular temple block provided the ideal model of a young nation desiring to establish instant monuments. Moreover, such a building was invested with romantic associations with the classical past, particularly in the mind of Jefferson: republican Rome. From this building on, the neoclassical temple would be a type repeatedly associated with public buildings and would come to symbolize authority, stability, and culture.

Jefferson's neoclassical buildings were used as models to promote an ideal architectural environment that would ennoble and improve the United States. Nowhere are his architectural ambitions better seen than in his design for the University of Virginia at Charlottesville (1817–1826). In contrast to the large, single institutional block of most colonial colleges, he broke up the university into a series of smaller units and called it his "academical village." His social aim was to create a small, ideal educational community that would encourage intellectual discourse between faculty and students. Faculty lived in two-story pavilions with their living quarters above and classrooms below; each pavilion illustrates a different example of classical architecture. One-story dormitories fronted by colonnades link the pavilions and form two ranges flanking a central quadrangular lawn. More student rooms and six "hotels" (for dining) were located in two outer ranges parallel to the two inner ranges. At the head of the lawn is the Rotunda (originally housing the library), modeled after the ancient Roman Pantheon. Jefferson had replaced the central role given to chapels in colonial college buildings and campuses by placing at the heart of his design a pantheon, dedicated not to religion or pagan gods, but to enlightened thought through books.

During the presidency of George Washington (1789–1797), the government decided to build a new capital city for the nation, reinforcing an often repeated theme during the first century of the United States, a theme of optimistic new beginnings on a generous and ever-enlarging land. A French engineer and architect, Pierre Charles L'Enfant, laid out the new federal city in 1791. He conceived of it on a truly monumental scale, and it was not until the twentieth century that Washington, D.C., began to approximate L'Enfant's original vision. L'Enfant's design is based upon baroque urban and garden planning, which accentuated sites for major buildings or fountains by use of radial avenues. He adapted

Architecture begins where engineering ends.

WALTER GROPIUS

The struggle to save New York's Grand Central Terminal and the failure to preserve Pennsylvania Station were early signs of the conflicts over the preservation of historic buildings in America.

PAGE 86

See also
Parades, Holidays and Public Rituals

principles that in Europe symbolized absolute power (such as in papal Rome or the gardens of Versailles) to create a democratic capital. This was a continual theme in American public architecture: appropriating architectural forms that were used in the past to represent dogmatic authority and recasting them for more republican purposes. At the end of a broad mall, two buildings were to be the centerpieces of this federal city: the President's House and the Capitol (in an arrangement not unlike Williamsburg).

The complicated history of the United States Capitol is one of multiple architects, an evolving design, political division, foreign invasion, civil war, and a key opportunity for a new nation to establish a dominant architectural symbol. A competition for the new building was held in 1792, and the surviving entries make clear the inability of most American architects and builders to think beyond the small scale of colonial examples. However, a late entry by William Thornton pleased the eyes of both Washington and Jefferson. Thornton was encouraged to continue work on a new design and during the mid-1790s the first design for the Capitol was developed. The composition was a hybrid of forms and motifs: a long palacelike block (to provide separate wings for the Senate and House of Representatives) was accentuated in the center with a low Pantheonlike dome and portico facing to the east and a much taller dome and semicircular colonnade on the west (mall) side of the building. How unified the various states wanted to be under a single federal government would be a debate that would continue throughout American society. Nonetheless, from the very start, the dominant architectural symbol for this gathering of the legislators would be the unifying containment of a circular dome (although Thornton in this early design had conceived of two domes).

After Benjamin H. Latrobe was appointed Architect of the Capitol in 1803, the competing domes were reduced to one (the tall, west dome was eliminated from the plans). During the War of 1812, the partially built Capitol and President's House were burned as the British tried to demoralize their former colonial possession by destroying its public buildings. Latrobe returned to rebuild the Capitol (1815–1817). As a European-trained architect and engineer Latrobe was able to design and build monumental and dignified classical spaces with masonry vaulting of a quality that had previously been unknown in America. He even invented new American orders of columns with capitals decorated with tobacco leaves or cobs of maize, one of the first attempts to create American architectural forms beyond the European tradition.

The Boston architect Charles Bulfinch finally brought the Capitol to completion in 1826. His major addition to the design was to change the building's dome from the low, saucerlike dome of previous designs into a taller, more prominent, and awkward dome. The building was completed, but by 1851 it had grown inadequate for the rapidly growing nation. In the late eighteenth century the future dimensions of the United States were vague and unpredictable. By the mid-nineteenth century it was necessary for the nation's major architectural symbol to undergo a radical alteration and expansion to stay in step with the new scale of the United States. The architect Thomas U. Walter added two large wings (1851–1859) to the ends of the original building to provide entirely new and much larger chambers for the House and Senate. To unify the sprawling breadth of the expanded Capitol, Walter built a new and much taller dome (1855–1863). Reminiscent of the domes of Renaissance-baroque churches (particularly Sir Christopher Wren's Saint Paul's Cathedral in London), it secularizes a long-used religious architectural form to symbolize the unity of many states under the single dome of the federal government. The dome was built in iron, reflecting the growing industrial capacity of the nation. Iron was certainly precious to the Union military cause during the Civil War, yet Abraham Lincoln insisted that construction of the dome continue during the war: "If people see the Capitol going on, it is a sign we intend the Union shall go on" (quoted in Hitchcock and Seale, *Temples of Democracy*, p. 141).

No other public building before the Civil War required the enormous size of the United States Capitol. The dominant image for a public building by the early nineteenth century was the classical temple, usually Greek in its inspiration. A Greek temple stimulated romantic thoughts of democracy and the beginnings of Western civilization. Greek Revival buildings were found throughout antebellum America from diminutive temples serving as county courthouses in rural Virginia to boldly scaled capitols in stone to serve the newly created states of the west, as can be seen in Columbus, Ohio, and Nashville, Tennessee. Such buildings proclaimed the arrival of an instant culture evocative of the greatest legacies of antiquity, yet could serve as the context for the workings of a grassroots democracy as exemplified by George Caleb Bingham's painting *The*

DEFIANT STYLE

*The Smithsonian Institution
(1846–1855), designed by
James Renwick in a medieval
and Romanesque style, defied
the nineteenth century tradition of neoclassical public
buildings.*
G. E. KIDDER SMITH / CORBIS

Verdict of the People (1854–1855), where election results are read to a community from the steps of a classical portico. Greek temples were used in nearly every building type, as seen in Philadelphia, where William Strickland based his design for the Second Bank of the United States (1818–1824) on the Parthenon in Athens, and Thomas U. Walter created a monumental Corinthian temple to serve as the central building at Girard College (1833–1847). Despite this compelling fashion for the Greek, a temple is a rather restrictive form, often poorly lighted because of shadowy colonnades. Both of these Philadelphia examples have interiors vaulted in the Roman manner to make them more functional.

In Washington, D.C., during the 1830s and 1840s several federal buildings were being built in the neoclassical manner by Robert Mills, who in 1836 had also designed the Washington Monument to be built at the heart of the city. This 555.5-foot (169.3-meter) monument (completed by Thomas L. Casey in 1884) in the shape of an ancient Egyptian obelisk is a prime example of the cult worship that arose around President Washington in the nineteenth century as the new nation sought to establish its own history of heroes and myths. This tribute to Washington seeks to outdo the structures of the most monumental builders of all time, the ancient Egyptian pharaohs.

In the mid nineteenth century a major exception to Washington's classical norm for federal buildings was built on a prominent location on the Mall. The architect James Renwick erected the Smithsonian Institution (1846–1855), a dark, brooding, asymmetrical pile of medieval towers and Romanesque arches, appearing like a picturesque cluster of buildings constructed over several generations. The head of the building committee, Congressman Robert Dale Owen published *Hints on Public Architecture* (1849) in which he promoted medieval revival architecture as more flexible, functional, and economical than Greek Revival temples. Other than the late-nineteenth-century Richardsonian Romanesque, classical styles with their civic and public connotations have tended to be preferred over medieval styles for major governmental buildings. Such styles as the Gothic Revival are more associated with religion, natural settings, and individuality.

An Expanding Land and the Gilded Age

In the early nineteenth century there was an explosive growth in the founding of new colleges, much of it fueled by the desire of various religious groups to have colleges established throughout an ever-growing land. In 1862, Abraham Lincoln signed the Morrill Act providing the means for all states to establish land-grant colleges. Rather than stressing a traditional curriculum of classical or theological education, these new, more democratic institutions were to be built around the pragmatic fields of agriculture, the mechanical

*Their buildings,
mostly beaux-arts,
renaissance, or
neoclassical, also
helped establish the
architectural style
believed appropriate
for cultural
institutions.*

PAGE 537

See also
Landscapes; Villages
and Towns

arts, and military science. Many of these land-grant colleges would be placed in isolated, rural locations, such as State College, Pennsylvania, and Urbana-Champaign, Illinois. Along with facilitating the agricultural mission of these schools, such a location reflected an often-repeated theme in American higher education; the need to create an ideal learned community of young adults uncorrupted by the temptations of the big city. Another advantage, to the nineteenth-century romantic mind, was life close to nature, with all of its moral and aesthetic advantages. The landscape architect Frederick Law Olmsted was a popular campus planner in the late nineteenth century. He advocated campuses designed like picturesque parks, with small buildings informally grouped. This represented a sharp break from the rigid classical arrangements of the past, which were dominated by a central, large building. Many campuses followed this more naturalistic approach, as can be seen in such diverse places as Smith College and the Kansas State Agricultural College (now Kansas State University); however, most of these colleges were still built with an Old Main dominating the grounds.

For most American children in the nineteenth century the architectural domain of education was the one-room rural schoolhouse. Although there were many variations, the archetypal rural school evoked the higher moral environments of the home and church. A houselike rectangular, gabled block often had such churchlike elements as a bell-tower, pure white color, and separate entrances for females and males. Most often, children of all ages were taught by one teacher, who encouraged the older children to help the younger. The building became a community gathering point for dispersed rural populations as they congregated for such events as a holiday pageant. To many immigrant families it represented assimilation into American society, for children met people from many backgrounds and were required to learn English. For Native Americans, though, a reservation school teaching only the knowledge, values, and language of white society represented a ruthless effort to eliminate their culture.

In the official realm, the restrictive form of a neoclassical temple often seemed too confining to the growing scale and bureaucracy of government in Victorian America. When the State, War, and Navy Building (1871–1888; now the Old Executive Office Building) was built in Washington by Alfred B. Mullett (the Treasury Department's Supervising Architect, 1866–1874), it dwarfed its surroundings, including the White House to the east. The chaste, democratic Greek Revival of the early nineteenth century was replaced by the fashionable neo-baroque elegance of Napoleon III's Second Empire in France. Mullett's sprawling palacelike block is animated with pavilions, mansard roofs, and a seemingly endless succession of columns.

This enlargement in scale can also be seen in state capitols. The modest Greek Revival Illinois State Capitol in Springfield by John F. Rague, built in the 1830s, was superseded by a much more grandly scaled and ornamented capitol by J. C. Cochrane (1867–1888), reflecting changes in how the people of Illinois thought of themselves. Their state was no longer a western outpost of ill-defined opportunities, but had become a rapidly growing agricultural, commercial, and industrial center for the Midwest, with more sophisticated tastes—as their new capitol made clear. By this time a common type had emerged for state capitols (although there were many individual departures and variations), where wings accommodating the two houses of the legislature flanked a central ceremonial space, usually a domed rotunda, fronted by a portico providing public access. This formula was first suggested by the U.S. Capitol in its various forms and found its first mature expression in a state capitol in Harrisburg, Pennsylvania (Stephen Hills; 1810–1821; now destroyed).

County courthouses, state universities, and capitols often played substantial roles in the competition among cities to predominate in their particular region. The question of which city was to be the county seat or home of the state university often led to major political struggles with long-term economic impact on the winning and losing communities. State capitals often moved in the nineteenth century following changes in population growth and convenience; as a result, capitol buildings often proved to be temporary dwellings of government, echoing the nature of a transient society filling a land of changing boundaries with an unpredictable future. On the other hand, state capitols and county courthouses were monumental symbols in the nineteenth century of the systematic taking of land from the Native Americans for the primary use of white Americans of European descent.

With the growth of cities in the nineteenth century, the responsibilities of municipal government grew markedly. The design for Philadelphia City Hall (1871–1901) by John McArthur, Jr., reflected a combination of the growing size of local government, city pride, and the excesses of

COUNTY COURTHOUSE

Tangible Evidence of Government

For many citizens, direct interaction with the state capitol or Washington, D.C., is minimal. The county courthouse is a more tangible presence of government that is involved in a person's legal relationship to a community, from marriage licenses to court trials. The courthouse is also the archive for the county, where such vital records as land deeds are kept. The workings of a civilized community living under laws is manifested in the county courthouse. It is a place where a community gathers on special occasions and builds memorials to its leaders and military dead. And it is occasionally the stage for landmark legal cases with implications well beyond the county, such as the courtroom struggle of William Jennings Bryan and Clarence Darrow in the 1925 Scopes trial in the Rhea County Courthouse at Dayton, Tennessee.

By the late nineteenth century the courthouse tended to be the dominant architectural landmark in its city. Often standing alone in the central square in town, a tower or dome proclaimed the building's preeminence over the local architectural environment. This pride-filled symbol of the booster spirit of a county seat was sometimes inflated in size and expense beyond what was truly appropriate for a particular county. One notorious example is the Macoupin County Courthouse (1867–1870) in Carlinville, Illinois, by Elijah E. Myers, the architect of several state capitols. Although the building was budgeted to cost $50,000, the final bill was for $1,380,000 due to graft and the extravagance of its classical design. It took over four decades for the county to pay off the debt.

political corruption. Filling the center square of Philadelphia, this heavily ornamented Second Empire masonry pile boasts a tower 511 feet (156 meters) high, topped by a 37-foot (11-meter) statue of William Penn. During this building's lengthy construction, a seminal public building was built in Pittsburgh: the Allegheny County Courthouse and jail (1884–1888), designed by America's most prominent architect of the day, Henry Hobson Richardson. Like the Philadelphia City Hall, Richardson's courthouse is a large pavilioned block culminating in a landmark tower. However, Richardson has calmed

down the exuberance and eclecticism of Victorian architecture. Unlike the Philadelphia building, ornament and picturesque effects do not dominate. Richardson concentrated on the essential masses, where the forms correspond to the functions within; the rusticated stone walls are articulated by the round arched openings of his distinctive Richardsonian Romanesque style. The Richardsonian romanesque, with its qualities of massiveness, stability, and functional clarity, made it one of the most popular architectural styles for public buildings at the end of the nineteenth century, from the Old Post Office Building in Washington, D.C. (1891–1899, by W. J. Edbrooke), to numerous courthouses built throughout Texas.

The American Renaissance versus the Skyscraper

A return to classical order at the end of the Victorian era was heralded by the 1893 World's Columbian Exposition in Chicago. This was a temporary city with white plaster walls organized around a central court of honor. Its classicism, inspired by the teachings of the École des Beaux-Arts in Paris, was one of richness and magnitude suggesting Roman imperialism in contrast to the Greek reserve and severity seen at the beginning of the century. America had moved from a democratic experiment to a world power with imperial aspirations. This world's fair presented a unified ensemble of generously spaced classical buildings that was in sharp contrast to the random development of the emerging skyscraper city in the congestion of downtown Chicago. Ibis illusionary "White City" of the fair would be a compelling model for public architecture for years to come.

Sometimes called the American Renaissance, the turn of the century often saw a desire to reform the center of a city into a unified classical vision, a "City Beautiful." The construction of Washington, D.C., in the nineteenth century had departed sharply from L'Enfant's original intentions. In 1901–1902, a Senate Park Commission advised a return to a modified L'Enfant plan that would be the basis for much of monumental Washington. Many City Beautiful plans were made, but few were fully realized; nonetheless, this planning movement had a major impact upon those model cities for Americla, the college campus. Cass Gilbert's 1910 master plan for the University of Minnesota, Minneapolis, reflected a revival of interest in Jefferson's plan for the University of Virginia, now greatly monumentalized in the Beaux-Arts classical manner.

Government buildings in Washington and their facsimiles in various state capitals set standards that were copied by counties, municipalities, and builders of commercial and residential structures.

PAGE 258

P

PUBLIC
ARCHITECTURE

*The American Renaissance
versus the Skyscraper*

*Good architecture
lets nature in.*

MARIO PEI

See also
Commercial Architecture

Many new state capitols were built during the American Renaissance, most reaffirming the domed, two-winged type, though now academically executed in a more knowing manner of classical and Renaissance sources (in contrast to the innocent simplicity of the Greek Revival and the free eclecticism of the Victorian era). Cass Gilbert's Minnesota State Capitol in Saint Paul (1895–1904) is one of the more refined examples, while Joseph M. Huston's Pennsylvania State Capitol in Harrisburg (1901–1909) was one of the most excessive (this building's financial scandal eventually landed the architect in jail).

The often-seen tendency of some communities to aggrandize their cities with public buildings of a scale and form associated with more important buildings is well represented by San Francisco's City Hall (1913–1915, by John Bakewell, Jr., and Arthur Brown, Jr.). Clearly mimicking the domed-palace-block form of Beaux-Arts classical state capitols, this building stands impressively at the heart of a unified civic center of buildings in the City Beautiful manner. However, many Beaux-Arts classical city halls are less dominant in their design, and appear to be just one classical block within a master plan, such as the understated Des Moines City Hall (1910–1911). This city hall was built for a progressive, commission form of city government: a large hall allowed the public to watch the city employees at work (no city bosses would be making deals behind closed doors).

The early development of modern architecture in America was not fought out in the conservative field of governmental architecture. One notable exception was the Woodbury County Courthouse (1915–1918) at Sioux City, Iowa, by the Prairie School firm of Purcell and Elmslie (for William L. Steele). It combines the abstract rectilinear geometry of Frank Lloyd Wright with the organic ornamentation of Louis H. Sullivan. Form follows function as the public offices and courtrooms are contained in the broad base. A skyscraper tower contains more private functions. Despite the radical nature of the building's aesthetic, Purcell and Elmslie did incorporate several traditional features: the series of piers across the front facade is reminiscent of a colonnade, the large lobby is capped with a dome, and the building establishes a landmark presence with its tower.

The skyscraper, that quintessential symbol of the modern American city began to have an impact upon state capitols by the 1920s and 1930s. Rather than the traditional Renaissance Revival dome, Bertram Goodhue's Nebraska State Capi-

tol at Lincoln (1922–1932) is topped with a soaring skyscraper tower. Louisiana governor Huey Long's political ego was monumentalized in a similar skyscraper capitol at Baton Rouge (1931–1932). Even some university campuses started to go vertical: most spectacularly, Charles Z. Klauder's forty-two-story Gothic Revival Cathedral of Learning at the University of Pittsburgh (1924–1937).

In the early twentieth century, there was a renewed interest in the Gothic style for college campuses. It offered an alternative to the sometimes cold and monumental classicism of the day. Architects like Ralph Adam Cram and such educators as Woodrow Wilson at Princeton advocated the English Collegiate Gothic and its monastic quadrangles as evocative of the original ideals of college life. This introspective turning toward an elite club of the intellectually and socially select reveling in things English was especially appealing to the private universities of the Ivy League, and is well illustrated by the cloistered confines of Princeton and Yale universities. Many state universities opted for a more open approach of generously spaced buildings, often in the more economical and "American" style of the Georgian revival, as can be seen in the early-twentieth-century architecture of the University of Illinois at Urbana-Champaign.

From the 1920s to the 1950s, most one-room, single-teacher schoolhouses were abandoned in favor of consolidated schools in town, an approach facilitated by the coming of the yellow school bus. The typical urban school of the early twentieth century was a large multiple-classroom building of several stories, where students were now divided by grade level and were taught in a building with a great variety of rooms, allowing for such diverse activities as shop and theater. The nineteenth-century image of a schoolhouse evocative of home and church was replaced by an institutional building whose modular regularity sometimes suggests a factory. Nonetheless, many schools were embellished with the forms and ornament of fashionable architectural styles, making them proud cultural monuments at the center of a community, as can be seen in the neo-Gothic Evanston Township High School in Illinois by Perkins, Fellows and Hamilton (1923–1924). Elegant school architecture could also symbolize the gross inequities of American society, as was played out on the steps of Central High School in Little Rock, Arkansas, when this exclusively white public school was ordered by the federal government to desegregate in 1957.

Washington, D.C., underwent tremendous growth during the twentieth century, including a number of national shrines as American society continued to sanctify its history The primary function of Henry Bacon's Lincoln Memorial (1911–1922) and John Russell Pope's Jefferson Memorial (1935–1943) is to contain a larger-than-life statue of a revered president; these structures come much closer than most neoclassical buildings to the original use of classical temples as the abode of a cult figure to a god. While the White House and the Capitol, the quarters for the executive and legislative branches of the federal government, have always been at the core of the plan of Washington and its buildings, the third major branch of government, the judiciary, did not have a building of its own until Cass Gilbert's Supreme Court Building was built (1928–1935) to the east of the Capitol. Since the 1860s the Supreme Court had been meeting in the Old Senate Chamber of the Capitol. Gilbert's white marble temple is one of the most imperial neoclassical buildings in America; to those who pass through its immense portico the building communicates the supreme authority and judgment of the country's laws. Perhaps the greatest impression of twentieth-century Washington, D.C., is not its monuments but the endless number of buildings that have been built for the country's bureaucracy, such as the Federal Triangle, where block after classical block was built during the 1920s and 1930s to accommodate various departments of the nation's government.

From the PWA to Modernism and Beyond

Franklin D. Roosevelt's New Deal ushered in a degree of federal involvement in local affairs previously unseen. Such traditional symbols of local pride as a city hall or a public library were now being built by the federal government under New Deal programs such as the Public Works Administration (PWA; 1933–1939). A PWA building often meant a significant upgrading of a local public facility. It was a tangible symbol of governmental stability during the Great Depression, as well as a symbol that the nation was going back to work. The styles of PWA buildings exhibited great variety, sometimes reassuringly using regional traditions such as a colonial revival post office in Delaware or a Pueblo-style courthouse in New Mexico. Some buildings were more radically modern, such as John Lloyd Wright's Coolspring School in Indiana. However, the style often associated with PWA buildings is stripped classicism,

as seen in Charles Z. Klauder's design for Pattee Library at Pennsylvania State University. This austere, more abstract approach to classicism was especially suitable for a nation in a depression desiring to build monumental buildings without ostentation.

In 1939, Ludwig Mies van der Rohe began to create a new plan for the Illinois Institute of Technology on the south side of Chicago. Several city blocks were replaced with a new campus consisting of glass, steel, and brick blocks that looked like carefully designed factories. In the era after World War II, modernism would triumph in American architecture creating a dilemma for public architecture. Civic architecture has often been conservative, reaffirming traditional architectural images of authority such as the portico, dome, or tower. Could a glass box convey such symbolism? Chicago's Richard J. Daley Center (1960–1966) is a steel-and-glass skyscraper containing 121 courtrooms for the city and Cook County. Nothing distinguishes its exterior from a corporate skyscraper other than its isolated location on an entire city block surrounded by an open plaza.

Some architects deemed the anonymous glass box insufficient as a model for a major public building. A striking alternative was offered by Kallmann, McKinnell, and Knowles's Boston City Hall (1963–1969). Influenced by the brutal concrete forms of Le Corbusier's late buildings, Boston City Hall represents a turning toward a monumentality of heavy masses and geometric shapes. The various functions find separate expression yet all are brought together into a unified whole, appearing a bit like an abstract classical temple. While this building is clearly a monument to modern Boston, other communities have de-emphasized the symbolic role of public architecture. Any functional, no-frills office building is sufficient to house the growing administrative nature of local government. A building that makes a major architectural statement can be construed as a waste of the taxpayers' money. The changing nature of local government can also be seen in city council chambers, which in recent times have tended to emphasize dialogue by having citizens face the council members in modestly scaled rooms, in contrast to the large, formal chambers of the past, where the audience looked down on the proceedings from balconies.

The baby boom years after World War II were naturally boom years for school architecture. The multistory, revival-style educational institutions of the early twentieth century were often replaced

The City Beautiful Movement sought to enhance urban life by improving civic design, the impetus coming from Chicago's Columbian Exposition which influenced public architecture.

PAGE 62

*The job of buildings
is to improve
human relations.*

RALPH ERSKINE

See also
The City

with sprawling one-story suburban schools where generously fenestrated modern geometric blocks were distributed in wings appropriate to their functions. An important early precursor to this development is the Crow Island Elementary School in Winnetka, Illinois (1939–1940), by Eliel and Eero Saarinen, and Perkins, Wheeler, and Will. School architecture in recent times has often reflected revisionist attitudes toward curriculum, such as the flexible open plans popular during the 1960s, which allowed for such approaches as team teaching.

At the end of his life, America's most noted modern architect, Frank Lloyd Wright, finally had an opportunity to design a major governmental building, the Marin County Civic Center at San Rafael, California (1957–1972). The building sprawls across its site, addressing the natural context in a manner characteristic of Wright. However, at its center he included a low dome and a separate tower; unlike much of his earlier work, Wright chose to link this building (though in an abstract manner) with the architectural traditions of its type: the American county courthouse.

Postmodernism has brought about a renewed interest in the tradition of building types and historical styles. Michael Graves's Public Service Building in Portland, Oregon (1980–1983), reflects a partial return to monumental classical forms and symbolic ornament, but with a mannerist manipulation of motifs evocative of the uneasy and disjointed links between contemporary life and the traditions of history. The growth of historic preservation has sought to save the public architecture of the past and to adapt sensitively and add on to existing landmarks. A case in point is the new Civic Center (1982–1990) that Charles Moore and the Urban Innovations Group integrated into the older complex of the 1932 Spanish baroque revival city hall in Beverly Hills, California. Old and new play off of each other as a popular new public place is created.

College architecture has been an arena for all major currents in architecture since 1945. When many new buildings went up to accommodate the explosive growth of colleges and universities from the late 1940s to the 1960s many unified Beaux-Arts classical or Gothic Revival campuses were violated by the ahistorical individuality typical of so many modern buildings. Campus planning became more open-ended where unpredictable growth was expected. Colleges and universities

sometimes became the experimental grounds for innovative architects. Charles W Moore and William Turnbull radically rethought a residential college into a playful village where such communal features as the laundromat were given landmark status in their design for Kresge College (1965–1974) at the University of California, Santa Cruz. Peter Eisenman in his Wexner Center for the Visual Arts (1983–1989) entered into a deconstructionist dialogue with Ohio State University's existing buildings, the aesthetics of demolished buildings, and the conflicting grids of Columbus, Ohio.

The past few decades have been an uneasy time for American monuments. When Venturi and Rauch created Franklin Court in Philadelphia (1972–1976) as a bicentennial tribute to Benjamin Franklin, they chose not to rebuild Franklin's house but to create a ghostly outline of it in stainless steel, with hooded openings in the pavement so that one could see what was left of the foundations. Instead of reconstructing history (like twentieth-century Williamsburg) they clarified what we do and do not know. Maya Lin's Vietnam Veterans Memorial (1981–1982) is the opposite of most of Washington's monuments; it is dark and abstract and recedes into the ground. Its two granite walls (inscribed with the names of the over 58,000 Americans who died in Vietnam) align with the Washington Monument and the Lincoln Memorial as a new example of public building continues the complex symbolizing of American society.

The public architecture of America provides a monumental chronicle of society's changing attitudes toward government and education. At first, colonial public architecture reflected in a diminutive manner the distant institutions of civilization in the homeland. With the founding of a new nation, instant monuments evocative of noble aspirations were sought. As the country grew, so did the scale of government, and the size and constituency of education. Historical forms and styles have often been appropriated for their symbolic associations. The modernist disdain in the mid-twentieth century with history in favor of function and structure created the paradox of creating useful buildings devoid of traditional meanings. Many public buildings in recent years have returned to a dialogue with the past, as one sees a renewal of interest in establishing a meaningful architecture for the public realm.

—CRAIG ZABEL

R

RADIO

In John Cheever's short story "The Enormous Radio" a young couple buy a new radio because they enjoy classical music. But the radio brings more than music into the Westcott home. The narrator describes the radio as "powerful and ugly" with a "mistaken sensitivity to discord" which allows Irene Westcott to eavesdrop on the arguments and troubles of the other families in her apartment building. The Westcotts get the radio repaired so that it again plays classical music, but it is too late to fix the damage done to the family's peaceful facade. Jim accuses Irene of wasting money, stealing from her dying mother, and having an abortion. At the end of the story, Irene turns to the radio:

> . . . *hoping that the instrument might speak to her kindly. . . . Jim continued to shout at her from the door. The voice on the radio was suave and noncommittal. "An early-morning railroad disaster in Tokyo," the loudspeaker said, "killed twenty-nine people. A fire in a Catholic hospital near Buffalo for the care of blind children was extinguished early this morning by nuns. The temperature is forty-seven. The humidity is eighty-nine." (Cheever, p. 41)*

Cheever describes how the introduction of radio changed American lives, a change which involved not only specific radio programs but also the relationships among people, and between people and the world around them.

Social historians interested in radio have tended to focus on three sites of change: radio audiences, and how they changed and were changed; the technological and organizational structure of the broadcasting industry and its profit-making operations; and particular programs. Radio has influenced how Americans interact with popular culture, with the government, with new technology, and with commercial culture. Yet only when the interactions among the three aspects of radio—programming, structure, and audiences—are considered, can we chart the importance of radio broadcasting in American life. The changes

brought by and to radio need to be considered in four time periods: prebroadcast radio; prenetwork radio; the golden age of network radio; and radio in the era of television.

Prebroadcast Radio

People first used radio to communicate with other individuals. Not until around 1920 did the idea of "broadcasting," sending one message to many individuals—one transmitter, many receivers—become possible and popular. But before anyone imagined radio broadcasting, a group of skilled hobbyists used radio to talk to each other across the country. Early radio listeners thought of radio as an active, rather than as a passive, medium. The first "hams" (middle-class, urban white men and boys) experimented with radio transmission and reception in the decade before World War I. Using inexpensive crystals as detectors, oatmeal boxes wound with wire as tuning coils, and telephones as headsets, the young hobbyists learned from each other, from magazines, from the Boy

HAM RADIO AFICIONADO

In the early era of radio, Ham radio operator James Henry Rogers wears headphones at the controls.
CORBIS-BETTMANN

After 1945, radio and film comedies continued to make their enormous audiences laugh.

PAGE 230

Scout Manual, and from trial and error to build their own equipment. They designed receivers and transmitters to pick up distant signals and to communicate with each other, using their varying skills at Morse code. The active participation of these young men in their new hobby influenced the shape of the radio industry.

Early in radio history, these amateurs set up a national relay or network, in order to send messages across the country. Connecting the various radio clubs, the American Radio Relay League (ARRL), founded in 1914, had two hundred stations from coast to coast within four months. The ARRL network, disbanded during World War I by government order but revived in 1919, allowed amateurs to engage in their favorite activity: communicating with other operators who lived far away. From the beginning, amateur radio operators were thrilled to be part of a group, an audience, separated by long distances.

Hams held contests to see who could transmit the fastest and the farthest. Susan Douglas showed that the mostly male amateurs used their hobby to forge a concept of masculinity measured by mastery of the new technology rather than by physical prowess. In the process, they proved that middle-class Americans wanted to know what people in different cities or states were like and showed that "these Americans had a feeling that there was more information available to them than they routinely received" (*Inventing American Broadcasting*, p. 206). Even before broadcast radio was conceived, then, the amateurs used radio to communicate across long distances, to find out what was happening across the country, and to make connections with other people in this country and abroad.

The days of amateurs receiving and sending signals across the country, however, were numbered. After World War I, corporations gained control of American radio and reduced the role both of amateur radio users and of government broadcasters. Unlike Great Britain and Europe, in the United States large companies, rather than individuals or governments, developed radio technology. While some inventors, like Lee De Forest, tried to set up companies to exploit their inventions, existing electrical companies moved quickly to control all patents except those held by the British Marconi Company. In 1919, the American government, in the guise of protecting national security, forced British Marconi to turn its American operations over to an American holding company, the Radio Corporation of America. RCA, a patent pool formed with the

help of the federal government by General Electric, American Telephone and Telegraph, Western Electric, and United Fruit Company (soon to be joined by Westinghouse), controlled radio receiver and transmitter manufacture. When broadcasting began, RCA scrambled to gain a place in that field of radio as well.

The end of World War I brought not only organizational changes but also technological changes to the radio industry which affected the composition of the radio audience. The development of the Audion, a new form of vacuum tube, and its availability to amateurs after World War I made the transmission of words and music possible. Listeners no longer needed to know Morse code, a skill that the young hams had enjoyed developing but which had limited the number of radio hobbyists. In addition, amateurs increasingly found transmitters more difficult to build than receivers as transmitter technology became more complex. When each radio fan did not need to be both a sender and a receiver, and when radio listeners could enjoy their hobby without learning Morse code, more people became interested in radio.

In 1919, when one of the hams, Frank Conrad, a Westinghouse engineer, began airing a regular program of recorded music from a well-made transmitter in his Pittsburgh garage, many people wanted to listen. They sent a son, or the boy next door, or the war veteran down the block who had learned about radio in the service, to buy the materials needed to build a radio receiving set. Conrad's employer, Westinghouse, noticed it sold more equipment when Conrad broadcast. In 1920, to encourage sales, Westinghouse moved Conrad's transmitter to the top of their factory, applied for a federal license, set regular transmitting hours, and named the station KDKA. Radio had changed from point-to-point communication into a potential mass medium.

In the almost seven years before the first radio network was formed in 1926, listeners and the large radio companies explored the possibilities for programming and financing radio broadcasting. These experiments illustrated interesting roads not taken in American media organization and proved that commercialized broadcasting was neither natural nor inevitable, but simply the easiest and most profitable solution for the corporations already involved in radio. By the time the first radio station went on the air in 1920, companies that manufactured radio equipment expected to profit from their radio operations, but they did not know where that profit would come from and how it would come. Options other than selling time on the air existed, as did nonprofit alternatives to commercial broadcasting. The particular commercial form American broadcasting took resulted from the interaction of several decisions and predispositions, beginning with a desire, on the part of both ordinary people and the radio industry, for national radio service.

As radio stations sprang up across the country, built by newspapers, feed stores, municipalities, colleges, and radio equipment manufacturers, many of the habits of the earlier hams carried over into radio listening. Because ready-made receivers were not yet available, new listeners to the recently established broadcasting stations needed help to assemble a receiving set. Much like the early hackers who helped spread an interest in computers, the prewar hams eagerly helped others build receiving sets and, in the process, indoctrinated new audience members into the culture of radio listening (including the thrill of receiving signals from distant places).

Prenetwork Radio

Early radio fans eagerly searched for faraway stations. In 1923, *Radio Broadcast* magazine identified one of the continuing attractions of broadcast radio as the "ability to astound our friends by tuning in a program a thousand miles away for their particular benefit" and concluded that there "is something fascinating about hearing a concert from a long way off, and the pleasure does not seem to wane with familiarity" (Morecroft, p. 361). A listener could bring distant events into the living room (or garage). In addition, the small, early radio stations programmed local "talent," and so it might be more entertaining to hear a station many miles away. A poem published in the *New Yorker*, and reprinted in the largest magazine for the new radio listeners, *Radio Broadcast* (May 1925), described long-distance listeners.

Eventually, long-distance listeners found themselves unable to overcome technological barriers—no amount of fiddling with the dials could banish static. By the mid-1920s, the radio audience turned away from distant broadcasts and returned to local stations, but quickly realized that local programs remained at an amateurish level and that they missed the thrill of listening in on faraway events. Listeners sought easily available and reliable radio service which featured both broadcasts from distant places and programming of sophisticated content.

Although the number of "distance fiends" dwindled, they left an important legacy. The collective memory of radio listeners contained the

---

THE DISTANCE FIEND

He was a distance fiend,
    A loather of anything near,
Though WOOF had a singer of opera fame,
And WOW a soprano of national name,
He passed them both up for a Kansas quartet
A thousand miles off and hence "harder to get."
    New York was too easy to hear.
    He was a distance fiend . . .

He was a distance fiend,
    Alas, but he died one day.
Saint Peter obligingly asked would he tell
His choice of residence—Heaven or Hell?
He replied, with a show of consistency fine:
"Good sir, you have hit on a hobby of mine,
    Which place is the farthest away?"
    He was a distance fiend.
                    ("The Distance Fiend," p. 35)
            published in the *New Yorker*, and
        reprinted in *Radio Broadcast* (May 1925)

---

possibility, and the excitement, of hearing distant people and events. Rural listeners knew of more varied programming available from urban stations and sought accurate market and weather information; people from the rural South who had moved to the urban North, including African Americans, sought familiar music; sports fans wanted to follow their teams on the road. The early radio fans "fished" for faraway stations and thus demonstrated the public's interest in national radio, over which the audience could hear programs from around the country.

Three technological options existed for providers of national radio service superpower, with a few powerful transmitters serving the entire country; wired networks, with programs sent over telephone wires from a single source for rebroadcast by scattered local stations; and shortwave rebroadcasting, which connected local stations to the programming source with radio waves instead of wires. The reasons for choosing one option rather than another went beyond the technological, even at the earliest experimental stage. The radio industry decided on wired networks because they proved technologically feasible, were part of a compromise hammered out among feuding radio patent holders, and avoided the appearance of a radio monopoly by using local stations to broadcast national programs. The choice of wired networks to provide national radio service was the

---

TV gives everyone an image, but radio gives birth to a million images in a million brains.

PEGGY NOONAN

See also
African American Music

deciding factor in the development of the organization, economics, and form of broadcast radio.

Network radio brought expensive wire line charges and thus the need for broadcasting, as well as receiver, sales to make money. By the 1920s, radio stations in large cities sold time for commercial messages, or accepted free programs provided by commercial enterprises, in order to raise money and cut expenses. Yet ambivalence about radio advertising started early and remained. From the beginning of the 1920s, listeners, government officials, and radio magazines complained about broadcast advertising and searched for alternative methods of financing radio. The omnipresent question "Who is to pay for broadcasting?" showed that many did not immediately accept commercialized broadcasting as the best answer. College, church, union, and municipal radio stations flourished. Broadcast advertising gained rich and powerful proponents when RCA founded the National Broadcasting Company in 1926, and the Columbia Broadcasting System began in the next year, both as for-profit concerns. The high quality of programming available on the new networks and network dominance and influence overrode some concerns, but the networks still worked to sell commercialized broadcasting to the public.

Contemporary American broadcasting presents itself as the "natural," sometimes even the inevitable, application of American capitalism to communication. Yet the American commercialized broadcasting system did not evolve naturally but rather grew out of a struggle over its form and content. During the first fourteen years of radio broadcasting, listeners, broadcasters, advertisers, and educators fought for control over radio. Listeners wanted national radio service. The provision of such service over wired networks resulted from a combination of technological, economic, cultural, and political factors. Wired networks brought with them a specific broadcasting structure and particular kinds of radio programs. The use of radio advertising to pay the expensive wire rentals brought early and continuing protests from educators and others who hoped radio would do more than sell products.

Broadcast advertising also faced other, more influential, skeptics. Potential advertisers and the advertising industry itself doubted that advertisements over the radio would be effective. Networks, and the promoters they hired, campaigned to convince doubters that broadcasting was the perfect advertising medium. The campaign to promote broadcast advertising worked to satisfy advertising industry that radio was a medium they could understand and use without difficulty. Promoters involved advertising agencies in radio broadcasting, began merchandising radio programs, and com-modified radio time. They then convinced broadcasters to change radio to conform to prevailing theories and practices of advertising. Like other advertising professionals, the promoters of radio advertising changed the product they had been hired to sell in order to make their job easier. For example, because advertisers had recently come to think of consumers as middle-class women, promoters of broadcast advertising depicted radio not as a boy's toy or a male-controlled entertainment medium but as an instructional tool staffed by home economists in order to enter the home during the day and sell to women. Broadcast advertising developed as a continuation and extension of widely accepted advertising principles. The attempt to sell radio advertising to advertisers and broadcasting's resulting acceptance of basic advertising ideas had important consequences for the form of both radio programs and radio broadcasting.

Wired networks and the development of broadcast advertising shaped radio programming. Other forms of national radio service might have presented different performers, formats, and material. The particular demands of national advertising led networks to drop local musicians in favor of vaudeville artists who had long performed for audiences across the country. They also replaced regional sponsors with large companies seeking a national market, companies that had the money to hire vaudeville stars. In one of the first sponsored programs, recording artists Billy Jones and Ernie Hare performed whimsical, nostalgic numbers as the Happiness Boys for the Happiness Candy Company (a northeastern manufacturer and distributor that also owned restaurants). Jones and Hare were soon replaced by hard-hitting vaudeville comedians representing huge companies.

The increasing commercialization and monopolization of the airwaves by the networks brought new complaints about the commercialization of radio broadcasting. A poem in *Radio Revue* (March 1930) illustrated some of the concerns:

SPONSORITIS

Dame nature has a "funny" way
Of spoiling our enjoyment
For everyone who lives today
Has his or her annoyment;

And each disease beneath the sun
Has diff'rent germs to bite us
Now RADIO's developed one—
They call it "SPONSORITIS".

It's thriving like a healthy weed
Or fungus newly grafted,
And mercenaries sow the seed
Wherever sound is wafted
The artists rave then grow morose
Because of laryngitis,
And "fans" then get a stronger dose
Of this same SPONSORITIS.

No use to try to save the wreck
Or prophesy disaster,
For he who signs the mighty check
Is boss and lord and master;
When there's a program spoiled or botched,
It's money bags who fight us,
With heavy hearts we've stood and watched
The spread of SPONSORITIS. . . .

In one important challenge to commercialized broadcasting, radio stations supported by colleges and universities worked for an amendment to radio regulatory legislation to guarantee 15 percent of all radio frequencies for nonprofit stations. They lost that battle, and the war.

Commercialized broadcasters moved quickly to smash the early 1930s backlash against broadcast advertising, and they succeeded in destroying most nonprofit alternatives. Under new regulations pushed by the radio industry, many educational stations ceased to exist because they found broadcasting too expensive. The 1934 Communications Act, which was supposed to regulate the industry, failed to mention advertising or networks. Broadcasting, as presented in the Communications Act, was made up of independent local units financed in whatever way they chose, even though most stations were commercial and used network programming for the entire broadcast day. The new law gave no protection to—indeed, continued the harassment of—nonprofit and educational stations.

The results of the acceptance of networks and broadcast advertising were evident as early as the 1930s. For example, affiliation with a network emphasized, for local broadcasters, the importance of time and illustrated the changes in programming that accompanied the organizational and conceptual changes involved in broadcast advertising. Unlike earlier radio performers who were urged to fill as much time as they could, a singer on an early network show remembered that "timing was the sword of Damocles hanging over our heads. We could not be ten seconds overtime without infringing on another sponsor's territory" (Dragonette, p. 104). Radio's growing commercialism brought about part of the increasing emphasis on time. Radio existed in time only and time was the commodity sold to finance broadcasting. One observer wrote that "a statue of radio Thespis would assuredly be blind and with a stopwatch in one hand, or perhaps in each" (Goldsmith and Lescarboura, p. 98). Network affiliation and the inclusion of advertisements brought a rigid form to radio. Each programming segment was carefully timed, and sponsors, who spent enormous amounts of money buying radio time, wanted the same programming formula (a certain number of jokes, so many songs in each segment) followed each week. Some of the artists used the rigid form as a spur to creativity, like poets working within a strict sonnet form, but for most it limited program possibilities.

Commercialized radio proved more responsive to advertisers than to listeners. Uncertainty over listener response (a continuing worry for the television networks, which distrust current ratings systems and experiment with people meters) forced advertisers to rely on their own impressions of what listeners liked. Advertisers and networks worried incessantly about offending listeners. Several years after Gertrude Berg went on NBC in 1929 with *The Rise of the Goldbergs*, a program about a Jewish immigrant family, the network and the sponsor (Pepsodent) became concerned that a program about Jews might alienate listeners. The NBC statistical department did a study in 1932 and reassured network executives and the sponsor "that there is a large audience for good programs of Jewish type"; that "the success of this program should make a telling argument for Jewish programs"; and that "an analysis of their mail receipts indicates that this popularity is not restricted to any geographic region." Further, the report quoted the Pepsodent advertising manager that "although the program concerns a Jewish family, the vast majority . . . of appeals to keep it on the air came from Gentiles." Unable to clearly identify what made a program popular or unpopular, advertisers relied on their instincts about what the public wanted. Such instincts often had more to do with the prejudices and predilections of advertisers than the wishes of the radio audience.

Most importantly, radio became a way to sell products. Programs filled the time between commercials, just as many critics feel that they do in

It's not true I had nothing on. I had the radio on.

MARILYN MONROE
IN TIME (1952)

See also
Humor and Comedy

391

current television offerings. Programs joined with commercials in trying—sometimes successfully, sometimes not—to manipulate the audience, not to entertain or educate or uplift, unless those actions would help sell.

The Golden Age of Network Radio

Despite its drawbacks, commercialized national radio did offer its audience some benefits. If listeners missed a sense of direct human connection with the voices they heard, if they had little control over programming, the performers who flocked to radio in the 1930s nonetheless brought the audience professional entertainment, some variety, and a sense of belonging to a national community. Entertainment programming, particularly comedy and drama, played an important part in the everyday life of most Americans in the 1930s and 1940s as radio entered what the industry liked to call its "golden age."

Vaudeville performers began to form the backbone of comedy programs in the early 1930s. In 1931, Eddie Cantor became the host of *The Chase and Sanborn Hour*, and by the next year new radio shows featured Ed Wynn, Burns and Allen, Jack Benny, George Jessel, Jack Pearl, and Fred Allen. The new programs took the form of the variety show, which in the 1920s had featured musical hosts such as Wendell Hall on the *Eveready Hour*, *Harry Reser of the Cliquot Club Eskimos*, Rudy Vallee on *The Fleischman Hour*, and Jessica Dragonette on the *Cities Service Concerts*. Now, however, comedians served as the stars and hosts of programs which featured comedy sketches.

Performers, subject matter, advertising, and the form of the entertainment remained interwoven, so that a change in one affected the others. Cantor, for example, was clearly a participant in the "new humor" brought by immigrants to the vaudeville stage. Albert McLean describes vaudeville's urban and ethnic (mostly Jewish) humor as based on verbal misunderstandings, rooted in stories of family life and of the underdog, and with a compressed and frantic form built around the joke (a modern invention). The compression and verbal basis of this humor made it a natural for radio. The radio comedians of the 1920s, coming from different personal and professional backgrounds, had relied on music and on what McLean calls the "relaxed whimsy of the minstrel show" (p. 116).

Cantor's programs featured jokes, skits, and stories about Ida Cantor and the couple's five daughters. Cantor's scripts, written by David Freedman (many of the writers, as well as the performers, came from vaudeville), depended on a

"joke factory" where young writers reworked old jokes to fit the week's subject. Programs with a midwestern, small-town flavor, including *Vic and Sade, Easy Aces,* and *Fibber McGee and Molly*, joined comedies which had come out of a Jewish and/or urban experience. Nevertheless, the influx of vaudevillians to radio in the early 1930s, and the good fit between the needs of radio and the form of the "new humor," determined the course of radio programming for many years.

Comedy, in a variety of formats, remained popular radio fare through the 1940s and into the 1950s. Comedians smoothly made the transition from gently spoofing the Great Depression to gently spoofing World War II, always mindful that the federal government regulated radio broadcasting and that major corporations paid the bills. By the 1940s, radio comedy, like all radio programming, featured more commercialized programs with heavy-hitting advertising, often as part of the program, produced by advertising agencies located in Hollywood. Several novels, including *The Hucksters* (1946) by Frederic Wakeman and Herman Wouk's *Inside, Outside* (1985), explained how the increasing commercialization of radio brought new pressures to bear on radio writers and performers.

Dramatic shows during radio's "golden age" grew out of the continuing comedy serials which began with *Amos 'n' Andy* and *The Rise of the Goldbergs* in 1929. By the end of the 1930s, network radio featured several dramatic anthology programs. The writers on such series, often drawing upon the left-wing political consciousness of the 1930s, experimented with radio's aural qualities and ability to deliver political messages. Plays had widely varied formats, and some featured musical montages and poetry. Norman Corwin, a writer for *Columbia Workshop* on CBS, wrote and directed twenty-six radio programs in as many weeks in 1940, in a series called *26 by Corwin*. The programs included plays about submarine crews, hillbilly harmonica players, a boy who searches for his dog in Heaven and in Curgatory, a soliloquy for one voice with a few sound effects, and a biblical trilogy. Corwin's next project, an exploration of the Bill of Rights entitled *We Hold These Truths*, took up patriotic themes which he had explored before. Broadcast just eight days after the attack on Pearl Harbor, the show illustrated how many of the radio writers of the late 1930s and early 1940s moved quite easily, both professionally and intellectually, into wartime radio.

World War II changed the nature of broadcasting. Radio made three contributions to the

THE VOICE OF AMERICA

As World War II began, the United States rushed to keep up with the Axis powers, which had begun using radio for propaganda in the 1930s. Americans knew the political power of radio, having heard President Franklin Roosevelt's effective use of radio during his Fireside Chats, but many remained fearful of the power of propaganda. Finally, in 1942, the president authorized the Overseas Branch of the Office of War Information to begin broadcasting over the Voice of America (VOA) to areas under Axis control. As Holly Cowan Shulman describes in *The Voice of America*, the broadcasts heard over the VOA changed as American foreign policy, war aims, domestic politics, and cultural climate changed over the course of the war. The first VOA broadcasts drew directly from the experimental programs of commercial radio in the 1930s. VOA programmers, including John Houseman, borrowed radio techniques from Norman Corwin to make their broadcasts appealing. As the war progressed, VOA broadcasts became more factual and detailed, and resembled news reporting more than modernist radio documentaries. In part, VOA programming responded to the progress of the war. When the VOA had no victories to report, it explained America's moral stance and described war production in imaginative terms. As Allied triumphs brought the shape of the postwar world into focus, direct reporting became more effective propaganda.

The VOA illustrated the division in broadcast programming that took place in the 1940s, a change given impetus by the war. Entertainment programming and news programming separated, and listeners came to believe that such a division was natural and preferable to the intermingling of fact and fiction that 1930s radio had featured. Contemporary critics disparage television "docudramas," which resemble Norman Corwin's and John Houseman's radio programs, for confusing television watchers about the difference between "truth" and "fiction." The VOA, at least in part to hide its propaganda aims, helped construct the broadcast convention that news programs were both objective and oppositional to entertainment programming.

---

war effort: news programs supported American intervention, propaganda broadcast over shortwave radio targeted Nazi-occupied Europe, and broadcasts to the troops via the Armed Forces Radio Service boosted morale. Yet such extensive news reporting was quite new to radio. Newspapers saw radio as a competitor, since radio news bulletins could reach people before newspapers could. In the "press-radio war" of the mid 1930s, newspapers in 1933 refused to allow the radio networks to broadcast wire service reports. CBS and NBC countered by establishing their own news departments. But neither network wanted to spend the money necessary to compete with the wire services, since few sponsors seemed interested in news programs.

A truce allowed radio announcers to "comment" on the news rather than report it, and the wire services again made their copy available for broadcast in 1934. The "commentators," as radio reporters came to be called, did just that until the Munich crisis of 1938, when H. V. (Hans Von) Kaltenborn, a former newspaper reporter, made 102 broadcasts in 18 days. Sleeping at the CBS studio, Kaltenborn, the son of German immigrants, translated the speeches of French and German leaders as they came over the shortwave radio and broadcast them to American listeners. With the help of radio broadcasts, Americans began to seek a connection to other parts of the world.

In *News for Everyman* (1976), historian David Culbert contends that between 1938 and the attack on Pearl Harbor, "radio emerged as the principal medium for combatting isolationism in America" and that "radio commentators played a major role in creating a climate of opinion favorable to an interventionist foreign policy though they did not directly make foreign policy" (Culbert, pp. 6, 7). Culbert describes how six radio newsmen—Kaltenborn, Boake Carter, Raymond Gram Swing, Elmer Davis, Fulton Lewis, Jr., and Edward R. Murrow—brilliantly and creatively invented broadcast journalism in the 1940s and demonstrated that such programming had commercial potential.

Another wartime radio activity, that of the Armed Forces Radio Service (AFRS), also influenced commercial radio programming. Radio was so much a part of American life that during World War II the armed forces arranged for soldiers in both Europe and the Pacific to listen in. Samuel Brylawski, a Library of Congress archivist in charge of the huge collection of AFRS record-

R

RADIO

*Radio in the
Era of Television*

FIRESIDE CHAT

ings, notes that by 1945 the AFRS sent fifty hours of radio programming weekly to overseas outlets—producing forty-three programs (fourteen hours) itself and distributing thirty-six hours of American commercial radio (with commercial messages deleted) each week. One program, *Command Performance*, began six months before the founding of the AFRS in August 1942 and used prerecorded programs, which made performers' lives easier and proved to the radio industry that the technology existed to edit radio programs and broadcast them from disks. The program supposedly reflected the desires of American soldiers who would receive a "command performance" from America's best-known radio and film stars. Radio producers recorded performers and edited together the best "takes," deleted off-color jokes and dated material, and sent shows out to AFRS stations on records for rebroadcast.

Recorded programs had long been anathema to the radio networks, which had the money to provide live performances and boasted about their live entertainment in the 1930s and 1940s. Even after the technology existed to play recordings over the air electrically, the networks had blocked their use. Recorded programs could be cheaper to produce and represented competition for live broadcasts over the networks. Bing Crosby's experience on *Command Performance* may have moved him to demand a transcription clause in his new contract with the American Broadcasting Company in 1946. That clause gave Crosby the right to record his program in Los Angeles at his convenience and ship it to New York for broadcast. The use of such recorded material paved the way for the rebirth of radio as a musical medium after the introduction of television.

As an alternative programmer in an industry controlled by networks, the presence of AFRS demonstrated a wider range of possibilities for ra-

dio than most people had imagined. For example, the ambivalent relationship between AFRS and commercialized broadcasting illustrated continuing listener dissatisfaction with radio advertising. While dependent on the networks for many of its most popular programs, the AFRS deleted all commercial references and advertising. AFRS even retitled programs that carried a sponsor's name. *Camel Caravan* became *Comedy Caravan;* *Maxwell House Program* became *Fanny Brice—Frank Aforgan;* and *Chase and Sanborn Hour* became *Charlie McCarthy.*

Brylawski notes a number of reasons for the "denaturing" of programs, including complaints by service personnel, the unfair advantages to those commercial programs used by the AFRS, and American agreements with the noncommercial British Broadcasting Corporation to use its transmitters to broadcast the programs. Most important, the advertisements seemed inappropriate for GIs in the field: "Troops fighting in the Pacific did not want to hear about 'refreshing Coca-Cola' nor did they appreciate the 'dangers of the common cold'" (Brylawski, p. 335). The radio industry had worked since the 1920s to make broadcast advertising seem natural and reassuringly American, but the contrast between wartime service and danger and the profit-making techniques of radio advertising showed that advertising was neither wholly accepted nor particularly patriotic.

Radio in the Era of Television

After the war, opposition to commercialized broadcasting resurfaced. Like the outbursts of anticommercial sentiment when broadcasting began in the 1920s and again just before the passage of the Communications Act in 1934, the criticism of broadcasting in 1946 appeared in a number of different forums. The Federal Communications Commission (FCC), usually the servant of the radio industry, issued a study of radio programming in March 1946 entitled *Public Service Responsibility of Broadcast Licensees.* The report said that station owners had not fulfilled the provisions of their licenses which mandated public service. In April, Charles Siepmann, a former employee of both the British Broadcasting Corporation and the FCC, reiterated the charge that radio stations had failed to serve the public interest in his book *Radio's Second Chance.*

The critique of broadcasting that reached the most people, however, was Frederic Wakeman's enormously popular novel, *The Hucksters* (1946). Wakeman, a former employee of the Lord and Thomas advertising agency, wrote a fictional ac-

See also
Communications and
Information Processing

count of his experiences producing radio programs and working for George Washington Hill, president of the American Tobacco Company, a large radio advertiser and a Lord and Thomas client. The book, and the movie of the next year, tell the story of a young advertising agency executive who works for an eccentric and demanding client. Wakeman presents funny pictures of the subservience of advertising and broadcasting professionals to their clients. In *The Hucksters*, selling Beautee Soap meant bowing to the wishes of the president of the company to present stupidly simple radio programs and ad campaigns. Wakeman blames the sorry state of radio programming on sponsors and clearly states that they controlled radio. Nevertheless, the ongoing resistance to commercialized radio represented by Wakeman's book and other protests had little effect because of the enormous power and influence of the radio networks.

After World War II, the story of programming, commercialization, and audience response continued to unfold in television, while radio changed dramatically. During the 1950s television quickly took over radio's central place in the living room, presenting news, entertainment, and educational programs for white middle-class families watching together in the evening and broadcasting programs aimed at women and children in special time periods. Radio, with its programming usurped by television, reinvented itself after the war. Technological changes (including the development of the transistor), programming changes begun during the war (including the use of recorded shows), and new ways of thinking about the audience on the part of both broadcasters and advertisers (including the rise of demographic research) turned radio into a commercialized music box programmed for particular audience segments.

RADIO AND ROCK 'N' ROLL

The first specialized radio stations, programmed for African-American listeners, attracted another audience as well. White teenagers found the music they heard on such stations so compelling in its form and content that they spent more and more time tuned in. Postwar broadcast radio had found its best audience: teenagers.

Teenage interest in radio grew out of a technological change as well as social and cultural factors. The invention of the transistor in 1947, like the introduction of the Audion after World War I, changed the audience for radio. The transistor acted like a vacuum tube in conducting, modulating, and amplifying radio signals, allowing radios to be cheaper, smaller, and more durable than prewar radios. With transistor radios, broadcast listening became a personal and portable experience. The smaller size and lower cost of the new radios allowed teenagers and others to own their own radios and to tune in without family interference. A teenager could listen alone in her bedroom, or with her friends gathered out-of-doors, to music that her parents might not enjoy or even condone. After the introduction of television and the transistor in the 1950s, radio became the medium of those marginalized by society.

Not many historians have looked at the connection between the development of rock and roll and radio in the 1950s. Clearly, rock and radio were made for each other. Based on musical styles derived (or stolen) from African Americans, rock and roll, broadcast over millions of radios, allowed young people to temporarily cross some class and racial lines. Record companies and radio stations, both struggling for a place in the entertainment industry after World War II, found that a relationship could be mutually beneficial. Record companies provided radio stations with hit songs and got free publicity. One estimate says that record sales nearly tripled from 1954 to 1959. Radio stations kept operating costs low by hiring a single performer (the disc jockey) to play recorded music, and found a new lease on life.

This kind of interaction, overlooked in many other industries, brought a government investigation into "payola" and charges that record companies paid disc jockeys to play certain records. Critics have seen the payola scandal as a racist attempt to limit the influence of rock and roll, since those prosecuted were primarily black or promoted black artists, while government investigators largely ignored white promoters and artists. Others simply point to the hypocrisy of the persecutions. One disc jockey, Alan Freed, commented, "What they call payola in the disc jockey business, they call lobbying in Washington." The payola investigations and prosecutions led to tightened controls by stations over play lists and cut off experimental, multicultural radio programming.

Most important, in response to television's popularity, radio stations adopted a strategy that they had previously rejected: specialization. Stations aimed at African Americans pointed to a new direction for radio. Television, taking up where radio had left off, offered programs aimed primarily at white, urban, upper-middle-class families. Many African Americans, uninterested in television and some not able to afford the new sets, turned to radio. Hoping for a new audience to replace those listeners lost to television, a few radio stations responded by playing recordings made for black audiences, so-called race records. "Negro radio" had important implications for broadcasting. The success of such stations showed that a segmented market approach could work for radio. Following up on the success of "Negro radio," broadcasters looked for other special-interest groups who had found little to interest them on television. Relying on specialized programming, radio "escaped direct competition with television and found it could profit without the evening audiences" (Fornatale and Mills, p. 17).

The FCC's reassignment of the FM spectrum in July 1962 opened a new venue for experimentation, delighting young radio listeners who remained interested in alternative music. After the war, the government tried to get consumers and broadcasters interested in a different set of radio frequencies in order to increase the number of radio stations available. Since most radios did not receive FM audiences and advertisers remained wary of stations that required the listeners to purchase new equipment. Many of the first FM stations were completely noncommercial, and commercial FM stations found sponsors difficult to find or keep. As a result, FM radio had few interruptions and could program longer pieces of music. The 1962 FCC ruling responded to the growth in the number of FM stations by assigning frequencies to particular communities, thus allowing for the orderly growth of FM.

Again the radio and recording industries developed together in the mid 1960s as rock 'n' roll performers began to focus on albums rather than singles. As AM radio became more rigid, listeners could hear experimental rock and roll on FM radio. The new FM stations had time for the music of the counterculture and to play entire rock and roll albums. Many listeners remember the days of progressive FM, free-form radio with the same fondness their parents reserve for radio programs of the 1930s. Contributing to FM's eventual success was its technical superiority. As rock and roll music became more complex, and as record play-

ers improved so that people found out how good records could sound, the fact that FM stations broadcast with better fidelity, in stereo, brought new listeners. As Fornatale and Mills explain it:

> *Progressive FM was killed by its own success: As it drew more and more advertising accounts it had to make changes in the format to retain them. As FM rockers demonstrated their hold on the 18- to 34-year-old market, advertisers fell all over themselves trying to get on the air. (p. 140)*

Increasing commercialization brought more conservative programming.

Radio's experimentation with new audiences and formats coincided with a reemphasis within the advertising industry on market research. As the market for consumer goods grew after the war, advertisers worked to sell more and more services to manufacturers. Advertising professionals found demographic information critical to targeting products for particular buyers. Radio and then television became, in David Marc's memorable phrase, "demographic vistas."

The 1970s and 1980s saw a proliferation of extremely specialized stations, many with automated play lists which gave responsibility for what music went over the air to the station's marketing department. An article by Ken Barnes on Top 40 radio called it "a fragment of the imagination" and listed twenty-four different station formats, including adult contemporary, album-oriented rock, beautiful music, big band, contemporary hit radio, country, easy listening radio, gold, and music of your life. The conservatism of music radio comes from the advertising professionals' belief that people like best the music they have heard before. With the introduction of cable television stations (such as MTV) that play video versions of top rock songs, much of the newest musical experimentation happens on television rather than radio. College radio stations remain the exception to this rule. Noncommercial since the 1920s, college stations serve as a key site for disseminating new music and introducing new artists.

The period since 1970 has brought both a revival of "noncommercial" radio and a boom in "talk" radio. The Corporation for Public Broadcasting, under the Public Broadcasting Act of 1967, funded National Public Radio (NPR) as both a production center for programming and a network linking member stations. Controversial NPR membership requirements kept out the small stations that had maintained the noncommercial radio option since 1920. Also, because most NPR stations are supported by listeners, programming is aimed at those most likely to contribute, and so the stations provide less diversity than the framers of the original legislation had hoped.

However, talk radio, in several different formats, has grown wonderfully diverse. Call-in shows, with listeners offering opinions or experts giving answers to questions, take radio back to its local roots. Debates on neighborhood issues fill local radio shows, and the hosts of such programs often become influential political figures in their communities. National variations of such programs exist (Larry King interviews celebrities and invites audience questions; Rush Limbaugh rants on conservative political issues; Bruce Williams dispenses business advice; and many doctors diagnose ailments from Alaska to Rhode Island). The local programs provide the audience and stations to host their national brothers and sisters.

Conclusion

In many ways the history of radio can be seen as a series of expansions and contractions. Technological developments (the Audion, networks, the transistor), social and cultural changes (brought by wars, migrations within the country, and the increasing commercialization of everyday life), and innovative programming brought radio listeners new possibilities for entertainment and education. Yet as each possibility has appeared, various factors have worked to close it off. Network radio brought the chance to hear national programs but turned listeners into passive rather than active participants in radio. Commercialization promised to provide radio programming free to listeners but introduced rigid programming options and too many advertisements. During radio's development, listeners and critics protested several times that commercialized broadcasting blocked the development of more interesting possibilities. Rock and roll on 1950s radio allowed teenagers to explore African American music and to participate in a youth culture, but the focus on demographics and the growth of automated Top 40 stations resulted in a homogenization that cut off the diversity young listeners had sought. At the same time, as new possibilities brought conservative responses, other avenues sometimes appeared. When AM radio became uninteresting, FM became the home of musical experimentation.

John Cheever is right that radio changed the Westcotts, but he shows them as helpless, much like the accident victims they hear about on their new receiver. Within the commercial considerations of large corporations which control broadcasting, radio listeners have found ways of using the medium in their own interests. Along with the Westcotts, the family in Woody Allen's film *Radio Days* (1987) represents radio audiences. They integrate radio into their everyday lives, using it to reinforce and underline their activities. Perhaps more important, the narrator of the film shows that radio provides the shape and content of his memories. Far from being victimized by broadcasting, he uses his radio memories to create a warm picture of his family life, where different members of his extended family enjoy different programs and music over the radio. The radio brings outside tragedies (a little girl dying from a fall down a well) into the home, but instead of inspiring fear, as the daily news does in the Cheever story, in *Radio Days* such news serves as a way to connect this one family with people all over the country. Allen has his narrator say, "Now it's all gone. Except for the memories." But it's not "all gone" as people continue to listen to and to use radio in varied ways and each generation remembers a different time as radio's "golden age."

—SUSAN SMULYAN

ROCK MUSIC

Background: The Early 1950s

Popular music of the early 1950s continued to embody trends from previous decades, incorporating Tin Pan Alley stylings, swing from the 1930s and 1940s, and tunes from Broadway and Hollywood musicals. Performed by full orchestras and vocal stylists such as Frank Sinatra, Perry Como, Nat King Cole, and Peggy Lee, most pop songs featured slow-to-moderate tempos, uncomplicated rhythms, and simple melodies and lyrics written by professional songwriters.

Pop music's homogenized sound, nonthreatening lyrics, and familiar themes appealed to middle-class listeners caught up in cold war politics and rapid social change. Good-time records like Teresa Brewer's "Music, Music, Music" (1950) and Patti Page's "[How Much Is] That Doggie in the Window?" (1953) continued pop's novelty-song tradition. Ballads such as Mario Lanza's "Be My Love" (1951) and Tony Bennett's "Because of You" (1951) focused on old-fashioned romance. Other traditional beliefs were advanced on numerous records in the early 1950s: Eddie Fisher's

Network radio programming gave way almost completely to television.

PAGE 476

"Oh My Papa" idealized the patriarchal family; Arthur Godfrey's "What Is a Boy?" reinforced traditional sexual stereotypes; Tony Bennett's "Rags to Riches" continued the Horatio Alger myth; and Frankie Laine's "I Believe" plugged into traditional religious beliefs. Even the structure of the pop music industry reflected the era's conservative attitudes toward race and gender. The pop field was dominated by white males, who did most of the songwriting, performing, producing, and marketing.

The Rise of Rock and Roll: 1954–1963

By the mid-1950s, an alternate style of pop music had emerged: rock and roll. Some experts claim the roots of the music can be traced to the backcountry ring shouts of African American slaves. Others maintain that rock sprang from black spirituals of the 1920s and 1930s. Still others claim that rock was an offspring of black rhythm and blues from the 1940s, noting that R&B songs such as Wild Bill Moore's "We're Gonna Rock, We're Gonna Roll" (1947) and Wynonie Harris's "Good Rockin' Tonight" (1948), with a cover by Roy Brown that same year, used the terms "rock" and "roll" as euphemisms for sexual intercourse.

Actually, rock and roll was more than just the offspring of African American music. It also descended from white country and western music and traditional white pop. By the late 1950s, three main rock styles were evident: R&B rock, country

rock, and pop rock. Each was a variation of the new idiom, blending R&B and country music with pop-style lyrics that appealed to teenagers.

R&B rock had the closest ties to rhythm and blues. Black R&B rockers such as Chuck Berry, Fats Domino, Little Richard, and Lloyd Price had begun their careers in the rhythm and blues field. When they crossed over to rock, they took their musical stylings with them, retaining the rhythm and beats found in their original music, but singing lyrics that were more pop-oriented than blues-oriented. For example, Chuck Berry combined teen-oriented pop lyrics with rhythm and blues and country and western to produce hits like "School Day" (1957) and "Sweet Little Sixteen" (1958).

The second style, country rock (also known as rockabilly), emerged from the country and western tradition of Hank Williams, Roy Acuff, and other Grand Ole Opry stars. Rockabilly artists such as Elvis Presley, Jerry Lee Lewis, Buddy Holly, and Carl Perkins used their country and western backgrounds to modify black rhythm and blues. Presley became the most successful purveyor of the new sound, which Carl Perkins described as "blues with a country beat." Legend has it that Sam Phillips, owner of Sun Records in Memphis, once remarked: "If I could only find a white man who had the Negro sound and the Negro feel I could make a million dollars." The young working-class singer from Tupelo, Mississippi, made Phillips a prophet, and in the process changed the course of American popular music. Although not the inventor of rock and roll, Elvis certainly did more than any artist to popularize it. His unique blend of country and western and rhythm and blues—evident on hits such as "Heartbreak Hotel" (1956) and "Hound Dog" (1956)—earned him 52 top thirty hits between 1956 and 1963, establishing him as the undisputed King of Rock and Roll.

The third type of rock music—pop rock—was performed mostly by young, white singers influenced by R&B rock, rockabilly, and traditional pop. At its best, when performed by pop rockers such as Ricky Nelson, Del Shannon, or Bobby Vee, pop rock authentically captured the spirit of rock and roll. Like rockabilly with its proletarian southern roots or R&B rock with its working-class black roots, this type of pop rock had its own socially based constituency. It was the music of white middle-class neighborhoods, in tune with white teenage culture. Less interpretive was the pop rock style of performers such as Frankie Avalon, Fabian, and Connie Francis, who were

THE KING

Rocking wildly in his trademark style, Elvis Presley did more than any artist to popularize black rhythm and blues with a country and western flavor.
THE NATIONAL ARCHIVES/
CORBIS

closer to the Tin Pan Alley stylings of 1940s and 1950s' pop singers like Perry Como.

The emergence of rock and roll was linked to social change of the post-World War II era, particularly the migration of blacks to northern and western cities; the rise of the baby boom generation; the growth of a consumer culture; and the rise of new technologies.

White America's sudden discovery of black rhythm and blues music was the result of the movement of large numbers of blacks from the South to large urban areas in the North and West during and after World War II. When blacks migrated northward to jobs in New York City, Chicago, Detroit, and other urban areas, they brought along cultural baggage, including rhythm and blues. For the first time on a large scale, whites living in cities outside the South could listen to black music in bars or record stores or on the radio.

By the early 1950s, R&B songs such as the Orioles' "Crying in the Chapel" (1953), the Crows' "Gee" (1954), Big Joe Turner's "Shake, Rattle, and Roll" (1954), and the Chords' "Sh-Boom" (1954) were attracting white audiences. Two of the first white performers to record rhythm and blues-influenced songs were Johnnie Ray ("Cry" and "The Little White Cloud That Cried," both 1951) and Bill Haley and His Comets ("We're Gonna Rock This Joint Tonight," 1952; "Crazy Man Crazy," 1953; and "Shake, Rattle, and Roll," 1954).

A white disc jockey named Alan Freed did much to popularize the new sound. In 1952, he began playing black rhythm and blues on his radio program in Cleveland, Ohio. To avoid the racial stigma associated with R&B, Freed called the music "rock and roll"—a phrase readily accepted by an unsuspecting white audience. Disc jockeys across the country followed Freed's lead, bringing the rock and roll sound to millions of white teenagers.

Public response to early rock and roll reflected racial tensions of the era. Prejudiced whites often condemned rock and roll as "African" or "race" music, fearing the allegedly lustful sound would lead to miscegenation. Several white congregations in the South even pushed for a ban on rock and roll in 1956, insisting the music was an NAACP conspiracy to corrupt white teenagers.

The practice of releasing "cover records" suggests more subtle forms of prejudice. The success of rhythm and blues artists on the pop charts by the early 1950s prompted major record companies to record white singers copying the black sound.

Many times a black R&B song hit the record charts, only to be quickly covered (re-recorded) by a white performer. For example, Pat Boone had hits with cover versions of Fats Domino's "Ain't That a Shame" (1955) and Little Richard's "Tutti-Frutti" (1956). Although covers usually lacked the artistic integrity of the originals, they were often more commercially successful for several reasons. Cover records were more familiar-sounding to listeners raised on traditional pop. They also appealed to whites who wanted to avoid black culture. Some covers "cleaned up" black songs that were deemed too crude or sexually suggestive for a white middle-class audience. For example, Etta James's 1955 rhythm and blues hit "Roll with Me, Henry," became "Dance with Me, Henry" when covered by white pop star Georgia Gibbs. Cover records, distributed nationally by major companies with connections in all the big cities, also had marketing advantages over the black originals, released on small, local labels.

Even the black artists who were able to crack the predominantly white pop charts felt the sting of racial prejudice. Chuck Berry, perhaps the most skilled singer/songwriter of the era, never received the public acclaim or movie offers accorded white performers such as Elvis Presley or Ricky Nelson, while black songwriters such as Little Richard and Maurice Williams were cheated out of royalties when their songs were covered by white pop singers.

If the birth of rock was linked to the emergence of blacks in American society, its growth was dependent upon another major demographic change in American society and culture—the coming of the baby boom generation. The boom began after World War II and continued until 1964, producing 76.5 million babies—one third of America's population. Rock music—like the baby boomers themselves—came of age after World War II. The new sound, with its distinctive beat and adolescent themes, was perfect for a new generation that considered itself unique.

Rock and roll became the boundary marker for the youth culture (and its various subcultures) that developed in the 1950s and early 1960s. The music contributed to teenagers' collective memory and identity, allowing members of the baby boom generation to clarify who they were by listening to the type of music that appealed to their particular subculture. Rock taught adolescents how to dance, how to talk, how to dress, and how to date. It also communicated group attitudes about school, parents, and everyday life. Ricky Nelson's phenomenal success on the rock charts depended

The new FM stations had time for the music of the counterculture and to play entire rock and roll albums.

PAGE 396

upon the bond between rock music and the teen audience. The young teen idol, who first gained television fame as the wisecracking youngster on *The Adventures of Ozzie and Harriet*, sang about young love on "A Teenager's Romance" (1957); described teen interests on "Waitin' in School" (1957); and explained how cars and curfews could cause problems on "It's Late" (1959).

The market for rock and roll expanded rapidly in the mid-1950s as teenage patrons contributed to the creation of a new culture of consumption. By 1963, young American consumers were spending $22 billion annually on rock and roll records, phonographs, transistor radios, clothes, and other products geared to the youth audience.

Technological advances further aided the growth of rock and roll. Prior to World War II, the recording industry had been limited to elaborate studios in New York City or Los Angeles. But by the 1950s, the introduction of magnetic

ROCK AND ROLL: MIRROR OF SOCIETY

Early rock and roll demonstrates that American society was anything but monolithic in the 1950s and early 1960s. The music carried different messages for various subcultures and classes. For some, rock and roll was a form of cultural rebellion. The 1955 movie *The Blackboard Jungle*, which depicted juvenile delinquency and featured Bill Haley and His Comets' "Rock Around the Clock" in its soundtrack, helped convince many Americans that rock music and rebellion went hand-in-hand.

To an extent, rock's rebellious image was true. Rock's close ties to black music were a direct affront to segregationist views of the era. Its working-class origins threatened white middle-class society. Some songs, such as Eddie Cochran's "Summertime Blues" (1958) or the Coasters' "Yakety Yak" (1958), raised the specter of teenage rebellion. Rock and roll's implicit sexuality and uninhibited nature also challenged the straitlaced, conformist attitudes of the 1950s and early 1960s. Elvis Presley, with his long sideburns and outrageous "cat clothes," epitomized the wild rock singer, while uninhibited dances like the twist made some parents wince. Fearful adults linked rock and roll to pornography, drugs, prostitution, alcohol, juvenile delinquency, organized crime, teen pregnancies, and even Communist subversion. Local officials banned rock and roll concerts and regulated teen dances and parties. Even the United States Congress investigated the financing of rock and roll in the notorious payola hearings of 1959–1960. Viewed from the 1990s, these attacks tell more about American paranoia of the 1950s and early 1960s than they do about the music.

In many ways, early rock and roll reflected more consensus than conflict between the generations. At times, dominant groups used rock to maintain cultural hegemony. A form of social engineering took place as traditional values and acceptable patterns of behavior were stressed on Dick Clark's popular TV show, *American Bandstand*, and numerous rock idols, including Pat Boone, Ricky Nelson, and Fabian, were marketed as safe role models for teenagers. Even Elvis Presley's rebellious image was homogenized as he portrayed all-American boys in various Hollywood films.

Rock and roll songs frequently expressed the values of the dominant culture. Hit records praising religion, marriage, the family, parents, individualism, and America abounded on the rock charts. Even America's cold war against communism was waged on the rock and roll front. For example, while President John F. Kennedy was steering America through cold war crises involving Cuba and Berlin, teenagers were listening to patriotic hits such as Johnny Burnette's "God, Country, and My Baby" (1961) and Miss Toni Fisher's "West of the Wall" (1962).

Early rock promoted the American belief in equality. Elvis Presley introduced many whites to R&B-influenced music, opening the door for black rock and rollers like Jackie Wilson, Lloyd Price, and Fats Domino. Rock music became a form of cultural integration, as white teenagers cheered on black performers, purchased records previously sold only to blacks, and even sat beside blacks at integrated concerts. At a time when segregation ruled many areas of the country, rock provided a public sphere for integrated groups such as the Crests and the Impalas, and it offered opportunity not just for black singers, but for white ethnics such as the Hispanics Ritchie Valens and Trini Lopez and the Italian Americans Frankie Avalon, Frankie Valli, and Bobby Rydell. Some hit records, for example Gene Chandler's "Duke of Earl" (1962) and Jay and the Americans' "Only in America" (1963), even expressed the belief that any person regardless of color, class, or wealth could find success in the United States.

tape and modern tape recorders (first developed in Hitler's Germany) enabled small, independent companies to record local rock and roll talent anywhere in the country. Sam Phillips and his Memphis-based Sun Records produced records by Elvis Presley, Carl Perkins, and Johnny Cash, while Norman Petty's tiny studio in Clovis, New Mexico, recorded Buddy Holly and the Crickets.

Rock and roll thrived on other technological innovations. New 45 rpm records with their wide hole in the middle gave the music a more distinct appearance, while portable record players and transistor radios allowed teenagers to carry rock and roll wherever they went. The rise of television programs such as *The Ed Sullivan Show*, *The Adventures of Ozzie and Harriet*, and Dick Clark's *American Bandstand* provided public forums for early rock and rollers. Radio stations showcased rock and roll through new formats featuring jive-talking disc jockeys. And the development of inexpensive car radios allowed teenagers to listen to all the latest hits as they cruised America's streets.

Rock and roll of the 1950s and early 1960s demonstrates that teenagers, like adults, were participating in the building of consumption communities based on the era's affluence, planned obsolescence, and conspicuous consumption. The commodification of American culture was advanced through records such as Elvis Presley's "Money Honey" (1956) or Barrett Strong's "Money (That's What I Want)" (1960). Fashions were advertised on numerous hits, including Carl Perkins's "Blue Suede Shoes" (1956) and the Royal Teens' "Short Shorts" (1958). And America's love affair with automobiles was mirrored in car songs like Chuck Berry's "No Money Down" (1956) and the Beach Boys' "Little Deuce Coupe" (1963).

Early rock and roll expressed other middle-class beliefs and stereotypes. Rock music—like American society itself—treated women as second-class citizens. Females were depicted as passive sex objects on numerous hits, including Buddy Knox's "Party Doll" (1957), Johnny Tillotson's "Poetry in Motion" (1960), and Eddie Hodges's "[Girls, Girls, Girls] Made to Love" (1962). Blacks were portrayed as comic figures on the Coasters' "Charlie Brown" (1959); they were depicted as lustful native dancers on Little Anthony and the Imperials' "Shimmy, Shimmy, Ko-Ko-Bop" (1959); and their alleged fondness for watermelon inspired Mongo Santamaria's "Watermelon Man" (1963).

Other racial and ethnic groups were similarly stereotyped by rock and roll, which, like society in general, was dominated by white males. Native Americans appeared as silly, cartoon characters on novelty hits such as Johnny Preston's "Running Bear" (1959) and Larry Verne's "Mr. Custer" (1960). Hispanics and Italians were ridiculed for their accents on Pat Boone's "Speedy Gonzales" (1962) or Lou Monte's "Pepino the Italian Mouse" (1962). And Arabs became the brunt of jokes about camels and sheiks on Ray Stevens's "Ahab, the Arab" (1962).

Rock music provides evidence that the mythic American West influenced people of all ages in the 1950s and early 1960s. While many adults watched TV Westerns like *Gunsmoke* and *Have Gun, Will Travel*, teenagers celebrated America's alleged frontier heritage through Duane Eddy's "Ramrod" (1958), Marty Robbins's "El Paso" (1959), and Johnny Cash's "Don't Take Your Guns to Town" (1959). California was frequently seen as the ultimate western paradise. The belief in the mythic West coupled with real economic opportunities convinced many Americans to move to California in the post-World War II decade. Rock music contributed to the era's glorification of the California dream. The Beach Boys' "Surfin' U.S.A." (1963) and Jan and Dean's "Surf City" (1963) plugged into images of the mythic West as a land of opportunity and happiness, focusing on the hedonistic pleasures to be found in California—the western Garden of Eden.

Early rock and roll was in harmony with the times. A product of technological change, it reflected major demographic shifts involving youths and blacks. It also mirrored the affluence and anxieties, as well as the conflict and consensus of America in the fifties and early sixties. But rock and roll—like the nation itself—was forever altered by the changes that occurred in the United States after the autumn of 1963.

Rock's Golden Decade: 1964-1974

The assassination of President Kennedy on 22 November 1963 sent shock waves throughout American society and culture. Teenagers who identified with the young president were particularly stunned by the incident. The bullets that killed Kennedy shattered the illusions of many youths, who had been taught that America was a land of freedom and opportunity and that good always triumphed over evil.

If Kennedy's death caused many baby boomers despair and disillusionment, the arrival of the Beatles (John Lennon, Paul McCartney, George Harrison, and Ringo Starr) just a few weeks later provided new hope. The English group and their

Rock and Roll emerged as a 1950s expression of rhythm and blues aimed initially at adolescent white audiences.

PAGE 28

♦ **Baby boomers**

Members of the generation born in the United States immediately following the end of World War II

*Music for the neck
downwards.*

KEITH RICHARDS

music projected optimism, enthusiasm, and fun. The four rock and rollers carried on like the Marx Brothers, spoofing the establishment and refusing to take themselves too seriously. Their light-hearted approach to life contrasted sharply with the seriousness and gloom of America after Kennedy's assassination. The Beatles, with their shaggy, mop haircuts, mod clothing, and outrageous chords and musical stylings, offered American youths a new identity, at a time when they desperately needed one. Prior to the fall of 1963, American teens had dismissed foreign rock stars as mere imitators of American rock and roll. But after November 1963, American youths, perhaps realizing that American culture did not have all the answers, turned eagerly to foreign approaches. The Beatles' first American hit, "I Want to Hold Your Hand," triggered a Beatle-mania craze in January 1964. Over the next two years, the Beatles earned nine additional number-one hits, making them the first non-American superstars in the history of rock and roll.

The Beatles' success launched a British rock invasion of the American pop charts. Some British groups, specifically the Dave Clark Five and Gerry and the Pacemakers, offered Beatle-esque pop rock that appealed to white middle-class teenagers. Others, like the Rolling Stones and the Animals, delivered less-polished, R&B-influenced music with greater working-class appeal. The British invasion altered the way American teenagers saw themselves and their world. Teenagers underwent rapid change as they adopted the British rockers' music, haircuts, and clothing styles. The foreign performers also provided the means for American teenagers to look beyond their own shores to see how others viewed the world.

British rock and pop rejuvenated American music, increasing record sales and altering styles. Initially the "new sound" from England was largely just a throwback to American rock and roll and rhythm and blues of the 1950s and 1960s. Many English performers even covered songs by Buddy Holly, Chuck Berry, and other early rockers. But eventually the British rock sound interacted with American music, as well as with social and cultural movements involving civil rights, the peace movement, and youth culture, to create a sense of experimentation in pop and rock.

One of the first new styles to emerge was folk-rock, which blended folk music's socially aware lyrics with British rock's electric guitars and drums. Two number-one records of 1965—the Byrds' "Mr. Tambourine Man" (written by Bob Dylan) and Barry McGuires "Eve of Destruction" (written by P. F. Sloan)—marked folk-rock's arrival. The Turtles, the Mamas and the Papas, Simon and Garfunkel, James Taylor, and Carly Simon also found success with the new style. Even established folksingers like Bob Dylan and Joan Baez added electric guitars and drums to their music.

Folk-rock in turn influenced the Beatles, the Rolling Stones, Donovan, and other British rockers, who began experimenting with complex musical arrangements and more meaningful lyrics about personal relationships, society, and politics. The Beatles revolutionized the pop music industry in 1967 with the release of *Sgt. Pepper's Lonely Hearts Club Band*. Instead of the ten or twelve unrelated songs normally included on pop albums, *Sgt. Pepper* wove together a series of songs telling the story of a make-believe band. The concept album broke new ground, inspiring other rock artists to experiment with complex music and lyrics.

American pop rock underwent similar changes as performers incorporated the English sound and folk-rock into their music. Pop rockers let their hair grow long, switched to mod clothing styles, and began singing message songs. Teen idol Bobby Vee typified the changes many American performers were going through. Having begun his career in the late 1950s singing rockabilly-influenced pop rock, Vee tried to capitalize on the Beatles' success in 1964 with an album entitled *The New Sound from England*. By the end of the decade, he was sporting a Beatles haircut and singing message songs such as "Come Back When You Grow Up" (1967) and "Maybe Just Today" (1968). In 1972 he recorded an entire album of original folk-rock songs under his real name, Robert Thomas Velline, completing his transformation from a 1950s teen idol to a mature singer/songwriter.

The rock and pop renaissance of the 1960s and early 1970s sparked an explosion of musical experimentation. Some groups developed an electrified blues sound, characterized by a driving rock beat and loud, power chords. This "hard rock" style produced mainstream rock classics such as the Kinks' "All Day and All of the Night" (1964) and Cream's "Sunshine of Your Love" (1968).

Other bands developed art rock or progressive rock. Building on the musical innovations of *Sgt. Pepper*, these groups blended rock with a variety of traditional music forms. The Moody Blues and Procol Harum combined rock with classical music, song cycles, and orchestras. Pink Floyd, Rick

See also
Concert Music

Wakeman, Keith Emerson, and Mike Oldfield experimented with synthesizers and electronic music. Oldfield's *Tubular Bells* (1973), featured in the soundtrack of *The Exorcist*, is an excellent example of the electronic music that came to be known as electro-rock or techno-rock. Jethro Tull, Chicago, and Blood, Sweat, and Tears mixed rock with jazz. Experiments in progressive rock also led to rock operas such as the Who's *Tommy* (1969) and *Quadrophenia* (1973), as well as rock musicals like *Hair* (1967) and *Godspell* (1971).

R&B rock was also influenced by musical experimentation and the changing times. The success of Berry Gordy's Motown Records was linked in part to the emergence of blacks in society. The Detroit-based company achieved phenomenal success with the Supremes, the Miracles, the Temptations, and other black groups who could deliver an appealing hybrid of rhythm and blues and pop to whites whose consciousness of black music and culture had been raised by the growing civil rights movement of the early 1960s. By the late 1960s and early 1970s, some Motown artists were blending R&B rock with socially relevant lyrics to produce Stevie Wonder's "Blowin' in the Wind" (1966) and Marvin Gaye's "Inner City Blues (Make Me Wanna Holler)" (1971).

As interest in African American culture developed in the mid-1960s, the market for more authentic-sounding black music expanded. The emergence of black pride contributed greatly to the advent of "soul music." James Brown, Wilson Pickett, Aretha Franklin, Otis Redding, and Sam and Dave found tremendous success with earthy, emotional songs that captured the spirit of black gospel and early rhythm and blues. Though less polished than the Motown sound, soul music more accurately expressed various aspects of black culture in the 1960s. The Impressions' "Keep On Pushing" (1964) mirrored the optimism of the early civil rights movement. Aretha Franklin's "Respect" (1967) became an anthem for racial equality. James Brown's "Say It Loud—I'm Black and I'm Proud" (1968) plugged into the emergence of black pride. Other songs communicated the emotional side of the African American experience: Wilson Pickett's "In the Midnight Hour" (1965), Arthur Conley's "Sweet Soul Music" (1967), and Sam and Dave's "Soul Man" (1967).

Country and western singers were also influenced by the changes occurring in rock music and American culture. Willie Nelson, Waylon Jennings, and others gained notoriety as "country music outlaws," because they adopted the longer hairstyles associated with the counterculture and incorporated rock beats and folk-rock lyrics into their music.

Even traditional pop singers were swept up by the currents of musical change. Frank Sinatra staged a comeback with the message songs "That's Life" (1966) and "Cycles" (1968). Shirley Jones and television's Partridge Family enjoyed a string

TINA TURNER

Rock and roll's Tina Turner
performs for a crowd.
NEAL PRESTON / CORBIS

R

ROCK MUSIC

Rock's Golden Decade: 1964–1974

See also
Adolescence

of formula pop rock hits. And, in the wake of the British rock invasion, English pop stars Tom Jones, Engelbert Humperdinck, and Petula Clark found enthusiastic audiences on American shores.

Rock and pop music addressed all the major social and cultural issues of the late 1960s and early 1970s, as numerous performers became active participants in social and political movements for equality, peace, and human rights. Joan Baez emerged as one of the era's most visible advocates of justice and nonviolence. She began her career singing traditional folk songs in small clubs in Cambridge, Massachusetts, eventually moving on to New York City's Greenwich Village. By 1963, Baez was one of the nation's most popular folksingers, with three albums on the best-selling charts and a *Time* magazine cover to her credit. With national attention riveted on the civil rights movement and an escalating war in Vietnam, Baez became increasingly involved with social protest. Pointing the way for other folksingers, she began marching and singing for civil rights, peace, and student rights.

Joan Baez also helped introduce the public to another young folksinger who would provide a major voice for social change in the 1960s and early 1970s—Bob Dylan. The Minnesota native had begun his career in the Midwest with a brief stint as a piano player in a backup band for pop rocker Bobby Vee. After moving to New York City to meet his idol Woody Guthrie, Dylan began singing in folk clubs, where he was discovered by John Hammond, a producer for Columbia Records. His early songs reflected main currents in the protest movements of the day. In 1962 Dylan wrote and recorded "Blowin' in the Wind," which became a best-selling hit record for Peter, Paul, and Mary in 1963, as well as an unofficial anthem of the civil rights movement. Dylan was among the first to herald the arrival of the baby boom generation with his seminal "The Times They Are A-Changin'" (1964). And he gave voice to the antiwar movement through songs such as "Hard Rain" (1963) and "Talkin' World War III Blues" (1963). After the Byrds had a number one record in 1965 with a rock version of Dylan's "Mr. Tambourine Man," Dylan surprised his fans by switching to an electric guitar and folk-rock. Throughout the rest of the 1960s, Dylan songs such as "Like a Rolling Stone" (1965), "Rainy Day Women #12 & 35" (1966), and "All Along the Watchtower" (1967) reflected the dissatisfaction, anger, and concerns of many troubled youths.

Bob Dylan not only gave a voice to the concerns of the Young generation, but he pointed the way for mainstream rock artists. John Lennon of the Beatles became one of the most important rock activists. By the late 1960s and early 1970s, he had thrown himself wholeheartedly into the peace movement, joining protests, staging "love-ins," and writing and recording the best-selling songs "Give Peace a Chance" (1969), "Imagine" (1971), and "Happy Xmas (War Is Over)" (1972).

Along with social and political protest, rock music became intertwined with the era's growing counterculture. By the mid-1960s, many youths (primarily from white middle-class backgrounds) felt alienated from American culture and society: Disheartened by the Vietnam War, distressed by society's treatment of minorities, and concerned about a culture which they felt was spiritually and morally bankrupt, these "hippies" advocated alternate means to structure society. The values and characteristics of this brave new world were detailed in rock music, which became the lifeblood of the counterculture.

While concerts such as the Monterey Pop Festival and Woodstock provided public spheres for communal celebration, recorded music expressed countercultural themes involving love, peace, youth solidarity, brotherhood, mysticism, and drugs. Scott McKenzie's "San Francisco (Be Sure to Wear Flowers in Your Hair)" encouraged members of the young generation to come to San Francisco for the 1967 "Summer of Love." The Youngbloods' "Get Together" (1969) preached harmony, brotherhood, and understanding. And the 5th Dimension's "Aquarius / Let the Sunshine In" (from the rock musical *Hair*, 1969) publicized the countercultural revolution that was allegedly creating a new age.

Countercultural fashions were adopted by most rock peformers and spotlighted on various songs. Even the names of some rock groups radiated the optimism of the counterculture. There were groups like the Sunshine Company, the Yellow Balloon, Parade, and the Peppermint Rainbow.

Many rock artists followed the hippies' lead and began experimenting with LSD and other drugs. At first, songs like the Byrds' "Eight Miles High" (1966) or the Beatles "Lucy in the Sky with Diamonds" (1967) cloaked drug references in allegedly innocent lyrics. But after Timothy Leary and other counterculture enthusiasts began publicly advocating the use of LSD as a means to heightened awareness and spiritual truth, rock music began dealing more openly with drug topics. Acid rock—a musical style that emerged in San Francisco—sought to emulate or heighten the LSD psychedelic experience through blatant lyrics, extended instrumental improvisations, and loud, electronically amplified music. Light shows featuring bright colors and strobe units added to the effect, as did longhaired performers dressed in wild-colored clothes. San Francisco became the counterculture's psychedelic capital, boasting groups such as Jefferson Airplane, Quicksilver Messenger Service, and the Grateful Dead. Their brand of acid rock or psychedelic rock spread nationally through Jefferson Airplane's "White Rabbit" (1967) and albums such as the Grateful Dead's *Anthem of the Sun* (1968). The style was furthered by non-San Francisco bands like the Doors and the Jimi Hendrix Experience.

Rock music followed the counterculture's lead in rejecting middle-class values. For example, songs such as the Rolling Stones' "Let's Spend the Night Together" (1967) promoted more open attitudes toward sex. The Beatles showed how far the music industry had come in just four years when they released "Why Don't We Do It in the Road?" (1968), a far cry from their 1964 hit, "I Want to Hold Your Hand." The alleged hypocrisy of middle-class adults was the subject of Joe South's "Games People Play" (1969). Materialism was the target of the Beatles' "All You Need is Love" (1966). And middle-class notions involving careers and planning for the future were rejected by the Grass Roots' "Let's Live for Today" (1967).

Along with reflecting social movements involving blacks and youths, rock and pop music of the late sixties and early seventies mirrored the changing role of women in American society. Whereas early rock and roll tended to treat women as dependent, passive objects, rock of the 1960s and early 1970s contained far more complex images in keeping with the changes occurring in American culture. Rock songs that treated women as second-class citizens or mere sex objects were still common, as evidenced by Roy Orbison's "Pretty Woman" (1964), the Rolling Stones' "Stupid Girl" (1966), or the O'Kaysions' "Girl Watcher" (1968). But by the mid-sixties and early seventies, alternative images of liberated women could be found in Gale Garnett's "We'll Sing in the Sunshine (Then I'll Be on My Way)" (1964); Lesley Gore's "You Don't Own Me" (1964); Nancy Sinatra's "These Boots Are Made for Walkin'" (1966); and Helen Reddy's "I Am Woman" (1972). The persona of strong-willed female singers such as Janis Joplin or Grace Slick of the Jefferson Airplane also reflected gains being made by women.

Rock and pop music furthered the cause of other groups during the late 1960s and early 1970s. The gay liberation movement gained publicity through the rise of glitter rock (or glam rock). The highly visual and theatrical style of presentation was pioneered by David Bowie, who appeared in women's clothes on the cover photo of his 1970 album, *The Man Who Sold the World*. Male glitter rockers like Bowie, Mott the Hoople, and the New York Dolls often wore eye shadow, makeup, tight-fitting jumpsuits, and platform shoes. In addition, songs such as Mott the Hoople's "All the Young Dudes" (1972) and Lou Reed's "Walk on the Wild Side" (1973) were interpreted as possible celebrations of homosexuality.

Native American rights were also advanced by rock and pop. As the American Indian Movement (AIM) gained momentum in the 1970s, the Raiders' "Indian Reservation (The Lament of the Cherokee Reservation Indian)" (1971) and Cher's "Half-Breed" (1973) appeared on the charts, while Floyd Westerman, a full-blooded Sioux, found success with an Indian-rights album based on Vine De-Loria's best-selling book, *Custer Died for Your Sins*.

By the late 1960s and early 1970s, the American public was deeply divided over women's liberation, the Vietnam War, the civil rights movement, and the counterculture. Hit records provided ample evidence of the polarization in the country. The Buffalo Springfield's "For What It's Worth" (1967) described a violent confrontation between student demonstrators and police in riot gear. Steppenwolf's "Monster" (1970) charged that a brutal, fascist government had taken over the United States. Crosby, Stills, Nash, and Young's "Ohio" (1970) found Richard Nixon guilty of the murder of four college students by the National Guard at Kent State University.

Even the rise of "heavy metal" music could be linked to the troubled times. The new brand of rock took its name from a phrase used in Steppenwolf's hit "Born to Be Wild" (which had borrowed the line from William Burroughs's novel *Naked Lunch*). The blues-based sound, which rock writer Ken Tucker called "angry music for angry times," featured extra-loud, repetitive chords and riffs played aggressively by young rockers screaming out their lyrics. Heavy metal artists, inspired by hard rockers such as the Who, the Kinks, Eric Clapton, and Steppenwolf, cranked up their amplifiers even louder to produce high-voltage records like Iron Butterfly's "In-A-Gadda-Da-Vida" (1968), Led Zeppelin's "Whole Lotta Love" (1969), and Black Sabbath's "Paranoid" (1970).

By the late 1960s, rock musicians, influenced by blues, jazz, and music from all over the world, were creating eclectic works.

PAGE 105

I declare that the Beatles are mutants. . . . They are the wisest, holiest, most effective avatars the human race has ever produced.

TIMOTHY LEARY
AS QUOTED IN SHOUT! THE
TRUE STORY OF THE BEATLES
BY PHILIP NORMAN

♦ **Avatar**

The embodiment of a deity or spirit in human form

If some songs reflected dissatisfaction with American society and culture, others mirrored public support. In 1965, the Spokesmen's "The Dawn of Correction" provided a patriotic response to Barry McGuire's "Eve of Destruction." The following year, Staff Sergeant Barry Sadler demonstrated that many Americans backed the Vietnam War with his number one hit, "The Ballad of the Green Berets." Records condemning the counterculture also appeared. Victor Lundberg's "An Open Letter to My Teenage Son" (1967) praised youths who upheld traditional American values, while Merle Haggard's "[I'm Proud to Be an] Okie from Muskogee" (1969) blasted hippies and student protesters.

By the early 1970s, rock and pop music—like the youth culture itself—seemed burned out. The Band's "The Weight"(1968), Dion's "Abraham, Martin, and John" (1968), and the Beatles' "Let It Be" (1970) showed signs of resignation. The Doors depicted the brooding, nihilistic side of the counterculture on their dark recording "The End" (1967). And Neil Young captured the somber, if not depressed, mood of the nation with his albums *Everybody Knows This Is Nowhere* (1969) and *After the Gold Rush* (1970).

Rock's Third Decade and Beyond: 1975–Present

By the mid-1970s, rock and pop were among the most successful forms of entertainment in the United States, sustained by the unprecedented level of discretionary income enjoyed by American teenagers. The Record Industry Association of America estimated total sales for 1976 at $2.7 billion. The following year, record sales increased to $3.3 billion. The expansion of the pop music field occurred during a time of rapid social change. The polarization of American society in the late 1960s and early 1970s gave way to fragmentation by the mid–1970s as public opinion splintered over myriad social, cultural, and political issues. Pop and rock also fragmented due to new subcultures with different beliefs, interests, and age groups.

Though rock and pop appeared to flow in numerous directions after 1974, most of the routes had been mapped out during the 1960s. With few exceptions, post-1975 rock and pop merely continued earlier styles such as blues-based hard rock, pop rock, traditional pop, country music, progressive rock, and R&B rock.

For example, the blues-based, hard rock style of sixties performers like the Rolling Stones, the Who, and Eric Clapton became even more popu-

PUNK ROCK

An even more outrageous offshoot of hard rock was the punk rock style developed in the mid-1970s and early 1980s by the Ramones, Iggy Pop, the New York Dolls, the Clash, and the Sex Pistols. Punk rock seemed to be rebelling against everything, including hard rock itself. Image was often more important than music, as punk rockers screamed out obscenities, stuck pins in their bodies, slashed themselves with razors, dyed their hair orange, and devised other means to shock audiences. By the early 1980s, punk rock had been transformed into a milder (and therefore more commercially viable) form known as "New Wave" by performers such as Elvis Costello, Talking Heads, the Police, and Blondie.

lar after 1975 with the emergence of talented hard rockers Rod Stewart, Bob Seger, and Bruce Springsteen. Heavy metal also gained in popularity after 1975 through the highly amplified music of aggressive metal bands such as Led Zeppelin, Rush, Mötley Crüe, and AC/DC.

Another 1960s style that prospered after 1975 was pop rock—a softer sound more acceptable to middle-of-the-road listeners. Post-sixties pop rock ranged from rock-influenced performers like Elton John, Paul McCartney, and Huey Lewis and the News to folk-influenced artists such as James Taylor, Paul Simon, and Billy Joel, all three of whom continued the singer/songwriter tradition from the 1960s.

Traditional pop also flourished after 1975, as singers like Barry Manilow and Debby Boone produced slow-to-moderate-tempo pop songs, spiced with light touches of rock. Perhaps the most significant development in 1970s pop was "disco"—a blend of pop, rock, and black music characterized by a pronounced dance beat and repetitive, electronically produced rhythms. Popular disco hits included George McCrae's "Rock Your Baby" (1974), Van McCoy's "The Hustle" (1975), and Gloria Gaynor's "I Will Survive" (1979). The Bee Gees, a popular rock group from the 1960s, soared to even greater heights in 1977 with dance hits recorded for the quintessential disco movie, *Saturday Night Fever*.

Another style which made a strong showing on the pop charts after 1975 was country music. Bob Dylan, the Band, Neil Young, Rick (former teen-rocker Ricky) Nelson, and the Eagles were among the first rock artists to experiment with blends of rock and country music. Their success paved the way for the country-influenced singers Glen Campbell, Linda Ronstadt, and Kenny Rogers, and enabled Willie Nelson, Waylon Jennings, Dolly Parton, and other country artists to cross over onto the pop charts. By the late 1980s, a younger generation of country artists, including Dwight Yoakam, Randy Travis, Steve Earle, and Alabama, were reaching a wide pop audience through their well-crafted blends of country, pop, and rock.

Art rock, which had roots in the 1960s, also flourished after 1975. Sixties groups such as the Moody Blues and Procol Harum continued to mix classical music with hard rock, while newer progressive rock bands like Emerson, Lake, and Palmer; Jethro Tull; and Pink Floyd experimented with blends of rock, jazz, and classical music. Blood, Sweat, and Tears and Chicago, early jazz-rock groups, continued to record excellent jazz-influenced rock music, while Miles Davis, Chuck Mangione, and Spyro Gyra moved even closer toward a fusion of jazz and rock.

R&B rock also built on trends from the 1960s and early 1970s. Tower of Power; Earth, Wind, and Fire; and MFSB mixed rhythm and blues with jazz. Stevie Wonder, Marvin Gaye, and Prince combined socially relevant lyrics with pop, rock, jazz, and R&B. Other black singers like Michael Jackson, Lionel Richie, and Diana Ross provided smooth mixtures of pop and rhythm and blues. The most innovative development in 1970s black music was hip-hop or rap music—a postmodern, rapid-fire, musical collage of rhyming lyrics; heavy drum beats; loud, thumping bass lines; polyrhythmic sounds; and musical sampling from other styles. Beginning in the late seventies and stretching into the nineties, rappers like Run-D.M.C., Hammer, and Public Enemy attracted a wide audience, encouraging later white imitators such as Vanilla Ice and New Kids on the Block.

The music industry reinforced pop and rock's tendency to remain within familiar musical forms after 1975. By the 1970s, six major companies dominated the recording industry: CBS, Polygram, RCA, Capitol-EMI, Warner Communications, and MCA. The high costs of recording coupled with a declining and more fragmented market made the major labels reluctant to record new groups or any music that was too innovative. Specialized radio programming contributed further to the trend toward proven musical styles. The fragmentation of American culture and pop-ular music resulted in a proliferation of radio formats aimed at particular segments of the splintered pop music audience. By the 1980s, listeners could choose among stations specializing in hard rock, soft rock, country-rock, oldies but goodies, dance music, rap, progressive rock, and heavy metal, in addition to country, classical music, rhythm and blues, jazz, big band, ethnic music, and Christian music. Musicians were constrained by these specialized formats, realizing their music would be ignored if it became too innovative.

Other market considerations made it even more difficult for new artists to be heard. By the late 1970s and 1980s, many performers were finding it unprofitable to tour due to rising costs for travel, sound equipment, stage lighting, and other tour-related items. Established acts with known box-office appeal were able to subsidize tour expenses through corporate sponsorship. Well-known performers could guarantee additional profits by marketing T-shirts, programs, and other concert souvenirs. The rise of MTV (the music television channel) in the 1980s also helped solidify the position of established stars, whose music videos guaranteed a viewing audience. Repeated exposure on MTV led to the rise of a cult of celebrity. Michael Jackson, Madonna, and George Michael, singer/dancers who could produce dynamic music videos of high visual quality, attracted huge audiences, enabling them to grab large shares of the rock and pop market.

Contemporary rock and pop have continued to address issues involving youth, race, ethnicity, class, and gender. Rock music has had much to say about the baby boom generation and youth culture. Pop and rock of the 1970s, 1980s, and 1990s recorded the passing of the baby boom into middle age. The older baby boomers' desire to hear music from their youth guaranteed the success of "oldies but goodies" radio formats, as well as middle-aged rock performers and nostalgia groups like Sha Na Na. Some songs, like the Four Seasons' "December, 1963 (Oh, What a Night)" (1976) and their lead singer Frankie Valli's solo record "Grease" (1978), looked back fondly at the past; while other hits, such as Bob Seger's "Against the Wind" (1980) and Don Henley's "The End of the Innocence" (1989), displayed more bittersweet nostalgia.

By the 1990s, rock music was no longer the sole property of the baby boom generation. As rock rolled toward the twenty-first century, it expanded its audience to include a new generation. Millions of post-baby boomers tuned in rock, as evidenced by second-generation rockers such as

Bob freed your mind the way Elvis freed your body.

BRUCE SPRINGSTEEN
SPEECH AT ROCK-AND-ROLL
HALL OF FAME INDUCTION
DINNER, REFERRING TO BOB
DYLAN AND ELVIS PRESLEY

Hearing him for the first time was like busting out of jail.

BOB DYLAN
COMMENT ON THE
ANNIVERSARY OF ELVIS
PRESLEY'S DEATH

*The life of a rock
and roll band will
last as long as you
look down into the
audience and can
see yourself, and
your audience looks
up at you and can
see themselves.*

BRUCE SPRINGSTEEN

Nelson (the twin sons of Ricky Nelson) and Wilson Phillips (the daughters of Beach Boy Brian Wilson and John and Michelle Phillips of the Mamas and the Papas). Teenage singers like New Kids on the Block, Menudo, and Debbie Gibson aimed their music directly at this youthful audience.

Contemporary rock and pop have addressed the plight of other minorities in American society. The oppression of Native Americans was explored on Neil Young's "Cortez the Killer" (1975), Robbie Robertson's "Showdown at Big Sky" (1987), and Europe's "Trail of Tears" (1988). Hispanics gained public recognition through performers such as Los Lobos, Freddy Fender, and Gloria Estefan, and records like Los Lobos' cover of "La Bamba" (1987) and Linda Ronstadt's *Canciones de mi padre* (1987). Gay liberation was furthered in the late 1970s and early 1980s by the Village People and Boy George of Culture Club, who acknowledged their homosexuality, and by disco clubs that provided a public arena for homosexuals.

Contemporary rock continues to express the hopes, needs, and fears of working-class people.

Bruce Springsteen's rise to superstardom in the mid-1970s and 1980s provided the most significant voice on the rock charts for middle- and working-class America. Capturing the sound and feel of his old neighborhood in Asbury Park, New Jersey, Springsteen sang about blue-collar life ("Factory," 1978); unfulfilled dreams ("The River," 1980); decaying cities ("My Hometown," 1984); unemployment ("Downbound Train," 1984); and other subjects of concern to ordinary Americans.

The plight of working-class Americans found expression in the music of other performers. The downturn of American industry in the seventies and eighties inspired Bob Seger's "Makin' Thunderbirds" (1982) and Billy Joel's "Allentown" (1982), while the depths to which many working-class people had fallen became the subject of John Mellencamp's "Down and Out in Paradise" (1987). The economic hard times that hit small farmers were portrayed on Mellencamp's "Rain on the Scarecrow" (1985) and Steve Earle's "The Rain Came Down" (1987). Performers led by Mellencamp and Willie Nelson even staged a benefit concert, "Farm Aid," to help farmers facing bankruptcy.

CONTEMPORARY ROCK AND THE AFRICAN-AMERICAN EXPERIENCE

Contemporary rock—like early rock and roll—has been greatly influenced by African American culture. While the problems of blacks and the civil rights movement seemed to fade from public view during the seventies, eighties, and early nineties, they remained an important subject for musicians. British rock bands such as the Clash and Sham 69 staged "Rock Against Racism" concerts in the late 1970s. Paul McCartney and Stevie Wonder's "Ebony and Ivory" (1982), U2's *The Unforgettable Fire* (1984), and Depeche Mode's "People Are People" (1983) stressed racial equality. And apartheid was the target of Peter Gabriel's "Biko" (1980) and the United Artists Against Apartheid's "Sun City" (1985).

Notions of black power and black pride have survived through Sister Sledge's "We Are Family" (1979), which became an anthem in many black communities. Rap music, which showcased inner-city African American culture, provided an even more important vehicle for young blacks to express views and concerns. Black pride surfaced on numerous rap hits in the 1980s, including Run D.M.C.'s "Proud to Be Black," Big Daddy Kane's "Young, Gifted, and Black," and Grandmaster Flash's "Freedom." Some rappers like Queen Latifah dressed in African-style clothes to demonstrate cultural pride. Others stressed black militancy. Members of the group Public Enemy expressed support for Louis Farakhan, and were accompanied on stage by uniformed guards carrying toy Uzi machine guns. Their aggressive image and enormous popularity among young, urban blacks caught the attention of the film director Spike Lee, who signed Public Enemy to record "Fight the Power" for his controversial *Do the Right Thing* (1989).

Rap music has provided a voice for specific concerns of the black community. Grandmaster Flash's "The Message" (1982) described inner-city poverty. Public Enemy's *Yo! Bum Rush the Show* (1987) explored urban violence. And N.W.A. (Niggaz with Attitude) dealt with police brutality and drugs in the late 1980s' songs "Straight Outta Compton" and "Dopeman."

Contemporary rock also reflects changing gender roles in the United States. The ubiquity of women in rock and pop after 1975 mirrored the emergence of liberated women in American society and culture. Independent women were featured on Mary MacGregor's "Torn Between Two Lovers" (1976), Pat Benatar's "Hit Me with Your Best Shot" (1980), and K. T. Oslin's "80s Ladies" (1987). The seventies, eighties, and nineties witnessed the growth of female rock bands such as the Bangles, the Go-Go's, and Heart; women rappers like Queen Latifah, MC Lyte, and Roxanne Shanté; and numerous women singers like Linda Ronstadt, Joan Jett, Tina Turner, Stevie Nicks, Cher, Aretha Franklin, Patti LaBelle, Janet Jackson, Rosanne Cash, Annie Lennox, and Sinéad O'Connor. But no singer better illustrates the new images of women in contemporary rock and pop than Madonna.

In many ways, Madonna is the antithesis of the women found in early rock and roll. Her many hit records, music videos, and roles in motion pictures serve as counterpoints to traditional female stereotypes. Whenever it is to her advantage, Madonna projects an innocent charm and sexuality (as in "Like a Virgin" or "Material Girl"). But, at the same time, Madonna always lets her fans know that she, and not the man, is in charge ("Papa Don't Preach" or "Who's That Girl"). En route to stardom in the eighties and early nineties, Madonna demonstrated that she could be as aggressive, dominant, and successful as any man. While her music and videos often portrayed males as sexual playthings and pushed social and cultural mores to the limits, Madonna's personal life attracted media attention because she pumped iron, used profanity in concerts, and had a brief but stormy marriage to badboy actor Sean Penn, followed by a well-publicized romantic fling with playboy Warren Beatty. Throughout it all, Madonna followed her own rules. For many female fans, she epitomized the new super-woman who could have it all: beauty, brains, career, sex, love, and freedom.

Like rock and roll of earlier decades, contemporary rock has potential for both liberation and repression. For some listeners, it remains a music of rebellion; for others, it provides a means to express traditional values or maintain cultural hegemony.

The fact that post-1975 rock music continued to be a voice for political and social protest suggests that the liberal politics of the 1960s did not die out as commonly believed. During the 1980s, numerous artists, including Talking Heads, the Ramones, Sting, R.E.M., Elvis Costello, and Midnight Oil, released records criticizing President Reagan and his policies. America's interventionist foreign policy was condemned by the Clash's "I'm So Bored with the U.S.A." (1977) and *Sandinista!* (1980); the haunting memories of the Vietnam War inspired Bruce Springsteen's "Born in the U.S.A." (1984); and Reagan's Star Wars project was ridiculed on INXS's "Guns in the Sky," (1987).

Rock and pop musicians went on record against conservative domestic policies that seemed to ignore major problems such as urban violence, drug abuse, the savings-and-loan scandal, pollution, and poverty. One of the most thorough indictments of government's mishandling of America's social problems was Neil Young's album *Freedom* (1989). The dark, brooding LP graphically described urban problems and social injustice, while lampooning President George Bush's "thousand points of light" approach to social problems.

Some singers, like modern-day muckrakers, exposed social problems and injustice wherever they found them, focusing on a wide range of topics such as domestic violence, bigotry, and greed. For example, Suzanne Vega's "Luka" (1987) uncovered child abuse, while Dire Straits' "Money for Nothing" (1985) satirized America's consumerism and the wealth of many pop stars.

Social-activist rock artists also criticized the rise of religious fundamentalism in the 1970s and 1980s. The Crass's "Asylum" (1978) questioned Christ's divinity. The sinister musical cover of the Cramps' *Songs the Lord Taught Us* (1980) hinted that religion had a dark side. And Bruce Springsteen's "Reason to Believe" (1982) suggested religion made people meek and fatalistic.

Social awareness and an international outlook remained integral elements of rock and pop music after 1975. African music influenced the Talking Heads' *Remain in Light* (1980) and Paul Simon's *Graceland* (1986). The expanded worldview of many Americans helped create a market for "world music," featuring artists such as Jamaica's Bob Marley and the Wailers, Brazil's Uakti, and South Africa's Ladysmith Black Mambazo. Global concerns also brought musicians together for a variety of causes during the eighties and nineties. Bob Geldof of the Boomtown Rats was nominated for a Nobel Peace Prize for organizing the "Band Aid" concert of 1985. The event, featuring superstars Paul McCartney, Eric Clapton, Mick Jagger, Neil Young, and Pete Townshend, raised millions of dollars for famine relief in Ethiopia, and led to numerous other benefit con-

Parents and Congress worried that a peer culture spread by comic books, television, radio, and the movies promoted delinquency and a disregard for family values.

PAGE II

**REGGAE'S BOB
MARLEY**

*The expanded worldview of
many Americans after 1975
created a market for world
music featuring artists like
Jamaica's Bob Marley.*
LIBRARY OF CONGRESS/
CORBIS

*The only
performance that
makes it, that really
makes it, is the one
that ends in
madness.*

MICK JAGGER

certs on behalf of the environment, human rights, and cultural understanding.

After 1975, numerous performers demonstrated that rock music was still on the cutting edge of cultural rebellion. If conservative listeners had been offended by the implicit sexuality of early rock and roll, they were shocked and appalled by the explicit sexual contents of contemporary rock. Donna Summer's "Love to Love You Baby" (1975), which featured the singer moaning and groaning in orgasmic ecstasy, led to the rise of what some critics called porno-rock. In the 1980s, Prince recorded several songs dealing with taboo topics: "Sister" explored incest; "Head" described oral sex; and "Jack U Off" focused on masturbation. Music videos on MTV during the eighties and early nineties also grew more and more daring: Madonna released videos depicting homosexuality, blasphemy, fornication, and sadomasochism; performers like Michael Jackson commonly grabbed their crotches while singing and dancing; the Divinyls' "I Touch Myself" (1991) celebrated female masturbation; and Chris Isaak's "Wicked Game" (1989) provided a soft-porn music video for home-viewing pleasure.

Contemporary rock's rebellious image was furthered in other ways. The creation of a Rock and Roll Hall of Fame in the 1980s institutionalized the "rock as rebellion" myth, canonizing rebellious figures like Elvis Presley, Jerry Lee Lewis, the Who, and the Rolling Stones. Rock grew even more outrageous as new performers—attempting to be more rebellious than the older ones—trans-

formed protest rock into "shock rock." Heavy metal groups kept cranking up the volume, and screaming louder and louder to be noticed; hard rockers and glitter rockers appeared in a variety of bizarre costumes; punk rockers pushed the outer limits of shock rock even further, shaving their heads, gashing themselves, biting the heads off chickens, and giving themselves names like Sid Vicious, Johnny Rotten, the Dead Kennedys, the Butthole Surfers, and the Circle Jerks. Records by Alice Cooper, Kiss, and Mötley Crüe voiced anger and aggression toward parents, teachers, and other authority figures. Songs by Ozzy Osbourne, AC/DC, Blue Öyster Cult, and Metallica suggested suicide as the ultimate form of rebellion. Other records by Venom, Iron Maiden, and Megadeth sought notoriety by dabbling in satanism and the occult. Still others, like Guns N' Roses' *Appetite for Destruction* (1987) and N.W.A.'s "F____k da Police" (1989), used profanity or violence for shock effect.

Despite the defiant image, however, contemporary rock may not be as rebellious as it appears. Some critics claim that heavy metal and shock rock merely allow teenagers to think they are outsiders, providing them with temporary escape from boring middle-class lives. By serving as safety valves for frustrated teenagers, these musical styles actually wind up defusing rebellion and inhibiting long-term change.

The rebellious image of contemporary rock should not obscure the conservative and even culturally repressive elements found in the music.

Materialism, patriotism, religion, attitudes toward technology, individualism, and other traditional beliefs and values continue to be expressed in post-1975 rock and pop. For example, America's consumer culture inspired Madonna's "Material Girl" (1985) and Run-D.M.C.'s "My Adidas" (1986), and powered the growth of the disco fad and MTV. Religion was celebrated on Bob Dylan's *Slow Train Coming* (1979) and Johnny River's *Not a Through Street* (1983). The individualistic spirit of the "Me Decade" was mirrored in 1970s rock and pop. Singer/songwriters James Taylor, Carly Simon, and Carole King produced introspective records that encouraged listeners to explore personal problems rather than social issues. Disco music allowed narcissists to dance in the spotlight, displaying themselves in ostentatious clothes and jewelry. Contemporary music also facilitated the quest for self-fulfillment by providing the soundtrack for church services, aerobics classes, jogging, walking, and a variety of other personal activities.

Contemporary rock and pop reflect Americans' long-standing ambivalence toward technology. After 1975 many musicians eagerly experimented with multiple synthesizers, keyboards, and other advances in electronic technology. The dissemination of the music changed due to the introduction of the music video, the "boom box," the compact disc, the Sony Walkman, and improved home and car stereos. At the same time, the ambivalent relationship between humans and machines might explain the rise of music and dance steps that treated humans like androids. Man and machine seemed to merge in the techno-pop style of Devo's "Whip It" (1980) or Neil Young's *Trans* (1981), while disco and break dancing popularized robotic dance steps.

After 1975 certain groups continued to use rock and pop music as the means to maintain cultural hegemony. The sexism of modern America is evident in music videos such as Robert Palmer's "Addicted to Love" (1986), which spotlighted zombie-like women gyrating to a hypnotic beat; or the Fabulous Thunderbirds' "Tuff Enuff" (1986), which featured long-legged female dancers dressed in hard hats and skimpy costumes. And racism can be found in remarks made in the late 1980s by white performers such as Elvis Costello, David Bowie, and Eric Clapton. Racial animosities heated up again in the 1990s, encouraged by groups such as Public Enemy and Guns N' Roses.

Contemporary rock also provided a public forum for conservatives in the 1980s. In 1985, the U.S. Senate, in response to groups such as the Parents' Music Resource Center founded by Tipper Gore (the wife of Tennessee Senator Albert Gore) and Susan Baker (the wife of cabinet member James Baker), opened hearings to investigate the alleged obscenity of rock lyrics. Ironically, the hearings occurred at a time when many rock and rollers were actually joining the conservative cause. Neil Young, Prince, and the Beach Boys were among the many rock stars who endorsed Reagan's presidency. Other performers advanced positions associated with the political Right: Sammy Hagar, lead singer for the heavy metal band Van Halen, advocated a strong military buildup; Alice Cooper praised the capitalistic features of rock music; Guns N' Roses, by their very name, provided implicit support for the National Rifle Association; and the rise of a host of Christian rock groups can be linked to the rise of religious fundamentalism. Syndicated columnist George Will even claimed Bruce Springsteen as a disciple of conservatism, insisting (despite the singer's objections) that "Born in the U.S.A." was a patriotic anthem.

When rock and roll music first appeared in the United States in the mid-1950s, it appealed mostly to various youth subcultures. But by the 1990s, rock music had become the dominant form of popular music in the United States, if not the world, making it one of the most important cultural developments in post-World War II America. Rock music now permeates almost every aspect of American society and culture. It has influenced country music, jazz, traditional pop, and other forms of contemporary music. It has been adopted by most social and economic groups. And it has become a fixture in everyday life. Rock music can be found on television, in movies, in commercials, at weddings, at funerals, at athletic events, and in schools, churches, community centers, senior citizen homes, or anywhere else where people gather. The music's relationship to millions of Americans, its ubiquitous position in modern society, and its potential as a source of information about recent American life and thought impart rock music with significance for social historians.

—RICHARD AQUILA

R

ROCK MUSIC

Rock's Third Decade and Beyond: 1975–Present

See also
Popular Music before 1950

SEXUAL BEHAVIOR AND MORALITY

Colonial America

Patterns of sexual life in the British colonies were shaped both by the social customs settlers brought with them and by conditions of migration and settlement in the New World. In the agrarian villages from which most colonists came, sexuality was linked closely to marriage and reproduction. Family survival in such preindustrial economies depended on the labor of children, which encouraged high birthrates. In the patriarchal household, which was the dominant family form in England at the time, the father controlled the labor and sexual lives of his wife, children, and servants in ways that best supported the family economy. Sons could be forced to delay marriage until fathers parceled out land or the homestead to them. The stability of the household demanded even greater control of the sexuality of wives and daughters. Children born out of wedlock threatened the limited economic resources of families and the need to ensure "legitimate" male heirs.

The agrarian communities of preindustrial England tolerated premarital sexual activity between betrothed men and women, however, because it was understood that marriage would follow. The religious beliefs of the colonists reinforced an ideal of marital, reproductive sexuality. Protestant churches placed strong prohibitions on sex outside of marriage and urged sexual moderation within marriage. Religious authorities considered sexual intercourse a marital duty of husbands and wives for the purposes of both procreation and pleasure.

English colonists in New England and in the Chesapeake colonies of Virginia and Maryland brought similar sexual customs and beliefs with them to America, but differing patterns of settlement, motives for migration, and economic and labor systems in the two regions created marked variations in family and sexual life during the seventeenth century. The Puritans, who settled the New England colonies in the 1620s and 1630s, successfully reestablished English patriarchal family structures and marital sexual relations there. They arrived in family groups and came from similar social backgrounds, primarily middling farm and artisanal families. They left England in search of land but were also motivated by a strong religious purpose. Dissatisfied with the Church of England, Puritans migrated to the New World to establish religious communities, modeled on their moral principles, for the rest of the world to imitate. Driven by this mission and aided by an abundance of land, they created orderly communities, a productive economy based on subsistence agriculture, and large, stable families.

Families, church, and civic authorities worked together to monitor the sexual behavior of young people and to channel sexuality into marriage and reproduction. Puritan fathers retained authority

SEX AND REPRODUCTION

The Puritan View

For both religious and economic reasons Puritans emphasized the necessity of sexual relations and reproduction in marriage. Failure to fulfill this conjugal duty could result in serious punishment. James Mattock, for instance, was expelled from the First Church of Boston because, among other offenses, "he denied Coniugall fellowship vnto his wife for the space of 2 years together vpon pretense of taking Revenge upon himself for his abusing of her before marryage." Most couples upheld the ideal of marital, reproductive sex. Families had an average of seven or eight children. This large family size, along with a relatively low mortality rate, led to rapid population growth. While they considered reproduction the central aim of marital sex, Puritans also believed that sexual relations should provide pleasure for husbands and wives. According to popular medical opinion of the period, orgasm by both partners was necessary in order for conception to take place.

*These members of
the male bachelor
subculture enjoyed
violent, socially
dysfunctional,
time-wasting
participatory
pleasures at
gambling dens,
groggeries, brothels,
cockpits, boxing
rings, and raucous
theaters.*

PAGE 56

◆ **Illegitimate**

*Not recognized as lawful
offspring; specifically, born
of parents not married to
each other*

over their children's labor and sexual lives. Though parents did not arrange marriages, they had a strong voice in determining the choice of a partner and the timing of marriage for their children. Traditional English courtship customs continued in New England. Through the practice of "bundling," couples were permitted to sleep in the same bed together as long as they remained clothed or kept a "bundling" board between them. Courting couples had little privacy and were seldom out of sight of family members in the small, crowded houses in which all members of the household often slept in the same room. If pregnancy did occur, family, community, and religious authorities made sure that marriage took place. The low rate of premarital pregnancy and illegitimacy indicates the effectiveness of moral regulation of youth in Puritan New England. In seventeenth-century New England less than one-tenth of all brides were pregnant at the time of marriage, and only between 1 and 3 percent of all births took place outside of marriage.

Very different patterns of family and sexual life developed among the European colonists who settled in the Chesapeake after 1607. Demographic, economic, and environmental conditions in this region inhibited the establishment of patriarchal family structures and marital sexual relations, at least for the first century of colonial development. Unlike the Puritans, the colonists who settled in the South came from varied social backgrounds, ranging from servant to nobleman, and did not migrate in family groups. The desire for profit from tobacco production, rather than a strong religious mission, motivated settlers in the Chesapeake. With this goal in mind, the colonial authorities recruited primarily young single men as indentured servants to provide cheap labor for tobacco plantations. As many as three-quarters of the early inhabitants were indentured servants. The focus on male labor resulted in a high sex imbalance in Virginia and Maryland, with men outnumbering women by four to one. The sex ratio, along with a high mortality rate, slowed population growth and inhibited the formation of families. Parents often died before their children reached adulthood and thus could not exert much control over their marital choices and sexual lives. Conditions of servitude further prevented stable family life, for servants were prohibited from marrying until they completed their period of service. The dispersed patterns of settlement, particularly in frontier regions, led many couples to live together and have children without civil or religious marriage.

The weak family ties and the skewed sex ratio in the Chesapeake contributed to a much higher incidence of premarital and extramarital sexual activity than in New England. Up to one-third of all brides were pregnant at the time of marriage among the immigrant population in the southern colonies. This situation presented both risks and advantages to women. The lack of family connections made them more vulnerable to sexual exploitation by masters and male laborers. Because of the shortage of women, however, premarital sexual relations and illegitimate births did not carry the same social stigma for southern women as they did in England or New England. As long as they were not bound in servitude, women with out-of-wedlock children could find husbands with relative ease in the Chesapeake colonies.

By the early eighteenth century, family and sexual patterns in New England and the Chesapeake were more similar, the result of changing demographic and economic conditions. The strict moral order maintained in seventeenth-century New England eroded somewhat with the growth of towns, the migration of children from their parents' homes to new settlements, and the decline of religious fervor that initially had bound community members together. As a result of these conditions, the premarital pregnancy rate in New England rose steadily throughout the eighteenth century. At the same time, family life became more stable in Virginia and Maryland, as the native-born population increased and the sex imbalance declined. By 1700, the sex ratio was three men to two women, which encouraged earlier marriages and thus increased marital reproduction. As in New England, white women in the Chesapeake now bore an average of eight live children and sometimes had ten or more pregnancies. With improved life expectancy, marriages lasted longer and more children reached maturity under their parents' care. Fathers were able to exercise greater control over their children's sexual lives and choice of marriage partners. The relative sexual and social autonomy young women had experienced in the early decades of settlement gave way to more traditional forms of regulation, leading to a significant decline in the rates of illegitimacy and premarital pregnancy.

Further hindrances to marriage and family formation among southern white colonists were removed by 1700 when slaves began to replace indentured servants as the dominant form of labor in the Chesapeake. At the same time, the introduction of slavery created new sexual patterns among the growing number of Africans imported to labor for white masters. As they had done with white servants, planters initially imported male slaves to work in the fields. This resulted in a high sex imbalance and seriously impeded the development of family life among slaves. The formation of families was made even more difficult by the fact that many Africans lived on small farms with a few slaves spread over a vast territory. Fertility rates remained low among African immigrant women due to high infant mortality rates, the trauma caused by forced migration and enslavement, and the African custom of long nursing periods, which delayed subsequent conception. By 1750 slave family and sexual patterns had become more stable as the native-born black population began to reproduce itself. The sex ratio had evened out, which allowed most slaves to marry, have children, and develop families and kinship networks. Birthrates increased steadily, so that by the late eighteenth century African American women bore an average of six children. In spite of these developments, the conditions of enslavement posed a constant threat to the family and sexual lives of African Americans. Masters frequently separated family members by selling them for profit or bequeathing them to married sons and daughters. Furthermore, slave women were subjected to sexual advances, rape, and impregnation by white planters and their sons.

Although colonial society attempted to channel sexuality into marriage and reproduction, illicit sex remained a constant problem. Communities regularly were confronted with cases of fornication, adultery, sodomy, bestiality, bastardy, rape, and interracial sex. Religious and civil authorities subjected sexual transgressors to a range of punishments including fines, whipping, branding, sitting in the stocks, and banishment. Certain offenses—sodomy, rape, bestiality, and adultery—were punishable by death, but in practice the courts only rarely resorted to execution. A central component of colonial punishment was public humiliation, which both chastised the offender and set an example for the rest of the community.

Colonial society punished women more harshly than men for engaging in premarital or extramarital sex. In the early years of settlement, the New England courts had attempted to treat men and women equally for the crimes of fornication and bastardy. Typically the offending couple was brought before the court, admonished for their sinful behavior, and persuaded to marry or punished with a whipping or a fine. By the early eighteenth century, however, the New England courts

were prosecuting primarily single women and not their male partners in fornication proceedings. Southern courts also punished women more diligently than men for premarital sex. Female servants in the Chesapeake paid a great cost for an unmarried pregnancy. They could not marry to make the birth legitimate unless someone paid their masters for the time they had left to serve. They were fined heavily or whipped and had to serve an extra twelve to twenty-four months in order to repay masters for lost labor during pregnancy and childbirth. The severe sanctions unmarried mothers faced in colonial society led some to resort to abortion or infanticide. Although the extent of infanticide is unknown, the practice may have become more common in the eighteenth century: every colony enacted legislation to punish the unmarried mothers of dead infants as murderers, unless a witness would testify that the child had been stillborn.

In part, colonial authorities prosecuted women more diligently for fornication and bastardy because pregnancy made the woman's guilt in the affair far easier to prove than the man's. More important, harsher treatment of female offenders stemmed from a double standard of morality that placed far greater value on female chastity because of the need to ensure the legitimacy of heirs in the patriarchal household. By custom and law a woman's chastity was not her own property but that of her father, if she were single, and of her husband, if she were married.

Colonial authorities considered sodomy, in contrast to fornication and bastardy, primarily a man's offense. It was punishable by execution, but as with other capital offenses, courts seldom resorted to the death penalty. Still, many received severe punishments for sodomitic acts. In 1636, when John Alexander and Thomas Roberts were "found guilty of lude behavior and uncleane carriage one [with] another, by often spendinge their seede one upon another," Alexander was whipped, burned with a hot iron, and banished from the colony, while Roberts, a servant, was whipped, sent back to his master, and forbidden to own land in the colony. The seventeenth-century concept of sodomy differs in important ways from the modern notion of homosexuality. Sodomy referred to nonprocreative sexual acts between two men, between a man and a woman, or between a man and an animal. It did not define a particular category of persons or an identity, in the way that the term "homosexuality" does. Typically, those convicted of sodomy did not become permanent social outcasts. If they acknowledged wrongdoing and accepted

Every time I'm about ready to go to bed with a guy, I have to look at my Dad's name all over the guy's underwear.

MARCI KLEIN
DISCUSSING CALVIN KLEIN
UNDERWEAR, NEWSWEEK
(SEPTEMBER 11, 1995)

*Mae West also
titillated audiences
with her witticisms
and sexual
allusions.*

PAGE 147

punishment, they could be reintegrated into the community just like other moral offenders.

In policing moral boundaries, colonial authorities also attempted to prohibit interracial sex. In the first half of the seventeenth century, interracial couples guilty of fornication, bastardy, or adultery faced the same sorts of penalties as white couples. As slavery became entrenched in the southern colonies, colonial governments began to enact more stringent laws against interracial unions, in an effort to strengthen control over the slave labor force and to maintain a fixed boundary between the races. In 1662 the Virginia legislature doubled the fines for interracial sex, and by the mid-eighteenth century all southern colonies, along with Pennsylvania and Massachusetts, had passed strict laws prohibiting interracial marriages and sexual unions. Ministers who presided over such unions were subject to punishment, and the guilty parties faced double fines and whippings as well as possible servitude and banishment from the colonies or both.

White masters, however, because of their social position and power, regularly violated the law with impunity by having sexual relations with female slaves. Planters' interracial liaisons did not threaten racial boundaries because mulatto children were generally confined to the status of slaves. This system contrasted sharply with that of the Spanish and Portuguese colonies, where planters often freed the children of their interracial unions. Far more threatening to the social order in the British colonies were sexual unions between black men and white women. This less common type of interracial union was punishable by castration. English colonists justified their sexual abuse and domination of slave men and women by constructing a stereotype of blacks as lewd, lascivious, and beastlike. According to the colonists' distorted reasoning, black women were always desirous of sexual relations, which absolved white men of blame; and black men lusted after white women and therefore required severe measures of control.

NATIVE AMERICAN SEXUAL CUSTOMS

The colonists constructed stereotypes of sexual depravity and immorality in response to Native American cultures. The many tribes that inhabited North America had varied marriage and sexual customs differing markedly from the colonists' ideal of marital, reproductive sex. In contrast with European cultures, many tribes did not have strict prohibitions against sex outside of marriage. They permitted sexual experimentation, including masturbation, among youth, and premarital sexual activity between opposite-sex or same-sex partners. Various Indian societies allowed trial marriages, practiced polygamy, and did not enforce strict monogamy within marriage. Among the Iroquois, Delaware, Montagnais, and numerous other groups, marriages were not contracted for life, as they were in European cultures. Married couples separated when either spouse desired to do so. Although divorce was common and easy to obtain, couples tended to stay together once they had children.

In contrast with Europeans, many Native American tribes granted women considerable sexual autonomy, both before and after marriage. They did not conceive of female sexuality as man's property and therefore did not stigmatize out-of-wedlock births or

women's extramarital affairs, a degree of permissiveness that greatly disturbed European colonists. Another aspect of Native American sexual life that aroused the hostility of colonists was the existence of *berdache* (from the French term for sodomite), men who dressed and acted as women and in some cultures had sexual relations with and married other men. Although they were not as common as cross-dressing men, some Indian women, too, primarily in the tribes of western North America and the Great Plains, lived as men and performed traditionally male tasks of hunting, trapping, and fighting. What particularly disturbed colonists was the acceptance and respect the *berdache* enjoyed within their tribal societies. Cross-gender men and women had a clearly recognized social status and often performed special ceremonial roles and economic functions for their people.

Using their own cultural and religious standards, the colonists condemned Native American divorce, polygamy, cross-gender identities, and extramarital sex as savage and barbaric. Throughout the colonial period European missionaries engaged in vigorous, often violent, but largely unsuccessful efforts to convert Indians to the Christian ideals of monogamous heterosexual marriage and female chastity.

♦ **Polygamy**

*Marriage in which a spouse
of either sex may have more
than one mate at the same
time*

The Nineteenth Century

VICTORIAN AMERICA. The social, economic, and demographic transformations accompanying the rise of industrial capitalism in the late eighteenth and early nineteenth centuries led to significant changes in sexual patterns, ideologies, and methods of regulation. The shift from an economy based on agriculture and artisanal labor to one based on commerce and manufacturing created a new and more stratified class structure with a middle class of businessmen, factory owners, and professionals and a class of wage laborers made up of both displaced artisans and farm laborers and newly arrived immigrants from England, Ireland, and Germany. The subsistence farms of the colonial period were increasingly replaced by commercial farming enterprises, a development fueled by an expanding transportation network of canals and railroads. Cities grew rapidly in the period after 1820, especially in areas where commerce and manufacturing created new jobs and economic opportunities. Industrialization and urban growth took place over a long period of time and occurred at different paces in the various regions of the country. By mid-century industrial capitalism was most advanced in the Northeast, while the South remained tied to a system of plantation agriculture and slave labor, and western frontier communities were based on family farm economies.

The shift to an industrial economy generated new family and sexual patterns. Within the emerging middle class, a nuclear family structure and an ideal of sexual restraint took hold. Different patterns and ideologies developed among working-class people, a topic that will be covered later. Among middle-class Americans, the patriarchal household of the colonial era was replaced by the nuclear family with its separate spheres of activity for women and men. Economic production increasingly shifted from household to factory, a development that sharpened the sexual division of labor within middle-class families. In the new capitalist order, husbands worked in offices and factories to earn the income that supported the family, while wives remained at home to take care of children and household duties. A doctrine of separate spheres was elaborated within the middle class during this period that posited distinctly different roles and characteristics for women and men. Women, characterized as gentle, selfless, pious, and pure, were to be the moral guardians of the home. Men, on the other hand, were defined as bold, aggressive, and competitive, best suited for the public world of politics, business, and war.

The role of children within the middle-class family also changed significantly. An economic asset as farm laborers in an agrarian economy, they became an economic liability in an industrial economy. Not only was middle-class children's labor power irrelevant, but their parents found it more difficult to secure their economic future. Instead of land, middle-class parents provided their children with education and character-building to enable them to succeed in the world. This demanded a much greater investment of parents' time, money, and attention, and encouraged families to have fewer children. Marital fertility rates show a marked decline over the course of the nineteenth century. By the end of the century, the average number of children in a family had fallen to four. Considering that high birthrates persisted among working-class, immigrant, and rural families, the decline among the urban middle class was even sharper than this figure indicates.

A new ideology of sexual restraint prevalent among middle-class Americans both facilitated the desire for fertility control and became a marker of class status. Disseminated by physicians, ministers, and health reformers in medical texts and advice literature, this ideology promoted male continence and female purity. Physicians and reformers urged men to avoid all sexual stimulation before marriage and to practice sexual control within marriage. They warned that exces-

When I'm good I'm very good, but when I'm bad I'm better.

MAE WEST

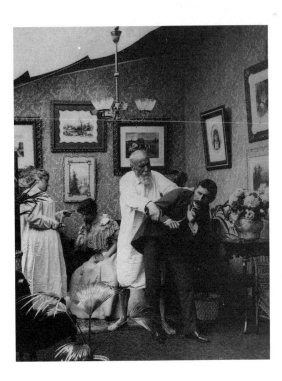

ROMANCE VICTORIAN STYLE

Victorian lovers reprimanded after stealing a kiss.
CORBIS-BETTMANN

*Socialist reformer
Emma Goldman
argued insistently
for equality and free
love, branded
marriage obsolete,
and advocated birth
control six years
before Margaret
Sanger began
her campaign.*

PAGE 124

sive sexual indulgence destroyed a man's physical and mental powers and undermined his ability to rule his family and compete successfully in the business world. Some advice manuals recommended that married couples limit coitus to once a month and then only for the purpose of procreation.

The "master vice" of masturbation was chief among the sexual indulgences warned against in men's advice literature. Although religious and medical authorities in earlier periods had written about the supposed harmful effects of masturbation, the early nineteenth century witnessed an intensification of anxieties and a voluminous production of antimasturbation literature. Lay and medical writers ascribed to this practice a host of ills from acne to insanity. According to the physician William Acton, the masturbator "cannot look anyone in the face, and becomes careless in dress and uncleanly in person. His intellect has become sluggish and enfeebled, and if his habits are persisted in, he may end in becoming a drivelling idiot or a peevish valetudinarian" (quoted in Marcus, p. 19). To guard against these adverse effects, health reformers Sylvester Graham, Reverend John Todd, and others recommended preventive measures such as cold baths and bland diets. Some also promoted more extreme measures, including surgery and mechanical restraining devices.

While men were encouraged to exert sexual control to uphold their role as breadwinner and head of the family, women faced an even more restrictive code of morality. Nineteenth-century sexual advice literature overturned an earlier image of women as passionate by claiming that women were inherently chaste and pure. They were expected to be the moral guardians of the home, to stem the lustful natures of husbands and sons. Many health and medical writers went so far as to deny that women experienced sexual passion at all. Dr. William Acton, a British physician whose work on female sexuality was widely read in the United States wrote that "The majority of women (happily for society) are not very much troubled with sexual feelings of any kind." According to Acton, "Love of home, of children, and of domestic duties are the only passions they feel" (quoted in Hellerstein et al., pp. 177–179).

Though other physicians expressed dissenting opinions about the nature of women's sexuality, female passionlessness became a dominant ideal within middle-class culture. Although promoted by male physicians and health reformers, the ideal of female purity was embraced by many middle-class women for their own uses. It granted women a position of moral authority within the family and society, and gave them a certain element of control in sexual relations by providing grounds for rejecting unwanted sexual activity and limiting reproduction. Given the dangers of childbirth and venereal disease, many women may have welcomed sexual restraint.

The notion of female purity may have offered some advantages to middle-class women, but it also served to intensify social censure of those women who did not adhere to the bourgeois conception of female respectability. Because women supposedly occupied a higher moral plane than men, their fall from virtue was seen as far more serious. Victorian society condemned, yet tolerated, illicit sexual activity on the part of men. Women who engaged in sex outside of marriage, however, were considered permanently "ruined."

Along with an ideology of sexual restraint, the middle class adopted a romantic ideal of courtship and marriage. While economic considerations remained important, middle-class Americans began to consider romantic love essential for a happy marriage. Unlike colonial couples, who expected to grow to love one another, middle-class couples expected to experience "true love" before they decided to marry. Middle-class courtship also became more private than it had been in rural settings. Courting couples usually met and exchanged intimacies in the parlors of middle-class homes, where they were expected to behave in a respectable manner.

The sexual practices of middle-class Americans did not always conform to the ideals of male continence and female purity promoted in sermons and medical literature. The letters and diaries of Victorian men and women sometimes describe the sensual pleasures they experienced in courtship and marriage. Other evidence, however, suggests that the proponents of sexual restraint had a decisive impact on their middle-class audience. The significant decline in the rate of premarital pregnancy suggests that young middle-class men and women had internalized norms of sexual continence and control. The rate dropped from 20 percent of all marriages in the 1830s to 10 percent in the 1850s. A survey of married women conducted by Dr. Clelia D. Mosher in the 1890s reveals the strong influence of, if not strict adherence to, Victorian sexual ideology. While many of the women interviewed acknowledged experiencing sexual desire, they also expressed feelings of guilt and confusion about their sexual lives. For the most part, they thought that sexual

See also
Adolescence

relations should be confined to marriage, and the vast majority believed that reproduction was the primary aim of sexual activity. The point is not that middle-class Americans invariably followed Victorian sexual standards in their daily lives, but that they often tried, and felt guilty when they failed.

The changing social and economic order required new methods of sexual regulation for middle-class Americans. Traditional forms of control were no longer effective in a rapidly growing, industrializing society. The community surveillance of individuals characteristic of the colonial era was difficult to maintain in expanding urban areas with highly mobile populations. In an increasingly secularized society, church leaders no longer had the authority to intervene in the moral lives of their congregations, although they continued to preach about moral issues. State involvement in the regulation of morals also eroded during this period. By the nineteenth century, legislatures and courts had backed away from the rigorous regulation of private morality they had practiced in the colonial period.

With the decline of traditional moral authorities, American society placed increasing emphasis on self-control and the internalization of sexual restraint. The characteristic feature of the new system of sexual regulation was the reliance on individuals, rather than external authorities, to police their sexual desires and behavior. The task of instilling sexual self-control rested primarily with the family, particularly mothers, who were held responsible for the proper moral upbringing of their children. Physicians also assumed a position as sexual authorities in the nineteenth century, publishing tracts, books, and pamphlets instructing people how to manage and control their sexual lives.

Victorian sexual ideals did face opposition. Some middle-class Americans experimented with alternative sexual systems and methods of regulation. Mormons, Shakers, Oneidans, and free-love advocates formed communities that departed from the dominant social order based on the nuclear family and marital, reproductive sex. Shakers, who lived in communal villages in New England, upstate New York, and the Old Northwest, practiced celibacy and tried to overcome physical desire by living a spiritual life. Instead of individual self-control, Shakers relied on close community surveillance to enforce sexual restraint among men, women, and children. The Mormon religion, founded by Joseph Smith in 1830, challenged Victorian sexual codes by permitting polygamy. Mormons formed cohesive patriarchal communities in the Great Salt Lake Valley in which men took multiple wives to enhance opportunities for reproduction, while women were bound by a strict code of chastity. John Humphrey Noyes and his followers explored other alternative sexual arrangements in the utopian community they formed at Oneida, New York, in 1848. Noyes urged Oneidan members to explore sexual pleasures outside of the confines of marriage and to practice "amative" over reproductive sex through coitus reservatus, a procedure in which the man withdrew without ejaculating.

The growth of industrial capitalism altered family life, sexual patterns, and methods of regulation among the expanding class of wage laborers, but in ways different from those experienced by the middle class. Laboring men and women did not experience the sharp separation between domestic and work spheres that characterized middle-class family life. Because of the instability of men's employment in a wage-labor economy

FREE LOVE
Challenging Victorian Moral Standards

Free lovers directly challenged the sanctity of monogamous marriage by arguing that love and attraction, rather than marriage, should be the basis for a sexual union. Frances Wright, one of the earliest and most outspoken advocates of free love, organized an interracial utopian community in Nashoba, Tennessee. Her radical positions on marriage and race sparked vehement opposition and sometimes violent riots. One writer accused her of trying to turn the world "into one vast immeasurable brothel." In the 1850s sexual anarchists established two short-lived communities—Modern Times on Long Island, and Berlin Heights, near Cleveland, Ohio. The free-love movement reached a broader audience after the Civil War, when Victoria Woodhull began voicing her radical sexual theories in public lectures and writings. Woodhull encouraged open sexual unions, not restricted by church or law. She rejected marriage as an institution that oppressed women and stifled love and sexual pleasure. Woodhull was joined by free lovers Ezra Heywood and Moses Harman, who wrote frankly about sexuality and protested women's sexual slavery in their respective journals, *The Word* and *Lucifer, the Light Bearer*.

Other books offered very specific information about the etiquette of necking and petting.

PAGE 270

My big trouble is that I always think whoever I'm necking with is a pretty intelligent person.

J. D. SALINGER
THE CATCHER IN THE RYE
(1951)

S

SEXUAL BEHAVIOR AND MORALITY

The Nineteenth Century

Sex. In America an obsession. In other parts of the world, a fact.

MARLENE DIETRICH

See also
Courtship, Marriage,
Separation, and Divorce

and the meagerness of wages, working-class families often depended on the economic contributions of all members of the household. In addition to caring for the home and children, working-class wives earned income through activities such as doing laundry, dressmaking, and piece work. Children continued to be an economic asset in working-class families, and consequently birthrates remained high. Parents sent children into the labor force as early as possible; those too young to be wage earners contributed to the family economy through street peddling, scavenging, and assisting mothers with income-producing work done in the home. In this context, working-class marriages were practical arrangements characterized by strong bonds of mutual support and sometimes fierce sexual antagonisms between husbands and wives. In contrast with middle-class marriages, an ideal of romantic love did not become an important aspect of conjugal relations among laboring men and women.

The experience of wage earning gave working-class youth greater social and sexual autonomy than they had known in preindustrial economies, where sons and daughters labored under the close supervision of parents in rural households or artisanal shops. Young working men and women met and courted openly in parks and city streets, often away from the watchful eyes of family and neighbors. It was not uncommon for working-class courtship to include premarital sexual activity. This stemmed from the rural practice of permitting sexual relations between betrothed couples in the expectation that marriage would take place if pregnancy resulted. In an urban industrial setting, however, this practice made unmarried women increasingly vulnerable to pregnancy and abandonment. In rural communities, young women could depend on family, neighbors, and church authorities to compel young men to marry them in the case of pregnancy. In large cities with highly mobile populations, the policing of male sexual behavior proved much more difficult. Most of the unwed mothers in the New York Anchorage, a nineteenth-century home for "wayward and erring girls," explained their situation as the result of broken promises of marriage by young men with whom they had become intimately involved.

Traditional forms of moral regulation had weakened significantly in working-class and immigrant communities, but they had not disappeared completely. Families and neighbors continued to monitor sexual behavior and to punish individuals who had violated community moral standards. But despite the existence of both distinct moral codes and the means of enforcing them, to middle-class observers the working-class communities appeared to be teeming with vice and sin. According to public officials and bourgeois reformers, working-class home life in crowded tenements encouraged overbreeding, promiscuity, and vicious habits among family members. Children who, according to middle-class standards, should have been carefully sheltered in the domestic sphere were sent out to labor in the streets, where, according to one moral reformer, "they graduate in every kind of vice known." Reformers expressed particular concern about the impact of industrialization and wage work on women's moral behavior. In a study of prostitution, William Sanger warned that "the employment of females in various trades in this city, in the pursuit of which they are forced into constant communication with male operatives has a disastrous effect upon their characters" (quoted in Stansell, p. 266). Inspired by evangelical Protestantism and a new ideology of sexual continence, middle-class men and women launched numerous efforts to reform the morals of laboring people. They established Bible societies and Sunday schools and organized temperance and antiprostitution campaigns, but in the end they had little success in converting working people to their standards of morality.

THE ANTEBELLUM SOUTH. The institution of slavery produced a distinct sexual system in the antebellum South for both white slaveholders and black slaves. Southern society, rooted in plantation agriculture and slave labor, did not experience the economic changes that generated new sexual patterns in northern cities and towns. The patriarchal household in which fathers exercised authority over wives, children, and slaves persisted in the South until the Civil War. Although most southern households did not have slaves, the patriarchal ideal served as a model for smaller farms as well. The household remained the central unit of economic production, in which all members had specific tasks and duties. Slaves performed domestic chores and backbreaking field work; wives oversaw the garden, dairy, and manufacture of clothing; husbands managed the plantation and conducted business and commercial transactions; and sons and daughters assisted parents with their respective tasks. White birthrates remained high in the agrarian South—up to seven children per family—for large families brought prestige and provided security for parents in old age. Planter parents continued to have a strong voice in the selection of mates for daughters and sons because the protection and consolidation of property and status rested on a wise union. In areas of the South not based on slave labor, families engaged in subsistence agriculture. Far less is known of the sexual lives of these groups, but traditional rural patterns of sexuality and marriage probably persisted, including high fertility rates, tolerance of premarital sex among the betrothed, and common-law marriages.

In the social context of the plantation South, Victorian sexual ideology developed only shallow roots. The southern moral code placed great value on female chastity both to ensure legitimate heirs and to protect family honor, but it neither denied female sexual desire nor promoted an ideal of women's passionlessness. Southern custom dictated that unmarried women remain virginal and that wives uphold moral decorum, but unlike the northern middle class, southerners thought that women, as well as men, were subject to sexual feelings. Women, in fact, were considered more prone to moral weakness due to their childlike, emotional natures. They were thought to be easily seduced and manipulated by scheming men.

The belief in women's moral vulnerability led families to watch their daughters carefully during the courtship period. Chaperons were present whenever daughters met with suitors, attended parties and balls, or visited friends and neighbors. Married women, too, were chaperoned to protect their reputations. Those accused of marital infidelity could face divorce, loss of their children, and physical abuse by their husbands.

While southern white women were hemmed in by strict moral codes, southern white men were permitted great sexual privilege, both before and after marriage. The qualities of male continence and self-control promoted among the northern middle class never became ideals for men in the antebellum South. Society tolerated, even expected, young men to engage in sexual affairs before marriage. Sexual experience was a point of honor for single men; male virginity aroused suspicion and ridicule. Married men could take mistresses or engage in casual affairs without damaging their reputations or family name. Such behavior could even enhance a man's prestige in the eyes of his companions.

Both single and married white men expected to have sexual access to enslaved women. Young men's sexual initiation often was with female slaves, and married men frequently took black mistresses and concubines. Southern men defended this practice by arguing that sex with female slaves protected the purity of southern white women. Because of their subordinate position within southern society, planters' wives did not openly acknowledge or oppose their husbands' interracial relations, but these affairs sometimes caused considerable strain in the marriages. According to one slave, her mistress "don't never have no more children, and she ain't so cordial with the Massa" after she learned of his relations with female slaves. Other planters' wives took out their frustration and rage on slave women, who were even more powerless to challenge white men's sexual demands.

When white Americans looked at slave family and social life, they saw only immorality and licentiousness. Slavery advocates claimed that African Americans were inherently depraved, while northern abolitionists argued that the institution of slavery had destroyed any semblance of family life and morality among black men and women. Contrary to the stereotypes perpetuated by whites, however, the slave community lived by distinct codes governing marriage, courtship, and sexual relations shaped by both African-American cultural traditions and the institution of slavery. Historian Herbert Gutman has argued that slave sexual and marital norms closely resembled practices of preindustrial cultures in the acceptance of premarital sex among the young, high fertility rates, and the tendency toward settled unions between men and women, often without legal marriage. One crucial difference is that African Americans had to adjust their sexual customs to the dictates of the slave system. Through various means, masters had extensive, though never complete, authority over the sexuality and family lives of slave men and women.

The courtship and marriage patterns of slaves demonstrate the combined influence of white masters and African American culture. Despite demanding work loads, young men and women found time for courting at church services, holiday celebrations, and plantation parties on Friday and Saturday nights. Courtships often lasted over an extended period of time, sometimes as long as a year, and were supervised by family and community members. Slaves accepted premarital sex among youth as part of the courtship process. In case of pregnancy, it was generally expected that marriage would take place. As an elderly male former slave explained, "If you fooled up a girl with a arm full of you, you had to take care of her." Although marriage followed most prenuptial pregnancies, slaves did not ostracize unmarried mothers but accepted and cared for them and their children as members of the community. Most of

That was the most fun I've ever had without laughing.

WOODY ALLEN
ALVY SINGER IN THE FILM
ANNIE HALL (1977)

Sex is to women's role in society as skin color and racist repression are to black personality.

PAGE 231

the women who had "outside" children eventually settled into long-term relationships with one man.

Despite the constant threat of separation posed by the slave system, slave men and women expected to form long-term, monogamous unions. Some couples had trial marriages, in which they lived together to determine if they were suitable for one another. Although legal marriage was prohibited under slavery, African Americans legitimized and celebrated their marriages in a variety of ways. Both black and white ministers or respected elders of the community conducted wedding ceremonies. Other couples cemented their union by jumping over a broomstick in the presence of friends and neighbors. Spouses did not always live together. Many had "abroad marriages" in which husbands lived on separate plantations and visited their families when they could, usually on holidays and weekend nights.

Once married, spouses were expected to be faithful to one another. Strong church and community sanctions existed to enforce marital and sexual norms. Black churches punished people guilty of sexual transgressions. The Beaufort Baptist Church in South Carolina suspended those who committed adultery for three months; a second offense resulted in a six-month suspension. Acceptance of the sinner back into the church required the approval of church members. Slaves in Darien, Georgia, adopted a West African custom of "putting on the banjo," singing about a young woman's inappropriate sexual behavior in order to warn her to reform.

The demands of the slave system shaped marriage, courtship, and sexual patterns within the slave community in a number of ways. Masters interfered with slave family life through the control of reproduction, sexual assault of women, and separation of family members. In addition to the production of commodities, slavery demanded the reproduction of the slave labor force, particularly after the slave trade was abolished in 1808. Thus, owners placed a premium on slave women's reproductive capacities and expected them to bear children often and as early as possible. Slave women usually began bearing children at around age nineteen, two years earlier than southern white women, and maintained high fertility rates. Plantation owners used a variety of means to ensure reproduction, both by offering inducements, such as lighter work loads or additional rations for pregnant slaves, and by compelling women to mate with men against their will.

In addition to forced unions with male slaves, women were sexually exploited by white owners and their sons. When resisted by slave women or their husbands, owners often resorted to force to satisfy their sexual desires and assert their dominance. Ruth Allen, the daughter of a white master and a female slave, stated, "My mammy didn' have any more to say about what they did with her than the rest of the slaves in them days" (quoted in Jennings, p. 62). Some women fiercely resisted their master's advances, but often at great cost. A cook named Sukie, who punched her master and pushed him in a tub of water when he tore off her

PORNOGRAPHY AND PROSTITUTION

Sexual Commerce in the Nineteenth Century

The mass production of pornographic literature began in the United States in the 1840s and grew rapidly after the Civil War with the dissemination of novels like *The Confessions of a Lady's Waiting Maid*, and prints and photographs of women in various erotic scenes and poses. Prostitution, which had developed on a small scale in seaport cities of the late eighteenth century, also expanded throughout the nineteenth century. The economic disruptions caused by industrial capitalism increased both the demand for and the supply of prostitutes, as cities and towns filled with young women in search of employment and single men living apart from families. By the end of the century an extensive market in prostitution catered to men of all economic backgrounds. Male customers could choose from fifty-cent "crib houses," one- and two-dollar brothels, and expensive parlor houses. A thriving prostitution trade also took root in western cattle and mining towns, where a severe shortage of women and an abundance of single men produced a great demand for sexual commerce. It is estimated that 20 percent of all women in California were prostitutes in the decade after the gold rush. A particularly exploitative system involving Asian prostitutes developed in some West Coast cities. Asian women who had been sold by their poor families or kidnapped were contracted to perform sexual services for a specified period of time, usually four to six years.

dress and attempted to rape her, avoided the assault but was sold to slave traders for her rebellious behavior.

Although reproduction did not require the existence of families, most owners encouraged settled unions among slave men and women for both moral and economic reasons. Southern ministers urged masters to do their Christian duty by promoting slave marriages and family life. The existence of families not only satisfied religious obligations but also facilitated owners' management and control of slaves. Masters could command obedience from slave men and women by threatening to whip or sell their children or spouses. Familial bonds also discouraged slaves from running away and leaving their loved ones behind.

The exploitation of family ties and women's reproduction made motherhood an ambivalent experience for slave women, who produced an additional source of profit for their owners each time they gave birth, and whose children might be whipped, assaulted, or sold to new masters. Some slave mothers responded by practicing birth control or abortion. Most women, however, did not resort to such measures. Whatever its dangers, they placed great value on motherhood, for it offered them a source of personal fulfillment that was denied in other areas of their lives.

SEXUAL CONFLICTS IN VICTORIAN AMERICA.

The late nineteenth century saw intense conflicts over sexuality and its regulation in Victorian America. With urban and industrial development, opportunities for sexual expression outside of marriage gradually expanded. This was most evident in the growing market for pornography and prostitution in cities and towns throughout the country. Social purity crusaders responded with aggressive campaigns to restore sex to a marital, reproductive framework.

The growth of sexual commerce inspired many middle-class women and men to organize social purity campaigns aimed at cleansing cities of vice and immorality. The earliest purity reform efforts began in Boston and New York in the 1820s, when Protestant clergy and businessmen conducted missionary work in poor neighborhoods to convert prostitutes to a moral way of life. Evangelical women, who formed the American Female Moral Reform Society, came to the forefront of the anti-prostitution movement in the 1830s and 1840s. They aimed not only to reform prostitutes but also to change male sexual behavior and eliminate the double standard of morality. Inspired by these goals, women campaigned for criminal sanctions against male seducers. They had little

success, however, and by the 1850s the original fervor of the movement had dissipated.

A second wave of purity reform that took shape in the 1870s attracted a national following and developed a more ambitious political agenda. Composed of temperance reformers, women's rights advocates, and Protestant clergy, the movement originally formed in opposition to the efforts of police and medical authorities to prevent the spread of venereal disease by licensing prostitutes. Arguing that such a system promoted vice and the double standard, reformers successfully defeated licensing attempts in Chicago, New York, and other cities.

After this victory, the purity movement expanded the scope of its activities and developed into a broad social crusade to abolish prostitution and to establish a single standard of morality for both sexes. Reformers used both educational and legislative methods to achieve these goals. They organized societies and clubs for young working women to provide wholesome amusements and prevent them from being lured into prostitution. Moral reformers in the Woman's Christian Temperance Union established White Cross societies to convert young men to the single standard.

Even as they used educational means, reformers increasingly called on the state to monitor and reform illicit sexual behavior. As a result of their activities, numerous vice and sex codes were enacted during this period. In an effort to shield young women from male vice, purity activists waged an effective campaign in the 1880s and 1890s to raise the age at which females could consent to sexual relations. Men who had sex with young women under this age would face criminal penalties, whether the women had agreed to have sex or not. By 1915, almost every state had raised the age of consent to sixteen or eighteen years. Other moral crusaders, under the leadership of Anthony Comstock, called on the state to prohibit the publication and dissemination of obscene literature. They achieved a major victory in 1873 when Congress passed the Comstock Law, forbidding the mailing of obscene and indecent materials, including articles that discussed contraception or abortion.

State regulation of sexuality was further expanded with the criminalization of abortion in the late nineteenth century. Prior to this time, the legal system did not consider the termination of a pregnancy before quickening (which occurs in the fourth or fifth month) a crime. In response to a vigorous campaign organized by American physicians, state legislatures throughout the country

*We do not go to bed
in single pairs . . .
we . . . drag . . .
with us the cultural
impedimenta of
our social class,
our parents' lives,
our bank balances,
our sexual and
emotional
expectations. . . .*

ANGELA CARTER
THE SADEIAN WOMAN (1979)

♦ Quickening

*To reach the stage of
gestation at which fetal
motion is felt*

passed laws that outlawed abortion at any stage of pregnancy and subjected both the abortionist and the patient to criminal penalties.

After 1900 the antiprostitution movement secured major legislative changes that seriously undermined the system of commercialized prostitution in American cities. With the growth of Progressive reform, the movement became a powerful political force that encompassed a wide range of social groups with varying agendas. Vice crusaders sought to rid the nation of immorality; municipal reformers aimed to rid cities of corrupt politicians who profited from the prostitution trade; physicians and social hygienists wanted to control the spread of venereal disease; and feminists saw the end of prostitution as central to women's emancipation. Much of the campaign focused on dismantling red-light districts through the enactment of red-light abatement laws, which enabled private individuals to file complaints against suspected places of prostitution. This law was first enacted in Iowa in 1909 and by 1917 had passed in thirty-one other states.

The Progressive campaign reached its peak during World War I, when the federal government enlisted the support of reformers in a major effort to eradicate prostitution and venereal disease among the armed forces. In order to "protect" soldiers from vice and disease, federal officials shut down red-light districts and ordered the arrest, compulsory testing, and quarantine of women suspected of infection. In the end, the Progressive campaign did not abolish prostitution but merely changed its structure in a way that made the profession more dangerous and precarious for women. The removal of brothels and red-light districts forced more prostitutes to turn to streetwalking and strengthened the control of pimps in the trade.

The Rise and Fall of Sexual Liberalism

Even as moral crusaders mounted an impressive campaign against prostitution, enormous social and economic changes were eroding the foundations of the Victorian sexual order they sought to uphold. In the period from 1870 to 1920, the pace of industrialization and urbanization accelerated rapidly, spread to new regions of the country, and changed basic patterns of life ever more drastically. The tremendous growth of the manufacturing and retail sectors of the economy created a great demand for labor filled by American men and women leaving the countryside and by millions of immigrants who entered the country, mostly from southern and eastern Europe. In the face of these developments, Victorian standards of sexual restraint and marital, reproductive sex began to break down. The production of a wide array of new consumer goods and the increased standard of living of many Americans led to a major reorientation of values within middle-class culture. A new ethic of consumption and self-

**FLIRTATION
OPPORTUNITY**

*Instead of the sex-segregated,
family-based entertainments of
the past, social spaces like dance
halls provided opportunities for
flirtation and intimate encounters with members of the opposite sex during the Victorian
era.*

LIBRARY OF CONGRESS/
CORBIS

gratification replaced the Victorian emphasis on thrift, sobriety, and self-denial. An industrialized consumer society increased opportunities for sexual commerce and erotic expression outside of marriage. The doctrine of separate spheres, and the ideal of female purity that it embodied, crumbled as middle-class daughters left home for college and professional careers and working-class daughters moved into jobs in factories, department stores, and offices. Black and white rural migrants and the immigrants who flocked to American cities challenged Victorian sexual conventions by participating in an urban world of commercialized leisure that promoted sexual pleasure and romance.

New forms of work and recreation in early-twentieth-century cities provided young people, particularly women, with greater freedom from family and community constraints. As women moved beyond the domestic sphere, they explored sexual experiences outside of marriage and procreation. Many middle-class daughters rejected marriage and domesticity altogether in order to attend college, pursue professional careers, and engage in social reform. Unable to combine careers with traditional family life, women professionals and reformers such as Jane Addams, Sophinisba Breckinridge, and Vida Scudder created alternative family arrangements by forming close and often lifelong relationships with other women. The nature of these relationships varied widely, but at least some involved sexual intimacy. One college-educated woman said that her female partner was "as much a real mate as a husband would be. I have come to think that certain women, many in fact, possibly most of those who are unmarried, are more attracted to women than to men."

Working-class and immigrant daughters also challenged Victorian sexual codes as they explored heterosexual pleasures in early-twentieth-century cities. The expansion and commercialization of leisure at the turn of the century created a youth-oriented, two-sex world of amusement that weakened traditional social controls and encouraged sexual and romantic relations. Instead of the sex-segregated, family-based entertainments of the past, young women and men attended dance halls, amusement parks, and movie theaters. These provided social spaces for flirtation and intimate encounters with members of the opposite sex, away from the watchful eyes of parents and neighbors. Within this world of urban amusements, young women dressed in the latest finery, attended dance halls and amusement parks un-

escorted, and often picked up young men to pay their way once they arrived. Dancing styles emphasized the heightened sexuality of urban youth culture. "Tough dances" such as the grizzly bear, the Charlie Chaplin wiggle, and the dip encouraged bodily contact and the shaking of the hips and shoulders. The sexual code of working-class female youth tolerated premarital sexual intercourse in certain social contexts. Some were willing to engage in sex with their "steadies." Others had sexual relations with male partners in exchange for gifts, dinner, or a night's entertainment, a custom known as "treating." Clearly among some young women, particularly Catholic immigrants, traditional codes of female chastity prevailed. Even so, the increased rate of premarital pregnancy—which rose from 10 percent in the mid-nineteenth century to 23 percent in the period between 1880 to 1910—suggests a growing incidence of sexual experimentation.

The new sexual mores first evident among urban working-class youth had spread to middle-class youth in a tamer form by the 1920s. In dress, mannerisms, and behavior, middle-class female youth of the 1920s adopted a freer and more provocative sexual style. Their shorter skirts, bobbed hair, rouge, and silk stockings defied the nineteenth-century image of female purity and innocence. New rituals of courtship among middle-class youth further undermined Victorian conventions. Instead of receiving male admirers in the parlor at home, young women went out on "dates" with their partners to parties, movies, or cabarets. By the 1920s a central component of the new practice of dating was the automobile, which one juvenile court judge called "a house of prostitution on wheels." Free of adult supervision, dating gave youth greater autonomy in their romantic encounters. Linked to dating was the practice of "petting," in which youth experimented with a range of erotic contacts short of intercourse, from casual kisses to physical fondling. Sexual studies by Alfred Kinsey and others indicate that middle-class women born after 1900 were more willing to engage in premarital petting and intercourse than those born in the nineteenth century.

In addition to new patterns of heterosexual interaction, the early twentieth century witnessed the growth of homosexual subcultures in American cities. Urbanization and the spread of a wage-labor economy enabled an increasing number of individuals to live independently of their families and to explore sexual desires that departed from the heterosexual norm. In large, anonymous cities, men and women pursued same-sex relations and

Two became briefly one but were required to remain two, even though the memory of briefly being one made being two and one concomitantly more difficult than ever before.

SCOTT SOMMER
STILL LIVES (1989)

See also
Manners and Etiquette

forged the beginnings of an underground homosexual community. They came to identify their erotic interest in the same sex as a characteristic that set them apart from the majority of people. Bars, cafes, and boardinghouse neighborhoods provided meeting places for gay men and lesbians. According to one commentator in 1908, in cities like Boston, Saint Louis, and New Orleans, "certain smart clubs are well-known for their homosexual atmospheres."

In the years before World War I, political radicals and bohemians in Greenwich Village launched an attack on Victorian codes of respectability through both their political writings and their personal lives. Influenced by the studies of Sigmund Freud and British sex theorists Edward Carpenter and Havelock Ellis, they rejected monogamous marriage and sexual self-restraint. Sex radicals experimented with open sexual unions based on emotional compatibility and attraction, rather than on legal marriage.

In response to the radical changes in sexual mores and attitudes in the early twentieth century, social experts, including physicians, psychologists, educators, and social scientists, attempted to explain and direct the new patterns of behavior. Unlike fundamentalists, Catholics, and other moral conservatives, they did not call for a return to the morality of the past. Instead, they constructed an ideology of sexual liberalism (the term used by historians John D'Emilio and Estelle B. Freedman in *Intimate Matters*) that viewed sexual desire as positive but attempted to channel it into heterosexual relations and marriage. Liberal sex reformers popularized an American version of the writings of Freud and Havelock Ellis. Although they rejected the Victorian ideal of sexual continence, they established new guidelines for acceptable male and female behavior and defined new categories of sexual deviance.

Sexual liberals of the 1920s decried the notion of sexual restraint. Ben Lindsey, one of the au-

THE FIGHT FOR REPRODUCTIVE FREEDOM

Margaret Sanger and Birth Control

Radical women in Greenwich Village and elsewhere further assaulted middle-class sexual conventions in their fight for reproductive freedom. The first organized efforts for women's reproductive rights had occurred in the late nineteenth century, when reformers called for voluntary motherhood and women's right to abstain from sexual relations. Radical women made a decisive break with their nineteenth-century predecessors by demanding artificial methods of birth control for the purposes of both fertility control and sexual pleasure. The anarchist Emma Goldman defied the Comstock Law by smuggling contraceptive devices into the country and disseminating pamphlets on birth control methods. Margaret Sanger, a socialist and public-health nurse, called for women's reproductive freedom in the journal Woman Rebel, which she edited and distributed at political meetings and labor union events. As a result, many working-class people wrote to Sanger seeking contraceptive information. After publishing several issues of the journal, Sanger was indicted under the Comstock Law. Rather than face jail, she left the country for England.

Sanger's writings and the subsequent arrest and conviction of her husband for distributing them gained widespread support and publicity for the birth control cause. Many middle- and upper-class liberals added their voices to the movement and organized to repeal the laws prohibiting the free distribution of contraceptive information. When Sanger returned to the United States after several months, the federal government dropped the charges against her to avoid further publicity.

During the next few years Sanger and other activists spoke widely on the issue of birth control, developed national support, and helped to establish birth control leagues and clinics staffed by women reformers. By the 1920s, however, the movement had shifted in a conservative direction. In response to political repression and the decline of feminism, Sanger and her followers distanced themselves from left-wing causes and increasingly sought the support of the medical profession. As physicians assumed a larger role, the movement advocated birth control as a matter of family planning and population control, rather than as a key element in the struggle for women's liberation. Nevertheless, birth control advocates made important gains during this period. By 1930 more than three hundred clinics throughout the country were providing contraceptive information and devices to American women. A major legislative victory came in 1936 when a federal appeals court overturned the anticontraception provisions of the Comstock Law.

thorities on modern marriage, criticized moralists who thought of sex as "ugliness, original sin, and fig leaves." Sexual repression, he and others argued, threatened to undermine marriage, the very institution it was designed to uphold, by causing frustration, anxiety, and illicit affairs. As one commentator warned, "Futile repression ends in volcanic upheaval and a fresh outbreak of license." Sex modernists proposed to deal with this crisis by "sexualizing" marriage. They promoted an ideal of companionate marriage that emphasized the importance of sexual pleasure for husbands and wives. Spouses were encouraged to be both amiable companions and pleasing sexual partners. Proponents advocated early marriage and the use of birth control to enhance sexual pleasure for couples without the fear of unwanted pregnancy.

The new ideal of marriage required new attitudes and behaviors from both sexes. Men were expected to demonstrate a vigorous sex drive; those who did not, appeared feeble and unmanly, and raised suspicions of homosexuality. Women were called on to keep the thrill in marriage by carefully maintaining their appearance. Films and advertisements, new shapers of sexual mores in the twentieth century, bombarded women with the message that "The first duty of woman is to attract." Sexual liberalism was intricately linked to consumer capitalism. To enhance their sex appeal, women were told they needed to buy cosmetics, mouthwash, stylish clothes, and a wide array of other consumer products. Even as modern sex reformers departed from an ideology of sexual restraint, they established rigid boundaries between "normal" and "deviant" behavior. Clear limits were placed on women's sexual behavior. They were expected to be sexually alluring but not promiscuous; to arouse male desire but not to initiate or control romantic relations; and, most important, to channel their sexual desires into marriage. Those who transgressed these boundaries faced serious consequences.

Even more than female promiscuity, sexual liberalism targeted homosexuality as a particularly deviant form of behavior. Drawing on the work of late-nineteenth-century physicians, modern sex theorists rejected the earlier view of homosexuality as sinful behavior of which anyone was capable, and instead characterized it as an abnormal or diseased condition associated with a particular type of individual. Initially medical authorities scrutinized the traits and life-styles of male homosexuals only, but with the new awareness of women's sexuality in the 1920s, they also identified lesbianism as a serious social problem.

Women's intimate friendships became increasingly suspect to those eager to channel female sexuality into heterosexual marriage. Physicians and psychologists debated whether homosexuality was an acquired form of mental illness or a congenital defect; in either case, they called for strict regulation and methods of correction. Homosexual men and women were subjected to a range of medical procedures designed to "cure" their condition, from psychotherapy and hypnosis to castration, hysterectomy, and lobotomy.

Blacks, too, were defined as sexual deviants who required careful monitoring and control. The stereotype of the black man as lustful aggressor continued to have great cultural force in white America even after slavery and was used to justify the murder and torture of blacks. Defenders of white supremacy continually raised the specter of the black male rapist assaulting the southern white woman. This became the most common defense for the widespread lynching of black men in the late nineteenth and twentieth centuries. Between 1889 and 1941 at least 3,811 blacks were lynched in the South. South Carolina senator Benjamin Tillman defended the practice before his colleagues in Washington in a typical fashion: "When stern and sad-faced white men put to death a creature in human form who has deflowered a white woman, they have avenged the greatest wrong, the blackest crime." In reality, few lynchings were associated with sexual assault. A 1931 study revealed that only one-sixth of the lynch victims between 1889 and 1929 were even accused of rape. The primary purpose of this brutal act was to instill terror in blacks and to maintain the system of white supremacy.

The stereotype of black female promiscuity also persisted into the twentieth century and shaped public policy in numerous ways. Birth control and family planning experts persistently portrayed black women as careless breeders and promoted contraception as a way to limit the reproduction of blacks and other "defective" groups. As Sanger argued at one point, birth control would produce "more children from the fit, less from the unfit." Many southern states, usually conservative on sexual issues, encouraged birth control in the 1930s to stem the tide of black population growth. Reproduction abuse of nonwhite women continued in the post–World War II era, when physicians and public health officials targeted poor black, Hispanic, and Native American women for sterilization, often without obtaining their informed consent. Contrary to the racist views that informed such policies, black fertility

There is nothing safe about sex. There never will be.

NORMAN MAILER

♦ **Lobotomy**
Surgical severance of nerve fibers connecting the frontal lobes to the thalamus for the relief of some mental disorders

**SEXUAL BEHAVIOR
AND MORALITY**

*The Rise and Fall of
Sexual Liberalism*

*If all the girls at
Smith and
Bennington were
laid end to end,
I wouldn't be
surprised.*

DOROTHY PARKER
HUMORIST, QUOTED IN
GEORGE S. KAUFMAN
AND HIS FRIENDS

rates declined steadily after the turn of the century; by 1945, black women bore an average of 2.5 children.

Clearly, the sexual behavior of Americans did not always conform to dominant liberal values. Alfred Kinsey's studies of male and female sexual behavior, published in 1948 and 1953, indicated a sharp conflict between sexual practices and publicly espoused ideals. Ninety percent of the men and 50 percent of the women surveyed had engaged in premarital intercourse, and half of the men and a quarter of the women had had extramarital relations. Kinsey's findings about homosexuality proved even more shocking to conventional values. Fifty percent of the men acknowledged feeling homosexual desire, and more than a third had engaged in homosexual activity as adults.

Despite the conflict between behavior and ideals revealed in the Kinsey reports, most Americans did not publicly question established sexual values and institutions. It was not until the 1960s, with the rise of the youth, feminist, and gay liberation movements, that many began to challenge the ideological dominance of sexual liberalism—acknowledgment of the importance of sexuality, as long as sex remained heterosexual, noninterracial, and largely confined to marriage—in the United States. Stirred by the civil rights struggle, middle-class college students engaged in protest movements to demand free speech on college campuses and to oppose the draft and the war in Vietnam. The student movement included a cultural as well as a political critique of American society. Youth in the 1960s rejected the mores of capitalist society to explore alternative life-styles and values. A hippie counterculture took shape in cities and university towns as young people experimented with new forms of dress and hairstyles, freer sexual behavior, rock music, and hallucinatory drugs. San Francisco's Haight-Ashbury district became a hippie mecca where thousands of "flower children" flocked during the "Summer of Love" of 1967. Some young men and women rejected traditional family arrangements by forming communes where they practiced open sexual unions and raised children in common.

Through their participation in civil rights and student protests, college women gained political skills and a radical ideology that led them to question established gender roles and sexual relations. As they applied the principles of democracy and egalitarianism to their own lives, women activists became increasingly dissatisfied with their marginal role within the student movement and society in general, and broke away to organize a movement for their own liberation. From the beginning, issues of sexuality lay at the heart of the women's liberation movement. Feminists called for a fundamental restructuring of marriage, family, and sexuality—those aspects of life which previously had been defined as private and personal. "The personal is political" became a rallying cry of the movement.

Feminists mounted a sharp critique of the widespread sexual objectification of women in American culture. In one of the first political acts of women's liberation, radical women protested the 1968 Miss America pageant in Atlantic City by crowning a live sheep as queen and throwing girdles, bras, high-heeled shoes, and curlers into a "freedom trashcan." Others challenged confining sexual images and roles by protesting bridal fairs and the distribution of *Playboy* on college campuses. Feminists redefined rape and sexual harassment as political problems that contributed to gender oppression. They ran seminars and established rape crisis centers to provide women with the resources and support to deal with sexual violence and abuse.

While they addressed sexual dangers, activists also called for enhancement of women's sexual pleasure. In a famous article, "The Myth of the Vaginal Orgasm," published in *Radical Feminism* (1973), Anne Koedt charged that women's pleasure had been defined in terms of men's needs and desires. She and other feminists drew on studies by Kinsey and Masters and Johnson that disputed Freudian theory by locating the source of the female orgasm in the clitoris rather than the vagina. Knowledge of the clitoral orgasm, Koedt contended, demanded greater attention to women's desires in heterosexual relations. More significant still, it challenged the very institutions of heterosexuality and marriage by indicating "that sexual pleasure was obtainable from either men or women, thus making heterosexuality not an absolute, but an option" (p. 206).

One of the central battles over sexuality was feminists' fight for reproductive freedom. The growing availability of birth control pills in the 1960s greatly facilitated women's ability to control their fertility, but the nineteenth-century criminal abortion laws remained a major barrier. In the early 1960s physicians and public-health officials organized to reform existing abortion statutes by broadening the conditions under which doctors could recommend abortion. In the late 1960s feminists decisively altered the terms of the debate by arguing that abortion was a woman's right and demanding the repeal of all restrictions on abortion. To build support for the cause, activists staged teach-ins, conducted petition drives, and engaged in civil disobedience by referring women to abortionists. An important legislative landmark was the Supreme Court decision in *Roe* v. *Wade* in 1973, which invalidated state laws that prohibited abortions in the first trimester and made abortions in the second trimester easier to obtain.

The central tenets of sexual liberalism were further challenged by the gay liberation movement, which flowered in the 1970s after several decades of change within gay communities. The gay subcultures and networks that had emerged in the early twentieth century expanded greatly during World War II, when millions of men and women left families, small towns, and farms to serve in the armed forces or to seek jobs in large cities. Living in sex-segregated environments outside of family contexts allowed many men and women to explore same-sex relationships for the first time in their lives. This period of discovery was followed by one of fierce repression during the McCarthy era. According to anticommunist crusaders, homosexuals posed a serious threat to both national security and the preservation of the traditional family. As a result of cold war politics, gay men and lesbians were purged from the armed forces and government jobs and subjected to increased criminal prosecution and police harassment. The severe repression disrupted and destroyed many lives, but it also forged a minority group consciousness among gays. With the founding of the Mattachine Society and the Daughters of Bilitis in the 1950s, a small political movement took root that aimed to secure better treatment and a more positive image of homosexuals in American society.

The feminist and gay liberation movements did not bring about a radical transformation of American society, but they did contribute to decisive shifts in sexual attitudes and behavior. After the 1960s, there was much greater tolerance for and incidence of nonmarital sexual activity. Youth were far more likely to have premarital intercourse than those of earlier decades, often with partners they did not expect to marry. The rate of premarital sex increased most sharply among women, due in part to the easier access to birth control and abortion. Compared with the 1950s, couples married later and had fewer children. Numerous couples chose to remain childless, and many others lived together openly without being married, an arrangement that earlier would have aroused great social condemnation, especially for women. De-

THE STONEWALL RIOT

Beginning of the Gay Rights Movement

The Stonewall Riot in June 1969 led to a radical change in the nature of gay politics. When police conducted a routine raid of the Stonewall Inn, a gay bar in Greenwich Village, customers and bystanders did not respond in a routine fashion. Instead of tolerating the arrests, they fought back by throwing beer cans and bottles, and rioting throughout the night. The Gay Liberation Front, formed in the wake of the Stonewall, dispensed with respectable politics and polite demands for equal treatment. Influenced by the tactics and ideology of feminism and the black power movement, activists made a bold call for "gay power" and the revolutionary transformation of existing social institutions, specifically the system of heterosexuality and the nuclear family structure that upheld it. Gay activists repudiated the pervasive conception of homosexuality as disease and declared that same-sex desire was a normal, human capacity that had been repressed by family and society. The gay liberation movement grew rapidly throughout the 1970s and led millions of men and women across the country to "come out," to publicly acknowledge and take pride in their gay identity. The movement also had a decisive impact on public policies and attitudes. By the end of the 1970s, half of the states had repealed their sodomy laws and numerous cities, including Houston, Los Angeles, Detroit, and Washington, D.C., amended their civil rights statutes to include provisions that prohibited discrimination on the basis of sexual orientation. In 1974 the American Psychiatric Association reversed a long-held position by removing homosexuality from its list of mental disorders.

clining fertility and marriage rates meant that motherhood did not occupy the central part of women's lives that it once had. The gay movement encouraged millions of men and women to live outside of the institution of heterosexuality altogether and to establish same-sex relationships. These various developments contributed to a marked decline in traditional nuclear family arrangements. By the 1980s, only about 10 percent of all American households adhered to the traditional model of two parents with two or more

See also
The Plantation

children at home and the husband as the sole breadwinner.

The vast changes in sexual mores and family life since the 1960s provoked a conservative political movement that aimed to restore traditional moral values and turn back the gains of feminism and gay liberation. The religious-based New Right organized a powerful political coalition around a "pro-family" ideology that defended traditional family and gender roles and opposed sexual expression outside of the marital, reproductive framework. New Right activists opposed sex education in the school, teenage sexuality, women's access to abortion, and gay rights. They enlisted the support of groups such as the fundamentalist Moral Majority and the National Right to Life Committee and called on television preachers Jerry Falwell, Pat Robertson, and Jim Bakker to mobilize the millions of evangelical Protestants behind their cause. In the 1980 election, presidential candidate Ronald Reagan actively courted the support of the New Right by endorsing its position on abortion and other "pro-family" policies. With Reagan's landslide victory, moral conservatives found strong support from the federal government.

New Right leaders specifically targeted abortion and gay rights as areas for enforcing their moral agenda. "Right-to-life" committees organized a national campaign for a "human life amendment" to the Constitution that would de-

clare the fetus to be a human person and thus make abortion equivalent to murder. Although this amendment was never enacted, the antiabortion activists did secure the passage of the Hyde Amendment in 1977, which prohibited the use of federal funds to pay for or promote abortions, thereby sharply curtailing poor women's access to abortion services. At the state level, many legislatures began to require parental or spousal consent before abortions were performed on unmarried minors or on wives.

The New Right also succeeded in restricting gay rights. Former beauty queen Anita Bryant led a successful campaign to repeal the gay rights ordinance in Dade County, Florida, in 1977. Encouraged by Bryant's victory, conservatives successfully defeated similar ordinances in other cities, including Saint Paul, Minnesota, Wichita, Kansas, and Eugene, Oregon. New Right activists also called on the federal government to prohibit the employment of gays in any "public sector" or "high visibility public jobs," and to prohibit federal funding of any organization which "suggests" that homosexuality "can be an acceptable lifestyle." They had less success in securing federal legislation, but they influenced President Reagan to appoint moral conservatives to the federal judiciary. In 1986 the Supreme Court expressed its New Right leanings by affirming the constitutionality of sodomy laws that prohibit homosexuality in the *Bowers* v. *Hardwick* decision.

The AIDS epidemic struck a further blow to gay communities in the United States. In 1981 physicians identified a deadly new disease among gay men who were dying from rare forms of cancer and pneumonia. Acquired Immune Deficiency Syndrome, or AIDS, as it is called, is the destruction of the body's immune system making the victim susceptible to life-threatening opportunistic infections. In 1983 medical researchers discovered and most medical professionals believed that the disease was caused by a virus transmitted through the exchange of blood and semen. With no cure in sight, the case-load grew at an alarming pace: from 225 in 1981 to 40,000 in 1987. Although gay men have constituted the great majority of AIDS sufferers, they are not the only ones at risk for the disease. Researchers have learned that the virus is also transmitted through heterosexual intercourse, blood transfusions, and the sharing of unsterilized needles by intravenous-drug users. The AIDS crisis has greatly curtailed sexual experimentation and casual encounters among both heterosexuals and gays.

American society has been sharply divided over how to respond to the epidemic. New Right leaders, claiming that AIDS is a divine retribution for homosexuals, supported proposals for the quarantine of those infected with the virus, the reenactment of sodomy laws in states where they have been overturned, and the removal of people with AIDS from schools, jobs, and housing. Strengthened by decades of activism, gay people vigorously protested such discriminatory policies and the inaction of the federal government in face of the crisis. Drawing on the resources of their own communities, gays have raised funds for AIDS education and research; recruited thousands of volunteers to provide services, counseling, and information for the sick; and organized effective "safe sex" educational campaigns. Even members of the conservative Reagan administration had conflicting ideas about how to deal with AIDS. Secretary of Education William Bennett called for educational materials that promoted sexual abstinence as the only effective means of preventing AIDS, while Surgeon General C. Everett Koop urged comprehensive sex education in the schools that informed youth about the effectiveness of condoms. The continuation of the AIDS epidemic ensures that sexuality will remain a divisive issue at the center of American politics for years to come.

The very notion of a history of sexuality challenges a long-held understanding of sexuality as a fixed biological instinct present in all individuals.

Such a conception cannot account for the wide variety of sexual patterns and meanings found within different historical periods and among different cultures. In American society, sexual behavior, ideologies, and methods of regulation have undergone major transformations from the seventeenth century to the present, a result of social, economic, and political developments. Patterns of sexual life have also varied in important ways according to class, race, ethnicity, and region. Throughout American history sexuality has been a site of struggle and conflict. Dominant groups in society have asserted political power and cultural authority over blacks, ethnic minorities, women, and gays through the control and organization of sexuality. These efforts have, in turn, met with resistance by subordinate groups and positive assertions of alternative sexual identities.

—MARY E. ODEM

SPORTS THROUGH THE NINETEENTH CENTURY

Sports as we know them are a very recent phenomenon. Not until the end of the nineteenth century did many of the features we take for granted become part of sports. Indeed, our usage of the word is rather new. In the eighteenth century, "sport" would more likely have been used in a phrase like "sporting man," or an individual might have been called a "sport." Both terms were less than flattering, for an individual so designated was likely a rake, a gambler, a man who lived by his wits. By 1900, however, "sports" connoted athletic games played by professionals or highly trained amateurs under clearly spelled out rules with masses of paying spectators cheering their favorites in specially built stadia. Events themselves were now supported by businesses or institutions (the National League, the sporting goods firm of A. G. Spalding and Brothers, Yale University, the National Collegiate Athletic Association, for examples), reported in mass-circulation newspapers, and evaluated with statistics. So severed from their folk origins had sports become that one game—basketball—had no past at all; it was simply made up in 1891 by one James Naismith, who worked at the Young Men's Christian Association Training School in Springfield, Massachusetts, as a way to keep athletes in shape between the baseball and football seasons. This essay will trace the

There is no joy in Mudville— mighty Casey has struck out.

ERNEST LAWRENCE THAYER
CASEY AT THE BAT:
A BALLAD OF THE REPUBLIC

♦ Rake

A dissolute person, marked by indulgence in things (as drink or promiscuous sex) deemed vices; a person who is unrestrained by convention or morality

International sport is war without shooting.

GEORGE ORWELL

See also

Parades, Holidays and Public Rituals

transformation of sports from folk games to modern spectacles.

The British Heritage

British colonists seem to have played mainly the games they remembered from their ancestral homeland. Of course North America was not "virgin land"; hundreds of thousands of Indians inhabited the continent. Eastern woodland tribes, for example, played a game colonists called stickball ("lacrosse" for the French), yet the British seem not to have adopted this or other Indian games. Perhaps they felt a need to keep intact all of their folk-ways in this strange land; and perhaps the Indian game was too alien to them, surrounded as it was by the various tribes' customs and observances. After all, Indians often played stickball and other games within a context of sacred dancing, chanting and drumming, shamanism, dietary restrictions, body painting, pipe-smoking, and other ritual practices, all part of a distinct religious worldview.

The English played various games on the eve of colonization, and they held a range of opinions as to the proper place of recreation. No single game was typical, but Richard Carew's description of "hurling" in Cornwall at the beginning of the seventeenth century gives us a sense of what was possible. The countryside for miles around could be the playing field, and the teams consisted of entire parishes:

> *Some two or more Gentlemen doe commonly make this match, appointing that on such a holyday, they will bring to such an indifferent place, two, three, or more parishes of the East or South quarter, to hurle against so many other, of the West or North. Their goales are either those Gentlemens houses, or some townes or villags, three or four miles asunder, of which either side maketh choice after the neernesse to their dwellings. When they meet, there is neyther comparing of numbers, nor matching of men: but a silver ball is cast up, and that company, which can catch, and cary it by force, or sleight, to their place assigned, gaineth the ball and victory.*

To gain the victory, however, men subjected themselves to brutal competition:

> *Whosoever getteth seizure of this ball, findeth himself generally pursued by the adverse party; neither will they leave, till . . . he be laid flat on Gods deare earth. . . . The Hurlers take*

> *their next way over hilles, dales, hedges, ditches; yea, and thorow bushes, briers, mires, plashes and rivers whatsoever; so as you shall sometimes see 20 or 30 lie tugging together in the water, scrambling and scratching for the ball. . . . (*The Quest for Excitement: Sport and Leisure in the Civilizing Process. *Edited by Norbert Elias and Eric Dunning [1986]).*

Whichever team carried the ball to their goal—a church, a manor, a parish seat—won the game.

Note that no restrictions on team size existed, that the playing field was the entire countryside for miles around, and that parish membership determined who played on each team. As Carew described it, the game was singularly violent, and such contests no doubt became ready opportunities to settle old personal grudges or larger community rivalries. Gentlemen arranged the matches, and they undoubtedly offered prizes for the winners, along with a feast for all after the game. These were great men, local nobility or gentry, patrons in the community, whose largesse helped secure the loyalty of their baseborn neighbors. Such games were a social glue, binding men together despite an intensely hierarchical social system. Carew added that hurling helped prepare men for war, for the game required that players know the terrain and anticipate their opponents' movements in order to ambush them. He concluded that hurling "put courage into their hearts, to meete an enemie in the face"; but while the game gave men fortitude, it also left them with bloody heads, broken bones, and injuries that might shorten their days. Though Carew did not mention it, hurling left them with something else—a sense of manhood. Sports like this one seem to have been primarily part of male culture. Implicitly, they defined masculinity—aggressiveness, courage, competitiveness—against femininity. This elemental conception of maleness characterized most sports through the nineteenth century.

Carew wrote his description just as popular recreations were becoming a controversial topic. On the one hand, there was the Renaissance tradition, which celebrated England's national love of play. But on the other, there was the rising tide of Puritanism, a theology suspicious of all worldly pleasures that threatened to divert people from their personal confrontation with God. Just when Jamestown, Plymouth, and Boston were settled the controversy boiled over. King James I issued his "Book of Sports" (1618) to reassure his subjects that the crown still approved their old entertainments:

Our pleasure likewise is, Our good people be not disturbed, letted, or discouraged from any lawful recreation, Such as dancing, either of men or women, Archery for men, leaping, vaulting, or any other such harmlesse, Recreation, nor from having of May Games, Whitson Ales, and Morris-dances, and the setting up of Maypoles, and other sports. . . . (quoted in Popular Recreations, *p. 7)*

The "Book of Sports" was a rebuke to the Puritans who insisted that the Sabbath must be spent solely in prayer and quiet introspection. Puritans responded that the very recreations the king praised led away from God to superstition and idolatry, to sin and wickedness. So powerful were the Puritans in many parishes that they refused to promulgate the king's decree. They enforced their pious Sabbath, and also banned as "corrupt" and "pagan" the festivals and saints days of the Catholic and Anglican calendars.

The middle decades of the seventeenth century saw the triumph of Puritanism under Oliver Cromwell, then its demise during the Restoration of the monarchy. The ideological battles fought in England were part of the heritage of those who initially settled the British colonies. Some who migrated were champions of Puritan piety, but others bore the tradition of country recreations, of feast days, cockfights, and ball games.

Early American Sports

In the Old World and the New, Puritans (or Calvinists) were suspicious of excessive worldly joys. Those who envisioned godly communities in the wilderness found human nature inherently untrustworthy, too much leisure dangerous, and work a holy endeavor. Sober religious folk were determined to keep amusements hedged within useful and moderate bounds, which threatened to constrict until they contained nothing at all. Yet others shaped their visions of the New World by the age-old ideal of a leisured paradise. These individuals dreamed of a toilless and bountiful life, and the English heritage of fairs, feast days, and sports became the palpable expression of the leisure ethic. The seeming boundlessness of the New World stirred their imaginations.

All of England's North American colonies inherited the dual-leisure tradition. Many colonial Virginians held Calvinist beliefs in original sin, predestination, and election; many came from pious middle-class stock. On the other hand, the Massachusetts Bay Colony was plagued by people who rejected Puritan hegemony, and by individuals who would rather play than work. But as a general rule, austerity was stronger in the North, while leisure found fuller expression in the South.

Early Virginia was disproportionately settled by men, and a boom in tobacco growing in the 1620s gave the colony the raucous tone of a mining camp. Drinking, gambling, and many of the pastimes of Old England flourished; with social status unclear and land abundant and unfenced, hunting, fishing and fowling, sports of the privileged back home, could be enjoyed by all. Within a generation, however, a gentry elite had established itself. Often from well-off families, these men controlled the labor of others through a system of indentured servitude, followed by black chattel slavery. By 1700, the southern colonies constituted a highly stratified society, with a planter elite that styled itself after the English country gentry, a middling group of white farmers, and a large body of black slaves.

The early boom economy, with its lack of settled domestic life, encouraged men's willingness to follow bouts of hard moneymaking with interludes of abandon. Later, the rhythms of the plantation, of sowing, tending, and harvesting, encouraged alternating periods of work and idleness rather than regular sustained labor. As the colony settled into a stable, highly stratified pattern late in the seventeenth century, the old English leisure ideal well served Virginia's social alignments. Men in this environment worked hard, but not with the Puritan's regularity, diligence, or sense of the transcendent godliness of labor. For the gentry on both sides of the Atlantic, to celebrate leisure, especially to do so with enormous wagers, was a way to identify themselves as members of a distinct ruling class, regardless of the poverty or ruthless competitiveness of their ancestors.

So several factors came together by the beginning of the eighteenth century to help make play a dominant southern value: the English leisure heritage, the erosion of the Calvinist notion of calling among the most influential men in the South, and the rise of the rural gentry to ruling-class status. But one more element was crucial. Black chattel slavery drove the final wedge between labor and leisure. How could men value hard work unequivocally once labor was inextricably associated with degraded, servile blacks? How pretend that work was ennobling, character forming, even sanctified in a society whose

Sports do not build character. They reveal it.

HEYWOOD BROWN

*Baseball is the very
symbol of the
outward and visible
expression of the
drive and push and
rush and struggle of
the raging, tearing,
booming nineteenth
century.*

MARK TWAIN
SPEECH (APRIL 1889)

hardest workers were seen as dangerous, half-civilized heathens, capable of nothing but brutish tasks?

For all of these reasons, sports and games became a major preoccupation in Virginia and the other southern colonies. Games and amusements were important to all classes, but by the end of the seventeenth century, the gentry had the time, motivation, and means for great displays of consumption and conviviality. As class lines became distinct during the new century, roughly two or three hundred tidewater families comprised Virginia's aristocracy. Knit together by kinship ties, they shared a gracious life in which leisure lay at the heart of their class style and identity. Horse racing, cock-fighting, and hunting were the great gentry passions. Men also eagerly participated in boating, wrestling, fencing, quoits (something like horseshoes), bowling, and cudgeling (fighting with long sticks).

Educated in England like so many young colonial men, the rich and accomplished William Byrd II (1674–1744), for example, participated in the whole panoply of English sporting customs on his enormous family estate at Westover, early in the eighteenth century. He played billiards, laid out a bowling green, competed in cricket, ninepins, and skittles. Wealthy Virginians like Byrd seized every opportunity for merrymaking, including dancing, partying, or gambling over a sociable bottle. Religion and law now buttressed rather than assailed these practices. Ministers of the Anglican church, whose congregations often depended on the patronage of local gentry, offered little resistance to the ethic of leisure, while county courts recognized gambling debts as legally enforceable.

Timothy H. Breen has demonstrated how a horse race among the Virginia gentry facilitated great displays of wealth, personal honor, and patriarchal prestige. The "merry-dispos'd gentlemen" of Hanover County who celebrated Saint Andrews Day in the 1730s with quarter-horse races did so to cultivate social solidarity, vent their competitiveness, and enjoy each others' company. Spectators could observe their betters, provided they "behave themselves with Decency and Sobriety, the Subscribers being resolved to discountenance all Immorality with the utmost Rigour." As Breen points out, however, what made horse races so central to southern culture was the dramatic tension between control and abandon. On the one hand, events should be orderly, reflecting the good harmony of the new society; they should be moderate, not leading men to licentiousness or excess;

and they should not become too distracting from productive endeavors. But on the other hand, sport as a vehicle for displays of prowess, wealth, and status encouraged men to compete recklessly, to drink, gamble, and assert themselves as if their very social position, even their masculinity, were in question. Time and again, governors and legislators inveighed against the disorderliness that accompanied horse races, but this failed to stop men from impulsively betting entire fortunes on a single race.

Before long, the southern gentry was building English-style circular tracks; importing thoroughbred horses; retaining breeders, trainers, jockeys, and stablemen (often blacks); and generally making racing a central symbol of upper-class life. The gentry, however, did not monopolize popular recreations. Various groups might mingle at a single event. Just as in the example of hurling by Richard Carew, great men would initiate contests, and lesser ones would receive their largesse. Thus, Elkanah Watson described a raucous cockfight in Southampton County, Virginia, at which there were "many genteel people, promiscuously mingled with the vulgar and debased" (*Men and Times of the Revolution; or, Memoirs of Elkanah Watson*, edited by Winslow C. Watson, 2d ed. [1856], pp. 300–301).

Yet on other occasions, events were more segregated. Observed Phillip Vickers Fithian one Easter, "Negroes now are all disbanded till Wednesday morning and are at Cock Fights through the County"; a week later he noticed "a ring of Negroes at the Stable, fighting cocks" (*Journal and Letters of Philip Vickers Fithian, 1773–1774*, edited by Hunter Dickinson Farish, new ed. [1957], pp. 91, 96). Blacks even continued some of the games of Africa in the slave quarters. Moreover, poor and middling whites claimed leisure space for themselves. They held their own races, cockfights, and bear baits; they hunted and fished for pleasure as well as game; they even staged their own ferocious eye-gouging battles. Nonregular working rhythms of plantations, farms, and market towns enabled individuals to find time for such activities. The hours taken in the middle of work could expand to days for annual events such as the "Public Times," held every spring and fall for court and assembly sessions at the county seats. Mid-eighteenth-century Williamsburg, for example, grew to three times its normal population during these events, as individuals watched or participated in horse races, plays, dancing, fiddling, acrobatics, wrestling, and other pleasures.

♦ **Gentry**
*upper or ruling class;
aristocracy*

Whether describing them as leisure-loving or lazy, many commentators have declared that southerners developed a distinct regional ethic, one which rejected labor as the all-consuming goal of life. When they esteemed commerce and enterprise at all, it was less because piling up wealth contained religious or moral value than because productivity facilitated the good life. While gentlemen-planters were not a hereditary aristocracy, they took their cue from great landed Englishmen, embracing sociability, gracious living, and personal polish as core values. Conspicuous consumption rather than rational saving was the hallmark of the region, because displays of luxury and fine living were markers of a man's status in society. Above all, we must not view the southern ethic as aberrant or unique. Nonregular working rhythms, conspicuous display, love of finery, and games and sports, all had deep roots in Western cultures. The compulsion to work steadily and regularly, to make leisure a subordinate value accepted only for its ability to increase one's capacity for labor, and to divide work and play into separate compartmentalized realms were the novel ideas.

Generally, however, conflicts over popular recreations took less dramatic forms. In 1621, Bradford had to deal with some new settlers who objected to working on Christmas Day (the Pilgrims of Plymouth, indeed, the Puritans in general, considered Christmas celebrations part of the pagan hangover of the Catholic church). The governor decided not to force these people to work against their consciences, but when he and the others returned from their labors that day, they found the newcomers "in the street at play, openly; some pitching the bar, and some at stoolball, and such like sports." Bradford took away their sporting toys, not because they played, but because they did so openly: "If they made the keeping of it (Christmas) matter of devotion, let them keep their houses; but there should be no gaming or revelling in the streets" (p. 97). At least the appearance of a godly community would remain, and the diligent not be tempted from their labor.

Dissenting Protestants, Puritans among them, did not object to all recreations. They allowed innocent amusements like simple ball games, played in moderation; hunting and fishing provided food; martial sports like cudgeling or swordplay taught skills useful to the defense of the settlements; sociable activities like cornhuskings, or spinning or quilting bees were encouraged. But they drew the line at recreations that violated the Sabbath, encouraged passion, or smacked of the old pagan excesses. The true test of recreations was their usefulness; proper leisure helped people live righteously by serving useful ends, ends which included refreshing them for work. Thus, even as he condemned profane or promiscuous dancing, Increase Mather observed, "The Prince of Philosophers has observed truly, that Dancing and Leaping, is a natural expression of joy: So that there is no more Sin in it, than in laughter, or any outward expression of inward Rejoycing" ("An Arrow Against Profane and Promiscuous Dancing," [1684] excerpted in Perry Miller and Thomas Johnson, *The Puritans: A Sourcebook of Their Writings*, vol. 2 [1938] p. 411).

This spirit of moderation grew out of the Puritans' dominant theology, Calvinism. After the fall from Eden, they believed, all humankind was tainted with sin. In his mercy, God, through Christ, saved a small number from eternal damnation. In other words, the Lord had predetermined the fate of all people, saving a few for reasons only He understood, damning the rest.

MORTON VS. BRADFORD
Recreation on Plymouth Plantation

Like southerners, the settlers of New England and the middle colonies were heirs to the dual-leisure tradition whose roots were in Western cultures. Yet the North proved a more austere climate for traditional recreations. About 1627, Thomas Morton, a renegade from Puritan society, led a band of like-minded settlers to the edge of Plymouth Colony, and there defied his pious neighbors. William Bradford (1590–1657), governor of Plymouth, accused Morton of atheism and paganism—categories that Puritans tended to conflate. Bradford described the renegades' revels: "They also set up a maypole, drinking and dancing about it many days together, inviting the Indian women for their consorts, dancing and frisking together like so many fairies, or furies, rather . . . as if they had anew revived and celebrated the feasts of the Roman goddess Flora, or the beastly practices of the mad Baccanalians" (*Of Plymouth Plantation: 1620–1647*, edited by Samuel Eliot Morison [1952], pp. 205–206). Morton taunted his Pilgrim neighbors, and they finally responded; in 1628 they cut down the maypole, arrested Morton for selling arms to the Indians, and shipped him back to England in irons.

Golf is a good walk spoiled.

MARK TWAIN

*When you come to a
fork in the road,
take it.*

YOGI BERRA

♦ **Deist**

*One who believes in deism:
a movement or system of
thought advocating natural
religion, emphasizing
morality, and in the 18th
century, denying the
interference of the Creator
with the laws of the
universe*

Since their fates were predestined, it followed that earthly efforts had no impact on people's futures. Nor could one know for sure whether one was among the elect. Still, through constant self-scrutiny, an individual might discover evidence of Christ's grace. Leading an upright life according to God's laws was a sign—albeit, a tenuous one—of salvation.

For the Puritans, an upright life meant far more than merely observing ritual forms. Their idea of "calling"—that laboring diligently in one's worldly occupation was a religious observation—infused daily business life with religious significance. The hardworking farmer or tradesman did the Lord's bidding as surely as the writer of sermons. Work was pleasing to God and it followed that success in one's earthly endeavors might just be a sign of inner grace. But even while individuals strove to succeed in the world, they must never overvalue the material fruits of success. Signs of salvation, not the good life, were what one sought in pursuing one's calling. Even as men's labor bore fruit, they must never overvalue the comforts of life, their eyes must always be on the Lord. Above all, the bond between piety and labor meant that play could never be unequivocally valued in its own right. Whereas southern life turned men away from seeing work as a transcendent value, northerners eyed leisure with suspicion.

It would be a mistake, however, to interpret northern ideas about sports, play, and leisure purely from the Puritan viewpoint. A more accurate depiction would see this cluster of Protestant ideas as a presence that sometimes dominated the northern colonies, sometimes was challenged by less than pious groups, but always made itself felt. In Massachusetts and New England, but also among the Dutch Calvinists of New York and the Quakers of Pennsylvania, ideas like calling and worldly asceticism tempered people's commitment to play. Moreover, the Protestant ethic did not simply fade with the seventeenth century, but rather it washed over communities in successive waves. The various religious awakenings that swept through people's lives from the mid-eighteenth through the early nineteenth centuries always contained a powerful element of Protestant self-control, an austerity that cast suspicious glances at those too immersed in the passions of the world. Indeed, even a deist and man of the world like Benjamin Franklin could not escape the earnest spirit of improvement, the suspicion of frivolity, that was his Protestant heritage.

Nonetheless, the English leisure tradition survived in the North: neither harsh frontier conditions nor Puritan hegemony obviated pleasures of the flesh. Crossroads taverns, community gatherings like elections or muste days, and marketing times tied to rural life were all loci of traditional games. What failed to emerge out of the old folkways was an ethos of leisure conferring social rewards, a cultural challenge to the Puritan work ethic, a way of life like that of the southern gentry which assumed that humans worked to play rather than played so they might work.

One exception to this rule emerged in the eighteenth century in cities like Boston, New York, and Philadelphia. Here an urban gentry began to form, consisting partly of British colonial officials and military officers, partly of newly prosperous merchants, and partly of men of landed wealth who lived and governed from the city. In Philadelphia, for example, such a group rivaled the pious Quakers in political clout. The Philadelphia gentry forged group identity through common membership in such organizations as the Mount Regal Fishing Club, the Dancing Assembly, the Gloucester Hunting Club, and the Jockey Club. In New York, too, balls, plays, dances, horse races, and cockfights were important venues where the new urban elite came to identify with each other. But not only the elites of growing cities were active in leisure pursuits. Tavern keepers, to attract customers, tradesmen and laborers among them, became pioneer promoters of recreations. They provided dart boards and bowling greens; they brought bulls and bears to confront pit bulls; they built rings for cockfights; and they held the stakes for various forms of gambling. By the mid-eighteenth century, then, cities were becoming the focus of a whole new realm of leisure. Here, where individuals were most oriented to the marketplace, recreations took their first steps toward commercialization.

Perhaps it is best to speak of various sporting heritages during the colonial era. By the last quarter of the eighteenth century, sporting events at their most organized might attract a few thousand spectators, rich and poor, mostly white, mostly male, watching thoroughbreds, for example, race for high stakes. Such an event would likely pit two local elites against each other, would be held on a track with grandstands built by a rich jockey club, would even be an annual occasion. But at the other extreme, and certainly more common, would be events centered in the countryside and small towns, where the vast bulk of the population lived. Most common were activities like hunting and fishing, where leisure and labor cannot even be distinguished from each other. The most likely form of "sport" might be simple ball games, played according to uncodified rules with available equipment in pastures or clearings. Folk games and recreations were part of communal preindustrial life; they grew out of face-to-face relationships, and expressed the tensions and cohesiveness of particular localities.

The Antebellum Era

In June 1802, the grand jury sitting in Philadelphia received a petition against Hart's racecourse, a local institution: "This English dissipation of horseracing may be agreeable to a few idle landed gentlemen, who bestow more care in training their horses than educating their children, and it may be amusing to British mercantile agents, and a few landed characters in Philadelphia; but it is in the greatest degree injurious to the mechanical and manufacturing interest, and will tend to our ruin if the nuisance is not removed by your patriotic exertions" (quoted in John Thomas Scharf and Thompson Westcott, *History of Philadelphia 1609–1884* [1884] p. 940). The petition was signed by fifteen hundred mechanics and twelve hundred manufacturers, which in that era generally meant craftsmen who worked in their homes or shops with the aid of families and perhaps an apprentice or journeyman.

The petition was filled with code words: Dissipated idle gentlemen who train horses rather than educate their children will ruin manufacturers without the jury's patriotic exertions. Here is a classic example of republican ideology, that set of ideas that helped drive the colonies to rebel against England, and to form a virtuous commonwealth. On one side, the idleness and dissipation of merchants and landed characters; on the other side, producers motivated by the spirit of hard work. Selfishness, luxury, corruption, in the republican lexicon, versus self-restraint, virtue, communal improvement. The racetrack became a symbol of a serious social and ideological schism.

Sports and leisure, as we have seen, had always had a conflicted history. During the revolutionary era, the Continental Congress outlawed games, sports, the theater, all of the usual amusements, as unfit for a virtuous people embarking on independence. Horse racing returned after the war, but the problem of proper versus improper amusement sharpened during the nineteenth century. The old republican tradition that had emphasized individual self-restraint in the name of communal welfare lived on long after the revolution. But as American society increasingly came under the sway of capitalism and the liberal ideol-ogy that accompanied it, sports and leisure were not immediately liberated from old prejudices. On the contrary, the newfound freedom of Americans to transact business during the antebellum era was accompanied by singularly stern cultural strictures that demanded rigid adherence to tough rules of personal conduct.

Historians have documented a transformation in the American economy that occurred largely during the first half of the nineteenth century. Agricultural production shifted from an orientation toward semi-subsistence and local consumption to market production. Especially with the opening of new lands, the development of inland waterways, and the building of new transportation systems, increasing numbers of farmers produced staples that they sold in national and international markets. Even more important for our purposes, cities burgeoned as centers of trade and manufacturing, while the methods of making goods were transformed. Machine production was part of this process, as was the increasing concentration of productive property in fewer hands, and the growing pull of the marketplace.

The Philadelphia petitioners against Hart's racecourse represented the old, preindustrial economy, in which apprentices learned a trade, and with luck, finally became skilled master craftsmen, and proprietors of their own shops. This system was part of a household economy that produced goods for local markets. Work and family were often contiguous: apprentices lived in the master's house, family members labored alongside the head of the household, and this patriarchal extended family was seen as the font of public order.

The new system was much more recognizably part of the modern capitalist order. Old words like apprentice and journeyman hung on, but working relationships were transformed: employers paid wages or piece rates (as low as they could get away with) to individuals who sold their labor for as much as they could command. Trades were rationalized, the size of firms expanded, and the possibilities of workers ever becoming independent property owners diminished. One tendency that accompanied these changes was the destruction of old craft skills; it was to owners' advantage to break down the production process into simple tasks that required cheap, easily replaceable workers. Moreover, entrepreneurs now found themselves much less burdened with fellow feeling for their employees; young workers lived in boardinghouses until they married and started their own families. The new order was based far less on cus-

Winning means everything! You show me a good loser and I'll show you a loser.

GEORGE STEINBRENNER
NEW YORK YANKEES OWNER

*The game isn't over
till it's over.*

YOGI BERRA

◆ **Dram**

*A small portion of
something to drink*

tomary or paternalistic relationships, much more on contractual ones.

This new organization of society—of productive relationships—had ideological implications. The old Protestant ethic was very serviceable in the new order. Protestantism's emphasis on stable, sober, dependable behavior was useful to a society whose organization of work increasingly demanded time, thrift, and intense specialization of tasks. Sheer productivity for its own sake had religious sanction, while landlords, speculators, and merchants were sometimes seen as manipuiators of markets, accumulators who produced nothing while living extravagantly. For the new middle class, delayed gratification and moral certitude were the cornerstones of society. The economies and social relationships in different parts of the country were not all transformed at once; but the total result, certainly by the middle of the nineteenth century, was a thoroughly changed society. By then, national markets, mass print media, telegraphy, steamships, railroads, voluntary associations, and above all, a powerful consensus of values bound most white, northern Protestant middle-class Americans together. For want of a better term, we can label the ascendant national culture that accompanied social and economic change Victorian.

Like the Puritans, Victorians would never argue that wealth was a sure sign of moral worth, but they did believe in a connection, or in the sociologist Max Weber's term, an "elective affinity", between prosperity and good morals. Capitalists and Evangelicals—often the same people— feared idleness, craved regularity, practiced self-control, and idealized usefulness. The millennial hopes of preachers, the belief in eternal life, in spiritual perfectibility, were as real to the saints as the profits that accrued from temperance, thrift, and hard work. Choosing Christ and controlling social stress were part of a single process; converting employees saved souls and secured a reliable labor force; establishing urban missions helped prepare for the millennium and assured a stable business climate. Business and religion were bound together with an earnest tone of moral certitude.

Victorianism, again like Puritanism, contained seeds of repression for popular recreations. Whereas for the Puritans a sociable dram or a local lottery for a good cause were acceptable, the new Evangelicals often condemned such practices as sinful, insisting on an unprecedented level of asceticism. Virtually every recreational outlet was condemned at one time or another, from cock-fighting to checkers, from horse racing to croquet. All leisure activities potentially fostered the evils of drinking, gambling, swearing, idleness, and Sabbath breaking. Declared a Congregational magazine, the *New, Englander,* in 1851, "Let our readers, one and all, remember that we were sent into the world, not for sport and amusement, but for labor; not to enjoy and please ourselves, but to serve and glorify God, and be useful to our fellow men." In a similar vein, William A. Alcott warned youthful readers in his *Young Man's Guide* (1833), "Everyman who enjoys the privilege of civilized society, owes it to that society to earn as much as he can, or in other words, to improve every minute of his time. He who loses an hour or a minute, is the price of that hour debtor to the community. Moreover, it is a debt which he can never repay." Even in the West, where the constraints of civilization supposedly were left behind, and the South, where the slave system encouraged an ethic of leisure, Victorianism found staunch adherents, and the wilder the sports, the more strenuous reformers were in suppressing all that stood in the way of the City of God and the progress of man.

Yet there were powerful countertrends. The same transformations that gave rise to the Victorian ethic of hard work and sober self-control also created an environment potentially conducive to popular recreations. By divorcing work from the extended family of shop and farm, the new capitalist order freed men and women not only to labor as best they could, but also to spend their leisure time according to their own lights. One of the constant refrains heard from antebellum reformers regarded the dangers of young people roaming the streets, free to go to theaters, gambling houses, dance halls, bars, and other places of recreation.

By midcentury a distinct working-class subculture had emerged in American cities, especially New York, and for young unmarried men, sports were an important part of that subculture. A cluster of images captures the scene: the volunteer fire companies where men gathered to drink, play cards, and occasionally display their heroics as fire fighters; ward-bosses in city politics who knew how to distribute largesse and secure elections with the aid of ballot-box stuffers and strong-arm enforcers; the Bowery in New York (and little Bowerys in other cities) where theaters packed in the crowds for melodramas, and working-class men donned the distinctive dress of the "Bowery B'hoy"; taverns where men treated each other to round after round of drinks, and where sporting events like cockfights, bare-knuckle boxing matches, or bull-baits were arranged or staged.

Beyond the working class and immigrant sporting underground, there were other factors contributing to the rise of sports. Steam-power printing, telegraphy, and the penny press all could be used to disseminate sporting news. America's first sporting magazine appeared in the second decade of the nineteenth century, and there were three new magazines in each of the next three decades, four in the 1850s, and nine in the 1860s. The *Spirit of the Times* became a main source of sporting news beginning in the 1830s, but before long, cheap working-class daily newspapers like the *New York Herald* covered sports with depth and regularity. Steamboats and railroads carried runners, or boxers, or thoroughbreds to matches; manufacturers marketed cricket bats, billiard tables, and archery equipment; telegraph lines flashed news of important contests. Perhaps most important, cities grew at an unprecedented pace during the antebellum era—nine had populations over one hundred thousand by 1860—creating a new potential market for popular entertainment like sports. Although America remained predominantly rural, cities, as nodes of production and distribution, had growing cultural influence.

Increasingly, recreation was transformed into entertainment, a sort of cultural goods to be purchased with earnings. Minstrel shows, melodramas, popular museums like P. T. Barnum's in New York (1842), circuses, pleasure gardens, and sporting events all became cultural commodities. Control of thoroughbred racing in this era passed from the hands of landed gentlemen to promoters who organized yearly meetings and standardized rules; boxing came into its own, as fight organizers coined money chartering trains and boats to transport fans to the scenes of battle; and by the 1850s the old folk game of baseball developed clubs and leagues which began charging admission to games and paying players. Pedestrianism, as foot racing was called, came as close as any sport to the modern athletic events of today. Wealthy socialite John Cox Stevens initiated the commercialization with a challenge in 1835 to pay $1,000 to the first man to run ten miles in under an hour. Roughly thirty thousand spectators showed up at the Union Race Course on Long Island to watch a field of runners take up the challenge. Over the next twenty-five years, crowds up to fifty thousand would cheer as runners competed for purses as large as $4,000. In an era when the average laborer earned something around $200 a year, the contests were irresistible to young athletic men, some of whom made a living traveling from race to race.

But athletics on this scale remained rare. Some sports, harness racing prime among them, displayed important "modern" characteristics—standardized rules, the keeping of statistics, regular schedules, and so forth—and some events attracted massive newspaper coverage and paid athletes handsomely. The $10,000 championship prizefight between Yankee Sullivan and Tom Hyer in 1849 is a good example. But mass spectator events remained rare. Professionalism was still unusual, profits secondary, organizations informal, and scheduling irregular. Sports as a commodity were in their infancy, far from the regular, profitable, well-managed, repeatable spectacles of the twentieth century.

Voluntary association more than money motivated this early stage of sports development. This was certainly true of most events in which working-class men watched or participated. Often

POPULAR ENTERTAINMENT

P. T. Barnum, of the popular New York museum bearing his name, poses for a photo with Tom Thumb, whom he sponsored.
CORBIS-BETTMANN

Sports may be what Americans talk about best.

THOMAS BOSWELL
WASHINGTON POST
COLUMNIST

their contests played out ethnic rivalries, especially Irish versus native-born. Similarly, young Germans who migrated to America after the abortive revolution of 1848 brought their Turner societies over from the old country. These organizations (the name comes from *Turnerbund,* literally "gymnastic society") blended nationalism, anticlericalism, and utopian socialism. As part of their program of universal education to prepare men for political and social democracy, the Turner groups placed great emphasis on gymnastic training and sponsored competitions of athletic skill. Similarly, Scottish immigrants in the 1850s replicated their track-and-field events in the Caledonian games. In these and other cases, ethnic

THE BIRTH OF BASEBALL

Like other sporting institutions, baseball also first became organized around the club ideal, and we still refer to multimillion dollar businesses as "ball clubs." Folk versions of baseball had been around for centuries, but in 1845, the New York Knickerbocker Baseball Club became America's first organized team. Merchants, professionals, clerks, and a handful of tradesmen were members of the club during its first fifteen years. By 1858, sixty teams affiliated together as the National Association of Base Ball Players. In part their goal was to prevent the sport from becoming a vulgar commercial spectacle. Early on, clubs tried to assure the social status of the game by excluding men lower down on the pecking order, by keeping the game open mainly to society's upper half. Certainly every mechanic and laborer could not take off whole afternoons for practice as the National Association clubs did, nor could they afford the elaborate banquets that followed games. But a ball, a bat, and an empty lot were easily procured, and before long, fire fighters, policemen, teachers, bartenders, and others organized their own clubs all over America. Some of the working-class teams were so good they began charging admission to their games and paying players. Betting, drinking, and boisterous cheering often accompanied these games. Distasteful as the low-caste game was, amateur clubs quietly conceded to professionalization when they purchased the services of "ringers."

groups helped perpetuate their identity through sports, even as outsiders sometimes attended competitions as spectators. Sports, then, could become a point of solidarity for foreign groups in an alien environment.

Men of the upper class, too, organized new sporting institutions. Metropolitan, university, and union clubs both symbolized and buttressed class prerogatives, reinforcing elite styles of dress, speech, and values, while creating new social and business networks. In the two decades before the Civil War, cricket, racquet, yacht, and rowing clubs began to spring up as exclusive men's organizations. The ubiquitous John Cox Stevens, for example, founded the New York Yacht Club in 1844, which attracted some of the city's leading men. When Stevens's yacht, *America,* defeated eighteen British rivals in the first America's Cup Race (1851), other cities quickly organized their own yacht clubs, and these spun out webs of social activities including balls and cruises. Boat clubs, crew teams, and regattas arose at prestigious Ivy League colleges, and in 1852, Harvard and Yale oarsmen competed in the nation's first—albeit informal—intercollegiate athletic contest. The embryonic alliance between sport and capitalism is especially clear in this example, because the Boston, Concord, and Montreal Railroad sponsored the regatta and paid all of the expenses as a business promotion.

By the Civil War sports had grown more prominent than ever in American life. Some of the games we recognize in the twentieth century—baseball, boxing, track and field prime among them—were no longer purely folk events. An occasional horse race, especially one pitting a thoroughbred from the North against one from the South, might even attract as many as fifty thousand people and dominate the news for a few days. But if sports proliferated in this era, they were neither highly organized nor well integrated into the larger society. The permanent arenas, regular schedules, massive coverage, compulsive record keeping, and high salaries we associate with modern sports were largely missing. Above all, still absent was an ideology of sports appropriate for a modern, capitalist, bourgeois society.

As the antebellum era came to a close, however, the outline of such an ideology was beginning to appear. The same nationalism that encouraged some to define American's mission as virtuous hard work caused others to wish for a nation of vigorous, physically fit men. Oliver Wendell Holmes, Sr., was one who sounded the alarm:

"I am satisfied that such a set of black-coated, stiff-jointed, soft-muscled, paste-complexioned youth as we can boast in our Atlantic cities never before sprang from loins of Anglo-Saxon lineage. . . ." ("The Autocrat of the Breakfast-Table," *Atlantic Monthly* 1, no. 6 [1858], 881). Like many others of the northern intellectual and social elite—Thomas Wentworth Higginson, Catherine Beecher, Horace Mann, Ralph Waldo Emerson, Walt Whitman among them—Holmes began calling for vigorous exercise for American youth. But these early sports advocates were careful to denounce raucous dissipations. The spirit of improvement, the progress of the race, the innocence of play were their ideals.

An avant-garde of clergymen, journalists, and reformers began the chant. Henry David Thoreau believed that "the body existed for the highest development of the soul" (Bradford Torrey and Francis H. Allen, eds. *The Journal of Henry David Thoreau*, vol. 1 [1962] p. 176), so he advocated not stuffy exercises like calisthenics, nor artificial games like baseball, but activities that immersed one in nature, such as walking, swimming, and rowing. Drawing on romantic faith in human perfectibility, men like Walt Whitman began to view the body as divine, and reformers like the Unitarian minister William Ellery Channing advocated wholesome recreations as part of the larger reform agenda. These early "muscular Christians," as they were sometimes called on both sides of the Atlantic, could advocate recreations with missionary zeal. Declared Frederic W. Sawyer in his influential *Plea for Amusements* (1847): "The moral, social, and religious advancement of the people of this country, for the next half century, depends more upon the principles that are adopted with regard to amusements generally, and how those principles are carried out, than to a great many other things of apparently greater moment" (p. 291). Sawyer argued that moral amusements could displace immoral ones, gymnasiums, for example, supplanting smoke-filled billiard halls. While more orthodox individuals scoffed at such suggestions, the tide seemed to be running in favor of liberal reformers and religionists. In colleges, the sons of America's elites began to participate in the earliest intercollegiate athletic competitions. Amherst, Brown, Yale, and Williams led the way. But in the popular imagination, too, bodily health took on new importance. The Cincinnati *Star in the West*, 6 December 1856, for example declared it equally sinful to neglect the body as the spirit or intellect: "God made man to develop all his faculties to the highest possible degree—to stand erect with broad shoulders and expanding lungs, a picture of physical and moral perfection."

These first glimmerings of modern sports were highly gendered—broad shoulders and expanding lungs were "manly" ideals—and while some reformers like Catherine Beecher recommended athletics for young women, the overwhelming emphasis of these early years was on sports for men. In important ways, the language of the new athletic advocates was infused with the rigid gender definitions of bourgeois culture. Sports, it was said, taught independence, self-reliance, courage, discipline—qualities valued in the rough-and-tumble world of business. In domestic ideology, so prominent in the popular culture of this era, women were to domesticate men, but this civilizing process, some feared, threatened to blunt masculine assertiveness in the social, political, and economic spheres. The same society that produced unprecedented quantities of consumer goods associated consumption with femininity and self-denial with manliness. Commercial success, love of luxury, soft living threatened to overwhelm masculine virtues in a sea of goods; spartan and manly sports, a few advanced thinkers seemed to be suggesting, might offer a way out of this trap. Advocating sports in the schools, the New York *Spirit of the Times* declared on 20 June 1857: "The object of education is to make men out of boys. Real live men, not bookworms, not smart fellows, but manly fellows."

So the antebellum era wove several strands of sporting life. In rural areas, gentry sports and country amusements continued. The growing cities witnessed the flowering of a working-class culture that highly valued athletic prowess especially when expressed in the form of ethnic rivalry. While the dominant chord of middle-class Victorianism, especially among Evangelicals, was in opposition to leisure and play, new voices were just beginning to be heard that advocated sports in the name of bourgeois ideals, and as a way to reform the unwashed masses. In the middle decades of the nineteenth century; then, the very structure of society, with its emerging classes, strict division of labor, glimmerings of a consumption ethic, and sharp separation of work time from nonwork time, opened up new opportunities for sports. And a justification for sports began to emerge, clustered around virtuous, bourgeois manliness: gymnastics gave men endurance, baseball promoted discipline, cricket taught self-control. In coming decades, such ideas would flood the nation.

♦ Bourgeois

Marked by a concern for material interests and respectability and a tendency toward mediocrity

Sports in the Gilded Age

In 1810, a free black American, Tom Molineaux, fought for the boxing championship of all England. Britons feared the prowess of this foreigner, yet were reassured by the skill of their champion, Thomas Cribb. The fight proved a great one, and the English press covered the event in minute detail. In America, on the other hand, the bout was scarcely noted. While boxing was the "national sport of England," few people on these shores had ever even heard of prizefighting; there simply was no interest in such an event here. Yet half a century later, when an American of Irish extraction, John C. Heenan, ventured to England to fight for the title against Tom Sayers, the American press exploded with coverage. Newspapers might condemn the illegal match (all prizefighting was illegal in this era), but they covered it round by round.

The interest in sports that characterized the antebellum era—an efflorescence of working-class events like boxing matches that at once expressed a class sensibility and ethnic divisions; the rise of baseball initially as a genteel middle- and upper-middle-class game; the very first intercollegiate athletic competitions between boys from elite schools; and harness races, which Oliver Wendell Holmes, Sr., praised for their democratic virtues, and which were distinctly modern in their emphasis on fixed rules, record keeping, and equality of entry—grew at an unprecedented pace during the Gilded Age. By the last decade of the nineteenth century, sports as we know them today had been born. And that birth was attended by the whole range of modern institutions we associate with urban-industrial America, bureaucratic structures, corporate organizations, capitalist ideologies, urban development.

THE "Y" MOVEMENT

The most important institutional form of the new healthful physicality was the Young Men's Christian Association (YMCA). Originally founded in England, the "Y" gave youths a refuge against the temptations of the metropolis. Here Christian fellowship, intellectual stimulation, and wholesome physical exercise supplanted the loneliness of boardinghouses and the evils of commercial amusements. Where urban life threatened good morals and communal order, YMCAs' and similar organizations upheld these old ideals. The "Y" represented a rejuvenated, muscular, middle-class ethos. By 1869, San Francisco, Washington, and New York City all had "Y" gymnasia; within twenty-five years, there were 261 YMCA gyms scattered across America. Religious leaders like Washington Gladden and Henry Ward Beecher praised the "Y" for offering sports like baseball, football, swimming, calisthenics, bowling, and weight lifting in a wholesome and clean atmosphere. The underlying assumption of "Y" programs was that supervised athletics promoted religious and moral goals. Simply put, it made more sense to teach physical training under Christian auspices, imparting the values of fair play, cooperation, and good sportsmanship, than to have young men roam the streets. Gymnasia countered the licentiousness of pool halls; men who did calisthenics did not bet on horse races; clean sports engendered leadership, discipline, and toughmindedness for capitalist society.

The "Y" movement was an early and prominent example of a widespread rehabilitation of sports that took place after the Civil War. Yet the proliferation of such urban institutions was testimony to the resiliency of the working-class ways that the reformers wished to change. No doubt, some laboring men were persuaded that the Christian athlete was on the road to bourgeois respectability and social mobility. Others probably participated in "wholesome" athletics some of the time, but also patronized beer gardens, dance halls, gambling parlors, saloons, burlesque houses, and the disreputable sports which were part of that culture. The public parks movement which swept the cities late in the nineteenth century provides a fine example of how men found their own paths. As antidotes to moral anarchy, vice, and corruption, city planners developed landscaped parks for public leisure. Clear brooks, lush trees, and blue skies were moral agents, they believed, which would improve the temperament of workers and elevate their thoughts. Parks could mollify class antagonism, planners argued, for here rich and poor came together in harmonious communion with nature. Unfortunately, rather than passively soaking up virtue, the urban multitudes came with beer, bats, and balls, ignored the "keep off the grass" signs, and had a rollicking good time.

By bringing men together in enormous numbers, the Civil War afforded unprecedented opportunities for sports. Between battles, men boxed, played baseball, and raced horses, often for the first time in their lives. More important, the war speeded the transformation of American society. The nation's capacity for manufacturing and distributing goods expanded, communication and transportation networks thickened, the organizational structure of society grew more sophisticated. As American capitalism matured with the century—as the division between those who owned the means of production and those who labored for wages grew deeper—images of stern competition, of winning the race of life, of survival of the fittest, took on enhanced ideological meaning. Athletics were readily enlisted in the cause of new social alignments.

The problem of moral sports in a Christian land did not go away. Some commentators maintained a hard line against all forms of frivolous amusements. More commonly, ministers and urban reformers gave renewed support to wholesome recreations. Thus, Henry Bergh (1811–1888) called for healthful and invigorating sports to replace cock mains, dogfights, bear baits, and boxing matches. Bergh substituted for the singular "sport"—a rowdy, one who defied social custom—the plural "sports", meaning rational and useful athletic activities. Dogfights and cock mains still found large and enthusiastic audiences, especially in the tradition-bound rural South and in polyglot cities like New York and New Orleans. The reformers never fully had their way with rural or working-class people. Nonetheless, new sports like baseball—not exactly a deacon's first choice, but better than prizefighting—grew extremely popular in working-class communities, as men organized countless teams and leagues.

But the efforts of neither the moral reformers nor their opponents ultimately were decisive in the rise of sports. More important was the commercialization of culture. Between the Civil War and the turn of the century, baseball became the acknowledged "national pastime," boxing under new rules exploded in popularity, football grew into a college mania, and basketball took firm root in urban athletic clubs. In addition, tennis, golf, and bicycling swept over the upper middle class in waves of popularity, while laborers started their own semiprofessional and amateur leagues in various team sports. Organizational and business structures arose to regulate and rationalize new activities. If sports in that era were rudimentary compared to today, the games themselves and the

structures that supported them were in place by the end of the nineteenth century.

Despite a vertiginous boom-and-bust cycle, this era left many workers with a little more disposable time and money than previously, especially those in the burgeoning white-collar sector. The old work ethic was in part a victim of its own success. As the economy slowly solved the age-old problem of insufficient productive capacity, and as work increasingly came to be thought of as a distinct realm of life, Americans were left with gaps of time to fill. Put another way, America's exploding productive capacity was changing people's perceptions of time. The dawning economy of potential abundance—where supply of aggregate goods and services might exceed demand—necessitated the stimulation of new wants and desires. The emergent ethos of play, of having fun, of "letting go" made a virtue of necessity.

New social conditions, then, transformed consciousness as well as material life. Production had shifted away from individuals' making objects for themselves and their communities, toward nameless workers' making goods for unseen others in return for cash. Now leisure more than ever revolved around the abstract concept of monetary exchange. Although Americans continued to create their own entertainment, the emergent national culture idealized the purchase of mass-produced commodities as a great human privilege and goal. Homegrown recreations competed for attention with mass entertainment, and the latter increasingly dominated and structured the former. To purchase leisure—to be a spectator at a ball game, or buy a bicycle or a baseball mitt—was to partake of a new cultural hallmark, the consumption of leisure. Entrepreneurs were quick to come in: A. J. Spalding began mass-producing sporting goods; newspaper tycoons like William Randolph Hearst for the first time printed entire sports sections; and authors like Gilbert Patten (creator of Frank Merriwell) coined money for himself and his publishers by churning out formula fiction.

Sports were integrally tied to the transformation of life in a mature capitalist economy. Cities became the foci of new activities not just because overcrowding militated against old traditional amusements, but because the city was where the commodification of life was most pervasive; in cities, people were already learning the cycle of desire, pleasure, and more desire that came with the ethic of consumption. Moreover, new technologies opened up recreational possibilities: pneumatic tires facilitated the bicycle craze of the 1880s and 1890s, motion pictures allowed count-

*Baseball is the key
to the emotional life
of millions of people.*

KENNETH L. BURNS
ANTHROPOLOGIST

S

SPORTS THROUGH THE NINETEENTH CENTURY

Sports in the Gilded Age

HEAVYWEIGHT CHAMP

A striking likeness of heavy-weight boxing champion John L. Sullivan. Symbolically, Sullivan espoused both Irish Nationalism and American patriotism.

CORBIS-BETTMANN

See also
Popular Entertainment before the Civil War

less fans to see prizefights, electric lightbulbs illuminated grand new downtown arenas. And sports were becoming firmly entrenched in American business culture. By the 1870s, for example, baseball had already been hit with strikes, blacklistings, and combinations to restrain trade. The team owners who founded the National League in 1876 soon wrested control of the game from the players, destroyed rival clubs, took over the apprenticeship system (the minor leagues), and instituted the reserve clause, which denied players the right to sell their labor to other franchises. Owners had, in short, attained what businessmen elsewhere strove for with varying degrees of success—controlled markets that minimized risk.

Both professional and amateur sports were part of the larger organizational revolution. League schedules were established, national rules promulgated, and regulatory bodies like the National Collegiate Athletic Association and Amateur Athletic Union formed. By the 1880s, professional baseball generated millions of dollars each year in revenue, and a prosperous franchise could draw five thousand spectators per game. Moreover, sports became interlocked with the larger world of business. A successful local team brought trade to hotels, restaurants, and bars; a new stadium meant jobs in construction, maintenance, and concessions. And sports replicated the structures of modernity. The keeping of statistics, the

rational measurement of means and ends, bureaucratic organizations, all permeated American life, including sports. Sports also articulated the dominant ideologies of an advanced democratic capitalist society—meritocracy, scientific worldview, equal competition, victory through brains, pluck, and hard work. Sports were a metaphor for life: that is, for the life of males in a modern capitalist country.

Still, it would be a mistake to view sports as simply one more manifestation of a modernizing juggernaut. Older, more traditional sports, such as boxing and cockfighting thrived in the late nineteenth century and appealed to ancient ideals of honor. Despite the structure of new professional and amateur sports, a subculture of raucous old pastimes continued to thrive. Modernization theory does capture the most striking trend in sports development—toward bureaucratic structures, rationalized play, quantifiable results. The problem is that these trends were often so mixed with seemingly antimodern ones. Richard Kyle Fox, for example, owner of the *National Police Gazette* during its heyday in the 1880s and 1890s used the most modern business techniques to promote traditional sport; his publication, brilliantly rationalized in production and distribution, was filled with misogyny and racism, hardly the stuff of an egalitarian society.

Indeed, while reformers argued that sports taught the ideal of equal opportunity, the fact is that the playing fields of athletics, like those of life, were never level. Exclusive organizations like the New York Athletic Club—and every major city had exclusive athletic clubs by the end of the century—allowed only the most wealthy and powerful men to join. While workers might become interested in the outcome of a Harvard-Yale football game, indeed, while those schools might even employ a "ringer" or two to assure victory, colleges remained elite institutions, effectively closed to the majority of Americans. To the extent that prestigious colleges did open up in this era, sports were part of the process by which the children of an industrial elite that was pushing its way into the most powerful positions in American life dispelled the boredom of the rigid old classical curriculum. Finally, the late nineteenth century saw the proliferation of exclusive country clubs and elite watering places like Newport, Rhode Island, and Saratoga, New York, that brought wealthy people together in play while excluding all lesser folk.

At high-amateur and professional levels, sports did admit whole new groups of people as spectators and participants. Yet a majority of Americans were largely left out. First, while there were some important gestures toward women's sports during this era, domestic ideology, notions of female delicacy, and lingering Victorian prudishness kept most women from active interest in things athletic. Gender roles still defined men as active, women as passive, and the operative metaphors of sports all tended toward patriarchy. Tough competition, physical violence, the importance of winning, teamwork—sports as metaphor did not just reflect masculine ideals, they helped constitute and define those ideals. Competing, achieving, and winning were at the very core of late Victorian notions of manhood, so sports not only excluded women, they helped define and give shape to a masculine world that feared, or devalued, or mystified all that it regarded as feminine.

Ethnically too, athletics in this era contained a strong streak of exclusivity While sports had become an important symbol of American culture, most men of the immigrant generation probably were not terribly interested as spectators, and if they played sports at all, it was more likely to be games from their homelands. The children of immigrants, however, found in athletics a powerful sense of belonging to the only culture they knew at firsthand. Symbolically, sports provided a sense of dual identity. Thus, heavyweight boxing champion John L. Sullivan espoused both Irish nationalism and American patriotism, and he literally cloaked himself in both the Stars and Stripes and the emerald green when he entered the ring. For Irish Americans who had long suffered severe discrimination, Sullivan represented not only glittering success, but also the possibility of identifying with both America and Ireland. In the twentieth century, baseball players like Joe DiMaggio and Hank Greenberg repeated this pattern for new immigrant groups.

The situation for blacks, however, was different. Despite the rhetoric of "may the best man win," by late in the nineteenth century, the openings that had existed in early professional sports closed down almost entirely. During the 1890s, African Americans were systematically barred from major league baseball, resulting in the formation of the all-black Negro leagues until Jackie Robinson reintegrated baseball after World War II. Moreover, heavyweight boxing champion John L. Sullivan simply refused to fight black opponents, though the strongest contender during the late 1880s was an Australian black named Peter Jackson. Even in the now obscure, but then quite popular, sport of bicycle racing, African American

Marshall W. "Major" Taylor was the best cyclist in the world during the 1890s, yet he was systematically barred from major races. So in the late nineteenth century—an era of lynching and Jim Crow legislation, of the most virulent racism since Reconstruction—the sporting meritocracy proved meretricious at best. Access to organized sports, then, was generally restricted by race and gender, and often by class.

Nevertheless, the sporting ideology that had become a commonplace of the late Victorian era was a powerful cement in American culture. Those excluded from the mainstream still created a sporting space with games and leagues of their own. Equally important, the ideas associated with sports—universal rules, fair play, utter seriousness in a frivolous cause, measurable performance, the joy of physical excellence, the tension of keen competition, the expertise of spectators—were constantly spreading into the larger national culture. Not for all Americans, but for increasing numbers of them, sometimes even crossing deep social chasms, sports were becoming a kind of national language or currency, a set of shared practices, values, and experiences so common as to become invisible as air.

In 1892, roughly a century after the illegal sport of boxing first appeared in America, William Lyon Phelps, professor of English at Yale, was reading the daily newspaper to his blind father, a Baptist minister. The old outlaw prizefighting was in the news, and Phelps read the headline "Corbett Defeats Sullivan," then turned the page, assuming the elderly Victorian gentleman would not be interested. Phelps Senior leaned forward and said to his son, "Read it by rounds."

—ELLIOTT J. GORN

SPORTS IN THE TWENTIETH CENTURY

During the 1890s, American sports were important experiences for two large groups of people: athletes and spectators. Millions of boys and men played baseball and football formally and informally, while girls and women practiced gymnastics, rode horses and bicycles, and played basketball. Millions of men, women, and children watched professional, college, and informal sports, from boxing to horse racing, college football to sandlot baseball games.

The bigger they come, the harder they fall

JOHN L. SULLIVAN

MODERN SPORTS

Central to American Culture

Consider these manifestations of modern sports:

—The best-known human being in the world during the 1970s and 1980s was an African American boxer and world heavyweight champion who joined the Nation of Islam, changed his name, and successfully defied the United States government's attempt to jail him for refusing to submit to the Vietnam-era draft.

—A commercially successful national cable television network broadcasts sports news and events twenty-four hours a day. In the words of a founder, "We believe that the appetite for sports in this country is insatiable."

—Major league teams in basketball, football, and baseball frequently field teams made up mostly of African American or Hispanic players.

—A major league baseball player signed a multi-year contract prior to the 1992 season worth twenty-nine million dollars.

—An upset in the women's 1991 Wimbledon singles championship match received front-page coverage in the *New York Times* and drew tens of millions of television viewers.

—"He was stiff-armed," announced the United States president in late 1990 when his secretary of state returned from the Middle East having failed to persuade Iraq to withdraw its troops from Kuwait. No reporter objected to the metaphor; instead, men nodded to themselves, remembering what it was like to feel the heel of a charging ball-carrier's palm at the end of a stiff, outstretched arm come thudding into one's chin, snapping back the head and momentarily scrambling neurons.

In 1890 these developments were inconceivable. Although organized sport could occasionally captivate the nation, it lacked the wherewithal to frame public discourse. One of many influential social and cultural institutions—political parties, organized religion, business corporations—sports had yet to reach its potential power at the center of American life, whether urban or rural, Protestant or Catholic; black or white; rich, poor, or middling.

A hundred years later, sports had come to influence and shape central institutions of American life: secondary and higher education; print and electronic media; the economic life of cities and suburbs. From a perch on the sidelines of American culture, sports began to structure the experience of culture in new ways signaling new patterns in the relations between sexes and races; the use and pursuit of leisure time; the networks by which social classes cohere and recreate themselves over time; even the language in which political leaders speak of politics, foreign policy, and war.

Before the administration of Theodore Roosevelt, no president would have used a football metaphor to describe a great matter of state. Such usage would have been met with confusion. It took both the conversion of the upper class to sporting ideology and the machinery of the mass media to popularize such concepts.

Nor is it only in talk of war that sports language dominates common discourse. It may be that the only common language of the public realm is now that of sports. A century ago people talked of Almighty God, of the help and intervention of Divine Providence. Today they: speak of aggressive coaches and celebrity athletes nailing slam dunks, hitting home runs, and taking hits.

These images and developments represent enormous changes in the past century. First, sports have become a pervasive fact of American life; sport grips hundreds of millions of people at the level of spectatorship. Second, sports comprise a multibillion-dollar business industry, driven by a logic that has little to do with the "play of the game." Third, with teams largely integrated along racial lines (though important exceptions remain) organized sport functions as a cultural icon of equal opportunity. Fourth, women athletes and coaches have achieved major significance in the competitive arena although gender segregation remains active. Finally, sports and television, consummating a marriage between media and athletics begun when sporting newspapers covered local events and pursued during the heyday of radio, may soon cease to be distinctly separate institutions.

During the past hundred years competitive participation and spectator attention have grown in many sports: the racing sports—horse, automobile, and bicycle; in team sports—hockey, vol-

See also
Radio

leyball, lacrosse, soccer; in individual sports—swimming, golf, bowling, track and field, skiing, ice skating; and many others. But nothing has captured the American imagination more than baseball. Since baseball has been the most popular and therefore most significant sport during the period, most of this essay focuses on the development of "the national pastime," while football, boxing, basketball, and tennis receive secondary attention.

The Sporting Landscape in 1890

The modern sports landscape dates from the 1890s. We begin with the national pastime. In the forty-five years since its formal "invention" in New York City, baseball had become the most widely played and most watched American sport. Two professional major leagues (three in 1890) distributed franchises in large and medium-sized cities east of the Mississippi and north of the Ohio rivers. Minor leagues (eight in 1884, nineteen in 1903), usually in smaller cities and towns spread throughout the country, included dozens of professional teams. Attendance of major league games probably totaled one to two million spectators per year, while another million or so attended minor league games. Hundreds, if not thousands, of organized and barely organized semiprofessional teams accounted for many more thousands of players and millions of active spectators.

Originally baseball culture perched at the border between respectability and low life, and still straddles that line somewhat to this day. In the past its two major leagues enforced policies at games designed to appeal to different segments of the urban population. National League teams charged fifty cents for admission, played no Sunday ball, and banned the sale of alcohol. The rival American Association sought poorer, working-class immigrant spectators by charging a quarter, playing on Sundays, and allowing the sale of liquor.

The popularity of the game received two blows in the 1890s. Long restive over the insertion of a "reserve clause" in player contracts (which effectively wiped out players' market bargaining power over salaries), the Brotherhood of Professional Base Ball Players convinced most of its members to break their contracts with National League clubs and join the new Players' League. The latter's management was to be shared between representatives of the players and the clubs' financial backers. A three-way battle erupted between the Players' League, the American Association, and the National League—whose "war committee"

chose to schedule games directly opposite those of the upstart league. Disaster nearly resulted for organized baseball. Despite purposely inflated figures, attendance at major league games, the lifeblood of professional sports, decreased from 1889 to 1890. Modern fans who lament that there's too much business news in the sports pages are part of a long tradition. That year, despite efforts of the Knights of Labor and the American Federation of Labor to promote the Players' League and boycott the National League, too many fans chose to avoid the ballparks altogether. The few remaining solid teams in the National League bought out the Players' League's financial backers and buried the most radical experiment in the history of American professional sports. Thereafter, the "reserve rule" was enshrined as the centerpiece of baseball's labor relations, and owners exercised virtually undisputed control over the baseball business until the mid 1970s.

While the "national game" remained overwhelmingly popular in the late nineteenth century, baseball's business side—battles between labor and management, labor discipline and blacklists and Pinkertons, franchise shifts, booms and busts, cartel agreements made and broken—rocked with the instability of much of Gilded Age business culture. Not until the rival American League, under the leadership of Ban Johnson, schemed and muscled its way into major league status and hammered out an agreement with the National League in 1901 did organized baseball settle down into a half-century of stable franchises and nearly uninterrupted growth.

Although baseball dominated the late-nineteenth-century sporting world, it was not the only pastime. By the 1890s football—college football—had moved beyond its Ivy League origins to public and private colleges and universities across the nation. The spread of this absorbing, extraordinarily violent game, however, carried controversy in its wake. While faculties worried that the competitiveness, violence, and hoopla of college football misdirected undergraduate energies, alumni sensed the game's potential publicity value and took control of its organization and administration. Collegiate football soon became a huge spectacle, and the main instrument of public relations for institutions of higher education. The annual Thanksgiving Day game in New York City between the two best college teams (usually Yale and Princeton during the 1890s) drew up to forty thousand spectators and served to kick off the winter social season. Paralleling and assisting the rise of the extracurriculum in American educa-

Football isn't a contact sport, it's a collision sport. Dancing is a contact sport.

VINCE LOMBARDI
QUOTED IN SPORTS IN AMERICA (1976)

**RUSHING
TEAMMATES**

*University of Southern
California football teammates
rush toward the camera on
September 19, 1931. From left
to right, R. Brown, Ernie
Smith, Aaron Rosenberg, and
Bob Hall.*

UPI / CORBIS-BETTMANN

tion, football became the principal means by which alumni, public relations, professionals, and fund-raisers gained control of American college life. For Theodore Roosevelt and like-minded men (such as Henry Cabot Lodge, Brooks Adams, and Alfred Thayer Mahan), football served as a key demonstration of the "strenuous life." Football as both experience and metaphor was used by these men in their campaign to reinvigorate the American elite. The game, they felt, would toughen and prepare children to exercise national power and wrest world leadership from effete old-world corruption.

If football was born in the heart of elite male culture, and baseball blossomed in the no-man's-land between urban working-class and middle-class sporting culture, basketball, which first appeared in this same decade, owed its creation to one of the principal institutions of middle-class evangelical reform: the Young Men's Christian Association (YMCA). Three pious young men, who wanted to do God's work but also enjoyed the somewhat less respectable (and apparently less godly) rough-and-tumble of physical sports, gathered at the YMCA training school (now Springfield College) in Massachusetts in the early 1890s. James Naismith, Amos Alonzo Stagg, and Luther Halsey Gulick soon saw themselves as missionaries come to preach the gospel of bodily health and exercise as well as the gospel of Jesus

Christ. Gulick even created the YMCA symbol, the inverted triangle of "mind-body-spirit."

Leading the effort to "reform" urban immigrant children, the YMCA wanted a vigorous sport that could be played indoors during the winter. Naismith invented the game in the winter of 1891, and basketball quickly took off, spreading first through the YMCA networks, then much more widely. Before the game had celebrated its first birthday, Luther Gulick exulted:

It is doubtful whether a gymnastic game has ever spread so rapidly over the continent as has "basket ball." It is played from New York to San Francisco and from Maine to Texas by hundreds of teams in associations, athletic clubs and schools. (Bernice Larson Webb, The Basketball Man: James Naismith *[1973], p. 72)*

Women, too, particularly college women, took up basketball, and before the end of the century special rules had been developed for the women's game.

Racial segregation in American sports had found its voice by the 1890s. In 1887 Adrian "Cap" Anson, the Hall of Fame first baseman and later manager of the Chicago White Stockings, one of the most talented and popular of nineteenth-century ball players, threatened not to play a match as long as the black player George Stovey remained on the opposing team. Anson had tried the same gambit four years earlier against a Toledo team and failed. This time he succeeded and Stovey withdrew. Over the next few years what became known as "organized baseball" became white baseball and stayed that way until 1946.

From its origins, organized sports in America depended on the press for publicity, for legitimation, and for communication with the mass of potential participants and spectators. Nineteenth-century reporters pretended to no ideology of objectivity and participated actively in the sporting worlds they chronicled. By the 1890s, however, the New York press was facing the competition of the popular "yellow" press of William Randolph Hearst and Joseph Pulitzer. Seeking massive working-class readership, these entrepreneurs introduced the modern tabloid sports pages. Increasingly, then, a pattern began that would be repeated with radio and television—spectator sports were reported and packaged as a way of selling newspapers.

Progressives, Reformed Play, and World War I

Psychologists' "discovery" of children's play and adolescence in the late nineteenth century invested urban reformers with a theory by which to approach the hordes of immigrant children swarming American cities during these years. Settlement houses made vigorous use of the new game of basketball, and gymnasia became important parts of their physical plants.

Luther Gulick organized the Playground Association of America (PAA) in 1906, a group of middle-class reformers, YMCA advocates, and socialites (Theodore Roosevelt was the group's first honorary president) dedicated to providing spaces for urban children to play. At least partly because of the PAA's prodding, the number of playgrounds in major American cities grew dramatically in the years before World War I. Between 1911 and 1917, PAA statistics for a large group of reporting cities showed that playgrounds had more than doubled, from 1,543 to 3,940.

While the PAA social workers had little influence on the course of spectator sports, they did provide an avenue along which middle-class Protestants adapted more and more to the idea and practice of play in American culture. Previously, sporting culture's least ambivalent adherents were either upper-class sportsmen like Theodore Roosevelt and the football players at elite colleges or the much less established working

classes—primarily men who sought display of skill and the experience of excitement in sporting events. The middle class joined America's sporting culture principally through basketball and the play movement—what might be called the domestication of sports. Sports were promoted and justified as character building, as uplifting, even as Americanizing. These qualified as no small virtues to native-born, middle-class Protestants, many of whom believed the national character was being drowned in a flood of foreign-looking, dirt-poor, and frequently incomprehensible immigrants who produced children at astonishingly high birthrates.

Progressives did help change American sports, though obliquely, at this moment. Pioneering the growth of bureaucracies in the administration of play, they developed science as a governing language to deal with the large number of children in urban settlements, and they helped organize America for World War I. For it was in the American effort in the Great War that the two streams in sports history—represented by college football and YMCA basketball—converged. Walter Camp, the former Yale football star who had become the czar of Yale's powerful football machine, joined the U.S. Navy Commission on Training Camp Activities as its athletic director. James Naismith joined the war effort as a "hygiene" lecturer, supporting YMCA efforts to look after the morals of the American Expeditionary Force.

World War I bureaucratized American culture as no event since the Civil War. It absorbed much of the progressive cultural agenda (scientific planning, rational social engineering, Americanization of immigrants) to oil the machinery of organized violence. Football always had been promoted at least partly because it appeared to strengthen the martial abilities of young, upper-class men, and World War I made use of that training and toughening. The military employed massive physical education and sports programs to condition recruits, in the process further legitimizing the mass ideology of sports. Ironically, World War I cemented the importance of organized play in the national consciousness. Public schools' adoption of physical education and athletic programs throughout the country followed on the heels of the war.

But the experience of sports themselves during this period was contradictory. Boxing, for instance, produced one of its great controversial champions in the decade before World War I—the African American heavyweight Jack Johnson. First, Johnson had to pursue the White title-

Quitters never win. Winners never quit.

ANONYMOUS TRADITIONAL ADAGE FOR FOOTBALL LOCKER ROOMS

♦ **Yellow press**

Featuring sensational or scandalous items or ordinary news distorted with shocking or lurid details

449

holder around the world until he got a chance to fight for the championship. When he defeated Tommy Burns in Australia in 1908, the stunned white boxing establishment went on a desperate search for a "Great White Hope" to take back the title. At last, in 1910, undefeated but retired former heavyweight champion Jim Jeffries announced he would take up the cause of the "portion of the white race that has been looking to me to defend its athletic superiority." Johnson crushed Jeffries, however, and that night racial violence claimed eight lives. Johnson's victory stuck in the craw of white America, and Johnson himself did nothing to make it easier to swallow.

In and out of the ring, Johnson thumbed his nose at white opponents and social conventions. He lived in the public eye, spending money on flashy clothes, fast cars, and the high life, including his three white wives and numerous white mistresses. Authorities pursued him on morals charges, finally securing a conviction in 1913. Johnson jumped bail and fled to Europe, then lost his title to Jess Willard in Cuba in 1915 (in a match that some, including Johnson, have claimed was fixed), and returned to the United States to serve his prison term in 1920.

The completely white game of organized baseball grew in popularity until 1909, when atten-

dance reached more than seven million, doubling the 1901 total. Though attendance declined somewhat before World War I, these first two decades of the twentieth century were the golden era of pitching, strategy, and what became known as "scientific" and "inside" baseball. Dominated by such pitchers as Christy Matthewson, Cy Young, and Mordecai "Three-Finger" Brown, and hitters such as Nap Lajoie, Honus Wager, and Ty Cobb, these years, some of the finest in the history of the game, only now are receiving their due from baseball historians.

If one player in particular expresses fully the social and cultural history of the period, he is Tyrus Raymond Cobb. In his long and extraordinary baseball career (1905–1928) Cobb set records which have stood for more than half a century, retaining the highest lifetime batting average through the late 1990s. Cobb's calculating, penetrating shrewdness made the most of any game situation. A proponent and the finest practitioner of "scientific baseball," Cobb analyzed, strategized, and bullied his way around the diamond. Consequently, Cobb was feared and disliked as much for his manner as his skill. An aggressive, vicious, racist brawler, on the field and off, Cobb also exemplified the character traits of the nineteenth-century American hero of production: acquisitive, self-reliant, normally under tight self-control, prepared for violence. A stingy, introverted loner who felt the world was against him, Cobb built his unremarkable physical skills and average means into exceptional baseball ability and a good-sized fortune. Cobb died a lonely millionaire after a long, bitter life, his funeral attended by just three people from organized baseball.

Cobb had no monopoly on mean-spirited acquisitiveness. The notorious penny pinching of Chicago White Sox owner Charles Comiskey helped lay the groundwork for the biggest scandal in American sports history—the fixed 1919 World Series. Even today, controversy swirls around the exceptionally complicated affair, as historians, novelists, and filmmakers promote competing versions of the fix, rearranging and reassigning varying levels of guilt, innocence, and blame. As many as eight players on the heavily favored White Sox were involved in a scheme to lose the Series to the Cincinnati Reds, in exchange for large sums of money from gamblers. The scandal, which did not even come to light until well into the following season, shook up baseball so terribly that owners surrendered much of their power over the game to a commissioner who promised to "clean up" the mess. Though the players were acquitted, Commissioner Kenesaw Mountain Landis banned the eight "Black Sox" from baseball for life. The fix itself provided baseball with a powerful myth of lost innocence. As the famous, and probably apocryphal, story goes, a distraught boy approached "Shoeless" Joe Jackson as the star outfielder came out of the grand jury room, and pleaded with his hero, "Say it ain't so, Joe." What helped baseball regain its popularity, and some of its ingenuousness, was a curious and riveting new phenomenon named George Herman "Babe" Ruth.

Sports and the Culture of Consumption

If Ty Cobb exemplified the character traits of the culture of production, Babe Ruth helped promote the newer economy and culture founded on consumption. A talented young pitcher and slugger with the Boston Red Sox, Ruth was purchased by the New York Yankees for the 1920 season and soon began hitting home runs at a faster pace than any previous player.

Ruth's contributions to twentieth-century sports, to the history of baseball, and to the culture of consumption were all enormous. First, though not single-handedly, he deflected a good bit of public attention away from the unfolding World Series scandal and into the ballparks themselves, where the shape of the game was changing dramatically. At the same time, Ruth showed what home run power could do to the game's offensive strategy. In fact, the home run hitting of Ruth and fellow players on the Yankees transformed the baseball strategy of the previous thirty years: one run at a time, base stealing, bunting, what Bill James has called "long sequence" offense. (For example: walk, hit and run, sacrifice fly—three successful at-bats to produce one run.)

Ruth's personality both fit and helped shape the period. Unlike Cobb, he appeared to play baseball "naturally," without calculation, almost (as the nicknames "the Babe" and "the Bambino" captured) with the manner of an overgrown child.

Like a child, Babe Ruth spent liberally—everything he had, in all senses of the term. A prodigious consumer of food, drink, clothing, and women, Ruth was himself an advertisement for consumption. He bought silk shirts dozens at a time, discarding them after a single wearing; he slept with hundreds, perhaps thousands, of women; he ate several dozen hot dogs at a sitting while gulping down beer by the quart. At ease surrounded by children, he had a notoriously bad memory for other people's names (even his own

teammates), which he made up for by calling them "Kid."

Ruth became that most modern of sports heroes, a celebrity. Created by the pioneering press agent Christy Walsh and sought after for public appearances, Ruth's persona became as important as the man, and Walsh sold it to endorse a myriad of products. Babe Ruth's life both helped bring about the culture of consumption and served as one of its most impressive creations.

But beyond individual players was the game itself. Perhaps more than any other institution in American society, baseball in the twentieth century brought together large numbers of people in one place for several hours at a time, thousands of times during a six-month period from April to October. Today, Major League teams play one hundred sixty-two games per season; the most successful franchises draw as many as two million paying spectators over the course of a season. (Professional and college football and basketball teams now rival baseball as audience creators, but only since the advent of television.) As a result, advertisers are as drawn to the ballpark as fans are to the game.

To all media—newspapers, radio, and television—sports spectacles are crucial providers of an essential element in a consumption economy: potential customers. That is why sporting events played such a huge role in the growth of media, first of the popular press, and then in the subsequent development of radio and television.

As the American economy exploded into consumer goods—and the need to sell them—after World War I, baseball, radio, and sports pages helped turn the cultural and economic trick. Radio carried Babe Ruth's stunning achievements to baseball fans across the country, and multi-station hookups carried many of the decade's big sports events: heavyweight boxing championships, baseball's annual World Series, football's Rose Bowl. Newspapers remained a key connection through which advertising was married to sports. But whereas a combination of society and sports pages had covered Ivy League football in the 1890s, the biggest fights or bowl games of the twenties got remarkable publicity, commercial sponsorship, and national attention. Sports pages themselves grew to enormous size at this time, while publishers and reporters frequently promoted organized sports.

The experience of sports became truly nationalized in the 1920s. That decade is known as, alternately, the Golden Age of Sport, and the Golden Age of Heroes. As disposable income

I zigged when I should have zagged.

JACK ROPER
EXPLANATION OF HOW
HEAVYWEIGHT CHAMPION
JOE LOUIS KNOCKED HIM OUT
ON APRIL 17, 1939

See also
Sports through the
Nineteenth Century

451

climbed and working hours declined somewhat, people spent more time and money on sports events, while the media created and promoted sports heroes into an elite galaxy of celebrities.

Babe Ruth shared the cultural limelight with boxers Jack Dempsey and Gene Tunney, college and professional football player Harold Edward "Red" Grange, golfer Bobby Jones, and tennis player Big Bill Tilden. All of these figures received a degree of public attention, publicity, and adulation inconceivable in the culture of thirty years before. Much of America's new mass culture focused on such people. More than one hundred thousand attended the second Dempsey-Tunney fight in Chicago's Soldier's Field; an estimated fifty million listened to the seventy-three stations on the NBC-radio hookup. Before this time it was literally impossible for so many people to give such intense, detailed, and simultaneous attention to a sporting event.

Leo Lowenthal's study of popular biographies in the early twentieth century noted a profound shift in the type of American hero that journalists held up for public adulation. At the beginning of the century magazine heroes tended to be men who had achieved recognition through productive work: businessmen, financiers, scientists, writers, artists, politicians or statesmen—what Lowenthal called "idols of production." Later, beginning in the 1920s, national heroes derived more from the world of entertainment: boxers, stars and starlets, baseball players, and the like—in Lowenthal's term, "idols of consumption." In the 1920s the distinctively modern convergence of sports and the entertainment business began. People, like Babe Ruth, Rudolph Valentino, and occasionally men like Charles Lindbergh, merged in the public mind; in the newsreels, in newspapers, on radio, and in advertisements, they all seemed to take part in the great national culture of fame and celebrity. The parties created by F. Scott Fitzgerald in *The Great Gatsby*, (1925) capture this facet of the Roaring Twenties perfectly: as department store magnates rubbed shoulders with Broadway performers and polo players, symphony conductors and athletes and movie actresses, the kaleidoscopic whirl of celebrity enfolded them all in its ephemeral embrace.

COLLEGIATE AND PROFESSIONAL FOOTBALL
The Myth of the Amateur

Professional football had a halting beginning in 1920, with the formation of the American professional Football Association, soon to be known as the National Football League (NFL). Populated mostly by working-class ethnics in grimy factory towns, the professional game boasted little of the glamour and respectability of the college game. In fact, professional football received most attention during this decade when the nation's most famous college player, Red Grange, sometimes called the "Galloping Ghost," finished his final season at Illinois and promptly joined the professional Chicago Bears. Managed brilliantly by the sports promoter Charles C. "Cash and Carry" Pyle, Grange became a phenomenal celebrity, barnstorming the country and collecting huge sums in product endorsements. But Grange was a rare exception. Not until the 1950s and especially the 1960s (under the skilled leadership of NFL Commissioner Pete Rozelle) would pro football shed its old image and begin to share the television and celebrity limelight with college ball.

The preeminence of collegiate football, however, was due mainly to the fact that it was a thoroughly professionalized operation run under the banner of amateurism. The amateur sporting ideal has always existed more in imagination than in reality in this country. Once players, spectators, managers, owners, or athletic directors got a taste of victory and its rewards—fame, publicity, money—they found it difficult to uphold principles which make winning less likely. But college football (for most of the twentieth century) and basketball (in the past few decades) claim allegiance to amateurism only as a matter of pious public relations. Between the efforts of alumni boosters, athletic departments, and the promotion-oriented intercollegiate governing bodies like the National Collegiate Athletic Association (NCAA), colleges have managed to create essentially professional programs which serve, frankly, as a farm system for professional leagues. They produce topflight athletes, exciting entertainment (in which television networks invest heavily), and occasional—and soon forgotten—scandals which suggest the genuinely professional nature of college sports (eligibility violations, gambling, recreational and performance enhancing drug use). The American sports public apparently prefers to believe in an ideal of amateur sports, despite overwhelming evidence that the reality has hardly, if ever, existed.

Sensitively attuned to the currents reshaping American culture then, Fitzgerald noted the New Woman's role in entertainment culture. Women, too, moved into the sporting world during the 1920s, particularly the individual sports of tennis, golf, and swimming. Because of the demands of this new publicity machine, they were taken up as celebrities as much as athletes: Mildred "Babe" Didrikson in golf, Gertrude Ederle in swimming, Suzanne Lenglen in tennis. That Fitzgerald makes his golfer Jordan Baker into a cheat suggests his discomfort both with the New Woman and with the hucksterism and dishonesty pervading the culture of entertainment—including sports. One of the men who fixed the 1919 World Series—the gambler Arnold Rothstein—appears in *The Great Gatsby*, metamorphosed into Meyer Wolfsheim, Gatsby's partner in business "gonnegtions." For Fitzgerald the surrounding culture of sports was omnipresent: Tom Buchanan's polo playing, Baker's tournaments, Wolfsheim's gambling, even Gatsby's odd term of endearment, "old sport." The sporting world's public hucksterism emerged full-blown in this decade, and we are able to glimpse the patterns of modern sports in the lives of Babe Ruth, Red Grange, and Babe Didrikson.

Baseball, Black and White

Barred from the white organized game, African American players and entrepreneurs nevertheless made baseball their "national pastime" as well. Professional clubs formed in the late nineteenth and early twentieth centuries as independent barnstorming (traveling) businesses. The star pitcher Rube Foster first put together the Chicago American Giants in 1911, and then, in 1920 founded the Negro National League composed of eight similar teams. The economics of black baseball worked against the league: spectators were poor and there were few sources of the capital required to back a professional team. With the onset of the Depression the league collapsed in 1931.

Then in 1933, W. A. "Gus" Greenlee, Pittsburgh's black numbers boss, reassembled the Negro National League around his heavily funded Pittsburgh Crawfords. Four years later a Negro American League joined the fray; both leagues lasted into the postwar years. While the Negro Leagues never provided much organizational or financial stability for players or owners, during their heyday in the 1930s and 1940s they did field some of the game's greatest players. During the Depression Greenlee's Crawfords included a re-

markable cast of future Hall of Fame players: pitcher Satchel Paige, catcher Leroy "Josh" Gibson, third baseman Judy Johnson, first baseman Oscar Charleston, and center fielder James Thomas "Cool Papa" Bell.

Black clubs continued to barnstorm the entire country since intra-league play could never make them enough money. They played white major leaguers frequently enough so that ballplayers and spectators could compare the best of both worlds. Although the overall level of Negro League play was probably below that of the white major leagues, the best black players were clearly at least the equals of their white counterparts. Negro League play differed somewhat from white baseball during these years. Major league baseball strategy had become more conservative, revolving principally around the home run. Black baseball, on the other hand, was not only more inventive and daring in organizational terms (opportunistic scheduling, pre-game entertainment, players excelling at more than one position), but also put a premium on speed, cunning, and risk-taking—what was known at the time as "tricky baseball."

Negro League baseball was central to African American culture throughout the United States. Ballplayers were well-known heroes, and baseball stories were staples of black newspapers' society pages. Opening-day celebrations could be extraordinarily elaborate, as in a 1937 Kansas City parade that included five hundred decorated cars, two marching bands, civil groups, politicians, and celebrities. Still, African American players and audiences knew that organized black baseball was the result of segregation, and they struggled to eliminate the very color barrier that had created the Negro Leagues.

Organized white baseball had achieved some real business stability by 1920. Attendance boomed to more than ninety million during the 1920s, as compared with fifty-six million the previous decade. These heights did not survive the Depression or World War II, when attendance averaged roughly a million spectators less per year. But in 1946, attendance surged to a record high, and the figure for the decade is nearly half again higher than it had ever been. Coinciding with this phenomenal growth in attendance was one of the most dramatic stories in the history of American sports, the racial integration of organized baseball.

The story begins with two characters: Jack Roosevelt Robinson and Wesley Branch Rickey. A California-raised African American, Robinson was one of the finest athletes in the country dur-

With the advent of television, the fans at home rather than those in the stands increasingly became the ultimate arbiters of which sports thrived and which ones failed.

PAGE 474

See also
Travel and Vacations

ing his college years (the first UCLA athlete ever to letter in four sports: football, baseball, basketball, and track). He fought segregation and racism from his earliest years. The army court-martialed him for defying the illegal segregation on a Fort Hood bus, but Robinson was acquitted. Branch Rickey was a shrewd, farsighted cigar chewing showman, occasional Methodist moralist, and general manager of the Brooklyn Dodgers. Rickey developed the farm system, fully integrating minor league teams into the major league club's player development strategies. He determined in 1945 to break baseball's unwritten but absolute color line by bringing a black player into the Dodger organization. After a nationwide search for the right combination of baseball talent and self-disciplined character, Rickey decided on Jackie Robinson, then a player with the Negro League Kansas City Monarchs.

Robinson accepted Rickey's offer to integrate organized baseball, promising not to retaliate against what both men expected to be torrents of racist abuse. After spending the 1946 season with the Dodgers' AAA Montreal farm club and leading his team to the championship of the minor league World Series, Robinson was promoted to the Brooklyn Dodgers in 1947. That season he became a national phenomenon, combining first-rate, exciting, aggressive diamond play with a dignified restraint in the face of vicious racism ranging from insults and catcalls to beanballs, hate mail, and death threats.

Robinson's obvious courage, pride, and determination drew the admiration of whites as well as blacks, and may very well have inspired fellow African Americans as they developed the theory and practice of nonviolence in the following decade. Also restrained and dignified, the African American response to Robinson demonstrated the black rejection of "separate but equal" strategies in favor of racial integration. Even before the Montgomery bus boycott began in late 1955, for example, black baseball fans in Shreveport and New Orleans, Louisiana, had organized boycotts of minor league teams that refused to hire black players.

Robinson's style of play combined the daring opportunism known as "tricky baseball" in the Negro Leagues, with an intimidating aggressiveness on the base paths. According to his manager Leo Durocher, "This guy didn't just come to play. He come to beat ya. He come to stuff the goddamn bat right up your ass." Named Rookie of the Year in 1947 and Most Valuable Player in 1949, Robinson established himself as perhaps the single most exciting player in the game.

African-American sportswriters focused attention on Robinson's achievements and the black players who followed him, thus encouraging the integration of professional football, tennis, and basketball. Consequently, the Negro Leagues, one of the most important institutions of twentieth-century, African-American cultural life during segregation, quickly began to lose players, spectators, and media coverage. Despite the relatively slow pace of racial integration in baseball—the New York Yankees and Boston Red Sox did not add a single black player until 1955 and 1959, respectively—the Negro Leagues had been reduced to four teams by the mid-1950s, and were dead by 1960. The paradoxical result was that there were

actually fewer opportunities for African Americans to make a living from professional baseball, a stark reality that may still prevail today.

This history of baseball's segregation and integration calls into question the simplistic idea that professional sport embodies the democratic promise of a meritocratic society. For over half a century the color line simply excluded hundreds, if not thousands, of players who could have performed creditably in professional baseball. Even when the color line began to be crossed, baseball talent and skill alone did not make the difference. Rickey's choice of Jackie Robinson, as opposed to any one of several dozen first-rate pros in the Negro Leagues, was political, commercial, and psychological. Rickey wanted a particular kind of ballplayer to be the pioneer. And because he held extraordinary power in the baseball world, he got his way. In sports as in other areas of American endeavor, background, education, class, and the ability to "fit in" counted quite as much as so-called pure talent. This is not to say that mediocre talent with the right connections could survive the world of topflight sports, but that topflight ability alone has never been sufficient for an athlete to reach the highest echelons. At least through the 1970s, black major leaguers, taken together, had consistently higher batting averages than comparable groups of white players. To make it in the big leagues and stay there, African-American players had to be better than their white counterparts. And despite more than forty years of baseball integration, African Americans remain disproportionately scarce in management and front-office positions, and no major league sports franchise is owned by a nonwhite.

The 1950s: Portents of Change

Modern cultural folklore, including that of organized sports, has settled on the 1950s as the decade of romantic inertia. If there was a certain glacierlike quality to international politics and the postwar revival of the cult of domesticity, there were also currents swirling underneath the surface that would crack the cultural monolith of the Eisenhower administration and the *Donna Reed Show* wide open.

Because spectator sports depend on a demographic base, the profound population shifts which began in the 1950s changed the shape of American sports. As suburbs mushroomed after World War II, drawing middle- and working-class families out of the older northeastern cities, the hometowns of some of the country's most venerable sporting franchises began a steady

You can't think and hit at the same time.

YOGI BERRA
REFERRING TO BASEBALL

♦ **Meritocratic**
Pertaining to a meritocracy, a system, in which the talented are chosen and moved ahead based on their achievement

*I identify with Babe
Ruth...a little
overweight and he
struck out a lot. But
he hit a lot of home
runs because he
went to bat.*

BILL CLINTON
U.S. PRESIDENT

process of decay. The gathering momentum of this self-feeding cycle—the more inner cities are abandoned, the less desirable they become as places to live and do business, so more people leave—had serious consequences for sports teams, many of whose facilities dated from the early part of the century. The African-American migration out of the South, a trickle beginning during World War I, became a flood in the years following World War II. To white suburbanites, who now made fewer trips into the cities they had abandoned, old stomping grounds began to look like unfamiliar territory, as poorer African and Hispanic Americans took their place. The combination of factors seriously reduced attendance at older ballparks located in central cities.

At the same time, Americans began a substantial internal migration to the Sunbelt cities of the South and West, a trend which continued well into the 1980s. Between 1940 and 1980 the population of the Sunbelt increased more than two and a half times as fast as that of the Midwest and Northeast, or frostbelt.

Television, a curiosity at the end of World War II, was fast becoming a dominant presence in American entertainment. In 1949 just under a million families owned a TV set; by 1951 the number had climbed to ten million, and two years later it doubled again. In 1955, two-thirds of American households owned a television, and by decade's end only 12 percent of households in the United States did not boast at least one.

Although TV networks neither invested heavily in sports programming in the 1950s nor claimed the kind of immense power in the sporting world they achieved two decades later, the new medium already began to influence patterns of sporting display and spectatorship. When fans could watch nationally televised, big-league baseball games, they stopped going to the hundreds of minor league parks in the country. Minor league attendance dropped precipitously, from forty-two million in 1949 to fifteen million in 1957.

Television changed boxing and other arena sports by first promoting them into new prominence, but then reshaping them in ways that contributed to their demise. During the brief "Golden Age" of boxing, for example, Gillette sponsored regular telecasts of Friday night bouts at Madison Square Garden. But in a development that foreshadowed TV's effect on other sports, boxing aficionados discovered that TV audiences, according to sponsors who presumed to speak for them, wanted a different kind of sport. They wanted offense—in this case slugging—and a lot

of it. Boxing strategy deteriorated, and local gyms and clubs found they couldn't compete with televised boxing. By the late 1950s half the nation's fight clubs had closed and only nominal audiences actually showed up for the broadcasts at Madison Square Garden.

The growth of TV, suburbanization, and the Sunbelt demographic shift helped to produce a decade of tremendous franchise movement in major league baseball. After fifty years of geographical stability, the Boston Braves moved to Milwaukee in 1953 and reversed its sorry fortunes. Two years later the Saint Louis Browns relocated to Baltimore, and the year after the Philadelphia Athletics moved to Kansas City. Then in 1958 the Brooklyn Dodgers, long a beloved symbol of working-class ethnic pride and home of baseball's "great experiment" with integration, departed their cramped and decaying quarters in Brooklyn for the suburban freeways of southern California. That same year the New York Giants accompanied their rivals west, to San Francisco.

It is a matter of some note that the Dodgers' relocation to Los Angeles still lives in sports mythology as an act of betrayal, second only to the fixing of the 1919 World Series. And yet owner Walter O'Malley's move was a thoroughly rational business decision: he was offered three hundred (120 hectares) acres of land near downtown, good access to highways, and the media market of the nation's third largest metropolitan area, factors which compared more than favorably with the thirty-five-thousand-seat Ebbets Field and attendance which had declined steadily for ten years despite excellent teams. Very little in the history of American capitalism suggests stability, and yet fans still felt that "their" team would stay put forever. This set of anomalies suggests the way that professional sport, unquestionably an entertainment business for almost a century, still occasionally offers a vision of relationships not wholly defined by the marketplace. There is, necessarily, a constant tension in professional sport in which business decisions frequently eclipse competing moral or emotional claims. Rational calculation of dollars and cents leaves little room for loyalty to neighborhood and peers.

Modern Times

The last generation of American sports history has been governed by five developments: TV's maturation into the single most powerful force in the sports business; the ascendancy of football; the fantastic growth of the financial stakes in professional sports; the rebellion of black and female athletes against condescension, segregation, and racial and sexual discrimination; and the changing power relations between owners and players. All of these were closely connected.

Roone Arledge, the most influential figure in televised sports in the past thirty years, through his productions *Wide World of Sports* (beginning in 1961) and ABC *Monday Night Football* (1970), transformed the way Americans thought about and watched sports on television. By using multiple camera angles, directional microphones, and striking close-ups, instant slow-motion replays, human interest crowd shots, and employing outspoken announcers with distinct personalities, Arledge repackaged football into an innovative sporting entertainment that crossed class, race, and gender boundaries. This novel program was meant to be comprehensible even to people who didn't know anything about football. As a result, professional football was able to shed its older image as a violent working-class sport perfectly suited to the grim realities of factory towns, and join—in fact, help create—a homogenous national culture of the managerial middle class. By the early 1970s professional football had surpassed baseball in TV, popularity, and had become the preferred sport of politicians. (Baseball's declining fortunes led owners to create divisions within leagues, to change rules in favor of the offense, and in the American League, to create a new position, the designated hitter.)

Monday Night Football, and Arledge's inspired broadcasts of the Olympics in the 1960s and 1970s, brought new groups of spectators to sports, audiences that advertisers were willing to pay for. More than ever before, the middle class, including women, watched the games and the ads. Until the 1980s, when networks faced intense competition from cable stations, the profitable partnership between sports and TV seemed to have no limit.

Television money has completed the transformation of college sports programs, particularly in football and basketball, into professional farm teams for the National Basketball Association and the National Football League. Colleges stand to earn so much money and publicity from topflight winning teams—one million dollars for each of the final four teams in the 1980 NCAA basketball tournament—that any remnant of an amateur ethos has little chance against the effort to subvert regulations against professionalism. Increasingly, heavily recruited high school athletes are being integrated into the same pyramid, with money and goods being supplied (on top of college scholarships) by advertisers like beer and sneaker companies.

Television also helped to create the careers, the financial base for, and, therefore, the symbolic power of black and female athletes in the 1960s, 1970s, and 1980s. The boxer Muhammad Ali, who first came to prominence as Cassius Clay, winning Golden Glove and Olympic championships in 1959 and 1960, had become the best known athlete in the world by the end of that decade. Combining unusual skill and energy in the ring ("float like a butterfly, sting like a bee," he characterized his style) with a quick outrageous wit and an extraordinary flair for self-promotion ("I am the greatest"), Ali outraged the sports world, after he won the heavyweight crown in 1964, by renouncing his "slave name" in favor of his new Muslim name.

Ali's vocal, unapologetic involvement with the separatist black nationalist Nation of Islam, and his 1967 refusal to be drafted into the army (on religious grounds) attracted enormous hostility from the white sporting and press establishment, but also gained him the adulation of more militant African Americans who admired his firm stance in the face of white disapproval. Ali evoked the memory of the first black champion, Jack Johnson, perhaps even more when he was indicted for refusing induction and the boxing authorities took his title away. Unlike Johnson, Ali fought his conviction until the Supreme Court overturned it in 1970. Then he won back the heavyweight title four years later.

Like Tommy Smith and John Carlos—American track stars who gave the black power salute on the victory stand at the 1968 Olympics and were summarily thrown out of the Games—Ali became a symbol for black athletes who struggled during the sixties and seventies to redress a history of unequal treatment in schools, sports programs, and on playing fields. Ali's success and power also owed much to TV, the medium which made him into a celebrity far beyond his ring exploits.

If the black revolt in sports saw some important gains—better salaries, more professional players, less public insistence that blacks conform to white cultural styles—significant discrimination remains to the present. African Americans are still overrepresented in certain sports (basketball, football) and positions within sports (outfielder, lineman) and underrepresented in other areas (tennis, swimming, quarterback, catcher), and there remain very few blacks in ownership, management, or front-office positions.

In America, it is sport that is the opiate of the masses.

RUSSELL BAKER
COLUMN IN THE NEW YORK
TIMES (OCTOBER 3, 1967)

See also
Television

Women's sports, too, underwent massive transformations in the past thirty years. Under the leadership of Billie Jean King, women's tennis vaulted to unprecedented levels of popularity, with purses to match. Through her outstanding tennis skills and articulate determination, King brought greater gender equality to women's tennis and also made the game of tennis more democratic, less dominated by the upper-class gentility of its origins. She brokered the successful marriage of women's tennis and television that brought money into her sport, and made her into a feminist heroine.

There have been other attempts to organize women's professional sports leagues—most notably in basketball and fast-pitch softball—but these have not yet found the financial backing necessary to survive in the world of televised professional sports. Although professional tennis remains the glamour sport for women, the women's movement of the late 1960s and 1970s had far-reaching impact on less visible sports. With the assistance of Title IX of the Educational Amendments Act of 1972 (passed through the efforts of women), females in school sports began to receive more funding.

TENNIS GREAT

Tennis pro Billie Jean King shakes hands with Bobby Riggs after defeating him in straight sets on September 20, 1973, in the so-called "battle of the sexes."

UPI / CORBIS-BETTMANN

The political controversies of the 1960s and 1970s—the civil rights and black power movements, the women's movement, even the anti-war movement—had important impact on the world of organized sports. While most of these were unsettling to the white men who continued to make up the largest part of the audience for professional and college sports, the one that perhaps provoked the most outcry was the changed relationship between players and owners in professional sports.

In the late 1960s and 1970s players in professional baseball, basketball, and football all organized newly aggressive unions and hired professional organizers. In 1975 a baseball arbitrator ruled that the game's "reserve clause" only held for a single year following the end of a player's contract, and that players could become "free agents" after that year. In one stroke players' market negotiating power was restored to a level not seen for a century. In the meantime, with TV contracts and new stadiums, the game had become much more lucrative. Players suddenly commanded extraordinary salaries.

Baseball salaries soared in the next fifteen years from an average of $46,000 annually in 1975 to $433,000 in 1988 to more than $850,000 in 1991. By the late 1980s the game's stars could command two and three million dollars per year, and Bobby Bonilla stunned the sports world when the New York Mets gave him a $29 million multiyear contract in the winter of 1991. Baseball owners fought back against the laws of supply and demand in ways reminiscent of more traditional industries. They stalled contract negotiations, staged lockouts, and—secretly and illegally—agreed among themselves to cap salaries. All of these strategies failed, as players shrewdly stuck together and outmaneuvered the owners. All the while, despite owners' periodic warnings of bankruptcy, the baseball business continued to prosper. Into the 1990s, franchises continued to mushroom in value, and after-tax balance sheets remained profitable.

Conclusion

Without television, neither Muhammad Ali nor Billie Jean King would have become powerful symbols or celebrities. Without TV, professional football probably would have remained a relatively class-bound, defensively oriented, unglamorous sport. Without the electronic media, beer and sporting goods companies would not have a pipeline through which they could pump hundreds of millions of dollars into the coffers of professional sports organizations and the pockets of athletes. And without the peculiar marriage of TV, sneaker companies, and the National Basketball Association, Chicago Bulls star Michael Jordan would not have become such a cultural and commercial icon in the black community.

As an entertainment business, modern sport seems to have inexhaustible potential. One of the central components of mass culture, sporting spectacles now appeal to nearly all demographic "markets." Even as late as the last quarter of the nineteenth century the sports audience was much more limited to working-class men and a significant minority from the middle and upper classes. TV's restless search for larger audiences with money to spend continues to domesticate and homogenize individual sports. And now the sports "seasons" that television created overlap and blend into each other almost without ceremonial pause—but not without pauses for commercials. With the assistance of sponsors, athletes have completed their transformation into celebrities, and now they are barely distinguishable from personalities on TV sitcoms or morning news/entertainment shows.

Ironically, the very nature of sport as business—the dream of riches it holds out to young athletes and hungry producers alike—guarantees it will remain intimately connected to the seedier side of culture and society: gambling, alcohol, drugs, and sexual promiscuity. The extraordinary pressures on athletes to succeed—to have a chance at the big money, or once having achieved it, to keep earning it—frequently lead them to the consolations of alcohol and other recreational drugs. Where so much depends on the proper functioning of a superbly trained body, performance enhancing drugs (painkillers and steroids, for example) seem to offer crucial assistance. And for men who have been emotionally coddled since adolescence the lure of sexual opportunism is hard to resist.

If Michael Jordan, known as "Air" Jordan (after the name of the shoes he sells for Nike) represents one image of modern sports, Pete Rose may stand for the other. For more than two decades Rose played baseball single-mindedly, passionately, and exceptionally well, fully earning the nickname Charlie Hustle. But Rose's gambling activities (which got him banished from the game in 1989) placed him firmly inside baseball's 150-year-old relationship with the culture and society of urban low-life.

By virtue of its inherent vitality, the modern sports business is drawn in competing directions, toward greater blandness and homogeneity in an effort to further broaden its televised appeal, while the promises it makes to potential participants encourage Faustian bargains. Along with the lottery and with about the same odds—the sports arena remains one of the last places in America where a person can strike it rich.

—WARREN GOLDSTEIN

THE SUBURBS

Images of suburbs underlie much of American culture today. Television sitcoms from *The Dick Van Dyke Show* to *Roseanne* have made a suburban setting familiar, funny, and resonant with their American audiences. A 1962 Malvina Reynolds song, "Little Boxes," characterized suburbs thusly:

> And the people in the houses
> All went to the university,
> Where they were put in boxes
> And they came out all the same.

In the early 1990s David Byrne sang of a suburban landscape full of Taco Bells and parking lots. Erma Bombeck's *The Grass Is Always Greener over the Septic Tank* (1976) is only one of many imaginatively titled volumes on suburban living that have been published since the 1950s.

American culture is suffused with suburban images because today it is overwhelmingly suburban. Kenneth T. Jackson, in his path-breaking synthesis of American suburban history, *Crabgrass Frontier* (1985), describes how the decades after World War II brought "the suburbanization of the United States." The evidence for such a process is manifold. Suburbs became the predominant home for Americans, with more than 40 percent of the population living in the suburbs, according to the 1980 census. Between 1950 and 1970, more than three-quarters of all new manufacturing and retail jobs were located in suburban areas. Overall between 1950 and 1970, 83 percent of the nation's total growth took place in suburbs. The overwhelming extent of this postwar suburbanization, with its trademark shopping malls, express highways, and industrial parks, leads many to assume that it *began* in 1945—which is not the case. Indeed, settlements on the fringes of cities are as old as the oldest American cities.

Early Suburbs

The earliest suburbs bore little resemblance to the ideal described by the famous landscape architect and planner Frederick Law Olmsted (1822–

Suburbs are things to come into the city from.

ART LINKLETTER
A CHILD'S GARDEN OF
MISINFORMATION

See also
The City

459

1903): "the most attractive, the most refined, and the most soundly wholesome forms of domestic life, and the best application of the arts of civilization to which mankind has yet attained" (quoted in Fishman, *Bourgeois Utopias*, p. 198). Before improvements in urban transportation transformed the "walking city," the most highly prized residential locations were close to the center of town. In Europe this was a centuries-old tradition: those with wealth and influence lived in town, while the poor and other outcasts lived outside city walls. In the United States similar forces were at work, and the word "suburb" had definite pejorative connotations. Early-nineteenth-century Philadelphians, for instance, forced unwanted businesses, such as slaughterhouses, and people of lower status to the outskirts of the city.

The suburban villa was an important exception to low-status outlying settlements. It was in many respects the antecedent of the modern suburb. From ancient Greece to eighteenth-century England, the wealthy elites of many societies have had country estates and houses. Such houses were located on the outskirts of cities—far enough away to avoid city problems but close enough for easy travel to and from town. These estates had many of the amenities available in city homes because large retinues of servants ensured the provision of basic comforts such as heated rooms, baths, and lighting. Elite families with many servants operated as self-contained islands—regardless of whether they were in the city or the country. It was not until the development of mechanical systems to provide services and amenities—and all of the socioeconomic changes the elite relied upon—that proximity to neighbors and a community became important to the comfort of a household.

The Suburb in the Industrial Era

In the nineteenth century, suburban communities developed across the United States as the demands of their residents—often newly transplanted from cities—for services and amenities came to resemble those of urbanites more than those of rural dwellers. Suburbs emerged from new communities as well as older rural settlements. Only after the emergence of uniquely urban services and amenities—which is to say, those unavailable in the countryside—did people feel a need for suburban governments, associations, or developers. Initially, transitional areas between the city and country contained some urban-oriented activities but had no special services to distinguish them from the adjacent countryside. As cities grew, though, they physically impinged

THE BIRTH OF THE SUBURB

Robert Fishman places the birth of suburbia in late-eighteenth-century London. The tremendous growth of London during that century led to an urban crisis. Some called for reforms such as urban squares and wide streets to alleviate congestion and disorder. However, a growing repulsion toward the city, especially by middle-class merchants, led many to establish weekend villas where their families could escape London's turmoil. These merchants prized "picturesque," naturalistic landscapes. By concentrating villas while still employing picturesque landscaping, they created the first romantic suburbs. As Fishman describes an early suburb at Clapham, outside London, "each property is private, but each contributes to the total landscape of *houses in a park*" (p. 55). Manchester's Victoria Park and Liverpool's Rock Park, both designed in the 1830s, are other examples of early British romantic suburbs.

A similar process took hold in the United States within decades. In antebellum Chicago, the word "suburb" often described an outlying community that was a small agricultural town or an industrial site. There were no commuters in these areas, but the residents were tied more closely to cities than were their more distant counterparts by farming for the city and by coexisting with noxious industries that city dwellers gave rise to but would not tolerate. Frequently, newspaper accounts used the term as an adjective—a "suburban" villa or "suburban" home. For instance, "suburban" served to describe the second home of a wealthy Chicagoan whose family spent summers and holidays away from the congestion and disease of the city. It also characterized the home of a Chicagoan who had retired from an active life in the city to become a gentleman farmer. As time went on, real estate developers planned romantic suburbs such as Chicago's Riverside and Lake Forest; these places combined rural living with urban amenities.

upon these formerly outlying communities, causing many to take on the features of a suburb—that is, a place that sought to combine the services and amenities of the city with country living.

The solitary country estate with an army of servants gradually gave way to suburban communities with mechanical service improvements. This transition from human to mechanical supports extended the option of suburban living, formerly reserved for the wealthy, to the middle classes. Lewis Mumford argued that the widening economic base of the suburban movement in Britain in the early nineteenth century, and in the United States later in the century, was the result of transportation innovations. While transportation advances were certainly important in making suburban living possible and affordable for more people, it was the extension of urban amenities to outlying communities that permitted the modern suburb. This is not to say that they negated disparities in wealth, though; transportation improvements did remain essential to the suburban option for all but the wealthiest. Until the 1830s, settlement in and around American cities was largely circumscribed by the distance a person could walk in an hour or so. However, the intro-

duction of the steam ferry (1811) and the omnibus (1830s), the railroad and the horsecar (from the 1840s), the cable car (1870s), and the electric streetcar (1880s) transformed the pattern of settlement within cities. For the first time people could live at some distance from their place of work and commute by means of public transportation.

This separation of work and home was integral to the modernization process in nineteenth-century cities. Facilitated by improving intracity transportation, it gave rise to urban residential areas based on class, ethnicity, or race. These residential areas no longer needed to contain a wide range of economic functions and types of people. Suburbs became an archetype of this segregation into residential areas homogeneous with regard to class. Sam Bass Warner, Jr., has ably explored the agglomeration of Boston's population by class in late-nineteenth-century streetcar suburbs. At the base of this segregation was a community, not an individual home. As Carol O'Connor explains in "The Suburban Mosaic," "early observers [of suburbs] note the existence of relatively homogeneous local units within heterogeneous suburban regions" (p. 245).

THE SUBURBS

The Suburb in the Industrial Era

ELECTRIC STREETCARS

A young boy leaps onto a moving streetcar as the conductor of another streetcar watches him. The electric streetcar revolutionized mass transit and opened up hundreds of locations for suburban development.
LIBRARY OF CONGRESS / CORBIS

461

*In the first half of
the twentieth
century, urbanites
had usually looked
to the inner city for
entertainment; those
residing in the
suburbs used street
railways to make
their way
downtown.*

PAGE 474

See also
Village and Town

Suburban dwellers were the first to take advantage of ferryboat services. A ferry connection between Manhattan and Brooklyn in 1814 made Brooklyn one of the first commuter suburbs in the United States. Commuters on ferries became a familiar sight by the late nineteenth century. And compact, built-up communities in New York and Philadelphia allowed horse-drawn omnibuses to proliferate in the early nineteenth century. By the second half of the nineteenth century, the railroad, too, had an important impact on suburbs by tying outlying areas more closely to the city center. Thus, the range of areas considered suburban expanded dramatically to include larger towns that served as trading centers for agricultural areas close to the city.

In 1888 the perfection of the electrified street railway (first tested in Richmond, Virginia) led to even more changes in suburban commutation patterns. By 1895, 85 percent of all street railways in the United States had been electrified. The electric streetcar revolutionized mass transit and opened up hundreds of locations for suburban development. No longer restricted to the radial patterns of commuter stops, suburban developers began to fill in the territory between stops.

The automobile took this filling-in process one step further. First visible in cities at the turn of the century, automobiles began to predominate by the 1920s. In 1920 there were over nine million cars in the United States; by 1930 this number had more than tripled to twenty-six million.

It is important to remember that the railroads, streetcars, and automobiles did not *create* these settlements on the outskirts of American cities. Rather, they expanded the area in which suburbs could appear and, as noted earlier, made suburban living affordable for more people. These transportation advances also worked to concentrate suburban settlement along their lines, particularly near railroad and streetcar stations.

Increasingly the term "suburb" was used to designate the settlement surrounding a railroad station. By the 1870s, the frequency and fares of trains to outlying areas were important factors in defining an area as suburban. The availability of relatively inexpensive commuter tickets was crucial for suburban development.

By the 1880s, many of these early suburbs tried to provide urban amenities. Suburbanites did not wish to forsake the society and comforts of the city, so parks, schools, cultural associations, and services like running water and sewer connections became part of the ideal suburban community. These improvements, of course, did not take place

overnight. In 1873 the existence of a waterworks in Irving Park, a community outside Chicago, was noted in advertisements for suburban homes. It was an amenity not available in many other suburban communities and was thus cause for special mention. By the 1890s the "model" suburban home was found in a community with paved streets, schools, good transportation, and other services usually available only in the city. This was a far cry from the antebellum picture of a "model" suburban home: an isolated country house to which a wealthy family retired.

This evolution was also evident in changes taking place in established rural towns, as the railroad and population growth pressed suburban expansion further from the city. The increasingly suburban character of many former agricultural towns can be traced in commuter schedules, inclusion of their residents in society registers, and the growing demands for urban services. These demands were met in part by community associations (or real estate developers in new areas), but more and more residents turned to local government for their provision.

In addition to residential development, industry and commerce had been a part of the suburban scene from the beginning. The hinterland was already home to market towns and noxious industries, and suburbanization simply engulfed many of these functions. Also, by the turn of the century, the owners of manufacturing establishments took advantage of relatively inexpensive land along railroad lines to establish suburban plants. For instance, George Pullman established his Pullman car works—and the model town Pullman—in south suburban Chicago in 1882. Glendale, near Cincinnati, was another such planned suburb.

The general trends outlined here were the result of thousands of individual decisions. In his study of Boston's nineteenth-century streetcar suburbs, Sam Bass Warner, Jr., notes "a building process which rested in the hands of thousands of small agents" (p. 117). One set of actors is particularly important to this process: the real estate developers who planned, built, and marketed suburban communities.

The most visible developers were those who created planned suburbs. In the nineteenth century Frederick Law Olmsted was among the most notable designers. He was joined in the twentieth century by developers such as Jessie Clyde Nichols, William Levitt, and James Rouse. Olmsted and his partner, Calvert Vaux, planned sixteen suburbs in the decades after the Civil War, among them Brookline and Chestnut Hill in Massachusetts, Sudbrook and Roland Park in Maryland, Yonkers and Tarrytown Heights in New York, and Riverside in Illinois.

Backed by the Riverside Improvement Company, Olmsted and Vaux sought in designing a suburb in 1868 to "unite at once the beauties and healthy properties of a park with the conveniences and improvements of the city" (Keating, *Building Chicago*, p. 73). Water and sewer mains, individual gas hookups, streetlamps, paved roads, parks, sidewalks, and a railroad depot were just some of the amenities offered. Deeds for lots sold in Riverside included restrictions on building lines, minimum prices for homes and the prohibition of fences; community parkland adjoined all lots. A contemporary account reminded potential residents that "parties buying at Riverside will have the satisfaction of avoiding the demand upon their resources for taxation in the way of improvements, so constant in all towns."

In the nineteenth and twentieth centuries real estate syndicates, land companies, and improvement associations opened thousands of subdivisions in suburban areas across the United States. Through these improvement companies, speculators sought to direct urban growth into the hinterland. Improvements to heighten marketability and attract settlement to particular subdivisions fell into two basic categories: those outside the subdivision and those within it. In the first category were extensions of streetcar and commuter rail lines, the construction of connecting highways, and the development of neighboring parks and boulevards. Among the improvements within subdivisions were commuter rail stations, industries and/or businesses, home construction, and infrastructure such as sidewalks, paved roads, electricity, and water and sewer lines.

While much suburbanization has been unplanned, there are notable exceptions; their influence, however, is debatable. In 1927 Clarence Stein

ORIGINS OF SUBURBAN GOVERNMENT

In the same way that the concept of a suburb evolved over the course of the nineteenth century, its government developed and changed. Early in the century a move to an outlying area was seen as a way of avoiding much of the intrusion of local government on one's life. By the 1870s this changed for many suburban areas, whose residents clamored for more government involvement in the provision of services.

Such demands, though, were not calls for the replication of urban forms. By the mid-nineteenth century, city government had acquired an unenviable reputation. An 1869 *Chicago Times* editorial (7 April) commented: "Municipal government in this country is a system of machinery to collect and consume taxes without returning anything like an adequate compensation. It has been refined, and expanded, and compounded to an extent that renders it next to unbearable." Outlying residents sought to obtain and to avoid city government; they needed a form of government somewhere between the urban and the rural.

The contrast between urban and rural government was strong from colonial settlement through the antebellum period. The chartered municipal form, drawn from British antecedents, gave special

rights and privileges to urban governments that other local governments did not receive. While the early nineteenth century saw the erosion of the special powers held by chartered cities, their governments were still easily distinguishable from those of rural areas. Suburban government emerged as a new form by the end of the nineteenth century, providing many of the services of chartered urban governments while being shaped by rural governments.

Robert C. Wood examined suburbs and their governments in *Suburbia: Its People and Their Politics* (1958). He felt that while suburbs were home for modern Americans, their governments were decidedly archaic: "They join the other suburban political units around our large cities in clinging persistently to the independence they received when they were isolated villages and hamlets in a rustic countryside" (p. 9). According to Wood and others, suburban government has hindered the development of metropolitan governments that could better serve urban areas. Such an indictment of suburban government goes back to the early years of the twentieth century, when political scientists began to criticize metropolitan governments, often in conjunction with reformers (or as reformers) advocating metropolitan consolidation.

S

*American City: A
place where by the
time you've finished
paying for your
home in the suburbs,
the suburbs have
moved 20 miles
farther out.*

EARL WILSON
AS QUOTED IN READER'S
DIGEST (JUNE 1956)

See also
Transportation and Mobility

and Henry Wright, under the financial sponsorship of Alexander Bing, planned Radburn, New Jersey, the first garden city in the United States.

During the New Deal the federal government directed the construction of three model suburban communities: Greenbelt, Maryland, near Washington; Greenhills, Ohio, near Cincinnati; and Greendale, Wisconsin, outside Milwaukee. Rexford Tugwell supervised these projects under the Resettlement Administration. Planning began in 1935, and construction was under way for the following three years. The three projects contained housing for 2,267 families. Tugwell believed there should have been not three but three thousand of these projects.

One of the purposes of the program was to demonstrate the advantages of resettling both urban and rural residents in a suburban environment where homes and jobs were located. There was to be plenty of light and many gardens and parks. Urban amenities such as good schools, public utilities, and job opportunities were included in the original plans for each town. But the greenbelt towns never worked out economically, and Congress authorized their sale in 1949 at just over $18 million, half of their $36 million total cost to the federal government.

Consolidation and Annexation

Annexation to the core city was a significant issue for suburbs until the early twentieth century; in some areas, notably those where development and increasing population have been more recent, it remains important. Core cities generally provided superior services and drew many early suburbs within their boundaries as suburbanites sought improvements. In addition, some suburban governments were successful while others were short-lived and soon abandoned; annexation often involved unsuccessful suburban forms.

Studies have identified several important factors in explaining the halt to annexations around the turn of the century. Jon C. Teaford and Kenneth Jackson have provided the most succinct discussions on this subject. Teaford explains:

> *By 1910 suburban America was a segregated collection of divergent interests, industrial and residential, Protestant and Catholic, truck farmer and commuter, saloon habitué and abstainer. . . . Each of these segments sought to escape from others and to achieve its goals by taking advantage of the state's willingness to abdicate its control over the creation of municipalities.* (City and Suburb, p. 12)

Jackson notes that this fragmentation heightened racial, ethnic, and class distinctions. Coupled with these divisions was the fact that by the end of the nineteenth century, incorporation as a suburban municipality was an easy process. Suburban municipalities, as well as special districts, dramatically improved the services available outside the city, thus eliminating what had been the strongest drawing card of annexation to the center city—better and less expensive services.

For instance, Brooklyn was incorporated as a city in 1834, and it later annexed two neighboring entities in 1855 and more territory in 1896. This process was spurred on by the introduction of a street railway network and the opening of the Brooklyn Bridge in 1883, both of which encouraged suburban settlement in its nearby rural townships. These townships, like those around Chicago, were composed of multiple settlements that competed for limited town funds. The fledgling suburban communities turned first to the rural townships with their demands for improvements, but they received only limited satisfaction. It was to receive better services and representation that the citizens of these townships agreed to annexation.

In New York the incorporated township and the incorporated village emerged in the closing decades of the nineteenth century to serve an increasing number of suburban communities. The forms were not unlike those found in Chicago: the contiguous townships that were providing suburban services were eventually annexed to the center city. At the same time that the adjacent townships were being absorbed by the city, a number of outlying suburbs began to incorporate as villages. Mount Vernon, just outside the Bronx towns that were annexed to New York City, incorporated in 1892 and avoided annexation. Nearby Bronxville was developed as an exclusive suburb after 1890; it incorporated as a distinct village in 1898, in order to facilitate the orderly development of the area. The end result of these annexations and incorporations was a metropolitan area composed of a central city surrounded by incorporated suburbs.

To the north, as Boston grew to metropolitan status, a similar process was taking place. The major difference was that village incorporation was not an option in Massachusetts. Many of these outlying townships possessed a unique, independent history until the mid-nineteenth century, when commuter railroads and streetcar lines drew them into a suburban orbit. Massachusetts's Charlestown, Cambridge, and Roxbury were among the towns that incorporated during the 1840s. Like the towns surrounding Chicago, they were composed of multiple settlements that were joined in a single incorporated government. The town of Cambridge, for instance, was composed of at least three settlements: Old Cambridge, Cambridgeport, and East Cambridge. Some of these modified rural governments became successful suburban forms, and Boston annexed others. As noted earlier, suburbanites created new townships that could more easily provide suburban services and representation. In contrast to New York City, Brooklyn, and Chicago, incorporated townships in Massachusetts became the most familiar suburban type as well as the form of government involved in annexations.

While the township was an important form for suburban governance in the nineteenth century (and beyond for Boston), it played virtually no role in metropolitan areas in the South and the West. For instance, California did not use the township except as a judicial unit. Townships did not serve as intermediate forms while cities like Los Angeles and San Francisco grew. Instead, the county was the basic unit of local government in California. There, as in some other western and southern states, a chartered county form evolved, which was employed in urban areas where more functions were demanded of local government.

The city and county of San Francisco were made coterminous in 1856, after the first spurt of urban growth; but no significant area has subsequently been annexed to San Francisco. Surrounding the city were chartered counties that absorbed further metropolitan growth. Within these counties, however, were incorporated villages and cities similar in scope to those in midwestern and Middle Atlantic metropolitan areas. In the Los Angeles metropolitan area today, numerous chartered counties form the basis of government, with incorporated suburbs and cities—including Los Angeles proper—serving parts of the counties.

Students of Suburbs

Late-nineteenth-century observers heralded the suburban community as the great hope for an industrializing world. One of the first to describe the suburb was Adna Ferrin Weber, in his 1899 study of urban growth, *Growth of Cities in the Nineteenth Century*. According to Weber, a suburb combined the healthfulness of the country with urban improvements. Weber's suburb had a lower population density than the center city and was distinguished from the surrounding countryside

by its city improvements, comforts, and society. Weber saw that the continued deconcentration of urban populations, even in an unplanned fashion, would greatly improve the daily lives of metropolitan residents.

Suburbs were seen by many early social scientists and reformers as a means of humanizing city life. Henry George, the popular nineteenth-century economist and social critic, promoted the benefits of the single tax, arguing that such a government levy on all land rents would make suburban living possible for more of the nation's population. George's 1879 *Progress and Poverty* argued that this would be a dramatic improvement for residents of metropolitan areas:

> *The destruction of speculative land values would tend to diffuse population where it is too dense and to concentrate it where it is too sparse; to substitute for the tenement house, homes surrounded by gardens, and to fully settle agricultural districts before people were driven far from neighbors to look for land. The people of the cities would thus get more of the pure air and sunshine of the country, the people of the country more of the economics and social life of the city. (p. 147)*

Visionary planners such as Ebenezer Howard of London sought to create garden suburbs that would allow as many people as possible to enjoy the benefits of suburban living. In his 1898 study *Garden Cities of Tomorrow* (1902; repr. 1945), Howard argued that "town and country *must be married*, and out of this joyous union will spring a new hope, a new life, a new civilization" (p. 48).

Howard's garden-city idea was essentially a plan for moving individuals, as well as industry, out from the city center to provide a more healthful environment. He proposed construction of a town-country magnet that would draw people from cities and rural areas alike. Natural beauty, social opportunities, high wages, and low rents would draw residents to new garden cities. The garden city would be economically self-sufficient yet be at one with nature. Population would be restricted, and all residents would be provided with jobs within the bounds of the community.

Like Weber and George, Howard called for further suburbanization (deconcentration) so that more metropolitan residents could take advantage of the benefits of suburban living. Also in agreement was the urban reformer Frederic C. Howe. In *The City: The Hope of Democracy* (1905), a study of the future of the city in American society, he ar-

America . . . always will have a suburban president . . . defined by the suburbs . . . where walking means driving, where talking means telephoning, where watching means TV, and where living means real, imitation life.

ARTHUR KROKER, DAVID COOK, AND MARILOUISE KROKER
CANADIAN SOCIOLOGISTS, IN PANIC ENCYCLOPEDIA (1989)

465

gued that suburbanization represented the democratic hope of the future.

As the first generation of academic social scientists began to examine and evaluate life in American metropolitan areas, they were struck with the improvements that suburbs brought to metropolitan life. During the 1920s political scientist Harlan Paul Douglass admired suburbs that combined the virtues of city and country: "It [the suburb] is the city trying to escape the consequences of being a city while still remaining a city. It is urban society trying to eat its cake and keep it, too" (*The Suburban Trend*, p. 4).

This is not to say that suburban living was idyllic. It was often lonely—especially for women—and the challenge of maintaining city standards in suburban areas was often overwhelming. William Dean Howells wrote of many of the pitfalls of suburban living in his 1875 *Suburban Sketches*: "In town your fancy would turn to the theaters; in the country you would occupy yourself with cares of poultry or of stock: in the suburb you can but sit upon your threshold, and fight the predatory mosquito."

Other critics of suburbs focused much of their attention on its governance. In 1933 Roderick McKenzie viewed suburban government as "little short of disastrous" and noted that "every great city now has around it a metropolitan area, one with it economically and socially but without

political unity" (*The Metropolitan Community*, p. 303). Many critics followed in his footsteps.

More recent historians have added a great deal to our knowledge of suburbs in the late nineteenth and early twentieth centuries. Many case studies have been completed. Warner's *Streetcar Suburbs* stands as a seminal work in the burgeoning subfield of suburban history. As Michael Ebner noted, it was "the first book by an urban historian to examine systematically the suburban tradition" ("Re-Reading Suburban America," p. 228). It served as an important model for subsequent studies.

Several of Warner's arguments were particularly important in setting an agenda for research in suburban history. First, Warner widened the scope of suburban research to include urban neighborhoods that were once suburban. He also felt that nineteenth-century Bostonians' desire for suburban homes was rooted in a rural ideal. In most basic terms, according to this ideal, the country is home to what is good about America, while the city harbors much that is bad. Second, Warner argued that the first suburbs in the United States emerged in the late nineteenth century, with the outward reach of streetcars that enabled the middle class to move from the city center. He argued that the streetcar suburbs were organized along class lines—not by the ethnic enclaves found within neighborhoods closer to the

SUBURBAN HOMES

The United States has become overwhelmingly suburban. Between 1950 and 1970, 83% of the nation's total growth took place in suburbs.
FRANKLIN MCMAHON/
CORBIS

city center. Warner also found that these suburban communities were the result of thousands of individual decisions—not some large-scale plan—to build and settle within the distinct areas of Dorchester, West Roxbury, and Roxbury. Finally, Warner lamented the passing of annexation movements and the rise of politically fragmented metropolitan areas.

Later studies, responding to Warner's arguments, often refined, and sometimes disagreed with, his interpretations. Some found patterns similar to those in Roxbury, Dorchester, and West Roxbury with the arrival of the streetcar and subsequent suburban development. Henry D. Shapiro and Zane L. Miller found that Clifton, a Cincinnati suburb, resembled Warner's suburbs, with growth tied to transportation advances and a subsequent annexation to the city. Joel A. Tarr traced the growing segregation of work and residence in nineteenth-century Pittsburgh, tying this closely to transportation improvements.

By looking at two Boston suburbs, Cambridge and Somerville, Henry C. Binford found that suburban growth took place decades before the arrival of the streetcar. Thus suburbanization there had not depended on the evolution of transportation. While Warner proclaimed the late nineteenth century "the first suburban era," Binford has shown quite convincingly that Cambridge and Somerville were suburbs and commuter havens in the decades before the Civil War.

Another study that focuses on Boston suburbs is *Shaky Palaces* (1984) by Matthew Edel, Elliott Sclar, and Daniel Luria. Taking issue with Warner's view that the building process was the result of thousands of individual decisions, these authors argue that "the building of homes is not the only phase of the building of suburbs. Providing transport access and utilities, and subdividing the farms and woods for small-scale builders to purchase, are also a part of the suburban process." Ronald Dale Karr examined yet another Boston suburb, Brookline, which contrasts strongly with Warner's suburbs. Its residents were wealthier and supported an activist government that rejected annexation. Karr found that the suburban government guided development by selectively withholding services, and that developers used restrictive covenants to shape the communities they were founding. These forces were not apparent in Dorchester, Roxbury, and West Roxbury.

Carol A. O'Connor, in her study of Scarsdale, New York, found that the village government was engaged in actively shaping the community through construction regulations. Zane Miller's study of Forest Park, a twentieth-century Cincinnati suburb, explored the important interaction between developers, local government, and residents in shaping the community.

Post-World War II Suburbs

Although suburbs do have a long history in the context of metropolitan areas across the United States, the explosion in suburban growth after World War II eclipsed much of the earlier growth. Between 1950 and 1970 the suburban population more than doubled, from thirty-six million to seventy-four million. In the fifteen largest metropolitan areas in 1980, the majority of the population lived in suburbs (with the exception of Houston, where only 45 percent of the population lived in suburbs).

There are many reasons for this tremendous growth. As in the earlier periods of suburban growth, transportation innovations spurred new outward expansion from city centers. The automobile and, more important, the superhighway transformed local transportation and settlement patterns across metropolitan areas. Although the federal highway program, including its capstone 1956 Interstate Highway Act, was aimed not at cities, but at connecting them with one another and with rural areas, subsequent highway development transformed the suburban landscape. Public transit went into a permanent decline as the ratio of citizens to registered passenger automobiles dropped from 1,078:1 in 1905 to 4:1 in 1950 to 2:1 in 1970.

Another important reason for the post-World War II suburban boom was the predominance of Federal Housing Administration (FHA) and Veterans Administration (VA) insured-loan programs, which made it less expensive to own a home than to rent in many metropolitan areas. Before the FHA began operation, individuals generally had to put down between one-third and one-half of the property cost. With FHA the down payment necessary for most homes dropped to under 10 percent, lowering a tremendous barrier to home ownership. Between 1934 and 1972 the percentage of American families owning homes jumped from 44 percent to 63 percent. In addition, although the FHA and VA did not lend money to developers, their loan assurances for home buyers allowed developers to borrow the extremely large sums of money necessary to construct large suburban tracts such as those of Levitt and Sons. The FHA also established minimum standards for home construction. Most homes built to FHA and VA standards had central heat-

Through the suburbs sleepless people stagger.

FEDERICO GARCIA LORCA
LINE IN "THE DAWN," IN THE
POET IN NEW YORK (1940)

They are the death of the soul.

J. G. BALLARD
TALKING ABOUT THE
SUBURBS IN
RE/SEARCH NO. 8/9

See also
Rock Music

*Slums may well be
breeding grounds of
crime, but middle-
class suburbs are
incubators of apathy
and delirium.*

CYRIL CONNOLLY
THE UNQUIET GRAVE

A POSTSUBURBAN ERA?

Does "suburb" remain a usable word in the 1990s? Many historians and journalists think not. "Exurbia," "outer city," edge city," and "technoburb" are among recently coined terms to describe recent varieties of suburbs and/or their predominant trends. The suburb, once a hallmark of modernity, may have become an anachronism.

No one better explores this question than Robert Fishman in *Bourgeois Utopias* (1987). He argues that "suburb" is no longer a useful description of contemporary America: "To me the massive rebuilding that began in 1945 represents not the culmination of the 200 year history of suburbia but rather its end. Indeed, this massive change is not suburbanization at all but the creation of a new kind of city, with principles that are directly opposed to the true suburb" (p. 183). In contrast with suburbs, which were closely tied to central cities, Fishman finds "technoburbs." A technoburb is a peripheral zone, possibly as large as a county, that operates as a viable socioeconomic unit. The boundaries of a technoburb are defined by the locations that can be accessed easily by car:

*Spread out along its highway growth
corridors are shopping malls, industrial
parks, campuslike office complexes, hospitals,
schools, and a full range of housing types. Its
residents look to their immediate surroundings rather than to the city for their jobs and
other needs; and its industries find not only*

*the employees they need but also the special-
ized services. (p. 184)*

While less definitive about the end of a "suburban era," Jackson also sees fundamental changes ahead, perhaps a postsuburban age. With urban gentrification and a rural renaissance, Jackson posits in *Crabgrass Frontier*, "that the long process of suburbanization, which has been operative in the United States since about 1815, will slow over the next two decades" (p. 297).

Whatever the future, the fact remains that the physical shell of suburbanization—including housing, schools, commercial centers, transportation, and other infrastructure improvements—will remain with us for years to come. Suburbanization as a process may come to an end, but we will continue to live with what past generations have built.

In addition, one of the most dramatic characteristics of suburbanization—its ability to create relatively homogeneous local units within larger heterogeneous regions—does not appear to be loosing its hold. The technoburbs that Fishman identifies no longer look to central cities, but they still purposefully exclude those enterprises, peoples, and activities deemed inappropriate by law and custom. Continued political fragmentation further strengthens the power of these relatively homogeneous local units, just as it did in the past. In short, while suburbs have changed dramatically, we will not soon be rid of their physical manifestations; nor has new outlying development abandoned all suburban characteristics.

ing, indoor plumbing, telephones, and several major appliances.

Both the FHA and VA insured-loan programs fueled new building in suburban areas. FHA insurance went to new residential developments, primarily in suburban areas (or outlying districts within some cities). In establishing criteria for underwriting home loans, the FHA made it virtually impossible to receive their insurance within older city neighborhoods. Jackson notes that in a sample of 241 new homes insured by the FHA in metropolitan Saint Louis (1935–1939), 91 percent were located in the suburbs.

This dramatic shift from city to suburb in metropolitan areas across the country affected many social and cultural trends. Young white people,

through the VA and FHA insured-loan programs, were able to purchase homes far away from their families in city neighborhoods. Women, however, were particularly isolated from the world of work and employment opportunities, as Gwendolyn Wright notes, and this led to many frustrations and problems. Perhaps no one has set out those frustrations more clearly than Betty Friedan in her 1963 book, *The Feminine Mystique*.

Another striking characteristic of suburban growth in the post–World War II period has been its racial segregation. That is, suburbs in metropolitan areas across the United States have been inhabited largely by whites. For instance, during the 1960s in Chicago, 287,000 white families moved to suburban areas; only 13,261 black fam-

See also

Landscapes; Commercial
Architecture

ilies obtained residences in a six-county area outside the city. This segregation persisted despite growing numbers of black families in suburban areas during the 1970s and 1980s. In 1980 the proportion of suburban blacks in the United States reached 23.3 percent.

This continuing segregation may stem in part from actions of the federal government. Jackson uncovered important connections between the FHA and VA insured-loan programs and residential segregation in the decades since 1930. He found that FHA underwriters "supported the income and racial segregation of suburbia" (*Crabgrass Frontier*, p. 13). Before racial covenants were outlawed by the U.S. Supreme Court in the 1948 *Shelley* v. *Kraemer* decision, the FHA openly recommended them. The FHA insurers also shied away from any neighborhoods that lacked "economic stability" or "protection from adverse conditions." These were means of redlining whole areas of center cities, many of which were minority occupied.

Compounding this residential segregation has been the shifting nature of occupational structure in metropolitan areas across the United States. While suburbs have been home to industry and business from their beginnings, there was a remarkable shift in manufacturing activity in the years after World War II. Between 1947 and 1967, 293,307 manufacturing jobs (4 percent) were lost by central cities in Standard Metropolitan Statistical Areas (SMSAs—areas with populations greater than one hundred thousand in 1960). At the same time, manufacturing employment in the suburbs increased by 3,902,326 (a 94 percent increase). The suburban share of SMSA manufacturing employment increased from 36 percent in 1947 to 53 percent in 1967. This suburbanization of certain job opportunities has been particularly disadvantageous for the minority groups, who have limited access to suburban residential areas.

—ANN DURKIN KEATING

Cut off from the mainstream of humanity, we came to believe that pink is "flesh-color," that mayonnaise is a nutrient, and that Barry Manilow is a musician.

BARBARA EHRENREICH
THE WORST YEARS
OF OUR LIVES (1991)

T

TELEVISION

No means of communication has equaled the capacity of television to reach large masses of people. With the launching of communications satellites in the 1960s, television could instantly transmit both sound and moving pictures to millions of people from anywhere on earth as well as from outer space. In 1969, for example, an estimated 723 million people, more than triple the population of the United States, saw a human first set foot on the moon. Subsequent improvements in transmission and the widespread ownership of receivers soon made it possible to reach more than half the world's peoples simultaneously.

Within less than a generation after its introduction in the late 1930s, television had woven itself completely into the fabric of all modern societies. By the 1990s, Americans spent about one-quarter of their lives watching television, and on average, American households had at least one set turned on for seven hours each day. For many people the rhythms of daily, weekly, and seasonal programming measured the passage of time as much as watches or calendars. Viewers frequently "knew" the actors, comedians, politicians, and news commentators on television better than their neighbors, friends, or co-workers. For most Americans, television replaced friends, the print media, radio, and the movies as their primary source of both entertainment and news. The "mediated" world of television, one framed by the technical limits of the medium and by what its controllers presented, also offered abundant cues for daily living. In particular, television programming and advertising suggested consumption as a therapy for feelings of impotency, loneliness, sexual deprivation, and meaningless work.

In the United States, program content was the product of varied social influences, government regulations, and, above all, the medium's economic character. Social influences included the experiences, aesthetic judgments, values, creativity, and artistic skills of those involved in program production; the industry's internal codes; the influence of media critics; and the varied pressures exerted by the television audience on program-

ming. Government regulations arose from television's dependence upon the airwaves for transmission. The Communications Act of 1934 mandated that, in exchange for receiving exclusive use of the airwaves, commercial television stations, along with radio stations, "operate in the public interest, convenience, and necessity." The degree to which the Federal Communications Commission (FCC), the federal agency assigned responsibility for enforcing the act and its subsequent modifications, exercised authority over program content and regulated other facets of the industry varied over time. (In the late 1970s and in the 1980s Congress and the FCC removed most of the accumulated government-imposed restrictions and guidelines.)

Except for public television, nothing ultimately determined program content as much as the industry's dependence upon receipts from advertising. Vigorous competition for advertising revenues among the local stations and their program suppliers (until the 1980s almost exclusively three national networks), as well as competition between television and other media, drove the industry to seek mass audiences. To obtain larger audiences, the program producers turned to entertainment. Entertainment, the use of virtually any technique to keep the viewer riveted to the receiver, thus became a salient characteristic of nearly all programming. The requirements of entertainment invaded even what were officially labeled as newscasts, sportscasts, and educational programming.

Television in the United States, in contrast with television in nearly all other nations, has been almost entirely a private rather than a public enterprise. In most nations, if there is a system dependent upon advertising, it must compete with a strong system subsidized by the public. In the United States, on the other hand, public television has received meager state support and has never drawn more than 5 percent of the total viewers. Of some 1,400 American television stations in operation in 1990, only 335 were public or educational stations. Until the 1980s nearly 90 percent of the privately owned stations were affiliated with one of the three giant commercial networks—

In television we have the greatest instrument for mass persuasion in the history of the world.

BUDD SCHULBERG
SCREENPLAY, A FACE
IN THE CROWD (1957)

See also
Journalism

the American Broadcasting Company (ABC), the Columbia Broadcasting System (CBS), and the National Broadcasting Company (NBC), which provided them with about two-thirds of their programming.

The Evolution of the Television Industry

In the 1920s and 1930s, the Radio Corporation of America (RCA), a giant company that manufactured radio equipment and owned NBC, was at the forefront in the development of American television. Hoping to profit from the sale of television cameras, transmission equipment, and receivers, RCA, under the direction of hard-driving David Sarnoff, spent an estimated fifty million dollars financing the continuing research of Vladimir K. Zworykin, a Russian-born American scientist, who in 1929 had demonstrated the first practical electronic system for both transmission and reception of images. Sarnoff also purchased valuable licensing agreements and patent rights from Philo T. Farnsworth, an American inventor. As early as 1936, RCA conducted tests of its all-electronic television system from atop the Empire State Building, broadcasting pictures at a rate of thirty complete pictures (frames) per second. In the same year, CBS purchased a system from RCA and installed it in the Chrysler Building,

near its radio studios in the Grand Central Terminal Building.

The year 1939 marked a series of firsts: NBC began regular telecasts in New York City with the opening ceremonies at the World's Fair and the network beamed the first televised baseball game, from Baker Field at Columbia University. In 1941, the FCC approved limited commercial broadcasting and accepted the television industry's recommendations for 525 lines per frame and 30 pictures per second as transmission standards, standards that are still in use today. During World War II, however, as engineers and their sponsors turned their energies elsewhere, improvements in television's technology came to an abrupt halt. Only six stations remained on the air, and they broadcast only locally, irregularly, and a few hours a day to fewer than ten thousand receivers.

After the war, a striking improvement in the television camera stimulated the industry's growth. To obtain what at best was a mediocre picture, Zworykin's iconoscope camera required great quantities of light. In response to the poor picture quality, Zworykin invented, and in 1945 RCA introduced, the image orthicon camera tube, which was even more sensitive to nuances in light and dark than most of the motion picture cameras of the day. "All of a sudden, we had an instrument

EARLY TELEVISIONS

Workers put together televisions on an RCA assembly line in the early days of TV.
CORBIS-BETTMANN

that reproduced a quality, picture with the atmosphere and mood that [Alfred] Hitchcock or [Ingmar] Bergman might require," recalled Worthington Minor, who at the time was CBS's manager of program development.

Abetted by the orthicon camera, by the FCC's decision to resume the licensing of new stations in 1945, by the resumption of the production of transmitters and receivers at the end of the war, by American Telephone and Telegraph's (AT&T) rapid construction of intercity coaxial cable links, by corporations eager to advertise their goods, and by consumers with accumulated savings, commercial television prospered, Taverns in particular rushed to acquire sets; groups made up mostly of men gathered around them nightly to watch wrestling, boxing, and other sports. In 1948, an estimated one million sets were in use, forty-eight television stations were in operation, and about seventy stations were under construction. Although an FCC freeze that had been imposed in order to bring some order to the chaotic industry halted the licensing of new stations between 1948 and 1952, the completion by AT&T of a transcontinental coaxial cable trunk in 1951 allowed the networks to inaugurate nationwide telecasts. Families owning sets skyrocketed from 50 percent of all families in 1953 to 90 percent in 1960.

Other technical improvements aided the industry's growth. The perfection of magnetic videotape in the late 1950s eliminated the contingencies of live programming and permitted endless reruns. In 1953 the FCC finally approved a color system compatible with black-and-white sets, but because of the additional costs in production, transmission, and receiving, color television grew slowly. Until 1965 only NBC, whose parent company, RCA, was the major manufacturer of color sets, showed more than a few programs in color. In 1965 a little-noted poll indicated that viewers had a decided preference for color, which led CBS to introduce a full array of color shows that fall; ABC announced that it would begin to transmit mainly in color in the fall of 1966. Within two years, monochrome network shows disappeared, the prices of color sets fell by about half, and color picture quality improved substantially. (The old black-and-white sets continued to receive broadcasts but still reproduced programs in monocolor.)

Apart from technical limitations, television operated within constraints imposed by the FCC, pressure groups, and advertisers. The Communications Act of 1934 guaranteed access to commercial television by those holding views not shared by the station ownership. In 1949, the FCC formalized the access concept with a set of procedures called the Fairness Doctrine. Although modified several times by the FCC, the courts, and Congress, in essence the doctrine required broadcasters to devote a reasonable amount of time to controversial issues of public importance and to give those with opposing viewpoints a reasonable amount of air time to express their positions. In practice, the doctrine may have been counterproductive. Neither the networks nor the stations relished giving "free" time and possibly reducing their audiences by the presentation of contentious issues, so they chose simply to reduce their coverage of controversial topics, thereby avoiding the need to give air time to unpopular subjects or personalities.

Self-regulation was a far more important restraint than FCC policies. Fearing the loss of sponsor support and alienation of a share of the audience, each network established a standards-and-practices department. These "network censors" acted as gatekeepers between program producers and the audience. They reviewed program concepts, story lines, scripts, and proposed footage in terms of what might give offense to sponsors or the audience. During the early cold war years of the late 1940s and the 1950s, the networks also blacklisted many performers and

Television programming is dominated by comedy shows, especially situation comedies.

PAGE 231

SPONSORS

Influence over Content

Sponsors, particularly in the early days of network television, exercised an exceptionally large and direct influence over program content. Until the late 1950s, a single advertiser frequently sponsored an entire program (as had been the practice in radio), which was typically produced by the sponsor's advertising agency. Sponsors could be explicit about what they wanted in a show. For example, writers for *Man Against Crime*, a show sponsored by Camel cigarettes, received mimeographed instructions to delete all scenes of "disreputable persons" smoking cigarettes; neither could cigarette smokers be shown coughing. But with rapidly escalating costs in the late 1950s, few advertisers could afford to purchase the time for an entire program. Multiple advertisers gave the networks far greater control over program content, though networks continued to remain sensitive to the responses of sponsors.

See also
Sports in the Twentieth Century

473

writers who had been charged by self-appointed investigators with being Communists or Communist sympathizers. Threatened by the withdrawal of sponsors, the media shamelessly fired or refused to hire persons found on such lists; they even employed their own "security checkers" and required employees to sign loyalty oaths. Blacklisting continued until the late 1950s, when the domestic anticommunist movement lost some of its momentum.

In the 1980s the near-monopoly once enjoyed by the "big three" commercial networks on the delivery of programs abruptly ended. In the 1970s and 1980s new competition arising from the rapid growth of independent stations, the appearance of "superstations"—stations that employed communications satellites to beam programs nationwide—the growth of cable television systems, and the mass marketing of videocassette recorders (VCRs) sharply reduced the proportional audience share and advertising revenues of the "big three" networks. The networks' audience share dropped from more than 90 percent in the 1970s to about 70 percent in 1990, and their proportion of total television advertising revenues fell by about one-fourth. Deregulation added to the television industry's instability. Beginning in the late 1970s and continuing through the 1980s, the FCC dropped many of its regulations, including the Fairness Doctrine (1987). In the 1980s, marketplace forces almost completely determined the industry's direction.

Effects on American Life

Although not easily isolable from other forces, television quickly, directly, and in some instances drastically affected American life. One of its most readily observable effects was on leisure. In the first half of the twentieth century, urbanites had usually looked to the inner city for entertainment; those residing in the suburbs used street railways to make their way downtown to shop or go to restaurants, movies, indoor arenas, saloons, concert halls, and the theater. Baseball parks, football fields, and amusement parks, though often located outside the central business district, could be reached cheaply by mass transit.

As millions moved to the sprawling suburbs after World War II and purchased their first television sets, they took their leisure activities with them. They made home repairs and worked in their yards, listened to music on high-fidelity phonograph records, and watched television. With television, each family had at its fingertips entertainment previously available only by going out to the theater, vaudeville, or the movies. "More than a year passed before we again visited a movie theater, recalled one man after the purchase of the family's first television set in 1950. "Money which previously would have been spent on books was saved for TV payments. Social evenings with friends became fewer and fewer still." Families went out less, slept less, and read less, and the children played outside less than before. That by 1970 comic book sales had plummeted to half the 1950 totals suggested the medium's power over children.

Novelty alone did not account for the medium's magnetism. With each subsequent decade, viewing time increased. People did not necessarily watch closely; studies indicated that family members frequently did other things while "watching" television, although they could often recall substantial amounts of program content. Viewing was consistently greater among children of elementary school age or younger than among high school or college-age youth; older people watched more than younger adults, blacks and Hispanics more than whites, and the less educated more than the better educated. Yet the discrepancy among these groups in viewing time typically averaged less than forty-five minutes a day, thus revealing the truly mass character of the new medium.

The shift of spare-time activities from public places to the privacy of the home nearly destroyed inner-city commercial leisure. In the 1950s and 1960s, movie theaters, bars, restaurants, dance pavilions, nightclubs, and amusement parks closed in great numbers. The large dance bands that had been so popular in the 1930s and 1940s all but disappeared. Attendance at inner-city high school sports events and at wrestling and boxing matches fell; none ever regained the prosperity that they had once enjoyed at the local level. In the 1950s both major-league and minor-league baseball attendance fell; the minor leagues never recovered, and even the big leagues never caught up proportionally with the population growth of the cities they served.

With the advent of television, the fans at home rather than those in the stands increasingly became the ultimate arbiters of which sports thrived and which ones failed. College and professional football fared much better on television than baseball. Baseball, with its multiple perspectives and wide vistas, did not translate well onto the small screen, whereas the more concentrated action and recurring drama in each series of downs

See also
Suburbs

made football an ideal sport for the new medium. The perfection in the 1960s of the instant replay and the slow-motion shot allowed fans at home to experience football in an entirely different way from those in the stands. The televised Super Bowl, a product of the merger of competing professional football leagues in 1966, eventually became an unofficial national holiday and a spectacle regularly watched by more than half of the nation's population. The exciting telecast from Munich of the 1972 Olympic Games, which included monumental blunders, sparkling heroes, and the tragedy resulting from the invasion of the Israeli compound by Palestinian terrorists, transformed the games into a worldwide quadrennial spectacle.

TELEVISION AND POLITICS

Shaping an Image

Television exerted a large influence on politics. In 1952, Richard M. Nixon's "Checkers speech" on television aided the senator in salvaging his shaky vice-presidential candidacy. In 1960, viewers and journalists alike proclaimed the handsome and relaxed John F. Kennedy the "winner" over a swarthy and wary Richard M. Nixon in the first televised debates between presidential nominees, but several studies agreed that the debates affected the final decisions of only a few voters. Nonetheless, because of the popular belief that the debates of 1960 had damaged Nixon, the better-known candidate and the front runner in the polls at the time of the first debate, no debates were held in 1964, 1968, or 1972. In 1976, both Jimmy Carter, a relative unknown, and Gerald Ford, an incumbent president who had been tied to Nixon's presidency and initially trailed badly in the polls, had reason to engage in televised debates. The decisions by Ford in 1976 and Carter again in 1980 to debate apparently set a precedent that made it difficult for any future incumbent to avoid a televised debate. Television debates among candidates for lesser posts also became commonplace.

Television, along with computers and public opinion polls, introduced what has been described as "the new politics." Candidates employed professional pollsters to gather the opinions of various constituencies, computers sorted the data, and finally media consultants plotted a strategy based upon the results of the polls. The media experts approached campaigns in terms of "selling a candidate," which entailed the same strategy as selling consumer goods to the public. Thus media people considered the management of images or impressions to be far more important to success than where the candidate stood on the issues. Richard M. Nixon's presidential campaign of 1968 was a classic example. Nixon's campaign staff put together a series of clever television advertisements that projected a "new Nixon," one who was more unflappable, relaxed, and skillful in dealing with controversy than he had been in the past. "Reason pushes the viewer back, it assaults him, it demands that he agree or disagree," explained one of Nixon's media consultants, while "impressions can envelop him, invite him, without making an intellectual demand."

The media consultants frequently resorted to images that appealed to primitive fears. During the 1964 election, President Lyndon Johnson's media people aired the "daisy" commercial aimed at his opponent, Barry Goldwater, who was accused of being too aggressive in relations with the Soviet Union. The commercial showed a little girl in white pulling the petals off a daisy. As she counted down to zero, the scene dissolved into an atomic explosion, and then a voice—by implication Johnson's—came on: "These are the stakes. To make a world in which all God's children can live, or go into the dark." Although political scientists repeatedly expressed skepticism about the efficacy of image manipulation, either their reservations were not shared by the candidates or the candidates were unwilling to take any chances. In the 1980s, appeals to raw emotions through image advertising became even more common.

Television refashioned politics in other ways. Candidates sought to say and do things that would maximize their coverage on television news programs. Presenting elections in terms of sporting contests, the medium increased the importance of the presidential primaries, especially the earlier ones, in the nominating process. Rather than serving as meetings to choose candidates, the national party conventions became carefully orchestrated television shows for acclaiming decisions already made. With television becoming the largest single item in campaign budgets, the costs of running for public office escalated to undreamed-of heights. Astronomical campaign costs generated a rising concern in the 1980s about the influence of large campaign contributors on the political process.

In the age of the postwar "baby boom," television quickly became a popular entertainment form.

PAGE 151

Television quickly altered the character of competing forms of entertainment. Network radio programming gave way almost completely to television; by the early 1960s few network entertainment programs remained on radio, and less than a third of the radio stations had a national affiliation. In the age of television, radio became a largely local medium, with each station aiming at a special audience. Confronted with competition from television, the movie industry either adjusted by making films for the new medium or aiming its fare at teenagers and young adults (those who watched television the least), a strategy that encouraged film content to become more experimental, violent, and sexually provocative.

Within a decade, *Life, Look, Collier's,* and *The Saturday Evening Post* had ceased to exist as mass-circulation weekly magazines. On the other hand, television, with its emphasis upon capturing a mass audience, left ample room for periodicals that appealed in depth to specialized tastes; in the 1970s and 1980s these magazines proliferated and prospered.

Television induced changes in the content of print media. Newspapers soon began to set aside regular allotments of space for columns on television and the listing of upcoming programs. *TV Guide,* founded in 1953 and completely devoted to television, became the largest circulation periodical in the United States; by 1976, it sold 20 million copies weekly. Blatantly copying formulas successfully employed by television, in the 1970s and 1980s the popular magazines *People, Us,* and several imitators featured short articles—nothing requiring more than a minute-and-a-half to read, ordered one editor—and abundant illustrations, all laced with titillating accounts of the activities of celebrities. *USA Today,* a national daily newspaper that imitated television news and talk shows, completed the cycle in 1980 when it syndicated its own television program, *USA Today: The Television Show.* By the 1990s newspapers throughout the country were beginning to ban stories that continued on another page, feature more celebrity stories, and employ more eye-catching graphics.

Early Programming

Even though nearly all commercial television programs were designed simply to entertain, they simultaneously disseminated information and suggested models for daily living. Apart from the news, the endless commercials, the tales of outlawry in the old West, of urban crime, and of international intrigue, the miniseries and the docudramas, and the antic tensions in situation comedies (sitcoms) all furnished viewers with implicit or explicit interpretations of the past and the present. With its enormous power to evoke images and fantasies, television also offered viewers visions of and strategies for achieving personal fulfillment.

Although changes in technology enlarged the medium's capabilities and the nation experienced great social upheavals during network television's first four decades, most program forms remained remarkably constant. The early morning news shows, soap operas, the late-night and midday talk shows, Saturday morning children's cartoons, evening news programs, game shows, sitcoms, and even the commercials all had their origins in the late 1940s and early 1950s. Only drama altered its essential character. In the early years, television presented drama live and, rather than weekly shows based upon the same set of characters and situations, viewers could see dozens of completely new productions each week.

Nothing that viewers saw on television was more pervasive or constant than commercials. In the late nineteenth century, advertisers had begun to sense the effectiveness of suggesting a causal relationship between consuming a particular brand of a product and being youthful, desirable, rich, powerful, or successful. Television gave advertisers the opportunity to convey the linkage between consumption and the satisfaction of personal needs in far more compelling, but at the same time more subtle, ways than had earlier media. The ads did not need to be explicit: in the 1950s viewers saw scores of cleaning products used in fifteen-thousand-dollar kitchens, and in the 1960s they saw countless soft-drink ads with the young engaged in exuberant play. Smoking a certain brand of cigarette seemed to promise excitement, romance, and ultimately sexual satisfaction. Ads not only appropriated lifestyles and held out consumption as a solution for personal needs, they also sold visions of America itself. Nothing distinguished the United States from other nations—not even democracy or respect for individual liberties—as much as its capacity to provide consumer goods. The ads depicted the United States as a consumer paradise.

Entertainment program content also reflected television's close ties to the consumer culture. During its first full season in 1949, television explicitly conjoined consumption and entertainment in such programs as *Kelvinator Kitchen* and *Missus Goes A-Shopping,* the latter a supermarket customer participation show. Debates over the purchases of goods for the home furnished the main story line for innumerable postwar sitcoms, and before FCC rules eventually prohibited the practice, news, quiz, and variety shows usually displayed the sponsor's name conspicuously on podiums, clocks, or walls so that it would be visible to viewers throughout the program. Shows in the 1940s and 1950s took the name of their sponsors: *The Kraft Television Theater*, *Camel News Caravan*, and *The Bell Telephone Hour*, for example. Variety show host Milton Berle's program was called *The Texaco Star Theater* and opened with service station attendants, outfitted in Texaco uniforms, singing "Tonight we may be showmen, but . . . tomorrow we'll be servicing your car!"

The variety show, a format that could be cheaply and easily produced, was a favorite of early television. Rooted in earlier vaudeville, circuses, and radio, the variety shows filled the screens with singers, dancers, magicians, jugglers, and animal acts. Comedians, including Sid Caesar, George Gobel, and Milton Berle, usually hosted the shows. Between 1948 and 1956, Milton Berle, a Catskills resort comedian and a child of vaudeville, earned the title of Mr. Television or, more informally, Uncle Miltie. Berle, who had not been a top performer in radio, found in television a perfect medium for the employment of his sight gags, outrageous costumes, and general buffoonery. A noncomedian, Broadway gossip columnist Ed Sullivan, hosted a far more enduring variety show. With a keen sense for presenting acts when they were of the most topical interest, he premiered both Elvis Presley (1956) and the Beatles (1964) on network television.

Variety shows soon lost their central place on prime-time television, however. Although Ed Sullivan, Jack Benny, and Red Skelton survived for more than a decade by employing a traditional format, competition with filmed series either ended variety shows or forced them to offer something distinctive. *The Smothers Brothers* succeeded in the late 1960s by offering comedy that was irreverent and antiestablishment, and *Rowan & Martin's Laugh-in* for a time (1967–1973) captivated audiences by fast-paced cutting from one scene to another and its more candid handling of sexual and political materials. But by the mid-1970s, except in non-prime-time hours, the variety show disappeared almost entirely from network television.

Sitcoms, a direct transplant from radio, were a far more enduring staple of prime-time television. Week after week the same basic cast of characters played in the same format. In the 1950s Jackie

I LOVE LUCY

The cast of TV's I Love Lucy *poses for a publicity photo. Pictured are: Vivian Vance, standing on left, next to Lucille Ball. Seated on left is William Frawley next to Desi Arnaz.*
UOI / CORBIS-BETTMANN

Gleason as Ralph Kramden, Phil Silvers as Sergeant Bilko, and Lucille Ball as Lucy Ricardo were all inclined to concoct elaborate schemes to advance their fortunes that in the end invariably miscarried. No other show exceeded the popularity of *I Love Lucy*. Featuring the beautiful, zany, and always scheming Ball, her shows ran almost continuously, with only short interruptions, on CBS from 1951 until Ball's retirement (with her ratings still high) in 1974. Even in the 1990s, viewers could find Ball reruns on stations throughout the world.

The family sitcoms of the 1950s communicated no simple, monolithic message. True, no shows equaled the sitcoms in their emphases upon the benefits of traditional family life, the suburbs, and the consumer culture. The lives depicted in the typical 1950s sitcoms mirrored the fantasies of a generation who sought to escape and forget the deprivations and turmoil that they had experienced in the Great Depression and World War II. Yet the dramatic tension required to attract viewers often revolved around the dissonance between the past and the present, between inner-city, ethnic, working-class family origins and the transformation of the family into homogeneous, middle-class suburbanites devoted to consumption. Ethnic working-class sitcoms, such as *The Goldbergs*, *Mama*, *The Honeymooners*, and *The Life of Riley*, presented families in inner-city neighborhoods and explored value conflicts that revolved around family identity, consumer spend-

See also

Humor and Comedy

T

TELEVISION

Early Programming

Disparagement of television is second only to watching television as a national pastime.

GEORGE F. WILL
"PRISONERS OF TV,"
THE PURSUIT OF HAPPINESS
AND OTHER SOBERING
THOUGHTS (1978)

See also
Film

ing, gender roles, ethnicity, and the nature of work and leisure.

Shows designed for children quickly became an integral part of network programming. Although children spent many hours watching whatever was shown, as early as 1947 NBC's *Howdy Doody* captivated them with its frenzied action. While Howdy Doody regularly promoted good behavior, Clarabell, the show's androgynous clown, regularly flouted adult authority. *Kukla, Fran, and Ollie* and *Captain Kangaroo*, both of which originated in the 1950s, had much more relaxed paces. By the mid-1960s, the three networks set aside Saturday morning entirely for children; then children could see made-for-television cartoons, all of which incorporated fast-paced action and most of them unending violence. The Saturday morning format remained in place for the next two decades.

Nothing about television programming caused as much widespread concern as its possible effects on children. In 1952 Senator Estes Kefauver held the first of many congressional hearings on the subject, and by 1990 more than 250 separate studies had been conducted on children's television. A consensus of the studies indicated that television watching encouraged short-term aggressive behavior and insensitivity to violence. Less debatable was the patent abuse of the child market by advertisers. The sponsors unrelentingly assaulted children with alluring advertisements for toys and nonnutritious foods. A 1991 study, for example, counted 222 junk food ads in one Saturday morning's set of cartoon shows. Critics also blamed the medium for a decline in College Entrance Examination Board scores (beginning in 1964), a decline in ability to think sequentially, encouragement of sensual gratification, and a general distrust of authority. All of the charges were plausible, but inventing a research design that could pinpoint the precise influence of television on such behaviors was impossible.

The 1950s achieved its vaunted and exaggerated reputation as the "golden age" of television through its live Broadway-like drama and public affairs programming rather than through variety shows, sitcoms, or children's shows. For a brief interlude, mainly from 1952 to 1955, live drama, with completely new shows ranging from thirty minutes to a hour and a half each week, was part of the regular nightly fare of network television. The shows offered opportunities for scores of talented young playwrights, producers, directors, actors, and actresses. The writers included Rod Serling, Gore Vidal, and Paddy Chayefsky. Chay-

efsky's *Marty*, later made into a movie, became a television classic.

Television's brief experimentation in the 1950s with live theater and large quantities of public affairs programming arose more from special circumstances than from audience preferences. Inadequate technology limited the possibilities of taped shows, and Hollywood, fearing competition from the new medium, initially refused to provide television with first-run movies. With CBS's near-monopoly on the stars in the 1950s, NBC had little choice but to experiment with live shows, even when they were expensive and their costs were not necessarily covered by advertising revenues. In addition, the longer live shows offered the networks an opportunity to gain greater control over programming. By 1960, packagers—companies that combined talent, production facilities, and program ideas—produced about 60 percent of television network programming, the networks about 20 percent, sponsors only about 14 percent, and individuals—like Lucille Ball—the rest.

In some instances, the absence of sponsorship fostered experimental programming. Several of the public affairs programs, including Edward R. Murrow's *See It Now* on CBS and *Today*, which was introduced in 1952 by NBC to fill a morning scheduling gap, initially had no sponsors. With Dave Garroway in Chicago as host, *Today* included an innovative magazine format, a combination of news, informational features, and light banter. Neither ABC nor DuMont (a short-lived fourth network) had many sponsors for daytime programming; hence they beamed the Army-McCarthy hearings of 1954 in full while NBC and CBS, with more sponsored daytime programming, carried only limited parts of the hearings.

The high-stakes, prime-time quiz shows contributed to the demise of the golden age. At the height of the fad, five shows were shown in a single day. In order to guarantee that popular contestants remained on the air, producers began providing them with answers prior to the show. When this practice was exposed in 1959, network executives denied knowing anything about the rigging, but they quickly canceled almost all of the shows. The scandal led to a congressional inquiry, the adoption of internal controls against deceit, steps by the networks to gain greater control over their programming, and the growing use of filmed series from Hollywood.

By the late 1950s, network competition had settled into a pattern that encouraged program standardization. CBS had demonstrated that, on the whole, the regular showing of familiar series was more popular than dramatic anthologies. NBC fired its chairman (and effectively, director of programming), Sylvester (Pat) Weaver, in 1956, the same year that CBS overtook NBC in the ratings, and named Robert Kintner, a past president of ABC, as its president; he had broken the Hollywood boycott by persuading Walt Disney in 1954 and Warner Brothers in 1955 to become makers of television programs. Kintner preferred the more predictable filmed series over live shows, and he inaugurated a new era in which Hollywood films became a staple of network programming.

Television News

Copying the format used in radio and without the resources to provide extensive film footage, the first television newscasts consisted of little more than a camera focused on a journalist reading from a script. In one of the few instances of clearcut "advocacy" news in the history of television, Edward R. Murrow in 1954 exposed the methods of Senator Joseph McCarthy, though the live telecasts of the Army-McCarthy hearings in the same year contributed even more to the senator's rapid fall from power. Even in the 1950s there were signs that obtaining high ratings depended

more on the personality of the person who delivered the news and the way the news was packaged—how entertaining it was—than on the network's effectiveness in presenting or analyzing events. Chet Huntley and David Brinkley's conversational and lighthearted treatment of the na-

---

TELEVISION NEWS IN THE 1960S

A Social Commentary

While nearly all Americans applauded television's handling of the space race and Kennedy's assassination, television's treatment of the divisive social issues of the 1960s soon embroiled the news media in controversy. Whether because of the "liberal" or "modern" values of television newscasters or because of the compulsion to make the news more entertaining—as critics charged—or simply by showing the savagery of white responses to peaceful demonstrations by blacks, televised newscasts added momentum to the civil rights movement. Simply by giving it coverage and by magnifying its size, television also abetted and shaped the character of the youth revolt of the 1960s. On the other hand, by its coverage of the burning and looting of urban ghettos during the "long, hot summer" of 1965 and the more violent and radical side of the youth rebellion in the late 1960s, the medium encouraged a widespread backlash against both movements.

For fifteen years (1961–1975), television newscasts brought to American homes the "living room war" in Vietnam. Although initially the networks stressed the value and the successes of the American military effort, no previous war had been so accessible to reporters. Reporters could cover and film almost anything they wished. While military press briefings consisted mainly of dry, "factual" material, including daily "body counts" of the enemy allegedly killed, the television reporters sent back vivid images—of body bags containing corpses, of angry, frustrated soldiers, of troops setting fire to a village with their cigarette lighters, of Vietnamese orphans, of Buddhist monks setting themselves on fire with gasoline. With the Tet offensive that was mounted by the enemy in 1968, journalists began to abandon remaining pretenses of neutrality. A decisive turning point in public support for the war came when, according to President Lyndon Johnson, Walter Cronkite urged on his evening newscast that the United States pull out.

All television is educational television. The question is: what is it teaching?

NICHOLAS JOHNSON

tional political conventions in 1956 transformed those newsmen into stars for NBC; that fall they became the hosts of NBC's evening news show. In 1962, Walter Cronkite, who conveyed an image of avuncular omniscience, began his tenure as anchorman and star of CBS's evening news program.

Television news came of age in the 1960s. With the expansion of nightly news from fifteen to thirty minutes in 1962 by both CBS and NBC, more exciting drama could frequently be found on the news programs than on prime-time entertainment shows. Television's reporting of the space race with the Soviet Union, beginning with John Glenn's orbital flight in 1962 and culminating with the moon landing in 1969, captivated millions worldwide. The assassination of President John F. Kennedy and subsequent events in November 1963 led the networks to cancel their regular schedules completely. For four days, as many as 93 percent of American homes watched television's intimate coverage of the events. In such times of crisis, the electronic media seemed to allay panic and ease the transition of power.

Entertainment Programming in the 1960s and 1970s

Throughout the 1960s entertainment programming reflected none of the great social upheavals found on the network news shows. Rather than family life in the suburbs or urban-oriented variety shows, rural, small-town, and western settings characterized much of the prime-time television fare from the late 1950s to the early 1970s. The Westerns entered their heyday; an astonishing thirty-two Western series were shown in the 1959–1960 season alone. Two of them—*Gunsmoke* (1955–1975) and *Bonanza* (1959–1973)—were among the longest-running shows in television history; their romanticization of the American West won them a worldwide audience as well. Dozens of family sitcoms, including *The Andy Griffith Show*, *Mister Ed*, *The Beverly Hillbillies*, *Green Acres*, *Petticoat Junction*, and *The Real McCoys*, reflected the appeal of non-urban settings.

Although frequently dismissed by television critics as trivial entertainment, Paul Henning's CBS sitcoms, *The Beverly Hillbillies*, *Green Acres*, and *Petticoat Junction*, satirized modern, urban America, especially its preoccupation with technology and consumption. *The Beverly Hillbillies*, a show rivaled in popularity only by *Bonanza*, returned to an ancient theme in American and European literature: the physical and moral superiority of pastoral or rural life over urban life. Although transplanted from the Ozarks to the

decadence and splendor of California's Beverly Hills, Jed Clampett, the male lead played by Buddy Ebsen, remained selfless, honest, fair, and incorruptible. He was, in the words of media critic David Marc, "a yeoman beyond the fantasies of Jefferson. Henning's *Green Acres*, a mirror reversal of *The Beverly Hillbillies* in that it placed city slickers amid rural people, brought into even sharper relief the fundamental conflict between America's past and its present.

While the Westerns did not frontally assault modernity, they were part of a wide-ranging and flourishing culture of compensation. In the 1955–1956 season, the "adult Westerns," such as *Cheyenne*, *Gunsmoke*, and *Tales of the Texas Rangers*, with their more complex plots and vivid renderings of violence, rode into prime time. Amid the daily network news programs depicting bitter internal divisions and the continuing perils of the cold war, the Westerns affirmed the continuing potency of the individual. The heroes came in different guises. Some were strong and brave, others dashing and romantic, and still others shrewd and comic, but in the end they all relied mainly upon their own resources to conquer villains. An urban counterpart to the adult Westerns was *The Untouchables*, an exceptionally violent show that starred Robert Stack as Eliot Ness, an incorruptible government agent who relentlessly and successfully pursued mobsters in the 1920s. Women may have found some compensation for their special plight in *I Dream of Jeannie*, *Bewitched*, or *The Flying Nun*, shows that portrayed women with magical powers. By implicitly drawing attention to the subordinate position of women, such shows may even have contributed to the coming of the women's liberation movement of the 1960s and 1970s.

The televised version of the bone-crunching game of college and professional football also furnished forceful images and fantasies of individual power. Television triggered a literal "takeoff" in football's popularity in the 1960s. While networks marketed the game as an endless array of spectacular collisions between padded giants, the perfection of slow motion, instant replay, and color increased audience appreciation of the sport's intricate plays, and the long completed pass and the breakaway run suggested the possibilities—at least on occasion—of the lone individual transcending the vast odds arrayed against him. Professional football even invaded prime-time television; in 1970 ABC inaugurated *Monday Night Football*, a program that almost at once absorbed the attention of millions of American men (and a number of American women) every Monday night in the fall.

The 1969–1970 season represented something of a watershed in television's programming history; not a single holdover from the 1968–1969 "top ten" series retained its position five years later. Westerns and rural sitcoms all but disappeared from regularly scheduled network programming. The programs looked different: blacks and ethnics suddenly became prominent, and hippielike hairstyles and clothing became common. The programs sounded different: a wave of greater permissiveness in language swept through the medium, and programs began treating previously taboo subjects such as interracial marriage, sexual impotence, and ethnic conflicts.

"Demographics," the industry's term for describing potential viewers in terms of such marketing characteristics as age, sex, and income level, rather than general audience ratings, dictated the sweeping program changes. The prevailing rural sitcoms and Westerns appealed to a broad constituency, but more to the young and the old than to the especially hard-to-reach young adults, those eighteen to thirty-four years old, who purchased the most goods and services. Under Robert D. Wood, CBS, the leader in network prime-time overall audience ratings, startled the industry by dropping a large number of still-popular shows—Jackie Gleason, Red Skelton, Andy Griffith, Ed Sullivan, *The Beverly Hillbillies*, *Green Acres*, *Hee-Haw*, and *Petticoat Junction*—and replacing them with urban-oriented shows that purported to have more "contemporary relevance."

Norman Lear's *All in the Family*, a sitcom based upon a popular show in Great Britain, led the way. Premiering in 1971, *All in the Family* not only leaped to the top of ratings charts but also revealed, for the first time on prime-time television, fundamental clashes between the young and the old, whites and blacks, men and women, as well as ethnic and religious divisions, and may have introduced a new synonym for "bigot"—"Archie Bunker"—into the language. The success of *All in the Family* led Lear to produce such spinoffs as *Maude*, whose heroine had an abortion and went through a long separation from her husband, and *The Jeffersons*, a show based on an upwardly mobile black family. "Relevancy," "realism," and "timeliness" became watchwords of sitcom producers in the 1970s.

In a fundamental sense, the new sitcoms were far less radical than they seemed. They incorporated and institutionalized the stresses and styles of the 1960s, thereby taming them and bringing them into the mainstream of popular culture. In the shows, family ties if not the family itself remained essentially conventional. Even *All in the Family* presented traditional marriages, an extended family living for most of the show's duration under the same roof, and the irascible Archie as an emotionally vulnerable person devoted in his own way to his wife and daughter. And sitcoms without fathers, mothers, or children invariably depicted the family as a critical source of strength and values. In *M*A*S*H*, *The Mary Tyler Moore Show*, *Barney Miller*, and *Cheers*, among other shows, family-like relationships with workmates served as effective surrogates for those of the more traditional family.

Only public television offered some kinds of programming not available on the commercial networks. In 1952 the FCC set aside channels for noncommercial television, but growth was slow until the late 1960s, when improved funding from foundations, federal and state governments, and viewer contributions encouraged the establishment of national programming services. No program established public television's visibility more than *Sesame Street*, a show introduced in 1969 to teach preschool-age children their numbers and letters. Using techniques employed by commercials, the show was an instant success and soon was shown in language-adapted forms in all the major countries of the world. In the 1970s and 1930s original series such as *The Adams Chronicles*, in-depth documentaries, and several series from Britain won the raves of critics and occasionally audiences equal to those of network programs in some cities.

The Effects of Deregulation and Increased Competition

The advent of deregulation of the networks and the fierce competition offered by cable systems and VCRs in the 1980s failed to produce dramatic changes in programming. True, cable provided viewers with around-the-clock news, weather, sports, music videos, religion, reruns, movies, and shopping programs, but none of the cable networks had the resources or promise of a big enough audience to justify spending large amounts of money on new programming. Except for quantity, cable entertainment shows looked much like their network counterparts. Influenced in part by the programming successes of public television, the networks presented more made-for-television movies, docudramas, dramatic specials, and miniseries. Television drama, with such shows as

In the age of television, image becomes more important than substance.

S. I. HAYAKAWA

See also
Radio

Hill Street Blues, Miami Vice, and *St. Elsewhere,* incorporated a more explicitly gritty realism, both visual and verbal, than had ever been shown before on network television. On the other hand, prime-time soap operas such as *Dallas* and *Dynasty* not only stoked desires for ostentatious consumption but also eclipsed in popularity. or drove off the air such urban, working-class shows as *All in the Family, Kojak,* and *Good Times. The Cosby Show,* which featured a black family of five children headed by a father and mother who were both professionals, proved that the traditional family sitcom could still command a huge audience.

In the last decade of the twentieth century television continued to be a defining characteristic of modern life. It affected leisure and political behavior, encouraged consumption, paradoxically both fostered and eroded traditional values, and created new galaxies of celebrities who were better known for their mere presence on television than for their actual deeds. Television, as Marshall McLuhan observed in 1964, increased the visual at the expense of the aural; it increased the importance of the vicarious at the expense of direct experience. With its own "language" it entertained, provided information, and served as a source of values while, as a secondary form of experience, it pared life of some of its poignancy, urgency, individuality, and subtlety.

—BENJAMIN G. RADER

THEATER AND MUSICAL THEATER

The social history of the American theater is an absorbing chronicle that has played against a dynamic backdrop of aesthetic, technological, economic, sociological, and political forces. The interactive and separate energies of these forces have informed a vibrant and galvanizing dialectic between audiences and theatrical practitioners—play-wrights, producers, directors, actors, designers, composers, and critics.

In American theater history, as well as in the chronicles of most other American arts, several significant motifs recur. First is the struggle between artistic aspirations and commercial realities. With few exceptions, the American theater has had to earn its own way at the box office. Therefore, the bulk of American theater productions have been carefully tailored to appeal to audiences willing to pay the price of admission for

being entertained, edified, or uplifted, or some combination thereof.

A second theme involves technology. The development of the transcontinental rail system after the Civil War, for example, helped establish New York City as the nation's preeminent theatrical center. No less significant was the introduction of industrially based entertainment media, such as the motion picture. Within the theater itself, the appearance of technologies such as dependable electrical systems drastically changed the aesthetic impact of theatrical lighting.

Another motif that has threaded through discussions of American arts and letters, including theater, can be described as a national artistic inferiority complex. Indeed, the debate between those who have argued for the cultural superiority of things European, especially British, and those who have insisted on the need for works of a distinctive American identity continues to rage. This dialectic has taken a variety of bipolar forms under such euphemisms as "elite" (European) versus "mass" (American) culture; high culture versus folk culture; high art versus popular art; and, especially in the twentieth century, art versus entertainment.

Theater, like the other arts, has tended to reinforce the ideology of the dominant ruling class. Composer Irving Berlin, in two extreme examples, used all-soldier casts to beat the drum of American patriotism for World War I in *Yip, Yip, Yaphank* (1918) and then again in World War II with *This Is the Army* (1942). The hegemony of white males in these two popular shows, both staged during the traumas of global conflict, reflects the racial-gender equation found, until only recently, in virtually all genres of American theater, and in American society itself. Since 1945, however, the American theater has opened itself up as never before to women, and to nonwhites and other minorities.

Tied to ideology is the question of politics and a manifest of issues relating to censorship. Here, the struggle has been joined by those advocating the freedoms of speech and expression enumerated in the First Amendment of the Bill of Rights and, on the other side, by those who believe that government has a legal right, indeed, an obligation, to define and enforce moral standards, a position reflecting the still potent puritanical heritage bequeathed by the early colonial settlers. Specific topics that continue to embroil the theater in controversy are the use of nudity and profanity and the depiction of characters seen by some as deviant, such as political radicals, hedonistic freethinkers, homosexuals, prostitutes, and wantonly violent criminals; similarly problematic are those dramatic situations, such as miscegenation, that have been deemed beyond the bounds of contemporary standards of propriety.

This, then, is the matrix against which the social history of theater in the United States has developed.

Colonial and Early National Periods

It should not be surprising that the earliest New World dramas reflected the national backgrounds of the various Europeans who came to conquer, subjugate, and settle. Some of the earliest dramas, in addition to providing a "touch of home" for transplanted Europeans, also served a proselytizing function. Spanish missionaries, for example, came with the Spanish conquistadores, and translated short, didactic religious plays into various Native American languages. In 1538 such playlets were presented in what is now Corpus Christi, Texas, as a prelude to baptisms of the newly converted. The Spanish influence, however, was most significant in Mexico and is therefore usually treated in histories of Latin American theater. In Quebec, the antecedents of a French tradition included a 1640 Jesuit school drama which in part provided religious instruction for indigenous Native Americans.

In the British settlements, London's influence was pervasive. In what would become the United States, the earliest theatrical productions reflected the substance and manner of the English Restoration and Georgian periods, but the formidable distances between population centers inhibited the development of any economically viable or sustained theatrical enterprises.

The greatest barrier to establishing a dynamic theater in the American colonies, however, was a persistent prejudice against the stage, an enmity associated with the Puritans of New England and the Quakers of Pennsylvania. In England, the Puritan bias against the theater's alleged immorality and frivolity reached a climax in the mid-seventeenth century. Then, civil unrest between Royalists and Puritans led to the establishment of Oliver Cromwell's Commonwealth and a Puritan-dominated Parliament which attempted to suppress dramatic activity. In 1649, Cromwell's Parliament even allowed the prosecution of actors as "rogues." In 1660, two year's after Cromwell's death, the Royalists finally prevailed, the English monarchy was restored and so, too, was theater. During the decades preceding and following the Cromwellian era, the Puritans were themselves persecuted, leading them to seek religious freedom in America. The Puritans and their political leaders like William Penn regarded theater as a threat to the kind of moral sobriety essential to maintain a well-run and conservative society. Given their own quest for liberty, the Puritans' unwillingness to sanction the rights of others to free expression demonstrates their paradoxical frame of mind, as well as the ideological basis for the still-contentious struggles between artistic freedom and censorship today.

The bias against theater was hardly limited to these regions. In Virginia, for example, the first known production of an English-language play in America, William Darby's *Ye Bare and Ye Cubb* (1665), resulted in charges against the actor-playwright and his cohorts. Although, after the cast gave a courtroom reenactment in costume, they were found "not guilty of fault," the incident marked the beginning of a pattern of judicial-legal interventions based on morality and taste; such issues of probity have continued to spur contentious debates on censorship that still clog court dockets and cloud the creative process.

Virginia and Maryland were the only two colonies that never formally prohibited theater, by either legislative or judicial fiat. Nonetheless, in 1752, when William Hallam sent his respected family troupe from London to Williamsburg, Virginia, it was necessary to secure Governor Robert Dinwiddie's permission to perform after assurances as to the propriety of their offerings had been made. After a successful stay of eleven months in Williamsburg, the Hallams and their troupe moved on to New York armed with a certificate of good behavior. This formality was necessary in order to counter the bad impressions created by another theatrical company's "roystering young men" with their "tricks and mischief." The early incident points up yet another source of the lingering prejudice against theater: "proper folks" were concerned about the moral fiber and behavior of actors and those who worked in the theater, a concern distinct from and yet linked to the plays and entertainments on which they labored.

The first American play published in the colonies was *Androboros* (1714), a three-act "biographical farce" authored by no less a figure than the governor of New York, Robert Hunter, whose intent was to pillory his obstructionist lieutenant governor. Fifty years passed before the next American play, *The Paxton Boys* (1764), was published. It, too, was a satire, but since it targeted Presbyterians, its author opted for anonymity. There is no evidence that either play was ever pro-

All good drama has two movements, first the making of a mistake, then the discovery that it was a mistake.

W. H. AUDEN

See also
African American Music

*A novelist may lose
his readers for a few
pages; a playwright
never dares lose his
audience for a
minute.*

TERENCE RATIGAN

duced, underscoring the fact that much colonial drama was "produced" in the theater of the mind, rather than on stage. Another sanctuary from the period's censorious and economic prohibitions was the university. *Gustavus Vasa*, written by undergraduate student Benjamin Coleman, was given one performance at Harvard College in 1690; in 1702, students recited a "pastoral colloquy" at William and Mary College.

As the American colonies approached the revolutionary war, an increasing number of plays by American authors, often writing on American subjects, appeared. Thomas Godfrey's five-act heroic tragedy in verse, *The Prince of Parthia*, first produced in 1767, is generally regarded as the first play by an American to be professionally produced in America. There was also a sympathetic portrayal of a tragic-heroic Native American, *Ponteach; or, The Savages America* (1766), by Major Robert Rogers, a veteran of the Seven Years' War (1754–63); in addition to its topical appeal, *Ponteach* (pronounced Pontiac) was significant in anticipating the wave of dramas on Indian themes that appeared over the next century.

Still, it was the British who largely set the pace. Restoration plays such as George Farquhar's *The Recruiting Officer* (1706) were favored by professionals and amateurs alike; in 1732, for example, Farquhar's comedy was the first play of record to be mounted in New York, which in less than a century would become the center of American theater activity. Several years later in Williamsburg, *The Recruiting Officer* was performed by amateurs attuned to the fashions of the London stage.

The first musical divertissement staged in America was the English ballad opera *Flora; or, The Hob in the Well*, which was mounted in Charleston, South Carolina, in 1735. The ballad opera form proved popular, particularly in less costly and abridged versions that served as "ballad after-pieces" to an evening's featured production.

It was Shakespeare, however, whose plays were most often produced in the colonies during the last half of the eighteenth century, accounting for a larger share of the American repertoire than that of Britain. But given the censorious pressures in the colonies, even Shakespeare, on occasion, had to be "sold." For example, when Hallam's Company of Comedians of London moved into New England in 1763 after a successful run in New York, the troupe was accused of trading in "vice, impiety, and immorality." To counter the claim, Hallam's Company hit upon the strategy of promoting its plays as "moral dialogues"; *Othello* was

transformed and touted as "a Series of Moral Dialogues in five parts/Depicting the evil effects of Jealousy and Other Bad Passions, and Proving that Happiness can only Spring from the Pursuit of Virtue." In the mid-1770s, however, the tensions between England and its American colonies exploded in armed hostilities, bringing to an end, by governmental decree, virtually all live theater in what would soon be the United States.

When the Second Continental Congress was summoned to Philadelphia in 1775 to make preparations for war with England, it passed a resolution recommending the suspension of "every species of extravagance and dissipation, especially all horse-racing, and all kinds of gaming, cockfighting, exhibitions of shows, plays, and other expensive diversions and entertainments" in order to encourage frugality and industry. In 1778, in the midst of the War for Independence, Congress greatly strengthened the earlier edict. Therefore, live theatrical entertainment, with the exception of amateur productions by British soldiers who occupied the majority of existing theaters, came to a virtual standstill.

With the formal signing of the Peace of Paris in 1783, the new nation and its theater embarked on what would prove to be a period of unprecedented growth and vitality. At first, however, the war's economic hardships discouraged most city

PAMPHLET PLAYS

During the War for Independence, patriots who espoused the cause of nationhood formally articulated in the Declaration of Independence of 1776 wrote "pamphlet plays" intended for publication rather than performance. Though the genre was dominated by satire, John Leacock's *The Fall of British Tyranny; or, America Triumphant, the First Campaign* (1776) was a highly popular "tragicomedy of five acts" tracing the causes of the Revolution; it also enjoyed the distinction of becoming America's first chronicle play and the first of many patriotic-historic dramas to feature George Washington as a character. Hugh Henry Brackenridge's *The Battle of Bunker's Hill* (1776) and *The Death of General Montgomery* (1777), as Felicia Hardison Londre observes in her masterful *History of World Theater* (p. 168), were unusual in that seriousness of tone and historical accuracy took precedence over satiric and propagandistic values.

See also
Concert Music

and state governments from repealing their wartime anti-theater laws. But the lifting of such prohibitions by Pennsylvania, the bastion of Quakerdom, in 1789 led to the legalization of theater everywhere. And though the process encountered pockets of resistance, it was clear that expressing the variegated saga of the American experience was a deeply felt need.

Royall Tyler's comedy *The Contrast* (1787), the first American comedy to be professionally staged, introduced "Jonathan," the prototype for a long line of theatrical Yankees. Imbued with honesty, common sense, plain talk, and, significantly, a passionate sense of himself as "a true blue son of liberty," Tyler's Jonathan captured a sense of the optimistic confidence coursing through the new nation. Yet, despite *The Contrast*'s success, and lingering animosities from the long war with Britain, the bulk of the repertoire of America's professional theaters was English.

Still, the unique enticements of the stage attracted aspiring American authors. William Dunlap, lured by the stage while studying painting in London in 1784 with Benjamin West, returned to New York and a sustained and influential career as both a playwright and a theater manager. Of Dunlap's approximately sixty plays, his most influential was *Andre* (1798), based on an actual event concerning a British spy in the revolutionary war. Dunlap, by dint of his translations of thirteen of the plays of the German playwright August Friedrich Ferdinand von Kotzebue, is also credited with initiating the turn-of-the-century American vogue for Kotzebue, then hailed across the Western world as "the German Shakespeare." Dunlap also wrote the significant *History of the American Theatre* (1832), the first attempt to chronicle the new nation's quixotic affair with live drama.

In the 1790s, opportunities for American playwrights writing on American themes increased. Susanna Rowson, one of America's first female playwrights, contributed *Slaves in Algiers; or, A Struggle for Freedom* (1794), a musical melodrama about American prisoners in Algiers, and *The Female Patriot* (1795); in treating the horrors of slavery and privileging the role of women in American history, Rowson focused on topics whose significance to American drama and culture would only continue to grow. John Daly Burk's patriotic *Bunker Hill; or, The Death of General Warren* (1797) anticipated the growing role of spectacle with an elaborately staged fifteen-minute battle scene without dialogue. These—as well as many of the plays by Margaretta Bleeker Faugeres, John Mur-

dock, and David Everett—anticipated such staples of nineteenth-century American melodrama as an emphasis on action and spectacle, a nationalistic spirit, and exotic locales.

This period also saw substantial growth in the American theater's infrastructure. During the 1790s, Philadelphia's Chestnut Street and New York's Park theaters vied for supremacy; even in Boston, the last bastion of Puritan values, sustained dramatic enterprise finally took hold with the opening of the Federal Street Theatre in 1794, while Charleston continued its preeminence in the South. With the construction of permanent theaters came the establishment of permanent theatrical companies and the emergence of strong-willed managers who attempted to balance commercial imperatives against artistic aspirations.

While British and Continental influences continued to be potent forces in the American theater, the melodrama soon became the most popular and culturally significant theatrical form. William Dunlap helped pave the way with Americanized adaptations of Kotzebue, including *False Shame; or, The American Orphan in Germany* (1799); inserting the word "American" in Kotzebue's *Falsche Scham* (1796) appealed to national pride, while the play's romanticism capitalized on the audience's appetite for drama made larger

---

JOHN HOWARD PAYNE

America's First International Playwright

John Howard Payne, best remembered as the lyricist of the still-popular ballad "Home Sweet Home," was smitten by the theater at an early age; when just fourteen, he published the critical journal *The Thespian Mirror* (1805–1806). His first play, the comedic melodrama *Julia* (1806), was produced at the prestigious Park Theatre in New York. Hailed as "a child prodigy" upon his 1809 acting debut in New York, Payne pursued a productive acting career for several years. But in the face of waning popularity he departed for London, where his plays attained popular and critical success. Payne wrote approximately sixty plays; the most significant—*Brutus* (1818), in which Edmund Kean acted the lead, and *Charles II* (1824), starring Charles Kemble—reflected European influences and won initial acclaim in London, thus making Payne America's first notable international playwright.

*It is the destiny of
the theater nearly
everywhere and in
every period to
struggle even when
it is flourishing.*

HOWARD TAUBMAN

See also
Film

than life. During the first decades of the new century, the popularity of the American "Yankee" grew to the point that actors such as James Henry Hackett could forge successful careers by specializing in variations of the role. Other popular topics included the American Revolution, the Native American, and the expanding western frontier. James Nelson Barker was the first to tackle another popular subject, the War of 1812; the propagandistic slant of his play *Marmion; or, The Battle of Flodden Field*, written in the midst of the conflict, helped focus Americans' anti-British sentiment.

Expansion and Diversification, 1812–1865

The successful conclusion of the War of 1812, while securing America's access to the world's great international sea-lanes, also opened the way for an unprecedented period of westward expansion and settlement. In 1803, President Thomas Jefferson concluded the purchase of the vast Louisiana Territory from Napoleon, thus adding France's lands west of the Mississippi River to the existing United States. Florida was added in 1819, and Texas, the Southwest, and California were annexed in the 1840s, so that by 1850, the United States, tripling its original size, now stretched from the Atlantic to the Pacific. Many kinds of people were attracted to the new territories—adventurers, settlers, soldiers, merchants, and actors.

The first significant touring company on the frontier was that of Samuel Drake, whose production of *Pizarro*, Richard Brinsley Sheridan's adaptation of a play by Kotzebue, was the troupe's most popular offering. Conditions on the road were rigorous. When Drake's company made a six-month tour that took it from Albany to Kentucky in 1815, its modes of travel included horse-drawn wagon, flatboat, and foot. Its scenery was designed to meet all possible venues, and the plays were altered to meet the particular circumstances of a given location. The capacity to improvise was a definite asset. Drake established one of the first regional circuits; though based around the Kentucky towns of Lexington, Louisville, and Frankfort, his troupe often made forays into Ohio, Indiana, Tennessee, and Missouri.

Drake's success encouraged competitors, including Noah Ludlow, a member of Drake's company who formed his own troupe in 1817. Ludlow toured regions of the South and Midwest (then the west) and is credited with establishing the first English-language theater in predominantly French-speaking New Orleans. After alternating between sundry management and acting engagements, including a failed tenure as manager of the Chatham Theatre in New York, Ludlow joined forces with Solomon Smith in 1835. Their successful partnership dominated the theater scene in the cities along the Mississippi, including Saint Louis. In 1853 Ludlow opted to retire; his highly regarded autobiography, *Dramatic Life as I Found It* (1880), written when he was in his eighties, provides a historically important portrait of America's frontier theater at the middle of the nineteenth century.

The move into the West was abetted by improvements in transportation. Canals and toll roads were built in the early decades of the nineteenth century. The first railroad appeared in 1830; others were soon constructed. The standard mode of travel, though, was water; thus it is not surprising that most frontier towns—and theaters—were located along the banks of the continent's interior river system. Small itinerant companies were found virtually everywhere, though few were located north of the Ohio River. Chicago, for example, did not host a professional production until 1833; its first professional theater was not established until 1847. The traveling companies set up makeshift stages in each town they visited. In 1831, however, the showboat was devised by William Chapman, an English actor who had come to America in 1827. Chapman's Floating Theatre made its maiden voyage in the form of a flatboat that docked for nightly presentations of Shakespeare or Kotzebue as it drifted downriver from Pittsburgh to New Orleans; at the end of voyage, Chapman would sell the boat for firewood, build another flatboat upriver, and start the cycle again. In 1836, after amassing enough savings to buy a steamboat with a twenty-foot-wide stage, Chapman was able to play the river in both directions. Though showboats continued regular runs (except during the Civil War years) until about 1925, the heyday of the genre was between 1875 and 1900.

With industrialization becoming a major force along the Atlantic seaboard after 1820, eastern cities and their theaters continued to grow. During the first decade of the nineteenth century, established theaters like the Chestnut Street in Philadelphia and the Park in New York were each enlarged to seat over two thousand spectators. Though Philadelphia and New York had vied for the honor of being the new nation's theatrical center since the end of the revolutionary war, by 1830, New York, by virtue of its four permanent and prosperous theaters, had become the dominant force. The largest of these, the three-thousand-seat Bowery, opened in 1826; at the same time, the number of shows per week was increased to six. With new theaters came new companies, so that by 1850 there were over fifty resident troupes nationwide performing on a regular basis. And with rapid expansion came competition, a battle for patronage that led to various strategies.

The most prominent stratagem, at least from the public's point of view, was the introduction of the star system. Impressed by the great success of British actor Edmund Kean's American tour of 1820–1821, entrepreneurs like Stephen Price made frequent trips to London to recruit performers. Among the growing number of stars to traverse the Atlantic were Charles Mathews the Elder in 1822 and 1833–1835; William C. Macready in 1826–1827, 1843–1845, and 1849; and Charles and Fanny Kemble in 1832–1834. Initially, tours were confined to the eastern states, but stars soon ventured to New Orleans and up the Mississippi. Eventually, the high salaries demanded by stars squeezed profits for those who organized their tours, but managers were reluctant to abandon the system because of high public demand.

The struggle to gain a competitive edge also influenced repertoire. Entr'actes increased in number and kind, as did novelties such as the employment of child actors and specialty actors and the use of animals. And though "quality" fare such as productions of Shakespeare continued to win favor among upper-class audiences, it was melodrama that captured the fancy of the middle and lower classes. Its suspenseful plots, theatrical effects, didactic moralizing, and the convention of the happy ending made it particularly appealing to unsophisticated audiences who supported live theater in ever-increasing numbers. It also was a form congenial to the insertion of commentaries on such contemporary issues as slavery, the rights of workers, and slum life. As a rule, better-educated and more sophisticated audiences looked to Europe for their standards; they also tended to give only condescending attention to native-born talent. As a result, American playwrights and actors usually won acceptance from the mass audience before winning approval from America's self-styled cultural elite. After 1830, this trend was ameliorated somewhat by the phenomenon of Jacksonian democracy, which increased pride in things American, and by the time the century was half over the number of American

plays produced on the American stage had increased from 2 percent to 15 percent.

American melodrama flourished in the work of a growing cadre of native writers. Capitalizing on the public's continuing fascination with the War of 1812, Mordecai M. Noah's *She Would Be a Soldier; or, The Plains of Chippewa* (1819) was a tightly plotted spectacle featuring a spunky heroine who disguises herself as a soldier, a noble Indian chief, and caricatures of a Frenchman, a foppish Englishman, and an American yokel; songs, dances, a military display, and a last-minute rescue enlivened the production. Noah prefaced this and his other patriotic spectacles with fascinating accounts of the American theater and with pleas for reducing "prejudices against native productions."

Actor Edwin Forrest, the first great tragedian of the American stage, encouraged American playwrights by sponsoring a series of nine playwriting contests. The first winner was John Augustus Stone whose *Metamora; or, The Last of the Wampanoags* (1829) provided Forrest, in the title role of the "noble savage" who lives and dies free of the "White man's bondage," one of the great roles of his illustrious career. Between 1825 and 1860, more than fifty Indian plays were produced for the American stage, many performed by Forrest. John Brougham's burlesque, *Po-ca-hon-tas* (1855), dealt a decisive blow to the genre through parody and satire which undermined the seriousness of the form's basic premises and conventions. Still, the character of the "noble savage" persisted until about 1870 before being abandoned.

The stock character of the American Yankee, though first introduced in Royall Tyler's *The Contrast* in 1787, did not flourish until 1824 with Charles Mathews's *A Trip to America*. Between 1830 and 1850 the Yankee had become such an important type that actors such as James Henry Hackett and George Handel Hill appeared regularly as common men who, though superficially simple and naive, eschewed pretense and deceit and embodied democratic values.

James K. Pauling's 1831 comic melodrama, *The Lion of the West; or, A Trip to Washington*, introduced the character of the backwoodsman, who became another important melodramatic type. The adventures of Pauling's central character, Colonel Nimrod Wildfire, were based on the exploits of Davy Crockett, the period's archetypal model for the practical, resourceful, self-taught American individualist. The mythologizing of Crockett reached its nineteenth-century apex with Frank Murdock's *Davy Crockett; or, Be Sure You're Right, Then Go Ahead* (1873), a melodra-

A further segregating of theater audiences occurred when avant-garde production companies were founded in the 1910s.

PAGE 542

T

**THEATER AND
MUSICAL THEATER**

*From Melodrama to
Realism, From
Commercialism to
Competition, 1865–1929*

*The theater needs
continual reminders
that there is nothing
more debasing
than the work of
those who do well
what is not worth
doing at all.*

GORE VIDAL

See also

Humor and Comedy

matic spectacle given over two thousand performances, with Frank Mayo in the title role.

The unprecedented success of a stage version of *Uncle Tom's Cabin* epitomized melodrama's ascendency as the dominant genre in nineteenth-century American theater. Indeed, the popularity of Harriet Beecher Stowe's novel, with its heartfelt aim "to awaken sympathy and feeling for the African race," inspired dozens of adaptations. These, though, had been opposed by Stowe, who feared abasement of her novel's moral intent—an indication of the low regard in which theater was held by the nation's literary and political Brahmins. Initially, Stowe's reservation seemed well-founded; the first stage version of *Uncle Tom's Cabin*, which opened in New York in 1852, was dismissed for its "bad taste" and "overdrawn characters." But George L. Aiken's six-act adaptation, which opened at Purdy's National Theatre on 18 July 1853, was hailed as "an agent for the cause of abolition" as well as a force for gaining new respectability for theater itself.

Although Aiken's version of Stowe's novel was regarded as a sensitive shaping of Stowe's characters and moral concerns, it also epitomized the basic elements of the melodramatic format with its archvillain, the viciously cruel Simon Legree; the suffering innocent, embodied by both Uncle Tom and Little Eva; thrilling spectacle, the chase across the ice floes on the Ohio River; comic relief, through the character of Topsy; and poetic justice, with the shooting death of Legree and the apotheosis of Uncle Tom. In keeping with the conventions of the day, the black characters were performed by whites in blackface. However, in many touring post-Civil War companies, *Uncle Tom's Cabin* employed blacks as chorus members for the plantation songs; therefore, the play is regarded as one of the first important vehicles for allowing black performers an entree into the mainstream of American theater.

The most popular American play of its era, Aiken's staging of *Uncle Tom's Cabin* is significant for the unique role it and Stowe's original novel played in raising the issue of abolition in the years immediately prior to the Civil War. Also, Aiken's production is regarded as the first play to have been offered on Broadway without an afterpiece or any other entr'acte or divertissement. The play's enduring popularity was similarly unprecedented. Indeed, *Uncle Tom's Cabin* enjoyed a continuous stage life of some ninety, years. There were forty-nine companies performing the play in 1879, and no fewer than a dozen touring troupes as late as 1927.

The Octoroon (1859), by Irish-born Dion Boucicault, also dealt with slavery. Based on Mayne Reid's novel *The Quadroon*, and incorporating events surrounding the murder of a slave from Albany Fonblanque's novel *The Filibuster*, Boucicault's play ridiculed southern racial laws by making Zoe an octoroon instead of a quadroon (that is, one-eighth instead of one-quarter black). Boucicault, though, attempted to balance sectional interests; while the characters and dialogue tilted sympathies to the South, the action was unmistakenly abolitionist. Boucicault, who lived in the United States between 1853 and 1860 and who thereafter divided his time between London and New York, was the most successful master of melodrama during the middle decades of the century. Boucicault's fondness for lavish special effects and his practice of borrowing freely from a variety of sources, including French melodrama (he had lived in France for a time), as well as his incorporation of the latest scientific devices into his plots, were all important influences on theatrical production.

From Melodrama to Realism, From Commercialism to Competition, 1865–1929

The end of the American Civil War brought new challenges and new opportunities. As a result of the issuance of Lincoln's Emancipation Proclamation and of the successful prosecution of the war by the North, slavery, as well as the influence of the rural South, had come to an end. Consolidated as never before, the United States embarked on a period of unprecedented territorial, economic, and political growth. The first transcontinental railroad was finished in 1869; by 1880 there were several more. Progress through discovery, invention, individual initiative, and uninhibited capitalistic exploitation were among the basic elements galvanizing the national psyche, as well as the country's political agenda and its policy of laissez-faire economics. These same elements also helped define the American theater as a clearly entrepreneurial, commercially based enterprise.

Immediately following the Civil War, one of the most significant theatrical forms to make its debut was the forerunner of what would eventually become the musical. In the United States, music—in forms such as the interpolated song, the entr'acte, and the afterpiece—had been a popular theatrical component since the colonial period. The American musical drama, though, came into its own in Charles M. Barras's *The Black Crook; An Original Magical and Spectacular Drama* in *Four Acts* (1866). Produced at the unprecedented cost of fifty thousand dollars, *The Black Crook*, was a melodramatic musical spectacular that played at Niblo's Garden in New York City for 475 performances. It was the first play to run for over a year, and with gross receipts totaling more than one million dollars, the most successful Broadway play up to that time. Though details are sketchy, the production was apparently made possible when a large French ballet troupe was deprived of a stage because of a fire that destroyed the New York Academy of Music, its scheduled venue. Though Barras was wary of having his metaphysical melodrama transformed into a musical spectacle, the penniless playwright agreed to the changes; some six months later he had already earned over sixty thousand dollars. The visual spectacles included transformations, phantasmagorias, displays of fire and water, and an eighty-strong bevy of chorines displaying much more of the female leg than had customarily been seen on stage. Excoriations from the pulpit and other bastions of moral rectitude only heightened interest in the "indecent and demoralizing exhibition." Revived regularly in New York during the rest of the century, *The Black Crook* spawned a host of traveling companies and such spin-offs as *The Black Crook Burlesque* and *The Black Crook Song Book*.

The success of *The Black Crook* inspired similar enterprises, including the 1869 appearance of Lydia Thompson and her "British Blondes," whose burlesques emphasized feminine attributes. Thompson and her imitators helped establish burlesque as a program of variety acts interspersed with musical production numbers featuring the allures of lovely young women. With its obvious sexual appeal, it is not surprising that burlesque attracted a primarily male audience. Though the form remained popular until the late 1920s, burlesque quickly degenerated in the face of competition from the then-new mass-mediated entertainments made possible by synchronized sound film and by network radio. Though the introduction of the striptease kept burlesque alive during the years of the Depression and World War II, burlesque had a tawdry existence mostly at the fringes of bourgeois middle-class values.

Modern vaudeville developed from the same movement toward popular mass entertainment. But in contrast to burlesque, which played primarily in concert saloons during the decades following the Civil War, vaudeville (or variety, as it was first called) found a home in regular theaters. This acceptance was due largely to the efforts of New

VAUDEVILLE PRECURSOR

Vaudeville evolved due to the popular trend toward mass entertainment in the decades following the Civil War. Elaborate dramatic sketches like this shared the stage with standard musical and novelty acts.
CORBIS-BETTMANN

York entrepreneur Tony Pastor, who attracted family audiences by promoting his Saturday matinees as occasions "when Ladies and Children can safely attend without escort" and by boasting of "selling no drink stronger than ice water." Pastor had additional influence through his practice of including elaborate dramatic sketches as well as the standard musical and novelty acts. Comedic parodies such as *The White Crook* (1867) and *Hamlet the Second* (1870), a send-up of Edwin Booth's then-current and acclaimed Shakespearean production, were representative of the "dramas" Pastor created. Through the years, Pastor continued to move his base of operations, always opening his latest theater further uptown. By 1881, when Tony Pastor's New 14th Street Theatre opened, the performer-turned-entrepreneur had at last succeeded in attracting women to evening performances and the term "variety" was being replaced by the more genteel-sounding "vaudeville."

Pastor's success was emulated with even more spectacular results by the theater-management team of Edward Franklin Albee and Benjamin Franklin Keith. In 1885, Albee helped reverse the declining fortunes of a run-down variety house managed by Keith in Boston. From this modest beginning, the combination of Albee's shrewd showmanship and Keith's sharp business practices resulted in the building of a theater chain that by the turn of the century dominated the East Coast.

T

**THEATER AND
MUSICAL THEATER**

*From Melodrama to
Realism, From
Commercialism to
Competition, 1865–1929*

*With television,
each family had
at its fingertips
entertainment
previously available
only by going out
to the theater,
vaudeville, or
the movies.*

PAGE 474

See also

Popular Entertainment
before the Civil War

Similarly powerful chains included the extensive West Coast–based Orpheum circuit, as well as the Loew's and Pantages groups. There were also hundreds of "small-time" and independent vaudeville houses. "Small-time" performers dreamed of breaking into the "two-a-day" performance schedule of the "big time"; another dream was to play New York's Palace Theatre, the Carnegie Hall of vaudeville until 1932, when it was converted into a movie house. Among vaudeville headliners who played the Palace and eventually went on to even bigger success as movie and radio stars were such ethnically and racially varied entertainers as the Marx Brothers, George Burns and Gracie Allen, W. C. Fields, Eddie Cantor, Ray Bolger, Will Rogers, Ed Wynn, and the black tap dancer Bill "Bojangles" Robinson. In contrast to mainstream society, show business offered opportunities for fame and fortune to Jewish and African American minorities.

The minstrel show, another uniquely American genre, also flourished in the decades following the Civil War. A paradoxical entertainment that exploited black musical and dance forms while creating opportunities for black performers, the minstrel show first appeared about 1830 when Thomas D. Rice, a white entertainer, performed various Negro tunes in blackface. The success of Rice's "Jim Crow" song and dance led to a number of imitators, including Dan Emmett, who in 1843 organized the Virginia Minstrels, a blackface ensemble whose fame took them as far as London; Emmett also composed a number of popular songs that remain standards in the American folk repertoire, including "Dixie," "The Blue Tail Fly," and "Early in the Morning." The minstrel show's definitive two-part form was established in 1846 by Edwin P. Christy's Christy Minstrels. In the first part, the entertainers formed a semicircle, with a tambourine player, "Mr. Tambo," at one end and a "bones" player, "Mr. Bones," at the other. The "Interlocutor," or middleman, hosted the proceedings and joked with the end men between musical selections. The second part, the "olio" as it was called, was given over to specialty routines performed in a freely improvised manner responsive to the tastes of individual audiences. In the decade before the Civil War, the minstrel show's widespread popularity exceeded even that of the legitimate theater.

After the Civil War, Charles B. Hicks, a black showman, established the Georgia Minstrels. This pioneering group opened the door for a number of "Simon Pure" or "genuine" minstrel companies that successfully toured throughout the northern United States. Billy Kersands, an alumnus of Hicks's troupe, later headlined with Haverly's Genuine Colored Minstrels in England during the 1870s. With the growing popularity of burlesque and vaudeville, however, the minstrel show declined steadily. In 1896, only ten companies survived, and by 1919 there were only three, mere curiosities from a bygone era.

Several black performers from the nineteenth century deserve mention. William Henry Lane, who performed as Master Juba, was known as the "father of American tap dancing." Sam Lucas helped open up other areas to black performers by dint of his extraordinary talents as a singer, composer, and actor. In 1878 he became the first black to play Uncle Tom in *Uncle Tom's Cabin*; he was also the first black to star in a motion picture, the 1915 version of Stowe's novel.

George Walker and Bert Williams, a popular turn-of-the-century, black song-and-dance team, were engaged by the top vaudeville houses and also produced their own musicals, including *A Lucky Coon* (1899) and the Broadway hit *In Dahomey* (1903), the first evening-length black musical to play a regular New York legitimate theater. In spite of mostly favorable reviews and many raves for Williams, *In Dahomey* was boycotted by many white New York theatergoers; in London, where prejudices against blacks were not so prevalent, *In Dahomey* ran for seven months.

In the years following the Civil War, as rail transportation became increasingly reliable and extensive, new modes of organizing the logistics of touring units appeared. In the immediate postwar period, the resident stock company was at its apogee; while an individual star often toured from one town to the next to perform a particularly well-known and celebrated role—as did Joseph Jefferson III, who portrayed Dion Boucicault's *Rip Van Winkle* (1865) more than 2,500 times—it was always with support from the local resident stock company. However, with the innovation of the "combination company"—a traveling unit complete with star, supporting players, and backstage personnel, as well as sets, costumes, and props—the fortunes of the resident stock company began to decline. In 1877, there were nearly one hundred combination companies traveling with full casts, scenery, and properties; by 1886, there were 282. The combination company, then, was a continuation of the nineteenth-century practice of the star system; now, however, the stars traveled with full companies. Between 1883 and 1902, English leading man Henry Irving made eight tours of America; Benoit Constant Coquelin, a star of the Parisian Comédie Française, toured three times between 1889 and 1900, and French diva Sarah Bernhardt, nine times between 1880 and 1918.

New York City, with its affluent and cosmopolitan audiences, became the nation's theatrical center, the city where the majority of the combination companies were booked and assembled. Edwin Booth, who began his theatrical career with his father, the noted actor Junius Brutus Booth, became one of America's greatest stars, with a reputation as a masterful interpreter of the classics. His production of *Hamlet*, in which he starred, ran for one hundred performances, the longest continuous run that Shakespeare's play had yet enjoyed. But after his brother, John Wilkes Booth, assassinated President Abraham Lincoln, Edwin retired for several years. When he returned to active production at his own Booth's Theatre, which he had built to his personal specifications, he introduced a number of innovations, including a level stage, hydraulic elevators, flying machinery (used to raise scenery from the stage into overhead space), and "free plantation," a system that allowed the placement of scenery anywhere on stage. Booth also eliminated the stage apron and used box settings, where the actors and action were enclosed for interior scenes by a semblance of three walls and often even a ceiling, to enhance the illusion of reality, an increasingly important theatrical trend at the time.

Augustin Daly was a New York drama critic who later gained recognition as a playwright, producer, and director. Although his many plays were largely derived from German and French sources, he is credited with nudging the theater toward a more realistic approach and with making the theater worthy of the support of the day's most refined citizens. Like Booth, he established a repertory company of talented performers whose youth made them amenable to Daly's then-unique concept of direction. For example, he discarded the practice of casting according to "lines of business," the traditional, four-tier system whose ranks included players of leading roles, players of secondary roles, players of third-line or "walking" parts, and general utility players. Daly also assumed the right to help shape his actors' interpretations, blocking, and stage business.

Playwright-manager Steele MacKaye was also concerned with a realistic approach to drama, as exemplified by his production of *Hazel Kirke* (1880), a melodrama that featured sympathetic characters who spoke with natural dialogue. MacKaye's most lasting influence, however, was

T

**THEATER AND
MUSICAL THEATER**

*From Melodrama to
Realism, From
Commercialism to
Competition, 1865–1929*

GREAT STAR

*Edwin Booth, who began his
theatrical career with his father
and became one of America's
greatest stars. He retired for
several years after his brother,
John Wilkes Booth, assassinated
President Abraham Lincoln.*
CORBIS-BETTMANN

as an educator. After training in Paris with François Delsarte, who had developed a "scientific" approach to acting in which the laws of stage expression were schematized like the laws of physics, MacKaye taught Delsarte's system in a variety of pioneering acting schools. His most significant training program, offered in 1884 at the Lyceum Theatre, established a curriculum that grew into the American Academy of Dramatic Art.

The trend toward realism continued in other arenas. Inspired by the popularity of "realist" novelists like Bret Harte and Mark Twain, dramas such as Bartley Campbell's *My Partner* (1879) exploited the details of frontier life. In contrast, Edward Harrigan examined urban life in a series of plays such as *Cordelia's Aspirations* (1883), which presented working-class life in relatively realistic, if comic, terms. These plays were an extension of the Bowery Boy tradition with its Dickensian focus on the adventures and tribulations of adolescent youngsters growing up in hostile and impoverished urban ghettoes.

Actor-playwright William Gillette, who wrote the Civil War dramas *Held by the Enemy* (1886) and *Secret Service* (1895), attempted to create the "illusion of the first time" at each performance by focusing on the moment-to-moment development of the action. In 1890 James A. Herne offered *Margaret Fleming*, often regarded as the outstanding realistic American drama of the nineteenth century. No New York producer would

A man in the theatrical business is allowed more liberties than his business brothers. His business demands it.

OSCAR HAMMERSTEIN I

See also
Radio

touch it, however, since its themes include infidelity and illegitimate pregnancy. Without a commercial backer, Herne had to produce *Margaret Fleming* with his own resources in relatively obscure venues. However, he recouped his financial losses with *Shore Acres* (1892), a successful play about an endearing New England character. A pattern had been set, or perhaps more accurately, reasserted. Realism was readily assimilated into the American theater as an element of scenography, or design. However, when realism implied adult themes and issues, it was often considered at best problematic and at worst subversive and downright un-American.

By 1900, commercial considerations had clearly come to dominate the American stage. Actors, for example, had become secondary to both directors and producers. With the ascendancy of the traveling combination company, they had to journey to New York, the home base of many of the companies, to secure employment. Actors were hired for the run of the play rather than by the season, and because there was no union to protect their interests, they received no salaries for rehearsals and might find themselves stranded far from home if a production suddenly closed on the road.

Another change involved the appearance of a new class of theatrical workers, the booking agents. The need for such middlemen arose because of difficulties experienced by theater managers outside of New York in arranging their seasons. The introduction of bookers was a matter of simple economics and of convenience; it was easier for local managers to engage touring productions of long-running New York hits for several nights than it was for a stock company to add a new play to its repertoire each week in order to draw area audiences. Nonetheless, the complexity of the combination system, even with the addition of booking agents, was still daunting. For example, when local managers met in New York each summer prior to the new season, managers had to negotiate with as many as forty different production representatives, each of whom was trying to configure the most closely plotted and lucrative schedule for their troupes as possible; double bookings and other devious practices abounded. One solution devised by theaters located along a single rail line was to hire one agent to represent them all; producers used a similar solution involving the hiring of a booking agent to represent a group of shows.

Such chaos paved the way for what became known as the Theatrical Syndicate. Emulating

the monopolistic oligarchs in the steel, railroad, and oil industries, six theater owners—Marc Klaw, Abraham Erlanger, Sam Nixon, J. Fred Zimmerman, Al Hayman, and Charles Frohman—joined to form the Syndicate in 1896. These men sought nothing less than total control of the American theater. At first, the Syndicate was welcomed. It did, indeed, create a new degree of order and stability for local managers. The only catch was that each manager had to sign an exclusive contract and take only those shows sent by the Syndicate, a monopolistic practice later imitated by the early movie moguls, who called the system "block booking." So powerful was the Syndicate that when a local manager refused to sign, the group simply built a rival theater, sent it star attractions, and charged artificially low prices until the competition withered and died. The Syndicate also took control of advertising, thus giving it a weapon to use against those artists who attempted to chart independent courses. *The New York Dramatic Mirror*, under the defiant editorship of Harrison Grey Fiske, opposed the Syndicate even though opposition meant the loss of advertising revenue; the Syndicate even tried to forbid its performers from reading the renegade newspaper.

In 1900, after being in existence for only four years, the Theatrical Syndicate controlled over 5,000 theaters, including virtually every first-class stage across the United States. Greed, however, led to severe cost-cutting, which in turn undermined the quality of the Syndicate's product. Audience complaints provoked managers to complain in turn to the Syndicate. *The New York World* openly accused the Syndicate of deceit and fraud for sending out "inferior companies, falsely representing them as the original casts of New York successes." Charles Frohman, though an original Syndicate member, was an honest showman; disgusted with the Syndicate's duplicity and increasingly shabby offerings, Frohman disavowed his participation in the association.

By 1915, the American theater, whatever its form or genre, was in decline. Many theater historians put a large measure of blame on the theater itself, particularly the Syndicate and the Shuberts, whose basic interests were commercial rather than artistic. Each organization's commitment to standardizing product for maximum public appeal and, therefore, profitability squeezed out most innovations except those of a technical nature. Similarly, the practices of blacklisting and block booking tended to squelch and marginalize alternative voices.

THE SHUBERTS, BELASCO, AND THE FISKES

Rivals to the Syndicate

Six theater owners called the "Syndicate" faced competition from ambitious new rivals like the Shubert brothers, who in 1905 began to build their own chain of theaters. The Shuberts profited from the favorable publicity and boffo box office take generated by Sarah Bernhardt's 1906 American tour. The Syndicate's stranglehold was finally broken in 1915. Ironically, the Shuberts, the big winners, proved every bit as autocratic as the Syndicate; in 1956, after decades of controlling "the road" and years of litigation, the Shubert organization was declared a monopoly in restraint of trade under the provisions of the Sherman Antitrust Act of 1885. However, because of the Syndicate's domination and its emphasis on profits in the early years of the century, the American theater became, and has remained, an extremely conservative commercial enterprise.

Other opponents of the Syndicate included David Belasco, a flamboyant playwright-manager who came into his own when he opened the Belasco Theatre in 1902. In addition to achieving realistic effects through his virtuosity with electric lighting, Belasco sought realism in stage design, even including the duplication of an actual Child's Restaurant for the concluding scene of his production of Alice Bradley's *The Governor's Lady* (1912). Belasco's singular productions were in such great demand that in 1909, the Syndicate agreed to a nonexclusive contract for Belasco's road-show bookings, a concession regarded as one of the first important breaks in the monopoly's power.

Actress Minnie Maddern Fiske, along with her husband, Harrison Fiske of the *New York Dramatic Mirror*, also opposed the Syndicate's stifling practices. Like other stars such as Sarah Bernhardt, who had resisted the monopoly, Fiske was subjected to negative reviews bought for and placed by the Syndicate in newspapers beholden to it because of its steady stream of advertising. In 1903, after being blacklisted and forced to play only secondary venues, Mrs. Fiske and her husband acquired the Manhattan Theatre. Here, they helped chart the course of modern theater by presenting a number of outstanding works with an emphasis on ensemble rather than star effects.

T

THEATER AND MUSICAL THEATER

From Modernism to Postmodernism, 1915 to the Present

The Marx brothers carried comic Jewish dialogues into vaudeville, brandishing madcap nihilism against established institutions.

PAGE 228

At the same time, the American theater faced increasingly potent competition from spectator sports, particularly baseball and boxing, and "the galloping tintypes," or motion pictures. Movies, which had started out as penny arcade "peep show" attractions in the form of Edison's hand-cranked kinetoscope in 1893, by 1915 had become big business. In that year, D. W. Griffith released the two-hour *Birth of a Nation*, his controversial—some believed racist—film drama about the American Civil War and Reconstruction. The work, described by President Woodrow Wilson as "history writ with lightning," attracted a huge audience willing to pay road-show, legitimate-theater admission fees and helped standardize the one- to two-hour feature film as the industry's basic unit. The 1914 opening of the first large-scale movie house, the 3,300-seat Strand Theatre in New York, inaugurated the era of the palatial "cathedral of the motion picture." Just before and after World War I, and throughout the 1920s, these trends continued unabated. Indeed, even the quintessential American show-business dream began to shift. Geographically, along with New York, there was now Hollywood; and with the immediate excitements of live the-ater, there was now the larger-than-life stardom offered by the movies. It would soon become clear, however, that Broadway and Hollywood also had much to share.

From Modernism to Postmodernism, 1915 to the Present

By 1915, the relative isolation of the American theater from European innovations—largely the result of the conservative and monopolistic business practices of America's principal theatrical entrepreneurs—was further exacerbated by the hostilities of World War I, then raging in Europe. Anti-German sentiment, for example, brought a quick end to the production of the Viennese operas that had dominated the American musical stage during the previous decade.

The United States entered the conflict in 1917, and the next year the long-stalemated struggle came to an end. With victory, America was on the verge of an unprecedented period of economic expansion and speculation. And in spite of the passage in 1919 of the Eighteenth Amendment prohibiting the manufacture, sale, or transportation of liquor, good times were about to roll. The syncopated rhythms of jazz provided the 1920s with a signature sound and spirit; indeed, the "jazz age" evoked an attitude of individual liberation and assertiveness, a turn of mind especially significant for women who had just won the right to vote with the passage of the Nineteenth Amendment in 1920.

Theatrically, the period's hedonistic yet stylish self-indulgence was probably best represented in the lavish entertainments produced by Florenz Ziegfeld. After a string of successful melodramas, such as *A Parisian Model* (1906), featuring his first wife, Anna Held, Ziegfeld presented *Follies* of 1907, the first of his famous series of revues featuring beautiful showgirls in sumptuous yet revealing costumes. With the addition of his name to the title and of even more lavish production values in 1911, the *Ziegfeld Follies* became the most fabled and longest-lived series of extravagant revues in show business history. Annual editions were mounted through 1925, with irregular stagings thereafter; even after Ziegfeld's death in 1932, the *Ziegfeld Follies* continued, since the name had been acquired by the Shuberts. Ziegfeld's idealization of feminine allures was underscored in 1922 when the revue acquired the subtitle "Glorifying the American Girl." Critic George Jean Nathan observed that Ziegfeld had transformed the vulgar leg show into "a thing of

grace and beauty, and symmetry, and bloom." The public agreed. Among the stars presented by Ziegfeld were Fanny Brice, Eddie Cantor, W. C. Fields, Marilyn Miller, Will Rogers, and Bert Williams.

Throughout the 1920s, the revue was Broadway's most dependable staple. Imitators of Ziegfeld's formula included the Shuberts' more daring *The Passing Show* (1912–1924) and the even more risqué *Artists and Models*, of which five editions appeared between 1923 and 1930. In 1919, George White, a former hoofer and musical-comedy juvenile, initiated his series of *Scandals*, and in 1923, the Earl Carroll Vanities began. The public's mania for revues led to late-night roof-garden shows such as Ziegfeld's *Midnight Frolic*, an adjunct to the Follies, atop the New Amsterdam, and the *Morris Gest Midnight Whirl* on the Century, Roof. The vogue for after-show entertainments proved strong enough to justify moving such programs to all-season, ground-level and basement locations; thus nightclubs supplanted the more elegant roof-garden cabarets. In addition to a gaudy array of singers, comics, dancers, skits, and novelty acts, revues featured the latest works of beguiling tunesmiths such as Irving Berlin, George and Ira Gershwin, Jerome Kern, Cole Porter, Richard Rodgers, and Lorenz Hart, all on their way to even more notable accomplishments in the 1930s.

There were also Harlem-bred revues. The most significant, since it was the first all-black potpourri to appear on Broadway since the turn-of-the-century, collaborations of Bert Williams and George Walker, was *Shuffle Along* (1921), the Noble Sissle—Eubie Blake success that yielded "I'm Just Wild About Harry." However, Lew Leslie's *Blackbirds* series beginning in 1928, earned the distinction of being the most successful of the Harlem-to-Broadway ventures. With their jazz-age syncopations and spirited tap dancing and their introduction of performers such as Bill "Bojangles" Robinson and Ethel Waters, Leslie's revues attracted both white and black theatergoers, itself a major breakthrough. The last edition appeared in 1939.

In Harlem during the 1920s, black writers and artists gathered in what became known as the Harlem Renaissance. In music, the lavish "sepia" revues at Harlem venues such as the Cotton Club attracted white socialites and intellectuals who helped tout the exuberant talents of the dancing Nicholas Brothers and composer-performers Duke Ellington, Cab Calloway, and Louis Armstrong. Thomas "Fats" Waller, another storied jazz

ENTERTAINER

Will Rogers in 1914, in a typical cowboy outfit with a rope over his shoulder.
CORBIS-BETTMANN

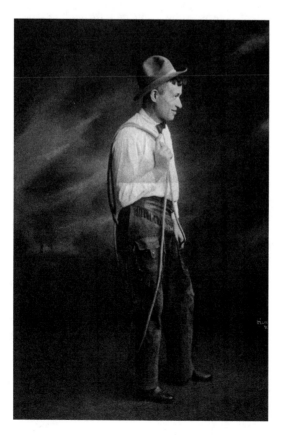

composer-player, penned the American classic "Honeysuckle Rose" for the all-black Broadway revue *Keep Shufflin'* (1928); for the Broadway-bound *Hot Chocolates* (1929), Waller and lyricist Andy Razaf produced "Ain't Misbehavin'." But by the mid-1930s, the Harlem-Broadway connection had withered, a victim of exacerbated racial tensions, and other forces unleashed by the Depression.

Though the operetta with its middle-European antecedents had suffered during the war years, it had a final fling during the 1920s. More important, *Show Boat* (1927), although in the tradition of the operetta, had special significance as the forerunner of the integrated musical in which song, dance, dialogue, and settings cohere to tell an essentially serious story. Based on the best-selling novel by Edna Ferber, it had a book by Oscar Hammerstein II and a catalog of indelible songs by Jerome Kern, including "Ol' Man River," "Can't Help Lovin' Dat Man," and "Make Believe." As the precursor of the modern American musical drama that reached maturity. with *Oklahoma!* (1943), *Show Boat* was perhaps most significant for having so effectively mined the American past and for Kern's adroit use of native American musical idioms.

In the post-World War I period, the most important alternative to the commercial theater of musical revues, operettas, and smart satirical burlesques was the so-called little theater movement. Inspired by Europe's independent theaters, Boston's Toy Theatre and the Chicago Little Theatre opened in 1912. They were soon joined by the Neighborhood Playhouse and the Washington Square Players in New York and the Provincetown Players of Provincetown, Massachusetts, all in 1915. By 1917, the number of such groups had reached fifty Though reflecting the passionate and idiosyncratic views of their respective founders, each theater group shared a common set of goals and methods. Dedicated to exploring advanced ideas and works from Europe, each company relied on unpaid volunteers for its personnel and upon subscribers for financial underwriting. In part, the impetus for the movement came from theater people disenchanted with the circumscribed conventions of the commercial theater; other supporters came from such newly established university drama programs as those founded by George Pierce Baker at Radcliffe and Harvard and Thomas Wood Stevens at the Carnegie Institute of Technology.

One of the little theater's greatest contributions was its encouragement of what became known as the "new stagecraft." Though reflecting a variety of influences, including the expressionistic approach popularized by the German Max Reinhardt, the American version of the new stagecraft eventually distilled itself into what might be called a simplified yet heightened realism. Instead of a literal reproduction of reality like that sought by Belasco, the new aesthetic of design simplicity tried to capture the spirit rather than the photographic detail of the script.

In 1916 Sheldon Cheyney of the Detroit Arts and Crafts Theatre launched *Theatre Arts Magazine*, until 1948 the most important American forum for new ideas concerning the theater. Foremost among these were the new theories of acting advanced by Richard Boleslavsky and Maria Ouspenskaya, veterans of the famed Moscow Art Theatre who in 1925 established the American Laboratory Theatre. There, they taught Konstantin Stanislavsky's "method," with its emphasis on enhancing the actor's imagination and memory.

The little theater movement is also significant for having supported a number of young American playwrights, including Eugene O'Neill. In 1914, five of his one-act plays were published with the support of his father, the legendary actor James O'Neill. At the same time, he began attending Baker's play-writing class at Harvard. The next year, he began his association with the Provincetown Players, who produced his first short plays and encouraged him to go to New York City, where the group itself moved in 1916. In 1921 the Players split, with O'Neill, producer-historian Kenneth Macgowan, and designer Robert Edmond Jones presiding over a branch committed to quality foreign and period plays as well as to the noncommercial works of O'Neill and others. In the meantime, O'Neill's first full-length play, *Beyond the Horizon* (1920), debuted on Broadway and won that year's Pulitzer Prize for the best play of the year. Not incidentally, the establishment of the Pulitzer Prize in 1918 for the best new American drama performed in New York, along with the initiation of the Drama Critics Circle Awards in 1936, were important factors in encouraging American playwrights as well as the American theater itself.

O'Neill, bucking the hegemony of the commercial theater's lighter musical and comic fare, scored an unprecedented string of critical successes with plays that continue to live in revivals around the world. *The Emperor Jones* (1920), *The Hairy Ape* (1922), *Desire Under the Elms* (1924), *The Great God Brown* (1926), *Strange Interlude* (1928), and *Mourning Becomes Electra* (1931) es-

The trouble with the theater is that it's no longer a way of life for an audience. It's just a way to kill an evening.

JESSICA TANDY

See also
Television

495

*A talent for
drama is not a
talent for writing,
but is an ability to
articulate human
relationships.*

GORE VIDAL

tablished O'Neill as a master of an essentially realistic and tragic approach probing the dark, convoluted aspects of human nature. After 1934, O'Neill withheld his works from production, although he continued to write prolifically. In 1936 O'Neill became the first and only American playwright to win the Nobel Prize for literature. He died in 1953. Though his reputation suffered during the 1940s, the successful 1956 mountings of *The Iceman Cometh* (1946) and *Long Day's Journey into Night* (1941) reestablished O'Neill's standing as America's foremost dramatist.

By 1930, although the energies and resources of companies like the Provincetown Players had dissipated due to the Depression and Broadway's commercialism, other independent groups had taken their place. The Group Theatre was formed in 1931 by Lee Strasberg, Harold Clurman, and Cheryl Crawford on the model of Stanislavsky's Moscow Art Theatre, with its ensemble approach. With a troupe that included Stella Adler, Morris Carnovsky, and Elia Kazan, it staged works by Paul Green, Maxwell Anderson, William Saroyan, Clifford Odets, and other promising young writers. Although it disbanded in 1941, the Group Theatre remained an important force due to the efforts of former members such as Strasberg and Adler, who disseminated Stanislavsky's system throughout the United States.

One of the most innovative responses to the Depression came in the mid 1930s with the establishment by Congress of the Federal Theatre Project (1935–1939). Designed to combat unemployment among theater workers, it put some five thousand professionals to work in New York City alone. It offered free and often quality performances of imaginative restagings of classics, as well as new works, including children's and foreign language plays.

In spite of its brief life, the Federal Theatre had a significant impact. In addition to the innovative multimedia experiments of the Living Newspaper and other richly varied enterprises that sprang up across the country, the Federal Theatre gave a boost to black drama through the Negro People's Theatre, a unit of the Federal Theatre headquartered at the Lafayette Theatre in Harlem and led by John Houseman. Among its successes were a seven-month run of Orson Welles's all-black, voodoo *Macbeth* (1935–1936), set in Haiti, and an ambitious *Doctor Faustus* (1937) with Welles in the title role. Also impressive was the Chicago production of *The Swing Mikado* (1938), which transformed the Gilbert and Sullivan operetta

THE LIVING NEWSPAPER
Innovation and Confrontation

Though pledged to provide adult and uncensored drama, the Federal Theatre ran into problems with *Ethiopia* (1936), the first production of its notable Living Newspaper series. A "theatrical documentary" probing Italy's attack on the African country, *Ethiopia* was deemed too volatile by the United States State Department which, despite Mussolini's aggression, did not want to offend the dictator. Indeed, the show's powerful multimedia mix of clips from motion picture newsreels, sound bites from topical radio speeches, projected headlines from the daily newspapers, and live and rhetorically charged dramatic vignettes was judged inimical to American foreign policy objectives.

Domestic issues tackled by the Living Newspaper series were at first less problematic. *One Third of a Nation* (1938), for example, took its title from President Franklin Delano Roosevelt's claim that one-third of the nation was ill-fed, ill-clad, and ill-housed. Like other editions of the Living Newspaper, the production used as its protagonist an "everyman" who, after raising the basic issue, was led through the background of the problem and its possible solutions. In 1939 congressional ire with the Federal Theatre's obvious pro—New Deal leanings led to a cutoff of appropriations.

into a celebratory display of dancing and singing set in the Caribbean. When the production moved to New York in 1939, its raves inspired showman Michael Todd to mount a hastily thrown together and Harlemized imitation, *The Hot Mikado* (1939), with Bill Robinson.

Also notable was the infamous nonstaging of composer Marc Blitzstein's *The Cradle Will Rock* (1938), a biting musical probe into the inherent conflicts in labor-management relations in a steel factory. When the Works Project Administration, the Federal Theatre's parent agency, ordered the play's postponement because of its perceived political volatility, an ad hoc, unsanctioned "rehearsal" performance was quickly arranged.

Provoked by the specter of federal censorship, Welles and Houseman, Blitzstein's producers, formed their own company, the Mercury Theatre, in 1937. In its short yet illustrious life, the Mercury presented vivacious updatings of plays by

---

See also
Urban Cultural Institutions

Georg Büchner, Thomas Dekker, George Bernard Shaw, and Shakespeare. Its greatest and most provocative stage success was a modern-dress rendition of Shakespeare's *Julius Caesar* (1938), fashioned as a sharp commentary on fascism with the conspirators garbed in uniforms resembling those of the German and Italian military. Welles and Houseman also took their dramatic acumen to the airwaves with the Mercury Radio Theatre, which produced the harrowing and historic Halloween night broadcast of *The War of the Worlds* (1938), which convinced a sizable portion of the population that Martians had landed in New Jersey. The troupe was soon lured to Hollywood where it scored its greatest triumphs, the watershed motion pictures *Citizen Kane* (1941) and *The Magnificent Ambersons* (1942).

The years between the two world wars were marked by an ongoing struggle between the stage's commercial productions and its more highbrow ambitions. Along with the era's frothy revues, there were musical comedies like *Of Thee I Sing* (1931), with a book by George S. Kaufman and Morrie Ryskind and music by George and Ira Gershwin, that pilloried presidential politics; like the satiric works of Gilbert and Sullivan, this American musical persuasively argued public issues by means of laughter. There were more self-consciously "serious" works by such talents as Clifford Odets, Elmer Rice, Maxwell Anderson, Robert E. Sherwood, John Howard Lawson, Paul Green, and Lillian Hellman. There were also sophisticated comedies such as Philip Barry's *The Philadelphia Story* (1939), the George S. Kaufman-Moss Hart collaborations *You Can't Take It with You* (1936) and *The Man Who Came to Dinner* (1939), and the whimsical meditations on the human condition offered by Thornton Wilder in *Our Town* (1938) and *The Merchant of Yonkers* (1938), rewritten in 1954 as *The Matchmaker* and adapted for the musical *Hello, Dolly!* in 1964. Ironically, one of the 1930s' towering theatrical and musical achievements, George Gershwin's American folk opera *Porgy and Bess* (1935), based on Dubose Heyward's book with lyrics by Heyward and Ira Gershwin, was not a commercial success.

The Second World War, like the first, ruptured the theater's normal patterns. Theater people, like their counterparts in the other entertainment arts, discovered that their talents had a unique value in helping to keep morale up. They toured army camps and visited stage-door canteens. Broadway developed a new élan and, in so doing, attracted an audience expanded by curious soldiers and civilians newly affluent from the prosperity generated by the all-out war effort.

Irving Berlin's *This Is the Army* (1942) represented the zenith of wartime revues. Opening with an all-soldier cast on the patriotic date of July 4, just seven months after Pearl Harbor, the show evoked fervent, red-white-and-blue support for United States troops everywhere. GIs identified with the sentiments expressed in "This Is the Army, Mr. Jones." But the showstopper came when three hundred soldiers trooped across the Broadway Theatre's stage to the insistent beat of their own feet marching in precisely choreographed close-order drills. The show was adapted successfully by Hollywood in 1944 and included a scene with heavyweight boxing champion Joe Louis in an obvious but no less sincere attempt to "include" American blacks in the patriotic pageantry.

The euphoria of victory was short-lived, for after World War II the United States entered into an era of international militarization and domestic conformity. The American theater responded with a sharp increase in the number of plays that explored the convoluted labyrinths of the human mind. In treating such basic and universal themes, many of America's most prominent and socially aware dramatists added poignancy and power to their works by the use of regional settings. Arthur Miller's *Death of a Salesman* (1949) and *A View from the Bridge* (1955), for example, reflected the playwright's blue-collar, working-class Brooklyn background; and Tennessee Williams's *A Streetcar Named Desire* (1947) and *Cat on a Hot Tin Roof* (1955) simmered with southern idioms.

Though an extension of the Group Theatre's approach first taught in the 1920s, it was the Actors Studio that became the postwar period's primary influence on acting. Established in 1947, the Actors Studio achieved its greatest impact with Lee Strasberg, who taught a performance approach based on the actor's individual psyche and emotional memory. The "method" attained its greatest notoriety with Marlon Brando's controversial characterization of Stanley Kowalski in Williams's *A Streetcar Named Desire*. As directed by Actors Studio co-founder Elia Kazan, Brando's Kowalski inflamed debate by popularizing an acting style that for some seemed to trade on boorish street talk, brutish behavior, and slovenly attire. While the novelty of the method's departure from tradition has mostly dissipated, it

You can't be boring. Life is boring. The weather is boring. Actors must not be boring.

STELLA ADLER
ACTING TEACHER, AS
QUOTED IN HER OBITUARY,
THE NEW YORK TIMES
(DEC. 22, 1992)

remains one of the touchstones of the contemporary theater both in America and abroad.

With the increasing postwar emphasis on cultural diversity, the American theater, like other national institutions, was opened to participants of all backgrounds, working in virtually all sections of the country. In part, such activity has been a reaction to Broadway's ever-increasing conservatism and the tendency of Broadway producers, reacting to multimillion dollar production budgets and escalating ticket prices, to try to lure mass audiences by relying on well-known and therefore presold stories and stars, many of them, ironically, from such competing media as movies, television, and popular music.

Women, though traditionally well represented as performers, did not begin to break into the front rank of playwrights until the 1930s. Among the first women to achieve celebrity as a writer was Clare Boothe, whose *The Women* (1936), with an all-female cast, and *Kiss the Boys Good-Bye* (1938) were among the decade's biggest hits. Even more prominent was Lillian Hellman, whose distinguished career included *The Children's Hour* (1934), *The Little Foxes* (1939), and *Toys in the Attic* (1960). More recently, contemporary playwright Beth Henley tapped into her southern roots for searing yet humorous explorations of family life with *Crimes of the Heart* (1979; Pulitzer Prize, 1981) and *The Miss Firecracker Contest* (1984). Wendy Wasserstein, who first attracted attention with *Uncommon Women and Others* (1977)

and *Isn't It Romantic?* (1981), won the 1989 Pulitzer Prize for *The Heidi Chronicles* (1988), the story of art historian Heidi Holland's twenty-five-year-long struggle to attain personal happiness and professional fulfillment and her development of a feminist perspective. Along with the rise of female writing talent, the 1980s witnessed a thriving feminist theater movement that included the Women's Experimental Theatre in New York, At the Foot of the Mountain in Minneapolis, and the Omaha Magic Theatre.

The first black female writer to have a play produced on Broadway was Lorraine Hansberry, whose *A Raisin in the Sun* (1959) won the New York Drama Critics Circle Award. It also featured Sidney Poitier, Claudia McNeil, Ruby Dee, and Diana Sands, a group of talented black players who would achieve further success in films and television, as well as on the stage. Though conventional in form, *A Raisin in the Sun* introduced a number of themes of continuing significance, such as the need for blacks to define their own aspirations, the importance of eliminating discrimination, and the place of African culture within the black American experience. A montage of excerpts from Hansberry's letters, notes, and plays was posthumously produced as *To Be Young, Gifted, and Black* (1971).

The first African American playwright to win the Pulitzer Prize was Charles Gordone for *No Place to Be Somebody* (1969), a tragic story of an illiterate black who attempts to emulate the Mafia as a means of vengeance against the repressive white world. Black anger against "the system" was perhaps most tellingly articulated by Imamu Baraka (LeRoi Jones) who, in arguing for racial separation, spurned New York's white cultural establishment to set up his Spirit House in the midst of the black ghetto of Newark, New Jersey. Baraka's militancy was most forcefully expressed in *Slave Ship* (1967), an epic collage of scenes depicting the black American experience. Charles Fuller's *A Soldier's Play* (1981), produced by the Negro Ensemble Company, is a poignant examination of racism in the army during World War II. Its successful Broadway run and a Pulitzer Prize took Fuller to Hollywood where his adaptation, *A Soldier's Story* (1984), proved one of the decade's best black-oriented films.

Inspired by the examples of Hansberry, Baraka, and Bullins, members of other minorities began to see the arts as uniquely effective forms for expressing their own cultural and political concerns. In 1965, for example, Luis Valdez, in cooperation with the National Farm Workers As-

AWARD-WINNER

Lorraine Hansberry, the first black female writer to have a play produced on Broadway, and whose Raisin in the Sun *won the New York Drama Critics Circle Award.*
UPI / CORBIS-BETTMANN

sociation, founded El Teatro Campesino (Field-worker's Theater), to dramatize the need for the unionization of farm laborers. After successfully achieving that objective, Valdez drew attention to the problem of discrimination against Americans of Mexican descent in *Zoot Suit* (1976) and *I Don't Have to Show You No Stinking Badge* (1987). The growth in Hispanic theater was documented in a 1985 survey that found over one hundred active regional troupes with specific ties to Chicano, Cuban, Puerto Rican, and other Spanish-speaking groups.

The increasing visibility of Asian Americans has most recently been reflected in the successful career of David Henry Hwang, whose concerns for East-West cross-cultural interactions are central to *FOB* (1979) and *The Dance and the Railroad* (1981). Hwang's most celebrated work, *M. Butterfly* (1988), is based on the actual case of a French diplomat who claimed that he did not know that the Chinese star of the Beijing Opera with whom he had lived for two decades was actually a man. In Hwang's absorbing recounting, the tale becomes a metaphor for the West's inability to see through its stereotypes of the East as exotic, feminine, and passive. Asian American theatrical efforts have received significant encouragement from institutions such as the Pan Asian Repertory Theatre in New York and the East-West Players in Los Angeles.

In addition to a dramatic increase in minority involvement in the theater throughout the 1960s, the decade also saw a strong movement toward decentralization of the theater. Fueled by growing disenchantment with the rampant commercialization of Broadway and its ever-escalating production and ticket costs, as well as by the foment provoked by the civil rights and women's movements and the protests against America's involvement in the Vietnam War, theatrical enterprises seemed to pop up everywhere.

On the streets, there were groups like the San Francisco Mime Troupe, created in 1959 by R. G. Davis. Combining a commedia dell'arte approach with the techniques of Soviet agitprop plays, the troupe systematically ridiculed everything and everyone in authority. In *A Minstrel Show, or, Civil Rights in a Cracker Barrel* (1966), the troupe savaged both racism and naive integration. One of the few radical theater groups born in the 1960s to have survived while sustaining its antiestablishment focus, the San Francisco Mime Troupe has kept its political drive alive in works such as *Steeltown* (1985), an examination of the marginalization of the labor movement and political left. The

Bread and Puppet Theater, founded in 1961 by Peter Schumann, literally used puppets or "living sculptures," some twelve feet tall, and bread given to the audience at each performance as part of a communionlike ritual. In parables such as *The Cry of the People for Meat* (1969), Schumann's ensemble depicted the imperialistic evils of the Vietnam War as a consequence of capitalism's proclivity, for violence.

Some of the most exciting experiments of the period were carried out by the Living Theatre Company. Though founded in 1947 by Judith Malina and Julian Beck to explore poetic drama and nonrealistic production strategies, it gradually began to incorporate the advanced techniques of theorists Antonin Artaud and Bertolt Brecht. By the 1960s, the Living Theatre traveled throughout the United States and Europe espousing revolution, anarchy, and freedom from the restraints of government and bourgeois convention. In works such as *Paradise Now* (1968), the traditional barriers between performers and audience were broken down in order to smash the heritage of theatrical illusionism and to establish a performer-audience solidarity for the revolutionary political tasks at hand. Despite its decline in the 1980s, the Living Theatre left a legacy that lives on in such strategies as the decentering of dialogue in favor of Artaudian and Brechtian techniques, the confrontational blitzing of audiences, and the whipping up of impassioned exhortations.

Though less politically radical, the Off-Broadway and Off-Off-Broadway movements provided a more varied but no less significant influence. Founded in 1951 by Jose Quintero and Theodore Mann, the Circle in the Square helped establish the careers of the actors Geraldine Page, Jason Robards, Jr., George C. Scott, and Colleen Dewhurst. Quintero had spectacular success with revivals of Tennessee Williams's *Summer and Smoke* in 1952, and Eugene O'Neill's *The Iceman Cometh* in 1956. During the 1950s, Off-Broadway theaters focused on repertory rather than experimentation; the goal was to attain a level of artistry more serious than that offered by Broadway.

At the start of the 1960s, Off-Broadway venues started feeling economic pressures similar to those affecting Broadway, including increased labor and overhead costs. Inspired by the opportunity created by Off Broadway's diminished offerings and growing caution, various bootstrap entrepreneurs began to offer plays wherever a room could be found. Joe Cino, who started using his Caffé Cino as an art center in 1958, is credited with initiating the Off-Off-Broadway phenome-

Soon motion pictures were running on the bill of vaudeville programs, where they followed comedy acts or song-and-dance skits.

PAGE 141

♦ **Agitprop**
Propaganda, especially political propaganda promulgated chiefly in literature, drama, music, or art

non that by 1965 had produced some four hundred plays by approximately two hundred different playwrights. The most significant Off-Off-Broadway producer was Ellen Stewart, who began offering plays in 1961 under the banner of the Café La Mama (later renamed La Mama Experimental Theatre Club). In the 1969–1970 season, La Mama alone presented more original plays than did Broadway.

Outside New York, yet paralleling the Off- and Off-Off-Broadway movements, a significant array of regional theaters developed. In 1947 Margo Jones established her Theatre 47 (the name changed with the coming of each new year) in Dallas. The Alley Theatre, also founded in 1947, was set up in Houston by Nina Vance, while the Arena Stage of Washington, D.C., was put into operation in 1949 by Zelda Fichandler. Women, indeed, were at the forefront of the regional theater movement. The establishment of the Missouri Repertory Theatre in Kansas City by

Patricia McIlrath in 1964 and Jo Ann Schmidman's Omaha Magic Theatre in 1969 were also significant.

A trend toward stabilizing such operations with resident companies was bolstered by the example of Tyrone Guthrie, who opened the formidable Guthrie Theater in Minneapolis in 1963. Substantial Ford Foundation grants available to those companies deemed likely to grow had also been a stabilizing force. Then, in 1965, the creation of the National Endowment for the Arts provided additional support. However, the challenge of financing American arts in general and American theater in particular has remained problematic, especially in view of the 1990 congressional debates on whether to continue funding for the arts endowment in view of controversies over tax-supported work that some have considered morally objectionable.

Still, regional theaters have remained strong. In 1990, there were more than two hundred such

**SHAKESPEARE
FESTIVAL**

Theatrical entrepreneur Joseph Papp established the New York Shakespeare Festival which in 1957 began offering free, city-supported performances in Central Park. This photograph of Shakespeare in the Park was taken on July 6, 1961.
UPI/CORBIS-BETTMANN

nonprofit professional operations collectively offering more than three thousand productions. Employment figures for actors were similarly striking. In 1966, for example, a survey revealed that for the first time in the twentieth century, more stage actors were employed outside New York than in it. By 1990, for every actor working on Broadway, there were four being paid by nonprofit regional theaters.

In many ways, regional theaters have functioned like subsidized European theaters, offering repertoires composed mainly of popular classic and contemporary titles. By 1990, however, some regional theaters had also become important supporters of new works. The Goodman Theatre of Chicago, founded in 1925 during the heyday of the little theater movement, took on this function in the 1980s by producing the American premieres of David Mamet's Pulitzer Prize-winning examination of real estate swindlers, *Glengarry Glen Ross* (1984), and David Rabe's excoriating probe of Hollywood, *Hurlyburly* (1984), both of which enjoyed successful Broadway runs. A number of theaters also established working relationships with playwrights; an example is the productive alliance between the Yale Repertory Theatre and August Wilson, whose insightful *Fences* (1985) and *The Piano Lesson* (1990) each earned a Pulitzer for the black playwright.

Entrepreneur Joseph Papp offered yet another alternative through his ability to forge successful links between the commercial, nonprofit, and educational theater worlds. In 1954 Papp established the New York Shakespeare Festival, which in 1957 began offering free, city-supported performances in Central Park; in 1962 the outdoor Delacorte Theatre was built to house the productions. Like jazz musician Billy Taylor and his Jazzmobile, Papp took productions as well as workshops into New York's ethnic neighborhoods. This was an important part of his lifelong ambition to "liberate" theater from its essentially bourgeois and intellectual middle-class orientation.

In 1966 Papp enlarged his operation with the acquisition of the Astor Library in downtown New York. Born again under the banner of the Public Theatre with five auditoriums, the old Astor Library got off to a rousing start with its inaugural event, Papp's production of the bellwether rock musical *Hair* (1967), with music by Galt MacDermott and book by Gerome Ragni and James Rado. It was the perfect vehicle for capitalizing on Papp's concern for expanding theater's demographic boundaries. Its characters were archetypal, youthful 1960s outsiders wrestling with racism, sexism, public attitudes toward homosexuality, the responsibilities of parenthood, drugs, poverty, and the Vietnam War. Significantly, and in contrast to the book musicals of the period like *Hello, Dolly!* (1964) and *Fiddler on the Roof* (1964), *Hair* features the pounding rhythms and amplified guitar licks of rock and roll, as well as the period's obscenity-laced, anti-establishment argot. Embraced by young people, the general public, and the critics, and widely publicized because of a nude scene, *Hair* moved to Broadway in expanded form to become the season's runaway hit. Catching the Zeitgeist of the period, it also caught the public's ear with such pop music hits as "Aquarius." Papp's comfortable embrace of everything from Shakespeare to rock music, as well as his openness to both conceptual and technical innovation, made him one of the American theater's most influential entrepreneurs.

A Postmodern Postscript

The breaking down of traditional assumptions and boundaries, though itself a long-standing tradition in the arts and human affairs, has in recent decades accelerated at unprecedented rates. Indeed, the speed and degree of change have been so great that the term "postmodern" is now commonly used in discussions of contemporary arts and culture to bracket the works of the late 1980s on from those of the immediately preceding "modern" era. Though a multitude of widely different styles prospered under the aegis of "modernism," each tended to adhere to a general set of characteristics that gave every work a signature relating it to such categories as surrealism or absurdism. In contrast, postmodern art has come to be characterized by a singular lack of consistency, either external or internal. In fact, the willful mixing and confusing of seemingly contradictory style, generic, and narrative elements has become a hallmark of the postmodern approach. Various manifestations of contemporary "performance art," with roots in European dadaism and surrealism of the 1920s as well as in the "happenings" and multimedia events of the 1960s, embody important aspects of the post-modern aesthetic. So, too, do the large-scale works of such contemporary artists as Robert Wilson, Richard Foreman, and the Wooster Group.

Related to postmodern production practice but focused on the role played in the artistic transaction by the spectator or reader is a group of theories grouped under the rubrics of poststructuralism and deconstruction. Based largely on the works of authors Jacques Derrida, Roland

T

THEATER AND MUSICAL THEATER

A Postmodern Postscript

It's one of the tragic ironies of the theater that only one man in it can count on steady work—the night watchman.

TALLULAH BANKHEAD

◆ **Bellwether**
One that takes the lead or initiative: leader; also an indicator of trends

*Our national flower
is the concrete
cloverleaf.*

LEWIS MUMFORD

Barthes, and Jacques Lacan, poststructuralism calls into question the basic assumption of structuralism—and, implicitly, all Western culture—that statements about truth and reality are independent of language. Poststructuralism argues that language profoundly influences its users to see and understand the world in very particular, language-inflected ways, invalidating or at least seriously compromising any claim to ultimate truth or objectivity. This destabilization of meaning has resulted in a condition, at least for postmodern critics and artists, that posits that, at best, truth is relative.

The critical-analytic process necessary to uncover the ideologic-linguistic values percolating just beneath a language's or work's surface structure has come to be known as deconstruction. The most ardent deconstructionists have been feminists, whose analysis of language has revealed various ways in which the values of white American and European men have tended to be privileged over those of women and people of color.

Today, the American theater is a richly variegated and lively enterprise. Like the other arts, it embodies and reflects the concerns and controversies of contemporary society. And though it is fashionable to declare Broadway a vast wasteland, itself a debatable proposition given the stylish and appealing successes of talents such as Neil Simon and Stephen Sondheim, it is far more accurate and revealing to conceive of the American theater as being in a dynamic steady state in which a dazzling array of forms, formats, and activities coexist. Furthermore, it should be recalled that in addition to Broadway, live theater abounds in regional, community, university, and even public school productions. Also, American movies and television might be considered in part as technological extensions of the American theater. Indeed, given the free and frequent movement of actors, directors, writers, producers, and composers among dramatic media, it may be overly restrictive to confine "theater" only to its live, stage-bound manifestations.

As the twenty-first century nears, the American theater will continue to evolve. And as it confronts society's and its own political, ideological, and technological upheavals, as well as its ever-increasing symbiosis with cinema and video, it may well be that part of its strategy for ensuring its capacity for adaptation and survival will revolve around attempts to deal with the pivotal question, "What is theater?"

—CHARLES MERRELL BERG

TRANSPORTATION AND MOBILITY

Mobility practically defines American social history. The march of Europeans and their descendants across the North American landscape, from 1607 to the present day, transforming the face of the land, reordering time and space, restlessly moving in search of wealth, freedom, and satisfaction—this story embraces the whole of American history. Immigration to America marks a common beginning for the earliest voyagers and the most recent arrivals. The potential for movement in America shaped and guided the lives of all who dared to take make the trip. In turn, the restless energies of these mobile voyagers fostered innovations that revolutionized the world in which Americans lived and worked—and moved.

There is nothing uniquely American about these habits of mobility and innovation, but their relentless influence placed a distinctive mark on the history of American society. For generations, Americans measured "progress" in terms of mobility, innovation, and technological "improvement." Most Americans have understood the exploitation of fossil fuels, and the assault on space and time, as natural, unambiguous triumphs. Critical assessment, on the other hand, may undermine our confidence in the virtue of these changes. Throughout this essay such value-laden terms as "progress" and "improvement" are meant to convey sentiments held in the past, whose merits, like all history, deserve scrutiny today.

Voyagers to the West

Fifteenth-century breakthroughs in navigation and ship design inaugurated Europe's conquest of the Americas. Beginning with the 1492 voyage of Columbus, square-rigged caravels and heavy galleons mastered the Atlantic waters, landing white adventurers (and their diseases) on New World shores, hauling treasure to the vaults of Europe, shuttling Africans into American slavery, and forging networks of commerce and communication that revolutionized the early modern world. Ranging in size from Columbus's *Santa María* (probably about 78 by 26 feet, drawing about 6 feet of water) to George III's three-decked men-of-war (up to 150 by 51 feet), these wooden ships with canvas sails serviced the world's first global empires. An age of restlessness had begun.

Atlantic crossings marked all immigrants to British America as voyagers, although individual experiences varied and the shock of transplantation differed according to one's expectations. Most early white settlers came from the restless classes of seventeenth-century England. Displaced agricultural laborers, unemployed urban workers, the "wandering poor" of Stuart England swelled the ranks of indentured servants who filled the Chesapeake colonies. West Country Puritans—spiritual voyagers before they became geographical pioneers—poured into New England. Younger sons of English gentlemen, uprooted by primogeniture from their ancestral lands, seized great estates in the new plantations. Restless entrepreneurs came to exploit a field for investment more open than Europe's markets ever would be.

The voyage itself often proved more grueling than adventurous. Crowded below decks with their livestock and luggage, immigrants suffered bad food, disease, and every discomfort for six to eight weeks or more—the longest trip on record lasted twenty-six weeks. Africans, of course, did not share even the bleakest hopes of the westering whites because they did not choose to move to America. Sold to Dutch, English, or Portuguese traders on the African coast, black slaves experienced a cruel deportation rendered positively demonic by conditions on the dreaded Middle Passage. Chained in tightly packed rows in dark, filthy holds, poisoned by the stench of wastes and death, hungry and terrified, black captives grieved for home and family, wondering what ghastly fate awaited them.

At the end of these immigrant voyages lay the North American coast. Mainland shores boasted ancient forests, sometimes rendered parklike by the Indians' annual burnings, but vastly deeper and more wild than the English had known. Because diseases that preceded the colonists—especially smallpox and influenza—had destroyed up to nine-tenths of the native population, the English saw what they were inclined to believe God and their sovereign had granted them: a bountiful paradise practically uninhabited.

Of course the North American coast actually sheltered thousands of native people. Dependent on hunting, gathering, and agriculture for subsistence, most Eastern Woodlands Indians pursued mobility patterns that inadvertently contributed to European myths about Indian life. Whereas Englishmen fixed their fortunes to the ground, moving people and things to suit their needs, Indians moved their communities to capture seasonal bounties within the natural environment. Their transience and lack of fixtures appeared to the English as simple indolence. Europeans who

defined themselves by attachments to property and place could only condemn as savages women and men who acquired little and roamed about in the wild forests.

The habits of the Indians nevertheless served the early colonists well. Indian trails marked overland paths for Europeans through the "trackless" New World forests. Indian canoes, dug out of logs or sewn together from white birchbark, extended navigation into much smaller streams than English ships could pass. Much of what white settlers learned of survival on North America's frontier they gleaned from Indian ways, and yet they never overcame their dread of these rootless, mobile natives. Even while they perfected their own penchant for moving around, the English viewed with suspicion any drift toward "savagery."

Colonial settlements first clustered near convenient landings, and the sea remained the primary highway for all transplanted Europeans. Gradually, as their numbers rose and they grew more familiar with the environment (and with native transportation), they spread along shorelines and up navigable streams, mastering the land as they came, fixing their claims to the ground in the form of clearings, buildings, fences, roads, docks, churches, and towns. Seventeenth-century colonists perfected their conquest of the coastal regions with little more for transportation than the natural waterways assisted by common roads. The latter were built, as in England, by local taxpayers, and the quality of these paths varied according to the ambitions of their users. In this primitive world most travelers walked or rode horseback, and goods moved in wagons or carts to town—or to the nearest waterway for more distant destinations.

In the eighteenth century the British plantations grew more prosperous and complex. Their populations expanded at unprecedented rates, from both natural increase and continued immigration, and the area of settlement quickly doubled. Eager to continue their successful assaults on the frontier, Anglo-Americans soon found development constrained by the limits of transportation over so large a field: if the fringes of colonial settlement were not to languish in wretched isolation, they must find ready communication with the centers of trade and culture. From this developmental necessity sprang the urge to improve transportation.

The Beginnings of Improvement

Improved transportation documented the triumph of English over Indian ways. Pioneers may have traveled light and borrowed Indian survival

. . . in many parts of the country the building of a highway has about the same result upon vegetation and human structures as the passage of a tornado or the blast of an atom bomb.

LEWIS MUMFORD
THE HIGHWAY AND THE CITY

See also
Travel and Vacations

and farming techniques, but they never intended to detach themselves from the lifelines of European empire. Settlers roamed the Shenandoah Valley, pushed through the Cumberland Gap into the valley of the Ohio, explored upstream along all the major rivers of the Atlantic seaboard, venturing however far, then crying out for improvement of the routes back to metropolitan centers. British policy in the Proclamation of 1763 discouraged this accelerating movement into Indian lands, but the American rebellion seemed to raise expectations even higher. With independence in 1783 came policies that encouraged the westward movement, and the formation of political union stimulated Atlantic communities to improve connections with each other and with the backcountry.

Internal improvements appeared almost everywhere in the first years of American nationhood. Coastal cities such as Boston, Providence, Philadelphia, and Baltimore chartered corporations to build turnpike roads, extending their trading networks deep into their hinterlands. Cleared of stumps (the largest were cut off at a foot or so), sometimes ditched and dressed with broken stone, turnpikes in the 1790s provided more or less all-weather roadways on which wagons and coaches transported goods, people, and information to bustling port cities. Improved post roads, especially north and east of New York, speeded the flow of newspapers and letters in the care of the new federal post office. Enterprising people

and corporations erected bridges where fords and ferries had delayed or endangered the traveling public. Bowing to the sensitivities of local citizens, turnpike charters sometimes exempted common farmers from paying the tolls imposed on commercial carriers; however, the customary rights of ferrymen and others who benefited from the lay of the land fell quickly to the ambitions of improvers.

Water transportation received equal attention as local enterprisers schemed to perfect the system of routes already laid down by nature. Certain canal projects immediately recommended themselves: across Cape Cod at Barnstable Harbor; from Boston to the Merrimack River; across the isthmus separating the Delaware River from Chesapeake Bay; through the Dismal Swamp of southern Virginia to North Carolina's Albemarle Sound. Gentlemen of grander vision dreamed of interregional canals from New York's Hudson River to Lakes Ontario and Champlain; from Philadelphia via the Schuylkill and Susquehanna rivers to Lake Erie; or the centerpiece of new American nationalism, a Potomac Canal linking the waters of the Ohio River system with the new national capital. American funds and engineering expertise could not sustain this first generation's designs, but canal fever persisted and the breakthrough was close at hand.

New York's Erie Canal, built between 1817 and 1825, repaid the frustrations of early improvers with spectacular success. Taking advan-

COMMERCE LINK

New York's Erie Canal, which was built between 1817 and 1825 and which helped New York City to broker American commerce the way London had served the British empire.
LIBRARY OF CONGRESS /
CORBIS

tage of a "water-level" route (rising some six hundred feet [180 meters]) as well as the fastest-growing city in the postwar United States, New York's DeWitt Clinton gambled the credit of the state against the hope of control over commerce with the American interior. After 1825, in part because the canal captured westering traffic and in part because fair prospects energized the metropolis's enterprising merchants, New York City brokered American commerce the way London had served the British Empire.

Much of the work of improving transportation involved making special vehicles. Pennsylvania wagon builders, for example, attached a boat-shaped box (which naturally centered its cargo) to a rugged undercarriage, producing a Conestoga wagon capable of traversing the punishing roads of the trans-Appalachian frontier. Interior merchants and farmers fashioned crude "arks" and flatboats on which they rafted lumber, whiskey, and surplus grain down the rivers to New Orleans. Long, narrow keelboats, when poled or pulled upstream, offered laborious (and expensive) returns for early pioneers of the Old Northwest. Canal transport via New York soon became so cheap that interior farmers often walked home empty-handed and bought supplies from the continuous downstream flow. Specially designed sailing packets linked New Orleans and other coastal ports with New York, rendering the selection of goods in the markets on Manhattan Island inevitably richer and fresher than almost anywhere else in the network.

Another important improvement required no hardware change whatever. Beginning in 1818, the Black Ball Line placed square-rigged ships on a regular schedule, sailing monthly between Liverpool and New York. Guaranteeing fixed departures, scheduled packets allowed American buyers and sellers to make a market predictably in England. Some scoffed as the first ships sailed with partial cargoes, but within a decade much long-haul business with the mother country was conducted on schedule. America's major export, cotton, found its best market in New York, far from southern fields, largely because scheduled shippers hustled to attract Liverpool buyers in order to fill their ships.

The cumulative effect of these and dozens of other specific improvements in the early American transportation environment produced a genuine revolution in commerce and mobility. Long-distance freight rates between New York City and the agricultural interior fell dramatically (often 95 percent or better). Exports of surplus food and fiber grew apace. Interior cities suddenly boomed. Rochester, New York, for example, grew in a decade from a village of fifteen hundred to a city of ten thousand. The farming frontier quickly pushed across the entire Old Northwest, and cotton planters seized fertile lands from Georgia to Texas. Responding to the excitement, settlers poured into Ohio, Indiana, Illinois, Michigan, Kentucky, Tennessee, Alabama, and Mississippi—all demanding more roads, canals, and transportation services in order to bring new wilderness lands into profitable communication with burgeoning American markets.

The social impact of this revolution in mobility proved no less dramatic. Boom towns like Rochester experienced unbelievable social disruption as thousands of transients came and went each year. The circulation of information increased astonishingly: New York news, which in 1790 took three weeks to reach Ohio, arrived in 1830 in six days or less. With the decline of frontier isolation, more Americans turned to pioneering with rising expectations. The operations of civil courts, the circulation of money and credit, the promises of campaigning politicians—all were transformed by this communications revolution. American habits by the 1830s appeared so hectic that foreign visitors experienced vertigo. Religious mission and reform societies reached out from New York and New England expressly to stir the fires of civilization among western residents, who seemed in danger of reverting to "savagery."

Far Western Frontiers

While American families consolidated their hold on eastern woodlands, frontiersmen scouted the sprawling continental wilderness beyond the Mississippi River. Here scarce water, harsh landscapes, and the rising hostility of displaced Indians rendered transportation both more difficult and more important to survival. Once again voyagers studied the ways of the Indians in order to master this new field for human mobility.

Forced by scant vegetation to range over much longer distances than their woodland neighbors, Indians of the dry plains stretched their patterns of movement over a grand terrain. At first dogs shared the burdens of nomadic life, but the spread of horses in the seventeenth and eighteenth centuries lent new speed, range, and power to migratory systems. Water, weather, and the habits of the bison set the boundaries of native life into the nineteenth century, when the relocation of eastern Indians and the approach of white traders crowded Indian lands and distorted these rhythms. As ear-

With progress in roads came more cars, more roads for the cars, and more cars for the roads that had been built to accommodate more cars.

"ONE FOR THE ROADS" REPORT ON U.S. HIGHWAYS AND SUPERHIGWAYS AS QUOTED IN TIME (OCT. 6, 1961)

See also
The City

lier in coastal forests, traffic in furs broached the cultural barrier separating Indians and whites, redirecting Indian patterns and initiating whites into the mysteries of this difficult land.

Like the adventurers at Jamestown two centuries before, explorers in the Far West received important assistance from a sponsoring "metropolis"—this time the infant United States. In 1803 President Thomas Jefferson sent Meriwether Lewis and William Clark on the first of many official expeditions, this one to open the Louisiana Purchase. The army officers Zebulon Pike and Stephen H. Long charted routes to the southern Rockies, and dozens of less famous individuals probed the mountains for passes. After 1820 private fur companies recruited mountain men—characters like Jim Bridger, Jedediah Smith, and Bill Sublette—who worked in the shadows between enterprise and expatriation, living among the Indians and gathering information on physi-

cal and cultural geography that would make American advances possible. The great trails that later carried emigrants to Santa Fe, California, and Oregon were blazed by these vagrant traders, and at mid century wagon trains still found refuge and succor among them.

Overland wagon trains delivered thousands of Americans to California and Oregon, but integration of the Pacific Coast into the United States depended on regular commercial transportation. Stimulated by California gold rush traffic after 1848, the United States Post Office; private contractors such as George Giddings and John Butterfield; and express companies like Wells Fargo, Adams Express, American Express, and National Express struggled to carry regular mail and passengers through the wastelands. Threatened with the loss of their final domain, mounted Indians in the three decades after 1850 preyed mercilessly on way stations where coaches stopped for water and fresh mules. To protect commercial carriers the U.S. Army took steps to "pacify" the Plains Indians, which in turn lured more travelers, traders, and settlers into the region. Ranchers assembled huge herds of longhorn cattle that, like the bison and the Indians before them, found water and grass where they could until they were driven to Kansas, the railhead, and the markets of the East.

Horse-powered transportation thus opened even the most forbidding American environments to the restless people of the United States. By the era of the Civil War they had planted settlers across a continent that their grandfathers believed would lie empty for ten generations. Three thousand miles (4,800 kilometers) between Jamestown and San Francisco had been subdued with the same transport technology that first brought Englishmen to Virginia: sailing ships, boats, and barges; wheeled wagons; mules, oxen, and horses. No celebration marked the achievement, though, because a more dramatic transportation revolution had captured center stage. On 10 May 1869, at Promontory Point, Utah, a justly proud assembly of capitalists witnessed the driving of the golden spike. The first transcontinental steam railroad was complete. The age of speed and power had begun.

The Impact of Steam Power

Steam power brought a new order of magnitude to changes in American mobility. Steam engines harnessed the energy of burning fuels to machinery that could overcome the natural forces of wind, water, and gravity; speed up the movement of vehicles; and sustain exertions for hours with-

THE WAY WEST

The Era of Overland Migrations

When overland migrations to Oregon and California quickened in the 1840s, emigrants organized themselves into trains that followed regular, tested procedures. Outfits consisted of sturdy covered wagons, two or three teams of oxen or horses, clothing, cooking equipment, food and water, perhaps a milk cow, and what tools and furniture could be wedged in beside the children. Starting after the worst spring floods, armed with one of many popular emigrants' handbooks or hand-drawn maps, or guided by a hired wagonmaster, several families bound for the same destination adopted rules of association and set out from Independence, Missouri. If equipment, animals, and weather held; if Indians did not attack; if maps and guides proved faithful; if men did not turn quarrelsome or illness become epidemic—if nothing delayed such travelers, they struggled through the mountains by late summer, descending toward the Pacific before September snows closed the high passes. For many, things did not go well: for the famous Donner Party of 1846–1847, small mistakes compounded into fatal disaster. Trapped by early snows in the high Sierras, most of these emigrants starved to death, and some were reduced to cannibalism. On the overland trails, the margin for error proved very small.

out rest or refreshment. Steam introduced dimensions of speed and power unimaginable ever before.

Successful steamboat navigation in the United States began in August 1807, when Robert Fulton's *Clermont* steamed up the Hudson River from New York to Albany. Quickly, side-wheel steamers appeared on the Atlantic coastal waters wherever contrary winds, downstream currents, or traffic congestion rendered sailing difficult. After 1817, specially designed shallow-draft steamboats (Henry M. Shreve's *Washington* was the first) revolutionized travel on the Mississippi and Ohio rivers. Over the next fifty years improvements in engine technology and boat design steadily increased speed (to over thirty miles [forty-eight kilometers] per hour), safety, and efficiency. Boats drawing little more than a foot of water probed the secondary rivers of the interior, and "floating palaces" adorned the lower Mississippi River. Steam engines' voracious appetites for fuel slowed their adoption on long-distance sailing ships, but by the 1840s transatlantic steam packets offered scheduled liners a measure of protection against delays in calm weather.

Improved water transportation facilitated interior settlement and economic growth, which in turn stimulated demand for even better transportation. Encouraged by England's first successful railway, the Stockton and Darlington (1825), American innovators quickly mated the steam locomotive with the flange-wheeled tramcar system used in mining operations. By the 1830s experimental railroads served Boston, Providence, New York, Baltimore, and Charleston, and chartered corporations projected routes all over the eastern United States. Still imperfect in hardware and operating procedures, early railways struggled for another decade, often bankrupting the promoters who hoped to harness this complex new technology. By 1845, however, the recognizably modern steam train, running on heavy iron "T" rails fixed to wooden cross-ties on raised, improved roadways, stood ready to "annihilate" space and time.

Unlike canals, which were public or mixed enterprises, American railroads were built by private profit-seeking corporations. This organizational difference restricted their access to public money, but it freed railroaders from the control of the local voting taxpayers whose demands often frustrated public-works projects. Railroad developers found that economies of scale favored carload lots, regular schedules, discrimination of freight by weight and value, discrimination of places by competition and traffic potential, integrated operations over long distances, and coordinated interchange with connecting roads. As hardware evolved and construction costs skyrocketed, outside capitalists displaced local investors. In the early 1850s, eastern railroad builders manipulated many short roads into operating trunk lines between New York and Chicago. By the time of the Civil War, American railroaders thought of themselves not as servants but as creators of interior markets.

High fixed costs for construction, equipment, expansion, and debt forced railroads to seek revenue more aggressively than any earlier carriers. They worked tirelessly to build up their territories and capture new ones to the west. Speed and all-weather service gave railroads some advantage over water and wagon competition, but their real transforming power lay in rate discrimination. Low rates for long hauls brought interior places artificially near the coasts, encouraging farming where there was no market. Special rates built up key towns as collection centers. Cutthroat competition drove prices below the normal profit margin on major routes; but much higher local rates recouped the losses incurred on service from points where competition was strongest. Pursuing their own strategies, interstate companies manipulated rates with apparent disregard for the traditional laws of trade.

This new power in the hands of absentee capitalists struck interior farmers and merchants as undemocratic and unfair: "If rates were a guide," quipped an Iowan in 1890, "Omaha was situated between Chicago and Iowa, Denver was on the Mississippi, and San Francisco on the Missouri, while the interior towns of Iowa and Nebraska were located on Behring [*sic*] Strait" (Larson, *Bonds of Enterprise*, p. 178). This capacity to redraw maps produced both regional benefits and local injuries that bewildered a generation. From the 1870s through the 1890s the popular Grange and other farmers' organizations protested this dilemma with demands for government regulation. State and federal laws mandating fairness in pricing brought some relief; but the struggle for control of the railroads produced more heat than light, and subsequent American transportation policies have been distorted by that bitter experience.

While producers and shippers wrestled with the new steam railroad network, American consumers enjoyed unimagined benefits. Cheap transportation may have injured the local shopkeeper, but it placed in his customers' hands quality goods at lower prices. In the two decades after 1880 urban wholesalers, followed by retailers,

The automobile changed our dress, manners, social customs, vacation habits, the shape of our cities, consumer purchasing patterns, common tastes, and positions in intercourse.

JOHN KEATS
THE INSOLENT CHARIOTS
(1958)

See also
Commercial Architecture

*The new freedom
afforded by the
invention of the
automobile was
reflected in the
1906 song "You
May Go as Far as
You Like with Me,
in My Merry
Oldsmobile."*

PAGE 357

See also
The Suburbs

penetrated the country trade. Drummers showed buyers their catalogs and samples, then relayed orders to cities like Chicago (often by electric telegraph), where jobbers and manufacturers shipped out the goods by railway. Giant department stores such as Marshall Field seized economies of scale by ordering large lots from manufacturers, limiting markups, and guaranteeing customer satisfaction; and mail-order houses such as Sears, Roebuck and Company, and Montgomery Ward eliminated the drummer and storekeeper alike, placing the contents of their warehouses within everyone's easy reach.

By the start of the twentieth century the railroads had established a comprehensive nationwide transportation network that bound Americans together in unprecedented ways. Railroads pioneered national advertising by promoting their crack passenger trains and by pulling private billboard cars that touted consumer goods by name. Railroads delivered the nation's mail in hours and days instead of weeks. The mail sacks bulged with newspapers and magazines advertising uniform, brand-name merchandise to the households of New York, Indiana, and Oregon. After 1886, when southern railroads changed their five-foot tracks to the northern standard gauge, passengers could travel on a through ticket to just about anywhere in the Union. In 1883 Congress adopted the four standard time zones, eliminating almost one hundred different local times and imposing artificial demarcations that symbolized the powerful integrative forces behind this transportation system. In the new century electric interurban cars offered clean, quick, inexpensive rides to a generation more affluent, restless, and rootless than any that came before.

Work itself changed in the railway age. Hundreds of employees worked for each large railroad firm, spread over many miles, some moving, some stationary, performing a wide variety of tasks. Impossible to supervise from a single venue, this army of workers coordinated a daily schedule of trains with sufficient precision to avoid delay, confusion, or accidental death. Early railroad managers invented bureaucratic procedures and systems of classification. Section gangs tended fifty-mile (eighty-kilometer) units of track. Train crews operated the moving trains. Stationmasters coordinated the interface between moving and stationary workplaces. Dozens of conductors, freight agents, and passenger agents sold the product of the firm, quoting rates from printed schedules (and deviating from those schedules according to corporate strategies). Auditors and

statisticians devised recordkeeping systems that kept all these variables in constant check.

Individuals hired by the railroads inevitably joined a bureaucratic class paid according to scale for type, rank, and perhaps time in service. For most workers, the boss was not their employer but another paid employee. At first, railway workers responded to these new conditions of employment by forming protective brotherhoods of engineers (1863), conductors (1868), and firemen and enginemen (1873); by 1900 specialized craft unions enrolled most of the individuals eligible to join. However, many classes of employees—track gangs, Pullman porters, baggage handlers (often black workers)—enjoyed no collective bargaining power. Railroad managers attacked all efforts at comprehensive labor organization, such as Eugene V. Debs's American Railway Union (1893), by blacklisting suspected labor radicals and calling in state or federal authorities to protect property from "communistic" strikers. Although everything about the railroad business assumed the character of class action, owners clung to the "free labor" fiction that every American deserved to negotiate for his own wage.

White-collar work found an early articulation on the railroads as well. Hundreds of men worked for wages by handling railroad money and information, with no stake in the ownership or profits of the firm. Some individuals found lucrative careers in the middle ranks of railroad management; but just as quickly as experienced professionals rose to positions of authority, ownership slipped into the hands of bankers and passive investors. "Heroic" entrepreneurs built nineteenth-century railroads, but the mature twentieth-century systems were controlled by salaried professionals—the first of their kind.

In the twentieth century, America's railroads paid for two generations of cutthroat capitalism. Government regulations limited railroad profits just when the industry most needed fresh capital to expand and refurbish the network. New competition from automobiles, trucks, buses, and airplanes cut into the railroads' monopoly on high-speed transportation, each new rival enjoying greater flexibility of operation (no fixed roadway) and generous public subsidies besides. Dieselization, streamlining, reorganization, and retrenchment kept the trains alive, though in steady decline, after World War II.

Urban Public Transportation

The rise and decline of the railroads can be seen compressed and intensified in the story of urban public transportation. Horse-drawn streetcars, first introduced in Manhattan in 1832 and in common use by the 1850s, exploded the integrated structure of the preindustrial "walking city." Relatively easy transportation allowed middle- and upper-class residents to live in parklike suburban neighborhoods away from the noise and filth of industry, the poverty of workers, and the ethnic cacophony that characterized post-Civil War inner cities. Tied to the freight lines of steam railroads, commerce and manufacturing remained tightly packed in downtown areas, creating a pattern of residential suburbs surrounding a business core that inverted the typical layout of colonial and European cities. The new structure inevitably concentrated problems of crowding, poverty, sanitation, crime, and disorder in a central district which could not easily expand or adjust. Industrial growth usually escaped these city cores along the lines of the major railways. Streetcar companies then extended lines to carry laborers out to the factories—or new working-class neighborhoods sprang up to rival the genteel suburbs.

Running below ten miles (sixteen kilometers) per hour and fouling the city streets with tons of waste each year, horsecars could not long keep up with the extraordinary rise of American cities. In 1888 Frank Sprague's electric trolley system in Richmond, Virginia, provided a model of quick and clean transportation capable of integrating much larger cities within easy commuting networks. During the surge of growth that followed the 1893 depression, Boston, New York, and

Chicago tried to relieve street congestion by elevating main trolley lines on stilts, creating hierarchical systems with rapid-transit service on the "elevateds" (or "els") and local feeder service at street level. Subways, pioneered in London in the 1860s, provided even faster high-volume transportation in Boston (1898) and New York (1904); however, the high costs and extraordinary disruption attending subways' construction limited their appeal.

Like steam railroads, most American street railways were built by private profit-seeking companies. City governments awarded franchises to developers who then installed tracks and electrical lines at corporate expense and operated the cars with a primary concern for revenue. This practice spared urban taxpayers the burden of paying for their streetcars directly, but it left them utterly dependent on private monopolies that frequently delivered poor service at rates many riders thought too high. Corrupt deals between traction magnates and city leaders further convinced early-twentieth-century riders that streetcars existed more to line the pockets of investors than to facilitate transportation in the city. Huge, consolidated steam railroad companies often purchased these traction franchises, cementing in the public mind a link between disappointing local service and the crimes of interstate "octopus" corporations such as the Southern Pacific Railroad.

By the 1920s, as their growth continued to choke the cities with more traffic than streets could handle, Americans looked for new solutions

SIXTH AVENUE EL

In order to relieve street congestion, New York built elevated train tracks called "els" in the late nineteenth century. This is the "el" platform at 6th Avenue and 34th Street.
LIBRARY OF CONGRESS/ CORBIS

Railroad iron is a magician's rod, in its power to evoke the sleeping energies of land and water.

RALPH WALDO EMERSON

to the problems created by their escalating habits of mobility. Two paths to a better future seemed imaginable. One path required planning that would regulate land use, industrial and commercial growth, and residential patterns of mobility. Hierarchically coordinated, fixed-rail rapid-transit systems fit nicely into the drawings of new professional urban planners who dreamed of laying down pathways before the people swarmed in to use them. The siren call of the private automobile marked the other path to the future. Freedom was the promise of a Ford: freedom from fixed-rail routes, schedules and timetables, inelastic fares, corrupt franchises, rude conductors, crowded cars, long waits—not to mention freedom from the planners of such systems, who would place new limits on enterprise, property rights, residential liberty, and personal freedom of movement. Since 1920, Americans have endured the interference of urban planners and traffic engineers—but they have fallen in love with their cars.

The All-American Auto

No people on earth took to the motorcar so quickly or so passionately as the Americans. Inventors such as Charles and (James) Frank Duryea (1893) and Elwood Haynes (1894) pioneered the American horseless carriage. By the turn of the century, dozens of small firms across the country designed and manufactured experimental cars. Gradually acquiring familiar features such as steering wheels, pneumatic tires, brakes, lights, electric starters, windshields, and closed bodies, modern automobiles took shape in the 1910s. Most early automobiles catered to a luxury buyer with a sporting sense of adventure; the real revolution in mobility came with the cheap, popular car.

In 1901 Ransom E. Olds produced the first successful cheap car, the Merry Oldsmobile. It fell to Henry Ford, however, to place the motorcar in the hands of ordinary working people. The first Model T sold in 1908 for $850. Sales nearly doubled every year, rising from twelve thousand in 1909 to a half million in 1916, while the price fell to $360. Ford's secret lay in the innovative moving assembly line that by 1914 cut assembly time from around twelve hours to just over two. Workers performed the same simple task on each unit as it passed—an efficient (and monotonous) use of labor that required less skill as machines became more automated. To lure and keep good workers, Ford advertised an astonishing five-dollar daily wage, but his terms included conformity to personal and moral habits so exacting that few workers actually qualified.

Ford consolidated his revolution in mass production with a parallel system of mass marketing. He located branch assembly plants in two dozen cities across the country and established dealerships (with parts and service) in almost every town. Aggressive marketing of this quality, low-cost automobile produced results: soon very ordinary, middle- and working-class families aspired to car ownership. By 1927 Americans had purchased fifteen million Model T cars and a like number of other models, and many cities reported automobile registrations nearly equal to the number of households.

Of course, the popular car stimulated urgent demands for better roads. Before the twentieth century, the United States had almost no hard-surfaced highways. Everywhere dirt roads choked travelers with dust or mired them in mud. If people were going to drive cars, they needed paved roads, but who should build and pay for them? Tradition laid the burden squarely on local authorities, who by the same tradition showed no initiative. In 1912 Carl Fisher, who owned the Indianapolis Motor Speedway, campaigned for a "Coast-to-Coast Rock Highway" (the Lincoln Highway) to be funded by private and corporate subscriptions. Henry Ford preferred tax-supported highways and threw his considerable influence against Fisher's proprietary road: "As long as private interests are willing to build good roads for the general public, the general public will not be very much interested in building good roads for itself" (Hokanson, *The Lincoln Highway*, p. 8).

Ford's commitment to public roads rekindled a jurisdictional debate that once had plagued canal-era internal improvements. Local authorities, indifferent to the plight of the motoring public, could interrupt any network of good roads by refusing to improve their own segments. On the other hand, national mandates for integrated systems offended local interests and state government sovereignty. Congress cautiously addressed this dilemma in the 1916 Federal-Aid Road Act, which placed seventy-five million dollars over five years at the disposal of the secretary of agriculture to improve rural post roads, the money to be disbursed through state highway departments. Many states created their highway departments in response to this measure, and subsequent federal initiatives encouraged construction of primary highways with offers of matching funds. Competition for scarce tax dollars, however, especially during the Great Depression, often thwarted the hopes of highway reformers.

See also

Landscape

The democratic promise of the private automobile lay in the freedom it allowed owner-operators to pick their routes and travel times according to personal convenience. Traffic jams, however, easily frustrated this potential. Railroads regulated traffic flow by rigidly adhering to closely timed schedules, but motorists insisted on freeing themselves from precisely that kind of control. Better roads eased congestion for a short time, but nicely paved routes simply encouraged motorists to use them more often. City streets, already crowded with carts, wagons, and streetcars, approached gridlock with the introduction of moving and parked cars. In 1926 Connecticut began planning the Merritt Parkway, one of the nation's first high-speed, limited-access roads designed to separate local and through traffic coming out of New York City. Similar expressways reduced congestion in Boston, Philadelphia, Chicago, and Los Angeles, imposing on the private motorist's universe concepts of hierarchy and discrimination typical of fixed-rail operations. Initially cheaper and more popular than subways or trains, expressways since 1945 have cut great scars through most American cities without really solving rush-hour crowding.

Trucks and buses made special contributions to the automotive revolution. Capable of moving freight from door to door on virtually any route, trucks combined the economies of rail transportation with the flexibility of automobiles. Quickly after 1910, trucks filled urban delivery networks, displacing handcarts and horse-drawn vehicles. Trucks made it possible for industries to locate farther away from fixed-rail services. Both trucks and buses brought motor transportation to rural places too small to support branch-line rail service. Gradually, as highways and vehicles both improved, buses and semitrailer trucks entered intercity and interstate markets wherever small lots, flexible scheduling, multiple deliveries, or other special needs rendered them advantageous.

As intercity traffic grew denser, rural expressways like the Pennsylvania Turnpike (1940) were created to eliminate conflicts between over-the-road vehicles and local folk. Built with public credit (bonds were serviced by tolls paid by the highway users), such long-distance, limited-access highways combined some of the benefits of a specialized railway with freedom for private motorists who could drive on these "tubes" if they chose. This integration of traffic-control principles into automotive transportation reached its logical culmination in the interstate highway system, launched in 1956 to provide a nationwide network of free expressways. Concerns over national defense gave Congress an excuse finally to seize the initiative in national highway planning, and the Highway Trust Fund, filled by user fees and taxes on fuels, tires, and vehicles, promised pay-as-you-go funding.

Automobile travel drove American mobility to even higher orders of magnitude. While cars, trucks, and buses stole some business from existing modes of transportation, the vast majority of car trips never would have been made by train, boat, or wagon. Americans of every class and occupation changed their lives to adjust to the car culture. Cars became a necessity, not a luxury, in the American household: even during the Great Depression, when new car sales plummeted, car use did not decline. Female motorists discovered behind the wheel a new measure of personal and geographical liberty (to the consternation of male commentators, who never tired of poking fun at "women drivers"). Young people—especially the college-age sons and daughters of the middle and upper classes—found in the automobile an instrument of escape, independence, and privacy particularly adapted to courting couples. Spontaneous, unscheduled movement made it easier than ever before for youngsters (or bootleggers, or bank robbers) to flout authority, elude capture, and undermine the conventions of society.

The car culture changed the face of cities and towns. Businesses deserted downtown, centered on its elegant railroad station, for the suburbs and shopping centers with plenty of parking. Hotels lost customers to new roadside motels. Diners sprang up along the highways, some resembling gleaming railroad dining cars, others wacky reproductions of giant coffee pots, milk bottles, or Dutch windmills. Billboards moved from the boxcar to the roadside. And gasoline filling stations took over prime corner lots in almost every American town.

In the 1950s, buoyed (and alienated) by postwar affluence, American teenagers constructed an entire youth culture around souped-up hot rods. Late-1950s-model Chevys with engines and suspensions customized for speed, painted with vivid colors, stripes, and flames, tuck-and-roll interiors, fuzzy dice suspended from the mirror, rock-and-roll on the radio, loaded with teens drinking Cokes and smoking cigarettes, cruised down evening streets in California, Iowa, and New Jersey, stopping at the drive-in, looking for girls, looking for challengers, ducking the cops, looking for trouble. Black, Chicano, and regional variations fed a youth car cult that remained fresh, im-

[The automobile] is a picture of the arrogance of wealth. . . . Nothing has spread socialist feeling more than the use of the automobile.

WOODROW WILSON
PRESIDENT OF PRINCETON
UNIVERSITY (1906)

mediate, and compelling to young people across the country. For a generation protected by the Salk vaccine and penicillin, late-night drag races and drunk driving kept death alive in the youth culture. Hit songs such as "Teen Angel" sentimentalized the fatal car crash, and James Dean and the young Marlon Brando modeled cool behavior on film. Later nostalgic films such as George Lucas's *American Graffiti* (1973) captured the bittersweet interior of a popular culture based on movement—going nowhere.

The Aviation Age

While American youth cruised summer streets in the 1950s and 1960s, the more affluent of their parents learned to "fly the friendly skies" on commercial airliners. Invented before World War I, the airplane found little acceptance for its risky and expensive services in early-twentieth-century popular markets. As a way of fostering an aviation industry, the federal government in 1918 initiated airmail service, first through the post office and then through subsidized private contractors. Scheduled passenger service began in California in 1925, and rising demand quickly overwhelmed the small planes in operation. Aircraft manufacturers scrambled to meet this small, high-value market, developing by 1935 excellent planes such as Douglas's twenty-one-passenger, 200-mile-per-hour DC-3.

Aviation development responded less to mass-market demands than to technological competition and government stimulation, always closely related to national defense. Almost all aviation services began with contracts to carry the mail. The federal government also assumed, in 1926, responsibility for navigational aids and safety systems, which spared the carriers enormous expense for ground facilities and traffic control. New Deal public-works programs funded airport, runway, and terminal construction in many cities and towns. Charges of collusion in the post office brought new regulatory reforms, culminating in a 1938 act that placed both safety regulation and economic control in the hands of the Civil Aeronautics Board (CAB). In 1958 the Federal Aviation Administration (FAA) assumed responsibility for airspace, navigation, and traffic control.

The strategies of the CAB and FAA fostered competition within a comprehensive regulatory framework. Clearly, the government wanted aviation to grow while still allowing the marketplace to determine service quality and price. After World War II, large reliable carriers received protection from the kind of cutthroat competition that once had deranged the railroad marketplace. Union labor enjoyed a measure of protection from regulators intent on keeping peace through arbitration. At the same time new carriers equipped with war-surplus DC-3s were allowed to extend passenger service into new markets. Major airlines responded with innovations, including jet service, which often enjoyed subsidies through government spending on research and development in the defense aerospace industry. Early jets consumed fuel so extravagantly nobody could afford to fly them; however, by 1958 practical jetliners such as the Boeing 707 and the Douglas DC-8 entered the fleets of international and interstate carriers.

Jet service required a new round of public investments in longer runways and huge private outlays for the planes. First associated in the early 1960s with jet-setter life-styles—skiing in Aspen, lunch in Las Vegas, dinner in Los Angeles—air travel soon became more affordable as the airlines targeted mass markets. Aggressive promotion and discount fares sold middle-class Americans on the comfort and convenience of flying. The successful democratization of flight called forth still more public investment in traffic control and passenger terminals.

In 1978, responding to public dissatisfaction with prices and service as well as a political revulsion against centralized regulation, Congress ordered deregulation of the airline industry. Over the next five years the CAB systematically dismantled the framework that shaped the industry, giving carriers their first experience in a relatively free market. Fares on some flights fell dramatically, and popular deep discounts ("super savers") have made certain preplanned trips cheaper than ever. Traffic patterns quickly changed from the trunk-line systems that resembled railroads into hub-and-spoke networks that concentrated passengers and planes in regional centers such as Chicago, Atlanta, and Dallas. Labor lost the fostering hand of government as aggressive operators, such as Texas Air's Frank Lorenzo, sought complete freedom over the wage bill. Union busting culminated in President Ronald Reagan's 1981 dismissal of striking air-traffic controllers, whose complaints included fear that deregulated airways were becoming unsafe. Even under deregulation, aviation remains uniquely privileged among American transportation industries: governments at various levels supply airport facilities, safety inspections, and navigation and traffic control, freeing airlines to fly planes.

See also
The Suburbs

Intersections with the Present

Mobility is part of the American self-definition. Personal liberty on a continental scale has required ready access to easy transportation, and Americans have come to assume that their right to unrestricted movement is as basic as the Constitution. Car ownership in America is more nearly universal than employment or adequate income. Most Americans equate automobility with independence. During the Arab oil embargoes of the 1970s, Americans exhibited an irrational preoccupation with keeping their gas tanks filled. Not just mobility but the potential for spontaneous flight seems almost as important as life, liberty, and the pursuit of happiness. Transportation has become an essential servant of the culture.

Because of this close association between liberty and movement, Americans favor the automobile over more structured or inflexible systems of transportation. Neither air pollution nor oil crises have seriously eroded the car culture, and much of the response to both problems has focused on making cars cleaner and more economical in order to keep driving them freely. Urban crowding continues to spawn expressway improvements far more often than developments in bus or fixed-rail transit. Only three new subway systems graced American cities since the 1970s: San Francisco's BART, Washington, D.C.'s METRO and Atlanta's MARTA. (The BART system barely survived a political opposition that condemned fixed-rail transit as undemocratic.) Buffalo's foray into rapid transit went broke. Chicago adopted an integrated, multimodal regional transit authority, coordinating rapid transit, commuter rail, and bus systems throughout the greater metropolitan area. Still, traffic on the Windy City's expressways congeals each morning and evening with hundreds of thousands of cars.

Why do Americans move so much? Primarily in response to perceived opportunities in social structures and economic markets. For early white Americans, mobility yielded enrichment and liberation. Their descendants wove the connection into a culture dominated by markets forces and people on the move. African Americans, Native Americans, immigrants from every land gradually adjusted traditional, more sedentary values to find a niche in American life. Eventually mobility became not just a means to liberation but something of an end in itself.

Has all this "progress" in transportation improved American life? Certainly each reduction in the barriers to movement opened up new opportunities for personal and economic achievement.

Just as certainly, each new "annihilation" of space and time has destroyed the virtues of original environments, small-scale communities, low-energy ways of life. Native American populations taught the first colonists how to get around in North America, but they were displaced relentlessly by successive waves of mobile newcomers. Africans became Americans against their will due to white mobility, but because of racial discrimination they have never received a fair share of the fruits of transportation improvements. All kinds of immigrants found homes in American communities, in part because Americans moved too much to defend effectively against intruders. In the generation of the 1990s, affluent white suburbanites race about so madly they cannot feel attachment to communities at all. The record clearly is mixed, but mobility remains at the center of American social history, propelling the story through time and shaping for good or ill the diverse narratives of a complex people.

—JOHN LAURITZ LARSON

TRAVEL AND VACATIONS

Americans spend a substantial proportion of their time in leisure activities, including the taking of vacations and associated travel. Travel away from the place of permanent residence is the critical factor distinguishing tourist or holiday vacation activity from other leisure pursuits. Vacations are clearly important in and of themselves to those taking them; thus the impetus behind them and the rewards of vacationing are examined here. In addition, the total flow of tourists is so great that it results in an economic sector, the tourism industry, that is of major importance to all states and innumerable localities. On an international level, tourism is projected to be the single leading economic sector by the year 2000. Holiday travel by Americans both within and outside the United States is a chief component of this emerging reality. Finally, tourism has consequences that include substantial social, cultural, and environmental effects, along with those that are purely economic.

Central to all of these concerns is how the notion of vacations has evolved and historically been practiced by Americans. First, however, it is necessary to delimit the subject of vacations and tourism. Precise definitions continue to be debated among researchers and organizations concerned with tourism. The efforts to standardize

By the 1920s the growth in real wages, the invention of the annual vacation, and broadening automobile ownership permitted the middle class to appropriate the national parks.

PAGE 276

T

TRAVEL AND VACATIONS

The European Background

One aspect of long-distance commuting has been the proliferation of second homes and seasonal housing in environmentally attractive locales within commuting range of major population centers.

PAGE 256

See also

Amusement and
Theme Parks

---

terminology and data collection are centered at the international level in the World Tourism Organization and within this country by such agencies as the United States Travel Data Center, the Bureau of the Census, and the United States Travel and Tourism Administration. The basic question is what makes a traveler a tourist, which is to say someone who is taking a vacation. Most define a person traveling away from home for pleasure as a tourist if the trip exceeds twenty-four hours in duration. Domestic tourism is usually thought of as travel that also exceeds some minimum distance from the normal place of residence, which is commonly set as fifty or one hundred miles.

The European Background

Travel for pleasure is usually thought to have begun in the sixteenth century, restricted to a small, privileged group. Prior to that time are recorded wanderings of early Greeks and Romans, along with larger numbers of people engaged in pilgrimages to the Holy Land or other sacred places. The latter part of the Renaissance was an era of great exploration and increasing knowledge about the world in which the affluent and the nobility, especially the English, engaged in travel to various preferred locales on the Continent. This flow soon resulted in the concept of the Grand Tour, a circuitous journey through a number of European cultural and social centers that became part of the background of the well-bred young Englishman. In addition, scholars and diplomats were frequent travelers along the same route. The Grand Tour initially had an educational focus, but it eventually shifted to a search for pleasure.

The notion of taking a respite from work or other obligations also has a long history. The term "holiday" derives from "holy days," days established as times of worship and ritual, free of daily toil and allowing for recreation time. Originally, such days were devoted primarily to making offerings and performing various rites and ceremonies; some of these days were based on world religions such as Christianity, whereas others had pre-Christian beginnings. In any case it seems probable that holy days had a strong linkage to natural events; that is, to the predictable, regular changes that occur in nature such as the daily and annual courses of the sun and the phases of the moon. Particular days having a natural origin thus might relate to the annual harvest periods and the beginning of the new year. Governments around the world have frequently formalized a number of these special days and, in effect, made them into national holidays. The latter effort has resulted in

some arbitrary shifts of dates to make certain holidays fall on Mondays, thus establishing periodic long weekends.

Many observers have identified health concerns as another factor in the establishment of vacation practices. As early as the seventeenth century, medical people in England and the Low Countries were recommending to wealthy patients that they "take the waters" at some spa. For nearly two hundred years more, communities possessing the appropriate resources flourished for this purpose, one of the most notable being Bath, England, which was used as a spa as early as the Roman period. Similarly, some people were steered to sea bathing as a curative for various ills. Brighton, some fifty miles (80 kilometers) to the south of London, became in 1754 the first seaside resort catering to this demand. It then became the model for numerous other seaside resort communities later. In the nineteenth century the English, clearly the first significant group of holidaymakers, reduced their travels to Continental locations as wars and other disturbances affected the attractiveness of their intended destinations. This resulted in the substantial growth of England's domestic resort industry at locations much as Margate in Kent and Scarborough in Yorkshire, and later at Blackpool, near Liverpool. More recently, in the late nineteenth and twentieth centuries the British have again returned to many Continental destinations in their search for desirable vacation settings.

The present-day desire for vacations among citizens of the more developed countries has evolved over the past two hundred years. The modern concept of taking periodic holidays is a product of the industrial revolution. Numerous economic and social changes resulted from its dramatic altering of the means and nature of production. Special days like Christmas, Easter, and Whitsuntide became recognized as days of nonwork in England, to which was added the August national bank holiday, observed on a Monday (thus creating a long weekend). These and other holidays often became formalized by agreements between employers and their employees. Through such processes a disassociation of holidays from their original religious roots took place. It also became increasingly recognized that, given the climatic regimen in western Europe, summer was to be preferred for vacations, because of the probability then of better weather. This factor has lost some of its importance in more recent times as mobility and affluence increased, permitting people to look farther afield for their vacation sites.

As countries' economies developed, an increasing share of their population moved into middle-income categories and the taking of vacations changed from being the nearly exclusive prerogative of the privileged to one being available now to the middle class. In time, with additional changes in society in the more developed countries, the taking of vacations has become available to a large part of national populations, and the notion of mass vacations and tourism has become common. For example, excursion trains for day trippers from large urban centers to reasonably nearby vacation centers went into operation in the 1840s. Resorts, both at the seaside and elsewhere, became very popular between 1870 and 1914. However, it was not until after World War II and the postwar recovery period that true mass tourism became the norm. At this time a great diversity of types of holidays and tourist facilities and systems emerged.

The Evolution of Vacation Travel

Several stages can be identified in the evolution of holiday-making by Americans since the Civil War. These steps, developed by scholar Carlton S. Van Doren, are based on such ever-changing variables as demographic, social, cultural, technological, income, time availability, and organizational and other realities and constraints. These stages may be described first as a period when only the privileged traveled for pleasure (the high society era, from 1860 to 1920), then a period when great numbers became participants (high participation, 1920–1958), followed by an extension of the previous period when travel became far faster and easier (high mobility, 1958–1973), and finally a period of change and adaptation after the energy crisis of 1973. The last period not only saw adjustments as a result of changing energy realities but also witnessed notable changes as a function of recessions in the early 1980s and 1990s and social factors such as the changing composition of the household. Let us examine first, however, the earlier period in which American leisure travel had its beginnings. In these descriptions of the evolution of vacation travel, I am indebted to Carlton S. Van Doren.

The Beginnings of American Leisure Travel

The roots of American holiday travel go back to the latter half of the eighteenth century and the first half of the nineteenth. This period saw the complete filling in of the lands east of the Appalachians and major movements into the interior lowlands to the west of that highland system. It also saw independence established and confirmed. These two events resulted in quite different stimuli for leisure travel. On the one hand, Americans tended to emulate Europeans, especially the British, while at the same time strongly identifying with and appreciating the land itself. In addition, technological developments contributed to fundamental changes in, for example, the developing national economy and transportation. However, conditions were still such that only the privileged could take advantage of the new options available for their leisure time.

Americans quickly copied the English practice of taking the waters for health purposes. A variety of locations possessing springs that offered presumed health benefits saw early resort development. Saratoga Springs, New York, may have been used by frontiersmen by the middle 1700s, and George Washington identified the possibilities of Berkeley Springs (later renamed Bath), on the eastern edge of the Alleghenies in 1748. Other spas developed, with those having the maximum accessibility by stagecoach routes to major population centers having the greatest importance. Bristol, Pennsylvania, was often described as the most attractive spa for the privileged of the time, because of its location on the main route from Philadelphia to New York City. These spas initially offered quite rudimentary facilities but responded rapidly to the desire for comfort by the rich. Simultaneously, coastal resorts with refreshing summer sea breezes and comfortable waters to attract the privileged had their beginnings in places such as Newport, Rhode Island, and Cape May, New Jersey. The practice of emulating the English also took the form of having young adults from wealthy families pay visits to European centers of culture in a direct copying of the Grand Tour concept.

The other influence upon early Americans' travel was their close link to the land. Most were rural or small-town dwellers who depended either directly or indirectly upon agriculture for their livelihoods. To these people the notion of a frontier beyond them was a factor that also steered their thinking toward the land and its attributes. Their knowledge of and appreciation for the land were also furthered by the reports of those to first penetrate beyond the Appalachians into the interior and later by the reports of early explorers and adventurers such as the mountain men who traveled through large areas of the mountain and plateau country of the West. These and other con-

Not just mobility, but the potential for spontaneous flight seems almost as important as life, liberty, and the pursuit of happiness.

PAGE 513

siderations have led historians to suggest that at an early stage Americans developed a meaningful part of their identity as a result of their relationship to the land and that a large measure of pride in the land and landscape of the United States is rooted in these early experiences and attitudes. An extension of this perspective is the idea that the land became a means of defining America as a place. Thus, in the years before 1860 Americans started to journey to and take holidays at various points in the Hudson and Connecticut River valleys and at inns in highland areas such as the Catskills, the Berkshires, and the White Mountains. The greatest landscape feature accessible to the affluent in these early days was Niagara Falls, New York, which had become the single most important tourist location by as early as the 1830s. As the Falls became progressively more important as a landscape feature, with its unusually great beauty and distinctive uniqueness, special holiday associations developed. Most prominently, by the late 1830s Niagara Falls had become a honeymoon destination, the result simply of newlyweds' going where everyone else was going.

This period also saw the rapid extension of benefits from scientific and technological advances, particularly as transportation was revolutionized. In the period from 1790 to 1820 a significant network of turnpikes and toll roads was developed throughout the settled East, followed by steamboats and railroads in the 1820s. Complementing the region's naturally navigable waterways was a rapidly expanded set of canals. Steamboats improved coastal and transatlantic transportation, aided in the early years, commencing in 1825, by the opening of a number of canals. The era of canals and rivers and lakes had only a brief life as a major mover of people, though, given the rapid growth of the faster and more spatially comprehensive railroad system. By 1860 a well-developed railroad net covered the eastern half of what was not yet a continentwide United States, with the West soon to be served by transcontinental links. In addition, the base for economic change was expanding as the rate of urbanization increased, the middle class began steady growth, and more comforts became available in accommodations catering to travelers. All these developments contributed over time toward a larger and larger part of the population having the attributes permitting holiday travel: adequate money, the time to pursue leisure activities, available transportation to reach the places of interest, and higher quality facilities and accommodations than previously available.

The century prior to 1860 saw only a small part of the American people engage in travel for leisure purposes. Those who did were primarily the handful of the affluent or those suffering from ailments for which mineral-spring spas or seaside resorts offered hoped-for cures to those able to afford them. More importantly, this period saw a number of fundamental attitudes about the land implanted in many Americans, which ultimately resulted in a great deal of vacation travel linked to appreciating the country's landscape. This trend can be seen in the awe Americans developed for the rough-and-tumble American West created by the explorations of Lewis and Clark and by the rapidly increasing body of travel writing. Thus, although those actually traveling during these times were few, the notion of distant places came to hold a strong fascination for the average mind.

The High Society Period: 1860–1920

The high society period provides an American parallel to the leisure-time practices of the privileged in England and elsewhere in Europe then. The vast majority of the population at this time were members of large families, had very long workweeks, continued to be rural or small-town residents except in the growing industrial centers of the Northeast, received hourly wages or were self-employed, and had little discretionary income and only limited mobility. They were typically imbued with a puritanical work ethic; for many, self-denial was implicit in their life-styles. These characteristics changed slowly for many groups in society, and it is only relatively recently that these deeply rooted attributes have altered to permit more and more people to have different perspectives on their time budgets.

Conversely, during this same era a rich group of industrialists, financiers, railroad magnates, and related professionals emerged, a group that engaged in acquiring summer and winter homes in pleasant locales, had family members who traveled to Europe, and developed various resorts and related facilities. During this period the communities that had already gotten a start, such as Newport and Saratoga Springs, took on even greater importance. Equally notable is the growth of innumerable new seashore and mountain resort communities in locations relatively accessible to East Coast population centers. The practice of taking regular vacations now became increasingly the norm. Destination preferences were divided into the return to some familiar holiday retreat as the most common, but with increasing interest in visiting new and different places.

This period saw the affluent come to appreciate the virtues of Florida's winter weather, which led to the emergence of a significant development of vacation locales in the central part of the Florida peninsula. High society eventually focused on the Palm Beach area on Florida's east coast. It was not long before the dreams of Henry M. Flagler and others led to southward penetration of railroads, with the erection of resort hotels at strategic locations. In the ten years following the end of World War I many of these developments came to fruition and the great tourist flow to Florida took off. Ultimately, Flagler's dream was to create an American Riviera along the East Coast south of Palm Beach. Similar kinds of

Thanks to the interstate highway system, it is now possible to travel from coast to coast without seeing anything.

CHARLES KURALT
ON THE ROAD (1980)

T

TRAVEL AND VACATIONS

The High Society Period: 1860–1920

railroad-hotel-linked developments occurred elsewhere, especially along the main lines that crossed the American West, making accessible a new set of environments. The Coronado Hotel in San Diego is often cited as an example of the accommodations available to a traveler having crossed the entire breadth of the United States in the new Pullman sleeping cars.

Numerous developments in the 1860 to 1920 period made travel simpler and less uncertain. The first telephone exchange in the United States went into use in New Haven, Connecticut, in 1878, making communications far more rapid both in dealing with travel needs and in maintaining contact with home and work. In 1865, Thomas Cook of Britain opened the first travel agency in this country, which was eventually followed fourteen years later by the first such agency opened by Americans. Then American Express Company employee Marcellus Berry, broadened the company's functions by introducing traveler's checks, in 1891. The American Automobile Association was established in 1902. And picture postcards became available, providing a strong impetus to those back home to visit places their friends or relatives had experienced.

Although the greater part of the population was not able to become actively involved in pleasure travel and vacations during this period, it was a time when many of the developments that would affect the whole population and its leisure activities in the future had their beginnings, as for instance the means of providing mass transportation, communication, and entertainment. While these developments were occurring, Henry Ford and other industrialists began implementing work-limiting procedures such as the five-day workweek and a shortening of the workday, so that discretionary time became far more widely available in periods of potential leisure. In this same period, government at all levels started to preserve open as well as recreational space, including the first national parks and forests. Of special importance were the identification and setting aside of the spectacularly beautiful Yosemite as first a state park (1864) then a national park (1890), the establishment of Yellowstone as the first formally created national park in 1872, and the increasing recognition of places of great natural beauty to be maintained for the general enjoyment of the people through time.

The high society period thus saw an evolution in the vacationing tendencies of the American people. The scale of tourism had clearly changed, by 1885 more Americans were enjoying holidays. The long-established Niagara Falls became the ultimate symbol of a tourist attraction, with something of a golden age in the late 1800s and early 1900s, although other attractions were also becoming prominent. Simultaneously and inevitably, holiday taking was becoming more commercialized, the places visited becoming centers of mass consumption. All these developments were further intensified by the expansion of communications with photography, the wireless, and the broader dissemination of newspapers, magazines, books, and eventually silent movies. Complementing these forms of information diffusion were such spectacular events as the Chicago fair of 1893 (formally called the World's Columbian Exposition), which assisted in bringing a new consciousness about places and things to far more people. This fair also saw the introduction of the

SUMMER CAMPS

Various special forms of holiday-making evolved during the nineteenth century. One example is the phenomenon of summer camps for young people that developed offering several-week outings for the young, providing training in a variety of sports and handicraft activities. Children from affluent families were served by a wide array of private camps, but the poor also were often able to participate, at church-related and YMCA facilities. Such camps, at first concentrated primarily in New England, were by the start of World War I attracting many thousands of girls and boys. Church-sponsored summer camps sprang up with many different denominations as sponsors, such as the Methodist facility at Ocean Grove on the New Jersey coast. By the 1880s, prominent New Yorkers led by Whitelaw Reid had developed a program to fund camp stays for children from the poorer neighborhoods of New York City, an idea that in slightly modified form continues to the present day. Summer camp holidays for the young received a further boost in the first decade of the 1900s with the 1910 incorporation of the Boy Scouts of America, and other youth groups with similar summer programs soon emerged. Increasingly, young people were exposed to places other than their immediate area of residence and became imbued with the practice of diverse leisure-time activities and travel.

midway concept, a feature included in many future developments.

The High Participation Period: 1920–1958

The high participation period witnessed continued expansion in the total population, increasing urbanization and, because of greatly improved communications, much greater public awareness of the whole country, especially the West. Changing attitudes toward free time encouraged leisure activities. Workweeks continued gradually to shorten (to the dismay of other industrialists, Henry Ford began closing his factories on Saturdays in 1926), paid holidays became more common, incomes rose, families grew smaller, and a much improved variety of recreational equipment became available. The Diner's Club became the first credit card designed for leisure-time use, appearing in 1949. Car ownership became far more widespread. Where the bulk of holiday travel had formerly been to a specific place, auto touring came into its own after 1920, resulting in a rapid expansion of facilities serving the motoring public.

Paralleling these changes was a surge in the number of attractions and facilities to entice and accommodate tourists. Seaside resorts, cottage communities on lakes and rivers, resort complexes near national parks, and specialized recreational communities developed into more common features of the tourist landscape. As services facilitating tourism expanded, previously introduced travel aids, including credit cards, traveler's checks, travel agents, and automobile clubs grew far more important. A flood of information about places to see and things to do was one product of the universal exposure to the mass media outlets that developed in this period. A gradual growth of holiday-making in all seasons occurred as people sought to escape the northern winter, enjoy the autumn foliage, open the spring fishing season, or hunt game during specified times. Paralleling participation in all these outdoor-oriented activities was a major flow of travelers to cities and other places where historic, cultural, spectator sport, shopping, dining, and other entertainments abounded.

This second period in the development of tourism was a tumultuous era in American history, with the Great Depression, World War II, and the recovery periods following both world wars. It was a time when Americans were learning more about their own country as the media extended through talking movies to television and a

NATIONAL TOURISM

Tourism emerged across the country. Florida became more and more of a mecca for those seeking a respite from cold northern winters. The population of Miami and its neighboring communities exploded with the completion of rail connections to the north in the 1890s and 1900s. Towns based on tourism that were located at strategic points grew in importance, such as Gatlinburg, Tennessee, and Jackson, Wyoming. Readily accessible beach resorts, such as Hampton Beach north of Boston and Virginia Beach, near Norfolk, became crowded. Cities developed the infrastructure and accommodations needed to satisfy the increasing numbers of tourists seeking urban amenities. Resorts serving religious and educational purposes, such as that at Chautauqua, New York, continued to be important, and the lake districts of northern New England and the Upper Great Lakes states became popular summer vacation areas. Motels, amusement parks, roadside restaurants, and the like grew and changed rapidly. For example, in the early 1920s tourist cabins phased out camping areas and were in turn gradually replaced by the forerunners of modern motels, from the late 1920s on. Each progression in the type of facility was marked by the provision of greater comfort and additional features. The accommodation industry eventually created its own trade journal, *Tourist Trade*, which appeared in 1932. Franchising contributed to the development of huge chains of motels, fast-food restaurants, and other kinds of facilities. By the end of this high participation period in 1958 an intricate array of facilities and tourist attractions existed across the country. Serving the leisure-time needs of the growing population had become a major economic activity as measured by the number of jobs created, the amount of income generated, and the alterations to the travel landscape. The now-familiar Holiday Inn logo appeared in 1958 in Memphis, Tennessee. Howard Johnson's opened its first ice cream parlor in Quincy, Massachusetts, in 1925, and entered the motel business in 1954 with an inn in Savannah, Georgia. Hertz Rental Cars opened in 1918. Disneyland, in Anaheim, California, introduced the theme park concept in 1955 and became a popular family destination. Club Méditerraneé (now known as Club Med) opened its first resort complex in 1950.

T

TRAVEL AND VACATIONS

The High Participation Period: 1920–1958

If we are always arriving and departing, it is true that we are eternally anchored. One's destination is never a place but rather a new way of looking at things.

HENRY MILLER
BIG SUR AND THE ORANGES
OF HIERONYMOUS BOSCH

See also
Landscapes

T

TRAVEL AND VACATIONS

The High Mobility Period: 1958–1973

Revivals were the nation's most popular regional gatherings and the ancestors of state fairs in the late nineteenth century and tourist attractions concocted by ingenious local boosters in the twentieth.

PAGE 307

♦ **Time-sharing**

Joint ownership or rental of a vacation lodging (as a condominium) by several persons with each occupying the premises in turn for short periods

deluge of information occurred. The late 1940s and the 1950s saw a satisfying of the material wants of a large part of the American people and newly available time and discretionary income that allowed increasing choices to be made in how leisure time was spent. Family vacations were now common, typically involving visits to relatives, touring part of the United States, or staying at a cottage or campground set up for recreational purposes. Holiday-making in the United States became both more common and more diverse in the activities undertaken and places visited as this period approached its end.

In addition to domestic travel, the 1920s and 1950s both saw many Americans travel abroad. Most of that travel was to Europe or to neighboring Canada and Mexico. For this international movement the earlier decade was still dominated by the privileged, while the post-World War II decade saw a far larger mass movement. The Depression and World War II had contrasting impacts on foreign travel. During these periods domestic as well as foreign travel was very limited, either because of economic or war-related conditions. Conversely, the events of these two stressful periods may be considered to have furthered a desire by the population in general to travel once conditions eventually permitted.

The closing date of this high participation period, 1958, was not chosen arbitrarily but rather because it reflected a convergence of events. In that year transportation was revolutionized by the opening of the first stretch of interstate highway, and the first commercial jet airliner flew then. At the same time, the postwar "baby boom" ended as the birth-rate peaked and started to decline. Many Americans had by then completed updating their personal household goods and automobiles, and many had moved out of the central cities into the rapidly growing suburbs. Nearly universal automobile ownership helped overcome one fundamental geographic fact about the United States: its sheer size. Amid increasing concern about the resources available to serve the American people, in 1958 President Eisenhower appointed the Outdoor Recreation Resources Review Commission, whose landmark report (released in 1962–1963) marked a new recognition of the importance of leisure time to Americans and helped stimulate a major expansion in the facilities and outdoor recreational lands available to the public.

The High Mobility Period: 1958-1973

The brief high mobility era was marked by continued growth in the volume and in the variety of

vacation taking by the American public. Several technical developments in transportation profoundly affected where and how fast people could travel and communicate. By the end of this period, the interstate highway system, which saw its first segment open in 1958, offered access to much of the country. Americans started making lengthy tours of large sections of the United States, Canada, and Mexico, as they suddenly were able to complete five hundred or more miles per day comfortably in their own cars. The introduction of the commercial jet airliner in 1958 made distant points readily available, and widespread access to rental cars permitted freedom of movement at one's destination. The development of the modern international air route system led to an enormous increase in the flow of Americans abroad, both to traditional destinations in Europe and to other continents, at seasons other than summer.

Widespread new travel services and amenities made vacation trips more attractive. Artificial control of local environments became far more common with the spread of air conditioning. Camping took on a new look as the number of tent campers was for the first time exceeded by those using a remarkable variety of recreational vehicles. Tollfree reservation systems came into widespread use, and the nature and variety of tourist attractions and accommodations expanded enormously. The federal government followed up on the recommendations of several important studies about the recreational needs of Americans by both expanding and diversifying the kinds of lands administered for the public's use. Existing national parks and monuments were now complemented by additional national lakeshores and seashores; scenic and wild rivers were identified and protected. In the service area, real estate practices became more diverse as the concepts of time-sharing, condominiums, and retirement communities became common. A great growth in the amount of travel literature and publicity accorded to vacation spots made an ever-growing part of the public aware of their vacation opportunities. Simultaneously, the travel industry began catering increasingly to all segments of society. Budget motels and fast-food restaurants contributed to a broadening of the potential travel market.

In the period of high mobility the destinations sought by holiday-makers became more and more diverse. Urban tourism continued to grow as the attractions of individual cities became more widely known. Every big city, had its own substantial amount of tourism, but tourist facilities of New York City, San Francisco, Los Angeles, Miami, New Orleans, and Washington, D.C., were especially notable. Cities and places with special resources or facilities became more important as better transportation made them more accessible, as for instance Reno and Las Vegas, which led in nightlife and gambling. Mountain communities that had once been important for mining were reborn as popular winter sport centers or meeting places, as was the case with Aspen and Vail. Special groups in the population came to identify their own favorite resort areas: college students descended upon such Florida beach cities as Fort Lauderdale and Daytona Beach; the retired and elderly sought a more friendly winter environment in Florida or Arizona. Specialized group tours became readily available to a vast array of places and areas. Cruise liners became more popular.

In effect, a revolution was occurring in the tourism and travel industry. Numerous entrepreneurs started to serve what they perceived as an immense market. Package tours became much more common. And the factors permitting holiday taking—the income needed, the time, and the desire—were increasingly being enjoyed by more and more of the population. All these new dimensions to the tourist industry were superimposed upon the traditional holiday-making activities, which continued unabated.

The high mobility era ended abruptly in 1973–1974 when an energy crisis swept the world as the major oil-producing countries established controls on their production and prices. Not only was the price of a gallon of gasoline or oil now much greater, but supplies became a problem, which intensified in a second stage of the energy crisis, in the late 1970s. The adjustments to travel practices that became essential for most individuals and families commonly resulted in greatly reduced holiday travel in the short run, then the making of conscious decisions to overcome the difficulties raised by the energy situation. These constraints upon mobility formed the basis for a fourth stage.

Change and Adaptation

After the new energy realities of the 1970s came into effect, numerous other forces also were at work. The federal government deregulated a number of major industries, including the airlines. Families continued to become smaller, more and more wives went to work outside the home, and the two-income family became common. More and more households were now headed by single parents, and the population as a whole was aging. Americans were seeking an incredibly di-

TRAVEL AND VACATIONS

Change and Adaptation

CONVENIENT AND COMFORTABLE

By the 1960s, recreational vehicle use exceeded the number of tent campers. Trailers like this made camping more convenient and comfortable.
CORBIS-BETTMANN

*A journey is like a
marriage. The
certain way to be
wrong is to think
you control it.*

JOHN STEINBECK
TRAVELS WITH CHARLEY:
IN SEARCH OF AMERICA
(1961)

verse range of leisure-time activities. For example, visiting distant places and participating in high-risk recreational activities, such as white-water rafting and hang gliding, became far more common. Vacation attractions and facilities expanded to meet this changing, growing demand. Such negative factors as high energy costs were offset by fuel-efficient smaller cars, and the two-income household helped meet rising costs.

Recent years have seen greater attention being paid to tourism by blacks and other minority groups. African Americans had rarely entered into the mainstream types of holiday-making and travel described previously. Continuing forces of segregation and discrimination along with their resultant low incomes, comparatively low levels of educational attainment, limited mobility, and the like help explain this phenomenon. Various studies suggest that blacks involved themselves in leisure activities that were the most likely to be relatively free of discrimination and were in familiar settings, meaning in effect that urban and near-to-home visits were the most usual. Such an urban orientation continues to this day, although an increase in the number of middle-income blacks is resulting in a level of holiday-making comparable to that of equivalent groups in the white population. Blacks have in the past not been frequent visitors to the national parks, a function of the factors previously noted and the fact that until recently there were few accommodations available along the routes to the west. Today, as can be seen in two issues of a popular magazine (*Ebony*, January and May 1991), blacks are seeking the sun in the winter and making other holiday journeys that suggest a convergence of their travel plans with white patterns. There is also a tendency among African Americans to take holidays that examine their black heritage. Festivals celebrating black culture are now common in the United States, but many also visit similar events in the U.S. Virgin Islands, the Bahamas, and Jamaica. Similarly, visits by blacks to museums, libraries, and historic places identified with the South and the civil rights movement have been common and are becoming increasingly so. The drive to discover one's roots is clearly an important one.

Since the start of the 1970s energy crisis we have been in a time of continuing adjustments. The energy situation has been augmented by other difficulties, including inflation, changes in the family and household structure, increasing withdrawal of the federal government from regu-

latory activity and social-service delivery functions, concern over the political stability of destination areas abroad, and a fluctuating value of the dollar relative to other currencies. Whether we are still in the postmobility phase is uncertain, although it seems increasingly clear that we are now less constrained in our mobility when compared to the late 1970s and early 1980s and are in a period when abundant choices and mass movements of people are quite common.

The Recent Past and the Present

In 1988, residents of the United States spent $318 billion traveling away from home. The great bulk of that sum, $294 billion, was spent on domestic travel. The total travel spending, both resident and foreign, within the United States represented 6.4 percent of the gross national product in 1988, enough to position those businesses serving tourists among the leading commercial economic sectors. Data collected by the U.S. Travel Data Center indicate that most travel was for vacations, visiting friends and relatives, entertainment and outdoor recreation, and weekend pleasure travel. Only a relatively small part of the total travel reported was for business and conventions. The primary destinations of Americans traveling within their own country, according to the U.S. Travel Data Center, in 1988 had the South Atlantic region clearly in the lead, with 231.9 million person-trips. It was followed by the Pacific Coast states, with 183.1 million person-trips; the Great Lakes region, with 165.3 million person-trips; the West South Central, with 138.4 million person-trips; and the Middle Atlantic states, with 125.4 million person-trips. It should be understood that these total figures do not indicate the relative role tourism plays in a particular region's economy. For example, the Rocky Mountain region ranks sixth in total person-trips, but of the six regions it is also the area with the smallest amount of other economic activity. In a relative sense, tourism is more important to that region than to any of the other eight regions. California, Florida, Texas, and New York, in that order, have the largest travel-generated employment among the states.

The major destinations of American tourists obviously indicate their vacation preferences. In 1986 Disney World, in Orlando, Florida, was the leading theme park in terms of attendance, which was nearly double that of its sister facility, Disneyland, and more than five times that of the third most popular park. Based on total sales, the Las Vegas Hilton was the leading resort hotel, fol-

See also
Parades, Holidays and Public Rituals

lowed by a number of comparable facilities in coastal, gambling, and special resource (e.g., theme park) settings. The leading ski resort in 1986 was Mammoth Mountain, California, with all but one of the next eleven ski resorts in popularity being in California, Colorado, or Utah. Only two of the top twenty skiing centers were east of the Rocky Mountains. The greatest number of nonresident fishing license sales were in Wisconsin, followed by Michigan, Montana, Colorado, and Minnesota. Montana, South Dakota, Colorado, and Pennsylvania had the most nonresident hunting license sales. This sampling reflects the diversity of America's tourism resources and helps explain the problems inherent in describing the landscape of tourism.

Americans seek many different things from their vacation travels. The most important single reason for such travel is likely being to visit friends and relatives. Such travel is difficult to measure and is not fully reflected in the available statistics. It is interesting that a substantial part of the volume of family and friend visits runs counter to the patterns of internal migration of Americans in the past few decades. That is, those who move away from an area frequently visit those who remain there. Equally difficult to obtain an accurate assessment of is vacation travel centered on cities. This is certainly a major sector of pleasure travel, but again it is often merged with the other indicators of economic activity for each metropolitan area. Nevertheless, when one thinks of vacation travel, visits to San Francisco, with its cable cars, Chinatown, Fisherman's Wharf, and so on; New Orleans, with its Bourbon Street and various residential districts; and New York, with Times Square, Central Park, museums, the Statue of Liberty, and the Empire State Building definitely symbolize the travel desires of a large proportion of Americans. By now a family visit to Washington, D.C., has become a must. Typically, thoughts on vacation destinations also center on national parks like Yellowstone, Great Smoky Mountain, and Yosemite or on favored Florida beach centers like Miami, Palm Beach, Daytona, and Fort Myers. The list is endless. When there is such a vast set of alternative destinations in a population where many can choose what suits them best, a remarkably intricate pattern of vacation travel destinations arises. It is also evident that, with the substantial changes that have occurred in the American economy in recent years, tourism looms ever larger in the thinking of local economic planners. The United States has now reached a point

where nearly every locality has begun competing for the tourist dollar.

A few examples may illustrate the complexity of contemporary vacation tendencies in an American society that has become more and more diverse. Some of the characteristics of this society have been pointed out earlier. For one thing, an increasing number of people, usually couples, find that their work schedules and other obligations make it ever more difficult for two people to get away at the same time for an extended holiday. The result is a strong tendency to take a number of short two- to five-day holidays scattered throughout the year. Many of these may be close to their residence and focus on participation in favored recreational activities. Other trips might involve a flight to a city or resort within or beyond the United States. A recognition of this evolving pattern is causing state development agencies as well as the private sector to push particular local attractions in competing for this sizable market. The increase in the number of single-parent households, single-person households, households containing a retired couple or widow or widower, and other combinations present still other kinds of needs for leisure-related travel.

The merchandising of vacation packages is now quite common, with the public being inundated with advertisements typically offering seven nights in a first-class hotel plus air fare plus excursions at a quite reasonable price in some population resort area like Cancun or Waikiki, or several days on a cruise ship, or a stay at a self-contained resort hotel complex such as the Greenbriar in West Virginia or the Broadmoor in Colorado. Similar kinds of attractions are offered to encourage the purchase of a second home, whether it be a condo, time-share units, or some other plan, in a resort community containing a remarkably broad array of facilities and services. The latter is particularly attractive to those who are retired; the Sun City, Arizona, image has become a major draw to many retired individuals and couples.

Resort developments cater not only to the elderly and retired, the sun worshiper and skier, but also to black Americans and other identifiable groups in the total society. In fact, the increasing ability to identify market segments has led to extremely focused targeting of publicity campaigns for the seemingly endless series of groups found within the larger society. Places attractive to each of these groups have been identified, to serve as symbols of what that specific element of the population may be seeking. Thus, the facilities for

By the mid 1800s, seaside resorts along the upper Eastern Seaboard, from the Jersey Coast to Maine, began to appear.

PAGE 31

INTERNATIONAL TOURISM

International tourism is important today both for Americans traveling abroad and for foreigners visiting this country. One estimate suggests that 1990 was the first year when the United States had a favorable tourism trade balance, with more spent in this country by visitors than was expended by Americans abroad. This major development is a consequence of a long-standing interest on the part of many foreigners in visiting this country, but it has been especially stimulated by the financial bargain the United States has come to offer to Europeans and the Japanese in the context both of actual costs and of exchange rates favoring foreign currencies. Most foreign tourist destinations are on the east and west coasts, with a few "islands" of particular interest in the interior, including certain national parks and New Orleans. The presence of foreign tourists is increasingly obvious to the casual observer of crowds at the Grand Canyon, in San Francisco, and in other favored spots. The United States is not yet the most convenient tourist destination for foreigners, as we are only beginning to develop more abundant currency exchange locations, tourist industry workers competent in foreign languages, travel guides and menus available in the languages of other countries, and the like. The continued growth in air connections, packaged vacations, and the attractiveness of American holidays to affluent foreigners suggest that their volume here will continue to grow. Foreign interests are also major investors in an increasing number of the facilities serving the tourist; for example, many large American hotel chains are currently owned by the Japanese. Japanese investors have also purchased the largest development and management company on California's Monterey Peninsula, an area extremely popular with tourists that contains several renowned golf courses, a sport for which Japan has a desperate shortage of facilities.

Americans also travel abroad in large numbers. Estimates for the late 1980s suggest that over 41 million Americans go out of the country for pleasure purposes each year. The total flow can be roughly divided into three streams, going to Canada, Mexico, and elsewhere in the world. Of the 14 million or more Americans who go overseas, about one-half visit Europe. The American tourist has long been characterized in often-unflattering terms, especially there. Nevertheless, U.S. travelers are vital to the economic well-being of many countries, and their business is pursued vigorously. In the early 1990s, travel to destinations other than Europe is increasing, as the number of Americans seeking new experiences expands. Many have already followed their own personal version of the Grand Tour or been on one or more package tours duplicating part of that itinerary. The growth in the flow to the Pacific Rim countries, Latin America, and elsewhere reflects this developing trend.

holiday-making run the gamut from very upscale to rudimentary.

Most recently, increasing attention is being paid to minimizing the impact of tourism on the environment. Ecotourism, a form of sustainable economic activity, has been one result. It represents an effort to encourage people to be ultrasensitive to their environment and to engage in activities to preserve the integrity of natural systems. These low-impact activities are frequently experienced in a natural setting and have their primary appeal to the allocentric tourist. Unfortunately, it has yet to be demonstrated that ecotourism can both satisfy its commendable environmental goals and simultaneously create sufficient economic benefits in the host area.

Two additional themes emerge from a consideration of pleasure travel by Americans. The first centers on the belief that many Americans may now be working largely to support their leisure rather than, as was historically true, placing primary emphasis on their work. This perception is for the most part based on the notion that increasing numbers of people seem ultimately to receive little real satisfaction from their work and that their fulfillment is to be sought in other directions. Given that premise, many people appear to be seeking meaning from their leisure-time activities, very frequently from their travels. This perspective is partly based on appreciating that more and more people may be overeducated and overtrained for the work they do, that the role of the individual in producing a product is becoming less and less visible given the nature of modern production and management methods, and that a growing dissatisfaction with contemporary bigness, particularly in business, may be taking place. Such perceptions are contributing to newer,

See also
National Parks and
Preservation

riskier forms of recreational activity on the one hand and to looking at our American heritage on the other. Both reactions contribute to significant tourist activity.

The second theme is also related to how very common an undertaking tourism is for the majority of the American people. It provides today, as it did for smaller groups in the past, common popular cultural experiences that help form our identity as a people. Where tourism was once the prerogative of the privileged, it is now shared in by members of all economic classes. As a result, travel has become a mass-consumption activity participated in by all the groups in the society. The development of a resulting "culture of consumption" is reflected in the remarkably diverse array of commercial outlets that surround and attach themselves to nearly all tourist attractions. Shopping malls have themselves become legitimate tourist attractions in some instances. Thus, we create distinctive manmade landscapes that may range from highway strip developments in many communities to the extremes typified by Reno and Las Vegas or Gatlinburg and the Outer Banks of North Carolina or the immense array of service outlets surrounding Disney World. Modern tourist attractions have come to symbolize major points of consumption. Thus, leisure is not only likely to attract more and more participation but is likely to have an ever-greater impact on our landscapes and habits, as well as being more significant as an economic activity.

—RICHARD V. SMITH

Travelling is like flirting with life. It's like saying, 'I would stay and love you, but I have to go; this is my station.'

LISA ST AUBIN DE TERÁN
OFF THE RAILS (1989)

U

URBAN CULTURAL

INSTITUTIONS

In his suggestive study *City People*, Gunther Barth argues that in America the "current of urban life stirred people into constant activity. It also left little opportunity for unrestrained adulation of traditional cultural expressions," which were challenged in the nineteenth century by exciting new forms like baseball, the metropolitan newspaper, the department store, and vaudeville. Whereas Europeans deemed it "a timeless affair . . . culture [the composer Jacques Offenbach noted] 'lives in America from day to day' " (p. 24). Still, the fine arts found permanent homes in American cities. The lyceum, the museum, the library, the theater, and the symphony orchestra were among the salient cultural institutions that appeared.

Urban cultural institutions began to take shape in colonial America, and by the end of the nineteenth century, most of the important, enduring ones were established. Their evolution reflected mixed purposes that included the stimulation and satisfaction of the curiosities of urban audiences, the conservation of the arts and ideas considered important, the making accessible to appreciative taste groups the pleasures offered by cultural activities, the affirmation of the status of patrons, and the effort to educate, tame, and uplift the minds and sensibilities of the uninitiated. First created because elites sought to replicate European cultural activities, American cultural institutions developed in response to native forces, experience, and needs. With the successful culmination of the Revolution, they continued to evolve in great part through the efforts of private promoters who offered the arts as entertainments to paying customers. Then, during the late nineteenth and early twentieth centuries, urban cultural institutions again fell under the control of elites and became important weapons of status definition, legitimizing of taste, and attempts at social control. By the mid-twentieth century, however, cultural institutions as well as artists ironically became co-conspirators in the mass marketing of art and the mind—an activity quite consonant with America's consumer, media reality.

What follows is a selective overview of the history of urban cultural organizations and spaces that Americans created to house, exhibit, and promote the expressive arts and ideas. Discussion touches upon a variety of activities and of necessity treats changing definitions of art as well as evolving notions of the purposes of art and the nature of artistic patronage and production.

Culture: Verb to Noun

During the nineteenth century, art and thought in its elite forms became identified with the term "culture." Prior to that, "culture" was a verb, associated with "growth or nourishment" and linked with a wide variety of things, including taste in the fine arts. Culture was associated with cultivation ("to cultivate"). Of course, the evolving European definition of the fine arts had elite connotations well before the nineteenth century, both because of the social structure of patronage (particularly in the fields of painting and music) and because of the establishment of institutions like Cardinal Richelieu's *Académie Française*, created in 1735, and the Royal Academy of Art founded by Sir Joshua Reynolds (1723–1792) in 1762. From the Renaissance onward, patronage initially came from the church and the aristocracy, though members of the mercantile classes eventually began to support artists, and as commerce and modern capitalism developed, the wealthy bourgeoisie emerged as major sponsors of the arts and intellect. Academies, in turn, were created for the purpose of controlling the definition of, and standards surrounding, fine art and intellectual production, establishing a support community of artists, teaching art and promoting connoisseurship, and facilitating the distribution of works and ideas. The standards and conventions codified became what has been termed the "cultivated tradition."

During the nineteenth century, the word culture evolved into a noun—culture became a thing itself and represented a body of works (usually drawn from painting, music, architecture, and belles lettres) that was believed to represent the best that had been created in the history of Western civilization. Raymond Williams explores the

See also
Urban Parks

527

U

URBAN CULTURAL INSTITUTIONS

Culture: Verb to Noun

Stuart Mill (1806–1873), Newman, and Matthew Arnold (1822–1888) to its modern elaborations by T. S. Eliot (1888–1965), Ivor Armstrong Richards (1893–1979), Frank Raymond Leavis (1895–1978), and George Orwell (1903–1950). Starting with Burke's generalized notions on the matter and Coleridge's particular idea of the need for a "clerisy"—a class of educated, thinking individuals who could apply their learning and tastes to evaluating and bettering society—culture took shape as an entity embodying a mission, an uplifting enterprise. It refined and civilized one. Signaling the possession of knowledge and taste of the proper kinds, culture became a legitimizing process, and its possessors, a distinctive and proud status group.

In *Democracy in America* (1835, 1840) Alexis de Tocqueville (1805–1859) considered the question of the state of the arts in the new republic. This was one among many aspects he explored during his 1831–1832 trip to the United States. He concluded that the arts would always be subject to the marketplace demand of a people who had no tradition of, and little time for, connoisseurship. Because of capitalism and a deeply held belief in equality, no cultivated leisure class would arise in America. Money and superficial taste would rule, pride in craft would disappear, and art would lack quality, substance, sentiment, and

evolution of that concept in *Culture and Society, 1780–1950,* tracing its origins in the thought of Edmund Burke (1729–1797), Samuel Taylor Coleridge (1772–1834), and William Cobbett (1763–1835) through its first clear formulation in the writings of John Ruskin (1819–1900), John

---

LITERATURE AND ENLIGHTENMENT
Cultural Institutions in the Colonial Era

During the colonial era a city was only of modest size, ten to fifteen thousand people. For most of the urban elite the city was an environment that, in keeping with the age of enlightenment, was culturally sophisticated: its institutions, formed through cosmopolitan thinking, tended to replicate those of the old world. Social organizations existed in surprising numbers before 1750 in cities like Boston, New York, Philadelphia, Baltimore, and Charleston, and in most instances they were privately supported. Typical institutions included an odd variety—coffeehouses, dancing assemblies, and fishing and hunting clubs as well as theaters, libraries, and galleries. The tavern or coffeehouse was especially important, for that was where much of the colonists' social life went on. Men's clubs met in taverns, and entertainments, exhibits of oddities and curiosities, and even book auctions took place there. Boston had its Physical Club, and Newport its Philosophical Society, but the best known of the clubs is

Franklin's Junto, formed in Philadelphia in 1727. Its members met to discuss politics, science, morals, and other intellectual and civic issues of the day. Given their interest in books, too, it is not surprising that the Junto founded the famous Library Company of Philadelphia in 1731, an idea soon replicated in other colonial cities.

The well-to-do, of course, kept private libraries housing books on subjects that ranged from gardening and architecture to literature, history, science, and philosophy. Because reading was so important to colonials, bookstores emerged as another prominent urban cultural institution, complementing the subscription library societies that had begun to be established. Cities like Boston, Philadelphia, and Charleston often had more than one bookseller who stocked local publications as well as the latest imported editions and magazines like the *Guardian* and the *Spectator*.

thought. Being quickly and easily made for profit, shallow in content, sensationalized, and transitory, American art would invariably be a diminished product. Tocqueville's observations were translated into English almost immediately and entered the discourse over the arts that was taking place. American artists, writers, intellectuals, and connoisseurs responded in a variety of ways to such charges and have been responding ever since.

Culture did indeed have to compete for attention in an increasingly egalitarian and materialistic atmosphere. American cultural forms could never be confined for long to the categories that elite arts producers, promoters, and taste groups sought to identify, delimit, and control, nor would the cultural institutions they established, supported, and worked through remain untouched by democracy and capitalism.

Cultural Growth

In *Cultural Excursions*, social historian Neil Harris identifies "four stages of cultural growth" that American cities have gone through: the colonial period; the national period from the end of the Revolution in 1870 or so; the period of rapid industrial growth between the 1870s and the Great Depression; and the 1930s through the present. His model offers a useful framework for a meaningful discussion of the types of cultural institutions that emerged, the changes in their shape, and the various purposes they espoused as well as practiced. Yet, because history is a kind of ebb and flow in which ideas and behavioral patterns appear and then seem to disappear only to reappear again in slightly different form, my discussion sometimes violates the boundaries of Harris's stages.

Music and the visual arts, though not as widely pursued as literature and ideas, were also of growing interest to colonists. Architecture and decorative gardens were important and enhanced the city by their presence. More public in intention were the picture sellers who set up shop. A notable example was William Price, whose "Picture Store" did business in Boston from about 1720 onwards. Such places enabled aspiring artists and connoisseurs to see and buy reproductions of European works and develop a taste for the visual arts. Indeed, the first American art exhibit occurred in such a store in 1730. Painter John Smibert (1688–1751), recently moved from Newport, set up a color-and-paint shop and studio in Boston, where he exhibited original paintings by himself and other Americans as well as copies he had made of works by Van Dyke and Reubens.

Smibert's studio became an art center for the colonies.

Urban culture during this period was dependent upon personal wealth, and the homes of the rich became places where cultural events were frequently staged. Both the visual arts and music benefited from private patronage. On the one hand, when artists like Robert Feke (c. 1705– c. 1750) visited a town to paint portraits of important persons and families, their presence provided the opportunity for private social events to be hosted by local patrons. However, social disapproval contributed to the fact that musical performances were more often held in private than in public. An annual subscription concert, for instance, was offered at Philadelphia's "Concert Room" in 1740, but after being attacked by Reverend George Whitefield (1714–1770), it had to be held privately as the "Musick Club." Still, successful public musical performances took place. The first public "Concert of Musick on Sundry Instruments" was given in Boston in 1729, and the "New Concert Room" there offered several instrumental and vocal performances during the early 1730s.

By midcentury, cultural institutions were playing an increasingly important role in town life. Greater sophistication was resulting from increased wealth and leisure time, further enhancing secular urban life and culture. Clubs continued to flourish at taverns. Coffeehouses also continued to provide space for an odd variety of entertainments—from the display of exotic animals, "A White Negro Girl," and the "Philosophical Optical Machine" to a highly popular show, the "Elaborate and Matchless Pile of Art, called the Microcosm, or the World in Miniature." Yet, despite the presence of such a mix of curiosities and entertainments, city people were taking seriously Joseph Addison's dictum, "A man that has a taste of musick, painting or architecture, is like one that has another sense" (quoted in *Cities in Revolt*, p. 192), and they pursued those and other arts with increasing vigor.

Theater, in particular, became established. Professional plays had been performed earlier (prior to 1737 in Charleston) and they were popular; but Reverend Whitefield had successfully put a damper on public play performances, too. Pious Quakers had also sought to do the same in Philadelphia, but the theater began to take root in spite of religious opposition. As it became more popular among the gentry during the 1750s, buildings were built or remodeled specifically for theater performances. Lewis Hallam, an actor and head

See also
Theater and Musical Theater

*Urban tourism
began to grow as
the attractions of
individual cities
became more
widely known.*

PAGE 520

of the "London Company of Comedians," built the Nassau Street Theater in New York; Charleston constructed a "new theater" on Queen Street; and Philadelphia put one up on Society Hill. The performances offered in these and other theaters by traveling companies included works such as Shakespeare's *Richard III*, Thomas Otway's *The Orphan* (1680), and John Gay's *The Beggar's Opera* (1728).

Music was a popular cultural pastime as well. More and more music sellers opened shops in cities, offering instruments, instruction, books, and music scores. Despite Whitefield's efforts to suppress them, concerts continued to occur in many cities with varying frequency. While these were still usually private, amateur affairs, the number of public concerts increased. As with the theater, music performances were an important part of the social life of an urban aristocracy after 1750. The American Company toured colonial towns, giving instrumental concerts and staging operas. Boston's Concert Hall housed subscription performances. New Yorkers could also attend subscription concerts as well as be entertained by touring companies, and some citizens successfully organized an amateur group in 1767 called the Harmonic Society. In Charleston, the Saint Cecilia Society was formed in 1762 to revive the interest in music that had been condemned by Whitefield, and it was successful in building a vital public music scene. Philadelphia could boast of holding an annual winter subscription series at the Assembly Room and of being the home of one of America's foremost colonial composers and music directors, Giovanni Gualdo, who ran a music shop and gave concerts that included the works of Bach and others as well as his own.

Museums emerged more slowly. No art schools or museums existed anywhere in the colonies before the Revolution. Harvard College began collecting curiosities in 1750, and they eventually built a display room for their artifacts but no artworks were among them. The first public museum, established by the Library Society of Charleston in 1773, had the purpose of gathering and exhibiting only natural history artifacts. The public would have to wait until after 1780 to see paintings displayed in public. Collecting was just beginning among the wealthy who could afford to have portraits painted by artists like Smibert, Feke, John Singleton Copley (1738–1815), Benjamin West (1738–1820), and Gustavus Hesselius (1682–1755). The wealthy also had opportunity to travel and acquire work done in Europe. A few notable private collections were put to-

gether. A Newport collector may have had a Van Dyke, and Charleston's Judge Egerton Leigh possessed some Italian masters like Veronese, Giordano, and Correggio. Two Philadelphia collectors owned copies of works by Correggio and Titian. The graphic arts, available at the picture shops, were collected, too; so were originals and copies of antiquities.

John Singleton Copley once lamented, "A taste of painting is too much Wanting to affoard any kinds of helps" for American painters. Partly for that reason, the most gifted of colonial America's artists, Boston's Copley and Philadelphia's Benjamin West, went to Europe before the Revolution and remained there. Yet, there was a climate of hope in the minds of some regarding the future of art. The painter and art promoter Charles Willson Peale noted in a 1771 letter to Benjamin Franklin, (1741–1827): "The people here have a growing taste for the arts, and are becoming more and more fond of encouraging their progress amongst them." Franklin agreed: "The Arts have always travelled westward, and there is no doubt of their flourishing hereafter on our side of the Atlantic, as the number of wealthy inhabitants shall increase . . . it appears that our people are not deficient in genius" (quoted in *Cities in Revolt*, p. 398). In important ways, the optimism of both Peale and Franklin was borne out. The arts and intellectual life continued to develop and expand in interesting and unexpected ways after America became a new republic.

Art in a Democracy

At the time America entered its early national period, art was distrusted by many because it was thought to reflect sensuality and luxury, traits associated with Europe and the danger of corruption. Of course, America's first order of business was to find an identity as well as solve the day-to-day problems posed by independence. The ideologies of republicanism, nationalism, and democracy conjoined in that effort and influenced the response to the question of the proper place of art in the new society. If the republican ideology helped create a fear of art, nationalism succeeded in undermining that fear. Not surprisingly, America's act of declaring its independence soon had an impact in the cultural realm.

The period between the end of the Revolution and 1870 witnessed an extraordinary expansion in the type and number of public cultural institutions as well as a change in the types of audiences that supported them. And, it must be reemphasized, the city was the natural place for this

See also
Public Architecture

growth to happen, since art could only thrive where there was a community of creative minds and patrons. Indeed, cultural institutions were established in cities located in all regions, and they often had the effect of popularizing the arts and intellect. "Libraries, historical societies, art unions, art academies, lyceums, theaters, and opera companies appear, not only in eastern cities," writes Harris, "but in the newer western towns such as Lexington, Cincinnati, Pittsburgh, Buffalo, and Indianapolis" (*Cultural Excursions*, p. 17). These institutions were still mainly in private individual hands, and though some, like Boston's Athenaeum, continued to be the preserve of local elites keeping alive the link between the wealthy leisured class and the fine arts, most were open to the public. And, in keeping with the newly emerging democratic ethos and the entrepreneurial spirit, their offerings—still a broad mix of things—were increasingly calculated to appeal to larger, more socially diverse audiences.

The museum—a place Dr. Samuel Johnson (1709–1784) called, in his 1775 *Dictionary*, a repository "of learned curiosities"—began to appear in America following the Revolution. The institution was first established in Europe after 1750. The British Museum (1751) and the Louvre (1793) established significant cultural precedents, the former because it offered treasures of science, literature, and art for the study of scholars, and the latter because it opened up the impressive private collections of the French kings to the public. While America, too, had witnessed the founding of Charleston's Museum in 1773 and Philadelphia's American Museum of Pierre Eugène Du Simitière (c. 1736–1784) in 1782, the earliest art museum appeared when Charles Willson Peale opened his "gallery of famous men" in 1782, showing portraits he had painted. Soon after, he opened a small public space in the annex of his Philadelphia home in 1785 and exhibited his collection of natural history specimens, Indian and South Seas island artifacts, as well as paintings (mostly his own). His collection grew so large that he moved it first to Philosophical Hall in 1794 and then in 1802 to Independence Hall. Though Peale's museum did not survive long after his death in 1827, it helped establish the museum as a popular urban cultural institution and was the first serious American effort to educate the public in history, science, and the arts, thereby promoting nationalism and republican values through the dispensing of knowledge. Peale's act also set a precedent for the philanthropic habit of giving private collections to public museums.

Museums began to spring up in cities like Boston, Salem, New York, Albany, Providence, Pittsburgh, Cincinnati, Lexington, and Saint Louis, and they usually followed the pattern of showing a variety of things. Daniel Bowen founded an early museum at Boston's American Coffee House in 1791, though it was moved and renamed the Columbian Museum four years later. It initially displayed wax figures of American political notables and then exhibited paintings and a living natural history collection until its collection was sold to the New England Museum in 1825. In New York the Saint Tammany Society began exhibiting some Indian relics in a room at the City Hall in 1790; Baker's American Museum, as the collection was soon named, wound up in the hands of John Scudder in 1802, who continued to expand its holdings. After he died in 1821, the American Museum remained in possession of his family and thrived for several years until, becoming troubled financially, it was bought by P. T. Barnum in 1841. Meanwhile in 1814, Peale's son Rembrandt (1778–1860) established a museum in Baltimore and displayed portraits along with other things until it closed several years later. Boston's Museum and Gallery of Fine Art was opened in 1841. Privately owned and charging

HISTORY AND SCIENCE

The Development of Specialized Collections

Specialized collections were made available to the public during the period between the end of the Revolution and 1870. Because history was very important to the national identity, some fifty historical societies were formed between 1823 and the Civil War. Science, too, was highly valued. America's first museum in Charleston displayed natural history objects, and scientific collections made up a large part of the eclectic displays in other early museums. Soon institutions like Philadelphia's Academy of the Natural Sciences (1812) were established, usually focusing on a single branch of science; for example, geology. What would become one of America's most significant museums was founded in 1816 in Washington, D.C. First named the Columbian Institute, it soon became the National Museum. A bequest of over a half-million dollars to the United States by Englishman James Smithson (1765–1829) enabled Congress to turn it into the Smithsonian Institution in 1846.

U

URBAN CULTURAL INSTITUTIONS

Art in a Democracy

A major city was expected to have several newspapers and such institutions of high culture as museums, a symphony, a public library, and universities.

PAGE 61

admission, it mingled art and entertainment that included concerts and plays but survived only as a theater. Most of these museums were open to the public on at least a part-time basis.

During this period, artists and collectors were very concerned about the role of art in a democracy. Besides creating museums that exhibited art, they formed arts organizations. The founding of an "American Academy of Painting, Sculpture, Architecture Etc."—the Columbianum—by Peale in 1795 was an early valiant but ill-fated attempt to bring artists together and exhibit only art objects. More successful was the creation of the Pennsylvania Academy of Fine Arts in 1805—Peale was again among its founders. In 1810 the Society of Artists of the United States was created, also in Philadelphia. Similar efforts occurred elsewhere. In New York prominent citizens formed the New York Academy of the Fine Arts in 1802. It became the American Academy of the Arts in 1808 and eventually constructed a building in 1831 for showing art. And in 1825 a group of New York artists founded a teaching and exhibiting organization that, the next year, was renamed the National Academy of Design. It functioned as a major force in the American art world until 1908. Boston's Atheneum, though founded as a library in 1807, began holding an annual, two-month-long art exhibition in 1826, charging twenty-five cents admission. The Atheneum subsequently installed a permanent picture gallery in its new building in 1845, though its art collection would eventually be loaned permanently to the Boston Museum of Fine Arts. Yale built the Trumbull Gallery in 1832, a space devoted solely to exhibiting art (they would acquire the James Jackson Jarves [1818–1888] collection in 1871). Finally, the National Institute opened an art exhibition space at the Washington Patent Office in the 1840s.

Still, the eclectic museum, housing a mixed collection of amusing objects and activities, persisted during the first half of the nineteenth century, and P. T. Barnum (1810–1891) was the quintessential figure who perfected its shape as a place of spectacle and pure entertainment. Beginning in 1841, Barnum's American Museums hawked a bizarre mixture of things: a copy of "the great picture of Christ Healing the Sick in the Temple, by Benjamin West, Esq., The Albino Lady; and 500,000 curiosities (quoted in *The Tastemakers*, p. 17). His fare delighted New Yorkers and frustrated early cultural custodians for nearly three decades before he abandoned his enterprise after his building burned a second time in

1868. Henry Tappan disdained Barnum's museum as "a place for some stuffed birds and animals, for the exhibition of monsters, and for vulgar dramatic performances—a mere place of popular amusement, and George Templeton Strong called it "an eyesore, with its huge pictures" as well as its "horrible little brass band . . . tooting in its balcony" (quoted in *Humbug*, p. 33, 17). But in *A Small Boy and Others*, Henry James fondly remembered the charm and fascination that the American Museum held for an impressionable child of the 1850s. Barnum, of course, was not the only promoter who vulgarly mingled art and enterprise. Perhaps the most shameless was Dr. Collyer. He described his New York establishment, "Palmo's Opera House," as "a new movement in the fine arts." Displayed was a *tableau vivant* advertised as "living men and women in almost the same state in which Gabriel saw them in the Garden of Eden on the first morning of creation" (Humbug, p. 19). Immensely popular, it drew people from all classes.

Of course, bread and circuses were not the only fare available to urban Americans. A loftier enterprise was the art union idea, launched by painter James Herring in 1838. First opening the Apollo Gallery in New York, and charging admission, he settled upon a scheme whereby he invited people to buy a five dollar annual subscription to the Gallery, renamed the Apollo Association in 1839. In return each "patron" got "a large and costly Original Engraving from an American painting" and a numbered ticket. At the year's end, a drawing was held and original paintings were given away to the holders of winning numbers. The lottery grew in popularity, and in 1844 it changed its name to the American Art Union. It became so successful that the union idea was copied by others; and it was so highly respected that it could make William Cullen Bryant one of its presidents. The Union continued to "give away" increasing numbers of paintings to subscribers; and, of course, those members who did not win paintings still had the consolation of collecting the engravings sent to them during the year. By the late 1840s, the Union had about 10,000 members and it was virtually in control of the art market, distributing more than 450 paintings a year worth $40,907, including Thomas Cole's (1801–1848) *Youth* (from *The Voyage of Life* series) and George Caleb Bingham's (1811–1879) *The Jolly Flatboatman*. It finally closed down only because it was declared illegal in 1851 as a lottery by the New York Supreme Court. During its entire life span, the Union estimated that it had "given away"

See also

Commercial Architecture

about 150,000 engravings and 2,400 paintings. Ironically, the final sale in 1853 of the Union's remaining collection was a failure.

The joining of democracy and education is perhaps best illustrated by another urban cultural institution that emerged in the 1820s—the American lyceum movement, founded by Josiah Holbrook (1788–1854) in 1826. Originated in England, the lyceum was imported to offer practical scientific knowledge to skilled workers through lectures and demonstrations. By 1846 it became a vehicle for offering lectures and lecture series on a variety of topics to a broadly based audience of townspeople. Its first chapter was established in Millbury, Massachusetts, but the Boston branch, founded in 1828, quickly became the center for what was soon to be a widespread national phenomenon. The American Lyceum, formed in 1831, caught on quickly in a political climate that had already allowed a widening of the franchise and favored the development of public schools and libraries. Lyceum branches were most prevalent in New England but also existed in cities such as Buffalo, Saint Louis, Richmond, Nashville, Mobile, Natchez, New Orleans, Little Rock, Louisville, Indianapolis, and Cincinnati. Of course, some chapters disappeared and new ones emerged; still, though the movement suffered

some decline during periods like the panic of 1837, it continued to grow until the 1860s.

From the beginning, the lyceum movement attracted the attention of well-known Americans like Daniel Webster (1782–1852), Caroline Beecher (1800–1878), Theodore Dwight (1822–1892), and Albert Gallatin (1761–1849), and its lecturers included intellectuals of the stature of Ralph Waldo Emerson (1803–1882), Henry David Thoreau (1817–1862), and Oliver Wendell Holmes (1809–1894). Support for it also came from those who participated in the public school and library movements. The lyceum offered programs ranging from adult education to pure entertainment. Theodore Parker (1810–1860) lectured on "The Political Destiny of America," Edgar Allan Poe (1809–1849) on "Selections from English Poetry with Critical Remarks," and Louis Agassiz (1807–1873) on "Glaciers," and E. P. Whipple (1819–1896) amused audiences with comments on "The Ludicrous Side of Life." Starr King (1824–1864) delighted them with his facile views on "Substance and Show," and Henry Ward Beecher (1813–1887) edified them with lectures like "Six Warnings" and "Popular Amusements." "The lyceum is my pulpit," Emerson once said; Starr King responded to the query about what he got from it with the answer, "FAME—fifty And My Expenses"; and Holmes ironically remarked, "a lecturer was a literary strumpet."

The lyceum movement did not survive long after the Civil War, though its traces reemerged in the Chautauqua movement that began in the 1870s as well as in certain urban institutions like New York's Ethical Culture School, the Educational Alliance, the People's Institute at Cooper Union, and the William Morris Club—all aimed at educating immigrants during the late nineteenth and early twentieth centuries. The popularity of the lyceum movement for nearly a forty-year period—and its rebirth under other names—suggests that Americans were starved for knowledge, even if they were not always discriminating regarding its content. The lyceum, moreover, bore an important relation to literature and the growing publication industry, for its lecturers were often literary men, and the platform it provided frequently gave birth to published work, Emerson's essays for example. And the growing literacy that the organization reflected and probably stimulated contributed to the development of the library movement then beginning to surface.

The museum and the lyceum were, of course, not the only urban cultural institutions reflecting the influences and pressures of democracy. Opera and theater did, too. The latter, a well-established institution in cities before the Revolution, suffered when the Continental Congress criticized "Plays" as well as "Cock Fighting" and "Horse Racing" in 1774 and when buildings were subsequently closed during the war. Still, theater survived this brief attack, and once again began to thrive in the cities after the Revolution. According to Lawrence Levine in *Highbrow/Lowbrow*, Shakespeare eventually "dominated the theater" in both the northeastern and southeastern regions (16). Tocqueville had noted the existence of Shakespeare in "the recesses of the forests of the New World," and the fact that Twain could include a delightful parody of Hamlet's soliloquy in *Adventures of Huckleberry Finn* suggests just how well-known Shakespeare was among common Americans. Of course, the bowdlerization of his plays indicated the types of performances insisted upon by appreciative but unruly audiences—bombastically acted lines, for example, interspersed with the singing of popular songs like "The Swiss Drover Boy." Theater's widespread popularity is further suggested by the fact that many traveling companies found it profitable to tour cities and towns throughout America during the nineteenth century—often playing in buildings that towns-

people had built especially for such performances. Whether put on in New York or Natchez, plays were attended by people from all classes, though audiences were often segregated in terms of their seating—"the dandies, and people of the first respectability and fashion" sat in the boxes, noted a contemporary spectator, while the "middling classes" were seated in the pit, and the working poor, prostitutes, and blacks in the gallery (24). Audiences continued to see a theater bill that mixed Shakespeare with plays like *Ten Nights in a Bar-Room* and multiple versions of *Uncle Tom's Cabin*.

Operatic, instrumental, and play performances were often given in places like the Chicago Museum, and the New York museums like the American and Peale's. In many cities, particularly in western towns, a distinct building was used for musical performances and plays. Sometimes, as in Beaver Dam, Wisconsin, it was called the Concert Hall; other times, as in Central City, Colorado, it was the Opera House or, in Portland, Oregon, the Casino Theater. Music was as popular among a broad social cross-section of the American people as theater. Opera had a wide following. Comic opera especially tended to be favored although grand opera gained a foothold among audiences by the 1840s. Italian operas like Vincenzo Bellini's (1801–1835) *La Sonnambula* became particularly popular, so much so that in 1851 George Templeton Strong exclaimed, "people are *Sonnambula*-mad. Everybody goes, and nob and snob . . . sit side by side fraternally on the hard benches" (25). As in theater, traveling companies put on performances all over America. Levine explains that opera, especially English translations of arias, remained part of popular culture until it began to be wrested from the people by elites during the late nineteenth century.

Culture: High and Low

American society and its economy changed radically during the 1800s. Industrial growth dominated the scene and contributed to an unprecedented urban population growth. A few cities reached over one million people by 1900, several others had one hundred thousand or more. By 1921 the majority of Americans lived in urban areas. The increase in population reflected not only a change in size but also a dramatic alteration in the ethnic mix of the people. The explosion of knowledge, vast increases in wealth, and sense of discontinuity that modernity was stimulating helped mold the new shape of the city, too. It was in this environment that popular cultural forms

See also
The City

like the department store, baseball, vaudeville, and the movies were born. Of course, the old cultural institutions—theater, concerts, and museums among them—continued to persist.

Despite the fact that during the first two-thirds of the nineteenth century many cultural institutions were patronized by audiences that cut across class lines, Levine argues that after 1870, culture became sacralized and segregated in terms of taste groups, and the gap between the fine and the popular arts widened. During the third stage in the evolution of American urban cultural institutions, "highbrow" culture became distinct from "lowbrow" culture. Profit-seeking entrepreneurs moved in the direction of creating entertainments that were put in the lowbrow category (vaudeville, burlesque, musical theater, and movies); elites established the highbrow. The cultivated tradition had its moment of triumph because it was implanted in institutions created by a whole generation of sons of old elites (men like Charles Eliot Norton [1827–1908]) and scions of new elites (individuals like Andrew Carnegie [1835–1919]), who began to exercise power and influence outside politics through organizations like the nationally based Sanitary Commission and Union League Clubs, founded during the Civil War, and the great cultural institutions formed afterwards. Such men worried about the course American civilization was taking. They believed that Americans suffered from degraded taste, that artists were unappreciated and unsupported, and that the spiritual and moral realms were threatened by materialism. They acted through the best means available to them: philanthropy replaced politics, and art and intellect were seized upon to correct wayward sensibilities. Given the seriousness of this mission, art and mind could neither be amusement nor decoration, only moral and aesthetic uplift.

The age of great new museums, opera houses, and symphonies was at hand. Of the museums established, most housed art, and these included: Washington's Corcoran Gallery (founded in 1859), Boston's Museum of Fine Arts and New York's Metropolitan Museum of Art (both 1870), the Philadelphia Museum of Art (1876), Chicago's Art Institute (1879), Saint Louis's Museum of Fine Arts (1879), Minneapolis's Institute of Art (1883) and Walker Art Gallery (1876), Cleveland's Museum of Art (1916), New York's Museum of Modern Art (1929) and Whitney Museum (1932), and Washington's National Gallery of Art (1941). The music organizations included the Boston Symphony Orchestra (1881), Boston

Pops (1885), Chicago Symphony Orchestra (1891), and the Philadelphia Orchestra (1900). New York already had a Philharmonic Society (1842), a musician-run orchestra, but another, the New York Symphony Orchestra, was founded in 1878; they would merge in 1928. New York's Metropolitan Opera appeared in 1883, and Chicago's Opera Society in 1910, though most resident opera companies appeared later than did symphonies and museums. They proliferated after 1900 in cities like Santa Fe, San Francisco, Kansas City, and Houston.

Libraries also began to be founded in great numbers during this period. Of course, private subscription libraries had been established in cities like Philadelphia and Charleston as early as the eighteenth century, and the Library of Congress (for the use of its members) had been in existence since 1800. However, the idea of a free library available to everyone was relatively new, and the establishment of the tax-supported Boston Public Library (1852) marked the beginning of the public library movement in America. Other cities quickly followed Boston's lead—Cincinnati in 1856, Saint Louis and Detroit in 1865, Cleveland in 1869, Louisville in 1871, and Chicago in 1873. The Enoch Pratt Free Library was founded in Baltimore in 1882, and Chicago's Newberry (a research collection whose public use was limited) appeared in 1887. The New York Public Library came along later in 1895. As was true of art museums and music organizations, wealthy individuals were important to the library's creation. The most famous library patron, Andrew Carnegie, donated forty-one million dollars between 1890 and 1917 to construct sixteen hundred library buildings in cities and towns throughout America.

In theory, these institutions were open to the public, but many were in fact closed to the majority by the price of admission, the elitist tone permeating the activity, or restrictions placed on their use. Together, opera and symphony societies, art museums, and many libraries took on a daunting aura. The art museum, a good example of the contradiction between the democratic ideal and exclusive reality, was made into a hallowed chamber into which all were invited—provided they came only at certain times, behaved properly, and either contemplated knowingly or struggled seriously to have their taste elevated and their sensibilities refined. Consider the Boston Museum of Fine Arts, incorporated in 1870 by the state legislature and opened in 1876. Though the rhetoric surrounding its creation and early administration insisted that it was "to be a popular institution," its practice

After World War II, American musicians saw this country's major cities, especially New York, as major cultural centers on par with the capitals of Europe.

PAGE 104

sanctified art instead of welcoming people. The museum secretary summed up its elitism early in the twentieth century: "A collection of science is gathered primarily in the interest of the real; a collection of art primarily in the interest of the ideal. . . . A museum of science is in essence a school; a museum of art is in essence a temple." For many years, Bostonians could only gain free admittance on Sundays. And though education eventually became more than a rhetorical mission at museums like Boston's, it was guided by docents carefully explaining the displayed works to viewers who were, in turn, watched by museum guards to ensure that they kept a proper distance from the art they were learning to worship.

At first the art museum's function seemed to parallel that of the modern public library movement: it appeared to be moving from being a "storehouse" to a "workshop," where anyone could pursue knowledge through the study of extensive collections of copies as well as a few original works. But those who wished museums to be storehouses for masterpieces won out. Museums increasingly benefited from gifts by wealthy collectors like Thomas J. Bryan (d. 1870), William W. Corcoran (1798–1888), James Jackson Jarves, Thomas B. Clarke (1848–1931), J. P. Morgan (1837–1913), Henry Clay Frick (1849–1919), and Henry Marquand (1819–1902). The gifts included art from China and Japan as well as Europe—and, eventually, America and Africa. The collections were housed in new buildings constructed in the "palace style" that clothed the artworks in a grand and hallowed aura and provided the city with an example of civilized urban space.

Of course, there were also museums featuring artifacts besides art, Washington's Smithsonian Institution and Chicago's Field Museum of Natural History being early examples. The latter grew out of the collections gathered for the 1893 Chicago Columbian Exposition; the Smithsonian had existed in one form or another since the early nineteenth century, but by 1870, it had given up its library and art collection, essentially concentrating on being a natural history museum but later adding cultural history to its purview (one historian has termed it America's "national attic"). Like the Field Museum, it was the beneficiary of gifts from a world's fair—the Philadelphia Centennial Exposition of 1876. As both institutions verify, world's fairs (which began in 1851 in London and continued through the nineteenth and twentieth centuries) were important in the development of the museum idea. In America, between 1876 and World War I, fairs took place every four or five years in cities like New Orleans, Chicago, Atlanta, Saint Louis, Nashville, San Francisco, Omaha, and San Diego. Attended by huge audiences (twenty-five million people visited the 1893 Columbian Exposition), fairs introduced Ameri-

PUBLIC LIBRARY

The New York Public Library at 5th Avenue and 42nd Street was built in 1895.
CORBIS-BETTMANN

cans to modern innovations like electricity and telephones and exposed them to art, often for the first time. Museums of "progress" (the exhibition of Western achievements), of "exotica" (the imperialist display of artifacts of subject nations), and of fine art (traditional Western masterpieces brought together under one roof), they exposed audiences to the wondrousness of the present, appealed to consumers, expressed national pride, and linked science, commerce, and high culture. Their buildings, mostly beaux-arts, renaissance, or neoclassical, also helped establish the architectural style believed appropriate for cultural institutions as well as necessary to bringing order to America's chaotic urban environment.

Unlike museums, libraries moved away from the storehouse to the workshop function. The shape of their collections and the mission they identified reflect a struggle that never ceased to take place during the nineteenth and twentieth centuries: the struggle over taste and the selection of works to be admitted into the realm of high culture. The motives for starting public libraries included a wish to collect and preserve important writings, a genuine commitment to educate people, and a desire to use books as a means of social control. Books, it was asserted, improved minds and taste. A debate emerged, however, regarding the issue of accumulation as opposed to use, and the motive of improving people took precedence over the "quality" of the collection. Tellingly, it was stimulated partly by the question of whether or not to collect popular fiction—a form that had become very important in the publishing industry. Uplift of the masses could only occur if the collections were used, it was argued, so the conclusion was drawn that libraries ought to house popular books to entice readers. Those favoring the inclusion of popular fiction won out, and recreation became one of the purposes of public library use.

Clearly, democracy was a phenomenon not wholly absent from the cultural scene between 1870 and the 1920s. The masses might be kept out of symphony halls and operatic performances by high ticket prices, an exclusive repertoire, and socially enforced etiquette. Hierarchy in the arts might separate classical from popular music and fine art from modern forms like photography, movies, commercial art, and industrial design. But the economic, political, and social landscapes were changing so dramatically by the turn of the century that elite cultural institutions could not remain untouched.

As already indicated, the quality of the works collected was increasingly a crucial consideration for art museums. They were abetted in their efforts to canonize artists by groups such as the National Academy of Design (1825) and the Society of American Artists (1877), which virtually controlled the exhibition of contemporary works and defined artistic standards. Like their European counterparts, American academies were conservative in taste and exclusive in the admission of artists to their ranks, and during their heyday, they were quite successful in promoting the work and status of their members. For the most part, academic artists were solidly bourgeois, widely recognized, highly respected, well supported, and sometimes wealthy and powerful (like their patrons). But the hegemony of the monied class and the fine-art academies was challenged during the first decade of the twentieth century by artists who exhibited independently. One of the most notable of these challenges occurred when "The Eight" made a rude disturbance by withdrawing their entries to the annual National Academy's exhibition and showed their works at New York's Macbeth Gallery in 1908.

The concept "culture," Raymond Williams reminds us, had undergone a revolution during the nineteenth century that made the artist into "a specially endowed person" at a time when he or she was in danger of becoming "just one more producer of a commodity for the market" and art was drawn into the cultural struggle to soften the jagged edges of a successful materialism. By the time of The Eight's show, however, culture had rejoined the class struggle, for a significant number of young artists and writers were beginning to see themselves as workers and social democrats. The Eight included Robert Henri (1865–1928) and several members of his group—John Sloan (1871–1951), George Luks (1866–1933), William Glackens (1870–1938), and Everett Shinn (1873–1958)—painters who, with the second generation of Henri students such as George Bellows (1882–1925) and Stuart Davis (1892–1964), were dubbed the "Ash Cans" in 1913.

What repulsed academicians were the Ashcans' subjects, which seemed to celebrate "lowlife" and immorality—urban scenes of slums and the tenderloin districts, portraits of working-class people and prostitutes. Their politics—democratic, in Walt Whitman's (1819–1892) sense, and socialist—were threatening, too. Sloan, for instance, not only lived in a New York City working-class neighborhood, but also ran for the state legislature as the Socialist candidate and, for a time, was art director of the radical *Masses* magazine. The Eight also repudiated the academic jury

If architecture were opera, this would be the ultimate prima donna.

PAUL GOLDBERGER
CRITIC, ON I. M. PEI'S
MEYERSON SYMPHONY
CENTER IN DALLAS, TEXAS

See also
Concert Music

ART IN THE TWENTIETH CENTURY

The revolt of a group of independent artists signaled the end of the academy as an art world power, yet it by no means put an end to that world's elitism and exclusiveness. While most artists remained poor, few held to a working-class commitment for long. Class-based warfare disappeared from the art scene by 1920, replaced by a bohemianism symbolized by New York's Greenwich Village. After a brief hiatus, political consciousness and engagement on the part of cultural producers reappeared with the creation of institutions like The New Playwright's Theater (1926) and the protest against the execution of Sacco and Vanzetti (1927). Artists and writers began to redraw their workers' banners, and proceeded to wave them in public for over a decade. The Artist's Union was formed in 1933; the League of American Writers grew out of the American Writers' Congress of 1935; and in 1936, the American Artists' Congress was founded. Through such organizations, artists and writers became, in Max Eastman's phrase, "artists in uniform." Just as influential in politicizing the fine arts were governmental agencies such as the Works Progress Administration (1935–1943) which, through programs like the Federal Art Project, Federal Theater Project, and Federal Writers' Project, hired thousands of artists at hourly wages to create works that would enhance the urban public sphere. These ranged from state travel guides and murals painted in public buildings to theater and dance performances. By the beginning of World War II, however, the issue of radical social change ceased to be important to artists, and they involved themselves in direct political action only sporadically thereafter.

system that rigidly selected and rejected works on the basis of conventional taste, the prize system that accorded honors to a few, and the hierarchical hanging order that placed the most favored works at eye level and the rest above or below. Their show had no jury, no prizes, and democratically hung every work at eye level.

During the first half of the twentieth century, museums rarely engaged in political activities. Indeed, a radical political viewpoint did not substantially affect most fine arts institutions until the 1960s, when museum workers began to or-

ganize, the Civil Rights and anti-Vietnam movements threatened the establishment, and feminism turned a mirror on the institutions' exhibiting practices. Then, the consciences of many arts community members were once again jarred, and individuals like the Metropolitan Museum's director, Thomas Hoving, the New York Public Theater's head, Joseph Papp, and the New York Philharmonic's conductor, Leonard Bernstein, entered the battle taking sides on causes, often bringing their institutions with them into the fray.

Modernity and Specialization

After the turn of the century, the fine arts community was increasingly challenged by modernity: complex, difficult science and technology, rampant industrialism, pervasive consumerism and mass media, disturbing new cultural forms and ideas, and a growing social-democratic thrust. That community also encountered unprecedented upheavals that included war, depression, and holocaust. And it collided with the phenomenon of modernism. Rather than hide, most artists, patrons, and cultural institutions faced the brave new world of the twentieth century and tried to deal with its realities as best they could. If arts institutions were able to resist for nearly six decades the pressures of the age's social and political upheavals, they were less successful at keeping modernism and modernity's component parts at bay.

The modern phenomenon of specialization really took hold in the museum world after 1920, and by the end of the first third of the twentieth century, fields such as art, history, and science were seldom mixed. Specialized museums included those devoted to an explicit category of art (modern or American or folk) and those that might be called living history museums. The latter, in which whole towns made up the exhibit, were begun in the 1920s: Old Deerfield Village, Massachusetts, was restored; Colonial Williamsburg, Virginia, was reconstructed; and Greenfield Village, Michigan, was fabricated entirely from old buildings brought together to create an ersatz place. Similar to the museums of living history were the botanical gardens, zoological parks, and aquariums featuring plants, birds, animals, and fish in simulated environments. Botanical gardens, originating with John Bartram's (1699–1777) 1728 garden near Philadelphia, began to appear in greater numbers. Living zoos, related to the stuffed-animal exhibits that had also been common since the eighteenth century, were established, too. One, the San Diego Zoological Park, grew out of the World's Fair of 1915–1916. Large

♦ **Social-democratic**

Relating to social democracy, a political movement advocating a gradual and peaceful transition from capitalism to socialism by democratic means

538

aquariums were founded later: Boston's, built during the 1960s, is perhaps the most famous of them.

Specialized art museums featuring contemporary styles and/or media, or American art, or folk art are especially significant, for they either rejected or affirmed modernity. American art and folk museums complemented the efforts of history museums by their nostalgic attempt to recover and legitimize cultural roots, while galleries like the Museum of Modern Art countered such efforts by privileging modernity over the past. The latter museum, MOMA, became one of the most powerful cultural institutions in twentieth-century America. Established in 1929, it was the first of several contemporary art museums to be established. Under the inspired directorship of Alfred Barr, MOMA not only highlighted a style of art that had been challenging the Academy since the 1870s but also featured the "arts" not traditionally associated with the word "fine." Besides departments of painting, sculpture, and architecture, MOMA also had departments of film, photography, and industrial design.

Through aggressively innovative exhibitions of modernist painting as well as topical shows like the *International Exhibition of Modern Architecture* (1932) and *Machine Art* (1934), MOMA argued that art, on the one hand, and modern science and technology, on the other, were not antithetical. Alfred Stieglitz (1864–1946) had already successfully convinced Buffalo's Albright Gallery to exhibit and purchase art photographs in 1910; the 1913 Armory Show had introduced modern art to audiences in New York, Boston, and Chicago; and Weimar Germany's Bauhaus had pioneered the merging of technology and art, beginning in 1919. But established museums were still wary of showing modern works. New York's Metropolitan, for example, did put on an exhibition of Postimpressionist art in 1921 but did so only under extreme pressure from patrons like John Quinn, Mrs. Havermeyer, and Lillie P. Bliss. The Met was so openly opposed to modern art that Quinn decided to sell his brilliant collection of paintings rather than bequeath it to a museum he believed would disdain it. Quinn was probably correct, since the Met on one occasion refused Gertrude Vanderbilt Whitney's offer of a gift of her extraordinary American art collection. Barr and MOMA benefactors Bliss, Abby Rockefeller, and Mrs. Cornelius Sullivan were challenging established definitions of fine art and taste, and their courage was amply rewarded. MOMA succeeded in changing the definition of art and became the most famous and respected contemporary art museum in the world. Moreover, it established a practice whereby museums functioned as active participants and patrons in the creation of contemporary art-works and movements. Eventually such established museums as New York's Metropolitan, Minneapolis's Institute of Art, and Chicago's Art Institute would follow suit.

Institutions devoted strictly to ethnic and national collections have been a fairly recent phenomenon, and have taken on new resonance of late. A few ethnic cultural institutions have already been noted—New York's Ethical Culture Society, for example. Others include the rich Yiddish theater that thrived in New York during the late nineteenth and early twentieth centuries. Jazz must be added to this list for, although a lowbrow form, it was eventually admitted to elite concert halls. The first such instance was African American bandleader James Reese Europe's (1881–1919) Clef Club "Concert of Negro Music," held in Carnegie Hall in 1912. Carnegie Hall also hosted musical performances by W. C. Handy (1924), by Paul Whiteman and George Gershwin (1928), and by Benny Goodman (1938). The Whiteman/Gershwin concert, "Experiment in Modern Music," premiered *Rhapsody in Blue* (1924). America's indigenous music had earlier been stimulated by New York's National Conservatory of Music when they invited Antonin Dvořák to become director in 1892. During his three-year stay in America, the great Czech composer wrote several pieces like the *New World* (1893) symphony that drew upon American folk music, including the African American tradition. By the 1950s, that tradition, by then called jazz, was established as one of the significant fine arts, and groups like the "Modern Jazz Quartet" appeared as guest performers with symphony orchestras. What was occurring, of course, was just the reverse of the nineteenth-century practice, exemplified by John Philip Sousa's band as well as orchestras like the Boston Pops, of mingling popular songs, marches, and "classical" excerpts at popular concerts.

MULTICULTURALISM. Other salient examples of the phenomenon that would later be termed multiculturalism occurred in the 1920s at the Harlem branches of the New York Public Library and the YMCA, both on 135th Street. At the former, librarian Ernestine Rose held poetry readings and discussions on books and culture. She also exhibited African sculpture. These cultural events were attended by individuals who became major African American artists, figures such as Countee Cullen (1903–1946), Langston

Six poets trying to write a poem.

PHILIP JOHNSON ARCHITECT, ON THE DESIGN TEAM FOR LINCOLN CENTER IN NEW YORK CITY

U

URBAN CULTURAL INSTITUTIONS

Modernity and Specialization

In 1954 Joseph
Papp established
the New York
Shakespeare
Festival, which in
1957 began offering
free, city-supported
performances in
Central Park.

PAGE 501

♦ Ethnology

*A science that deals with the
division of human beings
into races and their origin,
distribution, relations, and
characteristics; anthropology
dealing chiefly with the
comparative and analytical
study of cultures*

Hughes (1902–1967), and Jacob Lawrence. Rose also accumulated a major collection of African American studies materials with the help of the Carnegie Foundation, and this collection and library itself was later renamed the Arthur Schomberg Collection. As David Levering Lewis puts it, "the intellectual pulse of Harlem throbbed at the 135th Street library" (p. 105). Complementing the activities of the Library, the "Y" gave theater performances. There was also a Harlem Symphony. Though European arts were often featured at these places, African and African-American culture was of central concern. Harlem cultural institutions set a precedent that would be followed by museums like MOMA and the Metropolitan as well as specialized museums that eventually took African and African-American artifacts and cultural expression seriously by presenting them as art forms.

ETHNOLOGY. The interest in national, ethnic, and folk forms was first reflected in ethnology collections displayed in early museums like Peale's. World's fairs often included such artifacts, too. One of the earliest museums to departmentalize its ethnology collection was the Brooklyn Museum, in 1903. The idea of housing such collections in specialized exhibits was eventually adapted to entire museums, as exemplified by the establishment of Santa Fe's Museum of Navaho Ceremonial Art, and New York's Museum of Primitive Art and Museum of Early American Folk Art. A similar pattern occurred with regard to collections of national art and artifacts. Museums founded to highlight distinct national traditions included New York's Whitney Museum of American Art, Tulsa's Thomas Gilcrease Institute of American History and Art, Fort Worth's Amon Carter Museum of Western Art (featuring art and artifacts of the American West), Brooklyn's Jewish Museum, and Chicago's Polish Museum of America.

DISPLAY SPACES. The important shifts that occurred regarding collection emphases and practices clearly reflect the influence of modernity, with its machine and commercial landscape and its altered demographic patterns. These forces also effected changes in audiences and the way museums responded to them. Commerce and "mass media changed standards of receptivity," Neil Harris has argued, because they offered "images and information on a daily basis, fresh and immediate, easily available;" they made the museum, in particular, seem "stodgy and fatiguing" by comparison (*Cultural Excursions*, p. 144). Consider the influence of a popular modern urban in-

stitution, the department store. Harris correctly notes that the museum and the department store have shared several things: the time of their birth (the 1870s), their function (displaying artifacts), and techniques (the art of display). They even shared the same architectural style. Harris asserts that museums, fairs, and department stores served the ideal that valued continuity with the past. Each put art and beauty in a high position. But by the 1920s, museums were threatened by commerce: the department store was replacing the museum as an attraction and an arbiter of taste. While museums were dull, poorly lit, daunting, and uncomfortable, department stores had become innovators in the techniques of display and comfort as well as in the development of educational exhibits and demonstrations of various kinds, all to attract customers. Critic Forest H. Cooke, in a 1926 issue of *Century Magazine*, revealed the extent to which department stores had begun to set a standard for judging museums when he wrote, museum "rooms open to the public should be of great beauty as rooms, well ventilated, restful, and inviting leisure." Metropolitan Museum of Art president, Robert W. deForest, acknowledged the museum's failure when he admitted to a group of department store executives in 1930: "You are the most fruitful source of art in America." This competition pushed museums to move from being mere storehouses to becoming appealing display spaces.

As museums moved into the mid-twentieth century and beyond, they became part of the modern popular consumer reality through the use of modern display ideas and techniques borrowed from marketing and media. They created simplified spaces and backdrops for art, highlighted particular works, used dramatic lighting, emphasized advertising, promotion, and education, designed logos, and held blockbuster shows. Collections and exhibitions were made accessible to the public through special catalogues, tape-recorded tours, and slide-shows screened in special media rooms. Museums, theaters, and libraries became retailers of products linked to their collections and exhibitions. Most cultural institutions now contain stores that sell posters, reproductions, postcards, slides, books, T-shirts, and artifacts like earrings that reflect "good" design and the particular specialty of the organization. All these activities have reflected the increased pressure to draw mass audiences.

By the same token, businesses became more involved in culture. Corporations began to collect and display art at their home offices. Some, like the Philip Morris Company and Container Corporation of America, advertised themselves in magazines using works of art. Corporate sponsorship of increasingly expensive special exhibitions became common, too. During the early 1970s, Dayton's Department Store, in downtown Minneapolis, donated space on its top floor so that Walker Art Center could continue to exhibit while its new building was being completed. Such patronage not only advertised businesses but made them appear as good cultural citizens. The most dubious instance of this kind of collaboration occurred when several "historical" costume shows were put on during the 1980s at New York's Metropolitan Museum of Art, all curated by museum consultant Diana Vreeland, former fashion editor at *Vogue* and *Harper's Bazaar*. These exhibits were curiously linked with commercial activities occurring outside the museum. One pairing was the Met's "Chinese Imperial Robes" show and Bloomingdale's sales venture that featured "Imperial" Chinese artifacts and crafts. Others conjoined the Met with fashion entrepreneurs: "Twenty-five Years of Yves Saint Laurent" (1983), one of Mrs. Ronald Reagan's favorite designers, and "Man and the Horse" (1984), sponsored by Polo/Ralph Lauren. Such examples reflect blatantly what Debora Silverman has termed, a "movement of aristocratic invocation in 1980s American culture, whose participants combined representation from the worlds of the museum, the department store, fashion design, and media."

SUPPORT. American cultural institutions have been unique in the sense that most have been private organizations controlled and supported by private philanthropy. By contrast, Europe's great cultural institutions have been governmentally owned and supported. A few American cultural institutions like the Smithsonian, most public libraries, and more recently, urban arts complexes like New York's Lincoln Center and Washington's Kennedy Center (both created after 1960) provide an exception to this rule, though some—like Washington's National Gallery and Hirshorn Museum—have benefited greatly from private money. Government involvement in American art did not occur in any systematic way until the 1930s with the WPA's Federal Projects for Art, Writers, Theater, and Music; the Treasury Department's Arts Program; and the Farm Security Administration's History Section with its film and photography division. As already noted, the governmental arts projects of the 1930s stimulated the urban arts by putting artists to work, and making their productions available to the public;

but this died at the start of World War II. Government support for the arts did not again occur until the 1960s, when the National Endowments for the Arts and the Humanities were created in 1966. These agencies have been extremely valuable in helping urban cultural institutions meet the increasing costs of putting on exhibitions and programs. Indeed, without the Endowments, some arts organizations would have had to cut back or might have failed completely.

Postmodernism, Popular Culture, and Politics

Since the end of World War II, many new museums, repertory theaters, and opera companies have been established—institutions such as New York's Guggenheim Museum, the Los Angeles Museum of Contemporary Art, Atlanta's High Museum, the J. Paul Getty Center near Los Angeles, Minneapolis's Tyrone Guthrie Theater, the Vivian Beaumont Theater at New York's Lincoln Center, New York's Public Theater (its Shakespeare in the Park productions have been of unique importance in repopularizing the Stratford Bard), the Sante Fe Opera, and Montgomery, Alabama's Carolyn Blount Theater (home of the Alabama Shakespeare Festival). The number of orchestras continued to increase, too, as did ballet and dance companies. George Balanchine's New York City Ballet became the resident company at Lincoln Center; the Dance Theatre of Harlem appeared, as did other private companies

URBAN CULTURAL INSTITUTIONS

Postmodernism, Popular Culture, and Politics

All communities have a culture. It is the climate of their civilization.

WALTER LIPPMANN

CHOREOGRAPHER

Alvin Ailey, director of the Alvin Ailey dance troupe.
UPI/CORBIS BETTMANN

U

URBAN CULTURAL INSTITUTIONS

Postmodernism, Popular Culture, and Politics

. . . I derive genuine pleasure from touching great works of art. As my fingertips trace line and curve, they discover the thought and emotion which the artist has portrayed.

HELEN KELLER
BLIND/DEAF AUTHOR, THE
STORY OF MY LIFE

like those of Merce Cunningham, Alvin Ailey, and Twyla Tharp. Performance art, in particular, evolved new forms like "Happenings," and museums around the country began to expand their offerings to include live presentations of all kinds as well as film programs and poetry readings.

Most twentieth-century cultural institutions, with the exception of the theater, have tended to perpetuate a high-culture canon, but they have also striven to educate large audiences by courting popularity. Museums and theaters have been more receptive than symphony orchestras and opera companies to featuring modernist works. Concert-goers and opera lovers have been very conservative regarding the repertoire they support, though a few organizations such as the Saint Paul Chamber Orchestra have emphasized modern music. Theater, however, is more difficult to discuss in terms of the types of works offered and levels of taste.

Recall that the theater had been one of the most democratic art forms during the 1800s, and that Shakespeare was wrenched by elites from the popular domain during the second half of the nineteenth century. A further segregating of theater audiences occurred when avant-garde production companies were founded in the 1910s. Chicago's Little Theater appeared in 1912, and the Provincetown Players was begun in Provincetown, Massachusetts, in the summer of 1916, and moved to New York that fall. The picture was further complicated by the fact that "little theaters" cropped up in small cities all over America, but instead of offering an experimental fare, these "civic" theaters brought popular plays as well as serious "classics" to townspeople. Popular commercial theaters were thriving also, offering vaudeville, burlesque, conventional melodrama and farce, and a newly developing genre, the musical. Theaters with widely differing purposes continued to exist into the present; they range from New York's commercial Broadway houses, summer-stock playhouses, and dinner theaters to urban public theaters, amateur production companies, university groups, and experimental theaters (such as New York's Off-Off-Broadway houses and companies like New York's La Mama Experimental Theatre Club and Chicago's Steppenwolf Theatre Company).

The urban cultural scene of the past forty years has shown great flexibility with its variety of forms and styles and its openness to change. Postmodernism—the mode of pastiche, surface, and eclectic style—became the apt characterization for the creative output of much of the period. Highbrow art and low, popular culture and elite remained the categories around which discussions of art often centered, but they hardened *and* became increasingly slippery in their application. Beginning in the 1920s with the Frankfurt School thinkers, intellectuals sought to keep them theoretically separate and pure, but practically, they continued to be as amorphous as ever. Throughout the century, defining art and judging quality were complicated by the persistent challenges of the avant-garde artists like Alfred Stieglitz, Marcel Duchamp, John Cage, and Merce Cunningham; events like the Armory Show; and institutions like the Museum of Modern Art. New materials like welded steel, found objects, and neon light, and technologies like video, laser, computers, and synthesizers mixed things up. So did the appropriation (intact or in combination or through caricature) of discarded styles and motifs. And the fact that popular forms like the movies and jazz and pop music performances became thought of as art added to the confusion. By the 1960s, even rock and roll began to be taken seriously by cultural commentators like the critic Susan Sontag and composer Ned Rorem, and exhibitions touching upon popular culture were more frequently sponsored by museums—for example the Metropolitan Museum's "Harlem on My Mind" (1969) and MOMA's "High and Low (1990–1991)."

The art and literary worlds were also made to face certain absences that were inbred in their exhibition and publishing practices. Feminism, in particular, forced cultural institutions to admit that the work of women artists had been grossly neglected. Women had played significant roles in the American art world during the nineteenth century. The Women's Pavillion at the 1893 Chicago Columbian Exposition was a notable reminder of that fact. Women, moreover, were a prominent part of the avant-garde during the first third of the twentieth century. Harriet Monroe was the founder and editor of *Poetry* and Margaret Anderson headed *The Little Review*. Mabel Dodge presided over a salon that drew together some of the best artists and minds of the second decade of the twentieth century. Mary Cassatt, Gertrude Stein, Isadora Duncan, Amy Lowell, and Georgia O'Keeffe were well-regarded artists. Katherine Dreier, Lillie P. Bliss, Gertrude Vanderbilt Whitney, and Abby Rockefeller were patrons who were instrumental in the founding of distinguished museums. And the 1917 Independents' show in New York was an art exhibition where "women took center stage"—of the 1,235 artists exhibited, 414 were women.

Yet, though women continued thereafter to be distinguished in the American cultural world, they did not effectively challenge the essentially male power structure until the late 1960s. It would be another decade before the hard questions feminists were asking confronted the museum world in the guise of an exhibition: Judy Chicago's *The Dinner Party* (1973–1979) opened in March 1979 at the San Francisco Museum of Modern Art. The work, a large installation piece—a triangular-shaped table with embroidered tablecloths, porcelain plates, cups, and dinnerwear—was a collaborative effort that embodied the history and mythology of women through images, language (the names of famous women), and sculpture. Though the expensive production received about $40,000 in support from the National Endowment for the Arts, the only major museums that exhibited it were San Francisco's Modern and New York's Brooklyn Museum. Still, serious issues were raised and remain as an important part of the art discourse of the late twentieth century.

Once again, culture was politicized. By 1990, the battle lines were clearly drawn between a new set of custodians of elite culture like Allan Bloom and Hilton Kramer (supported by politicians such as Republican Senator Jesse Helms of North Carolina) and the new cultural radicals who were challenging the traditional (white, male) canon of artworks and fighting for feminist as well as gay rights and multicultural agendas. The conflict reached its most vocal level when the National Endowment for the Arts suddenly struck a cultural nerve by funding, among other things, a traveling exhibition of the work of Robert Mapplethorpe (1946–1989). Because Mapplethorpe was gay and his nude photographs were considered by some people to be obscene, the participating museums and the Endowment came under fire from the cultural and political Right. This time, major cultural institutions could not ignore the struggle. Some openly fought against the conservatives by refusing grants from a newly politicized NEA. Others capitulated by bowing to censorship. Funds for the Endowment were reduced by Congress, and so the agency ceased to underwrite proposals that might be controversial. The cultural war soon faded, but the fires that it generated still smolder.

Conclusion

In 1839 Alexis de Tocqueville could not predict the particulars of the course that the arts would take during the following century and a half. Yet, he was uncannily correct in his observations regarding the socio-economic forces and conditions that would influence the production and appreciation of art. Whether he was right in assuming that art would be degraded and appreciation shallow is still hotly debated. Of course, he could in no way have imagined the half-tone revolution and the invention of the movies that occurred in the 1890s, nor could he have had an inkling of the twentieth-century phenomena of radio, recorded sound, television, and the computer. Technological innovations as well as social changes have had an extraordinary impact on the arts and, thus, on the institutions that have promoted them. Regrettably, there has been too little space here to do more than survey broadly the development of urban cultural institutions and their influences. Missing, for example, is discussion of the moviehouse and the university, both of which have been important agencies in bringing culture to urban audiences. Still, I hope that the reader has at least a sense of the richness and complexity that is part and parcel of the evolution of American cultural life. Art has been alive and well in the United States for over two hundred years. Culture in the sense that Matthew Arnold defined it now touches more lives than ever before, and urban cultural institutions have contributed immensely to that result.

—RALPH F. BOGARDUS

URBAN PARKS

The word "park" originally had little connection with towns or cities. In medieval and early modern England, "park" described "an enclosed tract of land held by royal grant or prescription for keeping beasts of the chase." Such parks—often called deer parks in reference to the animals gathered in them—grew in number in the sixteenth century as English aristocrats and gentry families cleared and enclosed large tracts of land around their country estates, sometimes taking over entire villages and common fields. Eighteenth-century landlords continued the "imposition and theft" that characterized the English enclosure movement, the cultural critic Raymond Williams tells us. In the process the meaning of "park" shifted from a hunting woodland to an artificially constructed scenic landscape. With the help of landscape gardeners like Humphrey Repton and Lancelot ("Capability") Brown, these landlords created, as Williams writes, "the view, the ordered

One of the attractive things about flowers is their beautiful reserve.

HENRY DAVID THOREAU
JOURNAL (JUNE 17, 1853)

See also
The City

No town can fail of
beauty, though its
walks were gutters
and its houses
hovels, if venerable
trees make
magnificent
colonnades along
its streets.

HENRY WARD BEECHER
PROVERBS FROM PLYMOUTH
PULPIT (1887)

proprietary repose, the prospect"—"a rural landscape emptied of rural labour and labourers; a sylvan and watery prospect, with a hundred analogies in neo-pastoral painting and poetry, from which the facts of production had been banished" (The Country and the City, pp. 122–125).

The English gardeners' carefully crafted landscapes were intended to mimic or improve upon nature while making it appear as though no human hands had intervened. And since their work "was centered upon the great expanse of land and woods that in the typical large country place was simply called the Park," historian Norman Newton points out, their artificially natural landscapes became closely associated with the term "park" (*Design on the Land*, p. 20). English travelers readily extended this usage to the royal and aristocratic grounds of the Continent, where landscape gardeners initially adhered to a more formal style in arranging nature for human edification and enjoyment.

Only in the late eighteenth and early nineteenth centuries did parks become identified with cities. German towns, for example, turned old fortifications into public gardens. The London public had been conditionally admitted to royal grounds like Hyde Park from the seventeenth century, and gradually other royal lands were opened to public use. By the early nineteenth century, municipal and national governments in England and on the Continent had begun to establish and landscape new public parks that represented the romantic ideal of *rus in urbe*—country in the city.

Although this history closely linked the term "park" with designed natural landscapes, there has long existed an alternative, but more difficult to document, vernacular tradition associated with the concept of public open space, if not always the specific word "park." The cultural geographer J. B. Jackson contrasts "two types of park land": the " 'designed' parks" produced by landscape gardeners and " 'unstructured' playgrounds," where at least until the late nineteenth century "the common people and particularly adolescents, could exercise and play and enjoy themselves, and at the same time participate in community life." Jackson finds evidence of these unstructured areas in the churchyards of medieval Europe, in the stretches of undeveloped land outside the city walls or along riverbanks (what the French call *terrains vagues*), and in the "grove out in the country near the river" (*American Space*, pp. 127–130).

This same dual heritage of vernacular and designed public spaces marks the development of

urban parks in the United States. One strand of the vernacular tradition stretches back to the New England commons—spaces held by the community for shared utilitarian purposes (for example, grazing cattle or gathering fuel) as well as for public assemblies, particularly militia drills. Another strand included the eighteenth-century commercial proprietors who opened private parks, modeled on London's pleasure gardens, for outdoor entertainments. More elusive to historical recovery, though, are the innumerable open spaces appropriated by youths and adults for sports and games. In late-eighteenth- and early-nineteenth-century Baltimore, for example, boys played in a "public square," and Colonel John Eager Howard opened his private estate—"Howard Park"—as a recreational space for city residents. The city's springs provided another popular recreational spot. Early-nineteenth-century Brooklynites similarly turned the privately owned land along the bluffs of Brooklyn Heights into a popular setting for public promenades and socializing.

The growth of cities and the urban real estate market placed increasing pressure on these informal "common" spaces. In Baltimore, donations of land from the Howard estate for Lexington Market, the Baltimore Cathedral, and the Washington Monument gradually ate away at Howard Park until it had disappeared by the 1840s. As early as the 1820s, Brooklyn landowners "infected with the rage for improvement" eroded the "elegant walk" along Brooklyn Heights by tearing down trees and fencing their lands ("Promenade to Park," p. 532). In response, city officials increasingly marked out more formal, specialized, and publicly owned spaces and designated them as parks. New York's Common, for example, had served a diverse set of purposes in the seventeenth and eighteenth centuries—pasture ground for cattle, the setting for executions, the home of the almshouse and jail, and the site of public festivals and protests. But only in 1797—five years after it was enclosed for the first time—was it labeled "The Park" (rather than The Fields or The Common) on a city map. And the designations "City Hall Park" or "The Park" only became widely used in the first decade of the nineteenth century, when the area was landscaped during the construction of City Hall.

Other American cities also set aside open spaces—sometimes called parks but more often commons or squares. Drawing on English models, for example, William Penn's 1683 Philadelphia plan and James Ogelthorpe's 1733 Savannah plan reserved squares that were later surrounded

See also
Landscapes

by residences and institutions. Similarly, the 1811 street plan that established New York's famous grid street system set aside seven open spaces, most less than twenty-five acres (ten hectares). And in the next three decades, local real estate developers won city officials' sanctions to create private squares—Gramercy and St. John's parks, in particular—as the center of elite residential neighborhoods and promenades.

In the late 1830s and 1840s, wealthy and middle-class families also satisfied their desires for a public venue in which to see and be seen by resorting to "rural" cemeteries landscaped in the English romantic style. Cambridge's Mount Auburn, Philadelphia's Laurel Hill, and Brooklyn's Greenwood cemeteries helped to foster a taste for pastoral landscapes and a habit of urban picnickers and excursionists seeking "country," within the city. Urban gentry families also took up horticulture and hired landscape gardeners like Andrew Jackson Downing to improve their country estates.

Yet elite families still complained that their cities lacked proper parks, by which they meant large landscaped public grounds in the European tradition. Gentlemen merchants and their wives, who visited Europe for business and pleasure, bemoaned the contrast between European and American public spaces. *The New York Times* was "mortified" by the contrast between the grand parks of London, Paris, and Brussels and New York's "penurious" 145 acres (48 hectares) of public spaces (23 June 1853).

Nowhere was the pressure to imitate landscaped European public parks greater than in the nation's largest city, New York. Starting around 1850, the city's leading merchants and bankers—seconded by many of its newspaper editors—campaigned to create a grand, public park as a way of establishing New York's credentials as an international capital. Such a park, moreover, would provide appealing scenic vistas through which members of their class could ride their carriages.

As would be true in other cities, the movement for a large public park won support beyond the merchant class. Owners of land surrounding the proposed sites realized that such an amenity would greatly enhance the value of their property by attracting wealthy families to live near the park. And some social reformers believed that a park would improve the health and morals of the city's poorer citizens; it would serve as the "lungs of the city" and as an instrument of social improvement. Yet not all reformers agreed: leaders of the public health movement, for example, argued

that removing land for a large public park would only exacerbate the city's housing problems—the source of the most serious health ills. Moreover, many working-class New Yorkers argued that smaller, dispersed downtown parks would be less aristocratic and more democratic.

After two years of debate, in 1853 the state legislature authorized New York City to use powers of eminent domain to acquire more than seven hundred acres in upper Manhattan for Central Park. After a design competition in which politics figured prominently in the outcome, the park commissioners selected the Greensward Plan of the English-immigrant architect Calvert Vaux (who had also worked as a junior partner to Andrew Jackson Downing) and Frederick Law Olmsted, Sr., the park's superintendent. Vaux and Olmsted crafted their design largely according to the English pastoral tradition. The designers proposed open meadows and picturesque woodlands that would offer a refreshing antidote to the bustle and aesthetic monotony of city streets. They further separated the park from the city by sinking the four commercial roads that crossed the park beneath the surface so ordinary traffic would not interfere with the continuous movement of parkgoers' views.

In selecting the Greensward Plan for what would become the nation's most influential public park, the commissioners narrowed the definition of a park. They rejected those plans that worked within the more classical, continental design tradition with formal avenues and gardens. And they even more firmly ruled out the possibility that the park would be organized within the more eclectic, vernacular tradition of commercial pleasure gardens, which liberally mixed all styles of art and decoration to create recreational spaces answering popular desires for novelty and diversion.

As soon as Central Park opened to ice skaters in December 1858, it spawned imitators. The following year, according to David Schuyler, *The Horticulturalist* observed that parks were becoming "the great features in all cities of any importance" and credited "the great Central Park" for providing the "initiative" and the "conviction of their importance" (quoted in *The New Urban Landscape*, p. 101). By 1861, Philadelphia, Baltimore, Brooklyn, Hartford, and Detroit had begun to plan for their own landscaped urban parks. In 1865, Olmsted and Vaux designed Brooklyn's Prospect Park.

Philadelphia's Fairmount Park had been laid out earlier in the century to "ornament" the city's waterworks on the banks of the Schuylkill River;

I like trees because they seem to be more resigned to the way they have to live than other things do.

WILLA CATHER
O PIONEERS! (1913)

545

and in the mid-1850s, Philadelphia greatly expanded the park's area. In 1859—following the precedent set in New York—the park's designers (James C. Sidney and Andrew Adams) were selected in a competition. But the coming of the Civil War as well as further piecemeal additions meant that Fairmount Park was not entirely completed until the Centennial Exposition was held there in 1876.

Developments moved much more swiftly in Baltimore, which purchased a five-hundred-acre estate for Druid Hill Park in 1860. The landscape gardener Howard Daniels, who had won fourth prize in the Central Park competition, designed a romantic landscape. But design was not the only lesson that park-makers learned from Central Park: they also grasped the close and enduring connection between park development and real estate profits. Schuyler quotes the *Baltimore American*, noting the rise in property values around Central Park, and forecasting that the "cost of the entire park would be materially reduced by taking into consideration the probable enhanced value of the city property contiguous to its borders" (p. 109). One final lesson that Baltimore learned from New York was regulation: Druid Hill opened in 1860 with twenty-six carefully worded rules and regulations prohibiting everything from abusive language and gambling to the fast driving of carriages and picnicking without permission.

Despite the pervasive adoption of the pastoral landscape model for the nation's urban parks in the late nineteenth century, it would be a mistake to assume that the impulse to create these parks represented an equally pervasive antiurbanisrn—a Jeffersonian retreat from the city. As Daniel Blue-

URBAN PASTORAL

This 1961 photo of Central Park, the nation's most influential public park, illustrates the remarkable pastoral beauty within an urban setting achieved by designers Frederick Law Olmsted and Calvert Vaux.
CORBIS-BETTMANN

stone points out in his history of Chicago's park system, energetic park advocates were also the strongest boosters of the city itself. But in some cities park referenda revealed resistance to this pro-growth vision. In Saint Louis and Minneapolis, for example, working-class voters initially opposed proposals for large parks located far from their neighborhoods.

Still, in these cities as well as in Chicago the New York model proved influential. Illinois Lieutenant Governor William Bross credited his own interest in a grand landscaped space to a long discussion about Central Park that he had with Olmstead atop the Sierra Nevada. And in 1869, Chicago turned to Olmsted, Vaux & Company (which was simultaneously designing the nearby suburb of Riverside) to draw up the plans for the city's South Parks. What set Chicago apart from New York—but made it typical of cities from Buffalo to Boston—was that the 1869 bills establishing its parks created a citywide system, with six large parks connected by landscaped boulevards. Landscape architects like Horace W. S. Cleveland, who outlined a regional park system for Minneapolis and Saint Paul in 1883, anticipated the comprehensive city planning movements of the twentieth century.

As the park movement took hold in small as well as large cities, city residents continued to debate the definition of a public park. In 1870 Edward Winslow Lincoln became chairman of the Commission on Shade Trees and Public Grounds in Worcester, Massachusetts—an industrial city with about forty thousand residents. The city's parklands consisted of an eight-acre Common and a twenty-eight acre tract known as Elm Park. Imbued with the naturalistic aesthetic, Lincoln transformed the unsightly Elm Park into a mini-Central Park with broad stretches of lawn and artistically arranged trees and shrubs. He also sought to banish active and eclectic uses of Elm Park. Circuses, which had earlier lost their home on the Common, were banned in 1875. Three years later, the soon-to-be-familiar "keep off the grass" signs were given legal sanction. Baseball playing continued, but Lincoln hoped that this "dreary," amusement would soon be removed from his cherished Elm Park to specially designated playing fields in "different sections" of the city. The rowdy, exuberant, collective style of socializing that characterized many immigrant working-class communities in this era was the antithesis of what Lincoln wanted for Elm Park.

This clash between what J. B. Jackson calls "two distinct and conflicting definitions of the park"—"the upper-class definition with its emphasis on cultural enlightenment and greater refinement of manners, and a lower-class definition emphasizing fun and games"—continued throughout Lincoln's park regime (1972, pp. 214–215). When wealthy residents petitioned to triple the size of Elm Park, which was located adjacent to city's most affluent neighborhood, working-class Worcesterites objected. If Elm Park were to be expanded, they insisted, then the city must provide space for "the less favored children" in the city's working-class neighborhoods. Through their political mobilization they not only gained two parks for the working-class East Side but also won the designation of those parks as "playgrounds" rather than landscaped parks."

In some cities, class divisions over park use were less readily visible. For example, Saint Louis's Forest Park (opened in 1876) included numerous baseball and soccer fields as well as a racetrack for trotting matches, a feature deliberately excluded from many northern parks for fear of attracting mixed-class crowds of gamblers and sports. And unlike Central Park and other eastern parks, Forest Park regularly accommodated the large picnics of German and other ethnic fraternal associations. But Saint Louis park officials, like those in other border and southern cities, promoted racial segregation by defining the smaller Tandy Park as a "black park."

Late-nineteenth-century parks also accommodated middle-class Americans' growing enthusiasm for active sports. In the 1880s and 1890s, tennis courts were laid out on former meadows; by World War I most courts had been paved. In the 1890s, the bicycling boom erupted on park drives. By the first decade of the twentieth century, golf courses in city parks offered a new mode of communing with nature.

Some of these new sports altered patterns of socializing in parks. In the mid-nineteenth century, park officials had regarded women as a special class of parkgoers who required protection. By the 1890s, the visibility of women cycling and

THE PEOPLE'S PARK

In the late nineteenth century, political contests over the definition of a park intensified alongside skirmishes over patterns of day-to-day use. In Boston, for example, Stephen Hardy notes that many working-class residents and their representatives regarded much of the city's "Emerald Necklace" park system as "rich man's parks" accessible only to those who owned "elegant equipages" ("Parks for the People," p. 17). But residents of poorer neighborhoods traded their support for these landscaped parks in return for receiving playgrounds and small parks in their own districts. Their political pressure also won changes in restrictive park rules to allow active sports, merry-go-rounds, and refreshment stands within the city's parks.

A similar process reshaped New York's Central Park. In the 1860s, the park's first decade of operation, the city's wealthiest citizens, riding in their carriages, dominated the park, which was tightly regulated under rules set down by Olmsted and the park board president, Andrew Haswell Green. But as political changes after 1870 made the park's administration more susceptible to the rough and tumble of city politics, rules were gradually loosened, and the park's design became increasingly eclectic. Rules prohibiting walking on the grass, the use of the carriage drives by commercial vehicles, ball playing by boys over sixteen, and Sunday concerts were modified or less rigorously enforced. At the same time, restaurants, commercial amusements (goat and pony rides and a carousel), and statues honoring cultural heroes of the city's immigrant communities appeared within the pastoral landscape. An extremely popular zoo brought Barnumesque amusements and boisterous crowds to the previously genteel park.

An equally powerful force for change came from growing numbers of immigrant, working-class New Yorkers who now found the park more accessible and more to their liking. As immigrant and working-class New Yorkers spread out across the landscape, they animated its natural scenery. On Sunday, "every seat, every, arbor, every, nook was occupied, and the music of human voices and laughter drowned and silenced the precocious chirping and whistling of insects and birds," a newspaper reported. "In these crowded centres the illusion of country was completely lost" (*New York Herald*, 20 August 1877). By early next century, enormous crowds turned out to see flower displays in the park's conservatory, fly-casting exhibitions on the park's lake, and elaborate sound-and-light shows in the meadows. Thus, the nineteenth-century ideal of *rus in urbe* gave way to "urb in rus" spectacles.

See also
Parades, Holidays and
Public Rituals

New York's secluded 840-acre Central Park, designed in 1858 with rustic areas and formal gardens, became the model for future suburban parks.

PAGE 57

playing tennis in city parks established the image of the "new woman" freely playing outdoors and socializing with men. But new recreational facilities also sharpened other lines of social segregation. Although black and white groups were allowed to picnic in Forest Park, its tennis courts, golf course, and playgrounds were more rigidly segregated. When black residents of Saint Louis challenged this "separate but equal" policy in court, they won small concessions—for example, the right to use the Forest Park golf course before noon on Mondays.

New park uses and users in the early twentieth century stirred other debates about what constituted a proper park. One position, marked out by progressives and their working-class allies, defined parks as utilitarian recreational spaces rather than as pastoral landscapes. This impulse found its clearest expression in the playground movement that spread across the country in the early twentieth century, but it was also reflected in earlier movements to create small parks in the poorer districts of the city. The advocates of small parks and playgrounds—most often middle-class social reformers—argued that organized and supervised play would "Americanize" new immigrants and remedy many of the ills of the city, particularly crime and juvenile delinquency. Playground movement leaflets luridly asked: "Shall We Provide a Playground? Or Enlarge the Jail?" Reformers stressed the need for structured and directed play. "On the vacant lot we can do as we please," one playground advocate noted disapprovingly, but "when we have a fenced playground it becomes an institution" (quoted in *The Park and the People*, pp. 146–147).

As was true of the intentions of nineteenth-century landscape architects, the dreams of playground advocates were often frustrated by the social realities of the city. Playgrounds probably had little impact on juvenile delinquency. And although reformers had promised to turn playgrounds into melting pots, playground use seems to have followed existing ethnic lines. Some city children viewed the playground supervisors cynically: "They get on me nerves with so many men and women around telling you what to do," complained one eleven-year-old about the playground workers in his city (quoted in *The Park and the People*, p. 151).

But if working-class children sometimes found the playground supervisors annoying and their rules restrictive, they (and their parents) nevertheless appreciated the increased recreational facilities and programs. After all, working-class families had long been fighting for more recreational space. Thus, while these city dwellers and their political representatives did not always share the reform goals of the playground movement, they often enthusiastically backed proposals to increase the number and availability, of swings, ballfields, swimming pools, and similar facilities.

At the same time that some early-twentieth-century progressives sought to remake public space in a recreational mold, others threw their support behind efforts to create monumental public spaces and institutions in line with the City Beautiful movement. City Beautiful advocates wanted to bring order to a seemingly chaotic city by designing wide tree-lined boulevards and grand civic centers. Unlike Olmsted and Vaux and the first generation of park designers, the adherents of City Beautiful wanted to visually integrate parks with the city. San Francisco, for example, acquired Sutro Heights and the top of Telegraph Hill as parklands primarily because they offered superb views of the city. The City Beautiful aesthetic both influenced the design of particular park systems—for example, those in Kansas City and Seattle—and accelerated the trend to place important civic and cultural institutions, particularly museums, within parks.

While playground proponents and City Beautiful advocates argued for transforming the "rural" park in order to accommodate new urban realities (whether new immigrants, automobiles, or the new scenic vista of skylines), preservationists and landscape architects reasserted a mid-nineteenth-century vision of the pastoral landscapes that resisted rather than embraced the city. They organized societies to protect aging parks from the encroachment of playgrounds and museums. In the 1920s, they started preserving and publishing the papers and writings of the founders of the urban park movement, such as Olmsted and Vaux.

The result of these countervailing forces is difficult to map on a national level. Nevertheless, most urban parks became increasingly eclectic as they added recreation features that appealed to new constituencies. Moreover, other forces of change proved as powerful as the ideological agenda of either progressive reformers or preservationists. The new urban immigrants who took possession of city parks infused them with their own distinctive modes of socializing—collective picnics, for example. Parks competed with other centers of commercial entertainment—amusement rides, spectator sports, and the movies. But public parks were free, and as administrators permitted new sports and pageants, parks took on some of the attractions of the commercial city.

See also

Popular Entertainment before the Civil War

The automobile, which had such a profound impact on the structure of American cities, also reshaped urban parks. Between 1900 and 1930, the number of Americans who owned cars went from eight thousand to twenty-three million. By the 1910s and 1920s, cars whizzed along the formerly sedate carriage roads of the large urban parks. And the parks themselves were reconfigured to accommodate cars: drives were straightened and asphalted, and parking lots displaced pastures. Still, between 1910 and 1930, as park systems dramatically expanded with suburban growth and annexation, urban planners promoted parks as antidotes to traffic and congestion. Parkmakers like George E. Kessler, who designed park systems in Kansas City, Dallas, Salt Lake City, and Toledo, gained national reputations within the new professions of urban planning and park administration. Probably the most influential figure in adapting open spaces to the automobile was Robert Moses. Beginning in the 1920s Moses laid out an enormous park system in New York State that was accessible only by car.

In 1934 Moses became commissioner of New York City's park system and brought his car-centered and recreation-oriented approach to park-making directly within the city. With the assistance of huge appropriations of New Deal funds, Moses transformed the city's park system, adding three hundred playgrounds, fifteen swimming pools, seven golf courses, and eight thousand acres of parkland. Despite his autocratic management style, Moses dramatically democratized the city's park system by bringing recreational facilities within the reach of most city residents. (Most, but not quite all: black neighborhoods remained underserved even after his massive expansion of the park system.) The West Side Improvement, a $200-million transformation of Manhattan's Riverside Park and the nearby railroad tracks, was a typical Moses project. It gave priority to the automobile (the most spectacular views were reserved for the car driver rather than the parkgoer); it reversed the pastoral emphasis of Olmsted's original Riverside Park plan by introducing playgrounds and tennis courts; and, notably, it failed to cover the railroad tracks where they ran through Harlem.

Despite the limitations of Moses and his vision, by the end of the 1930s Americans had come to view access to open urban space and recreational facilities almost as a fundamental right. The words "basic," "universal," and "essential" were now frequently coupled with "public parks"—an indication that they were accepted as necessary public services. Parks and playgrounds were now also routinely linked with other institutions like schools and housing. In 1941, for example, San Francisco began coordinating the work of its Housing Authority with the recreation and park departments. By the late 1940s in cities like Saint Louis, black residents had also successfully begun to challenge the segregation of such public recreation facilities as golf courses and tennis courts. As the civil rights struggle gained momentum in the South in the late 1950s and early 1960s, its targets included segregated public parks, beaches, and pools.

In the post–World War II era, the nation's urban parks increasingly suffered some of the woes of the cities themselves. In the 1950s and 1960s, cities underwent a dramatic social transformation as millions of white middle-class residents retreated to the suburbs and new migrants from the rural South and from Puerto Rico and Central and South America took their places. Some of the social tensions that resulted from that shift were manifest in a heightened concern about urban crime. Although parks generally had a lower crime rate than other parts of the city, they were often perceived as especially threatening environments, particularly at night. One-liners on late-night TV shows—"It was so quiet in Central Park last night, you could have heard a knife drop"—encapsulated and fostered the association of parks and crime.

Despite the crime scares, city dwellers never abandoned their parks. Indeed, in the late 1960s urban park use seems to have increased. Youthful adherents of the counterculture and the antiwar movement claimed public parks as their assembly points. At times—for example, in the fight over Berkeley's People's Park—they even waged struggles to secure and increase public open space within the city. In addition, growing interest in the environment and in physical fitness—particularly the jogging craze that began in the 1970s—brought new groups of regular users into parks. Finally, many park officials embraced a broader agenda for the spaces under their command. They much more willingly tolerated the use of parks for active recreation, rock concerts, ethnic festivals, and even political protests.

But if urban parks retained a vital social constituency in the 1960s, 1970s, and 1980s, their political constituency substantially eroded. As cities lost important portions of their tax base to the suburbs, they faced recurring fiscal crises in the 1970s and 1980s. When faced with difficult choices, city officials usually opted to cut park fa-

I just come and talk to the plants, really—very important to talk to them, they respond I find.

CHARLES, PRINCE OF WALES
TELEVISION INTERVIEW
(SEPT. 21, 1986)

*Earth laughs in
flowers.*

RALPH WALDO EMERSON
POEMS (1847)

cilities and maintenance rather than police, fire, or welfare services. Moreover, as white middle-class families abandoned cities, various governmental policies and corporate practices encouraged private solutions to public problems. In the late twentieth century, the distinction between designed and vernacular public parks has taken on a new connotation. For example, private organizations have raised money to restore and maintain what had come to be seen as landmarks, such as Central Park—supplying more than half its budget in 1990. But the majority, of urban parks, like public schools and housing, are increasingly viewed, at least within mainstream discourse, as unsafe, poorly maintained, and second-rate. Such views foster inadequate public funding, which make such perceptions into realities.

The neglect of urban public parks has been most dramatic when they are in poor and especially in black neighborhoods. Boston's Franklin Park, designed by Olmsted and his stepson as the "jewel" in the Emerald Necklace, was allowed to deteriorate in the 1960s and 1970s as its surrounding neighborhoods turned largely black. In the early 1980s, city officials virtually abandoned the park, assigning no full-time workers to the maintenance of this five-hundred-acre park.

Despite uneven and inadequate public funding, urban parks retained a vitality, and excitement that reflected the cities in which they were located. Even in the worst times, black residents of Roxbury took advantage of the space afforded by Franklin Park, and interracial groups like the Franklin Park Coalition fought to win improved maintenance. At times, urban parks became the setting for clashes between warring ethnic and racial groups, which sought to defend their "turf." But parks could also serve as one of the few peaceful meeting grounds for diverse sets of urban residents. While acknowledging the "patterns of caste and class stratification and polarization throughout society as a whole," New York City Park Commissioner Gordon Davis argued in 1981 that Central Park reflected a profound form of social democracy, a degree of social and racial integration not found elsewhere in the city. In the face of the urban fiscal crisis, the recession of the 1990s, and the movement of more Americans to the suburbs, emerging coalitions of park activists and environmentalists have suggested new models for creating and administering open public spaces. They have suggested, for example, converting abandoned canal and railroad routes into parks and organizing regional park districts to overcome the political barriers between the suburbs and the city. Yet, in the 1990s and beyond, Americans—beset by profound social divisions and faced by daunting urban fiscal problems—would have to struggle with whether they could manage to maintain and expand the degree of social democracy that they had won in their most important urban public spaces over the past two centuries.

—ROY ROSENZWEIG AND ELIZABETH BLACKMAR

VILLAGE AND TOWN

The history of America can be traced through its towns and villages and hamlets. These have served as the primary cells of the body politic, outposts of a migrant, westward-moving people, embryos of cities, and repositories of the dream of community. The small town has engraved a durable image upon the American collective unconscious—in social myth, literature, historical memory, ideals. Perhaps in no other national culture do the words "small town" pulsate with such strong positive and negative emotional currents—especially among those who grew up in such places. They elicit a deep ambivalence: attraction and repulsion, affection and repugnance, nostalgia and frustration. In a mobile, individualistic, ever-urbanizing (and sub-urbanizing) society the small town (a nonmetropolitan place of as few as two or three hundred up to twenty-five to thirty thousand people) has shown a remarkable durability, despite the social and economic forces impinging upon it, and it continues to be a symbol of deeply held American values of roots and community.

The Colonial Era

European immigrants, mainly from England in the early seventeenth century, planted the precursors of the modern American town. When the tide of transoceanic migration reached these shores, it divided into two streams, one originating on the land of the Massachusetts Bay Colony and the other on the territory of the Virginia Company. These disparate environments further influenced the patterns of early urbanization.

The first settlers of both regions were adjured to form towns. The obvious reason for such instructions was to provide mutual protection against the "hideous howling wilderness." But the principals in England also saw commercial advantages in settling groups of people with complementary skills on a single site, thus providing a division of labor capable, it was hoped, of exploiting the putative riches of the New World. The owners also regarded collective settlement as a means of ensuring social control, to prevent these good English men and women from reverting to savagery.

VIRGINIA. The Virginia Company ordered the teams of "planters" it backed to found "handsome towns," later modified to "compact and orderly villages." But the investors' vision of rows of brick houses along cobbled streets quickly shattered on the reefs of reality. The first settlement, Jamestown, founded in 1607, was a collection of huts surrounded by a wooden palisade. It was sited in a marshy area, and malaria wiped out large numbers of its inhabitants; fires and Indian raids finished the job.

Subsequent colonizing efforts similarly failed, until the settlers found their salvation in the profitable cultivation of tobacco (*Nicotiana tabacum*). This single-crop economy favored a plantation system of agriculture rather than one centered in the agricultural villages of Europe that provided the model in Massachusetts. Under the dominance of the landed proprietor, plantations became self-sufficient communities with their own stores and artisans—and a labor force of indentured servants and later slaves. A sprinkling of small farmers and freed bond servants formed a loose society of neighborhoods—networks of people who lived close enough to one another that each might practice some specialized trade useful to the others as well as cultivate a crop for private profit.

The primary governing institution of planter society, aside from the colonial legislature, was the county court; in the courthouse the records of all-important land transactions were kept, property disputes were settled, and justice was dispensed. Those with legal business journeyed many miles and put up at nearby taverns. Court sessions were social as well as civic events; the planters clattered in astride their fine horses and wearing colorful coats and high boots, seeking diversion from isolated plantation life. Churches were similarly situated in open countryside; the parish was the basic unit of religious governance.

The first settlements in Virginia were ports to which planters brought their crops for shipment to England and where they purchased a wide range of supplies. These entrepôts, comprising a few houses and stores, their docks piled with bales of tobacco at harvest time, were located at the

Boom towns like Rochester experienced unbelievable social disruption as thousands of transients came and went each year.

PAGE 505

See also
The City

V

VILLAGE AND TOWN

The Midwest in the Nineteenth Century

In the small towns of the country, however, we found the hospitality of the residents all that we could desire, and more than we could desire, and more than we could enjoy.

J. S. BUCKINGHAM
THE SLAVE STATES OF
AMERICA, 1839 (1842)

See also

Landscapes

heads of the numerous inlets, bays, and estuaries that formed natural harbors along the coastline of tidewater Virginia and neighboring Maryland's Chesapeake Bay.

And so Thomas Jefferson wrote in his *Notes on the State of Virginia* (1781): "We have no townships. Our country being much intersected with navigable waters, and trade brought generally to our doors . . . has probably been one of the causes why we have no towns of any consequence." The result was a scattered society that to visitors from England seemed primitive and anarchic. The writer John Aubrey (1626–1697) described some squatters he happened upon as "mean people who live lawless, nobody to govern them, they care for nobody, having no dependence on anybody."

Another inhibition to urban development in the South was the tendency of new groups of settlers to split up and claim individual tracts of the fertile bottomland rather than to band together to found a town. Periodically, the British authorities complained about the slow pace of urbanization, and they sent detailed plans with each new contingent of emigrants. But nearly one hundred years after the settling of Jamestown, the historian Robert Beverly (1673–1722) wrote that the people of Virginia "have not any place of cohabitation among them that may reasonably bear the name of town."

MASSACHUSETTS BAY. In contrast, by 1717 the Massachusetts Bay Colony claimed more than one hundred towns. The people in the northern stream of settlement were largely Puritan dissenters organized into homogeneous congregations. The first civic act of these groups was to draw up a covenant, setting forth the rights and obligations of each inhabitant, which all the original grantees (proprietors) had to sign. Town and church were coterminous, and congregations were self-governing. That unique New England institution, the town meeting, evolved from a church body into a political assembly open to all property holders and dealing with secular matters. Town meetings were the first independent political units of colonial America. As Alexis de Tocqueville wrote, "the doctrine of the sovereignty of the people came out of the townships and took possession of the states."

The system of town-founding by congregations was codified in colonial law. A group of people wishing to "plant" a town was required to draw up a covenant and apply to the legislature for a land grant. The proprietors then apportioned their tract among themselves according to need and rank. They laid out their habitats in the im-

memorial pattern of the English agricultural village—a parallel row of houses along a single street with long, narrow strips of fields extending perpendicularly behind the houses. Common land was set aside for the church and for pastures and meadows—thus the New England village green, site of the square wooden meetinghouse with its cupola and bell (later replaced by a tall-spired church). Initially, plots of land were worked communally, with families living in the village. But gradually communal farming gave way to individual ownership and control, and the more independent souls moved farther out. They were disapprovingly called "out-livers," and it was feared that, deprived of daily surveillance by pious neighbors, their morals would degenerate. They were required to live within a day's travel so they could at least attend church on the Sabbath.

Under the tight lid of religious conformity, enforced by the minister and church elders, the Puritan towns were small theocracies. Beneath a surface harmony, they bubbled with tensions and spites. The religious authorities sought to mediate the resulting disputes, lawyers being anathema to the Puritans. There were also incessant theological arguments, and the bacteria of dissenters might fester and poison the Christian ideals of love, harmony, and cooperation. Eventually the infection came to a head, and the dissenters were excommunicated or won control of the town meeting or seceded in a body—"hiving off," it was called—to found a new church elsewhere.

Collective agriculture was soon abandoned, as the harder-working, more proficient farmers accumulated additional tracts of land. Disparities in landed wealth formed the basis of class divisions between rich and poor. At death, the father's property was divided among all the sons and daughters (as dowries). In an era when families of ten or twelve children were common, the third generation found its portions too small to provide a living. As a result, the young and ambitious looked north and west, where virgin land abounded. Also eyeing this territory were speculators in town plots—a new breed of entrepreneurs who bought up a tract and sold it off in parcels, setting aside church and school lots, to groups or individuals. Thus the covenant gradually gave way to the cash nexus.

The Midwest in the Nineteenth Century

After the war of 1812, the vast public domain west of the Appalachians, known as the Old Northwest Territory, was opened to settlement. Communal groups from New England founded towns much like the ones they had left, but Puritan-style theocracy did not take hold; there were too many competing sects on the frontier. Nor did the town meeting prosper in the villages founded by New Englanders. The states carved out of the Northwest Territory adopted the township-county system as a compromise between New England and Virginia. If the architectural emblem of the New England town was the church spire, in the Midwest it was the courthouse cupola, symbolizing a society governed by secular, legal norms rather than religious precepts.

Many southern pioneers retained their aversion to town life and cleared small farms in the vast forests. Although some scions of the landed gentry brought slaves with them, the plantation system itself did not take root for a variety of reasons, political, moral, and economic. Instead, wealthy speculators became the largest landholders, buying up huge tracts of the best soil and selling portions to settlers or hiring tenants to farm them.

Pioneer towns were little more than log cabins strewn helter-skelter along a single street. Gradu-ally they metamorphosed into rows of frame houses with porches and lawns and backyards, along shaded streets down which clopped the spring wagons of merchants. The bell of the trolley car might be heard as it meandered along its appointed route, stopping whenever anyone hailed it. In the business district office blocks of beef-red brick rose two or three stories, a modest but dignified vernacular architecture. New, more elaborate courthouses rose in the central squares—edifices of brick or limestone with an imposing tower, elaborate masonry trim, a statue of a Union or Confederate soldier nearby, and benches for the old men who whiled away their days talking and whittling.

Still, the typical midwestern town was on the whole an ugly place of slatternly false-fronted buildings and unpaved streets that were rutted or muddy in winter and dusty and reeking of garbage and horse dung under the summer sun. Nearly every town had been laid out with a main street, often officially called that, which became the main business and social artery. Through it flowed the lifeblood of the town—its strollers and shop-

THE PIONEER VILLAGE
Creating a Town in the Midwestern Wilderness

The pioneer villages of the Midwest sprouted around crossroads taverns, along wilderness trails, at ferry landings, on the sites of forts built during the Indian wars. A few sprang up near deposits of coal and iron ore and carried on elementary manufacturing. Many a town grew up around a gristmill to which farmers brought their corn to be ground, or a general store where they bartered pork and cornmeal for supplies.

Economic rivalry among the embryonic pioneer towns was endemic. Competition for designation as a county seat, which guaranteed an economic base of courthouse business, touched off the fiercest battles. New settlements energetically vied for the prize, using bribery, trickery, and sometimes violence to advance their claims. Communities also competed for the farmers' trade. Inevitably, the economic interests of farmers and town merchants began to diverge as the latter charged what the traffic would bear. Farmers complained that dealers' grain prices were too low, storekeepers' prices too high, and bankers' interest rates too dear.

The typical midwestern country town of the nineteenth century had been founded as a real estate proposition by a speculator. Streets and town lots were laid out in the ubiquitous gridiron or checkerboard pattern, which was best adapted to the sale of individual lots. The boomers' cries of a glorious future were taken to heart by those who settled there, and they became an article of faith of the gospel of growth. Civic pride was perverted into the admonition "Boost, don't knock," and ever-rising property values became the central goal.

Yet in those towns which survived the vicissitudes of pioneer days, people put down roots and acquired a sense of belonging; in the nineteenth century it was said that people were "born into" a town much as they were born into a church. Memories of pioneer days, when people helped each other out of necessity and when birth and status counted for little, were still alive, contributing to a spirit of community. In the postpioneer period, a rudimentary civic spirit veneered the raw acquisitive energy and survival drive that had dominated the early days. Women, in their traditional role as nurturers and promoters of domesticity and culture, became vocal, demanding the introduction of amenities. One of the first gestures to posterity in western towns was to plant trees along the unpaved streets.

*New town forms
developed with
characteristic new
housing types.*

PAGE 213

See also

The Frontier

pers, its parades and celebrations, its political rallies.

Every Saturday farmers parked their buggies along it and embarked on their weekly shopping trip. To them the country town was a Rome, a Paris, an urban oasis at which to refresh grim, isolated lives. Country folk chatted in the courthouse square, purchased necessities and a few simple luxuries in dimly lit general stores redolent of harness leather and kerosene, and blinked sleepily at the new electric streetlights before heading home.

Meanwhile, the townspeople created their own recreational and cultural life: band concerts, baseball teams, cotillions and at homes, reading clubs, lectures by itinerant savants, shows by traveling theatrical troupes at the new opera house, circuses, revival meetings. The public schools were a boon to the farmers' sons and daughters who could attend them. High schools encouraged social mobility; they were stepping-stones to college and the cities. Human capital became one of the chief exports of the small towns. Surveys showed a disproportionately high percentage of scientists, business executives, and writers came from small towns. But rural areas battered by the ups and downs of farm prices also shipped their surplus sons and daughters to factories in the cities.

So to many, the hometown became the place you were from, a focal point of nostalgia. To its residents, it provided status, identity, and support. It also encouraged an insular civic pride, partly based on rivalry with other places; people felt *their* town was somehow superior to the next one, though an outsider might see little to choose between them. Small towns also declared their superiority to the cities. Preachers and editorialists promulgated the official gospel of small-town goodness and neighborliness, and inveighed against metropolitan alienation, immorality, and corruption.

After the turn of the twentieth century, rising prosperity on the farms, the economic lifeblood of the country town, contributed to a smug sense that here was the good life. Trains arrived eight or ten times a day, wreathed in smoke, noise, and commotion, bringing news and goods and travelers from the city. The station was a favorite meeting place for locals, who watched the trains whizzing by "with the languid scorn a permanent fixture always has for a transient and the pity an American feels for a fellow-being who does not live in his town," as Booth Tarkington wrote in his novel *The Gentleman from Indiana*.

Blacksmith shops, livery stables, drugstores, and saloons were male bastions of somewhat shady repute. Women's lives centered on their homes; their labors were dawn to dusk, sweating over coal-burning stoves, pumping water, heating water for baths or laundry. The days of their weeks were structured by well-worn ritual: Monday, washing; Tuesday, ironing; and so on through Sunday, reserved for church and the heavy noon meal that followed. Women traditionally held the family together and dominated their homes; outside the home they specialized in religious, charitable, and cultural activities and watched over the morality of their husbands and children. Their husbands pursued their small-business dreams, though many found only a precarious living and sank into a dependent role of "diminished potency and power," in the words of historian Page Smith. A kind of small-town matriarchy prevailed, except in the male preserves of politics and commerce.

Every town had its rich families that dominated civic and economic affairs. They set the social tone and encouraged class distinctions; newcomers aspiring to acceptance found they must undergo a long vetting process. Even small villages had two rudimentary classes: those who worked and saved and went to church, and the rest, who were "no-accounts." The poor were blamed for their plight and formed a separate caste.

Such divisions clashed with the egalitarian ethos small towns still professed. There were invidious racial and ethnic distinctions as well, with blacks and foreigners segregated into "Bucktowns" and "Polish Towns," the poor to their shantytowns. Gossip was a potent weapon of social control, enforcing loosely articulated norms of morality and respectability. Yet the grapevine also carried news of sickness or a death in the family, bringing help from neighbors. Although there was a certain latitude for eccentricity, woe to those who willfully defied public opinion. The tyranny of the majority, which Alexis de Tocqueville identified as the drawback of democracy in America, was most pronounced in small towns, imposing a stifling dullness and provincialism. This, and the lack of economic opportunity for young people, save those who had a family business waiting for them, drove the best and the brightest to seek city lights.

Prairie Junctions: Mining Camps and Cow Towns

During the 1870s and 1880s, covered-wagon loads—later trainloads—of immigrants, many of them communal groups from Europe, poured into the Great Plains. The foreign immigrants had

been recruited by agents for the railroad companies, which needed to populate the huge land
grants along their rights-of-way. Railroads became the leading town promoters in the Far West.
They laid out villages along their tracks at regular
intervals, and named them in alphabetical order
after railroad employees. Existing towns were told
that they must pay a subsidy or be bypassed. Im-
pelled by economic imperatives, town officials
paid up, raising the money by bond subscriptions.
They knew farmers must ship their produce to the
cities and would take their trade to the town that
had a grain elevator and a depot.

Farmers led lives of unrelieved toil and hardship. Agriculture was a precarious venture on the
Great Plains because of the ferocious storms, low
rainfall, and plagues of grasshoppers, and this retarded the growth of country towns. Railroads
that gained a monopoly in their area added to the
struggling farmers' costs by charging exorbitant
freight rates, a cause of the Populist revolt of the
1880s and 1890s.

"Precarious" was the word for towns in the
gold and silver country of California, Arizona,
and the Rocky Mountains. Here, the mining
camp was the primary form of settlement; it appeared wherever the precious ore was found.
These disposable towns, dubbed "rag cities" because they consisted mainly of tents, plus a store
or two and a shack that served as saloon, lasted
only as long as the gold or silver held out. Nevertheless, they developed a legal system adminis-

tered by ad hoc miners' courts which awarded
claims, resolved disputes, and held criminal proceedings not far removed from lynch law. Still, the
miners kept order, belying the reputation for rowdiness that mining camps acquired in romantic
fiction.

Another type of town indigenous to the West
with an exaggerated reputation for bumptiousness
was the cattle town. Dodge City, Abilene, Wichita, and other Kansas towns served in turn as
shipping points for beef on the hoof that had been
driven in great herds from Texas to be transported
to the abattoirs of Chicago. With the cattle came
hordes of dusty, rowdy drovers eager for recreation
after months on the trail.

The city officials' way of dealing with the free-
spending cowboys was to quarantine them: all the
saloons, bordellos, and gambling halls were confined to one side of the railroad tracks that ran
down the main street, while the respectable folk
lived on the other, insulated from the hell-raising
and leading humdrum lives. The cattle towns took
a perverse civic pride in their lurid reputations, inflated by eastern reporters in search of "color."
Even in their heyday, the cow towns had schools,
elections, churches, reform movements, economic
conflicts; and after the cattle trade departed, officials repented their wickedness in an effort to attract the once-scorned farmers, who had "stood in
the way of progress" by fencing the open range.

In California, the miners who had opened up
the state were followed by farmers and town-

V

VILLAGE AND TOWN

The Revolt from the Village

The clean, bright,
gardened townships
spoke of country fare
and pleasant
summer evenings on
the stoop. It was a
sort of paradise.

ROBERT LOUIS STEVENSON
ACROSS THE PLAINS (1892)

See also

Housing

boomers. Some of the old Spanish pueblos, presidios, and missions grew into towns and cities. A few mining camps acquired stability when industrial mining operations sank shafts to systematically extract ore-veined rock deep beneath the surface. Others were resurrected as agricultural centers.

The Revolt from the Village

By the early twentieth century, the fortunes of country towns were closely tied to national markets. A long-term exodus from the farms, hastened by the agricultural depression after the boom of World War I, and sustained by the mechanization of farming, gradually eroded the traditional economic base of the country towns. The larger towns diversified by attracting industries, but industrialization brought with it city-style problems—pollution, hardening class divisions, the decline of craftsmanship and the advent of mass production, and the replacement of local owners by distant corporate control. Labor unions were banned and local politics was dominated by business elites bent on keeping wages low and "agitators" out.

Attracting industry had other drawbacks. Many growth-obsessed towns offered excessive subsidies in the form of tax concessions and infrastructure improvements to attract new factories. Small-town businesses became dependent on large corporate suppliers that served national markets. In his classic 1923 essay "The Country Town," the iconoclastic economist Thorstein Veblen described small-town shopkeepers as mere "tollgate keepers for the distribution of goods and collection of customs for the large absentee owners of business."

Standardization, industrialization, and the rise of mass culture through radio, movies, and nationally distributed periodicals exposed provincial towns that prided themselves on their self-reliance and resistance to urban ways. The 1920 census was a watershed; it revealed that for the first time in American history more than half of the population dwelled in urban places of 2,500 people and above. And in an increasingly urbanized society, small towns were damned by urban intellectuals (most of them escapees) as backward and provincial.

The intellectuals and urbanites regarded prohibition as small-town morality writ large. The temperance movement had grown from frontier beginnings into a national crusade, culminating in the moral fervor of World War I and the passage of the Eighteenth Amendment. Prohibition pitted rural America against urban America. Walter

THE FACADE OF THE SMALL TOWN

The damning of small towns by urban intellectuals was particularly visible in fiction. At the turn of the century, when the influx from the country to the city was accelerating, writers such as Booth Tarkington and Zona Gale celebrated the friendliness and folksiness of small towns; but in the 1910s and 1920s, a new critical realism focused a pitiless gaze on the emotional and cultural aridity of small-town life, giving rise to a literary movement called "the revolt from the village." In 1915, Edgar Lee Masters's *Spoon River Anthology* removed the facade of hypocrisy from small-town lives in terse epigrammatic poems. Sherwood Anderson's *Winesburg, Ohio* (1919), a series of linked, plotless stories tinged by Freudianism, displayed villagers as sexually repressed grotesques. The most stinging indictment was Sinclair Lewis's satirical *Main Street* (1920), which caustically evoked the social and cultural ugliness of Gopher Prairie, Minnesota.

Lewis wrote of his fictional town, "This is America—a town of a few thousand. . . . [I]ts Main Street is the continuation of Main Streets everywhere." To the village rebels, the small town was a metaphor for American culture—its provincialism, fundamentalism, anti-intellectualism, materialism, Fordism. Indeed, in 1922 an anthology edited by Harold E. Stearns appeared under the bland but ironically intended title *Civilization in the United States*. Louis Raymond Reed, the contributor of the essay "The Small Town" wrote: "The civilization of America is predominantly the civilization of the small town" (p. 286).

Lippmann saw it as "a test of strength between social orders. When the Eighteenth Amendment goes down, the cities will be dominant politically and socially as they now are economically." From the ramparts of his *American Mercury*, H. L. Mencken hurled thunderbolts of invective against small-town morality and hypocrisy. To progressive urban intellectuals, small towns stood for nativist opposition to labor unions, foreigners, and radicalism. And there was truth to the indictment, for small-town businessmen embraced the big-business—Republican party credo of laissez-faire and low taxes.

After the village rebels had raked over small-town America, a wave of probing sociologists descended on it. One of the first such studies was Robert and Helen Lynd's *Middletown* (1929), which found in Muncie, Indiana, the conformity and conservatism that the novelists had shown. It was followed by *Middletown in Transition* (1937), analyzing the impact of the Great Depression on Muncie. Other prominent studies included W. Lloyd Warner and associates' five-volume "Yankee City" series about industrialization in Newburyport, Massachusetts, and his *Democracy in Jonesville* (1949), Hollingshead's *Elmtown's Youth* (1949), Blumenthal's *Small-Town Stuff* (1932), and James West's *Plainville USA* (1955). As late as the 1960s, Arthur Vidich and Joseph Bensman, in their *Small Town in Mass Society* (1968), could proclaim that an upstate New York town was "a backwash" and "the last link in America to the nineteenth century and its values." The inhabitants of "Springdale" still proclaimed the old values of individualism, self-help, and autonomy, even though their town had become dependent on state and federal aid. Its politics were dominated by a self-perpetuating elite skilled at extracting subsidies from the state, and its small businessmen were at the mercy of their big corporate suppliers.

Towns in the Industrial Era

The Great Depression was a watershed, undermining the traditional rural values of self-help and individualism. The 1930s saw an unprecedented intrusion of the federal government into local government. Small-town and rural people had traditionally relied on charity and neighborliness to cope with troubles too big for the individual to handle; poverty was considered a disgrace, and ending one's days at the county poor farm was a fate to be dreaded. And so when unemployment struck, its victims sought to hide their disgrace. A common saying during the Depression was "if I have to be poor I want to be poor in a city where everybody doesn't know I'm broke."

Even in industrial towns the old individualism retained its hold. In Muncie, the Lynds noted, the factory workers were mainly farm boys and "thus close to the network of habits of thought engendered by the isolated, self-contained enterprise of farming." Consequently, they clung to the dream of going into business for themselves and achieving financial success, rather than joining together to assert their economic interests. Similarly, business-dominated, small-town governments, chronically resistant to change and "rocking the boat," averted their eyes from the rising tide of misery among their constituents and

chanted the mantra of "Boost, don't knock." But they could not forever ignore the fact that their miserly poor-relief budgets were inadequate to deal with the misery lapping at their doorstep. Eventually, they swallowed their principles and accepted Uncle Sam's helping hand. Federal largess financed a host of public-works projects, from post offices to bridges to new roads. These improvements would never have been made by traditionally parsimonious town fathers.

The Depression brought many people from the cities back to the land, even as the wave of bankruptcies drove others off it. But the countryside was the net loser in this exchange. The rural exodus was temporarily stalled by the agricultural boom of World War II, but it resumed at an even faster pace after the war. More than 8.6 million people departed for cities in the 1940s; the flight continued at the rate of a million per year in the 1950s, and three-quarters of a million annually in the 1960s. The flight of southern blacks from the land was a major component of this human tide, as the mechanization of cotton picking made their labor unnecessary. In 1940 the rural population made up 40 percent of the national population; by 1970 it was only 26.5 percent. In 1975 only 4 percent of the total population was engaged in farming.

Small towns suffered, perforce, from the loss of farmers. A favorite statistic of rural sociologists is the 1:5 ratio—for every five farmers who move away, one business in town goes under. The proof of this theorem was visible in the boarded-up stores along every Main Street. In the 1960s small-town businesses were decimated by a new invader—the shopping mall, often a gallery of stores set down in a former cornfield. The automobile had long been choking Main Street; shopping malls with acres of parking lots and "stripvilles" of establishments catering to the car culture "solved" that problem—at the expense of downtown merchants. Revitalization of central business districts became the challenge of the 1970s. One strategy was restoration of old buildings and the introduction of pedestrian malls and more ample parking facilities.

The "Rural Renaissance"

During the 1970s, there was a modest turnaround in the fortunes of rural America. Countering a trend of country-to-city migration nearly as old as the republic, rural counties showed a 15.4 percent gain in population—around four million people in all. The counties with the lowest population densities had the largest increases.

The increasingly suburban character of many former agricultural towns can be traced to commuter schedules, inclusion of residents in society registers, and the growing demands for urban services.

PAGE 462

*God made the
country, and man
made the town.*

WILLIAM COWPER
"THE SOFA," THE TASK (1785)

The rush to the countryside sparked a flurry of stories in the press about a "rural renaissance," and demographers scrambled to understand what had happened. Their main conclusions: First, many of the migrants were acting out of the long-standing preference among Americans, consistently shown in opinion polls, for small-town or country living—more for the latter. Second, and a seeming corollary to this, many of the rural immigrants cited "quality of life" as their primary reason for moving. Dissatisfaction with decaying, crime-ridden cities (and overgrown suburbs) was possibly an impetus, but the pull of areas affording natural beauty, space, and privacy was even more decisive. Third, although the usual incentive for moving, economic betterment, was not often cited, the availability of nonfarming jobs—professional, white-collar, and blue-collar—in rural areas made the move feasible for many. This development resulted from diverse causes, including decentralization of industry facilitated by improved communications; the relocation of governmental facilities to low-density areas; the energy boom in the Appalachians, the West, and the "oil patch" states; cheap gasoline; the aging of the general population and a growing number of longer-lived, more affluent retired people who preferred small-town life; the proliferation of community colleges, which alleviated cultural isolation; and the growth of the recreation and nursing-home industries. As commuters to city jobs moved farther out, a new postsuburbia proliferated in the rural fringes of metropolitan areas. The result was clusters of homes that were neither urban nor rural; sociologists christened them "countrified cities" or "linear suburbs" or "plug-in towns."

The migration to rural areas brought problems: environmental degradation, pollution, and the loss of irreplaceable farmland. Some developers did not provide adequate roads or sewage lines; many unincorporated villages tapped groundwater, which was insufficient for their population and polluted by agricultural pesticides. Newcomers roiled the stagnant waters of local politics by demanding urban-style services. The aging machinery of county government creaked under the strain of the demands for services—sewage, paved roads, water.

All this raised a larger question: Would the immigrants seeking quality of life end up degrading that same quality of life? And what of the impact on democratic participation of a diffuse population living in "plug-in cities"? Would the inhabitants shun involvement in local government?

See also
The Suburbs

Would they take part in community activities in nearby towns? Would they form communities of their own? Or would the open land spawn an alienated population of latter-day outlivers, with no ties to place other than the financial nexus of real estate values?

The Future of the Small Town

By the mid-1980s, the rural renaissance stalled and the movement to urban areas resumed. Mining regions, hit by falling energy prices, suffered a net loss of 1.7 percent in population; nearly half of all rural counties declined in population. Counties in which manufacturing was the dominant economic activity were shaken by deindustrialization—the restructuring of the national economy from one dominated by manufacturing to one primarily geared to providing services. In Ohio, the heart of the Rustbelt, eighty of eighty-four counties showed a net loss of people.

The economic malaise in the rural areas was starkly etched in unemployment figures. Between May 1985 and May 1986, agricultural employment fell by nearly 4 percent, mining employment by more than 16 percent, and manufacturing employment by 0.6 percent. The rural poor increased by 43 percent between 1978 and 1983, according to the Census Bureau. A Senate subcommittee reported that during the 1980s, net farm income averaged nearly 40 percent less than in the 1970s. More than one thousand rural counties had unemployment rates above 9 percent, compared with the national average of 5.2 percent. Some towns became "rural ghettos."

The farm crisis of the 1980s delivered a devastating blow to agriculturally based towns. More than 270,000 family farms disappeared in a wave of bankruptcies; the land was gobbled up by agribusinesses and consolidated into larger spreads. These corporate farming operations bypassed town merchants and made their bulk purchases in urban centers. They also imported hired laborers who, with no community ties and little hope of acquiring land of their own, formed a permanent underclass.

As town businesses closed their doors, the young and the able fled, leaving behind the poor and the nonaffluent elderly. In some small towns in the farm belt, the median age was over fifty, and many counties showed an excess of deaths over births. The fewer young workers who remained shouldered a heavier tax burden because of the need to provide health care for the oldsters, as well as to maintain schools and basic services.

Manufacturing towns that watched local industries go under to foreign competition or be bought out by conglomerates which cut the work force or shut the plants, found it harder to attract traditionally good-paying factory jobs. In the 1970s and 1980s, the phenomenon of "footloose" industries became more prevalent—establishments that were not tied to any site and left with little concern for the impact on the places they abandoned. Some towns sought to attract service industries, but the jobs often paid less than factory work. And the new factories that did relocate often hired outside workers rather than locals.

All this shuttered stores along Main Street. One study reported that in each decade since 1950 an average of 76 percent of towns of less than 2,500 population suffered a net loss of retail and service establishments—gas stations, grocery stores, lumberyards, hardware, farm implement, and furniture stores. This erosion was not due solely to loss of population; increased competition came from large chains, which offered goods and supplies more cheaply (and were not averse to monopolistic price-cutting). People drove to shopping malls to make their big-ticket purchases rather than buying at home. As a result, some towns could survive only as bedroom communities for cities some 50 miles (80 kilometers) away. Between 1983 and 1986, places outside a Standard Metropolitan Statistical Area (a densely populated area contiguous to a city of fifty thousand or more) suffered the greatest population declines.

Cutbacks in federal aid under the Reagan administration added to the woes of small towns already confronted by a dwindling tax base. They were starved for money to repair bridges and roads, and had to worry about city-style problems like crime, drugs, inadequate schools, air and soil pollution, toxic waste, AIDS, and polluted water tables. Federal crop-support payments to farmers continued, but much of the money went to large operators and the rest did not always help a town's economy, since it was used to pay off the big mortgages assumed during the 1970s rather than to make consumer purchases.

To be sure, many larger towns survived on a solid base of industry and farming and maintained basic services. But even they were hit by the loss of important amenities—a hospital, say, because Medicaid payments are lower for rural areas. The local bank might be taken over by a remote financial conglomerate that was less sensitive to local needs. Deregulation enabled air, rail, and bus lines to halt unprofitable local service, meaning that many towns were cut off from urban centers.

Town and Community

Yet, the crisis of the small town is not new; as we have seen, many of the trends are of long standing. The harsh judgment of history is that some small towns are doomed and others will survive only if they adapt to new circumstances. But self-help is often not enough. Governmental policies properly tailored to the needs of the one-quarter of the population in rural areas are needed. Measures designed to shore up the family farm, for example, would slow the small-town death rate in states like Iowa. The festering problem of rural poverty, which has been on the national agenda since at least the 1960s, must be addressed more decisively by the federal government in areas such as health care, housing, and small business assistance, instead of placing the entire burden on the states.

The picture is by no means uniformly bleak. Many towns are showing adaptability and planning moderate growth strategies. These municipalities, which sociologists call "entrepreneurial towns"—those with newspapers that air local issues, an activist political leadership, schools that emphasize academics rather than sports, and a citizenry willing to spend tax money on infrastructure improvements—have been able to revive fading local businesses or attract new ones to offset their losses.

A contemporary school of "neotraditionalist" city planners draws upon the classic small-town model in laying out new towns with low-traffic streets, local gathering places, sidewalks, pedestrian scale. Even shopping malls—those ravagers of so many small-town businesses—are being torn down and rebuilt as imitation Main Streets with small stores, community centers, and residential areas.

With enlightened leadership and planning, many towns can survive. But survival should not be judged by purely economic criteria or in terms of growth at any price; it should also include invigoration of the town's cultural life and preservation of its history and intangible values of community, smallness and human scale, face-to-face relationships over time, and a sense of place.

So we return to the ideal of community first declared by the early Puritans. John Winthrop described it eloquently in a sermon aboard the *Arbella*: "We must delight in each other, make oth-

The good thing about the country is…that we don't have there any bad weather at all— only a number of different kinds of good.

JOSEPH WOOD KRUTCH
"JUNE," THE TWELVE
SEASONS (1949)

V

VILLAGE AND TOWN

Town and Community

ers' conditions our own, rejoice together, always having before our eyes our commission and community in the work, our community as members of the same bond." New constellations of this old dream must be discovered that are appropriate for a heterogeneous, secular society.

—RICHARD LINGEMAN

WOMEN'S ORGANIZATIONS

Social reform has always played a major role in American history, and women contributed to this activity by building a vast array of voluntary organizations. During the nineteenth century, female reformers laid the groundwork for various organizations as they entered the public sphere, formed single-sex institutions, and gained the power to provide women with social and cultural resources. Initially these voluntary societies emerged as extensions of local charities and churches. As women changed their relationship to the state, these organizations set new goals. Even as "voluntary," associations, most organizations expanded their formal connections to government on municipal, state, and federal levels. Because of their persistent role as welfare agencies, women's organizations necessarily confronted a wide range of social problems; as class, ethnic, gender, and racial dimensions of the larger society changed, these groups modified how they defined their constituencies, reform practices, and policies. Women's organizations have always provided services to the community, but in significant ways these institutions also transformed the role and status of women in the American polity.

Women's Societies, 1800–1837

When women first organized benevolent societies after the revolutionary war, they were guided by a philosophy drawn from the eighteenth century. "Society" meant "polite intercourse" and "friendly visits" among the English well-to-do classes; it defined a special enclave that protected elites from the contamination of the world—or, the temptations of "the flesh, and the devil" (Spacks, p. 1). By adapting this view to a republican nation, reformers argued that societies could serve a civic and moral function in the public sphere. "Carnal talk," idleness, and fleshy indulgences could be mitigated through benevolent assistance and moral supervision. At the same time, the "love of society" instilled citizens with a sense of duty,

trust, and discipline, all the essential virtues necessary for a young Christian republic.

In their most basic form, the early societies represented an extension of the moral functions of the church. In 1818, when the Colored Female Religious and Moral Society organized in Salem, Massachusetts, its constitution made moral guidance a paramount concern, resolving "to be charitably watchful over each other, to advise, caution and admonish" (Scott, p. 14). In addition to rigid rules of moral discipline, societies also encouraged self-control as another useful virtue for their female constituency. Economic duties also defined the link between the church and most local women's societies. Disestablishment made most congregations dependent upon the proceedings of these organizations to maintain church facilities. Cent, mite, and sewing circles all engaged in raising money for various church projects. In Virginia, both black and white societies retained strong ties to particular churches and their biblical heritage, identifying themselves as the "Dorcas Society" and the "Good Samaritan Sisters" (Lebsock, pp. 216–217, 223).

Female charitable societies directed most of their finances toward subsidizing the welfare needs of women in the community: They not only knitted for the poor but they also solicited money and goods to organize Sunday schools, orphanages, workrooms, and asylum houses for training young girls as domestic servants. Programs often addressed the specific economic needs of women; for example, Mary Webb of Boston worked to establish a Fragment Society (1812) to clothe poor women and children, a Fatherless and Widows Society for indigent widows and abandoned women, and a Children's Friends' Society (1833) for caring for the babies of working women. In a practical way, these societies filled a gap in the available community services, especially when towns and cities reduced aid to the poor. These institutions also offered an alternative to the almshouses that benevolent workers felt represented the worst aspects of the "world."

One of the earliest societies in New York City was the Society for the Relief of Poor Widows

Films and advertisements, new shapers of sexual mores in the twentieth century, bombarded women with the message that "The first duty of woman is to attract."

PAGE 427

See also
Courtship, Marriage,
Separation and Divorce

> *It is hard to fight
> an enemy who
> has outposts in
> your head.*
>
> SALLY KEMPTON

with Small Children organized in 1797 by Isabella Graham (1742–1814) and her daughter, Joanna Bethune (1770–1860). This mother and daughter team laid the foundation for a series of organizations, such as the Orphan Asylum, which was incorporated in 1807 and given state funding as early as 1811. Following the War of 1812, they also established a House of Industry for women, and later they organized the Female Union Society for the Promotion of Sabbath Schools. Through her family and class connections, Bethune secured patronage from city officials. Through incorporation, these societies granted female directors legal powers not usually afforded women; they could own property, invest, sue, and manage institutions without the direct supervision of men. Most societies adopted standard business practices, assigning "managers" to visit people and "providential committees" to allocate goods and money (Scott, p. 14).

Benevolent women never actually claimed rights to political powers. Instead, they claimed the duty to protect women, especially such "respectable women" as widows, orphans, and deserving daughters of the middling classes. Much of the early charity work was aimed at widows, a group that symbolized the precarious nature of married women's economic dependency on men. Implicitly, then, benevolent women realized that the "protection" of women could not be left in the

hands of men alone. Prodigal husbands or greedy fathers could destroy a family, leaving even virtuous women destitute. Benevolent women valued and protected women and they learned to utilize the available community resources for moral and material purposes.

Women's Societies, 1837–1860

During the 1830s women shifted the scope and purpose of their organizations from local benevolence to collective campaigns for the moral regeneration of the nation. In response to the message of evangelical religion, female reformers replaced the older philosophy of guardianship with a new focus on transforming human behavior and attitudes. Conversion became the goal of most antebellum societies; members were called upon to spread the gospel of reform while they battled "sin" in all segments of society. Through the distribution of tracts and petitions, female reformers shaped "moral opinion" in a more visible and public way than their benevolent predecessors. At the same time, the eradication of sin called for more radical measures: the passage of more stringent laws, the holding of public events such as rallies and fairs, and the aggressive condemnation of a new enemy—immoral and unrepentant men.

What made this new generation of reformers "militant" was their explicit attack on male authority. When the New York Female Moral Re-

**FACING
HOMELESSNESS**

*Squatter camp of sharecroppers
who were evicted to allow the
landowners to keep promised
crop profits to themselves.*
UPI / CORBIS-BETTMANN

form Society formed in 1834, the organizers sought to eliminate prostitution through old and new measures: they would protect and "reclaim" their "fallen sisters" and they would "create a public sentiment" against the sexual double standard. Moral reformers called for the public humiliation of men who seduced "innocent" female victims, advocating criminal prosecution or exclusion from the company of "all virtuous female society" (Smith-Rosenberg, p. 201).

This new zeal reflected changes in the class composition of female reformers. Unlike the benevolent matrons with ties to elite members of the government, these moral reformers came from the artisan and middling ranks of society. Such class tensions emerged in their literature, which often portrayed the villains as powerful and influential men and their victims as women from poor but respectable families. Hostility toward aristocratic privileges emerged as a theme of other reforms, like temperance, in part because it reflected the social upheaval wrought by economic dislocation. One catalyst for the Daughters of Temperance was the depression of 1839–1843 that left many families destitute. For women, intemperate behavior came to symbolize male seduction, which changed "a kind and affectionate father" into a "terror" who abused his wife and children and left them impoverished (Tyrell, p. 139).

Like moral reform and temperance, the slavery issue aroused female reformers' sense of moral outrage, and, as in other causes, the unrepentant male slave-owner, driven by avarice, lust, and selfishness, was cast as the principal villain. Called to pray, write, and speak against this national sin, antislavery women aimed to battle slavery through education. By spreading the gospel of reform, they would reach the hearts and minds of American women. Indeed, they believed that the power of women's sympathies for the "oppressed female slave" could move the entire nation toward emancipation.

If salvation from sin was the end, then education provided the means for saving the American masses. Consequently, education loomed large as another major concern of antebellum female reformers.

Teaching became a sacred vocation, and women as well as men were needed for this redemptive work. In 1837, Mary Lyon (1797–1849) established Mount Holyoke Female Seminary on principles that differed from the previous female academies. Lyon's fund-raising strategies reflected her evangelical roots; she went door-to-door distributing circulars and recruiting pledges

for her school. Lyon also believed that not only the state but also the "Christian public" should finance her institution. That same public should supply students and converts from the "daughters of the church." By making Mount Holyoke a "school for Christ," Lyon also felt its goal was to "cultivate the missionary spirit among its pupils" (Sklar, pp. 198–199). As a result, her graduates would spread the gospel of moral reform while building new schools and forming a national network of female reformers.

The antebellum period, then, saw the rise of women's public activism as the basis for their organizations. Female reformers combined the evangelical quest for moral perfectionism with the democratic ethos of nation building. Whereas women shared many of the same techniques as their male peers, especially in their use of the media, they also surpassed men in such endeavors as raising money through fairs and collecting subscriptions. Antislavery women transformed the meaning of collecting petitions by organizing the first national political campaign that included the signatures of both men and women. Women not only contributed their "works" to these various reform causes, but their "words" in identifying how gender constructed power relations. Within this new climate, middle- and working-class women claimed reform as their arena for public service and political change.

Women's Associations, 1860–1890

WOMEN'S WAR RELIEF. The Civil War brought a new generation of women reformers into the field of benevolent work. These women were less concerned with moral reform than with coordinating a quasi-military organization for the relief of soldiers. In the North, the Woman's Central Association of Relief (WCAR) in New York organized in 1861; it recruited women of the urban elite with professional and business rather than evangelical aspirations. Unlike their antebellum counterparts, this new cohort of women sought a "partnership" with the government and they established close working relations with men involved in the United States Sanitary Commission.

Confederate women, like Union supporters, organized a variety of local sewing circles (Thimble Brigades in the South), Soldier's Friends Associations, and societies for relief. In 1862, Georgia women founded the Ladies Gunboat Association to collect funds for dwindling military supplies. In the North, civilian aid assumed a rigid and hierarchical structure. Local societies

Working women usually were still expected to take care of domestic chores and arrange for child care.

PAGE 120

See also
Nightlife; Sexual Behavior and Morality

WOMEN'S ORGANIZATIONS

Women's Associations, 1860–1890

During the silent film era, women were often able to find work as directors and editors in Hollywood.

PAGE 144

See also

Fraternal Organizations

sewed, canned goods, and prepared packages; the regional offices collected the supplies and sent them to railroad stations; and the central office distributed the items to agents and hospitals on the front. In 1863, the WCAR adopted the Boston Plan for Sectional Divisions, which called for associate managers to serve as intermediaries between the national and local branches. Managers kept the central office abreast of "the state of affairs in her neighborhood" (Ginzberg, p. 152). Success depended on the distribution of information as well as supplies, which required managers to keep detailed records and to maintain constant correspondence with their Washington supervisors. Such efficiency assumed a corporate model; good business management characterized women's war work.

After the war, northern women sought formal access to state governments through appointments to the charity boards. In 1872, Louisa Lee Schuyler (1837–1926) organized the State Charities Aid Association, which recruited city professionals and elites, promoted expert supervision of charity services, employed associate managers and visiting committees, and kept detailed records of recipients and resources. Clearly, the climate had changed in the postwar era, yielding both positive and negative results. Although these women paved the way for a more bureaucratic charity system, they also advocated a rather narrow vision of moral reform. Middle-class leaders of the New York Charities Association and state boards had little sympathy with alternative methods of reform, such as the Catholic Sisters organizations, which vied with Protestant groups for limited state resources. By imitating men so well, charity reformers often placed efficiency above the particular welfare needs of women, a strategy that aided the vast growth of the corporate state in the aftermath of the Civil War.

WOMEN'S MISSIONS AND THE CHRISTIAN TEMPERANCE UNION.

The missionary zeal of evangelical reform had not died by the postwar years. In 1861, Sarah Doremus (1802–1877) a leader in the Dutch Reformed Church, organized an ecumenical Woman's Union Missionary Society, which survived the war and laid the groundwork for the various denominational societies. Congregational, Methodist, Presbyterian, and Baptist women all formed foreign missions between 1869 and 1871. Combining local meetings with a national newspaper, the mission societies resembled their antebellum models. What had changed was a new sense of American exceptionalism and expansion that mission women both embraced and critiqued. Although they advocated the spread of Christianity in distant lands, they noted the harsh consequences of imperialism unmediated by women's religious influence. Mission women evoked a woman's point of view when evaluating foreign cultures; they focused on the troubling similarities between male authority afar and at home. Yet they did not escape their own cultural heritage, producing a literary and political message that combined exoticism with feminine empathy for their "heathen sisters."

YOUNG WOMEN'S CHRISTIAN ASSOCIATION.

Another kind of home mission work emerged in the cities during the nineteenth century. The Young Women's Christian Association (YWCA) started as a prayer society and blossomed into clubs, boardinghouses, and classes for working women. In 1858, the New York Ladies' Christian Association held prayer meetings in a Manhattan skirt factory and soon established a residence for twenty-one young women. Similar organizations formed in other cities, as founders embarked on city missionary work that aimed to provide "the influence and protection of a Christian home" for single laboring women (Scott, p. 104). Grace Hoadley Dodge (1856–1914), one of the leaders of the movement, established the 38th St. Working Girls' Society in 1884; by the following year, clubs in other cities joined forces to form the Working Girls' Association of Clubs. During the next ten years, nineteen clubs existed in New York City alone.

At first the clubs provided inexpensive housing for working women, but the goals of the association expanded to include cheap amusements, libraries, and gymnastic facilities. The YWCA sharply distinguished itself from charity facilities that provided welfare for the poor and instead it advocated self-support and self-improvement among working women. Instruction in vocational training was combined in most working girls' clubs with more traditional classes in home economics.

Although the organizers of the YWCA sought to cross class barriers, they did not always succeed. A gulf existed between working women and their middle-class benefactors, especially by the 1890s when factory women attempted to push the clubs toward labor activism. Too much supervision over working women's behavior also became a point of contention. Even the domestic ideology offered by YWCA leaders had little appeal for working women, in part because it suited middle-class and non-working-class households. And despite their appeals to diversity, the YWCA focused on

THE WOMEN'S CHRISTIAN TEMPERANCE UNION

Fighting the Demon Liquor

The very same organizational techniques and gospel message would emerge in the Women's Christian Temperance Union (WCTU), one of the most influential religious and political movements of the nineteenth century. Although temperance was not new, the WCTU made the campaign a woman's enterprise. Organized in 1873–1874, the initial crusaders adopted a militant style; they visited hotels and saloons, praying and singing, while asking the owners to stop selling alcoholic beverages. What began as revival quickly changed into a well-coordinated national campaign that drew women from different regions and denominations. The WCTU adopted the women's mission pattern for mobilizing a large, but locally based, network of female laborers. Early programs gained grass-roots support by signing pledges and calling for members to hold mass meetings. At an early stage, however, the WCTU functioned as both a "praying society" and an "activist organization" (Bordin, p. 13). It retained a stable and professional corps of national leaders and adopted a broad-based policy of "Do Everything" that gave autonomy to local unions. Like the mission movement, the WCTU relied on an extensive communication network and published its own newspaper, the *Union Signal*, whose circulation grew to 14,000 by 1884.

Frances Willard (1837–1898), serving as president of the national movement from 1879 until her death, gained prominence as a traveling ambassador and lecturer. In advance of most local union members, Willard combined the goals of temperance and suffrage under the rubric of "Home Protec-

tion." By praying and working for legislation, Willard argued that temperance women could preserve the tranquillity of the home. By adopting the theme of "maternal love," Willard assigned to women a special destiny as the divinely chosen guardians of human morality. Ultimately, the WCTU attempted to transform the state and civil society according to their vision of maternal virtue. To protect the home, women had to instill certain feminine ideals into the very fabric of all local, state, and national institutions.

FEMINIST AND SCHOLAR

Frances Elizabeth Willard, feminist, temperance worker, professor of natural science at Syracuse, and president of the Council of Federated Societies of American Women.
CORBIS-BETTMANN

American-born workers and rarely extended its services to foreign-born women. As a result, the YWCA may not have achieved all of its goals, but it did create an organization that recognized working women as actors and not simply as passive recipients of charity assistance.

WOMEN'S CLUB MOVEMENT. Working girls' clubs differed from the more prominent branch of the Club movement that began with the New England Women's Club and Sorosis in 1868. Through the initiative of Jane Croly (1829–1901), Sorosis aimed to provide an all-women environment that encouraged "self-culture" among its membership. A place for educated women "hungry for the society of women," Sorosis established four committees on literature, art, drama,

and music. Although Croly believed that women shared a special appreciation for "culture for culture's sake," she believed that club women should study culture's effects upon the welfare of women. At first, Sorosis functioned as an elite "think tank," recruiting the most talented professional women from the city. As a "kind of freemasonry among women," Croly hoped to establish a neutral gathering place for different reformers, making the club a forum for unity and discussion (Blair, pp. 20, 23, 25, 28, 31).

Sorosis meant "aggregation," and the New York club attracted women already involved in other reform activities. The New England Women's Club (NEWC) was active from its inception in political causes, nor did the group limit its membership to women alone. Ednah Dow Cheney (1824–1904), one of the founders, had been active in a variety of campaigns before the club's formation: she started the Boston School of Design (1851); served as secretary and president of the New England Hospital for Women and Children (1862); and she organized a teacher's program for the Freedmen's Bureau from 1867 to 1875. Perhaps the major advance of the NEWC was the organization of the Women's Education and Industrial Union in 1877, under the direction of Dr. Harriet Clisby. "Industriousness," not merely self-culture, served as their motto. They produced several reform experiments, including a women's store, lunchroom, health clinic, job registry, and legal assistance service (Blair, p. 80).

From the beginning, Croly sought to nationalize and centralize the club movement, calling a Woman's Parliament in 1869, forming the Woman's Congress and Association for the Advancement for Women in 1873, and organizing the General Federation of Women's Clubs in 1890. At the same time, black middle-class women organized the National Association of Colored Women (NACW) in 1896, the first national organization of black club women, which combined two older groups: the National Federation of Afro-American Women (organized under the aegis of the New Era Club of Boston) and the National League of Colored Women. Although

Josephine St. Pierre Ruffin (1842–1924) was the guiding force of the Boston black women's club, Mary Church Terrell (1863–1954) would inherit the leadership of the national organization. Like Sorosis, the NACW served as an informational clearinghouse of ideas from the "talented tenth" of the black community. The NACW also shared the domestic philosophy of the WCTU and the white women's club movement. Terrell advocated specific reforms that recognized the economic needs of black working women. Kindergartens, day nurseries, and mother's clubs became the principle items of their agenda. Their demand for "Homes, more homes, better homes, purer homes" reflected a specific urgency not found in the white women's club movement (Jones, p. 26). It indicated that black club women had to contend with racism as a force that permeated all aspects of the black community.

Through the end of the nineteenth century, clubs served a variety of purposes for their members. On the local level, women used the clubs for cultural activities, such as reading and study groups. Class status, religion, and even professional affiliation separated the membership of clubs in most communities and cities. Within each region or municipality, the clubs assumed a wider role in supporting community projects, such as the funding of memorials, playgrounds, and libraries. Black club women often focused their efforts on establishing health facilities, including hospitals and health clinics. Yet the clubs also served a third and decidedly political function: they provided a female training ground in "civics" for future political activists. By the 1890s, most clubs had joined forces with other organizations for the promotion of legislative and political reforms. Like the WCTU, club members claimed that society was an extension of the home and women had a special vocation for "Home Protection" and "Municipal Housekeeping."

Women's Associations, 1889–1930

SETTLEMENT HOUSES. While the clubs gained national prominence in the 1890s, another reform experiment emerged on the urban landscape, the Settlement House. The best-known settlement was Hull-House, organized by Jane Addams (1860–1935) and Ellen Gates Starr (1859–1940) in 1889, which was modeled on Toynbee Hall, a settlement formed by male university students in East London. By creating a distinctive "colony" of female reformers, the settlement house served both "objective" and "subjective needs," in the words of Addams: it offered

social services to the urban poor, mainly the foreign-born population, while it created a unique retreat for educated women with professional aspirations (Rousmaniere, p. 47). Most settlements duplicated the unique female culture offered in the women's seminaries and colleges. As a female community, Hull-House provided its members with an alternative to a more traditional family life. Equally important, as a separate female institution, the settlement offered women a supportive base within the larger community of Progressive reformers. Here women could establish networks with male activists, business leaders, and government officials without losing their influence as female activists.

Initially, the settlements resembled the urban clubs, offering literary and cultural activities. Soon the settlement became a more complex kind of reform agency that provided services for working women, day care for their children, rooms for social and political gatherings, and a training ground for educated women interested in the scientific study of urban problems. By 1910, Hull-House had expanded into a vast array of buildings filling an entire city block. Soliciting funds was part of Addams's duties as an administrator, and she served as a link between the settlement's workers and its financial backers. Similarly, but for different ends, the settlement mediated between the urban population and city institutions. It worked to bring needed services into the community while protecting the neighborhood from the encroachment of the ward bosses. Addams believed that Hull-House, as a model social democracy, integrated the political, economic, and cultural life of the city. In a unique way, the settlements placed a premium on human solidarity and diversity, recognizing that together the residents and reformers created a multicultural experiment in political democracy.

WOMEN'S LEAGUES. Interest in the problems facing working women led reformers in new directions during the late nineteenth and early twentieth century. Middle-class women recognized their prominent role as consumers and they mobilized their concerns into a new organization that would improve working conditions for women and children. Under the guidance of Maud Nathan (1862–1946) and Josephine Lowell (1843–1905) the Consumers' League was formed in 1890 in New York City. Its primary goal was to convince consumers to patronize those department stores that adhered to the "Standards of a Fair House," a guideline published by the League that promulgated fair wages, hours, and safe work-

ing conditions. As a pressure group, the League created a "White list" that identified those stores that met the League's standards. In 1899, the National Consumers' League was organized and spawned the formation of branch groups across the United States and abroad.

The National Consumers' League was not always successful in gaining the support of the labor unions. In 1904, the use of product labels triggered a clash with the International Ladies Garment Workers' Union. Yet another organization, the New York Women's Trade Union League (WTUL), made a more concerted effort to work with unions. Organized in 1903, the WTUL promoted the advantages of unions for female workers, supported the formation of several women's trade unions, and worked to convince male labor organizers to support their efforts. What made the WTUL different from other middle-class organizations was its commitment to unionization. Its other unique feature was the prominence of working-class women in leadership positions. By 1907, as the initial constitution had stipulated, three of the five board officers were working-class activists. One key member of the board was Leonora O'Reilly (1870–1927), a settlement worker and an early labor organizer for the Knights of Labor. The WTUL did not achieve a perfect alliance between working- and middle-class members. Nor did the leadership secure a harmonious relationship with male unionists. But the WTUL did gain publicity for a large number of strikes, such as the New York garment strike of 1909–1910. Similar to other women's organizations, the WTUL generated public opinion, offering a "radically" different perspective from "the accepted opinions and ideals of men" (Dye, p. 285).

Similarly, the Women's International League for Peace and Freedom (WILPF), formed from the membership of the Woman's Peace Party in 1915, followed this tradition and extended its influence into the arena of world politics and foreign policy. One of its principal organizers was Jane Addams, whose devotion to peace and international tolerance had its roots in her theories of social democracy. In 1899, Addams began lecturing against American imperialism, and in 1907 she published her lectures as *Newer Ideals of Peace*. Addams sought to change the meaning of heroism from a masculine and destructive principle to one based on harmony and justice, a shift she claimed was "the moral equivalent of war" (Degen, p. 20). The League symbolized the integral relationship between women's values and political action, demonstrating the view shared by most

WOMEN'S ORGANIZATIONS

Women's Associations, 1889–1930

Equality for women demands a change in the human psyche more profound than anything Marx dreamed of. It means valuing parenthood as much as we value banking.

POLLY TOYNBEE

See also
The Frontier

nineteenth-century reformers that women's influence could transform the world. The WILPF assumed that if women held more influence in the state, both domestic and foreign policy would change. Ultimately, the goal of the WILPF was to replace military conflicts with arbitration. Although this call for peace had little sway at the time, Addams's philosophy would reappear in later organizations and platforms, such as the United Nations and the Universal Declaration of Human Rights (1948).

ALUMNAE ASSOCIATIONS AND BLACK SORORITIES. The women's college associations and black women's sororities represented the last major advance in middle-class women's organizations during this period. Regional college associations first appeared in the Northeast and West in the 1880s, and eventually spread to the South in 1903. A national alliance organized in 1921 when the American Association of University Women formed. Both regional and national associations worked for educational legislation, to promote state teachers' pensions, uniform school attendance, and child labor laws. Conscious of their status as women and professionals, the college association advocated equal wages for women, calling for a "living wage" for college-educated employees (Talbot and Rosenberry, p. 229). One of its founders, Marion Talbot (1858–1948), represented a new generation of modern professional

women. Rejecting the conventional assumptions about women's nature, Talbot believed that women could not lay claim to any unique moral capacities. Rather than segregating the sexes, Talbot believed in coeducation and equal opportunities for women. Based on their educational experiences, the college association members hoped to create a new identity for professional women.

White and black sororities sought to supplement the college curriculum by educating women for their future roles as citizens. As a training ground for civic leadership, sororities advocated social responsibility and self-government. The first white sororities appeared in the late nineteenth century, and they established scholarship programs, funds for the creative arts, and social welfare projects. Typically, the female Greek societies followed the pattern of male fraternities: they built chapter houses, secured an endowment fund, published an official magazine, and organized alumnae chapters in major cities. In 1902, Alpha Phi summoned the Intersorority Conference that subsequently reorganized as the National Panhellenic Conference (Baird, p. 393).

Black women's sororities combined professionalism with their continued support for "racial uplift" and political activism against racism. Alpha Kappa Alpha Sorority, founded in 1908 at Howard University, provided funding and trained personnel for the campaign against lynching in

YWCA SUPPER

The Young Women's Christian Association begun as a prayer society, blossomed into clubs, boardinghouses, and classes for working women. Here a group of young women eat together at a weekly YWCA girls' club supper in the 1950s.
CORBIS-BETTMANN

1934, followed by a summer school for rural teachers and a nutrition clinic in 1940. The Black Public Health Movement gained much of its support from sororities, since many of the public health nurses used this organization as a communication and recruitment network.

These professional associations defined the trends in women's organizations. In the coming decades, women active in the leagues, clubs, and professions paved the way for both white and black women to play a significant role in state and even federal government during the New Deal era. Certain traditions continued as women's organizations focused on civic education, business policies, social welfare, issues of foreign relations, and the status of women. As middle-class women moved to the suburbs following World War II, local, municipal, and educational issues again became the preserve of women's reform efforts. Both environmentalism and antinuclear war sentiments drew on earlier peace efforts and conservation campaigns as well as the intellectual contributions of academic women like biologist Rachel Carson (1907–1964; author of *Silent Spring*, 1962).

A new wave of women's organization-building reemerged during the 1960s and 1970s. Sparked by the civil rights movement, female members of Students for a Democratic Society (SDS) participated in the foundation of Economic and Research Action Projects (ERAP) in order to build ties to the "urban poverty sector" (Sealander and Smith, p. 332). Organizing around two women's issues—welfare and schools—female activists helped mobilize Mothers for Adequate Welfare (MAW) and Citizens for Adequate Welfare (CUFAW), both of which contributed to the success of the National Welfare Rights Organization (NWRO) (Evans, pp. 142–143). Welfare mothers demonstrated a new militancy as active members of these groups; between 1967 and 1969, they staged sit-ins, demonstrations, and regular disruptions at welfare offices.

Middle-class women later applied the same techniques in protesting sexual discrimination against white-collar workers. By 1977, the National Women's Employment Project (NWEP) linked together a network of urban organizations that investigated businesses, produced case studies, and publicized violations of antidiscrimination laws (Sealander and Smith, pp. 325–327). Initially, the NWEP gained support from the federal government. The Presidential Commission on the Status of Women, for example, supported the passage of the 1963 Equal Pay Act. Public-pressure groups were needed to enforce the new federal legislation. One such group was the National Organization for Women (NOW), which mobilized in 1966 "to bring American women into full participation in the mainstream of American society *now*" (Woloch, p. 513). Although NOW focused on securing women's civil rights, it endorsed the broader grass-roots activities for women's liberation. In addition to establishing consciousness-raising groups, feminists turned to the federal government to fund a variety of women's centers. Often providing "a smorgasbord of services," centers like the one started in Dayton, Ohio, provided self-help classes, advocacy and referral services, political and personal counseling, a day-care cooperative, and a meeting place for a rape task force and a lesbian organization, Sappho's Army (Sealander and Smith, pp. 325–327).

Building on well-established traditions of women's organization-building, feminists also increased their dependence on federal funding, often curtailing the growth of a viable grass-roots base of community support. While the Dayton women's center used federal Model City monies, it relied less on dues and local funding from churches and other private institutions. Resistance to the tradition of women's "volunteerism" surfaced in NOW; in the 1970s, it challenged the pattern as "an extension of unpaid housework and women's traditional roles in the home" (Gittell and Shtob, p. 577). This philosophy, coupled with the decline in federal resources, eclipsed some of the more ambitious programs and goals of the women's movement. Even with these setbacks, women demonstrated their commitment toward building organizations, such as abortion clinics, rape-counseling centers, and abused-women's shelters, thus continuing the tradition of mobilizing women to solve women's welfare, economic, and political problems.

—NANCY G. ISENBERG

WOMEN'S ORGANIZATIONS

Women's Associations, 1889–1930

Of my two 'handicaps,' being female put more obstacles in my path than being black.

SHIRLEY CHISOLM

See also
Film

Glossary

a capella In music, to sing without musical accompaniment.

abatement A legal defense or plea to end an action, or law, on the grounds that a factual or technical error prevents the continuation of the action or law.

abattoir A slaughterhouse.

aboriginal A person, plant, or animal native to a biosphere. The term is used to distinguish the native from the imported, or immigrant.

acculturation The changes brought to the culture of a group or individual as the result of contact with a different culture.

activist A person involved in activities or action, often militant, who supports or opposes a social or political goal.

acumen A term that refers to the accuracy or keenness of a person's judgment or insight.

ad hoc A Latin phrase meaning only for the specific case or situation at hand. It is also used to mean impromptu, or improvised.

adjudication The hearing and settling of a legal case by means of judicial procedure.

adulation A term used to describe the excessive use of flattery or admiration.

affluent A term that refers to someone who has a generous supply of money, property, or possessions.

aficionado A fan, or devotee. The term is often used to refer to those with considerable or discerning knowledge of a particular subject.

afterpiece A short, usually comic performance that follows a play.

agglomeration An assemblage or collection of diverse parts into a single, sometimes jumbled unit.

agitprop A combination of the words "agitate" and "propaganda," a type of political propaganda used chiefly in drama or literature.

agrarian A sociological term used to refer to cultures or economies that are based on or derive their primary economic means from uses of the land, such as farming.

ahistorical Opposed to, or in conflict with history or historical precedent.

AIDS An acronym for acquired immune deficiency syndrome, a group of diseases or conditions that result from the weakening or suppression of the human immune system, brought on by the human immunodeficiency virus, also known as HIV.

alienation In psychological terms, an estrangement between one's self and the rest of the world; a feeling of not belonging.

alimony A sum of money, decided by a court, that is awarded to a former spouse after a divorce. The money is usually provided as a means of support for children, or to allow the former spouse to maintain a lifestyle similar to that of when the couple was married.

allegory The use of characters or events as representative of larger ideas or principals in a work or fiction or art.

allusion A literary term that describes the use of an indirect reference.

almanac A yearly publication in calendar form that contains weather predictions, astronomical schedules, and other factual data.

almshouse A poorhouse, or charitable establishment that serves the needs of the poor.

alto In music, the range between soprano and tenor.

altruism Selflessness, or concern for the welfare of others without thought of personal gain.

amalgam A combination of diverse elements or influences in a single entity.

amateur In sports, a player who does not receive compensation for his play.

ambient Surrounding or encircling.

ameliorism The act or process of making something better, or improving it.

Americans with Disabilities Act (ADA) Civil rights legislation, passed in 1990, that significantly reduced physical and legal obstacles for citizens with physical or mental disabilities, and prohibiting discrimination against the disabled in business, public accommodations, transportation, and telecommunications.

amplification The process of increasing the output or magnitude of sound or power. Musical instruments are often put through a process of amplification to allow a large audience to hear the music it is generating.

anabaptist A term used to refer to Protestant religious movements that were part of the Reformation during the 16th century and beyond. Meaning literally "one who baptizes again," the word refers to the practice of adult baptism that was representative of the variations or alterations that were introduced to the established Roman Catholic liturgy.

ancillary Subordinate to, or supporting, a larger central unit or organization.

android An artificial life form created from biological materials that resembles a human being.

anecdotal A type of conversation, oratory, or storytelling that makes use of short, humorous, or otherwise interesting incidents or stories.

animation In film, a motion picture created by photographing a series of drawings or paintings.

annexation The process of adding on to or joining various elements into a larger single unit.

antebellum Referring to the period before the American Civil War.

antecedent A preceding or prior representative example.

antedate To precede in time.

anti-Semitism The hostility, hatred, or practice of discrimination against Jews.

antihero In fiction or drama, a character lacking in traditional "heroic" virtues or attributes.

antiphony A form of participatory singing in which a leader will call a line or phrase, and the audience responds.

antithesis In direct contrast, or opposition to or of an idea or principle.

antiurbanism A policy of opposition to urbanization, or for the preservation of suburban and rural areas.

aphorism A maxim, or adage, intended to distill the essence of an idea into a short, memorable phrase.

aphrodisiac A food or drug that is intended to arouse or intensify sexual desire.

apogee The pinnacle or highest point. Often used to refer to the best, or most outstanding point achieved in drama or music.

apologist A person who writes or speaks in defense of someone or something. The term is often used to refer to a person who seeks to justify the actions of another, or to reconcile behavior or beliefs with established principles.

apotheosis An exalted, divine, or glorious example, or to raise to such status.

apprentice In modern terms, one who studies or learns a trade or skill under the supervision of a recognized or accredited master.

appropriation A set amount of public funds set aside for a specific cause or purpose.

arbiter One who determines or judges.

arbitration The process by which two opposing sides undergo to submit their views to an impartial person or group.

archetype A prototype, or original model, on which other things are based, or an ideal example of a type.

archvillain The archetype of a villain, or the leader of a group of villains.

argumentation The process of constructing, presenting, and elaborating an argument or opinion.

aria A musical term used to describe a solo vocal piece within an opera.

aristocracy From the Greek words *aristos*, meaning "best," and *kratos*, meaning "power," a term used either for a form of government ruled by a elite class or group, or to refer to the members of such a group.

Articles of Confederation The first constitution of the United States, ratified on March 1, 1781, by the Continental Congress, and in force until the adoption of the present U.S. Constitution on June 21, 1788.

artifact An archaeological term that describes an object that was created by a human, such as a tool or weapon.

artificial insemination The process by which donor spermatozoa are artificially introduced into the female genital tract for the purpose of reproduction.

artisan In architectural terms, referring to the work or style created by skilled manual laborers.

assimilation A sociological term referring to the process by which individuals or groups are brought and absorbed into a new and dominant culture.

atheism The lack of religious belief or belief in the existence of God.

attenuate To reduce in size, value, amount, or weaken in any way.

aural Of or relating to sound or the sense of hearing.

austerity A condition characterized as severe or stern, or without unnecessary adornment.

autoharp A musical instrument, similar to a zither, that is small enough to be held and is played by strumming the string and depressing chords.

autonomy From the Greek word *autonomos*, meaning self-ruling, autonomy is a lack of control by others, or self-governing.

auxiliaries Smaller, satellite groups that serve to support or supplement a larger central organization.

avant-garde A term used to describe the leaders in a given field, those noticeably ahead of most of the rest in the application and invention of new techniques. The term is often used in the arts, where those in the avant-garde are seen as the primary innovators and the first to try or introduce new ideas.

Baby Boom The collective name for the generation of American children born between 1946 and 1964. The term refers to the considerable increase in births following the end of World War II.

Baccalaureate A degree from a college or university signifying the completion of an undergraduate curriculum.

balcony In architecture, a platform projecting from the wall of a building above ground level, surrounded by a railing.

ballad In folk music, a type of song in the form of a narrative poem, comprised of simple stanzas and often a recurring refrain, and the music that accompanies it. The term also refers to a type of pop song, often slow and romantic.

barnstorming In sports, particularly baseball, a team that travels from location to location, playing exhibition games against local teams. The term derives from the post-World War I pilots who flew from place to place staging aerial shows and exhibitions, making use of available fields as landing sites.

baroque In architecture or design, an artistic style typified by elaborate and ornate decoration, popular in Europe during the late16th and 17th centuries. In music, a style consisting of strict forms and elaborate ornamentation, also of European origin, originating in the early 17th century.

barrelhouse In music, a style or genre of jazz, also called boogie-woogie, characterized by a repeated rhythmic and melodic pattern in the bass line.

barrio A district or within an urban area, most commonly used to describe a Spanish-speaking community.

bastion A stronghold or place of strength. Also used to refer to the projecting part of a fort or castle.

bathos The term for an abrupt and somewhat absurd transition from an exalted style to the commonplace. Also used to refer to overly sentimental pathos.

be-bop Also **bebop**. A style of jazz first made popular in the early 1940s by Charlie Parker. It is based on improvisation over chord progression, characterized by fast tempos, long phrases, and a greater emotional ranges than were common in jazz before that time.

beanball In baseball, a pitch thrown directly at a batter with the intention of hitting him.

bear baiting Also **bearbaiting.** A type of sport in which a bear was chained to a stake and attacked by a pack of dogs. The bear was most often savagely killed.

beaux-arts A French term meaning the fine arts.

behaviorism In psychology, a theory or science that studies the relationship between behavior (or response) and environment (stimulus) by strict experimental procedure. Behaviorism maintains that all complex forms of behavior are the result of muscular and glandular reactions to external stimuli that can be observed and measured.

bel canto From the Italian phrase meaning "beautiful song," a type of choral or operatic music popular in Europe from the mid-17th century through the mid-19th century, characterized by purity and evenness of tone production and a dexterous vocal technique.

belfry A bell tower, usually associated with a church or public building.

bestiality A deviant sexual behavior in which a human being engages in sexual relations with an animal.

bicameral Possessing two separate legislative branches, or chambers.

bifurcation An object that is forked, or divided into two separate branches.

bigamy In law, the crime of marrying one person while still legally wed to another.

bigot An intolerant, biased person, especially in matters of race or nationality.

biocentric management The management or operation of an enterprise, such as a park, that stresses the environment and the importance of the life forms it contains above all other considerations.

biocentrism The belief that life is more important, or central, than any other consideration.

biodegradable Matter that is capable of being broken down and decomposed through natural biological processes.

biota The inclusive term for all the plant and animal life of a particular region.

bipolar Literally referring to the two separate poles of a magnet, a term used to refer to a system with two opposite sides.

blackface A type of makeup, used by white performers to caricature black people, in a type of entertainment known as a minstrel show, developed in the United States in the early 19th century.

blacklisting A term used to refer to the restrictions, based on accusations of Communism, against hiring certain members of the entertainment industry during the 1940s and 1950s. The blacklist was based on the testimony before the House Committee on Un-American Activities (HUAC) of "friendly" witnesses from within the motion picture industry, who named those they believed to have Communist sympathies or connections.

blasphemy A religious crime or sin, in which one speaks of God or other sacred entity in an irreverent or disrespectful manner.

boll weevil A type of beetle less than one-fourth of an inch long whose larva is especially destructive to cotton plants. Infestations were first noted in Mexico in the mid-19th century, and later spread through the United States.

bondsmen A type of servant, much like a slave, forced or obligated to service without wages.

boom-and-bust cycle A phrase used in economics to refer to the repeating, not fully understood patterns in a country's economic fortunes.

Boston Tea Party The common name for a rebellious attack by American British colonials on December 16, 1773, on three British ships carrying 342 chests of tea. In protest of the British taxes on imports to the colonies, Boston citizens, led by Samuel Adams, boarded the ships and dumped the tea into Boston Harbor.

boycott A form of protest in which a person or group refuses to buy products from or support companies, individuals, nations, or other groups with which they disagree.

braggadocio A swaggering or cocky manner. Also used to refer to the pose of a braggart, or a person whose claims are empty or pretentious.

breechclout Also **breechcloth**. A loincloth.

broadside Also **broadsheet**. In publishing, a single, large sheet of paper or poster bearing printed matter. Because of their simplicity and highly visible size, they were ideal early vehicles for publishers.

brogue A strong, regional accent. Most often used to refer to an Irish dialect.

bureaucracy A general term for the employees and administrative structure of a company or organization, characterized by a specific hierarchy of authority or responsibility.

burlesque A type of vaudeville entertainment or comic art characterized by ridiculous exaggeration, racy humor, and displays of nudity.

cadre In politics, a tightly knit group of activists. The term also refers to the core or nucleus of a military organization.

calisthenics A formalized series of exercises designed to improve muscle tone and cardiovascular heath.

Calvinism A form of Christian belief or theology, a Protestant offshoot of the Catholic church, led by French reformer John Calvin (1509-64). It is characterized by belief in the absolute sovereignty of God, in predestination, and the absence of free will.

cameo In film, a brief, often minor appearance.

canon A religious term referring to a code or law that is established by a church council. The term also refers to a norm established for standards or judgments.

capital In architecture, the top part of a column or pillar.

capital punishment The use of the death penalty, or execution, as punishment for a crime.

capitalism The overall term for the economic system in which individuals and companies produce and exchange goods and services through a network of prices and markets.

capitol The building in which the legislature meets.

capstone In architecture, the top stone of a structure or wall. The term is also used to refer to the crowning achievement or pinnacle of a career.

caricature A representation, most often pictorial, of a person that exaggerates distinctive features with comic or mocking intent. Also used to refer to the process of such exaggerated imitation.

cartography The art, science, and study of maps and mapmaking.

caste system A type of social system arranged in hierarchical order, in which a person's status is determined by the caste, or level, into which he is born. A rigid caste system defines the worth or acceptability of an individual on the basis of their caste rather than individual merits or attributes, and personal advancement is often extremely difficult.

castration A surgical procedure that removes the testicles or ovaries. Used through the 19th century to produce or preserve the fine singing voices of young boys, or to provide guards for women's quarters, it has also used as a form of torture.

censor A person or group authorized to remove or edit objectionable material in work intended for public consumption. Also used to refer to the act of editing.

censure A formal or official rebuke or expression of criticism or blame.

cession A surrendering of territory to another country, that has been mandated by a treaty.

chapbook A term used to refer to a type of pamphlet or small book produced for popular reading.

charter In legal terms, a document issued or granted by a government, creating a business or political entity such as a corporation or colony, and defining its privileges and purposes.

chastity The abstention from sexual activity.

chivalry A rigid and clearly defined code of behavior that emphasized the protection of women and the weak. It is often associated with the Arthurian legends and knightly orders.

choral In music, a type of music written for a group, or chorus, comprised of a variety of voices and ranges.

chord In music, a combination of notes, sounded or struck simultaneously to produce a layered sound.

cinematography The art or science of motion picture photography.

cipher A code or other system of secret writing in which the meaning or message is disguised by means of a predetermined key.

circulation In publishing, a term used to refer in numerical terms to the readership of a periodical.

classicism A philosophy or attitude based on the forms and principles of ancient Greece and Rome. The term is used in a variety of artistic genres and often denotes simplicity and restraint of form.

clergyman A person who is a recognized member of the clergy, or ordained ministry, of a religion.

cloister A structure that is devoted to the study of religion, such as a monastery. In architectural terms, a covered walkway, open on one side, that runs along the outside of a building.

coalescence The coming together of diverse parts into a single entity.

coaxial cable A type of transmission line with two conductors. It is most often used to refer to the method of delivery used by cable television.

code duello A phrase used to refer to the formal arrangements or etiquette of duels.

cognoscenti The inner group, or those "in the know."

cohesion The process or device by which objects are held together.

coitus Sexual intercourse.

cold type A term used to refer to manual typesetting using precast metal characters.

collectivize To bring together assets and resources in the service and for the use of a group.

collusion In law, a crime in which two or more parties conspire secretly to achieve by their cooperation an illegal or deceitful purpose.

colonialism The theory and practice of extending the authority, political and economic control, of one nation over another, alien nation that has been conquered or settled.

colonist The term used to refer to an inhabitant or one of the original settlers of a colony.

commedia dell'arte One of the earliest and most influential forms of theater, originating in Italy in the 16th century, in which troupes of six to twelve actors improvised comedies based on stereotypical characters, masks, and broad gestures.

commingle To bring together, or mix.

commission A group or body, similar to a committee, assembled for the purpose of dealing with specific duties, tasks, or issues. Also used to refer to the legal document that confers the rank of military officer.

commodity A transportable article of trade of commerce. The term is often used to refer to agricultural products such as wheat.

commune A collective living arrangement or community, in which individual members contribute resources and labor to the group as a whole.

communism A political theory and model for a government system in which all resources, businesses, and means of production are jointly owned by all members of the community.

compendium A written list or compilation, often in short, detailed form. Also used to refer to a collection of items.

confederacy A political union, or league.

conglomerate A corporation created by the merger of a number of different companies with unrelated or complimentary specialties.

conjugal Of or relating to a marriage or marital relations.

connoisseur One who is an expert in a specific field, often referring to the fine arts.

conquistador From the Spanish *conquistar*, meaning conquer, the name given to the Spanish conquerors of Mexico, Central America, and Peru in the 16th and 17th centuries.

conservatory Most often used to refer to a school for music or drama.

constable A law enforcement official.

constituency The voters or district represented by an elected legislator.

Constitutional Convention The gathering of representatives from the thirteen U.S. states from May 25–September 17, 1787, during which the Constitution of the United States was drafted.

consumerism A political movement seeking to safeguard the rights of consumers by requiring honest packaging and advertising, guarantees, and higher standards. The term is also used to refer to a type of materialism.

contextualize To put something in its proper context, or relation to other factors.

Continental Congress The assembly of about 50 representatives from the American colonies that became the revolutionary government that initiated Declaration of Independence and the American Revolution. The First Continental Congress met in Philadelphia on September 5, 1774.

corporal punishment A type of physical punishment inflicted on the body of a person found guilty of a crime. Common types included flogging, branding, and mutilation.

correspondent A person, employed by print or broadcast media, who supplies news articles or stories.

cosmopolitan A trait that refers to something that is pertinent or common to the whole world.

counterculture A sub- or alternate culture or aesthetic that exists along with and in contrast to the dominant culture.

creed A belief, usually referring to religion or faith.

Creole A term used to refer to the American-born descendants of Europeans, especially in the West Indies or Spanish America. A white person whose ancestors were early French or Spanish explorers of the U.S. Gulf states, who preserve their language and culture, most especially associated with residents of New Orleans.

cricket An outdoor team sport, popular in Great Britain and its former colonies, involving 11 players and the use of bats, a ball, and wickets.

cul-de-sac A term used to describe a circular end to a street.

cultural aesthetic An expression used to define preferences that are determined by the consensus of a culture or ethnic group.

cupola An architectural term describing a domed roof or ceiling.

curriculum All the courses of study offered at an educational institution, or the related courses of one specific field of study.

curvilinear A term describing something that is curved or bound.

cutthroat To be relentless in competition.

debauchery An extreme indulgence or obsession with sensual pleasures.

decontextualization To take something out of its surrounding meaning, or context.

decorous A term describing someone who is proper.

decorum Polite behavior or appropriate conduct.

defoliation To cause the leaves to fall off a plant.

deism The belief in a God who created the universe, yet assumes no control over life or natural phenomena.

delegate A representative for another person.

delimit A term meaning to establish limits or boundaries.

delinquency A term referring to a failure to follow the laws or agreements that have been set.

democrat A member of a political party of the United States, or a general term used to describe someone who is an advocate of the political system of democracy.

democratization To place under the system of democracy, in which a country is ruled by its citizens, or representatives of the citizens, rather than by a monarchy or other nonelective system.

demographic A classification, often referring to a specific group or similarity of an area.

denaturing The process of changing the natural qualities of something, often resulting in the destruction of its beneficial use.

denomination A group or classification, often referring to a religion.

depravity Blatant and excessive moral degradation or corruption.

deracinated Displaced or removed from one's original environment.

deregulation The removal of government control or regulation.

desegregation The opposite of segregation, which separates one group from another, desegregation refers to the end of the separation. Most often used in reference to the civil rights struggles of the 1960s, which sought to end the forced segregation of blacks and whites.

dialectic A term classifying the specifics of language, including pronunciation, accent, and grammar.

diaspora The dispersion or separation of culture. The term is often used to refer to the pattern of immigration that spreads an ethnic group beyond their native land.

didactic Something that is intended to instruct or teach.

differentiation The process of distinguishing or perceiving the differences between two group or objects.

discotheque A nightclub that features music, dancing, and elaborate lighting.

discretionary income Money that is not allocated for necessities, such as food or shelter.

dishabille A term describing someone who is either partially, or casually, dressed.

displacement The process of moving someone, or something, from its environment or homeland.

disquisition A formal presentation of a subject, usually in writing.

dissonance A musical term meaning a sound that lacks harmony, consistency, or agreement in its composition or production.

diurnal An daily occurrence that happens in a 24-hour period, usually referring to events that occur during daylight.

diva A term used in opera to refer to the heroine or leading female character.

divertissement A break in a play or opera, in which a short performance is presented.

divination A supernatural ability to predict future events, or the process of predicting them.

domesticate The process of training or adapting something to home life; to tame.

domesticity The quality of, or devotion to, home life.

double entendre Also **double-entendre**. A word or phrase with two meanings, one of which is often risqué.

dowry A custom in which gift of land or money is given prior to a marriage, most often by the bride's family to the bridegroom or his family.

drawing room A large, private room on a railroad sleeping car. Also used to refer to a place within a home where guests are entertained.

dynamism A theory in which the universe is explained in terms of energy or force.

ecclesiastical A term describing something that relates to a church, as an institution.

echelon A social classification referring to the level of responsibility or authority of a specific class of people.

eclecticism The grouping of objects that have no relation to one another.

ecotourism A type of tourism in which the attraction is the native landscape, plant or animal life. It is often used to refer to trips to endangered ecologies.

edict A proclamation, that has the force of a law, that is issued by an authority.

effigy A derogatory figure used to represent a hated group or culture.

efflorescence The process of unfolding or developing, often referring to agriculture.

egalitarian The affirmation or one who affirms political, economic, and social equality for all people.

elan A distinctive, suave style or flair.

electorate A group of qualified voters.

embargo The government prohibition of certain or all trade with another nation.

emblematic A term referring to something that is symbolic of another.

embryonic Relating or comparing to an organism in its early stages of development, particularly before it has reached a recognizable form.

endowment A form of charity or philanthropy by which a wealthy individual or corporation provides property, money, or a source of income to an institution, or by donation causes an institution to be established, generally for the purpose of serving the common or public good.

Enlightenment A philosophical movement of the 18th century that emphasized the use of reason to question previously accepted practices.

ensemble A group of musicians, singers, dancers, or actors who perform together.

entr'acte A theatrical term used for a break between two acts during a performance.

entrepreneur A person who organizes and operates a business venture; commonly used to refer to people who seek business opportunities on their own rather than as part of an organization or corporation.

environmentalism A social awareness in which the protection of the environment from pollution and human destruction is the main focus.

ephemeral Something that lives or lasts for a very brief period of time.

epochal A classification for something that is highly significant, important, or momentous.

eponymous The process of naming or associating something, often a city or era, with the name of person.

escapism The process of removing oneself from reality or routine via fantasy or entertainment.

ethnicity A classification referring to one's ethnic character, background, or affiliation.

ethnocentric A mindset in which it is believed one's ethnic background is superior.

ethnology A subdivision of anthropology concerned with the study of cultures in their traditional form, and their adaptations to modern influences.

ethnomusicologist One who studies a style of music deriving from European classical tradition.

ethos The fundamental values or behaviors of a specific culture.

etymology The study of the origin and development of a language through its earliest known use, changes in form, and relation to other languages.

euphemism A term used to refer to or replace a more common or vulgar term.

evangelism The preaching or spreading of a religion, as with missionary work.

excoriation To tear, or wear off, the skin of something.

excrescences Abnormal growths or enlargements of the skin or surface.

exemplar A classification of something as a model or best example.

exhortation A speech or oratory that encourages, incites, or advises.

existential Relating to, or dealing with, the experience or existence of something.

expansionist One who practices the process of political or economic expansion.

expose To reveal or subject to a harmful element.

expressionism An artistic movement during the early 20th century that emphasized an artist's life experiences.

extramural An occurrence that takes place outside the normal boundaries or location of that setting. For example, a school function that takes place somewhere other than the school itself.

exurbanization The spread of a suburban or rural, often wealthy, residential area into the countryside surrounding a major city.

fascism A system of government that follows the principles of a centralized authority under a dictator, strict economic controls, censorship, and the use of terror to suppress opposition.

faction A group that separates itself within a larger group.

fallacy A false occurrence or statement.

falsetto A musical term used to classify a voice that produces tones in a range higher than the normal range.

Faustian bargain A legendary deal between the historical figure, fortune-teller, and magician Johann Faust (also referred to as Doctor Faustus, or Fausten, 1480?-1540?) and Mephistopheles, or the devil, in which Faust was given and increased knowledge of magic and 24 years of pleasure and power, after which his soul belonged to the devil. The term is often used to refer to a desperate bargain made on unequal terms.

federalist Originally referring to a member or supporter of the Federalist Party, the dominant political force in U.S. politics during the late 18th and early 19th centuries, the term is often used loosely to refer to a person who believes in or advocates a strong central government.

feminist A person who believes in the social, political, and economic equality of both sexes.

fertility rate The quantity of births within a class or group.

fiat A sanction or decree.

fidelity Faithfulness to one's obligation, duties, or observances, most often associated with the institution of marriage.

filial A term describing a relationship or object appropriate for a son or daughter.

film noir A cinematic genre in which black and white film is used to create a visual effect considered complimentary to a dark or gritty subject matter.

folio A publication on which the text is printed onto a large sheet folded into fourths that forms a small book or pamphlet.

foray A venture into an area or occupation that is outside one's usual area of expertise.

formative A term describing a time of formation, growth, and development.

forum A public meeting or open discussion used to voice ideas, often via television, radio, or newspaper.

fourth estate A journalistic term referring to a group of journalists or the public press.

franchise In its most common usage, a "franchise" refers to a business operation, often a retail store, that has been granted the right to use a company's name or to sell its goods and services.

free agent In sports, a player who is not under contractual obligation, and is free to negotiate with any team.

Freemason Also called a Mason, a member of the largest and most widely established fraternal order in the world. Freemasonry began in Europe as guilds originally restricted to stonecutters. In the 17th century they began to admit men of wealth, power, or social status, and over the years the guilds became more like societies, or clubs, devoted to general principles and ideals, such as fraternity, equality, religious toleration, and peace.

frontier A term often used to describe the end of civilized land, or the area just beyond it. In American mythology, the frontier represented the boundary of western expansion.

fugue A musical composition in which themes are expressed successively by a number of voices.

fulsome Offensive or insincere.

functional illiteracy A social classification referring to people whose reading and writing skills are insufficient for everyday life.

fundamentalism A social movement, or point of view, characterized by the rigid belief in the basic principles of one's society.

fusion Also **jazz fusion**. A musical style in which elements of jazz and rock are merged.

gable A triangular section of wall at the end of a pitched roof, or at the point where two slopes of the roof come together, often containing a window.

galvanize To induce an awareness or action.

gamut A complete range. In music, a series of notes.

gender A term categorizing an item by its sex or sexual identity as it relates to society or culture.

generic A term classifying something in a general group.

genre A literary classification of style linked by a common subject or theme.

genteel A social classification referring to one whose manners are refined and free from rudeness.

gentility A human character or trait possessing the qualities of being well-mannered and refined.

gentrification The process of restoring and upgrading a deteriorated urban property. The work is customarily performed or funded by the middle classes, which in turn forces the lower income residents out of the area.

gentry The upper or ruling class of a society.

gerontology The scientific study of aging. Factors studied include the biological, psychological, and sociological effects of old age.

ghetto An Italian term used originally to refer to a specific area of a city where Jews were required by law to reside, it has come to mean any section of a city, often depressed, occupied primarily by one or more minority groups, who live there because of social, economic, or legal pressure.

Gilded Age An era of especial wealth, culture, and good feeling. The arts are seen to flourish, money is being earned at high rates, and people are spending it extravagantly. In U.S. history the period around the end of the 19th century and the beginning years of the 20th century.

glossolalia Speaking in tongues.

golden age A historical era characterized by peace, prosperity, and happiness.

gospel A style of music, usually religious in lyrical content, sung by a choir or group of people.

gourmet One who is a connoisseur of fine food and drink.

graft To unite or join. In another context, the acquisition of gain (money) in dishonest or illegal ways.

grassroots A term used to describe people or a society living at a common, local level.

Great Depression The worst and longest economic collapse in modern industrial society, the Great Depression in the United

States began in late 1929 and lasted through the early 1940s, spreading to most of the world's other industrial countries.

halftone A cinematic term referring to light that is halfway between brightness and dark shadow.

hectare A metric unit used when measuring land. One hectare is equal to 2.471 acres.

hedonism The pursuit or devotion to things that provide pleasure, especially to the senses.

hegemony The predominant influence of one state over another.

hemp The fiber produced by the cannabis plant. Hemp can be woven to produce a strong sloth often used for tarps or sails, but can also be used for clothing.

heresy An opinion or belief based in religion. Most often heresy refers to the denials of the Roman Catholic church by a follower or believer.

heterogeneous Also **heterogenous**. A term meaning something made up of unrelated parts. The opposite of homogeneous.

hierarchy Most often used to refer to the structure of authority in a group or organization, ranked by authority or ability.

highbrow The highest class of a society. Often possessing the traits of being highly educated, cultured, and intellectual.

hinterlands A geographic term referring to land that is adjacent or just inland from a coast.

hippodrome An oval arena or open-air stadium used today for horse shows, but used in ancient times for horse and chariot races.

holistic A theory based on the principle that living matter is made up of whole parts, rather than the sum of its smaller parts.

homage To pay tribute to or honor, especially in a public setting.

homeopathy A medicinal style in which a disease or illness is treated with small doses of a drug that in larger quantities would produce symptoms of the disease.

homogamous From a biological term meaning an area that has only one type of flower or plant, often used to refer to an area of little or no cultural or ethical diversity.

homogeneity The state of things possessing similar qualities living together.

homophony A musical term characterized by a single melodic line that is accompanied by music.

honky-tonk A bar or dance hall in which loud music is played, usually classified as cheap or lower class. The term also refers to a type of ragtime music, characterized by the use of a tinny sounding piano.

hoopla A boisterous, public display of excitement.

hootenanny A musical term referring to an informal performance by folksingers, often including the audience's participation.

hostel A place of lodging, usually designated for young travelers, that is supervised and affordable.

hovel A small, run-down house, similar to a shack.

hucksterism A style of selling that includes bargaining or haggling over price.

Huguenots Members of a French Protestant culture that flourished in the 16th and 17th centuries.

humanism A philosophy or belief that emphasizes the dignity and worth of individual human beings.

humanizing To bestow the qualities or characteristics of a human to something inanimate.

hybrid Something that is made up of separate parts. In sociology, the term refers to the mixing of different cultures to form a new culture.

hydrology The scientific study of the properties, distribution, and effects of water and its uses.

hymn A religious song of praise or worship.

hyperbole A literary or oratory style that uses extreme exaggeration for emphasis.

hysterectomy The surgical removal of part or all of the uterus, performed to remove disease or to sterilize a woman.

iconoclastic A term used to describe an attack that made as an attempt to overthrow traditional or popular ideas or institutions.

iconoscope An early television-camera tube equipped with the ability to rapidly scan images and store them.

idealism The philosophy or practice of envisioning things in an ideal form. The term is often used to describe the subject of a piece of artwork or literature.

ideological A term referring to ideology, or relating to ideas.

ideology The collective term for the body of ideas and principles reflecting the social needs and aspirations of an individual, group, or culture.

idiom A literary term used to describe a word or expression that is peculiar to itself grammatically, or has no individual meaning. For example, *keeping tabs on.*

idiosyncrasy A peculiar or rare trait.

immigration The process of entering and settling into a country or region that is not one's native land.

imperialism The policy and practice by which a powerful nation extends and maintains economic and political control over weaker countries.

impressionism In art, a style or movement that developed in France in the late 19th century, characterized by nonrepresentational portrayals and such stylistic elements as the use of unmixed colors or small brushstrokes that simulate the reflection of light. Among the more prominent impressionist painters were Degas, Monet, and Renoir.

improvisation A theatrical style in which the performance is unrehearsed and unplanned.

inclusion The process or state of being included.

inculcate A term meaning to impress something on the mind of another by the use of repetition.

indentured laborers Workers who are bound to service as repayment for land or money.

indeterminacy The state of not being able to be determined, defined, or established.

indigenous A person or object originating and living in an area or environment.

indigent A social term referring to people who are impoverished or in need.

indigo A pea-type plant that produces flowers that are used to create a blue dye.

individualism The belief that oneself and one's personal independence is of primary importance before all others and things.

industrialism An economic and social system based on the development of large-scale industries and their productions. Other characteristics include mass production if inexpensive goods and the concentration of employment in urban factories.

inertia A state of laziness or lack of motion.

infanticide The act of killing an infant, often for the purpose of population or gender control.

innuendo An indirect or subtle comment, usually derogatory in nature.

inoculation A vaccine administered to protect people against a disease.

institutionalize To characterize as an institution or place a person in the care of institution. For example housing someone who is mentally ill into a mental institution.

insurgent Most often used in a political sense to refer to a person who revolts against civil authority, or a member of a political party who rebels against or challenges its leadership.

insurrection An act of open revolt against authority or a government.

integration The incorporation of diverse ethnic or social groups into a unified society.

interventionism In politics or national foreign policy, the process or policy of intervening in the affairs of another ruler or country.

isolationism A political policy or philosophy that advocates the belief that a nation's interests are best served by avoiding alliance or excessive contact with other nations.

itinerant A term referring to one who travels from place to place, especially as a means of finding work.

jeremiad A term used to refer to a lamentation, or cautionary or angry harangue.

jet-set A social class characterized by wealth who travel from one place to another.

Jim Crow laws A slang term describing the group of laws that enforced the segregation of blacks in the South.

journeyman A competent, tested worker in a skilled craft. Journeyman is the second stage in the structured learning process that begins with apprenticeship.

junto A small, secret group that is linked by a common interest or belief.

keelboat A riverboat with a keel or central beam, but without sails, that is used to carry freight.

kickback Money that is paid as a result of a secret agreement or coercion.

kinetograph Am early type of motion picture camera, developed by William K. L. Dickerson in 1891.

kinetoscope A device for viewing a continuous loop of film moved over a light source, with a rapidly rotating shutter to create the illusion of motion.

Ku Klux Klan A social group characterized as being white supremacists, who adhere to the belief that the white, Aryan race is superior, and that Blacks are inferior and unequal.

laissez-faire A French term meaning literally "let things alone," a policy of government nonintervention in individual or corporate financial affairs.

lament A song that expresses regret.

lampoon A humorous piece that ridicules or poke fun at a person, group, or institution.

legerdemain A show of skill or cleverness.

Levites Members of the Jewish tribe of Levi who are chosen to assist the Temple priests.

levy A term generally used to refer to the imposing or collection of taxes, or to the confiscation of property in default of an unpaid debt.

lexicon A group of terms used in a specific profession, often in the form of a dictionary.

libel The legal term for a written, published, or pictorial statement that maliciously damages another person's reputation.

licentiousness A term referring to characteristics that lack moral or sexual restraint.

limelight A focus of public attention.

lithography A style of publishing images in which the image is etched on a flat surface, often zinc or aluminum, treated with ink, and that transposed onto another surface such a paper.

liturgy A set of public forms followed in a Christian ceremony or ritual.

lobby A political term referring to a group of people whose goal is to influence legislators to favor a specific cause.

lobotomy An operation performed on the brain during which a portion of the brain is removed with the desired effect of altering a person's behavior.

locus A location characterized as the center or concentration of activity.

lowbrow A social classification possessing the traits of having unsophisticated preferences toward cultural events.

lyceum A Latin term for a hall where public lectures and concerts are presented.

lynching The execution, usually by hanging, of a person without a legal trial.

magistracy The position or function of a magistrate, or the district under their jurisdiction.

magistrate A public officer who possess the power to administer and enforce laws within a designated area.

mainstream A social term referring to the prevailing thoughts, influences, or activities of a specific area or period.

malaria An infectious disease, most often contracted from mosquitoes, that is characterized by chills and fever, and effects the operation of the liver, kidneys, and other vital organs.

mandate A law or command administered by a civil authority or ruler.

mandolin A musical instrument, similar to a guitar, that is played by depressing and strumming strings stretched from the base to the neck of the instrument.

mansard An architectural term referring to a roof, having two slopes on all four sides, with the lower slope being vertical and the upper slope being horizontal.

mantra A religious or sacred verbal prayer that is either sung or spoken in repetition.

marginalize A social classification characterized by confinement to a lower or outer limit or edge.

masochism A psychological disorder in which someone enjoys abuse and physical pain as a means of sexual gratification.

mass medium A broadcasting term referring to a means of public communication that reaches a large audience.

maternal A term referring to characteristics most often associated with a mother or motherhood.

matrilineal A sociological term referring to a society whose descendants follow a maternal ancestral line.

matrix A sociological term referring to a situation within which something else originates, develops, or is contained.

maypole A pole, used in the celebration of May Day, that is decorated with streamers that are wrapped around the pole as people dance around it.

McCarthyism A term used to refer to unsubstantiated accusations of communism or subversive activities. It derives from the actions of U. S. Senator Joseph McCarthy (1908-57), who led the aggressive campaign against communism's influence in the United States during the early 1950s.

mecca A place that is considered to be the center of activity or interest. The term derives from the Islamic holy city of Mecca, in Saudi Arabia, the birthplace of the Prophet Mohammed.

medieval A term used to describe someone or something as belonging to, or a part of, the Middle Ages.

medium A broadcasting term referring to a substance or item through which information is transmitted.

megaphone A device, shaped like a cone, that is used to amplify one's voice.

melodrama A theatrical term referring to an exaggeration of emotions or behaviors.

memorialist A literary term for a person who writes memoirs.

menagerie A collective display of live, wild animals.

Mennonites A social group whose members belong to the Anabaptist church and are characterized as living a simplistic, pacifistic, and nonresistant life.

mentor A teacher or counselor whose trust and wisdom are conveyed to the student.

mercantile A social classification characterized by the selling of goods and trade.

mercenaries People who are motivated by a desire for monetary or material gain. The term is usually used to refer to freelance soldiers who are hired by a foreign army to supplement or assist in training local troops.

meretricious A social trait that attracts attention by a display of vulgar behavior.

meritocracy A social system in which advancement is based on one's individual ability and achievements.

metaphysical Referring to a branch of philosophy concerned with the ultimate nature of reality and the relationship between mind and matter.

meter A musical or literary term referring to the rhythm that is produced as the lines are spoken or sung.

métier A trade, specialty, or forte.

metropolis A term referring to a large city, often with smaller cities or towns that thrive on the jobs generated by the larger city.

milieu A French term meaning an environment or setting.

militarism A glorification, or dominance, of the beliefs of a professional military class or its policies.

militia The term used to describe an army made up of ordinary citizens rather than professional or career soldiers. A militia would be intended to function as a reserve or contingent force, available to be called on in case of emergency.

millinery Articles, chiefly hats, that are produced by a milliner who is responsible for designing, making, trimming and selling.

minimalism A style of abstract painting that emphasizes extreme simplification of form and shape.

minstrel show A form of entertainment developed in the United States in the early 19th century, characterized by performances by white entertainers made up as blacks.

misanthropy A social belief of hatred and mistrust in mankind.

miscegenation The mixture, including cohabitation, marriage, and sexual relations, of different races.

missionary A member of a particular religious organization whose tradition is to "witness" by word and deed to the beliefs of their religion, so that others may come to know and understand it.

modality A tendency to conform to a general social pattern, or belong to a particular category or group.

modernism A state of being characterized by modern thought, character, or standards.

mogul A term used to refer to a rich or powerful person.

monogamy Within a relationship a term referring to being sexually involved with only one partner.

monographic A term referring to a written essay or book that is specific in length, often limited to one subject.

monologue A long speech delivered by one person.

monopoly An economic situation in which only a single company sells or produces an item or service, allowing them to control availability and pricing.

moral fiber A sociological term referring to the basic moral beliefs of a society, on which other behaviors are based.

moratorium A temporary suspension, often referring to criminal punishment or the payment of a debt.

mordancy A term used to describe behavior that is extremely sarcastic or painful.

Mormons Religious followers of a religion based on the message of an ancient prophet, who imparted a sacred history of the Americas to Joseph Smith. Smith became the founder of the religion and published the message as the Book of Mormon in 1830.

Morse code A form of communication developed by Samuel F. B. Morse, the inventor of the electric telegraph, in 1836, in which short tones (dots) and long tones (dashes) are transmitted and interpreted by the receiver.

motif An artistic or literary term referring to a dominant theme or central idea.

muckraker One who searches for and exposes the misconduct of those in public or political life.

mugwump A slang term that refers to someone who acts independently or remains neutral, especially with regard to politics.

mulatto A term used to describe someone with one white parent and one Black parent.

municipal A term referring to an area that is locally self-governed, rather than reliant on another city or town for government rule.

municipality A political unit, such as a city or town, that is self-governed. The term also refers to the body of officials who manage the governmental affairs of the city or town.

nadir An astronomical term for the point of the celestial sphere opposite the zenith, it is most often used to refer to the lowest point.

narrative A story or account, or the process of telling it.

nationalism The devotion to the beliefs and interests of a specific nation.

nativist A person opposed to the presence of foreigners and immigrants in the U.S.

naturalist A scientist in one of the fields of natural history, especially zoology or botany. The term also refers to a believer in naturalism.

navigation The process of steering or guiding a vessel. The term is most often used in reference to ocean travel.

neoclassical In art and architecture, a style or discipline that emulated classical Greek and Roman forms and motifs, popular in the late 18th century.

network In popular media such as television, a chain of stations whose programming is controlled and coordinated by a central organization.

New Deal The collective name given to a large-scale program of domestic government policies enacted under President Franklin D. Roosevelt, especially those intended to counteract the effects of the Great Depression between 1933 and 1938.

nickelodeon An early movie theater. The name derives from the 5-cent admission price.

nihilism A political or sociological belief that the destruction of present institutions is necessary for future growth or improvement. The term also refers to the philosophical belief that all values are arbitrary, and that nothing can be truly known or communicated.

nomad A member of a group or culture with no fixed home or homeland, which travels or migrates from place to place.

nonpartisan Business conducted without reference to political party, or an office, such as a judgeship, that requires no specific party affiliation.

nosology The science or study that deals with the listing or classification of diseases.

nostalgia A sentimental longing for the past.

novel In literature, a work of fiction of some length in which characters and situations are depicted within the framework of a plot.

nuance A small, subtle difference or change.

nuclear family A standard model for the family unit, consisting of a mother, a father, and one or more children under the age of majority living in the same household.

nullify To counteract or offset, or invalidate.

nurture A term that refers to the raising or support of the young.

obelisk A four-sided, tapering monolith with a pyramid or conical top. They were widely constructed by the Egyptian pharaohs, and were associated with sun worship.

obstructionist A person who blocks or delays a process or progress.

octoroon A person whose ancestry is one-eighth African American.

Odd Fellows A fraternal order, begun in England in the 17th century, that provides its members retirement, educational, and medical benefits.

oligarchy A form of government in which power is held by a small, select group of individuals that act in their own interests rather than those of the people they govern.

omniscience The state of being all-knowing, that is, knowing everything.

oracle The shrine of a prophetic deity, at which prophecy is revealed. The term is also used to refer to a person who has a history of accurately predicting future trends or events.

oral tradition The term used to refer to the preservation of personal or cultural history by word of mouth, without written document, usually in the form of epic songs, stories, or poetry.

oratory The art of speaking or speechmaking, especially speeches designed to influence the judgments or feelings of those listening.

original sin A Christian theological belief that holds that all humans are born with inherent sin, attributed variously to the fall of Satan or Adam's first sin in the Garden of Eden.

orthodoxy An accepted or established doctrine or creed, and the adherence to it. The term "orthodox" is also often used to refer to the most conservative or traditional element, especially of a religion.

pagan A follower of a religion or sect not Christian, Muslim, or Jewish.

pageantry Elaborate public spectacle or fanfare.

pamphlet A small, informal publication, often political in nature, used to express a specific viewpoint or opinion.

panoply A splendid or striking display.

paradigm An example or incident that serves as a pattern or model for all that follows.

paradox An apparently contradictory statement or example that seems impossible, but may be true.

parameters The limits or boundaries of any given definition. The term is often used to define the limits within which a problem or project must be accomplished.

parochial school A type of schooling for children, most often of grade school or high school level, that is sponsored by a religious institution.

pasteurization The process of heating food, most often a beverage or other liquid, to kill microorganisms in order to prevent disease and increase shelf life.

pastiche In literature or drama, a work that clearly and deliberately imitates or mimics the work of another artist.

pastoral Most often used to refer to a lifestyle or setting that is simple, serene, or idyllic, usually possessing elements of rural life.

paternal Of or relating to the father or male line.

pathos In literature, music, or art, a quality intended to arouse an emotional reaction such as pity, sorrow, or sympathy.

patriarchal A type of social system in which the father is the head of the household, and ancestry is determined through the paternal, or father's line.

patrilineal The determination or account of ancestry or lineage through the paternal line.

patronage The support of a cause by means of financial assistance.

pavilion A light, usually open-sided structure; a tent or in the form of a tent.

payola In radio, a term that refers to the payoffs given to certain disk jockeys or program managers to play or promote a certain record or artist.

pedantry The stressing or calling of attention to one's learning or education, or the emphasis on the trivial details of learning.

peer group A social organization consisting of a number of individuals with the same social standing or classification.

penology The science or study of criminal imprisonment, or prison culture. Penology seeks to determine the most effective use of imprisonment both as a deterrent to future criminal activity and as a rehabilitative process.

pension A sum of money that is paid on a regular basis, usually as a retirement benefit.

per capita A Latin term meaning "by heads," used to refer to the apportion of something per person.

periodical A publication, such as a magazine or newspaper, that is published on a regularly scheduled, or periodic, basis.

peripheral Located on a outer boundary. Also used to refer to related items of minor importance or relevance to a central item.

philanthropy In business, a term used to describe the ongoing practice or philosophy, usually of an individual, of giving to or establishing charitable or humanistic causes or foundations.

philosophy In general terms, a speculative inquiry into the source and nature of human knowledge, or the system and ideas based on such thinking.

photocomposition A printing process by which text or images are processed directly to film or photosensitive paper for reproduction.

photoemission The property of certain substances to emit electrons when exposed to light.

physiognomy Of or relating to the facial features, or the art or science of judging a person based on their facial features.

piedmont The land or landscape around the foot of a mountain or mountain range.

piety The demonstration of devotion and reverence to God or family.

pilgrimage The voyage taken by a pilgrim to a site of spiritual or political importance. Most often used to refer to a religious journey.

pillory In literature or drama, to expose to ridicule or abuse.

pimp A person who manages or procures customers for a prostitute.

pioneer The first to discover, found, or settle a particular land or scientific discovery. Widely used to refer to the early settlers of the American West.

pious Adamantly observant of religion and religious practices.

platform In politics, the collection of principles and policies agreed to and supported by all candidates of a party.

plebeian A slang or derogatory term for a person or style that is vulgar or common.

pluralism A philosophical belief that reality is made up of many different parts, and that no one theory or worldview is adequate for all aspects of life.

pneumatic tire A type of tire that is filled with compressed air. Also called a "balloon tire."

polarization The division of a group into two opposite and/or conflicting positions.

polemic In politics or literature, the art or practice of debate or causing deliberate controversy.

politicize To bring political considerations into an existing situation, or to make the situation a political event.

poll tax A type of tax levied on citizens when they are preparing to vote. It has occasionally been used as a political tool to prevent lower income citizens from voting.

polygamy A type of marriage made in which a husband or wife may have more than one spouse.

polyglot From the term for one with a knowledge of several languages, used to refer to a mix or collection of various cultures or influences.

polyphony A form of music made up of many different tones or voices.

populism A political belief that governmental power should be in the hands of the people, or population, rather than corporations or the rich.

portent An indication or foreshadowing of an event about to occur.

portico A porch or walkway with a roof supported by pillars or columns leading to the entrance of a building.

postbellum Referring to the period following the American Civil War.

postimpressionism In art, a series of movements and styles that followed and was influenced by impressionism. It was first used to refer to an exhibition of works by Cezanne, Seurat, and Van Gogh held in London in 1910.

postmodernism In architecture, a loose description of a group of design styles and tendencies that followed the modernist period. The term describes certain work dating from the mid-1960s, and remains a dominant trend in American architecture.

pragmatism The belief that the purpose of thoughts is to guide action, and that the effect of an idea is more important than its origin.

Pre-Raphaelite A descriptive term for a group of 19th-century English artists and critics whose work was inspired by medieval and Renaissance painters up to the time of the Italian painter Raphael (1483-1520).

precedent A previously established example used as a reference for a current situation or case.

predestination A religious or philosophical belief that man's fate or destiny is determined prior to birth.

prenuptial agreement A legal contract between the parties of a marriage agreed to in advance that determines the rights, usually financial, of each in the event of a divorce.

preservationism A social movement that focuses and advocates the preservation of natural areas, historical sites, and endangered species.

primordial A term referring to something happening first in a sequence of time, or the original or primary item of its kind.

principality An area ruled by a prince, or the position, authority, or jurisdiction of a prince.

privatism The social position of being concerned only with one's own interests and lifestyle.

probation In law, the act of suspending the sentence of a criminal on the promise of good behavior after freedom is granted.

probity A social term referring to a state of uprightness or confirmed integrity.

procreation The act of producing offspring.

progeny The offspring or descendant of a group.

progressive A social term referring to the belief in advancement, or proceeding in steps.

Prohibition The legal ban on the production and sale of alcoholic beverages. The Prohibition Act, also referred to as the Volstead Act, went into effect on January 15, 1920.

proletariat A low-income class characterized by a lack of possession in capital or production, and who make their living by selling their labor.

promiscuity The quality of being sexually indiscriminate in one's choice of partners.

propaganda Material distributed by the advocates of a specific cause to aid in influencing others to join their beliefs.

propinquity Proximity or nearness.

prose A literary term referring to spoken language, without metrical structure or rhyme.

protagonist The main character in a literary work, usually possessing good qualities. The protagonist is often the hero of the work.

Protestantism A religious term referring to a belief of the Protestant church, characterized by a belief that the Bible is the sole source of revelation and faith alone is justification to all believers. Protestantism is based on the theologies of Luther, Calvin, and Zwingli and was formed as a result of protest against the laws of the Catholic church.

provender Dry food used to feed livestock, including hay, oats, and wheat.

provincialism A society formed on the basis of people from the less sophisticated, unfashionable provinces of a region.

proxy A person who is authorized to act as a substitute for another, often supported by written authorization.

psalm Similar to a hymn, a religious or sacred song.

Psalter A religious book containing the Book of Psalms.

public weal A term for government assistance, or welfare.

pueblo A village inhabited by Native Americans in the southwestern United States. Contiguous flat-roofed adobe or stone houses in groups.

pugilism The skill, practice, and sport of boxing, or fighting with fists.

Pullman car A railroad sleeper car, designed by George M. Pullman (1831-97), in which the upper berths could be folded away, and the lower seats converted into sleeping berths. It was patented in 1863.

pulp magazines A popular term for a type of magazine or periodical, most often featuring sensationalist stories or popular fiction, such as mystery stories and science fiction. The term derives from the cheap paper the magazines were printed on.

pulpit A term, religious in reference, for an elevated platform or stand used for preaching or conducting a religious service.

punitive A term referring to inflicting or an intent to inflict punishment.

Puritan A member of a group living in the 16th and 17th centuries, made up of English Protestants who advocated strict religious discipline and the simplification of life and religious ceremonies.

pyre A funeral rite in which the body is placed on fire atop a pile of combustible material.

pyrotechnics The art of manufacturing fireworks, or a brilliant display of light.

quadroon A person whose ancestry is one-fourth African-American.

Quaker A member of the Society of Friends, a Christian denomination of the mid-17th century that rejected formal sacraments, creeds, priesthood, and violence.

quickening The process of the development of a fetus during pregnancy.

racism The belief that a racial or ethnic group is inferior due to their race or nationality.

radicalism A term that refers collectively to the actions or philosophies of radicals.

ragtime An American musical genre, mostly written for piano, that combined 19th century African-American musical styles with the chromatic harmonies of contemporary European music. It is characterized by syncopated melodies, usually in 2/4 time, over a regularly accented base.

rationalism A philosophical discipline that maintains that reason is the best guide for belief and action.

reactionary One who is opposed to progress, development, or liberalism.

realism A philosophical discipline inclined towards truth and pragmatism. In art, the representation of objects as they actually appear.

reciprocity A political policy in which the parties to a treaty or agreement are granted equally advantageous concessions.

Reconstruction The term used for the rebuilding plan established for the southern, formerly Confederate states following the American Civil War.

reformist A person with the political intent of bringing about change or reform.

rehabilitation The process of restoring something to usefulness, or to its former condition.

renaissance A rebirth or revival. Often used in art or music to refer to the renewed popularity of or interest in an older style or fashion.

reparation Most often used to refer to monetary compensation required from a nation defeated in war to allay or offset some of the costs of repairing the war damage.

repertoire The stock of performance numbers, such as songs or plays, performed by a player or company.

republican A member of a political party of the United States, or one who advocates a republican form of government.

repudiate To reject the validity of, or refuse to recognize or acknowledge.

reservation Land set aside by a government that provides a place for a specific group of people to live. This land is "reserved" for them to use. Most often used to refer to the areas used for the forced relocation of Native Americans during the settlement of the American West.

reserve clause An aspect of a baseball contract, in which the team reserved the exclusive right to automatically renew a player's existing contract, and bound the player to one particular team until retirement, or until traded or released.

revivalist Someone who revives or restores a belief no longer in use. Also used to refer to a minister or preacher who operates in a carnival-like atmosphere.

revue A theatrical term referring to a musical show consisting of skits, songs, and dances, often satirizing current events or trends.

rhetoric The study or art of the use of language and persuasion.

ringer A sports term referring to someone of much greater skill who is placed into a group of amateurs or less skills athletes.

ritualism The practice or observance of a religious ritual.

rotunda An architectural term for a circular building or dome.

royalty A fee paid to a writer or composer based on the profits of the piece's sales.

rubric A literary term describing the distinction of a letter or title from the regular text, often with the use of color or a larger font.

rural A term used to characterize people or life of or from the country.

rusticity A term used to describe life or people from the country, often characterized by a lack of sophistication or elegance.

Sabbath The first day of the week, Sunday, observed as the day of rest and worship by most Christians. The seventh day of the week from Friday evening to Saturday evening observed by Jews as a day of rest and worship.

sacred A term used to classify an object that is dedicated for the worship of a god.

sadomasochism The deriving of sexual pleasure from both sadism and masochism.

salacious Something that is appealing to, or stimulating, in a sexual way.

saloon An establishment where alcoholic beverages are sold and drunk, much like a tavern.

sanctify To reserve something for sacred use, or to grant something religious sanction with an oath or vow, such as marriage.

sanctions In political terms, restrictions or prohibitions, usually economic, against dealings or interactions with other countries.

satellite A device used to send and receive information.

satire A literary term used to describe a work in which a human vice or act of foolishness is attacked through irony, derision, or sarcasm.

saturation point The point at which something is completely engulfed or consumed by something else.

saturnalian A type of festival or celebration based on the Roman festival of Saturn, which began on December 17.

scatological A term used to describe anything relating to fecal matter.

schematize To develop a scheme or plan.

schism A separation or discord.

schismatic The process relating to, or to engage in, a schism.

secession The process of withdrawing from a union or branch. In American history, commonly applied to certain states in the South leaving the United States union.

sector A part or area, often relating to geographic locations and governmental bodies.

secular A term referring to an approach that does not relate to religious or spiritual views.

secularization The process of reforming without the contribution or control of religion.

sedition Behavior or language designed to incite rebellion against authority.

segregation To be separated, usually through force, from the mainstream for reasons of race or creed. The term is most often used to refer to the forced separation of blacks and whites, most notable in the southern U.S.

self-aggrandizement The act of enhancing or exaggerating one's own importance, power, or reputation.

seminal A term used to describe anything relating to, containing, or conveying semen.

seminary A school with the focus of training religious leaders such as priests, ministers, or rabbis. The term is also used to describe a private school of higher education for girls.

senescence The process of growing old and aging.

sensationalism A literary or political term describing the use and application of the sensational or extraordinary.

serial To form or arrange in a series, often referring to publications and television dramas.

sexism Prejudice or discrimination based on sex, most often used as those types of feelings toward women.

Shakers Members of a millenarian sect that originated in England in 1747, which practiced celibacy and an ascetic communal life.

sharecropper A person who is placed in a position of servitude by which he or she provides labor for the landowner in return for a share of the profits of the merchandise, usually an agricultural crop.

simulcast A broadcast via FM, AM, or television that is broadcast to the audience as the event is happening.

singularity A trait that marks someone or something as being different or peculiar.

social Darwinism A sociological principle based on the belief that humans compete in a struggle for existence in much the same way as animals and plants, in which the fittest are more likely to survive. The theory is based on the principles of natural selection outlined by Charles Darwin (1809-82) in his 1859 book, *On the Origin of Species*, which forms the foundation of modern evolutionary thought.

sodomy Sexual intercourse with a member of the same sex or with an animal; oral or anal intercourse with a member of the opposite sex. From the homosexual activities of the men in the biblical (Genesis) city of Sodom.

solo A composition or passage for an individual voice or instrument.

Sons of Liberty A secret patriotic organization, begun in 1765 in the American colonies to oppose the Stamp Act. After the act was repealed, the society continued to foster resistance against British colonial policy. Its leaders included Revolutionary War figures Samuel Adams and Paul Revere.

soprano A musical term used to classify a voice with the highest tonal range, usually achieved by a woman or a young boy.

souk An open-air market, most commonly found in an Arab city.

sovereignty A supreme power, especially over a political body.

spatial A term used to describe something relating to or involving the nature of space.

speakeasy A slang term for an illegal bar or club which served alcohol during the time of Prohibition.

spina bifida A congenital defect in which the spinal column is imperfectly closed so that part of the meninges or spinal cord protrudes, often resulting in hydrocephalus and other neurological disorders.

standardization The bringing of different parts or units to a uniform, or standard, level.

stanza One division of a poem, composed of two or more lines.

status quo The state of affairs as they exist.

stereotype A simplified or representative image of a type.

sterilization A medical procedure by which a man or woman is made sterile, or unable to bear or father children.

stigma A mark or other indication of infamy or disgrace.

stigmata In Christian thought, marks or wounds corresponding with those suffered by Christ at the crucifixion.

stillborn The medical term for the birth of a dead baby or fetus.

stimulus and response In psychological theory, a behavioristic phrase referring to human reaction to outside or environmental stimuli.

structuralism A method of language analysis based on physical attributes of speech and the underlying abstract system of language structure.

strumpet A colloquial or colorful term for a prostitute.

subculture A subgroup that exists within a larger cultural framework or system.

subsidy A form of financial assistance. The term is most often used to refer to financial support given by a government.

suburban The areas surround a centralized urban location or city.

suburbanization The process by which rural areas are incorporated or developed into a larger system of suburbs surrounding a major city.

subversive Policies or actions that are intended to undermine, or subvert, established systems. The term is most often used to refer to oppositional political activity.

succor Support or assistance, especially in time of stress or hardship.

suffrage The right or privilege of voting.

suffragette A person who advocates the right of women to vote.

surrogate A substitute or replacement.

syndication In arts such as television and journalism, the practice of offering an article, show, or other work for publication or broadcast simultaneously to a number of different venues.

symbiotic A relationship in which one part is dependent on another for its survival, or a mutually beneficial relationship.

symptomatic Showing evidence or symptoms of a known condition.

syncopation In music, a shift of accent or emphasis in which the weak beat is stressed.

syncretic A solution or hypothesis brought about by the combination of different types of beliefs of practices.

synthesize To bring together or make whole from a variety of different sources or elements.

taproot The main root of a plant that grows straight down from the stem. The term is also used to refer to the original or driving inspiration on which an idea or organization is based.

tariff A type of tax or duty imposed on goods that are imported from another country or locale.

temperance The organized efforts to temper or abstain from the use of alcoholic beverages.

tenement A form of housing characterized by multiple dwellings or living units within a single physical structure. The term has come to be associated with low-income housing.

tenor The highest natural male voice. The term is also used to refer to those who sing the tenor part or music written for it.

theocracy A theory or method of government in which a society is ruled by members of the priesthood or religious authority.

threshing A method of harvesting grains, such as wheat, by beating them with a machine or flail to separate the grain from the straw.

time-share A form of real estate ownership in which a person purchases the right to a property for a period of time. It is often used in vacation locales.

tonality The arrangement of notes or chords of a composition around a given note, called the tonic note.

tragicomedy A combination of the words "tragic" and "comedy," in literature or drama, a term used to describe a work possessing classic elements of both.

tramcar A cable car. The term is most often used to refer to the type that is suspended from an overhead cable.

transcendentalism A belief or philosophy that asserts the existence of a higher spiritual reality apart from the physical world.

transculturation The crossing over or mixing of elements from two or more separate cultures.

transgressive A term used to refer to something that goes beyond or over a set of boundaries or limits.

transient A person or phase that stays or lasts only a brief time, and then moves or passes away.

transitory Something that exists or stays only briefly.

treatise A detailed, usually well-researched written treatment of a specific subject.

trivialize To make or treat someone or something as insignificant or minor.

troubadour A term that refers to a member of the group or class of lyric poets in Provence, northern Italy, and northern Spain in the 12th and 13th centuries.

troupe An acting company. The term is often used to refer to a traveling or touring group of performers.

trundle bed A low bed mounted on wheels or castors that may be rolled under another bed for storage when not in use.

turnvereins A type of physical education or gymnastics club, associated with German and Swedish immigrants to the United States in the 19th century.

tutelary One who is in a guardian or teaching role. The term may also be used to refer to the role itself.

typesetting The process of setting individual characters into words for the purpose of publishing and printing.

typologically A system of language classification in which languages are grouped according to similarities and differences in structure.

typology The classification or organization of objects by type.

uglification The process by which something becomes or is made uglier. The term is often used to refer to the deterioration of neighborhoods or landscapes brought about by increased urbanization.

urban A classification of an area as, like, or constituting a city.

urbane Suave, sophisticated, and refined of manner or dress.

urbanite A person who lives in a city or who may be characterized by the influences of life in a city.

urbanization The process of building up an area and its subsequent development of the attributes of a city.

utilitarian Something defined or identified based on its usefulness rather than its esthetic appeal.

utopian Most often used to refer to ideas or examples possessing ideal elements, as in a so-called perfect world.

vaccination A medical procedure by which one is protected from possible infection by a virus or disease by the injection of a weakened or killed pathogen.

vanguard The leading or foremost element of a trend or movement.

variegated Something that has been changed or altered to provide variety. The term is often used to refer to the color markings of wild animals.

vaudeville A type of theatrical entertainment, most often made up of a variety of separate elements, popular in the United States in the late 19th and early 20th centuries.

venereal disease A disease or group of diseases transmitted through sexual intercourse.

venue In law, the locale where an illegal activity takes place. The term is also used to refer to the place from which the jury is drawn, and where the trial is held.

vernacular Most often used to refer to the native or local dialect or language of a particular geographic area, the term also refers to the vocabulary and references specific to an art or discipline.

vertigo A sensation of dizziness.

vibrato A musical term used to refer to a tremulous or pulsating effect in voice or instrument caused by slight, rapid variations in pitch.

vice In general, meaning wickedness or sexual immorality, the term is often used to describe the crimes associated with prostitution.

vignette In literature or film, a short, descriptive sketch or scene.

virtuoso Most often used to refer to a person with exceptional or masterful musical skills in instrument or voice.

visceral Intensely emotional.

vituperation Severe abuse of censure, most often with language or written commentary.

voluntarism The belief that people should give of their time to public, or volunteer, work.

WASP An acronym for white Anglo-Saxon Protestant. A slang term often used to refer generically to the suburban white middle class.

watershed Literally, a ridge of high land dividing two areas drained by different river systems. The term is often used to refer to a seminal or defining event, or turning point.

weaning The process by which children are taught to take nourishment other than by suckling. The term is also used to refer to a slow process of withdrawal, as from a habit or interest.

welfare A public assistance program providing at least a minimum amount of economic aid to individuals who earn less money than is needed to maintain an adequate standard of living.

white supremacy The belief that those of the Caucasian race are superior to all other races, especially blacks, and the opposition to inter-racial relations of any kind.

yeoman An antiquated term for a small, independent farmer.

yodel A type of singing or calling, most often associated with Scandinavian countries, in which the voice fluctuates between normal tones and falsetto.

zenith The peak, or highest point.

zoning codes In law, the division of a municipality or township into areas designated for residential or business use.

Index

A

A. T. Stewart Store, 81
a capella folksinging, 161
AARP. *See* American Association of Retired Persons
"Abbeys of Misrule," 326
Abbott, Robert S., 248, 254
ABC. *See* American Broadcasting Company
abolition, 95, 240, 563. *See also* slavery
aboriginal landscapes, 253
abortion, 123, 423–424, 428–429, 430
Abrams v.*United States*, 248
academic study
    of folk music, 162
    of landscapes, 259–260
    of motion pictures, 152–153
    of towns, 556–557
Académie Française (Richelieu), 527
academies, 527
Academy of the Natural Sciences, 531
Acadia National Park, 274
Acadians, colonial housing, 212
acid rock music, 404–405
Acton, William, 418
Actors Studio, 497
Acuff, Roy, 110
Adams, Abigail, 72, 119
Adams, Andrew, 546
Adams, Carol J., 176
Adams, Franklin P., 230
Adams, John Quincy, 92, 301–302
Adams, Samuel, 353
Addams, Jane, 144, 425, 566, 567, 568
Addison, Joseph, 529
Ade, George, 226
Adeler, Max, 226
Adler, Dankmar, 83
administrators, women as, 207–208
adolescence
    African American, 4, 7, 8
    automobile and, 511–512
    character of, 3
    colonial, 1–4, 413–414
    consumer behavior, 400, 401
    contemporary, 11–12
    definition of, 1
    delinquency, 2, 3, 6–7
    dependence on family, 6, 7–8
    education, 7, 8–9
    etiquette of, 270–271
    gender differences, 2, 3–4, 6
    in Great Depression, 11
    hippie counterculture and, 404–405
    in the Industrial Age, 7–10
    middle-class, 6, 7, 8–10, 11
    nightlife and, 290–291
    nineteenth century, 4–7

    organizations for, 9
    peer culture of, 9, 10–11
    post-war era, 11
    in the Progressive Era, 9
    Puritan, 1–3, 4
    radio and, 395, 396, 401
    rebellion, 1–2, 3, 6–7, 9, 10–12
    religion and, 2, 3
    in Revolutionary America, 4–5
    rock music and, 395, 396, 399–400, 401
    "scientific" understanding of, 8
    sexual behavior during, 9–10, 413–415
    of slaves, 4, 7
    social protest and, 428
    twentieth century, 7–12
    of women, 4–6
    working-class, 6–7, 9–10
    in World War II, 11
adornment, personal. *See* clothing; fashion; hair styles
adultery, 117, 415, 421
adulthood, transition to, 39–40
Adventure, Mystery, and Romance (Cawelti), 342
Adventures of Huckleberry Finn (Twain), 226, 534
advertising
    architecture as, 84
    art and, 540, 541
    of dime novels, 342
    of fiction, 350
    journalism and, 242
    magazine, 345–346
    newspaper, 243, 372
    political, 475
    radio, 110, 390–391, 394
    railroad and, 508
    sports and, 456, 459
    television, 471, 473, 475, 476
    tourism and, 522
    See also marketing
affluent. *See* wealthy
AFL. *See* American Federation of Labor
African-American literacy, 366
African Americans
    adolescence, 4, 7–8
    aging, 296–297
    art, 539, 540
    in baseball, 453–455
    black power movement, 66–67
    black pride, 403, 408
    celebrations, 12, 18, 19, 20, 310
    childhood, 41
    clothing, 74
    dance, 16–17
    discrimination, 61. *See also* racism; slavery
    emancipation, 20
    etiquette in nineteenth century, 268–269
    fraternal organizations, 177, 178, 179, 181, 182–183

African Americans (*continued*)
frontier and, 200
funeral customs, 18–19
hairstyles of, 77
Harlem Renaissance, 27
holidays, 311
humor, 225, 228
in industrial cities, 60–61
landscapes, 254
literacy among, 366
literature, 539–540
marriage, 122
as Masons, 177, 180
mortality, 132, 135
in motion pictures, 142–143, 153
music, 101–102, 104, 290, 356
African American identity, 13
African influences, 14–17
bebop, 29, 104, 290
blues, 23–25, 27–29
commercialization, 20, 24
as a communication tool, 19
development of, 20
gospel, 21–23, 27, 160
Gullah, 17
influence on rock music, 403
jazz, 25–27, 29
oral tradition and, 13–14
origin of, 15–16
prior to Civil War, 13–20
rap music, 407, 408
religious, 21–23, 27
rock, 28–29, 408
rock and roll, 398, 399
secular, 19–20
soul, 28, 29, 403
spirituals, 17–18, 21
twentieth-century, 101–102, 104
work songs, 19
newspapers, 245–246
nightlife, 286, 287–288
nineteenth-century urban, 58
Odd Fellowship, 179
population, 52, 65
press of, 240, 373–374
publishing and, 370
radio and, 395–396
religious revivals, 307
sexual stereotypes of, 427
as slaves. *See* slavery; slaves
in sports, 445, 446, 457
stereotypes in rock music, 403
suburban, 468–469
in theater, 488, 490, 494–495, 496, 498
travel, 522
urban migration, 399, 456
women, 561, 566, 568–569. *See also* women
African Methodist Zion Publishing House, 370
Africans, influence on music, 14–17, 409
AFRS. *See* Armed Forces Radio Service
"After the Ball," 356
aged. *See* aging; old age
aging
biology of, 293–294
economics of, 299–301
ethnic differences, 296–297

gender and, 296, 297
Greco-Roman cultural views, 294
historical views, 294–295
life expectancy and, 293–294
living arrangements, 298
marital status and, 298
nineteenth-century views on, 298–299
politics of, 301–303
population, 295, 296, 297
poverty and, 299–300
preventing, 293
retirement and, 300–301
stages of, 294
women and, 294, 298
See also old age
agriculture
crops, 314–315
cotton, 317–318, 322–323
indigo, 317
rice, 316, 318, 320, 323
sugar, 318, 323
tobacco, 315, 317
fairs, 329
Native American, 253
plantation. *See* plantation
selective harvesting, 253
technological advances in, 198
towns and, 558
See also cultivation; rural life
Aid to Families with Dependent Children, 50
AIDS, 430
Aiken, George L., 488
Aiken, William, 318, 320
Ailey, Alvin, 541, 542
AIM. *See* American Indian Movement
Ainsworth psalter, 352
airline industry, 512. *See also* aviation
airports, architecture of, 86
ALA. *See* American Library Association
Alabama, tribal lands, 194–195
Alaska, as frontier, 200
Alaska National Interest Lands Conservation Act (1980), 275
Albee, Edward Franklin, 489, 490
Albion's Seed (Fischer), 168
Albright Gallery, 539
alcohol, nightlife and, 281–283, 284, 289–290
Alcott, Bronson, 171
Alcott, William A., 438
Alexander, James, 362
Alfred A. Knopf (publisher), 374
Alger, Horatio, 341
Ali, Muhammad, 457
All in the Family, 481
All Saints Day, 312
All Souls Day, 312
All Things Considered, 250
Allegheny County Courthouse, 383
Allen, Nathan, 122
Allen, Ruth, 422
Allen, Woody, 233, 397
Allen, Zachariah, 81
Allestree, Richard, 264
Alley Theatre, 400
Almanacke for New England for the Year 1639, An, 338
almanacs, 222, 338, 339
Alpha Kappa Alpha, 568

Alpha Phi, 568
Alsop, George, 324
Altman, Robert, 153
AMA. *See* American Medical Association
Amateur Athletic Union, 444
amateur radio, 387–388
AME Book Concern, 370
American Academy of Dramatic Art, 491
American Academy of the Arts, 532
American Anti-Slavery Society, 240
American Art Union, 532
American Artists' Congress, 538
American Association, 447
American Association of Retired Persons, 302
American Association of University Women, 568
American Automobile Association, 518
American Bandstand, 400
American Bible Society, 366
American Broadcasting Company, 427
American Coffee House, 531
American Company, 530
American Education Society, 366
American Express, 300
American Express Company, 518
American Federation of Labor, 209, 210
American Folklife Center, 162
American Folklore Society, 162
American Giants, 453
American Graffiti (1973), 153, 512
American Independent Pictures, 152
American Indian Movement, 405
American League, 447
American Library Association, 373
American Lyceum, 532
American Magazine, 236
American Medical Association, 123, 201
American Mercury (Mencken), 556
American Minerva, 237
American Museum of Pierre Eugène Du Simitière, 531
American museums, 532
American News Company, 347, 374
American Newspaper Publishers Association, 243
American Psychiatric Association, 429
American Radio Relay League, 388
American Railway Union, 508
American Renaissance, 383–384
American Revolution. *See* Revolutionary War
American Society for the Prevention of Cruelty to
   Animals, 334
American Spelling Book (Webster), 338
American Sunday School Union, 366
American Telephone and Telegraph, 96, 473
American Tobacco Company, 395
American Tract Society, 366
American War for Independence. *See* Revolutionary War
American Way of Death, The (Mitford), 137
American Writers' Congress, 538
America's Cup Race, 440
Ames, Nathaniel, 222
Amos n' Andy, 230
amusement. *See* leisure; nightlife; popular entertainment; sports
amusement parks, 30–33, 35. *See also* theme parks
Anaheim, CA, 64
ANC. *See* American News Company
Ancient Arabic Order of the Nobles of the Mystic Shrine.
   See Shriners

Ancient Order of Hibernians, 181
Ancient Order of the United Workmen, 179, 184
Anderson, Eddie, 228
Anderson, Laurie, 105
Anderson, Margaret, 542
Anderson, Marian, 104
Anderson, Sherwood, 556
Anderson, Tom, 283
Andre (1798), 485
Androboros (1714), 483
Andrus, Ethel Percy, 302
Anheuser-Busch Brewing Company, 282
animation, 148–149, 229
annexation, suburban, 464–465
Anson, "Cap" Adrian, 448–449
anti-masonry movement, 178–179
Anti-Saloon League, 283
anti-urban bias, 254–255
Antiquities Act (1906), 276–277, 278
Apache Indians, 199
apartments, 214–215, 216–217, 218, 220
Apocalypse Now (1979), 153
Apollo Gallery, 532
Appalachian Mountains, as colonial border, 190
apprenticeship, 1–2, 40
Apte, Mahadev L., 231
Arbuckle, Roscoe "Fatty," 147
Arbuthnot, Mr., 230
arcades, shopping, 81
architecture
   American Renaissance, 383–384
   Beaux-Arts classical, 383–384
   Chicago School, 83
   City Beautiful movement, 383–384
   collegiate, 378, 379, 381–382, 384
   colonial, 78–79, 210–213, 378–379
   commercial, 78
      Art Deco style, 84
      for auto industry, 84
      in Chicago, 82, 83, 841
      colonial, 78–79
      dams, 85
      Gothic Revival, 81, 381
      Greek Revival, 79
      historic preservation of, 87
      Moderne style, 84
      Modernist influence, 85–86
      neo-Romanesque style, 83
      in New York, 82, 83, 84
      Palazzo style, 81, 82
      postmodern, 87
      suburban, 85, 86
      textile mills, 79, 81
      twentieth-century, 83–87
   effects of transportation on, 85
   of factories, 84
   Georgian, 378
   of Gilded Age, 382–383
   Gothic, 384
   Gothic Revival, 81, 381
   government standardization, 258
   Greek Revival, 79, 318–319, 380–381
   housing styles, 217
   industrial, 78–87, 83–87
   of malls, 86
   manifest destiny and, 79

architecture (*continued*)
    materials, 79, 81, 82
    modernist, 85–86, 385
    neo-baroque, 382
    neoclassical, 379, 382
    nineteenth-century, 79, 81–83, 380–383
    official, 258
    postmodern, 87, 386
    public
        of capital cities, 378–379
        collegiate. *See* architecture, collegiate
        colonial, 378–379
        county courthouses, 382, 383, 384
        educational institutions, 382, 384, 385, 386
        Gothic, 384
        as landmark, 382, 383
        of municipal government, 382–383, 384
        Republican, 379–381
        state capitols, 382
        symbolism in, 380–381
        urban, 383–385
        in Washington, DC, 379–381
    Richardson romanesque, 383
    skyscrapers, 59
    of state capitols, 384
    suburban, 85, 86
    of United States Capitol, 380–381
    urban, 59, 383–385
    See also housing
Archive of Folk Culture, 162
Archive of Folk Song, 162
aristocracy. *See* elite
Arizona, 298
Arledge, Roone, 457
Armed Forces Radio Service, 393–394
Armistead, Henry M., 119
Armour, Philip Danforth, 173
Armstrong, Louis, 25, 26, 102, 288
Army Corps of Engineers, 258
Army-McCarthy hearings, 478, 479
Arnaz, Lucy, 477
Arno, Peter, 230
Arnold, Benedict, 99
Arnold, Matthew, 543
art
    advertising and, 540, 541
    African American, 539, 540
    Ash Can school, 537–538
    avant-garde, 543
    capitalism and, 528–529
    censorship of, 543
    collections, 530
    colonial, 529, 530
    conservative criticism, 543
    corporate sponsorship of, 540–541
    exhibitions, 530
    fashion and, 541
    feminist, 543
    financial support of, 541
    galleries, 532
    lotteries, 532
    modern, 539
    museums, 531, 535, 539
    popular culture and, 528–529, 542
    Postimpressionist, 539
    regional, 540
    reproductions of, 529
    technological influences, 540, 542
    twentieth-century, 538
    Works Progress Administration support, 541
    See also arts; cultural institutions
Art Deco architecture, 84
art rock music, 402–403, 407
Artaud, Antonin, 499
Arthur, Timothy Shay, 119, 328, 335, 341
Arthur Schomberg Collection, 540
artists, women as, 542–543
Artist's Union, 538
arts
    colonial, 529–530
    democracy and, 530–531, 532
    modernism in, 539
    nineteenth-century, 531–537
    organizations, 531, 532
    philanthropy for, 535
    private nature of, 529
    Socialism and, 537, 538
    twentieth-century, 537–543
    women in, 542–543
    working-class, 538
    See also art; cultural institutions
Ashby, Hal, 153
Ash Can school, 537–538
Asian Americans, theater of, 499
Asimov, Isaac, 346
ASPCA. *See* American Society for the Prevention of Cruelty
    to Animals
assembly line, in automobile industry, 510
assimilation, 172–173, 177, 308–309
Associated Correspondents of Race Newspapers, 246
Associated Press, 241, 247
associations. *See* organizations; and individual association
    names
Astaire, Fred, 151
Astor, Caroline, 268
Astor Library, 501–931
Astor Place Opera House, 331
Athenaeum, 375, 531, 532
Athletics (baseball team), 456
athletics. *See* sports
Atkins, Chet, 111
AT&T. *See* American Telephone and Telegraph
AT&T Building, 87
attractiveness, twentieth-century standards, 76, 77
Aubrey, John, 552
automobiles, 510–511
    adolescents and, 511–512
    etiquette and, 269
    favored form of transportation, 513
    housing and, 219
    impact on architecture, 85
    impact on landscape, 256–257
    industry, 84, 510
    influence on public park, 549
    suburbanization and, 462, 467
    urban effects, 59, 511
    women and, 511
Autry, Gene, 109
avant-garde art, 543
aviation, 257, 512, 520
Avildsen, John, 153
Avon Books, 347, 348

B

B. Dalton, 350
Baby and Child Care (Spock), 48, 338
baby boomers, 48–49, 125, 399–400, 407
bachelor flats, 218
Back Street (1932), 147
backcountry, 168, 191–193, 224
Bacon, Henry, 385
Bacon, Lloyd, 147
Bacon's Rebellion (1676), 192
Baez, Joan, 164, 165, 404
Bailey, Beth, 122
Bailey, DeFord, 109–110
baked beans, 167
Baker, Ray Stannard, 247
Baker, Russell, 232
Baker Field, 472
Bakewell, John, Jr., 384
Bakker, Jim, 430
Baldwin, James, 310
Baldwin, Joseph, 224
Ball, Lucille, 477, 478
ballads, 155
ballrooms, 288
Baltimore, MD, 56, 544, 546
Baltimore and Ohio Railroad, 300
Baltimore Sun, 239–240
    Building, 81
Band Aid, 409
Bank of Pennsylvania, 79
Bannaker, Benjamin, 339
Baraka, Amiri (LeRoi Jones), 498
Barbary Coast, 280
Barker, James Nelson, 485
barn raisings, 324
Barnum, P. T., 332, 335–336, 439, 531
    American museums, 532
    as family entertainment, 335
    as popular entertainer, 328
Barr, Alfred, 539
Barras, Charles, 488, 489
Barrow, Bennet, 320
Barry, Phillips, 162
bars, 285, 289–290, 332. *See also* saloons; taverns
BART. *See* Bay Area Rapid Transit
Barth, Gunther, 527
Bartók, Béla, 104
Bartram, John, 538
Baruch, Bernard, 294
baseball, 444, 450–451, 456
    African American boycotts, 455
    as business, 458
    labor relations, 447, 458
    Negro Leagues, 453–864
    1919 World Series, 450–451
    nineteenth-century, 440, 447
    segregation in, 448–449, 453–455
    television and, 472, 474
    See also sports
Basie, Count, 27
basketball, 431, 448. *See also* sports
Bate, Humphrey, 110
Bath, England, 514
Battle of Bunker's Hill, The (1776), 484
Battle of Fallen Timbers, 191
Battle of Horseshoe Bend, 194

Battle of the Thames, 194
Battle of Tippecanoe, 194
Bay Area Rapid Transit, 513
Bay Psalm Book, The, 98–99, 338, 352, 353, 359
Beadle, Erastus, 371
Beadle, Irwin, 371
Beanland, Ephraim, 314
Beatles, 401–402, 404, 477
beauty, twentieth-century standards, 76, 77
Beauty Bound (Freedman), 77
Beaux-Arts classical architecture, 383–384
bebop music, 29, 104, 290
Beck, Julian, 499
bedroom communities, 559
Bee Gees, 406
Beecher, Catharine, 171, 441
Beecher, Henry Ward, 123, 442
beef, 166, 170–171
behaviorism, 46
Behrman, Martin, 61
Belasco Theatre, 493
Belden, H. M., 160
Belleville, IL, 179
Bellevue Hospital, 203
Bellini, Vincenzo, 354, 534
Bellows, George, 537
Benchley, Robert, 226
Beniger, James R., 88, 95
Benjamin, Park, 370
Benjamin Banneker's *Almanac*, 339
Bennett, James Gordon, 239, 243
Bennett, William, 431
berdache, 416
bereavement, 137–138
Berg, Gertrude, 391
Bergh, Henry, 443
Berkeley Springs, 515
Berle, Milton, 477
Berlin, Irving, 159, 482, 497
Berlin Heights, 419
Bernhardt, Sarah, 491, 493
Bernstein, Carl, 251
Bernstein, Leonard, 103
Berry, Chuck, 290, 398, 399
Berry, Marcellus, 518
Bessemer, Henry, 82
best-sellers, 347, 348
Bethune, Joanna, 562
Beulah (Evans), 344
beverages, 167, 168, 170
Beverly, Robert, 552
Beverly Hillbillies, The, 481
Biberman, Herbert, 150, 151
Bible, 22, 293–294, 338
bicycling, 443
Bier, Jesse, 226
Bierce, Ambrose, 226
Bierstadt, Albert, 195, 274
"Big Bear of Arkansas, The" (Thorpe), 224
Biglow Papers, The (Lowell), 222, 224
Bilko, Sergeant, 477
Bill Haley and His Comets, 290, 399, 400
Billings, Josh, 225, 226
Billings, William, 99, 352–353
Binford, Henry C., 467
Bing, Alexander, 464

Bingham, George Caleb, 380, 532
biocentric management, of national parks, 277
Biograph Company, 143
Biograph Girl, 141
biology, of aging, 293–294
Bird, Arthur H., 101
Birdseye, Clarence, 173
birth. *See* childbirth
birth control, 426, 428
    motion pictures advocating, 144
    nineteenth-century, 123
    twentieth-century, 124, 126
Birth of a Nation, The (1915), 142, 143, 261, 493
Birth of a Race, The (1918), 142
birth rate, 295, 296
Bishop, Henry R., 354
Black Ball Line, 505
Black Crook, The; An Original Magical and Spectacular Drama in Four Acts (1866), 488–489
black heritage, 522
Black Hills, SD, 199
Black Muslims, 169, 457
black power movement, 66–67
black pride, 403, 408
Black Public Health Movement, 569
Blackboard Jungle, The (1955), 400
blackface. *See* minstrelsy
blacklisting, 163–164, 473–474. *See also* censorship
blacks. *See* African Americans
Blackstone, William, 117
Blackwell, Henry, 119
Blake, Eubie, 25
Blake, Peter, 259
Bland, James, 356
blankets, in Native American fashion, 68
Blassingame, John, 326
Blatty, William Peter, 349
Blesh, Rudi, 357
Blitzstein, Marc, 103, 496
block booking, in theater, 492
blockbuster complex, in fiction, 351
Bloom, Allan, 543
bloomers, 73
"Blowin' in the Wind," 403
Blue Cross, 210
Blue Grass Boys, 112
blue yodel, 108, 109
bluegrass music, 112–113, 161
blues music, 23–25, 27–29
Bluestone, Daniel, 546
Bly, Nelly, 246
boardinghouses, 214
body, fashion emphasis on, 76, 77
Boeing 707, 512
Bogardus, James, 81, 82
Bok, Edward, 345
Bolden, Charles "Buddy," 25–26
Bolus, Ovid, 224
Bombeck, Erma, 231, 459
Bonanza, 480
Bonilla, Bobby, 458
Bonner, Robert, 341, 342
Bonnie and Clyde (1967), 153
Book of Martyrs (Foxe), 366
Book-of-the-Month Club, 374
"Book of Sports" (King James I), 432–433

booking agents, theater and, 492
Bookman, 374
books, 93, 340, 361. *See also* literature
bookselling, colonial, 340, 360–361
bookstores, 350, 375–376, 528
Boomtown Rats, 409
Boone, Pat, 399
Boop, Betty, 148
Booth, Edwin, 491
Booth, John Wilkes, 491
Booth, Junius Brutus, 491
Boothe, Clare, 498
Booth's Theater, 491
Borden, Gail, 174
Boston, MA
    annexation and, 464–465
    colonial, 52–55
        architecture, 78, 378
    "Emerald Necklace" park system, 547
    Franklin Park, 550
    suburban, 467
Boston Academy of Music, 331
Boston Braves, 456
Boston City Hall, 385
Boston Cooking School, 175
Boston Cooking School Cook Book (Farmer), 175
Boston Museum of Fine Arts, 535–536
Boston News-Letter, 55, 91, 235, 362
Boston Public Library, 369, 535
Boston Symphony, 100
Boston Symphony Orchestra, 102
botanical gardens, 538
Botein, Stephen, 236
Botkin, Benjamin, 162
Boucicault, Dion, 488
Boulanger, Nadia, 103
Bourgeois Utopias (Fishman), 468
Bow, Clara, 146
Bowen, Daniel, 531
Bowers v. *Hardwick* (1986), 430
Bowery, 280, 438
Bowery girls, 6–7
Bowery Theatre, 330, 333, 334, 487
Bowie, David, 405
boxing, 442, 449–450, 456
Boy George, 408
Boy Scouts of America, 518
Boyce, William, 353
boycotts, baseball, 455
Boylston, Dr. Zabdiel, 54
Brace, Charles Loring, 43
Bracken, Peg, 270
Brackenridge, Hugh Henry, 484
Bradbury, Ray, 346
Bradford, Andrew, 236
Bradford, William, 116, 166–167, 359–360, 362, 435
Bradlee, Benjamin C., 250
Branch Hotel, 332
Brandeis, Louis, 248
Brando, Marlon, 497, 512
Brant, Joseph, 190
Braves (baseball team), 456
Bread and Puppet Theater, 499
Brecht, Bertolt, 499
Breckinridge, Sophinisba, 425
Breen, Joseph, 147

Breen, Timothy H., 434
Br'er Rabbit, 225
Brewers, 282
Brick Market, 78–79
Brighton, England, 514
Brinkley, David, 479
Bristow, George Frederick, 99, 100
Britain
    colonial. *See* colonial America
    colonial journalism and, 237
    as colonizers, 189, 190–193
    communications with colonies, 90–92
    early suburbs of, 460
    economic boycott of, 237
    freemasonry in, 178
    parks, 543–544
    slave trade and, 315
    sports, 432–433
    theater, 483, 484
    traditional holidays, 514
    war with France, 190–191
British invasion, of rock music, 402
British Marconi Company, 388
British Museum, 531
"British Blondes," 489
broadcast journalism, 393
broadcast radio, 388–389, 394–395
broadsides, 156, 239, 338–339
Bronson, Bertrand, 155
Brooklyn Dodgers, 456
Brooklyn Museum, 540
Brooks, Mel, 233
Bross, William, 546
Brother Jonathan, 370
Brougham, John, 333, 487
Brown, Arthur, Jr., 384
Brown, James, 28, 403
Brown, Lancelot "Capability," 543
Brown, Richard D., 88, 94
Brown-Séquard, Charles E., 293
Brown v. *Board of Education* (1954), 49
Browne, Charles Farrar, 224, 225
Browning, Tod, 149
Browns, 456
Bruce, Lenny, 231
Bryan, William Jennings, 383
Bryant, Anita, 430
Bryant, William Cullen, 532
Bryce, Lord, 61
Brylawski, Samuel, 393–394
Buchwald, Art, 232
Buck, Dudley, 101
Bucklin, James C., 81
buffalo, 198–199, 506
buildings. *See* architecture; construction
Bulfinch, Charles, 380
Bull, Ole, 335
Bullets or Ballots (1936), 148
Bulls (basketball team), 459
bundling, 3, 116, 414
Bunker Hill; or, The Death of General Warren (1797), 485
Buntline, Ned, 341, 342, 371
Bunyan, John, 295, 366
Bureau of Indian Affairs, 199
Bureau of the Census, 514
Burgess, (Frank) Gelett, 226–227

burial practices. *See* funerals
Burk, John Daly, 485
Burke, Edmund, 527
Burleigh, Harry T., 104
burlesque, 333, 489
Burns, Tommy, 450
Burroughs, William, 405
buses, 511
business
    baseball as, 458
    central business districts, 59, 64, 82, 557
    newspapers as, 242–244
    role of information processing, 96
    sports as, 443–444, 458, 459
    suburban business districts, 86, 87
    in towns, 556
    See also economy; industry
Butler, Jon, 92
Byrd, William, II, 434
Byrds, 404
Byrne, David, 459

C
C-SPAN, 250
cabarets, 284, 285
Cable, George Washington, 224
cable channels, 482
Cable News Network, 250
Cadets of Temperance, 5
Caesar, Sid, 230
Café La Mama, 500
Cage, John, 104
Cagney, James, 148
Cahan, Abraham, 254, 268
Cain, James M., 149
Cajuns, foodways of, 169–170
Caldwell, Sarah, 105
Calhoun, John C., 322
California
    Anaheim, 64
    gold rush, 197
    Hollywood, 141, 143, 149, 150–152
    Los Angeles, 64, 465
    San Francisco, 384, 404–405, 428, 465, 513
    settlement of, 197, 401, 506
    towns in, 555–556
    urban development of, 465
calling, etiquette of, 267–268
Calloway, Cab, 286
Calvinism, influence on sports, 433, 435–436
Cambridge, Godfrey, 228
Camel cigarettes, 473
cameras, 139–140, 472–473
Camp, Walter, 449
camp meetings, 160
Camp Snoopy, 36–37
campaigns. *See* presidential campaigns
Campbell, Bartley, 491
Campbell, John, 235, 362
camping, 519, 520
camps, summer, 518
canals, 56, 504–505
Cane Ridge, KY, 307
Cannon, Sarah Ophelia Colley, 110
canoes, 503
Cantor, Eddie, 392

capitalism
  art and, 528–529
  fraternal organizations as response, 185
  railroad and, 507–508
  sports and, 443–444
Capitol Buildings. *See* state capitols
Capone, Al, 285, 287
Capra, Frank, 148, 151, 230
caravans, 195, 196
Carew, Richard, 432
Carey, Mathew, 369
Carnegie, Andrew, 535
Carnegie, Dale, 348
Carnes, Mark, 184
carousel, 32
Carpenter, Edward, 426
Carpenter, Samuel, 360
Carr, Benjamin, 99
cars. *See* automobiles
Carson, Fiddlin' John, 163
Carson, Rachel, 175, 569
Carson Pirie Scott Store, 83
Carter, A. P., 107
Carter, Betty, 29
Carter, Elliott, 105
Carter, Jimmy, 278, 475
Carter, Maybelle Addington, 107
Carter, Robert, 317
Carter, Sara Dougherty, 107
Carter Family, 107, 161
Cartier, Jacques, 189
Casey, Thomas L., 381
Cash, Johnny, 107
casinos, 288–289
Castle, Irene, 285
Castle, Vernon, 285
Catch-22 (Heller), 232–233, 350
Cathedral of Learning (University of Pittsburgh), 384
Catholics, 181–182, 308
Catlin, George, 195
Catskill Mountains, 230
cattle ranches, 198
cattle towns, 555
Cawelti, John, 342
CBS. *See* Columbia Broadcasting System
celebrations
  African American, 12, 17, 18–19, 20, 310
  colonial, 324–327
  Puritan, 433
  See also holidays; parades; rituals
celebrities, 141, 336, 487
  sports heroes, 95, 450, 451, 862
celibacy, 120, 419
cemeteries, 57, 133, 138, 545
censorship
  of art, 543
  in journalism, 248
  in motion picture industry, 143, 150–151
  of print, 373
  of television, 473–474
  See also blacklisting
"Centennial Hymn," 101
central business districts, 82, 557
Central High School (Arkansas), 384
Central Intelligence Agency, press and, 251–252
Central Pacific, 197

Central Park, 57, 545, 546, 547, 550
Century, 345
Chambers, Ephraim, 235
Champlain, Samuel de, 189
Chandler, Raymond, 346
chapbooks, 339
Chaplin, Charlie, 142, 145, 150, 229
Chapman, William, 486
charity, medical care as, 203–204, 205
charity. *See also* philanthropy; women's organizations
Charles, Ray, 29
Charleston, SC, colonial, 52, 53, 54
Charleston's Museum, 530
Chase, Gilbert, 354
Chase and Sanborn Hour, The, 392
Chautauqua, NY, as tourist spot, 519
Chayefsky, Paddy, 478
Checkers speech, of Richard Nixon, 475
Cheever, John, 387, 397
Cheney, Ednah Dow, 566
Cherokee Indians, 190, 191, 194–195, 369
Cherokee Phoenix, 240, 369
Chesapeake, colonial
  adolescence in, 2, 3
  family structure, 132
  information transmission in, 90
  mortality, 39, 132
  plantation and, 315
  sexual behavior in, 414–415
"Chester," 99
Chestnut Street Theater, 486
Chevalier, Michel, 120
Cheyenne Indians, 199
Cheyney, Sheldon, 495
Chicago, IL
  architecture of, 383
  commercial architecture, 82, 83, 84
  early suburbs of, 460
  music in, 27–28
  parks, 546
  public transportation in, 513
  theater in, 486
  vice in, 62
  World's Columbian Exposition (1893), 31, 62, 83, 383, 518–519, 536, 542
Chicago, Judy, 543
Chicago American Giants, 453
Chicago Bulls, 459
Chicago Daily News, 244
Chicago Defender, The, 245–246, 248
Chicago Orchestra, 101
Chicago School of architecture, 83
Chicago Symphony, 101
Chicago Times, 463
Chicago Tribune Tower, 84
Chicago White Sox, 450
Chicago White Stockings, 448
Chickasaw Indians, 195
Child, Francis James, 155, 162
Child, Julia, 176
child abuse, 43–44
Child ballads, 155
child labor, 43–44, 47, 48
child psychology, 46
childbirth, death in, 131, 133–134, 135
childrearing, 39, 42–43, 46, 47, 48

children
    African American, 41
    clothing, 72–73, 75, 77
    colonial, 39–41, 72–73
    in communications revolution, 94
    child labor, 43–44, 47, 48
    childhood, 39, 40
    education. *See* education
    frontier, 44
    gender roles, 42–43, 44, 47, 50
    during Great Depression, 47
    health of, 46, 49–50
    immigrant, 44–45
    juvenile justice and, 45
    leisure, 518
    loss of family members, 132, 135
    modern, 50–51
    mothers and, 42, 48, 50
    Native Americans, 40
    nineteenth-century, 41–45, 75
    in nontraditional families, 50–51
    playgrounds and, 548
    poverty and, 43–44, 47, 50–51
    psychological theories of, 46
    Puritan, 39–40
    of slaves, 41
    television and, 474, 478, 481
    theories of, 39, 40–41
    transition to adulthood, 39–40
    twentieth-century, 45–51, 77
    vacations, 518
    welfare of, 47, 50
    World War II and, 48–49
    See also adolescence; orphans
Children's Aid Society, 43
Chinese, 45, 176, 308
Choctaw Indians, 195
Christianity
    sport and, 441, 442
    women's organizations and, 561–563, 645–565
    See also Catholics; Episcopal church; religion; revivals
Christmas, 312
Christy, Edwin P., 490
Christy's Minstrels, 332, 490
Chrysler Building, 80
"church wrecking," 22
CIA. *See* Central Intelligence Agency
"Cider Making the Old-Fashioned Way," 334
Cimino, Michael, 153
Cincinnati Reds, 450
cinema. *See* motion pictures
cinématographe, 140
Cino, Joe, 499
CIO. *See* Congress of Industrial Organizations
circulating libraries, 368
cities, 51
    African Americans in, 58, 60–61
    anti-urban bias, 254–255
    architecture, 378–379, 383–385
    automobiles and, 59
    City Beautiful movement, 62, 83, 383–384, 548
    colonial, 52–55, 436
    crime in, 53–54, 57
    as cultural centers, 54–55
    cultural institutions, 527–543. *See also* arts; culture; libraries; museums

future of, 67
garden, 464
growth of, 55, 464–465
immigration and, 52, 58, 60
industrial, 59–63, 61, 62
inner, 66–67
manufacturing in, 60
mayors of, 61
multifamily housing, 214–215
nineteenth-century, 55–63
parks, 442, 543–550
popular entertainment in, 327–328
population, 52, 55, 56, 60, 63–64, 66
post-war development of, 63–64
poverty in, 53, 65–67
radial, 59–63
religion in, 54
role in Revolutionary War, 55
safety in, 57
sanitation, 54
social structure, 52–53, 56
suburban, 63–64
technological influences on, 255–257
tourism in, 520–521, 522
transportation and, 56, 59, 509–510
twentieth-century, 59–67
urban planning and, 62
urban reform. *See* reform
walking city, 55–58, 460
workers in, 60–61
See also suburbs; towns; urbanization
Citizen Kane (1941), 149
citizens, informed, 92–93
Citizens for Adequate Welfare, 569
City, The (Howe), 465–466
City Beautiful movement, 62, 83, 383–384, 548
city bosses, 61
City People (Barth), 527
City Tavern (New Amsterdam), 378
Civic Center (Beverly Hills, CA), 386
civic pride, in towns, 553
Civil Aeronautics Board, 512
civil death, 117
civil rights, 231, 250, 403, 549
Civil War
    humor and, 225
    mortality, 134
    music during, 356
    nostalgia for, 180
    public holidays during, 307
    rise of sports and, 441
    women in, 563–564
Civilian Conservation Corps, 277
Civilization in the United States (Stearns), 556
Claiborne, Craig, 176
Clampett, Jed, 480
Clapton, Eric, 24
Clark, Charles Heber, 226
Clark, Dick, 400
Clark, William, 193, 506
Clash, 408
class
    colonial fashion and, 70–71
    fraternal organizations and, 180–181, 185
    health care and, 206
    holidays and, 310–311

class (*continued*)
leisure and, 325–326, 433–434
medical care and, 204
popular entertainment and, 330–332
retirement and, 300
suburbanization and, 460
television depictions of, 481
theater and, 330, 534
in towns, 554
women's organizations and, 564–565
See also elite; middle-class; wealthy;
working-class
Clay, Cassius, 457
Clemens, Samuel. *See* Twain, Mark
clergy, dying and, 133
Clérisseau, C. L., 379
clerisy, 528
Clermont, 507
Cleveland, Horace W. S., 546
climate, housing and, 213
Cline, Patsy, 113
Clinton, DeWitt, 505
Clisby, Harriet, 566
Close Encounters of the Third Kind (1977), 153
clothing
of African American slaves, 74
children's, 72–73, 75, 77
colonial, 68–73
imported, 72
middle-class, 73–74
of Native Americans, 67–68
nineteenth-century, 73–75
Puritan, 69–70
regional differences in, 74–75
of slaves, 321
twentieth-century, 75–77
Club Méditeraneé, 519
clubs
comedy, 232
women's, 565–566
Clymer, George, 366
CNN. *See* Cable News Network
Coal Miner's Daughter (1980), 114
Cobb, Sylvanus S., 341, 342
Cobb, Tyrus Raymond ("Ty"), 450–451
Cobbett, William, 222
Coca-Cola, 170
Cocacolonization, 170
Cochrane, J. C., 382
cockfights, 434
code of honor, Southern, 264
codfish, 167
Coediquette, 270
coffeehouse, as gathering place, 528
cohabitation, 125
Cohen, Norm, 155
Colbert, Claudette, 148, 230
Colby, William, 251
Cole, Thomas, 298–299, 532
Coleman, Benjamin, 484
Coleman, Ornette, 29
Coleridge, Samuel Taylor, 528
collective bargaining, labor and, 210
College of New Jersey, architecture of, 378
College of William and Mary, architecture of, 378

colleges
architecture of, 378, 379, 381–382, 384, 386
medical, 202
sports in, 444, 447–448, 452, 457
Colliers, 346
Collins, Judy, 159, 164
Collyer, Dr., 532
Colonel Sanders' Kentucky Fried Chicken, 170
colonial America
adolescence in, 1–4
architecture, 78–79, 378–379
arts in, 529–530
building styles, 254
celebrations and, 324–325
children, 39–41
cities, 52–55, 436
clothing, 68–73
communications, 90–93
courtship, 70–71, 116, 414
cultural organizations, 528, 529–530
death, 131–132
economy, 53
education, 55, 360
elite, 52
etiquette in, 262–263
family size, 414
family structure, 132
foodways of, 166–169
frontier, 187–193
housing, 210–213
humor in, 221–222
journalism, 235–237
leisure, 436
libraries, 340, 361
literacy, 359, 360, 528
marriage, 116–117
media, 91
middle-class, 52–53
mortality and, 131–132
music, 98–99, 351–353
newspapers, 92–93, 235–237, 362, 364
popular entertainment, 323–324
popular literature, 338–340
postal system, 91
press, 359–360
printing, 339–340
public rituals, 324–325
reading in, 361–362, 364
roads, 504
sexual behavior, 413–416
sports, 433–437
theater, 483–485, 529–530
towns, 551–552
transportation, 503–504
warfare with Native Americans, 194–195
women in, 2, 4
working-class, 53
See also Chesapeake, colonial; New England, colonial; Puritans
colonization
British. *See* colonial America
Dutch, 189
French, 189, 190–191
of Ireland, 316
landscapes and, 253–254

Native Americans and, 187, 191, 194–195, 198–199, 503–504
Spanish, 188, 191
transportation and, 503–504
of West. *See* western expansion
See also frontier; settlement
color, in colonial wardrobe, 69
color television, 473
Colored American, 374
Colored Female Religious and Moral Society, 561
Coltrane, John, 29
Columbia Broadcasting System, 390, 427, 478, 480
Columbia University, Baker Field, 472
Columbian exchange, 165–166
Columbian Exposition (1893), 31, 62, 83, 383, 518–519, 536, 543
Columbian Museum, 531
Columbianum, 532
Comanche Indians, 199
comedy
clubs, 232
in fiction, 232–233
minstrelsy, 21, 228, 332–333, 356, 490
motion picture, 148–149, 228–229, 233
musicals, 233
radio, 230, 392
screwball, 148, 230
television, 230–231, 233, 477
theater, 489–491, 497
vaudeville, 110, 141, 392, 489–490
See also humor
comic strips, 231–232, 244
Coming Home (1978), 153
Comiskey, Charles, 450
Command Performance, 394
Commentaries on the Laws of England (Blackstone), 117
commerce, air, 505, 511, 512. *See also* commercialization; economy
commercial architecture. *See* architecture, commercial
commercialization
of foodways, 173–174
of holidays, 311–312, 519
of museums, 540–541
of music
country and western music, 107–109
folk music, 163–165
music industry, 407
popular music, 356–357
of publishing, 371–375
of radio, 390–391
of theater, 489–492
commercials, television, 475
Commission on Shade Trees and Public Grounds, 546
Committee for Industrial Organization. *See* Congress of Industrial Organizations
Common Sense Book of Baby and Child Care (Spock). *See* Baby and Child Care (Spock)
Common Sense (Paine), 237
commons, New England, 544
communications, 518
Federalist, 92–93
folk music as, 156, 158–159
history of, 88–91
mass, 338–339, 518
media and, 89–90

power and, 91–92
print, 358–377
regulations on, 97
revolution, 93–95
role in public rituals, 312, 313
technology, 89–90
theory, 88–90
Toronto school, 90–91
transatlantic, 91–92
and travel, 518
twentieth-century, 96–98
See also journalism; newspapers; publishing; radio; television
Communications Act (1934), 391, 394, 471, 473
Communism, 150–151, 473–474. *See also* McCarthyism; Socialism
communities, national, 94–95
commuter suburbs, 219, 558
streetcar suburbs, 204, 216, 461, 462
companionate marriages, and fraternalism, 185
company housing, 214, 218
Company of Comedians of London, 484
competition
among newspapers, 238, 240
among railroads, 507
in motion picture industry, 143, 145
Compleat Treatise of Singing (Tufts), 353
complex marriage, 120
composers, 99, 105. *See also* concert music
computers, 89, 96–97
Comstock, Anthony, 62, 423
Comstock Law (1873), 62, 123, 373, 423, 426
Concert Hall (Boston), 530
concert music, 103–105, 331–332, 529, 534, 535
influence of World War II, 102, 104
modern, 539
nineteenth-century, 99–102
subscription, 530
"Concert of Negro Music," 539
Concert Room (Philadelphia), 529
Conestoga wagons, 506
Coney Island, 30, 31–32
Confidence Men and Painted Women (Halttunen), 266
Congress of Industrial Organizations, 209, 210
Conlin, Joseph R., 170
Connecticut, divorce in, 117
Connecticut Wits, 222
Conrad, Frank, 388
conservation, 259, 275
conservatism, political, rock music and, 406, 411
conspicuous consumption
in diet, 169
fashion and, 69–70
holidays and, 311
nightclubs and, 290
in rock music, 401
See also consumption
Constitution Day, 309
construction
of interstate highways, 510, 511
technological advances in, 256
See also architecture; housing
Consumers' League, 567
consumption
adolescent, 400, 401
conspicuous, 69–70, 169, 290, 311, 401

consumption (*continued*)
railroad and, 507–508
sports and, 443, 444, 450–453
television and, 476–477
travel and, 525
contact zones, 187. *See also* frontier
Container Corporation of America, 541
contraception. *See* birth control
Contrast, The (1787), 485, 487
Control Revolution, The (Beniger), 88
Converse, Charles C., 101
conversion, religious, 3
Conzen, Michael, 259
Cook, Thomas, 518
Cook County, IL, juvenile justice in, 45
Cooke, Forest H., 540
cooking. *See* foodways
Coolspring School, 385
Cooper, Gary, 150
Cooper, James Fenimore, 195, 200, 324, 344, 367
Copland, Aaron, 103
Copley, John Singleton, 530
Copperton, UT, company housing, 218
copyright, publishing and, 370–371
Copyright Act of 1891, 344, 348
Coquelin, Benoit Constant, 490–491
Cordelia's Aspirations (1883), 491
Corman, Roger, 152
cornhuskings, 324
Cornish, Samuel E., 240, 370
Coronado, Francisco Vásquez de, 188
Coronado Hotel, 518
corporations
motion picture industries as, 152
sponsorship of art and, 540–541
Correspondents' Club, 246
corruption, in industrial cities, 61, 62
corsets, 69, 73
Corwin, Norman, 392, 393
Cosby, Bill, 228, 482
Cosby, William, 362
Cosby Show, The, 482
cosmetics, 70, 74, 76
Cosmopolitan, 247
cotton, 71, 72, 75, 318
cultivation of, 317–318, 322–323
Cotton Club, 286, 494–495
cotton gin, 75, 317
Coughlin, "Bathhouse" John, 283
counterculture
hippie, 290, 404–405, 428
motion pictures and, 153
counting rooms, 217
countrified cities, 558
country and western music, 288
bluegrass, 112–113
commerical success of, 107–109
country pop, 113–114
country rock, 398
Grand Ole Opry, 109–111, 112
hillbilly music, 106–107
honky-tonk, 112
rock music and, 398, 403, 406–407
social history of, 114–115
soloist in, 106

swing music, 111–112
themes in, 106, 108–109, 111, 114–115
Country Club Plaza, 85
country houses, 217
country life. *See* rural life
country pop music, 113–114
country rock music, 398
"Country Town, The" (Veblen), 556
Court, Franklin, 386
courthouses, county, 382, 383, 551, 553
courtship
of African American slaves, 421
calling and, 267–268
colonial, 70–71, 116, 414
definition of, 115
etiquette of, 269, 270
nineteenth-century, 122, 267–268, 418, 420
Puritan, 116
southern, 421
twentieth-century, 125
Victorian, 418
working-class, 420
See also marriage
"cover records," 399
Cowboy Songs and Other Frontier Ballads (Lomax), 162
cowboys, 158, 198
Coxe, Margaret, 119–120
Crabgrass Frontier (Jackson), 459, 468
Cradle Will Rock, The (1938), 496
Cram, Ralph Adam, 384
Cramps, 409
Crawfords, 453
Creek Indians, 190, 194, 195
cremation, 137
Creoles, foodways of, 169–170
Cribb, Thomas, 442
crime
in colonial cities, 53–54, 57
nineteenth-century cities, 57
organized, 285, 286
in urban parks, 549
Crisis, 374
Crocker, Betty, 174
Crockett, Davy, 223, 488
Croker, Richard, 61
Croly, Jane, 565
Cromwell, Oliver, 433, 483
Cronkite, Walter, 249, 479, 480
Crosby, Alfred W., Jr., 166
Crosby, Bing, 112, 394
cross-dressing, 416
Crow Island Elementary School, 386
Crowell-Collier, 375
Crucible, The (1953), 151
cruise liners, 521
Cry of the People for Meat, The (1969), 499
Crystal Palace, 36, 82
Culbert, David, 393
cultivation
cotton, 317–318, 322–323
indigo, 317
rice, 316, 318, 320, 323
sugar, 314–315, 318, 323
tobacco, 315, 317
Cultural Excursions (Harris), 529
cultural geography. *See* landscapes

cultural illiteracy, 376–377
cultural institutions
    colonial, 528, 529–530
    democracy in, 537
    elitist nature of, 527, 535–536
    financial support of, 541
    marketing of, 527
    modernism in, 539
    New Deal support of, 541
    nineteenth-century, 528–529, 531–537
    politics and, 538
    popular culture and, 542
    private, 529, 530
    specialization in, 538–539
    twentieth-century, 537–543
    urban, 527–543
    See also arts; libraries; museums; music; theater
cultural protest, in rock music, 403, 404
culture
    cities as centers for, 54–55
    feminization of, 333, 354–355
    folk, 338, 540. *See also* folk music
    four stages of, 529
    highbrow, 535
    knowledge and, 528
    lowbrow, 535
    as noun, 527–528
    popular. *See* popular culture
    See also cultural institutions; entertainment; literature; music
Culture and Society, 1780-1950 (Williams), 528
Cummins, Maria S., 344
Cure for Suffragettes, A (1913), 144
Currier and Ives, 299
Curtis, Cyrus H. K., 345, 373
Curtis, George William, 242
Custer, George Armstrong, 199
Custer's Last Fight, 282
Cyclopaedia (Chambers), 235
Cylopedia of Fraternities, 179
Cynic's Word Book, The (Bierce), 226

D ————————————————

Dalhart, Vernon, 106
Daly, Augustin, 491
dams, Tennessee Valley Authority, 85, 258
Dana, Charles, 243
dance, 541–542
    African American, 16–17
    clubs, 290
    country and western, 288
    dance halls, 284, 424
    musicals and, 151
    See also nightlife
Dance Theater of Harlem, 541
Daniels, Howard, 546
Darby, William, 483
Darrow, Clarence, 383
Darwinism, social, 154–155
dating, 269, 270, 425
Daughters of Bilitis, 429
Daughters of Rebekah, 177, 183
Daughters of Temperance, 563
Davis, Charles Augustus, 223
Davis, Gordon, 550
Davis, Jefferson, 322
Davis, Michael M., 207

Davis, Miles, 29, 104
Davis, R. G., 499
Davis, Richard Harding, 246
Davis, Stuart, 537
Davy Crockett; or, Be Sure You're Right, Then Go Ahead (1873), 487–488
Day, Benjamin, 93, 239, 368
Day, Charles William, 267
Day, Clarence, 230
Day of the Dead, 312
Daye, Stephen, 359
DC-8, 512
De Forest, Lee, 388
de Graff, Robert Fair, 374
De Priest, Oscar, 61
de Tocqueville, Alexis, 94, 528–529, 534, 554
    on art, 543
    on etiquette, 264
    on towns, 552
Deadwood Dick, 371
Dean, James, 151, 512
death
    acknowledgement of, 137–138
    children, 133
    colonial, 131–132
    cultural views after Civil War, 134
    institutionalized, 137
    during nineteenth century, 132–134
    Puritans and, 131–132
    during twentieth century, 134–138
    See also mortality
Death of General Montgomery, The (1777), 484
Debs, Eugene V., 508
decentralization, of theater, 500–501
decor
    of cabarets, 285
    of saloons, 282
Deer Hunter, The (1978), 153
Deerslayer, The (Cooper), 324
deForest, Robert W., 540
Delacorte Theater, 501
Delaware Valley. *See* Quakers
delinquency, 2, 3, 6–7, 43, 45
    playground movement and, 548
Delk, Edward Beuhler, 85
Dell (publisher), 348
Deller, Alfred, 164
Delmonico, Lorenzo, 176
Delsarte, François, 491
D'Emilio, John, 426
democracy
    arts in, 530–531, 532
    cultural institutions and, 537
    knowledge and, 94–95
Democracy in America (de Tocqueville), 94, 264, 528–529
Democrats, planter class as, 322
demographics
    post-war, 63–64
    television, 474, 481
    See also population
Demos, John, 1, 131
Demos, Virginia, 1
Dennett, Andrea, 36
department stores, compared to museums, 540
Depeche Mode, 408
Depression, 148

depressions. *See* Great Depression
deregulation
    of airline industry, 512
    of television, 474, 481–482
Des Moines City Hall, 384
desegregation, 49
Detroit, MI, riots in, 66–67
Deutsch, Karl, 88
development, urban, 64–65
Devil's Dictionary, The (Bierce), 226
Devil's Tower, 278
DeVries, Peter, 233
Dewey, John, 247
dialect humor, 222
dialogue songs, 157
Diamond, David, 105
Dicey, Edward, 237
Dick, Deadwood, 371
Dickinson, John, 237, 353
Dickson, William K. L., 139–140
Dictionary (Johnson), 531
Didrikson, Mildred ("Babe"), 453
Dies, Martin, 150
diet
    American, 176–177
    assimilation and, 177
    colonial, 166–169
    disease and, 170, 174
    immigrant, 171–173
    nineteenth-century, 169–173
    reform of, 176
    standardized, 173–175
    twentieth-century, 173–176
    See also foodways
Dike, Samuel W., 123
dime novels, 341–342, 346–347, 371
dinner parties, etiquette for, 266–267
Dinner Party, The, 543
Dinwiddie, Robert, 483
Dire Straits, 409
disco music, 406
discrimination, against African Americans, 61
disease
    diet and, 170, 174
    Native Americans and, 189, 503
    venereal disease, 424
Disney
    animated humor, 229
    motion pictures of, 148–149
Disney, Walt, 479
    as "friendly witness," 150
    theme parks of, 33–36
Disney World, 33, 35–362, 522
Disneyland, 33, 519, 522
"Dissertation on the Canon and Feudal Law" (Adams), 92
Distance Fiend, 389
distribution, of print materials, 369–371, 374
Divinyls, 410
division of labor, 417
divorce
    African American, 117, 118
    colonial, 117, 118
    contributing factors, 124
    definition of, 115
    nineteenth-century, 120–124
    no fault, 126

opposing societal views of, 122
    Puritan, 117
    twentieth-century, 124–125, 126, 127–128
    women and, 117, 121–122, 124
Dmytryk, Edward, 150
Do the Right Thing (1989), 153, 408
Doane, William C., 123
doctors
    as controllers of sexual desire, 418, 419
    as private practitioners, 206
    relationship with patient, 202
    relationship with trustees, 206
    See also hospitals; medicine
Dodge, Mabel, 542
Dodgers (baseball team), 456
Dollyland, 114
Dollywood, 35
Domestic Manners of the Americans (Trollope), 74, 265
Donen, Stanley, 150
Donizetti, Gaetano, 333
Donner Party, 506
Dooley, Martin, 226
Doors, 405
Doremus, Sarah, 564
Dorsey, Thomas A., 22
Doubleday, 374
Doucet, Jacques, 74
Douglas, Ann, 333, 354
Douglas, Stephen A., 197
Douglas, Susan, 388
Douglas Commercial, DC-8, 512
Douglass, Frederick, 240, 246
Douglass, Harlan Paul, 466
Downing, Andrew Jackson, 256, 545
Downing, Jack, 223
Dracula (1931), 149
Drake, Samuel, 486
drama
    education for, 491
    television programs, 481, 482
    See also theater
Dramatic Life as I Found It (Ludlow), 486
Dreamland, 32
dress. *See* clothing; fashion
driver, plantation, 320
drugs, recreational, 404–405
Druid Hill Park, 546
drum language, 15, 16
Drunkard, The (Smith), 335
Du Bois, W. E. B., 374
dueling, etiquette of, 264
dumbbell tenement, 215
Dumenil, Lynn, 184
DuMont, 478
Dunlap, William, 328, 485
Dunne, Finley Peter, 226
Durante, Jimmy, 286
Duryea, Charles, 510
Duryea, (James) Frank, 510
Dutch, as colonizers, 189
E. P. Dutton, 374
Dvořák, Antonin, 539
Dwight, John Sullivan, 100
Dwight's Journal of Music (Dwight), 100
Dyer, Mary, 54
Dyer-Bennet, Richard, 164

dying, 133, 137–138. *See also* death
Dylan, Bob, 164, 404
dyspepsia, 170

E

Earle, Alice Morse, 69
Eastern Woodlands Indians, 188, 503
Eastman, Max, 538
Eastman Kodak, 141
Easy Rider (1969), 153
Easy Street (1917), 145
eating, etiquette of, 263, 266–267. *See also* foodways
eating disorders, 176
Ebey's Landing National Historical Reserve, 279
Ebner, Michael, 466–467
Ebsen, Buddy, 480
ecology, 276
Economic and Research Action Projects, 569
economics
    of aging, 299–301
    of dating, 270
    of health care, 205–206
    home, 175
    of sports, 443, 444
economy
    antebellum American, 317–319
    colonial, 53
    cotton and, 317–318
    depressions. *See* Great Depression
    family structure and, 43–44
    markets. *See* markets, economic
    plantation, 314–319
    of scale, publishing and, 370–371
    South, manufacturing in, 322
    tourism and, 519, 522
    town, 556, 558, 559
    transportation and, 59
ecotourism, 524
Edbrooke, W. J., 383
Edel, Matthew, 467
Ederle, Gertrude, 453
Edison, Thomas A., 139–140, 141
editors, magazine, 345
education
    adolescent, 5, 7, 8–9
    architecture for, 384, 385–386
    colonial, 55, 360
    compulsory, 45
    desegregation, 49
    dramatic, 491
    of immigrants, 382
    literacy and, 360
    medical, 201–202
    for music, 353
    of Native Americans, 382
    nineteenth-century, 42, 554
    physical, 449
    of plantation elite, 322
    public, 58, 554
    schoolbooks and, 366–367
    as socialization, 42
    twentieth-century, 45, 49–50
Educational Amendments Act (1972), Title IX, 458
Edwards, Jonathan, 353
egalitarian friendships, 4
Eighteenth Amendment, 285, 493, 556. *See also* prohibition

eighteenth century. *See* colonial America
"Eight, The," 537–538
Eisenman, Peter, 386
Eisenstein, Sergei, 143
elder law, 299
elderly. *See* aging; old age
Election Day, 17, 325
elections, presidential, 475
electric trolley, 31, 255, 509
electronic age, publishing in, 376–377
elevated trolleys, 509
elevators, 82
Eliot, Samuel, 331
elite
    colonial, 52, 70–71, 317
    cultural institutions and, 527, 535–536
    frontier, 192
    ideal of football, 448
    leisure activities of, 331
    nineteenth-century, 55, 56, 444
    plantation, 318–319, 322
    sports, 440, 444, 447–448
    See also wealthy
Elks, 182, 184, 186
Ellington, Edward Kennedy "Duke," 26–27, 286
Ellis, Havelock, 426
Ellsberg, Daniel, 250–251
Elm Park, 546, 547
els, 509
Elssler, Fanny, 333, 335
Elton, G. R., 324
emancipation, African American, 20
"Emerald Necklace," in Boston parks, 546–549
Emerson, Ralph Waldo, 334
emigration. *See* immigrants; migration
Émile (Rousseau), 73
Emmett, Dan, 490
Empire State Building, 59, 84
Emporia Gazette, 245
emulators, 164
energy
    crisis, 521, 522
    hydroelectric dams, 85, 258
England. *See* Britain
English and Scottish Popular Bands (Child), 155
English Atlantic (Steele), 88
"Enormous Radio, The" (Cheever), 387
entertainment
    commercialization of, 327–332
    definition of, 323
    fraternal organizations as, 184, 186
    "free and easy," 332
    indoor family centers, 36–37
    mass, 30–31. *See also* amusement parks; theme parks
    newspaper as, 243–244, 372
    popular
        academic study of, 323–324
        class and, 330–332
        colonial, 324–327
        gender and, 325
        middle-class, 334–337
        Nationalist period, 324, 327–328
        nineteenth-century, 328–337
        philanthropic funding of, 328
        politics and, 334
        prior to Civil War, 323–337

entertainment (*continued*)
    popular
        religious revivals as, 327–328
        resorts, 331
        rural, 329
        seaside vacation, 331
        urban, 332–334
See also amusement parks; holidays; nightlife; parades; radio;
        rituals; television; theme parks; sports
environment, natural. *See* natural environment
environmentalism, 259
EPCOT Center, 33, 35–36
Episcopal church, 322
Equal Pay Act (1963), 569
Erenberg, Lewis, 285
Erie Canal, 55, 504–505, 776
Espionage Statute (1917), 248
Essler, Fanny, 335
E.T., 351
Ethiopia (1936), 496
ethnic humor, 227–228
ethnic museums, 540
Ethnic Press, 239
ethnic publishing, 369
ethnic radio, 392
ethnicity, television depictions of, 481, 482
ethnology, 540
etiquette
    adolescent, 270–271
    automobile and, 269
    British, 265
    of calling, 267–268
    colonial, 262–263
    of dating, 269, 270
    definition of, 261
    differences between North and South, 264–265
    dining, 263, 266–267
    as drama of democracy, 264–265
    gender roles and, 269–272
    middle-class, 261–262, 265–269, 269–272
    Native American, 262
    nineteenth-century
        immigrants and, 268
        literature, 266
        middle-class, 265–269
    prescriptive nature of, 261
    race and, 261
    as self-improvement, 265–266
    sexual behavior and, 266, 269, 270–271
    sincerity in, 267
    of slaves, 264
    as social control, 265
    social heirarchy and, 262–263, 266
    southern, 264
    telephone and, 269
    twentieth-century, 269–272
    urbanization and, 269
Etiquette in Society, in Business, in Politics, and at Home (Post),
        267, 271
Europe, James Reese, 539
Europe, travel to, 514, 515, 524
Europeans. *See* colonization
evangelism
    Great Awakening, 4, 160, 327, 353
    literacy and, 366
    revivals, 306–307, 308, 327–328

Second Great Awakening, 5, 17, 160, 307
Evans, Augusta J., 344
Evanston Township High School, 384
Everglades National Park, 277
Evolution of the Shopping Mall: Interiorization of Commer-
    cial Architecture, 86
Execution of Mary, Queen of Scots, The (1895), 140
executions, as public rituals, 305–306
Exorcist, The (Blatty), 349
exploitation
    of natural environment, 258–259
    of women, 7, 415, 416, 420, 422
exploration. *See* colonization; settlement; western expansion
exports, transportation and, 505
expressways, 511

F ————————————————————————

fabrics, 75
    colonial, 69, 71–72
    Native American, 67–68
Facade of the Small Town, 556
factories, 60, 84. *See also* industrialization; labor;
        manufacturing
Fairbanks, Douglas, 142
Fairlane Town Center, 86
Fairmount Park, 545
Fairness Doctrine, 473, 474
fairs, agricultural, 329
*Fall of British Tyranny; or, America Triumphant, the First Cam-
    paign, The* (1776), 484
Falsche Scham (1796), 485
False Shame; or, The Amerian Orphan in Germany (1796), 485
Falwell, Jerry, 430
families
    adolescents and, 6, 7–8
    of African Americans, 422, 423
    colonial, 2, 3, 116–118
    depiction in motion pictures, 151–152
    diversity in, 118–119
    economic constraints, 43–44
    nineteenth century, 6
    nontraditional, 50–51
    Puritan, 116–117
    reform of, 43–44
    single-parent, 51, 126
    size
        colonial, 414
        nineteenth century, 41–42
        twentieth century, 46, 48, 50
    of slaves, 422, 423
    suburban, 48–49
    television depiction of, 477
    "traditional," 115, 477
    transformation of, 50–51
    vacations, 520
    See also family structure
family entertainment centers, 36–37
family structure
    colonial, 132
    death and, 132, 135–136, 143
    housing and, 220–221
    of Native Americans, 115
    nineteenth century, 118–123
    patriarchal authority, 3, 5, 116–117
    Puritan, 116–117
    twentieth century, 220–221, 429–430

vacation activity, 521–522
See also families
family violence, in nineteenth century, 43–44
Faneuil Hall, 78
Fanny Hill (Cleland), 348
Faragher, John Mack, 170
Farakhan, Louis, 408
Farewell, Nina, 270
Farm Aid, 408
Farmer, Fanny, 175
farmhouses, 215–216
farming. *See* agriculture
Farquhar, George, 484
Farwell, Arthur, 102
fashion
    American, 75–77
    art and, 541
    class and, 70–71
    colonial, 68–73
    consumption and, 69–70
    day and evening, 72
    designers of, 74
    emphasis on body, 76, 77
    etiquette and, 263
    immodest, 69–70
    imported, 72, 74
    informality of, 75–76
    middle-class, 73–74
    nineteenth century, 73–75
    public and private, 74
    regional differences in, 75
    restrictive, 73
    twentieth century, 75–77
fast food restaurants, 174
Father Divine, 310
Fatherless and Widows Society, 561
fathers, 3, 5, 116
Faulkner, William, 347
FCC. *See* Federal Communications Commission
Federal-Aid Road Act (1916), 510
Federal Aviation Administration, 512
Federal Communications Commission, 394, 471, 473
federal government
    assistance programs, 136–137
        for housing, 467–468
        for towns, 557
    elderly and, 302
    health insurance and, 210–211
    and hospitals, 207
    housing and, 219–220
    journalism and, 238
    impact on landscapes, 257–258
    municipal government and, 63
    New Deal. *See* New Deal
    policy, on children and families, 47
    regulation
        of air traffic, 512
        of communications, 97
        of parks, 546
        of television, 471, 473–474
    standardization of foodways, 174–175
    support of suburbs, 464
    urban poverty and, 67
Federal Housing Administration, 467–468
Federal Street Theatre, 327, 485
Federal Theatre Project, 496, 538

Federal Triangle, 385
Federal Writers' Project, 530
Federalism
    communication policy of, 92–93
    journalism and, 238
Federalist Papers, The (Hamilton), 237
Feke, Robert, 530
Fels, Tony, 184
Female Patriot, The (1795), 485
Female Union Society for the Promotion of Sabbath
    Schools, 562
feme covert, 116
feme sole, 116, 117
feminization, of culture, 333, 354–355
Feminine Mystique, The (Friedan), 127, 468
feminism
    arts and, 543
    humor, 231
    National Organization for Women, 569
    sexual behavior and, 428–429
    theater, 498
Fenno, John, 237–238
Ferber, Edna, 495
Fern, Fanny, 341, 367
Fern Leaves from Fanny's Portfolio (Parton), 367
ferris wheel, 31, 32
fertility, 41–42, 295, 296, 417
Fetchit, Stepin, 228
FHA. *See* Federal Housing Administration
Fichandler, Zelda, 500
fiction
    comic, 232–233
    popular, 338, 340–345, 371–372
        best-sellers, 347, 348
        blockbusters, 349, 350–351
        dime novels, 341–342, 346–347, 371
        early criticism of, 340
        economics of, 342
        female audience, 344
        formulaic nature of, 342
        in libraries, 537
        magazines, 343–344, 345–347, 346–347, 349
        motion pictures and, 351
        paperbacks, 347, 348
        pulp fiction, 346–348, 350
        romance and, 350
        as social control, 342, 343
        social criticism in, 347
        story papers, 341–342, 346
        as subversive, 342–343
        television and, 351
        twentieth century, 348–351
    small towns in, 556
    See also literature
Field, Eugene, 226, 227
Field, Sara Bard, 124
Field Museum of Natural History, 536
Fields, W. C., 224, 229
Filibuster, The (Fonblanque), 488
film. *See* motion pictures
film noir, 149, 151
film school, 152–153
Finney, Charles Grandison, 328
fire fighting, 53, 57–58
fireworks, 310
First Blood, 351

Fischer, David Hackett, 167, 168
Fish, Mrs. Stuyvesant, 268
Fisher, Carl, 510
fishing, tourism and, 523
Fishman, Robert, 460, 468
Fisk Jubilee Singers, 104, 356
Fiske, Harrison, 492, 493
Fiske, Minnie Maddern, 493
Fithian, Phillip Vickers, 434
Fitzgerald, F. Scott, 452
Flagler, Henry M., 517
flags, display of, 258
Fletcher Henderson and His Orchestra, 26
Flexner Report, 202
flight. *See* aviation
Flint, Richard W., 31
Floating Theatre, 486
Flora; or, The Hob in the Well (1735), 484
Florida, 35, 517
    Miami, 519
    St. Augustine, 52
Flush Times of Alabama and Mississippi, The
    (Baldwin), 224
FM radio, 105, 396
folk culture
    museums, 540
    popular literature and, 338
folk music, 404
    a capella, 161
    aesthetics of, 161–162
    broadsides, 156
    Child ballads, 155
    commercialization of, 163–165
    cowboy ballads, 158
    dialogue songs, 157
    diversity in, 154
    folk rock, 402
    gospel music, 160
    governmental preservation of, 162
    left-wing political ideology in, 158–159
    lyrical songs, 155–157
    performance of, 161–162
    political content of, 163
    poverty and, 164
    religious, 160–161
    as representation of American culture, 154
    revival of, 164–165
    sentimental songs, 159–160
    social Darwinism and, 154–155
    topical songs, 158–159
    urban, 164–165
    work songs, 157–158
Folk Songs of North America (Lomax), 162
folklore, 162. *See also* folk culture; folk music
Folks, Homer, 302
Fonblanque, Albany, 488
food, 175, 176. *See also* foodways
food processing, 174–175
foodways
    American, 176–177
    assimilation and, 172–173
    chain restaurants, 174
    Chinese, 176
    colonial, 166–169
    Columbian exchange and, 165–166

    commercialization of, 173–174
    definition of, 165
    dining etiquette and, 263, 266–267
    gourmet, 176
    immigrant, 171–173
    livestock and, 166
    midwestern, 170–171
    Native American, 188
    nineteenth-century, 169–173
    politics of, 176
    post-war transformation of, 175
    reform of, 171, 175–176
    regional, 176
    religious observation and, 173
    southern, 168–170, 176
    Spanish influence, 165, 166
    standardization of, 173–175
    technology of, 173–174
    twentieth-century, 173–176
    World War II and, 175
    See also diet; food
foot racing, 439
football
    collegiate, 447–448, 452
    elite ideal, 448
    professional, 452
    television and, 456, 475, 480
    See also sports
Foote, Arthur, 101
"footloose" industry, 559
Ford, Gerald R., 233, 475
Ford, Henry, 84, 510, 518, 519
Ford, John, 145–146
foreign films, 152
foreign policy, rock music protest of, 409
forest fires. *See* fire fighting
Forest Park, 547, 548
Forest Park, OH, 467
forests, 258–259, 275, 518
Forrest, Edwin, 334, 487
Fortune, Thomas, 373
Foster, Rube, 453
Foster, Stephen Collins, 100, 299, 354, 355
Fountain of Youth, 293
"Four Hundred," at Patriarch's Ball, 268
Fourth of July, 309, 310–311
Fox, Richard Kyle, 444
Foxe, John, 366
Foxx, Redd, 228
Fragment Society, 561
France, 189, 190–191, 212
franchising, travel industry and, 519
Franciscans, 165
Frank, Henry, 369
Frankenstein (1931), 149
Frankfurt school, 337, 542
Franklin, Aretha, 28, 403
Franklin, Benjamin, 91, 222, 236, 362
    on arts, 530
    on cultural organizations, 528
    as journalist, 235
    libraries and, 361
    as printer, 340
Franklin, C. L., 22, 28
Franklin, James S., 222, 235, 362

Franklin Park, 549
fraternal organizations
    African American, 177, 178, 179, 181, 182–183
    class and, 180–181, 185
    decline of, 185–186
    as entertainment, 180, 184, 329
    ethnic, 181–182
    heterogenity of, 182
    initiation rites, 184
    as life insurance providers, 179, 184, 185
    masculinity and, 185
    military branches, 180
    nativism and, 181
    nineteenth-century, 177–180
    race and, 182–183
    religious expression and, 184, 185
    as response to capitalism, 185
    service organizations and, 186
    social change and, 183
    temperence and, 185
    women's auxiliaries, 177, 180, 183. *See also* women's or-
      ganizations
Freaks (1932), 149
Frederick Douglass' Paper, 240
free love, 419
Freed, Alan, 395, 399
Freedman, David, 392
Freedman, Estelle B., 427
Freedman, Rita, 77
Freedom's Journal, 240, 370
Freemasonry. *See* Masons
French, Alice, 225
French and Indian War, 190–191
Freneau, Philip, 238
Freud, Sigmund, 228, 426
Friedan, Betty, 127, 468
friendly witnesses, 150
Frohman, Charles, 492
frolics, 324
frontier
    African Americans and, 200
    bias and, 186–187
    cattle ranching, 198
    children and, 44
    colonial, 191–193
    defined, 187
    depiction in western films, 146
    emigration to, 195–197
    gender roles and, 195
    Great Plains, 197–198, 554–556
    housing, 213
    humor, 223–224
    intracultural conflict, 191–193
    landscapes, 254–256
    mining, 198
    Native Americans and, 187–191, 194–195, 198–200,
      505–506
    romanticism and, 195
    saloons, 282–283
    settlement of, 555–556
    slavery and, 197
    as symbol of freedom, 200
    technology and, 198
    television depictions of, 480
    towns, 555–556
    transportation and, 505–506
    See also colonization; western expansion
frontier thesis, 186–187
Fry, William, 99, 100
fuguing tunes, 352–353
Fuller, Charles E., 498
Fuller, Margaret, 119, 240
Fulton, Robert, 507
functional literacy, 376–377. *See also* literacy
funeral directors, 133, 137
funerals
    African American, 18–19
    colonial, 132
    nineteenth-century, 133
    Puritan, 132
    twentieth-century, 137

G

G-Men (1935), 147–148
Gable, Clark, 148, 230
Gabriel, Peter, 408
gag law, on press, 248
Galbraith, John Kenneth, 233
Gale, Zona, 556
galleries, art, 532
"Galloping Ghost," 452
gambling, 288–289
gang labor, 321
gangsters, 147, 286, 287
garden cities, 463
Garden Cities of Tomorrow (Howard), 465
gardens, 544
    botanical, 538
Gardiner, Stephen, 359
Garrison, William Lloyd, 240
Garroway, Dave, 478
Garvey, Marcus, 310
Gatlinburg, TN, 519
gay liberation, 405, 408, 429
Gay Liberation Front, 429
gay men, 425–426
Gazette of the United States, 238
Geer, Will, 163
Geldorf, Bob, 409
gender
    etiquette and, 269–272
    life expectancy and, 298
    popular entertainment and, 325
gender differences
    in adolescence, 2, 3–4, 6
    aging and, 296, 297
    childhood, 42–43, 44, 47
gender roles
    children and, 50
    division of labor and, 417
    etiquette and, 269–271
    on plantation, 314
    separate spheres, 425
    sexuality and, 427
    western expansion and, 195
General Magazine, 236
General Motors Building, 84
Genovese, Eugene, 326
genre fiction, 350
genteel culture, 265, 331

Gentleman from Indiana, The (Tarkington), 554
gentrification, 65, 220
geographic mobility, 327
    colonial, 503–504
    Great Depression and, 519
    landscapes and, 254
    Native American, 503
    nineteenth-century, 505–509
    social impact of, 505
    twentieth-century, 509–513
    See also settlement; transportation; western expansion
geography. *See* landscapes; natural environment
George, Henry, 465
Georgia, 194–195, 317
Georgia Minstrels, 490
Georgia Scenes (Longstreet), 224
Georgia Sea Islands, 17, 317
Georgian architecture, 378
Geriatrics (Nascher), 299
German Expressionism, influence on motion pictures,
    149, 151
German immigrants, 58, 193
    colonial housing, 212
    foodways of, 172
    fraternal organizations, 181
    newspapers of, 240, 245
    Turner societies, 440
gerontology, 299
gerousia, 294
Gerrish, Samuel, 353
Gershwin, George, 103
Gesell, Arnold, 48
ghettos, 66
Ghost Dance, 199
Giants (New York), 456
Gibson Girls, 74
Gideon, Miriam, 105
Gilbert, Cass, 83, 383, 384, 385
Gilbert, Henry F. B., 102
Gilbert, Ronnie, 163
Gilbert and Sullivan, 497
Gilded Age
    architecture of, 382–383
    sports, 442–445, 445, 446, 447–449
Gilder, Richard, 345
Gillespie, Dizzy, 104, 290
Gillette, William, 491
Gilliland, Henry, 106
Gilmore, Patrick Sarsfield, 101
Gilmore, William J., 88, 94
Ginsberg, Allen, 289, 290
Gish, Dorothy, 144
Gish, Lillian, 143
Gitlow v. *United States* (1925), 248
Glackens, William, 537
Gladden, Washington, 442
Glass, Philip, 105
Glassie, Henry, 259
Gleason, Jackie, 477
Glendale, OH, 462
Glover, Jose, 359
Gluckman, Max, 309
GM. *See* General Motors
Go Tell It on the Mountain (Baldwin), 310
"God Bless America," 159
Godey's Lady's Book, 74, 75, 94, 119, 239, 366, 367

Godfather, The (1972), 153
Godfrey, Thomas, 484
Godkin, Edwin Lawrence, 242
Godspell, 403
Goffman, Erving, 261
gold rush, 197
Goldberg, Herb, 125
Golden, Harry, 351
Goldman, Emma, 124, 426
Goldwater, Barry, 475
Goldwyn, Sam, 145
golf, 548
Gone with the Wind (1939), 149
Gone With the Wind (Mitchell), 348
Good Wives (Ulrich), 325
Goodman Theater, 501
Gordone, Charles, 498
Gore, Tipper, 411
Gorn, Elliott, 280
gospel music, 21–23, 160
Gothic architecture, 384
Gothic Revival architecture, 81, 381
Gottschalk, Louis Moreau, 100, 354
Gough, John, 335
gourmet food, 176
Gourmet, 176
government, federal
    assistance programs, 136–137
        for housing, 467–468
        for towns, 557
    elderly and, 302
    health insurance and, 210–211
    and hospitals, 207
    and housing, 219–220
    impact on landscapes, 257–258
    journalism and, 238
    municipal government and, 63
    New Deal. *See* New Deal
    policy, on children and families, 47
    press and, 251–252
    regulation
        of air traffic, 512
        of communications, 97
        of parks, 546
        of television, 471, 473–474
    standardization of foodways, 174–175
    support of suburbs, 464
    urban poverty and, 67
government, municipal, 463
    architecture of, 382–383
    colonial, 53
    criticism of in industrial cities, 62
    federal government and, 63
    machine-run, 61, 62
    metropolitian, 463–464
    nineteenth-century, 57–58
    reform, 62
    regulation, of parks, 547
    suburban, 463
Government Printing Office, 241–242
Graduate, The (1967), 153
Graebner, William, 9
Graham, Isabella, 562
Graham, Sylvester, 171, 418
Grand Canyon, 278
Grand Central Station, 82, 86

Grand Ole Opry, 109–111, 112, 170
Grand Terrace club, 287
Grand Tour, 514, 515
Grand United Order of Odd Fellows. *See* Odd Fellows
grandparents, 132, 135
Grange, 180, 507
Grange, Red, 452
Grateful Dead, 290
Graupner, Christian Gottlieb, 99
Graves, Michael, 33, 87, 386
gravestones, Puritan symbolism, 132
Gray Panthers, 302
Great Atlantic and Pacific Tea Company (A&P),
        173–174
Great Awakening, 4, 160, 327, 353. *See also* Second Great
        Awakening
Great Britain. *See* Britain
Great Depression
    adolescence during, 11
    childhood and, 47
    federal assitance and, 136–137
    health care during, 209–210
    housing during, 219
    humor and, 230
    motion pictures, 147, 148
    music, 103
    music in, 358
    nightlife and, 288
    poverty and, 136–137
    rural impact, 557
    travel and, 519
    urban impact, 63
Great Exhibition, 36
Great Gatsby, The (Fitzgerald), 452–453
Great Plains, settlement of, 197–198, 554–556
Great Smoky Mountains National Park, 274
Great Society, 67, 302
Great Train Robbery, The (1903), 141
Greco-Roman culture, views on old age, 294
Greek immigrants, 172
Greek Revival architecture, 79, 318–319, 380–381
Greek Slave, The, 266
Greeley, Horace, 123, 240, 242, 334
Green, Andrew Haswell, 547
Green, Archie, 158
Green, Johnny, 358
Green Acres, 480
Greenlee, W. A. ("Gus"), 453
Greenough, Horatio, 82
Greensward Plan, 545
Greenwich Village, 426, 537
Gregory, Dick, 228, 231
Gregory, James, 288
Greven, Philip, 131
Gridiron Club, 246
Griffith, David Wark (D. W.), 142, 143–144, 261, 493
Griffiths, Martha, 302
Grimké, Sarah, 119
Griswold, Rufus, 370
Grofé, Ferde, 103
Group Theatre, 496
Growth of Cities in the Nineteenth Century (Weber), 465
Gruen, Victor, 86
Gruening, Ernest, 301
Gualdo, Giovanni, 530
Gulick, Luther Halsey, 448, 449

Gullah music, 17
Gunning, Sarah Ogan, 163, 165
Gunsmoke, 480
Gustavas Vasa (1690), 484
Gutenberg, Johannes, 359
Guthrie, Woody, 103, 159, 163
Guthrie Theater, 500
Gutman, Albert, 421

H

Habermas, Jürgen, 362
Hackett, James Henry, 486, 487
Haggard, Merle, 112, 406
Hague, Frank, 61
Hair (1967), 403, 501
hair styles
    African American, 77
    colonial, 71
    Native American, 68
    nineteenth-century, 73
    Puritan, 70
    twentieth-century, 77
Hairston, Samuel, 318, 319
Hale, Sarah Josepha, 239, 367
Haliburton, Joseph, 328
Hall, David D., 90, 361
Hall, G. Stanley, 8, 299
Hall, Margaret Hunter, 263
Hall, Prince, 178
"Hall-Parlour" Houses: Permanent Dwellings in New
        England, 211
Hallam, Lewis, 327, 328, 529
Hallam, William, 483, 484
Halloween, 311
Halttunen, Karen, 266, 267
ham radio, 387–388
Hamilton, Alexander, 237
Hamilton, Andrew, 362, 379
Hamilton, Thomas, 237
Hamlet (Brougham), 333
Hammack, David, 62
Hammerstein, Oscar, II, 495
Hammett, Dashiell, 149, 346
Hammond, John, 326, 404
Handel and Haydn Society, 99
Handlin, Oscar, 131
Handy, W. C., 24
Hansberry, Lorraine, 498
Happiness Candy Company, 390
hard rock music, 402
Hardy, Oliver, 229
Hardy, Stephen, 547
Hare, Ernie, 390
Harlem, NY, 286, 310, 494–495
Harlem Renaissance, 540
    music of, 27
    nightclubs and, 286
    theater in, 494–495
Harlem stride, 25
Harlem Symphony, 540
Harlem's Hellfighters, 310
Harman, Moses, 419
Harmonic Society, 530
Harms, Thomas, 356
Harper and Brothers, 369

J. and J. Harper, 369
Harper's, 369
Harper's New Monthly Magazine, 367
Harper's Weekly, 232, 242
Harrigan, Edward, 491
Harrington, Michael, 67
Harris, Benjamin, 235
Harris, Charles K., 356
Harris, George Washington, 224
Harris, Joel Chandler, 225
Harris, Neil, 529, 540
Harrison, Peter, 78
Harrison, William Henry, 194
Hartsdale Canine Cemetery, 138
Harvard, John, 338
Harvard College, 54, 378, 530
harvest festivals, 329
Harvest Home, 324
Haverly's Genuine Colored Minstrels, 490
Haviland, John, 81
Hawks, Howard, 149
Hawthorne, Nathaniel, 120, 327, 336, 344, 345, 367
Hay, George D., 109–110
Haynes, Elwood, 510
Hays, Will, 147
Hazzard-Gordon, Katrina, 287–288
"head rolls," 71
Headhunters, 290
health
    of children, 45, 49–50
    in colonial cities, 54
    nineteenth-century, 57
    sanitation and, 133
    vacations as cure, 514
    water cures, 514
    See also health care; medicine
health care
    class and, 206
    community based, 206–207
    cost of, 205–206
    doctor-patient relationship, 202
    during Great Depression, 209–210
    health insurance, 208–211
    labor and, 209–210
    nurses and, 207, 208
    parallel systems of, 206
    professionalization of, 206–207
    women's roles, 207–208
    workers' benefits, 209–210
    See also health; hospitals; medicine
health insurance, 208–211
health maintenance organizations, 210
Hearst, William Randolph, 149, 241, 243, 244, 248, 372
heavy metal music, 405, 410
hedonism, motion picture depictions of, 146
Hee Haw, 113, 170
Heenan, John C., 442
Heidi Chronicles, The (1988), 498
Heilbut, Tony, 353
Heinrich, Anthony, 99, 100
heirarchy, social. *See* rank
Heller, Joseph, 232
Hellman, Lillian, 498
Helms, Jesse, 543
Hendrix, Jimi, 29

Henley, Beth, 498
Henning, Paul, 480
Henri, Robert, 537
Henry, Patrick, 169
Hensley, Virginia Patterson (Patsy Cline), 113
Hepburn, Katharine, 148
Herne, James E., 491
Herring, James, 532
Hersh, Seymour, 252
Hertz Rental Cars, 519
Hesselius, Gustavus, 530
Hetch Hetchy Valley, 275
Hewitt, James, 99
Heywood, Ezra, 419
Hibbs, Ben, 345
Hibernians, 181
Hicks, Charles B., 490
High Noon (1952), 146, 150
highbrow culture, 535
Highbrow/Lowbrow (Levine), 534
higher education. *See* colleges
Highway Trust Fund, 511
highways, 510, 511. *See also* roads
Hill, George Handel, 487
Hill, George Washington, 395
Hill, Joe, 158, 159
hillbilly music, 106–107, 108
Hilton, James, 347
Hindemith, Paul, 104
Hines, Earl "Fatha," 287
Hints on Etiquette and the Usages of Society (Day), 267
Hints on Public Architecture (Owen), 381
hippie counterculture, 290, 404–405, 428
Hispanic Americans
    aging of, 297
    Mexican Americans, 173
    rock music, 408
    in sports, 446
    stereotypes in rock music, 401
    theater, 498–499
    urban population, 65–66
historic preservation, 87, 220, 276–278
historic sites, 278
Historic Sites Act (1935), 277
historical societies, 531
History and Science: The Development of Specialized Collections, 531
History of New York (Knickerbocker), 222
History of the American Theater (Dunlap), 485–916
History of World Theater (Londre), 484
Hitchcock, Alfred, 152
"hiving off," 552
Hoadley, Grace, 564
Hobbit, The (Tolkien), 349
Hoboken, NJ, 331
Hodgkinson, John, 328
Hokinson, Helen, 230
Holbrook, Josiah, 533
Holiday Inn, 519
holidays
    British, 514
    Catholic, 308
    during Civil War, 307
    class and, 310–311
    colonial, 305–306, 324, 326

commercialization of, 311–312, 519
conspicuous consumption and, 311
creation through social dissention, 306
immigrant, 308–309
Super Bowl as, 311, 475
travel on, 514
violence and, 309–311
See also celebrations; travel; vacations; individual holiday names
Holliday, Billie, 27
Hollywood, CA
censorship of, 143, 150–151
motion pictures in, 141
threat of television, 151–152
during World War II, 149
Hollywood Ten, 150
Holmes, Mary J., 341
Holmes, Oliver Wendell, 222, 248
Holmes, Oliver Wendell, Sr., 440–441, 442
holy days, 514
Holy Land, pilgrimages to, 514
home, as refuge, 217, 565
"Home, Sweet Home," 354
home economics, 175
Home Insurance Company Building, 82
Home Life Insurance Building, 59
Homestead Act (1862), 197
homosexuality
AIDS and, 431
American Psychiatric Association and, 429
bar culture, 289
as deviant, 427, 829
early-twentieth-century, 425–426, 427
gay liberation, 405, 408, 429
gay men, 425–426, 427
Halloween costume parades, 311
Kinsey report findings, 428
lesbians, 10, 425, 426, 427
marriage and, 126–127
twentieth-century activism, 429
honky-tonk music, 113, 288
honor, southern code, 264
Hood, Raymond, 84
Hooper, Johnson Jones, 223
Hoover, Herbert, 97
Hopewell Indians, 188
Hopi Indians, 188
Hopkinson, Francis, 354
Hopper, Dennis, 153
horror films, 148, 152
horse racing, 434, 436, 437
Horstman, Dorothy, 115
hospitals, 203–207. *See also* doctors; health care; medicine
House Committee on Un-American Activities, 150–151
House of Industry, 562
house raisings, 324
"house wrecking," 22
Houseman, John, 393, 496
houses
country houses, 217
earth-fast, 211
farmhouses, 215–216
hall-parlor, 211
log, 213, 215–216
mail-order, 218

manufactured, 218
one-room, 211
wood construction, 255
See also apartments; architecture; housing
housing, 210–211
apartments, 216–217
automobile's influence on, 219
collective, 216
colonial, 210–213
company, 214, 218
diversity in, 213
family structure and, 220–221
federal assistance for, 219–220, 467–468
frontier, 213
gentrification, 220
historic preservation of, 220
industrialization and, 213–214, 218
inner city, 219–220
multi-family, 214–215, 218, 220–221
nineteenth-century, 59–60, 213–217
post-war, 64
public, 65, 219–220
single-family, 220
of slaves, 320
suburban, 216, 218–219
twentieth-century, 217–222
urban, 63, 214–215
urban renewal and, 220
utilities and, 218
working-class, 214–215
See also apartments; houses; suburbs
Housing Act of 1949, 65
How to Win Friends and Influence People (Carnegie), 348
Howard, Ebenezer, 465
Howard, John Eager, 544
Howard Johnson's, 174, 519
Howard Park, 544
Howard University, sororities at, 568–569
Howdy Doody, 478
Howe, Frederic C., 144, 465–466
Howe, Frederick, 309
Howe, George, 84
Howells, John Mead, 84
Howells, William Dean, 222, 345, 466
HUAC. *See* House Committee on Un-American Activities
Hucksters, The (Wakeman), 392, 395–396
Hughes, Langston, 230, 286
Hull-House, 566–567
Humana Building, 87
humor
African American, 225, 228
almanac, 222
backcountry, 224
civil rights and, 231
Civil War, 225
colonial American, 221–222
comic strips, 231–232
Davy Crockett myth, 223
dialect, 222
ethnic, 227–228
feminist, 231
frontier, 223–224
in Great Depression, 230
ironic, 232–233

humor (*continued*)
    Jewish, 227, 228
    minstrel, 228
    nineteenth-century, 222–226
    of oppressed peoples, 227–228
    political, 223, 224–225, 226, 233
    satire, 226–227
    scatalogical, 222
    study of, 221
    twentieth-century, 226–233
    See also comedy
Hunt, Richard M., 82
Hunter, Alberta, 285
Hunter, Richard, 327
Hunter, Robert, 483
hunting, sport, 324, 325, 326
Huntley, Chet, 479
hurling, 432
Hurst, Fannie, 147
Hurt, Mississippi John, 165
"hush harbors," 307
Huston, Joseph M., 384
Hutchinson, Anne, 54
Hutchinson Family Singers, 355
Hwang, David Henry, 499
Hyde Amendment (1977), 430
Hyde Park, 544
hydroelectric dams, 85, 258
hydropathy, 515
hymns, 353

I

I Am a Fugitive from a Chain Gang (1932), 148
I Love Lucy, 477
I Try to Behave Myself (Bracken), 270
"I Want to Hold Your Hand," 402
identity, American
    national parks and, 273–274
    nature and, 274
"idols of consumption," 452
"idols of production," 452
illegitimacy, 414
Illinois
    Belleville, 179
    Chicago, 27–28, 31, 62, 460, 486, 513, 546
        architecture, 82, 83, 84
    Cook County, 45
    Irving Park, 462
    Park Forest, 64
    Pullman, 60, 214, 462
    Riverside, 463
    State Capitol, 382
Illinois Institute of Technology, 385
illiteracy, 376–377. *See also* literacy
image orthicon camera tube, 472
immigrants
    aging, 297
    children of, 44–45
    Chinese, 45, 308
    colonial, 52
    diet of, 171–173
    education and, 382
    etiquette in nineteenth century, 268
    foodways, 171–173
    fraternal organizations of, 181

German, 58, 172, 193
    colonial housing, 212
    fraternal organizations, 181
    newspapers of, 240, 245
    Turner societies, 440
Greek, 172
holidays, 308–309
housing, 218
in industrial cities, 60–61
Irish, 58, 193, 282
Italian, 44–45, 172
Jewish, 45, 60, 172–173, 245, 308, 369
newspapers of, 244–245, 245
nineteenth-century, 58
parks and, 548
press of, 369
Scottish, 193
as settlers, 197–198
socialization of, 282–283
sports and, 440, 445–856
urban, 60
urbanization and, 58
voyages of, 503
West Indian, 173
immigration. *See* immigrants
IMP Girl, 141
imports, 72, 74, 167
Impressions, 403
Improved Benevolent and Protective Order of Elks. *See* Elks
Improvements in Longevity: A Twentieth Century Phenomenon, 296
In a Lonely Place (1950), 151
In Dahomey (1903), 490
indentured laborers, 2
Independence Hall, 379
Independent Motion Picture Company, 141
India, plantation pattern of, 314–315
Indian captivity narratives, 339
Indian Removal Act (1830), 195
Indiana, 194
    Muncie, 247, 557
Indianapolis Motor Speedway, 510
Indians. *See* Native Americans
indigo, cultivation of, 317
individualism
    manifestations in landscape, 254
    marriage and, 123
indoor family entertainment centers, 36–37
Industrial Age
    adolescence in, 7–10
    suburbs in, 460–464
    See also industrialization
industrial revolution. *See* industrialization; industry
Industrial Workers of the World, 158
industrialization
    factories, 60
    hospitals and, 203–205
    housing and, 213–214, 218
    leisure and, 518, 519
    of Midwest, 60
    nightlife and, 280–281
    publishing, 369–371
    sexual behavior and, 423–424
    towns and, 556, 557
    urban, 60–61

urbanization and, 56–57, 60–61
See also industry
industry
  agricultural. *See* agriculture
  airline, 512
  amusement, 35, 36–37
  automobile, 84, 510
  commercial architecture of, 84
  entertainment, 186
  "footloose," 559
  and labor. *See* labor
  motion picture, 139–154
  music, 24–25, 110–111, 357–358, 407
  radio. *See* radio
  railroad. *See* railroads
  television, 472–474
  tourism, 519
  See also industrialization
Infant and Child in the Culture Today (Gesell), 48
infant mortality, 39, 131, 133, 134–135
infanticide, 415
infectious diseases, 54
information
  access. *See* communications
  as different from knowledge, 95
  as entertainment, 95
  political power and, 91–92
  popular access to, 92–93
  processing, twentieth century, 96–98
  society, 95–98
  for tourism, 519
  transmission, 90–93
initiation, into fraternal organizations, 184
inner cities, 66–67, 549. *See also* cities
Innis, Harold A., 89
Inside, Outside (Wouk), 392
insurance
  health, 208–210
  life, 179, 184, 185, 186
integration
  of baseball, 453–455
  in rock music, 400
  of schools, 49
International Ladies' Garment Workers' Union, 209
International News Service, 241
International Tourism, 524
international travel, 520, 524
interpretive journalism, 247
interracial sex, 416, 427
Intersorority Conference, 568
Interstate Highway Act (1956), 467
interstate highways, 510, 511. *See also* roads
interviews, journalistic, 246
Intolerance (1916), 143
intracultural conflict, on frontier, 191–193
Invasion of the Body Snatchers (1956), 152
INXS, 409
Ireland, colonization of, 316
Irish immigrants, 58, 171, 193, 282
Irish music, 354
iron, in commercial architecture, 81–82
iron lever press, 365
ironic humor, 232–233
Iroquois Indians, 190
Irving, Henry, 490

Irving, Washington, 222, 367
Irving Park, IL, 462
Isaac, Rhys, 340
Isaak, Chris, 410
It Happened One Night (1934), 148, 230
"It Isn't Nice," 158–159
Italian Americans, 44–45, 172, 401
Italian music, 354
Ives, Burl, 163
Ives, Charles, 102
IWW. *See* Industrial Workers of the World

J

J. and J. Harper, 369
Jackson, Andrew, 194–195, 267
Jackson, John Brinckerhoff, 259, 544, 546
Jackson, Kenneth T., 459, 464, 468
Jackson, Mahalia, 22, 23, 353
Jackson, Michael, 29, 410
Jackson, Peter, 445
Jackson, William Henry, 274
Jackson, WY, 519
Jacobson Life Table, 132
James, Bill, 451
James, Elmore, 24
James, Henry, 345, 532
James I (king of England), 432–433
Jamestown, 190, 315, 551
Janis, Harriet, 357
January, Phillip B., 224
Jarves, James Jackson, 532
Jarvis, Anna, 308, 311
Jaws (1977), 153
Jay, John, 237
jazz age, 9–10, 285–288. *See also* Harlem Renaissance;
       prohibition
jazz music, 25–27, 29, 102, 103, 286–287, 539
Jazz Singer, The (1927), 147
Jefferson, "Blind" Lemon, 24
Jefferson, Thomas
  as architect, 379
  on exploration, 506
  on fashion, 72
  on food, 169
  on newspapers, 238
  purchase of Louisiana Territory, 193
  on Virginia, 552
Jefferson Airplane, 290
Jefferson Memorial, 385
Jeffersons, The, 481
Jeffries, Jim, 450
Jenney, William Le Baron, 82
jets, 520
Jewish Daily Forward, 245, 268
Jews
  humor, 227, 228
  immigrants, 60
    children of, 45
    foodways of, 172–173
    holidays, 308
    newspapers of, 245
    press of, 369
  radio programs, 391
Jim Crow, 355
Jimi Hendrix Experience, 290

job dissatisfaction, 524
jogging, 550
John Canoe festival, 17
John Street Theatre, 327
Johnny Guitar (1954), 146
johnnycake, 167
Johnson, Ban, 447
Johnson, George, 142
Johnson, Jack, 449–450, 457
Johnson, James Weldon, 228
Johnson, Jim Loftin, 62
Johnson, Lyndon B., 67
 daisy commercial, 475
 television coverage, 249
 on Vietnam War, 479
Johnson, Noble, 142
Johnson, Philip, 85
Johnson, Robert, 24
Johnson, Samuel, 531
Johnson Wax Administration Building, 85
Jolliet, Louis, 189
Jolson, Al, 147
Jones, Billy, 390
Jones, Evan, 172
Jones, George, 112
Jones, Inigo, 79
Jones, LeRoi, 498
Jones, Margo, 500
Jones, Samuel M., 62
Jones Valley, MD, 214
Joplin, Janis, 290
Joplin, Scott, 25, 102, 357
Jordan, Louis, 28
Jordan, Michael, 459
Jordan, Philip, 329
Josh Billings, His Sayings (Shaw), 226
Journal of the American Medical Association, 310
journalism
 abolitionist sentiment in, 240
 advertising and, 243
 broadcast, 393
 broadsides, 239
 censorship and, 248
 civil rights and, 250
 colonial, 235–237
 competitive, 238, 243
 corporate, 248–250
 editorial, 237–238
 ethnic, 240
 Federalist, 238
 government and, 251–252
 interpretive, 247
 mass, 244
 muckraking, 246–247
 nineteenth-century, 238–240, 242–247
 as political issue, 250–252
 politics and, 242, 247
 public relations and, 247
 sensationalism in, 244
 technological innovations in, 239–240, 242, 249
 television, 249–250, 479–480
 twentieth-century, 244–252
 use of interviews, 246
 Watergate and, 250–251
 yellow, 244, 449
 See also newspapers; press

journalists, 236, 246–247, 247–248, 252
Joy of Cooking, The (Rombauer), 175
Judson, E. Z. C., 341, 342, 371
Juneteenth, 20
Jungle, The (Sinclair), 174
Junto, 528
juvenile justice, 45

K

Kahn, Albert, 84
Kallmann, McKinnell, and Knowles, 385
Kaltenborn, Hans Von, 393
Kaminsky, Melvin, 233
Kansas, towns in, 555
Kansas City Monarchs, 453
Kansas-Nebraska Act (1854), 197
Kansas State Agricultural College, 382
Kansas State University, 382
Karloff, Boris, 149
Karr, Ronald Dale, 467
Kasson, John E., 30, 31, 261, 265
Kazan, Elia, 497
Kean, Edmund, 487
Keaton, Buster, 229
Kefauver, Estes, 478
Keighley, William, 147
Keillor, Garrison, 232
Keimer, Samuel, 235
Keith, Benjamin Franklin, 489, 490
Keith, George, 360, 361
Kellogg, Harvey, 171
Kellum, John, 81
Kelly, William, 82
Kelvinator Kitchen, 476
Kenna, Michael "Hinky-Dink," 283
Kennedy, Edgar, 229
Kennedy, John F.
 assassination, 250, 312, 401
 televised, 479, 480
 media and, 249–250
 on status of women, 127
 televised Presidential debate, 475
Kentucky, Cane Ridge, 307
Kentucky Fried Chicken, 170
Kern, Jerome, 358, 495
Kerr, Orpheus C., 225
Kersands, Billy, 490
Kessler, George E., 549
Kett, Joseph, 1
kinetograph, 140
kinetoscope, 140
King, Alexander, 351
King, B. B., 28
King, Billie Jean, 458
King, Larry, 397
King, Starr, 533
"King Cotton," 318
King George's War, 53, 316
King Kong (1933), 149
Kings County Hospital, 202
Kingsbury, Paul, 113
Kingston Trio, 164
Kinsey, Alfred, 425, 428
Kintner, Robert, 479
Kirby, Jack Temple, 106
Kiss Me Deadly (1955), 151

Kittredge, George Lyman, 162
Kiwanis, 186
Klauder, Charles Z., 384, 385
Knapp, Seaman, A., 323
Knickerbocker, Diedrich, 222
Knights of Columbus, 181–182
Knights of Labor, 180, 567
Knights of Pythias, 180, 183, 184
Alfred A. Knopf (publisher), 374
knowledge
    culture and, 528
    democracy and, 94–95
    as different from information, 95
Knowledge Is Power (Brown), 88
Kodak. *See* Eastman Kodak
Koedt, Anne, 428
Koop, C. Everett, 431
Kotzebue, August Friedrich Ferdinand von, 485
Kramden, Ralph, 477
Kramer, Hilton, 543
Krantz, Judith, 350
Kresge College, 386
Kroc, Ray, 174
Ku Klux Klan, 60, 143
    lynching, 181, 309, 427
Kübler-Ross, Elizabeth, 137–138
Kuhn, Maggie, 302
kultur, 102
Kwanzaa, 311

L

La Mama Experimental Theatre Club, 500, 542
La Salle, René Robert de, 189
labor
    agricultural. *See* plantation
    airline industry, 512
    child, 43–44, 47, 48
    collective bargaining and, 210
    female, 50, 207–208, 269, 564
    folk songs of, 158
    health care and, 209–210
    indentured, 2
    nineteenth-century, immigrants, 58
    unions, 447, 458, 508
    See also industrialization; manufacturing; slavery; urbanization; working-class
Labor Day, 308
labor unions, 447, 458, 508, 567
lacrosse, 432
Ladies Gunboat Association, 563
Ladies' Home Journal, 77, 345, 373
Lady Chatterly's Lover (Lawrence), 348
Laemmle, Carl, 141
Lafayette Theatre, 496
Lamb, Charles, 102
Lambert Air Terminal, 86
Lamplighter, The (Cummins), 344
land
    ownership, 253, 552
    public. *See* parks
    tribal, 194–195, 506
    See also property
land-grant colleges, 381–382
Landis, Kenesaw Mountain, 451
landmarks, architectural, 382, 383
Landscape, 259

landscapes
    aboriginal, 253
    academic approaches to, 259–260
    African American, 254
    anti-urban bias, 254–255
    automobile and, 256–257
    colonization and, 253–254
    environmental. *See* natural environment
    European transformation of, 253–254
    exploitation of, 258–259
    flag display and, 258
    frontier, 254–256
    garden, 544
    geometric, 257
    government impact on, 257–258
    influence of ideal on, 259
    New Deal's impact on, 258
    parks. *See* parks
    preservation of, 273–280
    railroad and, 255–256
    rural. *See* rural life
    South. *See* South
    technological impacts, 255–257
    transportation and, 255–257
    travel and, 516–517
    West. *See* frontier; western expansion
Lane, William Henry, 490
Lang, Margaret Ruthven, 101
Lanier, Sidney, 101
Lappé, Frances Moore, 171
Larcom, Lucy, 167
Lardner, Ring, 150, 230
Las Vegas, NV, 288–289, 584
Las Vegas Hilton, 522
Latino Americans
    aging of, 297
    Mexican Americans, 173
    music, 290, 408
    in sports, 446
    stereotypes in rock music, 401
    theater, 498–499
    urban population, 65–66
Latrobe, Benjamin Henry, 79, 380
Laurel, Stan, 229
Laurens, Henry, 314
law enforcement, 57, 147–148
Lawrence, Florence, 141
Laws, Malcolm, 155
laws. *See* legislation
Laws of the Indies (1873), 213
Leacock, John, 484
Leadbelly, 103
League of American Writers, 538
Lear, Norman, 481
learning. *See* education; literacy; schools
Lears, T. J. Jackson, 371
Leary, Timothy, 404
Leave It to Beaver, 272
Leaves of Grass (Whitman), 344
Lebowitz, Fran, 231
lecturers, lyceum, 533
Ledbelly. *See* Ledbetter, Hudie
Ledbetter, Hudie, 103, 163
Lee, Ann, 120
Lee, Spike, 153, 408
Leeds, Daniel, 222

Leeds, Titan, 222
left-wing politics, in folk music, 158–159, 163
Legion of Decency, 147
legislation
    on children and families, 47
    copyright, 370–371
    juvenile, 45
    municipal, 53
    for national parks, 275
    New Deal. *See* New Deal
    old age, 299
    sumptuary, 263
    zoning, 220
    See also government; United States Supreme Court
Lehr, Harry, 268
leisure, 311
    of children, 518
    class and, 325–326, 433–434
    in colonial South, 433–435
    consumption and, 525
    industrialization and, 518, 519
    middle-class, 519–520
    nineteenth-century, 56, 437–435
    Puritan, 326–327
    reform of, 327–328
    republican views of, 437–849
    television as, 474–476
    twentieth-century, 519–525
    urban, 56, 436, 437–439
    Victorian views of, 438–850
    of wealthy, 515, 517–518
    women and, 283–284, 325
    work and, 518, 524
    working-class, 438–440
    See also amusement parks; cultural institutions; entertain-
        ment; literature; motion pictures; music; nightlife; ra-
        dio; sports; television; theme parks; tourism
Leiter Building, 82
L'Enfant, Pierre Charles, 379–380
Lenglen, Suzanne, 453
Lennon, John, 404
Leopold Report, 277
LeRoy, Mervyn, 147, 148
lesbians, 10, 425, 426, 427, 569
Lescaze, William, 84
Leslie, Lew, 494
Letters from a Farmer in Pennsylvania (Dickinson), 237
Letters of Jack Downing, Major (Davis), 223
Letters on the Equality of the Sexes (Grimké), 119
Lever Building, 85
Levine, Lawrence, 228, 354, 534
Levittown, 64, 219
Lewis, David Levering, 540
Lewis, J. Vance, 41
Lewis, Meriwether, 193, 506
Lewis, Sinclair, 347, 556
libel, 250
liberalism, sexual behavior and, 426–427
liberation
    gay, 289, 405, 408, 429
    social, popular fiction as, 341–342
Liberator, 240
libraries
    circulating, 368
    colonial, 340, 361, 528
    mercantile, 368

nineteenth-century, 368–369
    private, 528
    public, 368–369, 535
        motives for, 537
        women in, 373
    publishing and, 369–370, 373
    subscription, 361, 368
Library Company of Philadelphia, 361, 528
Library of Congress, Archive of Folk Song, 162
Library Society of Charleston, museum, 530
licensing, of saloons, 283
Lieberman, Robbie, 159
life expectancy
    aging and, 293–294
    colonial, 132
    gender and, 134–135
    improvement of, 297
    maximum, 293, 294
    nineteenth-century, 132–133
    racial differences, 296–297
    twentieth-century, 134–135
life insurance, 179, 184, 185, 186
Life with Father, 230
Limbaugh, Rush, 397
Lin, Maya, 386
Lincoln, Abraham
    assassination of, 491
    etiquette of, 267
    Morrill Act and, 381
    press and, 241
Lincoln, Edward Winslow, 546
Lincoln Memorial, 385, 386
Lincoln Motion Picture Company, 142
Lind, Jenny, 335–336
Lindbergh, Charles, 452
Lindsey, Ben, 426–427
linear suburbs, 558
linen, 69, 71
Lion of the West, The; or, A Trip to Washington (1831), 487
Lippit Mill, 79
Lippmann, Walter, 247, 556
Lipsitz, George, 290
literacy
    African American, 366
    colonial, 90–91, 359, 360
    nineteenth-century, 365
    See also education
Literacy in the Colonies: Religious and Economic Necessity, 360
literary agencies, 371–372
literary agents, 350–351
literature
    African American, 539–540
    "American Renaissance," 344
    comic, 232–233
    distribution and marketing of, 374
    fiction, 340–345, 371–372
        best-sellers, 347, 348
        blockbusters, 349, 350–351
        dime novels, 341–342, 346–347, 371
        early criticism of, 340
        economics of, 342
        formulaic nature of, 342
        in libraries, 537
        magazines, 343–344, 345–347, 349
        motion pictures and, 351
        paperbacks, 347, 348

pulp fiction, 346–348, 350
    romance and, 350
    small towns in, 556
    as social control, 342, 343
    social criticism in, 347
    story papers, 341–342, 346
    as subversive, 342–343
    television and, 351
    twentieth-century, 348–351
lyceum and, 534
nineteenth-century, 367–368
poetry, 338
popular, 337–351
    almanacs, 338, 339
    bookstores and, 375–376
    broadsides, 338–339
    chapbooks, 339
    colonial through 1830s, 338–340
    criticism of, 337
    definition of, 337, 338
    fiction. *See* literature, fiction, popular
    Indian captivity narrative, 339
    marketing of, 350–351
    nineteenth century, 340–345, 367–368
    paperback and, 374
    twentieth-century, 345–351
religious, 366
travel, 519
See also magazines; newspapers; publishing
Literature and Enlightenment: Cultural Institutions in the
        Colonial Era, 528
Little, William, 353
Little Bighorn River, 199
Little Review, The, 542
Little Theater, 542
little theater, 495, 542
livestock, foodways and, 166. *See also* cattle
living history museums, 538
Living Newspaper series, in theater, 496
Living Theatre Company, 499
Livingstone, David, 246
Locke, David Ross, 225
Locke, John, on childhood, 41
Lockridge, Kenneth, 131
locomotives, steam-powered. *See* railroads
lodges. *See* fraternal organizations
log houses, 213, 215–216
Lolita (Nabokov), 232
Lomax, Alan, 162, 163
Lomax, John, 162
London Company of Comedians, 530
Londre, Felicia Hardison, 484
Long, Huey, 384
Long, Stephen H., 506
Longstreet, Augustus Baldwin, 224
Loos, Anita, 144
Lorenzo, Frank, 512
Lorimer, George Horace, 345, 372
Los Angeles, CA, 64, 465
Lost Horizon (Hilton), 347
Lott, Eric, 332
lotteries, art, 532
Louisiana
    New Orleans, 17
    plantations, 318
Louisiana Territory, 193

Louvre, 531
love, romantic, 119–120, 418
Lovecraft, H. P., 346
Lovejoy, Elijah P., 95
lowbrow culture, 535
Lowell, James Russell, 222, 224
Lowell, Josephine, 567
Lowell, MA, 57
    company housing, 214
    health care plan, 209
    Lowell Plan, 209
    national parks in, 273, 280
Lowenthal, David, 254
Lowenthal, Leo, 452
LSD, 404–405
Lubitsch, Ernst, 146
Lucas, Eliza (Pinckney), 316
Lucas, George, 152–153, 512
Lucas, Sam, 490
Lucy Did Lamm Her Moor, 333
Ludlow, Noah, 486
Luks, George, 537
Lumière, Auguste, 140
Lumière, Louis, 140
Luna Park, 32
Lundberg, Victor, 406
Luria, Daniel, 467
lyceums, 533–534
Lyman, Hannah, 70–71
Lynch, Silas, 261
lynching, 309, 427
Lynd, Helen, 247, 557
Lynd, Robert, 247, 557
Lynn, Loretta, 113–114
Lyon, James, 353
Lyon, Mary, 563
lyrical songs, 155–157

M

M. Butterfly (1988), 499
Mabley, Jackie "Moms," 228
McAllister, Ward, 268
McArthur, John, Jr., 382
Macbeth Gallery, 537
McCarthy, Joseph, 479
McCarthyism
    blacklisting, 163–164, 473–474
    folk music and, 163
    Hollywood and, 147, 150–151
    westerns and, 146
    See also censorship; Communism
McCartney, Paul, 408
McClure's Magazine, 247
MacDermott, Galt, 501
McDonald's, 174
MacDowell, Edward, 101, 102
McGuire, Barry, 406
McIlrath, Patricia, 500
MacKave, Steele, 491
McKay, Claude, 228, 286
McKenzie, Roderick, 466
McLain, George, 302
McLean, Albert, 392
McLuhan, Marshall, 89–90, 482
Macmillan Company, 375
Macon, Uncle Dave, 110

Macoupin County Courthouse, 383
Macready, William Charles, 335–336
macrobiotics, 175
Macy, Josiah, Jr., 299
Madden, Owney, 286
Madison, James, 92, 237
Madonna, 409
magazines, 367–368
    colonial, 236
    editorial formulas of, 345
    fashion, 77
    influence of television, 475
    nineteenth-century, 238
    popular, 343–344, 345–347, 349, 367–368
    sensationalism in, 372–373
    See also literature; newspapers; press
magnetic videotape, 473
Magnificent Seven, The (1960), 146
Mahal, Taj, 24
mail
    air delivery, 512
    postal system
        colonial, 91
        Federalist, 92–93
        reform, 96
mail-order, 218, 374
Main Street (Lewis), 556
mainstreaming, of folk music, 164–165
Malcolm X, 288
Malcolmson, Robert, 329
Malina, Judith, 499
Mall of America, 36–37
malls, 36–37, 81, 86
malnutrition, 170
Malone, Bill, 288
Mamet, David, 501
Mammoth Mountain, 522
Man Against Crime, 473
management, of railroads, 508
manifest destiny, 79, 194. *See also* frontier; settlement; western
    expansion
Manigault, Gabriel, 316
Mann, Theodore, 499
Mann Act (1910), 283
manners, 261, 263. *See also* etiquette
*Manual of Politeness, Comprising the Principles of Etiquette, and
    Rules of Behavior in Genteel Society, for Persons of Both
    Sexes, A*, 266
manufactured housing, 218
manufacturing
    in antebellum South economy, 322
    in cities, 60
    of houses, 218
    industrialization and, 60
    in South, 322
    in towns, 559
    urbanization and, 56–57
    See also agriculture; industrialization; industry; labor; ur-
        banization
maple sugar, 168
Mapplethorpe, Robert, 543
Marc, David, 396, 480
Mardi Gras, 324
Marey, Étienne-Jules, 139
Margaret Fleming (1890), 491
Marin County Civic Center, 386

Mark Twain's Library of American Humor (Twain), 222
market research, 345, 397
marketing
    of air travel, 512
    of cultural institutions, 527
    of Ford automobiles, 510
    of literature, 350–351, 374
    of news, 247
    of print materials, 369–371
    See also advertising
markets
    economic, domestic, 507
    for print media, 364–367
    real estate, 220
    rice, 316
Marley, Bob, 409–410
Marmion; or, The Battle of Flodden Field, 486
Marquette, Jacques, 189
Marquis, Don, 230
marriage
    African American, 117, 118, 421–422
    aging and, 298
    colonial, 116–117
    companionate, 119–120
    complex, 120
    definition of, 115
    diversity in, 128–129
    effect of Revolutionary War, 118–119
    individualism and, 123
    interracial, 122, 126
    love and, 119–120
    Native American, 416
    nineteenth-century, 118–123, 420
        alternatives to, 120
    prenuptual agreements, 119
    property and, 119, 120
    Puritan, 116–117
    reciprocity of, 119
    religion and, 123
    same-sex, 126–127
    sexual behavior in, 413, 418–419
    sexual liberalism and, 427
    of slaves, 117, 118
    in South, 117–118
    state regulation of, 118–119
    traditionalism, 125
    twentieth-century, 124–129
    in utopian societies, 120
    war and, 124
    women and, 127
    working-class, 420
    See also courtship; divorce; family structure; separation, marital
Marryat, Frederick, 265
Marsalis, Wynton, 29
Marshall Field Wholesale Store, 83, 508
Martin, Judith, 272
Martin, Sallie, 23
Martin, Scott, 329, 334
Marx, Karl, 240
Marx Brothers, 228
Maryland
    Baltimore, 56, 544, 546
    colonial, 212
    Jones Valley, 214
    plantations, 317
    See also Chesapeake, colonial

M*A*S*H (1970), 153
Mason, Lowell, 354
Masonic model, 178
Masons, 5, 177–179, 180–182
    African American, 180
    criticism of, 178–179
    lodges, 329
mass communication, 338–339, 518, 519. See also communi-
        cations; media; newspapers; radio; television
mass consumption. See consumption
mass culture, 11, 30–31. See also amusement parks; culture;
        cultural institutions; motion pictures; newspapers;
        popular culture; radio; sports; television; theme parks
mass entertainment, 30–31. See also amusement parks; enter-
        tainment; theme parks
mass journalism. See journalism; media
mass marketing. See marketing
mass media, 97–98, 244, 519
mass publishing, 371–375. See also mass media; newspapers;
        publishing
mass tourism, 515
mass transit, 56, 59. See also transportation
Massachusetts
    Boston, 52–55, 78, 378, 464–465, 467, 547, 550
    colonial, 2, 552
    Lowell, 57, 209, 214, 273, 280
    Somerville, 9
    Worcester, 546, 547
Massachusetts General Court, 263
Massachusetts General Hospital, 202
Masses, 537
Masters, Edgar Lee, 556
masturbation, 418
materialism. See conspicuous consumption; consumption
Mather, Cotton, 54, 99, 116
    library of, 361
    on music, 352, 353
Mather, Stephen Tyng, 276
Mathews, Charles, 487
Mattachine Society, 429
Mattock, James, 413
Maude, 481
Maxwell Communication Corporation, 375
May Day, 324
Mayer, Louis B., 145, 150
Mayo, Frank, 488
maypole, 435
Mazeppa (1831), 330
meat, in diet, 170–171
mechanical rides, 31, 33
media
    colonial, 91
    communications and, 89–90
    mass, 97–98, 244, 519
    proliferation of, 93, 94
    sports and, 451–452, 456
    See also journalism; newspapers; press; radio; television
Medicaid, 209, 302
medical schools, 202
Medicare, 209, 300, 302
medicine
    class and, 204
    education for, 201–202
    gerontology, 299
    hydropathy, 515
    nineteenth-century, 201–206

nurses and, 207, 208
    professionalization of, 206–207
    regional, 201
    surgery, 203
    twentieth-century, 49
    See also doctors; health care; hospitals
meetinghouse, 378
meetings, town, 552
Mellencamp, John, 408
Mellers, Wilfrid, 356
melodrama theater, 329, 330, 487, 488
melodramas, motion picture, 151–152
Melville, Herman, 344
memorial societies, 137
men
    clothing, 68, 71, 73, 75, 76
    fraternal organizations and, 185
    patriarchal authority, 3, 5, 116
    See also gender roles
Mencken, H. L., 227, 556
mercantile libraries, 368
Merchants' Exchange, 79
Mercury Theatre, 496–497
Merritt Parkway, 511
Merry Oldsmobile, 510
Mesa Verde National Park, 276, 278
Metamora; or, The Last of the Wampanoags (1829), 330, 487
method acting, 497
Metropolitan Museum of Art, 539, 541
Mets, 458
Mexican Americans, 173. See also Hispanic Americans
Mexico, 193–194
Miami, FL, 519
Michigan, 84, 194
    Detroit, 66
middle-class
    adolescence, 6, 7, 8–10, 11
    colonial, 52–53
    etiquette and, 261–262, 265–269
    hospitals and, 206
    housing, 217
    in industrial cities, 60
    nineteenth-century, 56, 60
        etiquette, 265–269
        fashion, 73–74
    popular entertainment, 334–337
    recreation, 276
    rock music audience, 399
    rock music's rejection of, 404–405
    sexual behavior, 417–420, 426–427
    sports and, 449
    travel, 519–520
    twentieth-century
        etiquette, 269–272
        sports and, 456
    vacations of, 515
middle colonies, housing, 211–212. See also colonial
        America
middlebrow, fiction, 345
Middlesex County, MA, 2
Middleton, Henry, 316, 317
Middletown (Lynd and Lynd), 557
Midway Plaisance, 32
Midwest
    foodways of, 170–171
    Great Plains, settlement of, 197–198, 554–556

Midwest (*continued*)
  industrialization of, 60
  nineteenth-century housing, 215–216
  settlement of, 195–196, 197–198, 552–554
  towns, 554
  township-county system of settlement, 553
  See also settlement
Mies van der Rohe, Ludwig, 385
migration, 193
  to frontier, 195–197
  urban, 106, 219
  westward. *See* western expansion
  See also frontier; settlement
military, fraternal organizations and, 180
Miller, Arthur, 151, 497
Miller, Samuel, 364
Miller, Walter, 144
Miller, Zane L., 467
Millinder, Lucky, 23
Mills, Robert, 381
mills, textile, 79, 81
Milner, Henry M., 330
Mingus, Charles, 29
minimalism, 86, 105
mining, 198, 555
  in folk music, 159
Minnelli, Vincente, 151
Minnesota, 192, 383, 384
Minnie Pearl, 110
Minor, Worthington, 473
Minstrel Show, A, or Civil Rights in a Cracker Barrel (1966), 499
minstrelsy, 228, 490
  blackface, 332–333
  music of, 21, 355, 356
Miss Manners, 272
Miss Manners' Guide to Excrutiatingly Correct Behavior (Martin), 272
Mission 66, 276
missionaries, 483, 564
Mississippi, 318
Mississippi Delta blues, 24
Mississippi Indians, 188
Mississippi River, exploration of, 189, 193
Missouri, 547, 548
Missouri Reperatory Theatre, 500
Missouri River, 189
Missus Goes A-Shopping, 476
"Mister Rogers," 128
Mitchell, Margaret, 149, 348
Mitford, Jessica, 137
mobile homes, 84
mobility. *See* geographic mobility; transportation; travel
Moby-Dick (Melville), 344
Model Cities program, 67
Model T, 510
Modell of Christian Charity, A (Winthrop), 262
modern art, 539
"Modern Jazz Quartet," 539
Modern Music, 103
Modern Sports: Central to American Culture, 446
Modern Times, 419
Modern Woodmen of America, 181, 184
Moderne style, in commercial architecture, 84
modernism, 85–86, 385, 539
Modernist architecture, 85–86, 385
modernization. *See* industrialization; urbanization

modernization theory, of communications, 88–89
Mohawk Indians, 190
Molineaux, Tom, 442
MOMA. *See* Museum of Modern Art
Monadnock Building, 83
Monarchs, 455
Monday Night Football, 456, 480
Monk, Thelonious, 104
monopolies, theatrical, 492
Monroe, Bill, 112–113
Monroe, Harriet, 542
Montgomery Ward, 508
Monticello, 279
monuments, national, 385, 386
Moody, Dwight L., 308
Moody, Eleazar, 263
moon, exploration of, 471, 480
Mooney, Hughson, 356, 357
Moore, Charles, 386
Moore, Thomas, 354
moral reform, 58, 443. *See also* reform; women's organizations
moral standards
  adolescence and, 5–6
  in colonial cities, 54–55
  cultural, 331–332
  sexuality and, 413–431
moralism, in folk music, 159–160
Moran, Thomas, 274
Morgan, Edmund, 168
Morgan, William, 178
Mormons, 118, 254, 419
Morrill Federal Land Grant Act (1862), 381
Morris, Ronald, 287
Morse, Samuel F. B., 88, 95, 96
Morse, Wayne, 301
mortality, 296–297
  of African Americans, 135
  in Civil War, 134
  colonial, 131–132
  infant, 39, 131, 133, 134–135
  nineteenth-century, 132–134
  racial differences, 296–297
  sanitation and, 133
  of slaves, 132
  twentieth-century, 134–138
Mortality Gap, 135
Morton, Jelly Roll, 25, 102
Morton, Thomas, 435
Moses, Robert, 549
Mosher, Clelia D., 418
Mosquito, La, 333
mother-in-law apartments, 220
motherhood, republican, 42, 119–120
mothers
  African American slaves, 423
  and children, 48, 50
  as controllers of sexual desire, 419
  nineteenth-century, 42
  republican motherhood, 42, 119–120
  twentieth-century, 48
Mother's Day, 308
Mothers for Adequate Welfare, 569
mothers' pensions, 136
Motion Picture Alliance for the Preservation of American Ideals, 150
Motion Picture Association, 152

motion picture industry
 African Americans in, 142–143
 censorship in, 144, 147, 150–151
 competition in, 143, 145
 corporate, 152
 early years, 141–145
 in Great Depression, 147–148
 Socialism in, 145
 women in, 144
 World War II and, 149
 See also motion pictures
Motion Picture Patents Company, 141
Motion Picture Producers and Distributors Association, 147
motion pictures
 academic study of, 152–153
 African Americans in, 142–143, 153
 animated, 148
 cameras, 139–140
 comedy in, 228–229, 233
 counterculture and, 153
 cult status of, 152
 European influence, 146, 149, 151
 film noir, 149, 151
 foreign, 152
 gangsters in, 147
 German Expressionist influence, 149, 151
 Great Depression, 147–148
 horror films, 148, 152
 independent, 153
 influence of television, 475
 law enforcement in, 147–148
 low budget, 152
 melodramas, 151–152
 musicals, 151
 New Wave influence, 152
 popular fiction and, 351
 in Progressive Era, 143–145
 public influence of, 143
 ratings for, 152
 screwball comedies, 148, 230
 sequels, 153
 silent, 141–145
 as social commentary, 143–145
 social influence of, 153–154
 sound in, 147
 special effects, 153
 talkies, 147
 theater and, 493
 video and, 153–154
 Vietman War in, 153
 western, 146
 women in, 151–152
 See also motion picture industry
Mott, Lucretia Coffin, 302
Mott the Hoople, 405
Mount, William Sidney, 334
Mount Auburn, 133
Mount Holyoke Female Seminary, 563
mountain resorts, 519, 521
movies. *See* motion pictures
MTV, 410
muckrakers, 246–247, 372
Muir, John, 200, 274–275
Mullett, Alfred B., 382
multiculturalism, 539–540

multifamily housing, 214–215, 218, 220–221. *See also* apartments
Mulvey, Christopher, 266
Mumford, Lewis, 461
Muncie, IN, 247, 557
Munday, Richard, 379
Muni, Paul, 148
municipal government, 463
 architecture of, 383
 colonial, 53
 criticism of in industrial cities, 62
 federal government and, 63
 machine-run, 61, 62
 metropolitan, 463–464
 nineteenth-century, 57–58
 reform, 62
 regulation, of parks, 547
 suburban, 463
Munsey, Frank, 346, 363
Munsey's, 247
Murdock, Frank, 487
Murrow, Edward R., 249, 250, 478, 479
"muscular Christians," 441
Museum of Modern Art, 539, 542
museums, 531
 American Museums, 532
 art, 531, 535, 538
 colonial, 530
 commercialization of, 540–541
 compared to department stores, 540
 as display spaces, 540–541
 ethnic, 540
 of folk culture, 540
 living history, 538
 natural history, 531, 532, 536
 nineteenth-century, 535, 536
 retail sales in, 540–541
 scientific, 531
 as storehouses, 536
 world's fairs and, 536, 537
 See also cultural institutions
music
 African American, 12–30, 100, 101–102, 104, 290, 356. *See also* African Americans, music
 African influences, 14–17, 409
 American national identity and, 102
 bebop, 29
 bluegrass, 161
 blues, 23–25, 27–29
 during Civil War, 356
 colonial, 98–99, 529, 530
  "fuguing tunes," 352–353
  hymns, 353
  "lining out," 352
  psalms, 351–353
  singing by note, 352
 commercialization of, 20, 24, 107–109
 concert, 98–105, 331–332, 529, 530, 534, 535. *See also* concert music
 country and western, 105–115. *See also* country and western music
 cultivated and vernacular, 98
 dance and, 16–17
 debate over "American," 98
 disco, 406
 European, 98

music (*continued*)
 folk, 154–165. *See also* folk music
 as genteel culture, 331
 gospel, 160
 in Great Depression, 103, 358
 hillbilly, 106–107
 honky-tonk, 288
 instruction of, 353
 jazz, 25–27, 29, 102–103, 286–287, 539
 Latino, 290
 Native American, 98
 New Age, 105
 of New Orleans, LA, 17
 nineteenth century, 99–102
 "old timey," 161
 opera, 331–332, 354, 535
 operetta, 495
 orchestral, 99–102
 patriotic, 100
 percussion, 15
 pop music, 406
 popular, 100, 397–398, 406, 542
  availability of sheet music, 356
  commercialization of, 356–357
  European influence, 357
  Irish, 354
  minstrelsy, 355, 356
  opera, 354
  prior to 1950, 351–358
  ragtime, 357
  rock influence on, 398–399
  Sacred Harp music, 354
  sentimentalism in, 355–356
  swing, 358
  Tin Pan Alley, 356
  twentieth-century, 357–358
 radio influence, 103, 357
 rap music, 407, 408
 religious, 160–161, 351–353
 revolutionary, 353
 rock, 397–411, 407. *See also* rock music
 secular, 354
 shape-note notation of, 328
 of slaves, 13–20
 soul, 403
 spiritual music, 17–18, 21
 synthesized, 104
 television and, 105
 See also cultural institutions; musical theater; nightlife
music industry, 24–25, 110–111, 357–358, 407
musical theater, 151, 233, 488–489, 490, 495, 497, 501, 542.
  See also music; theater
musicians
 stage presence, 108–109
 women as, 24–25, 27, 105, 113–115, 355
 See also music
musique concrète, 104
Musketeers of Pig Alley, The, 143–144
mutual benefit societies. *See* fraternal organizations
Mutual Film Corporation v. *Industrial Commission of Ohio*
  (1915), 144
Muybridge, Eadweard, 139
My Partner (1879), 491
Myers, Elijah F., 383
"Myth of the Vaginal Orgasm, The" (Koedt), 428

N

NAACP. *See* National Association for the Advancement of
  Colored People
Nabokov, Vladimir, 232
Nairn, Ian, 259
Naismith, James, 431, 448, 449
Naked Lunch (Burroughs), 405
Nasby, Petroleum Vesuvius, 225
Nascher, I. L., 299
Nash, Ogden, 230
Nashville: The Business of Popular Culture, 111
Nashville, TN, 106, 111
Nassau Hall (College of New Jersey), 378
Nassau Street Theater, 530
Natchez, MS, 318
Nathan, Maud, 567
Nation of Islam, 169, 457
National Academy of Design, 532, 537
National Association for the Advancement of Colored Peo-
  ple, 374
National Association of Base Ball Players, 440
National Association of Colored Women, 566
National Basketball Association, 457
National Broadcasting Company, 390, 472, 478, 480
National Collegiate Athletic Association, 444, 452
National Consumers' League, 567
National Council of Senior Citizens, 302
National Endowment for the Arts, 500, 543
National Football League, 452, 457
national forests, 275, 519
National Gazette, 238
national heritage corridors, 280
national historic parks, 279
National Historic Preservation Act (1966), 277–278
national historical reserves, 279
National Intelligencer, 241
National Labor Relations Act (1935), 209, 210
National League, 447
national monuments, 278, 386
National Organization for Women, 569
National Panhellenic Conference, 568
National Park Service, 273, 276–278, 277
national parks, 518, 520, 524
 and American identity, 273–274
 biocentric management of, 277
 conservation and, 275
 ecology of, 276
 historic preservation and, 276–278
 origins of, 273
 patriotism and, 273–274
 philanthropic donation for, 274
 recreation and, 276
 varieties of, 278–280
National Police Gazette, The, 244, 444
National Public Radio, 97, 250, 396–397
National Register of Historic Places, 276
National Right to Life Committee, 430
National Security League, 309
National Tourism, 519
National Welfare Rights Organization, 569
National Women's Employment Project, 569
nationalism, in music, 102
Nationalism and Social Communication (Deutsch), 88
Nationalist period, popular entertainment, 324, 327–328
Native American Balladry (Laws), 155

Native American Children: Producing Independent, Self Reliant Adults, 40

Native American Sexual Customs, 416

Native Americans
    aging and, 297
    agriculture, 253
    childhood, 40
    clothing, 67–68
colonization and, 187–191, 194–195, 198–199, 503–504.
        See also frontier; settlement; western expansion
    cross-gender behavior, 416
    disease and, 189, 503
    education of, 382
    etiquette, 262
    family structure of, 115
    foodways of, 165–166
    landscapes, 253
    marriage, 416
    missionaries and, 483
    music, 98
    press of, 240
    publishing, 369
    relations among, 188
    resettlement, 195, 198–199
    rock music and, 405, 408
    sexual behavior of, 416
    theatrical portrayals, 487
    tribal lands, 194–195, 506
    in Westerns, 146
    See also names of individual tribes
nativism, fraternal organizations and, 181
natural environment
    conservation, 259, 275
    environmentalism, 259
    nostalgia for, 274–275
    preservation of, 273–280
    travel and, 516–517, 518, 524
natural history museums, 531, 532, 536
nature. *See* natural environment
NBA. *See* National Basketball Association
NBC. *See* National Broadcasting Company
NCAA. *See* National Collegiate Athletic Association
NEA. *See* National Endowment for the Arts
Near v. *Minnesota* (1931), 248
Nebraska State Capitol, 384
Negro American League, 453
Negro Ensemble Company, 498
Negro National League, 453
Negro People's Theatre, 496
Negroes. *See* African Americans
Nelson, Ricky, 399–400
neo-baroque architecture, 382
neo-Romanesque architecture, 83
neoclassical architecture, 379, 382
neotraditionalism, in urban planning, 559
Ness, Eliot, 480
network radio, 389–390, 392–394. *See also* radio
network television, 471–472, 474
Nevada, 124
    Las Vegas, 288–289, 584
New Age, music, 105
New American Library, 348
New Deal, 63
    architectural programs, 385
    children and, 47

cultural institutions and, 541
historic preservation during, 277
impact on landscapes, 258
plantation system and, 323
public arts and, 538
urban supporters of, 63
New England, colonial
    church in, 552
    commons, 544
    foodways, 167–168
    holidays, 305–306
    housing, 211
    leisure, 326–327
    literacy, 359, 360
    mortality, 131
    sexual behavior, 413–414
    sports, 433
    theater, 327
    See also Massachusetts, colonial; Puritans
New England boiled dinner, 167
New England Courant, 235, 362
New England Primer, The, 338
New England Women's Club and Sorosis, 565
New Englander, 438
"new families," 50–51
New Federalism, 67
New Jersey, 331, 464, 518
New Male-Female Relationship, The (Goldberg), 125
New Masses, 103
New Mexico, 253, 378
"New" Morality, 124
New Orleans, LA, 17
New Playwright's Theater, 538
New Right, criticism of sexual behavior, 430
New Sound from England, The, 402
New Wave, 152, 406
New York
    Chautauqua, 519
    Harlem, 286, 310, 494–495. *See also* Harlem Renaissance
    Levittown, 64, 219
    New York City, 55–56
        annexation of suburbs, 464
        architecture, 82, 83, 84
        Central Park, 57, 545, 546, 547, 550
        commercial architecture, 82, 83, 84
        as commercial center, 505
        nineteenth-century, 55–56, 56
        parks, 545, 546, 549
        Riverside Park, 549
        suburbs, 464
        theater in, 486–487, 491
        urban planning in, 62
    Niagara Falls, 517, 518
    nineteenth-century theater, 330
    Rochester, 505
    Scarsdale, 467
New York Academy of the Fine Arts, 532
New York Age, 373
New York Anchorage, 420
New York Associated Press, 241
New York Central Labor Union, 308
New York City Ballet, 541
New York Daily Graphic, The, 242
New York Dramatic Mirror, The, 492
New York Evening Post, 237

New York Female Moral Reform Society, 562
New York Giants, 456
New York Herald, 239, 240
New York Hospital, 203
New York Journal, 244, 372
New York Knickerbocker Baseball Club, 440
New York Ledger, 341
New York *Medical Repository*, 239
New York Mets, 458
New York Philharmonic, 100, 105
New York Public Library, 535, 539
New York Shakespeare Festival, 501
New York *Sun*, 93, 368
New York Times, 244, 247, 372
New York Times Book Review, 349
New York Times v. *Sullivan* (1964), 250
New York Tract Society, 366
New York Tribune, 241
New York Weekly, 341
New-York Weekly Journal, 236
New York World, 242, 372
New York Yacht Club, 440
New York Yankees, 451
New Yorker, The, 230, 389
New York's Common, 544
Newell, Robert Henry, 225
Newer Ideals of Peace (Addams), 567
Newport, RI, 78–79
news, 241–242, 479–480. *See also* journalism; newspapers;
    radio; television
news agencies, 241–242
News for Everyman (Culbert), 393
newspapers
    advertising, 243, 372
    African American, 245–246
    as big business, 242–244
    chain, 248
    circulation of, 372
    colonial, 92–93, 235–237, 362, 364
    comic strips, 231–232
    competition among, 239, 243
    corporate, 248–249
    editorialism in, 237–238
    as entertainment, 244, 372
    ethnic, 240, 245, 246
    foreign-language, 245, 246
    illustrated, 242
    immigrants and, 244–245
    influence of television, 475
    marketing of, 247
    nineteenth-century, 238–240, 242–247, 364–365,
        439
    penny papers, 239–240, 243, 340–341
    politics and, 238, 242, 247
    Populist, 244–245
    proliferation of, 93, 94
    radicalism and, 248
    sensationalism in, 244
    sports coverage, 439, 443, 449
    Stamp Act and, 364
    technological innovations, 239–240, 242, 248
    See also journalism; press
Newton, Norman, 544
Nez Percé Indians, 199
NFL. *See* National Football League
Niagara Falls, 517,518

Nichols, J. C., 85
Nichols, Mike, 153
nickelodeons, 140
Nickelodeons: The First Movie Theaters, 140
Night of the Living Dead (1968), 152
nightclubs, 284, 290
nightlife
    adolescent, 290–291
    African American, 285, 286–287
    alcohol and, 285, 289–290
    ballrooms, 288
    bars and, 289–290
    cabarets, 284, 285
    dance clubs, 290
    dance-halls, 284
    diversity in, 290
    gambling and, 288–289
    gangsters and, 285, 286, 287
    Great Depression and, 288
    hippie subculture and, 290
    industrialization and, 280–281
    jazz music and, 286–287
    nightclubs, 284, 290
    1920's, 285–288
    nineteenth-century, 280–281
    post-war, 289
    racism in, 287–288
    role of alcohol, 281–283
    saloons, 281–283
    speakeasies, 285
    twentieth-century, 285–291
    urbanization and, 280–281
    vice districts, 280
    working-class, 280, 283
    World War II and, 288–289
    See also dance; entertainment; leisure; music
Nightline, 249
1984 (Orwell), 349
1950s, 455–456, 477–478, 511–512
1919 World Series, 450–451, 453
1920s, 9–10, 285–288
Nineteenth Amendment, 144
nineteenth century
    adolescence, 4–7
    architecture, 79, 81–83, 380–383
    arts, 531–537
    baseball, 440
    childhood in, 41–45
    cities, 55–63
    communications in, 95–96
    cultural institutions, 528–529, 531–537
    death in, 132–134
    divorce, 120–124
    education, 58, 554
    elite, 56
    families, 6, 118–123
    fashion, 73–75
    fertility, 41–42, 417
    foodways in, 169–173
    fraternalism during, 177–180
    housing, 213–217
    humor, 222–226
    journalism, 238–240, 242–247
    leisure, 437–445, 515–519
    libraries, 368–369
    literacy, 365–266

literature, 367–368
marriage, 118–123, 420
medicine, 201–206
middle-class, 56
museums, 535–536
newspapers, 238–240, 242–247, 364–365
nightlife, 280–281
opera, 535
periodicals, 365
popular entertainment, 328–337
popular literature, 340–345, 367–368
print in, 364–373
publishing in, 364–373
racial conflicts, 21
railroads, 56, 507–508
romantic love, 418
sexual behavior, 417–423
sport, 280
sports, 437–445, 446, 447–449
suburbs, 460–464
theater, 328–330, 485–492
towns, 552–556
transportation, 505–509
travel, 515–519
utopian communities, 120
vacations, 515–519
views on aging, 298–299
women's organizations, 561–568
working-class, 56–57, 419–420, 438–440
Nixon, Richard M.
    Checkers speech of, 475
    on country and western music, 111
    press and, 250–251
    television coverage, 249, 475
no-fault divorce, 126, 129
No Place to Be Somebody (1969), 498
Noah, Mordecai M., 487
nontraditional families, 50–51
North Carolina, 35
Northern Spectator, 240
Northland Center, 86
Northwest Ordinance (1787), 366
Norton, Charles Eliot, 535
nostalgia, rural, 110
Notes on the State of Virginia (Jefferson), 552
novels. *See* fiction; literature; popular literature,
        fiction
NOW. *See* National Organization for Women
Noyes, John Humphrey, 120, 419
NPR. *See* National Public Radio
nurses, 207, 208, 321
nutrition. *See* diet
Nye, Edgar Wilson, 226

O

Oakes, Urian, 263
obscenity, in rock music, 411
Ocean Grove, NJ, 518
Ochs, Adolph, 244, 372
O'Connor, Carol A., 461, 467
Octoroon, The (1859), 488
Odd Fellows, 5, 177, 178, 179, 180, 183, 184
Odyssey, 294
Oedipus at Colonus, 294
Oermann, Robert K., 113
Ogelthorpe, James, 544

Ohio, 33
    Forest Park, 467
    Glendale, 462
Ohrlin, Glenn, 165
oil, Arab embargo, 513
Ojibwa Indians, 191
Oklahoma, 195
Oklahoma! (1943), 358
old age
    benchmark age, 294
    Biblical views, 293–294
    legislation, 299
    philanthropy and, 299
    politics and, 301–303
    as problem, 299
    retirement and, 300–301
    social construction of, 294–295, 298–299
    stages of, 294
    See also aging
"Old Age" (Currier and Ives), 299
Old College (Harvard), 378
Old Colony House, 379
Old Creole Days (Cable), 224
"Old Drury." *See* John Street Theatre
Old Executive Office Building, 382
"Old Folks at Home" (Foster), 299
Old Northwest Territory, settlement of, 552–553
Old Post Office Building, 383
Old Sleuth, 371
Old State House, 379
Old Sugar, 224
Old Testament, on aging. *See also* Bible
"old timey" music, 161
Older Americans Act (1965), 302
"oldies" music, 407
Oldfield, Mike, 403
Olds, Ransom, 510
Oldsmobile, 510
Oliver, King, 26, 102
Olmsted, Frederick Law, 57, 83
    as campus planner, 382
    design of Central Park, 545
    on suburbs, 459–460, 462–463
Olympic Games, 457, 475
Omaha Magic Theatre, 500
O'Malley, Walter, 456
omnibus, 56
On Death and Dying (Kübler-Ross), 137–138
one-room houses, 211
one-room schoolhouses, 382
One Third of a Nation (1938), 496
Oneida Community, 120, 419
O'Neill, Eugene, 495–496
O'Neill, James, 495
Ong, Walter J., 89–90, 91, 358–359
opera music, 331–332, 354, 534, 535
    rock opera, 403
operetta, 495
Opry. *See* Grand Ole Opry
Opryland U.S.A., 111
orchestras. *See* concert music
Order of the Eastern Star, 177, 183
Order of the Sons of Italy, 181
Order of United Workmen, 179
Oregon, 194, 506
O'Reilly, Leonora, 567

organic food, 175
organizations
    adolescent, 9
    arts, 531, 532
    cultural. *See* cultural institutions
    fraternal
        African American, 177, 178, 179, 181, 182–183
        class and, 180–181, 185
        decline of, 185–186
        as entertainment, 180, 184, 329
        ethnic, 181–182
        heterogenity of, 182
        as life insurance providers, 179, 184, 185, 186
        masculinity and, 185
        military branches, 180
        nativism and, 181
        nineteenth century, 177–180
        race and, 182–183
        religious expression and, 184–185
        as response to capitalism, 185
        service organizations and, 186
        social change and, 183
        temperence and, 185
        women's auxiliaries, 177, 180, 183
        See also names of individual organizations
    women's
        academic, 568
        Christian, 561–563, 645–565
        class conflict in, 564–565
        clubs, 565–566
        feminist, 569
        fraternal auxiliaries, 177, 180, 183
        labor unions and, 567
        local nature of, 561
        management of, 564
        national reform efforts, 562–563
        nineteenth-century, 561–568
        prostitution and, 563
        sororities, 568–569
        See also names of individual organizations
organized crime, 285, 286
organized labor, 447, 458, 508
Origins of Suburban Government, 463
Ornaments for the Daughters of Zion (Mather), 116
Orphan Asylum, 562
orphans, 132, 135
Orwell, George, 349
Oswald, Lee Harvey, 250
Other America, The (Harrington), 67
Otis, Elisha, 82
Otis, Johnny, 290
Ottawa Indians, 190, 191
Outcault, Richard, 244
Outdoor Recreation Resources Review Commission, 520
outdoor theater, 501
overseers, plantation, 320
Owen, Robert Dale, 119, 120, 381

P

Pacific Northwest, 193
Padlock, The, 354
Paine, John Knowles, 101
Paine, Thomas, 237
Palace of the Governors, 378
Palazzo style, in commercial architecture, 81, 82

Pale Fire (Nabokov), 232
Palm Beach, 517
Palmo's Opera House, 532
pamphlet plays, 484
pamphleteers, 236
Pankhurst, Emmeline, 144
paperback books, 347, 348, 374
papermaking, 341, 365
Papp, Joseph, 501–931
parades, 308, 310, 311
Paradise Now (1968), 499
Paramount films, 145
Paramount Theater, 145
Parents' Music Resource Center, 411
Parisian Model, A (1906), 494
Park Forest, IL, 64
Park Theater, 486
Parker, Charlie, 29, 104, 290
Parker, Dorothy, 230
parks, national, 518, 520, 524
    and American identity, 273–274
    biocentric management of, 277
    conservation and, 275
    ecology of, 276
    historic preservation and, 276–278
    origins of, 273
    patriotism and, 273–274
    philanthropic donation for, 274
    recreation and, 276
    varieties of, 278–280
parks, urban, 442
    cemeteries as, 545
    City Beautiful movement, 548
    crime in, 549
    financial support for, 549
    immigrants and, 548
    influence of automobiles, 549
    inner city, 549
    recreation in, 546–549
    regulation of, 546, 547
    segregation, 547, 548, 549
    as socialization tool, 548
    sports in, 547, 548
    urban planning and, 548, 549
    working-class, 547, 548
    See also amusement parks; theme parks
parlor songs, 159–160
Partch, Harry, 104
Parton, Dolly, 114
Parton, Sara (Fanny Fern), 341, 367
Passages from the French and Italian Notebooks (Hawthorne), 336
pasta, 172
Pastor, Tony, 489
Patch, Sam, 223
paternalism, plantation ethic and, 314
patriarchal authority, 3, 5, 116–117
Patriarch's Ball, 268
patriotism, 273–274, 362, 364
Patrons of Husbandry, 180, 507
Pattee Library (Pennsylvania State University), 385
Paul Whiteman Orchestra, 103
Pauling, James K., 487
Paxton, Tom, 164
Paxton Boys, The (1764), 483
Payne, John Howard, 354, 485
payola scandal, 395, 400

PBS. *See* Public Broadcasting System
peace, music for, 404
Peale, Charles Willson, 328, 530
Pearl, Minnie, 110, 115
Peckinpah, Sam, 146
pedestrianism, 439
Peer, Ralph, 106–107, 163
peer culture, adolescent, 9, 10–11
Peiss, Kathy, 283, 284, 288
Penn, Arthur, 153
Penn, William, 483, 544
Pennsylvania
    colonial, 79, 211–212
        Philadelphia, 53, 56, 79, 382–383, 545
Pennsylvania Academy of Fine Arts, 532
Pennsylvania Evening Post and Daily Advertiser, 237
Pennsylvania Hospital, 203
Pennsylvania State Capitol, 384
Pennsylvania State University, 385
penny press, 239–240, 243, 340–341, 367, 368
pensions, 134, 136, 300
Pentagon Papers, 250–251
Pentecost Sunday, 17
People's Park, 547, 549
periodicals, 365, 367–368. *See also* magazines; newspapers
periwigs. *See* wigs
Perkins, Carl, 398
Perkins, Fellows and Hamilton, 384
Perkins, Wheeler, and Will, 386
permanent-press fabrics, 75
Perry, Lincoln, 228
persistence rates. *See* geographic mobility
personal adornment. *See* clothing; fashion; hair styles
Peter, Paul, and Mary, 165, 404
Peterson, Theodore, 345
"petting," 425
Petty, Norman, 401
Philadelphia, PA
    City Hall, 382–383
    colonial, 53
    colonial architecture, 79
    Fairmount Park, 545
    streetcars in, 56
Philadelphia Arcade, 81
Philadelphia Athletics, 456
Philadelphia Centennial Exposition (1876), 101, 536
Philadelphia Orchestra, 101
Philadelphia Public Ledger, 240, 368
Philadelphia Saving Fund Society, 84
philanthropy
    of Andrew Carnegie, 535
    arts and, 535
    old age and, 299
    popular entertainment and, 328
    See also women's organizations
philharmonic societies, 100–101
Philip Morris Company, 541
Phillips, David Graham, 247
Phillips, Sam, 398, 401
Philosophical Society, 528
photography
    cameras
        motion picture, 139–140
        television, 472–473
    fashion, 77
    trick, 140

Physical Club, 528
physical education, 449
physicians. *See* doctors
Pickford, Mary, 142, 146
picnic groves, 31
pie, 167
Pike, Zebulon, 193, 506
pilgrimages, 514
Pilgrim's Progress (Bunyan), 295, 366
Pinchot, Gifford, 275
Pinckney, Eliza (Lucas), 316
Pingree, Hazen, 62
Pinkster Day, 17
Pintard, John, 328
pioneer towns, 553–554
pioneers. *See* frontier; settlement; western expansion
Pirate, The (1948), 151
Pittsburgh Crawfords, 453
Pizarro, 486
pizza, 172
Plains Indians, 166
planning, urban, 62
    neotraditionalist, 559
    parks and, 548, 549
    planned communities, 64, 462–463
    role of transportation, 510
plantation
    agriculture, 315–319
        cotton, 317–318, 322–323
        indigo, 317
        rice, 316, 318, 321, 323
        sugar, 314–315, 318, 323
        tobacco, 315, 317
    antebellum, 317–319
    in Chesapeake, 316–317
    class and, 313–314
    colonial, 315–317
    culture of, 319–322
    drivers, 320
    economy, 314–319
    formative period of, 315
    gender roles and, 314
    legacy of, 322–323
    nurses, 321
    overseers, 318, 319
    paternalistic ethic of, 314
    pooling of resources on, 314
    sharecropping system and, 322–323
    social heirarchy of, 320–321
    social mobility and, 313
    system, 315, 323
    See also slavery; South
"platform" performances, 334
play, reform of, 449, 548
Playboy, 428
Players' League, 447
Playground Association of America, 310, 449
playground movement, 449, 548
Plea for Amusements (Sawyer), 441
plug-in towns, 558
Plunkitt, George Washington, 61
Po-ca-hon-tas (1855), 487
Pocket Books, 347, 348, 374
Pocket Library, 348
Poe, Edgar Allen, 367
poetry, 338. *See also* literature

Poetry, 542
police, 57
Police Gazette, 349
poliomyelitis, 49
political protest. *See* protest
politics
    advertising, 475
    colonial, 236–237
    conservative views of popular culture, 406, 411
    cultural institutions and, 538
    Democrats, 322
    folk music and, 158–159, 163
    of food, 176
    humor, 223, 224–225, 226, 233
    in industrial cities, 61, 62
    influence on television, 475
    information transition and, 92
    journalism and, 247
    left-wing, 158–159
    newspapers and, 238, 242, 247
    old age and, 301–303
    popular entertainment and, 334
    Populists, newspapers of, 244–245
    press and, 236–237
    saloon and, 283
    Whigs, press of, 240–241
    See also Communism; government; legislation; Presidential campaigns; Presidential elections; United States Supreme Court
Polk, James K., 194, 313
Polk, Leonidas, 322
polyester, 75
polygamy, 419
Ponce de León, Juan, 293
Ponteach; or, The Savages America (1766), 484
Pontiac, 190
poor. *See* poverty
Poor Richard's Almanack (Franklin), 222
pop music, 406
    pop rock, 398–399, 402, 406
Pope, John Russell, 385
popular culture, 534
    art and, 528–529, 542
    concert music, 542
    cultural institutions and, 542
    international influence, 336
    of 1950s, 511–512
    theater, 542
    urban nineteenth-century, 332–334
    See also cultural institutions; popular entertainment; popular literature; popular music
popular entertainment
    academic study of, 323–324
    class and, 330–332
    colonial, 324–327
    gender and, 325
    middle-class, 334–337
    Nationalist period, 324, 327–328
    nineteenth-century, 328–337
    philanthropic funding of, 328
    politics and, 334
    prior to Civil War, 323–337
    religious revivals as, 327–328
    resorts, 331
    rural, 329
    seaside vacation, 331
    urban, 332–334
    See also amusement parks; holidays; nightlife; parades; radio; rituals; television; theme parks; sports
popular literature
    almanacs, 338, 339
    bookstores and, 375–376
    broadsides, 338–339
    chapbooks, 339
    colonial through 1830s, 338–340
    criticism of, 337
    definition of, 337, 338
    fiction, 338, 340–345, 371–372
        best-sellers, 347, 348
        blockbusters, 349, 350–351
        dime novels, 341–342, 346–347
        early criticism of, 340
        economics of, 342
        female audience, 344
        formulaic nature of, 342
        in libraries, 537
        magazines, 343–344, 345–347, 349
        motion pictures and, 351
        paperbacks, 347, 348
        pulp fiction, 346–348, 350
        romance and, 350
        as social control, 342, 343
        social criticism in, 347
        story papers, 341–342, 346
        as subversive, 342–343
        television and, 351
        twentieth-century, 348–351
    Indian captivity narrative, 339
    marketing of, 350–351
    nineteenth-century, 340–345, 367–368
    paperback and, 374
    twentieth-century, 345–351
    See also literature; magazines; newspapers; publishing
popular music, 100, 397–398, 406, 542
    availability of sheet music, 356
    commercialization of, 356–357
    European influence, 357
    Irish, 354
    minstrelsy, 355, 356
    opera, 354
    prior to 1950, 351–358
    ragtime, 357
    rock influence on, 398–399
    Sacred Harp music, 354
    sentimentalism in, 355–356
    swing, 358
    Tin Pan Alley, 356
    twentieth-century, 357–358
popular sovereignty, 197
population
    African American, 52, 65, 318, 319
    aging, 295, 296, 297
    colonial, 52
    Hispanic Americans, 65–66
    minority, 65–66
    nineteenth-century, 55, 56, 60
    of slaves, 318, 319
    of small towns, 558
    structures, 295
    suburban, 63–64, 459, 467

urban, 52, 55, 56, 60, 63–64, 66
See also demographics
Populists, newspapers of, 244–245
Porcupine's Gazette, 237
pornography, 422
Port Folio, 239
Porter, Edwin S., 141
Porterfield, Nolan, 108
Post, C. W., 171
Post, Emily, 267, 271
Post, George B., 82
Post Office Act (1792), 93, 238, 239, 368
Post Office Act (1794), 238
Postal Reform Act of 1845, 96
postal system, 91
    delivery of mail, 504, 512
    Federalist, 92–93
    print and, 365
    reform, 96
postcards, 518
Postimpressionist art, 539
postmodernism
    architecture, 87, 386
    theater, 501
poststructuralism, 501–502
potato, 171
poteaux sur solle, 212
Potomac Canal, 504
Pottawatomi Indians, 191
poverty
    aging and, 299–300
    children and, 43–44, 47, 50–51
    colonial, 53
    feminization of, 51
    folk music and, 164
    Great Depression and, 136
    housing and, 219–221
    Puritan, 70
    rural, 558, 559
    urban, 53, 65–67
    widowhood and, 134
Powell, John Wesley, 102, 274
power, political, 91–92, 96
Powers, Hiram, 266
Prairie Home Companion, A, 232
prebroadcast radio, 387–389
preferred provider organizations, 210
pregnancy, premarital, 414. *See also* birth control; fertility
premarital sex, 2, 414, 415, 418
prenetwork radio, 389–392
prenuptial agreements, 119
preservation
    of folklife, 162
    historic, 87, 220, 276–278
    of natural environments, 273–280
presidential campaigns, 475
presidential elections, 475
presidents. *See* names of individual presidents
Presley, Elvis, 28–29, 290, 398, 400, 477
press
    abolitionist sentiment in, 240
    African American, 245–246, 373–374
    colonial, 236–237, 339–340, 359–360
        patriot sympathies, 362, 364
    ethnic, 240, 245, 246, 369

Federalist, 92–93
    freedom of, 362
    political reform and, 242
    proliferation of, 93, 94
    religious, 245
    rural, 245
    Spanish-language, 246
    Watergate and, 250–251
    See also journalism; newspapers; printing
Price, Stephen, 487
Price, William, 529
primary, in Presidential elections, 475
primitivism, 286
Prince, 29, 410
Prince Hall Masons, 178, 180, 182
Prince of Parthia, The (1767), 484
Princess Daisy (Krantz), 350
print
    censorship of, 373
    culture of ideas and, 362
    increased demand for, 364–367
    marketing and distribution of, 369–371
    public discourse and, 362
    technology and, 341
    television's influence on, 376
    transportation and, 365
    twentieth-century, 376–377
    See also media; literature; printing; publishing
printers, 237, 238
printing
    broadside songs, 156
    colonial, 236–237, 339–340, 360
    press, 359
        as communication method, 89
        technological improvements in, 238, 365
privacy, colonial, 263
private libraries, 528
private physicians, 206
privatization, of health insurance, 208–210
pro-life groups, 430
Proclamation of 1763, 191, 504
production. *See* agriculture; cultivation; manufacturing
Production Code, 147
programs, television, 471, 476–479, 480–481
    for children, 478, 481
    experimental, 478
progress, 513, 536–537
Progress and Poverty (George), 465
progressive rock music, 402–403
Progressives, 62, 310–311
    Progressive Era, 9, 134–145
    reform of Fourth of July, 310–311
    reform of sexual behavior, 424
    sports and, 449
    urban reformers, 62
prohibition, 285–287, 493, 556. *See also* temperance
Promontory Point, UT, 197, 506
propaganda, radio, 393
property, marriage and, 119, 120. *See also* land
prostitution, 283, 422, 423, 424
protest
    adolescent, 405, 428
    in music, 158, 159, 163, 404, 405, 408, 409
    of Sacco and Vanzetti trial, 538
    of Stamp Act, 306

Providence Arcade, 81
Provincetown Players, 495, 496, 542
Prudhomme, Paul, 170
Pruitt-Igoe housing, 220
Pryor, Richard, 228
psalms, 351–353
psychedelic music, 404–405
Psycho (1960), 152
psychology, child, 46
public architecture. *See* architecture, public
Public Broadcasting Act (1967), 396
Public Broadcasting System, 250
public education, 554
Public Enemy, 408
public health, 54, 57, 133. *See also* medicine
public housing, 65, 219–220
public lands. *See* national forests; national parks
public libraries, 368–369, 535
    motives for, 537
    women in, 373
public relations, journalism and, 247
public roads, 510, 511, 940
    colonial, 504
    expressways, 511
    highways, 510, 511
    toll, 517
    turnpikes, 504, 510, 517
Public Service Building (Portland, OR), 386
Public Service Responsibility of Broadcast Licensees, 394
public spaces, European, 544
public television, 481
public transportation, 509–510, 513
Public Works Administration, 63, 385
Publick Occurrences Both Forreign and Domestick, 235
publishing, 93, 349–351
    African American, 370
    centralization of, 341
    colonial, 359–361
    commercialism in, 371–375
    copyright law, 370–371
    in electronic age, 376–377
    ethnic, 369
    increase in, 364–367
    industrialization and, 369–371
    libraries and, 369–370, 373
    literary agencies and, 371–372
    marketing and distribution of, 369–371
    mass, 371–375
    nineteenth-century, 364–373
    religious, 93
    restructuring of, 349–350
    self-education and, 366
    story papers, 370
    transportation and, 365
    twentieth-century, 376–377
    writers and, 373
    See also literature; media; newspapers; press
pueblos, 188
Pulitzer, Joseph, 242–244, 372
Pulitzer Prize, for drama, 496
Pullman, IL, 60, 214, 462
pulp fiction, 346–348, 350
punk rock music, 406
Purcell and Elmslie, 384
Pure Food and Drug Act (1906), 174
Purim play, 227

Puritans
    "Abbeys of Misrule," 326
    adolescence, 1–3, 4
    childhood, 39–40
    cities, 52–55
    clothing, 69–70
    and conspicuous consumption, 69–70
    courtship, 116
    death and, 131–132
    family structure, 116–117
    "hiving off," 552
    holidays, 305–306
    leisure, 326–327
    marriage, 116–117
    music, 98–99
    sexual behavior, 413–414
    sport and, 435–436
    sports, 433
    towns, 552
    views on theater, 483
    women, 116–117
    work ethic, 436
Purnan, Lucy, 117
"Purple Cow, The" (Burgess), 227
Putnam's Monthly Magazine, 367
PWA. *See* Public Works Administration
Pyle, Charles C. ("Cash and Carry"), 452

Q

Quadroon, The (Reid), 488
Quakers, 168, 529
quarantines, of AIDS patients, 431
quick-freezing, of food, 173
quickening, 423–424
Quintero, Jose, 499
quiz shows, 478

R

Rabe, David, 510
race
    etiquette and, 261
    fraternal organizations and, 182–183
    nineteenth-century conflict, 21
    riots, 66, 143
racial covenants, suburban, 469
racial supremacy, in *The Birth of a Nation,* 143
racism
    in baseball, 453–455
    in boxing, 449–450
    in nightclubs, 287–288
    in rock music, 408
    slavery. *See* slavery
    in sports, 445
    suburbanization and, 468–469
    See also African Americans; minstrelsy; Native Americans; slavery; individual racial groups
Radburn, NJ, 464
radial cities, 59–63
Radical Feminism, 428
radicalism, in newspapers, 248
radio
    academic study of, 387
    adolescent audience, 395, 396
    advertising, 110, 394
    African American, 395–396
    broadcast, 388–389

comedy, 230, 392
commercialization of, 390–391
corporate control of, 388
country and western music and, 110–111
ethnic influences, 392
FM, 105, 396
folk music and, 163
hillbilly music and, 107
influence of, 103, 357
as market research tool, 397
network radio, 389–390
payola scandal, 395, 400
pre-recorded, 393–394
prebroadcast radio, 387–389
prenetwork radio, 389–392
rock and roll music, 395, 396
role in communications, 97
specialization in, 396
talk radio, 397
technological advances in, 388, 395
television and, 395–396, 475
vaudeville, 392
wired networks, 389–390
women and, 390
World War II and, 392–394
See also communications; entertainment; journalism; media; music
radio advertising, 390–391
Radio Broadcast, 388
Radio Corporation of America, 388, 472
Radio Days (1987), 387
Radio Revue, 390
Radio's Second Chance (Siepmann), 394
Rado, James, 501
rag cities, 555
Ragni, Gerome, 501
ragtime music, 357
Rague, John F., 382
railroad flats, 215
railroads
    advertising and, 508
    capitalism and, 507–508
    competition among, 507
    creation of towns, 555
    economic effects, 507–508
    fare prices, 507
    frontier and, 197
    impact on landscape, 255–256
    increased consumption and, 507–508
    management of, 508
    nineteenth-century, 56, 507–508
    suburbs and, 462
    transcontinental, 197, 507–508
    urbanization and, 56
Rainey, Gertrude "Ma," 22, 25
Raisin in the Sun, A (1959), 498
Raleigh Tavern, 378
Rambo, 351
Randolph, Edward, 316
Randolph, Vance, 160
rank, social, 262–263, 265–269
rap music, 407, 408
Rappe, Virginia, 147
Ray, Johnnie, 399
Ray, Nicholas, 146, 151
rayon, 75

RCA. *See* Radio Corporation of America
reading, 237
    colonial, 361–362, 364, 528
    nineteenth-century attitudes toward, 368–369
    television and, 349
    See also literacy
Reading Becomes a Necessity of Life (Gilmore), 88
Reagan, Ronald, 150, 301, 430, 512
real estate
    developers, suburbanization and, 463
    markets, 220
    metes and bounds system, 257
    rectangular pattern, 257
    tourism and, 520
    See also land
Realization of a Negro's Ambition, The (1915), 142
Rebel Without a Cause (1955), 151
rebellion, adolescent, 1–2, 3, 6–7, 9, 10–12, 400
record companies, black-owned, 24, 27
recreation
    national parks and, 276
    urban, 61–62, 546–549
    urban parks, 279
    See also entertainment; leisure; motion pictures; nightlife; radio; sports; television; travel
Recruiting Officer, The (1706), 484
Red, Tampa, 22–23
Reds, 450
Reed, Lou, 405
Reed, Louis Raymond, 556
reform
    diet and, 171, 176
    family, 43–44
    of foodways, 175–176
    of leisure activities, 327–328, 443, 449
    moral, 58, 443
    of play, 449
    political, press and, 242
    Progressive, 62
    of saloons, 283–284
    of sexual behavior, 423–424
    social, 43–44, 45–46, 443
    urban, 58, 449
    See also temperance; women's organizations
Reformation, 295
refrigeration, 173
regional art, 540
regional cooking, 176. *See also* foodways
regional theater, 500–501
regulation
    of air traffic, 512
    of communications, 97
    of marriage, 118–119
    of parks, 546, 547
    of sexual behavior, 423–424
    of television, 473–474
Regulator movement, 192
rehabilitation, juvenile, 45
Reich, Steve, 105
Reid, Mayne, 488
Reid, Whitelaw, 242
Reik, Theodore, 228
Reinagle, Alexander, 99
Reiner, Carl, 233
Reinhardt, Max, 495
Reliance Building, 83

religion
  adolescence and, 2, 3
  in colonial cities, 54
  declining role in holiday celebration, 311, 312
  foodways of, 173
  fraternal organizations and, 184–185
  fundamentalism, 409
  literature of, 366
  marriage and, 123
  religious conversion, 3
  religious music, 160–161. *See also* gospel; psalms; spiritual
    music
  revivals, 306–307, 308, 327–328. *See also* Great Awakening; Second Great Awakening
  of slaves, 17–18
  social rank and, 263
  See also Catholics; Christianity; Episcopal church; evangelism; Puritans
renewal, urban, 65
Renwick, James, 381
reporters. *See* journalists
reproduction. *See* childbirth; birth control; fertility
reproductive rights, 427, 428–429
Repton, Humphrey, 543
Republican America, public architecture of, 379–381
republican motherhood, 42, 119–120
reservations. *See* Native Americans, resettlement
resorts, 31, 331, 515, 519, 521, 524. *See also* spas
respectability, 265
restaurants, chain, 174
retirement, 297–298, 300–301
Retrospect of the Eighteenth Century (Miller), 364
Return of the Jedi, 351
Reuss, Richard, 159
Reuther, Walter, 210
revivals
  evangelical, 306–307, 308, 327–328
  Great Awakening, 4, 160, 327, 353
  Second Great Awakening, 5, 17, 160, 307
Revolutionary America
  colonial printers in, 237
  music, 353
  public rituals in, 306
  theater in, 484
Revolutionary War, 191
  celebration of, 306
  colonial cities and, 55
  effect on marriage, 118
revue, theater, 494
Reynolds, Joshua, 527
Reynolds, Malvina, 159, 459
Rhapsody in Blue (1924), 539
"Rhapsody in Blue," 103
Rhea County Courthouse, 383
Rhode Island, 78–79
Rhode-Island Almanack (Franklin), 222
rhythm and blues music, 398, 399, 407
Ricardo, Lucy, 477
rice, 316, 318, 323
Rice, Mrs. Isaac L., 311
Rice, Thomas D., 332, 336, 355, 490
Richard J. Daley Center, 386
Richardson, Henry Hobson, 83, 383
Richardson romanesque architecture, 383
Richelieu, Cardinal, 527
Richmond, VA, 379

Rickey, Wesley Branch, 453, 454–455
Riddles, Leslie, 107
rights, of women, 119–120, 427, 428–429
Riley, James Whitcomb, 226
ring tournaments, 326
riots
  Astor Place, 336
  colonial, 363
  over slavery, 197
  race, 66, 143
  Stonewall Rebellion, 289, 429
Rise of the Goldbergs, The, 391
rituals
  colonial, 324–325
  executions, 305–306
  Ghost Dance, 199
  lynching, 309
  religious revivals, 306–307, 308
  Revolutionary, 306
  in 1950s and 1960s, 312
  See also etiquette
rivers, 275
  Little Bighorn River, 199
  Mississippi River, 189, 193
  Missouri River, 189
  St. Lawrence River, 189
Riverside, IL, 463
Riverside Improvement Company, 463
Riverside Park, 549
Roach, Hal, 229
Roach, Max, 104
roads
  colonial, 504
  expressways, 511
  highways, 510, 511
  public, 510, 511
  toll, 517
  turnpikes, 504, 510, 517
roaring twenties. *See* 1920s
Robb, John S., 224
Robert Taylor Homes, 65
Robertson, Alexander Campbell "Eck," 106
Robertson, Pat, 430
Robeson, Paul, 104
Robinson, Earl, 103
Robinson, Edward G., 148
Robinson, Jack Roosevelt ("Jackie"), 445, 453–455
Robinson, John, 117
Robinson, Mary Jane, 119
Rochester, 228
Rochester, NY, 505
Rock and Roll Hall of Fame, 410
rock music, 28–29, 105
  acid rock, 404–405
  adolescent audience, 401
  African American influence, 398, 399, 403
  art rock, 402–403, 407
  baby boom generation and, 399–400
  British invasion, 402
  conservatism in, 406, 411
  conspicuous consumption in, 401
  contemporary, 411
  country and western music and, 403, 406–407
  country rock, 398
  "cover records," 399
  as cultural integration, 400

cultural values of, 400
disco, 406
folk music, 404
folk rock, 402
gay liberation and, 405, 408
golden decade of, 401–406
hard rock, 402
heavy metal music, 405, 406, 410
hippie counterculture and, 404–405
Hispanic, 408
influence of blues, 24, 28–29
musical experimentation in, 402
mythic West in, 401
Native American, 405, 408
New Wave music, 406
obscenity hearings, 411
payola scandal, 395, 400
pop rock, 398–399, 402, 406
progressive rock, 402–403
protest in, 404, 405
psychedelic, 404–405
punk rock, 406
racism in, 399, 401, 408
radio and, 395, 396
rap music, 407, 408
rhythm and blues rock, 398, 399, 407
rock and roll, 290, 395, 396, 398–401
rock opera, 403
sexuality and, 405, 410
shock value of, 410
social protest and, 405, 408, 409
soul, 403
stereotypes in, 411
techno-rock, 403
technological advances, 400–401, 411
television and, 401
women in, 405, 409
working-class sentiment, 408
world music, 410
See also music
rockabilly music, 398
Rockefeller, John D., national parks and, 274
"Rock Around the Clock," 400
Rocky (1976), 153
Rocky Horror Picture Show, The (1975), 152
Rocky Mountains, 193
Rodgers, Jimmie, 107–109
Roe v. *Wade* (1973), 429
Rogers, Anna B., 122
Rogers, Isaiah, 79
Rogers, James Henry, 387
Rogers, Jimmie N., 115
Rogers, Robert, 484
Rogers, Will, 226, 230
roles, gender. *See* gender roles
Rolfe, John, 315
roller coasters, 31–32
Rolling Stones, 24, 405
Rollins, Sonny, 29
romance fiction, 351
romantic love, 119–120, 418
romanticism, of frontier, 195
Rombauer, Irma S., 175
Romero, George, 152
Rookery Building, 82–83
Roosevelt, Eleanor, 302

Roosevelt, Theodore, 123, 275, 278
Root, John Wellborn, 82–83
Rorabaugh, William, 327
Rorem, Ned, 105, 542
Rose, Benjamin, 299
Rose, Ernestine, 539, 540
Rose, Fred, 112
Rose, Pete, 459
Rosenberg, Ethel, 312
Rosenberg, Julius, 312
Rosenzweig, Roy, 310
Rosita (1923), 146
Ross, Harold W., 230
Rossini, Gioacchino, 354
Rotary, 186
Roth, Philip, 233
Rousseau, Jean-Jacques, 41, 73
Rowan & Martin's Laugh-In, 477
Rowson, Susanna, 485
Royal Academy of Art, 527
Rozelle, Pete, 452
Ruby, Jack, 250
Ruddiman, Thomas, 361
Rudeness and Civility (Kasson), 265
Rudiments of the Latin Tongue (Ruddiman), 361
Ruffin, Josephine St. Pierre, 566
rural life
    country and western music and, 106
    Midwestern town and, 553–554
    parks, 544
    poverty and, 558, 559
    suburbanization and, 463
    towns and, 558
    unemployment, 558, 559
    See also agriculture; frontier; plantation; towns
rural press, 245
rural renaissance, 558
rus in urbe, 544, 547
Rush, Benjamin, 92–93, 328
Russell, Curly, 104
Russell, Henry, 354
Russwurm, John Brown, 240, 370
Rustbelt, 63
Ruth, Babe, 451
Rutman, Anita, 3
Rutman, Darrett, 3

S

Saarinen, Eero, 86, 386
Saarinen, Eliel, 84, 386
Sacco and Vanzetti trial, protest of, 538
Sacred Harp, 354
Sacred Harp music, 354
"Safe and Sane Fourth," 310–311
Sahl, Mort, 231
Saint Andrews Day, 434
Saint Augustine, FL, 52
Saint Cecilia Society, 327, 530
Saint Lawrence River, exploration of, 189
Saint Louis, MO, 547, 548
Saint Louis Browns, 456
Saint Paul Chamber Orchestra, 542
Saint Paul's Cathedral, 380
Saint Tammany Society, 531
St. Louis Post, 242

Salk, Jonas, 49
saloons, 281–284. *See also* bars; speakeasies; taverns
Salt of the Earth (1952), 151
San Diego Zoological Park, 538
San Francisco, CA
    Summer of Love, 404, 428
    transportation in, 513
    urban development of, 465
San Francisco City Hall, 384
San Francisco Mime Troupe, 499
Sanders, Harland, 170
Sanger, Margaret, 124, 426, 427
Sanger, William, 420
sanitation, 54, 57, 133
Santa Fe, NM, 378
Santa María, 502
Saratoga Springs, NY, 515
Sarnoff, David, 472
satire, 226–227, 497
Saturday Evening Post, 345, 346, 372
Saturday Night Fever (1977), 406
Savoy, 287
Sawyer, Frederic W., 441
Sawyer Observatory, 31
Sayers, Tom, 442
Scarborough, William K., 318
Scarlet Letter, The (Hawthorne), 120, 344, 345, 367
Scarsdale, NY, 467
Scharff, Virginia, 269
Scherman, Harry, 374
Schiller, Dan, 367
Schlereth, Thomas, 259
Schlesinger, Arthur Meier, 266
Schlesinger and Mayer Store, 83
Schmidman, Jo Ann, 500
Schönberg, Arnold, 102
School of Good Manners (Moody), 263
schoolbooks, 366
schoolhouses, 382
schools
    architecture of, 385–386
    desegregation, 49
    medical, 202
    nineteenth-century, 42
    public, in towns, 554
    See also education
Schudson, Michael, 367
Schuman, William, 105
Schumann, Peter, 499
Schuyler, David, 545
Schuyler, Louisa Lee, 564
science. *See* technology
science museums, 531
scientific housekeeping, 175
Sclar, Elliot, 467
Scopes Trial (1925), 383
Scott, Emmett J., 142
Scott, Learned, 81
Scottish immigrants, 193
screwball comedies, 148, 230
Scribners, 375
Scripps, E. W., 241, 244
Scudder, Vida, 425
sea, transport by, 502, 503
Sea Lion Park, 32
seafood, 167, 169

Seagram Building, 85
Seaman, Elizabeth Cochrane, 246
Sgt. Pepper's Lonely Hearts Club Band, 402
Sears, Roebuck, and Company, 218, 508
seaside resorts, 519
seaside vacations, 331
Second Bank of the United States, 79, 381
Second Great Awakening, 5, 17, 160, 307. *See also* Great
    Awakening
secularization, of holidays, 312
Sedgwick, Catherine, 265
Sedition Act (1918), 248
See It Now, 478
Seeger, Charles, 103
Seeger, Peggy, 163
Seeger, Pete, 163, 165
segregation
    in baseball, 448–449, 453–455
    in education, 49
    in parks, 547, 548, 549
    in towns, 554
Selection of Irish Melodies, A (Moore), 354
self-education
    lyceum and, 533–534
    as middle-class popular entertainment, 334–335
    role of print, 366
self-help literature, 127
self-improvement
    etiquette and, 265–266
    leisure and, 334–335
    sports as, 857–858
self-regulation, of television industry, 473–474
Selznick, David O., 145, 149
Seminole Indians, 195
senescence, 293. *See also* aging; old age
Senescence (Hall), 299
senex, 294
Sennett, Mack, 229
sensationalism
    in journalism, 244
    in magazines, 372–373
sentimentality
    holidays and, 308
    in popular music, 159–160, 355–356
separate spheres, 425
separation, marital
    colonial, 117, 118
    definition of, 115
    nineteenth-century, 120–121
    Puritan, 117
sequels, motion picture, 153
Sequoya, 369
Serra, Junípero, 165
service organizations, 186
Sesame Street, 481
Seton, Ernest Thompson, 274
settlement, 193
    colonial Virginia, 551–552
    experience of, 195–197
    of Great Plains, 554–556
    immigrants, 197–198
    of Midwest, 552–554
    Native Americans and, 187–191, 194–195, 198–199, 503–504
    transportation and, 507
    western, 555–556
    See also colonization; frontier; western expansion

settlement houses, 62, 566–567
Seven Cities of Cibola, 188
Seven Songs for the Harpsichord (Hopkinson), 354
Seven Years' War, 190–191
seventeenth century. *See* colonial America
Sewall, John, 120
Sewall, Samuel, 70–71, 91
sewing machines, 75
sexual behavior
    adolescent, 10–11, 413–414
    adultery, 415, 418, 422
    in antebellum South, 420–423
    colonial, 413–416
    etiquette and, 269, 270
    familial control of, 413–414
    feminist influence, 428–429
    gender differences in South, 421
    gender roles, 427
    illegitimacy and, 415
    illicit, 415. *See also* prostitution; sodomy
    industrialization and, 423–424
    interracial, 415, 427
    liberalism and, 426–427
    marriage and, 413, 418–419, 426–427
    middle-class, 426–427
    Native American, 416
    nineteenth century, 417–423
    premarital, 414, 415, 418
    Puritan view of, 413
    reform of, 423–424
    rock music portrayals, 405, 409–410
    of slaves, 415
    sodomy, 415
    state regulation of, 423–424
    twentieth-century, 425–431
        New Right criticism of, 430
    Victorian, 417–420
        alternatives to, 419
    of women, 427, 428–429
    working-class, 419–420, 425
    See also gender roles; homosexuality
sexual liberalism, 426–427
Sexual Politics of Meat, The (Adams), 176
Shakers, 120, 216, 419
Shakespeare, William, 484
Shaky Palaces (Edel, Sclar, and Luria), 467
Sham 69, 408
Shapiro, Henry D., 467
Shapiro, Laura, 175
sharecroppers, 170, 322
Sharman, Jim, 152
Shaw, Henry Wheeler, 225
Shawnee Indians, 191, 194
Shays' Rebellion, 192
She Would Be a Soldier; or, The Plains of Chippewa (1819), 487
sheet music, 356
Shelley v. *Kraemer* (1948), 469
Shenandoah National Park, 274
Sheppard-Towner Act (1921), 46
Sherwood, Mary Elizabeth, 268
Shinn, Everett, 537
Shippen, William, 378
shipping, colonial scarcity, 316
ships, 502, 505
shirtwaists, 74
shock value, of rock music, 410

Shootist, The (1976), 146
shopping malls, 36–37, 81, 86
Show Boat (1927), 495
showboats, 486
Shriners, 180
Shubert brothers, 493
Shulman, Holly Cowan, 393
Sidney, James C., 546
Siegel, Don, 152
Siegmeister, Elie, 103, 105
Siepmann, Charles, 394
"Significance of the Frontier in American History, The"
    (Turner), 186–187
silent pictures, 141–145
Silent Spring (Carson), 175
silk, 71–72, 75
Silverman, Kenneth, 306
Silvers, Phil, 477
Simitière, Pierre Eugène Du, 531
Simon, Neil, 233
Simon, Paul, 409
Simple, Jessie B., 230
sincerity, in etiquette, 267
Sinclair, Upton, 174, 302
Singin' in the Rain (1952), 151
singing, standardized, 99
single-parent families, 126, 136–137
Sioux Indians, 188, 199
Sirk, Douglas, 151
Sister Sledge, 408
sitcoms, 477
Sitting Bull, 199
situation comedy, 477
60 Minutes, 249
skyscrapers, 59, 84. *See also* architecture, commercial
Slater, Samuel, 79
Slaughter, Marion T., 106
Slave Ship (1967), 498
slavery
    territories and, 197
    theatrical depiction of, 488
    transportation of slaves, 503
    women and, 563
    See also abolition; plantation; slaves
slaves
    adolescence, 4, 7–8
    childhood, 41
    childrearing, 41
    in communications revolution, 94, 95
    courtship, 421
    divorce, 117–118
    drum language, 15, 16
    efficiency of, 321
    etiquette and, 264
    family life, 415, 422, 423
    family structure, 415
    foodways of, 168–169
    funeral customs, 18–19
    housing, 212
    as labor force, 313–314, 320–321
    leisure of, 326
    marriage, 117–118, 421–422
    mortality, 132
    music, 13–20
    on plantation, 313–314, 320–321
    population, 318, 319

slaves (*continued*)
    religious worship of, 17–18
    sexual behavior, 415
    sexual exploitation of, 7, 415, 416, 421, 422
    skilled labor, 319–320
    sport and, 434, 435
    See also abolition; plantation; slavery
Slaves in Algiers; or, A Struggle for Freedom (1794), 485
Sloan, John, 537
small towns. *See* towns
smallpox, 54, 131
Smibert, John, 78, 529, 530
Smith, Al, 61
Smith, Bessie, 25
Smith, Charles Henry, 225
Smith, Joseph, 419
Smith, Mamie, 24, 163
Smith, Page, 554
Smith, Robert, 378
Smith, Samuel Harrison, 241
Smith, Seba, 223
Smith, Solomon, 486
Smith, W. H., 335
Smith, William, 353, 362
Smith, Willie "the Lion," 287
Smith College, 382
Smithson, James, 531
Smithsonian Institution, 381, 531, 536
Smollet, Tobias, 361
Smothers Brothers, The, 477
Snook, John B., 82
social change, 106, 183
social control, popular fiction as, 342, 343
social criticism
    in popular fiction, 347
    of sports, 432–433, 435
    of suburbs, 466–467
    theater as, 496, 499
social Darwinism, 154–155
social history, country and western music as, 114–115
social issues, television treatment of, 479
social mobility
    etiquette and, 262–263, 265–269
    plantation and, 313
    as progress, 513
social protest. *See* protest
social rank, etiquette and, 263
social reform, 43–44
    child welfare and, 43–44, 45–46
    of sports, 443
    See also reform; women's organizations
social security
    aging and, 300–301
    old age and, 293
    Social Security Act (1935), 136, 209, 302
        Title II, 300–301
social structure, of cities, 52–53, 56
Socialism, 145, 537–538
societies, fraternal. *See* fraternal organizations
societies, women's. *See* women's organizations
Society for the Propagation of the Gospel in Foreign Parts,
    361
Society for the Protection of Cruelty to Children, 43
Society for the Relief of Poor Widows with Small Children,
    561–562
Society of American Artists, 537

Society of Artists of the United States, 532
sodomy, 415
softball, women's, 458
Sokolov, Raymond, 177
Soldier's Friends Associations, 563
Soldier's Play, A (1981), 498
Soltow, Lee, 366
Somerville, MA, 9
songs. *See* music
songsters, 156
Sonic Youth, 105
Sonnambula, La, 534
Sons of Liberty, 353
Sontag, Susan, 542
sororities, 568–569
Sorosis, 565
soul music, 28, 403
Sound of Music, The (1965), 152
Sousa, John Philip, 101, 356
South
    agriculture. *See* plantation
    colonial
        childhood, 39
        housing, 212–213
        lack of towns, 551–552
        marriage in, 117–118
        popular entertainment in, 326
        sports in, 433–435
    foodways of, 168–170
    inhibitions to urban development, 551–552
    leisure ethic in, 435
    plantation. *See* plantation
    rural life, 313–314
    slavery. *See* slavery
South Carolina
    antebellum class system, 314
    Charleston, 52, 53, 54
    colonial plantations, 315–319
    plantations, 318
South Carolina Gazette, 236
South Carolina Sea Islands, musical influence, 287
South Dakota, Wounded Knee, 199
Southern Honor (Wyatt-Brown), 264
Southern Living, 170
Southern Pacific Railroad, 509
Southwest, colonial housing, 212–213
Southworth, Mrs. E.D.E.N., 341, 367
Spaeth, Sigmund, 353
Spain
    building traditions of, 212–213
    as colonizers, 188, 191
    influence on foodways, 165, 166
    slave trade and, 315
Spam, 175
Spanish-language press, 246
spas, 515. *See also* resorts
SPCC. *See* Society for the Protection of Cruelty to Children
speakeasies, 285
specialization
    in cultural organizations, 538–539
    of radio, 396
Spielberg, Steven, 153
Spillane, Mickey, 149, 151
Spirit of the Times, The, 224
spiritual music, 17–18, 21
Spock, Benjamin, 48, 338

"Sponsoritis," 390–391
Spoon River Anthology (Masters), 556
sports
    advertising and, 457, 459
    African Americans in, 445, 446, 457
    animal fighting, 334
    in antebellum era, 437–441
    British traditions, 432–433
    as business, 443–444, 458, 459
    celebrities in, 451, 452
    Christianizing influences, 441, 442
    Civil War influence, 443
    collegiate, 444, 452, 457
    colonial, 433–437
    as common language, 446
    consumption and, 443, 444, 450–453
    in 1890's, 445, 446, 447–449
    elite, 440, 444
    in Gilded Age, 442–445
    "idols of consumption," 452
    immigrant traditions, 440, 445–856
    influence on modern life, 446
    masculinity and, 432, 441
    media coverage, 451–452, 456
    metaphors, 446
    middle-class participation, 449, 457
    modern definition of, 431
    moral opposition to, 432–433, 435
    newspaper coverage, 439, 443, 449
    in 1950s, 455–456
    nineteenth-century, 280, 437–445, 446, 447–449
    in parks, 547, 548
    Progressives and, 449
    Puritan, 435–436
    racism in, 445
    as self-improvement, 857–858
    slaves, 435
    social reform and, 443
    in South, 433–435
    suburbanization and, 455–456
    television and, 456, 474–475
    Turner societies, 440
    twentieth-century, 446, 449–459
    urban reform and, 449
    women in, 445, 453, 458
    World War I and, 449
    See also baseball; basketball; boxing; entertainment; football; leisure; softball; tennis
sportswear, 75
Sprague, Frank, 509
Springsteen, Bruce, 408, 409
Stack, Robert, 480
Stadt Huys, 378
stage manner, of musicians, 108–109
Stagg, Amos Alonzo, 448
Stallone, Sylvester, 153
Stamp Act (1765), 92, 306, 364
standardization
    of foodways, 173–175
    of medical care, 202
    railroad's effects, 255–256
    of television programs, 478–479
    of time zones, 508
standards, moral
    adolescence and, 5–6
    in colonial cities, 54

    cultural, 331–332
    sexuality and, 413–431
Stanford, Leland, 139
Stanhope press, 365
Stanley, Henry Morton, 246
Stanton, Elizabeth Cady, 123, 144
"Star Spangled Banner, The," 102
Star Wars (1977), 153
Starr, Ellen Gates, 566
stars
    in country and western music, 106–109, 111–114
    in motion pictures, 141
    in theater, 486
    See also celebrities
State, War and Navy Building, 382
State Capitol (Virginia), 377, 378–379
state capitols, architecture of, 379, 382–384. *See also* United States Capitol
State Charities Aid Association, 564
states. *See* individual state names
steam power, 507
Steamboat Willie (1928), 148
steamboats, 507, 517
Stearns, Harold E., 556
steel, in commercial architecture, 82
Steele, Ian, 88, 90, 362
Steeltown (1985), 499
Steeple-chase Park, 32
Steffens, Lincoln, 247
Stein, Clarence, 463–464
Steinem, Gloria, 114
Steppenwolf Theatre Company, 542
stereotypes, 401, 411. *See also* minstrelsy; racism
Stevens, Edward, 366
Stevens, John Cox, 439, 440
Stevenson, Adlai E., Jr., 231
Stewart, Ellen, 500
stickball, 432
Stieglitz, Alfred, 539
Stiverson, Cynthia Z., 340
Stiverson, Gregory A., 340
Stockton and Darlington railroad, 507
Stokes, Carl B., 67
Stolen Wife, The (Arthur), 119
Stone, John Augustus, 330, 487
Stone, Lucy, 119
Stone, Melville, 244
Stonewall Rebellion, 289, 429
Stories of Benevolent Assimilation (Ade), 227
story papers, 341–342, 346, 371
Storyville, 280
Stout, Harry S., 89, 92
Stovey, George, 448–449
Stowe, Harriet Beecher, 344, 488
Stravinsky, Igor, 103
Streetcar Named Desire, A, 497
Streetcar Suburbs (Warner), 466–467
streetcars, 56, 59
    horse-drawn, 509
    streetcar suburbs, 204, 216, 461–462
Strickland, William, 79, 381
strip malls, 86
Strong, George Templeton, 532, 534
Stuart, John, 316
stube, 212
Students for a Democratic Society, 569

Sturges, John, 146
subculture, adolescent, 11
subscription concerts, 530
subscription libraries, 361, 368
suburban government, 463
"Suburban Mosaic, The" (O'Connor), 461
Suburban Sketches (Howells), 466
suburbanization
    class and, 460
    federal assistance for, 467–468
    landscapes and, 255, 463
    public utilities and, 462
    racism in, 468–469
    real estate developers and, 463
    sports attendance and, 455–456
    transportation and, 461–462
    See also suburbs
Suburbia (Wood), 463
suburbs
    academic study of, 465–467
    African Americans in, 468–469
    annexation and, 463–464
    automobile and, 256–257, 462, 467
    business districts, 86, 87
    cities and, 63–64
    commercial architecture of, 87
    commuter, 219, 558
    development of, 85, 86
    early, 459–460
    family life in, 48–49
    federal support for, 464
    future of, 468
    government and, 463–464
    industrial, 60
    Levittowns, 219
    nineteenth-century, 216, 460–464
    planned, 462–463
    popular images of, 459
    population, 63–64, 459, 467
    post–World War II, 468–469
    railroad and, 462
    social criticism of, 466–467
    streetcar, 204, 216, 461–462
    technoburbs, 468
    transportation and, 467
    twentieth-century housing, 218–219
    women in, 468
    See also cities; suburbanization
subversion, popular fiction as, 342–343
subways, 59, 509
suffrage, 144
sugar, 314–315, 318, 323
Suggs, Simon, 222, 224
Sullivan, Ed, 477
Sullivan, Frank, 230
Sullivan, John L., 282, 444, 445
Sullivan, Louis, 83
Summer, Donna, 410
Summer Camps, 518
Summer of Love, 404, 428
sumptuary laws, 263
Sun Building, 81
Sun City, AZ, 298
Sunbelt, 63, 298
Sunday, Billy, 308
Super Bowl, 311, 475

supermarket, 173
Supreme Court. *See* United States Supreme Court
surgery, 203
surveying methods, metes and bounds system, 257
Susann, Jacqueline, 351
Sut Lovingood Yarns (Harris), 224
"Swanee River" (Foster), 299
Swift, Gustavus Franklin, 173
Swift, Zephaniah, 122
swing music, 358
Syndicate, 492,493
synthesized music, 104

T

tabloids, 349
Taking the Wheel (Scharff), 269
Talbot, Marion, 568
talk radio, 397
"talkies," 147
Talking Heads, 409
tall tales, 223
Talma, Louise, 105
Tammany Hall, 61, 247, 334
Tandy Park, 547
Tappan, Arthur, 366
Tappan, Henry, 532
Tarantule, La (Elssler), 333
Tarbell, Ida, 247
Tarkington, Booth, 554, 556
Tarr, Joel A., 467
task system, of labor, 320–321
Taubman Company, 86
taverns, 378, 528. *See also* bars; saloons
taxes, British, 191–192
Taylor, Cecil, 29
Taylor, Joe Gray, 170
Taylor, Marshall W., 445
teachers, women as, 563
Teaford, Jon C., 464
Teatro Campesino, El, 498–499
techno-rock music, 403
technoburbs, 468
technological advances
    in journalism, 248
    in printing, 365
    in radio, 388, 395
    in rock music, 400–401
    in television, 472–473
    in theater, 491
    in transportation, 507, 517, 520
    See also technology
technology
    culture and, 89–90
    of food preparation, 173–174
    impact on landscapes, 255–257
    influence on art, 540, 542
    influence on country and western music, 106
    journalism and, 238, 242
    print, 341
    rock music and, 411
    theater and, 482
    See also technological advances
Tecumseh, 194
"Teen Angel," 512
telegraph, 89, 96
telephones, 96, 269, 518

television
  advertising and, 471, 473, 476–477
  cable channels, 482
  censorship of, 473–474
  children and, 474, 478
  children's programs, 478, 481
  color, 473
  comedy, 230–231
  commercials, 475, 476
  as communication method, 89
  competition for motion picture audience, 151–152
  consumption and, 476–477
  demographics, 474, 481
  depiction of class, 481
  depiction of ethnicity, 481
  deregulation of, 474, 481–482
  drama, 481–482
  experimental programming, 478
  football coverage, 457, 480
  government regulation of, 471
  history of, 97
  image orthicon camera tube, 472
  industry, 472–474
  influence on magazines, 475
  influence on motion pictures, 475
  influence on newspapers, 475
  influence on radio, 475
  journalism, 249–252, 479–480
  leisure as, 474–476
  as mediated world, 471
  music and, 105
  networks, 471–472, 474
  news, 479–480
  1950s, 477–478
  political influence, 475
  popular fiction and, 351
  portrayals of women, 480
  print media and, 376
  program content of, 471
  programming, 476–479, 480–481
  public, 481
  quiz shows and, 478
  radio and, 395–396
  reading and, 349
  regulation of, 473–474
  rock music and, 401
  sitcoms, 477
  social effects, 474
  sports and, 456, 474–475
  standardization of programs, 478–479
  technological advances in, 472–473
  treatment of social issues, 479
  variety show, 477
  westerns, 480
  See also entertainment; leisure; media
temperance, 62, 283–284, 335
  fraternal organizations and, 185
  popular entertainment and, 335
  Women's Christian Temperance Union, 564, 565
  See also prohibition
tenements, 214–215, 219
Tennent, Gilbert, 39, 40
Tennessee, 35, 519
  Nashville, 106, 111
  See also Grand Ole Opry
Tennessee Valley Authority, 85, 258

tennis, 458, 548
Tenskwatawa, 194
Terhune, Virginia, 367
Terrell, Mary Church, 566
territories. See frontier; settlement; western expansion
Texaco Star Theater, The, 477
Texas, 35, 193–194
Texas Air, 512
text, of folk music, 161
textile mills, 79, 81
textiles. See fabrics
Thalberg, Irving, 145
Thanet, Octave, 225
Thanksgiving Day, 311, 447
Tharpe, Sister Rosetta, 23
theater
  African American, 488, 490, 494–495, 496, 498
  "American" distinctiveness, 482
  American Yankee in, 487
  Asian American, 499
  audience appeal, 482
  block booking and, 492
  booking agents and, 492
  British, 483, 484
  burlesque, 489
  changing audience, 329, 330
  class and, 330, 534
  colonial, 327, 328, 483–485, 529–530
  comedy, 489–491, 497
  commercialization of, 489–492
  decentralization of, 500–501
  depiction of slavery, 488
  education for, 491
  experimental, 499–500
  feminist, 498
  growth of infrastructure, 485
  in Harlem, 494–495
  Hispanic, 498–499
  in jazz age, 494–495
  little theater, 495, 542
  melodrama, 330, 486, 488
  method acting, 497
  minstrelsy, 332–333, 490
  missionary, 483
  monopoly in, 492
  motion pictures and, 145, 493
  musical, 151, 233, 488–489, 490, 495, 497, 501
  National Endowment for the Arts, 500
  Native American depictions, 487
  nickelodeons, 140
  nineteenth-century, 328–330, 485–492, 534
  Off-Broadway, 499, 542
  Off-Off-Broadway, 499–500, 542
  operetta, 495
  outdoor, 501
  patriotic, 485
  political controversy over, 482–483
  popular, 542
  post-war, 498
  postmodern, 501
  Puritan views on, 483
  realistic, 491–492, 495–496
  regional, 497, 500–501
  Revolutionary ban against, 484
  revue, 494
  satire, 497

theater (*continued*)
  Shakespearian, 484
  social issues in, 496, 499
  star system in, 487
  technological innovations in, 482, 491
  traveling, 486, 490–491
  travesty, 333
  twentieth-century, 493–502
  urban, 328–330
  vaudeville, 141, 489–490
  wartime, 482
  women in, 498, 500
  working-class, 333
  See also cultural institutions; leisure; motion pictures
Theatre 47, 500
Theatre Arts Magazine, 495
Theatrical Syndicate, 492
theme parks, 33–37
  definition of, 30–31
  Disney, 33–36
  Dollyland, 114
  malls as, 36–37
  Opryland U.S.A., 111
  See also amusement parks
Thimble Brigades, 563
38th St. Working Girls' Society, 564
This Is the Army (1942), 497
"This Land Is Your Land," 159
Thomas, Isaiah, 364
Thomas, J. Parnell, 150
Thomas, Theodore, 101
Thomas Jefferson: America's First Gourmet, 169
Thompson, Lydia, 489
Thompson, Roger, 2, 326
Thompson, Virgil, 103
Thompson, Wiley, 307
Thompson, William Tappan, 224
Thoreau, Henry David, on sport, 441
Thornton, William, 380
Thorpe, Thomas Bangs, 234
Thurber, James, 230
Ticknor, William Davis, 344
Tillman, Benjamin, 427
time zones, 508
Timothy, Elizabeth, 236
Tin Pan Alley music, 356
Tindley, Charles Albert, 22
titles, colonial, 262–263
tobacco, cultivation of, 315, 317
Today, 478
Todd, John, 418
Tolkien, J. R. R., 349
toll roads, 517
"Tom Dooley," 164
tomatoes, 172
Tommy, 403
Tonight Show, 351
Toombs, Robert, 322
topical songs, 158–159
Toronto school, of communications theory, 90–91
Toscanini, Arturo, 103
tourism
  advertising and, 524
  beginning of, 518
  definition of, 514
  economic effects, 522

economy and, 522
environmental effects, 524
in Florida, 517
group tours, 521
industry, 519, 521
international, 524
mass, 515
middle-class, 519–520
to national parks, 276
real estate practices and, 520
twentieth-century, 519–525
urban, 521, 522
vacation packages, 522
  See also amusement parks; theme parks; travel
Tourist Trade, 519
Town Hall (Boston), 378
town meetings, 552
towns
  academic study of, 556–557
  agricultural dependence, 558
  bedroom communities, 559
  business in, 556
  cattle towns, 555
  class distinction, 553
  colonial, 551–552
  definition of, 551
  economy of, 556, 558, 559
  entrepreneurial, 559
  ethnic segregation in, 554
  federal assistance for, 557
  fictional portrayals, 556
  frontier, 553–554, 555–556
  future of, 558, 559
  during Great Depression, 557
  in Industrial Era, 556–557
  industrialization and, 556, 557
  influence of railroad, 552
  intellectual criticism of, 556
  Midwest, 553–554
  mining camps, 555
  nineteenth-century, 552–556
  population, 558
  revitalization of, 558
  unemployment in, 558, 559
  urban migration from, 556, 557, 558
  See also cities; rural life; suburbs
Townsend, Francis E., 302
township, government of, 465
Toynbee Hall, 566
Trading with the Enemy Act (1917), 245
traditional families, 477
Traditional Tunes of the Child Ballads, The (Bronson), 155
traffic
  air, 512
  congestion of, 509, 510
Trail of Tears, 195
training, as holiday, 325
trains. *See* railroads
Transatlantic Manners (Mulvey), 266
transcontinental railroad, 507–508
transportation
  air, 512, 520
  architecture and, 85
  colonial, 503–504
  commercial, 505, 511
  economy and, 59

effect on nineteenth-century cities, 56
effects on travel, 517
exploration and, 504
impact on urban landscape, 255–257
increased comsumption and, 507–508
influence on amusement parks, 32–33
mass transit, 56, 59, 518
nineteenth century, 505–509
progress of, 513
public, 509–510, 513
scheduling of, 505
by sea, 502, 503
steam-powered, 507
suburbanization and, 461–462, 467
technological advances in, 507, 517, 520
traveling theater and, 487
twentieth-century, 509–513
urban, 56, 59, 509–510
in walking city, 509
water, 504–505, 507. *See also* canals; rivers; ships
western expansion and, 505–506, 507–508
See also automobiles; aviation; railroads; roads; streetcars; travel; trolley cars
travel
by African Americans, 522
agencies, 518
by air, 512
as common cultural experience, 524–525
communications and, 516
consumption and, 525
definition of, 514
effects of energy crisis, 521, 522
foreign, 520, 524
high participation period, 519–520
high society period, 517–518
holiday, 514
industry, 519, 521
middle-class, 519–520
nineteenth-century, 515–519
in Renaissance Europe, 514
summer, 518
transportation and, 517
twentieth-century, 519–525
of wealthy, 515, 517–518
See also entertainment; holidays; leisure; resorts; tourism; transportation
traveler's checks, 518
traveling theater, 486, 490–491
travesty theater, 333
Treatise on Domestic Economy, for the Use of Young Ladies at Home, and at School, A (Beecher), 171
Treaty of Fort Laramie (1868), 199
Treaty of Fort Stanwix (1784), 191
Treaty of Paris (1783), 191
trees, 255. *See also* forests
tribal lands, 194–195, 506. *See also* frontier
Tribune Building, 82
trickster humor, 225
Trip to America, A (1824), 487
Tristano, Lenny, 104
trolley cars, 31, 255, 509
Trollope, Frances, 74, 265
Trooper of Troop K, The (1916), 142
Tropic of Cancer (Miller), 348
Trumbull, Benjamin, 122
Trumbull Gallery, 532

trustees, hospital, 206
Tubb, Ernest, 109
Tubular Bells, 403
Tucker, Ken, 114
Tufts, John, 353
Tugwell, Rexford, 464
Tulley, John, 339
Turnbull, William, 386
Turner, Frederick Jackson, 186–187, 199, 274
Turner, Nat, 19
Turner, Ted, 250
Turner, Tina, 403
Turner societies, 440
turnpike roads, 504, 510, 517
TV Guide, 475
TVA. *See* Tennessee Valley Authority
Twain, Mark, 221, 222–223, 226, 534
twentieth century
adolescence, 7–12
arts, 537–543
childhood in, 45–51
cities, 59–67
clothing, 75–77
commercial architecture, 83–87
communications, 96–98
courtship, 125
cultural institutions, 537–543
death in, 134–138
divorce, 124–125, 126, 127–128
family size in, 46, 48, 50
family structure, 429–430
foodways, 173–176
housing, 217–222
humor, 226–233
journalism, 244–252
marriage, 124–129
medicine, 49
nightlife, 285–291
popular fiction, 348–351
popular literature, 345–351
popular music, 357–358
print and, 376–377
sexual behavior in, 425–431
social change, 106
sports in, 446, 449–459
theater in, 493–502
transportation, 509–513
travel, 519–525
Twenty-First Amendment, 285
26 by Corwin, 392
Tyler, Royall, 485, 487
Tympani Five, 28
typewriters, 269

U
U2, 408
Ueda, Reed, 9
Uhlenberg, Peter, 135
Ulrich, Laurel Thatcher, 325
Uncle Tom's Cabin, theatrical production of, 488
Uncle Tom's Cabin (Stowe), 344
unemployment
in Great Depression, 63
rural, 558, 559
urban, 67
Unfair Sex, The (Farewell), 270

Union Pacific, 197
unions, labor, 447, 458, 508
United Artists, 142
United Artists Against Apartheid, 408
United Auto Workers, 209
United Mine Workers of America, 209
United Press, 247
United Press International, 241
United States Capitol, 380–381
United States Gazette, 92
United States Supreme Court
    on abortion, 429
    architectural features, 385
    on desegregation, 49
    on freedom of press, 248, 250
    on homosexuality, 430
    on motion pictures, 144, 145, 152
    on publishing industry, 350
    on racial covenants, 469–877
    on tribal lands, 195
United States Travel and Tourism Administration, 514
United States Travel Data Center, 514, 522
United States v. *Paramount* (1948), 145, 152
Universal Instructor in All Arts and Sciences, The, 235
universities. *See* colleges
University of Pittsburgh, 384
University of Virginia at Charlottesville, 379
Untouchables, The, 480
upper class. *See* elite
urban beautification, 259
urban development, 64–65, 464–465
urban expansion, 64–65
Urban Innovations Group, 386
urban migration, 399
    African American, 456
    from towns, 556, 557, 558
urban parks
    cemeteries as, 545
    City Beautiful movement, 548
    crime in, 549
    financial support for, 549
    influence of automobiles, 549
    inner city, 549
    recreation in, 546–549
    regulation of, 546
    segregation in, 548
    sports in, 547, 548
    urban planning and
    working-class, 547, 548
urban planning, 62
    neotraditionalist, 559
    parks and, 548, 549
    planned communities, 64
    planned suburbs, 462–463
    role of transportation, 510
urban recreation areas, 278–279
urban reform. *See* reform
urban renewal, 65
urbanization
    and childhood, 43–45
    etiquette and, 269
    holidays and, 308–309
    immigrants and, 58
    industrialization and, 56–57, 60–61
    leisure and, 437–438
    manufacturing and, 56–57

    nightlife and, 280–281
    See also cities
USA Today: The Television Show, 475
USA Today, 248, 475
Utah, 197, 218, 506
utilities, public, 462
utilizers, 164
utopian communities, 120

V

VA. *See* Veterans Administration
vacations
    family, 520, 522
    for health, 514
    middle-class, 519–520
    nineteenth-century, 515–519
    package deals, 522
    See also entertainment; holidays; leisure;
        travel
vaccination, polio, 49
Vail, Theodore M., 96
Valdez, Luis, 498–499
Valens, Ritchie, 290
Valley of the Dolls (Susann), 351
Van Doren, Carlton S., 515
Vance, Nina, 500
Vanity Fair, 224
variety show, 477
vaudeville, 489–490
    Grand Ole Opry, 110
    motion pictures and, 141
    radio performances, 392
    See also comedy; humor; minstrelsy
Vaux, Calvert, 57, 462–463, 545
Vauxhall Gardens, 332, 335, 354
Veblen, Thorstein, 556
Vee, Bobby, 402
Vega, Suzanne, 409
vegetarianism, 176
Velline, Robert Thomas. *See* Vee, Bobby
venereal disease, 424
Venturi and Rauch, 386
Verdi, Guiseppe, 354
Verdict of the People, The, 381
Veterans Administration, 467–468
vice, 62, 280
Victorians
    leisure, 438–440
    music of, 159–160
    sexual behavior, 266, 417–420
        challenges to, 419, 424–425
videocassettes, 153–154, 481
Vietnam Veterans Memorial, 386
Vietnam War, 153
    deaths, 134
    folk music protest of, 404
    holidays during, 311
    media and, 250–251
    television coverage of, 479
Village People, 408
villages, 551–552. *See also* towns
violence, 43–44, 309–311. *See also* lynching; riots
Virginia
    backcountry, 193
    colonial, 168, 212, 551–552

Jamestown, 190, 315, 551
    plantations, 317
    Richmond, 379
    Williamsburg, 377, 378–379
Virginia Beach, 519
Virginia House of Burgesses, 263
Virginia Minstrels, 355, 490
VOA. *See* Voice of America
Vogue, 77
Voice of America, 393
Voice of America, The (Shulman), 393
Voice of the Negro, 374
von Stroheim, Erich, 146
Vonnegut, Kurt, Jr., 233
Voyage of Life, 298–299
Vreeland, Diana, 541

W
Wagner, Richard, 101
Wagner, Robert, 61
Wagner Act (1935), 209, 210
wagon trains, 195, 196, 507
Wagoner, Porter, 114
Wakeman, Frederic, 392, 395
Walden, or Life in the Woods (Thoreau), 344
Waldenbooks, 350
Walker, George, 490
Walker, T-Bone, 28
walking cities, 55–58, 460, 509
Waller, Thomas "Fats," 494
Walsh, Christy, 451
Walsh, Lorena, 3
Walt Disney World Resort, 33, 35–36
Walter, Thomas U., 380
war. *See* Civil War; Revolutionary War; Vietnam War; warfare, frontier; World War I; World War II
War News from Mexico (Woodville), 95
War of 1812, 380
War of Jenkins's Ear, 316
War of the Worlds, The (1938), 497
Ward, Artemus, 224–225
warfare, frontier, 189–191, 194–195
Warner, Jack, 150
Warner, Sam Bass, Jr., 461, 462, 466–467
Warner, Susan, 344, 345
Warner Brothers, 147, 479
Warren, Russell, 81
Washington, Booker T., 142
Washington, D.C.
    architecture of, 258, 379–381, 385
    tourism in, 522
    United States Capitol, 380–381
Washington, George, 72, 92, 238, 306
Washington, Martha, 72
Washington Bee, 373
Washington Monument, 381, 386
Washington Patent Office, art exhibits at, 532
Washington Post, 250–251, 252
Washington Temperance Society, 335
Wasserstein, Wendy, 498
water, transportation by, 504–505, 507. *See also* canals; rivers; ships
water cures, 515
Watergate, media coverage of, 250–251
Waters, Muddy, 24
Watkins, Carleton, 274

Watson, Elkanah, 329, 434
Watson, John B., 46
Watts, Isaac, 353
Way West: The Era of Overland Migrations, 506
Wayne, Anthony, 191
Wayne, John, 146
WCTU. *See* Women's Christian Temperance Union
We Hold These Truths, 392
wealthy
    elite. *See* elite
    housing, 217, 220
    leisure travel, 515, 517–518
    sponsorship of private cultural events, 530
Weavers, 163–164
Webb, Del E., 298
Webb, Mary, 561
Weber, Adna Ferrin, 465
Weber, Lois, 144
Weber, Max, 438
Webster, Noah, 237, 338
Weems, Mason Locke, 369
Weitzman, Lenore, 126
welfare, of children, 47, 50
Welles, Orson, 149, 496
Wesley, John, 353
West, 196–197, 401, 554–556. *See also* frontier; settlement; western expansion
West, Benjamin, 485, 530
West, Mae, 147
West Edmonton Mall, 36
West Indian Emancipation Day, 20
West Indian immigrants, 173
West Indies, plantation patterns, 315
Western Associated Press, 241
western expansion, 507–508
    exploration and, 193–195
    of plantations, 317
    transportation and, 505–506, 507
western music. *See* country and western music
western swing music, 111–112
Western Union, 82, 96
westerns
    motion pictures, 146
    television, 480
Westinghouse, 388
Wexner Center for the Visual Arts, 386
Whale, James, 149
Wharton, Anne Hollingsworth, 72
Whigs, press of, 240–241
Whiskey Rebellion, 191, 192
White, Alfred Tredway, 215
White, William Allen, 245
White Cross societies, 423
"white Indians," 193
White Sox, 450
White Stockings, 448
Whitefield, George, 92, 306, 327, 353, 529
Whitlock, Brand, 62
Whitman, Walt, 332, 335, 441
Whitney, Gertrude Vanderbilt, 539
Who, 403
Whole Booke of Psalmes, The. See Bay Psalm Book, The
Whole Duty of Man, The (Allestree), 264
Why? (1913), 144
Wide, Wide World, The (Warner), 344, 345
Wide World of Sports, 457

widows
    African American, 135
    assistance for, 562
    colonial, 132
    nineteenth-century, 134
    poverty and, 134
    twentieth-century, 135–137
"Wife of Usher's Well, The," 155
Wigglesworth Life Table, 132
wigs, 70, 71
Wild and Scenic Rivers Act (1968), 275
Wild Bunch, The (1969), 146
Wilderness Act (1964), 275
wildness, national parks as symbol, 274–255
Willard, Frances, 123, 565
Willard, Jess, 450
William and Mary College, theatrical productions, 484
Williams, Bert, 490
Williams, Bruce, 397
Williams, Hiram ("Hank"), 112
Williams, "Jonah Man," 228
Williams, Raymond, 527, 543
Williams, Tennessee, 497
Williamsburg, VA, 377, 378–379
Willis, Sara Payson (Fanny Fern), 341, 367
Wills, Bob, 111–112
Wilson, August, 501
Wilson, John Lyde, 95, 264
Wilson, Woodrow, 143, 384, 493
Wimbledon, 446
Winesburg, Ohio (Anderson), 556
Winslow, Anna Green, 71
Winslow, Edward, 352
winter resorts, 521
Winthrop, John, 167, 262, 559–560
Wise, Robert, 152
Witmark, M., 356
Wobblies, 158
Woman's Central Association of Relief, 563
Woman's Union Missionary Society, 564
women
    as abolitionists, 563
    as administrators, 207–208
    adolescence of, 4–6
    African American, organiations of, 561, 566, 568–569
    as artists, 542–543
    automobile and, 511
    as basketball players, 448
    benevolent, 562
    in Civil War, 563–564
    colonial, 2–3, 4
        sexual behavior, 415, 416
        wardrobe, 68, 71
    in communications revolution, 94
    composers, 105
    courtship and, 270–271
    divorce and, 117, 121–122, 124
    elderly, 294, 300
    exploitation of, 7, 415, 421, 422
    in fraternal organizations, 177, 180, 183
    frontier, 200
    gender roles. *See* gender roles
    home economics and, 175
    in hospitals, 207–208
    as journalists, 236, 252
    leisure and, 283, 284–285, 325
    marriage and, 127
    in Midwest towns, 554
    as missionaries, 564
    in motion pictures, 144, 151–152
    as musicians, 24–25, 27, 105, 113–115, 355
    "new woman," 547–548
    in 1920's, 10
    nineteenth-century
        adolescence, 4–6
        urban, 58
        wardrobe, 73
    on plantation, 314
    as playwrights, 498
    in politics, 302
    as popular fiction audience, 344
    property and, 120
    in public libraries, 373
    Puritan, 116–117
    radio and, 390
    restrictive fashions of, 73
    rights of, 119–120, 427, 428–429
    in rock music, 405, 409
    saloons and, 284
    sexual behavior, 421, 425, 426, 427, 428–429
        colonial, 415–416
        Victorian, 418–419
    as social reformers, 561–569
    in sports, 445, 453, 458
    suburban isolation, 468
    as teachers, 563
    television portrayals, 480
    in theater, 500
    twentieth-century, wardrobe, 76–77
    Victorian, 418–419
    war and, 124
    in workforce, 50, 207–208, 269, 564
    as writers, 344, 367
    See also abortion; birth control; childbirth; mothers
Women's Christian Temperance Union, 283, 423, 564, 565
Women's Education and Industrial Union, 566
Women's International League for Peace and Freedom, 567–568
women's organizations
    academic, 568
    Christian, 561–563, 564–565
    class conflict in, 564–565
    clubs, 565–566
    feminist, 569
    fraternal auxiliaries, 177, 180, 183
    labor unions and, 567
    local nature of, 561
    management of, 564
    national reform efforts, 562–563
    nineteenth-century, 561–568
    prostitution and, 563
    sororities, 568–569
Wonder, Stevie, 408
wood, 225
Wood, Charles Erskine Scott, 124
Wood, Robert C., 463
Wood, Robert D., 481
wood pulp, papermaking and, 365

Woodbury County Courthouse, 384
Woodhull, Victoria, 419
Woodland Indians, 432
Woodville, Richard Caton, 94
Woodward, Bob, 251
wool, 69, 72
Woollcott, Alexander, 230
Woolley, Edmund, 379
Woolworth Building, 59, 83–84
Worcester, MA, 546, 547
Worcester v. *Georgia* (1832), 195
work songs, 19, 157–158
workers
    child, 43–44, 47, 48
    female, 50, 207–208, 269, 564
    health care benefits, 209–210
    housing of, 214–215
    in industrial cities, 60–61
    leisure, 518, 519, 524
    See also labor; labor unions; slaves; working-class
Workers Song Books, 103
working-class
    adolescence, 6–7, 9–10
    arts, 538
    colonial, 53
    courtship, 420
    depiction in motion pictures, 144–145
    labor. *See* labor; labor unions
    nightlife, 283
    nightlife and, 280
    nineteenth-century, 56–57, 419–420, 438–440
        housing, 214–215
        leisure and, 438–440
        marriage, 420
        sexual behavior, 419–420, 425
    parks and, 547, 548
    rock music and, 408
    theater and, 333
    urban parks for, 548
    See also labor; slaves; workers
Works Progress Administration, 47, 163, 538, 541. *See also* New Deal
workweek, travel and, 518, 519
world music, 409–410
World Series, 1919 scandal, 450–451, 453
World Tourism Organization, 514
World War I, 424, 449
World War II
    adolescence during, 11
    deaths, 134
    divorce and, 127
    effects on childhood, 47–48
    foodways and, 175
    influence on motion pictures, 149
    influence on music, 102, 104
    mobility in, 519
    music of, 358
    nightlife and, 288–289
    radio and, 392–394
World's Columbian Exposition (1893), 31, 62, 83, 518–519, 536, 542
    architecture of, 383

world's fairs, 472, 536–537. *See also* Philadelphia Centennial Exposition (1876); World's Columbian Exposition (1893)
Worth, Charles, 74
Wouk, Herman, 392
Wounded Knee, SD, 199
WPA. *See* Works Progress Administration
Wren, Christopher, 380
Wright, Frances, 120, 419–420
Wright, Frank Lloyd, 84, 85, 386
Wright, Gwendolyn, 468
Wright, Henry, 464
Wright, John Lloyd, 385
writers, 344, 367, 373
Wroth, Lawrence C., 340
Wuthering Heights (Brontë), 347
Wyatt-Brown, Bertram, 264
Wyoming, 519

Y
"Y" Movement, 442
yachting, 440
Yale Repertory Theatre, 501
Yale University, Trumbull Gallery, 532
Yamasaki, Minoru, 86
Yankees, 451
"Yankee Doodle," 99, 100, 353
Ye Bare and Ye Cubb (1665), 483
yellow fever, 57
yellow journalism, 244, 449
Yellowstone National Park, 273, 274, 518
YMCA. *See* Young Men's Christian Association
yodeling, 108–109
Yorktown, 354
Yosemite National Park, 273, 274, 275, 518
Young, Lester, 27
Young, Neil, 406, 409
"Young Charlotte," 159
Young Man's Guide (1833), 438
Young Men's Christian Association, 284
    basketball and, 431, 448
    Comstock Law and, 123
    sports and, 442
    summer camps, 518
Young Wife, The, 119
Young Women's Christian Association, 284, 564–565, 568
Youngstown, 298
youth. *See* adolescence; children
Youth's Companion, 244, 367
YWCA. *See* Young Women's Christian Association

Z
Zenger, John Peter, 236, 362, 363
Ziegfeld, Florenz, 494
Ziegfeld Follies, 494
Ziegfeld's Midnight Frolic, 285
Zinnemann, Fred, 150, 151
zoning laws, 220
zoos, 538, 547
Zukor, Adolph, 145
Zuni Indians, 188
Zworykin, Vladimir, 472